# PC maintenance

## Preparing for A+ Certification

Faithe Wempen

**Developmental Editor** Michael Sander
**Cover and Text Designer** Jennifer Wreisner
**Desktop Production** Leslie Anderson
**Illustrator** Colin Hayes
**Photo Insert** Brad Knefelkamp, Riverside Color
**Copyeditor** Sharon R. O'Donnell
**Proofreader** Joy McComb
**Indexer** Nancy Fulton

**Publishing Team:** George Provol, Publisher; Janice Johnson, Director of Product Development; Tony Galvin, Acquisitions Editor; Lori Landwer, Marketing Manager; Shelley Clubb, Electronic Design and Production Manager.

**Acknowledgment:** The author and publisher wish to thank Roger Young, IT Department Chair, Davenport University, Granger, IN, for his academic and technical contributions.

**Dedication:** To Margaret, as usual

**Library of Congress Cataloging-in-Publication Data**

Wempen, Faithe
PC maintenance: preparing for A+ certification/Faithe Wempen.
p. cm.
Includes index.
ISBN 0-7638-1905-0
1. Electronic data processing personnel—Certification. 2. Computer technicians—Certification—Study guides. 3. Microcomputers—Maintenance and repair—Examinations—Study guides. 4. Computing Technology Industry Association—Examinations—Study guides. I. Title.

QA76.3 .W465 2004
621.39'16'0288—dc21 2002040841


Published by **EMC**Paradigm
875 Montreal Way
St. Paul, MN 55102

(800) 535-6865
E-mail: educate@emcp.com
Web Site: www.emcp.com



Printed in the United States of America
10 9 8 7 6 5 4 3 2 1

# BRIEF CONTENTS

# DETAILED CONTENTS

# INTRODUCTION

Are you considering the benefits of CompTIA A+ Certification for your career? You are in good company. To date, over a half-million people have become A+ Certified, demonstrating that they have the skills and knowledge to function competently as an entry-level PC technician.

If you plan to pursue multiple certifications, A+ is a natural place to start. Most computer technology programs at universities and vocational schools recommend that students become A+ Certified first, to gain a solid footing in computer hardware and software concepts.

## What Is A+ Certification?

A+ Certification is an entry-level certification that measures knowledge and skills based on six months of experience as a working PC technician. The exams are administered by CompTIA, a company that also offers many other certification programs including Network+, i-Net+, Server+, and Linux+.

The logo of the CompTIA Authorized Quality Curriculum Program and the status of this or other training material as "Authorized" under the CompTIA Authorized Curriculum Program signifies that, in CompTIA's opinion, such training material covers the content of the CompTIA's related certification exam. CompTIA has not reviewed or approved the accuracy of the contents of this training material and specifically disclaims any warranties of merchantability or fitness for a particular purpose. CompTIA makes no guarantee concerning the success of persons using any such "Authorized" or other training material in order to prepare for any CompTIA certification exam.

The contents of this training material were created for the CompTIA A+ Core Hardware Service Technician and A+ Operating System Technologies exams covering CompTIA certification exam objectives that were current as of January 2003.

### How to Become CompTIA Certified

This training material can help you prepare for and pass a related CompTIA certification exam or exams. In order to achieve CompTIA certification, you must register for and pass a CompTIA certification exam or exams.

In order to become CompTIA certified, you must:

(1) Select a certification exam provider. For more information please visit http://www.comptia.org/certification/test_locations.htm.

(2) Register for and schedule a time to take the CompTIA certification exam(s) at a convenient location.

(3) Read and sign the Candidate Agreement, which will be presented at the time of the exam(s). The text of the Candidate Agreement can be found at www.comptia.org/certification

(4) Take and pass the CompTIA certification exam(s).

For more information about CompTIA's certifications, such as their industry acceptance, benefits, or program news, please visit www.comptia.org/certification.

CompTIA is a non-profit information technology (IT) trade association. CompTIA's certifications are designed by subject matter experts from across the IT industry. Each CompTIA certification is vendor-neutral, covers multiple technologies, and requires demonstration of skills and knowledge widely sought after by the IT industry.

To contact CompTIA with any questions or comments:
Please call + 1 630 268 1818
questions@comptia.org

## Exam Content

A+ Certification is attained by passing two separate examinations: A+ Core Hardware Service Technician and A+ Operating System Technologies. The main topic areas, or domains, in each exam cover specific percentages of the total score.

**A+ Core Hardware Service Technician Examination**

| | | |
|---|---|---|
| 1.0 | Installation, Configuration, and Upgrading | 30% |
| 2.0 | Diagnosing and Troubleshooting | 30% |
| 3.0 | Preventive Maintenance | 5% |
| 4.0 | Motherboards/Processors/Memory | 15% |
| 5.0 | Printers | 10% |
| 6.0 | Basic Networking | 10% |

**A+ Operating System Technologies Examination**

| | | |
|---|---|---|
| 1.0 | Operating System Fundamentals | 30% |
| 2.0 | Installation, Configuration, and Upgrading | 15% |
| 3.0 | Diagnosing and Troubleshooting | 40% |
| 4.0 | Networks | 15% |

Within each of those domains are several individual objectives. For example, the Operating System Fundamentals category on the A+ Operating System Technologies exam has two objectives:

**Objective 1.1:** Identify the operating system's functions, structure, and major system files to navigate the operating system and how to get to needed technical information.
**Objective 1.2:** Identify basic concepts and procedures for creating, viewing and managing files, directories and disks. This includes procedures for changing file attributes and the ramifications of those changes (for example, security issues).

You will find a complete list of all of the objectives in each domain on the inside front cover of the book.

At the CompTIA Web site, a detailed document listing these objectives and what they cover is available in PDF (Adobe Acrobat) format. In this document you will see not only a listing of the individual objectives, but also lists of sub-objective content areas included in each one. These individual objectives are mapped to the chapters of this book in the "Guide to Examination Objectives" on page xxiii, following this Introduction.

The operating systems covered on the A+ Operating System Technologies examination are Windows NT 4.0, Windows 95, Windows 98, and Windows 2000. This book focuses mostly on those operating systems, but also includes discussion of Windows Me and Windows XP because you are likely to encounter them on the job. The Mac OS, Linux, and UNIX are not covered either on the exam or in this book.

## Understanding Adaptive Testing

Both A+ exams are adaptive, which means that the questions you are asked will vary depending on how you have answered previous questions. The differences in the questions involve both topic and difficulty. For example, suppose you give a correct answer to an easy question about printing. The testing software might then ask you a difficult question about printing. If you get that one right as well, it assumes you have "passed" the printing topic and moves on to something else.

This adaptive testing has two effects. One is to make it much more difficult to conceal a lack of knowledge in a certain area because the software will ask you more questions about a topic after you give an incorrect answer to a question in that area. The other is that the testing method weights the questions differently based on difficulty, so that two people who get the same number of questions right might end up with different scores. For example, if a test-taker gets most of the difficult questions wrong, the testing software gives that person more of the easier questions, whereas if a test-taker gets some of the more challenging questions correct, he or she will get more of the tougher questions.

Adaptive testing also means that different test-takers will have different numbers of questions on their exam—somewhere between 20 and 30 in most cases. Sometimes the testing software will make a score determination before asking the maximum number of questions, and will end the exam at that point.

## Other Exam Details

Each exam must be finished within 30 minutes, regardless of the number of questions asked. At the end of 30 minutes, the testing software will simply end the exam and calculate the score based on the number of questions completed.

The A+ exams are graded on a scale of 0 to 1300. To pass, you must receive at least a 596 on the Core Hardware exam and at least a 600 on the Operating System Technologies exam. You can take the exams at separate times or on the same day.

Each exam costs $139 to take (undiscounted price), so becoming A+ Certified will cost twice that, or $278, assuming that you pass each exam on the first attempt. Some preparation courses include exam vouchers in their prices, and some companies may be eligible for preferred pricing and/or volume discounts. See http://www.comptia.org/certification/new_pricing.htm for pricing information for countries other than the United States.

## What Are the Special Features of this Book?

By opening this book, you have taken the first step toward achieving two important goals: (1) preparing to pass both of the exams required to become A+ Certified, and (2) preparing to be a competent working PC technician.

Many A+ textbooks focus solely on passing the exams, teaching you only what you need to know to pass. But simply passing the exams will not necessarily help you succeed in a real job. By focusing equally on *both* goals, this book will prepare you not only for exam success, but also for a successful career as a professional PC technician.

For example, an A+ preparation textbook will tell you about Pentium II CPU cartridges. It will give you the precise dimensions of a cartridge, the range of operating speeds available in that CPU class, and the type of motherboard slot that supports them. But to succeed on the job you need more than that! You need to know that this style of CPU requires support brackets to be installed on the motherboard—and how to attach them. You need to know that such a CPU requires an active heat sink—and how to install one and connect its fan to the power supply. You need to know how to look up a Pentium II CPU's part number at the Intel Web site to find out its speed and specs. Can you pass the A+ exam without that information? Of course. But on the first day on the job as a PC technician you are going to look like a novice unless you know those things.

This book provides information in a variety of ways, with something to suit every learning style. Here is an overview of the major features of the text:

- **On the Test.** Each chapter begins by stating the CompTIA A+ exam objectives covered in that chapter. More information about these objectives is available at CompTIA's Web site at http://www.comptia.com.
- **On the Job.** At the beginning of each chapter is a quick review of the real-life job skills that correspond to the chapter content, so you can better understand how reading the chapter will translate into practical benefits in your career.
- **In Real Life boxes.** These side notes provide extra items of practical wisdom for applying chapter concepts on the job, or introduce useful options and features not covered specifically on the exams.
- **Warning boxes.** These side notes spotlight common mistakes made by beginners or problems that can occur in using certain hardware or software.
- **Try It! boxes.** Sometimes it is more interesting and useful to try a hands-on skill right away rather than waiting for the review at the end. These Try It! notes offer suggestions for quick activities using the equipment and features discussed in the chapter.
- **Vocabulary words.** New terms are defined in the margins, and also collected in a master Glossary at the back of the book.
- **Study Guide.** At the end of each chapter is a bulleted outline of the major concepts presented, for point-by-point study and review.

- **Practice Test.** Each chapter has 20 multiple-choice questions similar to those you might encounter on the A+ exams. There are also over 2,000 additional questions on the accompanying Encore Plus Companion CD (see below).
- **Troubleshooting.** Build your critical thinking skills with these problem-and-solution scenarios, useful for group discussion or individual study.
- **Customer Service.** Being a good technician means listening to a client and deciphering what is really going on, even when the client does not know the correct terms for what is happening. These critical-thinking scenarios test your ability to do just that.
- **Project Labs.** At the end of each major section of the book you will find a number of hands-on exercises you can perform in a computer lab or on an individual PC to build your confidence with handling hardware and installing, troubleshooting, and running software.
- **Internet Resource Center.** The IRC, at www.emcp.com, provides enriching material that reinforces the text, including links to numerous related Web sites.

Students in a formal classroom or lab environment will find that this book makes an excellent basis for group discussions and exercises, especially the Troubleshooting and Customer Service questions at the end of each chapter and the Project Labs at the end of each part.

## What Is on the Encore! CD?

This book includes an Encore! Companion CD that amplifies and enriches the content of the text. Chapter by chapter, this multimedia tool serves as a study guide and adds action to the images displayed in the book. *Tech Tutor* offers Flash animations of concepts that are presented in the text, while the videos in *Tech Demo* provide graphic demonstration of common PC maintenance tasks.

The Encore! CD also includes a *Test Bank* that provides guided preparation for taking the A+ exams. There are two levels of tests: book and chapter, and each level functions in two different modes. In the Practice mode you receive immediate feedback on each test item and a report of your total score. In the Test mode your results are e-mailed both to you and your instructor, highlighting the correct answers given in each of the domains contained in the exams.

In addition, the Encore! CD contains an *Image Bank,* with numerous colorful illustrations and photographs of selected objects and concepts discussed in the book, and a *Glossary* that includes graphic depictions as well as verbal definitions. Finally, the Encore! CD provides a link to the *EMC/Paradigm Internet Resource Center,* at www.emcp.com.

## What Is in the Workbook?

The Workbook that accompanies this book provides an opportunity to practice and demonstrate your mastery of the skills presented in the text. A series of projects for each chapter calls for hands-on demonstration of the practical tasks required of the PC technician. Written answers to pertinent questions about PC operations and systems, identification of parts in photographs of hardware, and your own drawings of various devices will reinforce your knowledge of the application of these skills. These activities, which can be performed by an individual or in varied group sizes, will add practical experience to your preparation for a career as a PC technician, and improve and deepen your understanding of the concepts to be mastered for the A+ Certification exams.

## Acknowledgments

Every publishing project is a team effort, and what a great team this book has had! Thanks to the staff at EMC/Paradigm for a job well done. The key players include:

**Tony Galvin, Acquisitions Editor,** arranged all the upfront details, ironed out contract details, and made sure that we all stayed true to the goal. Thanks for being so upbeat and positive and a good facilitator, Tony!

**Jan Johnson, Director of Product Development,** used her many years of knowledge about what teachers and students want to make sure that this book offered a complete package of benefits to the reader. Thanks for insisting on the highest quality, Jan!

**Michael Sander, Developmental Editor,** managed the editing and production process and was my primary contact at EMC/Paradigm. He answered all of my questions—even the dumb ones—and kept me on schedule and motivated. Thanks for being so well organized and responsive, Michael!

**Sonja Brown, Senior Editor,** was responsible for the awesome task of assembling the CD that accompanies this book, including contracting with videographers, photographers, and illustrators. Thanks for your creativity and attention to detail, Sonja!

**Roger Young, Technical Reviewer,** did a thorough review of the manuscript to make sure it was technically accurate. Thanks for your suggestions, Roger!

**Sharon O'Donnell, Copy Editor,** took my rough prose and polished it to make it easier to read, as well as pointing out to me when I just was not making sense! Thanks for making me sound so good, Sharon!

**Colin Hayes, Illustrator,** is responsible for all the drawings and diagrams in the book. If you could see the rough sketches and notes I turned in, you would understand what an awesome task this was. Thanks for putting your great talent to work, Colin!

# Guide to Examination Objectives

## A+ Core Hardware Service Technician Examination

| Objectives | Chapter or Appendix |
|---|---|
| **Domain 1.0 Installation, Configuration, and Upgrading** | |
| **1.1: Identify basic terms, concepts, and functions of system modules, including how each module should work during normal operation and during the boot process.** *Examples of concepts and modules:* | |
| System board | 1, 4 |
| Power supply | 1,3 |
| Processor/CPU | 1, 5 |
| Memory | 1, 6 |
| Storage devices | 1, 10, 13 |
| Monitor | 1, 16 |
| Modem | 1, 24 |
| Firmware | 9 |
| BIOS | 1, 9 |
| CMOS | 9 |
| LCD (portable systems) | 16, 20 |
| Ports | 7 |
| PDA (Personal Digital Assistant) | 1 |
| **1.2: Identify basic procedures for adding and removing field replaceable modules for both desktop and portable systems.** *Examples of modules:* | |
| System board | 4, 8 |
| Storage device | 11, 13 |
| Power supply | 3, 8 |
| Processor/CPU | 8 |
| Memory | 8 |
| Input devices | 17 |
| Hard drive | 11 |
| Keyboard | 17 |
| Video board | 8 |
| Mouse | 17 |
| Network interface card (NIC) | 22 |
| *Portable system components:* | |
| AC adapter | 20 |
| Digital Camera | 19 |
| DC controller | 20 |
| LCD panel | 16, 20 |
| PC Card | 20 |
| Pointing Devices | 20 |
| **1.3: Identify available IRQs, DMAs, and I/O addresses and procedures for device installation and configuration.** *Content may include the following:* | |
| Standard IRQ settings | 14 |
| Modems | 14 |
| Floppy drive controllers | 14 |
| Hard drive controllers | 14 |
| USB ports | 14 |
| Infrared ports | 20 |
| Hexadecimal/Addresses | 14 |
| **1.4: Identify common peripheral ports, associated cabling, and their connectors.** *Content may include the following:* | |
| Cable types | 7 |
| Cable orientation | 7 |
| Serial versus parallel | 7 |
| Pin connections | 7 |
| *Examples of types of connectors:* | |
| DB-9 | 7 |
| DB-25 | 7 |
| RJ-11 | 7 |
| RJ-45 | 7 |
| BNC | 7 |
| PS2/MINI-DIN | 7 |
| USB | 7 |
| IEEE 1394 | 7 |
| **1.5: Identify proper procedures for installing and configuring IDE/EIDE devices.** *Content may include the following:* | |
| Master/Slave | 11 |
| Devices per channel | 11 |
| Primary/Secondary | 11 |
| **1.6: Identify proper procedures for installing and configuring SCSI devices.** *Content may include the following:* | |
| Address/Termination conflicts | 11 |
| Cabling | 11 |
| Types (example: regular, wide, ultra-wide) | 11 |
| Internal versus external | 11 |
| Expansion slots, EISA, ISA, PCI | 11 |
| Jumper block settings (binary equivalents) | 11 |
| **1.7: Identify proper procedures for installing and configuring peripheral devices.** *Content may include the following:* | |
| Monitor/Video Card | 15, 16 |
| Modem | 24 |
| USP peripherals and hubs | 7 |
| IEEE 1284 | 7, 18 |
| IEEE 1394 | 7 |
| External storage | 10 |
| *Portables:* | |
| Docking stations | 20 |
| PC cards | 20 |
| Port replicators | 20 |
| Infrared devices | 20 |

| Objectives | Chapter or Appendix |
|---|---|
| **1.8: Identify hardware methods of upgrading system performance, procedures for replacing basic subsystem components, unique components and when to use them.** *Content may include the following:* | |
| Memory | 8 |
| Hard Drives | 11 |
| CPU 8 Upgrading BIOS | 9 |
| When to upgrade BIOS | 9 |
| *Portable Systems:* | |
| Battery | 20 |
| Hard Drive | 20 |
| Types I, II, III cards | 20 |
| Memory | 20 |
| **Domain 2.0 Diagnosing and Troubleshooting** | |
| **2.1: Identify common symptoms and problems associated with each module and how to troubleshoot and isolate the problems.** *Content may include the following:* | |
| Processor/Memory symptoms | 8 |
| Mouse | 17 |
| Floppy drive | 11 |
| Parallel ports | 7 |
| Hard Drives | 11, 13 |
| CD-ROM | 13 |
| DVD | 13 |
| Sound Card/Audio | 19 |
| Monitor/Video | 15, 16 |
| Motherboards | 8 |
| Modems | 24 |
| BIOS | 9 |
| USB | 7 |
| NIC | 23 |
| CMOS | 9 |
| Power supply | 3 |
| Slot covers | 8 |
| POST audible/visual error codes | 8 |
| Troubleshooting tools, e.g., multimeter | 3, 7 |
| Large LBA, LBA | 10 |
| Cables | 7 |
| Keyboard | 17 |
| Peripherals | 18 |
| **2.2: Identify basic troubleshooting procedures and how to elicit problem symptoms from customers.** *Content may include the following:* | |
| Troubleshooting/isolation/problem determination procedures | 8, 30 |
| Determine whether hardware or software problem | 30 |
| Gather information from user regarding, e.g., Customer Environment; Symptoms/Error Codes; Situation when the problem occurred | B |

| Domain 3.0 Preventive Maintenance | |
|---|---|
| **3.1: Identify the purpose of various types of preventive maintenance products and procedures and when to use them.** *Content may include the following:* | |
| Liquid cleaning compounds | 2, A |
| Types of materials to clean contacts and connections | 2, A |
| Non-static vacuums (chassis, power supplies, fans) | A |
| **3.2: Identify issues, procedures and devices for protection within the computing environment, including people, hardware and the surrounding workspace.** *Content may include the following:* | |
| UPS (Uninterruptible Power Supply) and suppressors | 3 |
| Determining the signs of power issues | 2 |
| Proper methods of storage of components for future use | 2 |
| *Potential hazards and proper safety procedures relating to Lasers:* | |
| High-voltage equipment | 2 |
| Power supply | 2 |
| CRT | 2 |
| *Special disposal procedures that comply with environmental guidelines:* | |
| Batteries | 2 |
| CRTs | 2 |
| Toner kits/cartridges | 2 |
| Chemical solvents and cans | 2 |
| MSDS (Material Safety Data Sheet) | 2 |
| *ESD (Electrostatic Discharge) precautions and procedures:* | |
| What ESD can do, how it may be apparent, or hidden | 2 |
| Common ESD protection devices | 2 |
| Situations that could present a danger or hazard | 2 |
| **Domain 4.0 Motherboard/Processor/Memory** | |
| **4.1: Distinguish between the popular CPU chips in terms of their basic characteristics.** *Content may include the following:* | |
| Popular CPU chips (Intel, AMD, Cyrix) | 5 |
| Characteristics | 5 |
| Physical size | 5 |
| Voltage | 5 |
| Speeds | 5 |
| On board cache or not | 5 |
| Sockets | 5 |
| SEC (Single Edge Contact) | 5 |

| Objectives | Chapter or Appendix |
|---|---|
| **4.2: Identify the categories of RAM (Random Access Memory) terminology, their locations, and physical characteristics.** | |
| *Content may include the following:* | |
| *Terminology:* | |
| EDO RAM (Extended Data Output RAM) | 6 |
| DRAM (Dynamic Random Access Memory) | 6 |
| SRAM (Static RAM) | 6 |
| RIMM (Rambus Inline Memory Module 184 Pin) | 6 |
| VRAM (Video RAM) | 6 |
| SDRAM (Synchronous Dynamic RAM) | 6 |
| WRAM (Windows Accelerator Card RAM) | 6 |
| *Locations and physical characteristics:* | |
| Memory bank | 6 |
| Memory chips (8-bit, 16-bit, and 32-bit) | 6 |
| SIMMS (Single In-line Memory Module) | 6 |
| DIMMS (Dual In-line Memory Module) | 6 |
| Parity chips versus non-parity chips | 6 |
| **4.3: Identify the most popular type of motherboards, their components, and their architecture (bus structures and power supplies).** | |
| *Content may include the following:* | |
| *Types of motherboards:* | |
| AT (Full and Baby) | 4 |
| ATX | 4 |
| *Components:* | |
| Communication ports | 4 |
| SIMM and DIMM | 4 |
| Processor sockets | 4 |
| External cache memory (Level 2) | 4 |
| Bus Architecture | 4 |
| ISA | 4 |
| PCI | 4 |
| AGP | 4 |
| USB (Universal Serial Bus) | 4 |
| VESA local bus (VL-Bus) | 4 |
| Basic compatibility guidelines | 4 |
| IDE (ATA, ATAPI, ULTRA-DMA, EIDE) | 11 |
| SCSI (Wide, Fast, Ultra, LVD [Low Voltage Differential]) | 11 |
| **4.4: Identify the purpose of CMOS (Complementary Metal-Oxide Semiconductor), what it contains and how to change its basic parameters.** *Example Basic CMOS Settings:* | |
| Printer parallel port—Uni., bi-directional, disable/enable, ECP, EPP | 9 |
| COM/serial port—memory address, interrupt request, disable | 9 |
| Floppy drive—enable/disable drive or boot, speed, density | 9 |
| Hard drive—size and drive type | 9, 10 |
| Memory—parity, non-parity | 9 |
| Boot sequence | 9 |
| Date/Time | 9 |
| Passwords | 9 |
| Plug & Play BIOS | 9 |
| **Domain 5.0 Printers** | |
| **5.1: Identify basic concepts, printer operations and printer components.** | |
| *Content may include the following:* | |
| Paper feed mechanisms | 18 |
| *Types of Printers:* | |
| Laser | 18 |
| Inkjet | 18 |
| Dot Matrix | 18 |
| *Types of printer connections and configurations:* | |
| Parallel | 18 |
| Network | 18 |
| USB | 18 |
| Infrared | 18 |
| Serial | 18 |
| **5.2: Identify care and service techniques and common problems with primary printer types.** | |
| *Content may include the following:* | |
| Feed and output | 18 |
| Errors (printed or displayed) | 18 |
| Paper jam | 18 |
| Print quality | 18 |
| Safety precautions | 2, 18 |
| Preventive maintenance | 18 |
| **Domain 6.0 Basic Networking** | |
| **6.1: Identify basic networking concepts, including how a network works and the ramifications of repairs on the network.** | |
| *Content may include the following:* | |
| Installing and configuring network cards | 21 |
| Network access | 22, 23 |
| Full-duplex, half-duplex | 24 |
| Cabling—Twisted Pair, Coaxial, Fiber Optic, RS-232 | 7, 21 |
| Ways to network a PC | 21 |
| Physical Network topographies | 21 |
| Increasing bandwidth | 23 |
| Loss of data | 23 |
| Network slowdown | 23 |
| Infrared | 23 |
| Hardware protocols | 21 |

## A+ Operating System Technologies Examination

| Objectives | Chapter or Appendix |
| --- | --- |
| **Domain 1.0 Operating System Fundamentals** | |
| **1.1: Identify the operating system's functions, structure, and major system files to navigate the operating system and how to get to needed technical information.** | |
| *Content may include the following:* | |
| *Major Operating System functions:* | |
| Create folders | 29 |
| Checking OS Version | 29 |
| *Major Operating System Components:* | |
| Explorer | 29 |
| My Computer | 29 |
| Control Panel | 28 |
| Contrasts between Windows 9x and Windows 2000 | 26 |
| ***Major system files: what they are, where they are located, how they are used and what they contain:*** | |
| *System, Configuration, and User Interface Files:* | |
| IO.SYS | 26, 27 |
| BOOT.INI | 26, 27 |
| WIN.COM | 26, 27 |
| MSDOS.SYS | 26, 27 |
| AUTOEXEC.BAT | 26, 27 |
| CONFIG.SYS | 26, 27 |
| COMMAND LINE PROMPT | 29 |
| *Memory management:* | |
| Conventional | 6 |
| Extended/upper memory | 6 |
| High memory | 6 |
| Virtual memory | 6 |
| HIMEM.SYS | 6 |
| EMM386.exe | 6 |
| *Windows 9x:* | |
| IO.SYS | 26, 27 |
| WIN.INI | 26, 27 |
| USER.DAT | 26, 27 |
| SYSEDIT | 30 |
| SYSTEM.INI | 26, 27 |
| SETVER.EXE | 28 |
| SMARTDRV.EXE | 26, 27 |
| MSCONFIG (98) | 26, 27 |
| COMMAND.COM | 26, 27 |
| DOSSTART.BAT | 26, 27 |
| REGEDIT.EXE | 30, D |
| SYSTEM.DAT | 26, 27 |
| RUN COMMAND | 28 |
| DriveSpace | 30 |
| *Windows 2000:* | |
| Computer Management | 12 |
| BOOT.INI | 26, 27 |
| REGEDT32 | 30, D |
| REGEDIT | 30, D |
| RUN CMD | 28 |
| NLDR | 26, 27 |
| NTDETECT.COM | 26, 27 |
| NTBOOTDD.SYS | 26, 27 |
| *Command Prompt Procedures (Command syntax):* | |
| DIR | 12 |
| ATTRIB | 29 |
| VER | 26 |
| MEM | 28 |
| SCANDISK | 28, 30 |
| DEFRAG | 28, 30 |
| EDIT | 6 |
| XCOPY | 29 |
| COPY | 29 |
| FORMAT | 12 |
| FDISK | 12 |
| MSCDEX | 13 |
| SETVER | 28 |
| SCANREG | 30 |
| **1.2: Identify basic concepts and procedures for creating, viewing and managing files, directories and disks. This includes procedures for changing file attributes and the ramifications of those changes (for example, security issues).** | |
| *Content may include the following:* | |
| File attributes—Read Only, Hidden, System, and Archive attributes | 29 |
| File naming conventions (Most common extensions) | 29 |
| Windows 2000 COMPRESS, ENCRYPT | 29 |
| IDE/SCSI | 12 |
| Internal/External | 29 |
| Backup/Restore | 29 |
| *Partitioning/Formatting/File System:* | 10, 12 |
| FAT | 10 |
| FAT16 | 10 |
| FAT32 | 10 |
| NTSF4 | 10 |
| NTSF5 | 10 |
| HPFS | 10 |
| *Windows-based utilities:* | |
| ScanDisk | 30 |
| Device Manager | 24, 30 |
| System Manager | 30 |
| Computer Manager | 30 |
| MSCONFIG.EXE | 30 |
| REGEDIT.EXE (View information/ Backup registry) | 30 |

| Objectives | Chapter or Appendix |
|---|---|
| REGEDT32.lEXE | 30 |
| ATTRIB.EXE | 29 |
| EXTRACT.EXE | 30 |
| DEFRAG.EXE | 30 |
| EDIT.COM | 6 |
| FDISK.EXE | 12 |
| SYSEDIT.EXE | 30 |
| SCANREG | 30 |
| WSCRIPT.EXE | 30 |
| HWINFO.EXE | 30 |
| ASD.EXE (Automatic Skip Driver) | 30 |
| Cvt1.EXE (Drive Converter FAT16 to FAT32) | 30 |
| **Domain 2.0 Installation, Configuration, and Upgrading** | |
| **2.1: Identify the procedures for installing Windows 9x, and Windows 2000 for bringing the software to a basic operational level.** *Content may include the following:* | |
| Start Up | 27 |
| Partition | 12 |
| Format drive | 12 |
| Loading drivers | 27 |
| Run appropriate setup utility | 26 |
| **2.2: Identify steps to perform an operating system upgrade.** *Content may include the following:* | |
| Upgrading Windows 95 to Windows 98 | 26 |
| Upgrading from Windows NT Workstation 4.0 to Windows 2000 | 26 |
| Replacing Windows 9x with Windows 2000 | 26 |
| Dual boot Windows 9x/ Windows NT 4.0/2000 | 26 |
| **2.3: Identify the basic system boot sequences and boot methods, including the steps to create an emergency boot disk with utilities installed for Windows 9x, Windows NT, and Windows 2000.** *Content may include the following:* | |
| Startup disk | 27 |
| Safe Mode | 27 |
| MS-DOS mode | 27 |
| NTLDR (NT Loader), BOOT.INI | 27 |
| Files required to boot | 27 |
| Creating emergency repair disk (ERD) | 27 |
| **2.4: Identify procedures for loading/adding and configuring application device drivers, and the necessary software for certain devices.** *Content may include the following:* | |
| Windows 9x Plug and Play and Windows 2000 | 14 |

| | |
|---|---|
| Identify the procedures for installing and launching typical Windows and non-Windows applications. (Note: there is no content related to Windows 3.1) | 28 |
| *Procedures for set up and configuring Windows printing subsystem:* | |
| Setting Default printer | 18 |
| Installing/Spool setting | 18 |
| Network printing (with help of LAN admin) | 23 |
| **Domain 3.0 Diagnosing and Troubleshooting** | |
| **3.1: Recognize and interpret the meaning of common error codes and startup messages from the boot sequence, and identify steps to correct the problems.** *Content may include the following:* | |
| Safe Mode | 27 |
| No operating system found | 27 |
| Error in CONFIG.SYS line XX | 27 |
| Bad or missing COMMAND.COM | 27 |
| HIMEM.SYS not loaded | 27 |
| Missing or corrupt HIMEM.SYS | 27 |
| SCSI | 27 |
| Swap file | 27 |
| NT boot issues | 27 |
| Dr. Watson | 30 |
| Failure to start GUI | 27 |
| Windows Protection Error | 27 |
| Event Viewer—Event log is full | 27 |
| A device referenced in SYSTEM.INI, WIN.INI, Registry is not found | 27 |
| **3.2: Recognize common problems and determine how to resolve them.** *Content may include the following:* | |
| Eliciting problem symptoms from customers | B |
| Having customer reproduce error as part of the diagnostic process | B |
| Identifying recent changes to the computer environment from the user | B |
| *Troubleshooting Windows-specific printing problems:* | |
| Print spool is stalled | 18 |
| Incorrect/incompatible driver for print | 18 |
| Incorrect parameter | 18 |
| *Other Common Problems:* | |
| General Protection Faults | 28 |
| Illegal operation | 28 |
| Invalid working directory | 28 |
| System lock up | 28, 30 |
| Option (Sound card, modem, input device) will not function | 14 |
| Application will not start or load | 28 |

| Objectives | Chapter or Appendix |
|---|---|
| Cannot log on to network (option—NIC not functioning) | 23 |
| TSR (Terminate Stay Resident) programs and virus | 28 |
| Applications don't install | 28 |
| Network connection | 30 |
| *Viruses and virus types:* | |
| What they are | 30 |
| Sources (floppy, e-mails, etc.) | 30 |
| How to determine presence | 30 |
| **Domain 4.0 Networks** | |
| **4.1: Identify the networking capabilities of Windows including procedures for connecting to the network.** *Content may include the following:* | |
| Protocols | 22 |
| IPCONFIG.EXE | 23 |
| WINIPCFG.EXE | 23 |
| Sharing disk drives | 23 |
| Sharing print and file services | 23 |
| Network type and network card | 22 |
| Installing and Configuring browsers | 25 |
| Configure OS for network connection | 25 |
| **4.2: Identify concepts and capabilities relating to the Internet and basic procedures for setting up a system for Internet access.** *Content may include the following:* | |
| *Concepts and terminology:* | |
| ISP | 25 |
| TCP/IP | 22, 25 |
| IPX/SPX | 22 |
| NetBEUI | 22 |
| E-mail | 25 |
| PING.EXE | 23, 25 |
| HTML | 25 |
| HTTP:// | 25 |
| FTP | 25 |
| Domain Names (Web sites) | 25 |
| Dial-up networking | 24 |
| TRACERT.EXE | 25 |
| NSLOOKUP.EXE | 25 |

# PART I

# Personal Computer Basics

# TEST OBJECTIVES IN PART 1

## A+ Core Hardware Service Technician Examination

- **Objective 1.1:** Identify basic terms, concepts, and functions of system modules, including how each module should work during normal operation and during the boot process.
- **Objective 1.2:** Identify basic procedures for adding and removing field replaceable modules for both desktop and portable systems.
- **Objective 2.1:** Identify common symptoms and problems associated with each module and how to troubleshoot and isolate the problems.
- **Objective 3.1:** Identify the purpose of various types of preventive maintenance products and procedures and when to use them.
- **Objective 3.2:** Identify issues, procedures, and devices for protection within the computing environment, including people, hardware and the surrounding workspace.
- **Objective 5.2:** Identify care and service techniques and common problems with primary printer types.

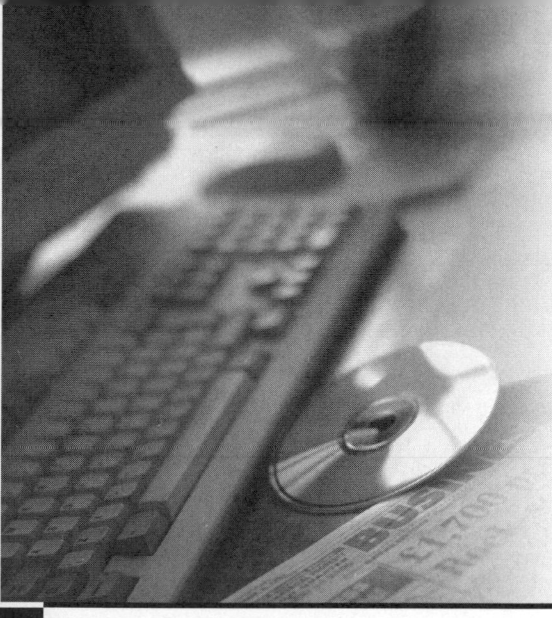

# 1 Computing Overview

## ON THE TEST

**A+ Core Hardware Service Technician Examination**

- **Objective 1.1:** Identify basic terms, concepts, and functions of system modules, including how each module should work during normal operation and during the boot process.

## ON THE JOB

Just as a long journey begins with a single step, your training to become an A+ Certified PC technician begins with gaining a basic understanding of the components that make up a typical PC.

If you are experienced with PCs, you might find that you are already familiar with some of the basic material in this chapter. It can serve as a convenient review for you. Starting with Chapter 2 you will begin learning the technical details to expand and amplify your knowledge about all of these components!

## What All Computers Have in Common

It used to be easy to say which devices were computers and which were not, but nowadays there are hundreds of types of computers, ranging from a traditional desktop PC to a computer inside a refrigerator that orders groceries for itself over the Internet. For the purposes of this book, when we talk about computers we mean *personal computers* (PCs) with which humans interact directly for business or personal tasks. The A+ exams cover three types of PCs—desktop models, laptop/notebook models, and personal digital assistants (PDAs)—but focus most heavily on desktop PCs.

**Personal computer (PC)**
A computer designed for the use of an individual.

Figure 1.1 lists what all computers have in common. The following sections look at some of these concepts in more detail.

- **Digital operation.** Computers work with digits—usually binary digits—rather than with analog data such as sound.
- **User input.** All computers have some way of accepting user input. On a PC this might be the keyboard or mouse.
- **Processing.** Each computer has a Central Processing unit (CPU) that performs math operations on the user input.
- **Output.** Each computer has a way of delivering the calculated data back to the user. On a PC this might be the monitor screen or the printer.
- **Hardware and software.** Each computer consists of some basic physical parts (the hardware) and some sets of instructions that specify how those parts should interact (software).

**FIGURE 1.1**
What All Computers Have in Common

## DIGITAL VERSUS ANALOG

**Analog**

Continuously variable data that has no precise numeric equivalent.

An *analog* device is one that can read and work with a continuously varying stream of data with no precise values, represented by the wave pattern in Figure 1.2. Sound waves are analog, and devices that work with sound such as radio and traditional telephone service are analog devices. For many years analog devices were the dominant form of technology in our society. Analog devices do not need to be absolutely precise in order to work well; some degree of error or data loss is an accepted part of the system. For example, when listening to an analog radio station, you might hear some crackles or hissing on the line if you get a bad connection, but you can still hear and understand the broadcast.

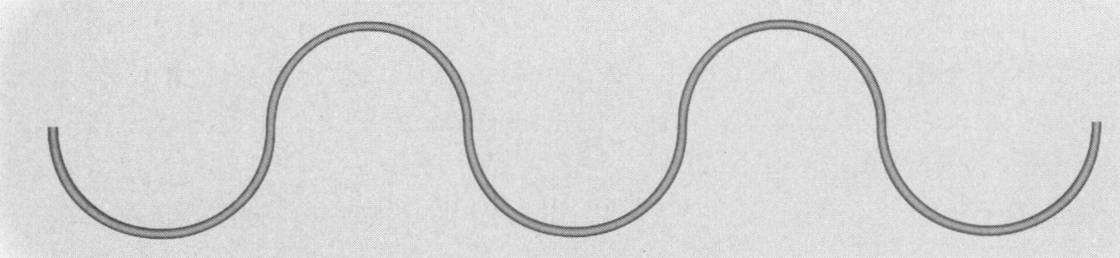

**FIGURE 1.2**
An analog representation of a string of data. Note the smooth transition from one value to the next.

**Digital**

Data precisely defined using numeric digits.

On the other hand, *digital* devices base their operation on exact numeric data. A pocket calculator is digital; it takes in numbers, processes numbers, and spits out numbers. With digital data, there is no "approximate," no room for even the tiniest variation or error. Further, most issues on a computer are yes/no propositions. The power is on or off; a formula is true or false (see Figure 1.3).

**FIGURE 1.3**
Digital data relies on precise transitions between values.

In the early days of personal computing, people continued to rely on analog devices for most activities involving sound. However, as computers became more powerful, they were able to use many more unique values per second to reproduce sound, resulting in sound that was virtually indistinguishable in quality from a smooth analog wave (see Figure 1.4). Digital sound had the advantage of being free of all the extraneous static and crackling to which analog sound was prone, and so became the most popular way of working with sound. Today, nearly all music is released on CD-ROM (a digital audio format) and nearly all telephone networks are digital rather than analog.

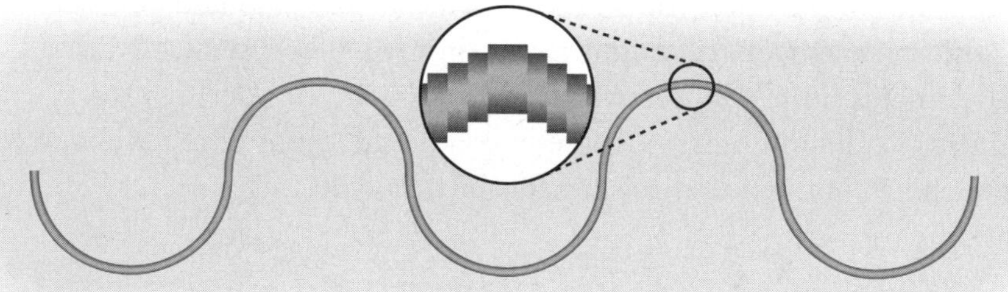

**FIGURE 1.4**
Today's computers can reproduce analog data in digital format very accurately.

## In Real Life

Have you heard commercials for cellular phone service providers that boast an "all-digital network"? What they are saying is that their service is run by computers that convert your voice to digital format for transmission, and then back to analog format at the other end so the other person can understand you. This is exactly what a modem does; the modem converts digital PC data to analog format and transmits it as sound. You will learn about modems in Chapter 24.

## Numbering Systems

**Decimal**

A numbering system based on ten digits. Can also refer to a period that separates digits, as in 1.2.

**Binary**

A numbering system based on two digits: 0 and 1.

**Bit**

A single binary digit.

**Byte**

A group of eight binary digits (bits).

**Hexadecimal**

A numbering system based on sixteen digits, 0 through 9 plus A through F.

If you have taken upper-level math classes, you know that there are numbering systems other than our standard decimal system. *Decimal* means base10; there are ten unique digits in our system, 0 through 9.

Computers use *binary* numbering to work with data at the most basic level. In a binary numbering system, there are only two digits: 0 and 1. This works well with digital hardware because the state of every electronic component is either 0 (off) or 1 (on). Each piece of data in computing is known as a *bit* (an abbreviation of *bi*nary digi*t*). Like the atom in traditional physics, it is the smallest meaningful unit with which to work.

Computers combine strings of bits into eight-bit chunks. A string of eight bits is called a *byte*. There are 256 unique combinations available with a string of eight bits: 00000000 through 11111111, each of which is assigned a number, letter, or symbol. That is how the computer turns binary data into human-readable programming.

Computers also use *hexadecimal* numbering for some tasks, such as defining memory addresses. Hexadecimal is base-16 (hex means 6 and decimal means 10).

With this system, not only do you have digits 0 through 9, but also six letters of the alphabet that function as digits. If you were to count from 1 to 17 in hexadecimal, the order would be 0, 1, 2, 3, 4, 5, 6, 7, 8, 9, A, B, C, D, E, F, 10. It is important to know about hexadecimal numbering because later in the book you will see numbers like 2EF8 and you will need to know that these are real numbers, not just some invented code. 2EF8 in hexadecimal is simply another way of writing 12024 in decimal (or 10111011111000 in binary). Sometimes a hexadecimal number has an h on the end to indicate that it is hexadecimal, so you might see 2EF8h; just ignore the h.

**TRY IT!**

**Use the Calculator in Windows (Start/Programs/Accessories/Calculator) to convert some numbers among decimal, hexadecimal, and binary. Display the Scientific features (View/Scientific), enter a number, and then click Hex, Dec, or Bin to convert to that format. The other option is Oct, for octal numbering (base 8).**

## Input, Processing, and Output

At their core, all computers are calculators. They accept numeric input, perform math operations on it, and produce output. A pocket calculator is a very simple computer. You press the buttons for the numbers you want to work with, press a button for a math operator such as plus or minus, and then press the Equals button to get the answer.

The computer on your desktop operates under the same basic principle. It accepts input from the keyboard or mouse, processes it, and sends it out to the monitor or other output device.

Of course, the data being moved through a PC is much more sophisticated than the data moving through a pocket calculator. Suppose, for example, that you key the letter K on the keyboard. Remember, each character is represented by eight bits (one byte), and the PC expects it to be in binary format. The keyboard converts the K to its binary equivalent and sends it on to the PC. The PC takes a look at the incoming K and figures out what to do with it—in this case, it needs to be routed to the video system. The video card receives the byte and tells the monitor to light up certain spots on the screen to form a shape that a human will recognize as a K; then you see a K on the screen (see Figure 1.5). The entire process takes only a few milliseconds, so it appears instantaneous.

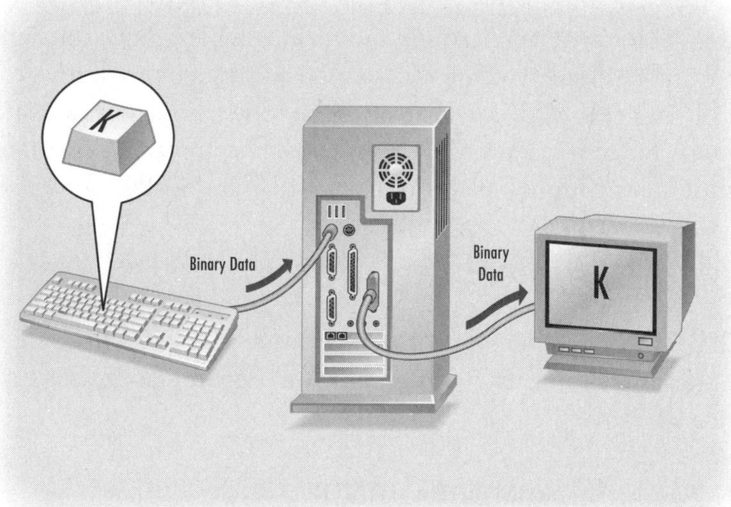


**FIGURE 1.5**
When you input a letter on the keyboard, the PC converts it to binary data, decides what to do with it, and produces output.

The input and output systems in a PC are very complex, and involve the cooperation of many hardware devices as well as several software programs. Some hardware can even function for both input and output (modems and network interface cards, for example). You will learn more about the flow of binary data through a PC and about specific input and output devices in later chapters.

### Hardware and Software

**Hardware**

Physical computer equipment such as drives, circuit boards, and silicon chips.

**Software**

Instructions that tell the hardware what to do, such as operating systems, device drivers, and applications.

**Firmware**

A combination of hardware and software, such as software that is permanently stored on a hardware chip.

The physical parts of the computer are known as *hardware*. The instructions that tell that hardware what to do are known as *software*.

In some computers the two functions are merged, with the instructions hard-coded into the hardware; this guards against the loss of the software in critical applications, and has been used successfully, for example, in NASA spacecraft. However, hard-coding the instructions into the hardware limits its flexibility, because you must get new hardware whenever you want it to do something differently.

A compromise between safety and flexibility is to include the instructions on a computer chip but make that chip replaceable or updatable with a special utility. This chip's instructions fall into an area between hardware and software that is known as *firmware*. Today's PCs use firmware to store certain critical startup data such as the Basic Input Output System (BIOS); most PDAs store their operating systems in firmware.

The majority of a PC's operations separate hardware from software entirely. When you start the PC, the BIOS tells the hardware to start and to copy the software into memory; then the software takes control of the PC and enables you to run applications and save data files. Since software is separate from hardware, you are free to buy and install new software without buying new hardware. There will be more about software later in this chapter, and also in upcoming chapters of the book. But first look at some of the most common pieces of hardware found in PCs today.

## A Look at a Typical Computer

This will be only a brief glimpse at the hardware that you will come to know in great detail in later chapters, but it is a good place to start if you are new to PC hardware.

### Looking at a PC from the Outside

Figure 1.6 shows a typical PC front view. From the front you can see:

- **Power button:** Turns the PC on/off
- **Floppy drive:** Accepts 3.5-inch floppy disks
- **CD drives**: Accept CDs of varying kinds
- **Power light:** Illuminates when the PC is on; remains lighted until it is turned off
- **Hard disk light:** Illuminates when the hard disk is being accessed; flashes while the hard disk reads or writes; goes out when there is no disk activity

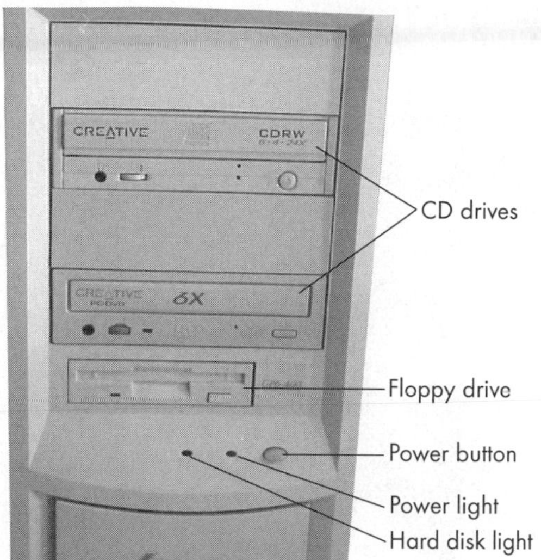


**FIGURE 1.6**
The Front of a Typical PC

Figure 1.7 shows the same PC from the back, from which you can see:

- **Fan vent:** Draws in air from the outside to cool the components inside
- **Power cord plug:** Accepts a standard three-prong power cord
- **Built-in ports:** Ports that come with the PC, for plugging in keyboard, mouse, and other standard devices
- **Expansion ports:** Ports that are added in expansion slots on the motherboard, not part of the base PC itself, such as video card or modem

## Removing the Cover

There are many PC case designs, each one with a cover that comes off a little differently. Especially in the last several years, major PC manufacturers have been using unusual case designs, so you may sometimes need to read the PC's manual to determine how to remove the cover.

On standard PC cases, however, you can usually remove the cover by removing screws around the edges of the PC—screws that appear to be holding the case on.

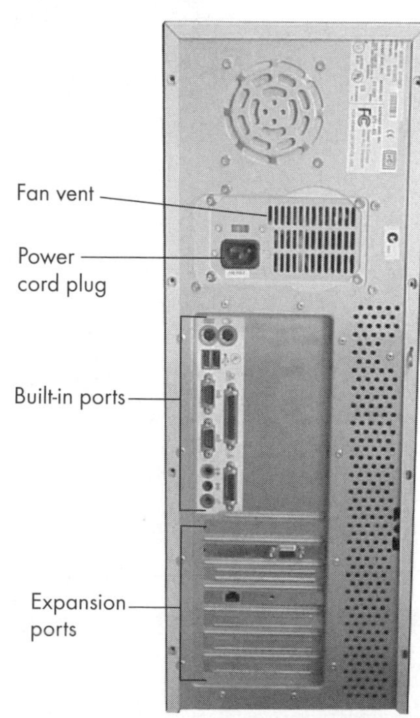


**FIGURE 1.7**
The Back of a Typical PC

For example, in Figure 1.8 you see many screws, but only one of them is on the cover.

This screw is holding the cover on

**FIGURE 1.8**
To remove the cover, first remove all screws holding it in place.

After removing any screws that are holding the cover, slide or lift it off. On some models you might need to slide it back a few inches and then lift. In Figure 1.9, for example, the cover has been slid back and is ready to be lifted off.

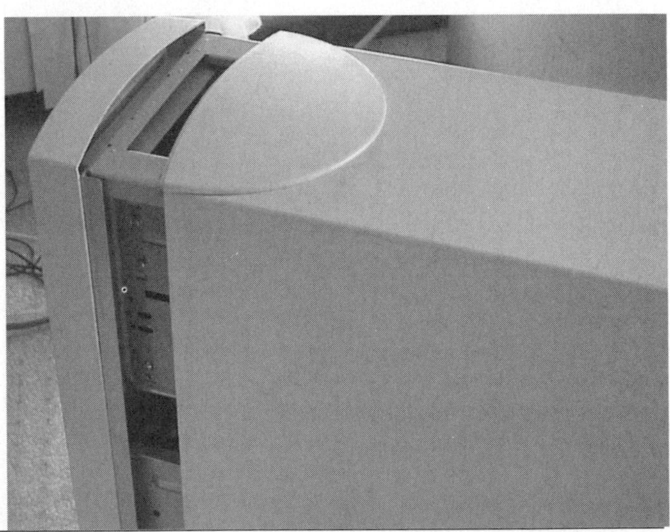

**FIGURE 1.9**
After removing the screws holding the cover, lift the cover off.

Some of the more modern cases use thumbscrews that don't require a screwdriver, or do without screws entirely. Some Dell PCs, for example, have buttons to push on the top and bottom of the case; when you push both simultaneously, the case pops open.

## In Real Life

Make sure you put the removed screws someplace safe and out of the way. You might want to place a small dish in your work area for holding removed screws.

## Identifying Key Components

When you remove the cover, you will find a complex system of circuit boards and cables inside, similar to those shown in Figure 1.10 and identified in Figure 1.11. The following sections will break down each area to show what each one contains.

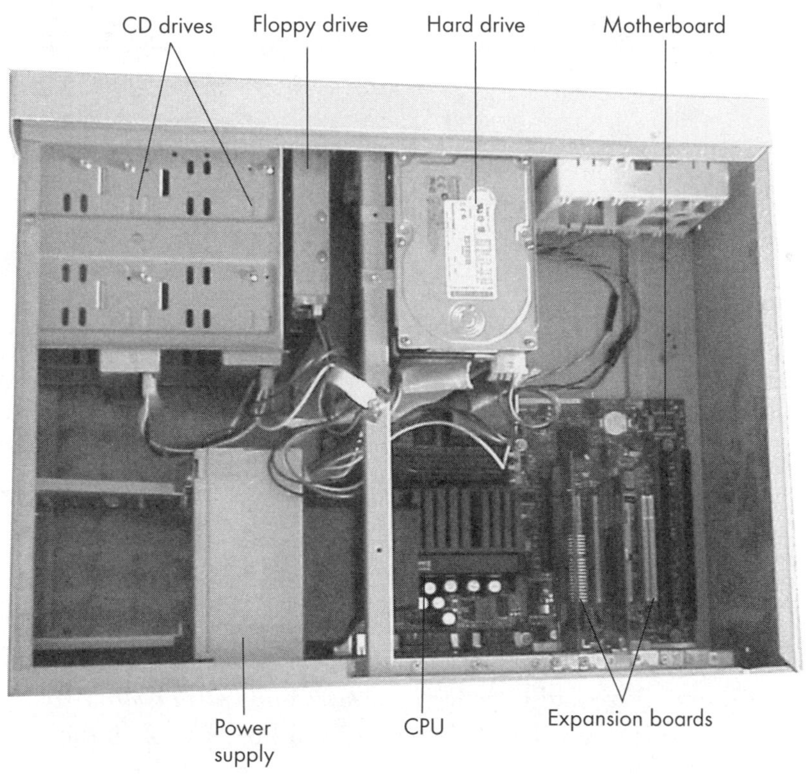


**FIGURE 1.10**
A Big-Picture View of the Inside of a PC

- **Motherboard:** This large circuit board is the focal point for the entire system. Everything else plugs into it. Also called system board.
- **Central Processing Unit (CPU):** This is the main chip on the computer; it performs all the math calculations for the entire system. In Figure 1.10 it is encased in a large rectangular cartridge. Also called microprocessor or processor.
- **CD and floppy drives:** These are accessible from outside of the PC, as you saw in Figure 1.5. Inside the PC, each drive is mounted in a drive bay.
- **Hard drive:** Not accessible from the outside, the hard drive can be mounted in any of several places in a case. At the bottom left corner of Figure 1.10 there is an empty rack that could hold several more hard drives.
- **Expansion boards:** Expansion boards fit into slots in the motherboard, adding capabilities to the system.
- **Power supply:** This large silver box converts the 110-volt AC power from the wall outlet to a variety of lower voltage DC specifications for various parts of the PC.

**FIGURE 1.11**
Parts Identified in Figure 1.10

The flat wide cables you see in Figure 1.10 are ribbon cables; these are used to connect drives to the motherboard. You will learn about them in Chapter 11, in the discussion about installing and configuring drives.

**TRY IT!**

Remove the cover from your PC and locate the components shown in Figure 1.10. Keep in mind that things might be arranged differently inside your PC than they are shown in the figure.

### *Motherboard*

**Motherboard**

The large circuit board in a PC that serves as the connecting point for all other components.

The large circuit board on the floor of the case is the *motherboard*, so called because all other components plug into it, and so are "children" of it. Other names for the motherboard include *main board* and *system board*.

It can be difficult to see the whole motherboard because of all the components installed on it, so Figure 1.12 shows a motherboard removed from the case, with only the CPU and memory installed. The components shown in Figure 1.12 are identified in Figure 1.13. You will learn more about motherboards in Chapter 4.

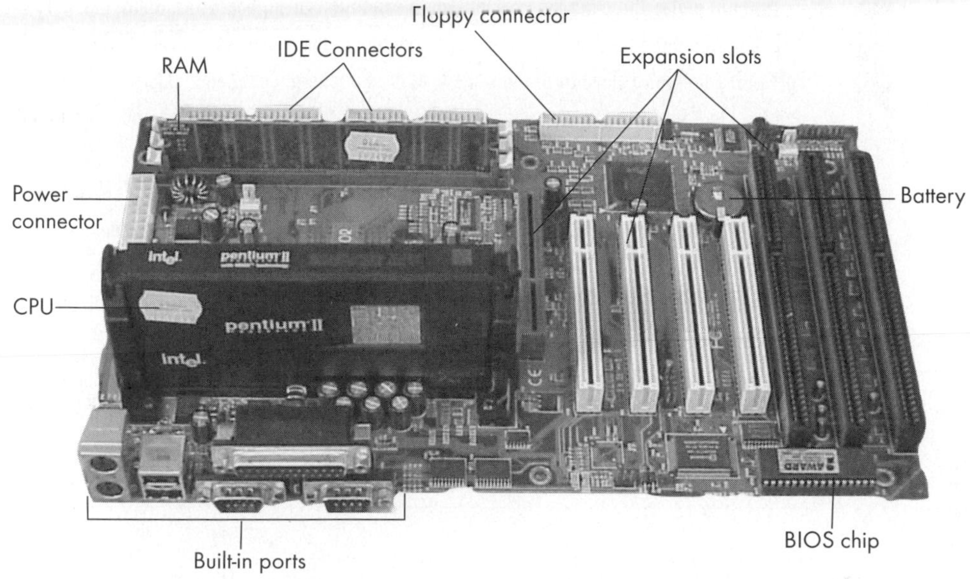


**FIGURE 1.12**
A Motherboard Removed from the Case

- **Power connector:** A group of wires runs from the power supply (see Figure 1.10) to this connection on the motherboard. Power supplies are covered in Chapter 3. Depending on the motherboard style, there may be a single connector with 20 wires or two connectors with six wires each.
- **Built-in ports:** These were also shown in Figure 1.7. As you can see, they are built directly into the side of the motherboard in this model. On some motherboards the ports are not physically built-in, but instead attach to the motherboard with cables. You will see the differences between motherboard styles in Chapter 4.
- **CPU:** The CPU cartridge in this example is a Pentium II. Other types of CPUs have very different packaging; some of them look like flat square chips, about 2 inches in size, mounted flat against the motherboard. You will learn more about CPUs in Chapter 5.
- **BIOS chip:** The BIOS, as noted earlier, is the software instruction used to start up the PC and interface with the hardware at a low level. That software is permanently stored on the BIOS chip. You can modify that instruction with a BIOS setup program, but your changes are not stored on the BIOS chip; they are stored on a separate complementary metal-oxide semiconductor (CMOS) chip. There will be more on this in Chapter 9.
- **Battery:** The battery provides a small amount of constant power to the motherboard, so that items that need to be always on (such as the system's date/time clock and the aforementioned CMOS chip) can stay that way even when the PC is unplugged. Motherboard battery issues will be addressed in Chapter 4.

**FIGURE 1.13**
Parts Identified in Figure 1.12

*continued*

- **Expansion slots:** These are the slots into which expansion circuit boards fit. Notice that in Figure 1.12 there are three types of slots. The single gray one in the center is an Accelerated Graphics Port (AGP) slot, for a video card. The white ones are Peripheral Component Interface (PCI) slots, and the black ones are Industry-Standard Architecture (ISA) slots. Not all motherboards have all of these slot types. Slot types are covered in Chapter 4.
- **RAM:** RAM stands for Random-Access Memory; this is the main memory in the PC. Most RAM today comes on mini circuit boards; the type shown in Figure 1.12 is a dual inline memory module (DIMM). You will learn about RAM in Chapter 6.
- **IDE connectors:** IDE stands for Integrated Device Electronics. A cable runs from an IDE connector to a CD drive or a hard drive. IDE devices are explained in Chapter 11.
- **Floppy connector:** A cable runs from the floppy connector to the floppy disk drive. Floppy drives are covered in Chapter 11.

**FIGURE 1.13**
***Continued***

## TRY IT!

Locate the parts shown in Figure 1.12 on your own PC. You might not have all of the same parts; for example, you might not have the same expansion slot types, and your CPU might look different.

### *CPU*

The CPU does all of the math calculations for the entire PC. Modern CPUs can process many millions of instructions per second; in Chapter 5 you will learn about the types of CPUs and their specifications.

There are two main shapes for CPUs—pin grid array (PGA) chips and single edge contact cartridges (SECCs). Figure 1.14 shows front and back views of a PGA chip; Figure 1.15 shows an SECC. The type you need depends on the type of motherboard you have.

FRONT

BACK

**FIGURE 1.14**
A PGA CPU. The back has a grid of pins that fit into holes in a socket on the motherboard.

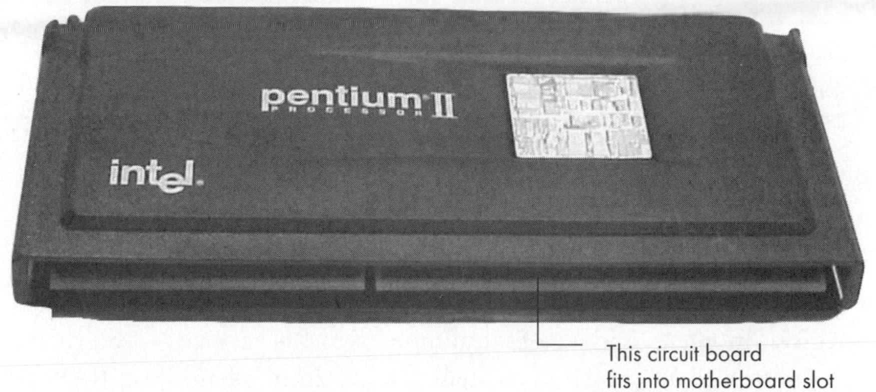


**FIGURE 1.15**
An SECC. Notice the circuit board sticking out of the bottom of the cartridge; it plugs into a slot on the motherboard.

When you are looking for the CPU on a motherboard, it might not look exactly like the ones shown in Figures 1.14 and 1.15 because there may be a cooling device attached to it. There are two main types of cooling devices: heat sinks and fans. A heat sink is a porcupine-like block that channels heat away from the CPU; a more familiar device is a small electric fan that cools the CPU. Some CPUs use a combination of both—a heat sink block with a fan mounted in the center. Figures 1.16 and 1.17 show the same CPUs shown in Figures 1.14 and 1.15, but with the heat sinks/fans attached.

**FIGURE 1.16**
A PGA CPU mounted on the motherboard, with a cooling fan on top.

**FIGURE 1.17**
An SECC CPU mounted on the motherboard, with a cooling fan and heat sink combination strapped to the side.

## TRY IT!

Locate your CPU. Which type of CPU does your PC have: SECC or PGA? Does it have a heat sink, a fan, or both?

### *RAM*

**Primary storage**

Short-term storage in a PC that is readily accessible, such as RAM.

**Volatile**

Not permanent; volatile storage loses its contents if it is not constantly refreshed.

Random-Access Memory (RAM) acts as short-term storage (also called *primary storage*) for the PC while it processes data. RAM keeps track of what programs and data files are open, what should appear on the screen at any given moment, and a great deal more. RAM is very fast—you can read or write from RAM much faster than you can from a hard disk. RAM is *volatile*, which means that whatever is stored there is only temporary; when you turn off the PC, RAM's content is erased. In Chapter 6 you will learn why this is so, as well as a number of other important details about RAM.

Physically, RAM on a motherboard looks like a small rectangular circuit board about 5.25 inches long. The type shown in Figure 1.18 is a dual inline memory module (DIMM); there is also an older, shorter kind called a single inline memory module (SIMM) that you might encounter in older PCs.

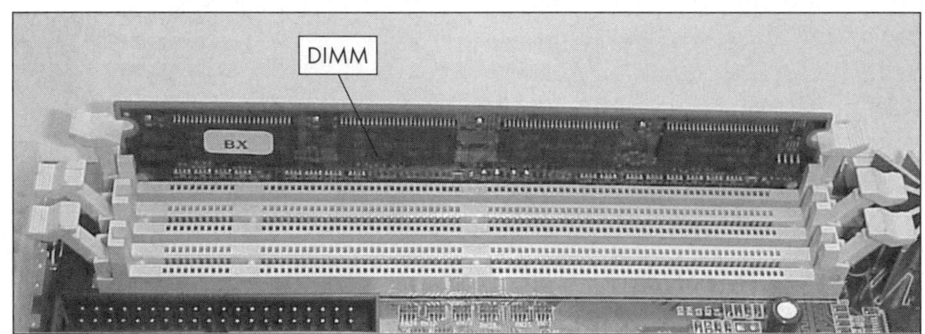


**FIGURE 1.18**
RAM is mounted in slots on a motherboard.

## TRY IT!

Locate the RAM in your PC. How many DIMMs or SIMMs are installed? How many slots for RAM are free?

### *CD Drive*

A CD drive is encased in a large silver box to prevent its drive mechanism from being damaged. Several types of CD drives are available on the market, including CD-ROM, DVD, CD-R, CD-RW, and so on, but they

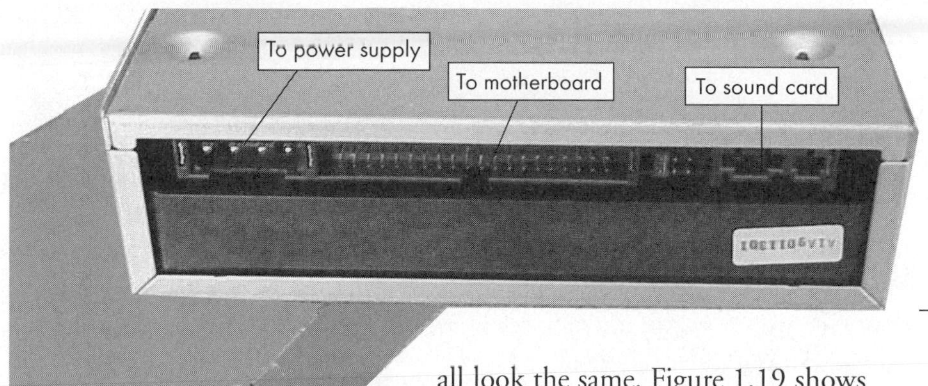


**FIGURE 1.19**
A CD Drive

all look the same. Figure 1.19 shows front and rear views of a CD drive removed from the case so you can get a better look at it. As noted in Figure 1.19, the back of the CD drive has several connectors. The drive receives power from the power supply, receives instructions from the motherboard, and plays audio CDs through the sound card. You can operate a CD drive without the audio cable running from the drive to the sound card, but it will not be able to play audio CDs. Chapter 13 is devoted to CD drives.

## In Real Life

CDs, floppy disks, and hard disks are all nonvolatile storage (secondary storage). In other words, whatever you place on a disk stays there, even after you shut off the PC. That is why it is important to save your work to disk before shutting down the PC—until you save, the data exists only in RAM. You probably already knew this, but it is worth remembering that not all the end users you will support as a professional PC technician will know it, so you will probably find yourself explaining it many times.

**Nonvolatile**
Permanent; non-volatile storage retains its data until it is explicitly changed; its content does not decay over time.

### *Floppy Drive*

The floppy drive is also encased in a metal box, but a smaller one than is needed for the CD drive. The modern 3.5" high-density floppy drive has been around for a long time, virtually unchanged for almost a decade in its appearance, specifications, and performance. A floppy drive has two connectors—one for the power supply and one that goes to the motherboard. The main difference between a floppy drive and most other drives is that the floppy drive uses a smaller type of four-wire power supply connector. Figure 1.20 shows both the front and rear of a floppy drive removed from the PC.

**Secondary Storage**
Storage in a PC that does not lose its content when the power goes off.

FIGURE 1.20
A Floppy Drive

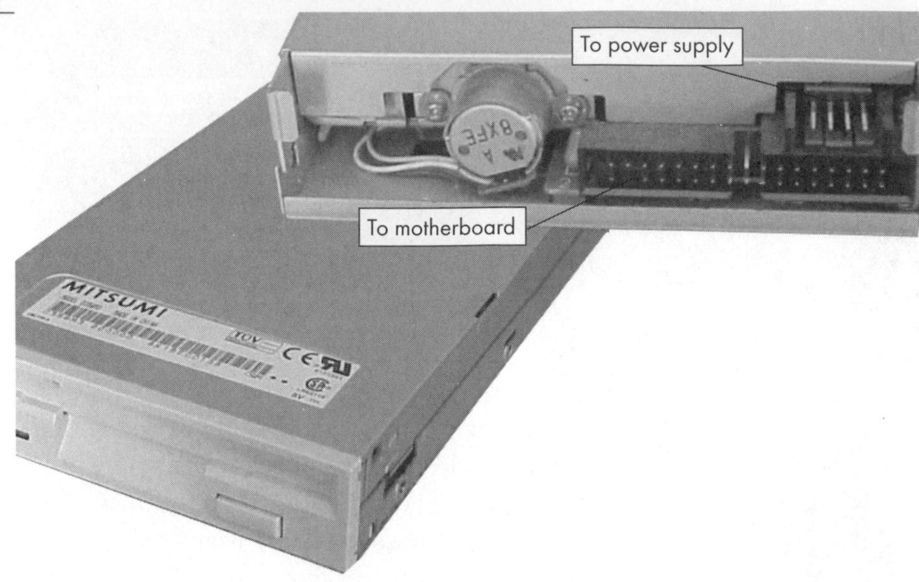


### *Hard Drive*

**Hard disk**

A stack of metal platters that store data; roughly synonymous with hard drive.

**Hard drive**

The read/write drive unit that controls a hard disk; roughly synonymous with hard disk.

A hard drive stores data inside the PC (except for external models, which are uncommon). Drives such as the CD and the floppy use removable disks, so the drive and the disk are separate. With a hard drive, however, you cannot remove the disk from the drive. You will often hear the terms *hard disk* and *hard drive* used interchangeably, or even *hard disk drive*.

Figure 1.21 shows the rear of a hard drive. It has the same connectors as the CD drive in Figure 1.19 except it lacks the connector for the sound card.

FIGURE 1.21
A Hard Drive

Hard drives look simple from the outside, but inside they are very complex; several chapters will be devoted to discussing them. See Chapter 10 for a general introduction to disk drives, Chapter 11 to learn about the interface between the motherboard and a hard drive, and Chapter 12 to learn how to configure and troubleshoot a hard drive.

Hard drives (and also CD drives) use two types of interfaces: Integrated Device Electronics (IDE) and Small Computer Systems Interface (SCSI). Most motherboards include IDE connectors, but not SCSI connectors; you must add an expansion card for SCSI device use. Most IDE hard drives are less expensive than SCSI drives, so the vast majority of systems have only IDE hard drives. SCSI drives tend to be faster and have advantages in situations where there are many hard drives on the same system, such as on file servers. You will learn about the differences between IDE and SCSI in Chapter 11.

## TRY IT!

**Locate and identify the various types of drives in your PC. Trace the cables that come out of them to determine what they are plugged into.**

### *Expansion Board*

Expansion boards are circuit boards that fit into expansion slots on the motherboard, adding some new or improved capability. Examples include modems, network interface cards, sound cards, and video cards. Figure 1.22, for example, shows a Network Interface Card (NIC). Notice that in addition to the circuit board, there is a metal backplate that fastens the card to the PC case, and on that backplate are any ports that need to be accessible. In the figure there is an RJ-45 connector for plugging in an Ethernet network cable. You will learn about network interface cards in Chapter 21 and network cables in Chapter 7.

**FIGURE 1.22**
**A Network Interface Card, an Example of an Expansion Board**

## In Real Life

The terms board and card are used interchangeably in the PC industry; both refer generically to any circuit board. You might hear an item called an expansion board, a circuit card, or any combination of those words; they are all the same thing.

The expansion board interacts with the motherboard according to the conventions of the type of slot it plugs into. As you saw in Figure 1.12, most motherboards include several different slot types (AGP, PCI, and ISA), and each slot type has its own pathway to the CPU, called an *expansion bus*. Chapter 4, which covers motherboards, will look at the various types of expansion slots in great detail, including their specifications and advantages/disadvantages.

**Expansion bus**

A pathway from the main system bus to an expansion slot such as an ISA, PCI, or AGP slot.

## TRY IT!

Identify as many as you can of the expansion boards installed in your PC. You probably have a video card; what else? Some systems do not have a video card; the video card capability is built into the motherboard.

### *Power Supply*

The *power supply* is essential because the motherboard cannot use 110-volt AC electricity. It requires a much lower voltage (around 3v to 12v), and it requires direct current (DC). The power supply takes in the electricity from the wall outlet, converts it, and sends the appropriate voltages to each device attached to it. Each different colored wire supplies a different voltage or performs a unique monitoring or management task. For example, all the red wires supply +5v current, and all the black wires are for grounding purposes.

**Power supply**

The electricity converter in a PC that steps down the voltage and converts the power to DC current for system use.

The power supply mounts inside the back wall of the PC case, so that its fan and plug stick out the back. Inside, a tangle of colored wires emerges from the power supply, leading to various types of connectors. In Chapter 3 you will learn about the types of power supplies, the types of connectors, and the voltages they supply. Figure 1.23 shows a power supply removed from the PC case, but you will probably buy the case and power supply as a set, with the power supply already installed.

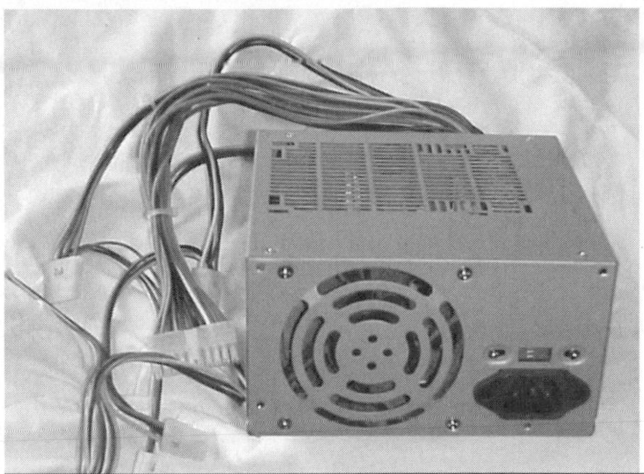

**FIGURE 1.23**
A Power Supply, Removed from the PC Case

## Notebook PCs

**Notebook PC**

A portable computer roughly the size and shape of a writing tablet or notebook.

*Notebook PCs* (also called portable or laptop PCs) have the same basic parts as their desktop equivalents, but everything is smaller and more lightweight (and also more expensive!). There are also some extra slots and sockets for laptop-only features such as PC Card devices. Figure 1.24 shows a typical notebook PC in overview; you will see this same PC in greater detail in Chapter 20, where you will also learn how to take it apart for upgrades and repairs. Some of the key features of the notebook PC are identified in Figure 1.25.

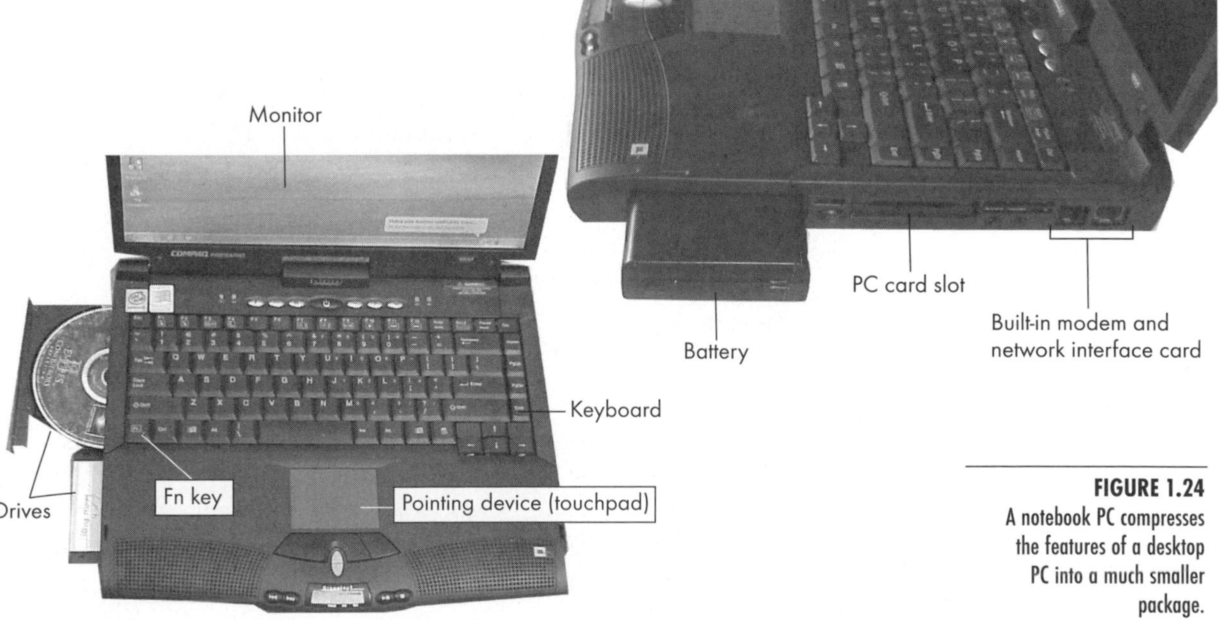


**FIGURE 1.24**
A notebook PC compresses the features of a desktop PC into a much smaller package.

- **Monitor:** Notebook PCs typically have a built-in Liquid Crystal Display (LCD) monitor; you can also attach external monitors.
- **Keyboard:** The keyboard of a notebook PC is also built in, but you can attach an external keyboard if you prefer. The keyboard contains a special function key, the Fn key, that you can press in conjunction with the normal function keys (F1 through F12) for machine-specific activities such as changing the display contrast.
- **Pointing device:** Instead of a mouse, most notebook PCs include some sort of mouse alternative. The model in Figure 1.24 has a touchpad; others have a pointing stick (which looks like the top of a pencil eraser) mounted in the center of the keyboard. You can attach an external mouse if you prefer.
- **Drives:** Almost all notebook PCs today have built-in floppy and CD drives; some older or ultra-lightweight models may have external drives that you attach only when you need them.
- **PC Card slot:** This interface enables the use of PC Card (PCMCIA) devices, which are like expansion boards but in the size and shape of a stack of credit cards.
- **Battery:** Notebook PCs have a battery for use when AC power is not available. A typical battery lasts about two to six hours on a charge.
- **Built-in devices:** Notebook PCs typically have devices built in that would be expansion boards in a desktop PC. These may include video card, modem, network interface card, and sound card. Figure 1.24 shows the modem and network plugs on the side of the notebook PC.

**FIGURE 1.25**
Some Key Features of a Notebook PC

## Personal Digital Assistants (PDAs)

**Personal digital assistant (PDA)**

A hand-held computer with a touch-sensitive screen, used for storing contact information, schedules, and memos, and for running simple applications.

*Personal digital assistants (PDAs)* are increasingly popular among people who need to perform simple computing tasks on the move. A PDA is a very small computer, even smaller than a notebook PC. Typically it has a touch-sensitive screen on which you write with a stylus. Most people do not try to use a PDA for any complex computing tasks. They use it for storing addresses and appointments and for jotting down memos, but it cannot rival a real PC in features. Figure 1.26 shows a Palm brand PDA and points out some of its physical landmarks.

So what is the difference between a PDA and a PC? Generally a PDA does not have a keyboard large enough to type on, while a PC does. This is just a guideline, however, because add-on keyboards are available for most PDAs and some models of notebook PC use a stylus rather than a keyboard. PDAs also use a different operating system than notebook and desktop PCs. There are two popular operating systems for PDAs today: Palm OS and Windows CE.

You do not need to know very much about PDAs to pass the A+ exam, beyond the basic anatomy and operation. Chapter 20 will provide all the facts you need to study.

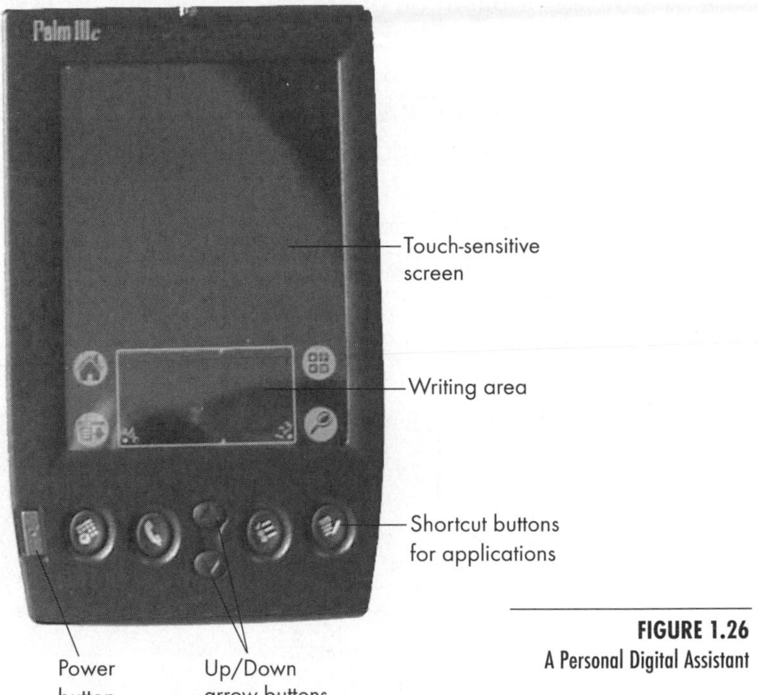


**FIGURE 1.26**
A Personal Digital Assistant

## Software

Earlier in the chapter you learned that hardware is the physical part of the computer—all the circuit boards, casings, silicon chips, and so on. Software is the logical part—the lines of instruction code that tell the hardware what to do when certain input occurs.

### BIOS

At the most basic level is the Basic Input Output System (BIOS). It is software in the sense that it is a set of instructions, but since it is permanently stored on a chip in the PC, technically it is firmware. The BIOS tells the PC some very basic facts about itself and provides instructions for handling the most elementary input and output functions, such as how to accept input from the keyboard. It also contains instructions for starting everything up when you press the Power button.

Periodically BIOS manufacturers release updates to their product. Since the BIOS instructions are permanently stored on the chip, in the early days of PC technology it was difficult to obtain the updates; you had to order a new chip and physically replace the old one. However, today a technology known as flashing can be used to run a special setup utility that updates the information stored on a BIOS chip. The BIOS chips with this capability are known as Electrically Erasable Programmable Read-Only Memory (EEPROM). Flashing, and BIOSes in general, will be examined in Chapter 9.

Another potential difficulty with BIOS was that it could not be modified by the end user to account for different hardware configurations. For example, the default BIOS settings tell the PC that it has one floppy drive; some systems have two. To allow for hardware changes, as well as modifications to the other default BIOS settings, a second chip was added to the mix: complementary metal-oxide semiconductor (CMOS). Any changes to the default BIOS settings are stored on the CMOS chip. Like regular RAM, the CMOS chip requires constant electrical power in order to maintain the information stored on it, but it employs a very small amount and can draw it from the motherboard's battery. Users can make changes to the BIOS settings through a BIOS setup program, like the one shown in Figure 1.27, and those changes are stored on the CMOS chip. When the PC boots, it first loads the settings from BIOS, and then applies any exceptions to them from the CMOS.

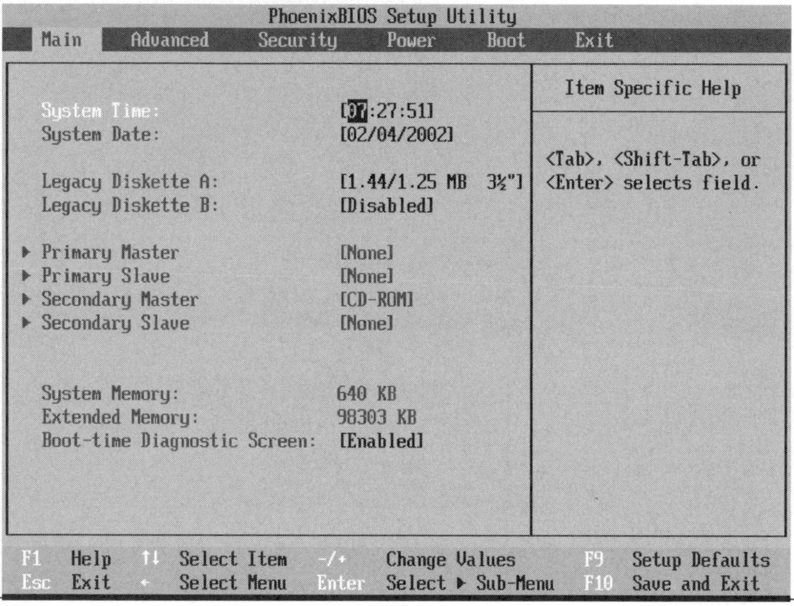

**FIGURE 1.27**

BIOS settings control the low-level software that interacts directly with the hardware.

## Operating System

The next level up is the operating system (OS). The OS keeps the PC running as you work and tells the devices what roles to play. It tells the video card what codes to pass on to the monitor for display in response to the input it receives from input devices. It tells the disk drives when to start and stop spinning and what data needs to be retrieved; then it tells the circuitry in the motherboard which data to store in memory and which data can safely be dumped. The operating system handles hundreds of critical housekeeping functions.

There are two basic types of user interfaces in operating systems: *command line* and *graphical user interface* (GUI). Microsoft Windows, shown in Figure 1.28, is a GUI interface; MS-DOS, shown in Figure 1.29, is a command line interface. A GUI operating system relies on pictures, menus, and a pointing device such as a mouse for user control. A command prompt requires the user to key text-based commands.

Although Windows' native functionality is as a GUI, you can also open a command prompt from within Windows, and key text-based commands there. This comes in handy when you need to issue certain commands that require a complex string of text to be keyed.

The A+ Operating System Technologies Examination focuses mainly on Microsoft Windows; Part 6 of this book is devoted to Microsoft Windows. However, you must also know some basics about working with command prompts for that exam; you will learn the essentials in Chapter 29.

**Command line**

A user interface based on keying text-based commands at a prompt; MS-DOS is one example. Can also refer to the command prompt itself.

**Graphical user interface (GUI)**

A user interface based on pictures and on pointing and clicking with a mouse; Windows is one example.

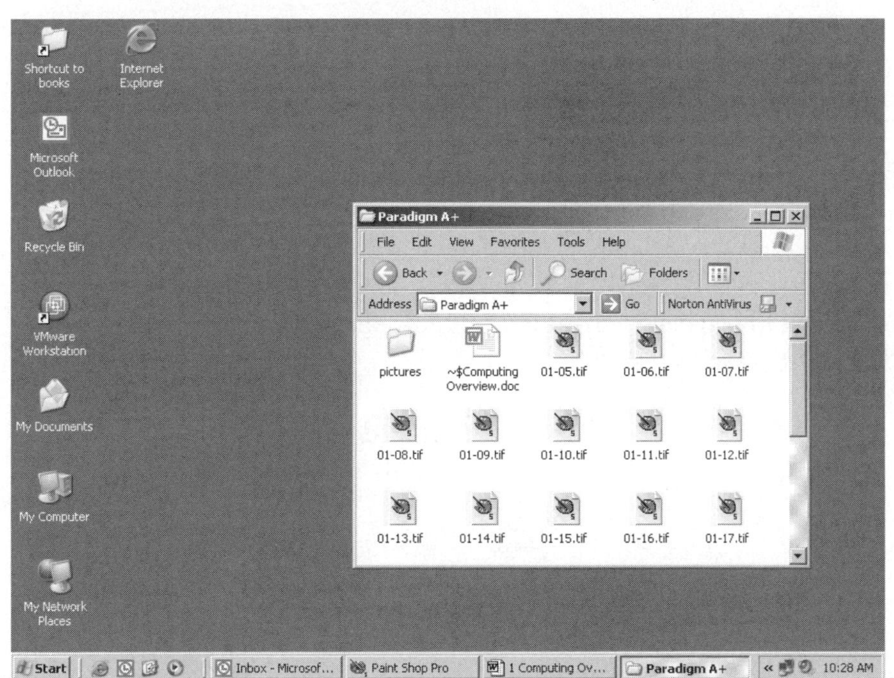


**FIGURE 1.28**
Windows is a GUI operating system.

```
C:\>cd ..

C:\>cd games

C:\games>dir /w
 Volume in drive C has no label.
 Volume Serial Number is 07D0-0815

 Directory of C:\games

[.]                     [..]                    BAM2.BAT
BAM2.BMP                GETKEY.EXE              INSTALL.BAT
INSTALL.PIF             bm2demo.zip             nh322NTi.zip
ASCIPUZL                CHKLIST.MS              HISCORES.3D
SOLWIN.EXE              WINBR.ZIP               WINCARDS.DLL
WINSPIDR.EXE            BAM2.PIF                elfbowl1.exe
snowcraf.exe            [BAM2DEMO]              [videopok]
[Frac]                  [GOLDMINE]              [WORDPUZL]
[WORDLE]                [TXTTRIS]               [TETRIS]
[SQUARE]                [RUM500.000]            [NEWGAMES]
[MONTECAR]              [MINERVGA]              [HUGECAVE]
[HEX]                   [DARNIT]                [CWDELUXE]
[CHINESE]               [Brkfre]                [BAKGAMON]
[astro]                 [Tyrreg]                [Adventure games]
[nethack 3.3]           [pokemon]               [Nethack for Windows]
[mameroms]              [wep]                   README.TXT
              18 File(s)      9,368,576 bytes
              30 Dir(s)  27,077,902,336 bytes free

C:\games>_
```

**FIGURE 1.29**
A command prompt is an older style of interacting with an operating system.

## APPLICATIONS

**Application**

Software that performs a useful end-user task such as creating a document or playing a game.

The final level of software consists of *applications*—programs that enable you to do something useful with the computer. The BIOS and OS are just overhead; the applications provide a reason for owning the PC. Applications can include word processors, spreadsheet programs, database programs, games, Internet browsers, e-mail readers, and so on. Figure 1.30 shows several applications running in Windows. To pass the A+ exam, you do not need to study any one application in particular, but you should know how to install and remove applications from Windows and how to troubleshoot problems in running applications. Chapter 28 can help you develop these skills.

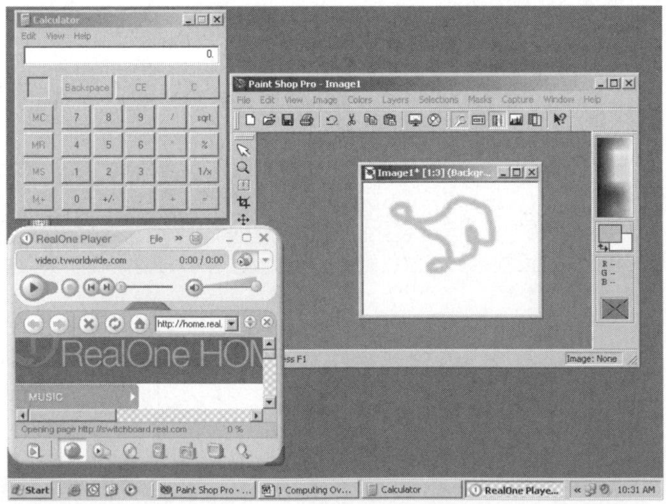


**FIGURE 1.30**
Applications run within the operating system.

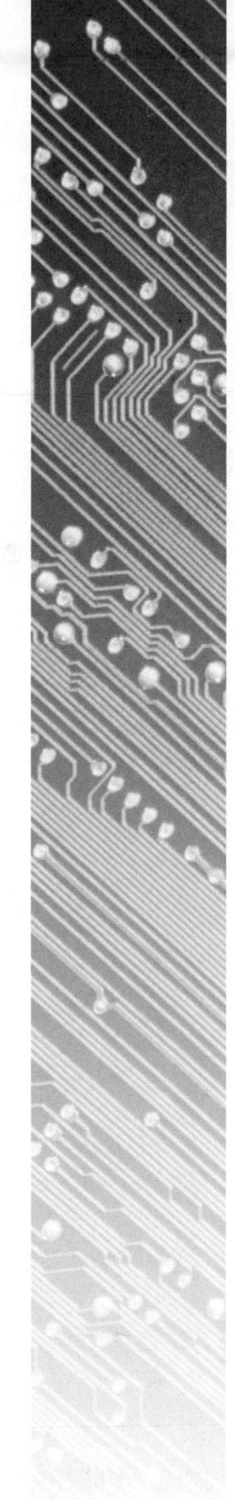

# STUDY GUIDE

This first chapter has provided a general overview of personal computers, to provide a review for those already familiar with the systems, and to introduce the subject to students who might not have had previous experience with computer hardware.

## How Computers Work

- Computers are digital; they rely on numbers for everything they do. The opposite of digital is analog.
- Data moving through a PC goes through three phases: input, processing, and output.
- The physical parts of a computer are hardware; the instruction sets that tell the hardware what to do are software.
- PCs do not use normal base-10 numbers; instead they use binary (base-2) numbers for data processing. Binary numbers consist of only 1s and 0s.
- PCs use hexadecimal numbers for memory addressing. Hexadecimal is base-16; in addition to normal digits these numbers also use letters A through F as digits. Sometimes people put an h on the end of a hexadecimal number to identify it as such.
- A bit is a binary digit—a single 0 or 1 in binary numbering. There are 8 bits in a byte.

## Computer Hardware

- To remove the cover from a PC case, you will probably need to remove some screws. Look for the screws around the edge of the case. Some cases do not use screws; one alternate system utilizes pushbuttons.
- The motherboard is the large circuit board inside the PC; everything else plugs into it.
- The Central Processing Unit (CPU) performs all the math calculations for the entire system. It can either be a 2-inch square chip (a pin grid array, or PGA) or a 5.5-inch long plastic cartridge (a Single Edge Contact Cartridge, or SECC).
- Random-Access Memory (RAM) stores data while the PC is turned on. It is stored on small rectangular circuit boards called dual inline memory modules (DIMMs) or single inline memory modules (SIMMs).

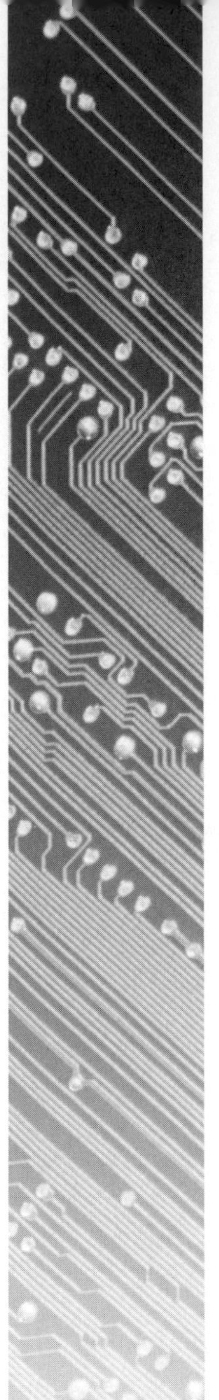

- The power supply converts 110-volt AC current from the wall to the much lower DC voltages required by the parts of the PC. Different parts require different voltages; each different colored wire provides a different voltage or service.
- Motherboards have expansion slots for plugging in expansion boards. These are circuit cards that add new capabilities to a system.

### Drives

- A CD drive receives power from the power supply and instructions from the motherboard. It also may have a cable that connects it to the sound card for playing audio CDs.
- A floppy drive uses a type of power supply connector different from most of the other drive types.
- A hard disk is similar in its connectors to a CD drive. Since its drive unit and disk are not separable, the terms *hard disk* and *hard drive* are synonymous.
- There are two types of hard disk interfaces: Integrated Device Electronics (IDE) and Small Computer Systems Interface (SCSI).
- Most motherboards have IDE connectors, but SCSI requires an expansion board.

### Types of Computers

- A desktop PC is the typical nonportable PC found in most homes and offices. The keyboard, pointing device, monitor, and case are all separate items.
- A notebook PC is a portable PC. It typically has a built-in monitor, a built-in pointing device, an Fn key, a PC Card slot, and a battery, none of which are present on a desktop PC.
- A personal digital assistant (PDA) is a hand-held computer with a touch-sensitive screen rather than a keyboard.

## BIOS

- BIOS stands for Basic Input Output System. The BIOS chip on the motherboard contains the startup instructions for the PC.
- The data stored on the BIOS chip is permanent, but if the BIOS chip is an Electrically Erasable Programmable Read-Only Memory (EEPROM) chip, it can be updated using a special utility program.

- Any exceptions to the BIOS's "rules" are stored on the complementary metal-oxide semiconductor (CMOS) chip on the motherboard. It draws a small amount of power from the motherboard battery to retain its settings.

### Operating Systems and Applications

- The operating system (OS) performs housekeeping tasks that keep the PC running and provides an interface between the end user and the hardware.
- Windows is a graphical user interface (GUI) operating system, which means it relies on pictures and a pointing device for user interaction.
- MS-DOS is a command line operating system. Users key text-based commands at a command prompt to tell the operating system what to do.
- Applications are software programs that perform specific useful functions for the end user. People buy computers in order to use applications to do such things as write letters, play games, develop spreadsheets, and so on.

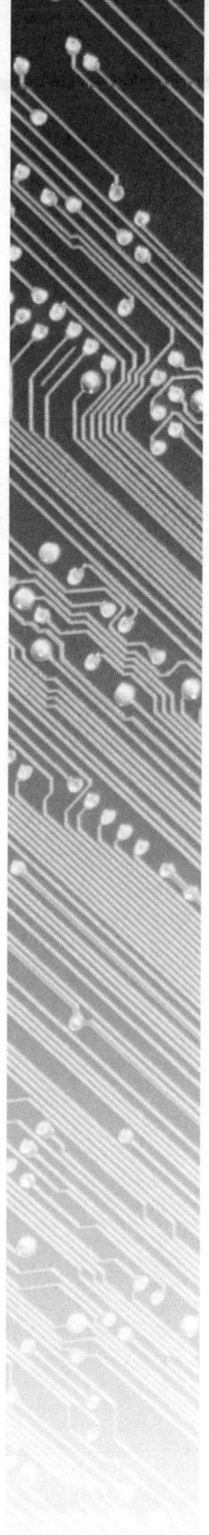

## PRACTICE TEST

On a blank sheet of paper, write the answers to the following multiple-choice questions and explain why the answer is correct.

1. When a modem sends data from the PC over a telephone line, what does it need to do in order for the phone line to be able to carry it?
   a. convert digital to analog
   b. convert analog to digital
   c. convert binary to decimal
   d. convert decimal to hexadecimal

2. Which of these are input devices?
   a. CPU and keyboard
   b. keyboard and mouse
   c. CPU and speakers
   d. CPU and keyboard

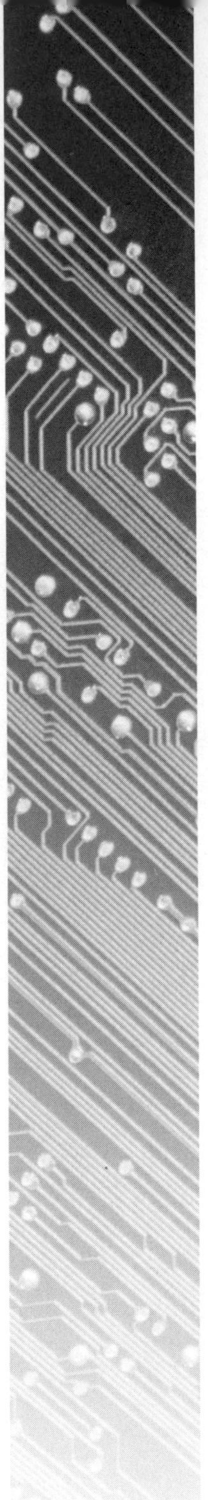

3. Which numbering system does the number 1001h use?
   a. binary
   b. decimal
   c. hexadecimal
   d. Cannot tell from information given

4. Which numbering system does the number 9837 use?
   a. binary
   b. decimal
   c. hexadecimal
   d. Cannot tell from information given

5. Which of these binary numbers has the correct number of digits to represent a whole, single byte?
   a. 0110101
   b. 11001
   c. 10101100
   d. 101110001

6. A light on the front of your PC flashes intermittently as the PC operates. What does that light represent?
   a. hard disk access
   b. power
   c. memory access
   d. video access

7. Firmware is
   a. software stored on a chip.
   b. software stored on a hard disk.
   c. another name for hardware.
   d. hardware that requires software to control it.

8. A heat sink
   a. draws heat from other components into the CPU, keeping it warm.
   b. draws heat away from the CPU, keeping it cool.
   c. converts AC current into heat, keeping the CPU warm.
   d. discharges negative icons that dissipate heat.

9. On an AT-style power supply you see several large four-wire connectors, two small four wire connectors, and two six-wire connectors. What do the six-wire connectors plug into?
   a. floppy drives
   b. motherboard
   c. hard drives
   d. None of the above

10. How is a hard disk different from a hard drive?
    a. A hard disk has a smaller capacity than a hard drive.
    b. A hard disk has a larger capacity than a hard drive
    c. A hard disk is removable from its casing; a hard drive is not.
    d. They are the same thing.

11. A CD drive and a hard drive both have the same power and IDE connectors; what does the CD drive have that the hard drive does not?
    a. an audio cable connector
    b. a floppy drive connector
    c. a capacity selector switch
    d. a voltage regulator switch

12. Which of these is not a type of slot for an expansion board on a motherboard?
    a. ISA
    b. IDE
    c. AGP
    d. PCI

13. Which of the following does a power supply do? Choose as many as apply.
    a. converts DC to AC power
    b. converts AC to DC power
    c. provides reduced-voltage (+12v and less) power to system devices
    d. both b and c

14. What is the purpose of the Fn key on a typical notebook PC?
    a. special activities in combination with the function keys (F1 through F12)
    b. special activities in combination with the numeric keypad (0 through 9)
    c. places the notebook PC in Suspend mode for battery savings
    d. toggles between internal and external keyboard

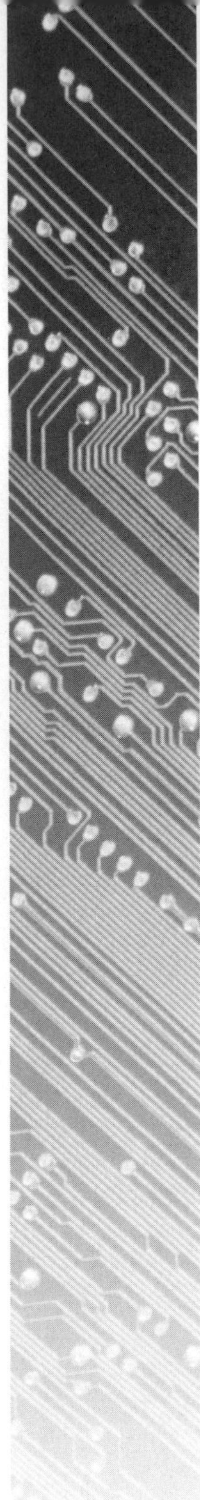

15. Notebook PCs provide support for PC Card devices. Which desktop PC feature is equivalent to the PC card slot on a notebook?
    a. battery backup
    b. processor
    c. RAM
    d. expansion slot

16. PDA stands for
    a. personal digital assistant
    b. personal device authority
    c. public digital authority
    d. pretty darn awful

17. Which is true about BIOS and CMOS?
    a. They both refer to the same chip.
    b. The BIOS setup program writes user changes to CMOS.
    c. The CMOS is updatable only through a BIOS update utility.
    d. The BIOS uses the motherboard battery to retain its content.

18. What is an EEPROM?
    a. a CMOS chip that is user-updatable
    b. a type of CPU
    c. a BIOS chip that must be physically replaced to update it
    d. a BIOS chip that can be updated using a special utility

19. GUI stands for
    a. graphical uninterruptible interface.
    b. general utility installation.
    c. general utility interface.
    d. graphical user interface.

20. Which of the following are nonvolatile storage?
    a. RAM and CPU
    b. hard disk and floppy disk
    c. RAM and floppy disk
    d. RAM and hard disk

## TROUBLESHOOTING

1. The display on your notebook PC is very dim, without much contrast. How would you adjust it?
2. You have an older PDA, one of the original Palm III devices. You want to install a program on it that requires a higher version of the operating system than it has. What could you do?
3. When you start up your computer, you see a message that says something about an error at a certain hexadecimal address. Which hardware component would you suspect first?

## CUSTOMER SERVICE

1. A friend just got a new computer, and you must explain to her over the telephone how to hook it up. Describe the connectors for keyboard, mouse, monitor, and speakers in a way that a novice would understand them.
2. The same friend now has the computer hooked up, but when she presses the power button, nothing happens. What kinds of things could you suggest to check?
3. Now the friend sees some text on the screen, and the PC seems to be starting up normally, but then a Keyboard Error message appears. What are some possible causes?

## FOR MORE INFORMATION

For links to Web sites that provide further information about the topics covered in this chapter, go to the EMC/Paradigm Internet Resource Center at www.emcp.com/College Division/Internet Resource Centers/PC Maintenance/For More Information.

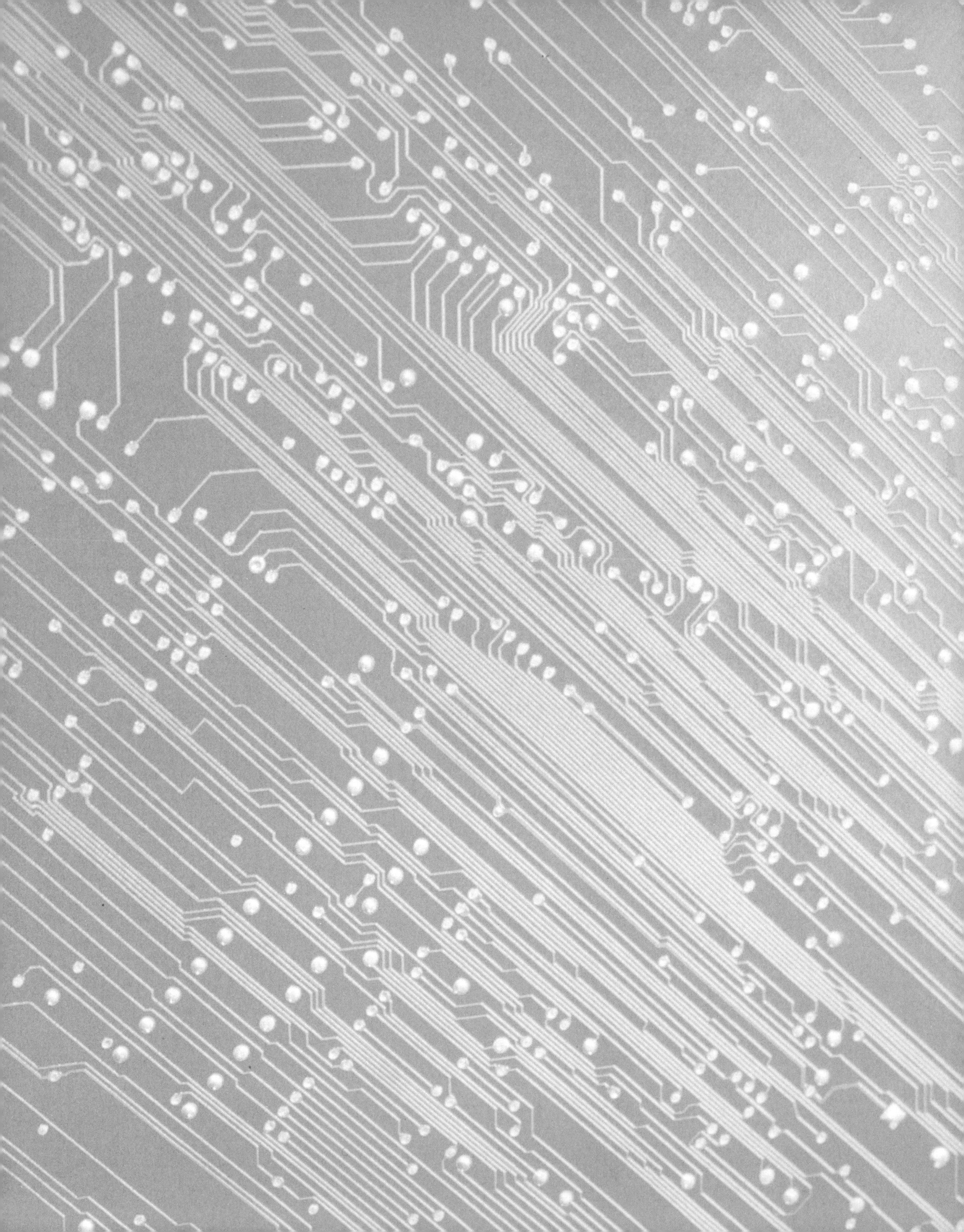

# 2 Safety and Preventive Maintenance

## ON THE TEST

**A+ Core Hardware Service Technician Examination**

- **Objective 3.1:** Identify the purpose of various types of preventive maintenance products and procedures and when to use them.
- **Objective 3.2:** Identify issues, procedures, and devices for protection within the computing environment, including people, hardware and the surrounding workspace.
- **Objective 5.2:** Identify care and service techniques and common problems with primary printer types.

## ON THE JOB

It is important to know how to handle, clean, and maintain PC hardware, not only because you, personally, will be doing those things but also because, as a professional PC technician, you will be the expert to whom others turn for advice on these matters. By learning the proper procedures for protecting yourself, the environment, and the PC components from harm, you can save yourself from costly and embarrassing mistakes.

Some of the tasks you might perform in this area include the following:

- setting up a safe work area for repairing PCs
- providing safety advice to end users
- troubleshooting cable problems involving electromagnetic interference
- cleaning PCs and related equipment

## Protecting Yourself from Electrical Shock

The most important precaution when working on PCs is simply to use ordinary care with electricity. Most people are aware of the basic rules:

- Keep fingers away from sockets.
- Make sure the power cord and all extension cords are in good repair.
- Do not string extension cords together to force a single outlet to support more devices than it can realistically handle (typically no more than six devices per two-plug outlet).
- Keep electrical devices away from water.

The voltage supplied to individual circuit boards inside the PC is very low, so touching circuit boards or chips will cause a person no harm. The only part of the PC that can deliver any noticeable shock is the power supply, which is discussed in the following section. The other major danger is from the monitor, discussed in the section after that.

### Power Supply Precautions

On a PC, the power supply (Figure 2.1) is the central point for electricity intake and distribution. A power cord runs from the wall outlet to the back of the power supply. The power supply stores the 110-volt current from the wall outlet in its *capacitors*, steps down the voltage, and apportions it to various system components. It is relatively safe for humans to interact with the power supply, as long as it remains assembled. Treat the power supply box as a single part—if anything about it goes bad, replace the entire power supply rather than try to disassemble and repair it. The reason for this is that the power supply's capacitors retain an electrical charge even after it is unplugged, and can deliver a nasty shock.

**Capacitor**

An electronic device that stores electrical charge and then releases it as needed.

**FIGURE 2.1**
A Power Supply from a Typical PC

Always unplug the power supply before working on a PC. Some technicians do not adhere to this rule; they leave the power cord connected because it has a grounding wire in it that can help prevent damage to the PC from electrostatic discharge (ESD), also known as static electricity. However, leaving the power connected can introduce new hazards to the PC because of the "on" state of some motherboard components whenever the PC is plugged in, and it can also leave a person more vulnerable to electrical shock. There are other ways of protecting the PC against ESD, which are covered later in this chapter.

## Monitor Precautions

The primary danger for electrical shock does not come from the PC itself but from the monitor. (The reference here is to regular monitors—the big boxy kind—not to flat-panel monitors like those in notebook PCs.) As mentioned earlier, the PC's power supply has capacitors that store an electrical charge of around 110 volts—enough to hurt a person, but usually not enough to kill. A monitor has a much larger capacitor, storing as much as 30,000 volts, and as with other capacitors, it doesn't lose its charge immediately when the monitor is unplugged. A monitor can remain unplugged for years and still retain a charge in the capacitor. Put simply, a person who gets shocked by the capacitor in a monitor is likely to die from it.

There is good reason, therefore, for the average PC technician to avoid working on monitors. This skill is not a requirement for earning the A+ certification or even to hold the vast majority of jobs in the PC repair field. If someone inexperienced must open up a monitor for repairs, the person should do so under the supervision of an experienced technician.

Unless something has been dropped down inside one of the vent cracks, there are very few reasons even to remove the cover from a monitor. There are some focus controls inside the cover that can be adjusted to correct a fuzzy display, but these can be difficult for an inexperienced technician to regulate effectively. Most good-quality monitors sold today have display controls that can be adjusted while the monitor is on and do not require removal of the cover. Chapter 16 discusses display quality problems and how to troubleshoot them.

WARNING

**Do not wear an antistatic wrist strap (covered later in the chapter) when working on monitors. These straps are designed to conduct static electricity through your body and away from the PC components, but can make it easier for dangerous high-voltage electricity to pass through the body as well.**

Inside a monitor, the critical part to stay away from is the suction cup with a wire running out of it. Beneath that suction cup is a high-voltage anode, which is the part that can deliver a death blow. Before work can be done on a monitor, this capacitor must be discharged. Though in theory all technicians should know how to do this, it is *not* a recommended practice. Chapter 16 discusses this further.

## Protecting Yourself from Other Dangers

There are other hazards besides electric shock when working on PCs. Figure 2.2 offers some safety tips.

- Do not wear jewelry made of metal that conducts electricity.
- Do not wear jewelry that dangles, such as hoop earrings or a necklace; it could get caught on something.
- Be careful not to stab or scratch yourself on the sharp metal pieces that stick out of many circuit boards.
- Avoid picking up a PC case by its frame when the cover is off, because some of the bars on the case might not be well secured and could come off.
- Because some PC cases have sharp metal edges inside them, use care when putting a hand down inside a PC case.
- Do not attempt to thwart built-in safeguards for laser devices. The lasers inside laser printers and CD drives can harm a person's eyes. Virtually all devices have safeguards built in so that the laser will not operate when the device is open or disassembled.
- Do not leave circuit boards lying on the floor where someone could step on them.

**FIGURE 2.2**
Safety Tips

## TRY IT!

Explore your work environment and look for possible hazards. Check your clothing, jewelry, and work area and identify and correct any problems you find.

## Putting Out Electrical Fires

Most technicians will never run into a fire caused by computer equipment, but it is always best to be prepared.

There are three classes of fire extinguishers:

- A for wood and paper fires
- B for flammable liquid, such as kitchen grease
- C for electrical fires

Of these, only the Class C extinguisher is appropriate for putting out a computer fire. Many fire extinguishers support multiple classes; it should not be difficult to find an extinguisher with an A-B-C rating that works on all fire types.

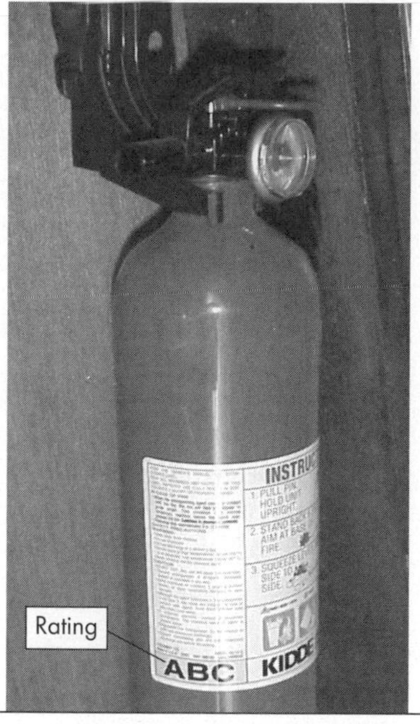


**FIGURE 2.3**
A Fire Extinguisher Rated for A, B, and C Class Fires

## TRY IT!

Locate the fire extinguisher nearest to your work area and read its label. What is its class rating?

## Protecting the Computer from Harm

Though warnings are necessary, do not be too disturbed by the discussion of fires and electrocution. Serious injury from working on a PC is actually fairly rare. It is far easier for a person to hurt the PC than to hurt himself or herself. The following sections explain some ways that humans can inadvertently harm computer components.

## Temperature

As a PC operates, certain components (such as the CPU) become hot, and cooling fans and heat sinks help channel the heat away. The cooler the room in which the PC sits, the easier it is for those components to stay cool. Do not make the room too cool, however, because at very low temperatures (below freezing) frost build-up becomes an issue. When the heat from the PC melts the frost, it creates water, and with water comes the possibility for short-circuiting. (Remember, electricity and water do not mix.)

In the past, computers were more sensitive to temperature than they are today. At one time it was common to find a "computer room" at a corporate headquarters where a raised floor kept cool air circulating, where the air conditioning was on high, and where employees dressed for winter all year round. Today these huge computers have been replaced by ordinary-looking PCs that do not require any special temperature treatment. The main reason PC cooling requirements are now less stringent is that today's CPUs run at much lower voltages than their ancestors (down to around 2 volts in some cases).

Still, it pays to remember that PCs like the cold more than people do. If the people are cold, the PC is probably comfortable. If the people are hot, the PC is probably *very* hot. Storage temperature for PC components is less of an issue than operating temperature, but extremes must still be avoided. Do not store your PC in an unheated shed in Minnesota all winter, and do not leave it baking in the back seat of a car in July.

When bringing a PC inside after it has been very cold or very hot, let it sit until its temperature is the same as that of the room. This is especially important when bringing it in from the cold, because condensation can create dampness inside the PC that can in turn cause short-circuits.

### In Real Life

I was once transporting a laser printer to a client in the middle of winter. When I got it there and hooked it up, the print quality was terrible. It had been great when I checked it before I left the office! After the printer sat inside and warmed up for an hour, the print quality was back to normal. The moral: Make sure that devices adjust fully to room temperature before spending time troubleshooting problems with them.

## Electrostatic Discharge (ESD)

*Electrostatic discharge*, or ESD, is the most common culprit for ruined PC parts, but many people have never heard of it. ESD is really just static electricity, the same thing that shocks a person on a low-humidity day.

**Electrostatic discharge (ESD)**

Static electricity, occurring when two items of unequal voltage potential touch.

ESD occurs when two items of unequal voltage potential come into contact with one another. The item with the higher charge passes electricity to the one with the lower charge to even out the voltage. As an analogy, picture two bodies of water meet; if one has a higher level, water will flow into the other one until they are the same. In the case of electricity, the equalizing happens quickly and the item of lower charge receives a rush of electricity that feels like a shock. You have experienced ESD firsthand if you have ever scuffed your socks on the carpet and then touched someone, giving the person a shock. You were not shocked yourself because in that case *you* were the item of higher charge.

Chapter 3 discusses electricity basics and amps and volts. *Voltage* is the amount of electricity; *amperage* is the rate at which the device draws the electricity. ESD is a high-voltage shock (3,000 volts or so), but it does not kill a person because it has very low amperage. The human body does not draw the electricity very strongly; it merely draws enough to equalize the charges and then stops. To damage a human body, there must be sufficient amps as well as volts. That is why a 110-volt wall outlet can hurt a person more than a 3,000-volt ESD shock.

**Voltage**

The strength of the electricity being delivered to a device. Standard household current is 110 volts.

**Amperage**

The rate at which a device draws electricity.

Electronic equipment is extremely sensitive to damage by high voltage, even when the amperage is very low. Humans notice ESD only when it reaches 3,000 volts, but ESD can damage a circuit board with less than 1 percent of that voltage. (Some experts say as little as one volt is enough to do some damage.) This means a person could touch a circuit board and destroy it with static electricity without even noticing. The next time the person tried to use that circuit board it would be dead, and she or he may have no idea why.

Further, ESD damage does not always show up immediately. It may cause the device to malfunction, or it may just weaken the device to the point that it fails a week or a month later. ESD damage can also create intermittent, tough-to-troubleshoot errors on a circuit board.

### *What Devices Are Most Susceptible to ESD?*

Generally speaking, any exposed circuit boards are targets for ESD damage, especially motherboards. Also at risk are microchips both on and off those boards—particularly RAM and CMOS chips.

Devices not particularly susceptible to ESD damage include those in which the circuit boards are never exposed—such as keyboards, mice, speakers, monitors, printers, and external modems—and those that do not contain circuit boards at all.

### *How to Prevent ESD Damage*

There are many ways to minimize the effect of ESD in the PC repair work area. Clothing is a good starting place. Synthetic materials such as nylon generate much more ESD than natural fibers like cotton and wool, so a technician should dress in natural fabrics whenever possible. Avoid working in stocking feet—wear rubber-soled shoes if possible.

Keeping the humidity high in the work area can also help considerably. The ideal humidity for working on PC hardware is 50 percent to 80 percent.

The work surface can make a difference. Try not to work in a carpeted area; a tile or linoleum floor is preferable. Carpet (especially nylon carpet) tends to generate ESD in the same way that nylon clothing does.

Grounding both the person and the equipment can eliminate ESD risk, because any ESD that builds up can bleed off to the ground harmlessly. To ground yourself, wear an antistatic wrist strap as you work, like the one in Figure 2.4. At your end of the strap is a Velcro bracelet containing a diode; at the other is an alligator clip that you attach to the grounding pin on an electrical outlet (the round, third hole) or to some other grounding source. If no grounding source is available, attach the clip to the PC's metal frame. Wear an antistatic wrist strap whenever working on a PC with the cover off, especially when handling circuit boards.

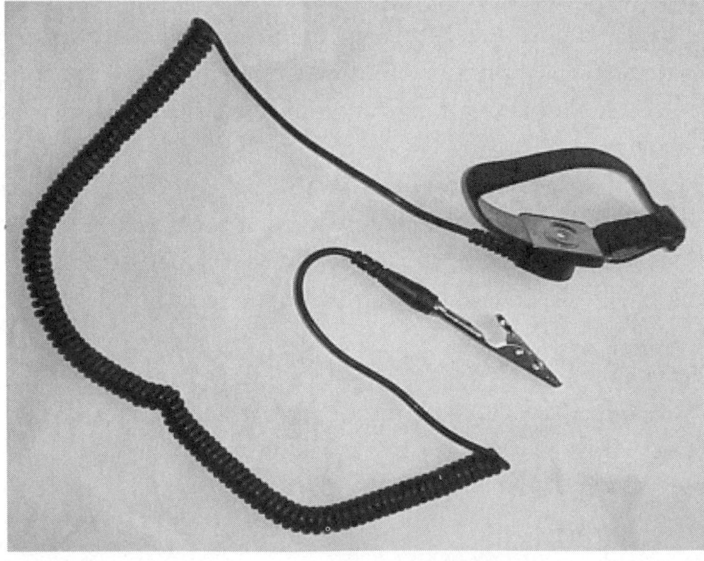

**FIGURE 2.4**
An Antistatic Wrist Strap

However, for personal safety, if there is a chance that you might come into contact with full fledged electrical current (not just the pesky ESD type), do *not* wear the wrist strap.

## TRY IT!

If you have an antistatic wrist strap, demonstrate its use by putting it on and connecting it to a ground plug.

Another way to minimize ESD risk is to frequently touch the metal frame or power supply of the PC as you work. This does not ground you, but it does equalize the electrical charge between you and the PC so that there is no difference in potential between you and the components of the PC that you touch afterward. Do this every few minutes to make sure no build-up occurs.

Antistatic mats are also available. These sit on the work surface and perform the same function for the parts on which the technician is working as the wrist strap does for the technician; the mat has a cord that attaches to the ground pin on an outlet.

Most new circuit boards come in an antistatic plastic bag. These bags have a coating that collects static charge on the outside of the bag, keeping it away from what is inside the bag. Circuit boards should always be stored in these bags when not in use. Computer stores sell extra bags, but most people accumulate a collection of them simply from buying and installing new hardware.

## WARNING

Never set a circuit board *on top of* an antistatic bag, because static charge accumulates there.

## TRY IT!

Examine an antistatic plastic bag. Feel the difference in texture between the outside and the inside of the bag.

Finally, there is antistatic spray you can buy that can minimize static charge in your environment. This is usually a colorless, odorless liquid in a pump bottle that you spray on the carpet and on your clothing.

## Electromagnetic Interference (EMI)

*Electromagnetic interference (EMI)* is caused when electricity passing nearby generates a magnetic field that interferes with the operation of a nearby cable or device. It occurs only when the PC is on, and goes away when the PC is off. It causes no permanent damage. EMI can come from unshielded cables, high-voltage power lines, radio transmitters, or other sources.

**Electromagnetic interference (EMI)**

Signal interference caused by the magnetic field building up around a cable through which electricity is passing.

Electricity passing through a wire generates a magnetic field, and magnetic fields generate electricity. Most computer cables move data via electrical pulses (fiber-optic cable is an exception), so a magnetic field builds up around the cable. When one cable runs next to another cable, each cable's magnetic field can interfere with data being sent along the other cable. Why? Because magnetic fields generate electricity, and the pattern of electricity through the cable is what forms the data being sent. When that pattern is altered, that data can become corrupted.

### *Symptoms of EMI*

EMI may be a problem when a data cable is not reliably carrying its data to the destination. For example, perhaps a printer is printing garbage characters interspersed with the normal characters, or perhaps a network connection keeps timing out due to transmission errors.

Power cables can also be susceptible to EMI; this can manifest itself as power fluctuation. Power fluctuations, in turn, can cause lasting damage to equipment, so in that sense EMI is capable of causing permanent damage.

### *Preventing EMI*

One way to avoid EMI problems from unshielded cables is to simply *not* run any cables next to one another and not allow a cable to be placed near any other cable. This is not often practical, because most computer users have a tangle of cables behind their PCs going in many directions. The best that most technicians can do is troubleshoot EMI problems as they occur by selectively moving cables that are causing problems.

Another way to minimize EMI is to select the proper cables to begin with. Shorter cables are less prone to EMI than longer ones, so use the shortest cable that will do the job in each case. Many cables sold these days are shielded, which means they have a special wrapping that minimizes EMI interference. Buying shielded cables can help greatly.

EMI problems caused by external sources such as power lines can be difficult to solve; sometimes moving the devices to a different area in the room or building can help.

## TRY IT!

Check your work area for potential EMI problems. Make any changes that you can to minimize the risks.

### Physical Trauma

Computers are not highly susceptible to physical trauma, but it is always best to handle them with reasonable care. Everyday bumps like inadvertently kicking a PC that is sitting on the floor will probably not cause any problems, but knocking a PC off a table while it is running can cause some damage.

There are two reasons why physical trauma is bad for a PC. One is that it causes parts to come loose. If someone drops a bare circuit board and it hits the floor just right, a wire connecting a chip or resistor to the board could come undone. Most people do not have the skill to repair a circuit board (it involves fine soldering), so a board with a broken connection is basically ruined. Connectors inside a PC can come loose as well. For example, the ribbon cables that connect drives to the motherboard can work loose, as can power supply plugs to drives. Circuit boards can also pop out of expansion slots, and chips can pop out of their sockets.

The other reason to avoid physical trauma pertains specifically to hard disks. A hard disk is something like a vinyl recording on a turntable. It has read/write heads that skim the surface of the drive. When the drive is subjected to physical trauma, those heads can bounce, scratching the surface of the drive and causing disk errors. On early hard disks this was a real problem even when the PC was turned off, but more recent models employ a system of head parking that positions the read/write heads in an unused area whenever the power is turned off. There need not be concern about bumping the drive while it is turned off, although knocking a PC around while the power is on can still cause some drive damage.

"Be careful" is the best advice to follow for avoiding physical trauma to the PC. If you do accidentally jar a PC so that it stops working, remove the cover and check that all the connections are snug. If it still doesn't work, try the troubleshooting procedures outlined in Chapters 8 and 30.

## TRY IT!

Examine your work area for hazards such as cords running across a path where people walk or devices sitting too near the edge of a table. Make any corrections you can to ensure a safer work area.

### MAGNETS

Magnets and computers do not mix—for several reasons. One has to do with magnetism and electricity. You learned in the discussion of EMI that magnetic fields generate electricity. A magnet can induce electrical charge in a component just by being near it, and that charge can harm the component either temporarily or permanently.

Magnets are also very hard on any disks that use metal particles for storage. These include hard disks and floppy disks; both have surfaces coated with metal particles, and the write heads on the drives change the magnetic polarization on areas of particles to write data. An external magnet placed anywhere near the disk can erase or corrupt the data on that disk.

To avoid magnet exposure:

- Do not use magnetized screwdrivers or other tools. If possible, use tools designed specifically for working on PCs.
- Keep disks away from unshielded speakers. Most speakers designed for PCs have shielding, but most home stereo speakers do not.
- Since some older telephones contain magnets, keep disks away from telephones, just to be on the safe side.

**WARNING**

The magnets in unshielded speakers can distort the image on a monitor if the speakers are too close to it. If there is distortion on the sides of the display, try moving the speakers farther away from the monitor.

**TRY IT!**

If you are not sure whether a screwdriver is magnetized, try picking up a screw with its tip. If it grabs the screw, the tool is magnetized.

## Cleaning a PC

People forget about cleaning inside their PCs. They tend to think that the PC case is a sealed unit into and out of which no dirt can pass, but of course that is not true: the power supply fan circulates air from the outside—complete with impurities—and those impurities settle inside the case. Over time, impressive amounts of dust can collect. Most computers will not malfunction specifically from being dirty, but the dirt can impede the free flow of air around components, causing them to run hotter and fail faster in the long run.

Users more commonly think about cleaning the outside of a PC, since that is the surface they interact with on a daily basis. People are much more likely to notice dirt building up on their keyboard than on their motherboard. Cleaning the outside parts might make some things run better (for example, cleaning a mouse can make it roll more smoothly), but this type of cleaning is primarily for the benefit of the user, not the PC itself.

The following sections outline some cleaning procedures. A competent technician should know these procedures, both for the technician's own use and in order to give appropriate advice to end users.

## Cleaning Supplies

Expensive special-purpose cleaning supplies are not required to clean a PC, but neither should a person use whatever products that happen to be lying around. Figure 2.5 shows a list of supplies to have on hand.

- a spray cleaning product, preferably one designed for computers
- several clean, dry, lint-free cotton towels
- a can of compressed air
- premoistened towelettes or a spray cleaner designed specifically for monitors
- cotton swabs
- denatured isopropyl alcohol (the pure kind, not rubbing alcohol)
- antistatic spray designed specifically for computer work areas
- *optional:* a small handheld vacuum designed for electronics (do not use a regular vacuum because the filter is not fine enough and because a regular vacuum can generate static that can harm the equipment)

**FIGURE 2.5**
PC Cleaning Supplies

## Cleaning the Surface of the Monitor

Always turn the monitor off before cleaning it. If any liquid gets inside, it can air dry without worries of short-circuiting. It is also much easier to see dirt and spots on the monitor screen when the screen is dark.

First, clean the outer casing of the monitor with a spray computer cleaning solution. Spray the cleaner on the cloth, not directly on the casing, to avoid spraying into vent holes.

Next, clean the glass using a cleaner designed specifically for monitors. This can be in the form of a spray or a towelette. Do not use ordinary cleaning products on monitor glass; they can leave streaks and harm the antiglare coating on the glass. Do not use regular glass cleaner, either, because it contains ammonia, which can also harm the coating.

**TRY IT!**

Clean your monitor.

## Cleaning Other External Surfaces

As with monitors, clean the outside casing of PCs, printers, scanners, monitors, and similar equipment with a computer cleaning spray product. Mild general-purpose spray cleaners also work. You can also use mild soapy water and a damp cloth to clean external surfaces only—not anything internal or with a vent or crack that leads inside.

**TRY IT!**

Clean all the external surfaces of your PC and peripherals.

## Cleaning a Keyboard

Since it is always at the forefront of activity, the keyboard can get very dirty. Though technicians may remind end users to keep their computing areas clean, more often than not people neglect to do so. They may type with unwashed hands, or eat, drink, smoke, and play with their pets while they work. All of this activity leaves dirt, oil, and other residue on the keyboard.

To clean a keyboard, first turn off the PC. (The keyboard need not be unplugged from the PC.) Then turn the keyboard upside down and shake it to remove any loose debris. What falls out—and the amount of it—is often surprising!

Use a cloth dampened with a spray cleaning solution designed for PCs to clean all visible surfaces. Get down between the cracks with a cotton swab or a bit of folded paper towel. Removing the keys is not recommended because it can be difficult to get them back on again, especially the spacebar, which has a couple of springs behind it. If you have access to one, a small handheld vacuum cleaner designed for working with electronics can be useful in sucking the debris out from under the keys.

**TRY IT!**

Clean your keyboard.

If liquid is spilled on a keyboard, unplug it immediately from the PC and try shaking it upside-down to release all of the excess liquid; then let it dry. If the liquid was plain water, the keyboard will probably be fine after it dries; just clean the outside as well as possible. But if the liquid contained sugar, the keyboard may never be completely clean again. Some people have successfully cleaned sticky keyboards in a dishwasher. To try this (there is little to lose with a keyboard that is otherwise on its way to the trash can), place the keyboard on the upper rack, wash it without using the heat-dry feature, remove it after the wash, rinse it, and set it in a dish drainer for several days to dry out.

## Cleaning a Mouse

A mouse, like a keyboard, gets very dirty because it is constantly being handled. In addition, a mouse has the added feature of the ball on the bottom, which rolls across the desk picking up dirt and lint and moving it up into the mouse. As a result, the rollers and sensors inside a mouse can become encrusted with dirt rather quickly, causing the mouse to malfunction.

When a mouse is dirty, the pointer on-screen may jump or stutter, or moving the mouse in one direction (vertical or horizontal) may result in no action at all. In addition, the mouse may become more difficult to roll across the desk or mousepad as more resistance builds up inside.

To clean a mouse, first wipe off the outside with mild soapy water, just as with any other external PC component. Then turn the mouse on its back and rotate the plastic plate that holds the mouse ball in place (see Figure 2.6). Turn the mouse over again and the ball and plate should fall into your hand.

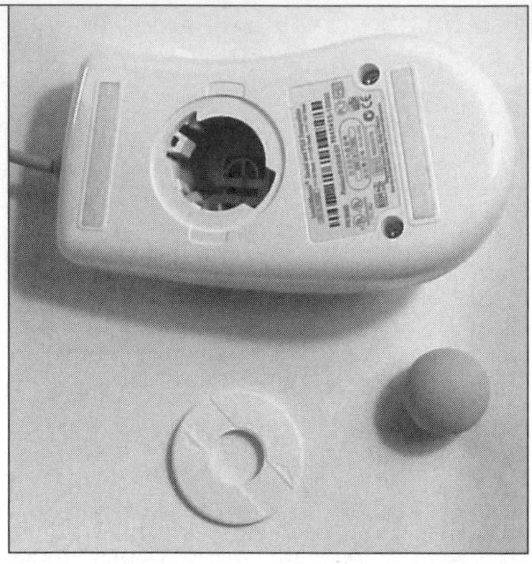

**FIGURE 2.6**
Remove the plate that holds the mouse ball inside the mouse.

Clean the ball with soap and water, then dry it with a lint-free cloth. Do not use alcohol on the mouse ball, because it dries out the rubber.

Next, clean the inside of the mouse with a cotton swab and alcohol, focusing on any rollers or sensors. Let the alcohol evaporate completely, then reassemble the mouse.

If you are cleaning a trackball instead of a mouse, the procedure is basically the same. Remove the ball (it may be necessary to remove some screws in order to do this; it depends on the model), and then clean inside the ball's cavity with alcohol and cotton swabs.

## TRY IT!

Clean your mouse or trackball.

## IN REAL LIFE

My favorite trackball is the Kensington Expert Mouse, which has a large ball in the center. However, the rollers inside get very dirty and clogged with lint and hair, and it can be difficult to fish all this debris out. I discovered that there were screws under a sticker on the bottom of the trackball that could be removed to open up the whole cavity, and I could then remove and clean each roller individually. You may discover special cleaning procedures such as this for your own favorite brands and models of hardware.

### CLEANING THE INSIDE OF A PC

Inside the PC there might be some big clumps of hair and dirt; just fish these out by hand and throw them away. Then check the motherboard and expansion boards for dust accumulation and blow it out with compressed air. (If possible take the computer outside or to an open area so you do not blow dust on the client's work area.) The board does not need to be sparkling clean; it just needs to have the major clumps of dust removed. A handheld vacuum designed for electronics can come in handy if one is available.

**WARNING**

**Hold your breath as you blast out the dust with compressed air or you will be coughing from all the dust flying around. It is best to do this job outdoors if weather permits. Keep in mind, too, that canned air generates a blast of cold, so do not blow it on yourself. (Some technicians use this side effect as a tool for cooling off overheated chips on a circuit board when troubleshooting problems.)**

For cleaning anything that involves circuit boards or chips, stay away from liquids, especially water, because of the danger of short-circuiting if the board is not completely dry when the PC powers up. If some kind of moisture is absolutely necessary, use alcohol on a cotton swab. Old circuit boards can build up deposits on the metal pins along the edge; these can be removed with alcohol and a cotton swab, too. Avoid touching any of the circuitry, chips, or resistors on a circuit board; it is easy to damage them. Handle circuit boards only by the edges.

Other parts that tend to accumulate dust include the fan on the power supply, the fan on the CPU (if present), and the air vents in the case itself. Wipe off the case's air vents with a damp paper towel. For the power supply, point the compressed air nozzle at an angle to the fan opening rather than blowing straight down into it, to avoid driving the dirt even deeper into the power supply box instead of blowing it out.

## Cleaning a Printer

Different types of printers require different cleaning procedures. If any of the following discussion is confusing, consult Chapter 18 to learn about printer parts.

### *Cleaning an Inkjet Printer*

Wipe the outside casing of an inkjet printer with a cloth dampened with cleaning fluid for PCs. This will not necessarily make the printer perform any better, but it will make for a nicer office environment.

The only parts of the inside that need cleaning are the inkjets, and these do not need to be cleaned by hand; a utility built into the printer cleans them.

The ink in an inkjet printer is liquid, and if the printer is not in frequent use, the ink dries out and bits of dried ink remain in the nozzles. The cleaning utility flushes out any dried-up ink from the nozzles. It uses up some ink to do this, so do not clean the nozzles unless the print quality has declined.

On most printers there are two ways to activate the cleaning utility: pressing a sequence of buttons on the printer itself or choosing a command from the printer's Properties box in Windows. To activate the utility in Windows, access it through the printer's driver:

1. Choose Start/Settings/Printers, then right-click the printer and choose Properties.
2. Look for a Utilities tab, or a tab that indicates tools or utilities. The name varies depending on the printer. Non-inkjet printers will not have this tab. As an example, Figure 2.7 shows the Utilities tab for an Epson inkjet printer.
3. After you select the tab in Step 2, click the Head Cleaning button (or whatever it is called for the specific printer) and then follow the on-screen prompts.
4. Use the Nozzle Check feature (or whatever it is called for the specific printer) to print a test that checks to make sure the nozzles are clean. If they are not, clean them again.

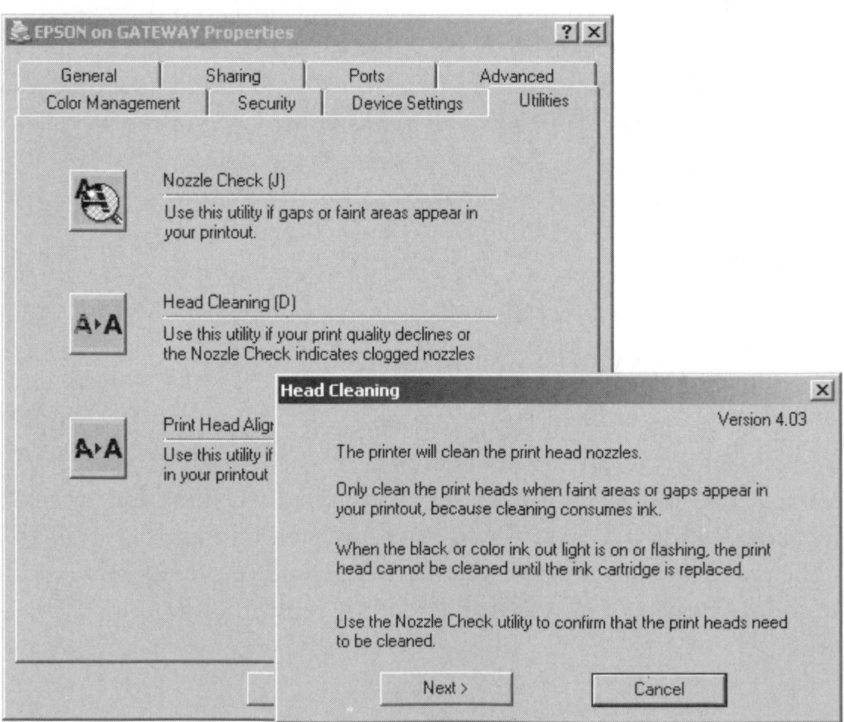


**FIGURE 2.7**
The Utilities tab for the printer contains buttons that run checks and clean the nozzles.

### *Cleaning a Laser Printer*

Laser printers use toner rather than ink. Since toner is a dry substance (a mixture of plastic resin and iron oxide), it does not clog things the way liquid ink does. However, toner is a loose powder that can scatter over clothing and the work area if the cartridges are not handled with care.

If toner spills, use a damp paper towel to clean it up. If it gets on clothing, get it out with a magnet, since toner is half iron. You can also suck it out with a special handheld vacuum designed for use around electronics. Do not use a regular vacuum cleaner. General-use vacuums do not have fine enough dust filters, and the toner particles can pass through them and into the air where they become a health hazard to breathe.

Several parts of a laser printer can accumulate toner, making them less effective over time. The following parts of a laser printer need cleaning:

**Corona wires.** These are individual wires strung horizontally across the inside of the printer. Most printers have two: the primary corona and the transfer corona. The latter is inside the toner cartridge on some models. Check the printer's manual to find out whether any corona wires can be cleaned. If so, clean them with a cleaning tool especially designed for that purpose, or an alcohol-dipped cotton swab. Be very careful not to break them. Some printers contain no corona wires at all; on others they are not user-accessible.

> **WARNING**
>
> **Inside the laser printer is a fusing unit that gets very hot. Read the printer's manual to find out where it is, and keep hands away from it until the printer cools down.**

**Drum.** Never touch the drum directly, because it scratches easily, and a scratched drum leaves a scratched image on every printout. Instead, use the printer's built-in cleaning utility program if there is one. Many Hewlett-Packard LaserJet printers have such a utility, which involves running a sheet of paper through so that a heavy layer of toner adheres to it, and then running the same sheet through again to pick up excess toner from the drum. If the printer does not have such a utility, the drum does not require cleaning. Some models include the drum in the toner cartridge; it is replaced with each new toner cartridge, so drum cleaning is not an issue.

**Cleaning pad.** On some printers there is a felt pad that cleans off excess toner. The pad is mounted on a hard plastic strip. If a new cartridge comes with a felt pad, it means that the printer has a felt pad somewhere that needs to be changed. Look in the printer's manual to determine the location of the pad and how to change it.

**Inside plastic parts.** If there is any paper debris or dust on the open plastic areas inside a printer, wipe it off with a slightly damp cloth.

**TRY IT!**

Clean your printer now. The steps will be different depending on whether it is a laser or inkjet printer, and depending on the model.

## Disposal of Hazardous Materials

Several parts inside a PC require special disposal procedures. It is important to know these, because the technician may need to arrange safe disposal of equipment; this information is also featured on the A+ exams. The PC parts requiring special disposal are identified in Figure 2.8.

- **Batteries:** A motherboard has a very small battery; a notebook PC has a large one as well. These batteries can contain lead, lithium, nickel cadmium, or mercury, all of which can seep into groundwater in a landfill.
- **Toner cartridges:** These cartridges from laser printers may contain traces of leftover toner, which can cause lung problems if breathed. Recycling companies buy some models of old cartridges.
- **Monitors:** These big plastic shells take up a great deal of space in a landfill, and they also contain phosphorus, mercury, and lead coatings on the back side of the monitor glass.
- **Circuit boards:** These contain small amounts of lead in the soldering.
- **Cleaning chemicals:** Some cleaning solvents used for PCs can pollute groundwater and soil. In addition, aerosol cans can release ozone-depleting chlorofluorocarbons (CFCs).

**FIGURE 2.8**
PC Parts Requiring Special Disposal Procedures

If the community has a hazardous waste disposal facility, take the hazardous materials there. Check the Environmental Protection Agency (EPA) Web site at www.epa.gov to find the location of your local facility.

All materials and equipment that pose an environmental hazard have an associated *Materials Safety Data Sheet (MSDS).* This document explains what hazards are present in the item and dictates the proper disposal and handling of the item. The manufacturer should be able to provide the MSDS on request, and these data sheets are also available from the EPA.

**Materials Safety Data Sheet (MSDS)**

A document containing information about the safe handling and disposal of an item that poses a personal safety or environmental hazard.

# STUDY GUIDE

Use the following summaries to review the information from this chapter.

## Protection from Electrical Hazards

- Use ordinary care when working with electrical appliances of any type, such as keeping them away from water.
- Do not overload an electrical plug with too many devices.
- Do not disassemble a computer's power supply.
- Do not remove the cover from a monitor unless you are experienced in working on monitors or are being supervised by someone experienced.
- If you do remove the cover from a monitor, keep well away from the high-voltage anode (under the suction cup).
- Do not wear an antistatic wrist strap when working on a monitor.
- Be aware that a Class C fire extinguisher is suitable for extinguishing electrical fires.

## Protection from Other Dangers

- Do not wear jewelry made of metal that conducts electricity.
- Do not wear dangling jewelry that could get caught on something.
- Be aware that there are sharp metal pieces sticking out of many circuit boards.
- Use care when putting a hand down inside a PC case; some cases have sharp metal edges inside.
- Be aware that laser printers and CD drives have lasers inside that can hurt your eyes.
- Do not leave circuit boards lying on the floor where someone could step on them.

## Work Environment Temperature

- PCs work best in a slightly colder environment than that preferred by human beings.
- Today's computers run much cooler than their predecessors because of lower-voltage chips.
- When bringing electronics into or out of the cold, allow them to come to room temperature before using them.

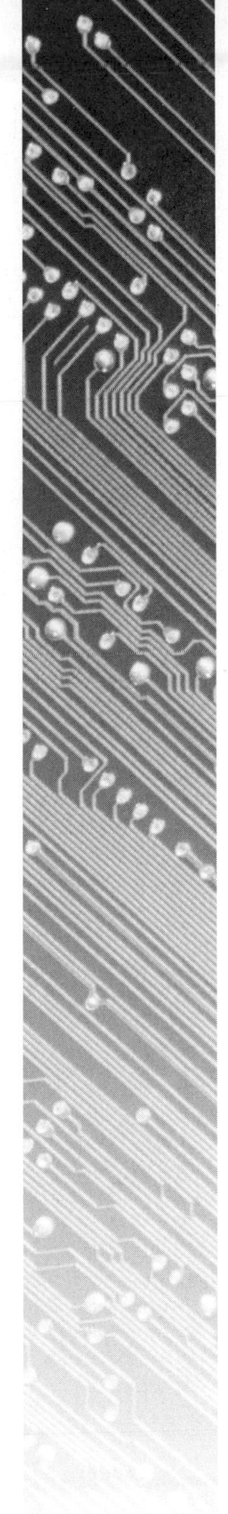

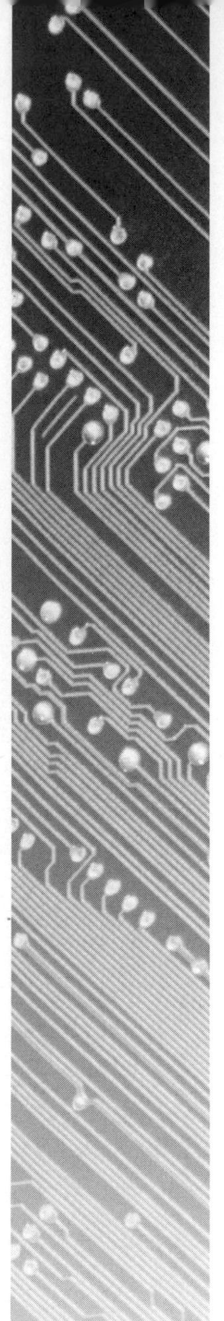

## Electrostatic Discharge

- Electrostatic discharge (ESD) is static electricity. It occurs when two objects with unlike voltage potentials touch; voltage passes from the one with higher potential to the one with lower potential.
- ESD can cause permanent damage to electronics. As little as one volt can ruin equipment, but humans do not notice ESD unless it is 3,000 volts or more.
- Components susceptible to ESD damage include circuit boards and microchips.
- High humidity (50 percent to 80 percent) in the work area can minimize ESD.
- An antistatic wrist strap and grounding mat can prevent ESD damage to components.
- Wearing natural-fiber clothing can minimize ESD.

## Electromagnetic Interference

- Electromagnetic interference (EMI) is data interference caused by a nearby magnetic field.
- The primary symptom of EMI is data corruption. When EMI occurs in a power cord, it can result in power fluctuation.
- EMI persists only as long as the interference exists; it does not cause lasting damage unless it creates power fluctuations that in turn cause some damage, or unless it is very strong and erases magnetically stored data.

## Physical Trauma

- If a PC is shaken or jolted, connectors can come loose inside.
- If a hard disk is jolted while the PC is running, the read/write heads can bounce against the disk surface and scratch it.

## Magnetic Damage

- Magnets can induce electrical charge in a sensitive electronic component, causing it to fail.
- Magnets can erase or corrupt data on a hard or floppy disk.
- Do not use magnetic tools when working on PCs.
- Keep disks away from unshielded speakers.
- Some older telephones contain magnets.

## Cleaning the Outside of a PC

- Dust and dirt on electronic components can reduce cooling effectiveness, causing chips to run hotter and decreasing their lifespan.
- To clean the outside of a PC and associated components, use a special cleaner designed for computer equipment, or a damp cloth dipped in mild soapy water if a cleaner is not available.

## Cleaning Monitor, Keyboard, and Mouse

- Clean a monitor screen only with a cleaner designed specifically for monitors; do not use regular glass cleaner or other general-purpose cleaners.
- To clean a keyboard, turn it upside down and shake it, then wipe off the keys with a damp cloth or paper towel dipped in mild soapy water.
- Removing the keys from a keyboard is not necessary, and is not recommended because reassembly can be difficult.
- A dirty mouse results in a jumping or unresponsive mouse pointer on-screen.
- To clean a mouse, remove the plastic panel on the bottom holding the ball in place, and then clean out the ball cavity with alcohol and cotton swabs.
- Wash the ball with soap and water. Do not use alcohol on it.

## Cleaning the Inside of a PC

- To clean the circuit boards inside the PC, blow the dust off with compressed air.
- Do not use water on circuit boards.

## Cleaning a Printer

- To clean an inkjet printer, use the printer's built-in utility to flush any dried ink out of the nozzles.
- If the printer uses corona wires, clean them carefully with an alcohol-dipped cotton swab.
- To clean a laser printer drum, run the printer's self-cleaning utility; however, many printers do not have them such a utility.
- Wipe spilled toner out of a laser printer with a damp paper towel.
- Replace the cleaning pad in a laser printer with every toner cartridge change.

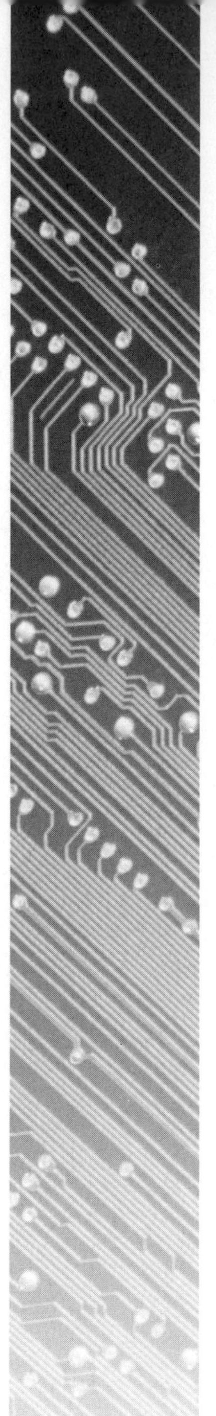

### Hazardous Material Disposal

- The motherboard has a small battery; a notebook PC has a large one as well. These batteries can contain nickel, lithium, and other metals.
- Toner cartridges can be sold to companies that refill them or returned to the manufacturer.
- Monitors contain phosphorus, mercury, and lead on the back side of the glass.
- Circuit boards contain small amounts of lead in their soldering.
- Hazardous items should not be placed in the regular trash because they can pollute the ground in a landfill. Take them instead to a hazardous waste disposal facility.
- A Materials Safety Data Sheet (MSDS) is a document that dictates proper procedures for safe handling and disposal of an item.

## PRACTICE TEST

On a blank sheet of paper, write the answers to the following multiple-choice questions and explain why each answer is correct.

1. A ________________ stores an electrical charge in a power supply or monitor even after the device is unplugged from the wall outlet.
   a. resistor
   b. voltage regulator
   c. current
   d. capacitor

2. Should you leave the power connected to a PC while working on it to keep the PC grounded and prevent ESD damage?
   a. Yes.
   b. No.
   c. It depends on the humidity level in the room.
   d. It does not matter either way.

3. Why are monitors dangerous to work on?
   a. The phosphors on the back of the monitor glass are highly radioactive.
   b. The high-voltage anode can deliver a 30,000-volt shock.
   c. The laser inside the monitor can hurt your eyes.
   d. There are many sharp wires sticking out of the picture tube.

4. Before working on the inside of a monitor, it is important to
   a. remove the base.
   b. discharge the capacitor.
   c. disconnect the electron gun.
   d. adjust the convergence.
5. It is important to wear an antistatic wrist strap when working with
   a. high-voltage equipment.
   b. ESD-sensitive components.
   c. high humidity.
   d. EMI-sensitive cables.
6. Which type of fire extinguisher would be appropriate for extinguishing a computer that was on fire?
   a. Class A
   b. Class B
   c. Class C
   d. Class D
7. Which humidity level would be most likely to cause ESD problems?
   a. 15%
   b. 25%
   c. 50%
   d. 75%
8. When two items of unequal voltage potential touch, which one receives a shock?
   a. the one having the higher voltage potential
   b. the one having the lower voltage potential
   c. both equally
   d. neither
9. What voltage of ESD can a human feel?
   a. 3,000 volts
   b. 300 volts
   c. 110 volts
   d. 30 volts
10. Why does static electricity not kill a person, given its high voltage?
    a. It lasts for only a millisecond.
    b. It is DC current rather than AC.
    c. The ohms are low.
    d. The amperage is low.

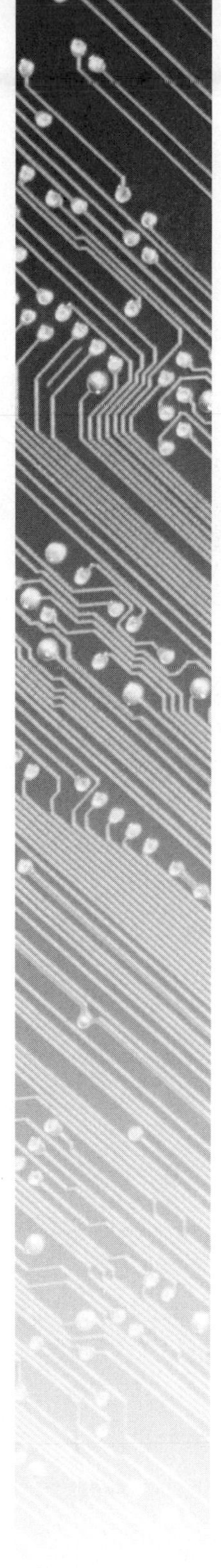

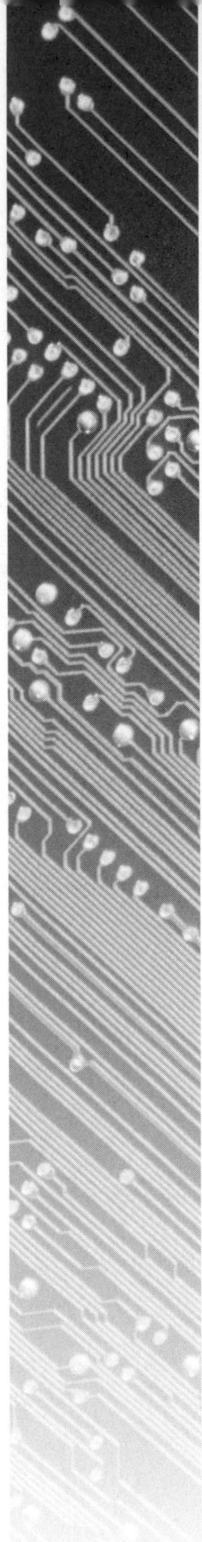

11. Which device can be most easily damaged by ESD?
    a. keyboard
    b. mouse
    c. monitor
    d. expansion board

12. How does an antistatic wrist strap prevent ESD damage?
    a. It grounds the wearer.
    b. It lowers the wearer's voltage potential.
    c. It sets up a magnetic field.
    d. It runs a constant low-voltage current through the wearer's body.

13. Rather than leave a circuit board lying on a worktable, is it better to set it on top of an antistatic bag?
    a. Yes.
    b. No.
    c. It depends on the type of circuit board.
    d. It does not matter; there are the same risks either way.

14. What might be the cause of EMI problems in an office environment?
    a. electrostatic discharge
    b. unshielded cables
    c. fiber-optic cabling
    d. magnetic tools being used to install circuit boards

15. Why is physical trauma to a hard drive more of an issue when the computer is running than when it is turned off?
    a. Electromagnetic interference causes data corruption.
    b. Electrostatic discharge builds up.
    c. The read/write heads are positioned over areas containing data.
    d. The circuit connectors are more likely to come loose.

16. Why should you not use a magnetic screwdriver to install a circuit board?
    a. The magnet will erase the data stored on a disk.
    b. The magnet can change the polarization on the connector.
    c. The magnet can generate an electrical charge.
    d. Electrostatic discharge can build up in the screwdriver.

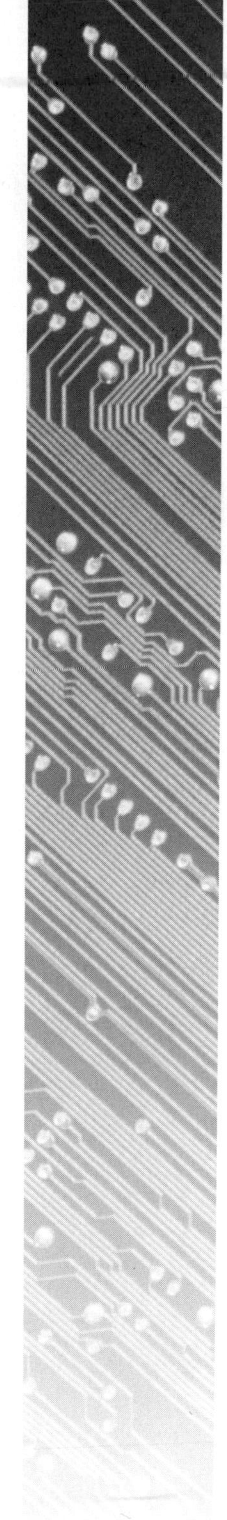

17. Why is ordinary glass cleaner not acceptable for cleaning monitor glass?
    a. It contains ammonia, which can damage antiglare coating.
    b. The pump spray of an ordinary cleaning product generates ESD.
    c. It contains water, and you should use only alcohol-based products.
    d. There is no reason you can't use regular glass cleaner.

18. What is the best way to clean the dirty keys on a keyboard?
    a. Pry off the keys with a screwdriver and run them through the dishwasher.
    b. Use cotton swabs or a bit of folded paper towel dampened with computer cleaning solution.
    c. Spray down the keyboard with an antistatic spray.
    d. Blow off the dirt with compressed air.

19. Which cleaning product is best for a mouse ball?
    a. soap and water on a soft cloth
    b. glass cleaner on a paper towel
    c. alcohol on a cotton swab
    d. spray lubricant sprayed directly onto the ball

20. What is the best way to clean the ink nozzles on an inkjet printer?
    a. Wipe with soap and water on a soft cloth.
    b. Apply alcohol on a cotton swab.
    c. Use the printer's built-in cleaning utility.
    d. They cannot be cleaned.

## TROUBLESHOOTING

1. A computer and printer that have always worked in one office begin to present problems when you move them to a different office. The printer prints correctly sometimes, but at other times it spits out page after page of garbage characters, sometimes in the middle of a print job. What would you check first?
2. On a service call, you find that you have forgotten to bring your anti-static wrist strap. You just need to replace a circuit board, so you do not want to go all the way back to your office. What are some things you can do to minimize the risk of ESD damage in this situation?

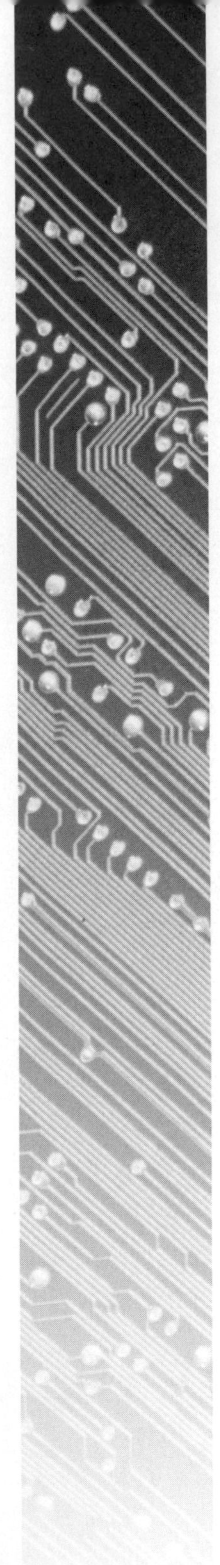

3. A friend of yours read an article on the Internet about cleaning circuit boards by putting them in the dishwasher. He washed all the circuit boards from his computer that way, and now he is worried that he should not have done it. He wants your help in reassembling his PC. What can you do to make the best of this situation?

## CUSTOMER SERVICE

1. A customer has commented to you that she has never heard of a problem's being caused simply by a computer being dirty. She asks you whether you think cleaning a PC is worth the trouble. What will your answer be, and why?
2. A customer complains to you about the high price of cleaning supplies that are made specifically for PCs. What are some lower-cost alternatives for case, monitor, and work area cleaning that you could suggest?
3. A novice customer complains that the mouse pointer jumps around on the screen in Windows. Explain in detail how you would instruct the person to disassemble and clean the mouse.

## FOR MORE INFORMATION

For links to Web sites that provide further information about the topics covered in this chapter, go to the EMC/Paradigm Internet Resource Center at www.emcp.com/College Division/Internet Resource Centers/PC Maintenance/For More Information.

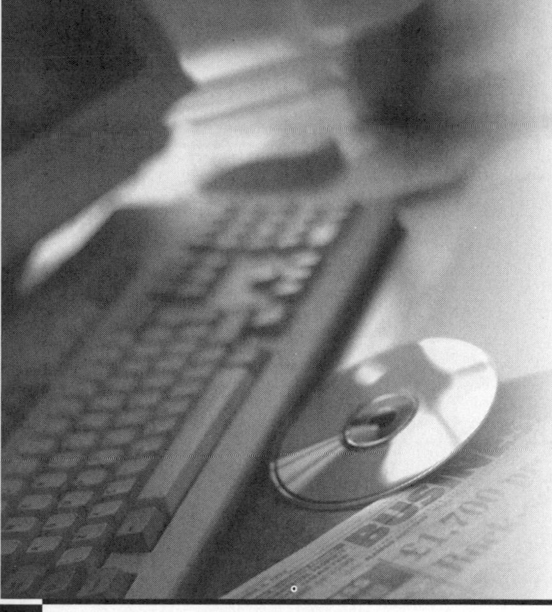

# 3 Case, Electricity, and Power Supplies

## ON THE TEST

**A+ Core Hardware Service Technician Examination**

- **Objective 1.1:** Identify basic terms, concepts, and functions of system modules, including how each module should work during normal operation and during the boot process.
- **Objective 1.2:** Identify basic procedures for adding and removing field replaceable modules for both desktop and portable systems.
- **Objective 2.1:** Identify common symptoms and problems associated with each module and how to troubleshoot and isolate the problems.
- **Objective 3.2:** Identify issues, procedures, and devices for protection within the computing environment, including people, hardware and the surrounding workspace.

## ON THE JOB

PC technicians are often called upon to replace the power supply in a PC; the power supply seems to fail sooner than many of the other parts. That means you will need to know how to select a new power supply that is compatible with the current motherboard and case, how to remove the old power supply, and how to install the one that will replace it.

Cases are replaced less frequently since there is little that can go wrong with them, but a technician might need to select a case for building a system from scratch. Technicians should also know about case specifications when choosing a replacement power supply.

Most technicians do not work much with electricity on a daily basis, but may occasionally need to test the electrical functioning of a cable, a power supply, or another device. The main reason to study electrical concepts and testing is to prepare for the A+ exam, which includes questions about them.

Some of the real-life tasks you might perform related to this chapter's material include the following:

- selecting a new case for a PC being built from scratch
- testing a power supply for proper electrical functioning
- selecting and installing a replacement power supply
- selecting and installing surge suppressors and UPS systems

# Working with Cases

PC cases lack the complexity of the other parts, and so they provide the ideal place to start an in-depth look at the parts of a computer system.

## Selecting a Case

There are actually many differences among cases, some of which can be significant. Anyone building a PC from scratch, or replacing the case on an existing PC, will need to know what differentiates one case from another. Computer stores sell cases ranging in price from as little as $40 to as much as $400 or more. The following sections describe the differences among cases.

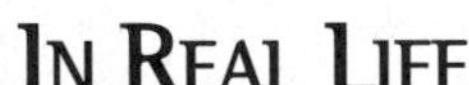

### In Real Life

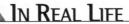

**You may run into some nonstandard case sizes and designs different from the models described here, especially if you work with older or proprietary systems For example, popular some years ago were "slim" cases that required a special type of motherboard with the expansion slots mounted on a separate card perpendicular to the motherboard. There are several varieties of these, and you will learn about them in Chapter 4.**

### *Construction*

The covers on inexpensive cases are made out of plastic; expensive ones are made out of metal. Though all cases have a metal frame inside, the frame on a lower-priced case is lighter and thinner and may have sharp, unfinished edges that can cut fingers.

### *Form Factors*

**Form factor**

The size and shape of a component, such as a motherboard or case.

*Form factor* as a generic term refers to the size and shape of something. In computer cases it refers to the size and shape of the floor—that is, the area in which the motherboard will be mounted. There are two form factors for cases: AT and ATX. (Not coincidentally, there are also two form factors of motherboards: AT and ATX.)

Two different case form factors are necessary because AT and ATX motherboards are different sizes and mount into cases at different orientations. In an AT motherboard the wide side runs perpendicular to the back of the case; in an ATX motherboard the wide side runs parallel to it. Figure 3.1 shows an example of an AT; it is deeper from back to front (left to right in this photograph) than it is from top to bottom.

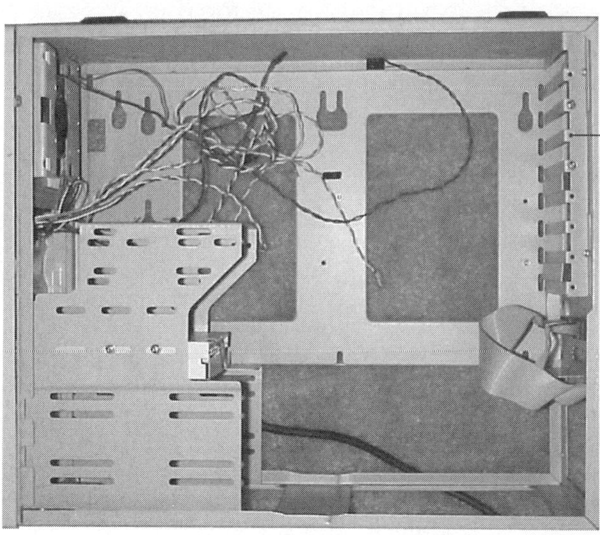


**FIGURE 3.1**
An AT Case

Some cases are large enough to accommodate either form factor, and may be marked as AT/ATX. Figure 3.2 shows a case that happens to be set up for ATX but, based on its form factor alone, could also accommodate an AT motherboard.

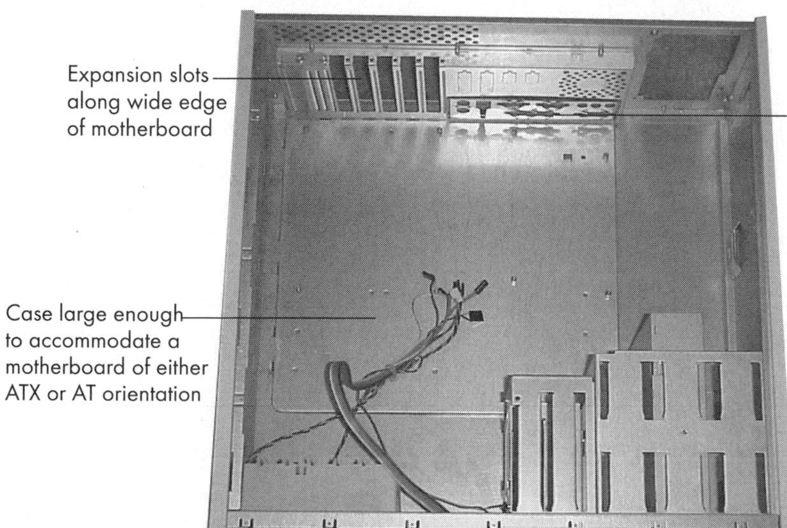


**FIGURE 3.2**
An ATX Case

In the preceding paragraph, emphasis on the words "based on its form factor alone" is important. While the size of motherboard that a case can take is one indicator of whether it is an AT or ATX case, there are several other, more significant indicators covered in the following sections.

There are also some other, nonstandard types of cases. One of the most common is the "slim" case. It has a space-saving design requiring a special type of motherboard that has only a single expansion slot into which a riser connects, with the rest of the expansion slots on the riser. This places the expansion cards parallel to the motherboard rather than perpendicular, so the case can be shorter than the height of an expansion card.

### *Power Supply Type*

With some cases a power supply comes preinstalled; with others it is sold separately. AT and ATX motherboards require different connector types to the power supply, so the power supply must be matched to the case and motherboard form factor.

When a case can be used with either AT or ATX, pay attention to which power supply type (if any) is installed in it, and make sure that the power supply has enough wattage to support the number of drives in the PC. See "Electricity Basics" (later in the chapter) to find out more about wattage, and see "Power Supply" (also later in the chapter) for more information about the power supply.

### *Connectors to the Motherboard*

The front of the case displays tiny lights. A pair of wires runs from each light to a small black connector, and that connector fits over a specific pair of pins on the motherboard (see Figure 3.3).

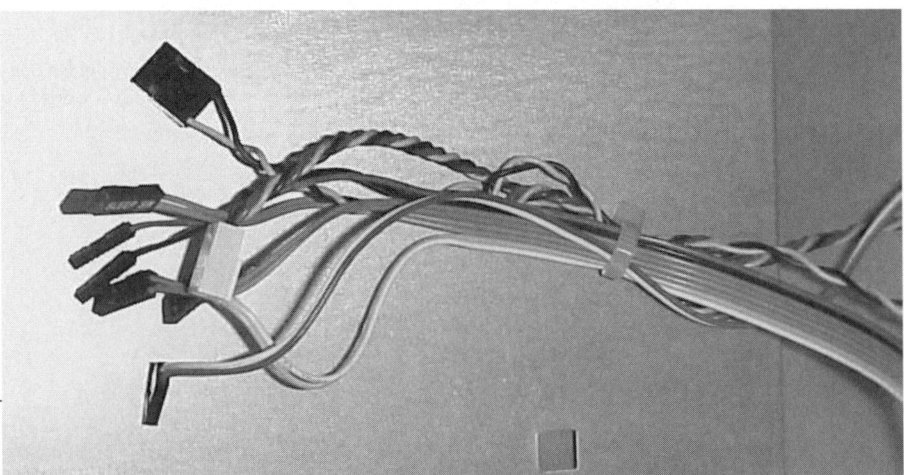

**FIGURE 3.3**
The Motherboard Connector Wires on a Typical Case

On an ATX system, the power button on the case also has some wires running out its back, along with a connector that plugs into the motherboard. On this system the power flowing from the power supply to the motherboard is "on" all the time when the PC is plugged in; the power button simply shorts the pins (that is, completes an electrical circuit between them) to which the button's connector is attached, telling the motherboard to turn on and the power supply's fan to start spinning. Figure 3.4 shows an example of this process.

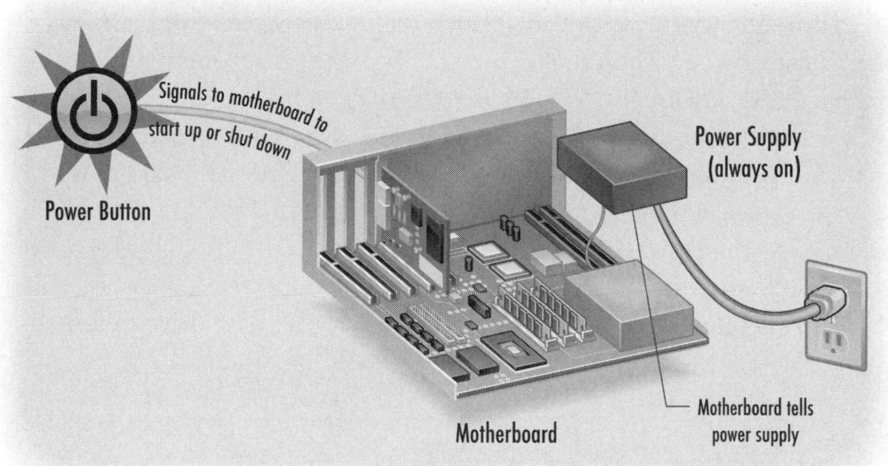


**FIGURE 3.4**
An ATX system's power supply is always on; the motherboard controls the PC's on/off state.

On an AT system, the case is not directly connected to the motherboard. Instead, there is a built-in power switch on the power supply or a set of wires coming from the power supply to which either a switch or a set of four metal leads is attached. This connects to the back of the power button on the case; when the user presses the button, the power supply turns on. Figure 3.5 shows an example of this means of turning power on and off.

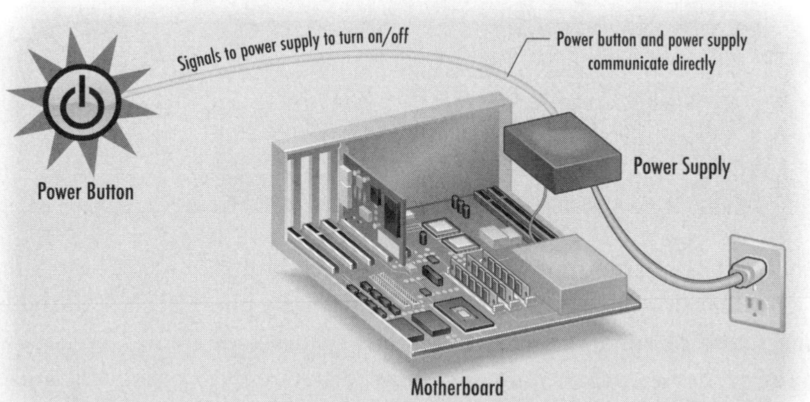

**FIGURE 3.5**
An AT system's power supply turns on and off with the power button on the case.

## TRY IT!

See if you can determine which type of case and power supply your PC has. If there are multiple PCs in your lab, see whether any of them are different from yours.

### *Bays*

**Bay**

A slot in a computer case for installing a disk drive.

Besides the form factor of the case, there is also its number of bays to consider. A *bay* is a holding area for a drive. The more bays a case has, the larger it is, and the more expandable the computer system will be. A large case with many bays should have a higher wattage power supply than a small case, because each drive installed in a bay will draw power.

Cases have internal and external bays. Internal bays are for hard drives (that is, drives that do not require external access). External bays are for drives that have removable disks, such as those for CDs or floppy disks. An external bay can be used for an internal device simply by leaving the plastic panel to cover up the hole in front, so having lots of external bays increases flexibility. Figure 3.6 shows some external bays with a CD drive mounted in one of them to demonstrate how drives would be oriented.

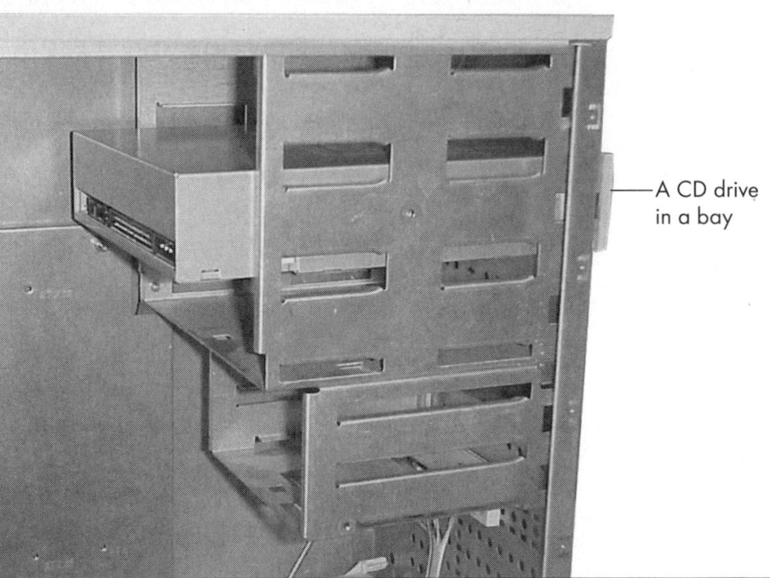


**FIGURE 3.6**
External Bays

Cases have two sizes of external bays: 3½-inch and 5¼-inch. These refer to the sizes of disks that the drives accept, not to the physical sizes of the bays themselves. The smaller-size drive bay is 4 inches wide, while the larger one is about 5¾ inches wide. Figure 3.7 shows a system with two of each size.

One of the smaller bays has a floppy drive in it; one of the larger bays has its cover removed and is ready to accept a large drive such as that for a CD.

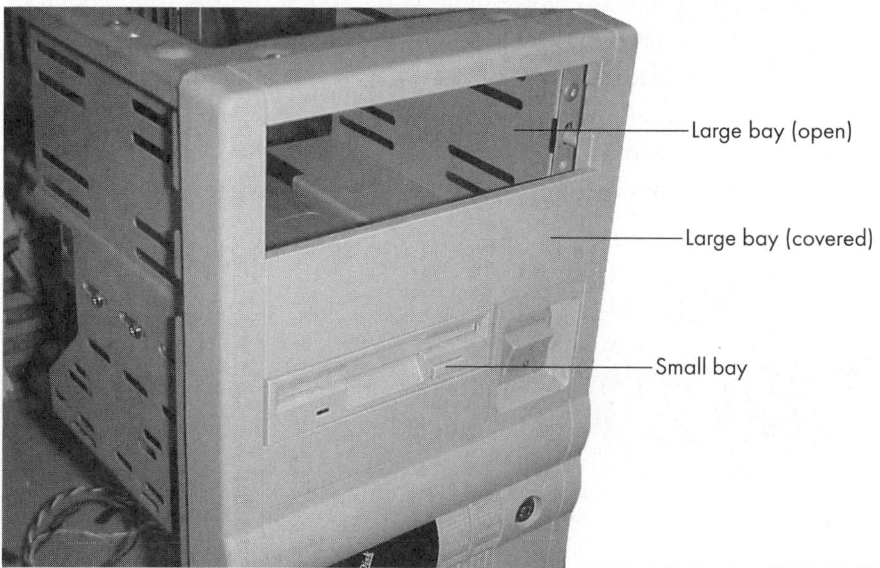


**FIGURE 3.7**
Two Sizes of External Bays

Different case manufacturers use various names to describe their products based on the number of drive bays they contain. *Tower* refers to a case that stands up on end rather than laying flat on the desk; flat-laying cases are called *desktop* cases. A small upright case with only a few bays (such as the one in Figure 3.7) is referred to as a minitower. A case with a few more bays (for example, at least three large and two small) might be called a midtower. A big case with four or more large bays is usually called a full tower. However, there is no standardization in naming—one manufacturer's midtower may have the same number of bays as another manufacturer's full tower. When reading the specs for a case, pay attention both to the internal and the external bays. For example, a case might have four large external, two small external, and four internal bays.

**Tower**

A PC case that sits upright, with its largest side perpendicular to the floor.

**Desktop**

A PC case that sits with its largest side flat against the desk.

## TRY IT!

**Count the number of internal and external bays contained in your PC. Also count the number of drive connectors on the power supply. Which would you run out of first: drive bays or power supply connectors for drives?**

## Preparing a Case for Use

A brand-new case will come with a bag of screws to be used for installing the motherboard and drives. Chapter 8 will cover installation of the motherboard and other basic components.

A new case will also come with a round speaker that has a couple of wires attached to it. This speaker conveys the system beeps and other base-level sounds the PC makes; it is not the same as the stereo speakers that attach to the sound card and deliver the sounds and music heard in Windows.

This speaker may already be mounted on the case; if not, it must be mounted prior to installing the motherboard because it contains a powerful magnet that can do damage to components if it is allowed to move around freely. Figure 3.8 shows two different types of speaker mountings.

**FIGURE 3.8**
Two Speaker Mountings

The holes where expansion slots will fit into the back of the new case are covered with scored metal panels. These panels pop out with a screwdriver. There is no need to release all of them; you may want to leave them in place until it is time actually to install the expansion cards. Any open holes must be covered with removable metal plates to keep the case's cooling system working efficiently, so if you are just going to cover the hole with a blank plate there is no reason to remove the metal panel. Figure 3.9 shows a case with most of the panels removed; only two remain.

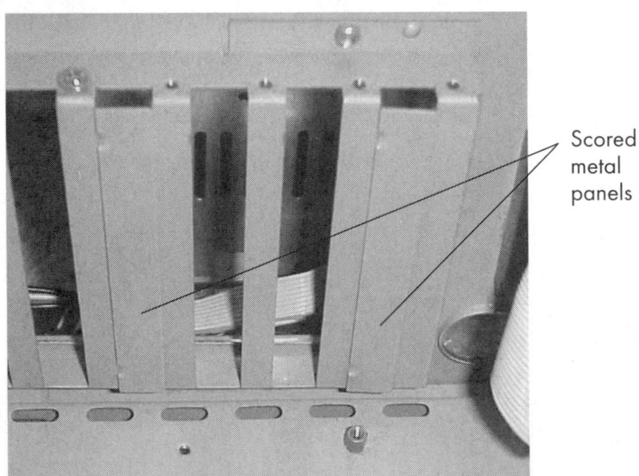


**FIGURE 3.9**
Scored Metal Panels Covering Openings for Expansion Cards

## TRY IT!

If there are any scored panels remaining on your case, pop one of them out and then cover the hole with a metal backplate.

Some cases (such as the one in Figure 3.10) also have pop-out metal panels behind the plastic panels that cover the drive bays. The metal panels can be removed with a screwdriver at any time.

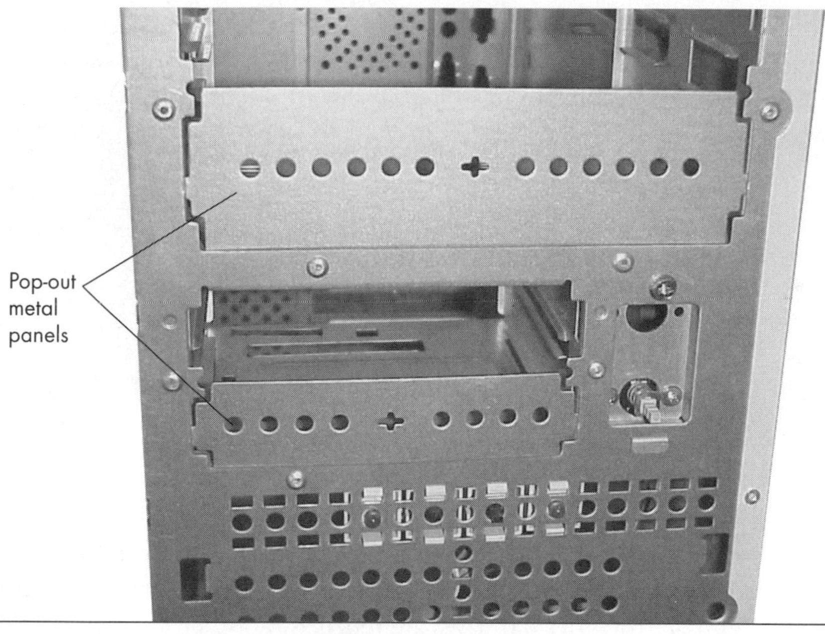


**FIGURE 3.10**
Metal Panels behind the Plastic Drive Bay Covers

As mentioned earlier and shown in Figure 3.3, a case will have a tangle of wires with small connectors coming out of the front. These will connect to various pins on the motherboard (Chapter 8 covers motherboard installation). As you follow the case preparation instructions, just move the wires off to one side for the moment.

At this point the case is ready for a motherboard (and power supply, if one is not already installed). See "Power Supply" later in this chapter if the case does not already have a power supply.

## TRY IT!

If you have a new case, prepare it for use by performing the activities just described, including mounting the speaker and removing the scored metal panels from any drive bays and expansion slots you think you will be using right away.

## Electricity Basics

The A+ Core Hardware Service Technician Examination includes several basic questions about electrical functionality and testing as they pertain to PCs. Though these concepts are not difficult to understand, they can be intimidating to many students and PC technicians whose everyday work does not include dealing with electricity.

When you plug an electrical device into a wall outlet, you will note that there are two prongs on the plug (plus an optional third prong for grounding). One prong is positive; the other is negative. Electricity flows into the negative prong, through the device, and then back out the positive prong into the socket, as shown in Figure 3.11.

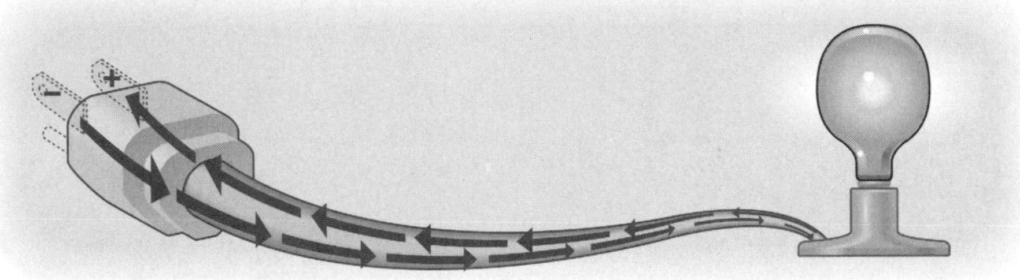


**FIGURE 3.11**
Electricity flows from the negative socket to the positive socket by way of the electrical cord plugged into the outlet.

Most textbooks explain electricity in terms of water flow, but there is another useful analogy: Think of positive and negative electrical charges as people who are attracted to one another, but separated. Positives and negatives are very attracted to one another, and are always looking for any opportunity to get together. Positives are repelled by other positives, and negatives are repelled by other negatives.

A large group of negatives start together in one socket of an electrical outlet. They do not want to be there together—they want to go out and find positives. So when an electrical cord is connected to the outlet, the negatives immediately travel down the path provided for them. They travel through the outgoing wire in the cable up into the electrical device; the flow of the negatives through the device is like a water current that turns a waterwheel. Then they travel down a second wire that leads back toward the outlet, but this second wire points directly into the positive socket of the outlet.

### Volts

The greater the difference in charge between the positives and the negatives, the greater the drive for them to get together and the more power the members of each positive/negative pair supply on their way to meet one another. This drive is measured in *volts* (v). Ordinary household electricity is 110 volts (110v) in the United States; in some other countries it is different (220 volts in most of Europe). It is important that the entire country have a standard voltage because electrical devices are designed to work only with a specific voltage. Too much voltage and a device will overheat and burn out; too little and it simply will not work.

**Volt**

A measurement of the strength of the electricity flowing through a circuit.

## AMPS

There is not just one positive/negative pair; there are billions of them, just as there are billions of water molecules in a rushing river. A single water molecule cannot turn a waterwheel, but when billions of them work together, they can make the wheel spin very fast. As with water flow, the rate of flow of electricity is called the *current*. It refers to how quickly the electricity flows through the path. Current is measured in *amperes*, or *amps* for short.

**Current**

The rate of flow of electricity.

**Ampere (amp)**

A measurement of current.

## WATTS

*Wattage* is the overall amount of power a device actually uses. It is determined by multiplying volts by the amps. For example, a 75-watt lightbulb uses 0.68 amps of 110v power (because 110 times 0.68 is approximately 75).

A lightbulb is a good example to look at here because bulbs of different wattages will work in the same light socket. For example, suppose someone replaces a 75-watt bulb with a 100-watt bulb; the device would still use 110 volts, but would draw about 0.91 amps.

This illustrates a point to remember for the test: the amperage is controlled by the device receiving the power. The device draws the amps it needs out of the outlet; the outlet does not push the amps onto the device proactively. When several different devices connect to the same extension cord, each one uses the same voltage but different amps, resulting in different wattages.

**Wattage**

The amount of electricity a device uses, derived by multiplying voltage by amperage.

## RESISTANCE

The positives and negatives always seek each other through the shortest, easiest path they can find—the path of least resistance. This is not just an old cliché; *resistance* is an electrical term that refers to the amount of

**Resistance**

The amount of obstacle placed in the electricity's path.

**Ohm**

A unit of measurement for resistance.

obstacle placed in the electricity's path, as measured in *ohms*. The Greek omega symbol (Ω) represents ohms as a unit of measure.

Resistance measurements are used to describe the path(s) that electricity can take. Given the opportunity, the electricity will always choose the lower resistance. Electricity needs a resistance of less than 20 ohms in order to be able to connect negative and positive. Infinite ohms, abbreviated with the infinity symbol (∞), would create total resistance—that is, no possible path.

Resistance does not have anything to do with any of the other factors discussed so far; it is a measure of the device itself. Resistance is always tested when the device is removed from any power source, because a device will always have the same resistance—that is, the same capacity for impeding electricity from passing through it freely—no matter what electricity is available to it.

**The primary reason to measure resistance would be to test a circuit suspected of being faulty. For example, suppose there is a cable that you suspect has a broken wire inside. You could test the resistance from one end of the cable to the other. If the wire is broken, the resistance measurement would be infinity (∞), meaning there is no connection at all. If the wire is intact, the resistance measurement would be a number (less than 20).**

## GROUNDING

Just as water is always seeking sea level and will flow downward until it gets there, electricity is always seeking the ground. When people get struck by lightning, the electricity takes a path to the ground through their bodies. When birds sit on an electrical line, they are not electrocuted because they are not touching the ground. The electricity has no reason to pass through the birds' bodies because the birds do not offer a path to the ground. If there were a way for a bird to put one foot on the wire and the other on the ground, the bird would be electrocuted, as would a human being.

Chapter 2 discussed the importance of grounding with static electricity. That same principle is in effect for the power coming from the wall outlet to the PC. The third prong on a connector (the round one) is a ground line; it plays no role in the normal in-and-out electrical flow through the socket. Instead, it is there to provide a path of very little resistance to the ground should one be needed (for example, if a short-circuit occurs, injecting a large amount of electricity into the system at once). It is a safety feature, nothing more.

### AC versus DC

Earlier you saw that, with an outlet, the negative electrical charges travel along the outgoing and ingoing wires looking for positives. In Figure 3.11 one prong is labeled + and the other -, but that is an oversimplification. In fact, the charged wires in the socket holes alternate between being positive and negative many times per second. The speed at which they alternate is measured in cycles per second, or hertz (Hz). Ordinary household electricity alternates at 60 Hz. This type of electrical delivery is called *alternating current* (AC). AC is an efficient way of sending power over wires, especially over long distances. When devices run on battery power, however, they use *direct current* (DC). With direct current, power always flows the same direction all the time—from negative to positive. Batteries use DC because they have no need to be far away from the devices they power and because this current requires lower overhead (which is desirable for a simple, battery-operated system).

PC components require DC power, but the wall outlet supplies AC, so one of the jobs of the power supply is to convert AC to DC. This will be discussed further under "Power Supply" later in this chapter.

**Alternating current (AC)**

A type of electrical delivery that changes the direction of the positive and negative charges many times per second (typically 60 Hz); used in household electricity.

**Direct current (DC)**

A type of electrical delivery in which the direction of the positive and negative charges does not change; used in batteries.

## Taking Electrical Measurements

Computer technicians use a device called a *multimeter* when taking electrical measurements. The "multi" part of the word refers to the fact that it is actually several meters in one: a voltmeter to measure volts, an ammeter to measure amps, and an ohmmeter to measure ohms. The meter has a dial or switch that can change among the different measurements.

There are two types of multimeters: analog and digital. As noted in Chapter 1, analog refers to continuously variable data. An analog multimeter has a gauge with a needle, which moves to show the measurement. It is *continuously variable*, meaning that there is no fixed division between one measurement and the next. A digital multimeter, in contrast, has a *light-emitting diode* (LED) screen that shows the measurement as a number; the division between one value and another value is mathematically quantifiable.

Analog multimeters are fine for some jobs, but digital devices are much better suited for working on computer equipment, for three reasons. First, the digital readout is easier to read accurately. Second, an analog meter does not show negative voltages; to test something with negative voltage, the probes must be reversed. Finally, and most important, when a multimeter

**Multimeter**

A meter for taking multiple types of electrical measurements, usually including voltage, amperage, and resistance.

**Continuously variable**

Having no fixed division between one measurement or value and the next.

**Light-emitting diode (LED)**

Semiconductor device that emits light when an electric current passes through it.

measures resistance, it sends a small pulse of electricity through the device being tested to see how much it impedes that pulse's progress. Analog multimeters must send a much stronger pulse because they need more electricity to move the needle. This stronger pulse of electricity can damage some sensitive electronic components. A digital multimeter, on the other hand, uses a much weaker pulse that will not do any harm. Figure 3.12 shows a digital multimeter.

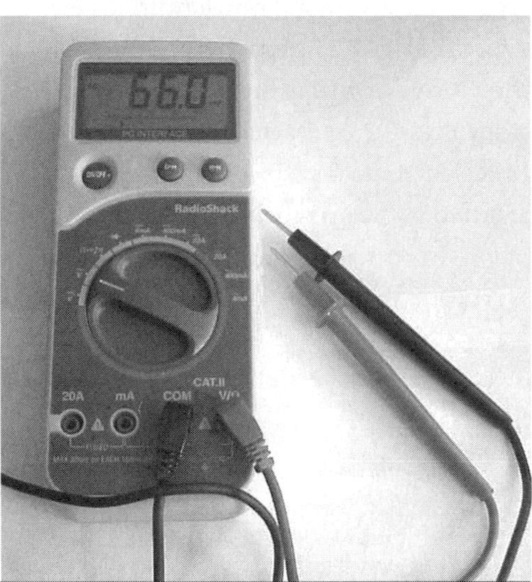


**FIGURE 3.12**
A Digital Multimeter

The multimeter has two long skinny probes, one red and one black. The red probe goes on the live wire and the black one on a ground wire, and the gauge reports the measurement. There are typically at least two dials or range selectors: one to switch among the various functionalities (ohms, amps, or volts) and one to switch among ranges. Some newer multimeters adjust the range automatically, so there is no manual selector required.

## Measuring Resistance

Resistance is the amount of obstacle that electrical current encounters in passing from point A to point B. The most common use of this measurement is to test the ability of current to flow through a conduit such as a cable or wire. If current should be able to pass from one end of a cable to another, for example, and the multimeter shows an infinite amount of resistance (that is, no flow at all), the wire probably has a break in it.

As mentioned earlier, resistance is measured in ohms. A measurement of 1 ohm means that 1 amp of current can pass through when 1 volt is applied.

To test resistance, set the multimeter to ohms and then place the probes on either end of the wire in question (either probe can go at either end). The multimeter sends some electricity through the red probe and measures the amount of electricity that comes back through the black probe. From this reading it determines a resistance measurement. Place either probe at either end of the cable; it doesn't matter.

Keep in mind that not every cable sends a wire straight through. In some cables a certain pin at one end corresponds to a completely different pin at the other end. Chapter 7 explains more about cables, including how to read a pin-out diagram that shows the pins at each end.

## Measuring Voltage

Recall that voltage measures the strength of the electricity being delivered. Standard 110-volt power passes to the computer's power supply, which steps it down considerably and delivers it to components requiring various voltages. For example, a typical floppy disk requires some power of +5v and some of +12v.

Voltage can be either positive or negative. Computer power supplies are capable of supplying both types to their components, but most components use only positive. When certain voltages used on a PC are referred to in this text, + and - signs will be included for clarity since it is possible for both to exist on different wires coming out of the same power supply.

The most common use of voltage testing for a PC technician is to measure the voltage from a wire coming out of the computer's power supply, in order to ensure that the correct voltages are being provided to components.

Voltage must be tested with the computer on. Since a connector must not be unplugged while the PC is running, you must stick the probe down into the back of the connector, where the wire comes into it. This is called *back probing*. For example, the red wires from the power supply should deliver +5v. To test that, set the multimeter to volts. Then place the red probe as far down as possible inside the connector where the red wire enters the plug, and place the black probe down inside where a black wire (a ground wire) enters the same plug. See Figure 3.13 for an example.

**Back probing**

A technique for taking electrical measurements while a device is running by sticking the probes in the backs of the connector holes.

### In Real Life

**Electrical testing is one of the few reasons for working on the inside of a PC while it is running. But you are not really working on it in terms of adding or removing anything—you are simply running a test. Besides, if you suspect voltage problems, the computer will probably not start up at all, so the fact that the power is on does not necessarily mean that the computer is operating.**

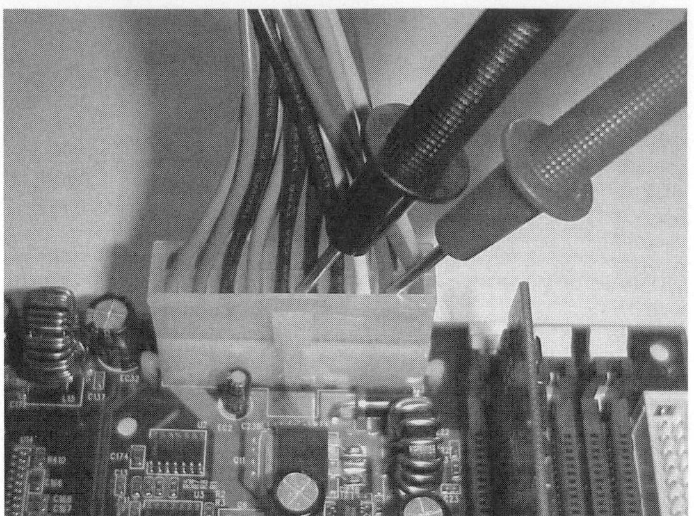

**FIGURE 3.13**
Back probing a connector tests the voltage on its wires while it is operating.

## TRY IT!

Test the voltage of the various wires in the power supply connector to the motherboard. Do *not* wear an antistatic wrist strap while doing this, to avoid the potential for electrical shock.

### Measuring Current

Current, the rate of flow of the electricity, is measured in amperes, or amps. For example, a typical floppy disk draws ½ amp of +5v and 1 amp of +12v. As with voltage, amperage must be measured with the power on. To test current, set the multimeter to amps and then place the probes in series with the device and turn on the power. In other words, instead of simply connecting the probes to the intact circuit, use the probes to make the multimeter a part of the circuit, so that the device cannot receive current without going through the multimeter. As the current flows through the multimeter and into the device, the multimeter measures the amps that the device pulls. This can be awkward or impossible to do with most PC components, which is why the average technician seldom (if ever) measures current in real-life work.

## Power Supply

Now that you are grounded (pun intended!) in basic electrical science, it is time to look at the power supply unit of a PC, that metal box with all the wires coming out of it.

The power supply takes wall current (110-volt AC) and converts it to an appropriate level of DC voltage for the various components in a PC. Depending on the component, this can be +3.3v, +5v, or +12v. Generally, the motherboard and any circuit cards use +3.3v or +5v, and fans and disk drives use +12v. Newer motherboards and processors tend toward +3.3v, while older ones are usually +5v. The CPU itself usually operates at an even lower voltage, but the motherboard handles the stepping down of the voltage from its own supply to whatever the CPU needs.

Many power supplies also generate -5v and -12v, but those negative voltages are rarely, if ever, used in modern systems, and some of the newer power supplies do not even provide -5v support. Support for -5v is part of the ISA standard, but new systems being produced today are almost all PCI-only, so they do not require such support.

Why do the plug(s) from the power supply to the motherboard have so many different pins and wires of different colors? This is to provide different voltages of power signal to the motherboard, which then passes them out as needed to connected devices. The motherboard itself uses only +5v. All the other plugs coming out of the power supply, called *Molex connectors*, are for drives, and they provide +12v (yellow) and +5v (red) power, plus two ground wires (black).

**Molex connector**

A connector from the power supply to a hard drive, CD drive, or 5.25-inch floppy drive.

## Types of Power Supplies

There are two basic types of power supplies, corresponding to the types of cases and motherboards: AT and ATX.

### *AT Power Supply*

The AT power supply can be distinguished from the ATX by two features:

- It has P8 and P9 connectors, each of them six-wire, for connecting to the motherboard. They may or may not be physically labeled P8 and P9, but can still be distinguished from all the other connectors because they are the only ones with six wires. P8 and P9 connectors are shown in Figure 3.14.
- On a modern AT power supply, in addition to all the colorful wires, there is an insulated black cable coming out of the power supply, at the end of which there is a power switch or there are four plastic-covered metal leads (for attaching to a built-in power switch inside the case). Figure 3.15 shows a switch cable and metal leads.

**FIGURE 3.14**
P8 and P9 Connectors to the Motherboard

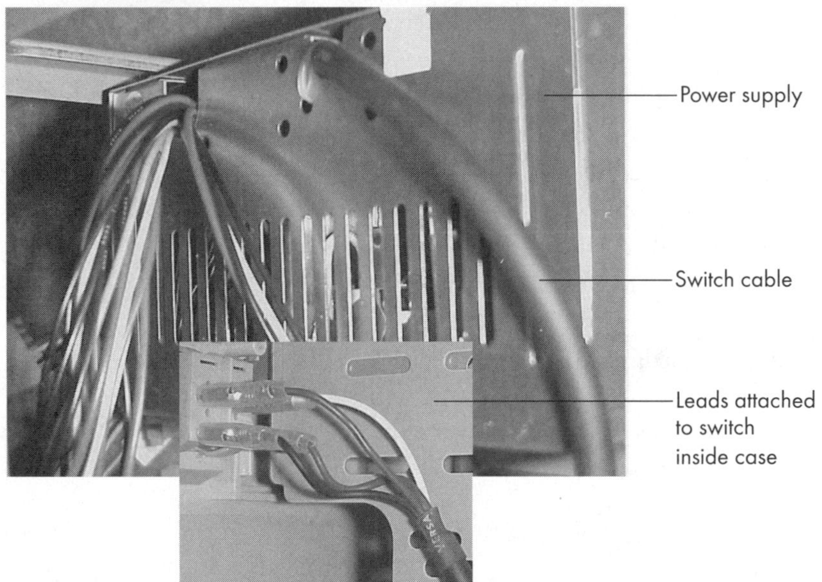


**FIGURE 3.15**
Leads for Attaching to the Power Switch inside the Case

The distinction concerning "modern" AT power supply is necessary because there have actually been several versions of the AT power supply over the years, some of which have had a power switch built into the side of the power supply instead of on the end of a black cable. In these early models a hole was cut out of the side of the case for the power switch to stick out. Table 3.1 shows the differences among the various AT power supply styles, but this information is not relevant to the test. The only type of AT power supply you will encounter in modern systems is the LPX, also known as the PS/2. The term "AT power supply" has come to be synonymous with the LPX style since it is the only one of the AT variants that is still being manufactured; however, it is useful to know that there are other variants.

| Type | Power Switch Type | Physical Size |
|---|---|---|
| AT Desktop | Built-in (side) | 8.35″ x 5.9″ x 5.9″ |
| AT Tower | External | 8.35″ x 5.9″ x 5.9″ |
| Baby AT | Built-in (side) | 6.5″ x 5.9″ x 5.9″ |
| LPX (PS/2) | External | 5.9″ x 5.5″ x 3.4″ |

**TABLE 3.1**
AT Power Supply Types

IBM's PS/2 computer, introduced in the late 1980s, was revolutionary in a number of ways, and introduced many new and improved connector types. Even though the actual PS/2 computer has been obsolete for a long time, the PC industry has made standard the PS/2 style of keyboard and mouse connector and the PS/2 style of AT power supply.

## TRY IT!

If you have an AT power supply, measure your power supply's outer dimensions and match them up with one of the types in Table 3.1. There are many proprietary designs in addition to the standard ones cited in the table, so do not be concerned if yours does not fit any of these specifications.

The P8 and P9 connectors fit into a single long bracket on the motherboard. Although it is physically possible to put them in any configuration, they must be arranged so that the black (ground) wires go toward the middle; otherwise the motherboard will be damaged. This possibility for damage is one reason the ATX power supply (a later design) uses a single connector to the motherboard. Figure 3.16 shows the proper installation for an AT power supply.

**FIGURE 3.16**
On an AT motherboard, make sure the black wires of the P8 and P9 connectors are together.

As mentioned earlier, the power supply steps down the voltage and provides power to the motherboard in a variety of voltages. The pins on the connectors are numbered 1 through 6, and each different-colored wire supplies something different. Figure 3.17 shows each pin number and its color and purpose. Notice how the wires of the same color have the same function. This will be discussed further under "How the Power Supply Starts the PC" later in the chapter.

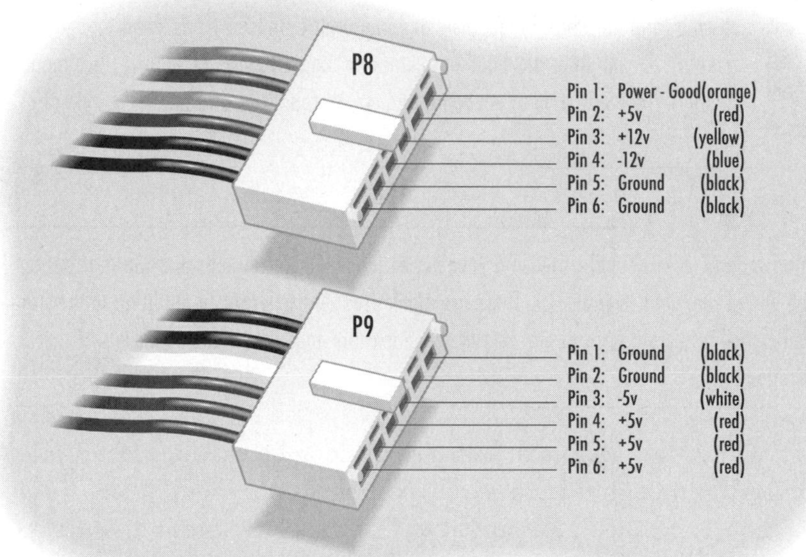


**FIGURE 3.17**
The Wires on P8 and P9 Connectors

### *ATX Power Supply*

The ATX power supply is a newer, improved model, and the standard for most systems built today (although AT power supplies are still readily available in computer stores).

The ATX power supply can be differentiated from the AT family in the following ways:

- It connects to the motherboard with a single 20-pin connector, shown in Figure 3.18.
- It has no power switch on the side or directly connected to it. As explained earlier in the chapter, the ATX design runs power on and off through the motherboard. Some ATX power supplies have a small rocker switch on the back of the power supply, but most have none.
- It has a wire that provides +5v standby power (purple) and a Power On wire (green). These two work together to enable features such as Wake on LAN that allow the PC to turn itself on when a device (such as a LAN connection or a modem) requests it.

- It adds support for +3.3v power, a lower voltage used by newer CPUs. Providing this lower voltage is advantageous because then the motherboard does not need a resistor to step down the voltage further for the CPU. Orange wires are used for this voltage.
- It uses a gray wire for Power-Good, whereas the AT power supply uses an orange wire for that. (Orange is already taken by +3.3v in the ATX.)
- The gray wire, Power-Good, is pin 8 on an ATX connector. Figure 3.19 shows the pin configuration for the connector.

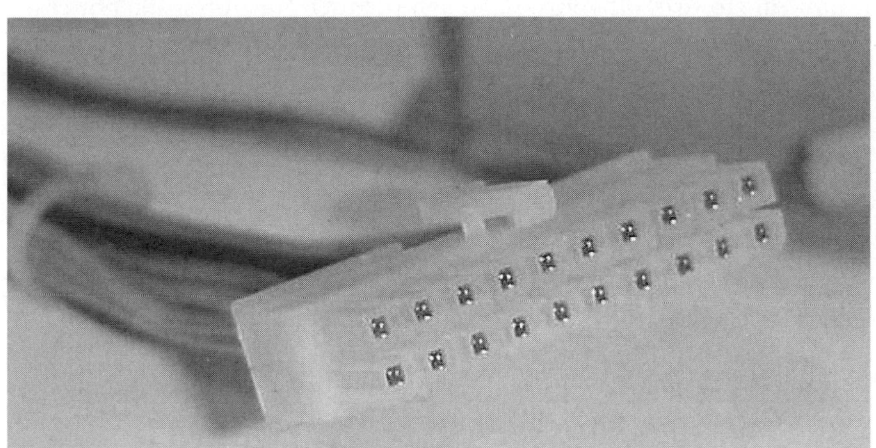

**FIGURE 3.18**
An ATX Connector to the Motherboard

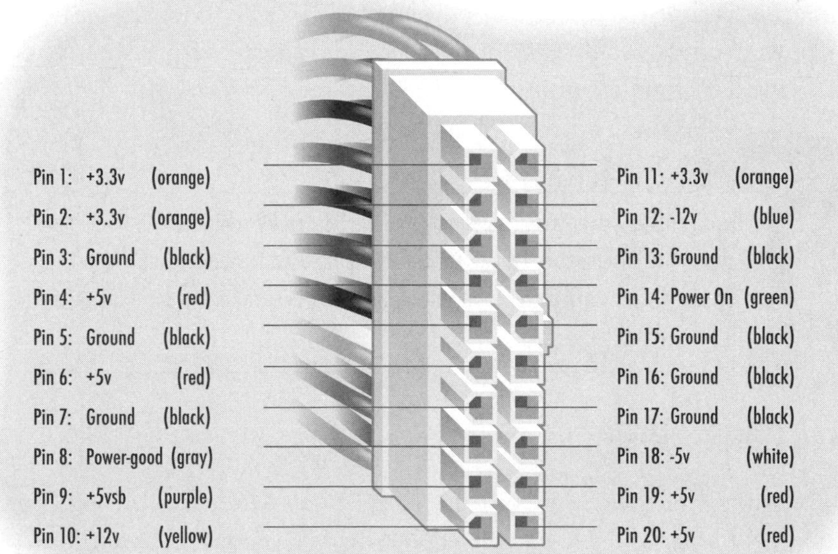


**FIGURE 3.19**
Pin Numbering on an ATX Power Supply

The ATX power supply has several advantages over the AT model. It is part of the larger ATX system type, so some of the benefits involve the tying together of various ATX components. For example, an ATX system is designed so that the CPU sits closer to the power supply than it does on an AT system, allowing the power supply fan to help cool it. The addition of +3.3v support is also an important benefit, as is the ability for the system to control its own power switch.

With an AT system, Windows shuts down and a message appears, saying "It is now safe to turn off your PC." Then the user must press the power button to turn it off. But on an ATX system, Windows shuts down and the PC turns itself off. This is because of those extra green and purple wires on the motherboard connector that handle standby and powering on and off through software.

Early ATX systems used a positive pressure system—a reverse flow fan on the power supply that sucked air *out* of the PC rather than into it. The idea was to place an additional fan or vent at the bottom of the case that pulled air in, and then let the power supply fan suck the air past the CPU and out the back. This would enable the CPU to be cooled with a passive heat sink rather than requiring a separate fan of its own. A filter could be installed over the intake area to keep the PC cleaner inside as well. There were some drawbacks, though. Such systems needed a more powerful fan in the power supply, and the CPU cooling was not as effective in real-life use as the designers envisioned. This type of power supply was abandoned, and the ATX power supplies sold today have the standard negative pressure system, with a fan that blows air into the case.

### In Real Life

**Since an ATX power supply does not have the P8 and P9 connectors to the motherboard, the designations P8 and P9 are free to be used by some other connectors. On my system's ATX power supply, for example, a Mini connector for a floppy drive is labeled P8.**

## Drive Connectors

**Mini connector**

A connector from the power supply to a 3.5-inch floppy drive.

A power supply has two types of drive connectors: Molex and *Mini*. There typically will be several Molex connectors (between four and seven) but only one or two Minis. The Minis are used for floppy drives; the Molexes are for all other drives (hard, CD, and so on). Both types of connectors deliver +5v on the red wire and +12v on the yellow. Figure 3.20 shows the two connector types.

**FIGURE 3.20**
Drive Connectors from the Power Supply: Mini (left) and Molex (right)

## How the Power Supply Starts the PC

When a user turns on a PC, the power supply starts itself, and waits until any startup spike or sag has passed and the power output has stabilized. Then it sends +5v through pin 8 (on an ATX connector) or pin 1 on the P8 connector (on an AT). This is called the Power-Good (or Power OK) signal. The motherboard looks for this signal, and if between +3.0v and +6.0v are passing through the Power-Good pin, it turns itself on and starts making use of the rest of the power coming through the other pins on the power-supply-to-motherboard connector.

If the motherboard is receiving power from the other pins but the right voltage is not coming through the Power-Good pin, it waits, continually resetting itself until it receives the correct voltage on Power-Good. This system helps prevent electrical damage to sensitive components from a malfunctioning power supply. The designers of the PC thought this was a very conservative system that would ensure freedom from power supply problems, but as any PC technician will tell you, power supply problems can and do still occur.

### In Real Life

The power supplies in PCs are of the switching type (as opposed to linear). Because of this, they do not run without a load—that is, without some device drawing power from them. If you turn on a power supply that is not connected to anything, it either will not work at all (best case) if it has protection circuitry built in, or will overheat and burn out within a few seconds (worst case) if it does not. Therefore, when testing power supplies, you should always have something connected to them, even if it is an old, out-of-date motherboard and an obsolete drive. How much do you need to connect? It depends on the age of the power supply. On modern systems, most motherboards draw the needed amount of current by themselves, but on older systems, or with larger power supplies, at least one disk might need to be connected as well.

## DETERMINING WATTAGE REQUIREMENTS

The wattage of the power supply refers to the maximum wattage of which it is capable. An extremely high wattage power supply in a lightly loaded system is a waste, because the system draws only what it needs in terms of amps. (That is not to say, however, that a high-*quality* power supply is a waste, because such power supplies can provide cleaner and more reliable power to a system and can help reduce sags and spikes from the wall current.)

Remember, wattage is voltage times current. Each individual drive and component draws a certain number of amps and uses a certain number of volts (supplied by the power supply). For example, a floppy disk has a connector from the power supply that supplies both +12v and +5v power. The drive draws .5 amp of +5v and 1 amp of +12v, for a total usage of 14.5 watts of power.

Each power supply generates a certain number of watts overall, but those watts cannot be accessed simply at will. There is a specific number of amps of various voltages. For example, a typical 250-watt AT power supply might break down like this (remember, an AT power supply does not supply +3.3V):

| | |
|---|---|
| +5v | maximum of 25 amps (125 watts) |
| +12v | maximum of 10 amps (120 watts) |
| -5v | maximum of .5 amps (2.5 watts) |
| -12v | maximum of .5 amps (2.5 watts) |

For a 235-watt ATX, the breakdown might be something like this:

| | |
|---|---|
| +5v | maximum of 25 amps (125 watts) |
| +3.3 | maximum of 14 amps (46.2 watts) |
| (+5V and +3.3V combined: maximum of 125 watts) | |
| +12v | maximum of 8 amps (96 watts) |
| -5v | maximum of .5 amps (2.5 watts) |
| -12v | maximum of .5 amps (6 watts) |

Notice that for the above specifications, the combination of +5v and +3.3v cannot exceed 125 watts. That allows for maximum power flexibility while still maintaining the 235-watt limit. Figure 3.21 shows the label on the ATX power supply with the preceding specifications. Not all power supplies have such labels, but those of better quality usually do.

Model : HP-235ATXAK
AC INPUT (60/50Hz): 115V~/6A , 230V~/3.5A
DC OUTPUT: +5V⎓/25A , +12V⎓/8A
-5V⎓/0.5A , -12V⎓/0.5A
MAX. OUTPUT POWER: 235W +3.3V⎓/14A
FUSE RATING: T6.3AH/250V +5VSB⎓/1A

**FIGURE 3.21**
Typical Power Supply Label Showing Voltage Breakdown

To determine the needed power supply capacity, make a list of all the devices in the PC and then total their power requirements. Some devices have these requirements printed on them; others may require estimation or a call to the manufacturer. For example, a motherboard might use 5 amps of +3.3v and .7 amps of +12v, for a total of about 25 watts. The various amps and volts for devices shown in Table 3.2 can be used for big-picture estimations.

| Device | Estimated Wattage |
|---|---|
| Motherboard | 20-30 watts |
| CPU (depends on CPU type): | |
| Pentium II | 30 watts |
| Pentium III | 34 watts |
| Pentium 4 | 65 watts |
| Athlon | 70 watts |
| AGP video card. | 20-50 watts |
| Average PCI circuit board | 5 watts each |
| Average ISA circuit board | 10 watts each |
| Floppy drive | 5 watts |
| CD drive | 10-25 watts |
| RAM | 8 watts per 128MB |
| IDE hard drive | 5-15 watts |
| SCSI hard drive | 10-40 watts |

**TABLE 3.2**
Wattage Estimation Chart

## In Real Life

The numbers in Table 3.2 came from the PC Power and Cooling Web site (www.pcpowerandcooling.com). This site is an excellent reference resource for PC power supply information, as well as a good place to buy high-quality replacement power supplies, cases, and cooling devices.

Consider this example: You are working on a Pentium III system with 256MB of RAM, an AGP video card, and three PCI expansion cards. There are two CD drives, one floppy drive, and two IDE hard drives. What size power supply is required? The answer: 136 (low estimate) to 226 (high estimate) watts. So a 235-watt power supply should be adequate, but a 200-watt power supply might not be sufficient. Remember that these numbers are general—they do not take into consideration the different voltages. It is possible for a power supply to have plenty of +12v capacity left but be maxed out in +5v, for example. To be precise, calculate the requirements for each individual device.

Most power supplies have a limited number of drive connectors, depending on their available wattage. A 300-watt power supply might have more drive connectors than a 175-watt model, for example. If you have more drives to hook up than connectors to supply them, you can buy a splitter plug (like an extension cord) that splits one plug into two. However, you should not do this more than once in a system, because the plugs are limited for a reason—the power supply has only a set amount of power it can give. It is better to replace the power supply with a higher-wattage model if there are many more drives to support than there are plugs available.

Several other measures exist of a power supply's performance, but these are not typically "shopping specs." A hardware enthusiast might want to compare the ratings of power supplies for features such as *MTBF*, input range, peak inrush current, holdup time, transient response, overvoltage protection, maximum and minimum load current, and so on.

**MTBF**

Mean time between failures, a measurement of the reliability of a device in terms of the average amount of time it can run before it fails.

## TRY IT!

**Make a list of all the devices in your system and use the guidelines in this section to estimate how many watts must be available to power it reliably.**

## Symptoms of a Faulty Power Supply

A failing power supply can cause all sorts of problems that do not appear to be directly related, leading the less experienced technician on a useless search through memory, processor, motherboard, and hard disk errors. When troubleshooting an intermittent problem that seems to jump around—for example, a memory problem that reports a different memory address as faulty each time, or spontaneous rebooting after a random amount of time—step back and consider the larger picture. There are three reasons a power supply can cause a problem: physical failure, overloading, and overheating.

**Physical failure.** In a failing power supply, the power supply is not generating its rated amount of power, or it is providing the wrong voltages on some wires. The PC generally will not start at all if such a condition exists. See "Testing a Power Supply" (below) for help in determining whether a power supply is working correctly. Replacing a faulty power supply is the best solution; repairing power supplies can be dangerous for all but the most experienced technicians, and is seldom cost-effective.

**Overloading.** There is not enough wattage to support all the devices plugged into an overloaded power supply. Problems on a system with an overloaded power supply will often occur at startup, when all the drives are spinning up, or when accessing a drive. See under "Determining Wattage Requirements" to calculate how much wattage the system needs. Then replace the power supply with a higher-wattage model if needed.

**Overheating.** Overheating occurs when the power supply fan (or sometimes the processor cooling fan) is not doing its job adequately, or when the system case's airflow is obstructed. Most computer cases are designed to pull fresh air through the case, across the major heat-producing components. The air flowing through the restricted space is very important. Removing the case cover, or leaving off empty-slot backplates, prevents the air from flowing as designed, and overheating can result. If the system starts up as it should but then begins to have problems after several minutes of operation, inadequate cooling is almost always the problem. Make sure that the airflow path is unobstructed, that the processor heat sink or cooling fan is in place and operational, and that the power supply fan is working quietly and correctly.

## Testing a Power Supply

Use a digital multimeter to test a power supply. Voltage is the measurement you are after, and remember that voltage must be tested with the power on. Further, remember that a power supply will function only when it has a load, so it must be tested while it is connected to a motherboard, and usually to a drive as well. This should not require any extra effort, since the power supply is probably already installed in the PC.

Review the section "Taking Electrical Measurements" earlier in this chapter if needed. Set the multimeter to DC-V (for DC current volts). If it is not an auto-ranging multimeter, set the range to 15 volts. Then place the black probe down inside a black wire hole, and the red probe down inside a hole of another color. Compare the multimeter's reading of the voltages to the numbers in Figures 3.17 or 3.19. If a voltage is within one or two volts of the target, that wire is functioning within an acceptable range. If not, the power supply has a problem.

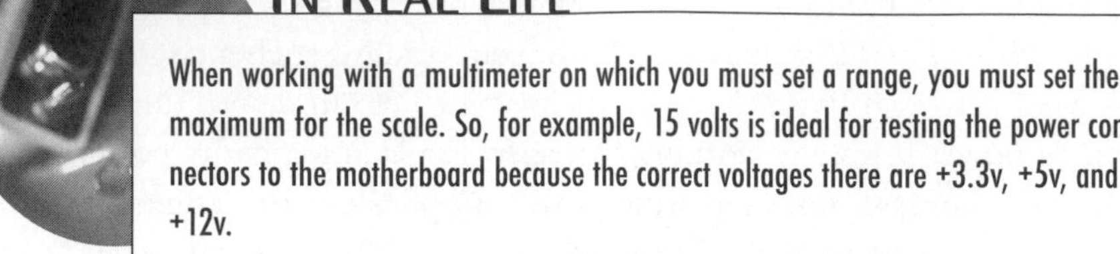

## In Real Life

**When working with a multimeter on which you must set a range, you must set the maximum for the scale. So, for example, 15 volts is ideal for testing the power connectors to the motherboard because the correct voltages there are +3.3v, +5v, and +12v.**

Next, test all the Molex connectors. If one is connected to a drive, use back probing; otherwise simply stick the probes down inside it. (Use one of the black wires on the connector for the black probe.) Remember, the yellow wire should test at +12v and the red wire at +5v.

If testing shows that the power supply is faulty, replace it (as described in the following section). Do not attempt to repair it; as you learned earlier in the chapter, it is dangerous to do so without specialized training.

## TRY IT!

**Test your power supply as described in this section.**

## Replacing a Power Supply

Removing a power supply is easy.

1. Make sure the PC is unplugged.
2. Disconnect the power supply from the motherboard.
3. If it is an AT model, disconnect the power supply from the case switch, or remove the switch itself if it is built into the power supply.
4. Remove the four screws on the back of the PC that hold the power supply in the case (see Figure 3.22). When you remove the final screw, have your hand ready inside the case to catch the power supply so it does not fall.

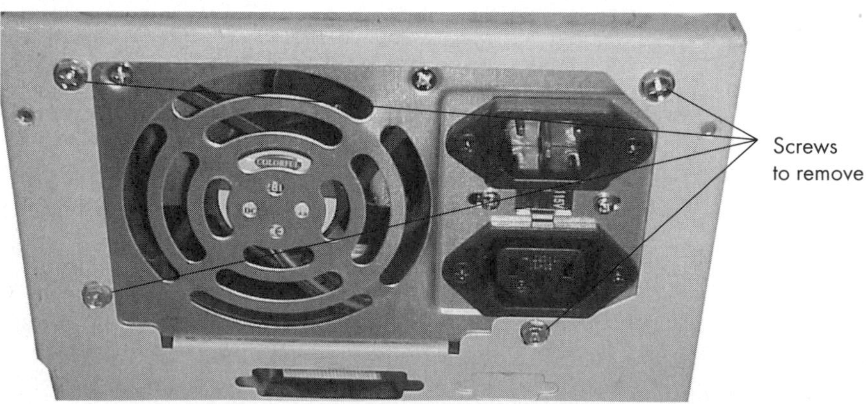


**FIGURE 3.22**
Four screws hold the power supply in the case.

Once the old power supply is removed, follow these steps to install the new one.

1. Insert the new power supply in the case and secure it with four screws.
2. If it is an AT model, connect the leads to the power switch in the case, or install the switch itself in the case if the switch is built-in.
3. Connect the power supply to the motherboard (using P8 and P9 connectors for AT or the long 20-pin connector for ATX).
4. Plug it in and try it out.

If the fan begins to spin when the power comes on, the power supply is installed correctly. If not, check the connector to the motherboard.

**TRY IT!**

**Remove and reinstall your system's power supply.**

## Surge Suppressors and Uninterruptible Power Supplies

Electrical devices rely on the power coming from the wall outlet to maintain a certain well-defined voltage range (around 110 to 120 volts). However, the actual range may differ from this because of problems with the local electricity provider, wiring in the home or office, or environmental conditions. Sometimes there are outages, power surges or spikes, and sags, all of which can inflict major damage to a PC's power supply.

A surge and a spike are basically the same thing: too much voltage. (The term "spike" is used to describe a more dramatic surge.) A sag is insufficient voltage.

External devices can help compensate for the various failings of household and office electricity. This section will review some of these devices and explain how they work and why you might want them.

**Surge suppressor**

An electrical device similar to an extension cord, containing a varistor that prevents too much voltage from passing through to the devices plugged into it.

### Surge Suppressors

A *surge suppressor* is basically an extension cord, but inside it is a metal oxide variable resistor *(varistor),* sometimes abbreviated MOV, that can absorb any excess power during a surge or spike, preventing it from reaching the plugged-in devices. An occasional power surge can be the result of poor electrical service, but the really damaging power spikes almost always come from lightning strikes.

**Varistor**

A variable resistor, also called an MOV (metal oxide varistor), which creates resistance against current flow when the flow exceeds a certain level. Used in surge suppressors to prevent overvoltage conditions.

The varistor works by depleting its own ability to resist, so over time a surge suppressor loses its effectiveness in protecting the PC from power overage. With an inexpensive model there is no way of gauging the hits that the suppressor has taken or the remaining effectiveness. Some of the better models, like the one shown in Figure 3.23, have lights that indicate the surge suppressor's "ready" status.

Some surge suppressors also include a pass-through for a telephone line, adding surge protection to it as well. This is valuable because a lightning strike can come through a phone line and destroy a modem. Modems are one of the components most often damaged by power surges, because phone lines are frequently left unprotected. A surge suppressor does nothing to help with power sags or outages; for that you need a UPS (see below).

**FIGURE 3.23**
A surge suppressor prevents devices from being damaged by power surges.

## Uninterruptible Power Supply

**Uninterruptible power supply (UPS)**

A battery backup for a computer or other electrical equipment.

An *uninterruptible power supply* (UPS) is a combination surge suppressor and battery backup. It handles power surges in the same way that a surge suppressor does, but it has the added bonus of being able to power the PC for a few minutes when a power outage occurs. This is very useful because it helps avoid problems that appear when a PC is shut down incorrectly, such as disk errors. (See Chapter 30 to find out about disk errors and how to correct them.)

In most cases a UPS includes power conditioning, so it protects against undervoltage situations (*brownouts*) as well as complete power failures. Every UPS does not have this feature, so watch for it when shopping for one.

**Brownout**

An undervoltage condition in which a device is receiving less than the normal amount of electricity.

Some UPS devices have a cable that connects to a PC (usually via serial port) that allows Windows to interact with the UPS. With this feature enabled, the UPS can signal to Windows when the battery is being used, and Windows can shut itself down automatically. This is useful for people who leave a PC running when away from home or overnight at the office.

There are two types of UPS devices. An *online UPS* runs the PC off of the battery at all times. The power comes into the battery and charges it continuously, and the PC draws its power from the battery. If power stops coming from the wall outlet, the PC simply continues running on the battery as long as it can. This type of UPS is rather expensive. Some call it a "true UPS."

**Online UPS**

A UPS that runs off of the battery continuously as the battery is continuously recharged.

The other type is a standby UPS. It works as a surge suppressor most of the time, passing the wall outlet current straight through to the devices plugged into it. The battery stays charged, but is not in the main loop. When the wall outlet stops providing power, the UPS quickly switches the devices over to the battery. There is a momentary skip when the power changes over, but it is so brief that most devices will continue working without interruption. This type of UPS is the model that local computer stores typically carry for sale, and is much more affordable. However, some experts argue that it is not a real UPS, but rather a *standby power supply* (SPS).

**Standby power supply (SPS)**

A UPS that passes regular AC current directly through to the attached devices as long as AC current is available, switching to battery when AC is not supplied.

A UPS typically has between four and six plugs, not all of which are tied into the battery. For example, the Back-UPS Pro 650 has three plugs that use the battery and three others that have only surge suppression. This enables a person to use the UPS as an extension cord/power strip for more devices than the battery itself can support.

A UPS is much larger and heavier than a surge suppressor, mainly because of its big battery. Figure 3.24 shows a typical UPS. Its battery will last for many years, but it is replaceable if it ever does go bad. The UPS has self-testing routines and lights that show the battery's status, and will report when it is time to replace the battery.

**FIGURE 3.24**
A UPS contains a large battery.

## Power Sources for Notebook PCs

Notebook PCs have more complex power systems because they are dual-mode. They run on regular AC current when plugged in, and on a DC battery when not plugged in. Further, they are able to switch back and forth between power sources instantly without interruption of any computing tasks.

### AC Adaptation

Most notebook PCs have a voltage converter and an AC-to-DC converter built into a transformer in the power cord, so they do not require a separate power supply unit inside the PC, which saves space and weight. As a result, unlike cords from desktop computers, power cords on different models of notebook computers are not interchangeable.

### Battery

All notebook PCs have a battery that supplies power for running the PC; some have two. The most common substances used in computer battery packs are nickel cadmium (NiCad), nickel-metal hydride (NiMH), and lithium ion (LIon).

Nickel cadmium is a material used in the battery packs for many notebook computers. NiCad batteries can provide considerable power, but must be recharged every three to four hours. A full recharge can take as long as 12 hours, but some batteries can be recharged in a shorter period.

The nickel cadmium batteries found in some older laptops work best when they are allowed to run completely down before recharging. If laptops using such batteries are left plugged in most of the time and used on battery power only briefly, in time the batteries lose their ability to retain a full charge. Even with full drainage, all batteries can be recharged only a limited number of times. The maximum for most NiCad batteries is about one thousand recharges.

Unlike NiCad batteries, NiMH batteries do not use heavy metals that can have toxic effects. In addition, NiMH batteries can store up to 50 percent more power than NiCad batteries, and do not suffer from loss of functionality by partial draining and recharging.

LIon batteries are composed of lithium, the lightest metal and a metal that has the highest electrochemical potential. It is also, however, unstable, so LIon batteries are made using lithium ions from chemicals. Because of their lightness and high energy density, LIon batteries are ideal for portable devices, such as notebook computers. In addition, LIon batteries are not affected by partial draining and recharging, and do not use poisonous metals such as lead, mercury, or cadmium. The only disadvantage to LIon batteries is that they are more expensive than NiCad and NiMH batteries.

Windows can communicate with the battery to find out how much power is left, and can apply power management rules to conserve that power as much as possible. Chapter 20 explains more about portable PCs.

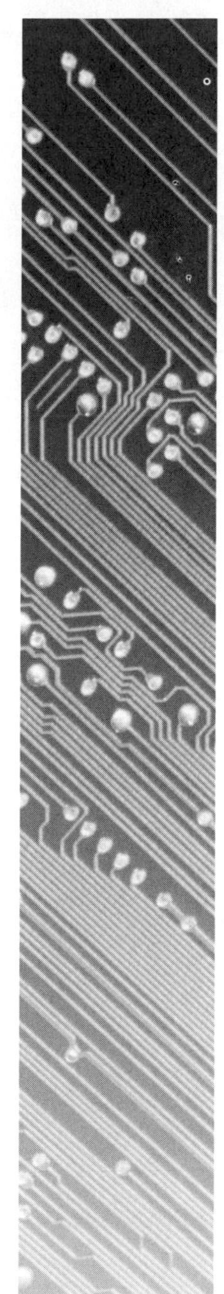

# STUDY GUIDE

Use the following summaries to review the content of this chapter.

## CASES

- A case can be either AT or ATX. This designation refers to the size and orientation of the area in which the motherboard will be mounted. Some cases are large enough to accept either an AT or an ATX motherboard.
- A case typically comes with a power supply already installed. The power supply must match the motherboard (AT or ATX).
- A technician may occasionally encounter a slim case that requires a special kind of motherboard containing no expansion slots.
- The power button on the case of an ATX system connects directly to the motherboard; the power button on an AT system connects to the power supply.
- Cases have internal and external drive bays. An internal bay can hold a drive such as a hard drive that does not require removable media. An external bay is necessary for floppy and CD drives.
- Cases have two sizes of external bays. The smaller ones are good for floppy drives and a few other drive types; the larger ones are for CD drives.
- A case can sit either on end (a tower case) or with its widest side flat on the desktop (a desktop case). Desktop cases typically have fewer external drive bays.
- Tower cases with few drive bays are known as minitowers. The next step in size and number of bays is a midtower. The tallest of the cases, with the most drive bays, is a full tower.
- When preparing a new case, you must mount the speaker, remove the bag of screws (to be set aside for later use), and remove the access panels for any drive bays or expansion slots you plan to use.

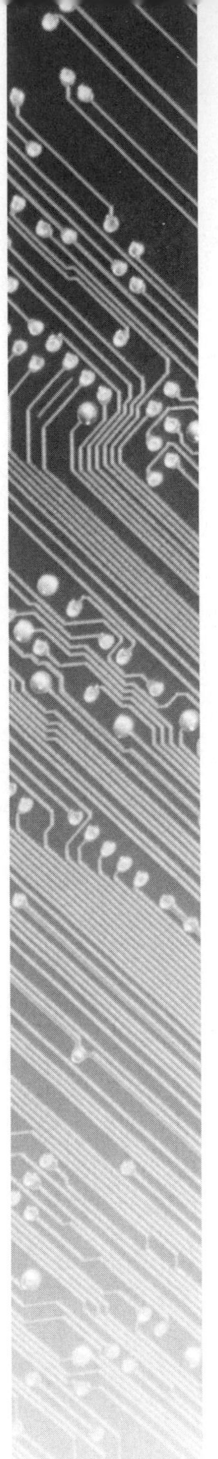

## Electricity

- Positive and negative charges are drawn together; this attraction creates the flow of electricity.
- Voltage (abbreviated as *volts* or *v*) is the measurement of the difference in charge between the positive and negative. The higher the voltage, the greater the difference. Standard AC wall current in the United States is 110v.
- Amperage (abbreviated as *amps* or *a*) is the measurement of the rate of flow of the electricity. Another name for it is current.
- Wattage (abbreviated as *watts* or *w*) is the overall amount of power a device actually uses. It is determined by multiplying volts by amps.
- Resistance is the blockage preventing the free flow of electricity through a particular path. It is measured in ohms (Ω).
- If there is no electrical path between two points, it is said to have infinite resistance, abbreviated as ∞.
- A ground connection enables excess electricity to bleed off harmlessly to the earth. The black wires on a power supply connector are ground wires. On standard electrical devices, the ground is the round prong between the two flat ones.
- AC stands for alternating current; it refers to the reversal of which socket is positive and which is negative in a wall outlet. This alternation happens thousands of times per second and is measured in hertz (Hz). Ordinary household current alternates at 60 Hz.
- DC stands for direct current; it refers to electricity that flows in one direction only and does not reverse. It is the type of electricity provided by batteries. PC components require DC, so the power supply converts AC to DC.

## Taking Electrical Measurements

- Separate meters are available to measure voltage, amperage, and resistance, but it is handier to have a multimeter, which can measure all three.
- There are analog and digital multimeters; a digital one is best for working on PCs.
- A multimeter has two probes: red and black. To measure resistance, place the probes at opposite ends of a cable or other conduit. Check resistance with the power off.

- Resistance is measured in ohms. Higher numbers mean more resistance and less electrical conductivity. At higher than 20 ohms, electricity cannot be reliably conducted.
- To measure voltage, the power must be on. Use back probing to check circuits in place.
- To test current, the multimeter must interrupt the flow of electricity so that the power flows through the multimeter to complete the circuit.

## Power Supply

- The power supply takes 110-volt AC and converts it to various levels of DC—between +3.3v and +12v for the components in a PC.
- Although the power supply can generate -5v and -12v, these negative voltages are not used in modern systems.
- Each color of wire from the power supply produces a different voltage. The black wires are for grounding.
- The larger of the two types of drive connectors on a power supply are called Molex; they run CD and hard drives. The smaller ones are called Mini; they run floppy drives.
- A power supply can be either AT or ATX. The primary differences are the connector to the motherboard and the connection to the power switch.
- On an AT power supply, P8 and P9 connectors, each with six wires, connect to the motherboard.
- An older AT power supply may have a built-in power switch. Modern AT power supplies have an insulated black cable that has either a built-in power switch or four plastic-coated leads to connect to a power switch.
- Another name for an AT power supply is LPX, but LPX actually refers only to the most modern AT power supply, not the early models.
- The ATX power supply has a single 20-pin connection to the motherboard. It has no power switch connected to it; instead it has a two-wire connector that attaches to the motherboard to control the PC's on/off state.
- The ATX power supply provides +3.3v power, so the motherboard does not need to step down the voltage further to support +3.3v CPUs.
- ATX provides extra wires (purple and green) for use with Wake on LAN and Wake on Modem, if the BIOS supports it.
- When a PC starts up, the power supply sends a +5v signal to the motherboard (on pin 8 for an ATX or on pin 1 of P8 for an AT). If the motherboard receives the signal, it knows the power supply is good and it starts up. If it does not, it keeps resetting itself until it receives the correct voltage.

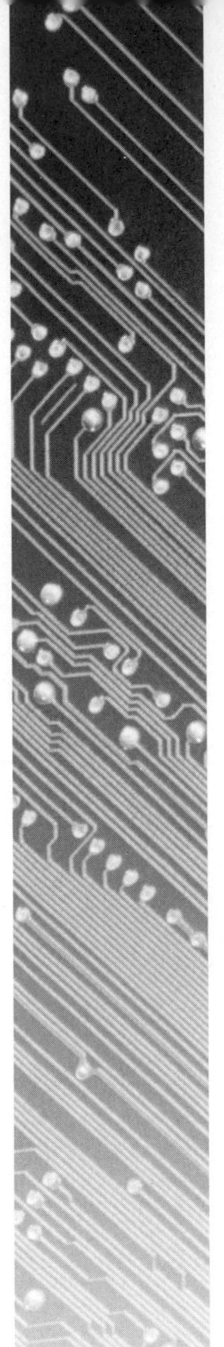

## Wattage Requirements

- Each device connected to the power supply (or to the motherboard) draws a certain number of amps of one or more voltages.
- Voltage times amperage equals wattage, so each device has a certain wattage of power it requires.
- The power supply has a maximum wattage it can provide, such as 200 watts. It provides specific maximums for various voltages; this means it cannot, for example, supply 200 watts of +5v and no watts of some other kind.
- An AT power supply is fairly evenly divided between +5v and +12v, offering about 120 watts of each in a typical 235-watt model. It also offers a small amount of -5v and -12v.
- An ATX power supply offers a combination of +5v and +3.3v, not to exceed a fixed combined amount. It also offers +12v and a small amount of -5v and -12v.
- Not all power supplies of the same wattage are identical. High-quality power supplies can produce more stable, reliable voltages and can offer features that improve the quality of the power provided.

## Power Supply Troubleshooting and Replacement

- A malfunctioning or underpowered power supply can cause seemingly random system errors that may mimic memory, hard disk, or motherboard problems.
- A power supply may malfunction because of physical failure, because it does not have enough wattage to support all attached devices, or because of overheating.
- To test a power supply, use a multimeter to test the voltage on each of the wires of each of the connectors.
- To remove a power supply, disconnect it from the motherboard and remove it from the case. On an AT model, disconnect it from the power switch as well.
- To install a power supply, attach it to the case, attach it to the power switch (if it is an AT), and connect it to the motherboard.

## UPS and Surge Suppressors

- A surge suppressor is a power strip that absorbs excess voltage spikes to protect equipment.
- An uninterruptible power supply (UPS) is a battery that supplies power to the PC when normal power is not available.

- Most UPS devices include power conditioning, so they protect against undervoltage situations as well as complete power failures.
- Some UPS devices have a cable that connects to the PC, enabling Windows to interact with the UPS so it can shut down automatically when a power outage occurs.
- An online UPS runs the PC off of the battery at all times.
- A standby UPS switches to the battery only when normal AC power is not sufficient.

### Notebook Computer Power

- A notebook computer has an AC adapter that includes a voltage converter and an AC-to-DC converter in a transformer block in the power cord.
- A notebook battery can run the PC for up to several hours without AC power. The most common battery types are NiCad, NiMH, and LIon.
- A NiCad (nickel cadmium) battery is the oldest type. It can run three to four hours on a charge. A full recharge can take up to 12 hours.
- NiCad batteries are subject to "memory" problems, which means that if they are not allowed to run down completely before recharging them, they eventually become unable to hold a full charge.
- NiMH (nickel metal hydride) batteries are superior to NiCad because the metals are less toxic. They can also store up to 50 percent more power and do not suffer from memory problems.
- LIon (lithium ion) batteries are light and long-lasting, but can be more expensive than the other types. They are not affected by memory problems and do not use poisonous metals.

## PRACTICE TEST

On a blank sheet of paper, write the answers to the following multiple-choice questions and explain why each answer is correct.

1. Which components must all match one another in both AT and ATX models?
   a. CPU, hard disk, and motherboard
   b. motherboard, power supply, and case
   c. memory, hard disk, and CPU
   d. power supply, case, and hard disk

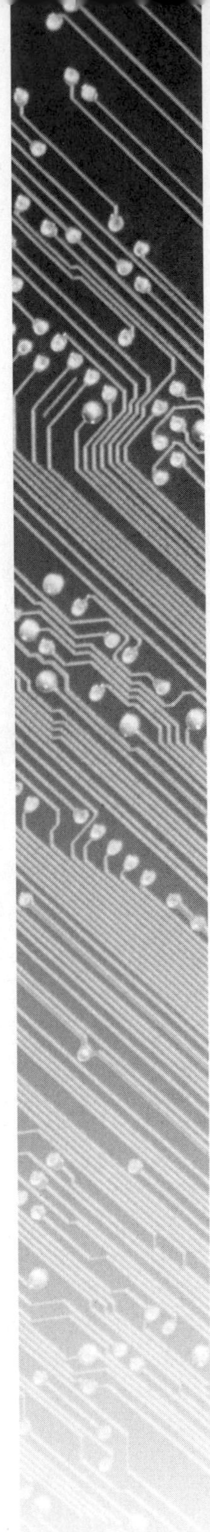

2. An AT power supply connects directly to
   a. the motherboard.
   b. an internal bay.
   c. the power button on the case.
   d. the hard disk.

3. A technician wants to build a PC that has two hard disks, two CD drives, and a floppy drive. How many external bays are needed?
   a. two
   b. three
   c. four
   d. five

4. What is the voltage of common household AC current in the United States?
   a. +5v
   b. +12v
   c. 110v
   d. 220v

5. What two factors must be multiplied by one another to calculate watts?
   a. amps and ohms
   b. ohms and volts
   c. amps and volts
   d. hertz and volts

6. What is the unit of measure for resistance?
   a. amps
   b. ohms
   c. volts
   d. hertz

7. At what frequency does common household current alternate?
   a. 60 amps
   b. 60 ohms
   c. 60 hertz
   d. 60 volts

8. Direct current (DC) is distinguished from AC in that it
   a. is provided by a wall outlet.
   b. does not alternate between positive and negative.
   c. has a much lower voltage.
   d. has a higher amperage.

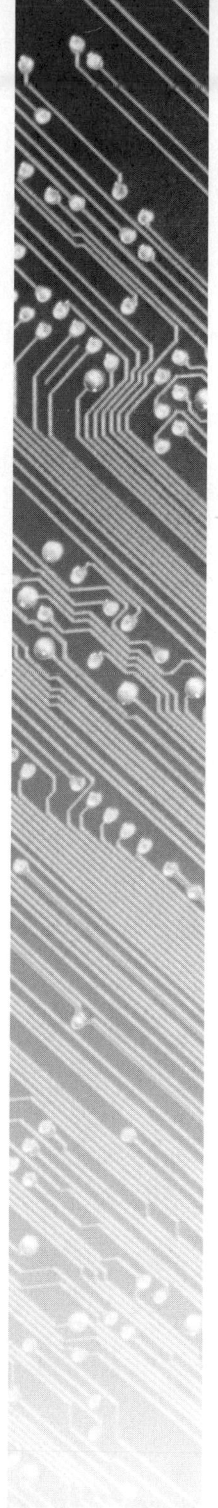

9. Which type of multimeter uses a needle gauge and is continuously variable?
   a. analog
   b. digital
   c. both
   d. neither

10. Which probe on a multimeter goes on the ground wire when testing voltage?
    a. the red probe
    b. the black probe
    c. either probe
    d both probes

11. Which probe on a multimeter goes on the live end of a cable when testing resistance?
    a. the red probe
    b. the black probe
    c. either probe
    d. both probes

12. When connecting the power supply to an AT motherboard, how should connectors P8 and P9 be attached?
    a. black wires at the ends
    b. black wires together
    c. red wires together
    d. wires in any configuration

13. Which devices require a Molex connector to the power supply?
    a. hard disk and floppy disk
    b. floppy disk and CD
    c. CD and hard disk
    d. AGP video and chipset

14. A switching power supply
    a. is another name for a linear power supply.
    b. uses alternating current.
    c. generates alternating current.
    d. will not run without a load.

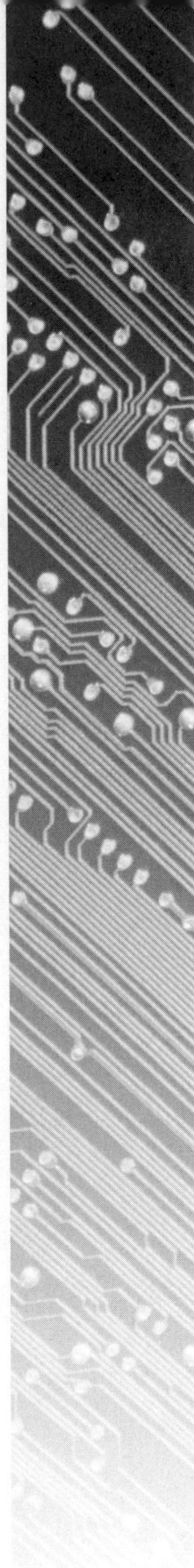

15. How many watts does a device need if it requires 0.5 amps of +12v and 3 amps of +5v?
    a. 21 watts
    b. 20.5 watts
    c. 17 watts
    d. Impossible to tell from information given
16. How many amps of +3.3v power does a 200-watt AT power supply provide?
    a. 8
    b. 14
    c. 25
    d. none
17. What component in a surge suppressor absorbs power spikes?
    a. capacitor
    b. varistor
    c. resistor
    d. None of the above
18. What component in a surge suppressor absorbs power sags?
    a. capacitor
    b. varistor
    c. resistor
    d. None of the above
19. Which type of UPS runs off of the battery full-time and so does not need to switch over to the battery when a power outage occurs?
    a. standby UPS
    b. online UPS
    c. offline UPS
    d. None; all types switch to battery only when needed
20. Which type of notebook PC battery suffers from problems with "memory" if it is not discharged completely each time before recharging?
    a. NiMH
    b. NiCad
    c. LIon
    d. alkaline

# TROUBLESHOOTING

1. You are having a problem with a device, and you wonder whether the cause may be a bad cable. You can take the time to test the old cable with a multimeter, or you can just buy a new cable and try swapping it with the old one. What are some of the factors involved in deciding which to do?
2. You have an AT power supply that works only intermittently. Sometimes when you press the power button you hear a faint humming noise inside the power supply and the fan does not spin; at other times it spins just fine. What will you do?
3. A PC's case has plenty of drive bays available, but there are no more power supply plugs to connect to drives. What are your options?

# CUSTOMER SERVICE

1. You are building a PC from scratch for a client, and it will cost about $75 more for an ATX motherboard, case, and power supply than for an AT. What can you explain to the customer about the advantages of an ATX system so the client can decide whether to spend the extra money?
2. Suppose a client lives in an area where the electrical power is very inconsistent, with many surges and sags and brief power outages. The client wonders about buying a surge suppressor. What would be your advice?
3. You are trying to walk a client through the process of installing a new CD drive over the phone, but the client says that there is no opening for the drive to slide into. What is going on, and how would you instruct the client?

# FOR MORE INFORMATION

For links to Web sites that provide further information about the topics covered in this chapter, go to the EMC/Paradigm Internet Resource Center at www.emcp.com/College Division/Internet Resource Centers/PC Maintenance/For More Information.

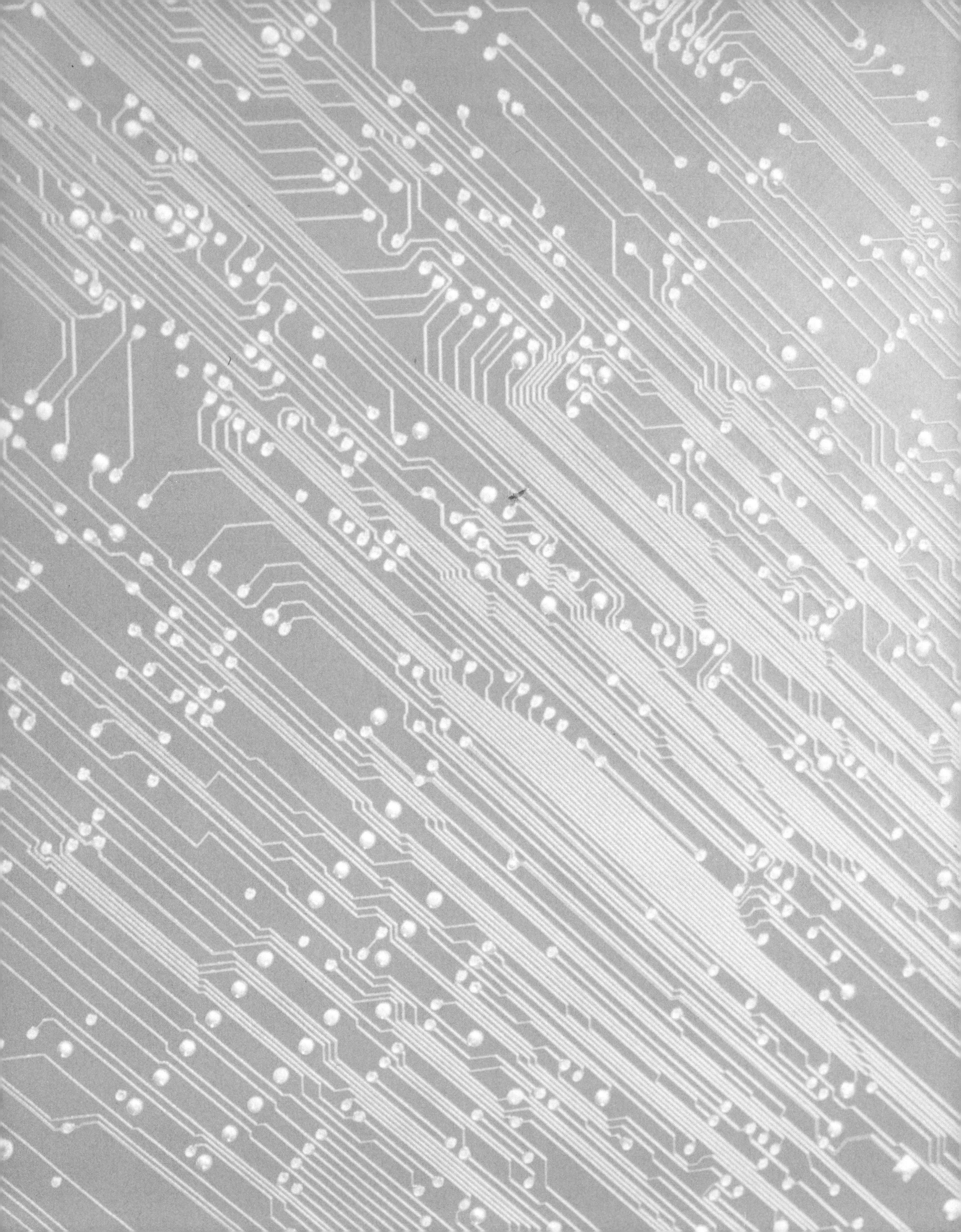

# Project Lab, Part 1
## Personal Computer Basics

### Project #1: Creating a Safe Workspace for Disassembling PCs

1. Create a checklist for avoiding ESD damage to a workstation. Refer to Chapter 2 if needed.
2. Evaluate your own workstation against the checklist you created, correcting any potential problem areas.
3. Is there any equipment you can recommend to buy that would make your workstation safer from ESD exposure? If so, what? How can you work around your current lack of that equipment and still be safe?

### Project #2: Physically Inspecting the Inside of a PC

1. Disconnect all external cables from your PC. Make notes about which connector goes where if you think you might not be able to remember where each one goes. For example, the mouse and keyboard plugs may be physically interchangeable on some PCs; how will you remember which goes where?
2. Remove the PC cover and identify the following components, drawing a diagram to indicate their positions:
   - CPU
   - RAM
   - Motherboard
   - IDE drive interface
   - Floppy drive interface
   - Power supply
   - Video card
3. Trade PCs with a classmate who has a different type of PC, and draw a diagram identifying the components from step 2 in the other PC.
4. Make a list of the differences you observed between the two PCs, if any. Is the CPU different? Which components are in different spots? Does the video card fit into a different type of slot? Are some components built into the motherboard versus being on expansion boards?

5. Replace the PC cover and reconnect all external cables in the correct places.

## Project #3: Cleaning a PC

1. Assemble the cleaning tools and supplies needed to clean the PC, printer, and other peripherals. Are there any tools or supplies you don't have that would be helpful? If so, how will you work around not having them?
2. Clean each of the following components, and write down what cleaning supplies you used on each one and what you did with them. Note the results: How well did the cleaning products work?
   - Monitor glass
   - Monitor, plastic parts
   - Outside of PC
   - Inside of PC
   - Mouse
   - Keyboard
   - Printer

## Project #4: Working with the Power Supply

1. Locate the PC's power supply. What is its wattage capacity? Is it an ATX or an LPX (AT)?
2. Trace the cables from the power supply to each of the attached drives. How many drives are drawing power from it?
3. Turn on the PC and measure the voltage on one of the red wires on the connector to the motherboard. What is the voltage reading?
4. Write down a checklist of safety precautions for working with power supplies and working inside the PC in general.
5. Trade lists with a classmate or discuss in small groups to make sure your checklist is complete.
6. Observing all the safety precautions on your checklist, completely remove the power supply from the PC. Write down the steps you took to do so.
7. With the power supply removed, compare it to that of another classmate. Are the wattages the same? Is there the same number of drive connectors? Are they the same form factor?

8. Reinstall the power supply, and reattach all connectors to it. Then start up the PC to make sure it is working. If it does not work, retrace your steps to determine where errors may have been made. Document your steps and the results.

## Project #5 (Challenge): Notebook PC Basics

1. Make a list of the external parts of a notebook PC that differ from those found on a desktop PC.
2. Draw a diagram showing the location of the following items:
   - Battery
   - Floppy drive
   - CD drive
   - External monitor port
   - External keyboard/mouse port
   - Pointing device
3. Remove the battery from the notebook PC. What information can you determine about the battery from its label? Then reinstall it.
4. Turn on the notebook PC while it is plugged into AC power; then unplug it and watch the notification area in Windows. What change do you observe there? How might you use a notebook PC differently when it is running on its battery versus running on AC power?
5. Create a safety checklist for working with notebook PCs, and then check yourself to make sure you are following all of them.
6. Open up the notebook PC and locate the area where you would add more RAM. Is there already RAM in the slot? What can you determine about it, if anything, from the writing on it?
7. Disassemble the notebook PC enough that you can see the hard disk. Draw a diagram showing how it connects to the rest of the system. What is the capacity of the hard disk, based on the information on its label?
8. Reassemble the PC, and turn it on to make sure it still works. If it does not work, retrace your steps to determine where errors might have been made. Document your steps and the results.

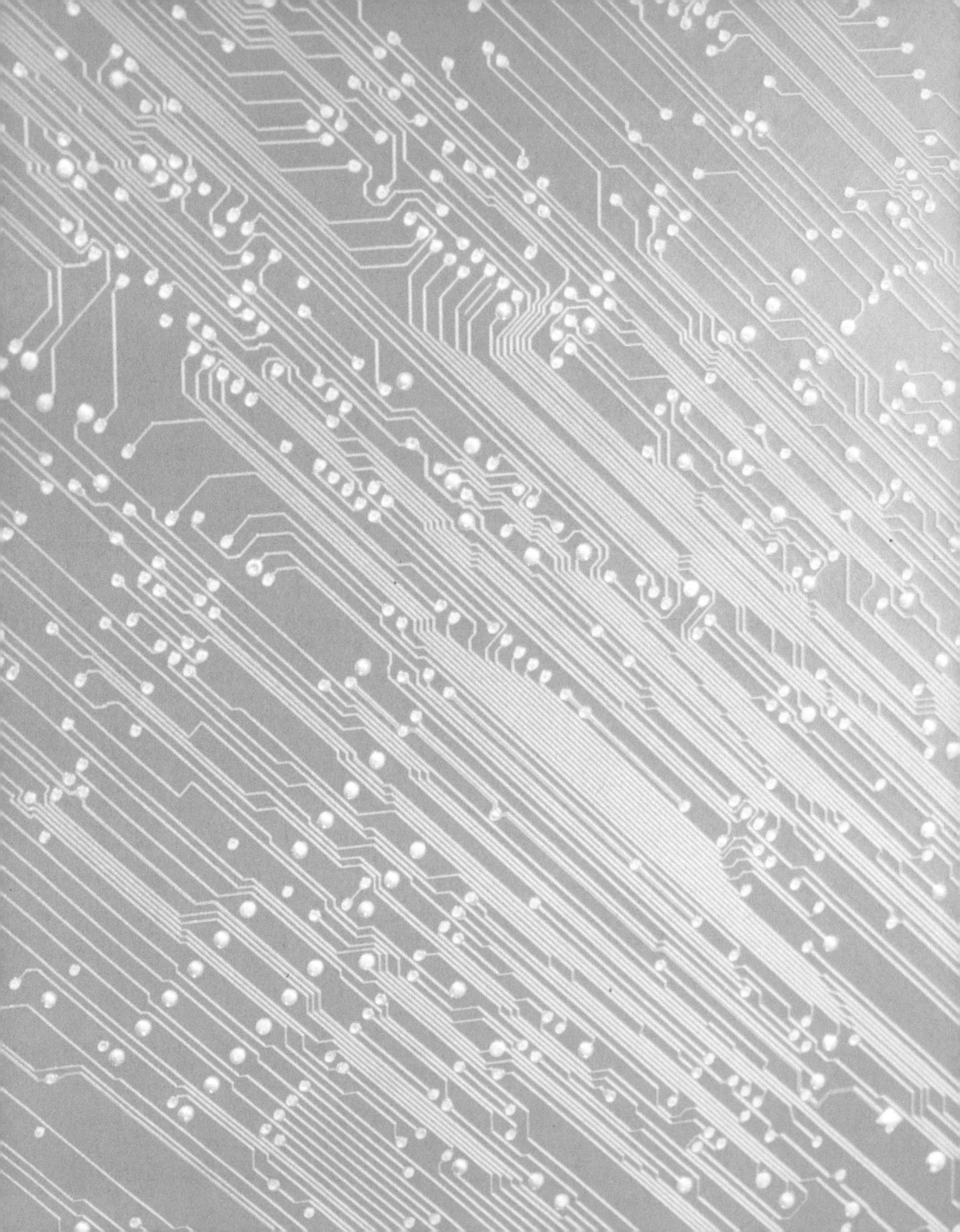

# PART 2

# Processing and Memory

# TEST OBJECTIVES IN PART 2

## A+ Core Hardware Service Technician Examination

- **Objective 1.1:** Identify basic terms, concepts, and functions of system modules, including how each module should work during normal operation and during the boot process.
- **Objective 1.2:** Identify basic procedures for adding and removing field replaceable modules for both desktop and portable systems.
- **Objective 1.4:** Identify common peripheral ports, associated cabling, and their connectors.
- **Objective 1.7:** Identify proper procedures for installing and configuring peripheral devices.
- **Objective 1.8:** Identify hardware methods of upgrading system performance, procedures for replacing basic subsystem components, unique components and when to use them.
- **Objective 2.1:** Identify common symptoms and problems associated with each module and how to troubleshoot and isolate the problems.
- **Objective 2.2:** Identify basic troubleshooting procedures and how to elicit problem symptoms from customers.
- **Objective 4.1:** Distinguish between the popular CPU chips in terms of their basic characteristics.
- **Objective 4.2:** Identify the categories of RAM (Random Access Memory) terminology, their locations, and physical characteristics.
- **Objective 4.3:** Identify the most popular types of motherboards, their components and their architecture (bus structures and power supplies).
- **Objective 4.4:** Identify the purpose of CMOS (Complementary Metal-Oxide Semiconductor), what it contains, and how to change its basic parameters.
- **Objective 6.1:** Identify basic networking concepts, including how a network works and the ramifications of repairs on the network.

## A+ Operating System Technologies Examination

- **Objective 1.1**: Identify the operating system's functions, structure, and major system files to navigate the operating system and how to get to needed technical information.

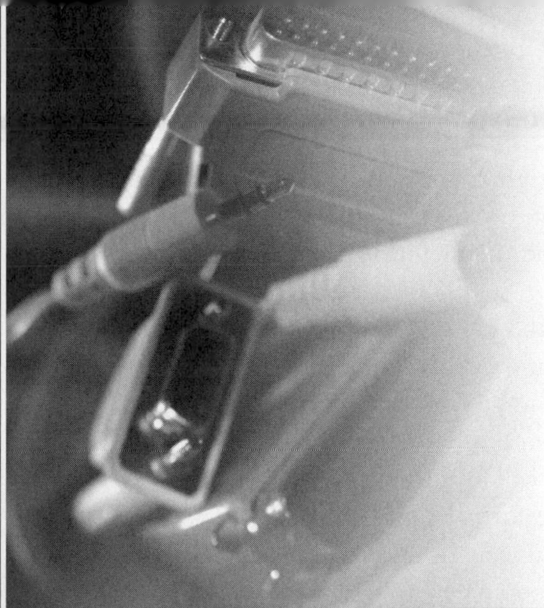

# 4 The Motherboard

## ON THE TEST

**A+ Core Hardware Service Technician Examination**

- **Objective 1.1:** Identify basic terms, concepts, and functions of system modules, including how each module should work during normal operation and during the boot process.
- **Objective 1.2:** Identify basic procedures for adding and removing field replaceable modules for both desktop and portable systems.
- **Objective 2.1:** Identify common symptoms and problems associated with each module and how to troubleshoot and isolate the problems.
- **Objective 4.3:** Identify the most popular types of motherboards, their components, and their architecture (bus structures and power supplies).

## ON THE JOB

The motherboard is the central piece of hardware in a PC; everything else plugs into it. When the motherboard fails, nothing else can work either. Therefore, it is essential for a technician to understand how the motherboard functions, what can go wrong with it, and what differentiates one motherboard from another.

Some of the tasks you may be called upon to perform involving motherboards include:

- selecting a new motherboard for a newly built PC
- selecting a replacement motherboard for an existing system
- identifying a motherboard's chipset
- setting jumpers on a motherboard
- choosing expansion boards that will fit into the available slots on a motherboard
- choosing memory and CPU upgrades for a motherboard
- replacing the motherboard's battery

## Overview of the Processing Subsystem

In simplest terms, the processing subsystem is the part of the PC that routes and calculates data. It is the middle part, between input and output. It includes the motherboard, the CPU, and the memory, plus the operating system software.

**Motherboard**

The large circuit board in a PC that serves as the connecting point for all other components.

The *motherboard* holds the memory and the CPU, and contains circuits that connect them. It also contains circuitry that connects various input/output ports, so data can come and go from outside the PC. The motherboard's traffic-directing abilities and other features depend on its *chipset*. Motherboard and chipset types will be covered later in this chapter.

**Central Processing Unit (CPU)**

The main processing chip in a PC that performs the math calculations.

The *Central Processing Unit* (CPU) performs math calculations. It receives instructions to add, subtract, multiply, divide, or one of thousands of other functions, and it also receives the data upon which to perform its calculations. Then it does the work and outputs the result. Chapter 5 covers CPUs.

**Memory**

Computer chips that act as short-term storage for data.

The *memory* (also known as Random-Access Memory, or RAM) acts as a temporary storage area for data. The CPU itself cannot hold very much data inside; memory provides a much larger work area in which the operating system can keep track of the instructions and results of programs. Chapter 6 discusses memory.

**Operating system**

The software that starts up the user interface on a PC, keeps it running, and processes user commands.

The *operating system* is the software portion of the processing subsystem. It contains the instructions that tell the other components what to do and in what order. Windows is the most popular operating system, but there are many others. Chapters 26 through 32 contain most of the specifics about Windows, but other chapters cover certain features of Windows as well.

## How a Motherboard Works

The motherboard's primary job is to manage the flow of data among components. Data travels through the motherboard, as it does through all other parts of the computer, through patterns of electrical pulses that represent binary numbers. A pulse is a 1; a lack of pulse is a 0. The essential components of this data transfer system are the buses, which are the "roads" that carry the data, and the chipset, which is the set of controller chips that manage the data flow.

### Buses

**Bus**

A data pathway between chips, slots, or other components on a circuit board.

Each motherboard has a system of data pathways called *buses* that run between the ports, slots, and sockets into which other components connect.

There are different buses for different connections. For example, data moves between the CPU and RAM on the *address bus*. Sometimes data must travel through more than one bus to reach its destination. For example, for data from an Industry-Standard Architecture (ISA) expansion card to reach the CPU, it must go through the ISA bus (which is like a country road), through the chipset (which is like a transfer station), to the system bus (which is like a high-speed freeway). Figure 4.1 shows an extremely simplified version of a typical system's major bus lines.

**Address bus**

The data pathway that runs between the CPU and the RAM.

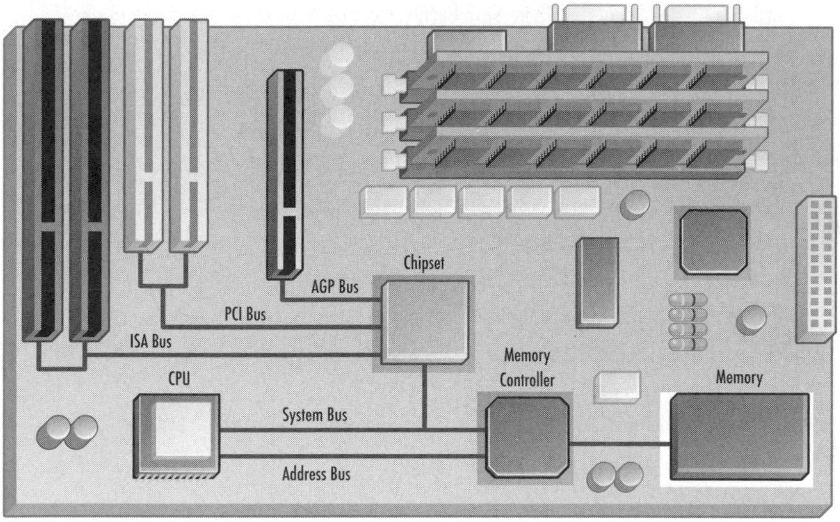

**FIGURE 4.1**
A typical motherboard has several buses.

Figure 4.1 shows the chipset as a single chip, whereas in reality it is usually at least two or more separate chips. Chipsets are explained in more detail in the next section. Notice also in Figure 4.1 that the memory does not connect directly to a bus; instead, a *memory controller chip* (MCC) connects to the bus and processes all instructions pertaining to memory.

**Memory controller chip (MCC)**

The chip that controls data flowing into and out of RAM.

Just as on a regular highway, each bus has both a width and a speed. The width is the number of "lanes" of traffic the bus can transfer at once; the speed is the rate at which the data is transferred on that bus. The faster the speed and the greater the width, the higher the overall data flow for that bus. The different types of buses are identified in Figure 4.2.

**System bus**

The bus that connects the address bus (the CPU and memory's bus) to the chipset on the motherboard. Also called external data bus or processor bus.

**AGP bus**

The bus that connects the AGP expansion slot to the motherboard chipset.

**PCI bus**

The bus that connects all of the PCI slots in the motherboard to the chipset. Also called local I/O bus.

**ISA bus**

The bus that connects any ISA slots in the motherboard to the chipset. Not present in the newer models of motherboards.

- **System bus:** A 64-bit bus that connects the CPU and MCC to the chipset, it is also known by several other names, such as external data bus or processor bus. The system bus is synchronized with the CPU speed, which is usually a multiple of the system bus speed; for example, the system bus might run at 133 megahertz (MHz) and the CPU might run at 1.3 gigahertz (GHz) (10 times the system bus speed).
- **Address bus:** Connects the CPU and the MCC, which in turn connects to the memory. It runs at the same speed as the system bus in most systems, but may have a different width.
- **AGP bus:** A 32-bit bus that runs between the Accelerated Graphics Port (AGP) expansion slot on the motherboard (for a video card) and the chipset. A video card is the only type of expansion card an AGP slot will accept. There have been several versions of the AGP standard since its introduction; the earliest version (AGP 1x) ran at 66MHz, while the latest, most expensive version (AGP 8x) runs at 533MHz. Some older systems do not have this bus.
- **PCI bus:** A 32-bit bus that runs at 33MHz. Sometimes called the local I/O bus, it connects the PCI expansion slots in the motherboard to the chipset. PCI slots are used these days for most expansion board devices, such as modems, network cards, and sound cards. PCI devices are preferable to ISA because of the higher bus speed and the capability of sharing system resources with other PCI devices. Chapter 14 discusses system resources in more detail.
- **ISA bus:** A 16-bit bus running at 8MHz that connects ISA expansion slots to the chipset. It is becoming obsolete, and many new motherboards do not have it.

**FIGURE 4.2**
Types of Buses on a Typical Motherboard

The section titled "Expansion Slots" later in this chapter provides more information about the various types of expansion slots associated with the buses.

Why don't all buses use the highest speed and the greatest width? It is primarily a backward compatibility issue: The ISA bus remains on some motherboards these days so that users can continue to use ISA expansion boards. Those boards expect a 16-bit bus that runs at 8MHz, so the ISA bus must limit itself to that speed and width. The same applies to the PCI bus. It could easily run faster than 33MHz, but the PCI standard dictates that it use that speed. To break that 33MHz limitation when video cards needed to be faster, the AGP bus was created. AGP started out as 66MHz, but eventually it became possible to make it faster. Rather than creating yet another new bus, PC manufacturers simply decided to update the AGP standard to increase the speed.

## In Real Life

It is important to know about these buses and their capacities and speeds because many add-on devices for a PC can be purchased in different versions that work with different buses. For example, modems are available in both ISA and PCI models. Since the PCI bus is faster and wider, a PCI modem would be a better choice if the PC had an open PCI expansion slot. Similarly, video cards come in both AGP and PCI models. An AGP model is a better choice if the motherboard has an AGP slot because the AGP bus has a faster speed than PCI.

## Chipsets

The exact routes of the various buses, and the components tied into each one at certain points, depend on the chipset of the motherboard. The *chipset*, as the name implies, is a set of chips mounted on the motherboard that direct the flow of traffic along and between the buses. Two motherboards with the same chipset are functionally identical, even if the motherboards have different manufacturers. Intel is the largest maker of chipsets; some other manufacturers include Via Technologies and Silicon Integrated Systems (SiS).

**Chipset**

A set of chips that together control the traffic flow along and between buses.

A chipset can consist of a single chip, but usually involves two or more chips working together. There are two basic architectures for chipsets in motherboards: north/south bridge and hub. The A+ exam does not specifically cover chipset architecture, but it is useful to have a basic understanding because so many of the other components depend on it.

### *North/South Bridge Chipsets*

*North/south bridge* is the older of the two architectures for Intel chipsets, and is still used for most of the non-Intel chipsets. It is typical of Socket 7 systems such as the Pentium, and of Slot 1 systems such as Pentium II. It breaks down the chipset duties into three categories:

**North/south bridge**

A chipset architecture that divides operations among three chips: north bridge, south bridge, and super I/O.

- **North bridge:** This chip acts as a connector between the system bus (the fastest bus) and the other relatively fast buses (e.g., PCI and AGP). In some very old systems, up to three separate chips make up the north bridge.
- **South bridge:** This chip acts as a connector for many of the slower bus devices, such as the ISA bus, the IDE interface, and the USB ports. The IDE interface under this architecture runs at 33 megabytes per second (MB/sec). (Chapter 11 covers IDE in more detail.)

- **Super I/O:** The super I/O chip interacts with built-in ports on the motherboard, such as parallel and serial, and communicates with the floppy drive controller and the keyboard and mouse ports. This chip is an auxiliary part of the chipset, and may have a manufacturer and model number different from the others. It connects to the south bridge via the ISA bus.

The system clock and the BIOS and CMOS can be connected to the south bridge or the super I/O depending on the chipset model. Figure 4.3 shows a typical north/south bridge architecture.

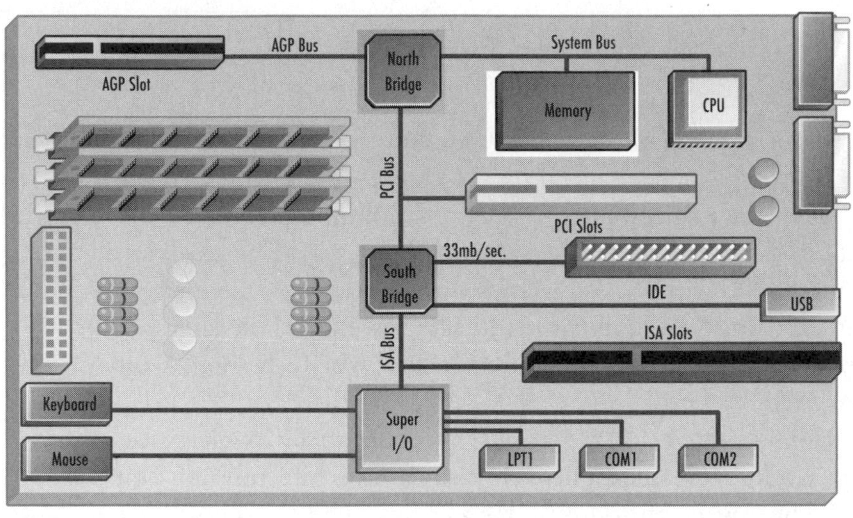


**FIGURE 4.3**
Chipset That Uses a North/South Bridge Architecture

There is a variant (used for AMD Athlon/Duron systems) that has a super south bridge that combines the functions of the south bridge and the super I/O into a single chip. In such systems the IDE interface can run at up to 100MB/sec, which means faster hard disk performance.

The north and south bridge chips often have different model numbers. This is because the south bridge chips are less expensive and more standardized to manufacture, so the same south bridge chip can be used with a variety of different north bridge chips to form unique chipsets. The defining feature of the north/south bridge architecture is that the north and south bridges are connected via the PCI bus. This forces the PCI bus to carry both its own expansion slot traffic and the rest of the chipset traffic as well.

**Hub chipset**

A motherboard chipset that divides operations among three chips: memory controller hub, I/O controller hub, and super I/O.

### *Hub Chipsets*

The newer Intel chipsets (800 and above) arrange the components in a *hub chipset*. Pentium III and higher systems usually have this architecture (see Figure 4.4), which includes three main chips: memory controller hub, I/O controller hub, and super I/O. The main difference from the north/south bridge is that the first two are not connected via the PCI bus, but rather through their own high-speed hub interface bus that operates at 266MB/sec.

- **Memory controller hub:** This is the equivalent of the north bridge. The CPU, memory, AGP bus, and PCI bus all feed into it.
- **I/O controller hub:** The equivalent of the south bridge, the IDE and USB interfaces connect to the I/O controller hub, and the IDE interface runs at up to 100MB/sec. In systems that have them built-in, sound and/or local-area network (LAN) interfaces are connected here.
- **Super I/O:** This chip performs the same as it does with a north/south architecture.

Separating the PCI bus from the north bridge means that the PCI bus is free to handle the traffic from PCI devices; it does not need to carry all the south bridge traffic as well. Most of the hub chipsets do not support ISA slots. Instead, they connect the super I/O chip to the I/O controller hub with a low pin count (LPC) bus.

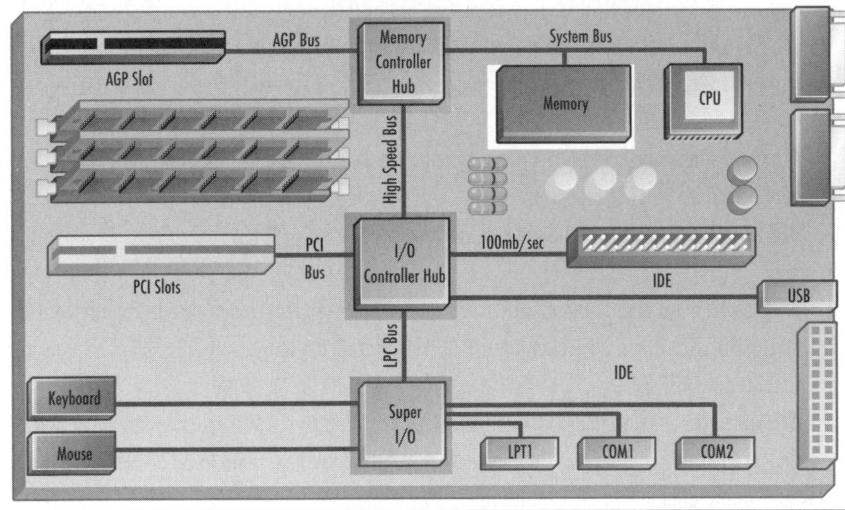


**FIGURE 4.4**
Chipset That Uses a Hub Architecture

### *Single-Chip Chipsets*

Certain types of chipsets, especially those made by Silicon Integrated Systems (SiS), combine the functions of multiple chips into a single chip. Some of them even combine additional functions such as built-in video card functionality, sound card functionality, and/or network interface functionality into that single chip. The north/south bridges are still there, but they are contained in a single chip rather than spread out.

### *Comparing Chipset Features*

A motherboard's chipset determines almost everything about its functionality. That is why it is important to select a motherboard with a chipset that includes the features desired for a particular PC system.

Although this chapter cannot detail the specifications of every chipset that a technician might encounter, that information is not important for studying for the A+ exam. But when one is shopping for a new motherboard, it is useful to know the features of some of the chipsets that are for sale today. Some of the shopping points are shown in Figure 4.5.

- **System bus speed:** Faster is better. The latest chipsets will run at 400MHz or higher. Older sets may run at 66, 100, or 133MHz.
- **CPUs supported:** Look for a motherboard that supports whatever CPU type and speed you plan to use.
- **Dual CPUs:** If this feature is important to you, look for a chipset that supports it. The feature is widely available on most chipsets made since late 1999. The motherboard itself must have two CPU sockets in order for the feature to be enabled.
- **Memory types:** Modern motherboards support either SDRAM or RDRAM. (Chapter 6 covers memory in detail.) RDRAM is more expensive, but faster.
- **Memory speeds:** SDRAM comes in either PC100 or PC133 speeds. Its speed must match the system bus speed. RDRAM comes in only one speed: PC800. Its speed is double that of the motherboard's system bus.
- **Maximum memory:** The latest chipsets support between 2GB and 4GB of memory; older sets may be limited to 512MB or less.
- **PCI specification support:** Older chipsets may support only PCI 2.1; newer sets will support PCI 2.2.
- **AGP slot:** If you plan to use an AGP video card (recommended), make sure the motherboard has an AGP slot. There have been several AGP standards; the latest is AGP 4x. Older chipsets may support only AGP 2x.
- **IDE support:** The latest hard disk can transfer data at up to 100MB/sec or more, but only if the chipset can support that rate. Older motherboards' IDE may be limited to 33 or 66MB/sec. For more information about IDE transfer rates, see Chapter 11.
- **USB support:** All motherboards today should include support for at least two USB ports; some support four.
- **ISA support:** If you plan to use old ISA expansion cards in the system, make sure the motherboard has some ISA slots and chipset support for them.
- **Power management:** The chipset should support Advanced Configuration and Power Interface (ACPI) power management features if you plan to use power management to conserve power usage.

**FIGURE 4.5**
Shopping Points for Chipsets

### *Identifying the Chipset*

On most motherboards it is fairly simple to find the chipset: look for the two largest chips besides the CPU and read the writing on them. (The super I/O chip is not always readily identifiable, but there is no need to locate it because it is not a component unique to the chipset.) For example, in Figure 4.6 the motherboard uses a two-chip chipset manufactured by VIA. The upper chip is the north bridge, and its model is VT82C598MVP. The lower chip is the south bridge, and it is VT82C586B.

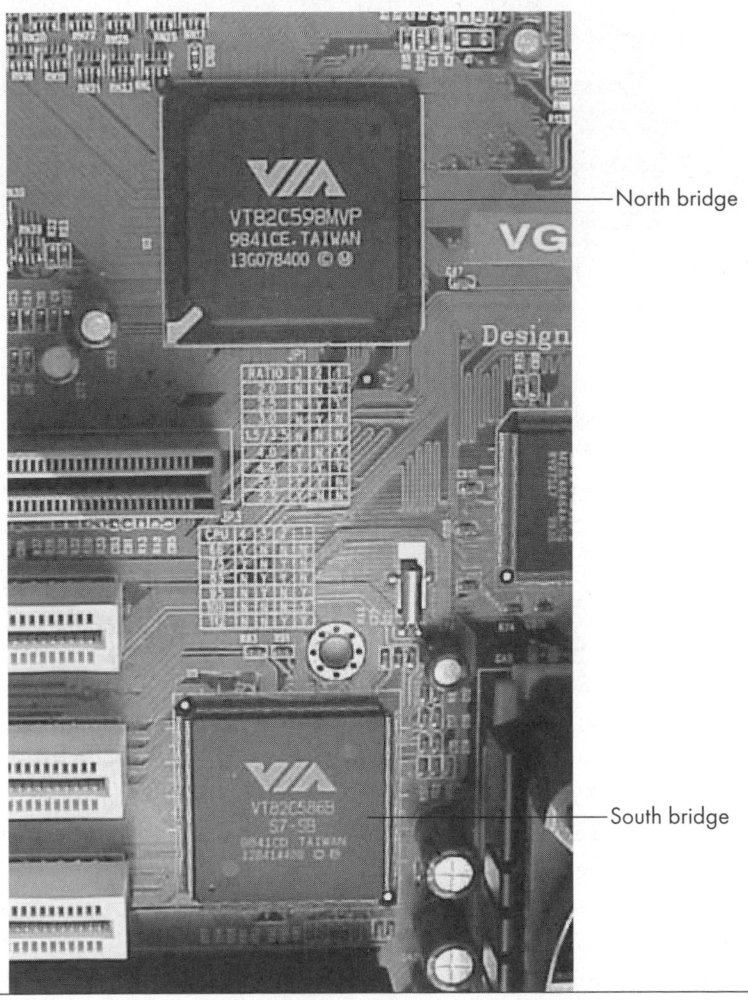


**FIGURE 4.6**
A VIA Chipset

On some systems a heat sink is glued onto the north bridge or memory controller hub chip, as in Figure 4.7, so that you cannot read its name. Short of removing the heat sink (and then having to reglue it), there is little way of identifying such a chipset. The lettering on the south bridge or I/O controller hub chip may not be indicative of that on the north chip because, as indicated earlier, sometimes the same south chip is used with different north chips.

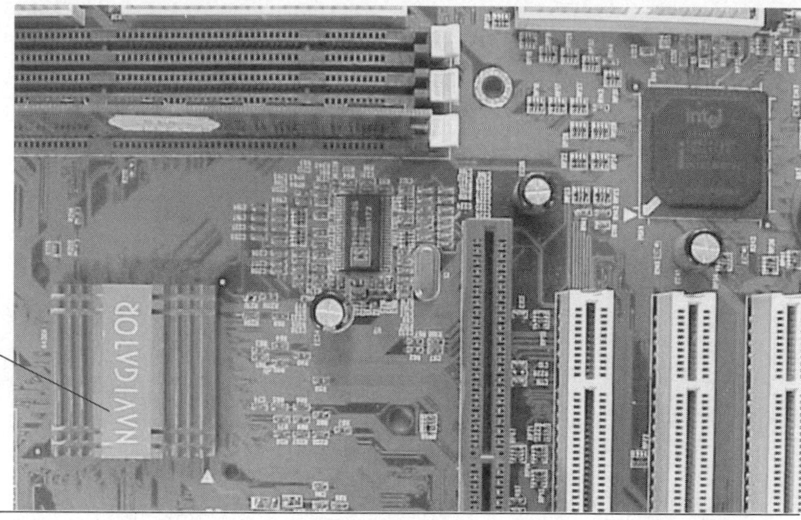


**FIGURE 4.7**

Intel Chipset with One Chip Covered by a Heat Sink

## TRY IT!

**Find as much information as you can about your motherboard's chipset. Start with the motherboard manufacturer and check that company's Web site. If you cannot determine the motherboard's manufacturer, try to identify the chipset manufacturer and try that company's Web site.**

## JUMPERS AND SWITCHES

Some motherboards can work in a number of different ways, for maximum flexibility. For example, a particular chipset might be capable of supporting several different CPUs, running the system bus at different speeds and supplying one of several different voltages. On modern systems these settings are configured through software, through the BIOS setup program to be discussed in Chapter 9. In older systems these settings are configured through jumpers or switches on the motherboard.

**Jumper**

A metal bridge surrounded by a plastic cap; when the jumper is placed across two pins, it completes a circuit between them and changes the flow of electricity on the circuit board.

A *jumper* is a metal bridge surrounded by a plastic cap. When you place a jumper across two metal pins, it creates a path for electricity to flow between them, changing the overall flow through that circuit board. When you remove the jumper, you disable that electrical path.

For example, suppose there is an electrical pathway that carries power from the motherboard's power connector to the CPU socket. This particular motherboard can support CPUs that require either +5v or +3.3v. A set of three pins determines which voltage the CPU receives. When a jumper is placed over pins 1 and 2, the power flows through at +5v. When the jumper is moved to pins 2 and 3, a voltage regulator steps down the voltage to +3.3v and then continues on to the CPU socket. So if you needed to install a +3.3v CPU in the motherboard, you would set the jumper cap to cover pins 2 and 3 (see Figure 4.8; there are actually two jumpers in Figure 4.8, but only the top one is for the voltage.)

**FIGURE 4.8**
**Voltage-Regulating Jumper**

Figure 4.8 shows a simple example, but sometimes more pins are required because there are more than two possible settings. For example, in Figure 4.9 there are seven sets of pins. Some sets have no jumper at all, some have a jumper over both pins, and others have a jumper on only one pin. Having the jumper on one pin and having no jumper at all have the same effect; the jumper caps are just being stored when they hang off a single pin. In Figure 4.9 the setting is Off/On/Off/On/Off/Off/Off. To determine what this means, you must consult the manual for the motherboard or look for an explanatory chart printed on the motherboard. There is such a chart, shown in Figure 4.10. From the chart you can determine that the first setting of Off/On/Off/On means that the motherboard is set for a ratio (that is, a clock multiplier) of 4.5. (Clock multipliers will be covered in Chapter 5.) You can also determine that the last setting of Off/Off/Off means that the system bus is operating at 100MHz. By multiplying those two settings, you can conclude that this motherboard is set up for a 450MHz CPU.

**FIGURE 4.9**
A Set of Jumpers

| Ratio | 1 | 2 | 3 | 4 | BUS CLK | 5 | 6 | 7 |
|---|---|---|---|---|---|---|---|---|
| 3.0 | ON | OFF | ON | ON | 112MHz | OFF | ON | OFF |
| 3.5 | ON | OFF | OFF | ON | 100MHz | OFF | OFF | OFF |
| 4.0 | OFF | ON | ON | ON | 83MHz | ON | OFF | ON |
| 4.5 | OFF | ON | OFF | ON | 75MHz | ON | ON | OFF |
| 5.0 | OFF | OFF | ON | ON | 66MHz | ON | OFF | OFF |
| 5.5 | OFF | OFF | OFF | ON | CPU CLK=BUS CLK*Ratio | | | |



**FIGURE 4.10**
Charts Explain Jumpers in Figure 4.9

To change a jumper position, lift the jumper cap off the pins; you can use your fingers or a tweezers. Then move the jumper cap to the desired pins and gently press it down over them.

## In Real Life

It is not always possible to determine what every jumper does on a motherboard unless you have a manual for it. If you do not have a manual, try to obtain one from the motherboard's manufacturer, or try the Web site http://www.motherboards.org.

**Switch**

An alternative to a jumper, in which tiny on/off switches substitute for jumper caps.

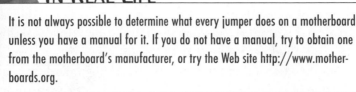

Some older motherboards may have *switches* instead of jumpers. Switches serve the same purpose as jumpers, and were popular in the early days of computing, but have faded in popularity because of manufacturing cost. Switches typically exist in banks of multiples (see Figure 4.11). In the figure all of the switches are set to Open (or On). Notice the designation SW1 to the left of the bank of switches; if you had the motherboard manual, you could look up SW1 to find out what these switches were for. To change the position of a switch, use any small, pointed object such as a nail, paper clip, or ink pen.

**FIGURE 4.11**
A Bank of Switches

## TRY IT!

Make a note of the position of a jumper on your motherboard; then set it to a different position. Make sure you put it back the way you found it when you are finished practicing.

## Selecting a Motherboard

A wide array of motherboards has been manufactured over the years. When you are looking at a system with an eye toward replacing its motherboard, or using its motherboard as a replacement in some other system, it helps to understand the factors that differentiate one motherboard from another. Chipsets, one of the most important factors defining the capabilities of a motherboard, have already been discussed. The following sections look at some other features.

### Form Factors

Chapter 3 introduced the two main form factors for PCs: AT and ATX. The case, power supply, and motherboard are all either one type or the other. A few other variations of motherboards exist, but AT and ATX are the most popular.

#### *AT Motherboards*

The IBM Advanced Technology (AT) computer was the first 80286 CPU to gain popularity. (Chapter 5 covers the 80286 and many other CPU types.) The AT had a number of improvements over earlier IBM PCs, which were known as XTs. Even though the original 80286-based AT computers are obsolete, the basic design layout for their motherboards remains a part of the AT standard.

The original AT motherboard was rather large—12 by 13 inches. In later PC models this size was reduced to 8.5 by 13 inches, or about the size of a sheet of legal paper. This was known as *Baby AT* size. Today's AT motherboards are even smaller, measuring only 8.5 by 9.5 inches.

**Baby AT**

A small AT motherboard, measuring 8.5 by 13 inches or less.

The easiest way to distinguish an AT motherboard from an ATX is to look at how the expansion slots are oriented. On a modern AT motherboard (see Figure 4.12) the expansion slots are parallel to the wide edge of the board; on an ATX motherboard they are parallel to the narrow edge. (On an 8.5 by 9.5-inch model it may require a second glance to determine which is the wide edge, since there is only 1 inch of difference.) Notice in the figure that the CPU sits behind the expansion slots. When the motherboard is mounted into a case, the expansion slots point toward the back, and the CPU points toward the front.

**FIGURE 4.12**
An AT Motherboard

An AT motherboard has an AT-style keyboard connector, as shown in Figure 4.13. It is larger than the PS/2-type connector used on ATX systems.

**FIGURE 4.13**
An AT Keyboard Connector

The AT motherboard also has an AT-style connector for the power supply. Figure 4.14 shows the connector with 12 pins sticking up out of it. Earlier figures in Chapter 3 showed the power supply connectors, P8 and P9, that hook into the connector.

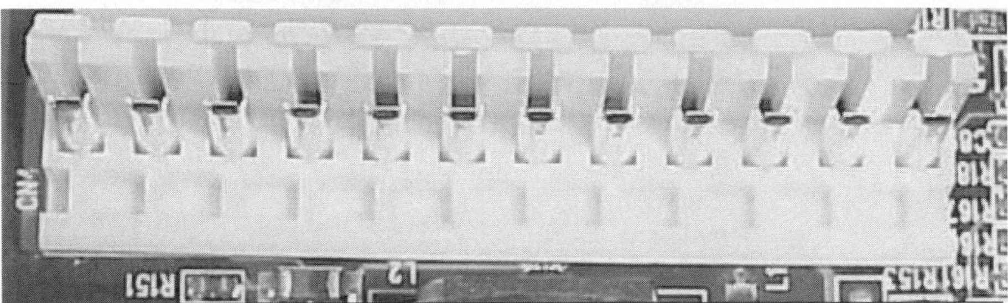

**FIGURE 4.14**
Power Supply Connector on an AT Motherboard

Another unique feature of the AT motherboard is that it does not have any connectors built into its side except that for the keyboard. The mouse port, COM ports, and LPT port all connect via ribbon cable to the motherboard, with plugs for them mounted to the case with backplates (see Figure 4.15).

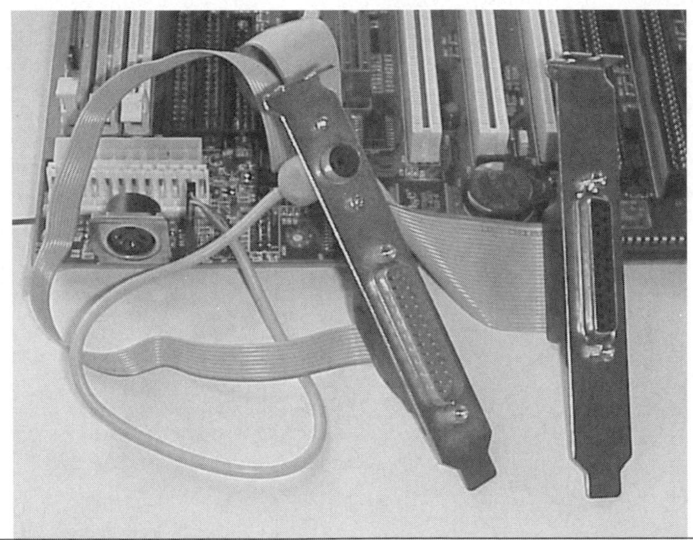

**FIGURE 4.15**
Ports on an AT computer must be mounted to the case with backplates.

The ATX motherboard, the more modern type, will eventually replace the AT style altogether because of its many advantages. However, in your work as a PC technician you will likely continue to encounter AT motherboards for years to come.

### *ATX Motherboards*

The ATX motherboard is the type you will find in almost all new PCs, including the mainstream brands like Dell and Gateway. An ATX motherboard is larger than an AT, measuring 12 by 7.5 inches. The expansion slots run parallel to the narrow edge, which means the wide edge of the board runs across the back of the PC case when installed. Notice that the CPU on the ATX motherboard shown in Figure 4.16 is next to the expansion slots. This enables the CPU to sit closer to the power supply fan, providing improved cooling.

This edge goes to back of case.

**FIGURE 4.16**
An ATX Motherboard

Notice also that the ports are all built into the motherboard on an ATX model (Figure 4.17), so no connectors and cables are required to hook up the parallel, serial, and mouse ports. The keyboard connector on the ATX is the smaller, PS/2 style rather than the large round plug found on the AT.

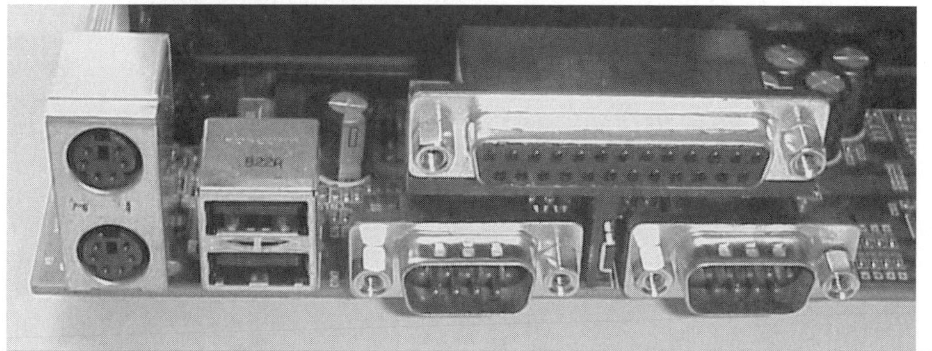

**FIGURE 4.17**
Built-In Ports on an ATX Motherboard

As discussed in Chapter 3, the power supply connector on an ATX is a 20-pin female connector. Since it is all one piece, there is no possibility of switching the plugs accidentally as there would be on an AT (see Figure 4.18).

**FIGURE 4.18**
Power Supply Connector on an ATX Motherboard

### *Slimline Motherboards*

In their quest to produce less bulky PCs, over the years computer manufacturers have come up with several nonstandard motherboard types. One of these, the LPX, contained no expansion slots. Instead it had a single slot into which users plugged an add-on circuit board (a daughterboard) that contained the expansion slots, enabling the expansion boards to run parallel to the motherboard rather than sticking up perpendicularly and resulting in a shorter PC. This *slimline* form factor, as it was called (see Figure 4.19), was later replaced by a smaller, similar design called NLX. These slimline systems are not very popular today because they have limited expansion potential. The system shown in Figure 4.19, for example, has only three expansion slots.

**Slimline**

A type of PC case in which the expansion boards are mounted on a riser board so they sit parallel to the motherboard rather than perpendicular to it. Modern versions are known as NLX.

**FIGURE 4.19**
An LPX Motherboard, with Expansion Slots on a Separate Card

## TRY IT!

**Identify which form factor your motherboard uses. If there are different PCs available, check all of them and compare form factors.**

## EXPANSION SLOTS

Earlier in this chapter there was a discussion of buses and the differences among them. You learned, for example, that a PCI expansion board is preferable to an ISA model because of the higher speed and larger width. Now look at buses from the perspective of the expansion slots in the motherboard.

Expansion slots hold expansion boards that add capabilities to the PC. For example, you could add a modem, a network interface card, a sound card, a SCSI controller, or any of dozens of other devices via an expansion board.

There are two types of expansion devices: internal and external. When a device exists on an expansion board, it is known as *internal* (e.g., an internal modem). Internal devices draw power from the motherboard. *External* devices, on the other hand, have their own power supplies (e.g., an external modem, which connects via cable to a COM port).

**Internal**

A device that fits inside the PC case, such as in an expansion slot or drive bay.

**External**

A device that works from outside the PC case, rather than being installed inside it.

### *ISA*

In early PCs there was only one type of expansion slot: *Industry-Standard Architecture* (ISA). As mentioned earlier in this chapter, the standard ISA input/output (I/O) bus is limited to 16-bit width and 8MHz speed. The original ISA bus was 8-bit, but the specification was later expanded to 16-bit. On some older PCs there might be a couple of shorter 8-bit slots and a couple of longer 16-bit slots; on more modern PCs they are all 16-bit. Figure 4.20 shows three 16-bit ISA slots. The 16-bit slots can accommodate both 8- and 16-bit boards.

**Industry-Standard Architecture (ISA)**

An older type of expansion slot that transfers data 8 bits at a time at 8MHz; now nearly obsolete

Expansion boards that do not transfer a large volume of data, and that do not require high speed, will usually work just fine in an ISA slot. A modem is a good example; it is limited to 56 kilobytes per second (Kbps) data transfer rate

**FIGURE 4.20**
ISA Slots on a Motherboard

anyway, so it is not impaired by the ISA slot's limitations. However, the ISA bus has some other drawbacks, including an inability to share system resources with other devices. System resource and sharing will be addressed in Chapter 14. The ISA bus is being phased out, and is no longer common in new motherboards. It is also becoming more difficult to locate ISA expansion boards; almost all expansion boards sold today are for a PCI slot.

**TRY IT!**

**Count the number of ISA slots on your PC's motherboard, if any. Are they all 16-bit slots?**

### *Early Attempts at a Better Bus*

Although PCI is the current standard for expansion buses, there have been some earlier attempts by PC manufacturers to improve upon the ISA bus by creating a bus that was faster, wider, or both. Even though you do not need to be knowledgeable about these buses for the A+ exam, you should at least be aware of them in case you come across them in an older PC.

**Microchannel Architecture**

An early attempt by IBM at improving the ISA bus. Used a disk-based precursor to Plug and Play. Now obsolete.

**MCA.** *Microchannel Architecture*, or MCA, was developed by IBM and used almost exclusively in IBM-branded PCs. It was popular in the late 1980s but soon faded into obscurity because other PC makers did not share IBM's enthusiasm for it. It was designed to replace the ISA bus, and included a number of improvements, but lacked backward compatibility for ISA devices.

MCA had an early, experimental version of Plug and Play; there were no jumpers or switches on the motherboard or any of the expansion cards. Instead, the motherboard was configured with a Reference floppy disk that was unique to that model of PC. An Option disk unique to each expansion board was also required. Users would run the setup programs on these disks to set or change configuration parameters. Without these disks, the MCA system could not be configured. (IBM retains a library of these disks available for download at ftp://ftp.pc.ibm.com/pub/pccbbs.)

**Enhanced Industry-Standard Architecture (EISA)**

A now-obsolete early attempt at a 32-bit version of ISA.

**EISA.** *Enhanced Industry-Standard Architecture* (EISA) was an attempt by the rest of the PC industry (that is, everyone except IBM) to make a better, faster bus without having to pay royalties to IBM to use MCA. It was essentially a 32-bit version of ISA, whereas MCA was a totally different system. It required a setup disk, like MCA; however, an advantage of an EISA system was that an EISA motherboard also had 8-bit and 16-bit ISA slots, for backward compatibility with older adapter cards. Although the 32-bit EISA slot was wider than traditional ISA, it was not faster; it ran at only 8MHz. EISA, like MCA, never really caught on, and soon faded into obscurity. In Figure 4.21 notice the three different sizes of ISA slots in the EISA motherboard: 8-bit, 16-bit, and 32-bit.

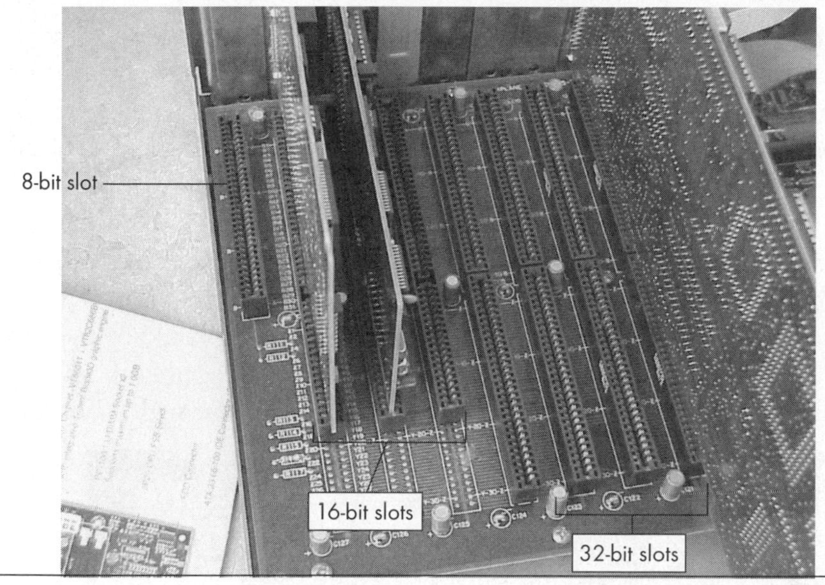


**FIGURE 4.21**
An EISA Motherboard

## *Local Buses*

The original ISA, which hooked directly into the system bus, ran at 8 MHz, as did the CPU. However, as CPU speeds began to increase, system designers were forced to separate the ISA bus from the system bus so each could run at a different speed. The ISA bus stayed slow as CPUs got faster and faster. This meant that the ISA bus was a poor choice for devices that moved a lot of data, such as video cards.

The MCA and EISA buses were both 32-bit, but they were still quite slow. PC manufacturers therefore looked for a way to make a faster bus. If they simply sped up the ISA bus, there would have been no backward compatibility; expansion boards designed for the slower ISA bus would not have worked. Lack of backward compatibility was one of the reasons MCA failed, and nobody wanted to repeat that fiasco. Therefore a whole new bus was needed.

The bus that was developed was a *local bus*, which meant that its bus tied directly into the system bus. This enabled the new type of slot to be not only wide (32-bit), but also fast.

**Local bus**

A bus tied directly into the system bus, not relying on the ISA bus for data conveyance.

**VESA local bus (VLB)**

The first commercially popular version of a local bus, found in many 486-class PCs. Now obsolete, replaced by PCI.

**VESA Local Bus.** The first attempt at a local bus was the *VESA local bus* (VLB, sometimes written as VL-Bus). VLB was introduced in some of the later 486 PCs, and remained popular for about a year until it was supplanted by the PCI slot still in use today.

The Video Electronics Standards Association (VESA) developed the standard. The VLB ran at the same speed as the system bus (which at that time was the same as the CPU speed; this was before clock multipliers were popular), resulting in very high data flow potential. When clock-multiplied 486 CPUs became available, the VLB continued to run at the base, unmultiplied speed of the system bus.

Physically a VLB slot was just a 16-bit ISA slot with an extra slot added to the end. (The extra slot was usually brown, whereas the main ISA slot was black.) This meant that the ISA portion of the slot could be used alone for an ISA board, or both of the sections could work together to accept a VLB expansion board. Figure 4.22 shows a motherboard with VLB slots.

**FIGURE 4.22**
A Motherboard with VLB Slots

VLB was very popular in 486 systems, but by the time the first Pentium systems were produced, most motherboard manufacturers had switched to PCI as the local bus standard. Occasionally you may encounter a Pentium system with a VLB or a 486 system with PCI, made during the brief transition period.

**Peripheral Component Interface (PCI)**

The current standard for local bus operations on a typical motherboard, connecting PCI expansion slots to the chipset.

**PCI.** *Peripheral Component Interface* (PCI) is the modern standard for general-purpose local bus expansion slots. Most motherboards have at least four of them (although there may be fewer if the motherboard also has a few ISA slots). The PCI bus is sometimes called a mezzanine bus because it added a whole new bus to the mix. Notice in Figure 4.3 how the PCI bus connects the north and south bridges. It lies physically between the system bus and the ISA bus. As discussed earlier in this chapter, the PCI bus is a 32-bit bus that runs at 33MHz—faster than the ISA but slower than the system bus.

PCI slots are used for a wide variety of expansion boards—virtually every expansion board made today comes in a PCI version. The greater width and speed of the slots enable expansion boards in PCI slots to run much better and faster than they would in ISA slots. PCI devices can also share system resources with one another, so a fully loaded system does not run out of resources such as interrupt request lines (IRQs). (Chapter 14 details how to manage IRQ assignments.) As shown in Figure 4.23, PCI slots are almost always white, although a motherboard manufacturer could make them in any color.

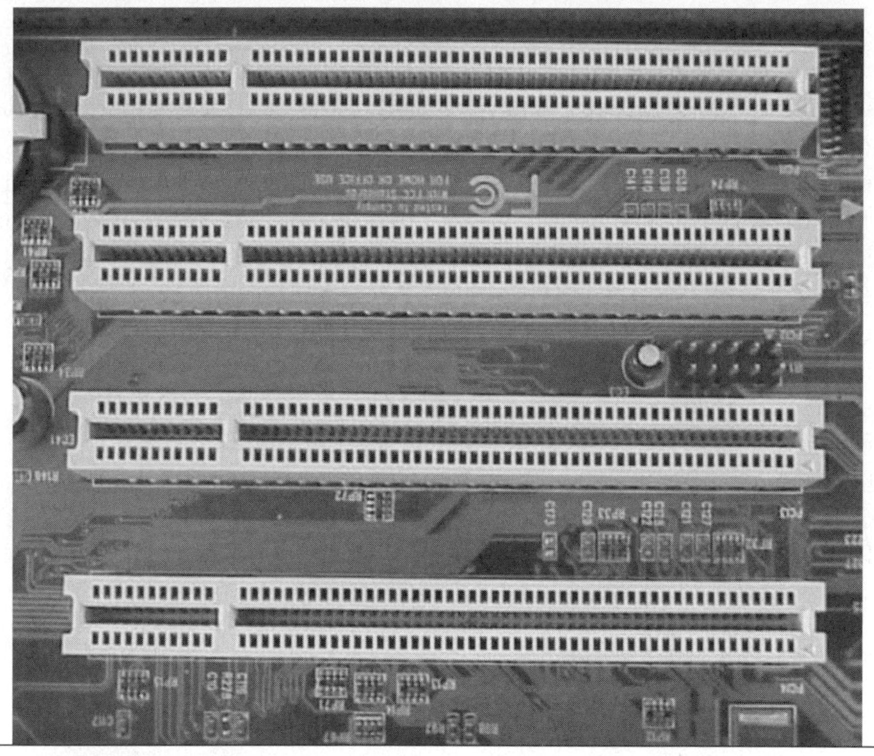

**FIGURE 4.23**
PCI Slots on a Motherboard

## TRY IT!

Count the number of PCI slots on your PC's motherboard. How many are filled by expansion cards and how many are free?

**Accelerated Graphics Port (AGP)**

A high-speed local bus designed exclusively for video card use.

**AGP.** *Accelerated Graphics Port* (AGP) is a high-speed bus reserved for video use only. Most motherboards have an AGP expansion slot, as shown in Figure 4.24. It is typically brown, slightly smaller than a PCI slot (and keyed differently), and indented toward the center of the motherboard about 1 inch more than the PCI slots.

**FIGURE 4.24**
An AGP Slot on a Motherboard

Motherboards have only one AGP slot, but there may be cases in which it is useful to have more than one video card in the PC (for example, in order to use several monitors at once in an operating system that supports them). In such instances a PCI video card can be used as the secondary card. PCI video cards can also be used in systems that do not have an AGP expansion slot.

Some motherboards have built-in AGP video as part of the chipset. On such systems the motherboard has a pin connector to which you attach a small ribbon cable connected to a loose video port connector. The video port is then mounted to the case, and from the outside of the PC it looks as if there is a real video card installed. The built-in AGP video can be disabled in the BIOS setup, so that a separate video card (PCI model) can be used instead of the built-in. This enables the system to keep working if the built-in video goes bad, and provides the flexibility of upgrading to the latest video card technology without discarding the entire system.

## TRY IT!

**Look at your motherboard to see whether it has an AGP slot. Is there an AGP video card in it?**

## MEMORY SLOTS

There are many different types and specifications of memory. (Chapter 6 describes memory in detail.) Most motherboards are limited in the types of memory they will accept: the memory must be physically compatible with the memory slots in the motherboard, and it must also match the speed and feature set that the chipset requires.

On all modern systems you will find three 168-pin dual inline memory module (DIMM) slots for memory, as shown in Figure 4.25. These consist of small troughs, keyed asymmetrically so that the memory fits into them only one way. At either end of each trough are fasteners that hold the memory in place. These DIMM slots are not Zero Insertion Force (ZIF): that is, they require some pressure to insert the memory.

**FIGURE 4.25**
DIMM Slots on a Motherboard

On older systems you may find single inline memory module (SIMM) slots as well. These slots are shorter (30- or 72-pin) and the memory may sit at an angle to the motherboard instead of perpendicular to it. There are many kinds of SIMMs, so if a system requires them, be sure to read Chapter 6 before making the purchase. Figure 4.26 shows an assortment of SIMM slot types over the years.

**FIGURE 4.26**
Examples of Types of SIMM Slots

## TRY IT!

**Identify the number and type of memory slots in your PC.**

## Slot or Socket

The CPU must be matched to the motherboard, both physically (slot or socket size) and in terms of the chipset's capability. As discussed earlier, the chipset controls the system bus speed and the available multipliers for the CPU, so the chipset determines what speeds of CPUs may be employed. If you use an unsupported CPU speed, the CPU may not work at all or the motherboard may force it into one of its supported speeds. (The latter is less likely to happen in newer systems that have overclocking prevention.)

There are two basic types of CPU slots in a motherboard: socket or slot. (Chapter 5 provides a more detailed look at the various types of CPU slots and sockets.)

**Pin grid array (PGA)**

A square or rectangular socket consisting of concentric rings of holes into which the legs on a PGA-style CPU fit.

The socketed type of CPU is called a *pin grid array* (PGA). It is a ceramic chip with a grid of pins on the bottom that fit into a matched grid of holes in the motherboard. Different CPUs have different numbers of pins and holes in different arrangements. In Figure 4.27, which shows a typical PGA CPU and its socket, the CPU has been flipped on its back so the pins are visible. Notice also in the figure that the CPU chip itself is on the bottom, surrounded by the pins. The area on which the pins are mounted is just a ceramic shell that helps conduct heat away from the CPU. PGA sockets are used in 486, Pentium, Pentium Pro, Pentium III, and Pentium 4 systems.

**FIGURE 4.27**
A PGA Socket and a CPU

The slotted type of CPU is called a Single Edge Contact Cartridge (SECC), as mentioned in Chapter 1. The CPU is mounted on a circuit board encased in a plastic shell, and that circuit board fits into a slot in the motherboard. An SECC slot on a motherboard looks much like a regular expansion slot but sits at a 90-degree angle to the other expansion slots. It has brackets that fit around it for supporting the CPU.

There is only one physical size of SECC slot, but there are two different internal designs: Slot 1 (for Intel CPUs) and Slot A (for AMD CPUs). These are competing brands, and the motherboard's design determines which one it supports. SECC slots are used in PCs that use Pentium II CPUs, as well as some systems that use Celeron and Athlon CPUs. Figure 4.28 shows an empty SECC slot on a motherboard, with the support brackets installed.

**FIGURE 4.28**
An SECC Slot on a Motherboard

## TRY IT!

**Identify the type of CPU in your motherboard. Is it a PGA or an SECC?**

## Built-In Components

An earlier section mentioned that AGP video is sometimes built into the motherboard. Other capabilities can be built in as well, such as sound support, a network interface card, or a modem. Building these capabilities into the motherboard is a money-saving measure for PC manufacturers. Although it costs a little more to manufacture the motherboards, the systems do not require expansion cards for any of the built-in functions, so the PC makers save substantially in that area.

For end users with very basic needs, built-in components can be sufficient. For example, a business user who works primarily on spreadsheets does not need a high-end sound card; the built-in sound in a motherboard is adequate. However, built-in components are seldom as full-featured as stand-alone expansion board models. In addition, if the user ever wants to use an expansion board for that capability, he or she must disable the built-in capability through the BIOS setup program, and not all end users are comfortable doing that. Chapter 9 explains how to disable a built-in component in BIOS setup.

If you are not sure whether a motherboard has any built-in capabilities, look for chips that may indicate a built-in item, as in Figure 4.29, or consult the manual.

**FIGURE 4.29**
A Built-In Video Controller on a Motherboard

## In Real Life

If your motherboard has built-in components, you will probably need to locate a driver for them for Windows. If the motherboard came with a CD containing the needed drivers, but you cannot locate it, you can probably download the drivers from the PC manufacturer's Web site, or from the motherboard's manufacturer if you built the PC yourself. Look on the motherboard for writing on a chip that might indicate its model number, as in Figure 4.29. If you cannot find any, look up the chipset ID number.

## TRY IT!

Determine whether your motherboard has any built-in components. Which ones does it have, if any?

## BATTERIES

As Chapter 9 will explain, each motherboard has a BIOS setup program that shows the default settings for the motherboard and enables users to make changes to these settings. Those changes are stored on a *nonvolatile RAM* (NVRAM) chip on the motherboard, along with a *real-time clock* (RTC) that keeps track of the current date and time. This chip, sometimes called the RTC/NVRAM chip, is a *complementary metal-oxide semiconductor* (CMOS) chip.

**Nonvolatile RAM (NVRAM)**

A type of RAM that does not need to be continually refreshed in order to maintain its contents.

**Real-time clock (RTC)**

A clock/calendar chip that keeps track of the current date and time on a PC.

**Complementary metal-oxide semiconductor (CMOS)**

A type of electronic chip that stores and recalls nonvolatile software programming.

A CMOS chip can store data even after the PC has been turned off, but it requires a small amount of power to do so. This power comes from the motherboard's battery. When a PC's RTC starts losing time, or when the PC forgets its configuration each time it shuts off, the battery may be dying.

Early motherboards used a barrel-type battery that was permanently soldered to the motherboard. When the battery failed, it had to be disabled and an external battery pack added. Figure 4.30 shows one of these old batteries. Notice the pins to the left of the battery labeled + Jbt -. These pins are for an external battery to be connected in the event that the original battery dies. The external battery pack will have a connector that fits down over these pins.

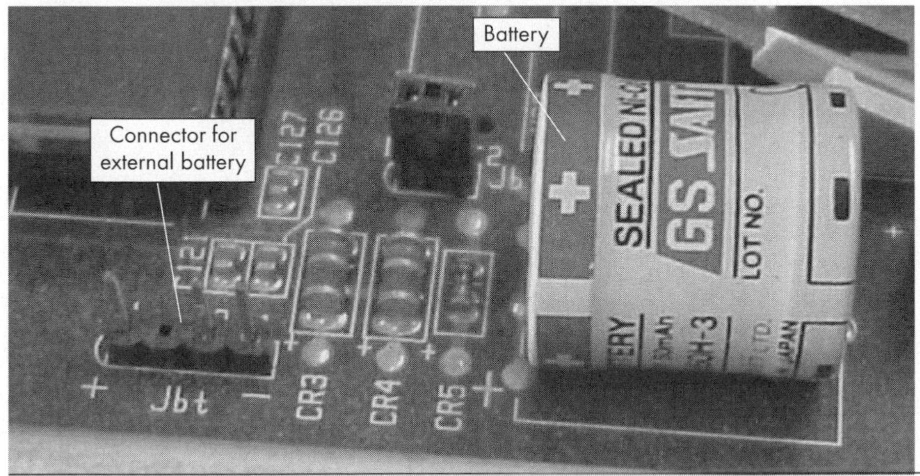


**FIGURE 4.30**
A Barrel-Style Battery

The next generation of motherboards used a replaceable battery with a size and shape similar to the ordinary alkaline batteries used in household devices. These are not conventional batteries, however, and you cannot use conventional batteries in such sockets if the original dies. It must be replaced with a special battery from an electronics store. See Figure 4.31 for an example.

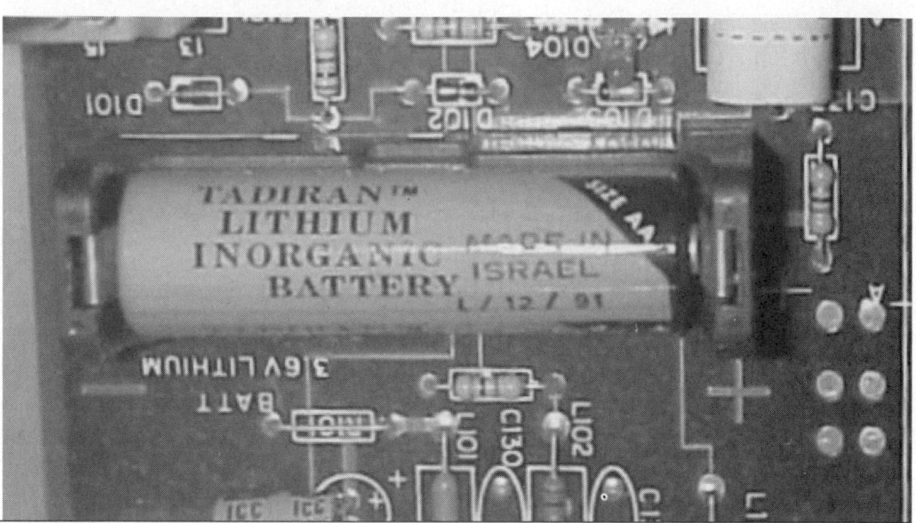


**FIGURE 4.31**
An Early Removable Motherboard Battery

Later motherboard models switched to a replaceable battery that looks like a thick coin or a very large watch battery. It is held in place by a clip, and can easily be removed and replaced (see Figure 4.32).

**FIGURE 4.32**
A Coin-Style Battery

Some systems do not have a battery at all, or have a battery built into the CMOS chip itself. If you cannot locate the battery on a motherboard, consult the motherboard manual or the PC manufacturer's Web site to find out where the battery capability resides. On systems with a combination battery and CMOS chip you must replace the chip when the battery dies. On systems with no battery at all, there is a capacitor on the motherboard that charges whenever the PC is plugged in; to charge the battery, simply leave the PC plugged in for a while.

## TRY IT!

**Locate the battery on your motherboard. If there is no battery, determine the source of the battery capability.**

## I/O Ports

*Input/Output (I/O) ports* are fairly standard in motherboards these days. Most include one or two COM (serial) ports, one LPT (parallel) port, a keyboard port, two USB ports, and a mouse port. Depending on the motherboard design, these may be built into the side of the board (ATX, Figure 4.33) or attached via small ribbon cables (AT, Figure 4.34).

**Input/Output (I/O) ports**

Ports designed to transfer information into and out of the PC. Examples include serial (COM) ports and parallel (LPT) ports, as well as USB ports.

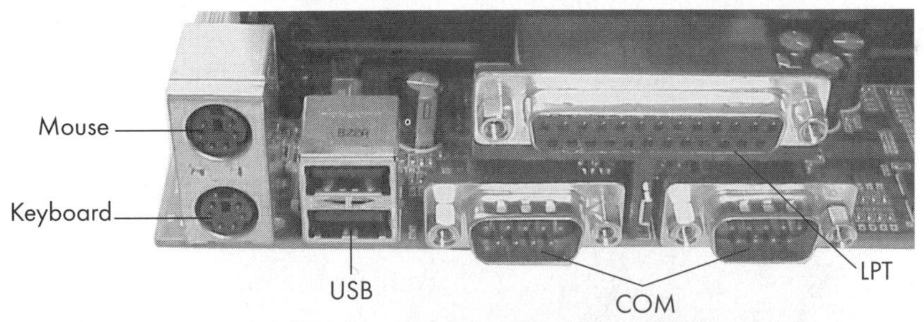


**FIGURE 4.33**
Built-In I/O Ports on an ATX Motherboard

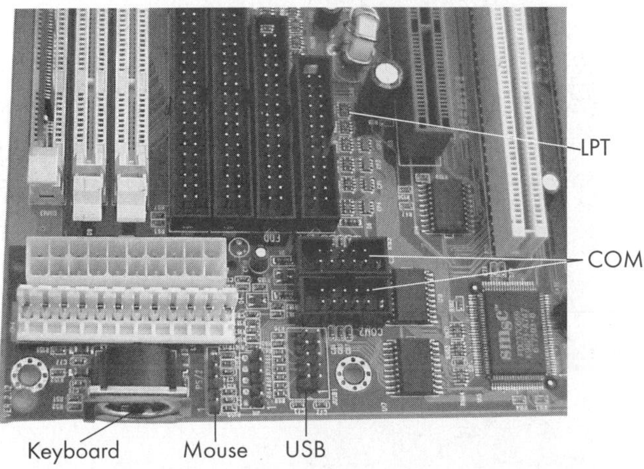


**FIGURE 4.34**
I/O Port Connectors on an AT Motherboard

**COM port**

Short for Communications port. A generic type of serial port built into most motherboards.

Older motherboards may not have a PS/2 style mouse port, because originally the mouse was a serial device and plugged into a *COM port.* Only in the last 10 years has the standard been for the motherboard to provide a separate port for the mouse. When you buy a mouse, it may come with a serial adapter that can change a PS/2 plug to a DB-9 plug if the motherboard does not have a mouse port.

The COM ports themselves may be either 9-pin or 25-pin. In Figure 4.33 they are both 9-pin. The two sizes are functionally equivalent; you can use an adapter to make one into another whenever needed. On an AT motherboard, the COM connectors (shown in Figure 4.34) are not size-aware; you can connect a ribbon cable with either size of connector to them.

**TRY IT!**

**Make a list of all of the I/O ports that your motherboard supports. On an AT system, I/O ports require external connectors to be connected via ribbon cable, so it is possible that not every port that the motherboard supports will have a connector hooked up for it.**

## Drive Connectors

**Primary IDE**

The first IDE interface on the motherboard or expansion board.

**Secondary IDE**

The second IDE interface on the motherboard or expansion board.

All motherboards sold today come with a standard set of drive connectors: two IDE and one floppy. The IDE connectors might be labeled IDE0 and IDE1, or IDE1 and IDE2 (see Figure 4.35). The lower of the two numbers is the *primary IDE*; the other is the *secondary IDE.* Chapter 11 discusses IDE in more detail.

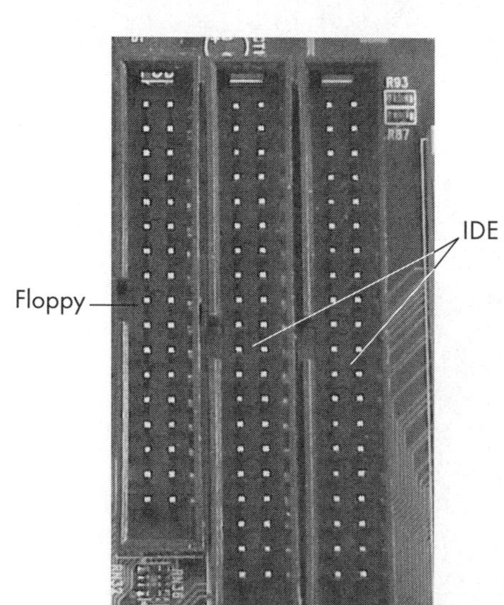


**FIGURE 4.35**
The IDE and Floppy Drive Connectors on a Motherboard

Older motherboards did not always have these drive connectors. Some motherboards required an I/O expansion board to add the drive connectors (and the connectors for COM and LPT ports as well). Figure 4.36 shows an LPX motherboard that has not only the ISA expansion slots on a daughterboard, but also the IDE and floppy connectors.

**FIGURE 4.36**
The IDE and floppy connectors might be on a separate board on an older or slimline system.

## Troubleshooting Problems with Motherboards

This section outlines some common problems that involve motherboards, including their symptoms and solutions.

### Dead Motherboard

A dead motherboard and a dead power supply can present exactly the same symptoms: nothing happens. The power supply fan may not spin, but that does not necessarily mean the power supply is at fault. So when a system appears completely dead, first eliminate the power supply as a suspect, either by testing the power supply with a multimeter or by swapping it out with a power supply known to be good.

If the problem is not the power supply, check the following configuration issues with the motherboard:

- Is the right type of CPU installed? Is it installed correctly? (See Chapter 5.)
- Is the right type of RAM installed? Is it installed correctly? (See Chapter 6.)

If the power supply fan runs but there is no video on-screen, the motherboard is still a suspect. Check the following:

- Is there a video card installed? Is it in the right type of slot and completely seated? (See Chapters 8 and 15.)
- Is there a monitor connected to the video card? Is it turned on?
- Does a different video card solve the problem?

If you see text on the screen—anything at all, even an error message—then you know the motherboard is working. You will learn how to assemble a basic PC system in Chapter 8.

If you do not see anything, perhaps a *POST card* will help (POST stands for Power On Self Test). A POST card is a circuit board that you insert into an expansion slot in the motherboard. As the PC boots, an LED on the board displays a digital numeric code indicating the status of the boot process. If it stops on a particular number, you can then look up that number in the reference manual for the POST card to determine what is wrong. POST cards are available in both ISA and PCI models, and are sometimes called POST testers.

## Beeping

If the speaker is connected to the motherboard, you may hear a pattern of error beeps if something is wrong with the motherboard. These are called *beep codes*, and the number and length of the beeps are significant. For example, on an AMI BIOS, five beeps means a CPU error and two beeps indicates a memory parity error. The actual codes depend on the BIOS manufacturer and model. Two Web sites that provide full listings of the codes are http://www.ami.com (AMI BIOS) and http://www.phoenix.com (Phoenix or Award BIOS).

## Dead Battery

When the PC's real-time clock (RTC) starts losing time (anywhere from a few minutes a day to total stoppage), or the BIOS setup program loses the custom settings you have entered, the motherboard battery probably needs to be changed. The average motherboard battery lasts between three and six years, so if a PC is older than that, it is on borrowed time.

As shown in Figure 4.30, a motherboard with a built-in battery will usually have a connector for attaching an external battery. On a motherboard with a coin-type battery, just release the battery from its clip and take it to an electronics store for a replacement.

### In Real Life

The old battery can be left in place. Some technicians prefer to remove an old battery to ensure that it does not leak; to do so, cut the wires holding the battery in place. This is not really necessary, because the type of battery used in a motherboard seldom leaks. You do need to watch the external battery pack used for the replacement, however; these use ordinary alkaline batteries and are prone to leakage.

## Dead Built-In Component

Although it is uncommon, occasionally a built-in component in a motherboard may fail, leaving the user with a dilemma: replace the entire motherboard with a new one containing the same built-in component, or add an expansion card for the component. The latter is usually the more economical solution.

The built-in component might need to be disabled in the BIOS setup program before the system will recognize an expansion card of that same type, but in most cases this is not necessary because most motherboards will accept multiple instances of a device type (two network cards, two video cards, two sound cards, and so on). However, the old device may continue to use system resources unless it is disabled in BIOS.

If the PC runs Microsoft Windows 95 or higher, the old device can be disabled through Device Manager so that it does not take resources away from the functioning devices; see Chapter 14 for details.

## Malfunctioning Expansion Slot

If an expansion board does not work in the motherboard, it is always a good idea to try it in a different expansion slot. If the device works in the new slot, the problem may be a bad slot (uncommon, but it does occur). If it still does not work, try a different, known-good board.

The problem may also be related to the BIOS setup program. Depending on the settings, the BIOS setup program may retain information about PCI devices; this is called Extended System Configuration Data (ESCD). It is like Plug and Play, but at the chipset level, and is only for PCI devices. If an expansion slot is not working, try clearing the ESCD. The option may be called Config Data or something similar. Figure 4.37 shows a BIOS setup program with this option set to Yes. See Chapter 9 for more information on BIOS setup.

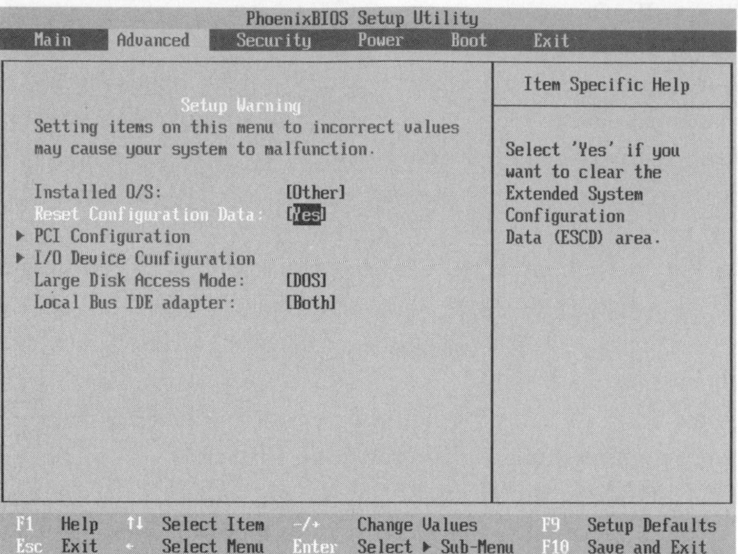


**FIGURE 4.37**
Resetting the Extended System Configuration Data can sometimes clear up a problem with an expansion slot.

## Bad Jumper Settings

Wherever there are motherboard jumpers, there is the potential for bad jumper settings. Depending on the motherboard, there may be jumper settings for the CPU speed, system bus speed, CPU voltage, and many more parameters.

It is critical that the jumper for CPU voltage be set correctly. It is set when installing the CPU, and never needs to be changed unless a different CPU is installed. The wrong voltage setting can damage a CPU. The CPU speed and system bus speed jumpers are also important, but incorrect settings will not immediately damage the CPU; they might prevent it temporarily from working, or make it work at the wrong speed. Refer to the earlier section "Jumpers and Switches" in this chapter.

## Bent Pins

A bent pin on the motherboard can cause problems by creating unintended electrical flow patterns. For example, if two pins that are supposed to be separate are bent so that they touch, that is like adding a jumper between them. A bent pin on a connector, such as the connectors where ribbon cables for drives plug in, can cause the connectors not to be fully seated and the drives unable to work. Check all the pins on the motherboard to make sure they are upright; if they are not, gently bend them back into place with fingers or a small tool.

# STUDY GUIDE

Use the following summaries to review the key concepts of this chapter.

## The Processing Subsystem

- The motherboard holds the memory and CPU and contains circuits that connect them. It also provides connections to input/output ports.
- The Central Processing Unit (CPU) is a chip that performs math calculations.
- Memory, also called RAM (for Random-Access Memory), acts as a temporary storage area for data as a work area.
- The operating system is the software that tells the CPU, memory, and motherboard what to do and in what order. Windows is the most popular operating system.

## How a Motherboard Works

- The motherboard's primary job is to manage the flow of data between computers.
- Data travels through a motherboard via patterns of electrical pulses that represent binary numbers.
- Buses are pathways that carry data between ports, slots, and sockets.
- The chipset is the set of chips that directs the bus traffic.

## Buses

- A motherboard has several buses, each with its own width and speed.
- Buses range in width from 16-bit on the ISA bus to 64-bit on the system bus.
- Buses range in speed from 8MHz on the ISA bus to 133MHz or higher on the system bus.
- The system bus connects the CPU and the memory controller chip (MCC) to the chipset. It is also called the external data bus. It is synchronized with the CPU.
- The address bus runs between the CPU and the MCC.
- The Advanced Graphics Port (AGP) bus is a 32-bit bus that runs between the AGP expansion slot (for the video card) and the chipset. It runs at 66MHz or higher, up to 533MHz on some systems.
- The PCI bus is a 32-bit bus that runs at 33MHz. It is the standard bus for expansion boards in modern motherboards.
- The ISA bus is a 16-bit bus running at 8MHz. This bus is becoming obsolete.

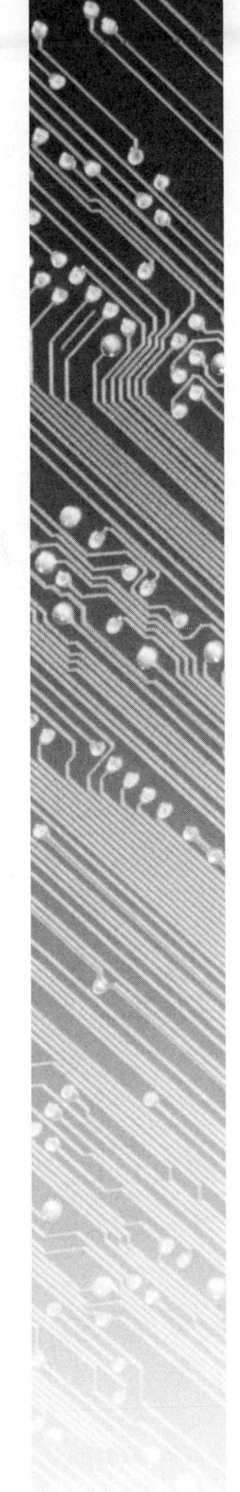

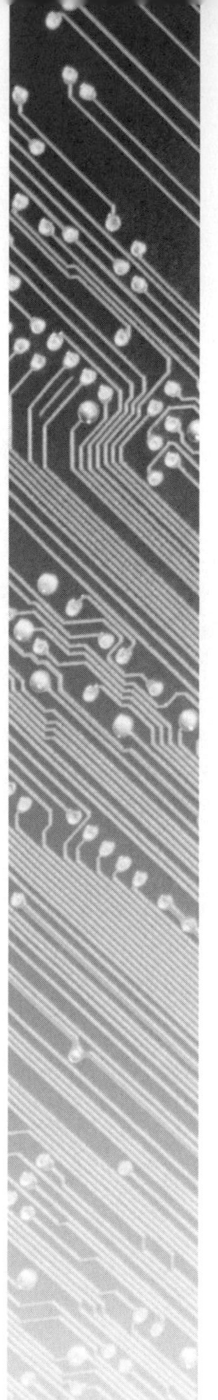

## Chipsets

- A chipset is a set of chips mounted on the motherboard that directs the flow of traffic along and between the buses.
- Two motherboards with the same chipset are functionally identical, even if they are made by different companies.
- Intel is the largest maker of chipsets; other manufacturers include Via Technologies and Silicon Integrated Systems (SiS).
- A chipset can be a single chip, but it is usually two or more chips working together.
- The chipset controls almost everything about the motherboard's operation, including the bus speed, the supported CPUs, and the amount and type of memory supported.
- There are two basic architectures for chipsets: north/south bridge and hub.
- On a north/south bridge chipset, the PCI bus functions as the connection between the north and south chips. The ISA bus functions as the connection between the south bridge and the super I/O chip.
- On a hub chipset, the memory controller hub and the I/O controller hub are connected via a proprietary high-speed connection. This keeps the PCI bus free for data transfer.
- On systems that do not have an ISA bus, the connection between the south bridge (or the I/O controller hub) and the super I/O chip is via an LPC bus.
- To identify the chipset, look for large square chips soldered directly to the motherboard with writing on them that indicates a model number.

## Jumpers and Switches

- A jumper is a set of pins that can accept a metal or plastic cap to bridge them.
- When the jumper cap is on, the pins are bridged; when the jumper cap is off, they are not.
- A jumper cap hooked over only one pin is the same as having no jumper cap at all.
- A switch performs the same function as a jumper but works like a light-switch toggle.
- Switches are uncommon in most equipment because they cost more than jumpers to manufacture.
- To change a switch's position, use any small pointed object such as a nail, paperclip, or ink pen.

## Form Factors

- There are two main types of motherboards, denoting both size and shape: AT and ATX.
- The motherboard, case, and power supply must all be of the same type.
- An AT motherboard has a large keyboard plug, with the expansion slots parallel to the wide edge of the board.
- An ATX motherboard has a PS/2 style keyboard plug, with the expansion slots parallel to the narrow edge of the board.
- An AT motherboard has connectors for I/O ports such as COM, LPT, mouse, and so on; an ATX motherboard has those ports built directly into the side of the board.
- An AT motherboard uses two-part power supply connectors (P8 and P9); an ATX motherboard uses the single-part power supply connector.
- ATX motherboards are considered superior because of their design advantages.
- Slimline motherboards, seldom seen in new systems, fit the components into a smaller than normal case by mounting the expansion slots on a card that sits perpendicular to the board. There have been two designs for these: LPX and NLX.

## Expansion Slots

- ISA expansion slots were the original type of expansion slot. Early motherboards had two lengths: 8-bit and 16-bit. Later models had only the 16-bit type.
- MCA was an early attempt to improve on ISA. It was a 32-bit slot, but because of licensing issues with IBM, MCA never became popular. MCA systems do not accept ISA expansion boards.
- Enhanced ISA (EISA) was a competitor to MCA. An EISA slot is a 32-bit ISA slot, but still suffers from ISA's speed limitations. EISA never proved popular.
- The first local bus expansion slot type was VESA local bus, or VLB. It was designed to run at the same speed as the system bus (around 33MHz at that time) and to be 32-bit.
- VLB was quickly replaced by a superior design called Peripheral Component Interface (PCI). PCI is still the standard for local bus expansion slots.
- AGP is a high-speed bus designed solely for video card usage. The AGP bus is able to operate at up to 533MHz, depending on the system and the version of AGP in use.

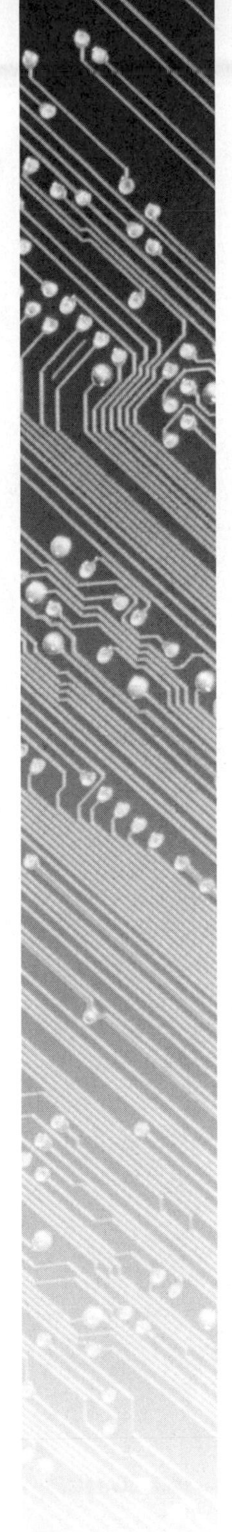

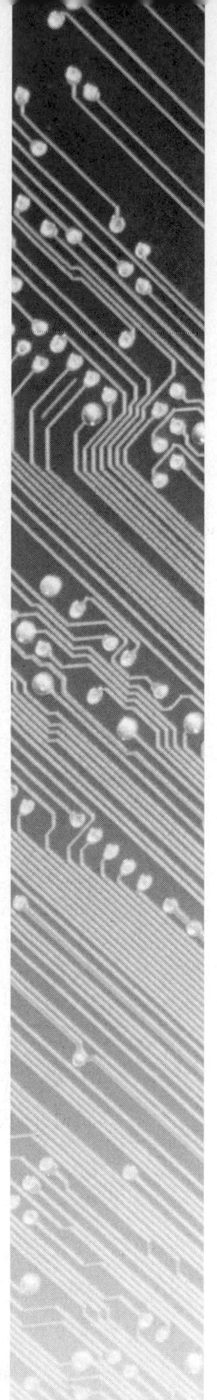

- Modern motherboards have dual inline memory module (DIMM) slots for memory. Older motherboards used single inline memory modules (SIMMs).
- There are two types of CPU designs found today: pin grid array (PGA) and single edge contact cartridge (SECC).
- A PGA slot has holes into which pins on the back of the CPU can fit. CPUs using PGA have included the 486, Pentium, Pentium Pro, Pentium III, and Pentium 4.
- An SECC slot is like an expansion card slot but oriented differently, and holds a CPU mounted on a circuit board and encased in a plastic cartridge. The SECC type of slot is used on Pentium II, Celeron, and Athlon systems.

## Built-In Components

- Some motherboards have built-in video, sound, and/or network card capabilities.
- Such systems are typically less expensive to manufacture since they do not require expansion boards for those functions.

## Batteries

- Most motherboards have a battery that keeps the CMOS chip powered so that it retains the date/time and BIOS setup information.
- Originally batteries were soldered to the motherboard, but later models have had removable and replaceable batteries.
- Batteries in modern motherboards are coin-type, like giant watch batteries.

## I/O Ports and Drive Connectors

- Most motherboards include two COM ports, one LPT port, a keyboard port, two USB ports, and a mouse port.
- On an ATX system these ports are built into the side of the motherboard; on an AT system there are connectors on the motherboard for cables that lead to ports mounted on the case.
- COM ports may be either 9-pin or 25-pin; both function the same.
- Most motherboards have two IDE connectors and one floppy drive connector.
- On some systems, especially slimline models, the IDE and floppy connectors are on a daughterboard.

## Troubleshooting Problems with Motherboards

- A dead motherboard and a dead power supply can appear exactly the same. If the power supply fan does not spin, first check the power supply, then suspect the motherboard.
- Make sure the right type of CPU is installed, and that it is installed correctly.
- Make sure the right type of RAM is installed, and that it is installed correctly.
- Make sure there is a working video card installed correctly, and that a working monitor is connected to it and turned on.
- If text appears on the screen, the motherboard is working.
- If the speaker is hooked up and you hear a series of beeps, it may be a BIOS beep code. Check the BIOS manufacturer's Web site for the meaning of the code.
- A POST card is an expansion card that monitors the boot process and shows a numeric code telling at what point the boot process locks up.
- If the PC's clock loses time or it forgets its BIOS settings, the battery may be going dead.
- If a built-in component on the motherboard fails, disable it in BIOS or in the Windows Device Manager and then add a replacement on an expansion card.
- If an expansion slot is not working, use a different one.
- Sometimes resetting the Extended System Configuration Data in BIOS setup can clear up a problem with a PCI slot.
- Double-check jumper and switch settings against the charts in the motherboard manual if there is any question about the settings.
- Bent pins on the motherboard can cause problems; straighten any pins that appear bent.

# PRACTICE TEST

On a blank sheet of paper, write the answers to the following multiple-choice questions and explain why each answer is correct.

1. The processing subsystem consists of which hardware components?
   a. CPU, memory, and hard disk
   b. memory, motherboard, and expansion cards
   c. CPU, memory, and expansion cards
   d. CPU, memory, and motherboard

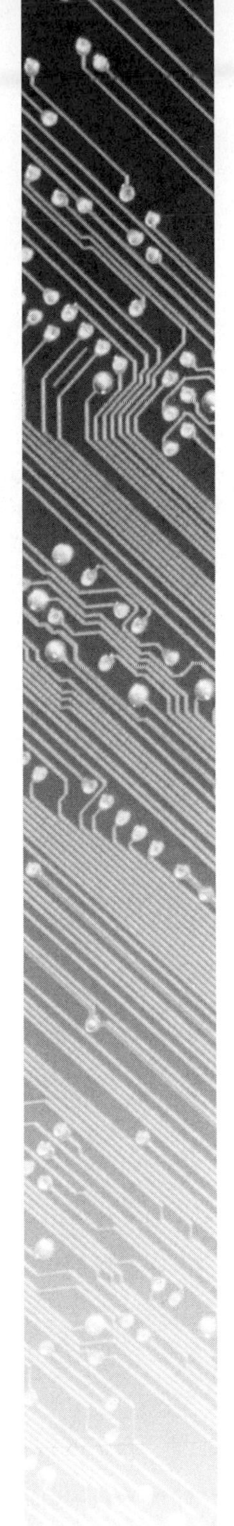

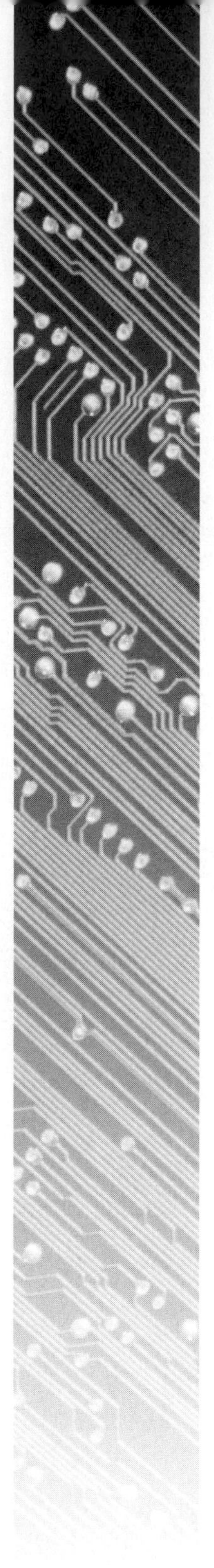

2. The data pathways within a motherboard are its
   a. chipsets.
   b. buses.
   c. buffers.
   d. I/O ports.

3. Which bus connects the CPU to the chipset?
   a. address bus
   b. system bus
   c. AGP bus
   d. PCI bus

4. The ISA bus is a ____bit bus that runs at ____ MHz.
   a. 32, 16
   b. 32, 8
   c. 16, 16
   d. 16, 8

5. Which bus connects the north and south bridges in a north/south bridge chipset?
   a. AGP
   b. system
   c. ISA
   d. PCI

6. Which part of a hub architecture chipset corresponds to the north bridge in a north/south bridge architecture?
   a. memory controller hub
   b. Super I/O
   c. I/O controller hub
   d. PCI bridge

7. Which of these is *not* determined by the chipset in the motherboard?
   a. system bus speed
   b. memory type
   c. ISA bus speed
   d. IDE support

8. What happens when a jumper cap is placed over two pins?
   a. The electrical path between them is broken.
   b. The electrical path between them is completed.
   c. The voltage changes.
   d. Nothing, unless a switch is also activated.

9. Which motherboard form factor orients the expansion slots on the motherboard parallel to the short edge of the board?
   a. LPX
   b. NLX
   c. AT
   d. ATX

10. Which motherboard form factor(s) have the COM, LPT, keyboard, and mouse ports permanently mounted to the side of the motherboard?
    a. AT only
    b. AT and ATX
    c. ATX only
    d. LPX and NLX

11. Which of these is a slimline motherboard?
    a. AT
    b. ATX
    c. NLX
    d. LPT

12. Which of these buses is *not* obsolete?
    a. MCA
    b. EISA
    c. VLB
    d. They are all obsolete

13. Which of these is a local bus?
    a. VLB
    b. ISA
    c. EISA
    d. MCA

14. Which of these expansion board devices could be used in a PCI slot?
    a. modem
    b. video card
    c. sound card
    d. All of the above

15. Which of these expansion board devices would work in an AGP slot?
    a. modem
    b. video card
    c. sound card
    d. All of the above

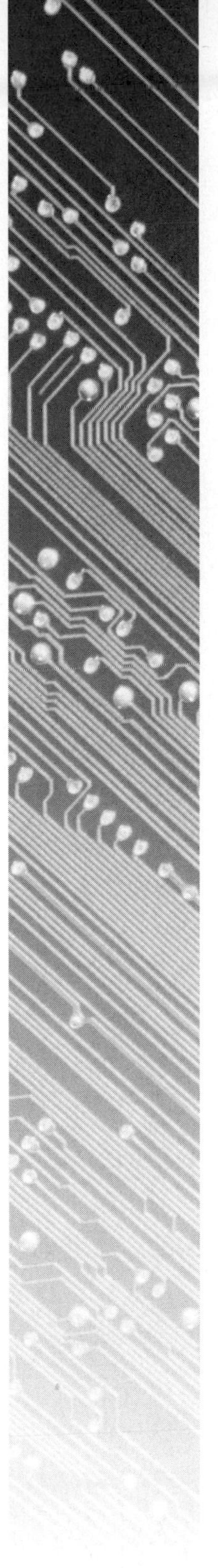

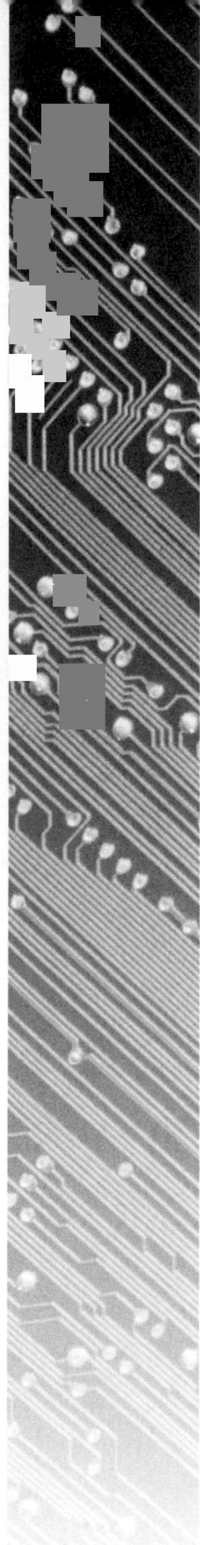

16. The type of CPU slot that consists of a grid of holes is
    a. PGA.
    b. VGA.
    c. SECC.
    d. Slot 1.

17. Which of these is not a common built-in I/O port in a modern motherboard?
    a. COM
    b. LPT
    c. FireWire
    d. USB

18. A typical motherboard has how many IDE connectors?
    a. 1
    b. 2
    c. 4
    d. None

19. Which of these is *not* a symptom of a dead battery in the motherboard?
    a. BIOS setup loses any custom settings you have entered.
    b. There is no video display.
    c. RTC is inaccurate.
    d. All of these are symptoms of a dead battery.

20. To disable a malfunctioning built-in component on the motherboard, such as a sound or video adapter, what should you do?
    a. Turn off the device in BIOS setup.
    b. Remove the chip by desoldering.
    c. Remove the component with wire cutters.
    d. None of these are correct; the motherboard must be replaced.

# TROUBLESHOOTING

1. Someone gives you a motherboard, but has no information about it. Describe how you would go about deducing some facts about it and figuring out in what type of system it might work.
2. A new motherboard was tested at the store and worked properly with the store's power supply, CPU, memory, and video card. When you get it back to your workshop and put it in a PC, it does not work anymore. The power supply fan spins, but there is no video on the

screen. Describe the troubleshooting procedure you would go through.

3. When you pick up a motherboard, a jumper cap falls to the floor. Describe how you will figure out where that jumper came from on the motherboard and what its correct setting should be.

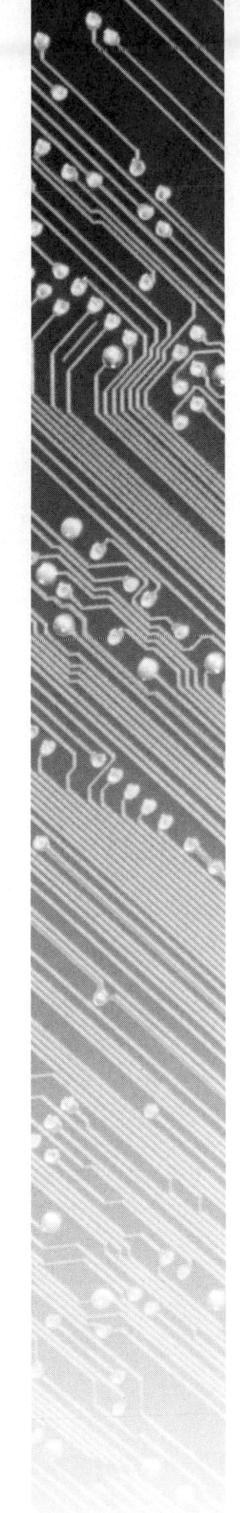

# CUSTOMER SERVICE

1. You are talking on the telephone to a novice-level client who wants you to install a new video card. You would like to pick up the video card on the way to the client's home, but do not know anything about the computer. Describe the directions you would give the client and the questions you would ask to determine the bus type for the video card, and the cautions you would issue to the client so he did not harm anything while doing it.
2. A client has a very old computer, and at some point someone has replaced the old barrel-type battery with an external battery pack with an alkaline battery. That alkaline battery has leaked all over the motherboard, but the motherboard still appears to work. What are this client's options?
3. A client has a motherboard with built-in video card, but Windows will not recognize the video model through Plug and Play; it sees it only as Standard VGA. You have determined that the chipset on the motherboard is an SiS 540. What are this client's options?

# FOR MORE INFORMATION

For links to Web sites that provide further information about the topics covered in this chapter, go to the EMC/Paradigm Internet Resource Center at www.emcp.com/College Division/Internet Resource Centers/PC Maintenance/For More Information.

# 5 CPUs

## ON THE TEST

**A+ Core Hardware Service Technician Examination**

- **Objective 1.1:** Identify basic terms, concepts, and functions of system modules, including how each module should work during normal operation and during the boot process.
- **Objective 4.1:** Distinguish between the popular CPU chips in terms of their basic characteristics.

## ON THE JOB

It is important to be able to identify CPUs and to determine which CPUs will work for a particular purpose. Of course the fastest, most modern CPU will provide the best performance in any PC, but only in a perfect world will every client have a completely up-to-date system. In real-life PC technician work, you will probably encounter many types of CPUs of various ages and capabilities.

Some of the activities you might perform using the skills in this chapter include:

- selecting a replacement CPU for a system whose CPU has gone bad
- setting the jumpers on a motherboard for the correct voltage and speed of CPU being used
- selecting a motherboard with the right kind of slot or socket for a CPU you plan to use in it
- explaining to a client why one CPU is better than another for a given use

This chapter does not deal with the specifics of installing a CPU in a motherboard; that will be covered in Chapter 8.

# How a CPU Works

**Central Processing Unit (CPU)**

The main processing chip in a PC that performs the math calculations.

As you learned in Chapter 1, the only job of the CPU, or *Central Processing Unit,* is to perform mathematical calculations. The operating system sends the CPU instructions that include the numbers to calculate and the formulas to use upon them, and the CPU does the job and provides the result.

**WARNING**

**The CPU works very closely with the motherboard's chipset, and each motherboard has a short list of a few CPU models and speeds that it will work with. Therefore, it is important to select the motherboard with the CPU in mind, and vice versa.**

## How Data Moves In and Out of the CPU

Begin by looking at how data moves from the motherboard's circuitry to the CPU and back out again. Chapter 4 explained the process from the perspective of the motherboard; now the emphasis is on the CPU.

Data comes into and out of the CPU on the system bus, as noted in Chapter 4. Another name for the system bus is the external data bus, because it is external to the CPU. The pins on a CPU chip each carry an electrical charge, and the data enters and exits the CPU by patterns of electrical pulses—the same way it travels through the motherboard.

**Register**

Storage area in the CPU where it places bits as it is performing calculations on them.

Inside the CPU are work areas called *registers.* These are storage grids in which the CPU can temporarily place numbers for calculation. Since data comes in bit by bit, all of the data for a calculation might not arrive all at once; the registers enable the CPU to remember data long enough to answer the question posed to it.

**Low-order bits**

The bits sent to the CPU that represent the data to be calculated.

**High-order bits**

The bits sent to the CPU that represent the instructions for calculating the low-order bits.

When data comes in, a part of that data is the number to be calculated and a part is a code representing the instruction for the action to be performed on it. The CPU knows the codes for many different math operations, from the simple multiply, divide, add to much more complex procedures, and it recognizes the code for each one as a request to execute it. In an 8-bit CPU, data comes into the CPU eight bits at a time. The first four bits are the *low-order bits* that represent the data; the second four bits are the *high-order bits* that represent the instruction.

For example, 0111 is the number 7 in binary, and 0010 is the number 2. Assume that 1000 means to move a number into a certain register, 1001 means to move a number into a different register, 1100 means to add the two registers' contents, and 1110 means to place the result of that calculation on the external data bus. The operating system sends the following instructions to the CPU:

1. 10000111 (Move the number 7 into Register A)
2. 10010010 (Move the number 2 into Register B)
3. 11000000 (Add Register A and Register B and place the result in Register C; notice four 0000s used for filler)
4. 11100000 (Place the content of Register C on the external data bus; again four 0000s used for filler)

**Low-order bits**

The bits sent to the CPU that represent the data to be calculated.

**High-order bits**

The bits sent to the CPU that represent the instructions for calculating the low-order bits.

Figure 5.1 illustrates these four steps, which constitute a very low-level program written in machine language. This is an example of an 8-bit instruction; it talks to the CPU eight bits at a time. Today's CPUs are 32-bit or 64-bit. The advantage of having more bits to work with is not only that more data can be conveyed in the low-order bits, but also that more math functions can be represented in the high-order bits. Notice that there is not always output for every input operation; in Figure 5.1 there are four lines of input but only one of them (the last one) results in any output.

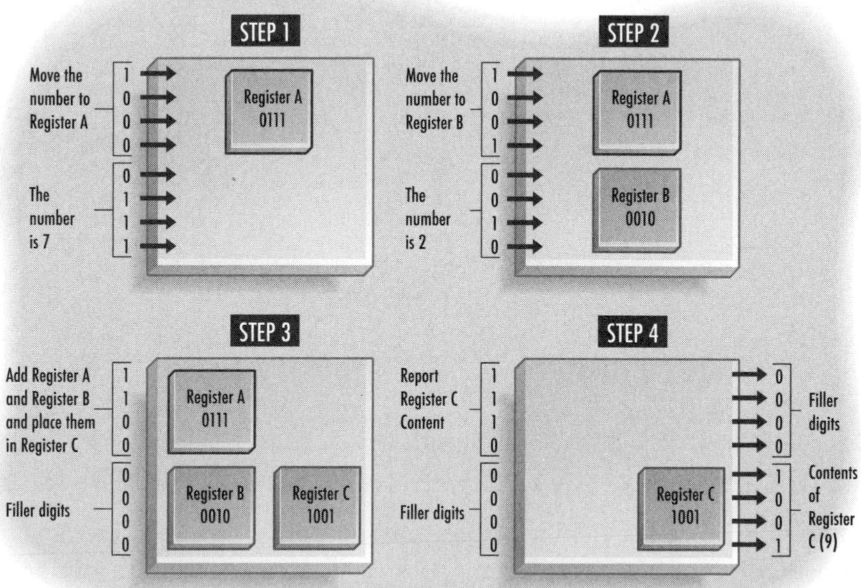


**FIGURE 5.1**
Data Flowing Into and Out of a CPU

**Machine language**

The set of commands that the CPU understands for high-order bits.

*Machine language* is the set of commands (conveyed through the high-order bits) that the CPU understands. In order to speak to a CPU, the operating system needs to know the codes for all of the instructions that the CPU knows, so it can send the appropriate commands in the high-order bits. Part of the job of an operating system is to interface with the chipset to determine what commands the CPU can accept and then to translate all of the commands that the user issues into machine language instructions. Each CPU has its own machine language, although new generations of CPUs usually have machine languages that are built upon a core set of commands from previous generations. That is why a given chipset can support only a select list of CPUs, not every CPU that has ever been made.

## Data Processing Speed

**System crystal**

The timekeeping unit on the motherboard that controls the pace of data entering and exiting the CPU.

**Clock cycle**

One tick of the system crystal's clock, resulting in one data movement into or out of the CPU.

Data does not flow freely into and out of the CPU at any speed; there is an orderly cadence to the process. The tempo is set by the *system crystal* (Figure 5.2), which is a timekeeping unit on the motherboard similar to that in a modern wristwatch except that it ticks much faster. Each tick of the system crystal is a *clock cycle*, and data movement occurs in rhythm with this ticking. The system bus operates at the same speed as the system crystal. On modern motherboards, 100 or 133MHz are common system crystal speeds.

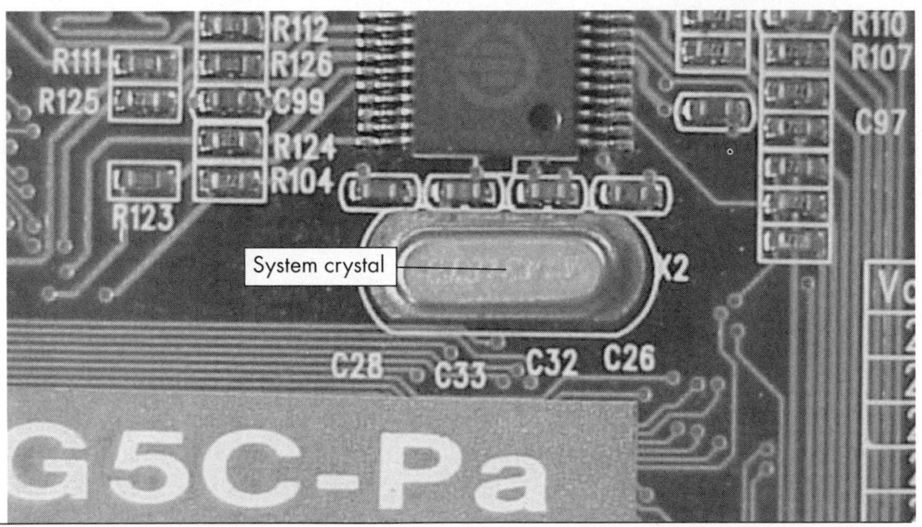


**FIGURE 5.2**
A System Crystal

Every time the clock ticks, an opportunity occurs for data to enter and exit the CPU. Look back at Figure 5.1; each of those steps occurs during a different clock cycle.

Each CPU has a rated speed at which it can reliably operate, measured in megahertz (MHz). This speed, representing the number of clock cycles per second that the CPU can handle, is known as the CPU's *internal speed.* However, it is the system crystal, not the CPU, that determines the speed at which the PC operates. The actual speed at which the CPU operates as directed by the system crystal is its *external speed.*

**Internal speed**

The speed at which the CPU can reliably operate, measured in MHz.

**External speed**

The speed at which the CPU actually operates, regulated by the system crystal.

The CPU speed on very old computers was slower than the system crystal. On an 80286 PC, for example, an 8MHz CPU on a motherboard might be coupled with a 16MHz system crystal. As CPUs became more powerful and efficient, they began to keep up with the system crystal and run at the same speed. By the time the 486 CPUs were popular, the CPUs were outstripping the motherboard crystals in speed. (That is where clock multipliers come in, described later in this chapter.)

Some motherboards have a system crystal that operates at only one speed; others have jumpers that enable the user to change the system crystal speed to accommodate different speeds of CPU. The motherboard in Figure 5.3 has a chart printed on it showing jumper settings for different external speeds.

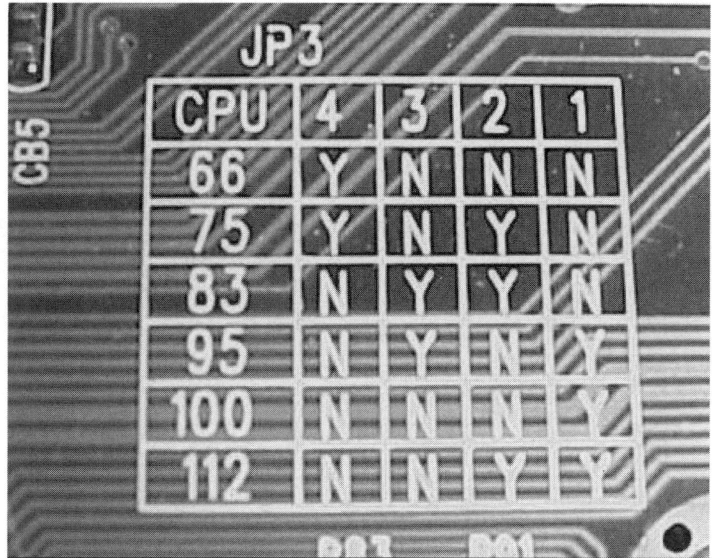


**FIGURE 5.3**
Some motherboards allow different external speeds to be set by changing jumper positions.

**Underclocking**

Running a CPU at a lower external speed than that of which it is capable.

**Overclocking**

Pushing a CPU to run at a higher external speed than that for which it is rated.

### *Overclocking and Underclocking*

A CPU can work reliably on a motherboard with a slower external speed than its own top internal speed, but it will run at the crystal's speed. This is called *underclocking*. It does not do any harm, but it limits the CPU's capabilities. When a user sets the system crystal to push the CPU faster than its rated speed, that is called *overclocking*. It can result in faster system performance, but it can also cause overheating and instability.

Overclocking is possible because of the manufacturing process for CPUs. A company that makes CPUs makes them all in the same assembly line. Some turn out better than others, so as part of the manufacturing process they are put through their paces at various speeds. When a CPU is pushed beyond its speed capabilities, it starts to overheat or generate errors. The CPUs are sorted based on the speed at which they failed, and then marked for sale with a speed rating based on that testing. Usually the manufacturer allows a comfortable cushion for error in the labeling, so a CPU that is rated at 1.6GHz may actually have proved reliable up to 1.8GHz or even higher. In addition, sometimes chip makers turn out too many good-quality CPUs and not enough that fail at the lower speeds, so they take some of the good ones out of the high-speed bin and label them at the lower speeds. When you buy a CPU, you never know the actual top speed without testing it through a series of overclocking speeds.

An overclocked CPU can overheat and sometimes be damaged during overclocking. Overclocking a CPU also voids its warranty. The latest CPUs have overclocking protection built in. This protection is not in the CPU chip itself; it is part of the CPU packaging. The CPU is set to operate only at a certain internal speed, and refuses to be pushed higher.

The average user should avoid overclocking because of the risk of generating errors and damaging hardware. In addition, technical support professionals should discourage the end users they support from overclocking because it can result in more technical support being required.

### *Clock Multipliers*

**Clock multiplier**

The multiplier by which the CPU's internal speed exceeds its external speed.

Today's PCs run a lot faster than the external speed of the average motherboard. In other words, the internal speed of a CPU is many times greater than the external speed of the motherboard (as dictated by the system crystal). This is accomplished with a *clock multiplier*.

On 386 computers and earlier, the internal and external speeds were the same, but on later PCs a technology was developed that made it possible for the CPU to execute two or more instructions per clock tick. This is known as clock doubling (or tripling, quadrupling, and so on), and the multiplier by which the internal speed exceeds the external speed is the clock multiplier. The clock multiplier need not be a whole number. For example, a 333MHz CPU might have an external speed of 95 and a multiplier of 3.5.

Some motherboards include jumpers that enable the user to set the clock multiplier manually. Figure 5.4 shows a chart printed on a motherboard that enables multipliers of between 2.0 and 5.5. On other motherboards there is only one multiplier possible, or the motherboard automatically chooses a multiplier based on the CPU installed.

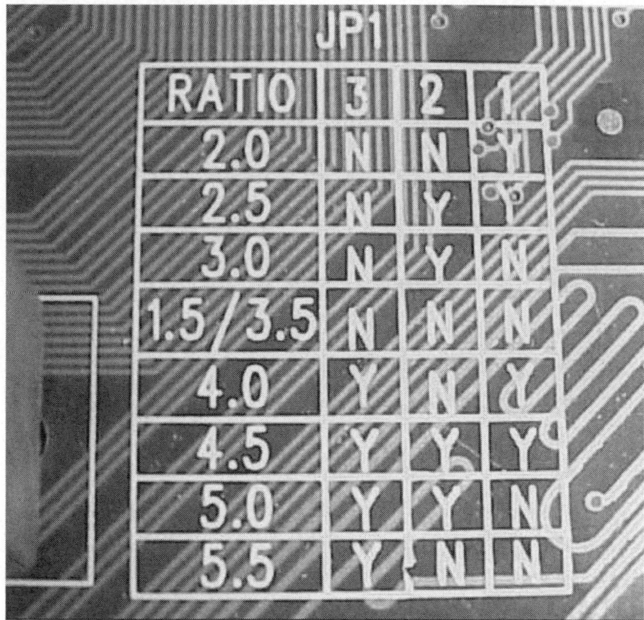

JP1
RATIO 3 2 1
2.0 N N Y
2.5 N Y Y
3.0 N Y N
1.5/3.5 N N N
4.0 Y N Y
4.5 Y Y Y
5.0 Y Y N
5.5 Y N N


**FIGURE 5.4**
Table on a Motherboard Describing Available Clock Multiplier Settings

## TRY IT!

**Look on the motherboard(s) available to you to see if any have jumpers for clock multipliers like the one shown in Figure 5.4. Check the setting to confirm that it is appropriate for the installed CPU, if there is one.**

## Core Voltage

Just like any other device, a CPU requires a certain power voltage to operate. This is its *core voltage*. The older the CPU, the higher the core voltage; early CPUs required +5v, while the latest CPUs use +2.8v or even less. A voltage regulator on the motherboard steps down the voltage provided by the power supply before it reaches the CPU socket. Lower

**Core voltage**
The electrical voltage that the CPU requires to operate.

voltage is advantageous because it allows the chip to run cooler, so it is less sensitive to overheating and requires less aggressive cooling methods. CPU cooling is discussed later in this chapter.

Some motherboards have a variable voltage regulator that makes them capable of supporting CPUs of different voltages. The user selects the voltage of the installed CPU with a jumper, as in Figure 5.5.

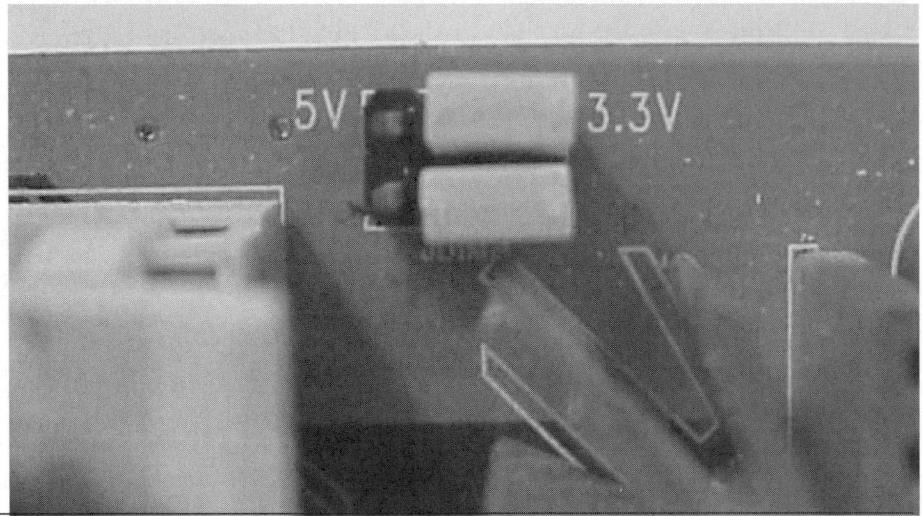


**FIGURE 5.5**
A Jumper for Selecting CPU Core Voltage on a Motherboard

**TRY IT!**

**Look on the motherboards you have available to see whether any of them have voltage-regulating jumpers. Identify the current setting and confirm it is appropriate for the installed CPU, if there is one.**

## Cache Usage

The CPU is the fastest component in the system. The RAM, the external data bus, and all of the other components that interact with the CPU do not even come close. Therefore, bottlenecks often occur when data is entering or exiting the CPU.

**L1 cache**

The module that holds data waiting to enter the CPU. Also called front-side cache.

On the front side (that is, the side going into the CPU), delays often occur when the CPU needs data that must be retrieved from RAM. It takes several clock cycles for the data to be retrieved from RAM and sent to the CPU via the external data bus; meanwhile, the CPU sits idle. To help prevent such bottlenecks, modern systems include an *L1 cache* (also called a front-side cache). A cache is an area of reserved, extremely fast memory with a fast connection to the CPU. Data that the CPU is likely to need in the near future (say, the next several millionths of a second) is stored in the L1 cache so that when the CPU does call for it, it is readily available.

Modern CPUs are more adept than their ancestors at predicting what data the CPU will need, so they are better able to keep the L1 cache stocked with the correct data for fastest performance. In addition, modern CPUs have the L1 cache built right into the CPU packaging, so no external bus is required to transfer data to the CPU.

On the back side (that is, the side leaving the CPU), delays occur when the CPU has more processed data to dump back onto the external data bus than the bus can handle at the moment. This results in data being unable to leave the CPU promptly, which means that new data is halted because there is no room for it. To solve this problem, an *L2 cache* (also called a back-side cache) is employed to store excess output from the CPU until the external data bus can catch up with it. On early systems the L2 cache was a separate memory module mounted in a special RAM slot on the motherboard. A mini circuit board containing RAM is known as a "stick" in PC slang, so this type of L2 cache was known as a Cache on a Stick, or COAST (see Figure 5.6). Modern CPUs integrate the L2 cache into the CPU packaging.

**L2 cache**

The module that holds data that has exited the CPU as it waits to be delivered back to RAM. Also called back-side cache.

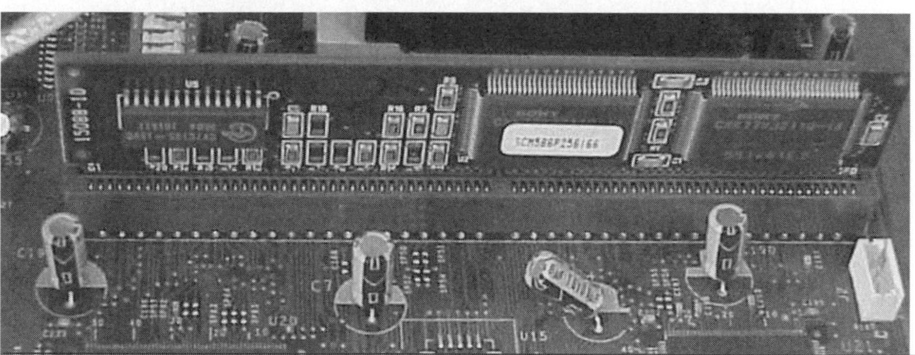

**FIGURE 5.6**
A Cache on a Stick (COAST) Module on an Older Motherboard

## Cooling Methods

CPUs generate heat as they operate, and if left alone they quickly overheat and shut down. A variety of cooling techniques have been developed over the years to prevent that from happening.

As mentioned earlier, one way to make a CPU run cooler is to decrease the core voltage. The newer CPUs have lower core voltages than their predecessors.

Another way to cool off a chip is to place a *heat sink* on it. A heat sink is a metal or ceramic plate with spikes that channel heat away from the CPU, causing the heat to gradually dissipate into the air. On some systems the

**Heat sink**

A block of heat-conductive material placed on a CPU to channel heat away from it, either with or without a fan.

**Passive heat sink**

A heat sink that does not have a fan.

**Heat sink compound**

A heat-conductive adhesive used to mount a heat sink to a CPU.

power supply's fan blows or sucks air across the spikes, further aiding the cooling. Plain heat sinks, like the one shown in Figure 5.7, are often called *passive heat sinks* because they do not have any moving parts. These are usually fastened permanently to the CPU using a gluelike *heat sink compound* that transfers heat very efficiently. (You can buy it at a computer store.)

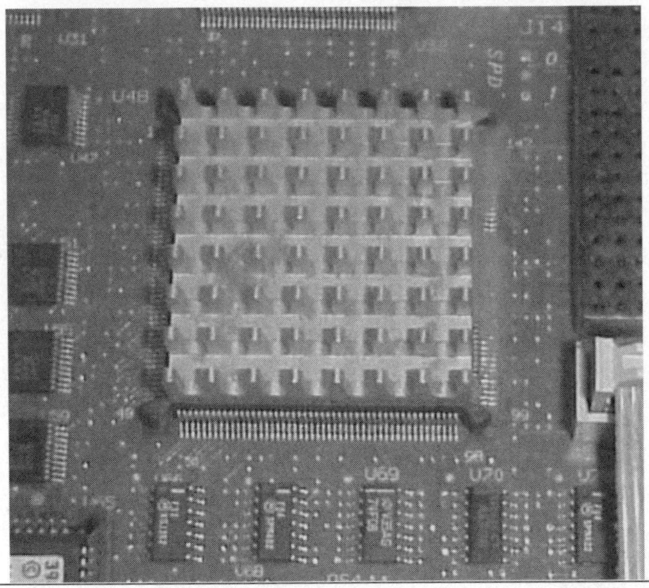

**FIGURE 5.7**
A Passive Heat Sink on a CPU

**Active heat sink**

A heat sink that includes a fan.

If a heat sink has a fan attached to it, it is an *active heat sink*. CPUs that run too hot to be properly cooled by a passive heat sink alone will often employ a heat sink/fan combination (see Figure 5.8). These usually attach to the CPU via a clip so that they are removable, rather than being bonded with a heat sink compound. Fans can go bad, and you would not want a broken one to be permanently attached to your CPU. Their increased cooling effectiveness makes it possible for them to operate just next to the CPU, rather than being glued to it.

**FIGURE 5.8**
An Active Heat Sink/Fan Combination

## In Real Life

Many intermittent problems with computers freezing up turn out to be problems with the CPU's not being adequately cooled. If a PC works fine for a few minutes and then locks up, check to make sure the heat sink is securely fastened to it and that, if there is a fan on it, it is spinning.

## TRY IT!

Identify the cooling methods used on the systems available to you.

# Types of CPUs Prior to Pentium

To understand modern CPUs, it is helpful to study earlier models that were less complex and can be explained using simpler concepts and terminology. Then as you learn about each successive generation of CPU, you can build on your knowledge of the simpler models for a fuller understanding. CPUs prior to the Pentium are not explicitly covered on the A+ examination, but it is useful to learn about them because their workings illustrate basic CPU concepts that you need to know.

Although this chapter focuses mostly on Intel-brand CPUs because Intel has long been the industry leader, there are other CPU manufacturers as well, such as Advanced Micro Devices (AMD). We will discuss a few of the most popular AMD CPUs as well.

## 8086 AND 8088 CPUs

In the mid-1970s there were several competing brands of CPUs for computers—all of them very high end and expensive, with no standardization among them. They had 8-bit internal registers and used an 8-bit external data bus and 16-bit address bus, and could use a maximum of 64KB of RAM (2 to the 16th power).

**8086**

An early CPU with 16-bit internal registers, a 16-bit external data bus, and a 20-bit address bus. Never widely used or produced.

Intel Corporation, which was not yet the powerhouse it is today, came out with a revolutionary CPU called the *8086* in 1976. It used 16-bit internal registers, a 16-bit external data bus, and a 20-bit address bus, so it could use up to 1MB of RAM (2 to the 20th power). This was clearly a better chip than all of the others, but initially nobody wanted it because a system that used it would have been prohibitively expensive. Motherboards of that time had 8-bit designs, and this 8086 chip would have required an entirely different motherboard.

**8088**

An early CPU with 16-bit internal registers, an 8-bit external data bus, and a 20-bit address bus. Used for the original IBM PCs and PC XTs.

Next, Intel released a stripped-down version of the 8086 called an *8088*. This CPU kept the 16-bit internal registers and 20-bit address bus, but the external data bus was 8-bit so it could work on existing motherboards. It was still clearly superior to competitors' chips because it was a 16-bit chip, and could process 16-bit software instructions and access more memory, so IBM (which was a huge company even back then) chose the 8088 for the original IBM Personal Computer, released to the public in 1981. It was available in clock speeds ranging from 4.77MHz in the original IBM PC to 10MHz in the IBM PC XT.

### *8088 Packaging*

The 8088 CPU (Figure 5.9) was a rectangular chip with "legs" on two sides. This type of packaging, called Dual Inline Pin Package (DIPP), was also used for the memory in early motherboards. Although some chips still come in this packaging today, it has been phased out of CPU use because it was too easy to bend and break the legs.

**FIGURE 5.9**
An 8088 CPU (Photo courtesy of Intel Corporation)

### *8087 Math Coprocessor*

Figure 5.1 showed a single operation (producing the sum of two numbers) that took four steps, or clock cycles. The average real-life operation in an 8088 PC took about 12 clock cycles to complete. Part of the problem with early CPUs was that they lacked the large instruction sets that are included in today's CPUs. They supported very few math operations, so more complex math had to be handled laboriously with many clock cycles' worth of activity. To help improve the situation, a *math coprocessor* chip was introduced: the 8087. This chip took over the high-level math operations, freeing the main CPU to perform the functions it did best. Another name for a math coprocessor is a floating-point unit (FPU).

**Math coprocessor**

An extra processing chip that works with the CPU to support math calculations. Also called a floating-point unit (FPU).

## 80286 CPUs

The next generations of Intel CPUs were the 80186 and 80188, but they were never commercially popular. The next generation to be widely employed in PCs was the 80286, which was used in the IBM Advanced Technology (AT) computer.

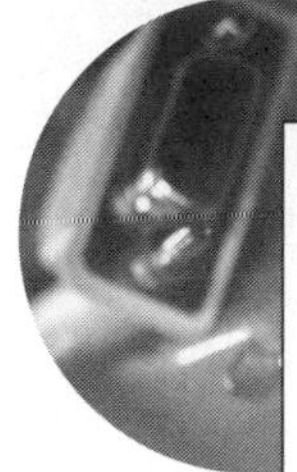

### IN REAL LIFE

**IBM's PC AT computer had several non-CPU advantages over its predecessors, including the basic AT layout for the motherboard that is still used in AT motherboards. It also introduced an improved keyboard layout that remains in use for many of today's keyboards.**

### *286 Features*

The 80286 could run programs designed for the 8088 because it understood all the instructions that the 8088 understood; it also added many new instructions and was more efficient at executing them. Whereas the 8088 required an average of 12 clock cycles per instruction, the 80286 required only about 4.5. This made it more than twice as efficient even if clock speed differences were not taken into account. The 80286 also had a faster clock speed, up to 20MHz.

**Protected mode**

An operating mode on 80286 and higher CPUs that enables the CPU to access more memory than just the first 1MB.

The 286 had some advanced features that made it much better than the 8088, but in order to use them, the computer had to be switched to *protected mode*, which was incompatible with all of the programs written for the 8088. Therefore, 286 computers also could function in *real mode*, which provided backward compatibility. In real mode the 286 functioned essentially as a high-powered 8088.

**Real mode**

An operating mode on 80286 and higher CPUs that simulates the 8088 CPU.

The 8088 could use only 1MB of RAM, but in protected mode the 286 could use up to 16MB, provided the operating system could support that much memory. (MS-DOS could not. Some versions of UNIX could, as could the early OS/2 product.) Protected mode also offered the ability of switching back and forth between two or more running programs simultaneously loaded in memory.

**Pin grid array (PGA)**

A square or rectangular socket consisting of concentric rings of holes into which the legs on a PGA-style CPU fit.

### *286 Packaging*

The 80286 chip used a different type of packaging than the 8088; it was mounted on a square ceramic block with pins on its bottom that fit into a socket on the motherboard containing concentric rings of pins. This design is known as *pin grid array* (PGA), and variants of it are still used for CPUs today. Figure 5.10 shows the underside of an 80286 CPU and its motherboard socket.

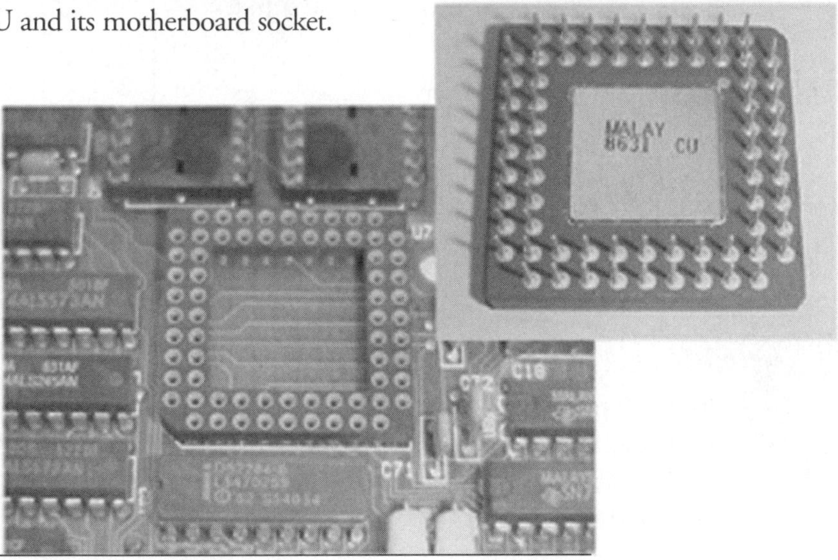

**FIGURE 5.10**
An 80286 CPU and Its Motherboard Socket

### *287 Math Coprocessor*

The 80286 CPU performed basic math functions very well, but like the 8088 it struggled with more complex math. An 80287 math coprocessor chip was available as an add-on for those who used their computers for activities involving advanced math. Shaped much like an 8088 chip (DIPP packaging) but of a slightly different physical size, the 80287 chip fit into a special socket in the motherboard. Figure 5.11 shows an 80287 coprocessor installed on a motherboard.

**FIGURE 5.11**
An 80287 Math Coprocessor

## 80386 CPUs

The next generation of Intel CPU was the 80386, also known as the I386.

### *386 Features*

The Intel 80386 CPU represented a huge leap in performance because it was a 32-bit chip with 32-bit internal registers. That meant it could run 32-bit applications, which were just beginning to become available.

Like the 80286, the 80386 could run in protected mode, but the 386 had two different protected modes available: 286 protected and 386 protected. In 386 protected mode it supported some new features, including virtual memory and virtual 8086.

*Virtual memory* made it possible to use part of a hard disk to simulate extra RAM; a computer was therefore able to run programs that required more DRAM than it physically possessed. *Virtual 8086* made it possible to multitask—that is, run several programs at once—by creating multiple virtual 8086 processors and running a separate program on each one. Even though each processor could run only a single program at a time, collectively a 386 system could run a number of programs at once.

**Virtual memory**

A scheme for using part of a hard disk to simulate additional RAM.

**Virtual 8086**

A method of simulating multiple 8086 CPUs on a single 80386 or higher PC.

### *386SX and 386DX*

The computer industry did not immediately embrace the 80386 CPU because of the high cost of 32-bit motherboards. Many consumers were not ready to pay the price for a true 32-bit system when there was very little 32-bit software available. So as a marketing compromise, the 80386 was manufactured in two styles: the 386DX and the 386SX.

The *386DX* chip was designed for 32-bit motherboards with 32-bit external data bus and 32-bit address bus. The *386SX* chip was internally identical to the 386DX, but it used a 16-bit external data bus and a 24-bit address bus (so it could be used on a less expensive motherboard). That meant that a 386SX could run 32-bit applications but the data transferring into and out of the CPU could travel in only 16-bit chunks, so it took twice as long for each input and output operation. If the user was running a 16-bit application, there was no difference between CPUs.

**386DX**

A full 32-bit 80386 CPU with 32-bit address bus and 32-bit external data bus.

**386SX**

An 80386 CPU with a 16-bit external data bus and a 24-bit address bus.

Because of the smaller address bus (24-bit instead of 32-bit) on the 386SX, the 386SX was limited to 16MB of RAM, whereas the 386DX could have up to 4GB of RAM. Back in the days of the 386, however, 16MB was sufficient.

### *386 Packaging*

The 80386 CPU was in a physical package different from either of its predecessors; it was a square chip permanently soldered to the motherboard (it did not use a PGA socket). It was also the first CPU to be used with a heat sink, so when you encounter 80386 CPUs on motherboards, you will probably find them with a heat sink permanently affixed to them. That is one of the ways of identifying the CPU chip—look for the chip with the heat sink. Figure 5.12 shows a 386SX with a heat sink (left) and without it (right).

**FIGURE 5.12**
An 80386 CPU, with and without a Heat Sink

### *387 Math Coprocessor*

As with the 286, a math coprocessor was available for the 80386, called the 80387. Designed from scratch to optimize math operations for 386 systems, it was a flat square chip with wires wrapped on all four sides. It fit tightly into a special high-sided square socket, as shown in Figure 5.13. Intel manufactured its own 80387 chips, but several competitors also produced them, so you might find different brand names on them as seen in the figure.

**FIGURE 5.13**
An 80387 Math Coprocessor

WARNING

It is easy to orient these 80387 coprocessors incorrectly. One corner of the chip is usually a little different from the others–perhaps rounded. Look for a corner of the socket that looks different (for example, with an arrow or of a slightly different shape) and orient the odd corner of the chip to match it. They can also be tricky to remove; you may be able to work one loose gradually by lifting gently on the edges with a flat-heat screwdriver.

### *Competitors to the Intel 386*

With the 386 family, Intel faced its first serious competition from other CPU makers. AMD and IBM both produced 386-type CPUs, and in fact AMD produced the fastest 386 chip available: a 40MHz model. Intel's own 386 CPUs ran at a maximum of 33MHz, as did the 80387 math coprocessors. Intel changed the naming scheme from a plain number to a copyrightable designation: I386. The *I* stands for Intel, and most 80386 chips made by Intel are labeled as such.

AMD 80386 CPUs had their own type of motherboard that did things a little differently from the standard made-for-Intel models. For example, the math coprocessor used a different kind of socket (a PGA type similar to an 80286 CPU, the middle socket in Figure 5.14). There was also an upgrade socket on some motherboards for future expansion (the socket on the left in Figure 5.14).

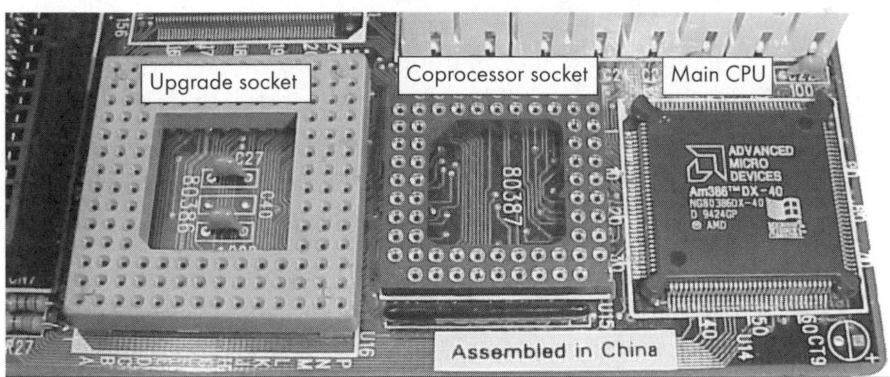


**FIGURE 5.14**
An AMD 40MHz 386 CPU (right) with Coprocessor Socket (center) and Upgrade Socket (left)

## IN REAL LIFE

The upgrade sockets in 386 motherboards, like the one in Figure 5.14, are useless today unless you can find a compatible upgrade chip. During the early 1990s much was made of a motherboard's "upgradeability" features, meaning it had an extra slot that was planned for use with some improved CPU that would come out in the future. However, these upgrade slots were almost never employed because it was more economical in the long run to buy a whole new motherboard/CPU combination such as an i486.

## 80486 CPUs

For its 80486 CPU, Intel maintained the *I* naming convention but switched to the lowercase *i,* probably because the uppercase *I* was getting confused with the number 1; this CPU was called the i486.

### *486 Features*

The i486 was a 32-bit all-around chip (32-bit external data bus, registers, and memory address bus), like the 80386, but it contained a built-in math coprocessor and an 8K L1 cache. It also contained some new functions and commands that reduced the amount of instruction that had to be sent to the CPU for a given operation, thereby improving overall data flow. The average instruction took only 2 clock cycles; the 286 and 386 both averaged about 4.5 cycles per instruction. Because of this, clock speeds being equal (that is, comparing a 40MHz 386 to a 40MHz 486), the 486 was about twice as efficient at processing data, and appeared to be running a program about twice as quickly. The actual clock speeds of 486s ranged from 25 to 120MHz. (The higher speeds were offered by competitor AMD, rather than Intel.)

The 486 systems were the first to have faster speeds for the internal data bus than for the external one. As you learned earlier, when the CPU is faster than the motherboard's bus, a multiplier allows the CPU to execute multiple instructions per clock cycle. Early attempts at this process were called clock-doubling because they multiplied clock speed times two; the later 486s used 2.5x or 3x multipliers. Notice in Figure 5.15 that one of the CPUs is marked DX2; that refers to a 2x clock multiplier. When a 2x clock multiplier is used, the average instruction takes only 1 clock cycle.

### In Real Life

**If a DX2 runs at two times the clock speed, you would think that a DX4 would run at four times, wouldn't you? Actually, DX4 CPUs run at anywhere from two to three times the clock speed. So, for example, on a 33MHz bus motherboard, a DX4 might run at somewhere between 66 and 100MHz.**

Like the 386, the 486 operated in real mode or protected mode; it could also run in virtual real mode, which simulated multiple 8086 CPUs running simultaneously.

The 486 CPU was significant to the industry because it was the first CPU with enough power to make graphical user interfaces such as Windows usable. Windows would run on a 386, but Windows-based applications were noticeably slower than the more nimble DOS versions. Finally with the 486, the PC hardware caught up with the software demands and made Windows-based programs run quickly enough for the user not to become annoyed with the delays.

### *486SX and 486DX*

The 386 line made consumers accustomed to having a choice of CPU prices, with the SX line being less expensive than the DX line. To satisfy consumer demand for an economy model, Intel released the i486SX CPU. It was the same as the regular 486 (that is, the 486DX), except its internal math coprocessor had been disabled. It did not cost Intel any less to make a 486SX than a DX; it was just a marketing means of selling more CPUs, some at lower profit margins than others.

**Zero Insertion Force (ZIF)**

A type of chip socket that has a lever that raises and lowers to secure or release the chip, so that no pressure is required to insert or remove it.

### *486 Packaging*

There were several packaging styles for the 486 CPU, as various motherboard manufacturers experimented to find the best method. Some were permanently soldered to the motherboard like the 386; others were removable PGA chips held tightly in place by the socket, like the 286. Still others used an entirely new style of packaging called the *Zero Insertion Force (ZIF)* socket, with a handle that raises to remove the CPU and lowers to secure it.

Figure 5.15 shows three different 486 packaging styles. Both of the removable models are the same 168-pin PGA package, but placed into different styles of motherboard. The nonremovable model is also 168-pin, except there are not really "pins" in the traditional sense, but rather wire connections to the motherboard. Most of the 486 CPUs were +5v, although a +3.3v version was made for use in notebook PCs.

Nonremovable

Removable but not ZIF

ZIF

**FIGURE 5.15**
Three Packaging Styles for i486 CPUs

### *OverDrive and Upgradeability*

Many 486 motherboards had an extra PGA socket for future expandability. One early use for this extra slot was to install a 487 coprocessor chip for 486SX systems (which lacked a built-in coprocessor). The 487 chip was actually a full-blown 486DX chip that simply disabled the main CPU and took over all of its functions.

Another use for the extra PGA socket was to install an OverDrive CPU. An OverDrive CPU, like the 487, disabled the main CPU and took over its duties. OverDrive CPUs not only added a coprocessor (that is, they were DX rather than SX) but they also, in most cases, were clock-doubled (DX2 models) so they could, for example, make a 25MHz system into 50MHz. Figure 5.16 shows an example of an OverDrive socket that was found next to a nonremovable 486SX CPU. Notice the early ZIF design in which a bar rather than a lever secures and releases the chip.

**FIGURE 5.16**
A 486 Motherboard's OverDrive Socket

An OverDrive socket can be distinguished from a regular CPU socket by its having 169 holes rather than the usual 168. The original OverDrive processors were 169-pin, so you could use them only in these special OverDrive sockets; you could not buy one for use in a new system.

Separate OverDrive sockets were necessary only on motherboards with nonremovable main CPUs. On systems where the CPU could be easily removed and replaced, the sockets were simply wasted space. Therefore, some later 486 motherboards have a single ZIF CPU socket labeled OverDrive Ready (see Figure 5.16), meaning it can accept regular or OverDrive CPUs equally well.

**FIGURE 5.17**
An OverDrive-Ready Main CPU Socket

### *486DX4 CPU*

Chip makers had such success with the clock-doubled DX2 models that they decided to take it further and create DX4s that could run at 2x, 2.5x, or 3x the motherboard's speed. These chips had a problem, however: they required +3.3v rather than +5v, so they could not be used in +5v motherboards. Their other problem was heat: they required a special heat sink to stay cool.

To circumvent this issue, some motherboards of this era included voltage regulator jumpers or switches enabling users to choose which voltage they wanted. (Such motherboards used Socket 7 sockets; see below for details.) Intel also introduced a DX4 OverDrive CPU, a 3x DX4 that had the voltage regulator and heat sink built in and could run on any 486 motherboard with either a separate OverDrive socket (as in Figure 5.16) or an OverDrive Ready socket (as in Figure 5.17).

### *Pentium OverDrive for 486*

Toward the end of the 486 life cycle, the release of Pentium systems began. Intel came out with an OverDrive chip for 486 systems that was supposed to increase their performance to Pentium levels and would work in any Socket 2 or Socket 3 system. (See the next section for more on socket numbers.)

The Pentium OverDrive chip was a +5v CPU that incorporated as many of the features of the real Pentium as possible into a packaging that would work on a 486 motherboard. For example, it included a 32KB built-in L1 cache and superscalar architecture. (You will learn more about those features later in this chapter.) However, in real-life performance it tested slightly worse than the fastest 486 CPUs of the day (120MHz DX4), and therefore was not a great commercial success.

### *Zero Insertion Force (ZIF) Sockets*

Since average end users were now tinkering with their motherboards and replacing their CPUs, it became more important to make the CPU insertion and removal process as foolproof as possible. To achieve this, the Zero Insertion Force (ZIF) PGA socket was invented. Rather than trying to insert a CPU's 150+ little pins into separate holes by force, the ZIF socket enables users to drop the CPU effortlessly into loose holes and then lower a lever to tighten the grip on the pins. Figures 5.16 and 5.17 both show ZIF sockets, as does one of the images in Figure 5.15.

There have been several designs of ZIF sockets over the years. Each one has a number, starting with Socket 1 (Figure 5.16), the original OverDrive socket with 169 pins. Socket 2 (Figure 5.17) was also an OverDrive socket, but it was larger because Intel planned that it be able to accept Pentium OverDrive chips as well. (More on the Pentium shortly.) It had 238 pins.

#### In Real Life

There is an easy way to tell a Socket 1 from a Socket 2: count the number of pins along the bottom. A Socket 1 has 17 pins; a Socket 2 has 19 pins.

Socket 3 was very popular because, depending on the motherboard on which it was installed, it could be used for either +3.3v or +5v CPUs and either a 486 or a Pentium CPU. A Socket 3 socket (Figure 5.18) differs from a Socket 2 in the number of pins in the keyed corner (the bottom left in these figures). Socket 3 has an additional single hole.

**FIGURE 5.18**
A 486 in a Socket 3 ZIF Socket

**WARNING**

**Remember, the CPUs that a motherboard can support depend on its chipset and voltage. Not every motherboard that is physically capable of accepting a certain CPU in its socket can support that CPU.**

Socket 4 was a 273-pin, +5v-only socket used exclusively for the original 60 and 66MHz Pentium CPUs. Pentiums and 486s overlapped for a while, so the early Pentiums came out before the later 486s. The idea of using a variable-voltage socket (Socket 3) actually became popular *after* the design was completed for the Pentium.

Socket 5 was a 320-pin socket, also for Pentiums, but for higher speed (75 to 100MHz) and lower voltage (+3.3v) models. Socket 5 was the first to use a staggered pin grid array (SPGA), in which the rows of pins are offset to fit more pins into the grid without greatly increasing its size. The lower voltage made the CPUs much less prone to overheating.

## IN REAL LIFE

**Pentium CPUs that fit into Socket 5 actually have only 296 pins, not 320. The extra holes are for use by a Pentium OverDrive chip.**

Socket 6 was designed for the 486DX4 and the 486 Pentium OverDrive CPU (which upgraded a 486 to approximate Pentium performance). It is very much like Socket 3, but has two extra pins and accepts only 3.3v CPUs.

Socket 7 (Figure 5.19) was very much like Socket 5 but had one extra pin, for a total of 321. Motherboards that included Socket 7 had a voltage regulator module (VRM) that the user could change with a jumper so the motherboard could accept CPUs of either +5v or +3.3v. This made it possible for a single motherboard to support a wide variety of CPUs simply by setting a few jumpers. Recall that Socket 3 sockets could also accept different voltages, but not on the same motherboard; the flexibility with Socket 3 was in manufacturing only.

**FIGURE 5.19**
A Socket 7 Socket

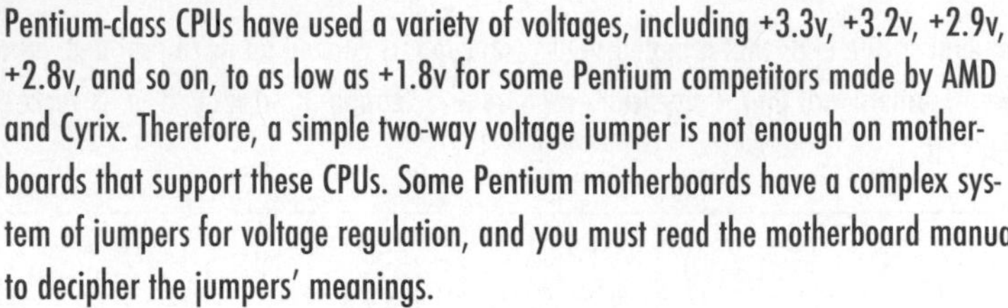

## In Real Life

Pentium-class CPUs have used a variety of voltages, including +3.3v, +3.2v, +2.9v, +2.8v, and so on, to as low as +1.8v for some Pentium competitors made by AMD and Cyrix. Therefore, a simple two-way voltage jumper is not enough on motherboards that support these CPUs. Some Pentium motherboards have a complex system of jumpers for voltage regulation, and you must read the motherboard manual to decipher the jumpers' meanings.

A Super Socket 7 (Super7) is an enhanced Socket 7 socket and motherboard, used for later Pentium-class motherboards and motherboards designed for non-Intel competitor chips. It looks like a regular Socket 7, but the motherboard's chipset is different. The improved chipset supports faster interaction with the CPU, and provides support for the AGP video bus and UltraDMA hard disk controllers, and for advanced power management. It also supports chips that use a split-voltage scheme that allows them to run internally at a lower voltage (+2.8 or +2.9v) while they continue to communicate with the rest of the system at +3.3v. A Super7 motherboard can accommodate almost any Socket 7-compatible CPU, whether or not it employs split voltage.

Other ZIF sockets are discussed in the next several sections on more modern CPUs. The improvements they offer over the first seven socket designs will be easier to understand in context.

## TRY IT!

If you have a motherboard available that has a ZIF socket, remove the CPU and then replace it, making sure it stays oriented the same way.

### *Competitors to Intel i486*

Intel was not the only company to make 486-type CPUs. Advanced Micro Devices (AMD) and Cyrix also made 486-compatible CPUs that worked in most 486 motherboards.

The AMD models were called AM5x86, which was somewhat misleading because the *5* implied that it was somehow better than the 486, which was not necessarily true. It did have some minor improvements. The 5x86 had a higher clock multiplier than the 486DX4, in that it truly did run at four times the motherboard speed, unlike the 2.5x to 3x of the DX4. (The higher speed required a capable motherboard, of course.) It also had a 16KB write-back cache and a 133MHz internal speed, and performed at about the same level as a 75MHz Pentium. It required a 33MHz motherboard bus and a Socket 3 socket. (It would work in a Socket 1 or Socket 2 with a voltage adapter installed.) The 5x86 ran hot, and required a cooling fan.

The Cyrix 486DX2 and DX4 CPUs were similar to the AMD models and came in speeds up to 100MHz.

# Pentium CPUs and Succeeding Generations

The original Pentium was released by Intel in 1993, incorporating many CPU technology improvements over the 486.

## Pentium CPUs

The Pentium has the same 32-bit address bus width as the 386DX and the 486, but it has a 64-bit data bus, so it can move twice as much data to and from the CPU per clock cycle. The 64-bit data bus is split up into two 32-bit data buses, which enables the CPU to process two separate sets of instructions at the same time (called *dual pipeline* or superscalar architecture). Inside the Pentium are 32-bit registers, so it is still processing data in 32-bit chunks, but it is doing two chunks simultaneously, as if two 486 chips were built into a single Pentium chip. Earlier CPUs ran a certain number of clock cycles per instruction; the Pentium, because of superscalar architecture, can run multiple instructions per clock cycle.

**Dual pipeline**

A CPU that is able to process two sets of instructions at the same time. Also called superscalar architecture (although technically that term also refers to quad pipeline).

Another improvement implemented in the Pentium is branch prediction, a scheme in which the cache stores both sides of a yes/no branch. For example, suppose a line in a program says "If X = 1, go to line 100 in the program. If not, go to line 200." With branch prediction, both line 100 and line 200 would be loaded into the cache, so either way the needed data would be readily available. Another important feature of the Pentium is its improved caching.

### *First- and Second-Generation Pentium*

The term "Pentium" actually refers to two different CPUs: first generation and second generation. The first generation of Pentiums were +5v, 273-pin models that ran at either 60 or 66MHz and fit into Socket 4 motherboards. They had some problems, like any new product, mostly involving the tremendous amount of heat they generated.

The second generation of Pentiums (Figure 5.20) ranged in speed from 75 to 200MHz. They were +3.3v CPUs that drew fewer amps than their +5v cousins, resulting in fewer heating problems. They were 296-pin models that fit into Socket 5 or Socket 7 motherboards. There was also a third generation of Pentium, the Pentium MMX, described later in this chapter.

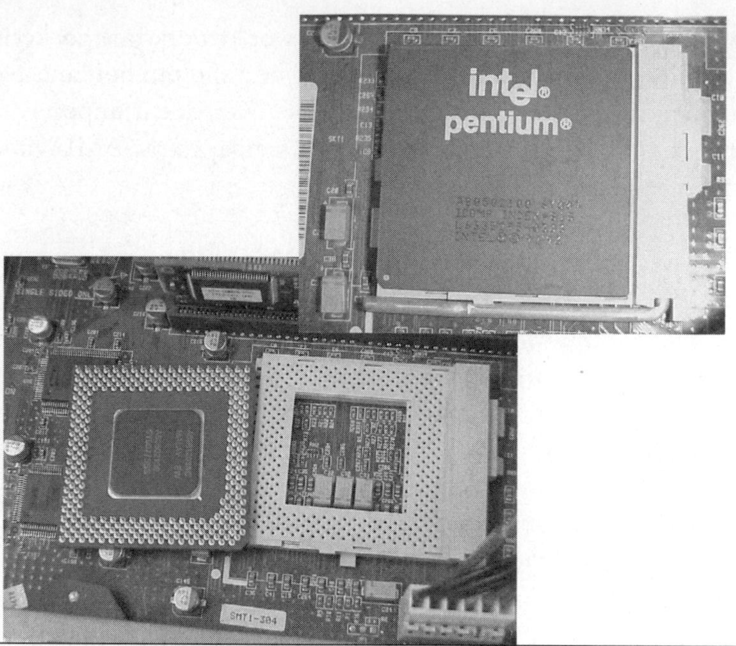


**FIGURE 5.20**
A Second-Generation Pentium Chip

### *Pentium Clock Multipliers*

Since Pentium motherboards had a bus speed of either 60 or 66MHz, the second generation of Pentium CPUs included clock-multiplying technology so the CPU could outstrip the motherboard's bus speed. For example, a 200MHz Pentium runs at a 3x multiplier on a 66MHz motherboard. The multiplier used by a Pentium chip is determined by its bus frequency (BF) pins. Some Pentium CPUs have the bus frequency hard-wired into them so they only work at a certain multiplier. Others allow jumpers on the motherboard to control the BF, making it possible to overclock them.

### *Pentium Pro*

**Quad pipeline**

A CPU that can process four instructions in a single clock cycle.

The Pentium Pro was Intel's attempt to produce an improvement to the Pentium. It included *quad pipelining* (so it could process four instructions at once) and an on-chip L2 cache. Because the L2 cache was on the chip, there was no bottleneck between it and the CPU itself. This cache was available in 256KB, 512KB, or 1MB sizes, depending on the model. The chip design was known as a dual-cavity PGA, referring to the fact that it had two compartments: one for the CPU itself and one for the on-board L2 cache.

**Dynamic processing**

A CPU function in Pentium Pro and higher that allows commands to run out of queue order to minimize CPU idle time.

Another improvement the Pentium Pro offered was *dynamic processing.* This allowed it to run commands out of queue order whenever it was stalled waiting for something else to happen, thereby optimizing overall throughput.

The Pentium Pro was optimized for 32-bit operating systems, and worked well with them, but with a 16-bit operating system like MS-DOS it was actually slower than a regular Pentium. This made it unpopular in consumer-level PCs and, along with its inability to support MMX (described in the next section), ultimately led to its demise. The Pentium Pro required a special, oblong-shaped PGA socket called Socket 8, +3v, with 387 pins.

### *Pentium MMX*

Third-generation Pentiums (1997 and after) added a new feature called *multimedia extensions* (MMX). The MMX addition helped the CPU with graphic-intensive applications such as games, but only those that were specifically written to take advantage of MMX. Pentium MMX CPUs were available in speeds of 166, 200, and 233MHz. These Pentiums work only in Socket 7 motherboards.

**Multimedia Extensions (MMX)**

A set of CPU command features that improve the operation of multimedia-intensive programs that are designed to take advantage of MMX functionality.

Pentium MMX chips are very much like second-generation Pentiums, but they have a few new features, including a 16KB write-back cache (as opposed to 8KB), more transistors, and a pipelined MMX unit. They also operate at a lower voltage (+2.8v), which means they would not be compatible with first- and second-generation Pentium motherboards unless there was a VRM that could go down as far as +2.8v. Because it seemed as if CPU voltages were continually changing, a new type of voltage regulator was introduced on new motherboards at this time. It was a socket next to the CPU that could accept a removable, replaceable VRM that supplied the correct voltage for whatever CPU was to be installed.

This MMX feature helps process repetitive loops of instructions that are common to graphics-intensive games. For example, suppose that a game displays the walls of a room as you move through it. For each step the character takes, the walls change a little, but the vast majority of each wall stays the same from one second to the next. MMX takes some of the burden off the CPU to keep processing the pictures of those walls in full with each change. At the time not many games were written to use MMX, so the MMX feature of these third-generation Pentiums went unused in most systems.

### *Competitors to the Pentium*

The main competitor to the Intel Pentium was the AMD K5. It was compatible with the Pentium both physically and in circuitry, so it worked in most Pentium motherboards. It was slightly less expensive than the real Pentium and offered some modest technical improvements over it.

The marketing of the K5 used a misleading numbering system that did not reflect the actual clock speed of the CPU. AMD claimed that the internal advantages of a K5 made it unfair to compare it to an Intel CPU of the same clock speed, so it gave the chips numbers that matched what it considered the "true speed"— the clock speed of the comparable Intel model. For example, the AMD PR166 supposedly offered the same performance as the Intel 166MHz Pentium, but actually had a clock speed of 117MHz. The K5 operated at +3.52v, and did not work very well on a motherboard that supported only +3.3v CPUs. However, as indicated earlier, there were many different voltages used for the various Pentium generations, so many Pentium-class motherboards have a wide variety of voltage settings they can accept.

## Pentium II CPUs

The next generation of Intel CPU was the Pentium II. These have not been manufactured since the late 1990s, but are still in widespread use in homes and offices, so PC technicians will likely spend quite a bit of time working on Pentium II systems.

### *Pentium II Features*

The Pentium II is basically a fast Pentium Pro with MMX added. Both the Pentium Pro and the Pentium II are based on a design called P6. (The Pentium III, which is discussed later in this chapter, is also considered a P6 chip.)

Pentium II CPUs have an internal speed ranging from 233 to 450MHz, and run on external buses of either 66 or 100MHz. Like the later split-voltage Pentiums, they have an internal voltage of +2.8v and an external voltage of +3.3v.

In addition to being faster overall than the original Pentium, the Pentium II includes a set of technologies called Dynamic Execution which is in three parts:

- **Better branch prediction:** The original Pentium could predict the flow of data and have the next probable bit of data ready for use; the Pentium II can do this through several branches, keeping the pipelines full so there is no waiting for data retrieval.
- **Data flow analysis:** This enables the CPU to execute instructions out of queue order, so that they can be processed in whatever order provides the best performance.
- **Speculative execution:** This improves performance by guessing what instructions are going to be called for and executing them in advance.

The end result of these three technologies is that the CPU is kept busy constantly preparing data that might be needed for program execution. It makes the CPU more proactive.

The other improvement of Pentium II over the original Pentium is the Dual Independent Bus (DIB). The CPU has two data buses: one truly external, for the motherboard, and one partially external (that is, external to the main CPU but internal to the CPU package), for the cache. This enables the bus between the CPU and its cache to be faster than the motherboard's bus.

As you recall, the Pentium Pro was not commercially successful because it was optimized for 32-bit programs and did not offer very good speeds at 16 bits. The Pentium II has this same limitation, but by the time the Pentium II was introduced almost everyone was running the 32-bit version of Windows (Windows 95 and higher).

### *Pentium II Packaging*

The biggest difference between the Pentium II and the original Pentium from an everyday installation-and-usage perspective is the packaging. Frustrated with competitors making low-priced, compatible alternative CPUs, Intel set out to design an entirely new CPU package for the Pentium II. The result was the Single Edge Contact Cartridge (SECC), shown in Figure 5.21.

**FIGURE 5.21**
An SECC Pentium II Cartridge

The SECC mounts the CPU on a circuit board, along with several L2 cache chips, and then encases that circuit board in a plastic shell for protection. The circuit board sticks out of the bottom of the shell and plugs into the motherboard, in a slot similar to an expansion slot but sized and oriented differently. The slot itself is called Slot 1, and is trademarked by Intel so competitors cannot develop compatible CPUs for it. Figure 5.22 shows a Slot 1 slot with the plastic mounting brackets for a Pentium II SECC already installed. The cartridge slides down into the brackets and its circuit board edge fits into the slot.

**FIGURE 5.22**
A Slot 1 Slot, Ready for an SECC to Be Installed

The SECC design has several advantages besides its trademark status. Since the Pentium II's L2 cache does not need to be a part of the same die used to stamp the CPU, the Pentium II can be manufactured more inexpensively. Intel can also acquire cache chips from other vendors so it does not have to manufacture them, and it can use L2 cache memory that runs at half the speed of the CPU itself, saving yet more expense. The L1 cache always runs at the same speed as the CPU because it is built into the CPU chip.

There are disadvantages as well, and these disadvantages eventually returned later CPUs (Pentium III and Pentium 4) to a PGA packaging. The main disadvantage is the amount of space the SECC takes up on the motherboard. It must sit upright, so braces are required and no slimline design is possible. (Those braces also cost money, dissipating the cost advantages mentioned earlier.) Another disadvantage is that the SECC generates quite a bit of heat, and cooling is made awkward by the fact that the hot elements are encased in a plastic box. This requires more aggressive cooling methods, usually including a large passive heat sink with a fan mounted in the center of it. Figure 5.23 shows a Pentium II mounted on a motherboard with heat sink and fan installed.

**FIGURE 5.23**
A Pentium II on a Motherboard, with Heat Sink and Fan Installed

### *Pentium II Voltage*

Different voltages were used during the lifespan of the Pentium II, ranging from +2.8v on the 233MHz model to +2.0v on the 450MHz model. Knowing the individual voltages is not essential; the important fact to remember is that different releases of the Pentium II require different voltage settings on the motherboard. Some motherboards can automatically detect the voltage required and supply it; others require the user to set jumpers.

### *Celeron: Low-Budget Pentium II*

Intel uses the name Celeron for its low-budget Pentium II model. (It uses the same name for its low-budget Pentium IIIs.) The Celeron Pentium II came out after the Pentium II had been perfected, so its performance is actually better than the early Pentium II, even though it is less expensive.

The main difference between the Celeron and the Pentium II is the packaging. Like the Pentium II, the original Celeron was a chip mounted on a small circuit board that fit into a Slot 1 socket. However, the Celeron's circuit board lacked the outer plastic cartridge, so the overall effect was of a PGA-style (inline, not staggered) socket mounted to a circuit board that was inserted in Slot 1. This type of packaging was called *Single Edge Processor* (SEP). It cost less to manufacture than SECC because it did not have the plastic outer shell, and it was also easier to cool since the fan could be attached more directly to the CPU.

**Single Edge Processor (SEP)**

A variant of SECC that leaves the circuit board on which the CPU is mounted exposed, rather than encasing it in a plastic cartridge.

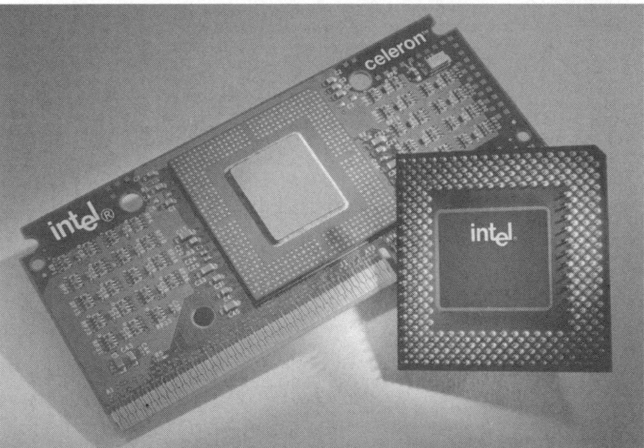


**FIGURE 5.24**
A Celeron with SEP Packaging (Photo courtesy of Intel Corporation)

The SEP design was used for most Pentium II-based Celerons, but as competitors began having success with a 370-pin PGA socket chip with Pentium II-level performance, Intel switched the Celeron to that style of socket. You might expect this socket to be called Socket 9, to go along with the earlier numbering scheme, but it is known as the Socket 370 or PGA-370.

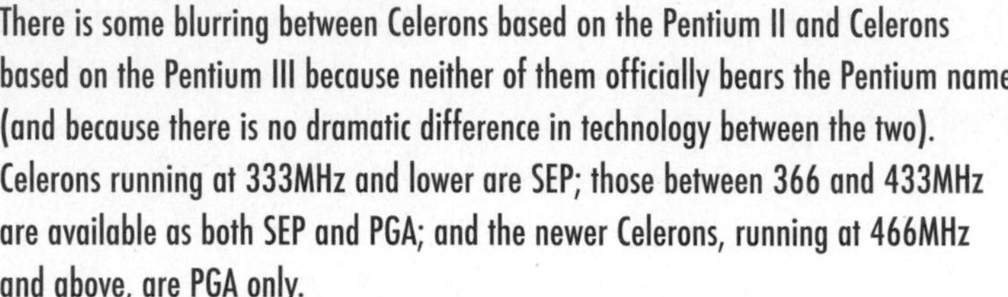

## In Real Life

There is some blurring between Celerons based on the Pentium II and Celerons based on the Pentium III because neither of them officially bears the Pentium name (and because there is no dramatic difference in technology between the two). Celerons running at 333MHz and lower are SEP; those between 366 and 433MHz are available as both SEP and PGA; and the newer Celerons, running at 466MHz and above, are PGA only.

**FIGURE 5.25**
A Pentium II Xeon CPU (Photo courtesy of Intel Corporation)

### *Xeon*

At the other end of Intel's Pentium II spectrum is the high-end Xeon CPU. While the Celeron was a lesser version of the Pentium II, the Xeon is an improved version. It has more L2 cache memory (up to 2MB), and the L2 cache runs at the same speed as the CPU itself. This larger, higher speed cache is the primary reason the Xeon is more expensive. It comes only in an SECC package, and it fits into a different type of slot: Slot 2.

### *AMD K6*

Intel's primary competition for the Pentium II market has been AMD with its K6 CPUs. The K6 offers performance somewhere between the Pentium and Pentium II, and comes in a Socket 7 type of PGA chip.

The inside of the K6 chip is like a Pentium II but outside (that is, in its connection to the motherboard) it resembles a Pentium MMX. There have been three versions of the K6:

- **K6:** The original, with speeds of between 166 and 300MHz.
- **K6-2:** Faster internal speed (266 to 475MHz), and works on motherboards with bus speeds of 66 to 100MHz. Also adds 3DNow technology, a new multimedia instruction set that is an improvement on MMX. Figure 5.26 shows a K6-2 installed in a Socket 7 motherboard.
- **K6-3:** Speeds of 400 or 450 MHz, and adds a full-speed L2 cache on the same die as the CPU, making it more closely integrated than the L2 cache on the Pentium II.

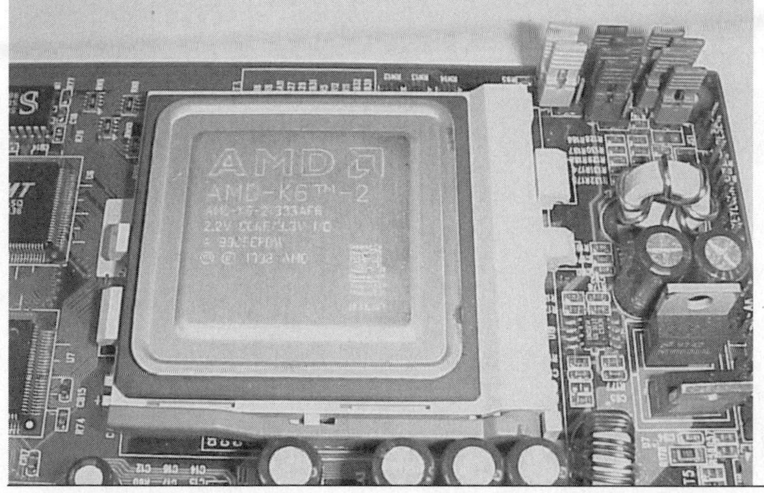


**FIGURE 5.26**
A K6-2 CPU

The K6 chips tend to run hot, so they require high-quality cooling fans. They also have complex voltage requirements, so should be used only in motherboards specifically designed for them.

## Pentium III CPUs

The Pentium III and Pentium 4 (Intel changed its numbering convention from Roman to Arabic) improve on the Pentium II design: better performance, faster speeds, more cache memory. There are no revolutionary new features in these models; the difference lies in fine-tuning and improving existing concepts.

### *Pentium III*

The Pentium III comes in speeds from 450 to 1,000MHz (1GHz). It includes a 32KB L1 cache and a 512KB half-speed or 256KB full-speed L2 cache.

The feature of the Pentium III that attracted the most attention when it was released was its ability to report its processor serial number to applications that request it, enabling security programs to identify systems. Consumers objected strongly on privacy grounds, so methods of disabling the serial number reporting were quickly introduced. Most Pentium III systems have a setting in the BIOS that turns the CPU serial number feature on and off.

Some Pentium III CPUs use an improved version of SECC called SECC2 (see Figure 5.27); others use a Socket 370 PGA packaging. The main innovation in this packaging was to place the Pentium III CPU on the top of the ceramic PGA package rather than on the underside, so it could be

**Flip chip**

A CPU design that places the CPU on the top of the ceramic PGA package rather than on the bottom, for easier cooling.

closer to the cooling fan. This is called *flip chip* (FC), and its packaging is known as *FC-PGA* (see Figure 5.28).

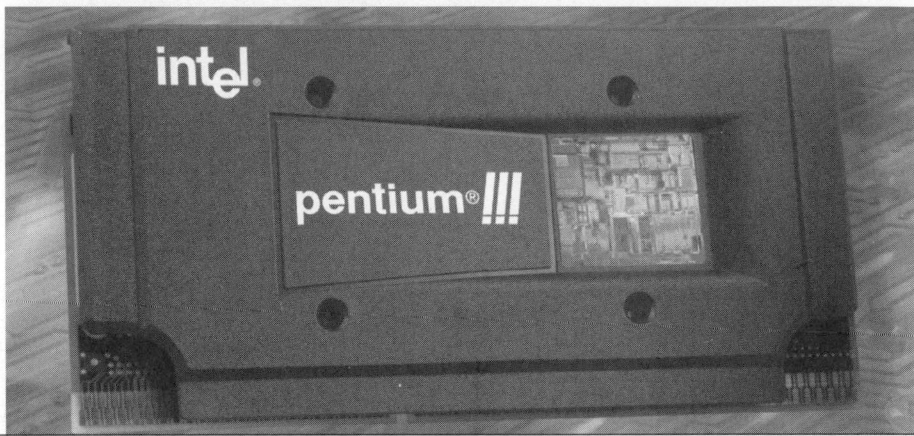


**FIGURE 5.27**
A Pentium III in SECC2 Packaging (Photo courtesy of Intel Corporation)

**FIGURE 5.28**
A Pentium III in FC-PGA Packaging

The SECC2 version of the Pentium III has fewer cryptic markings than the Pentium II cartridges did. The first line of its coding tells the speed, cache size, bus speed, and voltage; for example, 600/512/100/2.0v. It also has an *S*-spec, which appears as *S* followed by four characters.

As with the Pentium II, a budget version of the Pentium III is available under the Celeron name and a high-end version under the Xeon name.

### *AMD Athlon and Duron*

AMD's Athlon CPU is its competitor to the Pentium III. It runs at between 550MHz and 1GHz. The first Athlons used an SECC packaging like the Pentium II that fits into a different kind of slot called Slot A. It is physically the same size as Slot 1, but not pin compatible, which means that motherboard manufacturers can use the same physical parts for constructing the motherboards for the two systems, but the same motherboard cannot support both CPUs.

Later versions of the Athlon (see Figure 5.29) used a PGA style rather than the SECC, and the socket was called Socket A. It is physically the same as Socket 370 but the pin functions are different, so, as with Slot A, motherboard manufacturers can use parts they already have but consumers must buy a motherboard specifically for the CPU.

The first Athlons had a 512KB half-speed L2 cache on a separate chip in the cartridge, but later Athlons use a 256KB full-speed cache directly built into the CPU die.

The AMD Duron CPU is a low-budget Athlon with less L2 cache memory. Everything else is the same as the Athlon. Duron CPUs use the PGA-style Socket A.

Motherboards for the Athlon and Duron have a 200 or 266MHz front-side bus, a very high-end bus for a consumer PC, which contributes to their high performance.

**FIGURE 5.29**
A Socket A Athlon (Photo courtesy of Advanced Micro Devices)

## PENTIUM 4 AND BEYOND

At this writing, the popular CPU in the industry is the Pentium 4 (Figure 5.30). Its speeds range from 1.3 to more than 2.2GHz, and ever-increasing speeds are being made available.

**FIGURE 5.30**
A Pentium 4 CPU (Photo courtesy of Intel Corporation)

The Pentium 4 is not yet covered on the A+ examinations because it was not invented when the latest revision of the exams was introduced. However, here are a few key facts about it:

- It is smaller and more powerful than any previous CPU.
- It is based on a new architecture called NetBurst.
- The processor bus is 64-bit, 100MHz quad pipeline, resulting in 400MHz 64-bit bus performance.
- It has a 20KB L1 cache and a 256KB full-speed L2 cache.
- It uses a new type of PGA socket called Socket 423, with 324 pins in a 39x39 SPGA arrangement. There is also an alternate packaging that has 478 pins and uses a 478-pin socket.
- The motherboard has an automatic voltage regulator module.

AMD also continues to improve its CPUs, and a Pentium 4-type Athlon XP is available.

Intel has a very high-end CPU called the Itanium available at this writing. It is expensive, and used only in the most powerful servers. Designed for 64-bit systems, the Itanium does not run regular 32-bit software; a special 64-bit version of the operating system is required.

## TRY IT!

**Now that you are familiar with the different CPUs, identify all of the CPUs in all of the motherboards available to you. Collect as much information on them as you can, including type, speed, and core voltage.**

# STUDY GUIDE

Use the following summaries to review the key concepts of this chapter.

## HOW A CPU WORKS

- Data comes into and out of the CPU on the system bus, also known as the external data bus.
- Inside the CPU are work areas called registers that store data while the CPU operates upon it.
- High-order bits represent the instructions to the CPU; low-order bits represent the data.
- Machine language is the language that the CPU understands. Each CPU has its own machine language.

## CPU SPEED AND VOLTAGE

- The system crystal sets the timing for data moving through the system bus. Each tick of the system crystal is a clock cycle.
- The external speed is the speed dictated by the system crystal. The CPU's internal speed is the number of clock cycles per second that it can handle.
- Overclocking is pushing a CPU to operate at a faster speed than it is rated for.
- The clock multiplier is the number of internal operations in the CPU that occur for each clock tick of the external speed.
- The core voltage of the CPU is the voltage it requires to operate. Lower voltages are advantageous because of cooling issues and because of the amps drawn.
- The higher the voltage, the hotter the chip. A heat sink channels heat away from the CPU. A passive heat sink has no moving parts; an active heat sink has an electric fan.

## CPU CACHING

- The front-side cache, or L1 cache, stores data waiting to enter the CPU.
- The back-side cache, or L2 cache, stores data waiting to go somewhere else after leaving the CPU.
- A Cache on a Stick (COAST) was an early method of incorporating an L2 cache into motherboards. Today's L2 caches are built into the CPU itself.

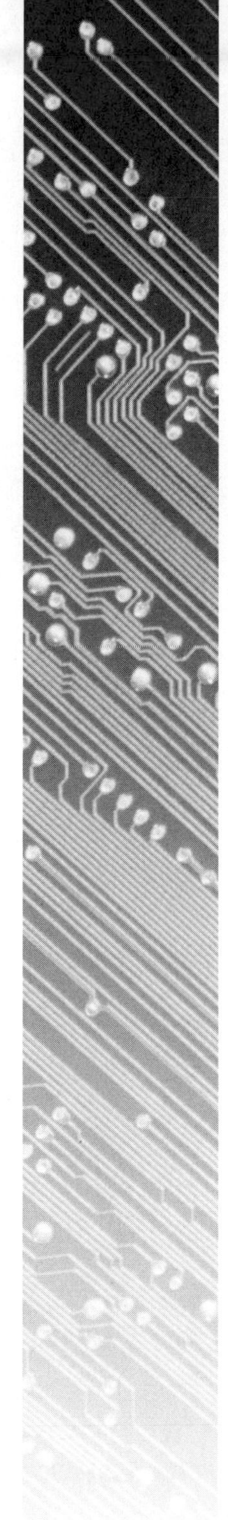

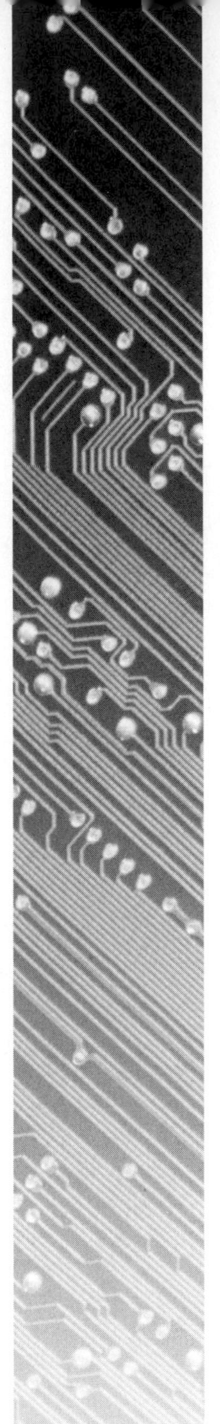

## 8088 CPUS

- The CPU in the original IBM PC was the 8088. A faster version of this CPU was also used in the IBM PC XT.
- The 8088 was a rectangular chip with legs on two sides. This packaging is called Dual Inline Pin Package (DIPP).
- A math coprocessor chip (also known as a floating-point unit) is an add-on to the main CPU that helps it perform high-level math operations. The 8088's math coprocessor was called the 8087.

## 286 CPUS

- The 80286 CPU was used in the IBM PC AT. The 80286 had two modes: real mode (for backward compatibility) and protected mode (for more modern applications).
- In protected mode, the 80286 could access up to 16MB of RAM. However, MS-DOS did not support protected mode, so only a few applications could use it.
- The 80286 CPU introduced a pin grid array (PGA) packaging consisting of a square ceramic chip with concentric rings of pins that fit into holes in the motherboard.
- The 80286 had a math coprocessor option available called the 80287.

## 386 CPUS

- The 80386 CPU was a 32-bit CPU, which meant it could run 32-bit applications.
- The 80386 had three operating modes: real mode, 286 protected mode, and 386 protected mode. In 386 protected mode, it could use virtual memory and virtual 8086.
- The 386SX was a version of the 386 designed to work in less expensive, 16-bit motherboards. It could run 32-bit applications, but the data traveling to and from the CPU used a 16-bit bus.
- The full version of the 386 was called the 386DX.
- The math coprocessor for the 80386 was the 80387.

## 486 CPUS

- The i486 CPU had a built-in 8K L1 cache and a built-in math coprocessor.
- The 486 systems could have faster internal data buses than external, made possible by clock multipliers.

- The 486DX was the standard model; the 486SX lacked the coprocessor and the L1 cache.
- There were several packaging styles for the 486. Some were built into the motherboard, like the 386s. Others were removable PGA models like the 286s.
- A new type of CPU socket called Zero Insertion Force (ZIF) was introduced with the later 486s. It had a handle that lifted to release the CPU from the PGA socket and lowered to secure it there.
- Intel produced a variety of upgrade chips for 486 PCs under the name OverDrive. Some motherboards had separate sockets for OverDrive CPUs; others could accept them in the main CPU socket.
- ZIF sockets have different numbers of pins and different names, such as Socket 1, Socket 2, and so on. The 486 CPUs used Socket 2 or Socket 3.
- Advanced Micro Devices (AMD) has been a major competitor to Intel. Its 5x86 chip competes with the i486.

## PENTIUM

- Pentium CPUs have a 64-bit data bus, split into two 32-bit data buses so they can process two sets of instructions at a time (dual pipeline). This makes them approximately twice as fast as a 486 at the same clock speed.
- Pentiums incorporate branch prediction and have improved caching.
- First-generation Pentiums were +5v, 273-pin, ran at 60 or 66MHz, and used Socket 4.
- Second-generation Pentiums were +3.3v, ran at 75 to 200MHz, and used Socket 5 or Socket 7.
- The Pentium Pro was a commercially unsuccessful update to the Pentium. Most of its new features eventually were incorporated in the Pentium II.
- The Pentium Pro excelled at running 32-bit programs, but for 16-bit programs was slower than a regular Pentium.
- Later Pentium models incorporated MMX (multimedia extensions) technology for better performance in playing 3-D games.
- The AMD K5 CPU was a strong competitor to the Pentium.

## PENTIUM II, III, AND 4

- The Pentium II is much like a fast Pentium Pro with MMX. Pentium IIs were made in speeds from 233 to 450MHz, using external buses of 66 or 100MHz.

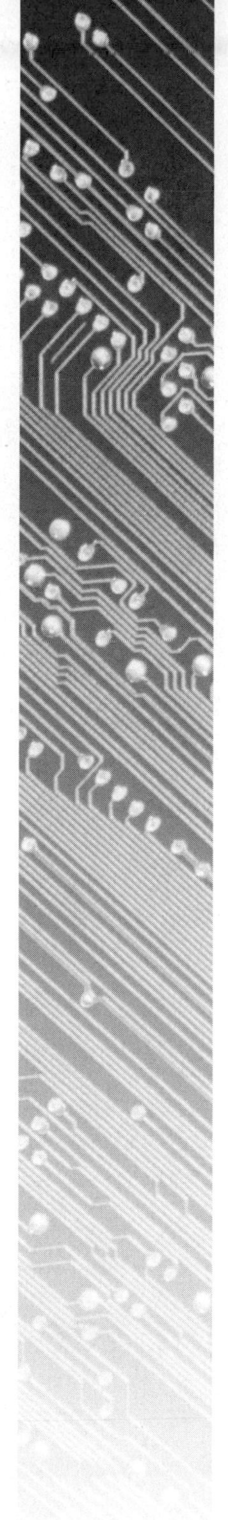

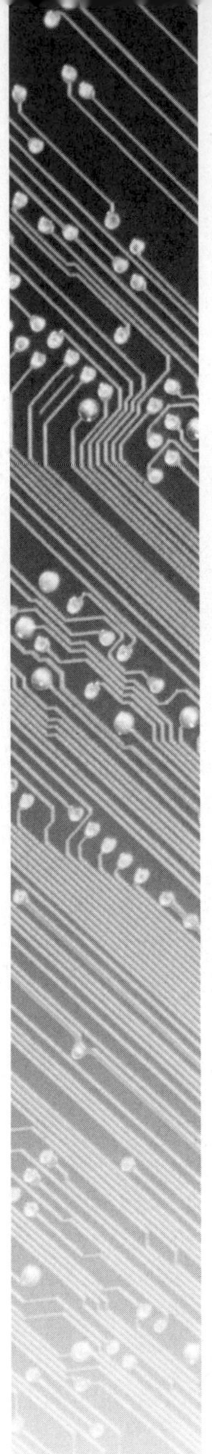

- Pentium II CPUs used a new type of packaging, Single Edge Contact Cartridge (SECC), which consisted of a plastic cartridge with a circuit board inside that fit into a Slot 1 motherboard slot.
- The Pentium II features a Dual Independent Bus, in which the bus for the CPU's connectivity to the Internet is separated from the bus between the CPU and the cache.
- Celeron is Intel's name for low-budget Pentium II and Pentium III CPUs. Some Celerons use a variant of the SECC called a Single Edge Processor (SEP).
- AMD's competitor to the Pentium II is the K6, available as the K6, K6-2, and K6-3.
- The Pentium III comes in speeds from 450MHz to 1GHz.
- Pentium IIIs used SECC2 or Socket 370 PGA packaging.
- AMD's competitors to the Pentium III are the Athlon and the Duron. Both use a Slot A SECC packaging. Slot A is physically compatible with Slot 1, but the circuitry is different.

## PRACTICE TEST

On a blank sheet of paper, write the answers to the following multiple-choice questions and explain why each answer is correct.

1. Data comes into and out of the CPU on the
   a. ISA bus.
   b. system bus.
   c. local I/O bus.
   d. south bridge.

2. Inside the CPU are work areas that store data temporarily while it is being processed. These are called
   a. low-order bits.
   b. high-order bits.
   c. registers.
   d. binary bits.

3. Machine language is
   a. the set of commands that the CPU understands.
   b. the set of low-order bits that the operating system sends to the CPU.
   c. the operating system language.
   d. the BIOS language.

4. The ________________ determines the speed of the external data bus.
   a. CPU's internal speed
   b. operating system
   c. real-time clock
   d. system crystal

5. Overclocking is
   a. replacing the system crystal to increase the external data bus speed.
   b. pushing the motherboard to run faster than its rated external data bus speed.
   c. setting the clock multiplier to a higher multiple than the motherboard's rated maximum.
   d. setting the motherboard to push the CPU into a faster internal speed than it is rated for.

6. On a 66MHz motherboard, what would the clock multiplier be for a 200MHz CPU?
   a. 2.5
   b. 3.0
   c. 3.5
   d. 4.0

7. Another name for the L1 cache is
   a. front-side cache.
   b. back-side cache.
   c. disk cache.
   d. Cache on a Stick.

8. A heat sink that includes an electric fan is known as a(n)
   a. active heat sink.
   b. passive heat sink.
   c. grounded heat sink.
   d. Super7 Heat Sink.

9. The CPU used in the original IBM PC was the
   a. 8086.
   b. 8087.
   c. 8088.
   d. 80286.

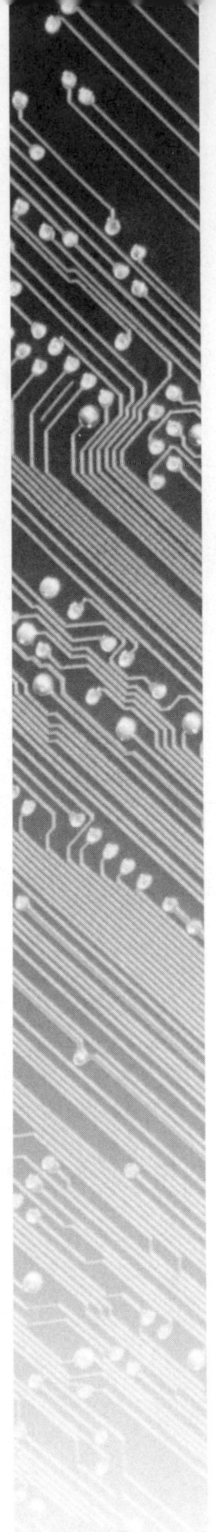

10. A DIPP chip is
    a. a square ceramic chip with concentric rings of pins on the bottom.
    b. a rectangular chip with metal legs on two sides.
    c. a chip soldered permanently to a circuit board.
    d. not really a chip at all, but a plastic cartridge that sits perpendicular to the motherboard.

11. Another name for a math coprocessor is
    a. floating-point unit (FPU).
    b. OverDrive chip.
    c. RAM extension.
    d. system crystal.

12. Which CPU was used in the IBM PC AT, and could operate in either real or protected mode?
    a. 80186
    b. 80188
    c. 80286
    d. 80287

13. What CPU mode is backward-compatible with programs written for the 8088?
    a. real mode
    b. protected mode
    c. compatibility mode
    d. 386 enhanced mode

14. A PGA socket is
    a. a rectangular socket with holes on two sides for chip legs.
    b. a slot for an SECC cartridge.
    c. a square socket with wire contacts around three sides.
    d. a square socket with concentric rings of holes.

15. The difference between the 386SX and 386DX is
    a. the DX has a wider external data bus.
    b. the DX has a built-in coprocessor.
    c. the DX has an on-board L2 cache.
    d. None of the above

16. The difference between the 486SX and 486DX is
    a. the DX has a wider external data bus.
    b. the DX has a built-in coprocessor.
    c. the DX is dual pipelined.
    d. None of the above

17. A ZIF socket is a type of _____ socket.
    a. SECC
    b. DIPP
    c. PGA
    d. coprocessor

18. A CPU with dual pipelining capability, such as the Pentium, can
    a. activate two IRQs at once.
    b. accept data on two separate 32-bit data buses simultaneously.
    c. communicate on a different bus with the motherboard than with the L2 cache.
    d. use the L1 and L2 caches simultaneously.

19. What feature of the Pentium II did the Pentium Pro lack?
    a. dual pipelining
    b. Dynamic processing
    c. multimedia extensions (MMX)
    d. None—it had all of these features

20. What is an Athlon?
    a. Intel's high-end Pentium II and III line
    b. Intel's low-end Pentium II and III line
    c. AMD's 64-bit competitor to Intel's Itanium
    d. an AMD CPU that competes with the Pentium II and III

# TROUBLESHOOTING

1. You find a motherboard with a ZIF PGA socket labeled Socket 7. It has two jumper setting charts on it: one for Ratio, running from 2.0 to 5.5 in increments of 0.5, and one for Speed, with available values of 66, 75, 83, 95, 100, and 112. What range of CPU speeds would you expect it to support? What general class of CPUs would such speeds fall under?
2. You decide to try a 300MHz AMD K6-2 CPU in the socket described in the above question. How would you set the ratio and speed jumpers?
3. You find an SECC slot motherboard and an Athlon SECC CPU. Can you assume that they will work together? Why or why not?

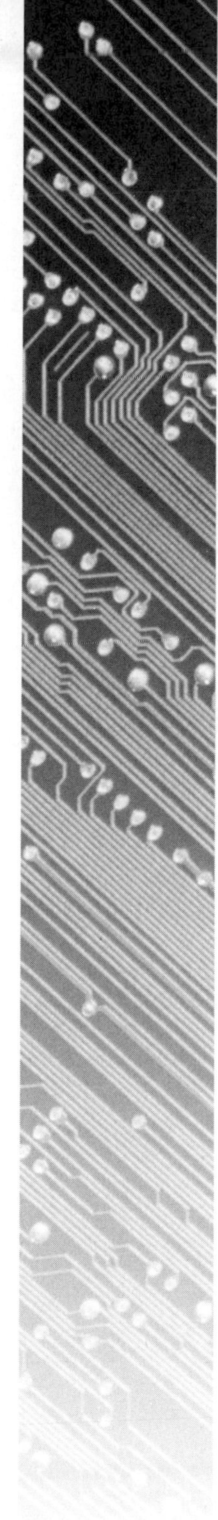

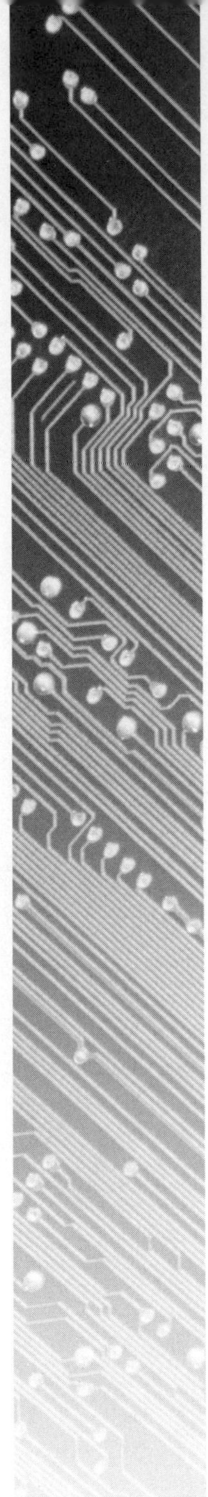

## CUSTOMER SERVICE

1. A client wants to upgrade a 120MHz 486DX4 computer, and says that she has found a Pentium OverDrive for 486 chip for sale on an auction site online. She asks your opinion as to whether she should buy it. What would be your advice to her?
2. A client with a 400MHz Pentium II system is dissatisfied with the way his PC runs 3-D games. He would like to upgrade his CPU because he has heard that MMX will make his games run better. What advice can you give him?
3. A client with a 1GHz Pentium III system spends most of her time doing word processing and accessing the Internet via a 56Kbps modem. She has clipped an ad for a Pentium 4 PC to show you, and asks whether it would improve her Internet connection speed if she upgraded. What would you tell her?

## FOR MORE INFORMATION

For links to Web sites that provide further information about the topics covered in this chapter, go to the EMC/Paradigm Internet Resource Center at www.emcp.com/College Division/Internet Resource Centers/PC Maintenance/For More Information.

# 6 Memory

## ON THE TEST

**A+ Core Hardware Service Technician Examination**

- **Objective 1.1:** Identify basic terms, concepts, and functions of system modules, including how each module should work during normal operation and during the boot process.
- **Objective 4.2:** Identify the categories of RAM (Random Access Memory) terminology, their locations, and physical characteristics.

**A+ Operating System Technologies Examination**

- **Objective 1.1**: Identify the operating system's functions, structure, and major system files to navigate the operating system and how to get to needed technical information.

## ON THE JOB

Memory works closely with the CPU and the motherboard; those three items together form a trinity that stores, transfers, and processes the data that makes the whole PC run. A PC technician must be thoroughly familiar with the purposes, types, and potential problems with RAM in order to handle such tasks as these:

- selecting RAM for system upgrades
- selecting RAM to match a new motherboard
- determining whether old RAM on-hand can be used in a new system
- understanding and diagnosing OS-based memory problems
- optimizing memory usage on a system with a limited amount of RAM

# Types of Memory

**Memory**

A generic term meaning any electronic device (usually a microchip) that stores data in binary format.

When they hear "memory" most people think of Dynamic Random-Access Memory (DRAM), the main memory of a PC that stores the operating system and applications as they are running. There are other types of computer memory as well. Generically, the term *memory* can mean anything that stores data. You have got your own memory in your brain, for example. In computer terms, however, *memory* refers to a device (usually a microchip) that stores data in binary format.

Computer memory can be broadly divided into two categories: Read-Only Memory (ROM) and Random-Access Memory (RAM). RAM can be further subdivided into Static RAM (SRAM) and Dynamic RAM (DRAM). The following sections look at each in more detail. Figure 6.1 summarizes some commonly used terms related to memory, which will also be discussed later in the chapter.

- **Conventional memory:** The first 640KB of RAM. Used to run real-mode applications.
- **Upper memory:** The 360KB of memory between 640KB and 1MB. Reserved for system use, but with the help of EMM386.EXE can be used to run parts of MS-DOS.
- **High memory:** The first 64KB of extended memory (above the 1MB mark). Can be used to run parts of MS-DOS with the help of HIMEM.SYS.
- **Expanded memory:** Extra memory above 1MB added to an 80286 system on an ISA expansion card.
- **EMS:** Stands for Expanded Memory Specification; a standard for expanded memory usage.
- **LIM:** Stands for Lotus-Intel-Microsoft; the same as EMS.
- **Extended memory:** Extra memory above 1MB on 80386 systems and higher (that is, systems that use SIMMs or DIMMs).
- **XMS:** Stands for eXtended Memory Specification; a standard for extended memory usage.
- **HIMEM.SYS:** A driver loaded at startup that manages extended memory and converts it to XMS format for use with protected-mode programs. Also enables the DOS=HIGH command to load part of MS-DOS in high memory.
- **EMM386.EXE:** A driver loaded at startup that makes extended memory able to emulate expanded memory and also enables the DOS=UMB command to load part of MS-DOS in upper memory blocks.

**FIGURE 6.1**
Memory Terms

# Read-Only Memory (ROM)

*Read-Only Memory (ROM)* is just what the name sounds like: memory to which you cannot write new data. It retains whatever data is originally stored in it, and that exact same data can be recalled time after time. Another term commonly used for ROM is firmware because it is not really hardware and not really software.

**Read-Only Memory (ROM)**

Memory that can be read but not written to.

ROM is nonvolatile, which means it does not lose its data when the power goes off. However, this is not a differentiating factor between ROM and RAM per se because there is a type of RAM (Static RAM) that is also nonvolatile. What distinguishes ROM from RAM is that you cannot change data stored in ROM without a special tool or utility program, whereas any application can make changes to data stored in RAM.

The most common use of ROM on a PC is to store the Basic Input Output System (BIOS) data. The BIOS contains the startup instructions for the PC at a very low level—that is, the diagnostics for the CPU, RAM, and motherboard and the instructions to seek out and load an operating system from disk. If these instructions were improperly modified, the PC would not be able to start, so storing them on a ROM BIOS chip makes good sense. This type of BIOS chip was originally called *Programmable Read-Only Memory* (PROM).

**Programmable Read-Only Memory (PROM)**

A type of ROM BIOS chip that cannot be modified after its initial creation.

As the PC industry matured, it became inconvenient that the data on a ROM BIOS chip could never be changed. A new type of PROM was introduced, called *Erasable PROM (EPROM),* which could be erased with an ultraviolet light PROM eraser. The average consumer did not have a PROM eraser, but this development made things easier for the PC manufacturers. An EPROM (see Figure 6.2) can be easily identified by the clear window in its top, which allows the light to come in.

**Erasable Programmable ROM (EPROM)**

A type of PROM that can be erased with ultraviolet light and then reprogrammed to contain different data.

**FIGURE 6.2**
An EPROM Chip with Window to Allow Erasure by Ultraviolet Light

**Electrically Erasable PROM (EEPROM)**

A type of ROM that can be erased or edited with electrical pulses. Also called flash ROM

Technology continued to develop. As new hardware devices were produced, consumers wanted their computers to be able to work with them. But this required replacing the BIOS chip, and many end users lacked the skill and nerve to pull a chip out of the motherboard. To get around this problem, chip manufacturers introduced a type of ROM chip called a *flash ROM* that could be erased with electrical pulses. It was soon replaced by a variant that allowed the ROM to be edited by making each bit individually erasable with electrical pulses, rather than fully erased and rewritten each time. Both of these are known as *Electrically Erasable PROM* (EEPROM). The term *flash ROM* has come to mean either of them as well. Figure 6.3 shows two different types of EEPROMs. The chip on the left has a DIPP package, which you have already learned about in Chapter 5. The chip on the right has a Plastic Leaded Chip Carrier (PLCC) package. The DIPP package is standard in modern systems.

## In Real Life

**Do not confuse flash ROM with flash RAM (which is usually referred to as flash memory). Flash memory is nonvolatile, rewritable memory similar to SRAM (covered in the next section). It functions as a combination hard disk and memory on small devices such as digital cameras, cellular phones, and PDAs.**

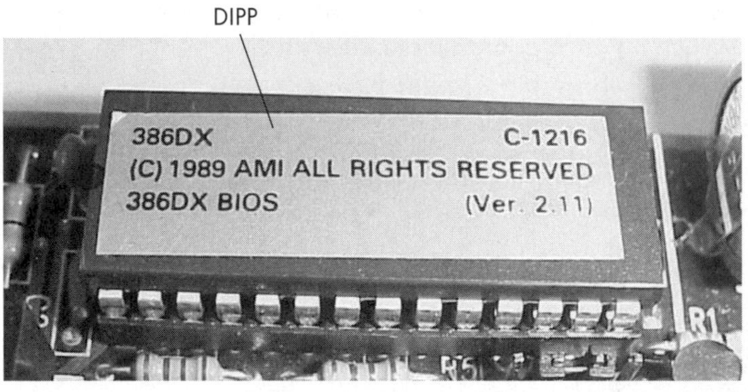

**FIGURE 6.3**
Two Different Packages for EEPROMs

EEPROM, found in almost all motherboards today, makes updating the BIOS a simple task. You download a BIOS update from the system manufacturer and place it on a bootable floppy disk, and then boot from that floppy to run the utility that writes the new BIOS data to the EEPROM chip. You will learn more about that in Chapter 9.

The BIOS is not the only use for ROM. In many handheld PDA computers the entire operating system is stored on a ROM chip. To get a new operating system, you download it from the device manufacturer and then run a special utility to update the ROM chip's content.

# Random-Access Memory (RAM)

RAM is much more flexible than ROM because it can be both read and written to with equal ease. The designation "random access" comes from the fact that one address in RAM is just as easy to access as any other. Files in RAM are not necessarily stored contiguously; pieces of them may be scattered throughout the physical storage area. Hard disks are like that, too, as you will see in Chapter 10. In contrast, a cassette tape player is *not* random access; the machine has to rewind or go fast forward to get to a desired spot.

## SRAM AND DRAM

There are two kinds of RAM: Static RAM (SRAM) and Dynamic RAM (DRAM).

DRAM is "regular" RAM, the type that PCs use as their main memory. This type of RAM is volatile, meaning it constantly needs to be refreshed in order to retain the data stored in it. Inside a DRAM chip is a grid of tiny capacitors, each of which can store an electrical charge for a couple of milliseconds. When a capacitor is charged, it holds a 1 value; when it is not charged, it holds a 0 value. When the power goes off, the capacitors stop receiving electricity and they all revert to a 0 state, wiping out whatever was stored there. The advantage of DRAM is that it is inexpensive, so a PC can have many megabytes of DRAM without prohibitive cost.

In contrast, SRAM holds whatever you put into it until it receives different instructions. It is not ROM; it readily accepts new input, and holds onto that input without requiring electricity to maintain it. This makes it very fast because of the low overhead; it does not expend any effort in retaining its content. A computer could use SRAM for all memory, but it would be extremely expensive.

SRAM is used in the L1 and L2 caches that support the CPU. In the latest CPUs these SRAM caches are built into the die for the CPU itself; in older systems they were separate, as you saw in Chapters 4 and 5. Both SRAM and DRAM are slower than the CPU. SRAM is the faster of the two, making it the likelier candidate for use in the cache.

**Extended data out (EDO)**

A type of DRAM that requires refreshing less frequently than normal RAM.

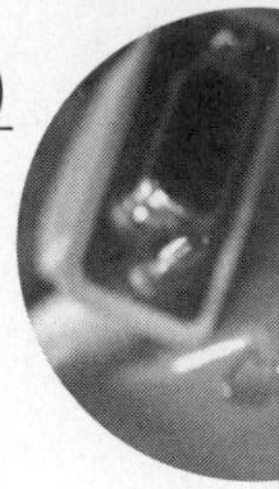

## IN REAL LIFE

RAM manufacturers have experimented over the years with different ways of making DRAM more like SRAM without raising its cost too much. One such method was *extended data out (EDO)*. EDO DRAM is DRAM in which the capacitors need to be refreshed less often, resulting in lower overhead. EDO DRAM was popular in the late 486 and early Pentium period, but it is now obsolete.

## HOW RAM STORES DATA

Each RAM chip has a width and a depth, in the same way that a spreadsheet has a certain number of rows and columns. For example, a RAM chip might be 4 columns wide by 1,024,000 rows deep (see Figure 6.4). Another RAM chip might be 1 column wide by 256,000 rows deep. At each of the intersections of row and column is a tiny capacitor that can be charged to hold a 1 or uncharged to hold a 0.

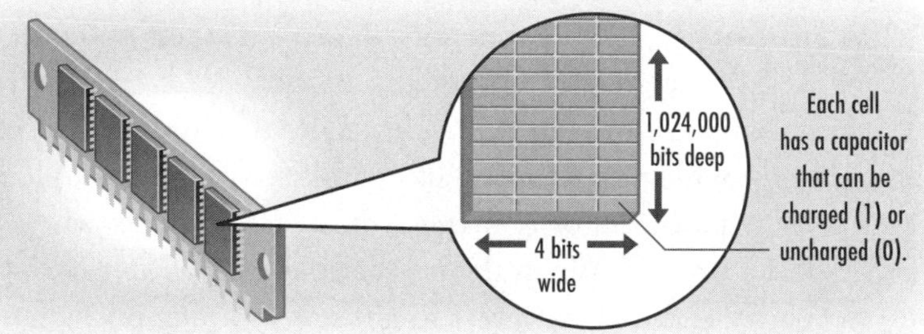


**FIGURE 6.4**
Each RAM chip has a width and a depth.

## IN REAL LIFE

When referring to the depth of RAM chips, you typically round the off number and use Kb for a thousand bits (kilobit) and Mb for a million bits (megabit). So, for example, 1,024,000 would be referred to as 1Mb. The small b means "bits." Sometimes the b is dropped, as in 1M. When an abbreviation uses a capital B, it means byte (8 bits). For example, a hard disk's capacity might be expressed in megabytes (MB) or gigabytes (GB).

The width of the RAM chip is significant because the CPU must address the system RAM in units matching the width of the address bus. On the oldest PCs the width was 8 bits (1 byte); on modern PCs it is 64 bits. That means a single 8-bit RAM chip cannot interact with the CPU on a 64-bit address bus. It must be combined with enough other identical RAM chips to produce the needed width. For a 64-bit address bus, that would mean eight 8-bit RAM chips (see Figure 6.5).

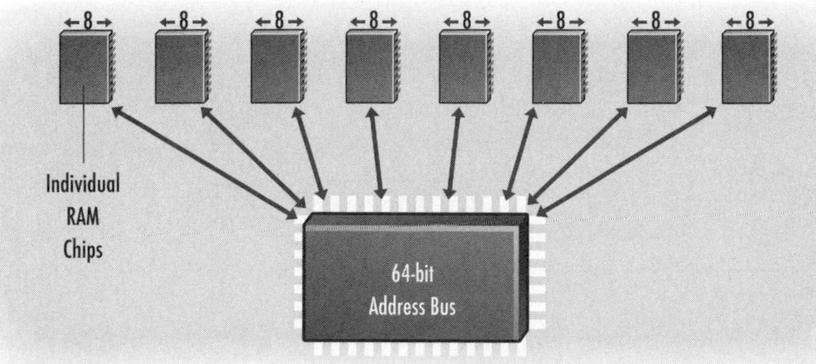


**FIGURE 6.5**
Multiple RAM chips combine to create the needed width to communicate with the address bus.

## RAM Packaging

In the earliest PCs, RAM chips had DIPP packaging and mounted directly to the motherboard. They were organized in rows to create the needed widths. Figure 6.6 shows an example.

**FIGURE 6.6**
Single-Bit RAM Chips in DIPP Packaging in an 80286 Motherboard

**Single inline memory module (SIMM)**

A type of RAM stick with 30 or 72 pins that fits into a SIMM slot on a motherboard. Now obsolete, replaced by DIMM.

This system quickly became impractical, because of the increasing numbers of chips needed to form a row as address bus widths increased, and because it was easy to bend or break the legs of the delicate DIPP chips. A new packaging was developed, the *single inline memory module* (SIMM), in which several RAM chips were mounted on a small circuit board. That circuit board then fit into a slot in the motherboard. Each of

**Stick**

A small circuit board on which one or more RAM chips are mounted.

these circuit boards was known as a *stick* of RAM. The early SIMM sticks were 30-pin models (see Figure 6.7), which meant they had 30 individual metal contacts running along the edge of the circuit board. Each 30-pin SIMM's RAM chips added up to 8 bits in total.

**FIGURE 6.7**
A 30-Pin SIMM

These early SIMMs had wider bit widths than individual RAM chips, but they were still not wide enough to interact individually with the CPU. Therefore groups of SIMM slots were combined on motherboards into *banks*. A bank is a group of SIMM slots (although technically a single slot can be a bank) that combine their widths to interact as a single unit with the CPU via the address bus. For example, suppose you have an 80386 CPU with a 32-bit address bus. You would need a bank of four 8-bit SIMMs to interact with it, as in Figure 6.8.

**Bank**

One or more memory slots on a motherboard that combine to be treated as a single logical unit when addressed by the CPU.

**FIGURE 6.8**
A Bank of Four 8-Bit SIMMs Making Up a Single 32-Bit Width

Notice in Figure 6.8 that there are two banks: one full and one empty. To add more memory depth (that is, more rows in which to store data), additional banks could be filled. If there were no empty banks to be filled, the existing SIMMs could be removed and replaced with deeper ones. Although all the SIMMs in a single bank had to be of equal depth, the SIMMs in different banks could be different depths.

Over time it became unwieldy to have so many SIMM slots in a motherboard, so a new type of SIMM was introduced: the 72-pin SIMM. These were about 1 inch longer than the 30-pin variety, and had smaller, more closely spaced pins. Each 72-pin SIMM was 32-bit, so only one SIMM was required to make up a 32-bit bank. In Pentium and higher systems, where the address bus was 64-bit, two 72-pin SIMM slots could be combined to make up a 64-bit bank.

The number of chips on a SIMM is not indicative of its capacity, and the chips on a SIMM are not necessarily all the same. Different SIMM manufacturers combine different RAM chips (all with the same depth, of course) on a single stick. Figure 6.9 shows four different 72-pin SIMMs, all of which are 32 bits in width.

**FIGURE 6.9**
Four Different 72-Pin, 32-Bit SIMMs

With the advent of the Pentium, 64-bit address buses became the norm and a new type of memory packaging was introduced: the *dual inline memory module* (DIMM). The DIMM is longer than a 72-pin SIMM and has 168 pins across the bottom. The "dual" in the name means it is double-sided; there are 84 pins on each side. DIMMs are 64-bit, so only one DIMM slot is required to make up a bank. A system with only three DIMM slots can have three complete banks, making for more memory depth expandability. (Remember, it is the depth that determines the memory capacity.) In Figure 6.10 notice that there are a couple of offset notches in the bottom; this makes the DIMM "keyed" so it cannot be inserted the wrong way.

**Dual inline memory module (DIMM)**

A type of RAM stick that has 168 pins and fits into a DIMM slot on a motherboard.

**FIGURE 6.10**
A 168-Pin, 64-Bit DIMM

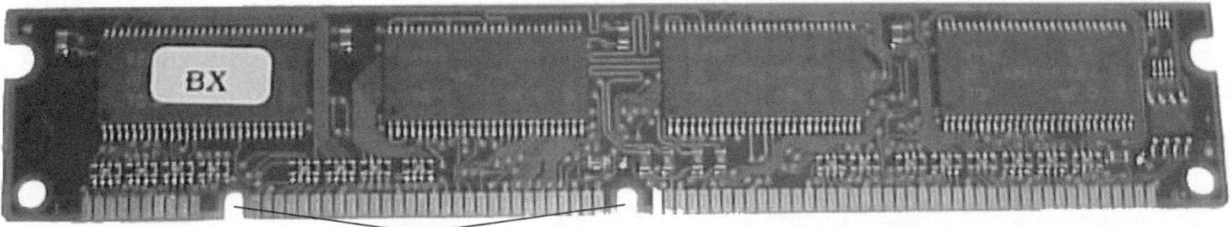

Table 6.1 summarizes the widths of RAM and the number of sticks required for a bank.

| Address Bus Width | RAM Type | Sticks Per Bank |
|---|---|---|
| 386 or 486 (32-bit) | 30-pin SIMM (8-bit)<br>72-pin SIMM (32-bit) | 4<br>1 |
| Pentium and up (64-bit) | 72-pin SIMM (32-bit)<br>168-pin DIMM (64-bit) | 2<br>1 |

**TABLE 6.1**
Number of SIMMs or DIMMs Needed for a Bank

There is one more RAM package type: the RIMM. This is a high-speed RAM packaging available in high-end PCs. The *R* stands for Rambus; the official name is Direct Rambus technology. Costing over four times as much as a DIMM, the RIMM fits into a 184-pin custom RAM slot. It transfers data at up to 800MHz over a narrow 16-bit bus. RIMM packaging is not covered on the A+ exam.

**TRY IT!**

**Examine as many different PCs as you can and determine what packaging the RAM in each one uses.**

## Parity versus Nonparity

**Parity chip**

An extra RAM chip on a stick that functions as an error checker.

Some SIMMs have a 1-bit-wide chip on them called a *parity chip*. Even though it stores no data, it is included as a sort of "sanity check" to ensure the accuracy of the data storage. It compares the number of 1 values stored in a particular byte with the number of 1 values found when accessing that byte. If the values are the same, the data is assumed to be correct. If the values are not the same, a parity error occurs and you see an error message. Parity makes RAM more accurate, but also adds overhead so it slows it down just a bit.

Although it was stated earlier that the number of chips on a SIMM is not an indicator of its capacity, a SIMM with nine chips on it is generally assumed to be a parity SIMM (eight chips for data and one for parity). Figure 6.11 shows two 72-pin SIMMs: one with eight chips (nonparity) and one with nine chips (parity).

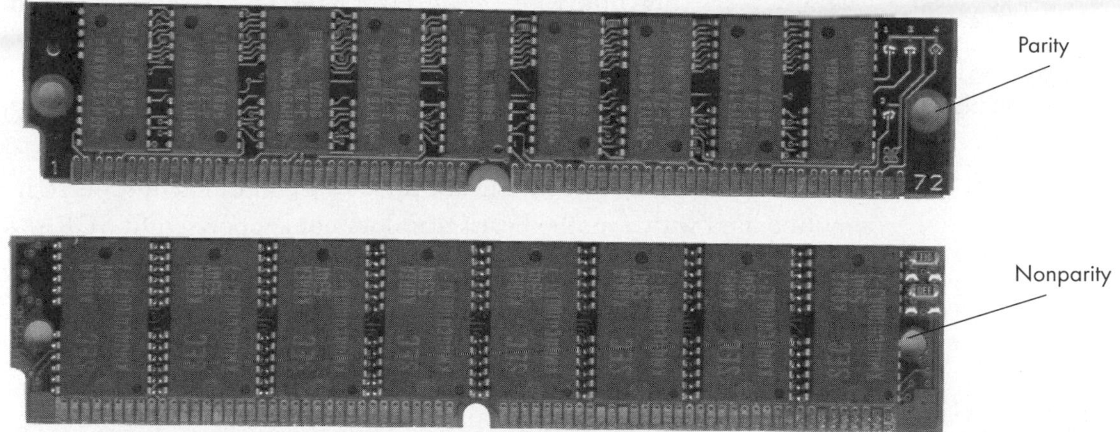


**FIGURE 6.11**
Parity versus Nonparity SIMMs

Today parity RAM is uncommon because memory technology has improved to the point where RAM is much more reliable. A variant of a parity bit called Error Code Correction (ECC) enjoyed a period of popularity in the late 1990s, but is now obsolete because it requires a motherboard to be capable of ECC, making the system more expensive.

## TRY IT!

If you have any 72-pin SIMMs available, count the number of chips on them. Do any of them have eight or nine chips? What does that tell you about them? Eight chips is definitely a nonparity SIMM, while nine chips is definitely parity. If the SIMM has some other number of chips, you cannot be sure.

## RAM Speeds

Early systems used *fast page mode* (FPM) RAM, which was measured in nanoseconds (ns) of delay in retrieving data from it. Lower numbers were better; for example, 60ns RAM was faster than 70ns RAM. Each motherboard had a specific speed of RAM it would accept. You could use faster RAM than it required, but not slower. You also had to be careful not to mix RAM speeds in the same motherboard, because this could cause intermittent memory storage glitches.

**Fast page mode (FPM)**

A type of RAM found in older PCs, with speed measured in nanoseconds (ns) of delay.

In today's systems, however, the RAM's speed is synchronized with that of the system bus. This is called *synchronous dynamic RAM* (SDRAM). The RAM in the motherboard must match its bus speed; for example, if the motherboard has a 133MHz bus, you need 133MHz RAM (also known as PC133). As with FPM RAM, you can use a higher speed than the motherboard requires, but not a lower speed.

**Synchronous dynamic RAM (SDRAM)**

A type of RAM that operates at the same speed as the system bus.

**Double Data Rate (DDR) SDRAM**

A type of RAM that operates at twice the system bus speed.

Most new systems come with *Double Data Rate (DDR) SDRAM*, which adds a multiplier to the RAM in the same way that clock multipliers do for CPUs. For every tick of the system bus the RAM can perform two operations, giving it an overall rate of 200 or 266MHz on a 100 or 133MHz system bus, respectively. DDR SDRAM is physically the same size and shape as a regular DIMM, but the notches are in different spots so it cannot be used with a motherboard that does not support DDR SDRAM.

Rambus RAM (which comes in RIMMs, as mentioned earlier) is even faster; it can run at up to 800MHz. It is very expensive, however, and not currently found on most mainstream PCs. This may change in the next few years, or Rambus RAM may die out.

## RAM Labeling

In the days of 30-pin SIMMs, RAM was typically marked with two measurements: the first number was the bit depth (in millions) and the second number was the bit width. So, for example, you might have a 4 x 8 SIMM that was four megabits deep and eight bits (one byte) wide. That would be considered a four-megabyte SIMM. On a 30-pin SIMM, the first number tells you the number of megabytes of capacity (you multiply 4 by 8 to get the number of megabits, and then divide by 8 to convert the megabits to megabytes).

On 72-pin SIMMs you may also see two numbers, but they do not mean the same thing as on the 30-pin models. The first number is still the bit depth, but all 72-pin SIMMs are 32 bits in width. The second number can be either 32 or 36. If it is 32, it is a nonparity SIMM; if it is 36, it is parity. So, for instance, you might have a 4 x 32 or 4 x 36 SIMM, both of which would be the same capacity: 16MB.

To determine a 72-pin SIMM's capacity, you multiply the first number by 4 because it is a 32-bit model (8 bytes times 4). Alternatively, you multiply the first number by 32 (because of the 32-bit width), and then divide it by 8 to convert bits to bytes. That ends up the same as if you had simply multiplied it by 4.

Both 30- and 72-pin RAM may also have the speed labeled. For example, the individual RAM chips may have lettering on them that ends with a dash followed by a number such as 80, 70, or 60. That number is the RAM speed in nanoseconds.

SDRAM DIMM capacity is expressed as a single number: the number of megabytes of storage, such as 64 or 128MB. Speed is expressed as "PC" plus a number (usually 100 or 133).

## TRY IT!

Examine the labeling on as many different SIMMs and DIMMs as possible. Make a list of the facts you can determine from the labeling. Also note the specifications that you are not sure about based on the labeling alone.

# Selecting RAM

Selecting RAM for a motherboard can be a challenge because, as you have seen, there are so many types and variants of RAM. The best way to determine what type of RAM a motherboard can accept is to look at its manual. If you do not have a manual, you can try looking up the motherboard's specifications on the Internet (one source is www.motherboards.org). Another way is to examine the existing RAM in the system to see whether you can determine its specifications from the labeling. Installing RAM will be covered in Chapter 8.

You need to be aware of certain specifications when buying RAM in order to match the RAM's specs to that of the motherboard:

- **Physical size:** 30-pin SIMM, 72-pin SIMM, 168-pin DIMM, or 184-pin RIMM
- **Capacity:** expressed in megabytes
- **Speed:** expressed in nanoseconds (ns) for FPM or in megahertz (MHz) or PC rating for SDRAM; DDR or non-DDR for DIMMs
- **Refresh technology:** EDO or non-EDO (72-pin SIMMs only)
- **Parity:** Parity or nonparity, ECC or non-ECC (72-pin SIMMs only)

There is one other factor that has not been mentioned: the metal used in the pins. It can be either gold (yellow) or tin (silver). Some PC professionals feel that you should not mix unlike metals because it encourages corrosion, so you need to match the metal used in the RAM to the metal used in the RAM slot on the motherboard. However, most technicians agree that by the time the metals begin corroding, the system will be obsolete, so this is not an important consideration.

## TRY IT!

Pick a motherboard from among those you have to work with in your lab, and try to determine what kind of memory it would require. Use any available means of finding out, including looking up its model number on the Internet, investigating a manual that came with it, and/or examining SIMMs or DIMMs already installed on it.

# RAM Interaction with the Operating System

Now that you know the hardware side of RAM, we will look at how it interacts with the operating system. The operating systems we will discuss here are MS-DOS and Microsoft Windows because those are the systems covered on the A+ exams. The following sections explain how the operating system addresses RAM and how different generations of PCs were able to use RAM to run programs.

## Understanding Memory Addresses

**Memory address**

The address of a particular logical memory byte.

A *memory address* is the address of a particular byte of memory in storage. It does not refer to a fixed physical location in memory, but rather a logically assigned location, much as a telephone number refers to a phone line at a certain address.

The width of the address bus determines the maximum number of unique memory addresses a system can have. For example, the 8086 CPU (see Chapter 5) had a 20-bit address bus, which made for $2^{20}$ unique combinations (about 1 million); therefore, it could address up to 1MB of RAM. A 32-bit address bus has 32 wires and each can send a 1 or a 0, which means there can be $2^{32}$ of unique memory addresses described in binary numbering (just over 4GB of RAM).

Memory addresses are not written in binary, however, but rather in hexadecimal; in binary they would be too long and confusing. A binary number is converted to a hexadecimal in four-bit chunks, because there are 16 possible combinations for a four-digit binary number. Each of these 16 combinations is assigned a digit in hexadecimal: 0 through F (see Table 6.2).

| Binary | Hexadecimal |
|---|---|
| 0000 | 0 |
| 0001 | 1 |
| 0010 | 2 |
| 0011 | 3 |
| 0100 | 4 |
| 0101 | 5 |
| 0110 | 6 |
| 0111 | 7 |
| 1000 | 8 |
| 1001 | 9 |
| 1010 | A |
| 1011 | B |
| 1100 | C |
| 1101 | D |
| 1110 | E |
| 1111 | F |

**TABLE 6.2**
Converting from Binary to Hexadecimal

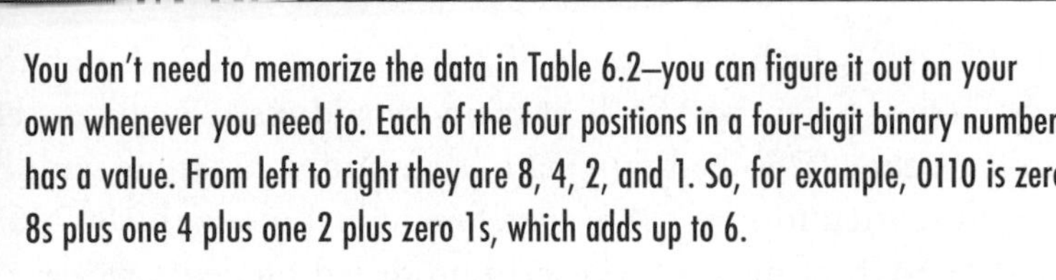

## In Real Life

**You don't need to memorize the data in Table 6.2—you can figure it out on your own whenever you need to. Each of the four positions in a four-digit binary number has a value. From left to right they are 8, 4, 2, and 1. So, for example, 0110 is zero 8s plus one 4 plus one 2 plus zero 1s, which adds up to 6.**

To express a binary memory address in hexadecimal, you break it down into four-digit chunks and then convert each chunk to a hexadecimal digit; for example, 10100000000011111111 would be A00FF. This makes memory addresses much easier to read.

## The First 1MB: Conventional and Upper Memory

**Conventional memory**

The first 640KB of RAM, used for running real-mode programs.

**Upper memory**

The RAM between 640KB and 1MB, reserved for system use.

The designers of the original IBM PC and the MS-DOS operating system made some strategic decisions about memory management that stayed with the entire PC industry for over a decade and still affect computing today. Perhaps the most significant of these was the creation of conventional and upper memory.

The 8086's 20-wire address bus allowed for 1MB of RAM to be addressed. The operating system for the PC, MS-DOS, divided this 1MB of RAM into two logical sections. (It was divided only in a software sense; there was no physical divider.) The first 640K was *conventional memory*, and the rest was *upper memory* (see Figure 6.12).

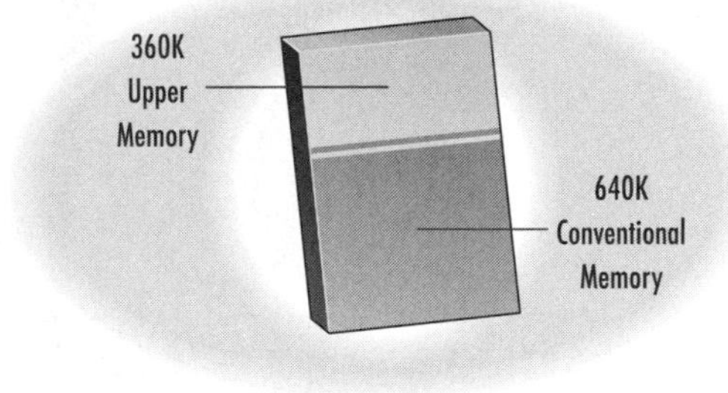


**FIGURE 6.12**
Conventional and Upper Memory

The operating system and the files for running programs could be loaded into conventional memory only; upper memory was exclusively for system use. One system use was to copy the BIOS information from the motherboard and various other I/O cards into this area of RAM for quick access. This is called *ROM shadowing*, and PCs still do it today. Another system use was to provide a staging area for copying data to and from the RAM on the video card. However, a good deal of the upper memory was not utilized.

**ROM shadowing**

Copying the contents of ROM into RAM for faster access to it.

This system worked well in the days when applications were small (100 to 200KB or so). But as programs got bigger, they began to require nearly the full 640K for themselves. If any other programs or utilities were loaded into conventional memory, such as a mouse driver, these large programs would not be able to run. There was usually additional memory available in upper memory, but it was reserved and the programs could not get to it.

## Expanded Memory

IBM's PC AT (which used Intel's 80286 CPU) had a 24-bit address bus, which allowed for up to 16MB of memory addresses. As discussed in Chapter 5, the 80286 had to remain backward-compatible with the programs written for the 8086; therefore in real mode the 80286 was still limited to 1MB of memory usage. In protected mode, however, the 80286 could take advantage of add-on *expanded memory* boards. The first 1MB was still on the motherboard, but up to 15MB extra could be added on an ISA expansion card.

**Expanded memory**

A means of providing more than 1MB of RAM to 80286 and higher systems by swapping data into and out of upper memory.

**Page frame**

A reserved 64KB area in upper memory used for swapping data into and out of expanded memory.

**Expanded Memory Specification (EMS)**

The standard for expanded memory usage. Also called LIM.

This expanded memory was divided into 16KB pieces called pages. In protected mode the operating system reserved a 64KB area in upper memory called a *page frame* that could hold four of these 16KB pages at a time; data would get swapped into and out of this upper memory area from the expanded memory (see Figure 6.13), enabling the PC to access the full amount of the expanded memory (typically about 2MB, but up to 15MB was possible). The standard for expanded memory was called *Expanded Memory Specification* (EMS); another name for it was Lotus-Intel-Microsoft (LIM), for the three companies that jointly developed the standard.

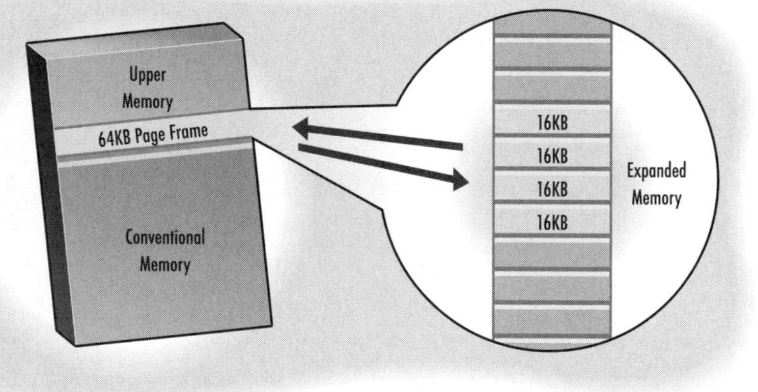

**FIGURE 6.13**
Expanded memory swaps pages in and out of the page frame in upper memory.

## Extended Memory

Starting with the 80386 systems, motherboards began using SIMMs for memory and were able to accept multiple megabytes directly on the motherboard. This extra memory above the 1MB mark was called *extended memory*. Applications became available that could take advantage of extended memory using a specification called *eXtended Memory Specification*

(XMS). To use extended memory, a PC had to load a driver called *HIMEM.SYS* in the CONFIG.SYS file. This driver enabled protected-mode applications to use extended memory. A side benefit of HIMEM.SYS was that it enabled the DOS=HIGH command to be used in CONFIG.SYS. This command loaded part of MS-DOS into the first 64KB of extended memory above the 1MB mark, known as *high memory*, freeing up a few kilobytes of conventional memory for programs that ran in real mode.

During the transition period between 80286 and 80386, application developers produced some programs that required EMS memory and others that required XMS memory. A utility called *EMM386.EXE*, also loaded in CONFIG.SYS, enabled MS-DOS to make the extended memory provided by the SIMMs appear to be whatever type was needed—either EMS or XMS.

EMM386.EXE also has a side benefit on 386 PCs and higher. When HIMEM.SYS loads part of DOS into high memory, EMM386.EXE takes the leftover portions of DOS that could not load into high memory and places them in upper memory, further freeing up conventional memory. To enable this benefit, you would add DOS=UMB in the CONFIG.SYS file. You can combine DOS=HIGH and DOS=UMB into a single line: DOS=HIGH,UMB.

Windows 95 and higher handles all memory management and automatically provides conventional, LIM, and XMS memory to applications as they need them; therefore, you do not have to set up memory management drivers in CONFIG.SYS on modern PCs. They are included here only for historical purposes. Later in this chapter you will learn how to set up CONFIG.SYS for an MS-DOS system.

**Extended memory**

Memory above 1MB in 80386 and higher systems.

**eXtended Memory Specification (XMS)**

A standard for managing extended memory.

**HIMEM.SYS**

A utility for managing extended memory and making it available to protected-mode programs.

**High memory**

The first 64KB above the 1MB mark.

**EMM386.EXE**

A memory management utility in DOS and Windows that enables extended memory to simulate EMS or XMS.

# Examining and Optimizing Memory Usage

The following sections explain how to check memory usage in MS-DOS and Windows and how to improve upon it, if possible.

## MS-DOS Memory Management

The current revision of the A+ exam does not require that test-takers know how to optimize memory under MS-DOS. In real life, however, a good technician should be familiar with the procedure for doing so, in case he or she ever needs to work with an MS-DOS system.

To check the amount of memory in the system, key **MEM** at a command prompt (you can key MS-DOS commands in upper- or lowercase characters). This tells the amount of conventional memory, the amount of extended memory, and how much of that extended memory has been converted to XMS format (see Figure 6.14).

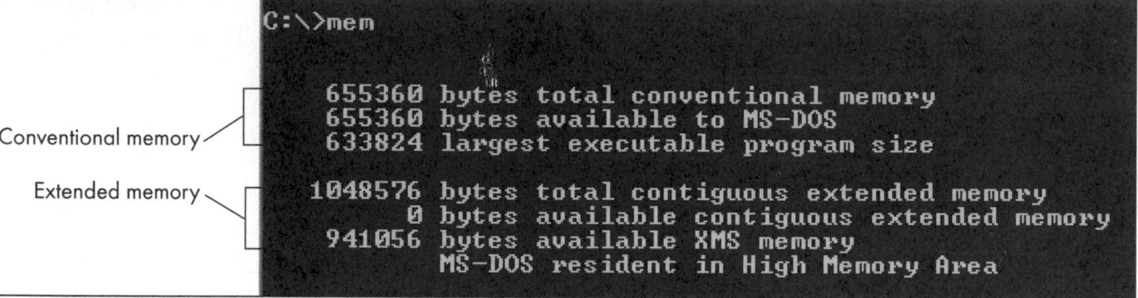
C:\>mem
655360 bytes total conventional memory
655360 bytes available to MS-DOS
633824 largest executable program size
1048576 bytes total contiguous extended memory
0 bytes available contiguous extended memory
941056 bytes available XMS memory
MS-DOS resident in High Memory Area
Conventional memory
Extended memory

**FIGURE 6.14**
**The Results of the MEM Command**

For more complete information you can add the **/C** switch, but the information will scroll by very quickly; add the pipe command **| MORE** to see it one page at a time. The complete command would be MEM /C | MORE. This more complete version shows exactly what is loaded into conventional and upper memory (see Figure 6.15).

Programs and drivers occupying space in conventional memory

```
C:\>mem /c | more

Conventional Memory :

  Name                 Size in Decimal       Size in Hex
  ----------------     ---------------------  -------------
  MSDOS                  12080      ( 11.8K)      2F30
  KBD                     3296      (  3.2K)       CE0
  HIMEM                   1248      (  1.2K)       4E0
  COMMAND                 3696      (  3.6K)       E70
  FREE                     112      (  0.1K)        70
  FREE                  634752      (619.9K)     9AF80

Total  FREE :           634864      (620.0K)

Upper Memory :

  Name                 Size in Decimal       Size in Hex
  ----------------     ---------------------  -------------
  SYSTEM                176112      (172.0K)     2AFF0
  MSCDEXNT                 464      (  0.5K)       1D0
  DOSX                   34848      ( 34.0K)      8820
  MOUSE                  12528      ( 12.2K)      30F0
  REDIR                   2672      (  2.6K)       A70
  FREE                     880      (  0.9K)       370
  FREE                    6640      (  6.5K)      19F0
  FREE                   27824      ( 27.2K)      6CB0

Total  FREE :            35344      ( 34.5K)

Total bytes available to programs (Conventional+Upper) :      670208   (654.5K)
Largest executable program size :                             633824   (619.0K)
Largest available upper memory block :                         27824   ( 27.2K)

    1048576 bytes total contiguous extended memory
          0 bytes available contiguous extended memory
     941056 bytes available XMS memory
            MS-DOS resident in High Memory Area
```

**FIGURE 6.15**
**The MEM command with the /C switch shows the contents of conventional and upper memory.**

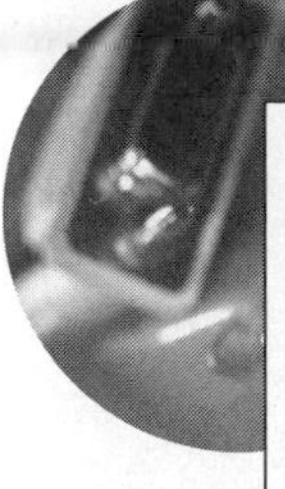

## In Real Life

The pipe symbol (a straight vertical line) is located in different spots on different keyboards. Follow it with the word MORE to make a long listing appear screen-by-screen. Some MS-DOS commands support a /P switch that does the same thing, and in some versions of MS-DOS, the MEM command serves that purpose. The | MORE trick works in all versions.

## TRY IT!

Try the MEM and MEM /C commands at a command prompt, either from MS-DOS or from a prompt within Windows. If possible, try it from both places and compare the results. You can get to a plain DOS prompt from a Windows 9x system by pressing F5 at startup when you see the message *Starting Windows.*

The main goal of memory management under MS-DOS is to keep conventional memory free for running programs. The secondary goal is to make the system's extended memory available to programs that require either EMS or XMS memory. Both of these goals are accomplished by editing the startup configuration files CONFIG.SYS and AUTOEXEC.BAT (in DOS 5.0 and above). These are both plain-text files that you can edit in a text editing program.

In DOS 6.0 and higher there is an automated utility called MEMMAKER that can make the edits to your startup files described in the following section. MEMMAKER is useful to know about because it is fairly easy to run and it can correct problems that inexperienced users introduce by trying to adjust memory management settings manually. However, students preparing to be professional PC technicians should learn the manual method of making the edits rather than relying on MEMMAKER, because the utility is not available in DOS 5.0, and because making the edits manually can often free up a little more conventional memory than MEMMAKER can accomplish.

### *Using EDIT*

MS-DOS comes with a text editor called EDIT that works well for editing CONFIG.SYS and AUTOEXEC.BAT. To start it, key **EDIT** at the command prompt. To edit a particular file, enter its path and name after the EDIT command; for example, EDIT C:\CONFIG.SYS. If the file already exists, it opens; otherwise EDIT creates a new file with that name.

EDIT works just like a regular word processing program, but it is even simpler because there is no formatting. The only inconvenience is that if

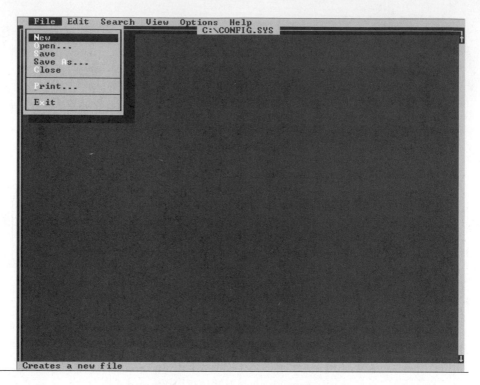


**FIGURE 6.16**
Hold down Alt plus a bold letter to open a menu or select a command with the keyboard in EDIT.

you do not have a DOS-based driver for your mouse, you must use the keyboard to control the menu system. To open a menu, hold down the Alt key and press the key for the bold letter in the menu name; to select a command from a menu, key the bold letter in its name (see Figure 6.16). When you are finished, save your work with the File, Save command (Alt + F, S) and then exit with the File, Exit command (Alt + F, X).

### *Editing CONFIG.SYS*

Open CONFIG.SYS in EDIT and then perform the following actions to optimize memory management under MS-DOS:

- If the line DEVICE=C:\DOS\HIMEM.SYS does not already appear, add it at the top of the file, on its own line. If it appears but with some other location than DOS (for example, WINDOWS), leave it.
- If the line DEVICE=C:\DOS\EMM386.EXE does not already appear, add it directly beneath the HIMEM.SYS line. Again, if WINDOWS appears in the path instead of DOS, that is all right.
- If the line DOS=HIGH,UMB does not appear, add it directly beneath the EMM386.EXE line.

Now save your work, exit EDIT, and reboot. These changes have loaded DOS into high and upper memory as much as possible, freeing up some conventional memory. They have also paved the way for loading device drivers into high memory, which you will do next. But first you need to know what drivers are currently taking up space in conventional memory and how much space they are taking. Use the MEM /C | MORE command again and make a note of the contents of conventional memory. Jot down the names of the files in order from largest to smallest. For example, you might have a list like this:

| | |
|---|---|
| OAKCDROM | 35K |
| MSCDEX | 23K |
| MOUSE.SYS | 12K |
| ANSI | 4K |

Ignore MSDOS, HIMEM, and EMM386; do not include them on your list. Now go back to EDIT C:\CONFIG.SYS and find the line corresponding to the first item on your list (that is, the largest one). It will probably look something like this:

```
DEVICE=C:\CDROM\OAKCDROM.SYS
```

Change the word DEVICE to DEVICEHIGH, so it looks like this:

```
DEVICEHIGH=C:\ CDROM\OAKCDROM.SYS
```

Save your work, exit EDIT, and reboot; then use MEM /C | MORE again to see whether the line you modified caused that driver to be relocated to upper memory. Go through the whole process again, moving on to the next-largest driver that was in conventional memory, until you run out of room in upper memory. The reason you progress from largest to smallest is because each driver requires contiguous blocks of memory and you want to fill up the big spaces first with the big drivers and then try to wedge the little ones in the remaining niches.

## TRY IT!

**If you have access to a PC with MS-DOS 5.0 through 6.22, try the procedure outlined in this section for freeing up conventional memory. Do not try it on a Windows 95 or higher system, however, because those utilities and settings could interfere with Windows' automatic memory management.**

### *Editing AUTOEXEC.BAT*

Some of the items on the list you made from MEM in the preceding section did not appear in CONFIG.SYS because they are loaded in AUTOEXEC.BAT instead. CONFIG.SYS loads first as the system starts up, and then AUTOEXEC.BAT loads. The two files have different functions: CONFIG.SYS contains drivers that must load at startup, while AUTOEXEC.BAT is a batch file that runs a list of commands that should be run at startup but could conceivably be run at any time from a command prompt.

MS-DOS mouse drivers can be loaded in either place. If loaded in CONFIG.SYS they use the .SYS version: MOUSE.SYS. If loaded in AUTOEXEC.BAT they use the .COM version: MOUSE.COM.

Go through the same process with AUTOEXEC.BAT as you did with CONFIG.SYS, except instead of changing DEVICE to DEVICEHIGH, change LOAD to LOADHIGH or LH. If there is no LOAD command in front of a line in AUTOEXEC.BAT, simply add LOADHIGH or LH and then a space in front of it. So, for example, a line like this:

```
C:\MOUSE\MOUSE.COM
```

would become this:

```
LOADHIGH C:\MOUSE\MOUSE.COM
```

The end result of all this is the freeing of more conventional memory, which enables you to run larger MS-DOS programs without getting out-of-memory error messages.

## Windows Memory Management

Windows 95 and higher does a fairly good job of optimizing memory usage, especially on a system with enough RAM. ("Enough" RAM is somewhat subjective, but there are guidelines for each Windows version.)

### *Checking Memory Usage in Windows*

There are several places in Windows that report the amount of memory a system has and how it is used. To find out how much memory in general a PC has installed, right-click *My Computer* and choose Properties; then look on the General tab (see Figure 6.17). The figure shows Windows 98, but the report is similar in all versions.

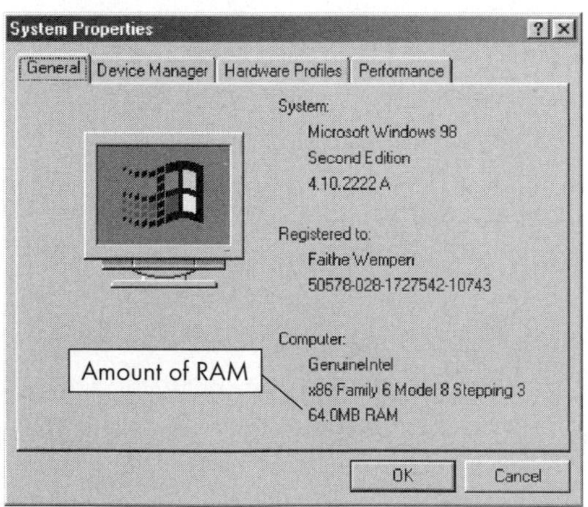


**FIGURE 6.17**
The General tab reports the amount of memory installed.

Much more detailed information about memory usage is available through the System Information utility (Start/Programs/Accessories/System Tools/System Information). Choose System Summary at the top of the folder tree, and then look at the memory specifications reported in the right-hand pane (see Figure 6.18). This figure shows Windows XP, but again the report is similar in all versions. The virtual memory and paging file shown in this figure are discussed in the next section.

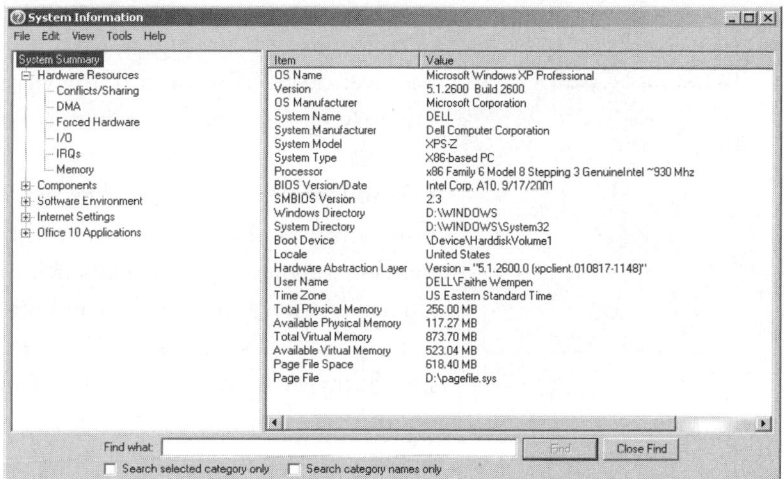


**FIGURE 6.18**
The System Summary in System Information reports the amount of physical and virtual memory.

## TRY IT!

Use System Information to find out how much memory your PC has installed.

### *Virtual Memory*

Recall from the discussion in Chapter 5 that 80386 and higher PCs can support virtual memory, a scheme for using part of the hard disk to simulate memory so that a program thinks it has more memory available than it actually has. Data is swapped into and out of the physical RAM from a *paging file* (also called swap file) on the hard disk. It is slower than regular memory, but it works.

**Paging file**

An area on the hard disk reserved for use as virtual memory. Also called a swap file because the OS swaps data into and out of main memory from it.

All versions of Windows make extensive use of virtual memory; without it Windows runs much more slowly and might not even run at all on systems without an ample amount of physical RAM.

## IN REAL LIFE

Windows 3.1 is not covered on the A+ exam, but here is a key fact about virtual memory in it: By default it sets up the swap file to be Temporary, but you will get much better performance by changing the setting to Permanent.

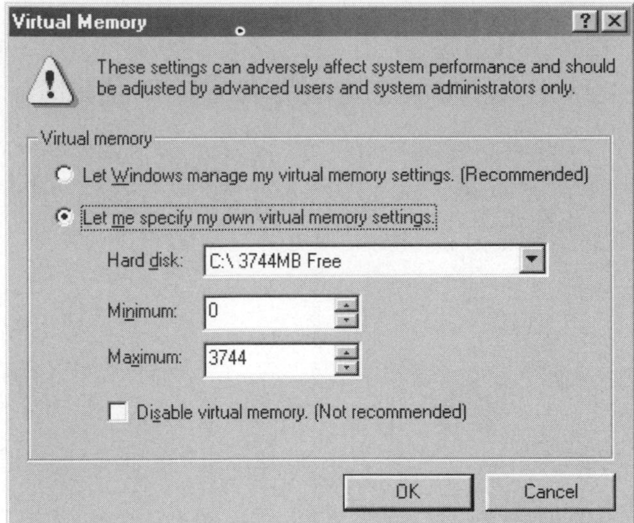


**FIGURE 6.19**
Virtual Memory Settings in Windows 95/98



**FIGURE 6.20**
Virtual Memory Settings in Windows 2000

The default virtual memory settings in Windows 95 and higher should seldom need to be modified. System Information reports the size of the paging file and the virtual memory usage, as you saw in Figure 6.18. In case you ever do need to modify the virtual memory settings, however, here is how to do it.

- **Windows 95/98:** Right-click *My Computer* and choose Properties. Select the Performance tab and then click the Virtual Memory button. To configure the settings manually, choose the Let me specify my own virtual memory settings option and then enter a location, minimum, and maximum (see Figure 6.19).
- **Windows 2000:** Right-click *My Computer* and choose Properties. Select the Advanced tab and then click the Performance Options button. Click the Change button under the *Virtual Memory* heading, and then select the drive and size options from the Virtual Memory dialog box (see Figure 6.20).
- **Windows XP:** Right-click *My Computer* and choose Properties. Select the Advanced tab and then click the Settings button in the Performance section. Select the Advanced tab in the Performance Options dialog box, and then click the Change button in the Virtual memory section. The dialog box that appears is the same as the one shown in Figure 6.20.

You might modify the virtual memory settings to place the paging file on a different drive than the default, for example. If the paging file is on your primary hard disk, and it is running out of room, relocating the paging file to a new, empty drive could make it perform better and could free up space on your primary hard disk for other uses.

# STUDY GUIDE

Use the following summaries to review the key concepts of this chapter.

## ROM

- ROM stands for Read-Only Memory; its content is permanent.
- Some types of ROM can be changed by using a special utility; this type of ROM is called flash ROM.
- There are two types of flash ROM: Erasable Programmable ROM (EPROM), which can be modified with ultraviolet light, and Electrically Erasable Programmable ROM (EEPROM), which can be modified with electricity.
- Another name for the programming on a ROM is firmware since it is between hardware and software.

## SRAM AND DRAM

- RAM stands for Random-Access Memory. It can be both read and written to freely.
- There are two types of RAM: Static (SRAM) and Dynamic (DRAM). Static RAM is used primarily for caches; Dynamic RAM is what most people mean when they talk about RAM.
- DRAM stores 1 values in charged capacitors. The capacitors must be constantly refreshed or they revert to 0 values.
- EDO DRAM is a type of DRAM in which the capacitors do not need to be refreshed as often, resulting in lower overhead.

## RAM STORAGE

- Each RAM chip has a width and a depth, like a spreadsheet.
- The width of a bank of RAM must be the same as the width of the address bus. Several RAM chips must be combined in order to achieve this width.
- RAM chips are combined on single inline memory modules (SIMMs) and dual inline memory modules (DIMMs). Each module is called a stick of memory.
- In some systems multiple sticks of memory work together to make up a single memory bank.
- SIMMs come in 30- and 72-pin varieties. A 30-pin SIMM has an 8-bit width. A 72-pin SIMM has a 32-bit width.

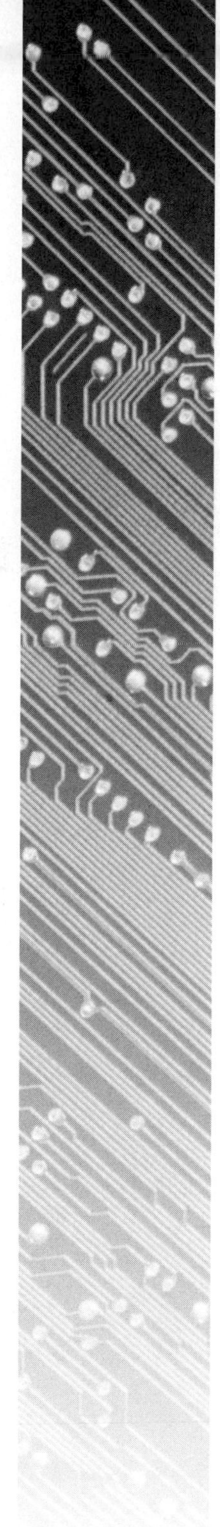

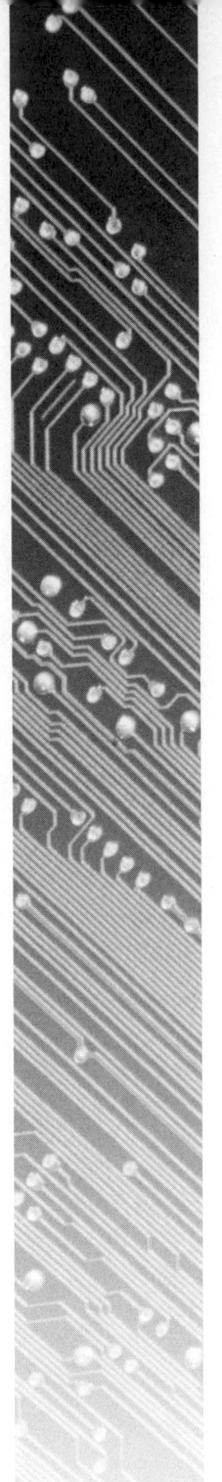

- DIMMs are 168-pin and have a 64-bit width.
- Some 72-pin SIMMs have an extra memory chip that functions as a parity bit for error correction purposes.
- SIMMs are usually fast page mode RAM, with speed measured in nanoseconds of delay in retrieval.
- DIMMs are usually synchronous dynamic RAM (SDRAM), with speed coordinated with the speed of the system bus.
- When selecting RAM for a motherboard, you must consider physical size, capacity, speed, parity, and any special technologies such as EDO.

## RAM INTERACTION WITH THE OPERATING SYSTEM

- A memory address is the address of a particular byte of memory in storage. It is logically assigned rather than assigned to a fixed physical location.
- The address bus width determines the number of available memory addresses on a system.
- To calculate the number of addresses, take 2 to the *n*th power where *n* is the bus width.
- Memory addresses are expressed in hexadecimal rather than binary numbering because it is easier to read. Four binary digits are converted to a single hexadecimal digit.
- The first 1MB of memory is divided into 640KB conventional memory and 360KB upper memory. This convention originated with MS-DOS.
- The 80286 PCs could accept expansion boards containing memory. This is expanded memory and the standard governing it is EMS (Expanded Memory Specification), also known as LIM (Lotus-Intel-Microsoft).
- The 80386 PCs and higher have memory above 1MB mounted on the motherboard through SIMMs and DIMMs. This is extended memory, and the standard governing it is XMS (eXtended Memory Specification).
- The first 64KB above the 1MB mark is high memory.
- The HIMEM.SYS driver manages extended memory and makes the high memory area available for storing part of DOS as it runs.
- The EMM386.EXE driver makes memory available in either XMS or EMS format as required and enables the upper memory area to store part of DOS as it runs.

## MEMORY MANAGEMENT IN MS-DOS

- To check memory usage in MS-DOS, use the MEM command at a prompt. For detailed information, use MEM /C.

- To increase conventional memory available in MS-DOS, edit CONFIG.SYS and AUTOEXEC.BAT to load as many drivers and utilities as possible into upper memory.
- MS-DOS comes with a text editor program called EDIT that can be used for editing these files.
- In CONFIG.SYS, load devices high by preceding the device name with DEVICEHIGH rather than DEVICE.
- In AUTOEXEC.BAT, load devices and programs high by preceding the device or program name with LOADHIGH or LH.

## MEMORY MANAGEMENT IN WINDOWS

- In Windows 9x and higher, you can check the amount of memory through the System Properties or through System Information.
- In most cases you should not modify the default virtual memory settings in Windows, but if you do need to do so, it is accomplished from System Properties. The exact steps depend on the Windows version.

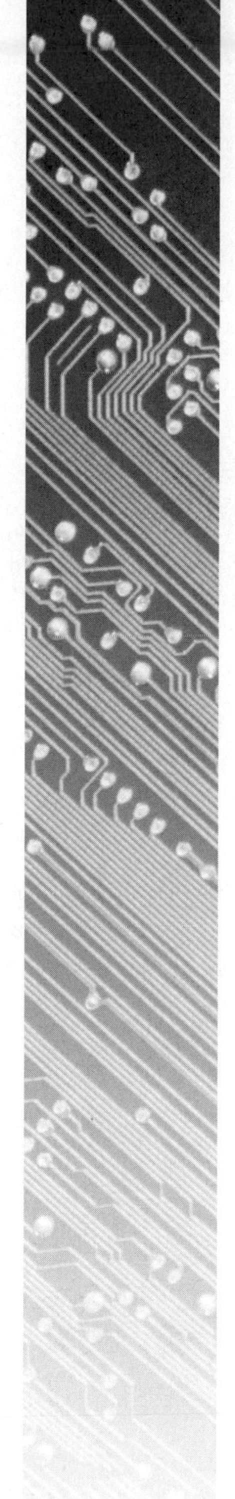

# PRACTICE TEST

On a blank sheet of paper, write the answers to the following multiple-choice questions and explain why each answer is correct.

1. What is the difference between ROM and RAM?
   a. ROM is volatile; RAM is nonvolatile.
   b. RAM is volatile; ROM is nonvolatile.
   c. ROM is read-only; RAM is writable.
   d. RAM is read-only; ROM is writable.

2. What does *nonvolatile* mean when referring to memory?
   a. It is programmable with ultraviolet light.
   b. It does not require constant refreshing of its capacitors to retain data.
   c. It stores BIOS setup data.
   d. It loses its data when you turn off the power.

3. Which of these memory types is volatile?
   a. ROM
   b. EEPROM
   c. SRAM
   d. DRAM

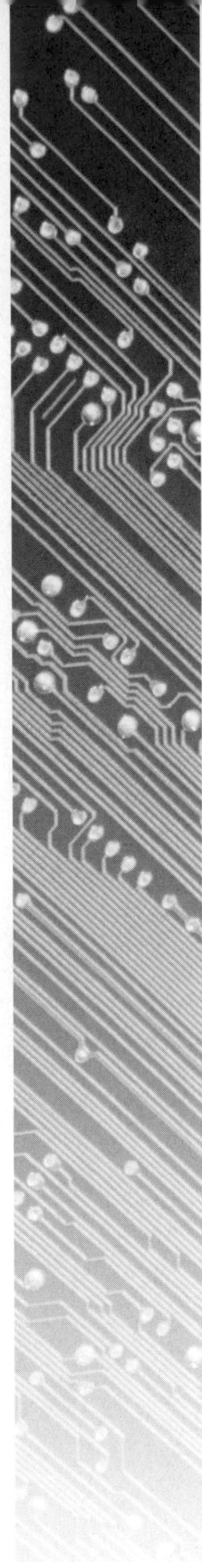

4. EEPROM is a type of ROM that
   a. can be erased and rewritten with electrical charges.
   b. can be erased and rewritten with ultraviolet light.
   c. can be erased only with a special ROM eraser tool.
   d. cannot be erased once it is created at the factory.

5. What is a common use for SRAM in a PC?
   a. ROM BIOS
   b. video RAM
   c. L2 cache
   d. main memory on motherboard

6. The width of a _________ of RAM must correspond to the width of the address bus.
   a. chip
   b. stick
   c. SIMM
   d. bank

7. How many physical RAM chips are there in a stick of memory?
   a. 3
   b. 8
   c. 9
   d. Can be any of the above

8. How many pins are on a DIMM?
   a. 30
   b. 72
   c. Can be either 30 or 72
   d. 168

9. What is the purpose of a parity bit?
   a. It speeds up transfer of data into RAM.
   b. It speeds up retrieval of data from RAM.
   c. It improves storage and retrieval reliability.
   d. All of the above

10. Which type of RAM measures its speed in nanoseconds of delay, with lower numbers being faster?
    a. FPM
    b. RIMM
    c. DIMM
    d. DDR SDRAM

11. Which of these RAM types is the fastest?
    a. FPM
    b. RIMM
    c. SDRAM
    d. DDR SDRAM

12. What is the capacity in megabytes of a 72-pin 16 x 36 SIMM?
    a. 16MB
    c. 36MB
    c. 64MB
    d. Cannot tell from information given

13. What is the capacity in megabytes of a 64-bit PC133 DIMM?
    a. 32MB
    b. 64MB
    c. 133MB
    d. Cannot tell from information given

14. Which of these would be a choice you would make when choosing SDRAM DIMMs?
    a. EDO versus FPM
    b. DDR versus non-DDR
    c. parity versus nonparity
    d. ECC versus non-ECC

15. What is the RAM limit for a system with a 32-bit address bus?
    a. 20MB
    b. 160MB
    c. 4GB
    d. 32GB

16. What hexadecimal character is represented by the binary number 1101?
    a. 11
    b. B
    c. C
    d. D

17. The first 1MB of memory in a DOS-based operating system is divided into two sections: conventional and
    a. upper.
    b. high.
    c. extended.
    d. expanded.

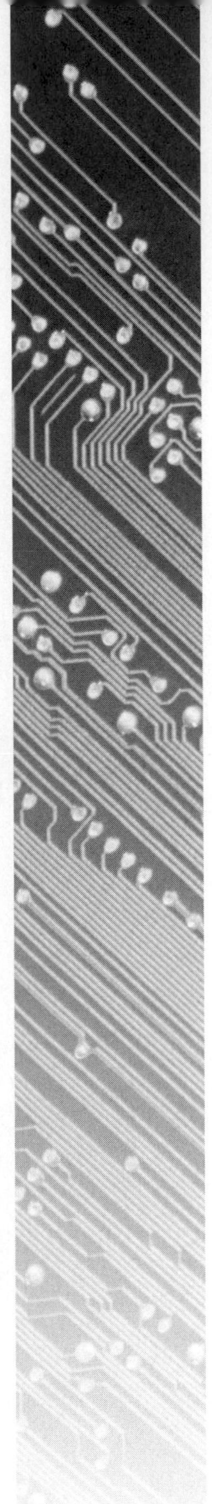

18. XMS is a standard for using what type of memory?
    a. extended
    b. expanded
    c. EMS
    d. high
19. To simulate EMS in MS-DOS for an application that requires it, you must load EMM386.EXE in
    a. AUTOEXEC.BAT.
    b. CONFIG.SYS.
    c. HIMEM.SYS.
    d. MEMMAKER.
20. Virtual memory is a method of simulating
    a. hard disk space by using memory.
    b. memory by using hard disk space.
    c. expanded memory by using extended memory.
    d. extended memory by using conventional memory.

# TROUBLESHOOTING

1. You are upgrading the memory on a Pentium motherboard. It currently has two 72-pin SIMMs, 8MB each, for a total of 16MB, and two empty 72-pin SIMM slots. You have a single 16MB SIMM that has been removed from a 486 motherboard, and it appears to be the same speed and type as the others already in the Pentium machine. Can it be used in one of the empty SIMM slots? Why or why not?
2. You are upgrading the memory on a Pentium III motherboard. It currently has two 32MB DIMMs labeled PC100. You have a 128MB DIMM labeled PC133 you would like to use in this system instead; will it work? Why or why not?
3. A client complains that his Windows 98 PC is running very slowly. Upon questioning, he admits that he has been tinkering with the system settings. You suspect he has probably done something to the virtual memory. How would you check this, and fix it if needed?

# CUSTOMER SERVICE

1. You get a phone call from a client requesting that you come to her office and upgrade the memory in her PC. What information can you gather from her over the phone that will help you bring the right type of memory with you?
2. A client asks you whether you think he needs a memory upgrade. He does not know how much RAM he currently has or what Windows version he is running. When questioned further, he does say that it is a Windows version that has a Start button in the lower left corner, so you know it must be at least Windows 95. Describe the steps you would walk him through over the telephone to determine how much RAM is installed.
3. You happen to have the original manual for a PC that needs a memory upgrade, and the manual specifies that the PC requires 60ns EDO RAM. You check all of the local computer stores, but nobody sells that anymore. What are your options?

# FOR MORE INFORMATION

For links to Web sites that provide further information about the topics covered in this chapter, go to the EMC/Paradigm Internet Resource Center at www.emcp.com/College Division/Internet Resource Centers/PC Maintenance/For More Information.

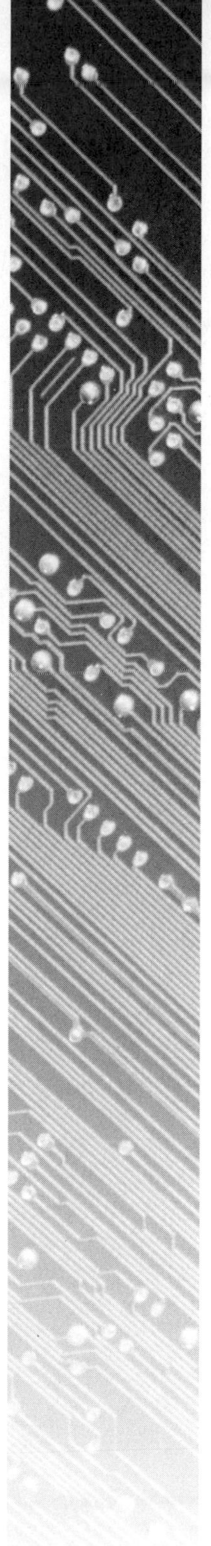

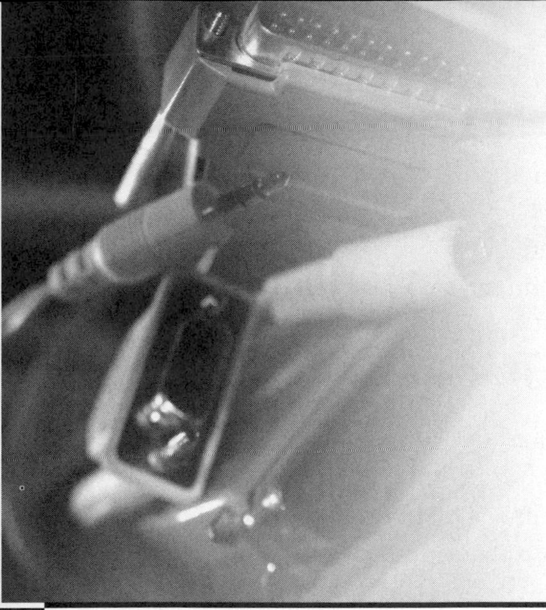

# 7 Cables

## ON THE TEST

**A+ Core Hardware Service Technician Examination**

- **Objective 1.1:** Identify basic terms, concepts, and functions of system modules, including how each module should work during normal operation and during the boot process.
- **Objective 1.4:** Identify common peripheral ports, associated cabling, and their connectors.
- **Objective 1.7:** Identify proper procedures for installing and configuring peripheral devices.
- **Objective 2.1:** Identify common symptoms and problems associated with each module and how to troubleshoot and isolate the problems.
- **Objective 6.1:** Identify basic networking concepts, including how a network works and the ramifications of repairs on the network.

## ON THE JOB

Computers have two ways of moving data. One is buses, which we have talked about extensively in the last several chapters. The other is cables. Whenever data has to leave a circuit board for any reason, it travels via cable. There are many types of cables, and part of a PC technician's job is to identify and install the correct cables for each purpose.

Sometimes the correct cable to use is obvious; the connector on the cable and the connector on the device match up perfectly. That is not always the case, however. Sometimes a cable with the wrong connector can be used along with an adapter; sometimes it cannot. And sometimes two cables with seemingly identical connectors can be very different when it comes to performance.

The information in this chapter may help you in these situations:

- choosing a ribbon cable for a high-speed hard drive
- connecting an external device to a serial port
- setting up a new printer
- changing the number of pins on a serial connector with an adapter
- advising end users about the length limitations of certain cable types

## Serial and Parallel Data Transmission

**Serial**

Transmitting one bit at a time.

**Parallel**

Transmitting several bits at the same time.

Cables transmit data with electrical pulses, just as buses do. Some cables transmit data *serially*—that is, one bit after another. Other cables transmit data in *parallel*—multiple "lanes" at a time. The following sections briefly explain these concepts. We will look into them in more depth later in the chapter when discussing specific types of cables.

### In Real Life

**When talking about a particular cable, it is tempting to blur the lines between a particular pin or wire in the cable and the purpose assigned to it. But try to keep in mind that a particular cable does not by itself transfer data in any particular way; a cable is just a bundle of wires strung together with connectors on the ends. The standards that govern the hardware and the operating system determine how the data is transferred. Although in this chapter we will cover the most common assignments for various pins and wires, be aware that a number of other possibilities exist.**

### Serial Data Transmission

In a serial cable, only one wire sends data in a certain direction at once, so data is sent in a single-file fashion. No two bits ever arrive at the same destination simultaneously (see Figure 7.1).

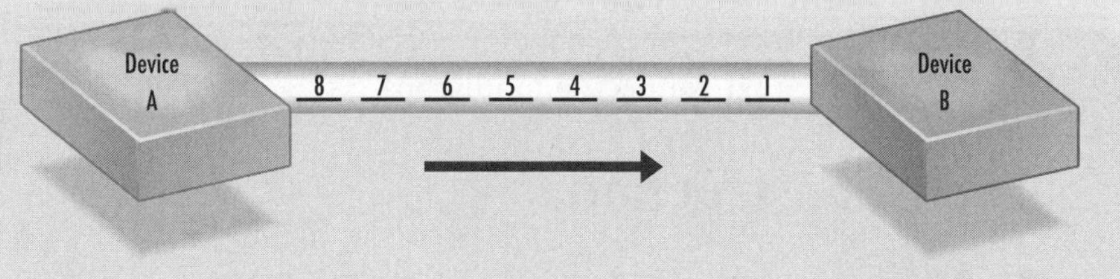


**FIGURE 7.1**
Serial Data Transmission

A typical serial cable has multiple wires in it, but each one has a different purpose. For example, there might be a wire for sending data, a wire for receiving data, a wire for detecting the presence of a device at the other end, a wire to signal to the other device that it is okay to start sending, a grounding wire, and so on.

The COM ports on the motherboard, and the cables that connect to them, are the most common serial connectors, to the point where the terms *COM port* and *serial port* have informally come to be synonymous. However, there are actually other types of serial cables and connectors, such as USB and FireWire, which we will look at later in this chapter. Some use the term *legacy* to differentiate the old COM style of serial connection from the more modern ones, so a COM port on a motherboard might be referred to as a legacy serial port.

## Parallel Data Transmission

A parallel cable has eight wires for transmitting data, each one carrying one bit of data at a time (see Figure 7.2). That means that, all other factors being equal, a parallel data cable could transmit data up to eight times faster than a serial cable. (That is assuming, of course, that the two are sending and receiving at the same speed, which is not necessarily the case.)

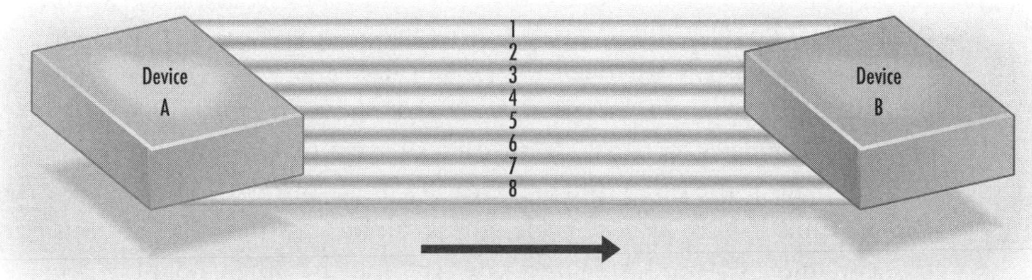


**FIGURE 7.2**
Parallel Data Transmission

A printer cable that attaches to an LPT port is the most common type of parallel cable. However, there are other parallel-type cables as well, such as the ribbon cable that connects a motherboard to a drive.

## Cable Construction

All cables have at least four parts: the connectors on each end, the conduit between them, and the casing or sheath surrounding the conduit that protects it from damage (see Figure 7.3).

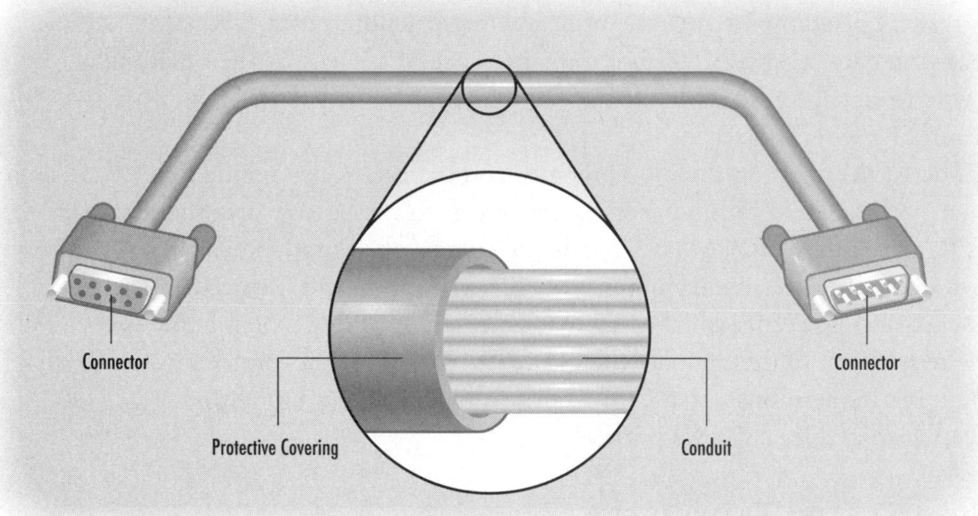


**FIGURE 7.3**
The Construction of a Typical Cable

**Male**

A connector having pins that fit into holes or slots in a female connector.

**Female**

A connector having holes or slots into which a male connector fits.

**Gender changer**

An adapter that switches between male and female connectors.

The conduit is usually metal wire because of its ability to carry electricity efficiently. However, some types of cable, such as fiber-optic, transfer data via light pulses rather than electrical pulses and use a conduit that is light conductive (tiny strands of glass fiber, for example) rather than electricity conductive.

Some cables have the same connectors at both ends; others have different connectors. For example, a printer cable has a different connection for connecting to the PC than for the printer itself.

Cable connectors can be either *male* (that is, having pins) or *female* (having receptacles for pins). Most cables have a male connector at one end and a female at the other, but some cables break this general rule; a parallel printer cable is male at both ends, for example: a 25-pin DB connector at one end and a 36-pin Centronics connector at the other. Adapters are available that can change a connector between male and female (for example, to create an extension cable); these are called, appropriately, *gender changers*.

The protective sheath can be as simple as some clear plastic, as with a typical telephone cord. If a cable's covering protects against EMI (electromagnetic interference), it is called *shielded* cable. If it is there only to keep out water, dirt, and other normal environmental pollutants, it is *unshielded* cable. Later in the chapter, when you learn about twisted pair cabling, you will see that this distinction can be important.

**Shielded cable**

A cable with an outer covering that reduces or eliminates EMI.

**Unshielded cable**

A cable without EMI shielding.

## Pin-Out Diagrams

The connectors match up the strands from the conduit to pins or tabs that match up with the connector on a device. The arrangement of specific wires to specific pins is called the pin-out. To determine what each pin on a cable does, you must consult a *pin-out diagram* for that cable.

**Pin-out diagram**

A diagram that tells the purpose of each pin or hole on a connector.

There are two parts to a pin-out diagram: the picture of the connector with numbered pins, and a table telling the purpose of each pin (Figure 7.4). The picture is necessary in order to know where the numbering starts. On a female connector, the numbering usually runs from left to right; on a male connector, it is usually right to left. When you plug one into the other, the pins must match up.



| Pin | Name | Description |
|---|---|---|
| 1 | CD | Carrier Detect |
| 2 | RXD | Receive Data |
| 3 | TXD | Transmit Data |
| 4 | DTR | Data Terminal Ready |
| 5 | GND | System Ground |
| 6 | DSR | Data Set Ready |
| 7 | RTS | Request to Send |
| 8 | CTS | Clear to Send |
| 9 | RI | Ring Indicator |

**FIGURE 7.4**
A Pin-Out Diagram for a 9-Pin Serial Port

In Figure 7.4 the pin-out is the same at both ends of the cable. On some cables, however, this is not the case. For example, a parallel printer cable has different connectors at each end, and the wires do not match up one-for-one from end to end. Another example is a serial cable that has 9 pins on one end and 25 pins on the other; the extra 14 pins are unused. To test such a cable, you would need a pin-out diagram showing which pins on the 25 end correspond to which pins on the 9 end, as illustrated in Figure 7.5. The pins with the same purpose are physically connected by the cable conduit; the conduit wire crosses over inside the cable, so that the position at one end is not representative of the physical position at the other.

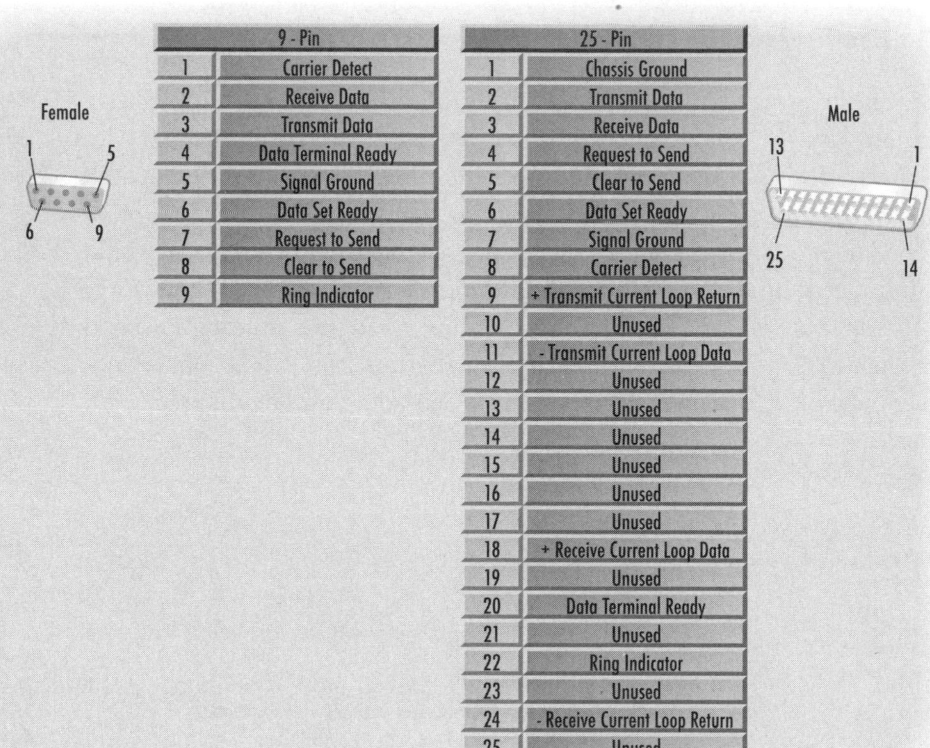


| 9 - Pin | |
|---|---|
| 1 | Carrier Detect |
| 2 | Receive Data |
| 3 | Transmit Data |
| 4 | Data Terminal Ready |
| 5 | Signal Ground |
| 6 | Data Set Ready |
| 7 | Request to Send |
| 8 | Clear to Send |
| 9 | Ring Indicator |

| 25 - Pin | |
|---|---|
| 1 | Chassis Ground |
| 2 | Transmit Data |
| 3 | Receive Data |
| 4 | Request to Send |
| 5 | Clear to Send |
| 6 | Data Set Ready |
| 7 | Signal Ground |
| 8 | Carrier Detect |
| 9 | + Transmit Current Loop Return |
| 10 | Unused |
| 11 | - Transmit Current Loop Data |
| 12 | Unused |
| 13 | Unused |
| 14 | Unused |
| 15 | Unused |
| 16 | Unused |
| 17 | Unused |
| 18 | + Receive Current Loop Data |
| 19 | Unused |
| 20 | Data Terminal Ready |
| 21 | Unused |
| 22 | Ring Indicator |
| 23 | Unused |
| 24 | - Receive Current Loop Return |
| 25 | Unused |

**FIGURE 7.5**
The pin-out diagram for a cable with two different connectors shows which pins match up with one another in purpose.

## Connector Types

Next consider the physical types of connectors that a cable can have. The connector determines with what type of device a cable is physically capable of connecting. These do not necessarily correspond to a particular type or purpose of data transmission, although some of them happen to be used for only one cable type.

### TRY IT!

Find as many different connector types as you can on the PCs and peripherals available to you, and connect and disconnect each type to practice its use.

## BNC

*BNC* stands for British Naval Connector, or Bayonet-Neill Connector, depending on whom you ask. It has a metal ring with threads that tighten to hold the metal core of a coaxial cable in a socket (see Figure 7.6). The most popular use for it is for cable television, but it is also used for 10Base-2 Ethernet networking (now mostly obsolete; see Chapter 21). BNC connectors are used only on serial cables.

**BNC**

A type of connector with a metal core and heavy outer covering. A cable television cable is one example. *BNC* stands for British Naval Connector or Bayonet-Neill Connector.

**FIGURE 7.6**
A BNC

## D-sub (DB)

A *D-sub connector*, also called a DB, gets its name from the fact that the metal ridge around the pins is shaped like a capital D. It is the most common type of connector for PCs, and is found on the parallel and serial ports as well as on the video card, MIDI port, and joystick port. These are usually described as "DB" plus the number of pins, and identified as either male or female. For example, a typical serial cable that plugs into a PC's COM port is DB-9 or DB-25 female. A D-sub connector can be used for either parallel or serial cables (see Figure 7.7).

**D-sub connector**

A type of connector with a D-shaped metal ridge around multiple rows of pins or holes (usually two or three rows).

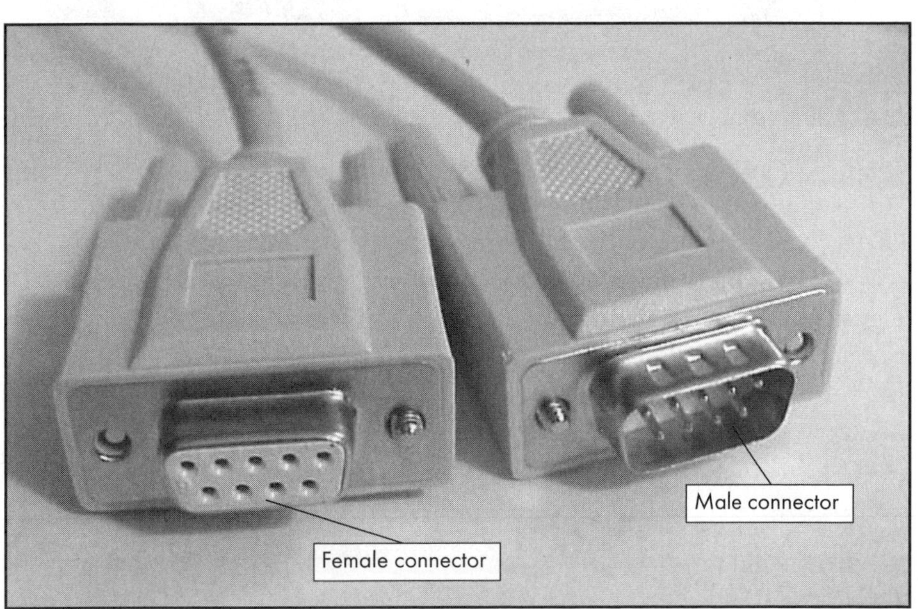


**FIGURE 7.7**
DB-9 Connectors (Female and Male)

## CENTRONICS

**Centronics**

A type of connector consisting of a solid bar with pins on either side that fits into a trough-style connector and is secured with wire loops.

*Centronics* is a parallel type of connector most typically used to connect a parallel printer cable to a printer, but also used for some types of external SCSI (Small Computer Systems Interface) devices (see Chapter 11). The male Centronics connector (on the cable) has a plastic bar on which rows of flat metal pieces are mounted. These are called pins just as on a DB connector, even though they are not pointed. The female Centronics connector (on the device) has a channel for that plastic bar, and inside the channel are more metal pieces that correspond to those on the cable (see Figure 7.8). On both ends of the female Centronics connector are wire loops for holding the male connector in place.

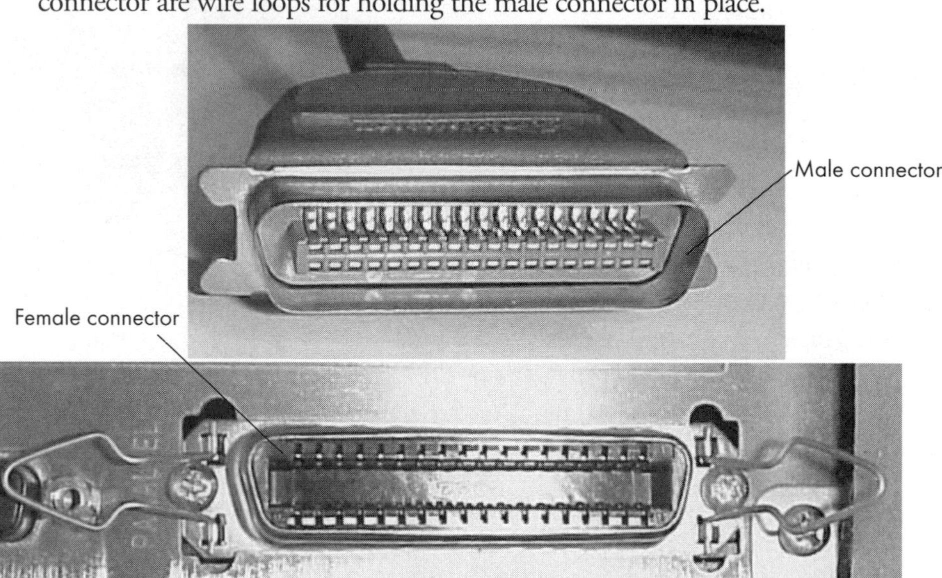


**FIGURE 7.8**
Centronics Connectors (Female and Male)

## RIBBON CONNECTORS

At each end of the ribbon cable is an identical connector consisting of a grid of holes; these plug into a grid of pins on a circuit board or drive. Figure 7.9 shows a typical ribbon cable connector. Ribbon cables are discussed in more detail later in this chapter.

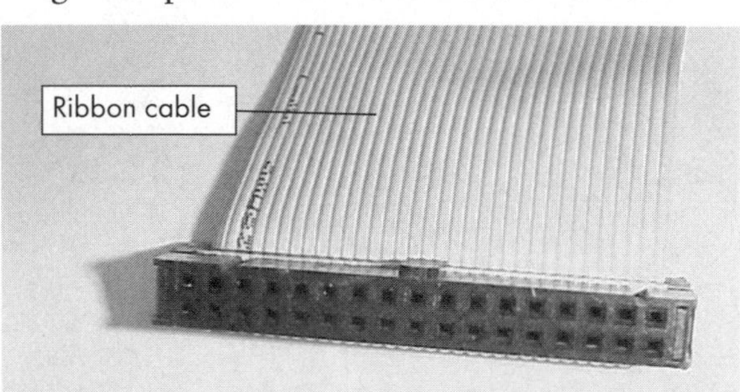


**FIGURE 7.9**
A Ribbon Connector

## RJ

Nearly everyone has seen RJ connectors, but perhaps did not know what they were called. A telephone cable is an RJ-11 (single-line) or RJ-14 (dual-line). A similar type of cable called RJ-45 is used for Ethernet networking; it is just like a telephone cable but slightly wider. RJ cables transfer data serially.

### In Real Life

Some people do not make a distinction between RJ-11 and RJ-14; they call them both RJ-11.

Figure 7.10 shows all three types of RJ connectors. Notice that the RJ-11 cable has only two metal wires in its connector, while the RJ-14 has four and the RJ-45 has eight. Even though there are multiple wires, these are still serial cables; they send only one bit of data at a time in either direction. This type of cable is known as *twisted pair;* you will learn more about it later in this chapter.

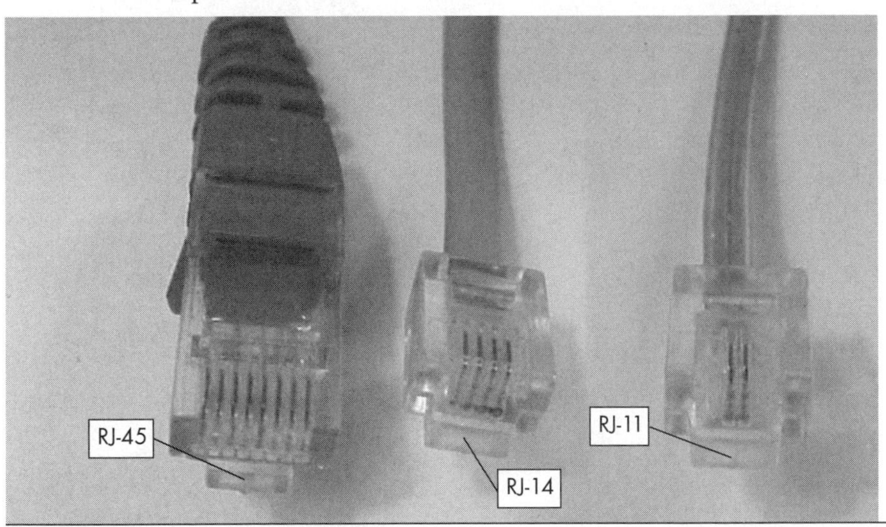


**FIGURE 7.10**
RJ-45, RJ-14, and RJ-11 Connectors

## DIN and Mini-DIN (PS/2)

**DIN connector**

The standard five-pin connector for an AT-style keyboard. *DIN* stands for Deutsche Industrie Norm.

A *DIN* connector is a keyboard connector on an AT-style motherboard. *DIN* stands for Deutsche Industrie Norm, which was the German committee that came up with the standard. It has five pins, with the male end on the cable and the female end on the motherboard. The pin

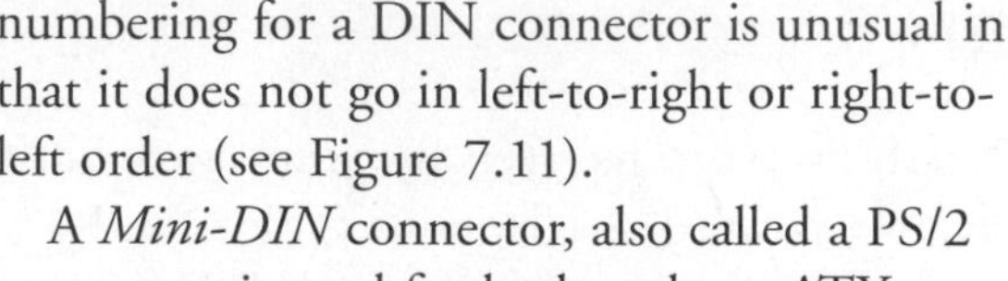

numbering for a DIN connector is unusual in that it does not go in left-to-right or right-to-left order (see Figure 7.11).

A *Mini-DIN* connector, also called a PS/2 connector, is used for keyboards on ATX motherboards and also for the PS/2-style mouse (see Figure 7.12). The standard type has six pins, and is smaller than a regular DIN (hence the name Mini-DIN). There is also a four-pin variety used for video in home theater systems, but it is not common in PCs.

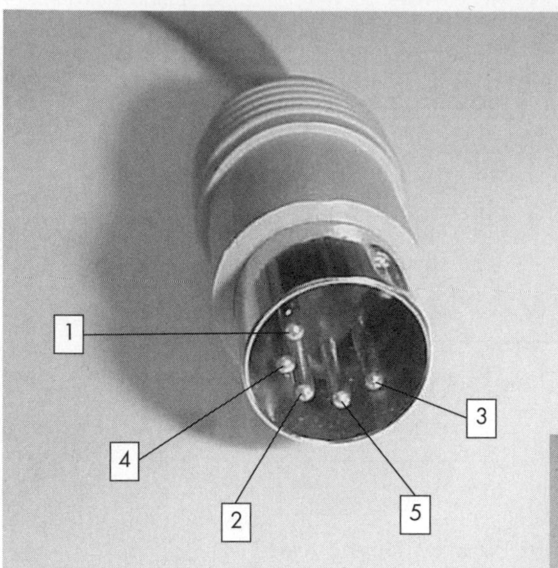


**FIGURE 7.11**
A DIN Connector on a Keyboard Cable

**FIGURE 7.12**
A Mini-DIN Connector on a Mouse Cable

**Mini-DIN**

Another name for the PS/2-style connector, a round connector with six pins, smaller than a DIN connector.

Keyboards come with DIN or Mini-DIN connectors, but it is the same keyboard either way; you can buy an inexpensive adapter that will change between a DIN and a Mini-DIN plug.

## Audio Connectors

There are two types of audio connectors for a PC: internal and external. An internal audio connector is a small plastic connector that helps a few wires run from the sound card or motherboard to the CD drive; it enables you to play audio CDs through the PC's speakers (see Figure 7.13).

**FIGURE 7.13**
An Internal Audio Cable's Connector

An external audio connector hooks up the microphone and speakers to the sound card. It looks like the plug on a pair of headphones you would plug into a stereo system (see Figure 7.14).

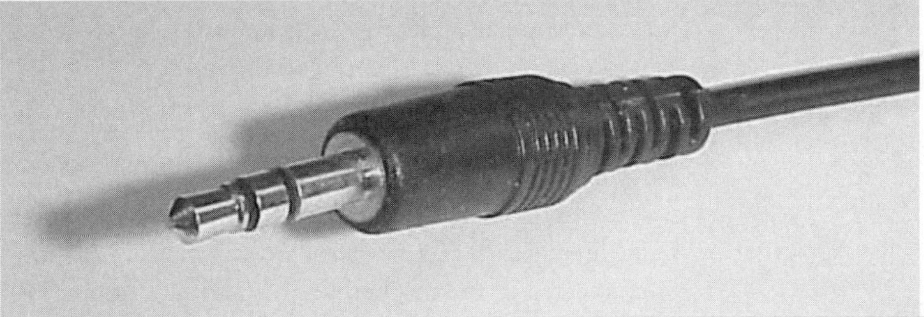

**FIGURE 7.14**
An External Audio Cable's Connector

## High-Speed Serial

There are two standards for high-speed serial data transfer: FireWire and Universal Serial Bus (USB). The connectors are different for each, and the cables have different connectors on each end. What they all have in common is that they are small, rectangular, box-shaped connectors. Figure 7.15 shows one end of a USB cable. FireWire and USB cabling are discussed in detail later in this chapter.

**FIGURE 7.15**
High-speed serial cables such as USB have rectangular connectors like this.

## Power

You are probably already familiar with both ends of the power cord that connects the PC to the AC outlet, as illustrated in Chapter 3. In that chapter we also covered the internal plugs on a power supply, both Molex and Mini.

Occasionally you may find a few other small power connectors in a computer system. For example, the fan on a CPU heat sink requires a power connector. A plug for it is usually built into the motherboard near the CPU slot or socket. The three-pin female connector on the fan looks like a small version of the Mini connector on the power supply (see Figure 7.16). If there are no pins on the motherboard through which to connect it, you can buy an adapter for a Molex connector that will step down the voltage to the appropriate running level.

**FIGURE 7.16**
The connector for the CPU fan is a miniature version of the Mini connector.

# Serial Cables and Ports

Now that you are familiar with the general sizes and shapes of connectors, let us look more closely at some of the most popular cables. We will start with serial cables—cables that send data one bit at a time.

## Legacy COM Ports and Cables

A typical PC has at least one built-in COM port, either built directly into the motherboard (in an ATX system) or connected to the motherboard via a small ribbon cable (in an AT). The COM port has been the most popular type of serial port in PCs for so long that the term *serial port* has come to be virtually synonymous with *COM port* and *serial cable* synonymous to *COM cable*. Only in the last several years have higher speed serial ports such as USB and FireWire become so widespread as to eclipse the popularity and universality of the COM port. Today these old-style COM ports are called "legacy." They are in the process of being phased out, so new systems that are bought in the next several years may not include them.

Early PCs had DB-25 COM ports, but not all of the pins were used. Later models had one DB-25 and one DB-9; modern PCs have only DB-9. The connector on the motherboard is male. The cable has one male end and one female end. Look back at Figure 7.4 for the pin-out of a DB-9 serial cable, and at Figure 7.7 for a photo of it.

The most common use for a COM port these days is to connect an external modem to a PC; other uses might include connecting the synch cradle for a PDA or connecting a "smart" UPS that is able to interface with Windows. Cables and converters are available to go from 9 to 25 pins or vice versa, depending on what connectors the PC and the device have. Figure 7.5 showed the pin-out for a 9-to-25 adapter cable.

**Universal Asynchronous Receiver Transmitter (UART)**

A controller chip for a COM port, determining the port's maximum throughput rate.

A COM port's maximum speed depends on the *Universal Asynchronous Receiver Transmitter (UART)* chip controlling it. This is usually built into the chipset of the motherboard for a built-in COM port. The standard UART on most motherboards these days is the 16550A, which can transfer data at up to 115Kbps. This is faster than a 56Kbps modem, so it works fine for a regular external modem. However, if you have a higher speed device such as an Integrated Services Digital Network (ISDN) terminal adapter, the limitation of the 16550A UART can inhibit the device's performance. There are two possible solutions: change to an internal version of the device that can run from a PCI expansion card, or add an extra COM port on an expansion card that has a higher speed UART. If you decide to do the latter, shop for a 16650, 16750, or 16850 UART. The difference among these three is the buffer size, and they can support speeds of up to 230Kbps, 460Kbps, or 920Kbps, respectively.

**There is no easy way to determine the UART that a serial port uses in Windows 2000/XP. In Windows 9x you can use the Diagnostics tab in the Modem Properties dialog box to check the properties for each COM port. A hardware diagnostics and testing program will probably report the UART type; see "For More Information" on the Internet Resource Center for this chapter to find some Web sites that sell hardware diagnostics programs.**

Since the latest devices are increasingly being developed for USB or FireWire interface rather than COM port, most users will never run out of COM ports on their PCs. However, if that does occur, you can add a PCI or ISA expansion card containing extra COM ports. Conversely, if you do not need all of the built-in COM ports in your system, you can disable one or all of them in the BIOS setup program to free up for other purposes the IRQs (Interrupt Requests) and I/O addresses assigned to them.

## USB

As stated earlier, *USB* stands for Universal Serial Bus, a high-speed serial port that is quickly replacing many of the older port types. USB versions of keyboards, mice, scanners, digital cameras, and many other devices are now available.

**Universal Serial Bus (USB)**

A high-speed, Plug and Play, hot-pluggable type of serial port found in most modern PCs.

USB has several advantages over the regular serial COM port. Some of the main benefits are:

- USB is faster. Whereas ordinary COM ports are limited to around 128Kbps, USB can run at between 12Mbps (USB 1.1 standard) and 400Kbps (USB 2.0 standard).
- Unlike legacy COM port devices, USB devices are hot-pluggable, so you can connect and disconnect them without turning off the PC.
- USB devices are fully compatible with Plug and Play, so Windows should recognize them automatically and immediately.

- You can chain up to 127 USB devices off a single USB port on a PC, and they will all share a single IRQ and I/O address. To do so, connect a multiport hub to the PC, and then connect devices or other hubs to that hub.

USB ports may be labeled USB, but more likely they will have a USB symbol to identify them, shown in Figure 7.17.

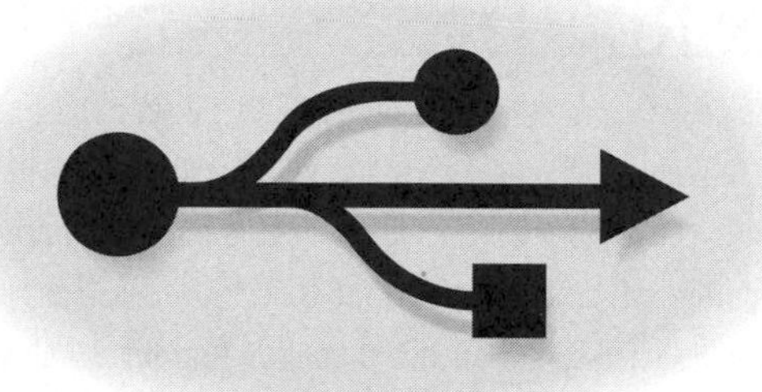

**FIGURE 7.17**
The Symbol for USB

A USB cable has four wires, and sends data by a method called No Return to Zero Invert (NRZI) encoding. With most cable connections, as with electricity, there are separate pins for the data lines and their grounding return lines. Look back at Figure 7.5, for example. With NRZI, there are two levels of electrical voltage: high and low. When the voltage changes, that is a 0. When it does not change, that is a 1.

USB cables typically have two different ends. On one end is the standard flat rectangular plug that fits into the USB connector on a PC or a hub; on the other end is a small square connector, slightly rounded on one side, that plugs into a USB device (see Figure 7.18). If you have a USB cable that has the flat plug on both ends, it is probably an extension cable that would run from hub to hub rather than a cable for a device.

**FIGURE 7.18**
A Typical USB Cable for a Device

One of the useful things about USB is that you can connect a hub to the PC's USB port and then shoot off multiple devices from that hub, so that all of those devices in effect share that single PC port. You can chain one hub to another, up to five levels deep. Inside the PC's chipset is the starting point hub for the USB connectivity, called the *root hub*. Each of the USB ports on the PC is considered a port on that hub. Some USB devices have both an input and one or more output ports, so they can serve as mini-hubs. For example, the keyboard in Figure 7.19 has two USB output ports in addition to being a USB device itself.

**Root hub**

The base-level USB hub in a system, usually built into the motherboard, into which all USB devices or hubs connect.

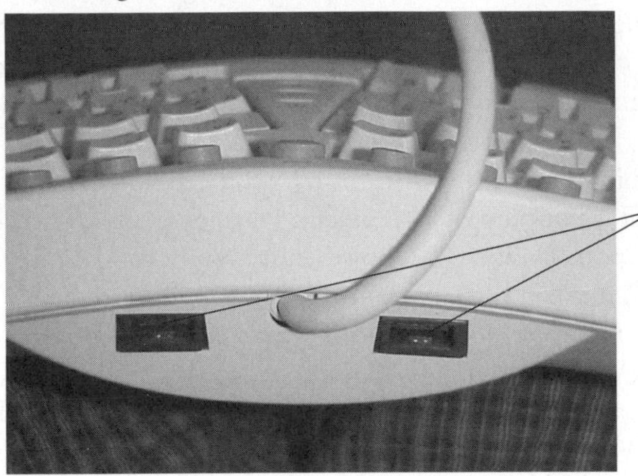


**FIGURE 7.19**
This USB keyboard also has two USB output ports, so it functions as a mini-hub.

A *USB hub* is different from a regular USB device (referred to as a *USB function*) because it acts as a repeater, strengthening and passing along the signals it receives. It also can function as a power source for small USB devices, so they do not need their own power supplies.

**USB hub**

A USB device whose function is to allow other USB devices to connect to the root hub. A USB hub is like an extension cord for USB.

**USB function**

A USB device that performs an end user function rather than simply acting as a hub.

There have been two standards for USB. The original was 1.0, which was quickly followed by 1.1. Older computers that have USB ports conform to this standard, which can support data transfer of up to 12Mbps. The current standard is USB 2.0, which is 40 times faster than USB 1.x and is fully backward compatible. At this writing, drivers and devices supporting USB 2.0 are just beginning to become available. You can mix and match USB devices and hubs of the two standards freely and everything will still work, but any 2.0 devices that are downstream from a USB 1.x hub will be limited to 1.x speeds.

## In Real Life

**Windows 95 does not support USB (except Windows 95c, an OEM version that came on some PCs). If a customer has a USB port but Windows cannot see it, check the Windows version number. Upgrade to Windows 98 or higher if needed.**

## TRY IT!

**With Windows running, disconnect a USB device. Then reconnect it and watch Windows redetect it automatically. This is hot-pluggable Plug and Play.**

## IEEE 1394 (FireWire)

**IEEE 1394**

A high-speed serial connection used to connect video equipment such as digital video cameras to a PC. Also called FireWire.

*IEEE* (Institute of Electrical and Electronics Engineers) is a standards board that establishes the specifications for new technologies. As technologies emerge, they are often called by their IEEE specification numbers until a catchier name is invented. This was the case with IEEE 1394 for so long that the standard number is almost as popular as the identification as FireWire.

FireWire is a lot like USB in that it is a high-speed serial type of connection that is hot-pluggable, Plug and Play-compatible, and chainable on a single PC port. Unlike USB, however, it has not caught on with mainstream PC makers, and support for it is not built into most motherboards. Therefore, to use it you need a PCI expansion card containing FireWire ports.

The primary advantage of FireWire is its speed; it can transmit data at up to 400Mbps. (Recall that the fastest the USB interface could achieve was 400Kbps.) Because of this high-speed capability, FireWire has been embraced by the digital video industry, and most digital camcorders have a FireWire port for transferring their data to a PC. Because of the tremendous size of digital video files, FireWire's ability to transfer a lot of data quickly makes it the best available choice for this purpose. There are new FireWire standards being proposed at this writing that will increase its speed even more, to up to 1,600Mbps or even higher.

FireWire PC adapter cards typically support 200Mbps data transfer, but most FireWire devices actually send and receive data at only 100Mbps. (That is still very fast.) FireWire allows for up to 63 chained devices from a single interface; devices can be *daisy-chained* without a hub (unlike USB).

**Daisy chained**

Connected from one device to the second, the second to the third, and so on.

The cables use six wires: four for data and two for power. The connectors are different on the two ends of the cable—the connector that goes into the PC's expansion card is tall and rectangular with a rounded end; the connector that goes into the device is small, short, and square or rectangular (see Figure 7.20).

## Parallel Cables and Ports

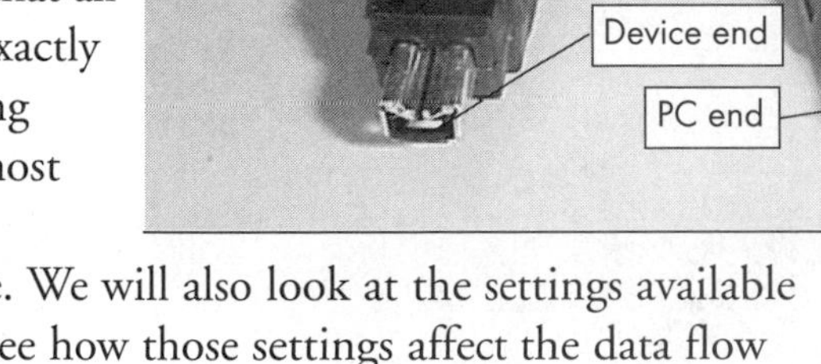

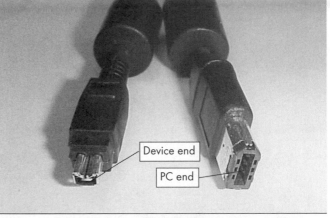

**FIGURE 7.20** This FireWire cable is designed to connect a digital camcorder to a PC.

As discussed at the beginning of this chapter, a parallel cable carries multiple bits of data simultaneously. It therefore must have more wires than a serial cable (generally speaking), and have a means of synchronizing the data bits so that all of the bits for one byte arrive at exactly the same moment. In the following sections we will look at the two most popular serial cables in a PC: the ribbon cable and the printer cable. We will also look at the settings available for the built-in parallel port and see how those settings affect the data flow through a parallel cable.

### Ribbon Cables

A *ribbon cable* gets its name from the fact that it is flat and wide like a piece of ribbon. A ribbon cable encloses each individual wire in its own plastic channel, minimizing interference between wires and enabling the cable to transmit the data at higher speeds than if the wires were simply jammed up against one another.

**Ribbon cable**

A parallel data cable in which the wires are arranged side-by-side and each wire is separated in its own plastic-covered channel.

Ribbon cables are used almost exclusively inside a PC; you will seldom see one that runs outside the case. Ribbon cables connect disk drives to the motherboard or to a controller card. Figure 7.21 shows a ribbon cable for connecting a typical IDE hard drive. Chapters 10 through 12 cover drives and their ribbon cables in more detail.

**FIGURE 7.21** Ribbon cables connect drives to the motherboard or interface card.

Different drive interface types use ribbon cables with different numbers of pins and holes. A floppy drive, for example, uses a 34-pin cable, while an IDE drive uses a 40-pin cable. The number of wires in the cable does not always match the number of holes or pins on the connectors; high-performance IDE drives use an 80-wire ribbon cable, for example, that is pin-compatible with 40-pin connectors.

Ribbon cable pins are numbered, as on the DB-style connectors shown earlier in this chapter. However, the pins are not numbered row-by-row, but rather column-by-column, so that 1 and 2 are at one end of the connector and 39 and 40 are at the other. Figure 7.22 shows the pin-out diagram for an IDE cable.

| Pin | Name |
|---|---|
| 1 | Reset |
| 3 | Data Bit 7 |
| 5 | Data Bit 6 |
| 7 | Data Bit 5 |
| 9 | Data Bit 4 |
| 11 | Data Bit 3 |
| 13 | Data Bit 2 |
| 15 | Data Bit 1 |
| 17 | Data Bit 0 |
| 19 | Ground |
| 21 | DMA request |
| 23 | Write strobe |
| 25 | Read strobe |
| 27 | I/O ready |
| 29 | DMA acknowledge |
| 31 | Interrupt request |
| 33 | Address Bit 1 |
| 35 | Address Bit 0 |
| 37 | IDE CS0 (1F0-1F7) |
| 39 | Drive Active/Slave Present |

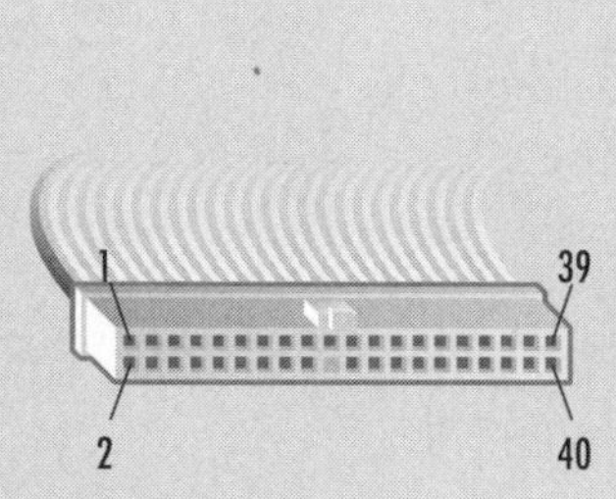


| Pin | Name |
|---|---|
| 2 | Ground |
| 4 | Data Bit 8 |
| 6 | Data Bit 9 |
| 8 | Data Bit 10 |
| 10 | Data Bit 11 |
| 12 | Data Bit 12 |
| 14 | Data Bit 13 |
| 16 | Data Bit 14 |
| 18 | Data Bit 15 |
| 20 | Key (pin missing) |
| 22 | Ground |
| 24 | Ground |
| 26 | Ground |
| 28 | Cable Select/Spindle Synch |
| 30 | Ground |
| 32 | Reserved/IO ChipSelect 16 |
| 34 | Passed Diagnostics |
| 36 | Address Bit 2 |
| 38 | IDE CS1 (3F6-3F7) |
| 40 | Ground |

**FIGURE 7.22**
Pin-Out for an IDE Cable

**Pin 1**

The first numbered pin in a connector. On connectors that can physically fit in either direction, locating Pin 1 and matching it to the Pin 1 indicator on the other connector ensures that the cable is oriented correctly.

Most ribbon cables have a specific orientation for use; they will not work if you plug them in upside down. However, the connectors on a ribbon cable can be physically oriented either way in most cases. To help eliminate the confusion, a ribbon cable has a red stripe along one edge; this red stripe designates *Pin 1*. On the connector into which it plugs, there will be a tiny "1" to indicate Pin 1; the cable must be plugged in so that the red stripe and the "1" are together.

As further improvement, a cable key was added, which is a little bump on the surface of one of the flat sides that fits into a notch in the connector so it is nearly impossible to connect the cable the wrong way. Another improvement was to plug up one of the holes on the connector (Pin 20) and remove the corresponding pin from the male connector. That makes the cable physically incapable of being connected upside down.

## In Real Life

On some older or less expensive systems, Pin 20 might not be missing from the IDE connectors on the motherboard. On such systems a cheaper, unkeyed IDE ribbon cable is used that does not have Pin 20 blocked out. If you have only a keyed cable to use with such a system, you can either break off Pin 20 from the IDE connector on the motherboard (a scary proposition because of the risk of bending or breaking other pins), try to pop out the spacer in the hole for Pin 20 on the cable, or use a different cable.

We will look at the cables that connect IDE and floppy drives in greater detail in Chapter 12.

## TRY IT!

Check the ribbon cables on all of your IDE drives to see which ones are keyed and which ones are not.

### Printer Cables

The terms *printer cable* and *parallel cable* have come to seem synonymous in popular usage, but a parallel printer cable is actually only one of many types of parallel cables. (Some printers can use a serial interface, too, like a legacy serial port or USB.) Therefore, it is somewhat misleading to call the legacy parallel port in a PC a "printer port."

A parallel printer cable has 25 pins at the PC end, and connects to a DB-25 female connector there. At the other end it has a male 36-pin Centronics connector. In Figure 7.23, which shows the pin-out for a parallel printer cable, notice that the purposes of the pins do not directly align even when they have the same purpose. Pins 1–14 are the same for both, but Pins 18–25 on the 25-pin end correspond with Pins 20–27 on the 36-pin end. Notice also that on a parallel printer cable, both ends of the connector are male (that is, they have pins rather than holes).

13 1
25 Male 14

| Pin | DB-25 Parallel |
|---|---|
| 1 | Strobe |
| 2 | Data Bit 0 |
| 3 | Data Bit 1 |
| 4 | Data Bit 2 |
| 5 | Data Bit 3 |
| 6 | Data Bit 4 |
| 7 | Data Bit 5 |
| 8 | Data Bit 6 |
| 9 | Data Bit 7 |
| 10 | Acknowledge |
| 11 | Busy |
| 12 | Paper End/Out |
| 13 | Select |
| 14 | Autofeed |
| 15 | Error |
| 16 | Initialize |
| 17 | Select in |
| 18 | Data Bit 0 Ground |
| 19 | Data Bit 1 Ground |
| 20 | Data Bit 2 Ground |
| 21 | Data Bit 3 Ground |
| 22 | Data Bit 4 Ground |
| 23 | Data Bit 5 Ground |
| 24 | Data Bit 6 Ground |
| 25 | Data Bit 7 Ground |
| 26 | |
| 27 | |
| 28 | |
| 29 | |
| 30 | |
| 31 | |
| 32 | |
| 33 | |
| 34 | |
| 35 | |
| 36 | |

18 1
36 Male 19

| Pin | Centronics 36-pin |
|---|---|
| 1 | Strobe |
| 2 | Data Bit 0 |
| 3 | Data Bit 1 |
| 4 | Data Bit 2 |
| 5 | Data Bit 3 |
| 6 | Data Bit 4 |
| 7 | Data Bit 5 |
| 8 | Data Bit 6 |
| 9 | Data Bit 7 |
| 10 | Acknowledge |
| 11 | Busy |
| 12 | Paper End/Out |
| 13 | Select |
| 14 | Autofeed |
| 15 | Not used |
| 16 | Logic Ground |
| 17 | Shield Ground |
| 18 | +5v DC |
| 19 | Strobe Ground |
| 20 | Data Bit 0 Ground |
| 21 | Data Bit 1 Ground |
| 22 | Data Bit 2 Ground |
| 23 | Data Bit 3 Ground |
| 24 | Data Bit 4 Ground |
| 25 | Data Bit 5 Ground |
| 26 | Data Bit 6 Ground |
| 27 | Data Bit 7 Ground |
| 28 | Acknowledge Ground |
| 29 | Busy Ground |
| 30 | Reset Ground |
| 31 | Reset Ground |
| 32 | Fault |
| 33 | Signal Ground |
| 34 | Not used |
| 35 | +5v DC |
| 36 | Select In |

**FIGURE 7.23**
A Pin-Out Diagram for a Parallel Printer Cable

## Parallel Port Modes

**IEEE 1284**

The specification governing parallel printer ports, outlining SPP, Bidirectional, EPP, and ECP modes.

The *IEEE 1284* standard (Standard Signaling Method for Bidirectional Parallel Peripheral Interface for Personal Computers), released in 1994, defined the modern standards for legacy parallel ports and modes. This standard defines four possible operating modes for a parallel port, listed in Figure 7.24.

- **SPP (Standard Parallel Port):** The original parallel port mode, designed primarily for output. It has eight-bit output at 150KB/sec and four-bit input at 50KB/sec.
- **Bidirectional:** An improved version of SPP that uses eight bits for both input and output. Other names for it are PS/2 or Extended. It transfers data at 150KB/sec in both directions.
- **Enhanced Parallel Port (EPP):** A faster standard for bidirectional parallel communication, this mode transfers eight-bit data at up to 2MB/sec. It was developed to support nonprinter parallel devices such as tape backup drives and external disk drives, but also works with printers.
- **Enhanced Capabilities Port (ECP):** Another fast standard, the same as EPP in speed and bit width but designed primarily for printers and scanners rather than external drives. It requires a Direct Memory Addressing (DMA) channel in addition to an IRQ (which all modes require).

**FIGURE 7.24**
Operating Modes for a Parallel Port

All computers sold today support at least the latter three modes listed in Figure 7.24. You can choose which mode you want the port to use by changing its setting in BIOS setup (see Chapter 9), as shown in Figure 7.25.

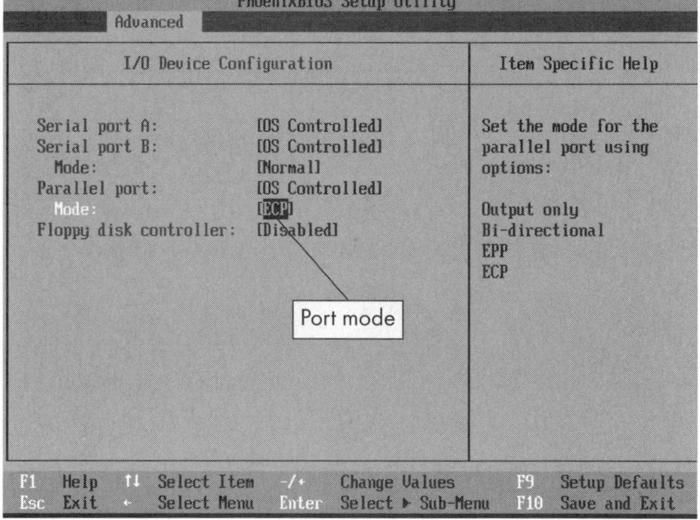


**FIGURE 7.25**
Changing the Parallel Port Mode in BIOS Setup

How do you know what mode to use? Here are some tips:

- Start out with ECP mode. It offers the best performance.
- If you are running low on DMA channels and cannot spare one for ECP mode (see Chapter 14 for details), switch to EPP mode.
- If your printer and scanner or other device are sharing the printer port using a pass-through and you are having problems with either device, switch to Bidirectional.
- If you are currently using Bidirectional and are having problems with devices sharing the port, try EPP and then ECP in turn to see whether either of them resolves the problem.

## Direct Parallel Cables

A direct parallel cable, also called a parallel pass-through cable, is just like the 25-pin male end of a parallel printer cable (see Figure 7.23) except it is the same pin-out for both ends. Both ends are usually male, and this type of cable is typically used to connect two PCs directly via their parallel ports. This enables users to create a makeshift "network" for transferring data when there are no network interface cards available. The parallel port is good for such a purpose because it can transfer multiple bits of data at once, but is not widely used for networking because it has a range limitation of about 10 feet.

Windows includes a utility called Direct Cable Connection that sets up such a connection. To use it, connect both PCs via a direct parallel cable and then run the Direct Cable Connection Wizard on each PC and follow the prompts. In Windows 9x you will find Direct Cable Connection on the Accessories/System Tools submenu of the Start menu. If it is not there, try using Add/Remove Programs to install it. In Windows 2000 and XP, you use the Network Setup Wizard to establish a direct cable connection.

**TRY IT!**

Connect two PCs with a direct parallel cable and then try establishing a connection between them with the Direct Cable Connection Wizard in Windows. Transfer a file from one PC to another using this connection.

## Network Cabling

In Chapters 21 and 22 you will learn how to set up a network, but look now at the types of cables used in a network. All of these are serial cables.

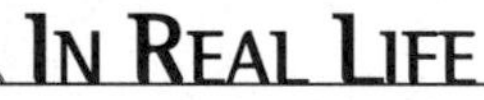

**IN REAL LIFE**

The following sections introduce several types of network cables, but in real-life usage the vast majority of today's networks use a single type of cabling: UTP (Unshielded Twisted Pair) Category 5. You will learn what that is later in this chapter.

**TRY IT!**

If you have a network set up in your work area, identify which type of cabling it uses.

### THICK ETHERNET

Originally networks all used thick coaxial cable ("co-ax"), about .5 inch in diameter. Coaxial cable is the type of cable used for cable and satellite TV connections; it has a center wire core covered by insulation, and then wrapped in a wire-mesh outer casing that acts as an EMI shield.

This original type of network cabling is still used in some old networks. The most common use for it is in a *10Base-5* Ethernet network. (Ethernet is a type of network, and the 10 refers to the bits per second it can transfer: 10Mbps. This will be explained in greater detail in Chapters 21 and 22.) Because of the size of the cables, this type of cabling is known as *thick Ethernet* or *thicknet.* It can carry data up to 1,640 feet (500 meters).

One feature of thick Ethernet cable is that it has a mark on it every 8.2 feet (2.5 meters) indicating where devices must be connected. This minimum amount of spacing per device is required to keep line noise to a minimum.

Devices do not connect directly to the thick Ethernet cable; a single cable stretches through the whole network segment. Each device uses a "vampire" connector, a transceiver that pierces the cable (you attach it at one of the marked spots) to tap into it. The transceiver box has a cable with female DB-15 connector that attaches to the network interface card in the PC.

Thick Ethernet cabling is rare these days; most of it has been replaced by network cabling of a newer technology.

**Thick Ethernet**

An older type of Ethernet network cabling, consisting of .5-inch coaxial cable. Also called thicknet.

**10Base-5**

An older type of Ethernet network capable of transmitting data at up to 10Mbps and using thick Ethernet cabling.

## Thin Ethernet

*Thin Ethernet* cable is also called *thinnet.* It is still coaxial cable, but a thinner type, more like the type used for television cable, making it easier to work with. Another name for this type of networking is *10Base-2.* The 10 refers to the speed: 10Mbps.

**Thin Ethernet**

A type of coaxial Ethernet cable used for 10Base-2 networking. Also called thinnet.

**10Base-2**

An older type of Ethernet network capable of 10Mbps and using thin Ethernet coaxial cabling.

### In Real Life

**Coaxial cable designed for cable or satellite television is a different grade from the type used in networking; they are not interchangeable. Television cable is RG-6 rated, and will not work for networking (at least not very well). Thinnet cable is RG-58. It will work for television, but it is expensive so there is little reason to use it for that.**

A 10Base-2 network uses BNC connectors to connect each PC rather than a vampire transceiver, so it is much easier for a beginner to run the cabling. A T-shaped connector is attached to a network card, and separate pieces of cable connect to either side of the T so that the network signal passes through it.

Thin Ethernet is not as robust a network cabling system as thick Ethernet. It supports only 30 devices on a segment (thicknet supports 100), and the segments must be shorter (607 feet [185 meters] as opposed to

1,640 feet [500 meters]). Consequently, its use has traditionally been limited to smaller networks. Like thicknet, thinnet is becoming obsolete because faster types of cabling with greater range are supplanting it.

## Twisted Pair

**10Base-T**

A type of Ethernet network capable of transmitting data at up to 10Mbps using unshielded twisted pair cables.

**100Base-T**

A type of Ethernet network capable of transmitting data at up to 100Mbps using unshielded twisted pair cables.

Twisted pair cabling is by far the most popular type used for networking today. It consists of one or more pairs of color-coded 22- to 26-gauge wire, twisted around one another at certain intervals within the cable sheath. The most common use for twisted pair cables is in a *10Base-T* or *100Base-T* network. It is also used for telephone lines, both regular and ISDN. This type of cabling is also called RJ, although RJ more accurately refers to the connectors at the ends of the cable rather than the cable itself. In Figure 7.10 you saw several types of RJ connectors. They differed in the number of tiny metal wire prongs in the connector. Each of those prongs represents a wire in the cable; for example, a cable with four pairs in it would have an eight-wire, RJ-45 connector on each end.

### *Shielded or Unshielded*

**STP**

A type of network cabling with EMI shielding. Stands for shielded twisted pair.

**UTP**

A type of network cabling with no EMI shielding. Stands for unshielded twisted pair.

Twisted pair cables can be either shielded or unshielded. Shielding has to do with the protection from EMI, not the physical protection from the elements. Cable with a thick rubber coating could still be considered unshielded cable. Shielded twisted pair cabling is often abbreviated *STP;* unshielded is *UTP*. Most network cable is UTP because the shielding makes it more expensive. Therefore, STP is used only in situations where EMI is a problem.

### *UTP Categories*

There are various categories of UTP cabling (refer to Figure 7.26). IT professionals refer to cable as "Cat" plus a number, as in Cat5 or Cat6. Higher categories are more expensive, but carry data farther and faster. It is important to know about these categories so you can select the best combination of cost and performance for a given project.

- **Category 1:** Traditional telephone cable, consisting of one or two twisted pairs. Cannot be used for networking because it cannot transmit data, only analog sound.
- **Category 2:** Four twisted pairs. Can transmit data up to 4Mbps.
- **Category 3:** Four twisted pairs, each twisted three times per foot. Can transmit data up to 16Mbps.
- **Category 4:** Four twisted pairs. Can transmit data up to 20Mbps.
- **Category 5:** Four twisted pairs. Can transmit data up to 100Mbps.
- **Category 6:** Four twisted pairs. Can transmit data up to 155Mbps.

**FIGURE 7.26**
Categories of UTP Cabling

You can use a higher category than required for a particular job, but not a lower one. For a 10Base-T network, which needs to be able to carry data up to 330 feet (100 meters) at up to 10Mbps, you need Cat3, Cat5, or Cat6. For a 100Base-T network you need Cat5 or Cat6, to carry data up to 330 feet (100 meters) at 100Mbps.

## In Real Life

In most networking applications only two of the four pairs of wires are actually used: one pair for sending and one pair for receiving The extra two pairs exist to cover the bases for future expandability. Therefore, two-pair cable theoretically would be adequate for networking, except that the only two-pair cabling sold today is Cat1, which is unsuitable for data in other ways.

### *UTP Wire Colors*

The "pins" in a UTP connector are numbered from right to left as you are looking at the plug with the release tab facing the floor (see Figure 7.27).

There are two standards for the wire colors in cables: EIA/TIA 568A and EIA/TIA 568B, established by the Electronics Industries Association/Telecommunication Industries Association. The two standards prescribe slightly different wire colors inside a UTP cable, as shown in Table 7.1.

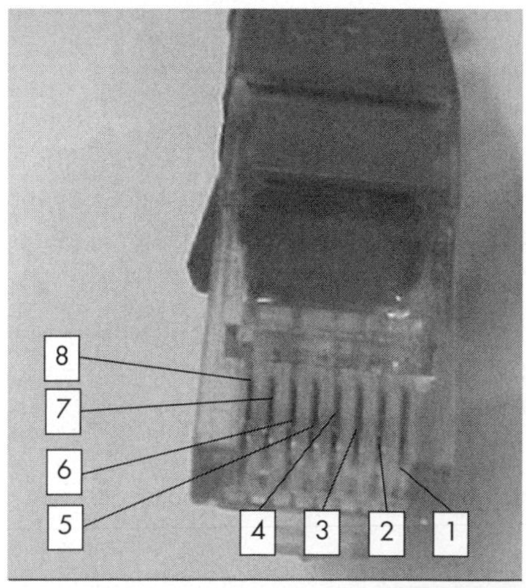


**FIGURE 7.27**
Pin Numbering for an RJ-45 Connector

| Pin | 568A | 568B |
|---|---|---|
| 1 | White/Green | White/Orange |
| 2 | Green | Orange |
| 3 | White/Orange | White/Green |
| 4 | Blue | Blue |
| 5 | White/Blue | White/Blue |
| 6 | Orange | Green |
| 7 | White/Brown | White/Brown |
| 8 | Brown | Brown |

**TABLE 7.1**
Wire Colors for UTP Cable

### *STP Categories*

Shielded twisted pair (STP) cable does not get much discussion in most hardware texts because it is seldom used anymore. In Chapter 21 you will learn about a network type called Token Ring, which is virtually the only remaining use for STP cabling, and even it does not require STP; it can work with UTP if needed.

Figure 7.28 lists several types of STP cable defined by IBM.

- **Type 1:** The most common STP cable type. Contains two pairs.
- **Type 2:** Like Type 1, but adds two pairs of voice wires.
- **Type 3:** Contains four pairs.
- **Type 6:** Patch cable, used for connecting token-ring hubs.
- **Type 8:** A flat type of STP cable used for running under carpets.
- **Type 9:** A two-pair, high-grade type of STP.

**FIGURE 7.28**
Types of STP Cable

**Hermaphroditic connector**

A connector that can plug into any other connector of the same type, male or female.

The unusual thing about STP cabling is that it usually does not have an RJ-45 connector on it like UTP. Instead it has a *hermaphroditic connector* on one end for connecting to the token-ring network. Neither male nor female, this type of connector can plug into any other connector of the same type. On the other end it has a DB-9 connector that attaches to a token-ring network interface card in a PC. See Chapter 21 for more information about token-ring networks.

## Fiber-Optic Cables

*Fiber-optic cables* are just beginning to gain some usage in PC networking (see Figure 7.29). They are expensive and difficult to work with because they break easily, but they transfer data at very high rates of speed. Fiber-optic cables use pulses of light rather than electricity; they are unaffected by

EMI, static, or electrical problems. They also have a much greater range (up to 6,500 feet [2,000 meters]). Because of the expense, fiber-optic cables are usually used only for the central portions of a network; connections to individual resources typically employ regular Cat5 UTP cable. Fiber-optic cable is also used with FDDI and ATM types of networks, which we will cover in Chapters 21 and 22.

**Fiber optic cable**

A cable that transmits data via light pulses at high speeds but is rather fragile and expensive.

Fiber-optic cable used in an Ethernet network is 62.5/125 multimode cable. Each fiber-optic Ethernet connection needs two of these cables, one for sending and one for receiving. Just as there are two speed standards for regular Ethernet (10Base-T and 100Base-T), there are two speed standards for fiber-optic Ethernet: 10Base-FL and 100Base-FX.

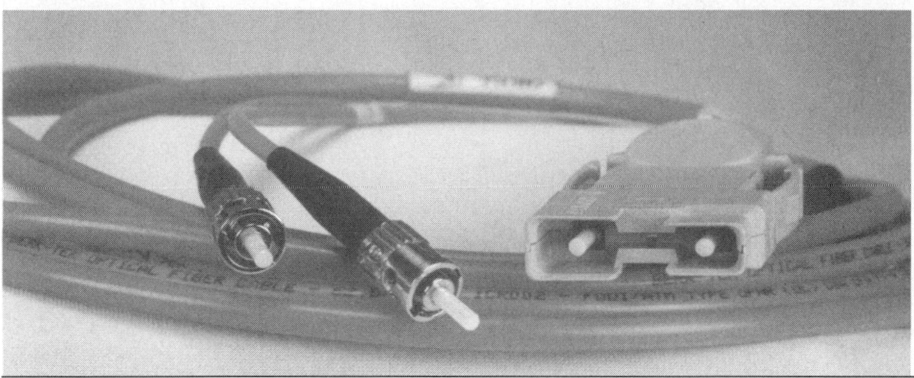

**FIGURE 7.29**
Fiber-Optic Cable

# Troubleshooting Cable Problems

Cable problems are fairly straightforward to diagnose. If data is not getting from point A to point B, one of the following must be true:

- The connectors are not snugly plugged in.
- The port controller at one end or the other is not accepting the data from the cable.
- The cable has a break in it, in one or more wires.

Checking the connectors is the first thing to try—make sure they are snug. Then start troubleshooting using the guidelines in the following sections.

## Checking Port Status in BIOS Setup

If data is not coming in or going out on a certain port, check to make sure that port is operational.

First, if it is a legacy parallel or serial port or a USB port, check in the BIOS setup to make sure the port is enabled. Some PC technicians turn off a port that is not being used in order to free up an IRQ; then some other technician will try to use the port and cannot figure out why it will not work.

You will learn how to work with the BIOS setup program in Chapter 9. Briefly, though, you just look for the port (it may be under I/O Device Configuration or Integrated Peripherals) and make sure it is not set to Disabled (see Figure 7.30).

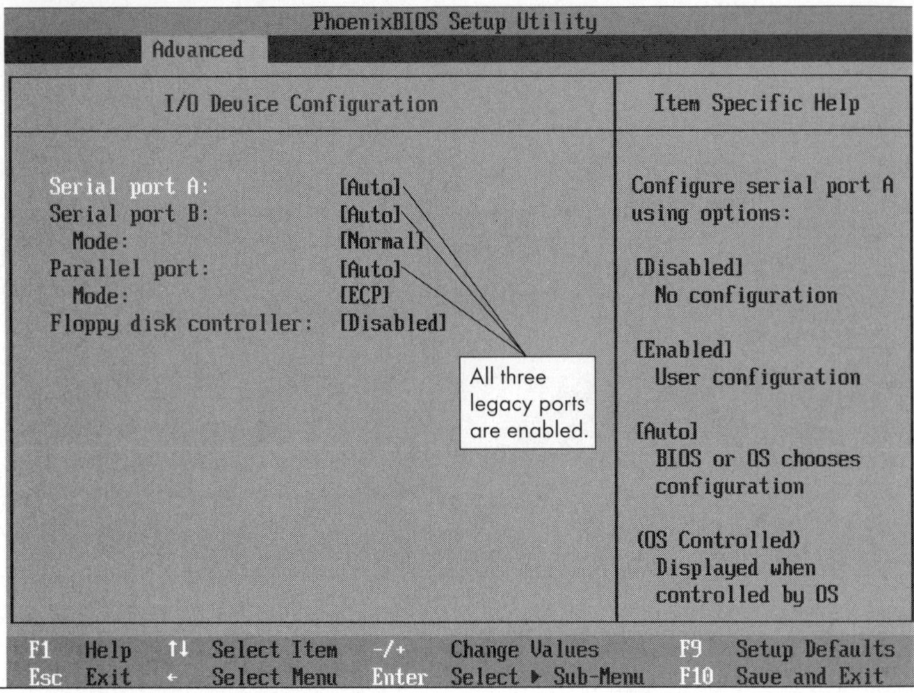


**FIGURE 7.30**
Port Status in BIOS Setup

## TRY IT!

**Enter your BIOS setup program and check the status of your legacy parallel and serial ports.**

## Checking Port Status in Windows

If the port shows up in BIOS setup, or if it is not a built-in port, the next place to look for the port is in Device Manager in Windows.

- In Windows 9x, to access Device Manager, right-click *My Computer* and choose Properties, then click the Device Manager tab.
- In Windows 2000/XP, right-click *My Computer* and choose Properties, select the Hardware tab, and then click the Device Manager button.

To check for a built-in COM (serial) or LPT (parallel) port, look in the Device Manager window for a category called Ports, and click the plus sign next to it to open that category. Then double-click the port to see its Properties box and check on the General tab for a message that reports the device is working properly (see Figure 7.31). If there is a problem with the port, see Chapter 14 for troubleshooting help.

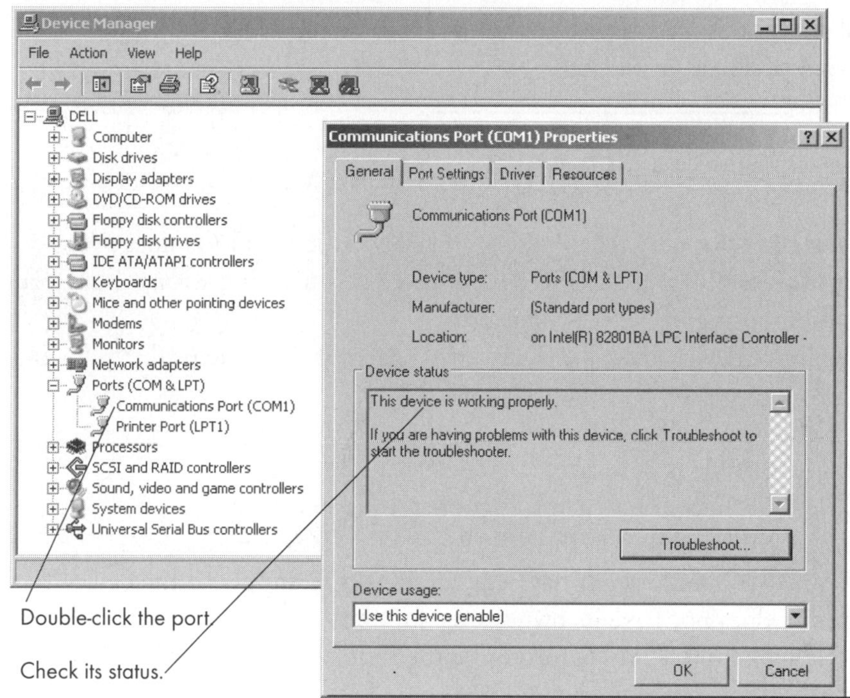


**FIGURE 7.31**
Checking the Status of COM1 in Device Manager

**TRY IT!**

**Open Device Manager and check the status of each legacy parallel and serial port, plus any other ports listed.**

## Testing Legacy Parallel and Serial Ports

To confirm that a legacy parallel or serial port is working, you can use a *loopback plug* and some diagnostic software. A loopback plug connects to the port and redirects the outgoing data back into the same connector instead of sending it to the opposite end of a cable. When used with diagnostic software, a loopback plug is an effective tool for checking all of the individual pins on the port connector at once.

**Loopback plug**

A plug that connects to a parallel or serial port and routes outgoing data back into the connector for diagnostic purposes.

There are many hardware diagnostic programs on the market today, and they all use the same type of loopback plug for their testing, so you can buy a generic plug for parallel or serial port use and be confident it will work with your software. "For More Information" for this chapter on the Internet Resource Center lists some companies that make testing software.

Although parallel and serial ports are the most common type tested with loopback plugs, loopbacks are also available for USB, audio, and joystick ports.

**TRY IT!**

**If you have a hardware diagnostic program and a loopback plug available, use it to test your legacy parallel and/or serial ports.**

## Troubleshooting USB Device Problems

USB devices are very reliably Plug and Play, so if Windows does not immediately recognize a USB device, there is something wrong. Start your troubleshooting in Device Manager.

Does the device appear in Device Manager? If not, one of the following is true:

- The device itself is defective.
- Its USB cable is defective.
- The USB hub into which it is connected is defective.
- The USB capability in the PC's BIOS setup has been disabled.
- The USB hub does not have enough power to supply to the device (if the device does not have its own power supply).
- The USB hub is not connected to the root hub (if the device is not directly connected to the PC).

To check out the USB hub situation, look in Device Manager under the Universal Serial Bus Controllers category. There should be at least these two entries:

- USB Root Hub: This is the internal hub in the motherboard.
- [Motherboard chipset manufacturer] [model number] Controller: This is the controller for the root hub, built into the motherboard chipset. This is the only USB item that uses any system resources (such as an IRQ), and it is the only one to have a Resources tab in its Properties box.

Both of these devices should show no errors (that is, no yellow exclamation point or red *X* through them), and when you view their Properties, the Device status on the General tab should report "This device is working properly." If you have an external USB hub, it should also be listed in Device Manager. In Figure 7.32, for example, it is listed as Generic USB Hub.

If there are no USB hubs listed in Device Manager, try entering the PC's BIOS setup program and checking whether the onboard USB support has been disabled. (See Chapter 9 for more information about BIOS setup.)

To check the available power for a hub in Device Manager, view its Properties and look on the Power tab, as in Figure 7.33. It reports how much power is being drawn by USB devices. If there is a lack of power, it will show up here. You can solve this by moving a USB device to a different hub that has more available power or by connecting it directly to the PC.

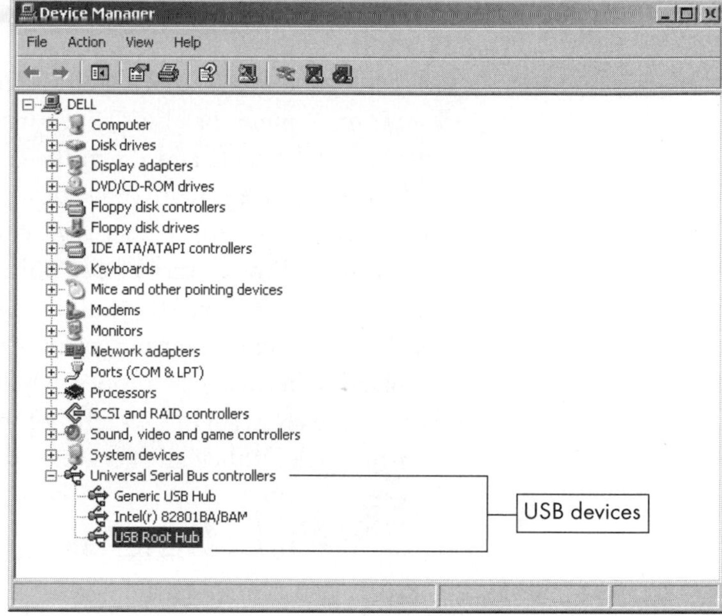


**FIGURE 7.32**
**USB Devices in a System with an External USB Hub as well as the Built-In Hub on the Motherboard**

If lack of power is not the problem, try a different USB cable, or try moving the USB device to a different port in the hub, or to a different hub entirely.

## TRY IT!

**Check the status of all USB devices in Device Manager. If you have one or more external USB hubs, identify the path from each USB device to the root hub through the external hubs.**

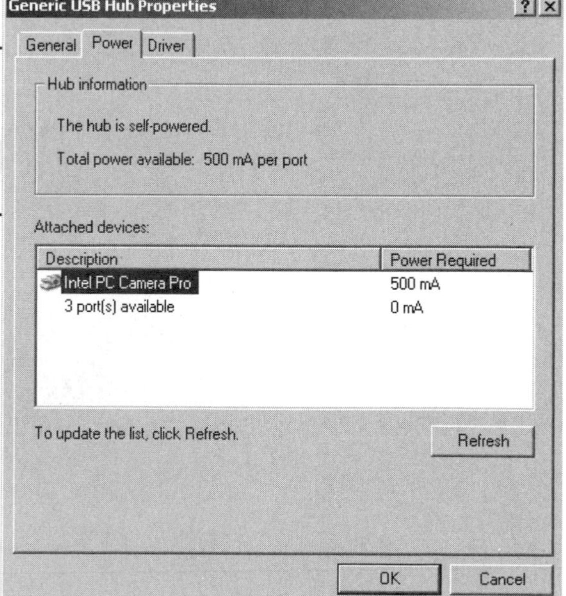


**FIGURE 7.33**
**Power Usage for a USB Hub**

## Checking Cables for Broken Wires

Because cables are fairly inexpensive and most technicians end up with a drawer full of extra ones, it is often easier to swap out a cable with another one rather than going to the trouble of testing it. If the new cable works, you know the old cable was bad; if it does not, you know the cable is probably not the problem.

However, if you do not have an extra cable available and you do not know whether the cable is the problem, you might want to test a cable. To do so you will need a pin-out diagram; if both ends are not identical, the diagram must show both ends so you can match up the pins to test.

Get out your digital multimeter, which you learned about in Chapter 3, and set it to ammeter or ohms. Then insert one probe in a hole in the female end of the cable and touch the corresponding pin at the male end with the other probe. Figure 7.34 shows a very short cable being checked; this particular connector, with a PS/2 connector at one end and a DB-9 at the other, is used to convert a PS/2 port to be used with a serial mouse. If the resistance is less than 20 ohms, the wire is doing its job of carrying the signal. If the resistance registers at infinity, or higher than 20 ohms, there is no connection between the probes, which means either that the wire is broken or you are trying to test the wrong pin. Repeat the process for every wire in the cable; if they all check out, the cable is okay.

## IN REAL LIFE

**Depending on the size of the holes in the female end of the cable, you might need to use smaller probes with your multimeter; you can buy a set of small probes at your local electronics store.**

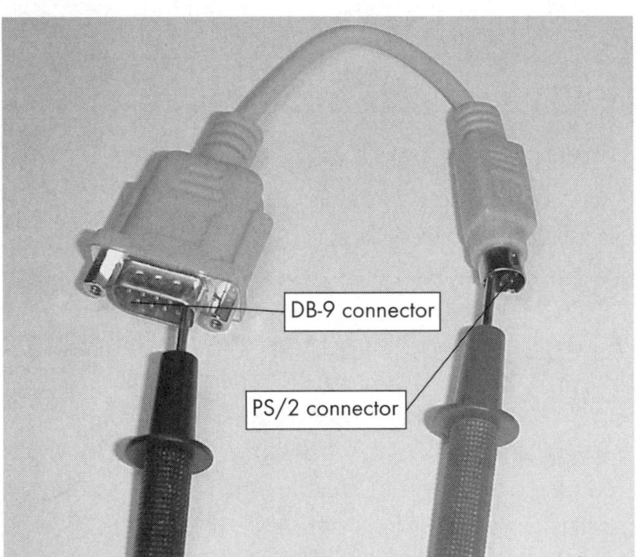


**FIGURE 7.34**
Testing a Wire in a Cable

## TRY IT!

Test each wire in a cable to verify that the cable is fully operational.

# STUDY GUIDE

Use the following summaries to review the key concepts in this chapter.

## SERIAL AND PARALLEL DATA TRANSMISSION

- Serial cables transmit data one bit at a time. Only one wire carries data in each direction; other wires are for overhead functions.
- Examples of serial cables include legacy serial port cables, networking cables, USB, and FireWire.
- Parallel cables transmit data several bits at a time (usually eight bits, or one byte).
- Examples of parallel cables include legacy parallel printer cables, direct parallel pass-through cables, and IDE and floppy drive ribbon cables.

## CABLE CONSTRUCTION

- All cables have connectors on each end, a conduit containing wires that carry data from one end to the other, and some sort of protective coating around the wires.
- The conduit is usually metal because it conducts electricity well.
- Fiber-optic cable transfers data via pulses of light rather than electricity, and is made of light-conductive glass fibers.
- Cable connectors can be either male (having pins) or female (having receptacles for pins).
- Most cables have one connector of each kind, but some cables are male or female at both ends.
- Gender changer adapters are available to switch a connector between male and female.
- If the conduit covering protects against EMI, it is called shielded cable. If not, it is unshielded.

## PIN-OUT DIAGRAMS

- A pin-out is a description of the purpose of each pin on a connector. It is usually accompanied by a picture of the connector showing the pin numbering.
- Pin numbering for male versus female connectors is reversed in diagrams, so that a pin plugs into a hole with the same number.

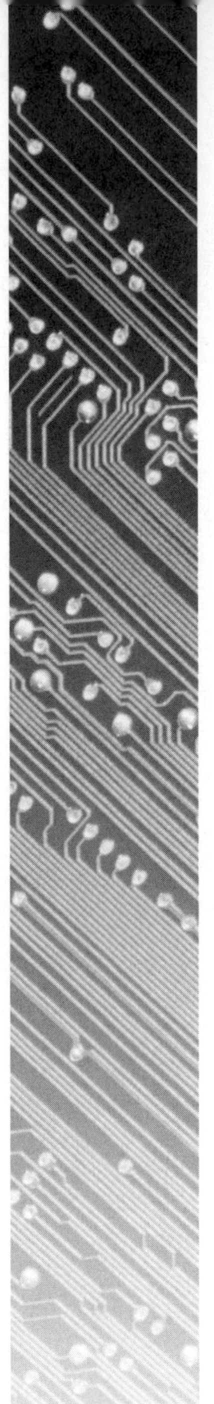

## Connector Types

- A BNC connector is typically used with coaxial cable, a for 10Base-5 Ethernet or cable TV.
- A D-sub connector, also called DB, is a D-shaped metal connector with rows of holes or pins inside it. It is used for legacy parallel and serial ports on a PC, as well as joystick and video ports.
- A Centronics connector has a plastic bar with rows of metal tabs on it. It is used to connect a parallel printer cable to a printer and also for some types of external SCSI devices.
- A ribbon cable connector is a plastic bar with two rows of holes in it that fit over rows of pins on a circuit board.
- An RJ-11 connector is the type of connector used for telephone lines. A plastic block with metal contacts for each wire in the cable, it is used with twisted pair wiring.
- An RJ-45 connector is a wider version of an RJ-11, used for 10Base-T and 100Base-T Ethernet.
- A DIN connector is an AT-style keyboard connector. DIN connectors have five pins in a semicircle.
- A Mini-DIN connector is a smaller version of DIN used in PS/2 ports. It has six pins.
- There are two types of high-speed serial ports: FireWire and USB. Each one uses a small, rectangular blocklike connector. Each one has different shaped connectors, and each one is different at the PC end versus the device end.
- A Molex connector attaches the power supply to an IDE drive. A mini-connector attaches the power supply to a floppy drive.

## Serial Cables and Ports

- The serial port built into a PC is known as a COM port or a legacy serial port. It is a DB-9 or DB-25 male connector on the PC. Common uses are for an external modem or a synch cradle for a PDA.
- You can convert between DB-9 and DB-25 with an adapter plug.
- A COM port's maximum speed depends on the UART chip in the chipset. UART stands for Universal Asynchronous Receiver Transmitter.
- Most motherboards have a 16550A UART, which can transfer data at up to 115Kbps.
- High-performance serial port UARTs are available on expansion cards, such as 16650, 16750, and 16850. These can support speeds of up to 230Kbps, 460Kbps, or 620Kbps, respectively.

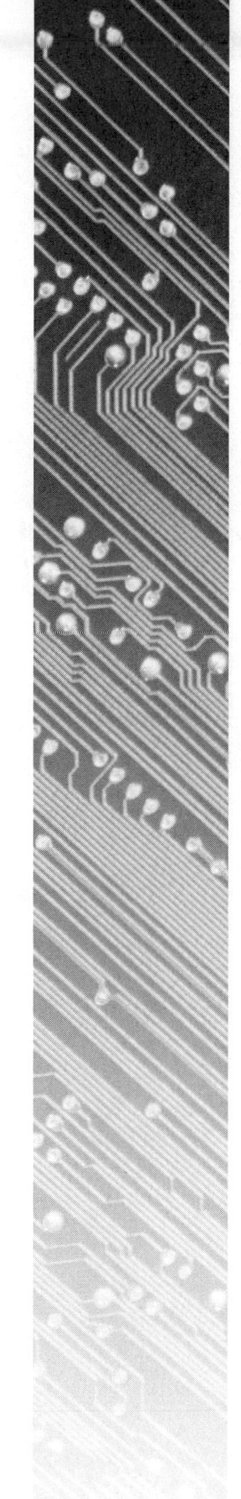

- USB stands for Universal Serial Bus. USB ports are built into most modern motherboards.
- USB versions of many different devices are now available, including keyboard, mouse, scanner, and digital camera.
- There are two USB standards: 1.1 and 2.0. USB 1.1 can transmit data at 12Mbps; USB 2.0 transmits at up to 400Kbps.
- USB devices are hot-pluggable and Plug and Play-compatible.
- You can chain up to 127 USB devices off a single USB port using a series of hubs up to 5 hub levels deep.
- The starting point USB hub in the PC is the root hub.
- IEEE 1394, also known as FireWire, is a competitor to USB for high-speed serial communications. It is also hot-pluggable, Plug and Play-compatible, and chainable.
- FireWire ports are not built into motherboards; you must buy a PCI expansion card containing FireWire ports.
- FireWire can transmit data up to 400Mbps, making it very useful for transferring digital image files.

## Parallel Cables and Ports

- Ribbon cables are flat and wide like a piece of ribbon. They enclose each wire in its own plastic-covered channel, minimizing interference.
- Ribbon cables connect disk drives to the motherboard or to a controller card. Different drive interface types use cables with a different number of pins/holes.
- High-performance IDE drives use an 80-wire ribbon cable that has only 40 holes/pins; the extra wires are for buffering between the active wires to cut down on interference.
- All ribbon cables have a red stripe along one side; this stripe must align with pin 1 on the connector.
- Some ribbon cables are keyed with a raised piece so they fit into a connector only one way. Some IDE ribbon cables have pin 20 blocked off, with the same pin missing from the connector on the motherboard.
- A parallel printer cable has a 25-pin male connector at the PC end and a 36-pin Centronics male connector at the printer end.
- Most BIOSes support several choices of parallel port modes, including Bidirectional, EPP, and ECP.
- Bidirectional is the standard operating mode for modern parallel printer ports. It transfers 150KB/sec in 8-bit chunks.
- EPP stands for Enhanced Parallel Port. It is a high-speed port mode used for nonprinter devices such as external drives. It transfers data at up to 2MB/sec.

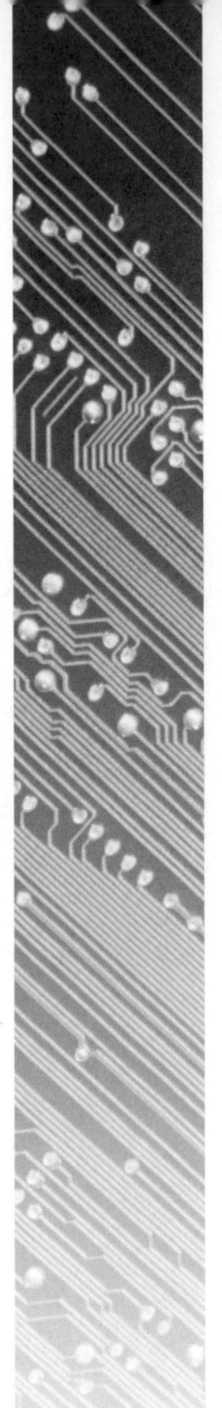

- ECP stands for Enhanced Capabilities Port. It is a high-speed port mode used for printers. It requires a DMA channel to be assigned to it.
- A direct parallel cable is the same at both ends: a male DB-25 connector. It connects the parallel ports on two PCs to one another for transferring data. Windows includes a Direct Cable Connection application for managing such a connection.

## Network Cabling

- Thick Ethernet cabling (thicknet) is used in 10Base-5 Ethernet networks. It is a thick coaxial cable with marks every 8.2 feet (2.5 meters). Devices connect to it using a vampire connector at the marks. It is now virtually obsolete.
- Thin Ethernet cabling (thinnet) is a thinner coaxial cable that looks like television cable but is actually a higher grade type. Used in 10Base-2 Ethernet networks, the specification for it is RG-58. It is becoming obsolete since it is limited to 10Mbps.
- Twisted pair cabling comes in shielded (STP) or unshielded (UTP) versions.
- 10Base-T and 100Base-T Ethernet networks use UTP cables.
- UTP cables are rated in categories, with higher categories supporting faster data transfer rates. 10Base-T requires category 3, 5, or 6; 100Base-T requires 5 or 6.
- STP cabling is used in Token Ring networks. This type of cabling uses a hermaphroditic connector that can connect to any other connector of the same type without worrying about male or female. On the other end of the cable is a DB-9 connector that attaches to the token-ring network card in the PC.
- Fiber-optic cables are used for high-speed network backbones. Their price makes them unsuitable for use between individual PCs.

## Troubleshooting Cable Problems

- First, check that the connectors are snugly plugged in.
- Next, make sure Windows sees the port in which the cable is connected. If it does not, check in BIOS setup to ensure the port is enabled.
- If the port is active, try swapping out the cable with a known good one.
- You can test a cable pin-by-pin for breaks using a multimeter set to ohms, but it is time-consuming to do so.
- A loopback plug attaches to a port and enables a diagnostic application to send data into and out of it to test it for proper operation.
- For problems with USB connections, check the USB hub status in Device Manager in Windows.

# PRACTICE TEST

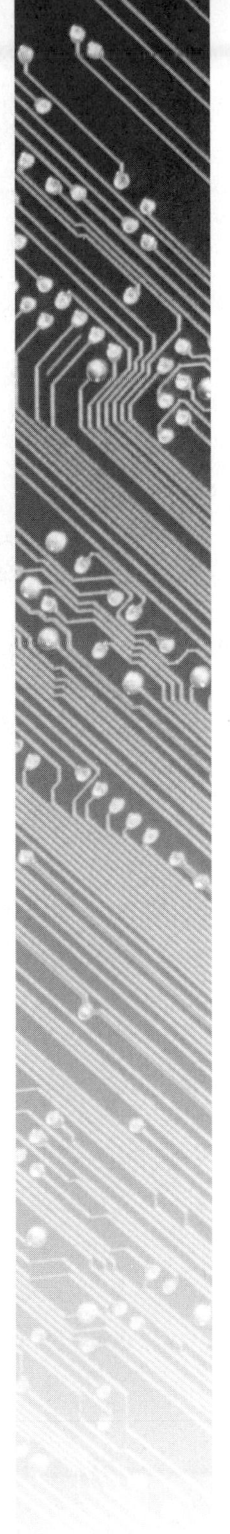

On a blank sheet of paper, write the answers to the following multiple-choice questions and explain why each answer is correct.

1. Which of these is *not* a serial port?
   a. USB
   b. legacy COM port
   c. LPT port
   d. FireWire

2. A shielded cable is different from an unshielded cable in what way?
   a. It has a protective plastic or rubber coating on the conduit.
   b. It contains EMI shielding.
   c. It contains ESD shielding.
   d. All of the above

3. What type of connector is at the printer end of a parallel printer cable?
   a. DB-25 male
   b. DB-25 female
   c. female 36-pin Centronics
   d. male 36-pin Centronics

4. What type of Ethernet uses a thinnet coaxial cable with a BNC connector?
   a. 10Base-T
   b. 100Base-T
   c. 10Base-2
   d. 10Base-5

5. A male DB-9 connector has
   a. flat metal tabs.
   b. a hermaphroditic block.
   c. holes.
   d. pins.

6. Which type of RJ connector and cabling would be suitable for 10Base-T Ethernet?
   a. Cat5 UTP cable with RJ-45 connector
   b. Cat2 UTP cable with RJ-14 connector
   c. Cat4 STP cable with RJ-45 connector
   d. Cat1 UTP cable with RJ-11 connector

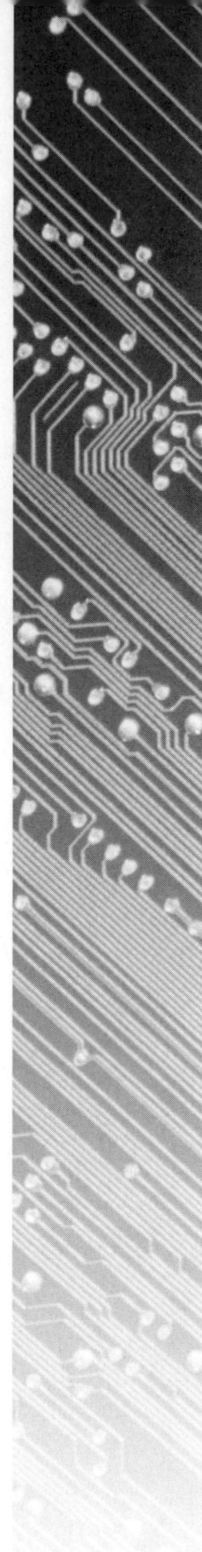

7. Which of the following cable/port types could *not* be used to attach a mouse to a PC?
   a. legacy serial port (DB-9)
   b. USB
   c. Mini-DIN PS/2
   d. DIN

8. Which statement is true of USB?
   a. It supports more devices on a single PC interface than FireWire.
   b. Its top data transfer rate is faster than that of FireWire.
   c. It is not typically built into the motherboard, but requires an add-on card.
   d. Devices can be daisy-chained together from one device to another without using a hub.

9. The IEEE standard number for FireWire is
   a. 1284.
   b. 1384.
   c. 1294.
   d. 1394.

10. On a keyed IDE ribbon cable, which hole number is blocked, and which corresponding pin is missing on the motherboard connector?
    a. 1
    b. 20
    c. 21
    d. 40

11. Which of these is not a legacy parallel port mode?
    a. Bidirectional
    b. EDP
    c. ECP
    d. EPP

12. On a direct parallel cable, what are the connectors?
    a. DB-25 male and DB-25 male
    b. DB-25 male and DB-25 female
    c. DB-25 female and 36-pin Centronics
    d. 36-pin Centronics and 36-pin Centronics

13. What category of cabling would you buy to create a 100Base-T Ethernet network?
    a. Cat2
    b. Cat3
    c. Cat4
    d. Cat5

14. How many twisted pairs are there in Cat3 cabling?
    a. 1
    b. 2
    c. 3
    d. 4

15. What type of network uses Type 1 STP cabling?
    a. 10Base-2
    b. 10Base-5
    c Token Ring
    d. NetWare

16. Why is fiber-optic cabling not used for entire networks?
    a. It is not fast enough.
    b. It is expensive.
    c. It is not compatible with Ethernet.
    d. It cannot be used with a router.

17. Why would someone turn off a port in BIOS setup?
    a. to free up an IRQ
    b. to free up memory
    c. to free up hard disk space
    d. None of the above

18. Where in Windows would you check a port's status?
    a. System Manager
    b. System Restore
    c. Device Manager
    d. Port Manager

19. Which USB item uses an IRQ?
    a. root hub
    b. USB controller
    c. generic USB hub
    d. All of the above

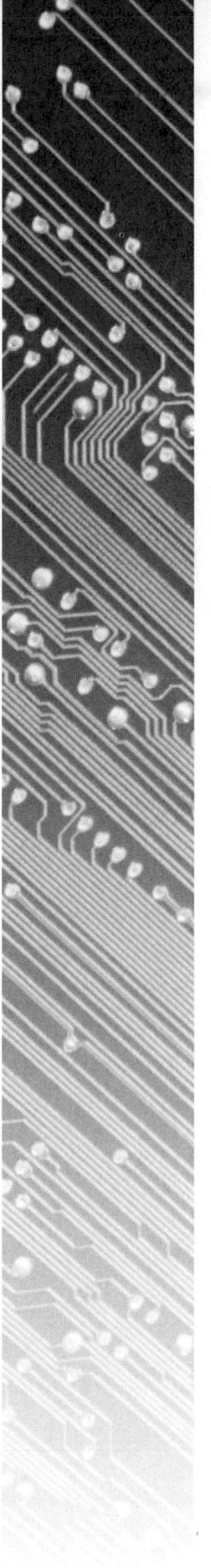

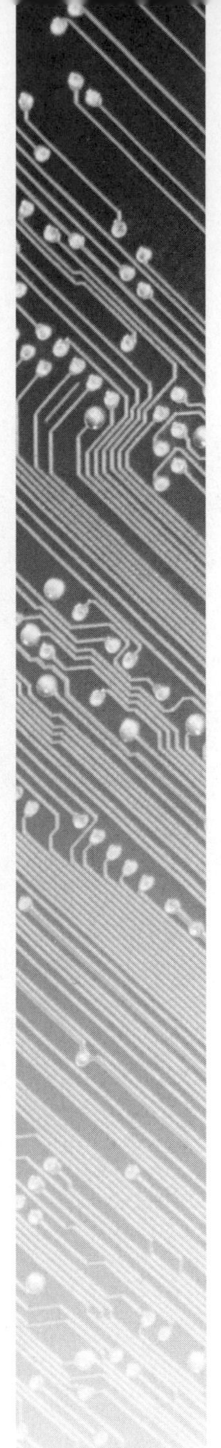

20. To check a cable for broken wires, set your multimeter to
    a. amps.
    b. volts.
    c. ohms.
    d. watts.

# TROUBLESHOOTING

1. Your computer has two legacy serial ports. You can connect a serial mouse to one of them and it works perfectly, but when you connect it to the other one, it appears totally dead. What would you check, and in what order?
2. You are working with an older PC that does not have a USB port. You install one on a PCI expansion card, but Windows cannot see it. What is likely to be the problem?
3. A client with an inkjet printer attached to the legacy parallel port wants to hook up a parallel interface scanner that has a printer pass-through. You hook them up, but the scanner does not work. When you connect the scanner directly to the port, it works just fine; the printer does too. They just do not seem to be able to share the port. What could you try?

# CUSTOMER SERVICE

1. You need to give a client directions over the telephone for hooking up a ribbon cable between a motherboard and a drive. What tips and advice can you give to make sure the client gets it oriented correctly at both ends?
2. You are instructing a client over the telephone to connect a cable from an external modem to a legacy serial port, but the client claims it won't fit. What is wrong, and what can you suggest?
3. A friend wants to hook up a secondhand keyboard he has acquired to his PC, but the keyboard has a DIN and his system has a Mini-DIN. What do you recommend?

# FOR MORE INFORMATION

For links to Web sites that provide further information about the topics covered in this chapter, go to the EMC/Paradigm Internet Resource Center at www.emcp.com/College Division/Internet Resource Centers/PC Maintenance/For More Information.

# 8 Installing and Troubleshooting the Basic Components

## ON THE TEST

**A+ Core Hardware Service Technician Examination**

- **Objective 1.2:** Identify basic procedures for adding and removing field replaceable modules for both desktop and portable systems.
- **Objective 1.8**: Identify hardware methods of upgrading system performance, procedures for replacing basic subsystem components, unique components and when to use them.
- **Objective 2.1:** Identify common symptoms and problems associated with each module and how to troubleshoot and isolate the problems.
- **Objective 2.2:** Identify basic troubleshooting procedures and how to elicit problem symptoms from customers.

## ON THE JOB

As a PC technician, you will need to know how to build a PC from scratch and how to add and remove parts. In the last several chapters you have learned about the specifications and terminology pertaining to the motherboard, CPU, memory, case, and power supply, but until now we have put off the discussion of how to physically assemble and disassemble these parts. This chapter covers that physical assembly.

Some situations in which this chapter's information might be applied include:

- assembling a new PC
- building a functional PC out of parts
- installing a motherboard in a case
- replacing a defective or out-of-date motherboard
- installing a CPU on a motherboard

- setting up a motherboard to accept a different type of CPU
- removing and replacing RAM
- adding more RAM to an existing system
- troubleshooting PC startup problems

**TRY IT!**

**This entire chapter is a "Try It!" exercise, because it deals with the hands-on process of PC assembly. Students are encouraged to try out everything that they can in this chapter with the hardware they have available.**

## What You Need

You can assemble a PC anywhere, but the best possible place would be a work area designed specifically for working on PCs, with an antistatic mat, a handy grounded AC outlet, and a humidity-regulated environment free of synthetic fiber floor covering. When you are ready to test your PC, a grounded AC outlet is a must.

In most cases you will need only one tool: a small Phillips-head screwdriver. Depending on the case and motherboard you may need a few other tools as well, such as a flathead screwdriver to pop out metal plates or a nut driver to remove an I/O port from a backplate and mount it on the case wall. A basic PC toolkit from any computer store should suffice. You should also have an antistatic wrist strap. See Appendix A, "The Computer Technician's Toolkit," for more information about tools.

## Preparing the Case

In Chapter 3 you learned how to get a case ready to accept a motherboard. The key steps are to punch out the metal panels for the expansion slots and drive bays you plan on using and to install the system speaker. Do these things now if you have not done them already.

## Configuring a Motherboard

As discussed in Chapter 4, most motherboards have jumpers that can be set to make them operate in different modes. For example, some motherboards have jumpers that control the bus speed, the clock multiplier, the CPU core voltage, the amount and type of RAM, and so on. The older the motherboard, the more complex its system of configuration jumpers will be. Some very old motherboards may even have switches instead of jumpers.

WARNING

Take antistatic precautions when assembling a PC, as discussed in Chapter 2. This may include using an antistatic wrist strap and an antistatic mat, and working in a room with high humidity. See "For More Information" for this chapter on the Internet Resource Center for some Web sites where you can buy antistatic mats and straps.

Most technicians find that it is easiest to set the jumpers on the motherboard before installing it in a case. (The same is true for installing the CPU and RAM.) If the motherboard is already installed in a case, you do not need to remove it to set its jumpers, but the jumpers may be easier to see with the motherboard outside the case.

The best source for jumper setting information is the manual that came with the motherboard. If you bought the motherboard as a separate part, it almost certainly came with a manual. If you bought it as part of a prebuilt PC, the PC probably came with a manual (which may or may not have the jumper settings listed). If you do not have a manual, try looking on the motherboard itself or checking the motherboard maker's or PC manufacturer's Web site. Many manufacturers have manuals available for free download from their Web sites.

Figures 8.1 and 8.2 show representative pages from a motherboard manual. Figure 8.1 shows a diagram of the motherboard with all of the components labeled. Jumpers have "JP" names such as JP1. Figure 8.2 shows tables that describe each jumper's purpose and setting.

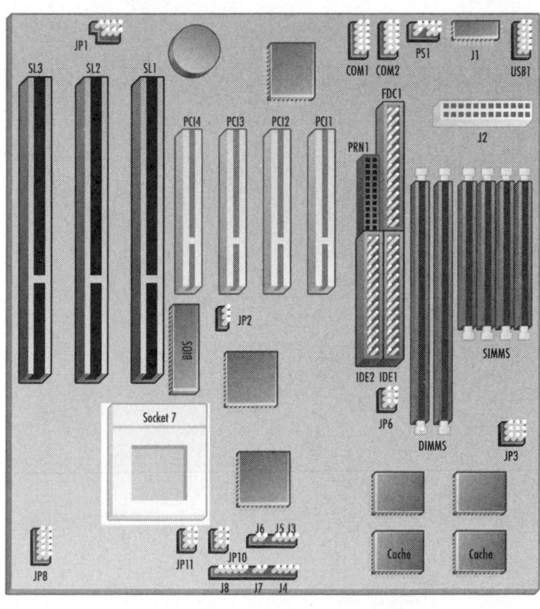


**FIGURE 8.1**
Diagram of a Motherboard Layout

| JP1 - Clear CMOS | |
|---|---|
| Setting | Description |
| Open | Normal (default) |
| Close | Clear CMOS |

| JP2 - Flash ROM | |
|---|---|
| Setting | Description |
| P1, P2 | 12v Flash ROM (default) |
| P2, P3 | 5v Flash ROM |

| JP3A, B, C - CPU Speed Selectors | | | | | |
|---|---|---|---|---|---|
| Settings | 50MHz | 55MHz | 60MHz | 66MHz | 75MHz |
| A | P2, P3 | P1, P2 | P2, P3 | P2, P3 | P1, P2 |
| B | P2, P3 | P2, P3 | P2, P3 | P1, P2 | P2, P3 |
| C | P2, P3 | P2, P3 | P1, P2 | P2, P3 | P1, P2 |

| JP6 - DIMM Module Voltage | | |
|---|---|---|
| Setting | 5v | 3.3v |
| A | P1, P2 | P2, P3 |
| B | P1, P2 | P2, P3 |

| J7 - System Reset | |
|---|---|
| Setting | Description |
| 1 | Ground |
| 2 | Reset System |

| JP8 - CPU Voltage Selectors | | | | | |
|---|---|---|---|---|---|
| Settings | 3.5v | 3.3v | 3.2v | 2.9v | 2.8v |
| Close | A | B | C | D | E |

| JP10 - CPU Type Selectors | | |
|---|---|---|
| Settings | P54C | P55C |
| A | P1, P2 | P2, P3 |
| B | P1, P2 | P2, P3 |

| JP11A, B - CPU Internal Clock Speed Selectors | | | | |
|---|---|---|---|---|
| Setting | 1.5X | 2.0X | 2.5X | 3.0X |
| A | P1, P2 | P2, P3 | P2, P3 | P1, P2 |
| B | P1, P2 | P1, P2 | P2, P3 | P2, P3 |

**FIGURE 8.2**
Tables Describing Jumper Settings

If no manual is available, look on the motherboard itself to see whether there are any clues as to the correct jumper settings. For example, in Chapter 4 we looked at some charts printed on a motherboard that described the settings for various system bus speeds and clock multipliers. Figure 8.3 shows these charts again.

| Ratio | 1 | 2 | 3 | 4 | BUS CLK | 5 | 6 | 7 |
|---|---|---|---|---|---|---|---|---|
| 3.0 | ON | OFF | ON | ON | 112MHz | OFF | ON | OFF |
| 3.5 | ON | OFF | OFF | ON | 100MHz | OFF | OFF | OFF |
| 4.0 | OFF | ON | ON | ON | 83MHz | ON | OFF | ON |
| 4.5 | OFF | ON | OFF | ON | 75MHz | ON | ON | OFF |
| 5.0 | OFF | OFF | ON | ON | 66MHz | ON | OFF | OFF |
| 5.5 | OFF | OFF | OFF | ON | CPU-CLK=BUS CLK*Ratio | | | |

**FIGURE 8.3**
Charts printed on the motherboard itself may provide clues as to the correct jumper settings.

Some of the settings you might need to change on the motherboard may include:

- System bus speed
- CPU clock multiplier
- CPU voltage
- CPU type
- RAM voltage
- Flash ROM voltage
- Enable/disable on-board video and/or sound

Newer motherboards (Pentium II and higher) will not have many jumpers because they have the capability of detecting and configuring many of these factors automatically, and/or of setting them through BIOS setup.

## Installing the CPU

Installing the CPU is easier when the motherboard is not installed in the case, so you will probably want to do it early in the process.

In Chapter 5 we covered the many different CPU packages that have been used over the years, but in modern systems you will encounter only two: ZIF PGA and SECC. The following sections show how to install each of these kinds of packages.

Before you install the CPU, find out what type of cooling device it requires (such as a passive heat sink or a heat sink with fan) and make sure you have one. If you are not sure, ask at your local computer store or check the Web site for the CPU manufacturer.

If you will be attaching a passive heat sink, you will need some heat sink compound (basically a heat-conductive glue). If you will be attaching an active heat sink with a fan, it will probably clip on without the compound. You do not want to use compound when attaching an active heat sink to a CPU because you might need to remove it later; the fan might go bad and need replacement.

## Installing a PGA CPU

As you will recall from Chapter 5, *PGA* stands for pin grid array, a type of CPU that consists of a flat ceramic chip with concentric rings of pins on the bottom. These pins plug into a socket on the motherboard with corresponding holes. All PGA CPU sockets these days are Zero Insertion Force (ZIF). They have a handle on one side that lifts to release and lowers to tighten.

To install a PGA CPU:

1. Lift the handle on the PGA socket, opening it to receive a chip (see Figure 8.4).

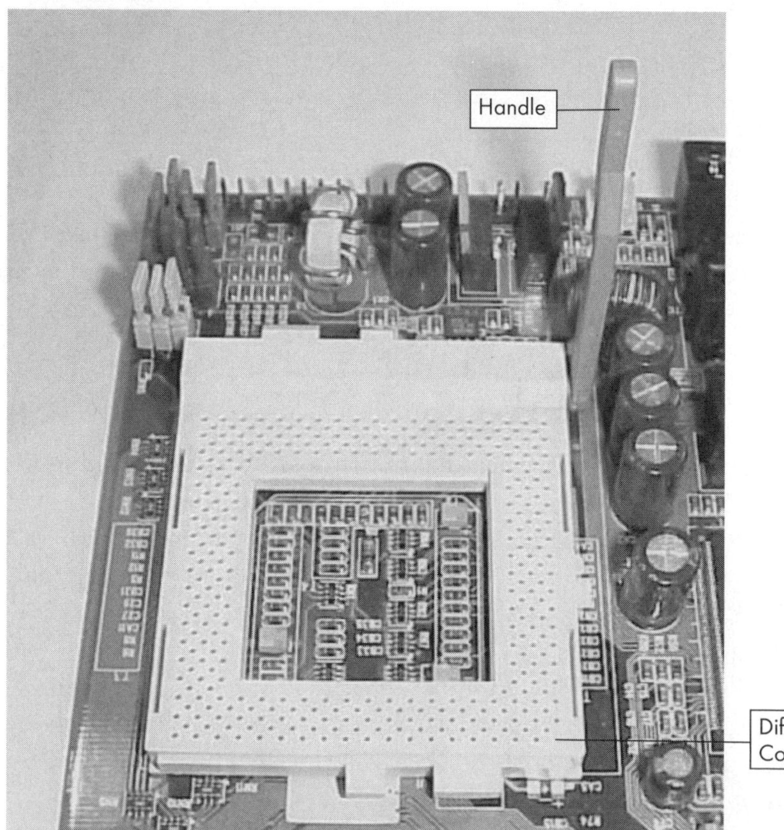


**FIGURE 8.4**
When the handle is lifted, the socket is open.

2. Look at the chip and at the socket. Notice that on both one corner is different from the others; perhaps it is missing a pin or has a rounded edge. Orient the CPU so that those keyed corners line up. In Figure 8.5 the keyed corners are at the bottom right for both the socket and the chip.

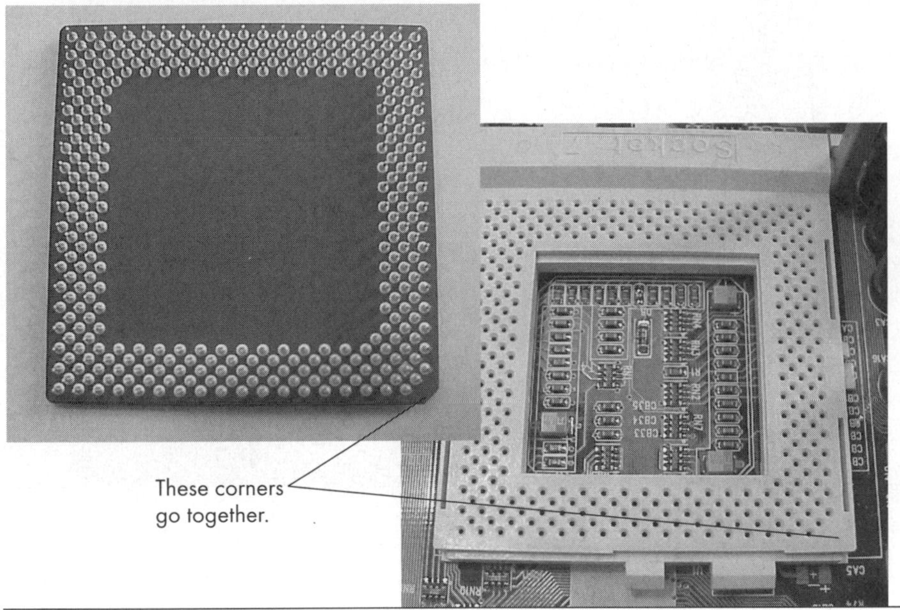
These corners go together.

**FIGURE 8.5**
Look for the corner that is different from the other three on both socket and chip.

**WARNING**

**In some cases the chip will not fit if you do not orient it correctly, but in other cases it will fit even if it is wrong. Running the CPU in the wrong orientation can destroy it.**

3. Place the CPU chip into the socket, fitting its pins down into the holes. Do not force it; it should drop in effortlessly. If you need to apply pressure, it is oriented incorrectly or you do not have the handle fully raised.
4. Lower the handle, securing the CPU. There is a ridge in the socket that the handle should tuck underneath to secure it; you might need to pull the handle outward slightly to get it under this ridge (see Figure 8.6).

**FIGURE 8.6**
A PGA CPU Properly Installed

5. Next, attach the heat sink. If it is a passive heat sink, apply a thin layer of heat sink compound to the top of the CPU and then affix the heat sink to it, allowing time for it to dry (see Figure 8.7). Heat sink compound serves two purposes: it attaches the heat sink to the CPU, and it creates greater conductivity between them so that the CPU can more effectively channel its heat into the heat sink where it can be dissipated.

**FIGURE 8.7**
Attaching a Passive Heat Sink

## In Real Life

Some people attach a passive heat sink before they install the CPU; it is your choice.

If it is an active heat sink, it has a clip with loops that fit under tabs on the sides of the socket. Slip one loop under a tab and then press the other side down until it hooks over the clip on the opposite side (see Figure 8.8).

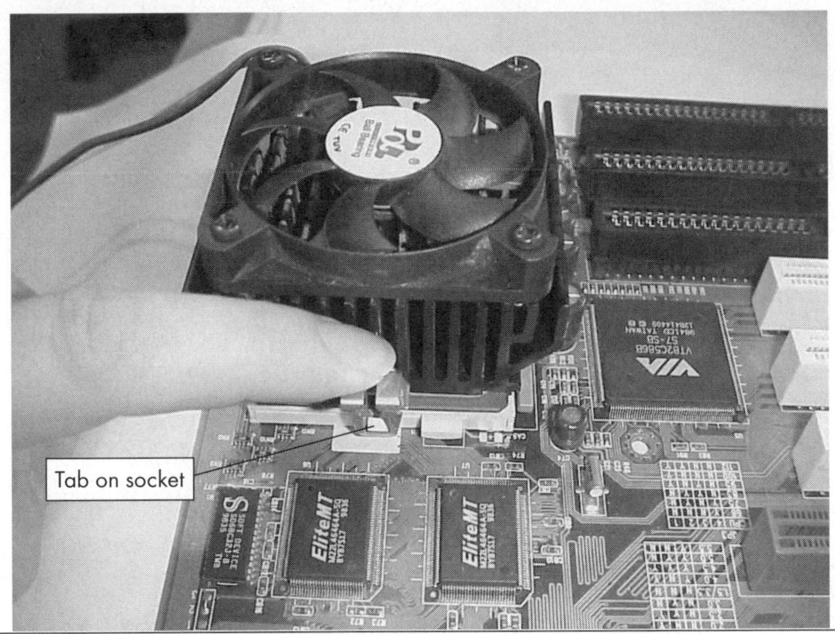


**FIGURE 8.8**
Attaching an Active Heat Sink-Fan Combination for a PGA CPU

6. If you are using an active heat sink, plug in the fan's power cord. On most motherboards there is a three-pin connector near the CPU for this purpose, as shown in Figure 8.9. If your motherboard lacks this connector, you can buy an adapter that will allow you to plug the power cord into a Molex or Mini connector for a drive.

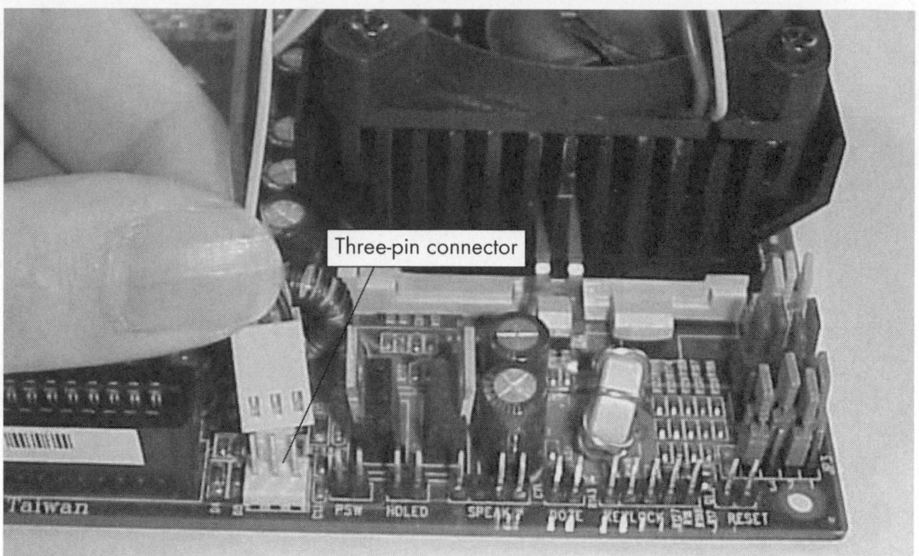


FIGURE 8.9
Attach the power cord for the CPU fan to the motherboard

## INSTALLING AN SECC CPU

As you learned earlier, *SECC* stands for Single Edge Contact Cartridge, the type of CPU that comes in a plastic cartridge that fits into a slot in the motherboard. Here is how to install one.

1. Attach the support brackets to the motherboard. These brackets come with the board and fit down over the CPU slot. On less expensive motherboards these push down into holes with umbrella-style fasteners, but on most motherboards these days they are held in place by screws inserted through the bottom of the motherboard. In Figure 8.10 screws are being used.

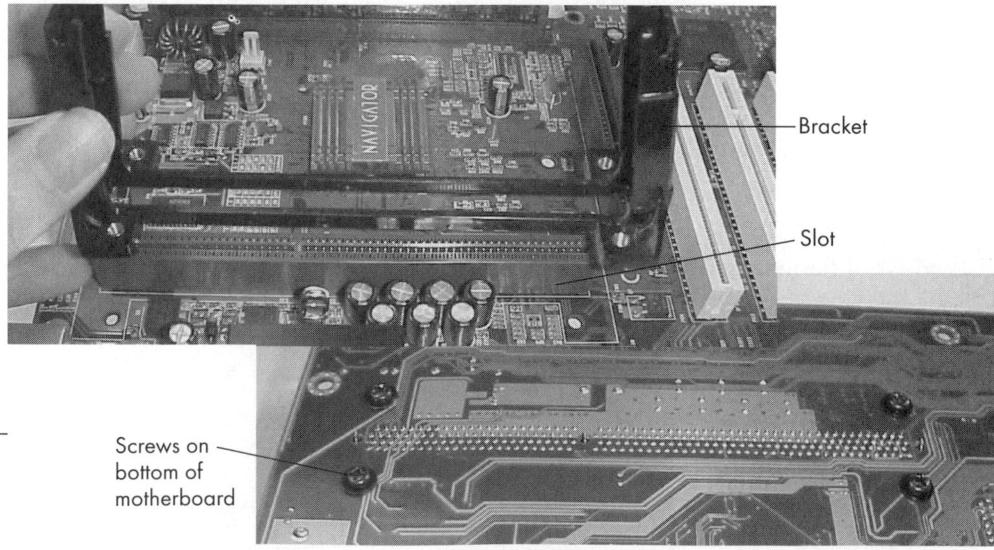


**FIGURE 8.10**
Attach the support brackets to the CPU slot.

2. Check the bottom of the cartridge and the slot in the motherboard, and make sure the cartridge is facing in the right direction to fit down into the slot. The separator is offset so it fits only one way.
3. Slide the cartridge into the support brackets and press it firmly into the motherboard as far as it will go. When it is completely seated, the clips on the ends of the cartridge will lock into the bracket (see Figure 8.11).

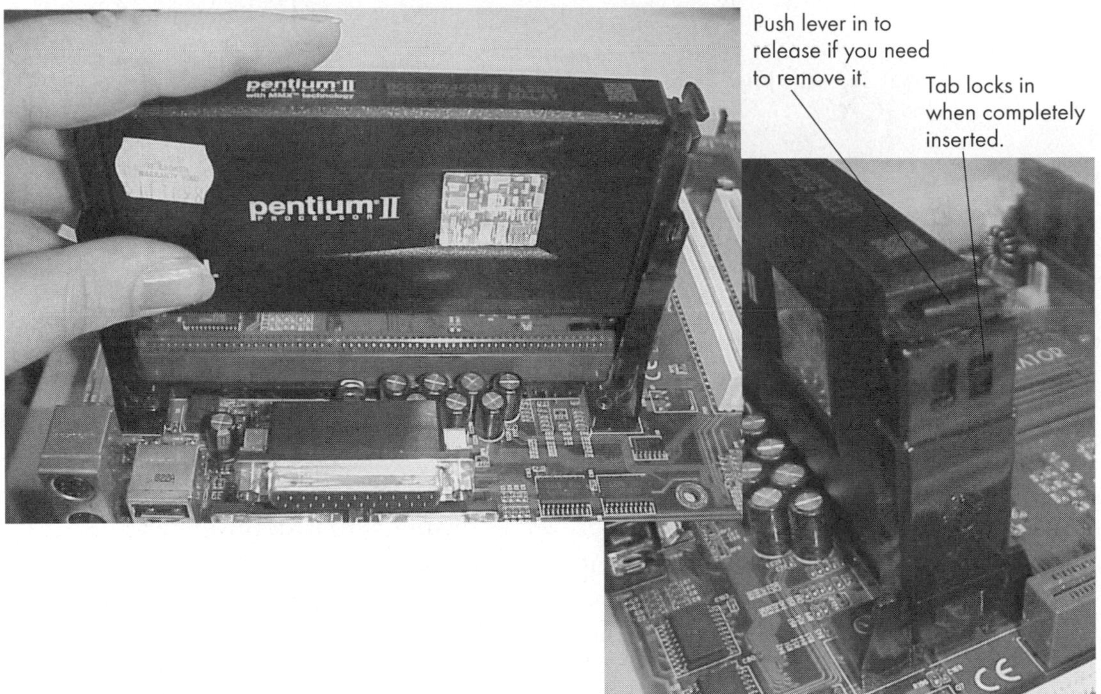
Push lever in to release if you need to remove it.
Tab locks in when completely inserted.
pentium II
pentium II PROCESSOR

**FIGURE 8.11**
Insert the cartridge into the slot.

4. Nearly all SECC CPUs use active heat sinks with fans; these clip onto the CPU. Align the fan so that the metal tabs fit into the holes on the cartridge, and then raise the fastener bar to tighten the fan into place (see Figure 8.12).

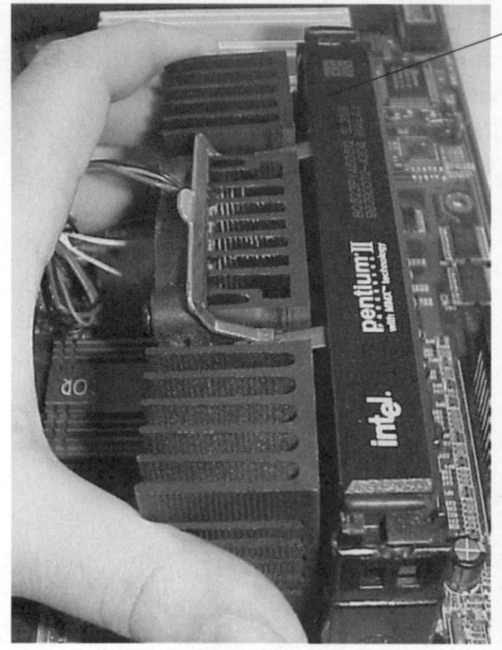
Hang the clips
off the holes in
the cartridge
pentium II
intel

Pull bar up
toward CPU to
secure heat sink.
pentium II
intel

**FIGURE 8.12**
Clip the heat sink-fan combination onto the cartridge.

5. Attach the fan's power cord to the motherboard, the same as with a PGA unit (refer to Figure 8.9).

## Installing RAM

The older the motherboard, the more likely its manual will contain complex rules on the installation of RAM (Random-Access Memory). You might have to set a jumper on the motherboard for the RAM's voltage, and you might be able to install only certain kinds of RAM and only in certain banks. Pay close attention to the manual in selecting RAM and deciding which banks you will place it in.

For example, the instructions shown in Figure 8.13 come from a Pentium-class motherboard that has two DIMM slots and four SIMM slots. Recall that on a Pentium system, each DIMM is a bank by itself but SIMMs must function in banks of two. Therefore, this system has a total of four banks. However, these instructions state that SIMM slots 3 and 4 and DIMM slot 1 cannot both be used at once; this means they are the same bank as far as the motherboard is concerned. You can use one or the other, but not both. So you really only have three banks to work with. The only way to know this is to read the motherboard manual. That is why it can be difficult to choose RAM for a motherboard without a manual, simply by guessing at the correct RAM specifications and settings.

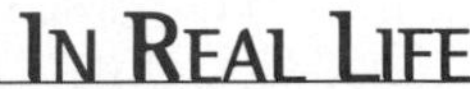

## IN REAL LIFE

Notice the poor grammar in Figure 8.13. This is typical of motherboard manuals. Most motherboards are produced in countries where English is not widely spoken, and the people who write the manuals are seldom native English speakers.

| MEMORY BANK | | |
|---|---|---|
| Bank 0/1 | Bank 2/3 | Bank 4/5 |
| DIMM 2 | SIMM 1,2 | SIMM 3/4 |
| | | DIMM 1 |

*SIMM 3,4 and DIMM 1 cannot be used at the same time. When using SDRAM, JP6 must be set to 3.3v position and make sure the SDRAM is with buffer.

**FIGURE 8.13**
Instructions for Selecting and Installing RAM from a Motherboard Manual

If you are adding more RAM to an existing system, you might be able to find information at the manufacturer's Web site regarding the type of RAM to buy and the slot(s) to install it in. For example, Figure 8.14 shows the instructions provided by Dell Computers for a Dimension 4100 system. Notice that it specifies the type of RAM required: non-ECC PC133 SDRAM.

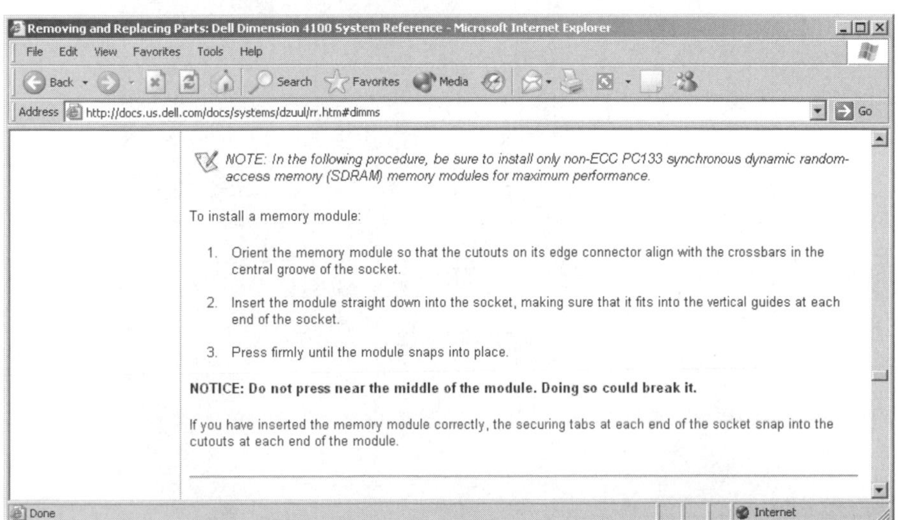

Removing and Replacing Parts: Dell Dimension 4100 System Reference - Microsoft Internet Explorer

File Edit View Favorites Tools Help

Back Search Favorites Media

Address http://docs.us.dell.com/docs/systems/dzuul/rr.htm#dimms Go

*NOTE: In the following procedure, be sure to install only non-ECC PC133 synchronous dynamic random-access memory (SDRAM) memory modules for maximum performance.*

To install a memory module:

1. Orient the memory module so that the cutouts on its edge connector align with the crossbars in the central groove of the socket.
2. Insert the module straight down into the socket, making sure that it fits into the vertical guides at each end of the socket.
3. Press firmly until the module snaps into place.

**NOTICE: Do not press near the middle of the module. Doing so could break it.**

If you have inserted the memory module correctly, the securing tabs at each end of the socket snap into the cutouts at each end of the module.

Done Internet

**FIGURE 8.14**
Online instructions may be available for newer PCs, as are these instructions for a Dell PC.

## Installing a SIMM

As explained in Chapter 6, *SIMM* stands for single inline memory module, the older type of RAM. It is used in Pentium and older systems. (Pentium was actually the breaking point where SIMMs were phased out and DIMMs were introduced, so a Pentium system could have either or both depending on the motherboard.)

SIMMs usually fit at an angle to the motherboard and then tilt up to perpendicular when they are installed. On some very old systems they remain tilted when installed, but this is the exception. Both 30- and 72-pin SIMMs install the same way.

To install a SIMM:

1. Slide the SIMM into the SIMM slot at an angle.
2. With your fingers, push the SIMM up until it is perpendicular to the motherboard and the metal clips on either end snap into place to hold it there. If the SIMM will not go in, or the clips do not hold it firmly, you might have it backwards; try it in the other direction. Figure 8.15 shows three SIMMs already installed and a fourth one ready to be pushed up.

**FIGURE 8.15**
Installing SIMMs in a Motherboard

### Installing a DIMM

DIMM (for dual inline memory module) is the more modern type of RAM. It is used in later Pentium systems and almost all systems built since then.

DIMMs fit straight down into a slot; you do not have to tilt them as with SIMMs. They also require a bit more physical pressure to insert them, especially in a brand-new motherboard that has never had DIMMs inserted before.

To install a DIMM:

1. Select the slot, and match the orientation of the DIMM with the slot. It will fit only one way because of the notches in the slot.
2. Firmly press the DIMM straight down into the slot, until the clips on both ends fit down over the notch in the DIMM. If the clip does not snap into place, the DIMM is not fully inserted (see Figure 8.16).

Tab locks into DIMM when fully inserted
BX

**FIGURE 8.16** Installing a DIMM in a Motherboard

## Installing a Motherboard in a PC Case

Installing the motherboard in the case is most technicians' least favorite job. It involves manual dexterity and fiddling with tiny screws and washers. But it is important to mount the motherboard in the case properly because an improperly mounted motherboard can easily short-circuit.

The motherboard must be mounted so that it does not directly touch the case in any way. The case is made of metal, and electricity could arc from one spot on the motherboard to another by passing through the case.

To ensure that the motherboard does not touch the case, a network of plastic and/or brass spacers is installed on the case floor. These are called

**Stand-offs**

Brass or plastic spacers that hold the motherboard away from the metal floor of the PC case.

*stand-offs* because that is their purpose—they help keep the motherboard standing off the floor. On ATX systems brass stand-offs are used; AT systems use plastic or a combination of plastic and brass.

When you buy a PC case, it comes with a bag of assorted screws and stand-offs, as described in Figure 8.17 and shown in Figure 8.18.

- **Plastic stand-offs:** These white plastic pieces look like stacks of tiny buttons. On one end is an umbrella tip that fits into a hole in the motherboard, then expands once it is through the hole to keep it there. You might not need these for an ATX motherboard.
- **Brass stand-offs:** These little brass screws have a nut on the top, and within that nut are screw threads. These install in the floor of the case and serve two purposes: they keep the motherboard raised and they provide threaded holes for the screws that attach the motherboard to the case. You might not need these for an AT motherboard.
- **Small metal screws:** These screws attach the motherboard to the case. You can recognize them by the extra metal ring around the main head of the screw, and by the fact that they are small in diameter and shorter than some of the other screws.
- **Paper washers:** These washers go between the motherboard and the screws mentioned above, to make sure there is no electrical arcing if a screw hole is close to a metal area on the board. They are usually dark red or brown.

**FIGURE 8.17**
Items for Installing a Motherboard

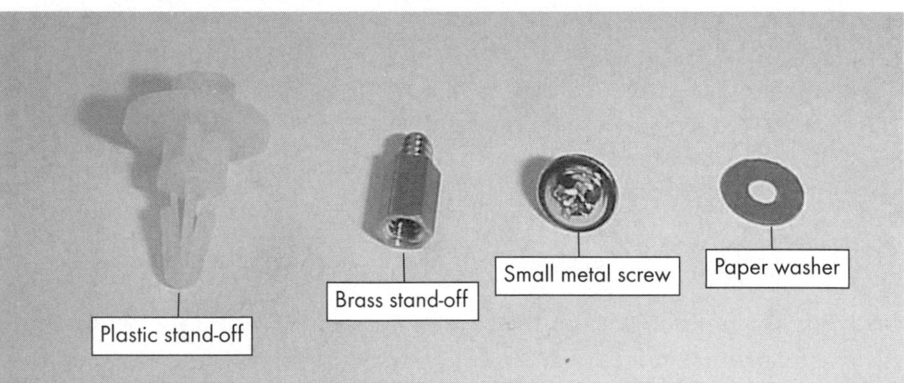


**FIGURE 8.18**
Items Needed to Attach the Motherboard to the Case

## Removing the Case Floor

If the floor comes out of the case, remove it. It will be much easier to install the motherboard on the floor if it is separated from the case. On many cases the floor is held in place by two or three screws.

## Installing the Stand-Offs

Next, set the motherboard on the case floor and make a note of the holes in the floor that match up with holes in the motherboard. These are the areas where you will attach stand-offs.

### *Plastic Stand-Offs*

A plastic stand-off attaches to the motherboard first, and then the bottom fits into a channel in the case floor and the entire motherboard slides to one side to lock the stand-offs into the channel. Plastic stand-offs are usually used only with AT motherboards because only AT-style cases have these channels in the floor (see Figure 8.19). Notice that the channels are wider at one end; that is where the stand-offs will be inserted. Then the motherboard will slide toward the narrow end.

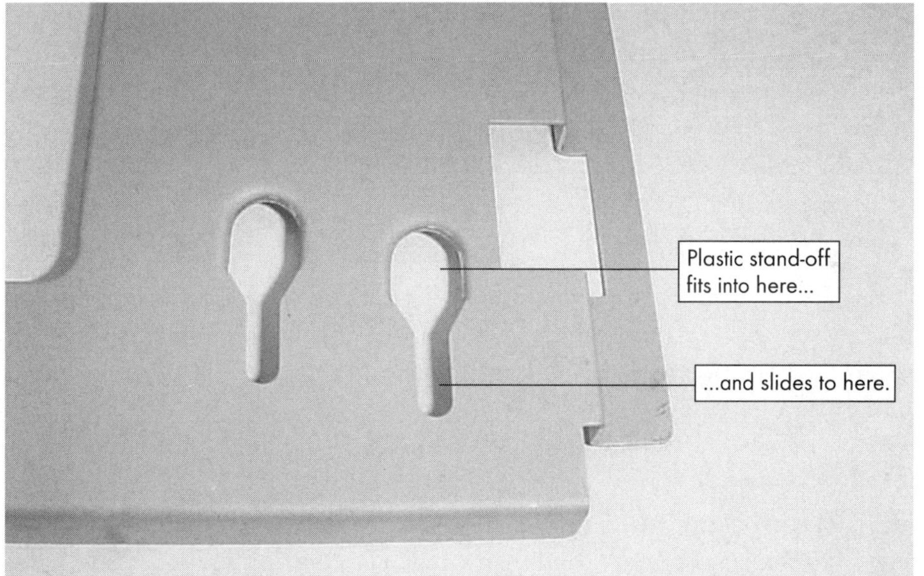
Plastic stand-off fits into here...
...and slides to here.

**FIGURE 8.19**
Channels for Plastic Stand-Offs in the Computer Case Floor

Identify the holes in the motherboard where plastic stand-offs should be installed, and then poke the umbrella tip of the stand-off through the hole so that the wide end of the stand-off is at the bottom of the motherboard (see Figure 8.20).

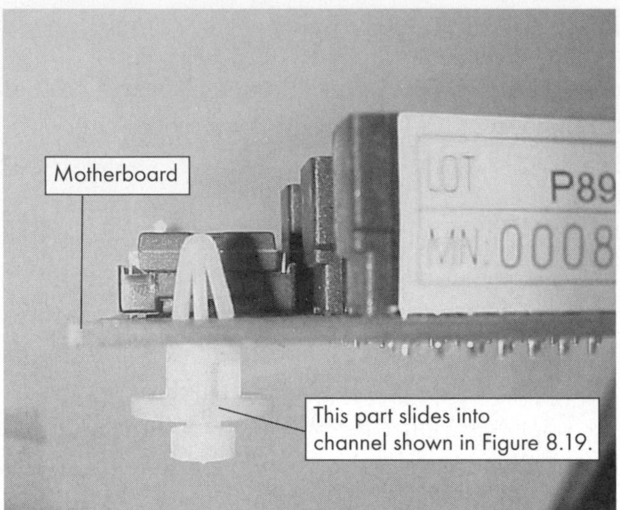
Motherboard
LOT P89
MN:0008
This part slides into channel shown in Figure 8.19.

**FIGURE 8.20**
Attach plastic stand-offs to the motherboard.

If you make a mistake and need to remove a plastic stand-off, use pliers to compress the umbrella tip of the stand-off so it will fit back through the hole. Then pull it back through. This is not easy to do—you need to apply some force. So be certain where you want the plastic stand-offs before you install them.

## In Real Life

**Most cases have many more stand-off holes than you will need to accommodate different sizes and designs of motherboard. A typical motherboard requires no more than four stand-offs.**

### *Brass Stand-Offs*

Brass stand-offs are used for all ATX and some AT motherboards. They attach to the case floor first, and then screws attach the motherboard to them.

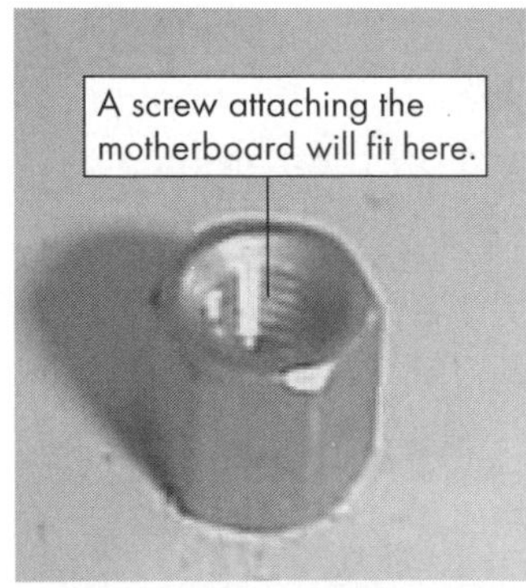
A screw attaching the motherboard will fit here.

**FIGURE 8.21**
Attach brass stand-offs to the case floor in spots where there is a corresponding hole in the motherboard.

To determine where to place brass stand-offs, place the motherboard on the floor and note where holes in the motherboard match up with screw holes in the case floor. Then screw brass stand-offs into those holes. You will know that they are installed correctly when you set the motherboard on the case floor and you can see the screw threads inside each brass stand-off through the holes in the motherboard. Figure 8.21 shows a brass stand-off installed on a case floor.

## Attaching the Motherboard to the Case Floor

The next step is to attach the motherboard to the case floor:

1. Place the motherboard on the case floor. If using plastic stand-offs, set down the motherboard so that the stand-offs fit into the wide part of the channels, and then slide the motherboard until the stand-offs slide into the narrow part and are held there. If there are no plastic stand-offs involved, simply set the motherboard on the floor.
2. Check to make sure that the screw holes in the motherboard align with the holes in the brass stand-offs. If they do not, remove the motherboard and reposition the brass stand-offs.
3. Place a paper washer over each screw hole in the motherboard, and then tighten a screw into each one (see Figure 8.22). The motherboard is now attached to the case floor.

**FIGURE 8.22**
Place a paper washer over each screw hole and then insert a screw into it.

### In Real Life

**Do not tighten any one screw until all screws have been loosely inserted. That way you can adjust the motherboard so that all the screw holes line up well enough to accept a screw.**

If the case floor was removable from the case, reinsert it into the case at this point and attach any screws that you removed earlier to hold it in place.

## Attaching Case Wires to the Motherboard

A tangle of colored wires with two-pin or three-pin connectors emerges from the inside front of the case; these wires must be attached to specific pins on the motherboard. They control such functions as the power light, the hard disk activity light, the speaker, the Reset button, and so on. On an ATX system, one of them also controls the power switch (typically labeled PWR SW). Figure 8.23 shows several case wires connected to the motherboard.

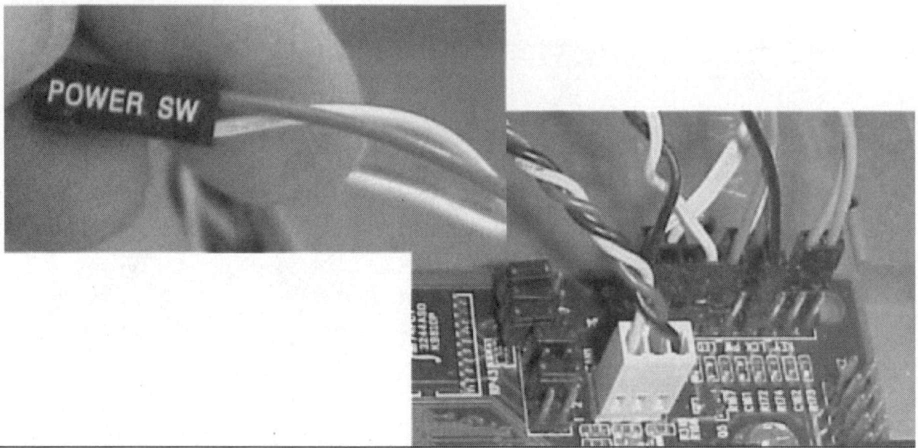


**FIGURE 8.23**
Case wires connected to the motherboard enable the lights and buttons on the case to communicate with the motherboard.

### In Real Life

If you are using an older case with a newer motherboard, some of the wires will not need to be connected. For example, some older cases had a Turbo switch and a Turbo light with wires and connectors, but most motherboards today do not have pins for that. This Turbo feature was a way of placing a PC into high-performance or low-performance states for running specific programs. For instance, some older games ran better when the computer ran more slowly. The Turbo feature is now obsolete.

Printed on the motherboard in tiny letters you might find abbreviations for the purposes of certain pins, and on the connectors themselves there might be corresponding abbreviations, so it is possible to match up the connectors to the right spots by following that lettering. However, it is much easier if you have a chart in the motherboard manual from which to work. Figure 8.24 shows charts from a motherboard manual specifying the positions of the pins for each connector, including the orientation of Pin 1 for each one, and explaining the purpose of each wire. Notice that the drawing shows two connections that do not appear in a chart: J5 and J6. These are for Turbo. The pins are there because it was easier for the motherboard manufacturer to include them than to remove them, but they are not implemented in this particular motherboard and thus do not appear in the charts.

**J3 - HDD LED Connector**

| Pin | Description |
|---|---|
| + | +5v DC |
| - | Active Low |

**J4 - Speaker Connector**

| Pin | Description |
|---|---|
| 1 | Data Out |
| 2 | N.C. |
| 3 | Ground |
| 4 | +5v |

**J7 - System Reset**

| Pin | Description |
|---|---|
| 1 | Ground |
| 2 | Reset System |

**J8 - Keylock & Power LED Connector**

| Pin | Description |
|---|---|
| 1 | LED Output |
| 2 | N.C. |
| 3 | Ground |
| 4 | Keylock |
| 5 | Ground |

TB-SW TB-LED HD-LED
J6 J5 J3
Keylock RST Speaker
J8 J7 J4

**FIGURE 8.24**
Charts in a Motherboard Manual Specifying the Case Connector Positions

Connect the connectors to the motherboard as described in the manual for your motherboard, or rely on the writing on the motherboard and on the connector plugs if needed. Do not forget to connect the system speaker.

## Connecting I/O Ports

This next step is for AT motherboards only; ATX models have built-in I/O ports on the side of the board.

An AT motherboard comes with at least one serial and one parallel port and a PS/2 port on backplates, with narrow ribbon cables leading away from each one. There may also be backplates with USB ports, a video port, and sound card ports if any of those features is built into the motherboard's chipset.

To install the ports:

1. Consult the motherboard manual to determine which sockets on the motherboard are for which connectors.
2. Plug them in, taking care to orient the red stripe on each ribbon cable to Pin 1 (see Figure 8.25). The diagram in the motherboard manual should identify the location of Pin 1, or a number or arrow should be stamped onto the motherboard identifying it. The parallel and serial ports will use narrow ribbon cables, and the PS/2 cable will be a set of bare or wrapped wires with a thin, flat connector like the ones that you connected for the speaker and lights in the preceding section, except with five holes (one of which may be filled in for keying purposes). Attaching the cable for the PS/2 port backward can short out the board, so confirm the proper orientation in the motherboard manual.

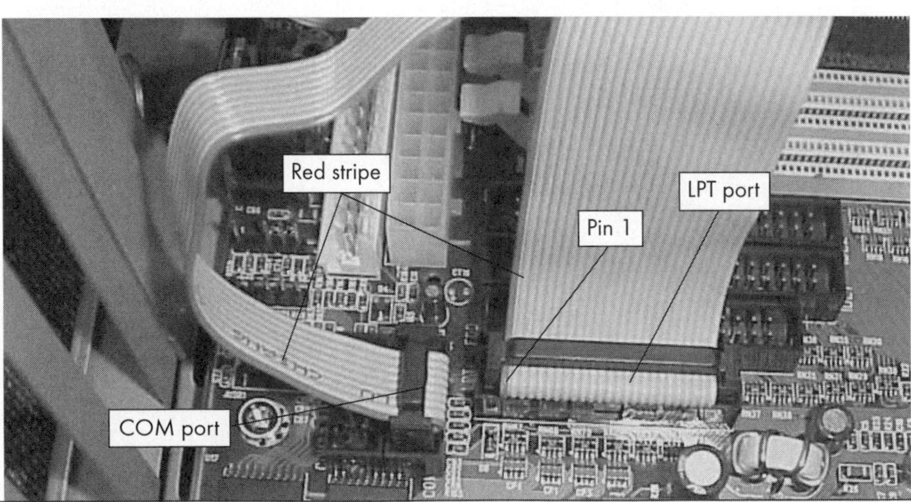


**FIGURE 8.25**
Attach the connectors for the I/O ports to an AT motherboard.

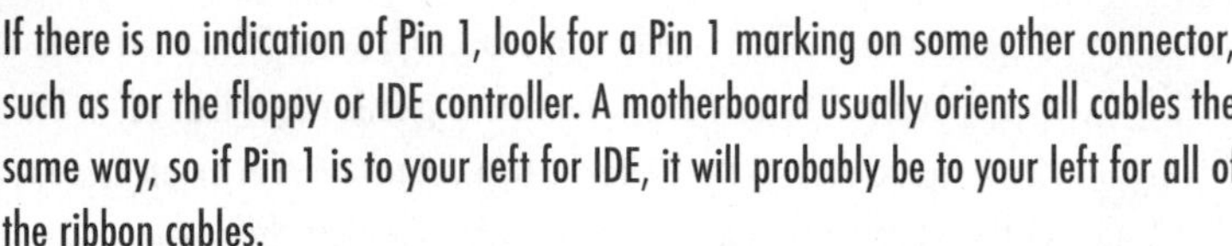

## IN REAL LIFE

If there is no indication of Pin 1, look for a Pin 1 marking on some other connector, such as for the floppy or IDE controller. A motherboard usually orients all cables the same way, so if Pin 1 is to your left for IDE, it will probably be to your left for all of the ribbon cables.

3. Attach the backplates to the case with screws. If you need to pop out a perforated metal panel on the case to make room for the backplate, do so with a flathead screwdriver as discussed in Chapter 3.

Some cases have holes in them designed for mounting ports. If yours does, you can remove the ports from the backplate and mount them on the case instead.

## CONNECTING THE POWER SUPPLY

Next, you attach the power supply's motherboard connector(s). On an AT-style motherboard there are two connectors, labeled P8 and P9. Attach them to the motherboard, making sure that the black wires are together (see Figure 8.26).

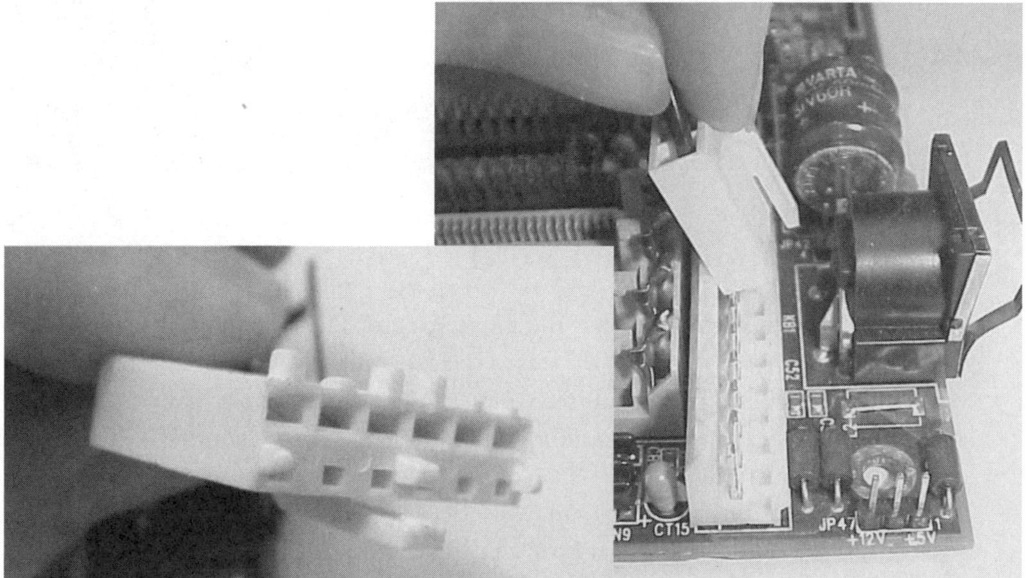


**FIGURE 8.26**
An AT-style power supply connection to the motherboard has two sections: P8 and P9.

## In Real Life

Beginners sometimes struggle with attaching P8 and P9 connectors to the motherboard, because the connectors have some plastic ridges that get in the way. The secret to success is to start with the connector slanted at an angle, toward the back of the connector. This lets those ridges fit down into the grooves. Then after the first half-inch or so, stand it up perpendicular.

An ATX power supply has only one connector to the motherboard, and it is keyed to fit only one direction. Plug it in there, as shown in Figure 8.27.

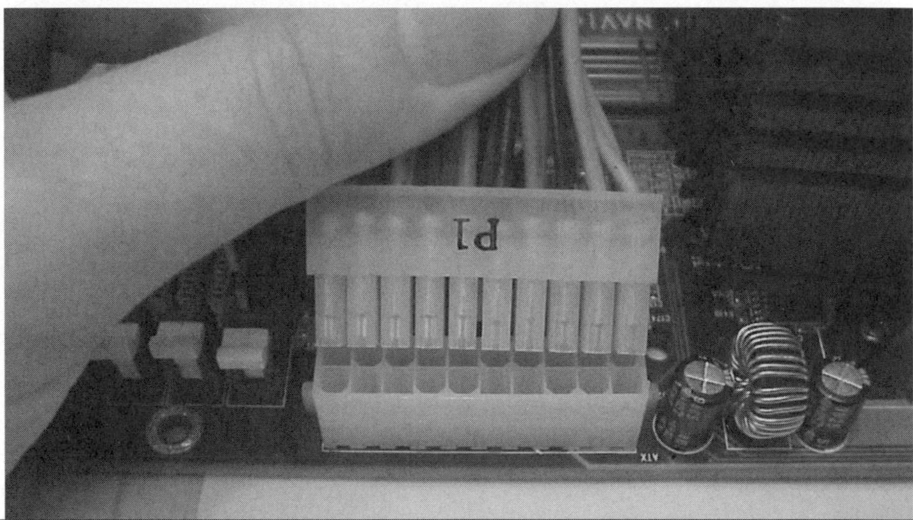


**FIGURE 8.27**
An ATX power supply connector is one large block.

# Installing a Video Card

Now you need to verify that the motherboard, CPU, and memory are working. The best way to do this is to install a video card and hook up a monitor. That way you can see whether any text appears when you turn on the PC. If text appears, you know that all of the components you installed so far are working.

If your motherboard has built-in video, you hooked up a video port when you installed the I/O ports earlier in this chapter. If not, you must install a video card in an expansion slot. You will learn about video cards in detail in Chapter 15, but for now any video card will do. If the motherboard has an AGP slot, an AGP video card would be best, but a PCI video card or even an ISA card will work for this test.

To install a video card:

1. Remove the backplate behind the slot in which you will install the video card.
2. Handling the expansion card only by its edges, press it down into the expansion slot until it is completely seated (see Figure 8.28).
3. Attach the card's backplate to the back of the PC with a screw. Set aside the blank backplate that you removed, in case you need it later.

**FIGURE 8.28**
Installing a Video Card

## Testing the Installation So Far

Plug a monitor into the video card, and turn on the monitor. Now you are ready to test. Turn on the PC's power. If everything is working, you should immediately hear the power supply fan spin up; the fan on the heat sink (if there is one) should spin too. Wait a moment for the monitor to warm up and you should see text on the screen. You will probably see a warning about not having a keyboard installed; ignore it. You may also hear a single beep from the system speaker as it tests itself.

If things happened as described above, congratulations; you are ready to move on to installing the rest of the components—keyboard, mouse, drives, and so on. If not, consult the following sections for troubleshooting advice.

## TRY IT!

If you are working in a classroom with other students, and each of you has a PC, try simulating some errors and then having other students troubleshoot and correct them. For example, you might loosen a cable or change a jumper setting. Do not do anything that would potentially damage the hardware, however, such as orienting a PGA CPU incorrectly or switching the P8 and P9 connectors on an AT motherboard.

## No Power Supply Fan

If nothing happens when you turn on the PC—no power supply fan spinning, no activity at all—then the power supply either is not receiving electricity or is not operational.

### In Real Life

Most power supplies will not operate without a load, so if you plug in a power supply without hooking it up to a motherboard, it probably will appear totally dead, with no fan spin-up, even though it is actually fine. For accurate results, you must test a power supply with a current-drawing device attached to it.

To troubleshoot a completely dead PC, first trace the path of the electricity from the wall outlet to the power supply, making sure that

- the plugs are all snug
- the surge suppressor is not turned off
- the power cord is good (test with a multimeter or swap it with a known good one)
- the voltage switch on the power supply is set to 110v or 115v, not 220v

If none of that helps, the power supply itself is probably bad. Try swapping it with a new or known good one as described in Chapter 3.

### In Real Life

An essential part of a PC technician's troubleshooting arsenal is a selection of parts that you know to be good, such as power supply, video card, and so on. Many times the only way to positively confirm that a part is bad is to swap it with one that you know is good and observe the results.

WARNING

Usually swapping parts is a great way to isolate a problem, but there is one exception. If you suspect a power supply is bad, do not try the questionable power supply in a PC you know is good. A bad power supply has the potential to damage a motherboard.

## Beep Codes

As the PC starts up, a single beep from the speaker is normal. This signals that the PC has passed its internal tests. However, multiple beeps signal problems, as mentioned in Chapter 4. The exact number and pattern of the beeps depend on the BIOS manufacturer and version, and on the specific type of problem. These are called beep codes.

Without a reference guide, and without knowing the BIOS manufacturer, it is impossible to tell exactly what is wrong with a PC by listening to the beeps. However, the vast majority of real-life beeping comes from bad, incompatible, or improperly installed RAM, so check that first when you hear multiple beeps.

You can find reference guides for the various BIOS manufacturers at the Web sites listed on the Internet Resource Center.

## No On-Screen Text

Troubleshooting situations in which the power supply fan operates but no text appears on the screen can be frustrating because there is so little to go on. A no-video situation can have many different causes. Check the following:

- Make sure the RAM you have installed is compatible with this motherboard and is correctly installed.
- Make sure that the motherboard is configured to accept the CPU that you have installed. Make sure any jumpers have been appropriately set for system bus speed, clock multiplier, and, most importantly, CPU core voltage.
- Make sure the CPU and memory are properly installed.
- Check that the CPU is correctly and completely installed. A PGA CPU might be oriented the wrong way; an SECC CPU might not be completely pushed down into its slot.
- Check the motherboard manual to make sure that you are not violating any rules regarding the placement of RAM in the banks.

- Make sure the video card is completely inserted in the correct slot type, that the monitor is firmly attached to it, and that the monitor is turned on and its contrast turned up.
- If it is an AT motherboard, make sure the P8 and P9 connectors are plugged in with the black wires together.

One more thing to try is to look for a Reset jumper on the motherboard. If the BIOS's CMOS data has become corrupted, it could cause a no-video situation. Start the PC with the Reset jumper in Clear, Erase, or Reset position (wording depends on model). Leave it on for 10 seconds, then turn it off and put the jumper back to Normal position.

If you have no luck after checking all of these things, try a different video card. If that does not work, start swapping out components—CPU, memory, and motherboard—one at a time with known good ones until you find the problem.

If you do not have extra known good parts to swap out, try a POST (Power On Self Test) card. As you will recall, a POST card is a circuit board that fits into a PCI or ISA expansion slot in the motherboard. As the PC boots, it displays numeric codes showing the progress of the various internal self-tests that occur before the first text appears on the screen. When the boot process locks at a certain point, the numeric code freezes on the POST card. You can then look up that numeric code in a reference book (which comes with the POST card) to determine what is wrong. POST cards are available at stores that cater to the professional PC technician. A list of some Web sites that sell them appears on the Internet Resource Center.

## TRY IT!

If you have access to a POST card, insert it in a PC and watch the numbers change as the PC starts up. It need not be a defective PC. Look up one of the numbers you see on the card to find out what it means.

# STUDY GUIDE

Use the following summaries to review the key concepts of this chapter.

## CONFIGURING A MOTHERBOARD

- Take antistatic precautions when working with a motherboard, as described in Chapter 2.
- Set jumpers on the motherboard before installing it in the case because they will be easier to see. Consult the motherboard manual to determine jumper positions.

## INSTALLING THE CPU

- For an SECC CPU, install support brackets on the motherboard.
- Insert an SECC CPU into its slot until the tabs on the ends lock into the support brackets.
- For a PGA CPU, align the different corner on the CPU with the different corner on the socket. For example, one corner may be rounded or a pin or hole may be missing.
- Raise the arm on the PGA socket to open it. Drop in the CPU, and then lower the arm.
- Attach a passive heat sink with heat sink compound, a gluelike substance. Attach an active heat sink (that is, one with a fan) with its built-in clip.

## INSTALLING RAM

- Consult the motherboard manual to determine the type and placement of RAM. Some motherboards will accept only certain kinds of RAM.
- Handle RAM only by the edges, just as you would handle a circuit board.
- Insert SIMMs at an angle and then tilt them into perpendicular position. Metal clips lock them into place when they are completely seated.
- Insert DIMMs straight down into their sockets. Clips snap into place at both ends when they are completely seated.

## INSTALLING THE MOTHERBOARD IN THE CASE

- Remove the floor from the case if it is removable; this will make it easier to install the motherboard on it.

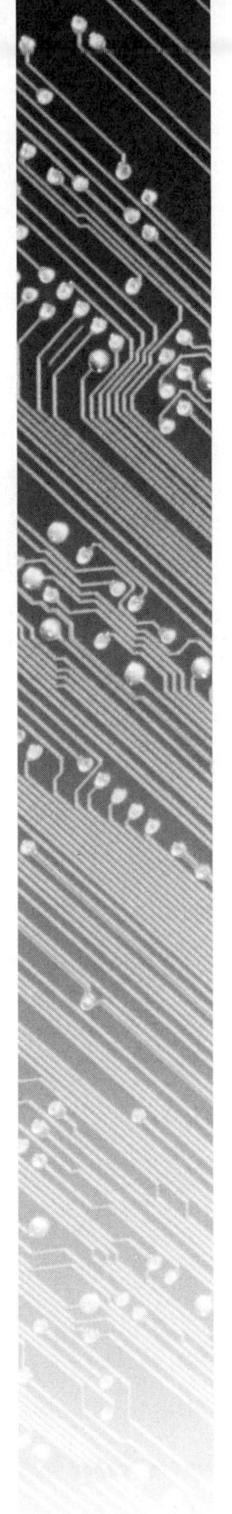

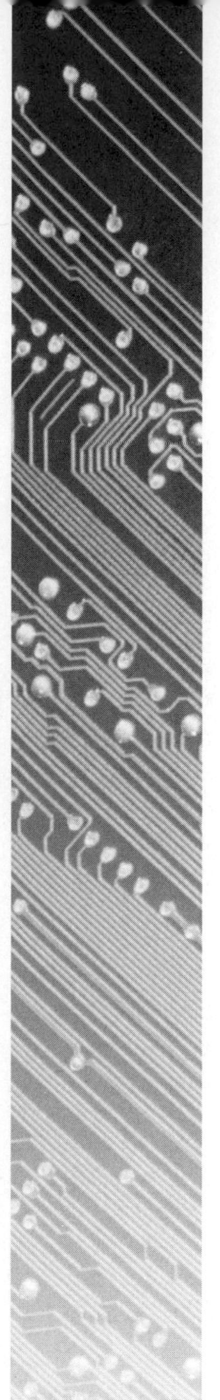

- Set the motherboard on the case floor and notice where the holes and channels line up. Those are the spots where you will install stand-offs.
- Install plastic stand-offs on an AT motherboard in spots that match the channels in the case floor.
- Install brass stand-offs on the case floor in spots that match up with screw holes in the motherboard.
- Attach the motherboard to the case floor using screws, screwing them into the sockets on the brass stand-offs. The motherboard must not directly touch the case floor in any spot.

## Attaching Ports and Cables

- Case wires run from the front of the case and from the system speaker. Each is a set of two or more wires with a small black connector. Attach these to the motherboard as dictated by the motherboard manual.
- If the motherboard manual is not available, read the labeling on the motherboard and on the connectors to try to match them up.
- On an AT system, connect the cables for the I/O ports (parallel, serial, USB, PS/2 mouse) to the motherboard and then mount their connectors, either on backplates or directly on the case.
- When connecting ribbon cables for ports, align the red stripe with Pin 1. Consult the motherboard manual to determine which is Pin 1, or look for a 1 on the motherboard near the connector.
- On an AT system, connect the P8 and P9 power supply connectors to the motherboard so that the black wires are together. On an ATX system, connect the single 20-wire P1 connector to the motherboard.

## Installing a Video Card

- Installing a video card is necessary for testing purposes.
- Handle the video card only by the edges. Insert it into an expansion slot in the motherboard and secure it to the case with a screw.
- Plug a monitor into the video card's port, and turn on the monitor.

## Testing and Troubleshooting

- If you do not see video on-screen when you turn on the PC, start troubleshooting.
- First, check all connectors to make sure they are snug.
- Recheck the settings for the motherboard and confirm that the CPU and RAM used are of the correct type.

- Confirm that the monitor is plugged in, turned on, and connected to the PC.
- If you do not hear any power supply fan, try a different power supply.
- If you hear multiple beeps from the system speaker, look up the pattern of beeps at the BIOS manufacturer's Web site.
- Swap parts with known good ones to narrow your search for the defective part, or try a POST card if one is available.

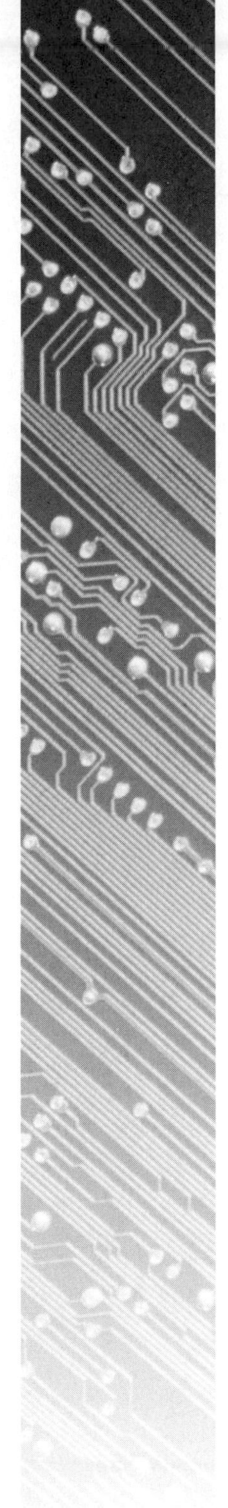

# PRACTICE TEST

On a blank sheet of paper, write the answers to the following multiple-choice questions and explain why each answer is correct.

1. Which of the following would *not* be set by a jumper on the motherboard?
   a. CPU core voltage
   b. on-board sound and video
   c. clock multiplier
   d. boot order

2. Which of these would *not* be a potential source of information about the correct jumper settings on the motherboard?
   a. Web site of BIOS manufacturer
   b. motherboard manual
   c. writing on the motherboard itself
   d. Web site of motherboard manufacturer

3. Why is heat sink compound not used with an active heat sink?
   a. It would inhibit the heat sink's ability to conduct heat away from the CPU.
   b. It would cause the fan to go bad faster because of the greater heat transfer.
   c. It makes it harder to remove the fan if it goes bad.
   d. There is no reason; heat sink compound is routinely used with an active heat sink.

4. What is the significance of a rounded corner on a PGA CPU?
   a. The chip must be oriented with that corner pointing toward the power supply connector.
   b. It identifies the orientation of the CPU.
   c. The chip must be oriented with that corner facing the joint of the handle on the socket.
   d. There is no significance; it might simply mean the chip is worn from handling.

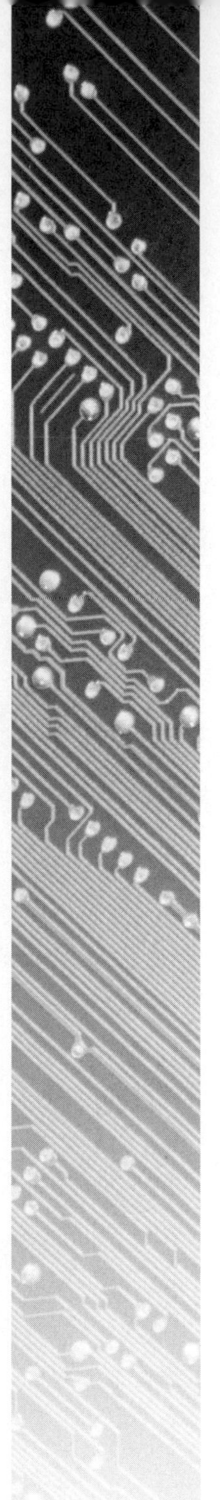

5. When do you attach an active heat sink for a PGA CPU?
   a. before installing the CPU on the motherboard
   b. after installing the CPU on the motherboard but before starting the PC
   c. only after the initial testing confirms that the CPU is operational
   d. It makes no difference when you install it.

6. The fan for an active heat sink draws its power from
   a. the CPU.
   b. the motherboard battery.
   c. the motherboard or power supply.
   d. nowhere; it is self-powered with its own internal battery.

7. Support brackets for an SECC CPU are installed
   a. on the motherboard before the CPU is installed.
   b. on the motherboard after the CPU is installed.
   c. on the CPU itself before it is installed on the motherboard.
   d. on the CPU itself after it is installed on the motherboard.

8. When installing an SECC CPU
   a. you must be careful to get the cartridge oriented correctly because if you install it backward and then start up the PC, damage will result.
   b. the cartridge is the same on both ends, so it will work fine installed with either side facing either way.
   c. the correct orientation of the cartridge depends on the model; Pentium II fits one way and Athlon fits another way.
   d. It is impossible to insert the cartridge backward in the slot because the slot is keyed.

9. Which type of RAM is always a separate bank for each slot regardless of the type of motherboard and CPU?
   a. 30-pin SIMM
   b. 72-pin SIMM
   c. 168-pin DIMM
   d. Both b and c

10. Which of these is *not* used in mounting an ATX motherboard to its case?
    a. brass stand-offs
    b. plastic stand-offs
    c. paper washers
    d. metal screws

11. The purpose of a paper washer is to
    a. prevent electrical arcing between the metal screw and the motherboard.
    b. create an EMI barrier between the case and the motherboard floor.
    c. add physical spacing needed for proper motherboard alignment.
    d. All of the above

12. A plastic stand-off is installed
    a. on the motherboard before attaching it to the case floor.
    b. on the case floor before attaching the motherboard to it.
    c. on the motherboard after attaching it to the case floor.
    d. on the case floor after attaching the motherboard to it.

13. A brass stand-off is installed
    a. on the motherboard before attaching it to the case floor.
    b. on the case floor before attaching the motherboard to it.
    c. on the motherboard after attaching it to the case floor.
    d. on the case floor after attaching the motherboard to it.

14. When you attach screws to hold the motherboard onto the case floor, what do they screw into?
    a. the case floor
    b. plastic stand-offs
    c. brass stand-offs
    d. either b or c, depending on the motherboard type

15. On an AT motherboard, which of these case wires must be connected to the motherboard in order for the power switch to turn on the PC?
    a. PWR SW
    b. TURBO SW
    c. Power LED
    d. None of the above

16. Which of these would be built into an ATX motherboard and not require a connector to be attached to the motherboard during installation?
    a. USB port
    b. PS/2 mouse
    c. legacy parallel port
    d. All of the above

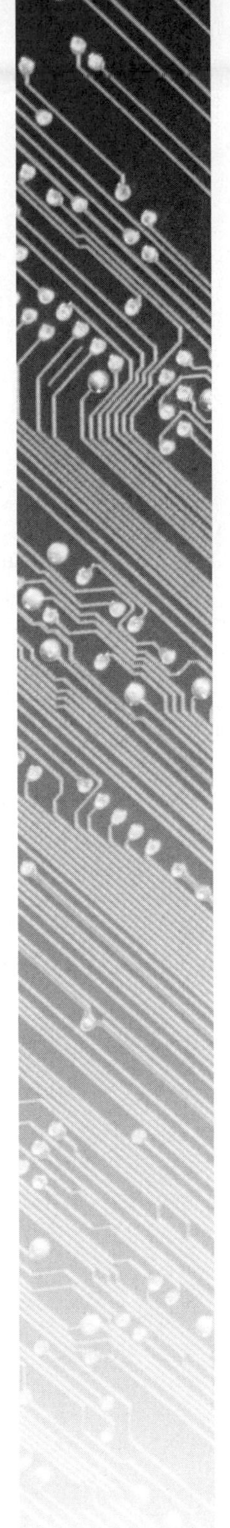

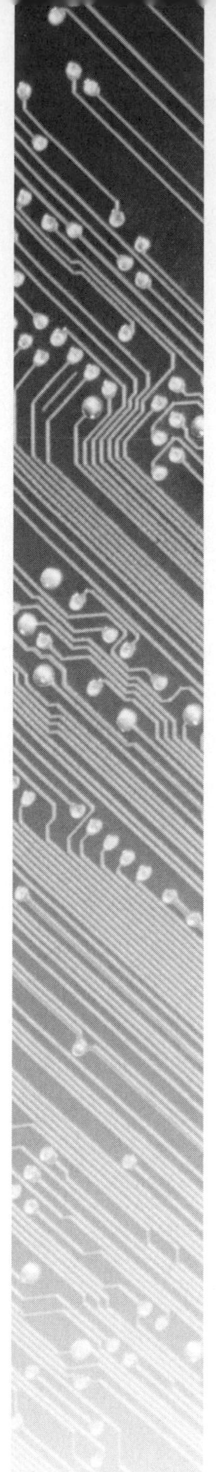

17. When attaching AT power supply connectors to the motherboard, how should P8 and P9 be oriented?
    a. red wires together
    b. black wires together
    c. black wires facing out
    d. It does not matter.

18. Which type of video card is required to make sure the motherboard, CPU, and memory are operational?
    a. ISA
    b. PCI
    c. either PCI or AGP
    d. Any that will fit into any expansion slot.

19. If the power supply fan does not spin up when you press the Power button, which of these could *not* be the reason?
    a. It is not plugged in.
    b. It is not connected to the motherboard.
    c. The floppy drive cable is backward.
    d. The power supply is defective.

20. The power supply fan spins but you see nothing on the screen and hear no beeps. Which of these could *not* be the problem?
    a. The CPU is installed incorrectly.
    b. The wrong type of memory is installed.
    c. The video card is defective.
    d. The system speaker is defective.

# TROUBLESHOOTING

1. You have just assembled the PC parts described in this chapter and pressed the Power button on the PC case, but nothing happens; it is totally dead. Describe what you would check first.

2. After fixing the problem that was causing the complete lack of power in #1 above, you try again. When you press the Power button, you immediately hear a series of loud beeps coming from the system speaker. Describe what you would do.

3. After fixing the problem that was causing the beeping in #2 above, you hear no beeps but you also get no video on-screen. Describe what you would do.

# CUSTOMER SERVICE

1. A customer has bought a secondhand motherboard with an SECC slot, and wants you to install memory and a CPU in it and use it to upgrade his old computer. What are some questions you should ask him over the phone to make sure you bring the correct parts with you?

2. A customer has removed her PGA CPU to look at it, and now she cannot get it reinstalled. Describe how you would instruct her to reinstall it over the phone.

3. Yesterday you built a system for a friend, and today the friend calls you to say that the Reset button does not work. What have you probably forgotten to do, and how could you instruct your friend over the phone to correct it so you do not have to make another trip to her home?

# FOR MORE INFORMATION

For links to Web sites that provide further information about the topics covered in this chapter, go to the EMC/Paradigm Internet Resource Center at www.emcp.com/College Division/Internet Resource Centers/PC Maintenance/For More Information.

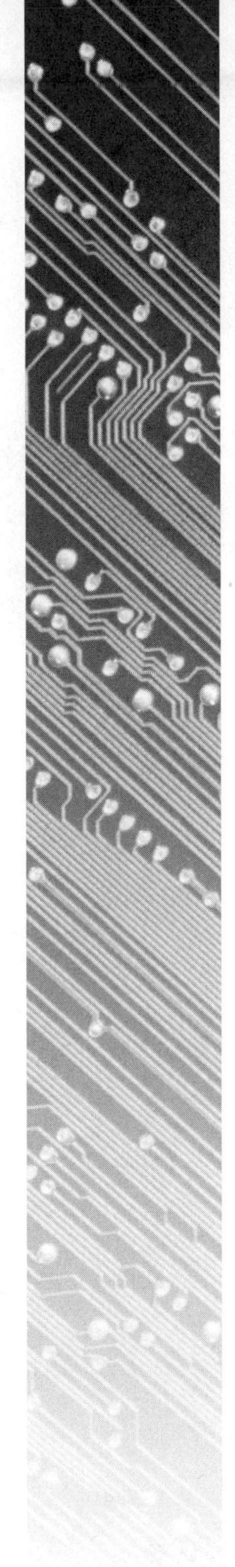

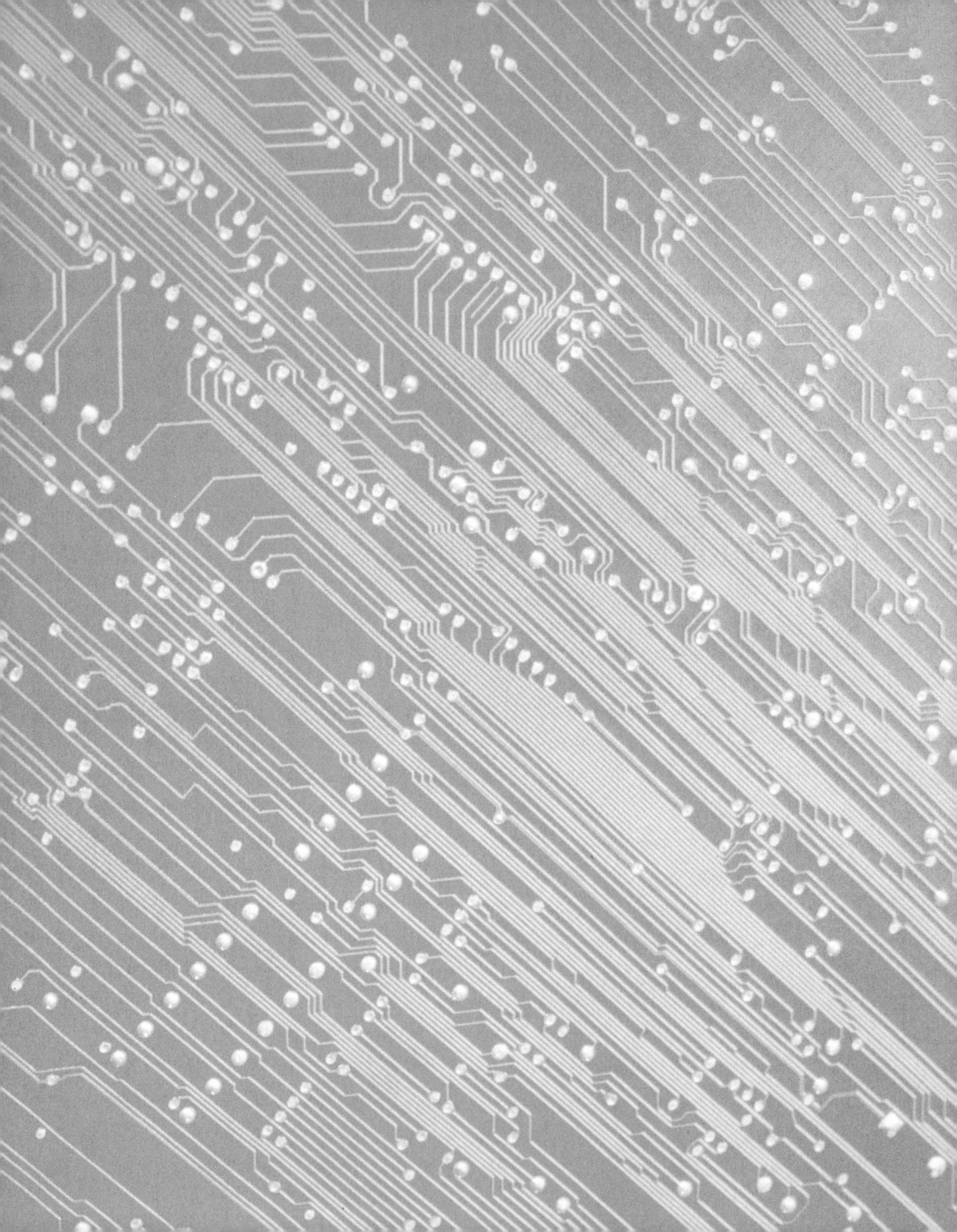

# 9 Working with the BIOS Setup Program

## ON THE TEST

**A+ Core Hardware Service Technician Examination**

- **Objective 1.1:** Identify basic terms, concepts, and functions of system modules, including how each module should work during normal operation and during the boot process.
- **Objective 1.8:** Identify hardware methods of upgrading system performance, procedures for replacing basic subsystem components, unique components and when to use them.
- **Objective 2.1:** Identify common symptoms and problems associated with each module and how to troubleshoot and isolate the problems.
- **Objective 4.4:** Identify the purpose of CMOS (Complementary Metal-Oxide Semiconductor), what it contains and how to change its basic parameters.

## ON THE JOB

The BIOS setup program provides a way to change the base-level hardware settings for the motherboard's chipset. Understanding how a BIOS works and being able to edit BIOS settings can be useful in the following situations:

- enabling or disabling I/O ports such as legacy parallel and serial and USB
- controlling chipset-based power management settings
- configuring settings for disk drives
- specifying a boot order among the available drives
- manually assigning IRQs and I/O addresses to I/O ports
- setting an operating mode for a legacy parallel port

- enabling or disabling chipset-based Plug and Play
- setting or clearing an administrator password
- updating a BIOS to the latest version

# Understanding BIOS and CMOS

In Chapter 3 you learned about the Basic Input Output System (BIOS) and complementary metal-oxide semiconductor (CMOS). The following sections review that information briefly.

## BIOS

As previously discussed, the low-level programs that help hardware start up and communicate with other pieces of hardware are stored on ROM chips on the circuit boards themselves. That way they can never be accidentally erased or changed. These sets of low-level programs are called *Basic Input Output Systems* (BIOSes). The BIOS for the motherboard is the *system BIOS*, which is stored there on a ROM BIOS chip. Another name for BIOS is firmware, although firmware is actually a bit broader term; BIOS is simply the most common use for firmware.

**Basic Input Output System (BIOS)**

The low-level startup instructions for a component, stored on a firmware chip on the component's main circuit board.

**System BIOS**

The motherboard's BIOS.

The BIOS programs do not need to be altered on a day-to-day basis. For example, the instructions for sending and receiving data from the chipset to the CPU are the same every time you turn on the PC. However, over the years, as new hardware is introduced, it can be helpful to have a way of updating the system BIOS to support the latest devices and add-ons. The original ROM BIOS chips were completely unalterable, but today's EEPROM BIOS chips can be changed with a BIOS update utility program.

## CMOS

As you learned earlier, CMOS (for complementary metal-oxide semiconductor) is a type of RAM chip that requires very little electricity to retain its data. A CMOS chip theoretically could be used for many different purposes, but in real-life usage the term has come to be virtually synonymous with a particular application: storing changes and additions to the data stored on the system BIOS chip.

Most motherboards sold today do not have a CMOS chip. Any changes that need to be made to the ROM BIOS are made directly to the BIOS chip itself. This is possible because today's BIOS chips are EEPROMS

(Electrically Erasable Programmable ROMs) that can be modified with electrical pulses, and the BIOS Setup program can generate the needed pulses to write the changes.

In earlier days, however, all motherboards had both a ROM BIOS chip and a CMOS chip. The ROM BIOS chip held the core set of settings—the "house rules" for the motherboard. The end user could then enter a BIOS Setup program to specify any changes to those rules, and those changes would be stored on a CMOS chip. Then each time the PC started up, first the BIOS data would load, and then the CMOS data would load on top of it. Whenever the CMOS data differed from the BIOS data, the CMOS version would win. So, for example, if the BIOS specified that there was one floppy drive and the CMOS specified that there were two, the system would believe it had two.

CMOS is not ROM; it is *nonvolatile RAM* (NVRAM). It needs a small amount of electricity to retain its data, and draws it from the motherboard battery. Some CMOS chips have a built-in long-life battery of their own (nonchangeable), so that they do not rely on the motherboard battery. Some motherboards do not have a battery at all.

**Nonvolatile RAM (NVRAM)**

A type of RAM that retains its data without needing to be continually refreshed.

Today's motherboards combine the functions of the ROM BIOS and the CMOS into a single EEPROM chip. Such chips may have a long-life battery built in or may rely on a separate motherboard battery.

## Interaction with Memory

In Chapter 6 you learned that the first 1MB of a PC's memory is broken down into two sections: conventional and upper. Upper memory consists of 360KB of RAM that is set aside for system use. One of these system uses is to provide memory addresses for interacting with the BIOS.

Reading data from ROM is slow compared with reading from RAM. Therefore, some systems copy the contents of the BIOS into that reserved area of RAM as the PC starts up, resulting in faster access to that BIOS data as the PC operates. This is called *ROM shadowing* or BIOS shadowing. On some systems it can be enabled or disabled in the BIOS Setup program (see Figure 9.1).

**ROM shadowing**

Copying the contents of ROM into RAM for faster access to it.

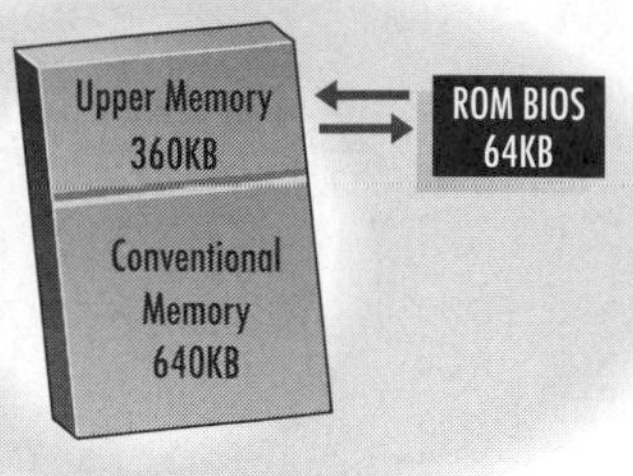


**FIGURE 9.1**
ROM BIOS interacts with RAM through the reserved system area in the top 360KB of the first megabyte.

### In Real Life

ROM shadowing is useful on a system that is running a 16-bit operating system such as MS-DOS, but with a 32-bit operating system it does not do much good because the operating system uses its own 32-bit virtual device drivers (VxD drivers) rather than referring to the 16-bit BIOS instructions for the devices as it runs. On such a system the BIOS instructions for communicating with the devices are read only once, at startup.

## Accessing the BIOS Setup Program

All motherboards ship with default settings defined in the BIOS. These default settings should enable the system to start up and run through its initial self-tests. However, since the motherboard manufacturer cannot anticipate all of the customization that a given user will perform, the end user needs to be able to modify the BIOS settings. This modification is performed through the BIOS Setup utility.

The exact procedure for entering the BIOS Setup utility varies depending on the PC. As the PC starts up, a message briefly appears on-screen telling you what key to press to enter Setup, something like this: *Press F2 for Setup.* The key could be F1, F2, Delete, or any other key, depending on the BIOS manufacturer and version. It is always one of the function keys or special-purpose keys and not a regular letter or number.

## In Real Life

Since you know that the regular numbers and letters are excluded, it is a manageable process of elimination to find the key that enters BIOS Setup on a system where no message appears on-screen to help you. Just start pressing all of the non-character keys quickly as soon as you see text on the screen until one of them takes you to Setup.

If you do not press the specified key, the message goes away after several seconds and the PC proceeds to boot normally. If you press the named key while the message is still on the screen, however, a Setup program stored on the BIOS chip appears (see Figure 9.2).

```
PhoenixBIOS 4.0 Release 6.0
Copyright 1985-2000 Phoenix Technologies Ltd.
All Rights Reserved
Copyright 2000-2001 VMware, Inc.
VMware BIOS build 212

CPU = Pentium III  933 MHz
640K System RAM Passed
15M Extended RAM Passed
256K Cache SRAM Passed
Mouse initialized
Fixed Disk 0: IDE Hard Drive
ATAPI CD-ROM: IDE CDROM Drive





Press <F2> to enter SETUP
```

**FIGURE 9.2**
A message flashes on-screen at startup letting you know what key to press to enter BIOS setup.

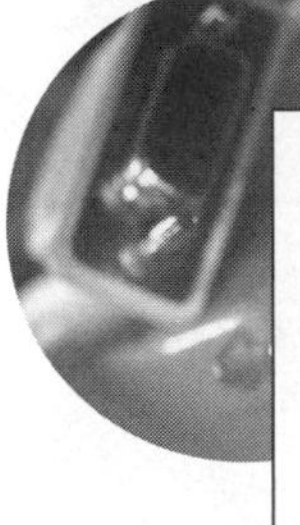

## In Real Life

On today's systems, you can enter the BIOS Setup program only during startup. On some older systems, however, you could enter it at any time. Such systems typically required a multikey combination to enter the program, such as Ctrl + Shift + F10. Even older systems did not have the BIOS Setup program built into the BIOS chip; the motherboard came with a separate setup utility on a floppy disk. If you have such a motherboard and you do not have the floppy disk, you might be able to download the files needed for the floppy disk from the manufacturer's Web site, or you might be able to get into the BIOS Setup through some third-party utility program.

There are many different types of BIOS Setup programs, some of them radically different from others. Some programs are graphically based and enable mouse use; others are keyboard-only and consist of screens of text-based menus. Today the vast majority of PCs use the text-based type, so that is what will be covered in this chapter.

With any BIOS Setup program, on-screen instructions tell how to move between settings and how to change values. In Figure 9.3 you can see that the left and right arrow keys move between pages, the up and down arrow keys move between settings on the same page, Enter opens a submenu (indicated by a right-pointing triangle), Esc exits, and the + and - keys change the values.

Notice also in Figure 9.3 that help is available for the selected setting in the right pane of the screen. The text here changes depending on the option selected.

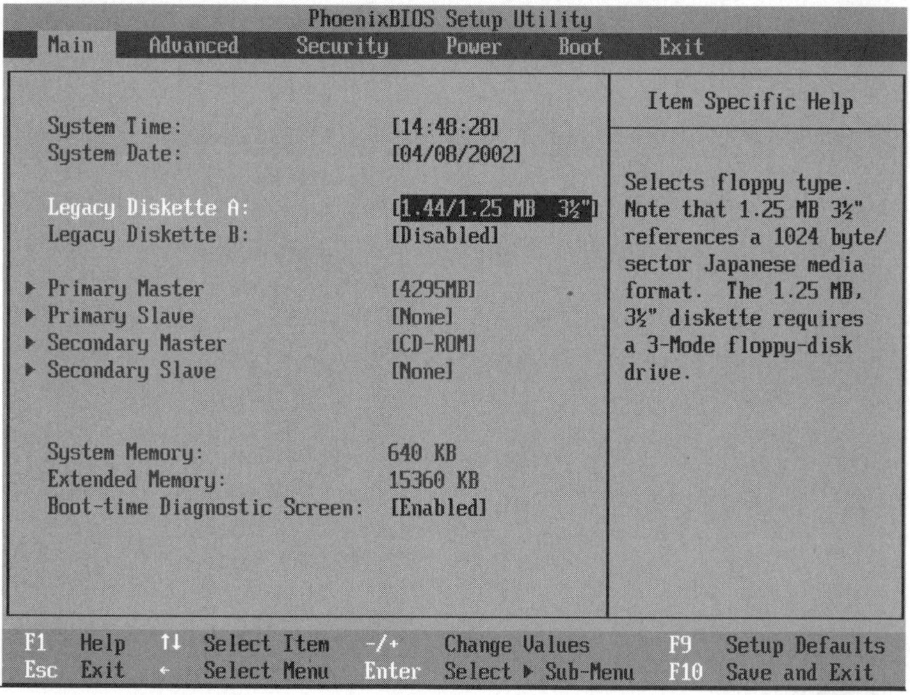

**FIGURE 9.3**
A Typical BIOS Setup Program

Your BIOS Setup program might not look just like the one in Figure 9.3, and might not work exactly the same way, but it will contain on-screen instructions that can help you figure it out. You also may be able to get help with the program by pressing the F1 key.

A common convention in most BIOS Setup programs is for the F10 key to save changes and exit and for the Esc key to exit from the current screen. If the current screen is a top-level menu, pressing Esc usually opens a dialog box asking whether you want to exit the BIOS Setup program itself and discard or save changes.

**TRY IT!**

Start up a PC and enter its BIOS Setup program. Use any means necessary to determine the key(s) to press in order to do this. Once you get into the program, explore the options available there. Move from page to page and option to option. Then exit from the program, discarding changes. If possible, do this on several different PCs so you can get an idea of the differences among BIOS Setup programs.

## Common Adjustable Settings in the Setup Utility

The following sections describe some of the settings you can adjust in a typical BIOS Setup program. Not all motherboards' BIOSes will have all of these settings; some BIOS Setup programs are much more feature-rich than others.

The settings covered in the following sections are by no means comprehensive. We have purposely excluded many of the settings found exclusively on older systems and many of the settings that rarely need to be adjusted. The settings described here should be more than adequate in gaining a general understanding of the scope of BIOS Setup.

**WARNING**

The names of the settings given here are not necessarily the names by which your BIOS Setup program will call them. Different programs use different names for many features. For example, one BIOS Setup program might call a feature Wake on Ring, while another might call the same feature On Modem Ring. So how do you know? Utilize the Help system built into your BIOS Setup program, and if you are ever in doubt about a setting, leave it set to its default.

### Date and Time

All BIOS Setup programs enable you to change the system date and time. This is necessary because as the motherboard's battery ages, it begins to lose time, so the clock does not stay accurate. At the top of Figure 9.3 notice the System Time and System Date editable fields.

There are other ways of setting the date and time that do not involve BIOS Setup. You can do it from Windows by double-clicking the clock in the bottom right corner. You can also do it from a command prompt (such as MS-DOS) by keying **date** or **time** and then pressing Enter, and the values in the BIOS Setup program will change too.

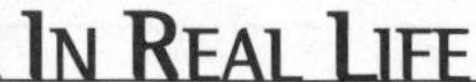

## In Real Life

On PCs with Internet access, software can be used to retrieve the current date and time from an Internet time server and automatically update the system clock. Windows XP has such a feature built in; with other Windows versions you can get third-party products that do the same thing.

## TRY IT!

Change your PC clock's time to one hour ahead using the BIOS Setup program. Then use the Time command at a command prompt to set it back to the actual time. Boot into Windows and confirm that the time is correct in the date and time properties there.

## Processor Configuration

In the vast majority of BIOS programs, there are no adjustable settings for the CPU. Its speed and type appear in dimmed letters, meaning they are for information only. You might also see the Front Side Bus Speed (the system bus speed) and the amount of built-in cache memory it has. Figure 9.4 describes some other settings you might encounter that deal with the CPU.

- **ECC Cache Support:** Enables error correcting in the L2 cache. Enable this only if your CPU supports it. More modern motherboards autodetect this.
- **Serial Number:** Pentium II and higher CPUs have a built-in serial number that can be used for tracking. Many users see this as an intrusion on their privacy. Choose Enable to allow it to be read, or Disable to prevent it.
- **CPU Warning Temperature:** Some computers contain a monitoring system that constantly takes the CPU's temperature and lets you know if it gets too hot. Set the temperature threshold here for a warning to appear.
- **CPU Shutdown Temperature:** Set the temperature threshold here for the PC to automatically shut down from overheating.
- **Current CPU Temperature:** If present, this is a read-only field that reports current temperature.
- **CPU Internal Cache and CPU External Cache:** These are the L1 and L2 caches, respectively. Normally they remain enabled; you might disable them when troubleshooting memory problems.

**FIGURE 9.4**
CPU-Based Settings

## TRY IT!

Explore the settings for the CPU in your PC's BIOS Setup. Do not make any changes to them. Check these settings on several different PCs if possible to get a feel for the range of difference among programs.

## DRIVE CONFIGURATION

One of the primary purposes of BIOS Setup is to define the types of drives installed in the PC. There is no way for the motherboard's chipset to be preprogrammed with this information because every system has different drives. Therefore, after you install a new drive, the BIOS Setup must be configured to recognize it. Depending on the BIOS age and version, this might be done automatically or might require some user participation.

Floppy disks are not usually autodetected by Plug and Play; you must go into the BIOS Setup program and specify the type and capacity of floppy drive you are installing. However, by default the Setup assumes that a 3.5-inch high-density floppy drive is installed, so if that is what you have you should not need to make any changes to BIOS Setup. Figure 9.5 shows the choices of floppy drive types available in the example BIOS Setup program; you may have slightly different choices.

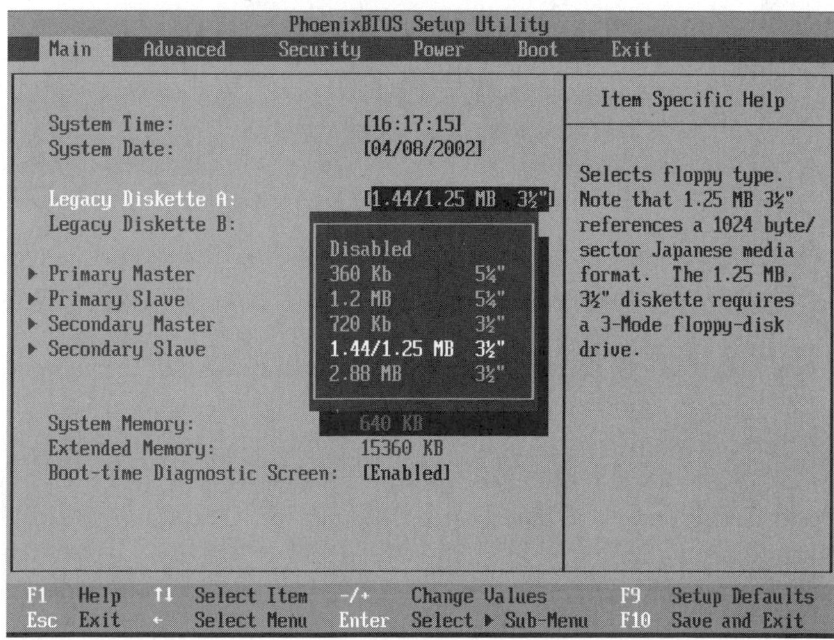


**FIGURE 9.5**
Specify a floppy drive size and capacity.

IDE drive setup depends on the BIOS version. Newer computers (post-1998 or so) support Plug and Play technology so if you add a new IDE drive, it will be detected and configured invisibly without even entering the BIOS Setup program. You may see a brief message on-screen listing the detected drives, as in Figure 9.2.

### In Real Life

**Floppy drives that run on the IDE interface, such as an LS-120 drive, are treated like other IDE devices in the BIOS and are automatically detectable.**

Most computers that lack true Plug and Play support have an alternative means of detecting IDE devices built into the BIOS Setup program. The exact name varies, but it is usually something like Detect IDE or Drive AutoDetect. This utility queries all IDE channels, asking the drives about their type and size, and reports that information back to the BIOS Setup program. This feature was introduced with the ATA standard for IDE devices in 1988. You will learn about IDE standards in Chapter 11.

### In Real Life

**PCs that support Plug and Play usually have an Auto setting as the default for each IDE device position (Primary Master, Secondary Master, Primary Slave, Secondary Slave), so they can automatically detect IDE devices. If a PC is not automatically detecting IDE devices but you believe it to be Plug and Play compatible, check to make sure the IDE devices are set to Auto rather than None (turned off) or User (manually user-defined).**

For very old computers that do not have any way of detecting an IDE drive's settings, you must manually enter a hard drive's settings, such as the number of cylinders, heads, and sectors. This data is often abbreviated as *CHS* (cylinders, heads, sectors). Another name for it is the drive geometry. (See Chapter 10 for more information.)

**CHS**

Cylinders, heads, and sectors, three specifications for a drive that collectively determine its capacity and geometry.

CD-ROM drives do not have these settings in BIOS Setup; set the IDE channel to ATAPI or CDROM if you want it to support a CD drive. Very old motherboards may not have built-in support for IDE CD-ROM drives (this support was introduced in 1996 with the ATA-2 standard). On such systems you cannot hook up an IDE CD-ROM drive directly to the motherboard; you must use an expansion card with IDE support.

The drive geometry information is usually clearly marked on the drive's label, as shown in Figure 9.6. Note the settings listed and then set the IDE channel in BIOS Setup to User or Manual setting.

Figure 9.7 lists a few other drive-based settings you might encounter.

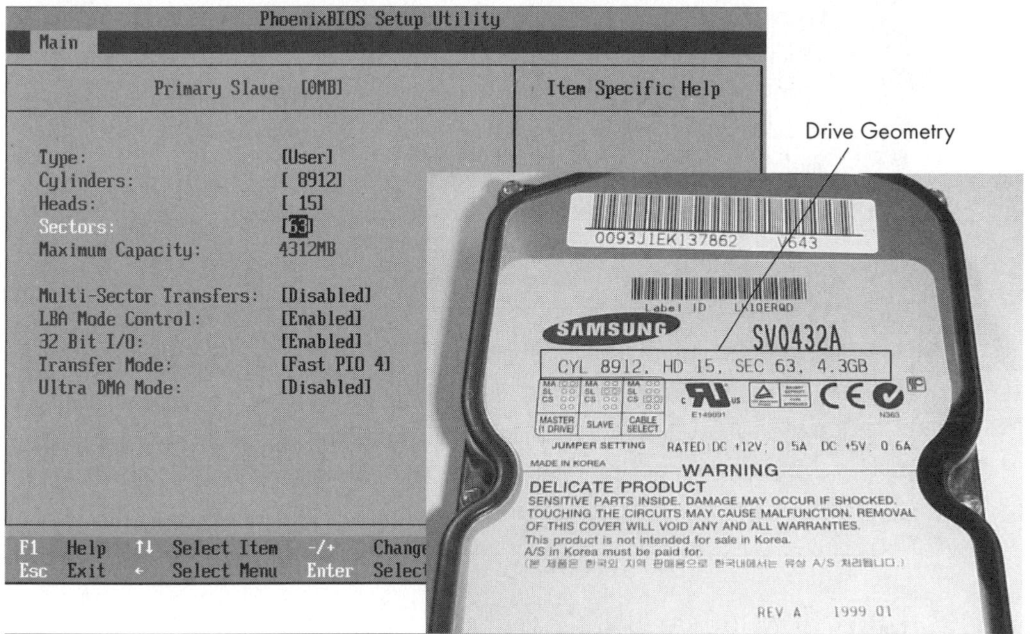


**FIGURE 9.6**
Most BIOS Setup programs have a utility that can automatically detect the proper settings for IDE devices.

- **Floppy Drive Swap:** Makes the floppy drive that is ordinarily drive A into drive B and vice versa.
- **IDE Controller:** Usually set to Both, which enables both IDE controllers on the motherboard. You can set it to Primary or Secondary to enable only one of the IDE controllers, possibly freeing up an IRQ.
- **Hard Disk Pre-Delay:** An amount of time to pause after system startup before the PC tries to read anything from the hard disk. It allows the hard disk the time to get fully up and running. Some hard disks report an error if you do not allow them this time. An average setting is six seconds.
- **Floppy Controller:** Enables or disables the floppy drive controller. If you are using an IDE-based floppy drive such as an LS-120, you might want to disable the "regular" floppy controller to free up the IRQ.
- **Multi-Sector Transfers:** Specifies how many sectors are in a block that moves from hard disk to memory. Use the setting recommended in the drive's specifications. If you autodetect the drive (and 99 percent of the time you will), this will be set automatically.

*continued*

**FIGURE 9.7**
Drive-Based Settings

- **LBA Mode Control:** Enables or disables Logical Block Addressing. Should be enabled for most modern hard drives. We will look at LBA in more detail in Chapter 10.
- **Transfer Mode:** Your choices here are Fast PIO Mode 1 through 4 or DMA Mode 1 or 2. The mode specifies a scheme of transferring data; we will look at it in Chapter 10.
- **UltraDMA:** Can be set to Disabled or to Mode 0, 1, or 2. This is another specification for data transfer, also addressed in Chapter 10.
- **SMART Capability:** Enables the SMART system (self-monitoring analysis and reporting technology) to report impending hard disk crashes and other problems for IDE drives. This technology is implemented on drives that conform to ATA-3 and higher standards. You will learn about ATA standards in Chapter 11.

**FIGURE 9.7**
*continued*

## TRY IT!

1. If your BIOS Setup has a separate IDE Detect utility, use it to redetect all of your IDE drives. If not, make sure all of your IDE drive positions are set to Auto.
2. If there is a Floppy Drive Swap option in your BIOS Setup, enable it, and then boot to a command prompt and try accessing your A drive by keying B: and pressing Enter. Then reenter BIOS Setup and turn off the feature again.

## Boot Configuration

At startup the BIOS looks for an operating system on an attached disk. If more than one attached disk contains a valid operating system, it chooses one over the other according to the settings you specify in the BIOS Setup program.

The default setting is usually to check the floppy drive first and then the Primary Master IDE (sometimes called IDE 0,0). This enables a bootable floppy to be used to bypass the hard disk boot for troubleshooting purposes when needed. However, some users frequently leave nonbootable floppy disks in the drive, which produces an error when the system restarts, so it might be advantageous on some systems to change the boot order so that the hard disk is checked first, and then the floppy drive only if no operating system is found on the hard disk.

In most setup programs you can also specify that you want the CD to be included in the list of bootable drives. That makes it possible to boot from a bootable CD disc. Microsoft Windows Me, 2000, and XP come on bootable CD, for example, so you can boot from the CD and begin the Windows setup process without needing a bootable floppy.

The interface for setting boot order varies widely among BIOS Setup programs. In some it is a free-form list of drives that you can rearrange, placing your preferred drive(s) at the top of the list. In others it is a multiple-choice drop-down list. Figure 9.8 shows a BIOS Setup program that lists drive types by category in the order that the user prefers. As you can see in the instructions at the right side of the screen, the plus and minus keys move a drive up or down on the list, and Shift + 1 enables or disables a drive from being bootable.

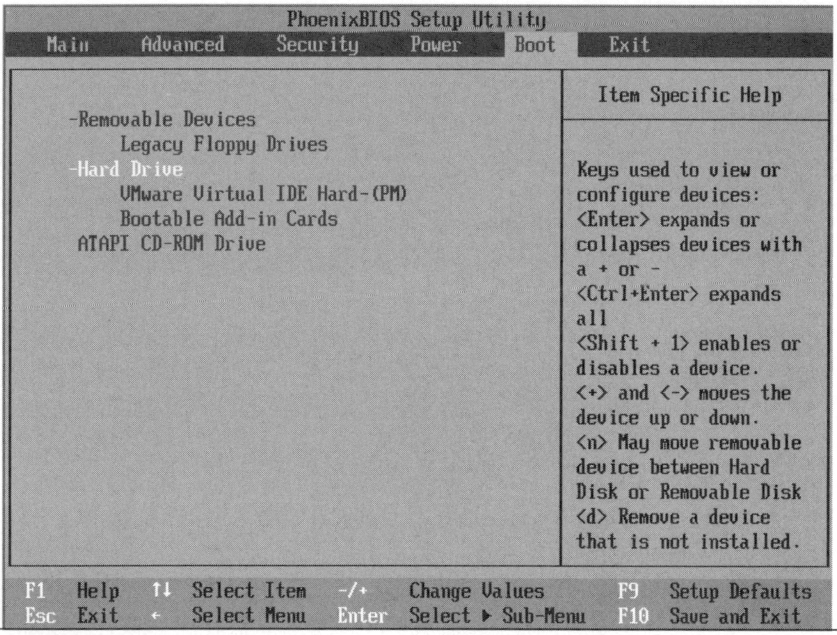

```
PhoenixBIOS Setup Utility
Main   Advanced   Security   Power   Boot   Exit

                                        Item Specific Help
  -Removable Devices
      Legacy Floppy Drives
  -Hard Drive                           Keys used to view or
      VMware Virtual IDE Hard-(PM)      configure devices:
      Bootable Add-in Cards             <Enter> expands or
   ATAPI CD-ROM Drive                   collapses devices with
                                        a + or -
                                        <Ctrl+Enter> expands
                                        all
                                        <Shift + 1> enables or
                                        disables a device.
                                        <+> and <-> moves the
                                        device up or down.
                                        <n> May move removable
                                        device between Hard
                                        Disk or Removable Disk
                                        <d> Remove a device
                                        that is not installed.

F1  Help  ↑↓ Select Item  -/+   Change Values        F9  Setup Defaults
Esc Exit  ←  Select Menu  Enter Select ▸ Sub-Menu    F10 Save and Exit
```

**FIGURE 9.8**
Select the drives that should be bootable and specify in what order they should be checked.

## In Real Life

Do not be confused by the controls shown in the example figures in this chapter. BIOS programs vary widely. They all do the same thing, but in very different ways. For example, the controls for specifying the boot order in the BIOS Setup program you are working with may look more like the floppy drive type selector shown in Figure 9.5.

## TRY IT!

1. In BIOS Setup, set up your CD drive to be bootable and to be preferred over all other boot devices.
2. Insert a Windows Me, Windows 2000, or Windows XP CD in the drive and restart. The setup program for that operating system should load.
3. Remove the CD, restart, and go back into BIOS Setup.
4. Set the boot order so that the hard disk and floppy disk are both preferred over the CD drive in booting.
5. Restart the PC again and allow it to boot normally.

Figure 9.9 shows some other boot options you might encounter.

- **Quick Boot or Quick POST:** Makes booting quicker by skipping extended memory testing. Useful for systems that are frequently rebooted; not useful for brand new systems in which you are not sure whether there are memory errors.
- **Quiet Boot:** Turns off the display of most of the system startup messages, instead displaying a logo from the company of manufacture. Usually turned on by default in brand-name computers such as Dell; can be turned off if you are interested in seeing the boot messages (helpful for troubleshooting).
- **Restore on AC/Power Loss or After Power Failure:** Determines whether the system will attempt to restart itself after a power outage or will stay off. Available only on ATX motherboards. The default is Last State, which means if it was off it will remain off; if it was on it will turn back on again.
- **Scan User Flash Area:** A few motherboards enable user programs to be stored in Flash BIOS and run at startup. To use one of them, set this to Enable; otherwise, leave it at Disable for security.
- **Boot Up Floppy Seek:** When this is enabled, the BIOS checks the floppy drives to see whether they are double density or high density. Since double-density drives have been obsolete for at least 10 years, you can safely leave this disabled to save time at startup.

**FIGURE 9.9**
Boot Options

## TRY IT!

If your PC has Quick Boot and/or Quiet Boot settings, try booting with them both on and off to observe the difference. When finished, leave them set to whichever setting you prefer.

## Memory Usage

In very old PCs you might be able to specify the amount of RAM installed, and when you install new RAM you might need to enter the BIOS Setup program to do so. However, in most PCs made in the last decade, the amount of installed RAM is automatically reported and you cannot change it. If the amount of memory is inaccurately reported, the RAM may be installed incorrectly or of the wrong type, or a jumper on the motherboard might need to be changed.

### In Real Life

During a transition period in the early 1990s, many BIOS Setup programs automatically detected RAM, but only when you opened up the BIOS Setup program itself. In other words, if you installed more RAM, you would see an error at startup, and that error would keep recurring until you entered—and then exited—the BIOS Setup program. Saving your changes and exiting BIOS Setup would update the RAM setting and eliminate the error.

Figure 9.10 details other settings you may encounter related to memory.

- **ECC or DRAM Data Integrity Mode:** Set to ECC when using ECC memory; set to Non-ECC otherwise.
- **EDO DRAM Speed Selection:** If using EDO RAM, enables you to set its speed.
- **System BIOS Cacheable:** When enabled, allows the system BIOS data from ROM to be cached (shadowed) at the address F0000h-FFFFFh in upper memory.
- **Video BIOS Cacheable:** When enabled, allows the ROM on the video card to be cached at address C0000h-C7FFFh in upper memory.
- **Video RAM Cacheable:** When enabled, allows video memory to be cached at address A0000h to AFFFFh in upper memory.
- **Gate A20 Option:** Choose Fast to allow the chipset to control the connection between the CPU and extended memory (the A20 gate). Choose Normal to grant this control to a part of the keyboard controller. Fast is the default, and the preferred setting because it improves system speed.

**FIGURE 9.10**
Memory Settings

## Plug and Play

Figure 9.11 shows some settings that pertain to a motherboard's Plug and Play capabilities.

- **PnP Compatible OS or Plug and Play OS:** If the operating system is Plug and Play compatible (Windows 95 and higher, for example), set this to Yes to let the operating system handle Plug and Play resource assignments and force the chipset's Plug and Play capabilities to take a back seat. If using a non-Plug and Play operating system such as Windows 3.1, Unix, or MS-DOS, set this to No and the chipset will take a more active role.
- **Reset Configuration:** When set to Yes, this resets all of the resource assignments that the BIOS has created using its own Plug and Play capability. Then it automatically resets the setting to No. Setting this to Yes might be useful as a troubleshooting technique in a system in which the IRQ and address resource assignments seem to be functioning incorrectly. See Chapter 14 for more information about resource assignments.
- **Assign IRQ for USB or USB Support:** Turn this on if you plan to use the built-in USB support from the motherboard; turn it off to free up the resources.
- **DMA, Address, and IRQ assignments:** This is not a single setting, but a whole category of settings. If you turn off Plug and Play, you can set specific IRQ, DMA, and I/O addresses for specific devices. However, this is not recommended on a Plug and Play system because the automatic assignments can change automatically as needed but your manual settings cannot.

**FIGURE 9.11**
Plug and Play Settings

## Expansion Bus Management

Most BIOS programs enable you to adjust the way the expansion buses (AGP, PCI, and ISA) work to support various types of expansion boards.

- **Resource Configuration:** Some BIOS Setup programs enable you to set aside specific addresses in upper memory, as well as specific IRQs, for the use of legacy ISA devices. Most users can ignore this; it is useful chiefly for coaxing an ISA expansion card that requires a specific I/O address and IRQ into working in an otherwise Plug and Play system (see Figure 9.12).

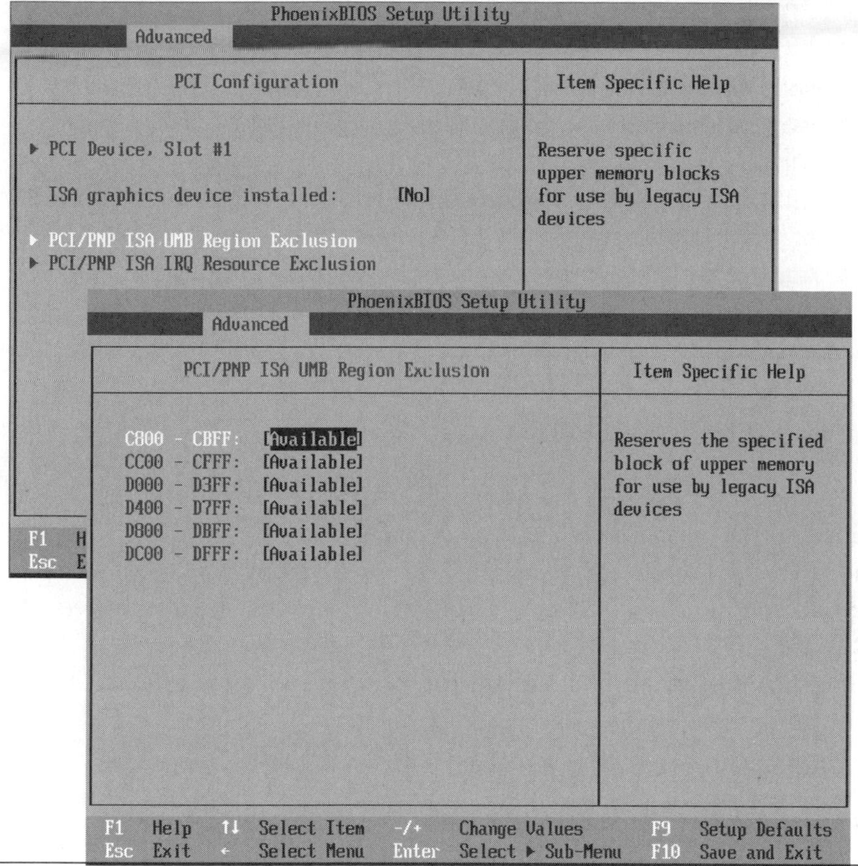


**FIGURE 9.12**
Reserving System Resources for Legacy ISA Device Usage

- **PCI IRQ Sharing:** As you learned earlier, PCI expansion cards can share IRQs. Some BIOS programs enable you to specify the maximum number of IRQs to be devoted to PCI devices. Setting this to a low number would ensure that plenty of IRQs were left over for ISA devices. Setting this to a high number, or to Auto, would minimize IRQ sharing among PCI devices as much as possible, so that each PCI device could have its own IRQ if available.
- **Palette Snooping:** This enables a PCI video card to share a common palette with an ISA video card. Normally this should be disabled, but you might turn it on if you want an ISA-based multimedia expansion card to be able to read data from your video card's RAM.
- **AGP Aperture Size:** The aperture is a range of PCI memory addresses dedicated to serving the AGP bus. In most cases the default setting is the best. There may also be a setting for Primary Video Adapter. On a system with an AGP bus, this should usually be set to AGP, signaling that the AGP slot will be used for the primary video card.

## TRY IT!

1. Boot to Windows and use System Information to see what IRQs your PCI devices are using.
2. Restart, go into BIOS Setup, and change the setting for PCI IRQ sharing (if you have such a setting).
3. Restart again and boot to Windows. Go back to System Information and see whether any IRQ assignments have changed.
4. Restart, go into BIOS Setup, and restore the original setting for PCI IRQ sharing.

## Integrated Peripherals

Integrated peripherals consist mainly of the legacy parallel and serial ports built into the motherboard. The parallel and serial ports require addresses and IRQs, and the BIOS Setup enables you to specify which ones they receive. You can also completely disable each port individually to free up IRQs for other uses.

For each port you can choose one of the following settings in BIOS Setup:

- **Disabled:** Turns it off completely.
- **Enabled:** Turns it on and allows you to specify what resources it uses.
- **Auto:** Turns it on and automatically assigns resources (usually the best setting).

In Figure 9.13, for example, Serial port A is completely disabled, and Serial port B is enabled with manual resource assignment. The menu for choosing its Base I/O address is open. The menu in Figure 9.13 assigns only the I/O address, but some BIOS programs also let you assign the interrupt (IRQ).

Parallel port A is set to Auto, which enables the BIOS to assign its resources automatically. Notice also that the parallel port's mode is set to ECP; you learned about the various types of parallel port modes in Chapter 7.

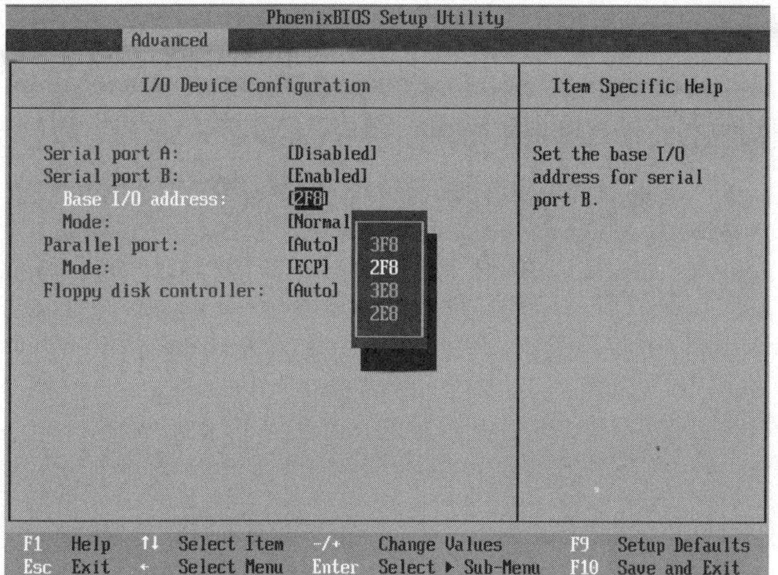


**FIGURE 9.13**
Defining Resource Usage and On/Off Status for the Legacy I/O Ports

## TRY IT!

1. Look on the back of your PC and identify a legacy port that has nothing plugged into it (either parallel or serial).
2. In BIOS Setup, disable that port.
3. Boot to Windows and look in Device Manager to confirm that the port does not show up there.
4. Reboot and reenter BIOS Setup. Reenable that port with Automatic resource assignments.
5. Reboot to Windows and watch Windows redetect the port at startup. Then look in Device Manager for the port, and check its resource assignments.

Figure 9.14 describes some other settings for integrated peripherals.

- **Legacy USB:** This is *not* for USB usage overall; it is a specialized setting that pertains only to USB keyboards and mice. Normally USB usage is controlled by the OS, but if you have a USB keyboard or mouse, you might not be able to start the OS because the OS will think there is no keyboard or mouse present. Turning on Legacy USB support in the BIOS enables these USB devices to interact with the system independently of the operating system so that they work even when you are not using a USB-aware OS.
- **Audio:** If you have built-in sound support on the motherboard, you will have a BIOS control for it. Enable assigns system resources to the built-in sound card; Disable does not.

**FIGURE 9.14**
Integrated Peripheral Settings

## Power Management

Most PCs these days have power management features built into the BIOS. The standards for PC power management are part of the Energy Star set of specifications; devices that conform to that standard will display an Energy Star logo or sticker.

**Power management**

PC features that shut down certain components or put them in low-power mode after a specified period of inactivity.

*Power management* features enable the PC to use less electricity by shutting down certain high-consumption parts after a specified period of inactivity. These parts may include the hard disk motor and the display monitor. Power management can also include placing the PC in a low-power Standby or Suspended state after lengthier periods of inactivity to reduce the power consumption even more.

**Advanced Power Management (APM)**

The original standard for PC power management, now obsolete.

**Advanced Configuration and Power Interface (ACPI)**

The modern standard for PC power management and Plug and Play peripheral resource assignment.

There are two standards for power management: *Advanced Power Management* (APM) and *Advanced Configuration and Power Interface* (ACPI). The BIOS supports one or the other. APM is the older technology, and is less sophisticated and more prone to conflicts with operating system's power management settings. On some systems a BIOS update (covered later in the chapter) may be available that will change the BIOS over to ACPI, which is desirable. See Chapter 14 for more information about ACPI.

### TRY IT!

**Look around in your BIOS Setup to see whether there is any indication of which power management standard your motherboard supports: APM or ACPI.**

Your BIOS might support one or more of these modes, which the PC enters automatically after a specified period of inactivity:

- **Doze Mode:** Decreases the CPU clock speed to around 10 to 25 percent of its normal speed during inactivity.
- **Standby Mode:** Stops the CPU clock, the hard disk, and the L2 cache during inactivity.
- **Suspend Mode:** Stops everything listed above for Standby mode plus other system devices as well during inactivity.
- **Hibernate Mode:** Saves the contents of RAM to disk, and then shuts everything down, so the system uses no power at all. At wakeup it restores memory contents, making for a quicker startup than with a full shutdown.

These various power-saving states are explained in more detail in Chapter 20, which discusses notebook PCs, since they are most useful on a computer that runs on a battery and therefore has a limited amount of power to expend.

Figure 9.15 shows a BIOS Setup program with a few simple power management settings available. On a notebook PC the BIOS settings for power management will likely be more extensive.

Some of the other settings you might encounter for power management in the BIOS Setup are shown in Figure 9.16.

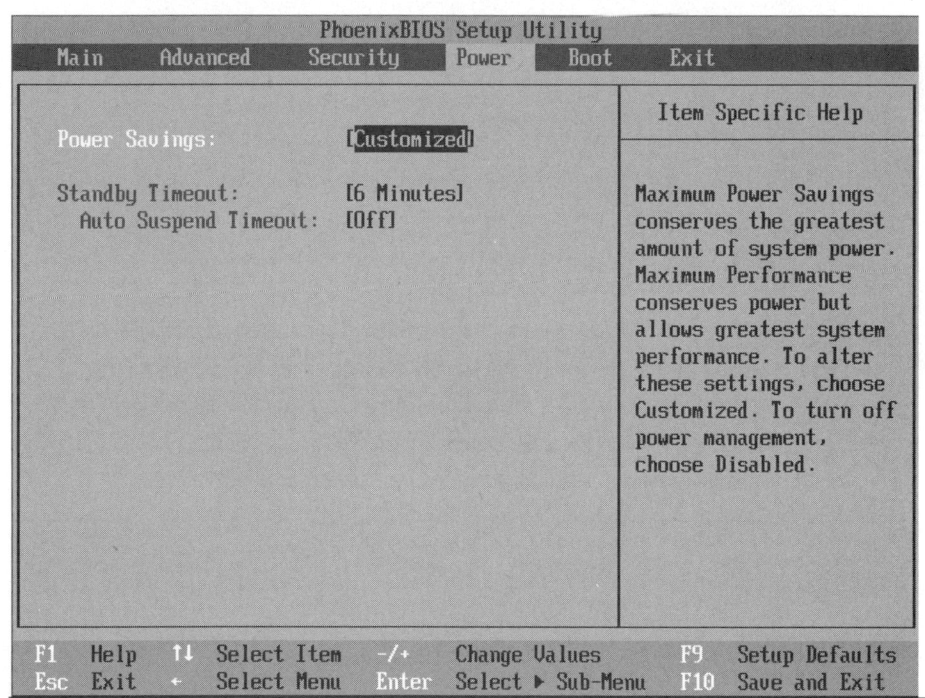


**FIGURE 9.15**
Power Management Settings in BIOS Setup

- **Power Savings or Power Management:** There might be an overall setting for power management that lets you choose among Disabled, Custom, Maximum Power Savings, or Maximum Performance. If you choose Custom, other settings appear in which you can customize the wait time before certain power-saving features take effect.
- **Inactivity Timer:** This goes by a lot of different names, but it is the amount of idle time that should elapse before power management activates.
- **Hard Drive:** When enabled, allows the power management utility to turn off the hard drive after the specified interval.
- **VESA Video Power Down:** When enabled, allows the power management utility to turn off the monitor after the specified interval.

*continued*

**FIGURE 9.16**
Power Management Settings

- **Fan Always On or CPU Fan Off in Suspend:** Controls whether the CPU fan will remain running even when the PC is in a low-power state.
- **ACPI Function:** This setting will be present only on a motherboard that supports ACPI. When enabled, allows the use of ACPI power management.
- **DPMS Support:** Enable this for a system with a monitor attached that supports the Display Power Management Signaling (DPMS) standard.
- **HDD Power Down:** When enabled, allows IDE hard disks that support the ATA-2 specification or higher to handle their own power management.
- **Wake on LAN:** Determines whether the PC will resume from Standby when data is requested from it over the LAN. Available for ATX motherboards only.
- **Wake on Ring:** Same as Wake on LAN, except it applies to a modem.

**FIGURE 9.16**
*continued*

## In Real Life

Windows 95 and higher has power management features built in. These are supposed to work in cooperation with the features in the BIOS, but in practice they often conflict. Such conflicts can result in the PC's not being able to "wake up" from its suspended or standby state. To avoid these conflicts, you can shut off the BIOS power management features entirely and rely only on those in Windows.

## Security

Some BIOSes have built-in security measures. Depending on the BIOS, they may enable you to specify a user password, which must be entered in order to boot the PC, and/or a supervisor password, which must be keyed in order to enter the BIOS Setup program. Use these passwords with care, and only on systems where they are necessary; it is very easy to forget a password and render a system useless. Some motherboards have a jumper you can use to clear the BIOS password, along with any BIOS setting changes. See "Recovering from Bad BIOS Setting Changes" later in this chapter.

In Figure 9.17 you see a box for entering a supervisor password. It asks you to key it twice to make sure you do not make any typos.

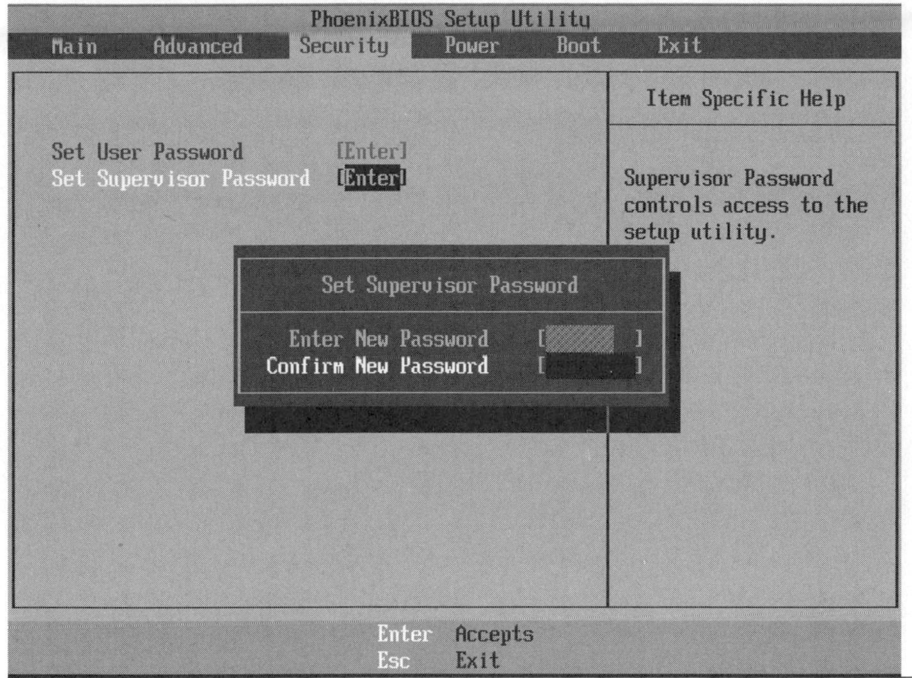


**FIGURE 9.17**
Security Settings on a Typical BIOS Setup Program

## TRY IT!

1. If your BIOS Setup includes security, set both a supervisor and a user password.
2. Boot the PC and test the user password.
3. Reboot the PC and reenter BIOS Setup, using the supervisor password to do so.
4. Remove both passwords by changing them to blanks.
5. Reboot and confirm that it does not prompt you for either password.

# Exiting the BIOS Setup Program

In almost all BIOS Setup programs, pressing Esc from a main screen takes you to the Exit menu, from which you can choose to exit and either save or discard your changes. In most BIOS Setup programs, pressing F10 is a shortcut for exiting and saving changes (see Figure 9.18).

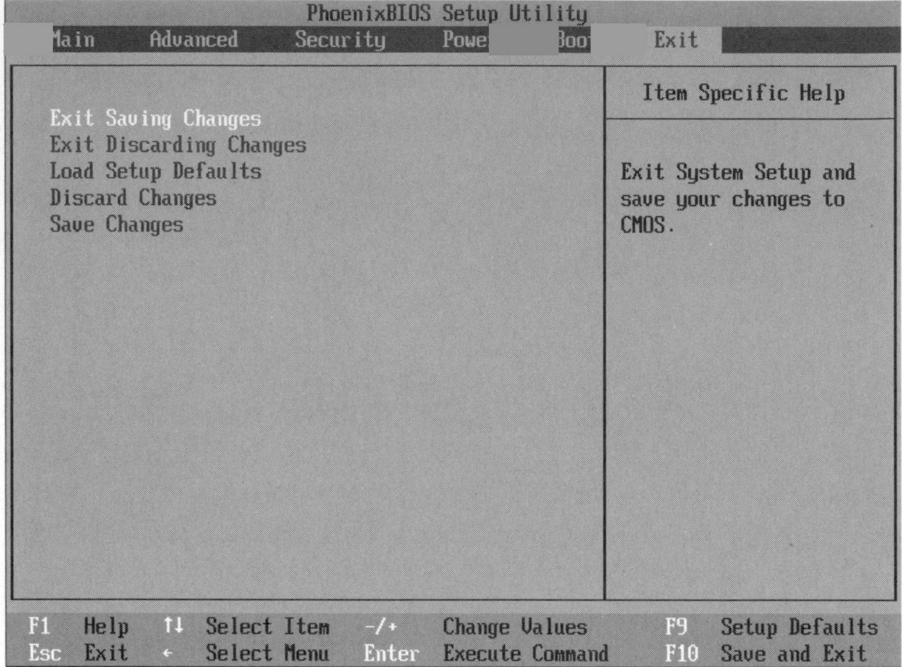


**FIGURE 9.18**
Exiting the BIOS Setup Program

# Recovering from Bad BIOS Setup Changes

If you make BIOS Setup changes that turn out to hinder the system's performance, you can easily undo them. But if you make a great many changes, it may be difficult to know which one is the problem. One easy way to fix things is to reload the default settings. In most BIOS Setup programs you can press F9 to do so. There is also likely to be a menu option for reloading defaults.

But what if you have disturbed things so badly that you cannot enter BIOS Setup? In such cases it is often possible to clear out all of your custom settings and reload the defaults with a Reset or Recovery jumper:

1. Locate the jumper on the motherboard for resetting the BIOS, and change it from Normal to Reset (or Recover) position.
2. Power on the system and leave it on for 5 to 10 seconds.
3. Turn off the power and put the jumper back to Normal position.

**TRY IT!**

This exercise is optional. It deletes all of your BIOS Setup custom settings, so do not do it if you have settings you want to keep. Make sure you have notes on the hard drive settings before doing it.

1. Locate the jumper on the motherboard that resets the BIOS.
2. Set the jumper to Reset position and restart the PC to wipe out all BIOS settings.
3. Wait 5-10 seconds and then turn off the PC and reset the jumper to Normal.
4. Restart and reenter the BIOS Setup program to confirm that all of the settings are back at the defaults.
5. Restore any custom settings as needed, such as redetecting IDE devices or configuring I/O and port settings.

## Installing a BIOS Update

Modern BIOSes are all EEPROMs, which means you can update them using flash BIOS utility rather than having to replace the BIOS chip physically. Reasons for updating the BIOS might include getting support for a new type of device, getting ACPI power management support, or correcting a persistent bug in the BIOS programming.

**WARNING**

There is a small risk of disabling the entire PC whenever you do a BIOS update, so do not do it unless you have a problem you are trying to correct.

First, acquire the update. It will consist of two parts: an updating utility program and the update data file. You can download them as a set from the motherboard or PC manufacturer's Web site. Usually the file you download is an executable file that creates a bootable floppy disk containing the needed files. Run it and create the floppy disk.

To find the correct update you might need to know the number of your existing BIOS. (This will also tell you whether the update you are downloading is any more recent than the version you already have.) One way to identify the BIOS version is to watch the screen as the PC boots; it will probably appear very briefly at the top of the screen at the beginning of the boot process. Copy it down quickly; you might need to reboot several times to get it all. Or try pressing the Pause/Break key to pause the boot process while you write it down.

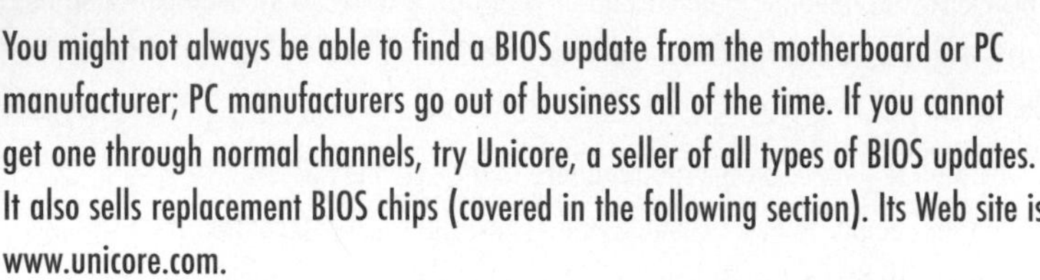

**IN REAL LIFE**

You might not always be able to find a BIOS update from the motherboard or PC manufacturer; PC manufacturers go out of business all of the time. If you cannot get one through normal channels, try Unicore, a seller of all types of BIOS updates. It also sells replacement BIOS chips (covered in the following section). Its Web site is www.unicore.com.

Next, restart the PC and let it boot from the floppy disk. The BIOS update utility starts automatically; follow the on-screen prompts to update the BIOS. Some of these utility programs enable you to save your old BIOS so you can revert to it later if needed; that is a good precaution to take if it is available.

**WARNING**

As the BIOS updates, a message appears on-screen warning you not to shut off the PC during the update. Take this warning very seriously. If you lose power during the update, it could disable the BIOS completely. If that happens, you will probably need a whole new motherboard. On some systems there is a last-resort method that can restore the BIOS to working order in this situation. To try it, set the BIOS reset jumper to Reset or Recover and then boot again from the floppy created for the BIOS update. If the light on the floppy drive comes on, it is recovering the BIOS. Wait until the light goes off, and then turn off the power and put the jumper back to Normal position.

**TRY IT!**

Search the Web to see whether a BIOS update is available for your PC. If it is, download it. Check with your instructor, and if he or she approves, install it.

## Replacing a BIOS Chip

If a motherboard's BIOS is not an EEPROM, or if no update is available for it, your only alternative may be to replace the BIOS chip. This procedure is seldom performed anymore because it is much easier to update the BIOS with a utility program, and because ROM BIOS chips are often soldered to the motherboard on modern systems.

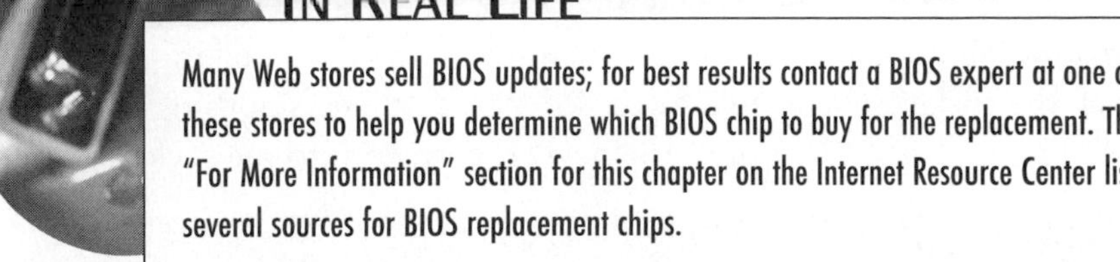

## In Real Life

Many Web stores sell BIOS updates; for best results contact a BIOS expert at one of these stores to help you determine which BIOS chip to buy for the replacement. The "For More Information" section for this chapter on the Internet Resource Center lists several sources for BIOS replacement chips.

You can pry the chip out of the motherboard with any hard flat object, like a flathead screwdriver tip, but for best results (i.e., not breaking the chip legs off in the socket) you should use a chip puller tool. This is like a pair of tweezers with hooks on the end that slip under the chip. Be careful not to damage the motherboard or the socket with your metal tools (see Figure 9.19). Then insert the new chip by aligning the legs and then carefully pressing the chip into the socket.

**WARNING**

Like all chips, Dual Inline Pin Packages (DIPPs) are extremely sensitive to ESD damage. Make sure you use antistatic protective measures.

**FIGURE 9.19**
Removing a DIPP-Style BIOS Chip

On some very old motherboards the BIOS chip is not a DIPP, but a Plastic Leaded Chip Carrier (PLCC). Pry one of these out with a small pointed tool like a bent paperclip or the tip of a small awl, taking care not to crack the socket. There are no exposed legs, so there is nothing to break off (see Figure 9.20). Then press the new chip down into the socket.

**FIGURE 9.20**
A PLCC-Style BIOS Chip

## TRY IT!

The following exercise is optional. You might not want to do it on a working motherboard because of the potential for damaging the BIOS chip. If you have an old scrap motherboard to practice on, try this exercise on it.

1. Remove the BIOS chip with a chip puller tool.
2. Examine it, and then put it back in again.

# STUDY GUIDE

Use the following summaries to review the key concepts of this chapter.

## BIOS and CMOS

- BIOS stands for Basic Input Output System. It is the set of programs that work at a low level to start up the PC and interface with hardware.
- BIOS is stored on a Read-Only Memory (ROM) chip.
- Another name for BIOS is firmware because it is somewhere between hardware and software.
- Today's ROM BIOS chips are EEPROMS (Electrically Erasable Programmable ROMs), which are software-updatable with a special utility. However, in earlier systems they were unchangeable.
- You can change the BIOS settings with a BIOS Setup program. The changes you make to the default BIOS settings are stored either in the EEPROM itself or in a separate CMOS chip.
- CMOS stands for complementary metal-oxide semiconductor. It is a type of nonvolatile RAM chip that retains its settings through a small amount of power from the motherboard battery.

## BIOS Interaction with Memory

- BIOS instructions for dealing with hardware are accessed through upper memory (the top 360KB of the first 1MB).
- Some motherboards support ROM shadowing, which copies the data from ROM into upper memory so it is more readily available.
- In 32-bit environments such as Windows 95 and higher, ROM shadowing is less important since the 32-bit device drivers deal with the hardware directly rather than going through the 16-bit BIOS instructions for them.

## Working with a BIOS Setup Program

- On most motherboards the only way to access the BIOS Setup program is to press a specific key during the boot sequence. The name of the key to press appears on-screen briefly at startup. F1, F2, and Delete are keys commonly used.
- BIOS Setup programs vary greatly in their interface and options.
- In most BIOS Setup programs, Esc returns to the previous menu or exits the program if already at a top-level menu.

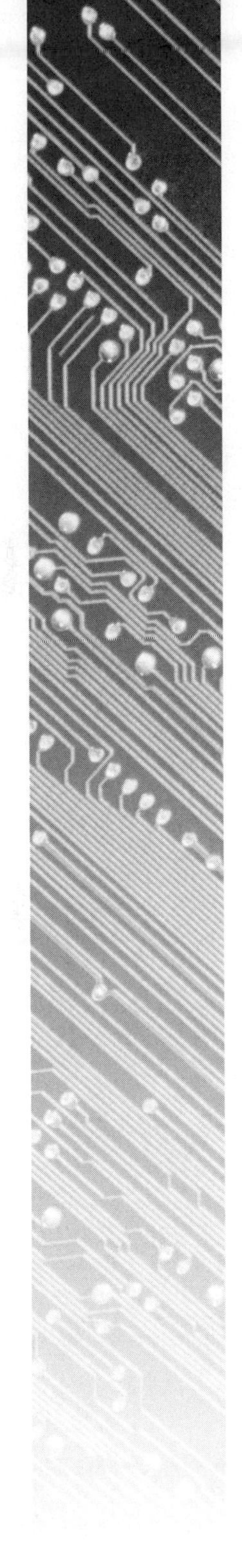

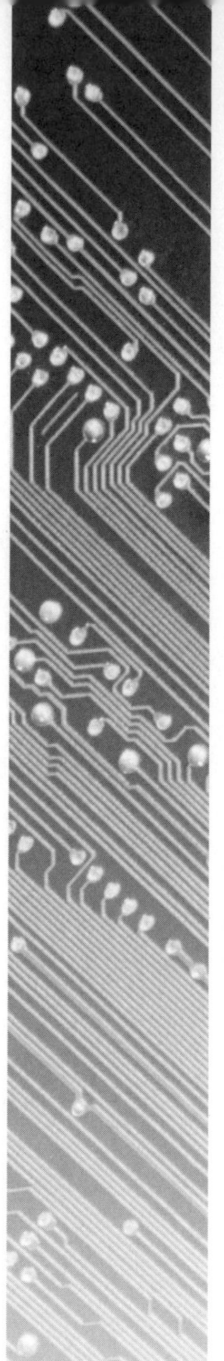

- The up and down arrow keys usually move between options on a page, and the right and left arrow keys move between pages.
- Some values can be changed by pressing Enter and then selecting from a list that appears. Other values are changed by pressing the + or - key.
- F10 is usually the key that exits the program and saves changes.

## Common Adjustable Settings

- The date and time can be set from BIOS Setup. They can also be set from within Windows or at a command prompt.
- Most of the settings involving the CPU are read-only.
- IDE and floppy drive controllers can be enabled or disabled through BIOS, and the drives connected to them can be defined.
- A floppy drive must be configured manually in BIOS for the type of drive installed.
- Most BIOS Setup programs can automatically detect IDE devices and use the correct settings for them. You might not even need to enter BIOS Setup after installing a new drive.
- On a very old system you might need to manually enter the settings for a drive. The key settings for a drive are cylinders, heads, and sectors (CHS). Another name for this is the drive geometry.
- Most BIOS Setup programs enable you to specify which drives are bootable and in what order they should be checked.
- The amount of memory the BIOS Setup reports is read-only on modern systems. After installing new memory, entering and then exiting the BIOS setup program is enough to update its records to the new amount.
- A system with Windows 95 or higher installed should be set up as having a Plug and Play-compatible OS in BIOS Setup.
- Legacy serial and parallel ports can be enabled or disabled in BIOS Setup, and their resources manually or automatically assigned.
- Some BIOS Setup programs have power management features that shut down certain parts of the PC after a period of inactivity to save energy.
- Some BIOSes have built-in security measures. Depending on the BIOS, they may enable you to specify a user password, which must be entered in order to boot the PC, and/or a supervisor password, which must be keyed in order to enter the BIOS Setup program.

## Recovering from BIOS Setup Changes

- To go back to the default settings for the BIOS, look for an option in the BIOS Setup program that allows you to do so. In many programs it is the F9 key that does this.
- If you cannot get into BIOS Setup, try using the Reset jumper on the motherboard. Move that jumper to Reset position, restart the PC for about 10 seconds, and then turn it off and move the jumper position back to Normal.

## Updating the BIOS

- For an EEPROM, acquire a BIOS update by downloading it from the motherboard or PC manufacturer or a third-party vendor. Use that downloaded program to make a bootable floppy disk.
- Boot the system with your bootable floppy disk and follow the instructions on-screen to update the BIOS.
- If no software-based BIOS update is available, you can investigate the availability of a replacement BIOS chip.

# PRACTICE TEST

On a blank sheet of paper, write the answers to the following multiple-choice questions and explain why each answer is correct.

1. *BIOS* stands for
   a. Base Information Output System.
   b. Base Input Output Service.
   c. Basic Input Output System.
   d. Boolean Industry Output Service.

2. *CMOS* stands for
   a. common metafile output service.
   b. common metal-oxide silicon.
   c. complementary metal-oxide semiconductor.
   d. cooperative metafile output system.

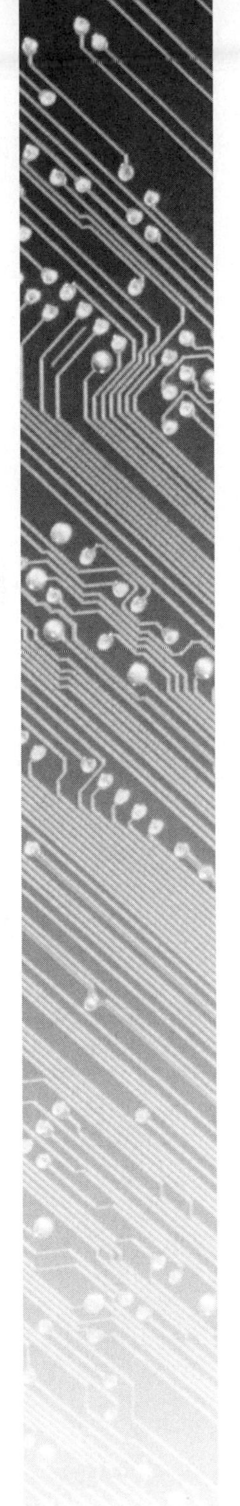

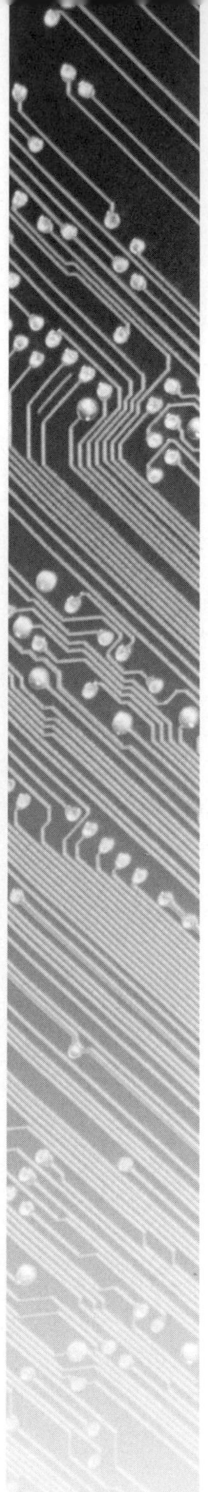

3. What happens during booting when data stored in CMOS differs from data stored in ROM BIOS?
   a. ROM BIOS settings prevail.
   b. CMOS settings prevail.
   c. The settings with the most recent update date and time prevail.
   d. The system looks to the operating system to mediate the conflict.

4. A CMOS chip draws the power it needs from
   a. nowhere; it does not require any power.
   b. the CPU socket, which receives power from the power supply.
   c. its own socket on the motherboard, which receives power from the power supply.
   d. the motherboard's battery.

5. What is ROM shadowing?
   a. Data from RAM is copied to ROM.
   b. Data from ROM is copied to RAM.
   c. Data from ROM is stored in CPU registers.
   d. Data from RAM is stored in a cache on the hard disk.

6. Why is ROM shadowing not important on most systems today?
   a. The 32-bit operating systems do not need 16-bit hardware access.
   b. The 64-bit operating systems do not need 32-bit hardware access.
   c. There is no CMOS chip.
   d. There is no ROM.

7. Which of these is *not* likely to be the key to press to enter BIOS Setup at startup?
   a. Delete
   b. F2
   c. Page Down
   d. S

8. What function key opens Help text in some BIOS Setup programs?
   a. F1
   b. F2
   c. F9
   d. F10

9. What function key exits BIOS Setup and saves changes in most BIOS Setup programs?
   a. F1
   b. F2
   c. F9
   d. F10

10. Which of these is *not* a way to set the current date on a PC?
   a. BIOS Setup program
   b. Date command at DOS prompt
   c. double-clicking clock in Windows
   d. All of these are ways to set the date.

11. Which type of floppy disk can a modern BIOS automatically detect?
   a. floppy disk interface drive
   b. IDE LS-120 floppy drive
   c. SCSI floppy drive
   d. None of the above

12. Which of these is *not* a factor in a drive's geometry in BIOS setup?
   a. tracks
   b. cylinders
   c. sectors
   d. heads

13. Which of these drive types can be set to be the first boot device in BIOS Setup?
   a. CD-ROM
   b. floppy disk
   c. hard disk
   d. All of the above

14. When a BIOS is set to cache the system BIOS and/or video BIOS, in what area of memory is it cached?
   a. conventional
   b. upper
   c. high
   d. extended

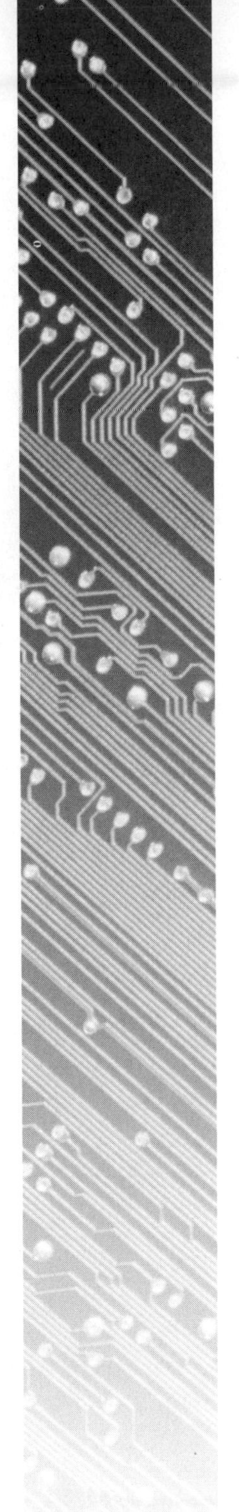

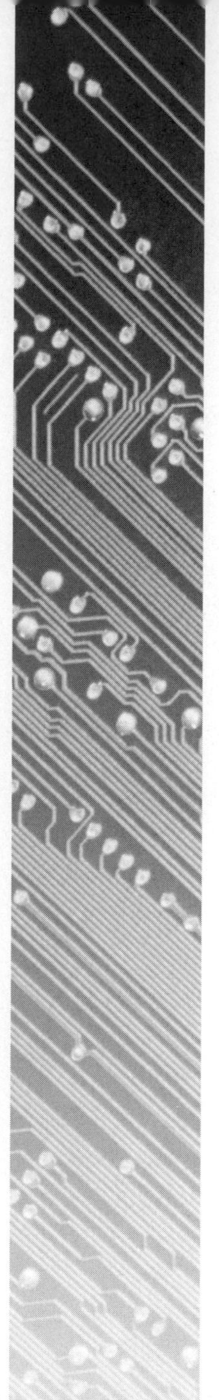

15. For which of these operating systems should BIOS Setup be configured for a Plug and Play operating system?
    a. Windows 3.1
    b. Windows 95
    c. MS-DOS
    d. Unix

16. Which of these power management modes saves the contents of RAM to disk and then shuts off all hardware?
    a. Doze
    b. Standby
    c. Suspend
    d. Hibernate

17. What can you restrict by setting a supervisor password in the BIOS Setup program?
    a. PC booting
    b. Windows booting
    c. access to the BIOS Setup program
    d. disk formatting tools

18. After setting the Reset jumper on the motherboard to Reset position and powering on the system, how long do you need to wait before turning it off again and resetting the jumper to Normal?
    a. 5 to 10 seconds
    b. 15 to 30 seconds
    c. 30 to 60 seconds
    d. 5 to 10 minutes

19. What is the correct procedure for installing a BIOS update on an EEPROM?
    a. Remove the BIOS chip and replace it with a flashed chip.
    b. Download a utility program and run it from within Windows.
    c. Download a utility program and use it to create a boot disk, then boot from that disk.
    d. None of the above

20. When removing a DIPP-style BIOS chip, you must be careful to
    a. avoid ESD.
    b. avoid breaking the legs off the chip.
    c. avoid damaging the socket as you pry out the chip.
    d. All of the above

# TROUBLESHOOTING

1. You have a PC with a nonworking internal modem that is configured to be COM2. You replace it with a known good external modem and attach it to a legacy serial port on the PC. What will you probably need to change in BIOS Setup in order for it to work?
2. You install a new CD-ROM drive as the Secondary Slave but it is not automatically detected. What can you do in BIOS Setup to make the system see it?
3. You install a new hard 16GB hard disk but BIOS Setup autodetects it as an 8GB drive. What can you do to make it see the full 16GB?

# CUSTOMER SERVICE

1. A client mentions that he does not want to upgrade his computer system because he is concerned about privacy issues involving CPU serial numbers on newer models. What can you tell him about this issue?
2. While troubleshooting a problem with a drive over the phone, you ask the client to watch as the PC boots and let you know what IDE devices are being detected. The client claims that no such information appears. What can you do?
3. A client has just bought a USB keyboard to replace a broken AT-style keyboard, but cannot get the PC to recognize it. What BIOS settings would you check?

# FOR MORE INFORMATION

For links to Web sites that provide further information about the topics covered in this chapter, go to the EMC/Paradigm Internet Resource Center at www.emcp.com/College Division/Internet Resource Centers/PC Maintenance/For More Information.

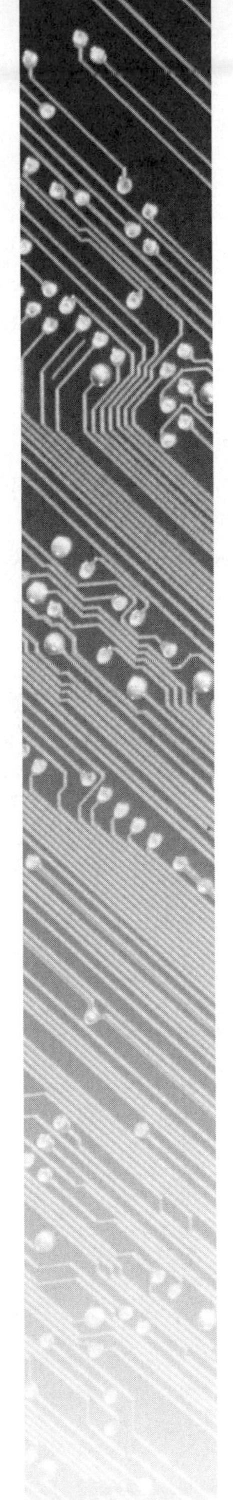

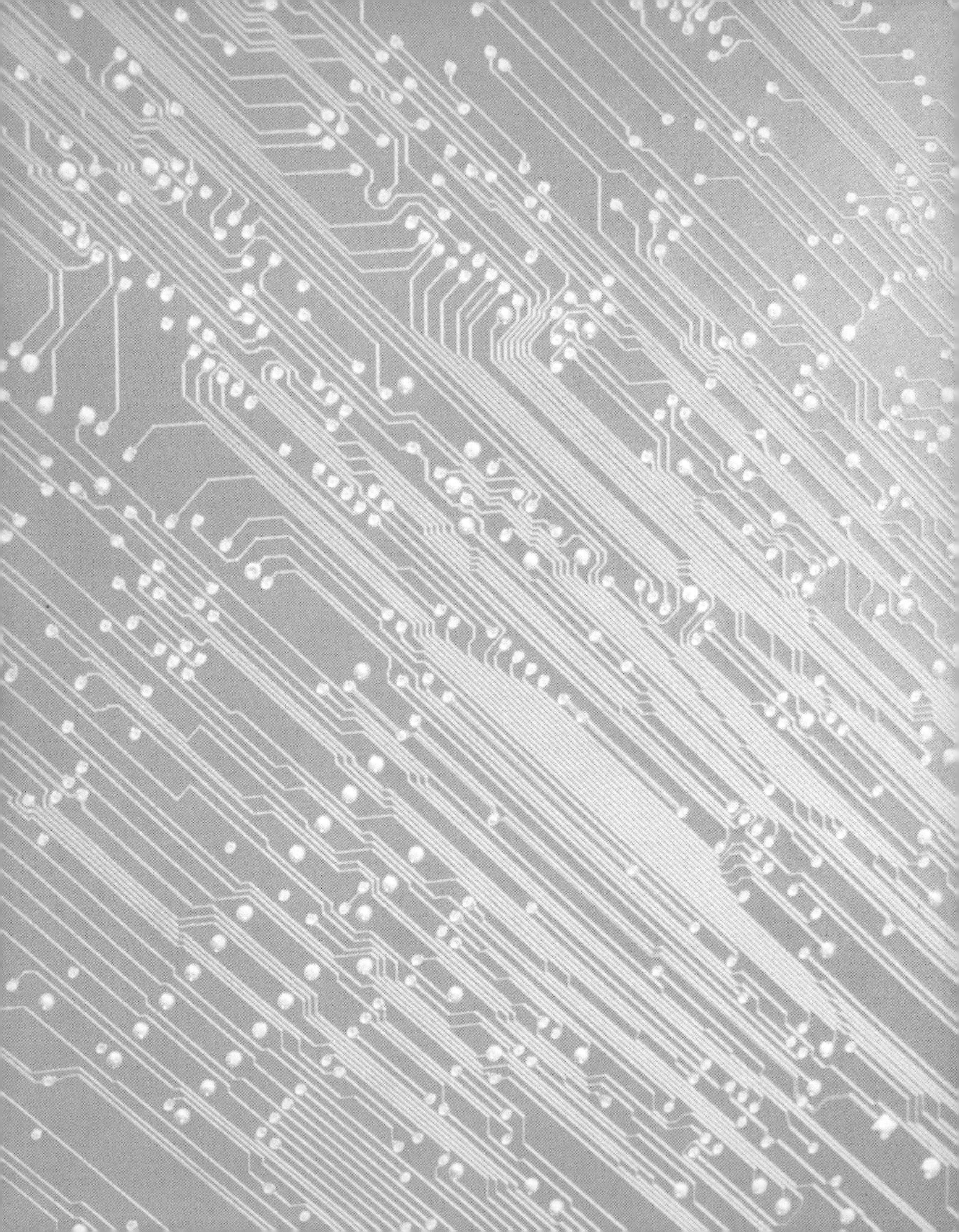

# Project Lab, Part 2
## Processing and Memory

In all of these projects, make sure that you take appropriate precautions to avoid ESD and other damage to components.

### Project #1: Installing and Removing a PGA-Style CPU

1. Examine the CPU. What can you tell about it? Can you determine its speed? Its type? How many pins are there? Does it use standard PGA or SPGA pin arrangement?
2. Examine the motherboard. If a manual is available for it, look up the CPU in it. Make any jumper setting adjustments required for the CPU you have. Document what settings you changed.
3. Install the CPU in the PGA socket. How do you know which way to orient it? How can you tell if it is completely inserted?
4. Install an active heat sink and connect the heat sink's fan power cable to the motherboard or power supply.
5. Trade workstations with another student and check his or her work, including checking any jumper settings made.
6. Return to your own workstation and remove the CPU.
7. Swap CPU chips with a classmate. Will the new CPU work in your motherboard? How did you make the determination? If the new CPU will work, install it in your motherboard; otherwise swap with another classmate until you find one that will work (or until you determine that no compatible CPUs are available).

### Project #2: Installing and Removing an SEC-Style CPU

1. Examine the CPU. What can you tell about it?
2. Check the motherboard, looking for any jumper settings that might need to be changed. Consult the motherboard manual and set any jumpers as needed.
3. Install the CPU support brackets on the motherboard.

4. Install the CPU on the motherboard. How do you know which way to orient it? How can you tell if it is completely inserted?
5. Install an active heat sink including a fan, and connect its power cord to the motherboard or power supply.
6. Trade workstations with another student and check her or his work.
7. Return to your own workstation and remove the CPU.

## Project #3: Installing and Removing RAM

1. Look in the motherboard's manual to determine its RAM requirements. How many slots make up a bank? What physical size, capacity, speed, and other specifications does your motherboard require?
2. Select from the available RAM in your lab RAM that is appropriate for your motherboard. If none is available, find the closest match you can and then write down why it is unsuitable.
3. Install compatible RAM in one bank. How can you tell that it is completely inserted?
4. Trade workstations with another student and check his or her work.
5. Return to your own workstation and remove the RAM.

## Project #4: Installing a Motherboard in a Case

1. Install the CPU, heat sink, and RAM on the motherboard.
2. Select an appropriate case for the motherboard. What considerations did you use to make the selection?
3. Install the motherboard in the case, using whatever stand-offs are appropriate.
4. Connect the case wires to the motherboard for the power and reset switches and any LEDs on the front of the case. Draw a diagram showing which connectors go on which pins on the motherboard. Refer to the motherboard manual as needed.
5. Connect the power supply to the motherboard.
6 Plug in a keyboard and mouse to the computer.
7. Install a video card, and connect a monitor to it.
8. Double-check all the connections and inserted items from steps 4 and 5. Then turn on the PC. What happens?
9. If you do not see any text on the screen, troubleshoot the problem. With each try, document the changes you make and the results you observe.

## PROJECT #5: CHANGING BIOS SETTINGS

Complete project #4 first, so that you have an operational computer.

1. Enter BIOS Setup.
2. Check the system date and time, and change them if they are not accurate.
3. Check the CPU information reported in BIOS. What CPU does it say you have? Is that accurate? If it is not, why do you think it is not accurate? For example, you might have a speed or clock multiplier jumper set incorrectly on the motherboard. Make the necessary corrections.
4. Set the boot order so that the PC boots first from the CD, then from the floppy, then from hard drives.
5. How much RAM does the BIOS report that you have. Is that accurate? If it is not, troubleshoot.
6. How many COM ports does the BIOS report that you have? If you have two, disable the first one and set the second to be COM1.
7. Set the printer port to ECP mode.
8. Turn off BIOS-based power management.
9. If there is a BIOS-based security/password feature, set the password to CLASS.
10. Exit, saving your changes.
11. Reenter BIOS Setup, typing the password as needed to enter. Then remove the password and exit, saving your changes.
12. Reenter BIOS Setup to confirm that the password is no longer required; then exit again, discarding your changes.

## PROJECT #6 (CHALLENGE): TROUBLESHOOTING PRACTICE

Complete project #4 first, so that you have an operational computer.

1. Disable or change something on your motherboard that will cause a problem with it. (Don't do anything that will physically damage the hardware.) For example, you might loosen a cable, change a jumper setting (other than voltage), or remove an item.
2. Swap PCs with a classmate, and troubleshoot the problem, with the goal of bringing the PC up to operational level (text appearing on-screen when turned on). Document the steps you take and what you observe with each try.

## Project #7: (Challenge) Resetting the BIOS Password

1. Set a password for entering BIOS Setup. Write it down, but keep it a secret.
2. Swap PCs with a classmate. Figure out how to override the password protection on the PC's BIOS Setup, and enter BIOS Setup. Possible resources for this information may include the motherboard manual, the motherboard or BIOS manufacturer's Web site, or a Web search.
3. Write down where you found the instructions and how you did the reset.

# PART 3
## Data Storage

# TEST OBJECTIVES IN PART 3

## A+ Core Hardware Service Technician Examination

- **Objective 1.1:** Identify basic terms, concepts, and functions of system modules, including how each module should work during normal operation and during the boot process.
- **Objective 1.2:** Identify basic procedures for adding and removing field replaceable modules for both desktop and portable systems.
- **Objective 1.5:** Identify proper procedures for installing and configuring IDE/EIDE devices.
- **Objective 1.6:** Identify proper procedures for installing and configuring SCSI devices.
- **Objective 1.7:** Identify proper procedures for installing and configuring peripheral devices.
- **Objective 1.8:** Identify hardware methods of upgrading system performance, procedures for replacing basic subsystem components, unique components and when to use them.
- **Objective 2.1:** Identify common symptoms and problems associated with each module and how to troubleshoot and isolate the problems.
- **Objective 4.3**: Identify the most popular type of motherboards, their components, and their architecture (bus structures and power supplies).
- **Objective 4.4:** Identify the purpose of CMOS (Complementary Metal-Oxide Semiconductor), what it contains and how to change its basic parameters.

## A+ Operating System Technologies Examination

- **Objective 1.1:** Identify the operating system's functions, structure, and major system files to navigate the operating system and how to get to needed technical information.
- **Objective 1.2:** Identify basic concepts and procedures for creating, viewing, and managing files, directories, and disks. This includes procedures for changing file attributes and the ramifications of those changes (for example, security issues).
- **Objective 2.1:** Identify the procedures for installing Windows 9x, and Windows 2000 for bringing the software to a basic operational level.

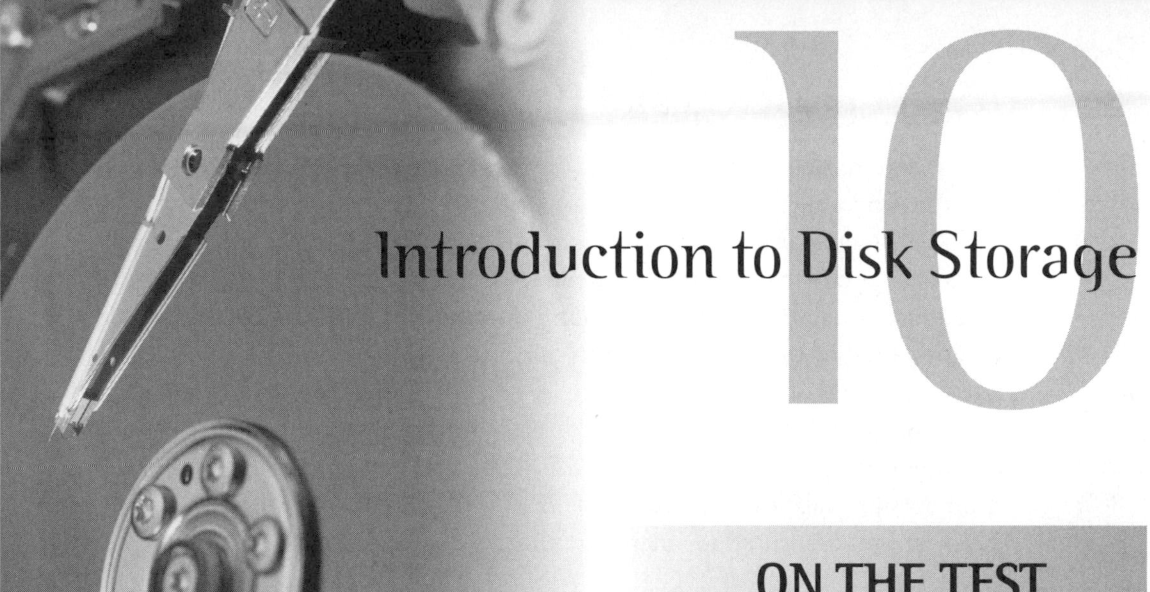

# 10 Introduction to Disk Storage

## ON THE TEST

**A+ Core Hardware Service Technician Examination**

- **Objective 1.1:** Identify basic terms, concepts, and functions of system modules, including how each module should work during normal operation and during the boot process.
- **Objective 1.7:** Identify proper procedures for installing and configuring peripheral devices.
- **Objective 2.1:** Identify common symptoms and problems associated with each module and how to troubleshoot and isolate the problems.
- **Objective 4.4:** Identify the purpose of CMOS (Complementary Metal-Oxide Semiconductor), what it contains and how to change its basic parameters.

**A+ Operating System Technologies Examination**

- **Objective 1.2:** Identify basic concepts and procedures for creating, viewing, and managing files, directories, and disks. This includes procedures for changing file attributes and the ramifications of those changes (for example, security issues).

## ON THE JOB

On the surface, learning the technical details behind disk drives might not seem to be of much benefit to the hands-on PC technician. But having a good grasp of the key concepts makes it much easier to troubleshoot problems and make informed setup decisions. Information about disk drive operation and data storage will serve you in situations like these:

- selecting the best drive for a system
- interpreting information about a disk's properties
- understanding disk error messages
- figuring out why a certain disk is not bootable

## ASCII Characters and Data Storage

Disks store data as binary numbers. Each character can be uniquely described by a certain combination of 1 and 0. The set of codes that defines which character corresponds to which number is called ASCII (American Standard Code for Information Interchange). It was developed in the 1960s to achieve some standardization among different types of data processing equipment. The numbers and letters familiar to our written language are known as the *ASCII character set.*

**ASCII character set**

The 128-character set of numbers, letters, and symbols defined by the American Standard Code for Information Interchange.

The original ASCII standard called for 7-bit codes, so there were 128 combinations possible. In 1981 IBM introduced for use on the IBM PC an 8-bit version, called the *extended ASCII character set,* which added another 128 combinations used for math, graphical, and foreign language characters, for a total of 256.

**Extended ASCII character set**

An expanded version of the original ASCII character set, adding 128 other characters.

Although humans need to see data in ASCII format, computers need to see it in binary. So if you key **dog**, for example, it is immediately translated for the computer's use into 1100100 1101111 1100111. There are different codes for uppercase versus lowercase letters, so *DOG* would be different from *dog.*

### In Real Life

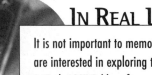

It is not important to memorize the binary equivalents of each number, but if you are interested in exploring them, or in translating text to binary manually, try the AriTech ASCII Table software (see "For More Information" on the Internet Resource Center). It is a free Windows program that translates between ASCII characters and various numbering systems. Appendix E also contains an ASCII-to-number translation table.

### TRY IT!

Spell your name in binary numbers. Use Appendix E, *ASCII to Numeric Conversion Table,* as a reference.

## How Disks Store Data

Disks can store data either magnetically or optically. We will look at those technologies separately in the next few sections.

Both of these storage methods are based on transitions. There are two possible states for a particular spot on the surface of a disk. On a magnetic disk it is positive or negative magnetic charge; on an optical disk it is reflective versus nonreflective. Those two types of spots do not represent the 1s and 0s directly, though. Instead, the drive's read/write head looks for the spots where the disk changes from one state to the other, and then sends an electrical pulse to the drive controller that indicates a 1. If no pulse is sent, that indicates a 0 (see Figure 10.1).

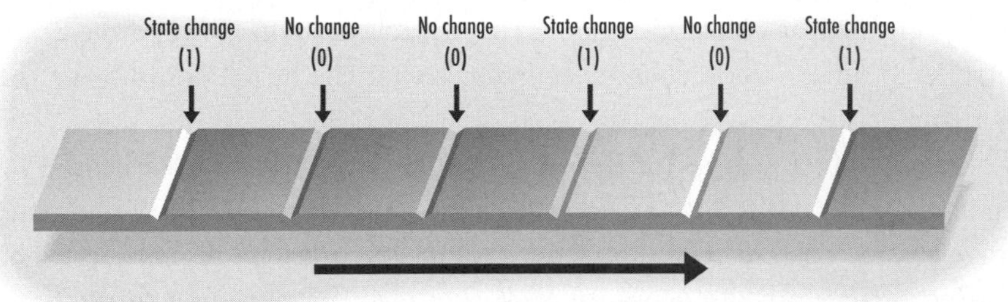


**FIGURE 10.1**
Ones and zeroes are stored on a disk with changes to the state of the disk surface.

As you can imagine, this system requires a high degree of precision. The drive controller must know the exact amount of time that should pass between receiving two 1s in a row. If it does not receive any pulse within that time, it interprets that as a 0. If the drive timing is off even a little bit, too many or too few 0s will be registered in a long string of 0s. To ensure that all of the parts are working in synchronization, a separate pulse called a *timing signal* keeps the beat. This timing signal is conveyed with transition bits as well. This introduces an important point: not all of the bits stored on a disk are for data; some of them are for overhead functions and disk management.

**Timing signal**

A signal in a drive that dictates the amount of time that should pass between two 1s in a row.

The drawing in Figure 10.1 shows the basic concept, but in practice it is a little more complicated; drive makers have found that they can greatly improve a drive's read/write efficiency by employing schemes that minimize the number of transitions to be read. These are *encoding schemes*, and they employ complex sets of rules for determining when a timing signal bit must be present. Run-length limited (RLL) is the standard scheme used on most drives today; earlier schemes included frequency modulation (FM) and modified frequency modulation (MFM).

**Encoding scheme**

A method of minimizing the numbers of transitions involved in data storage on a disk. The most common is run-length limited (RLL).

## In Real Life

**The drive timing and encoding scheme are set by the drive manufacturer; the PC technician and end user have no control over it. You should be aware of these factors not so you can change them, but so you can understand what is happening when something goes wrong.**

## How Magnetic Storage Works

**Polarity**

A positive or negative magnetic charge.

Magnetic storage creates transitions by magnetizing areas of the disk with either a positive or negative *polarity*. It then reads the transitions between the positive and negative areas as 1s and the lack of transitions as 0s. Floppy and hard disks are examples that use magnetic storage technology.

The read/write head, although it is a single unit, actually performs two different functions: it magnetizes areas of the disk with positive or negative polarity, and it reads changes in polarity and relays them to the drive controller. The drive controller specifies whether the head should be reading or writing at any given moment.

The disk surface (Mylar for floppies or metal for hard disks) is coated with a thin layer of iron oxide particles. The read/write head in a magnetic storage system has a wire coil around it, and electricity passes through that coil. Recall from our discussion of EMI that electricity passing through a wire generates a magnetic field, which is exactly what happens here. The magnetic field polarizes the surface of the disk as either positive or negative. The flow of electricity through the wire then reverses, changing the polarization and creating a transition point on the disk. In magnetic storage this is known as a *flux transition* since the transition is in the electrical flux (see Figure 10.2).

**Flux transition**

The transition on a magnetic disk between positive and negative polarity.

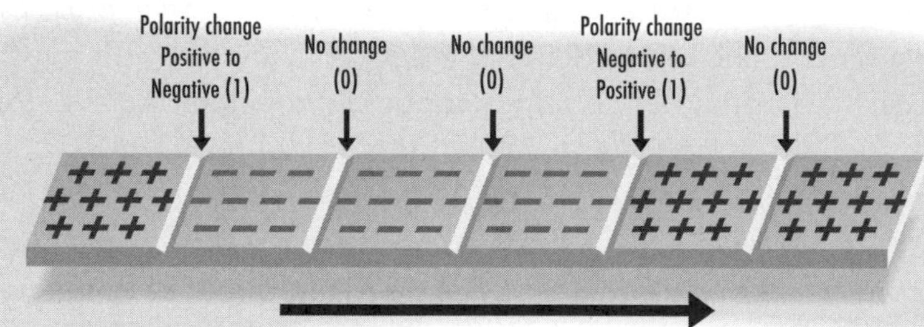


**FIGURE 10.2**
**Magnetic data storage reads transitions between areas of positive and negative polarity.**

## How Optical Storage Works

Whereas magnetic storage uses polarity to differentiate one area of the disk from another, optical storage uses a difference in surface reflectivity. CDs are the most common example of optical storage.

**Land**

An area of reflectivity on an optical disk such as a CD.

**Pit**

An area of lesser reflectivity (less than a land area) on an optical disk.

An optical disk is divided into areas of great reflectivity called *land* and areas of lesser reflectivity called *pits*. The drive's read/write head shines a laser beam onto the disk and then measures the amount of light that bounces back. From this measurement it determines whether the area is land or pit. When the read/write head detects a change in reflectivity—either from more to less or from less to more—it sends a pulse indicating a 1 value. When it does not detect a change, it sends a 0 value (see Figure 10.3).

This chapter calls a CD drive's head "read/write," but in reality not all CD drives are capable of writing. Most are read-only. Chapter 13 explains the technology behind CD writing.

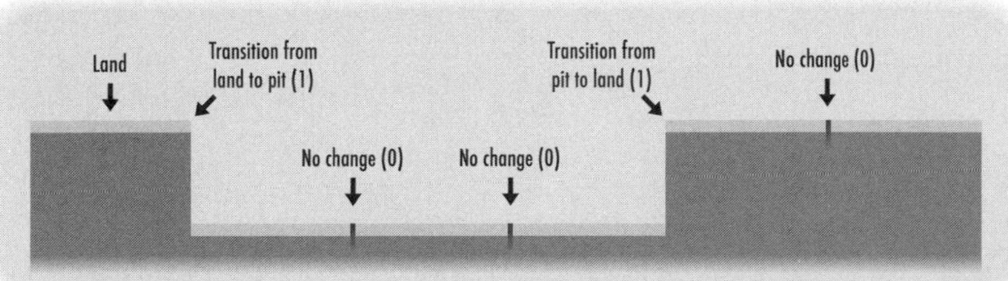


**FIGURE 10.3** Optical disks store data through transitions between areas of greater and lesser reflectivity.

## Disks versus Drives

The terms *disk* and *drive* are often used interchangeably, but they are not really the same thing. A *disk* is the platter or set of platters on which the data is stored; a *drive* is the mechanical unit that reads and writes the disk.

Some disks are removable from their drives, like floppy disks and CDs. Other disks are built permanently into the drive unit, like hard disks. For this latter type, both *disk* and *drive* are equally appropriate terms to use since the two are inseparable, and often the terms are used together, as in *hard disk drive*.

**Disk**

A platter or set of platters on which data is stored.

**Drive**

The mechanical unit that reads and writes a disk.

## How Disk Space Is Organized

When a disk is manufactured, its surface is one large area. Before the disk can accept any data, an organizational structure must be imposed that uniquely names each physical location on the disk; that way, the drive controller can specify the exact physical spot where a given bit of data should be written or retrieved.

The following explains the organizational units into which a disk can be broken down.

**Heads.** Almost all magnetic disks are double-sided. There is a separate *read/write head* for each side; for example, a floppy drive has two heads. On hard drives there are usually multiple stacked platters inside the casing, each with a top and bottom head (see Figure 10.4). The numbering starts at the bottom side of the bottom platter with 0. An average number of heads for a hard disk today is 16.

**Read/write head**

The mechanism in a disk drive that retrieves and stores data on the disk. Most magnetic disk drives have multiple heads, from 2 to 16. Optical drives usually have only 1.

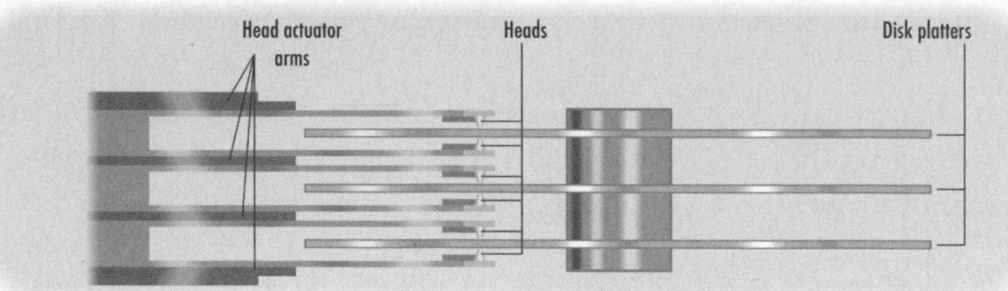


**FIGURE 10.4**
Multiple Heads on a Multiplatter Drive

## In Real Life

The number of heads is important only on hard disks, since floppy drives can usually be assumed to have two heads (one for each side of a single-platter disk) and CD drives can be assumed to have one head. The number of heads is the same as the number of disk platter surfaces available for writing data.

**Track**

A concentric ring on a disk surface.

**Tracks.** Each disk side is organized into concentric rings called *tracks*, like the rings on a cross-section of a tree. In a multiplatter or multiside disk, each side has its own separate tracks. Figure 10.5 illustrates the concept, although on a real disk there would be many more tracks than shown in the figure. A 1.44MB floppy disk has 40 tracks per side, whereas a large hard disk can have tens of thousands.

**FIGURE 10.5**
A track is a ring around a disk at a certain in/out position.

**Cylinder**

All areas of a disk at a certain in/out head position, on all disk sides combined.

**Cylinders.** The heads move in and out on a single actuator, so that all of the heads are in the same position at all times. The stack of tracks accessible at a given position constitutes a *cylinder* (see Figure 10.6). The number of cylinders a drive has is the same as the number of tracks on a single disk side.

**FIGURE 10.6**

A cylinder is a group of tracks at the same head position.

**Sectors.** The surface of the disk is further divided into pie slices made by lines that cross over the track lines. Where these lines intersect the track lines, they create small segments called *sectors*. Modern 1.44MB floppy disks use 36 sectors per track; a typical IDE hard drive usually has 63, although it can vary. A high-performance SCSI hard drive can have 600 or more per track. Each sector holds exactly 512 bytes of data.

**Sector**

A segment of a track on an individual disk surface.

## In Real Life

SCSI hard drives usually have fewer heads and more sectors per track than IDE hard drives, which makes them faster because the actuator arm does not have to negotiate positioning among so many platters. They are also more expensive because having more sectors per track means the read/write mechanism must be finer and more precise. You will learn more about SCSI and IDE in Chapter 11.

**FIGURE 10.7**
A sector is a segment of a track created by dividing lines through the center of the disk platter.

## Low-Level Formatting

**Low-level formatting**

The creation on a disk of logical organization units such as tracks and sectors.

This slicing up of the disk surface into logical organizational units such as tracks, sectors, and so on, is accomplished by a procedure known as *low-level formatting*. Low-level formatting determines the number and spacing of the tracks and the number and spacing of sectors per track. Together these two factors determine the total number of sectors on the disk, and therefore its storage capacity (because each sector holds 512 bytes). Low-level formatting also assigns a unique number to each sector for addressing purposes.

Hard disks are low-level formatted at the factory. A label on a hard drive casing reports the number of cylinders, heads, and sectors for the disk, sometimes abbreviated CHS. Another name for the drive's organizational characteristics is *geometry*. BIOS Setup requires this information in order to communicate with the drive. Most hard disks can report their geometry to BIOS automatically, but you can also enter the data manually in BIOS Setup, as you saw in Chapter 9.

**Geometry**

The definition of the number of cylinders, heads, and sectors in a disk drive. Also called CHS (for cylinders, heads, sectors).

### TRY IT!

**Find the CHS information on your hard disk's label. Calculate the capacity of the drive based on the number of cylinders, heads, and sectors (multiply cylinders by heads by sectors, and then multiply that result by 512 bytes per sector).**

Low-level formatting is not the same as the formatting you do in an operating system (with the Format command, for example). When you format a hard disk through your operating system, you are doing a high-level format, which we will discuss in more detail later.

Floppy disks are not low-level formatted at the factory. For a floppy disk there is no separation between low-level and high-level formatting. Both are performed simultaneously when the user formats a disk in the operating system (for example, with the Format command at a command prompt).

### In Real Life

**Utilities are available for redoing a low-level format on a hard disk. You must acquire the utility from the drive manufacturer, because different manufacturers use different low-level formatting parameters. Technicians are seldom called on to do any low-level formatting.**

## Zoned Recording and Sector Translation

Notice in Figure 10.7 that as you get closer to the center of the disk, the sectors get smaller. This is a problem because, as mentioned above, each sector must hold 512 bytes. The ones in the center are barely large enough to do so, while those at the outer edges have wasted space. This is especially an issue on hard disks since they have many more tracks and sectors than floppies. To solve this problem, *zoned recording* on hard disks was introduced. It allows different tracks to have different numbers of sectors. Figure 10.8 shows a more realistic picture of the sector distribution. There are usually about 10 zones per drive (that is, 10 different numbers of sectors per track), starting with the fewest in the center and the most at the edges.

**Zoned recording**

A means of creating fewer sectors per track on the inner parts of a disk and more on the outer parts.

**FIGURE 10.8** Zoned recording allows tracks closer to the edge of the disk to have more sectors per track.

Virtually all hard disks sold today use zoned recording. However, the technique does throw one quirk into the mix—the motherboard's BIOS expects each track to have the same number of sectors. So a *sector translation* scheme must be built into the on-board controller on the drive. The scheme makes the drive pretend that certain sectors are located on tracks other than those on which they physically exist, so that the numbers will come out even per track. The CHS geometry listed on a hard disk's label, therefore, is for logical addressing purposes only, and does not directly correspond to the physical sector layout on the disk.

**Sector translation**

A conversion scheme for translating the unequal number of physical sectors per track on the disk (due to zoned recording) to an equal number of logical sectors per track.

# BIOS Drive Support

This chapter has discussed the physical storage of data on a disk, but when you save or retrieve files on a disk through the operating system, you are operating several layers removed from that physicality.

The first level up (for hard disks only) is the sector translation done by the drive controller to account for zoned recording, as discussed in the preceding section. The sectors that the drive controller reports to the PC's

BIOS come from a translation table in the drive controller, and do not directly correspond to the physical sectors on the disk.

The next level up is the motherboard BIOS. It recognizes a variety of drive types that connect to it, and issues requests for data storage and retrieval on behalf of the operating system. Depending on the drive type and the BIOS version, it may also perform some translations of its own.

You learned about the BIOS Setup program in Chapter 9, so you should be familiar with its operation. The following sections show examples of drive setup in a sample BIOS Setup program, but keep in mind that the BIOS Setup program associated with the motherboard(s) you are working with may function differently.

## Floppy Drive BIOS Support

A typical motherboard has one built-in floppy drive connector, with a cable attached that can support up to two floppy drives. As mentioned in Chapter 9, most BIOSes do not automatically detect a newly installed floppy drive. You must enter BIOS Setup and set that floppy drive to the size and type of drive you have installed. (However, if you are replacing an old floppy drive with a new one of the same type, the BIOS setting will remain the same and you should not have to make any changes.)

There will be many choices in BIOS Setup for the floppy drive because there have been many types of floppy drives manufactured since the original IBM PC. However, only the 1.44MB 3.5-inch floppy is still manufactured today; all other types have been obsolete for years. Figure 10.9 shows a BIOS Setup program being configured to accept a 1.44MB 3.5-inch floppy drive.

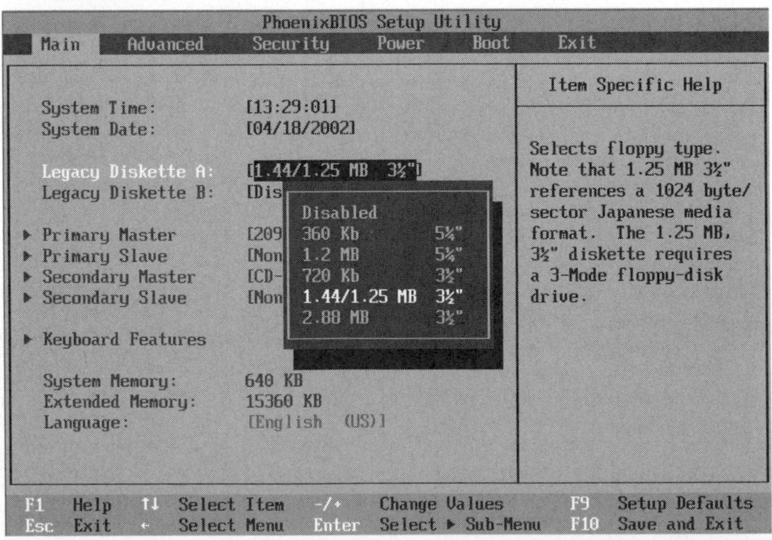


**FIGURE 10.9**
Configuring a Floppy Drive in BIOS Setup

A floppy drive is straightforward in terms of the translation of physical sectors into logical sectors that the operating system can address. It is basically a straight pass-through with the BIOS making no changes. A 1.44MB 3.5-inch floppy has 80 tracks (40 on each side) and 36 sectors per track.

## CD-ROM Drive BIOS Support

A typical motherboard has two built-in IDE connectors, each of which can support up to two drives on a single cable. Motherboards that support ATA-2 or higher will allow any or all of those four IDE devices to be CD-ROM drives.

Another name for IDE is Advanced Technology Attachment (ATA). You will learn more about that in Chapter 11. There have been several revisions to the ATA standard over the years, and ATA-2, introduced in 1996, added Advanced Technology Attachment Packet Interface (ATAPI) support. It allows other drive types besides hard drives to work on an IDE interface. Such drives might include CD-ROM drives, tape backup drives, LS-120 SuperDisk drives, and IDE-based Zip drives. If your motherboard was manufactured in 1996 or later, its BIOS probably includes CD-ROM drive support. If it does not, you might be able to get a BIOS update, as described in Chapter 9.

ATA-2 compliant BIOSes also support automatic drive detection, so the BIOS might automatically detect a newly installed CD-ROM drive and set it up with no user intervention required. If it does not, you can go into BIOS Setup and configure the IDE channel to accept a CD-ROM drive. Depending on the BIOS Setup program, you may have one or more of the settings shown in Figure 10.10 to choose from.

- **Auto:** This is the first setting you should try. Automatic configuration is always a good idea as a first try because then the drive can report its information directly to the BIOS, saving you from having to guess at it.
- **CD-ROM:** This is the obvious next choice for a CD-ROM drive, but it is not available in some BIOS Setup programs.
- **ATAPI Removable:** Choose this if the BIOS Setup does not have a CD-ROM setting. It refers generically to any ATAPI device, but that could include a CD-ROM.
- **IDE Removable:** Choose this if the BIOS Setup program does not have either of the above choices. It refers generically to any IDE drive that has a removable disk. It could include ATAPI, but it could also include removable hard drives.

**FIGURE 10.10**
BIOS Setup Program Settings for Configuring a CD-ROM Drive

Figure 10.11 shows a CD-ROM drive being configured in BIOS Setup using the CD-ROM setting. Notice that there are several options shown, such as Multi-Sector Transfers, LBA, and so on. These options pertain primarily to hard disks, might not even appear in your BIOS Setup program for a CD-ROM drive, and are normally left set to Disabled for CD-ROM. See the section "Hard Disk BIOS Support" in this chapter for an explanation of the options.

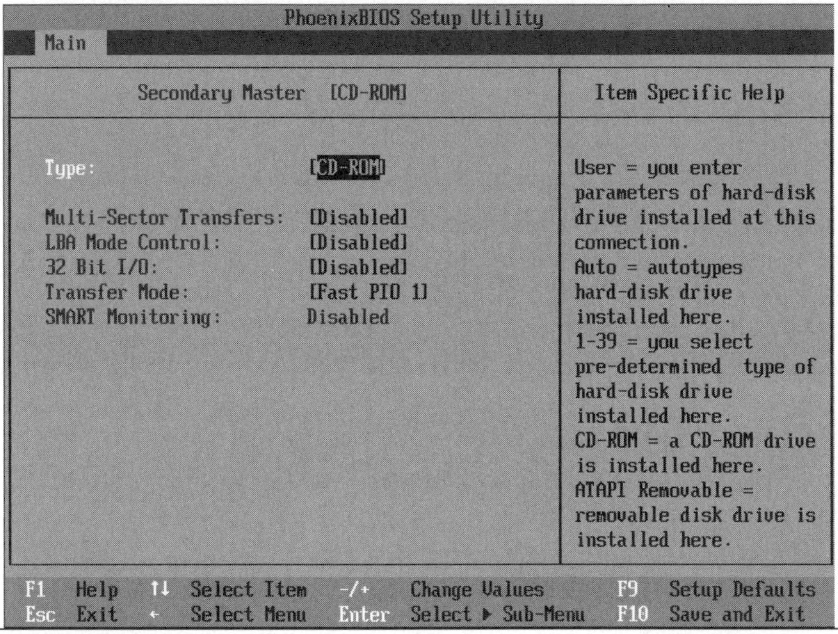

```
                      PhoenixBIOS Setup Utility
 Main
        Secondary Master   [CD-ROM]             Item Specific Help

  Type:                       [CD-ROM]          User = you enter
                                                parameters of hard-disk
  Multi-Sector Transfers:     [Disabled]        drive installed at this
  LBA Mode Control:           [Disabled]        connection.
  32 Bit I/O:                 [Disabled]        Auto = autotypes
  Transfer Mode:              [Fast PIO 1]      hard-disk drive
  SMART Monitoring:           Disabled          installed here.
                                                1-39 = you select
                                                pre-determined  type of
                                                hard-disk drive
                                                installed here.
                                                CD-ROM = a CD-ROM drive
                                                is installed here.
                                                ATAPI Removable =
                                                removable disk drive is
                                                installed here.

 F1  Help   ↑↓ Select Item   -/+   Change Values        F9  Setup Defaults
 Esc Exit   ←  Select Menu   Enter Select ▸ Sub-Menu    F10 Save and Exit
```

**FIGURE 10.11**
Configuring a CD-ROM Drive in BIOS Setup

The BIOS treats the CD-ROM drive's data the same as it does floppy drive data—it passes it straight through with no translation performed on it.

If the BIOS does not support ATAPI devices, you can still use your CD-ROM drive on an IDE interface but you will not be able to boot from a CD-ROM and you will need to load drivers for the CD-ROM drive in your CONFIG.SYS and AUTOEXEC.BAT files. These real-mode drivers may force Windows 95 and higher to operate in a compatibility mode that cripples its performance, so it would be a definite plus in such a system to update the BIOS to get ATAPI support.

## Other IDE Removable Drive BIOS Support

Figure 10.10 described several BIOS Setup settings for IDE drives that are not hard drives. Not every BIOS Setup program has all of these, but those that do typically use them for devices such as tape backup drives, cartridge-based removable hard drives, and Zip drives.

Some BIOS Setup programs have a special setting for LS-120 drives, which are like super floppy drives. They look and work like regular floppy drives, but they also can accept special 120MB floppy disks (called SuperDisks by some manufacturers). If there is no special setting in BIOS for one of these drives, the best choice is ATAPI Removable.

## Hard Disk BIOS Support

Now we enter the complex area of BIOS drive support. Most of the drive options that can be set in BIOS Setup apply exclusively to hard drives. The following sections focus on IDE hard drives; SCSI drives do not interact directly with the motherboard BIOS. You will learn more about SCSI and IDE in Chapter 11.

### *Hard Disk Type and Size*

A BIOS Setup program typically has drive types numbered from 1 to 39 that you can select for a hard drive interface. In the early days of personal computing, there were very few different sizes and types of hard disks, so BIOS makers thought they would be able to identify them all by a numeric value. However, hard drive technology grew so quickly and so many different manufacturers were producing all kinds of drives that this simple identification style proved impossible. As a consequence, these drive types are rarely used anymore. They are included in BIOS Setup only for backward compatibility.

The more popular setting for a hard drive is Auto, which allows the drive to report its settings to BIOS automatically, including its CHS (cylinders, heads, sectors) and its preferred settings for other values (described in the next few sections). If Auto does not work, you can try setting it to User and then filling in the CHS values yourself. However, if Auto does not work, there is probably an external reason, such as bad jumper settings or cabling on the drive or a nonworking drive. Figure 10.12 shows a 2GB hard drive with automatically detected settings.

```
                    PhoenixBIOS Setup Utility
 Main
           Primary Master  [2097MB]                  Item Specific Help

 Type:                       [Auto]                  User = you enter
 Cylinders:                  [ 4334]                 parameters of hard-disk
 Heads:                      [ 15]                   drive installed at this
 Sectors:                    [63]                    connection.
 Maximum Capacity:           2097MB                  Auto = autotypes
                                                     hard-disk drive
 Multi-Sector Transfers:     [16 Sectors]            installed here.
 LBA Mode Control:           [Enabled]               1-39 = you select
 32 Bit I/O:                 [Disabled]              pre-determined  type of
 Transfer Mode:              [Standard]              hard-disk drive
 SMART Monitoring:           Disabled                installed here.
                                                     CD-ROM = a CD-ROM drive
                                                     is installed here.
                                                     ATAPI Removable =
                                                     removable disk drive is
                                                     installed here.

 F1   Help   ↑↓  Select Item   -/+    Change Values        F9   Setup Defaults
 Esc  Exit   ←   Select Menu   Enter  Select ▶ Sub-Menu    F10  Save and Exit
```

**FIGURE 10.12**
A Hard Drive Configured with the Auto Setting

Jot down the current settings for your primary hard disk and then set it to User in BIOS Setup. Manually enter the settings to match the settings you wrote down. Then, since this exercise was just for practice, set it back to Auto again.

### *BIOS Methods of Increasing Capacity*

On the original IDE specification, the size limit was 540MB. It was not that the drive individually or the system BIOS individually could not handle more, but that the combination of the two could not. The drive could physically have a lot more cylinders than the BIOS could keep track of. The BIOS's limit is 1,024 cylinders, but there is no fixed limit for hard drives; some have upward of 16,000. On the other hand, the BIOS could keep track of many more heads than the drive could physically contain. It supports up to 256 heads, but most drives have only 16 or so, and cannot handle more without increasing their external dimensions.

To overcome this limitation, the ATA-2/Enhanced IDE (EIDE) standard, developed in 1996, enabled the BIOS to translate the addresses coming in from the drive controller into different addresses it could convey to the software. For example, if the drive actually has 8,000 cylinders and 16 heads, it can tell the software that it has 1,000 cylinders and 128 heads.

There are three possible settings in most BIOS Setup programs, as shown in Figure 10.13.

- **Standard CHS (Normal):** The addressing is the same coming into and going out of the BIOS—a straight pass-through. This setting turns off any translation and limits the drive size to 528MB.
- **Extended CHS (ECHS, also called Large):** This was the original type of translation. It accepts the CHS data from the drive and divides the number of cylinders by whatever number is necessary to get it under the 1,024 limit. Then it multiplies the number of heads by the same amount, so you end up with the same total number of sectors as before. Finally, it conveys this translated sector data to the software. This would still be an appropriate setting for a drive that did not support LBA, described below, but is becoming obsolete.
- ***Logical Block Addressing* (LBA):** When communicating with the drive, the BIOS assigns a number to each sector and deals with each on a sector-by-sector basis rather than according to cylinder and head. However, the operating system still requires CHS values, so it creates a CHS table to match the operating system's requirements. When communicating with the drive it uses a 28-bit binary number, which gives a maximum capacity of 128GB, but when communicating using CHS it is limited to 8.4GB, for an effective maximum of 8GB.

**Logical Block Addressing (LBA)**

A means of sector translation that assigns a number to each sector and works with each individually, using a CHS table for conversion to CHS values as needed.

**FIGURE 10.13**
Bios Setup Program Sector Translation Settings

Some BIOS programs, especially more recent ones, do not offer ECHS; instead they have an on/off setting for LBA (see Figure 10.14 for an example).

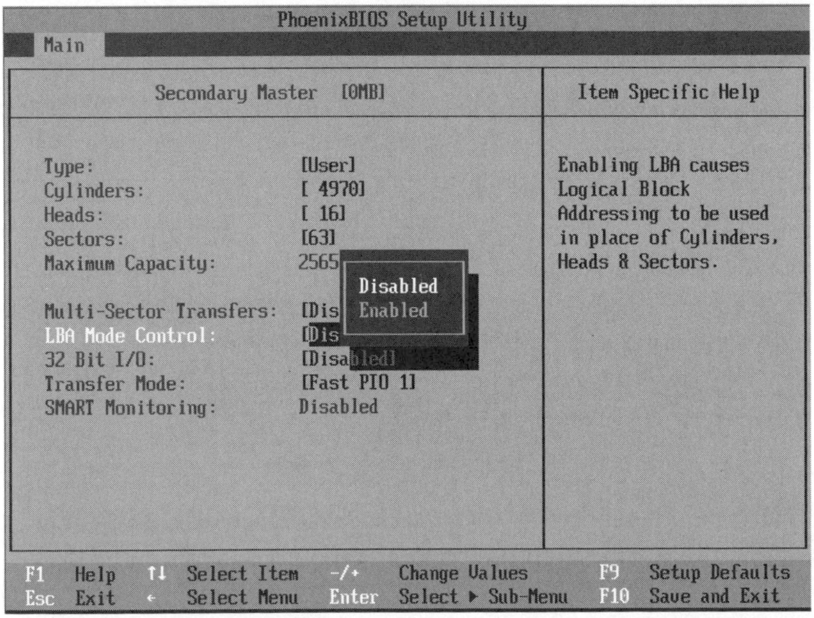

```
PhoenixBIOS Setup Utility
Main

Secondary Master   [0MB]                    Item Specific Help

Type:                     [User]            Enabling LBA causes
Cylinders:                [ 4970]           Logical Block
Heads:                    [ 16]             Addressing to be used
Sectors:                  [63]              in place of Cylinders,
Maximum Capacity:         2565              Heads & Sectors.
                               Disabled
Multi-Sector Transfers:   [Dis Enabled
LBA Mode Control:         [Dis
32 Bit I/O:               [Disabled]
Transfer Mode:            [Fast PIO 1]
SMART Monitoring:         Disabled

F1  Help  ↑↓ Select Item  -/+   Change Values        F9  Setup Defaults
Esc Exit  ←  Select Menu  Enter Select ▶ Sub-Menu    F10 Save and Exit
```

**FIGURE 10.14**
Turning On/Off LBA Addressing for an IDE Drive

As you know, today's hard drives are much larger than 8GB, so how do they manage LBA support? The 8GB barrier is broken by an extension to BIOS called *Enhanced BIOS Services for Disk Drives*, which was introduced in 1998. This is a BIOS feature, not a drive feature, and it supports up to 18 trillion gigabytes. However, the ATA standard for IDE drives limits drive size to 137 gigabytes, so that is the real maximum at this writing.

**Enhanced BIOS Services for Disk Drives**

A BIOS extension that enables LBA support for drives of over 8GB.

A BIOS made before 1996 probably will not have support for ECHS or LBA, so whatever drive you put in such a system will be seen as no larger than 528MB in size. A BIOS update might solve this problem. A BIOS made between 1996 and 1998 might support LBA but not have Enhanced BIOS Services for Disk Drives support, so a drive connected to such a system would be limited to 8.4GB. Again, this probably can be overcome with a BIOS update. You could also overcome it by adding an IDE controller expansion card (which has its own BIOS) and connecting the drive to that controller card rather than directly to the motherboard.

**WARNING**

The FAT16 file system, which is your only choice under MS-DOS and most versions of Windows 95, limits the size of an individual volume to 2.1GB, so if you install a large hard disk in such a system, you must use partitioning to carve it up into logical drives of 2.1GB or less in order for the operating system to be able to access all of the disk space. We will discuss this further in the "Disk Partitions" and "High-Level Formatting" sections later in this chapter.

**IN REAL LIFE**

If you install an old drive that has been using Standard CHS into a new system that autodetects it and sets it up to use LBA, you could lose access to the existing data on that drive. In such a case you would manually configure the drive in BIOS to use Standard CHS, retrieve its data, and then switch it over to LBA and repartition it.

**TRY IT!**

In your BIOS Setup program, experiment with the different translation settings for your primary hard drive to see which types your BIOS supports (Large, LBA, and so on). Make sure you set the drive back to its original setting when you are finished experimenting.

### *Transfer Mode*

The transfer mode selected in BIOS Setup for a drive determines how quickly the BIOS will attempt to send and receive data on that drive.

The most common transfer mode type is *Programmed Input/Output* (PIO). There are five different PIO modes, numbered 0 through 4, ranging from 3.3MB/sec for PIO 0 to 16.67MB/sec for PIO 4. Nearly all drives today can support PIO 4, but if you use a PIO mode that is higher than the drive can handle, data corruption may result. Check the drive label or, if there is no information about PIO mode there, check the drive's specifications on the drive manufacturer's Web site.

**Programmed Input/Output (PIO)**

A transfer mode (actually five different modes, PIO 0 through PIO 4) for increasing the speed at which the BIOS attempts to send and receive data for a drive.

An alternative transfer mode to PIO is *Direct Memory Addressing* (DMA). DMA transfers data directly between the BIOS and memory without going through the CPU. This helps improve overall system performance since the burden on the CPU is less. There are two kinds of DMA: regular and bus mastering. Regular DMA uses the DMA controller on the motherboard, the same one that handles DMA functions for slower speed items like the keyboard and sound card. Bus mastering DMA has higher speed DMA functionality built into the south bridge of the chipset so it can take advantage of the PCI bus for DMA transfers. There are three bus mastering DMA modes, 0 through 2, ranging from 4.16 to 16.67MB/sec.

**Direct Memory Addressing (DMA)**

An alternative to PIO (actually three different modes, DMA 0 through DMA 2) for transferring data directly between the BIOS and RAM, increasing data transfer rates.

Both of these transfer types have become nearly obsolete because of the introduction of *UltraDMA* (UDMA), also called UltraATA. UltraDMA modes are supported on motherboards that conform to the ATA-4 or higher IDE standard. That includes most motherboards manufactured after mid-1998. UltraDMA modes support transfer rates of from 33MB/sec (ATA-4) up to 100MB/sec (ATA-6), faster than even the fastest PIO and DMA modes. Some BIOSes enable you to choose which UltraDMA mode to use; for others you simply enable UltraDMA and it does the rest. You will learn more about UltraDMA in Chapter 11, when we look at the IDE interface in more technical detail.

**UltraDMA**

A high-speed transfer mode for disk drives that improves upon DMA and allows transfer rates of up to 100MB/sec.

**WARNING**

**When a modern BIOS autodetects a modern IDE drive, it will set the PIO/DMA Mode to Disabled because it employs UltraDMA instead. You should not attempt to enable PIO or DMA on such a drive because it will only slow it down.**

## TRY IT!

**If you have a disk utility program that can test the performance of a hard disk and report a numeric measurement for it, try testing your hard disk when it is set to several different transfer modes (UltraDMA, various PIO modes, etc.). Which gives the best performance? Do any of them cause the drive not to work at all? Make sure you return to the original setting when finished experimenting.**

### *Other Settings*

If you use Auto as the drive type, all of these other settings will be configured automatically. However, if you are setting up the drive's definition manually, you will need to know the correct settings to use for the following:

- **Multisector transfers:** This specifies the number of sectors in each block transfer from the hard drive to memory. The BIOS settings available are Disabled, 2, 4, 8, or 16. For today's hard drives 16 is usually the right setting, but check the hard drive's specs if in doubt.
- ***Self-Monitoring and Reporting Tool* (SMART):** Introduced with the ATA-3 standard in 1997, SMART is a technology that monitors the drive's performance, watching for performance degradation that could signal an impending failure. The BIOS setting is Enabled or Disabled. Enable it if your drive supports it. See Chapter 11 for more details.

**Self-Monitoring and Reporting Tool (SMART)**

A technology for monitoring drive performance and reporting any irregularities or changes that might signal impending failure.

## Disk Partitions

**Logical drive**

A drive letter that has been assigned to a portion of a physical disk.

The operating system does not deal directly with physical hard disks. Instead, it deals with logical drives. A *logical drive* is a drive letter that has been assigned to a portion of a physical disk. A single physical disk can have multiple logical drives. The operating system might see a C drive, a D drive, and an E drive, for example, all of which are part of a single physical disk drive.

Some users like having multiple logical drives because it gives them more storage flexibility; it also enables them to install multiple operating systems on a single PC, each on its own logical drive. Others prefer to have a single large logical drive for each physical drive so they do not have to worry about running out of room on one logical drive while another one has space to spare.

The operating system's file system limitations may also force you to create some logical drives in order to access all of the available space on a large physical hard drive. If the operating system supports only the FAT16 file system (MS-DOS and Windows 95, for example), you must create logical drives no larger than 2.1GB. To understand why, see "Clusters" later in this chapter. This limitation is one reason that many people upgrade to Windows 98 or higher.

Because partitioning is covered in more detail in Chapter 12, this chapter does not include "Try It!" exercises on the topic. Instead, this chapter focuses on the theory behind partitioning, so you will have a conceptual understanding of how it fits into the disk management picture.

## In Real Life

There were several releases of Windows 95 after the original release: Windows 95A, Windows 95B, and Windows 95C. Windows 95B and 95C support the FAT32 file system and allow logical drives to be larger than 2.1GB; Windows 95 original and Windows 95A do not. To determine which version of Windows 95 is installed, choose Help, About Windows 95 from any file management window.

## Primary and Extended Partitions

To create these logical drives, you first must create partitions. At a minimum you need to create a *primary partition* in which you use all of the space on the entire physical drive, or else you can set aside some of the space. If you do set aside space, you can create an *extended partition* and then create logical drives on that extended partition. An extended partition differs from a primary partition in that (1) it is not bootable, and (2) it can have multiple logical drives within it, whereas a primary partition can have only one logical drive letter. Figure 10.15 shows one way that disk space might be divided up into logical drives.

**Primary partition**

A bootable partition on a hard drive that can have only one logical drive letter.

**Extended partition**

A nonbootable partition on a hard drive that can have multiple drive letters assigned to it.

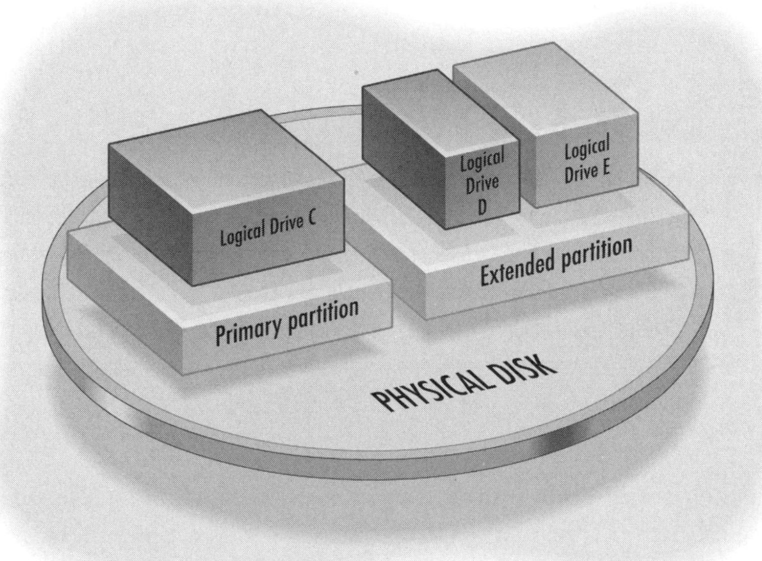


**FIGURE 10.15**
A single physical drive can have multiple logical drives.

The FDISK partitioning program that comes with MS-DOS and Windows 9x/Me allows only one primary partition per physical drive; all other partitions must be extended. However, Windows 2000's Disk Management program enables you to create multiple primary partitions on a single physical drive. Chapter 12 covers the specifics of disk partitioning under MS-DOS, Windows 9x, and Windows 2000.

## Active Partition

**Active partition**

The primary partition that is set up to be checked for boot instructions at startup.

In order for an operating system to boot from a partition, it must be a primary partition, and it must be the *active partition*. This second condition is necessary because it is possible for a drive to have more than one active partition, as mentioned above. FDISK or any other partitioning program can make a partition active. When a PC boots, the BIOS searches the active partition for startup files, so setting a particular partition to be active makes the operating system boot from that partition. In most cases, since there is only one primary partition, it is automatically set to be active.

## Master Boot Record

**Master boot record (MBR)**

The information about the way a drive is partitioned.

The information about the physical drive's partitions is stored in a *master boot record* (MBR) written to the first sector of the first cylinder (Cyl 0) of the first head (Hd 0). It persists there no matter what high-level formatting is done to the drive.

### In Real Life

**The fact that the MBR is impervious to high-level formatting means that if a virus infects the MBR, reformatting the drive will not get rid of it. To re-create the MBR, use the command FDISK /MBR at a command prompt, or use the FIXBOOT command in the Windows 2000/XP Recovery Console. See Chapter 12 for further discussion of FDISK, and see Chapter 27 for more information about the Recovery Console.**

## Clusters

**Cluster**

A group of sectors treated as a single storage unit.

Since a single sector holds only 512 bytes, very rarely would a file occupy only one of them. In the vast majority of cases a file occupies many sectors. Therefore, to cut down on the overhead involved in sending instructions to a drive, high-level formatting creates multisector *clusters*. The operating system then works with those clusters rather than with individual sectors. Another name for clusters is allocation units. (Allocation units is actually the preferred Microsoft terminology as of MS-DOS 4.0, but popular usage has stayed with clusters.)

The partition-creation process defines the cluster size for a logical drive. FDISK does this automatically based on the size of the drive and the file system (FAT16 versus FAT32, discussed later in the chapter). Some other partitioning programs enable users to choose a cluster size.

The best cluster size depends on the size of the disk. It is a trade-off between performance and storage space: the larger the clusters, the more efficient the file system because it has fewer units to address. However, large clusters waste disk space. A cluster can hold data from only one file, so if it contains even one sector's worth of data, it is considered completely full. Rarely is a file exactly the same size as a cluster, so there is the likelihood of many half-full clusters with wasted empty space. The larger the cluster size, the more pronounced this problem becomes.

Defining cluster size is an issue primarily with drives under 2GB using the FAT16 file system. Table 10.1 lists some hard disk sizes and the recommended cluster size for each. Notice that the largest number of sectors per cluster is 64. Because FAT16 uses 16-byte entries to reference clusters, there can be only 65,536 clusters. That is the basis of the 2.1GB limit per logical drive for FAT16 partitions: 65,536 clusters times 32,768 bytes per cluster.

| Drive Capacity | Cluster Size |
|---|---|
| 16MB to 128MB | 4 sectors (2,048 bytes) |
| 128MB to 256MB | 8 sectors (4,096 bytes) |
| 256MB to 512MB | 16 sectors (8,192 bytes) |
| 512MB to 1GB | 32 sectors (16,384 bytes) |
| 1GB to 2 GB | 64 sectors (32,768 bytes) |

**TABLE 10.1**
Default Hard Disk Cluster Sizes for FAT16 Partitions

With the 32-bit FAT32 file system the maximum number of clusters increases to 268,435,456. That means a single logical drive that uses FAT32 can be up to 2 *terabytes* in size, so there is no need to break a single physical hard disk into multiple logical drives with FAT32.

**Terabyte**

One trillion bytes.

Using FAT32 changes the default cluster size. On small drives FAT32 employs small cluster sizes for maximum storage space, but on larger drives it uses large clusters for maximum access efficiency. Table 10.2 lists the default cluster sizes for FAT32 partitions.

| Drive Capacity | Cluster Size |
| --- | --- |
| Up to 260MB | 1 sector (512 bytes) |
| 260MB to 6GB | 8 sectors (4,096 bytes) |
| 6GB to 16GB | 16 sectors (8,192 bytes) |
| 16GB to 32GB | 32 sectors (16,384 bytes) |
| 32GB to 1TB | 64 sectors (32,768 bytes) |

**TABLE 10.2**
Default Hard Disk Cluster Sizes for FAT32 Partitions

The NTFS file system uses smaller clusters than FAT. Table 10.3 lists the default cluster sizes for NTFS.

| Drive Capacity | Cluster Size |
| --- | --- |
| Up to 512MB | 1 sector (512 bytes) |
| 512MB to 1GB | 2 sectors (1,024 bytes) |
| 1GB and up | 4 sectors (2,048 bytes) |

**TABLE 10.3**
Default Hard Disk Cluster Sizes for NTFS Partitions

# High-Level Formatting

After you create the logical drives, the operating system sees them but cannot read and write them because they have not yet been high-level formatted. *High-level formatting* lays down an organization system that is compatible with the specific operating system installed.

**High-level formatting**
Preparing a disk for use by a particular operating system by creating a file system such as FAT or NTFS.

Although the principle is the same, the details of high-level formatting are different for File Allocation Table (FAT) file systems versus the New Technology File System (NTFS). The following sections address each separately but focus on FAT because it is more heavily emphasized on the A+ exams.

This chapter covers the concepts behind high-level formatting; Chapter 12 explains the formatting procedures involved in various operating system versions.

## FAT Formatting

FAT file systems include FAT16, which is used in MS-DOS and Windows 95, and FAT32, which is used in Windows 98 and Windows 2000. We will use the term *FAT* generically when a concept relates to both FAT16 and FAT32.

High-level FAT formatting does the following:

- Creates the *volume boot record*, which provides information about the partition and stores boot file(s) if the drive is bootable. It is written to the first sector in that logical disk, known as the *boot sector*.

**Volume boot record**
Information about a particular partition and its boot files if bootable.

**Boot sector**
The first sector on a logical disk.

- Creates a *file allocation table* (FAT), which is like a table of contents for the disk, right next to the volume boot record. Then it creates a second identical copy of the FAT right next to the first for redundancy.
- Checks the data obtained during the low-level format about any tracks and sectors that are physically unusable, and blocks off those sectors in the FAT so that the operating system will not use them.
- Creates a blank *root directory* into which all other directories (folders) that you later create on the drive will be placed.

**File Allocation Table (FAT)**

A table of contents for a disk, listing the contents of its root directory.

**Root directory**

The top-level directory (folder) on a logical disk.

One way to format a drive is from a command prompt: key **FORMAT** and then the drive letter and press Enter (for example, **FORMAT C:**). You can also issue a Format command from within Windows by right-clicking the drive icon in My Computer and choosing Format. You will have a chance to try this in Chapter 12.

The following sections explain some of these terms in more detail.

### *Volume Boot Record*

Every logical drive must have a volume boot record even if it is not going to be bootable. The volume boot record contains information about the drive's capacity, number of sectors, and volume label (if any). If the drive is bootable, it also contains the first boot file (which would be IO.SYS for MS-DOS and Windows 9x). At startup the BIOS looks at the volume boot record on the active partition; if it finds a boot file, it uses it to start loading an operating system.

### *Root Directory*

A directory and a folder are the same thing; the term *folder* has replaced *directory* in popular usage because it is used in Windows. A directory is an organizing unit for files, much like a tabbed folder in a file cabinet is an organizing unit for individual papers. Directories make it easier to manage large numbers of files on a single disk by allowing them to be arranged into and managed as groups. The root directory is the top-level directory on a disk, the directory in which all other directories reside.

**Directory**

A logical unit that organizes files into groups for easier management. Also called folder.

### *File Allocation Table (FAT)*

The FAT is a map of the contents of the root directory. It is a small database that reports where the first cluster of each item stored in the root directory is located.

The FAT does not keep track of entire files, but only of the first cluster of each file. In that first cluster, in addition to the data stored there, is the name of the second cluster in the file. The second cluster then points to the third, and so on, until the last cluster of the file, which contains an end file marker. Because of this chain-link organizational structure, a single error, if it occurs in one of the first few clusters of the file, can cause almost an entire file to be "lost." In Chapter 12 you will learn about some utility programs that can help recover the contents of files that become lost due to FAT errors. FAT errors are infrequent, however, because there are two copies of the FAT and they error-check one another. An exception is when a program terminates abnormally or Windows shuts down unexpectedly while information is being written to the FAT. Those are the most common sources of FAT errors.

Besides the file's name and the location of its first cluster, the FAT also keeps track of any attributes associated with the file or folder (such as Read-Only), the date/time of the last modification, the size, and the location of the first cluster in which the file is stored. The exception: It does not report the size of a folder because all folders are exactly the same size (32 bytes).

The FAT stores information only about the root directory; it does not keep track of the contents of subdirectories. Instead it remembers the names and locations of the subdirectories, and directs any requests to the subdirectory in question. The subdirectory maintains its own content listing.

### *FAT16 and FAT32*

FAT16 is the original type of FAT. As its name implies, it uses 16-bit binary numbers to uniquely identify each cluster on the logical drive. (See the earlier discussion under "Clusters" for further details.) FAT32 is a 32-bit variant that uses a 32-bit binary numbering system for cluster identification.

FAT32 is supported by Windows 95C and higher only, so a FAT32 drive cannot be read in MS-DOS or the original version of Windows 95. Therefore, if you have a drive that requires MS-DOS for access, you need to use FAT16.

Otherwise, there are many good reasons to use FAT32. As mentioned, FAT32 makes it possible to have much larger logical drives; if you want a logical drive to be larger than 2GB, you must use FAT32. FAT32 also enables drives to have smaller cluster sizes than an equivalent-sized drive under FAT16. There are other minor improvements. For example, FAT32 synchronizes the two copies of the FAT much more intelligently than FAT16, so there is less chance of corruption and error.

Windows 95C supports FAT32 partitions but has no conversion utility; it can only create new, blank FAT32 partitions. Windows 98 comes with a

FAT32 Conversion Wizard, accessible from the System Tools menu. There are also third-party programs, such as Partition Magic, that can perform a conversion without losing data.

### *FAT Bootable Disks*

For a FAT disk to be bootable under MS-DOS or Windows 9x, it must contain three files:

- **IO.SYS:** Loads the operating system interface to the hardware. In Windows 9x it also loads the operating system kernel.
- **MSDOS.SYS:** In MS-DOS this file loads the operating system kernel; in Windows 9x it is simply a text-based configuration file containing settings for IO.SYS to use.
- **COMMAND.COM:** The command line interpreter. In MS-DOS this is the command prompt interface at which you key commands. In Windows 9x it must be loaded but remains behind the scenes while Windows loads on top of it. This is one of the basic differences between Windows 9x and Windows NT: Windows NT does not have any part of MS-DOS running behind it.

The first two files are hidden, so they do not appear in a directory listing for the drive. COMMAND.COM is not hidden, and appears in the root directory.

## NTFS Formatting

*New Technology File System* (NTFS) is an entirely different file system developed specifically for Windows NT. It has some advantages over FAT16 and FAT32, such as the support of enormous partition sizes (up to 16 *exabytes*) and more sophisticated security permission capabilities on an individual file level. For example, the version of NTFS that comes with Windows 2000 (NTFS 4) enables files to be encrypted based on user certificates.

**New Technology File System (NTFS)**

A file system for Windows NT, 2000, and XP that offers advantages over the traditional FAT file system.

**Exabyte**

A trillion megabytes.

### *Compatibility Issues*

Why don't all PCs automatically use NTFS? It is primarily an issue of compatibility. Drives formatted with NTFS can be used only with Windows NT 4, Windows 2000, and Windows XP. If you have a PC set up for dual-booting with MS-DOS or Windows 9x, any partitions formatted as NTFS are not visible when you use those operating systems.

Another drawback of NTFS is that, since its partitions cannot be read under MS-DOS, you cannot boot from a DOS or Windows 9x startup disk and access that partition. When troubleshooting a system problem that prevents Windows from starting normally, it is sometimes advantageous to be able to access the disk via command prompt and copy some of the files onto floppy disks to save them. You cannot do that with an NTFS partition. (You can, however, use the Windows 2000/XP Recovery Console to access certain system folders on an NTFS partition if Windows will not boot normally. Chapter 27 covers Recovery Console usage.)

## In Real Life

**The operating system must support NTFS, but when accessing an NTFS partition over a network, the remote PC need not have an operating system that supports it directly. That is because the request for file access passes through the local operating system, which converts it to network packets. The fact that the file was retrieved from an NTFS partition is of no concern to the remote PC.**

NTFS is only for hard disks; floppy disks use FAT exclusively, so they are universally compatible with all MS-DOS and Windows PCs.

### *Master File Table (MFT)*

Remember that when you partition a physical drive, it creates a master boot record that contains information about each partition and logical drive. NTFS partitions are listed in that MBR, along with any FAT partitions. Each NTFS logical drive also has a volume boot record (in a slightly different format from one on a FAT drive) and a root directory.

The steps that occur when you high-level format an NTFS drive are nearly the same as those explained earlier for a FAT drive. The big difference is that instead of a FAT, an NTFS partition has a *Master File Table* (MFT). It is similar to a FAT in concept, in that it contains pointers to the starting clusters of files and folders. The main differences between a FAT and an MFT include the following:

**Master File Table (MFT)**

The equivalent of a FAT for the NTFS file system. Stores data about the starting clusters of files and folders stored on the disk.

- The MFT does not store file attribute information such as Hidden, System, and so on. These are part of the files themselves under NTFS. There are more attributes available under NTFS than under FAT.
- The MFT contains a descriptor that reports information about the MFT itself; there are two copies of it, and they occupy the first two record positions in the MFT.
- The MFT contains a log file that tracks all NTFS operations. This log file can be helpful to a disk repair program in the event of a disk error.

- If a file is very small (under 1,500 bytes), the entire file is stored within the MFT itself rather than in a separate cluster on the disk.

You can format a new partition with NTFS when installing Windows NT 4.0, 2000, or XP, as part of the setup program. You can also format NTFS partitions from within Windows 2000 or XP using the Disk Management tool. You can also right-click on a drive icon in My Computer and choose Format.

You can change a FAT partition over to NTFS by reformatting it, but it will lose all its data. To convert a partition from FAT to NTFS and preserve the data, you can choose that option during Windows Setup or use the CONVERT utility at a command prompt afterward.

### *NTFS Bootable Disks*

Creating a bootable NTFS partition is not quite as straightforward as creating a FAT partition. There is no stand-alone command interpreter like COMMAND.COM in NTFS, so not only must the key startup files (such as NTLDR and NTOSKRNL) exist on the disk, but a user interface program must also exist. This could be Windows itself, the Windows Setup program, or the Windows Recovery Console. Therefore, a bootable NTFS disk must contain Windows (NT/2000/XP) or the Windows Setup program. Chapter 27 discusses in detail the boot sequence in various Windows versions.

This does not mean you are locked out of an NTFS drive when Windows will not boot normally. You can boot from the Windows 2000 or XP CD-ROM, for example, and then use its setup program to repair an existing Windows installation or reinstall it completely. You will learn more about that in Chapter 27.

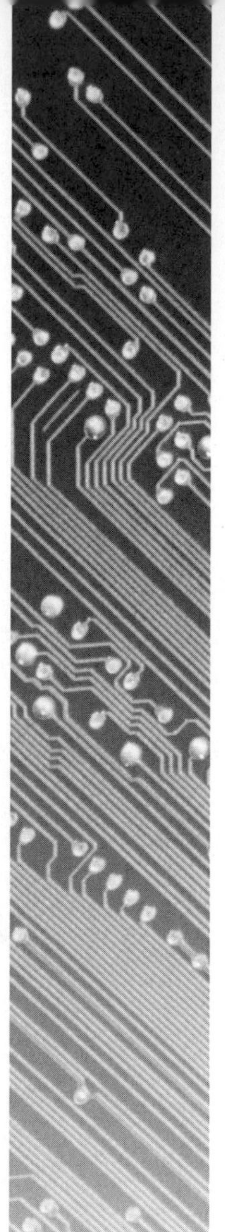

# STUDY GUIDE

Use the following summaries to review the key concepts of this chapter.

## ASCII Characters and Binary Storage

- Each letter, number, or symbol can be uniquely described by a binary number. The code set that defines which character maps to which number is called ASCII.
- The original ASCII standard used 7-bit codes, which resulted in 128 possible characters. IBM introduced an 8-bit version in 1981 called Extended ASCII.

## How Disks Store Data

- Data is stored on a disk as binary code.
- This storage is based not on the actual 1s and 0s being written to the disk, but on transitions.
- A disk surface can have two possible states. A 1 exists wherever there is a transition from one of the states to another. A 0 exists when there is no transition.
- With magnetic storage (floppy disks, hard disks), the transition is between positive and negative magnetic polarity.
- With optical storage (CD, DVD), the transition is between areas of great reflectivity and areas of lesser reflectivity.
- Each drive has a timing signal that dictates the time that should elapse between two transitions in a row (that is, two consecutive 1s). If no transition occurs within that time, the drive interprets that as a 0.
- Encoding schemes are used to cut down on the number of timing signals required, increasing disk efficiency. The most popular encoding scheme is run-length limited (RLL).

## Magnetic Storage

- Hard and floppy disks use magnetic storage.
- The disk is either Mylar (floppy) or metal (hard disk). It is coated with a thin layer of iron oxide particles.
- The read/write head has a wire coil around it through which electricity passes, generating a magnetic field.
- When the electrical flow reverses, the magnetic polarity changes between positive and negative.

- When the magnetism of the particles on the disk change, it is known as a flux transition. When the read/write head reads a flux transition it sends an electrical pulse to the drive controller, which interprets it as a 1.

## Optical Storage

- An optical disk has areas of great reflectivity called land and areas of less reflectivity called pits.
- The drive's read head shines a laser onto the disk and measures the light bouncing back. From this measurement it can distinguish between land and pit.
- Whenever there is a transition between land and pit, the read head sends an electrical pulse to the drive controller, which interprets it as a 1.

## How Disk Space Is Organized

- Almost all magnetic disks are double-sided, and each side has its own read/write head.
- Most hard disks have multiple disk platters, with a separate head on each side of each platter. The number of heads in a drive is one of the ways of describing it.
- An average number of heads for a hard disk today is 16.
- Each disk side is organized into concentric rings called tracks. The same track on a whole stack of platters/sides is called a cylinder. The number of cylinders in a drive is another way of describing it.
- Each track is divided into segments, each of which holds 512 bytes. The number of segments per track is yet another way of describing a disk.
- The CHS of a disk is the cylinders, heads, and sectors. You can calculate a disk's capacity by multiplying these three numbers together. Another name for CHS is geometry.

## Low-Level Formatting

- Low-level formatting determines the drive's CHS specifications by creating the tracks and sectors.
- Zoned recording is a means of creating more sectors per track on the outside of a disk than on the inside.
- The IDE interface requires that each track have the same number of sectors, so drives that use zoned recording provide sector translation between the physical drive and the IDE controller.

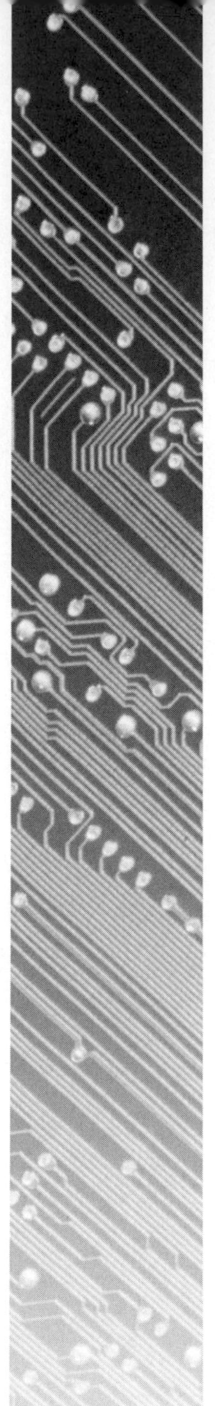

## BIOS Drive Support

- Most BIOS Setup programs automatically detect the correct settings for various drive types and set them up for you.
- One exception is floppy drives; you must configure them manually in BIOS.
- CD-ROM drives are usually detected either as CD-ROM or as ATAPI.
- ATAPI refers to any IDE device other than a hard disk. It includes CD-ROMs, tape backup drives, and IDE-based high-capacity floppy drives.
- Older BIOS Setup programs might include Detect IDE utilities that you must run to detect the IDE drives; newer BIOS Setup programs detect the drives automatically without your even having to enter the setup program.
- Most BIOS Setup programs offer 39 numbered hard disk types preconfigured; all of these types are long obsolete.
- They also offer User or Manual choice for you to enter the drive CHS and other settings manually.
- Auto is the best choice for a hard disk whenever possible.
- Most BIOS Setup programs support translation modes that allow larger hard disks to be used in a PC.

## BIOS Methods of Increasing Disk Capacity

- The original IDE specification had a 540MB limit on hard disk size, due to the limitations when combining the BIOS and the drive capabilities.
- The drive can have many more cylinders than the BIOS can recognize, and the BIOS can have many more heads than the drive can physically contain.
- To overcome this limitation, the ATA-2/Enhanced IDE standard allows the BIOS to translate the addresses coming in from the drive to different addresses it can convey to the software.
- The BIOS sees all of the cylinders on the drive, and reads from them, but it tells the software that there are fewer cylinders and more heads. It does this by maintaining a translation table.
- The original translation table type was enhanced CHS, also known as Large. It handles the translation with simple math.
- An updated version is Logical Block Addressing (LBA). It assigns a number to each sector and then references sectors by number rather than by CHS when dealing with the drive. It creates a virtual CHS for the software's benefit.
- Originally LBA was limited to 8.4GB because that is the largest virtual CHS table it can create for sending data to the software.

- A BIOS extension called Enhanced BIOS Services for Disk Drives, introduced in 1998, helps LBA support much larger drives, up to 18 trillion gigabytes. The ATA standard, however, limits drive size to 137 gigabytes.

## Transfer Mode

- The transfer mode determines how the BIOS interacts with the drive to transfer information from it. The most common type is Programmed Input/Output (PIO).
- There are five PIO modes (0 through 4), ranging from 3.3 to 16.67MB/sec. Nearly all drives can support PIO 4.
- An alternative to PIO is Direct Memory Addressing (DMA). DMA bypasses the CPU to help improve system performance. It is less commonly supported than PIO.
- Bus-mastering DMA uses the PCI bus for DMA transfers. There are three modes, 0 through 2, topping out at 16.67MB/sec.
- Both PIO and DMA are old technology; the newer one is UltraDMA (UDMA). It was introduced in 1998 and allows disk transfers at much higher speeds.
- UDMA speeds range from 33 to 100MB/sec.
- SMART monitoring watches for degradation in disk performance as a signal of impending drive failure.

## Disk Partitions

- A physical disk must have at least one partition (primary partition). The primary partition is then formatted as a single logical drive letter.
- A disk may also have an extended partition, which may be divided into one or more additional logical drives.
- A primary partition differs from an extended one in that it is bootable (and can be set to be active) and that it can contain only a single logical drive.
- With the FAT16 file system, logical drives must be no more than 2.1GB.
- The FDISK program in MS-DOS and Windows 9x manages disk partitions.
- In Windows 2000/XP the Windows Setup program sets up partitions, as does the Disk Management tool within Windows.
- Information about the physical drive's partitions is stored in a master boot record (MBR). It persists no matter what high-level formatting is done.

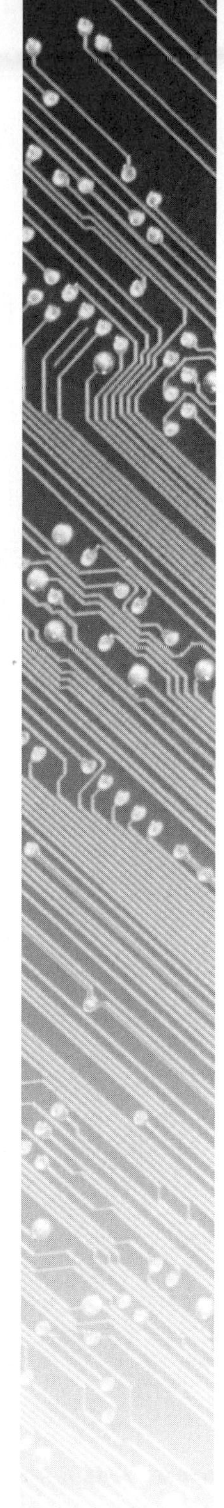

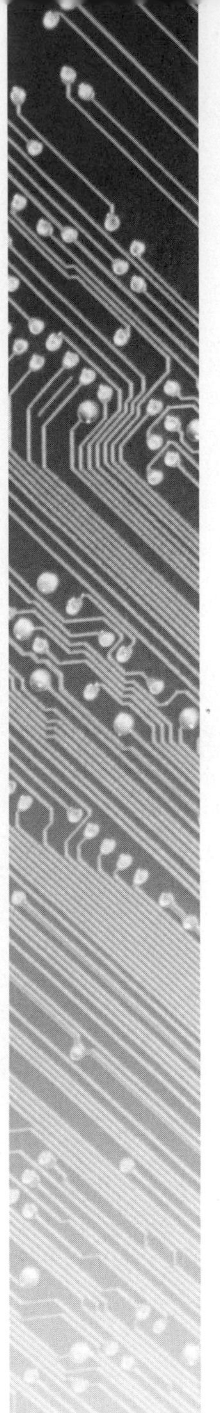

- A cluster is a group of sectors. Cluster sizes range from 4 to 64 sectors. The operating system addresses clusters, rather than individual sectors, to cut down on address overhead.
- Partitioning defines the cluster size for a logical drive. FDISK does this automatically based on the size of the drive and the file system.
- Large clusters mean a more efficiently operating file system, but also more wasted disk space.

## High-Level Formatting

- High-level formatting can use FAT16, FAT32, or NTFS.
- FAT16 works with all operating systems (MS-DOS or Windows). FAT32 works with Windows 95C and higher, but not with MS-DOS, Windows NT 4.0, or the original version of Windows 95.
- NTFS works only with Windows NT 4, Windows 2000, and Windows XP.
- All file systems have a volume boot record, which contains data about the drive's capacity, number of sectors, and volume label. If the drive is bootable, it also contains the first file needed for booting.
- All file systems contain a root directory, which is the top-level directory into which all others are placed.
- All file systems scan the disk during high-level formatting for any bad sectors identified during the low-level format and block them off to prevent their use.
- A FAT file system uses a File Allocation Table (FAT) for keeping track of the contents of the root directory; NTFS uses a Master File Table (MFT) for this purpose.
- FAT16 uses 16-bit binary numbers to uniquely identify each cluster. FAT32 uses a 32-bit numbering system.
- To be bootable, a FAT disk must contain IO.SYS, MSDOS.SYS, and COMMAND.COM.
- The NTFS file system is more sophisticated and feature-rich than either FAT system, but for compatibility reasons it cannot be used on every PC.
- You cannot create an NTFS boot disk, but you can boot from a Windows 2000 or XP Setup CD-ROM to access NTFS partitions if Windows will not start normally.

# PRACTICE TEST

On a blank sheet of paper, write the answers to the following multiple-choice questions and explain why each answer is correct.

1. ASCII characters are
   a. binary numbers 1 and 0.
   b. the numbers, letters, and symbols familiar to our written language.
   c. the numbers 0 through 9.
   d. symbols that you cannot type on a standard keyboard but that programs use to execute.

2. How many characters can there be in the 8-bit extended ASCII character set?
   a. 128
   b. 160
   c. 256
   d. 512

3. How are 1s represented in magnetic disk storage?
   a. positively charged metal particles
   b. negatively charged metal particles
   c. transitions between positive and negative particles
   d. nonreflective pits

4. On an optical disk, a land area is
   a. a reflective spot.
   b. a nonreflective spot.
   c. a transition between a reflective and a nonreflective spot.
   d. an area of neutral charge.

5. The number of disk heads on a drive is the same as the number of
   a. platters.
   b. sides.
   c. cylinders.
   d. tracks.

6. The number of tracks on a single side is the same as the number of
   a. cylinders.
   b. tracks.
   c. platters.
   d. sides.

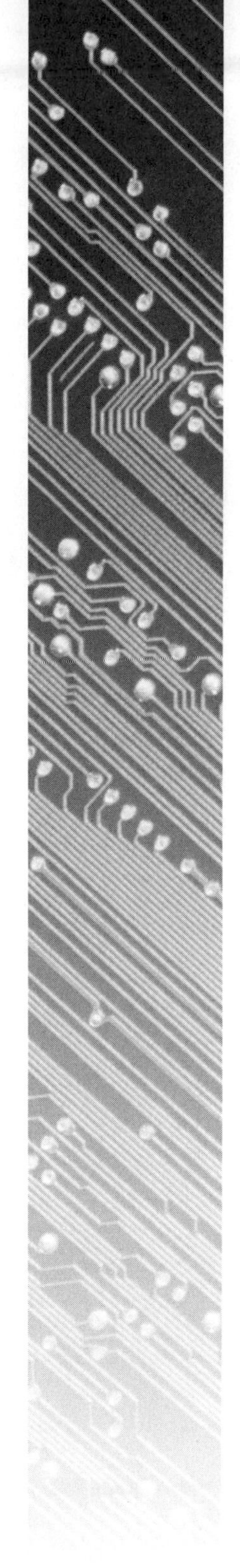

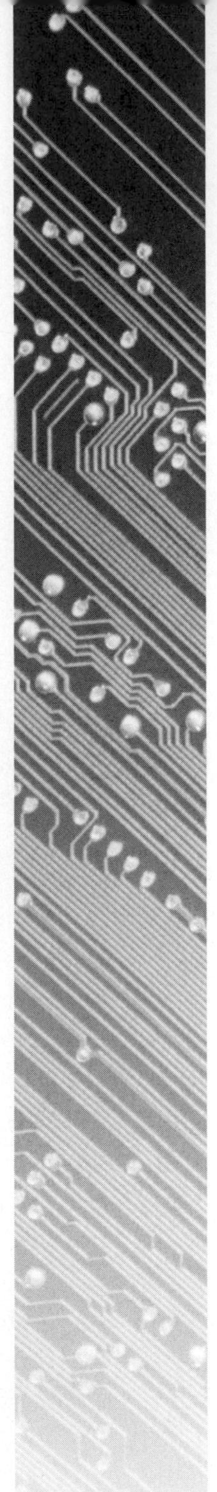

7. Each track is divided into multiple
   a. cylinders.
   b. heads.
   c. zones.
   d. sectors.
8. Low-level formatting
   a. creates the drive geometry.
   b. sets up Logical Block Addressing.
   c. defines the partitions.
   d. selects between FAT and NTFS file systems.
9. How many bytes are stored per sector?
   a. 16
   b. 128
   c. 512
   d. It depends on the cluster size.
10. An end user should low-level format a hard disk with the
    a. FDISK command.
    b. LLF command.
    c. FORMAT command.
    d. Not applicable; the end user does not do low-level formatting.
11. When using the FORMAT command on a floppy disk, which type of formatting is accomplished?
    a. low-level
    b. high-level
    c. both
    d. neither
12. What is zoned recording?
    a. Different amounts of data are stored per sector on inner versus outer tracks.
    b. Different numbers of sectors are created on inner versus outer tracks.
    c. Data is compressed for storage on inner tracks.
    d. Different cluster sizes are used on inner versus outer tracks.
13. Which of these drive types would not be considered ATAPI?
    a. tape backup drive
    b. CD-ROM
    c. hard drive
    d. They are all ATAPI drives.

14. What is the size limit for hard drive BIOS support under standard CHS addressing?
    a. 540MB
    b. 2.1GB
    c. 8.4GB
    d. 137GB

15. What is the purpose of LBA?
    a. to enable the BIOS to recognize larger hard drives than standard CHS allows
    b. to enable FAT16 partitions to overcome the 2.1GB size limit
    c. to enable FAT32 partitions to overcome the 8GB size limit
    d. None of the above

16. Which of these results in the fastest data transfer performance?
    a. PIO
    b. bus mastering DMA
    c. UltraDMA
    d. Depends on the mode being used

17. Which type of partition can have multiple logical drives on it?
    a. primary
    b. active
    c. secondary
    d. extended

18. The default cluster size for a 2GB hard disk under FAT16 is ____________ the default cluster size for the same drive under FAT32.
    a. larger than
    b. smaller than
    c. the same as
    d. Cannot determine from information provided

19. Which of these items is not created by high-level FAT formatting?
    a. File Allocation Table
    b. Master File Table
    c. root directory
    d. volume boot record

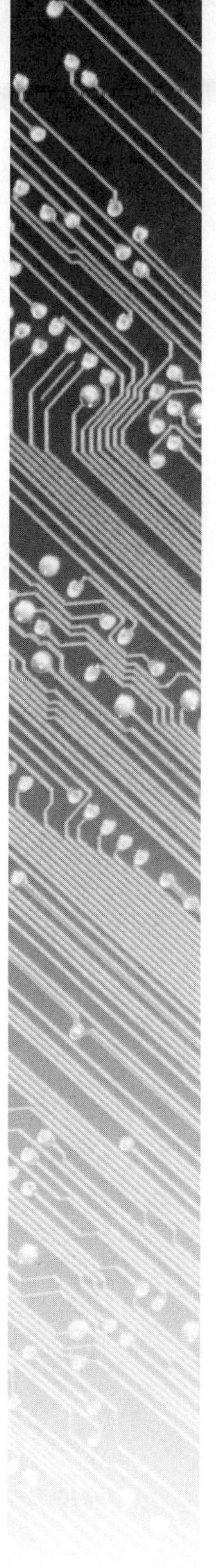

20. Which of these operating systems does not support NTFS?
    a. Windows 98
    b. Windows NT 4
    c. Windows 2000
    d. Windows XP

## TROUBLESHOOTING

1. A client has removed his old floppy drive and installed an LS-120 IDE floppy drive, but the new drive has been assigned the drive letter B. The A drive letter seems still to be assigned to the old floppy drive, which is physically nonexistent. How can you fix this?
2. A client has just bought a new 60GB hard drive, but her BIOS Setup program sees it as 540MB. What can you do to help?
3. You have successfully configured the BIOS in #2 to see the full 60GB, but when you try to partition the drive using FDISK it limits you to 2.1GB logical drives. What can you do to enable larger logical drives?

## CUSTOMER SERVICE

1. A client wants to know why you advise her to clean a CD with a soft cloth when the drive has problems reading it, but you tell her not to clean a floppy disk that way. What explanation can you give?
2. A client read an article on a Web site about how using a PIO mode 4 can increase a drive's performance. He goes into BIOS Setup and notices that PIO is set to Disabled for his primary hard drive. He wants to know whether you think he should enable it. What do you answer?
3. A client is having trouble with her PC, which she recently upgraded from Windows 98 to Windows XP. You advise her to try booting from a startup floppy that she created under Windows 98, but when she does so, her hard drive is inaccessible. What is going on, and how could you advise her to gain access to it?

## FOR MORE INFORMATION

For links to Web sites that provide further information about the topics covered in this chapter, go to the EMC/Paradigm Internet Resource Center at www.emcp.com/College Division/Internet Resource Centers/PC Maintenance/For More Information.

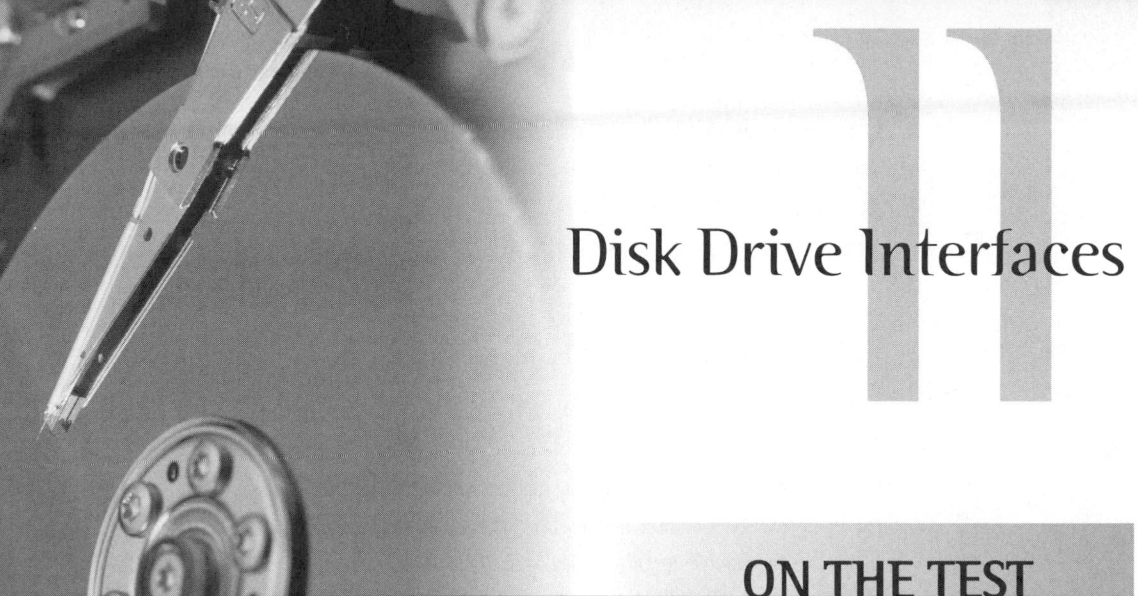

# 11 Disk Drive Interfaces

## ON THE TEST

**A+ Core Hardware Service Technician Examination**

- **Objective 1.2:** Identify basic procedures for adding and removing field replaceable modules for both desktop and portable systems.
- **Objective 1.5:** Identify proper procedures for installing and configuring IDE/EIDE devices.
- **Objective 1.6:** Identify proper procedures for installing and configuring SCSI devices.
- **Objective 1.8:** Identify hardware methods of upgrading system performance, procedures for replacing basic subsystem components, unique components and when to use them.
- **Objective 2.1:** Identify common symptoms and problems associated with each module and how to troubleshoot and isolate the problems.
- **Objective 4.3:** Identify the most popular type of motherboards, their components, and their architecture (bus structures and power supplies).

## ON THE JOB

The preceding chapter grounded you in the theory behind disk drives; in this chapter you will delve into the practical skills involved in installing and configuring those drives. In order to configure hard drives, you need to understand the principles behind the two most popular drive interfaces: IDE and SCSI. We will look at those, as well as how to install and troubleshoot a drive.

Skills related to this chapter's material include:

- selecting the best drive type to meet a specific storage need
- setting IDE drive jumpers
- selecting ribbon cables that will support a drive's full capabilities

- setting SCSI ID and termination
- installing a drive in a PC
- troubleshooting interface-related drive problems

## Drive Interface Overview

This chapter begins by looking at the various drive interfaces a PC can support and their relationships to the motherboard's BIOS. Figure 11.1 briefly describes each type.

- **Floppy:** The term "floppy disk" originally referred to the early removable disks that were made of extremely thin Mylar encased in a flexible plastic jacket. They would flop around a bit when handled, thus the name floppy disk. Today's floppy disks are not floppy at all; they are encased in hard plastic square sheaths. When most people talk about floppy drives, they mean any removable disk drive, including Zip and LS-120 (SuperDrive). From a drive interface perspective, some of those drives are actually IDE rather than floppy. A true floppy drive is a drive that connects to the motherboard's floppy disk drive (FDD) parallel interface via a 34-pin ribbon cable.
- **IDE:** IDE, for *Integrated Device Electronics,* is the most popular interface for hard drives, as well as a variety of other drive types such as CD, Zip, LS-120, tape backup, and DVD. An IDE drive connects to the IDE interface on a motherboard via a 40-pin parallel ribbon connector. You can also buy expansion boards that add more IDE interfaces. IDE is popular as a drive interface because the drives are fairly inexpensive (in comparison to SCSI) and because motherboards support up to 4 IDE drives with no add-on interface required.
- **SCSI:** SCSI, for *Small Computer Systems Interface,* is an alternative to IDE for connecting hard drives and other devices that require quick throughput. SCSI has some performance advantages over IDE, but has never caught on with mainstream PC users because of its higher cost. It has no direct relationship to the motherboard chipset; the SCSI controller card has its own BIOS. Almost all drive types available as IDE are also available in SCSI versions; SCSI is a parallel interface.
- **USB:** USB, for *Universal Serial Bus,* is a high-speed serial interface, used mostly for connecting external devices to a PC. Some external drives use the USB interface, but since drives are usually internal, USB is not a common interface for drives. The USB interface has a single USB point of connection with the motherboard chipset, and many different USB devices can share it at once.

**FIGURE 11.1**
Types of Drive Interfaces

**Integrated Device Electronics (IDE)**

A drive interface that has the drive controller built into the same unit as the disk drive itself.

**Small Computer Systems Interface (SCSI)**

A type of drive interface that allows chaining of several drives from a single interface.

**Universal Serial Bus (USB)**

A high-speed, Plug and Play, hot-pluggable type of serial port found in most modern PCs.

Figure 11.2 shows conceptually how the various drive interfaces connect to the motherboard chipset. Notice that IDE, floppy, and USB have integrated support on the motherboard, but SCSI requires an expansion card that goes through the PCI (or ISA) bus.

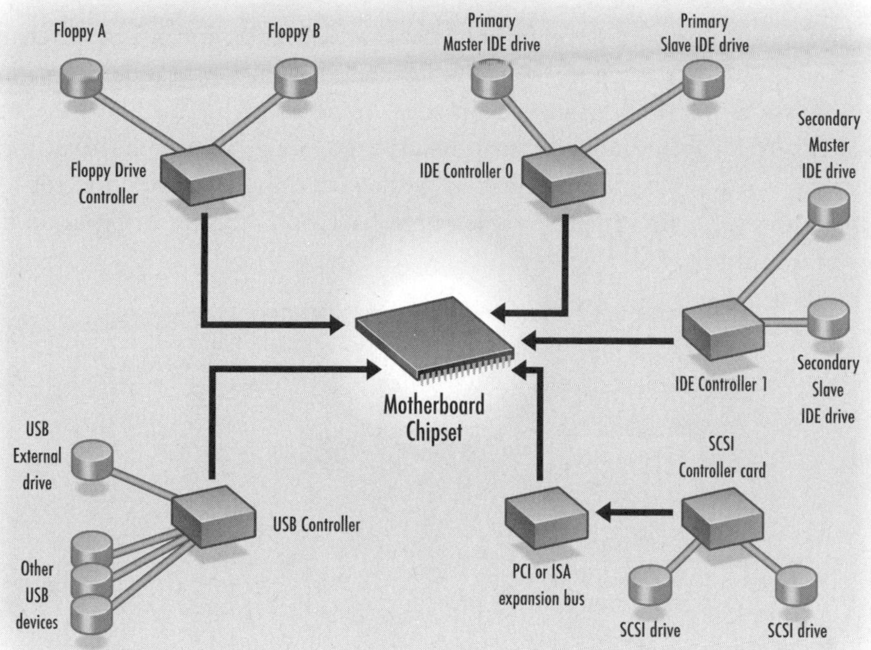


**FIGURE 11.2**
How Various Drive Interfaces Relate to the Motherboard Chipset

**TRY IT!**

Identify the drive interface types in use on your PC. How many of each type of drive do you have? Are the IDE devices connected directly to the motherboard, or through an expansion board?

## Floppy Interface

The floppy disk interface is a 34-pin connector and ribbon cable. The end that plugs into the motherboard is a standard pin connector, shown in Figure 11.3.

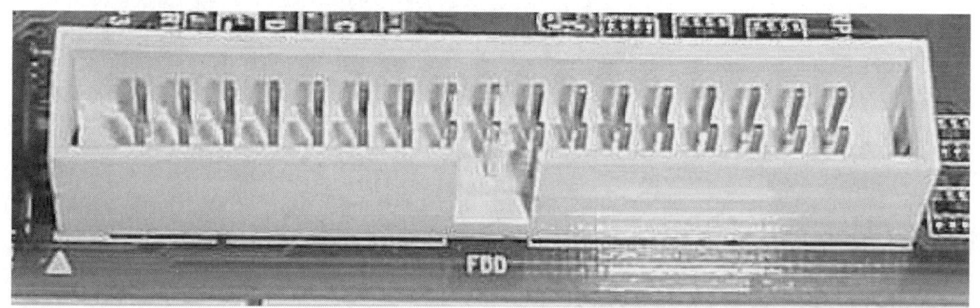


**FIGURE 11.3**
The Floppy Drive Interface on the Motherboard

The connectors on a floppy ribbon cable are different for 3.5-inch versus 5.25-inch drives (see Figure 11.4). A 3.5-inch drive uses a standard pin connector; a 5.25-inch drive uses an edge connector, which is like a sheath that fits over a metal-tabbed circuit board edge. Since 5.25-inch drives are nearly obsolete, most technicians will work with only the pin connector type. However, a floppy drive cable might have both connector types on it for maximum flexibility.

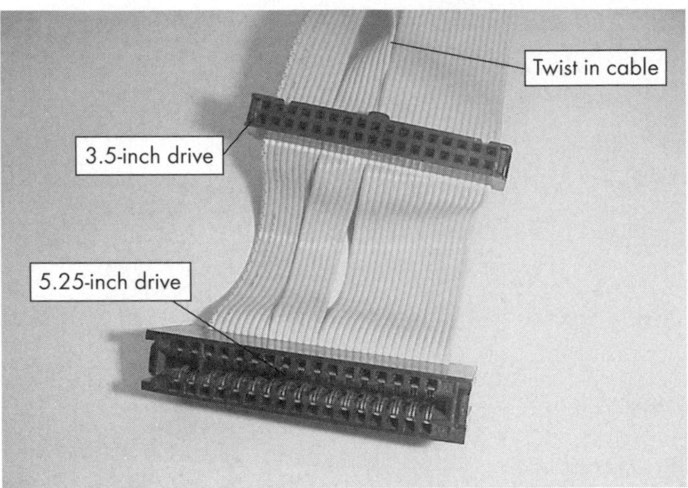


**FIGURE 11.4**
Floppy Drive Connectors for 3.5-Inch Drives (top) and 5.25-Inch Drives (bottom)

A floppy drive ribbon cable can be distinguished from an IDE ribbon cable not only by the number of holes in the connectors (34 versus 40), but also by the twist in a few strands of the wire. This twist occurs between the drive connectors. The drive plugged into the far end of the cable (after the twist) will be drive A; the drive plugged into the center of the cable (before the twist) will be drive B. Notice the twist in the cable in Figure 11.4.

A 3.5-inch floppy drive uses a *Mini* power supply connector, whereas a 5.25-inch floppy drive uses a full-size *Molex* connector. You learned about these in Chapter 3; Figure 11.5 shows them as a reminder.

**Mini**

A type of power supply connector used to provide power to 3.5-inch floppy drives.

**Molex**

A connector from the power supply to a hard drive, CD, or 5.25-inch floppy drive.

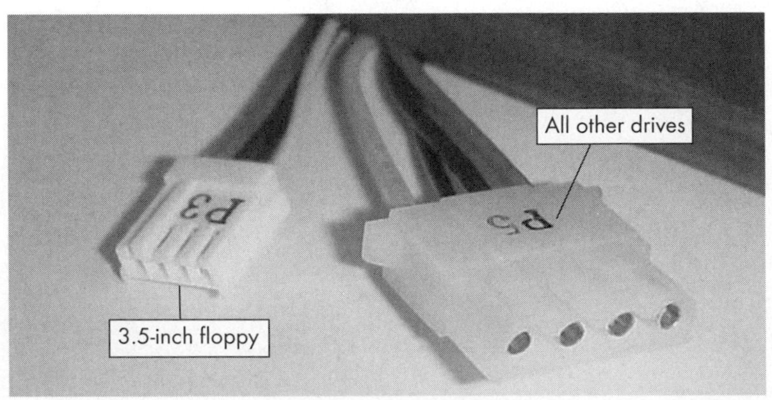


**FIGURE 11.5**
A 3.5-inch floppy drive uses a Mini power connector (left); a 5.25-inch floppy drive uses a Molex connector (right).

## TRY IT!

**Locate the floppy drive cable on your PC, and trace it from the drive to the motherboard.**

The two connectors shown in Figure 11.4 are a mutually exclusive pair; you can use one or the other of them but not both. You can tell because the twist in the cable occurs before the pin-type connector. Any connector that comes after the twist is automatically the A drive connector, and since there can be only one A drive, those two connectors can be assumed to be mutually exclusive. On such a cable there will be four connectors, rather than the usual three. There is another connector in the center of the cable for the secondary (B) floppy drive. Figure 11.6 shows the full cable, with all four connectors: one for the motherboard, one for the B drive (middle), and two for the A drive, only one of which can be used.

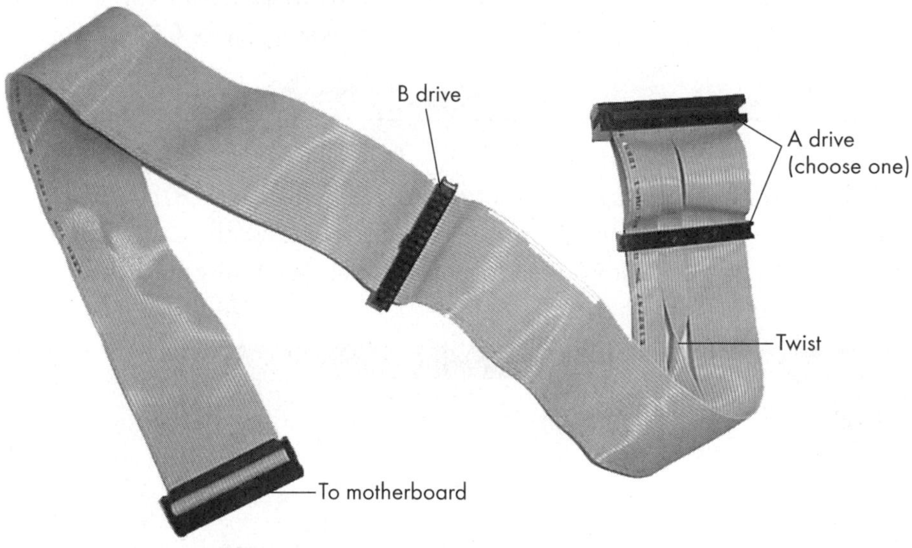


FIGURE 11.6
On this floppy cable with four connectors, the two at the right are a mutually exclusive pair.

# IDE Interface

IDE is a generic term that refers to a disk drive with a built-in controller. The full name, Integrated Device Electronics, reflects the fact that the controller for the drive is built into the drive unit itself rather than on a separate board. In the earliest days of hard disk technology, the hard disk and its controller were two separate pieces. With an IDE drive, however, the drive controller is part of the package. You have probably noticed that a hard disk has a little circuit board strapped to the bottom; that is the integrated drive controller.

IDE was a real revolution in PC technology. It meant that drive makers did not have to make their drives compatible with a particular controller standard, so they could develop higher performance drive/controller combinations that spoke their own proprietary language between them.

There have been three different versions of the IDE interface over the years, as described in Figure 11.7.

- **XT IDE (8-bit ISA):** This was the original IDE standard for XT computers (8086 models). It used a 40-pin connector.
- **MCA IDE (16-bit Micro Channel):** This was a proprietary standard developed by IBM for its Micro Channel Architecture PC bus, a great idea that failed in the marketplace and quickly became obsolete. It used a 72-pin connector.
- **ATA IDE (16-bit ISA):** This standard, originally developed for the 80286 system, is still found in systems today. It uses a 40-pin connector, but not the same type as the XT IDE.

**FIGURE 11.7**
IDE Drive Interface Versions

Each of these used a different cabling, so you could not mix and match them on the same bus. Of the three, only ATA remains; the other two have been obsolete for at least 10 years. Figure 11.8 shows a 40-pin ATA IDE connector on a motherboard.

**FIGURE 11.8**
An ATA IDE Connector on a Motherboard

## ATA Versions

**Advanced Technology Attachment (ATA)**

A set of standards for IDE drives that govern their speed, performance, and interface.

*ATA* stands for *Advanced Technology Attachment,* a reference to the fact that it was originally developed for the IBM AT computer (of which the 286 was the first model).

An organization called the National Committee on Information Technology Standards (NCITS) sets the standards for ATA, so that all drive and PC manufacturers have a common set of rules from which to work. The original ATA standard has been updated several times over the years, adding new features and capabilities, but each version retains basic backward compatibility. Therefore, any IDE device that conforms to any version of the ATA standard should be able to operate with at least basic functionality on any system that supports any version of ATA. This makes ATA devices universally compatible with almost any PC.

### *ATA-1*

The original ATA, ATA-1, was developed in 1988 and introduced the 40-pin connector and ribbon cable, and the master/slave/cable select configuration options. It also provided specifications for signal timing for PIO and DMA modes, and CHS and LBA drive parameter translations.

ATA-1 introduced the Identify Drive command that the BIOS Setup program uses to autodetect the drive specifications. In earlier hard disks, you had to manually set up the drive type in the BIOS program, either by a numeric drive type or by entering the number of cylinders, heads, and sectors. On ATA drives, however, the drive can send this information to the BIOS Setup program upon request.

### *ATA-2*

ATA-2 came out in 1996, adding support for storage devices other than the hard disk on an ATA interface. It also allowed for faster PIO and DMA transfer modes, support for *PC Card* (PCMCIA) drives, and support for power management schemes that allowed the hard disk to spin down after a certain period of idleness to conserve power (especially battery power on a laptop). Finally, it defined LBA translation for drives of up to 8.4GB. Other names for ATA-2 included Fast-ATA, Fast ATA-2, and *Enhanced IDE* (EIDE).

**PC Card**

A standard for connecting peripherals to notebook computers via a credit card-sized plug-in interface. Also called PCMCIA.

**Enhanced IDE (EIDE)**

An improved version of the original ATA standard, also known as ATA-2.

## In Real Life

The term "EIDE" has come to be almost as generic as IDE. Technically it refers to any IDE device that conforms to ATA-2 standard or higher, which includes virtually every IDE drive available.

### *ATA-3*

**Self-Monitoring and Reporting Tool (SMART)**

A technology for monitoring drive performance and reporting any irregularities or changes that might signal impending failure.

A minor 1997 update, ATA-3 added support for *Self-Monitoring and Reporting Tool* (SMART) error detection technology, added a security mode for password protection, and eliminated the 8-bit DMA transfer protocols. ATA-3 drives are also referred to as EIDE.

### *ATA-4*

This 1998 revision introduced the original version of UltraDMA (UDMA), with transfer modes up to 33MB/sec. This is commonly referred to as UDMA/33 or UltraATA/33. UltraDMA/33 operates at twice the speed of the fastest PIO or DMA mode. (To take advantage of it, both the drive and the motherboard or I/O card must support UltraDMA/33 or higher.)

**Crosstalk**

Interference between adjacent wires or cables caused by electromagnetic interference (EMI).

ATA-4 also introduced support for an optional 80-wire, 40-pin ribbon cable that helped cut down on noise resistance *(crosstalk)*, and integrated the ATAPI standard (AT Attachment Packet Interface), which had formerly been a separate standard. This allowed CD-ROM drives, tape drives, and other removable storage devices to work under a common interface standard, making it easier for the BIOS Setup to autodetect ATAPI devices.

### *ATA-5*

This standard, introduced in 1999, offers UDMA/66, providing transfer modes up to 66MB/sec. The only catch (and it is a minor one) is that you need an 80-conductor cable to take advantage of the higher transfer rate. If you have only a standard IDE cable, the drive will operate at UDMA/33 speeds. The drive automatically detects the type of cable in use. Again, the drive and the motherboard or I/O card must be capable of UDMA/66 in order to get the top speeds.

### *ATA-6*

This standard, released in 2000, offers UDMA/100, with transfer rates of up to 100MB/sec. As with ATA-5, you must have an 80-conductor cable; otherwise the drive will revert back to UDMA/33 performance. Again, the motherboard or I/O card must be UDMA/100 capable; if it is not, the drive will revert to the top speed that it does support—UDMA/33 or UDMA/66.

## Slave/Master Jumpers

There can be either one or two IDE devices per interface. Most motherboards have two IDE connectors, so you can have a total of four

IDE devices directly connected to it. (You can also add an cxpansion card with more IDE connectors.)

Each IDE interface has one drive that is designated the *master*. It is the primary drive on that interface, and it takes control of all traffic on that cable. If there is a second drive on the same interface, it is designated as the *slave*.

**Master**

The main drive on an IDE interface cable, which takes control of all incoming instructions.

The main difference between the two is the amount of traffic to which it pays attention. The master listens for all traffic, decides what data should be passed along to the slave drive, and then passes it along. The slave drive listens only for data coming from the master drive.

**Slave**

A drive on an IDE interface cable, in addition to the master, which receives instructions from the master only, not directly from the interface.

Any IDE drive can function either as master or as slave, but you cannot have two slaves or two masters on the same cable; there must be one of each. A single IDE drive on an interface, with no second drive, is automatically the master.

A drive's master/slave status is controlled by a jumper. Depending on the drive, this jumper might be on the bottom of the drive (on the circuit board) or at the back of the drive next to the ribbon cable connector.

On most IDE drives the jumper positions are apparent. Letters next to the jumper pins designate a pair of pins for a certain setting, or a label on the drive shows diagrams of the positions. In Figure 11.9, the diagrams are rotated 90 degrees clockwise from the jumpers. Figure 11.10 describes the most common settings.

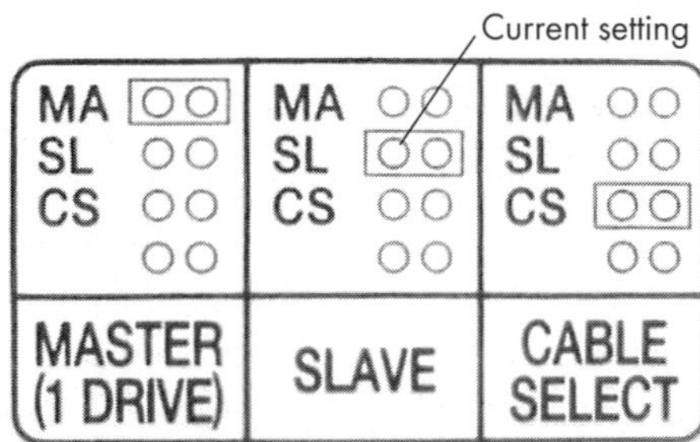

**FIGURE 11.9**
IDE jumper positions control master/slave status.

- **Master:** Use this setting when there are two drives on the interface and this one should be the master, or when the drive is alone on the interface. Often abbreviated MA or MS.
- **Single:** Not all drives have this setting, but if present it should be used instead of Master for a drive that is alone on the interface.
- **Slave:** Use this setting when there are two drives on the interface and this one should be the slave. Often abbreviated SL.
- **Cable Select:** Use this setting when you are using a special type of IDE ribbon cable that enables the drive's master/slave status to be determined by its position on the cable. Often abbreviated CS.

**FIGURE 11.10**
Common IDE Interface Jumper Settings

**Cable Select**

A means of determining an IDE drive's master/slave status by its position on the ribbon cable.

If using *Cable Select*, the master drive should be connected to the far end of the ribbon cable (farthest away from the motherboard interface) and the slave should be connected in the middle. Cable Select works only if the controller and both drives support it, if both drives are set to Cable Select, and if the right type of cable is used (a Cable Select-capable 80-wire cable).

**TRY IT!**

Check the jumper settings on all of the IDE devices in your PC.

## IDE Ribbon Cable Selection

As mentioned, UDMA/66 and UDMA/100 work only with an 80-wire ribbon cable. Such a cable has only 40 holes on the connectors, but it has extra wires between each of the "live" wires in the cable that reduce crosstalk interference between the wires. Figure 11.11 shows the difference between the two types. If you use a 40-wire cable on a drive that is capable of UDMA/66 or higher, the drive will be limited to UDMA/33 performance levels.

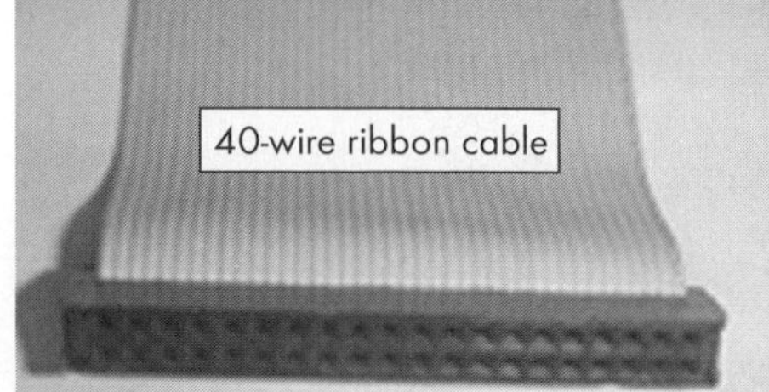


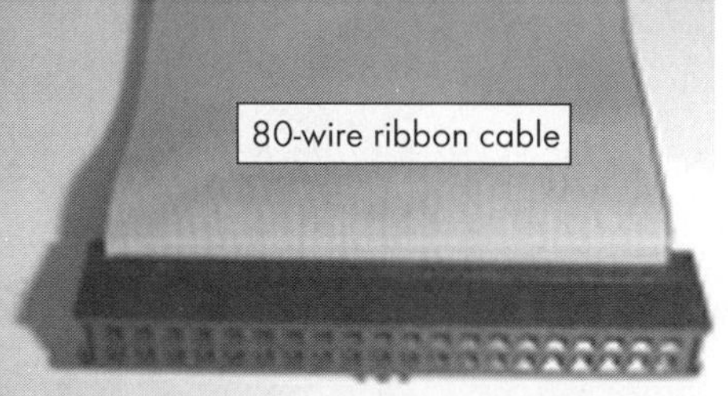


**FIGURE 11.11**
Examples of 40-Wire and 80-Wire Ribbon Cables

## TRY IT!

**Locate the IDE cables in your PC, and determine whether they are 40-wire or 80-wire models.**

### MIXING IDE DRIVE TYPES ON A SINGLE CABLE

When two IDE devices share a ribbon cable, UDMA performance level will be limited to the maximum that the two devices can agree upon. For example, if a UDMA/33 and a UDMA/100 hard drive are sharing a cable, both will operate at 33MB/sec.

If possible, a fast hard drive should be on its own ribbon cable, on a separate IDE interface from slower drives. If the system is "full" with four IDE devices, the choices are to (1) be satisfied with lesser performance from the high-speed drive, or (2) add an IDE expansion card with a high-performance IDE interface that can be devoted to the high-speed drive.

If sharing is unavoidable, make the faster drive the master, and if possible make a CD drive or other less frequently accessed drive its slave. This will enable as much high-speed performance as possible for the drive. A reduction in performance of a UDMA/66 or UDMA/100 drive is not as big a drawback as one might think, because on most systems a transfer rate of 33MB/sec is adequate to keep up with the rest of the components.

## SCSI Interface

Small Computer Systems Interface (SCSI) is the other important type of hard drive interface. SCSI used to be very popular in high-end systems such as file servers because of the problems and limitations of IDE. However, IDE has improved over the years to the point where it is almost as good as SCSI, so there is less reason to seek out SCSI equipment.

SCSI has always been less popular than IDE, for three reasons. One is that the drives themselves cost more, and price-sensitive consumers have been unwilling to spend the extra money for them. Second, most motherboards do not natively support SCSI, so you must add a SCSI controller card to your system in order to use a SCSI drive. Finally, SCSI device manufacturers have not done a very good job of educating the buying public about the advantages of SCSI over IDE.

Even many computer professionals are not sure why SCSI is better, although they have heard that it is. Here are some reasons:

- SCSI has a higher overall throughput rate than IDE in some cases.
- You can chain more drives onto a single interface (at least seven, as opposed to only two with IDE). Since each interface requires system resources (such as IRQs), using SCSI drives can be an advantage if you are worried about running out of IRQs.
- Multiple drives on the same bus share bandwidth more gracefully than with IDE. If two or more devices on the same SCSI chain need to be used at once, there is less likelihood of a bottleneck than with IDE.

Are these significant enough to warrant the extra cost? That is a question to answer on a case-by-case basis. Generally speaking, SCSI is most advantageous in situations in which many drives are operating simultaneously, such as on a file server with RAID or mirroring (covered in Chapter 12). Home users with a single hard drive will not see much extra benefit from SCSI.

## Types of SCSI

SCSI has been available for several years, and like ATA has gone through a number of changes. Here are the three main types of SCSI:

- **SCSI-1:** The original used an 8-bit expansion card, and its bus operated at 5MHz. It could support up to seven devices on a chain. The standard was very loose, and as a result, proprietary SCSI devices proliferated, each with its own proprietary expansion card. It is now obsolete.
- **SCSI-2:** Introduced in 1990 as a way to standardize SCSI so that devices could use common interfaces, SCSI-2 came in two speeds: standard (5MHz) and fast (10MHz). It also came in three bit widths: 8-bit (standard or narrow), 16-bit (wide), and the less common 32-bit (also called wide).
- **SCSI-3:** Fostering improved SCSI standards when operating at higher speeds, SCSI-3 comes in three speeds: 20MHz, 40MHz, and 80MHz, and two widths: 8-bit (narrow) and 16-bit (wide). Also called Ultra SCSI.

There are many descriptors in use for SCSI specifications, but they can all be grouped into one of the three types above. For example, if you see "Fast Wide SCSI," you can assume it is a 10MHz, 16-bit SCSI-2. If you see "Ultra-20 wide SCSI," you can assume it is a 20MHz, 16-bit SCSI-3.

One of the key advantages of SCSI is that it allows chaining together of multiple devices off a single expansion card. Most SCSI variants will work compatibly with other variants on the same chain, so if you have a SCSI-3 expansion card you can use it to run SCSI-2 and SCSI-1 devices as well. However, these older standard devices are limited, and will slow down the data access to any devices that follow them in the chain.

## SCSI ID

Up to seven SCSI devices can be chained together so they run off the same interface. (Seven is the limit for "normal" SCSI but, as you will see in Table 11.1, some different subtypes of SCSI have different maximum device limitations.) Internal SCSI devices usually run off one long ribbon cable with multiple connectors on it; external SCSI devices usually have both an "In" and an "Out" port, so you can run one cable into the device and another cable out of it.

Because all of the devices share an interface, there needs to be a way to keep the traffic for each device separate. In IDE this is the master/slave setup; in SCSI it is an ID number assigned to each device. When a message comes from the operating system to the expansion card, it is accompanied by an identifier that tells to which device number the message should be delivered. Each device listens only for its own ID number, and ignores everything else; therefore, it is important that you set each device to a unique ID number. Some devices are set with jumpers, whereas others have a thumbwheel or a counter that increments when you press a button on it.

On devices that use jumpers to set the ID, the jumper settings are not nearly as obvious as those on an IDE device. You might see three pairs of jumper pins, as you saw in Figure 11.9. In Figure 11.12, pin sets 1 and 4 are jumped, which adds up to a SCSI ID of 5. Some SCSI devices today conform to standards that support more than seven devices on a single chain; on such devices there will be an extra jumper (labeled 8) so more different IDs are possible.

The expansion card usually takes the SCSI ID 7 for itself, leaving IDs 0 through 6 for attached devices. (Some cards take 0, leaving 1 through 7 for device use.) If you are going to boot from a SCSI hard drive, you should set its IDE to 0 (or 1 if the adapter has taken 0 for itself) so that it is the first device on the chain. Other than that, the ID numbers can be used in any order. A Wide SCSI chain can include up to 15 devices.

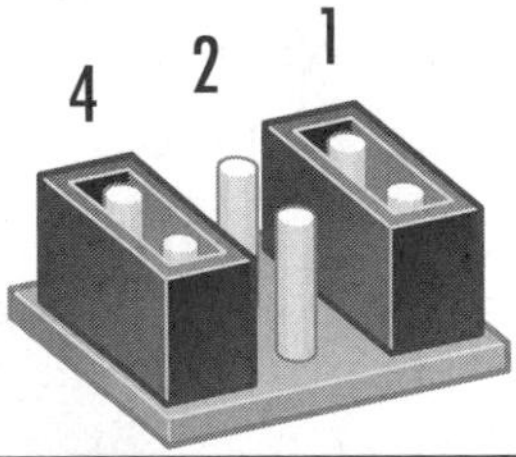

4 2 1

**FIGURE 11.12**
Jumper positions like this on a SCSI device would indicate a SCSI ID of 5 (4 + 1).

### TRY IT!

If you have SCSI devices in your PC, identify the SCSI ID setting for each of them.

## SCSI Termination

**Terminate**

To cap off a SCSI chain so the data signal stops traveling down the cable and bounces back a signal that it has reached the end.

Both ends of a SCSI chain must be *terminated*—that is, the chain must be capped or blocked, either with physical plugs or with jumpers, to indicate that there are no more devices. Usually the SCSI adapter is the beginning of the chain, so it is terminated (generally with a jumper). However, it is not necessarily the beginning; if both internal and external SCSI devices are connected to the same SCSI adapter, the ends of the chain will be the last external and last internal devices.

There are different kinds of termination. Figure 11.13 shows some of the ways to define the process.

**Passive termination**

Termination achieved with resistors.

**Active termination**

Termination achieved with voltage regulators.

- **Passive versus active:** *Passive termination* works with resistors driven by the small amount of electricity that travels through the SCSI bus. *Active termination* employs voltage regulators inside the terminator. Active termination is much better, and should be used whenever there are fast, wide, or Ultra SCSI devices on the chain and/or more than one or two SCSI devices on the chain. It may not be apparent from looking at a terminator whether it is passive or active.
- **Built-in versus separate:** Some devices have terminators built in that you can turn on and off with jumpers or switches. These are almost always passive terminators.
- **Internal versus external:** An internal terminator terminates an internal SCSI chain (inside the PC case); an external terminator terminates an external chain.
- **SE versus LVD versus HVD:** In the next section you will learn about three varieties of SCSI: Single-Ended (SE), Low-Voltage Differential (LVD), and High-Voltage Differential (HVD). Each requires its own type of terminator, although some terminators support both SE and LVD.

**FIGURE 11.13**
Methods of SCSI Termination

Figure 11.14 shows several types of terminator blocks. These fit onto connectors in a SCSI cable or onto a connector on the SCSI device itself. (Some SCSI devices have both in and out connectors so the SCSI signal can pass through them.)

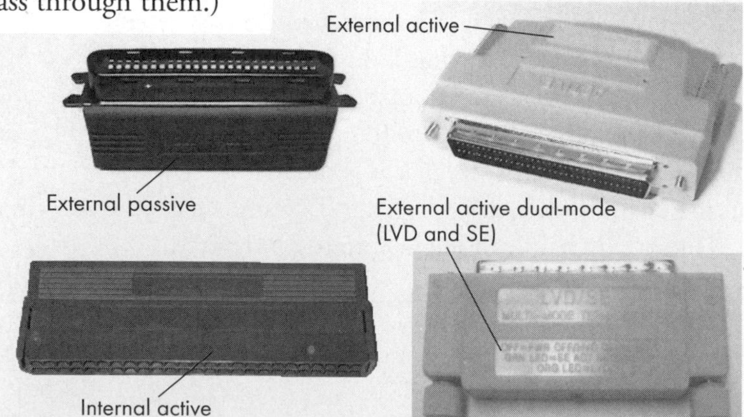


**FIGURE 11.14**
SCSI Terminators

## TRY IT!

Determine how the SCSI chain in your PC is terminated (if you have SCSI devices). Identify the termination method being used.

There are many other termination variants. Although you will not be called upon to know them for the A+ examination, you may be curious about them or interested in using them in your work as a PC technician. Figure 11.15 shows some of the most common. All of these are active terminators.

- **LVD/SE terminators:** These terminators sense when SE or LVD is being used and adjust themselves accordingly. They are very popular (more so than regular active terminators or any of the other types listed below) because they are fully backward compatible with all SE SCSI but allow for flexibility in future planning.
- **Feed-through terminators:** These are special-purpose terminators for use when for some reason you cannot terminate a chain at its end. They attach immediately before the last device in the chain, and provide termination that "passes through" to one last device.
- **Active negation terminators:** These are active terminators used with Ultra SCSI (SCSI-3) devices in SE mode.
- **Forced perfect terminators:** These are used with Fast SCSI in SE mode; they have the advantage of providing extra distance capability.
- **High-byte terminators:** These are not really terminators in the traditional sense. They are used when transitioning from the last wide device in the chain to a narrow device; they terminate the bits used only by the wide SCSI interface, allowing the remaining bits needed for narrow SCSI to continue on through.

**FIGURE 11.15**
Types of Active Terminators

## SCSI Interface and Connectors

A SCSI interface card adds the needed port(s) to the computer to support SCSI drives. Drives are not the only type of SCSI device; there are also SCSI scanners, CD drives, and so on. As noted previously, a single SCSI interface card can support up to seven different SCSI devices.

SCSI devices can be either internal or external. Internal devices are those that connect to the SCSI interface from inside the PC, including any drives, such as hard or CD. External devices are those that sit outside the PC and plug into it via an external cable. A scanner and an external backup tape drive are examples. Many SCSI interface cards have both internal and external connectors, so you can use both types of devices.

There are two types of internal SCSI connectors that you might find on SCSI interface cards. One is the SCSI A cable; it looks just like an IDE ribbon cable except that it has 50 wires instead of 40. It is used for 8-bit SCSI-1 and SCSI-2. The other is the SCSI P cable; it has 68 wires and a D-shaped connector (but there are the same number of pins in both rows, unlike a traditional D-sub connector). There is also an 80-pin variant called SCA.

The external connector type depends on the SCSI type. SCSI-1 always has a 50-pin Centronics external connector (as on a parallel printer), and SCSI-3 always has a 68- or 80-pin female D-sub connector. However, a SCSI-2 card could have a 25-, 50-, or 68-pin female D-sub, depending on the model.

There are still further variations of SCSI standards, as shown in Figure 11.16. You can tell what variation a device conforms to by the SCSI symbol on its label (see Figure 11.17).

- **Single-Ended (SE) SCSI:** This is standard SCSI. Assume a device is this type if it does not state otherwise.
- **Low-Voltage Differential (LVD) SCSI:** This SCSI variant produces greater speeds, and allows more devices and a greater maximum distance for a chain. To take advantage of LVD, all devices in the chain must support LVD and the chain must use LVD termination; otherwise all devices revert to normal (SE) performance.
- **High-Voltage Differential (HVD) SCSI (also called Differential SCSI):** This is a special type of SCSI incompatible with the other two types. It allows for greater maximum distances (up to 82 feet [25 meters]). HVD SCSI devices cannot be combined with other SCSI devices on a chain, and must use HVD termination.

**FIGURE 11.16**
SCSI Standard Variations

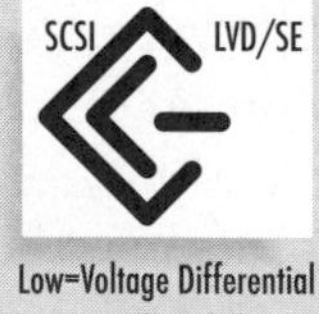


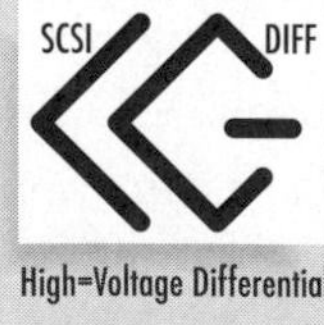


**FIGURE 11.17**
Symbols for SE, LVD, and HVD SCSI

## TRY IT!

Look for one of the symbols from Figure 11.17 on each of your SCSI devices. What types of devices do you have?

Part of the reason more people do not use SCSI is that the number of connector types, standards, and specifications can be bewildering. Table 11.1 summarizes the types of SCSI, the connectors they use, and their limitations on chain length and number of devices. Where there is a difference between SE and LVD, the table notes the LVD specification with an asterisk (*).

| SCSI Type | Bits | Number of Pins | Maximum Number of Devices (excluding adapter) | Maximum Distance | Speed |
|---|---|---|---|---|---|
| SCSI-1 | 8 | 25 | 7 | 20 feet/39 feet* (6 meters/12 meters*) | 5MB/sec |
| Fast SCSI | 8 | 50 | 7 | 10 feet/39 feet* (3 meters/12 meters*) | 10MB/sec |
| Fast Wide SCSI | 16 | 68 or 80 | 15 | 10 feet/39 feet* (3 meters/12 meters*) | 20MB/sec |
| Ultra SCSI | 8 | 50 | 3 / 7* | 10 feet/39 feet* (3 meters/12 meters*) | 20MB/sec |
| Ultra SCSI | 8 | 50 | 4 to 7 | 5 feet/39 feet* (1.5 meters/12 meters*) | 20MB/sec |
| Wide Ultra SCSI | 16 | 68 or 80 | 3 | 10 feet/39 feet* (3 meters/12 meters*) | 40MB/sec |
| Wide Ultra SCSI | 16 | 68 or 80 | 4 to 7 / 15* | 5 feet/39 feet* (1.5 meters/12 meters*) | 40MB/sec |
| Ultra2 SCSI* | 8 | 50 | 7 | 39 feet (12 meters) | 40MB/sec |
| Wide Ultra2 (Ultra 160) | 16 | 68 or 80 | 15 | 39 feet (12 meters) | 80MB/sec |
| Wide Ultra3 SCSI* | 16 | 68 or 80 | 15 | 39 feet (12 meters) | 160MB/sec |
| Ultra320 SCSI* | 16 | 68 or 80 | 15 | 39 feet (12 meters) | 320MB/sec |

**TABLE 11.1**
SCSI Interfaces and Connectors

## TRY IT!

Find each of your SCSI devices in Table 11.1.

### Using Different SCSI Types on the Same Chain

There are some complex rules for which SCSI types can share a chain with other types; these are the most important:

- SE and LVD can share with one another, but all devices will revert to SE standards in a mixed environment.
- HVD cannot share with anything else.
- Adapter plugs can be used to convert from one number of pins to another.
- Wide and narrow SCSI devices can share a chain, but you should try to position the wide devices closest to the adapter. In addition, after the last 16-bit (wide) SCSI device in the chain, you must apply a high-byte terminator to terminate the top 8 bits but allow the bottom 8 bits to continue on to the narrow SCSI devices further out.
- Fast and slow SCSI devices can share a chain, but you should try to position the fast devices closest to the adapter.
- The higher speed Ultra SCSI devices work best when on an LVD-only chain, although they will also work with SE devices.

## Installing a Drive

Installing a drive is fairly simple. The following sections outline the process.

### Setting Up the Drive

Before installing the drive, you must set it up. The setup depends on the drive type:

- Floppy: No setup required.
- IDE: Set master/slave jumpers.
- SCSI: Set SCSI ID jumpers and termination (if required).

To determine the correct setting for the drive, you will need to look at other drives already installed. For example, if there is already an IDE device on the same IDE interface cable that the new drive will use, check its master/slave status and set the new one to the opposite. If installing a SCSI drive, check the SCSI IDs of all other devices in the chain to make sure the new drive's ID is unique.

It is important to set up the drive first because once it is in a drive bay, it will be difficult to access the jumpers. If you find that you need to change the jumper positions you will probably have to remove the drive from the bay to do so.

## Mounting the Drive in the Bay

First, choose the bay. Hard drives are internal, so you do not need one of the externally accessible drive bays for it. Look for a bracket inside the area where the existing hard drive (if there is one) is mounted; there is probably room for another hard drive above or below it.

If there is an existing hard drive, notice how it is held in place in the case. It may be installed in a metal cage that can be removed from the rest of the case. You might need to remove the cage in order to attach the screws on the far side of the new drive. The cage is usually held in place by one or two screws.

All other drives are external. If installing an external drive, pop off the plastic faceplate in front of an available drive bay. (It is usually easiest to push it out from the back if you can reach your hand inside that far.) If there is a metal plate behind the plastic one, pop it out with a screwdriver.

Next, slide the drive into the bay. If you are working with a removable cage for a hard drive, attach the drive to the cage with screws and then replace the cage in the main case. If you are installing the drive in a bay that is part of the main case, simply set the drive loosely into the bay for the moment; you can attach it with screws after you have run the cables. It is easier to fit your hand into the tight spaces where the cables connect if the drive is not already secured with screws. You insert an internal drive from the inside of the case, and an external drive from the outside (see Figures 11.18 and 11.19).

**FIGURE 11.18**
Inserting an Internal Drive in a Bay

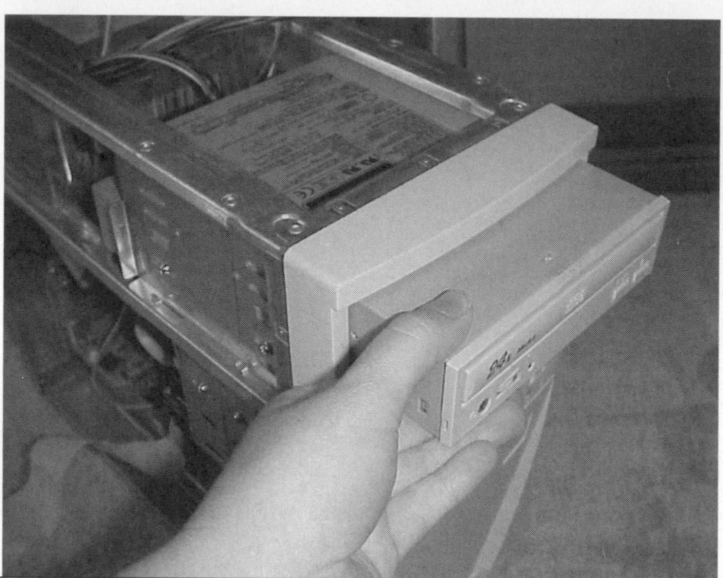

**FIGURE 11.19**
Inserting an External Drive in a Bay

Some cases do not use screws to hold drives in place; instead they use mounting rails that fasten to the sides of the drive and snap the drive into the case. Such cases typically come with sets of rails, but you can also buy the rails separately.

To place a small drive (such as a 3.5-inch floppy) in a large bay, you will need mounting brackets that fill in the extra space. You will also need a faceplate with a bezel around it that can cover the extra hole in the front of the bay.

**TRY IT!**

If you are not sure whether a drive is good, you might not want to install it in a drive bay right away. You can connect it to the motherboard and the power supply and then turn on the PC to try it out with the drive sitting anywhere that is convenient. Then, after you confirm that the drive works, you can turn off the PC and install it properly.

## Installing the SCSI Adapter (SCSI Only)

If you are installing a SCSI drive and you do not already have a SCSI adapter installed, insert one in an ISA or PCI expansion slot in the motherboard. This is the same as installing any other expansion board; look at the instructions in Chapter 8 for installing a video card for details.

### Connecting the Drive to the Motherboard or Expansion Card

If this will be the first device on the cable, you must connect the cable to the motherboard or expansion card. Select an appropriate ribbon cable for the drive type: a 34-pin floppy cable for floppy, a 40-pin IDE cable for IDE, or a 50-, 68-, or 80-pin cable for SCSI. If using SCSI, install any converter plugs that might be necessary for going from one number of pins to another.

**In Real Life**

**Recall from Chapter 7 that some IDE cables and connectors are keyed, with Pin 20 blocked out. If the hole for Pin 20 is blocked out on the IDE cable you have, make sure that Pin 20 is missing on the motherboard. If it is not, use an unkeyed cable.**

Find the end of the cable that is farthest from the other connectors on the cable. This is the end that connects to the motherboard or expansion card. Plug it in so the red stripe on the cable points to Pin 1 (see Figure 11.20). If both IDE connectors are available on the motherboard, use the one with the lowest number. Sometimes they are numbered 0 and 1, sometimes 1 and 2. The numbers are usually stamped on the motherboard next to the connectors, and/or printed in the motherboard manual.

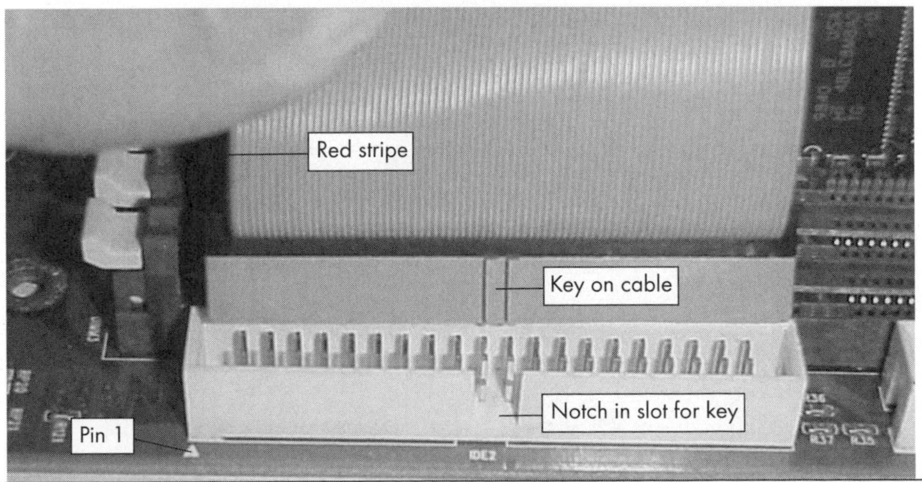


**FIGURE 11.20**
Connect the ribbon cable to the motherboard or expansion card.

Then connect one of the other connectors on the cable to the drive (see Figure 11.21). Choose the connector according to the following rules:

- If using a SCSI cable, choose any connector that lies between the SCSI expansion board and the terminator block (if there is one).
- If using an IDE cable, use the connector at the far end of the cable first. In reality you can use either connector unless you are defining master/slave position via Cable Select, but it is a good habit to acquire.
- If using a floppy cable, connect the drive that is to be the primary floppy (A) to the far end. Use the middle connector for a second floppy drive (B).

**FIGURE 11.21**
Connect the ribbon cable to the drive.

Again, the red stripe on the cable must align with Pin 1 on the drive. Most drives have a label that identifies Pin 1, but in almost all cases it is the end that is closest to the power supply connector (see Figure 11.22).

**FIGURE 11.22**
Pin 1 is usually the end closest to the power connector.

### In Real Life

Sometimes IDE cable length can be insufficient for every connector to reach between a drive and the motherboard, and you might have to use whatever connector will reach. You might even need to change the drive bay in which drives are installed to make the cables reach.

### Connecting the Power Cable

Next, connect any available power plug from the power supply to the drive. As was shown in Figure 11.5, there are two types of plugs; choose the one that fits the drive you are installing. If you cannot fit your hand far enough into the space to get the drive connected, loosen the screws holding the drive in place and slide it forward slightly.

**TRY IT!**

Remove all of the drives from your PC and reinstall them.

### BIOS Configuration

Depending on the drive and the BIOS, the BIOS may detect the drive automatically when you start up the PC or it may require you to enter BIOS Setup and change a setting or two. You learned about configuring drives in BIOS in Chapter 10, so return to that chapter if you need a review of that material.

At this point the drive is ready to use, at least from an interface perspective. If it is a removable disk drive, Windows (98 and higher) should recognize the drive automatically. MS-DOS will require a driver to be loaded for a CD-ROM drive. (A floppy disk containing MS-DOS drivers and a setup utility for them should have come with the CD-ROM drive.)

If it is a hard disk, the operating system will not immediately recognize the drive; you must partition and format it first. Chapter 10 discussed the concepts of partitioning and formatting; you will learn the procedures in Chapter 12.

## Troubleshooting Drive Interface Problems

Interface problems usually cause the drive not to appear correctly in BIOS Setup or the drive to physically malfunction (no light, light on all of the time, data not transferring correctly, and so on). If the drive appears physically healthy and shows up correctly in BIOS Setup, see the troubleshooting sections in Chapters 12 and 13. Otherwise, check the following troubleshooting aids.

### DEAD DRIVE

If the drive does not spin and its light does not come on at all, it is either not receiving power from the power supply or is not configured in BIOS Setup. Check the following:

- Make sure power and ribbon cables are snug.
- Make sure drive is enabled in BIOS Setup.
- Try a different power supply connector.
- Try a different ribbon cable.
- Try a different drive.

If none of the above works, the problem is likely the drive interface in the motherboard itself. Try installing an expansion board that includes a drive controller for that drive type and then disabling the motherboard's built-in controller in BIOS Setup.

**IN REAL LIFE**

**You can tell whether a hard drive is spinning by resting your palm flat against the top of the drive. You can feel vibrations if the drive is spinning.**

### BIOS DOES NOT SEE DRIVE (IDE)

The BIOS Setup should automatically detect and list IDE devices. If the BIOS Setup does not see a particular drive, it may be due to one of the following problems:

- Power supply connector is not snug.
- Ribbon cable connectors are not snug.
- Jumper setting is incorrect.
- Drive is physically defective.
- It has an old BIOS version, unable to detect the new type of drive.

To narrow down the problem, try a different drive of the same type using the same cables.

### Floppy Light Remains On

This is almost always the result of the ribbon cable's being plugged in backward either on the drive or on the motherboard. It could also result from the cable's being offset on the connector by one or two pins, or from a defective cable.

### Old Contents in Floppy File Listing

This error manifests itself as "phantom" disk content. You swap one floppy for another in the drive, but Windows or DOS still shows the content of the previous disk.

This is usually a cable problem. Pin 34 on a floppy ribbon cable is the disk change line; if that wire is broken, the operating system will not receive the message that the disk has changed. It could also be a defective drive, however, or the wrong drive type chosen in BIOS Setup.

## STUDY GUIDE

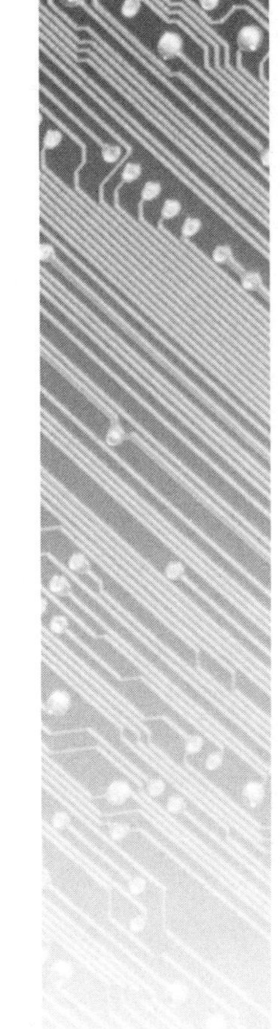

Use the following summaries to review the key concepts of this chapter.

### Drive Interface Overview

- The floppy drive interface in a PC is for standard floppy drives only, not for special high-capacity removable disk drives such as LS-120 or Zip drives.
- The floppy drive uses a 34-pin ribbon cable. A typical motherboard can support up to two floppy drives on a single ribbon cable.
- IDE (for Integrated Device Electronics) is the most popular interface for hard drives, as well as a variety of others such as CD and tape backup.
- IDE uses a 40-pin ribbon cable. A typical motherboard can support up to 4 IDE devices, two per ribbon cable.
- SCSI (for Small Computer Systems Interface) is an alternative to IDE for connecting hard drives and other devices that require quick throughput.
- SCSI uses a variety of interfaces depending on the subtype, ranging from 25 to 80 pins.
- USB (for Universal Serial Bus) is a high-speed serial interface for external devices, and is sometimes used for external hard drives.

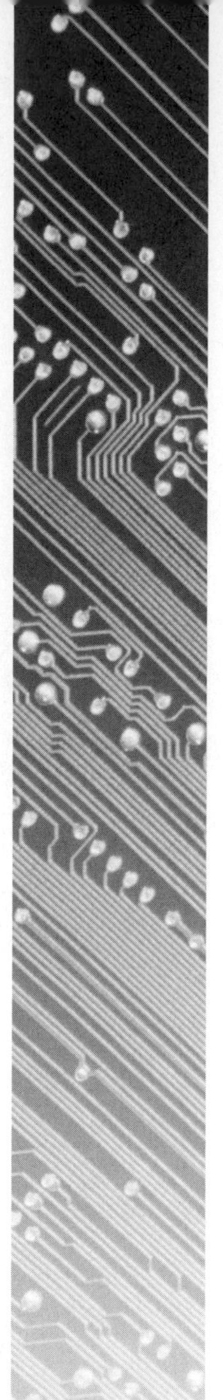

## Floppy Interface

- The connectors on a floppy ribbon cable are different for 3.5-inch versus 5.25-inch drives.
- If a floppy cable has four connectors, the different one and the one nearest to it are a mutually exclusive pair, for connecting either a 3.5-inch or 5.25-inch drive.
- A floppy cable has a twist in several of the wires at one end.
- The drive plugged into the connector after the twist is the A drive. The drive plugged into the middle is B.
- The connector farthest away from the end with the drive connectors connects to the motherboard.

## IDE Interface

- IDE generically refers to any drive with a built-in controller. However, in practical use today, IDE is synonymous with the AT Attachment (ATA) standard.
- There have been six versions of ATA since its original introduction in 1988.
- ATA-2 is also called Enhanced IDE or EIDE. It introduced LBA translation for drives of up to 8.4GB.
- ATA-3 introduced SMART error detection technology.
- ATA-4 introduced UltraDMA (UDMA), with transfer modes of up to 33MB/sec.
- ATA-5 increased UDMA speed to 66MB/sec with an 80-conductor cable.
- ATA-6 increased UDMA speed to 100MB/sec (again with an 80-conductor cable).
- You should avoid mixing drives with different UDMA speeds on the same cable because performance will be limited to the slower of the two.
- Drives that support ATA-5 or ATA-6 will be limited to ATA-4 performance with a 40-wire cable.
- Each IDE device must be set to be either master or slave. The drives use jumpers for this setting.
- Some drives have a separate jumper setting for Single; others use the same setting for both Master and Single.
- The Cable Select setting enables the drives to determine their own master/slave status based on their position on the ribbon cable. The drive at the far end is the master; the drive in the center is the slave. This requires a special cable.

## SCSI Interface

- SCSI is a higher end drive interface with some performance improvements over IDE. It requires a controller card, and the drives are more expensive.
- Many SCSI devices can be chained off a single interface (at least seven, as opposed to two with IDE).
- Multiple SCSI drives can share the same bus more effectively than IDE devices can, making SCSI a good choice for situations where multiple drives are used simultaneously.
- There have been many SCSI standards and variants over the years.
- SCSI-1 was the original. The standard was very loose, resulting in many proprietary models incompatible with one another.
- SCSI-2 was the first standardized SCSI interface. It came in two speeds: Standard (5MHz) and Fast (10MHz). It also came in three widths: 8-bit (narrow), 16-bit (wide), and 32-bit (also called wide, but less common).
- SCSI-3 is also called Ultra SCSI. There are three speeds: 20MHz, 40MHz, and 80MHz, and two widths: 8-bit (narrow) and 16-bit (wide).
- Each SCSI device must have a unique ID in the chain. The ID is set with jumpers or with a thumbwheel or pushbutton counter.
- The last device in the chain must be terminated. Termination can be passive or active; active is better.
- Termination can be built into the device and controlled with a jumper or switch, or can be a separate block plugged into a connector.
- A high-byte terminator is used after the last wide device on a SCSI chain when there are still narrow devices after it. It terminates the bits that do not need to be passed further along the chain, letting the remaining bits pass through.
- There are three varieties of SCSI standard: Single-Ended (SE), Low-Voltage Differential (LVD), and High-Voltage Differential (HVD). The last is also called Differential SCSI.
- SE and LVD can be mixed on the same chain (although performance will be limited to SE level); HVD must stand alone.

## Installing a Drive

- Before installing the drive, set its jumpers as needed. IDE and SCSI drives have jumpers; floppy drives do not.
- Mount the drive in the bay, but do not tighten its screws until you have connected all the cables, so you can reach the connectors more easily.

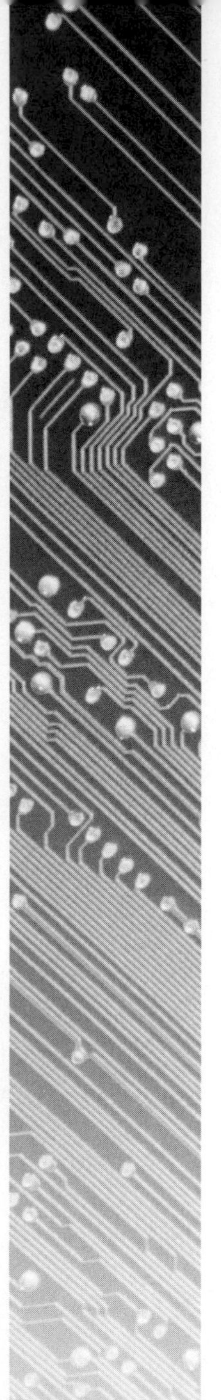

- Connect the drive to the motherboard or expansion card with a ribbon cable. Make sure Pin 1 on the connector aligns with the red stripe on the cable.
- Connect the power supply to the drive. Floppy drives (3.5-inch type) use the small connector; all other drive types use the large Molex type.
- Configure the drive in BIOS Setup if needed. Many BIOSes will detect new drives automatically.

### Troubleshooting Drive Interface Problems

- If the drive does not spin and its light does not come on, it is either not receiving power from the power supply or not configured in BIOS Setup.
- The BIOS Setup should automatically detect and list IDE devices. If it does not, check all connectors and check jumper settings.
- A BIOS update can help an old BIOS recognize a new drive type.
- If the floppy drive light stays on, the cable is reversed.
- Phantom disk content on a floppy disk after changing the disk can indicate a faulty cable.

## PRACTICE TEST

On a blank sheet of paper, write the answers to the following multiple-choice questions and explain why each answer is correct.

1. Which of the following is a parallel interface?
   a. floppy
   b. IDE
   c. SCSI
   d. All of the above

2. Given its advantages over other interfaces, why is USB not the dominant interface for drives?
   a. It lacks the speed of the IDE interface because it is a serial connection.
   b. USB is for external devices, and most disk drives are internal.
   c. Most motherboards do not have built-in USB support, so you need an adapter.
   d. All of the above

3. Which type of floppy drive uses a Mini power connector rather than a Molex?
   a. 3.5-inch
   b. 5.25-inch
   c. both 3.5-inch and 5.25-inch
   d. neither 3.5-inch nor 5.25-inch
4. Which drive letter is represented by the floppy drive connector in the middle of the floppy ribbon cable?
   a. A
   b. B
   c. depends on jumper setting
   d. depends on whether Cable Select is used
5. If you have a hard disk labeled EIDE, you can assume that it conforms to which ATA standard or higher?
   a. ATA-1
   b. ATA-2
   c. ATA-4
   d. ATA-6
6. On a system with two IDE ribbon cables, each with one drive connected to it, what should be the jumper setting for the drive on the secondary IDE channel's cable?
   a. Single if available, otherwise Master
   b. Master (not Single)
   c. Slave
   d. does not matter
7. If using Cable Select to determine IDE drive master/slave status, where should a single drive be connected?
   a. middle connector
   b. connector farthest from motherboard
   c. does not matter as long as CS jumper is set
   d. does not matter as long as SL jumper is set
8. How many wires (conductors) are there in an IDE cable designed to be used with a UDMA/100 drive?
   a. 34
   b. 40
   c. 68
   d. 80

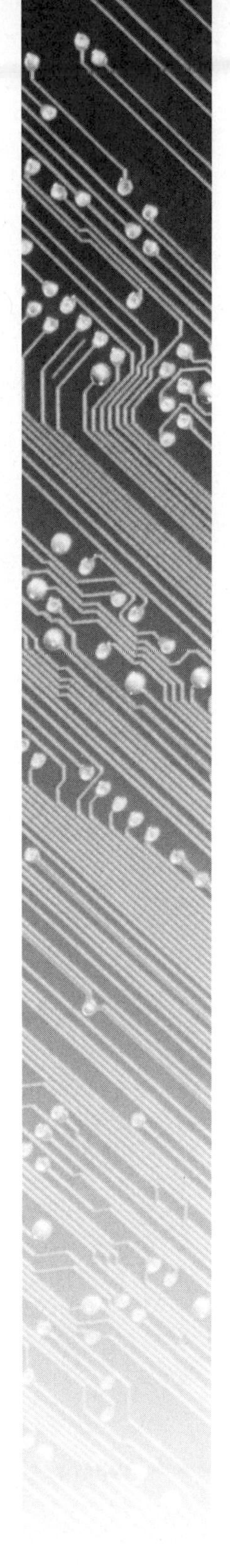

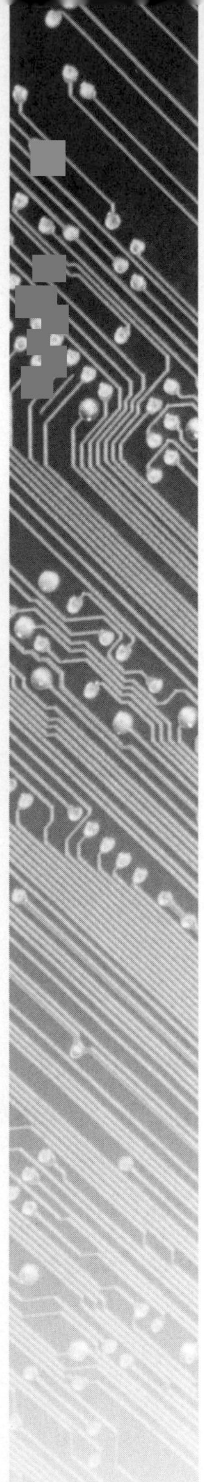

9. What is the purpose of the extra 40 wires on an 80-wire IDE cable?
   a. carry additional data for increased overall transfer volume
   b. reduce crosstalk between wires
   c. split off to handle additional drives
   d. All of the above

10. Which of these is an advantage of SCSI over IDE?
    a. better sharing between devices on same interface
    b. built-in support on most motherboards
    c. less expensive
    d. drives formattable into larger partitions

11. Which of these drive types would be considered SCSI-3?
    a. Ultra SCSI
    b. Wide Ultra SCSI
    c. Ultra3 SCSI
    d. All of the above

12. If you have a 10MHz 16-bit SCSI-2 device, which of these is an accurate descriptor of it?
    a. Fast Narrow
    b. Fast Wide
    c. Ultra SCSI
    d. Ultra Fast Wide

13. What is the purpose of a high-byte terminator?
    a. It terminates the device that follows it; it is used in cases where there is no available connector following the last device.
    b. It provides passive termination to internal SCSI devices only.
    c. It provides active termination to fast SCSI-2 in SE mode.
    d. It terminates 8 bytes after the last wide SCSI device in a chain, allowing the other 8 bytes to continue on to any narrow SCSI devices following it.

14. Which type of interface uses a 50-pin ribbon cable for internal drives?
    a. floppy
    b. IDE
    c. SCSI
    d. USB

15. Which type of SCSI cannot be used with any other type of SCSI?
    a. SE
    b. LVD
    c. LVH
    d. HVD

16. Which drive type does not require jumper configuration prior to installation?
    a. floppy
    b. IDE
    c. SCSI
    d. They all require jumper configuration.

17. Where would a SCSI adapter typically be installed?
    a. drive bay
    b. AGP slot
    c. PCI or ISA slot
    d. either b or c

18. Which of these could *not* be the cause of a BIOS failing to recognize an IDE drive?
    a. Master/slave jumper is not set correctly.
    b. Ribbon cable is defective.
    c. Ribbon cable is backward.
    d. These are all possible causes.

19. What is probably the cause of the floppy drive light's remaining on all of the time?
    a. There is a problem with Pin 34 on the cable.
    b. The ribbon cable is backward.
    c. The floppy drive controller is disabled in BIOS Setup.
    d. None of these would cause that problem.

20. How many A drives can a system have?
    a. 1
    b. 2
    c. 3
    d. 4

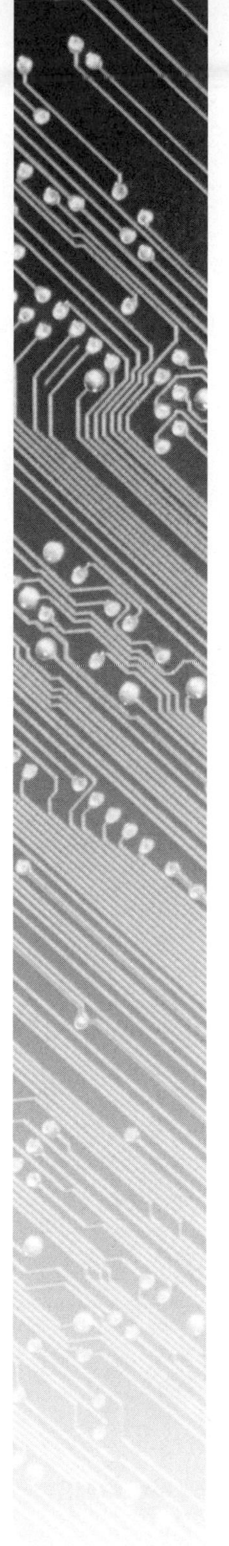

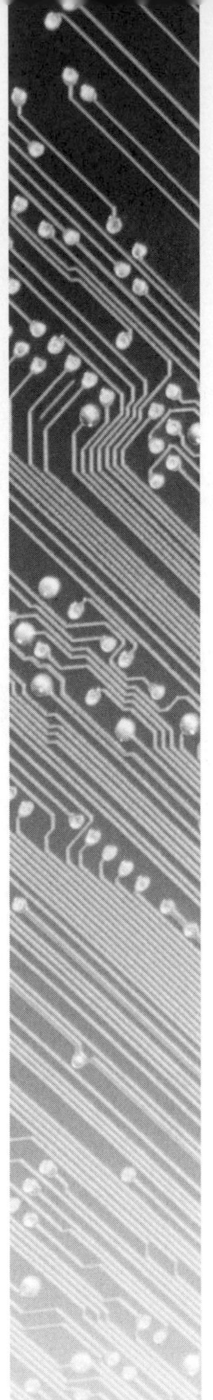

## TROUBLESHOOTING

1. You are installing a second hard drive in a PC that currently has two CD drives and one hard drive. The primary IDE interface has the existing hard drive on it, and the secondary interface has both of the CD drives. For performance reasons, you have decided to put one hard drive and one CD drive on each interface. Describe the jumper settings and cabling changes you would need to make.
2. You currently have a SCSI adapter in a PCI slot, with an internal SCSI hard drive and internal SCSI CD drive connected to it in a single chain. The SCSI adapter's ID is set to 7, the hard drive to 0, and the CD drive to 1. You have connected an external SCSI scanner to the card, but the PC does not see it. Why not, and what can you do to fix it?
3. A client wants you to install a new hard drive in her system but there are no available internal drive bays. What are your options?

## CUSTOMER SERVICE

1. A friend has an old IBM XT that he wants to fix up, and wants your help choosing a hard drive to put in it. What type of hard disk would you recommend?
2. A client who uses her computer primarily for Internet and word processing asks whether you think she should buy an IDE or a SCSI CD drive for her system. She does not currently have any SCSI devices. Which would you recommend to her and why?
3. You are walking a client through the installation of a new CD drive over the telephone. The new drive came with its own ribbon cable, and he is trying to plug it into his motherboard's secondary IDE connector, but he claims it will not fit. What is going on, and what can you suggest?

## FOR MORE INFORMATION

For links to Web sites that provide further information about the topics covered in this chapter, go to the EMC/Paradigm Internet Resource Center at www.emcp.com/College Division/Internet Resource Centers/PC Maintenance/For More Information.

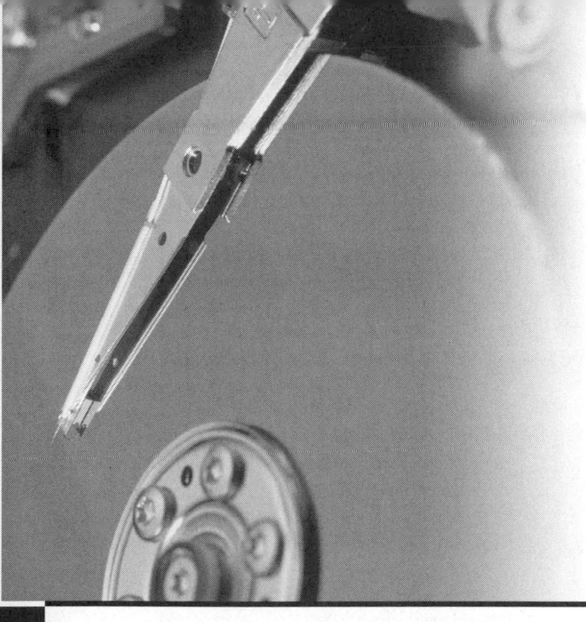

# 12 Performing Disk Management Tasks

## ON THE TEST

**A+ Core Hardware Service Technician Examination**

- **Objective 2.1:** Identify common symptoms and problems associated with each module and how to troubleshoot and isolate the problems.

**A+ Operating System Technologies Examination**

- **Objective 1.1:** Identify the operating system's functions, structure, and major system files to navigate the operating system and how to get to needed technical information.
- **Objective 1.2:** Identify basic concepts and procedures for creating, viewing, and managing files, directories, and disks. This includes procedures for changing file attributes and the ramifications of those changes (for example, security issues).
- **Objective 2.1:** Identify the procedures for installing Windows 9x, and Windows 2000 for bringing the software to a basic operational level.

## ON THE JOB

This chapter introduces many hands-on skills for working with disks in an operating system. You will learn how to care for floppy disks, how to partition and format hard disks, how to troubleshoot hard drive problems, and how to use disk management tools to optimize disk performance and set up multidisk volumes.

Real-life skills related to this chapter's material include:

- using and caring for floppy disks
- partitioning a new hard drive
- restructuring the partitions on a hard drive
- formatting a partition with FAT16, FAT32, or NTFS
- determining a disk's capacity and available space
- troubleshooting hard drive problems

## Understanding the File Storage Hierarchy

**Logical drive**

A drive letter representing part of a physical hard disk.

**Directory**

A logical unit that organizes files into groups for easier management. Also called folder.

**Root directory**

The top-level directory (folder) on a logical disk.

In Chapters 10 and 11 you learned about the physical aspects of disk storage, such as the magnetic or optical means of placing the files on the disk and the partitioning of a single physical drive into multiple *logical drives*. Within a logical drive, however, there is yet another hierarchy, involving directories (also called folders). It is essential that you understand this system of *directory* hierarchy, because as a PC technician you will likely need to explain it to others.

The *root directory* on the disk stores some individual files, but it also stores directories. Each of those directories is a database of information about certain files stored on the drive. For organizational purposes, those files are said to be "in" that directory, but they are not physically contained in it. Only the file management information about those files, such as their size, date modified, attributes, and cluster address, is stored within that directory. The files themselves can physically be anywhere on the disk.

In Figure 12.1, the physical structure of the disk shows items scattered all over, in random arrangement. (Figure 12.1 assumes for simplicity's sake that the physical drive is set up as a single primary partition with a single logical drive.) Physically, disk storage is a jumble of data clusters including both files and directories.

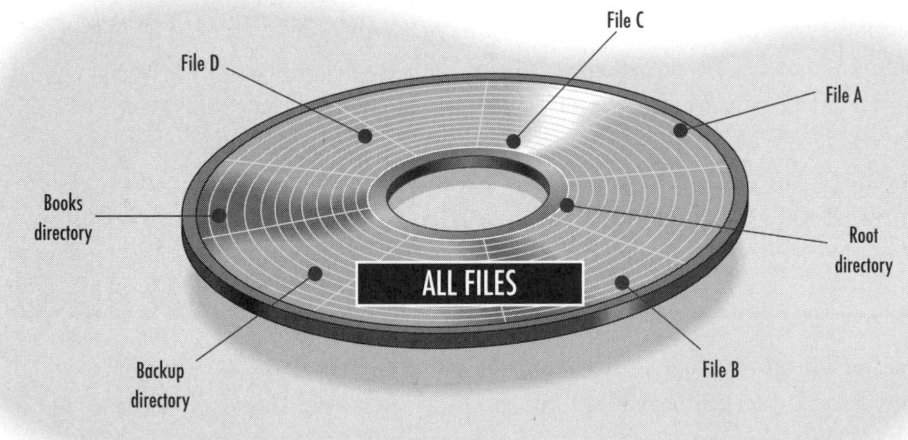


**FIGURE 12.1**
**Physical File and Directory Storage on a Disk**

Physically, the root directory is a small file containing a database listing the other directories on the disk plus any files that are not assigned to any of the other directories. Logically, in the operating system it appears as the top-level folder in a hierarchical tree of folders. Figure 12.2 shows a logical diagram of the disk content from Figure 12.1. In Figure 12.2, the root directory's content includes the Books directory and File A.

The Books directory is also physically a database file listing the files and directories assigned to it. Figure 12.1 shows it as a file stored in a random location on the drive. Logically, however, the operating system sees the Books directory as a container that holds File B and File C and the Backup directory, as shown in Figure 12.2. The same goes for the Backup directory. Figure 12.1 shows it as a file in a random location, but Figure 12.2 shows that it is a container within the Books directory that holds File D.

## In Real Life

**If you are experienced with Windows, you might find the term *directory* foreign, because in Windows directories are called folders. The two terms are synonymous. Later in the book, when we begin to work with Windows extensively, we will use *folder* rather than *directory*.**

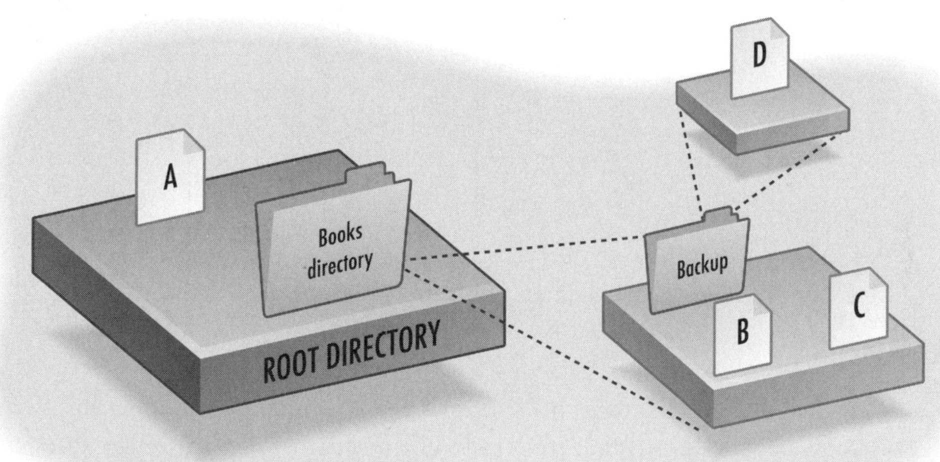


**FIGURE 12.2**
Logical Representation of the File Storage System, as Seen through the Operating System

Within an operating system, each directory appears as a folder containing the files listed within it. Figure 12.3 shows the hierarchy represented in Figure 12.2 when displayed in Microsoft Windows XP. Chapter 29 provides more details about working with files and folders in Windows.

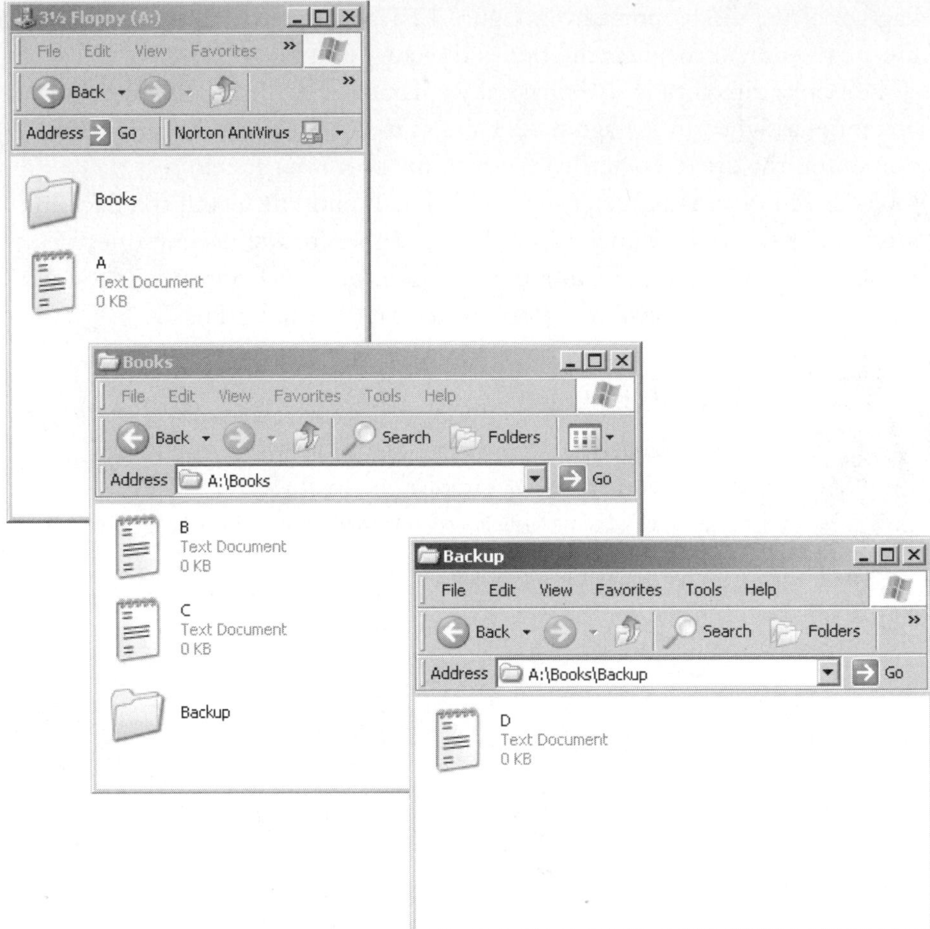


**FIGURE 12.3**
Folders nested within one another in Windows represent the logical directory structure.

One of the advantages of Windows over command-line operating systems such as MS-DOS is that in Windows it is much easier to see the directory structure. In Figure 12.3, for example, you can see all three directories' contents at once, in three separate windows. At a command prompt you can "see" only one directory, and even then you would have to issue the DIR command to view the list of its contents. In Figure 12.4, for example, you can tell that the Books directory is the active directory because its name appears in the prompt (A:\Books>). The DIR command has been issued to display the list of items in Books.

```
A:\Books>DIR
 Volume in drive A is 502570
 Volume Serial Number is 7400-3CAC

 Directory of A:\Books

04/30/2002  01:30 PM    <DIR>          .
04/30/2002  01:30 PM    <DIR>          ..
04/30/2002  01:52 PM             3,374 B.txt
04/30/2002  01:52 PM            20,244 C.txt
04/30/2002  01:31 PM    <DIR>          Backup
               2 File(s)         23,618 bytes
               3 Dir(s)       1,432,576 bytes free

A:\Books>
```

**FIGURE 12.4**
At a command prompt you do not see the full picture of the directory hierarchy.

### IN REAL LIFE

Open Windows Explorer and examine the folder hierarchy on the C drive. How many levels deep is the deepest folder structure there?

## Floppy Disk Management

In earlier days floppy disks were essential to PC operation. Originally most PCs did not have hard disks, so they stored everything on floppies. Even when hard disks became common, most new programs came on floppy disks, and most backup programs backed up to floppy disks.

Today the CD-ROM is the most popular format for distributing new software, but floppy disks continue to be a part of almost all new PCs manufactured. People still use floppies for quick transfers of small files from PC to PC, for archiving important files for backup, and for countless other routine purposes.

### TYPES OF FLOPPY DISKS

For the last several years, the dominant floppy disk standard has been double-sided, high-density 3.5-inch disks. However, a decade or so ago it was common to find several other types of floppy disks in use as well.

There have been two sizes of floppy drives in PCs: 5.25- and 3.5-inch. The measurements refer to the diameter of the disk, not to the physical size of the drive. The 5.25-inch size disk is the older style. The oldest version was a double-sided double-density disk that held 360KB of data; an updated high-density version held 1.2MB of data. The 3.5-inch disk is the newer style. The original 3.5-inch disk type was double-density and held 720KB of data; the modern version (high-density) holds 1.44MB.

The drives themselves also came in both double-density and high-density models. High-density drives can read double-density disks, but not vice versa. There is no easy way to distinguish a double-density from a high-density drive physically unless there is a label on the drive stating its capacity.

As a PC technician today, the main thing you need to know about these older styles of disks is how to recognize them. It is easy to tell the difference between a 5.25-inch and a 3.5-inch disk, of course; Figure 12.5 shows both types so you can compare.

**FIGURE 12.5**
Examples of 5.25- (left) and 3.5-Inch (right) Disks

Unless a 5.25-inch disk states its capacity on its label, there is no foolproof method of distinguishing a double-density from a high-density model. However, on many high-density 5.25-inch disks the center hole is reinforced with a band, while on double-density disks it is not. The band is definitive proof of high-density, but the lack of band does not necessarily mean it is double-density.

On a 3.5-inch disk it is much easier to distinguish double-density from high-density. On a high-density disk there are square holes in two corners. One has a sliding plastic tab on it (for write-protecting the disk); the other is open all of the time. On a double-density disk there is only the write-protect hole; the other is missing (see Figure 12.6).

## In Real Life

In the early days of high-density 3.5-inch disks, the high-density disks were expensive, so users would buy double-density 3.5-inch disks and use a special punch to make the extra hole in the corner so the PC would identify the disks as high density. However, not all double-density disks were of good enough quality to work reliably as high-density disks, so users often had a problem with losing data. If you ever see an old disk with a round second hole instead of the usual square, that is the explanation.

## Write-Protecting a Floppy Disk

**Write-protect**

To protect a disk from having its contents erased or modified.

*Write-protecting* a modern 3.5-inch disk is easy—just slide the plastic tab in the corner so that the hole is exposed. An open hole means the disk is protected; a closed hole means it is writable (see Figure 12.7).

Write-protecting a 5.25-inch disk is somewhat more involved. The disk has a notch in one side of it; you must cover this notch with a sticker to write-protect the disk (see Figure 12.8). Boxes of blank 5.25-inch disks came with sheets of black stickers for this purpose, but you can use any type of sticker (such as a piece cut out of a self-stick mailing label).

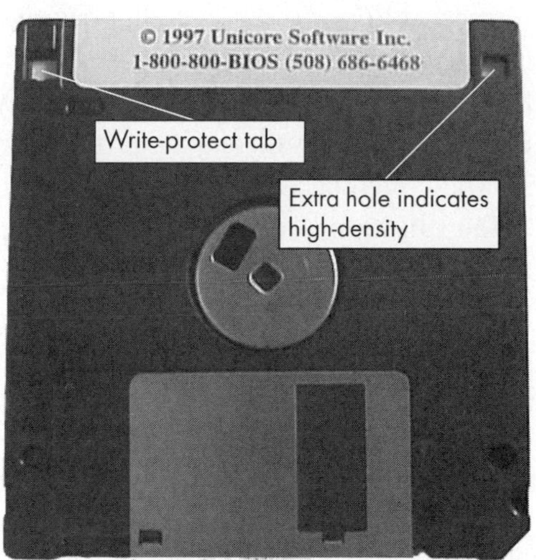


**FIGURE 12.6**
A high-density 3.5-inch disk has two square holes in the corners.

**FIGURE 12.7**
Write-protect a 3.5-inch disk by sliding the tab so the hole is open.

## TRY IT!

1. Delete everything from a floppy disk, and then write-protect it.
2. Try copying a file to the floppy disk. What error message appears?
3. Remove write-protection and try copying the file again.

**FIGURE 12.8**
Write-protect a 5.25-inch disk by covering its notch with a sticker.

## Formatting a Floppy Disk

As you learned in Chapter 10, when you format a floppy disk, you perform both a high-level and low-level format simultaneously. The Format command in the operating system directs the drive to do both.

If you buy preformatted floppy disks, you do not need to reformat them. You can reformat a disk at any time, but formatting it will cause it to lose any data that it contains. If a disk is formatted for Macintosh and you need it to be IBM-compatible, reformatting will achieve that (and vice versa). Other than that, there is no compelling reason to reformat an already-formatted floppy disk. In earlier days users would reformat a floppy disk that was beginning to develop surface errors in order to isolate those errors, but floppy disks are so inexpensive today most people throw away a floppy disk when it starts displaying errors. Some people reformat a disk as an alternate method of deleting all of the files from the disk.

You can format a floppy disk either at a command prompt or from within Windows.

### *Formatting a Floppy at a Command Prompt*

To format a floppy disk at a command prompt, run a program called Format.exe (which is included in MS-DOS and also on emergency startup disks you create in Windows 9x/Me). The syntax is

**FORMAT *drive*:**

So, for example, to format the disk in the A drive, key

**FORMAT A:**

If you want to make the newly formatted disk bootable, you can add the /S switch (which stands for System). This copies the startup files IO.SYS, MSDOS.SYS, and COMMAND.COM from the current disk to the named disk. To transfer the system files from the hard disk to a floppy, you would key

**FORMAT A: /S**

If the disk has already been formatted and you are reformatting, you can skip the check for bad sectors by adding the /Q switch, which stands for Quick. It would look like this:

**FORMAT A: /Q**

To format a floppy, do the following:

1. Key **FORMAT**, press the spacebar once, then key the drive letter and a colon. Add any switches desired, then press Enter.
2. A message appears prompting you to insert the disk to be formatted. Do so if you have not already, and press Enter to continue.

3. Wait for the format to complete. It takes about one minute. After the format has completed, the program will prompt you for a volume label. This is an internal label for the disk; it does not necessarily correspond to any label on the outside, and it is totally optional.
4. Key a volume label and press Enter (11 characters maximum, no spaces) or just press Enter to skip it.

If you ever want to change the disk's volume label, you can do so from a command prompt with the Label command:

1. Key **LABEL A:** and press Enter. A prompt appears asking for the new label.
2. Key the new volume label and press Enter.

## TRY IT!

**Open a command prompt window from within Windows, and format a floppy disk from it.**

### *Formatting a Floppy in Windows*

When you format a floppy in Windows, there are no commands or switches to remember because all of the available options are incorporated in the Format dialog box. To format a floppy in Windows (any version), do the following:

1. Open My Computer.
2. Insert the floppy in the drive. Right-click the drive icon and choose Format. The Format dialog box opens; it looks slightly different in various Windows versions. Figure 12.9 shows the Format dialog box for Windows 98; Figure 12.10 shows it for Windows 2000.
3. *Optional:* Choose a quick format if the disk has been formatted before. In Windows 98, select Quick under Format type; in Windows 2000, click the Quick Format check box under Format options (see Figures 12.9 and 12.10).

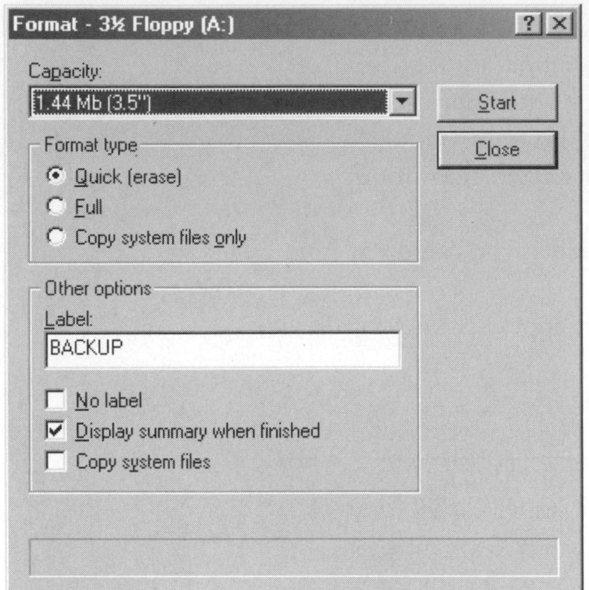


**FIGURE 12.9**
The Format Dialog Box in Windows 98

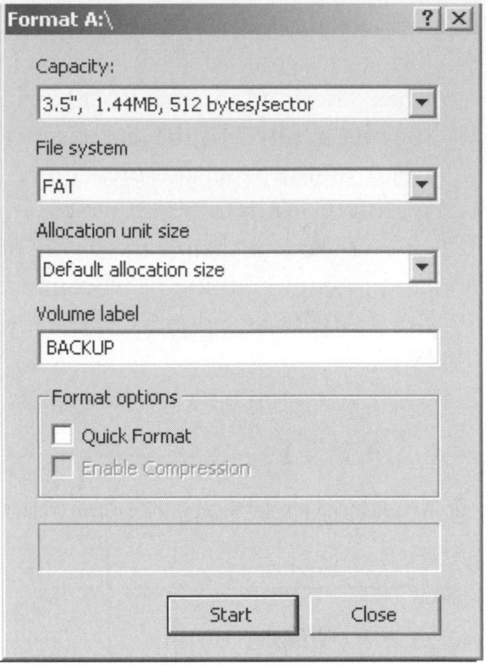

**FIGURE 12.10**
The Format Dialog Box in Windows 2000

4. Leave the File system and Allocation unit size settings at their defaults. These settings are used in Windows 2000 only, not Windows 9x.
5. *Optional:* If you want to make the disk bootable (Windows 9x only), click the Copy system files only check box option under Format type. This makes the disk bootable but does not format it. These are not options in Windows 2000 because, as discussed earlier, Windows 2000 (and all Windows NT variants) does not allow you to start up from a floppy.

## In Real Life

Windows XP's Format dialog box is like the one for Windows 2000 shown in Figure 12.10, except it includes an extra check box called Create an MS-DOS startup disk. That option creates a plain MS-DOS bootable disk, not the same kind of emergency startup disk with utilities that Windows 9x can create. The resulting disk contains only MSDOS.SYS, IO.SYS, and COMMAND.COM.

6. *Optional:* Key a volume label in the Label or Volume Label box if desired.
7. Click the Start button in the dialog box. The formatting begins.
8. If a warning appears telling you that formatting will erase everything on the disk, click OK to continue.
9. When the formatting is completed, if a summary message appears (Windows 9x only), click OK to clear it.

**TRY IT!**

Format a floppy disk from Windows using the Quick option (Windows may not allow this if, for example, the floppy disk has not been formatted before).

## Selecting and Caring for Floppy Disks

Shopping for floppy disks used to be challenging when there were many different kinds, but today you will find only two choices: formatted or unformatted. Buying preformatted disks saves you time you might spend in formatting. MS-DOS and Windows users should buy the type formatted for IBM-compatible PCs.

Figure 12.11 shows some tips for caring for floppy disks.

- Store them away from magnets. Any magnetic storage medium (hard disk, floppy disk, and so on) is susceptible to data corruption if exposed to a strong magnet. Remember that there are magnets in other places besides the obvious; for example, a speaker has a magnet in it.
- Keep disks out of extreme heat and cold.
- Do not get a disk wet. If you accidentally do get it wet, let it dry completely before you try to use it.
- On a 3.5-inch disk, do not open up the sliding metal panel to expose the disk surface. On a 5.25-inch disk, do not touch the exposed disk surface.
- Keep 5.25-inch disks in dust jackets at all times when not in use. The 3.5-inch disks do not require dust jackets, although some people store them in plastic sleeves as extra precaution against spilling liquid on them.

**FIGURE 12.11**
Floppy Disk Care

## Partitioning and Formatting Hard Disks

From Chapter 10 you already understand the purposes of partitioning and formatting. Now we will deal with actually performing those tasks.

The method to use depends on your operating system version. There are two classes of operating systems: those based on DOS (which includes Windows 95, 98, and Me) and those based on Windows NT (which includes Windows 2000 and Windows XP). The systems based on DOS use a utility called FDISK for partitioning and a utility called FORMAT for formatting. The systems based on NT have partitioning and formatting utilities built into Windows Setup, and also in the Windows-based Disk Management utility. The following sections address the two operating system classes separately.

### From a Command Prompt in MS-DOS or Windows 9x

The following sections address how to set up FAT partitions in DOS and Windows 9x and how to format the logical drives.

#### *Partitioning with FDISK*

**FDISK**

A utility program for creating and managing FAT partitions. Short for Fixed Disk.

You can use *FDISK* to create and delete partitions. FDISK.EXE is located in the C:\DOS directory in MS-DOS, or on the startup disk you create in Windows 95, 98, or Me (and also in the C:\WINDOWS\COMMAND folder in those OSes). To start FDISK, key **FDISK** and press Enter at a command prompt. You can also use third-party partitioning programs such as Partition Magic, which are more feature rich and easier to operate, but FDISK is free.

> **WARNING**
>
> **Simply running FDISK will not affect any existing partitions or any data on them, so you can use FDISK to check the partitions at any time. However, make sure you do not delete any partitions through FDISK that contain data you want to keep.**

DOS and Windows 95 support only FAT16 partitions, but Windows 98 and Windows Me support both FAT16 and FAT32. In those latter two OSes, you choose whether you want FAT16 or FAT32 by your answer to a question about enabling large disk support when FDISK starts (see Figure 12.12). After starting FDISK, and answering Y or N to the question shown in Figure 12.12 if it appears, the main FDISK menu opens, shown in Figure 12.13. The options on this main menu are described in Figure 12.14.

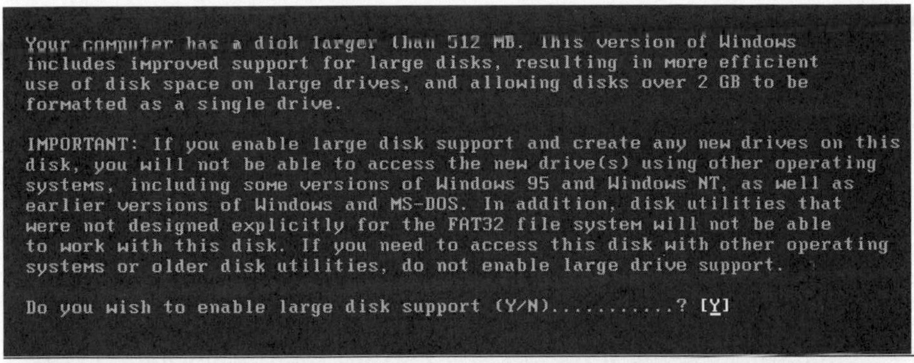

```
Your computer has a disk larger than 512 MB. This version of Windows
includes improved support for large disks, resulting in more efficient
use of disk space on large drives, and allowing disks over 2 GB to be
formatted as a single drive.

IMPORTANT: If you enable large disk support and create any new drives on this
disk, you will not be able to access the new drive(s) using other operating
systems, including some versions of Windows 95 and Windows NT, as well as
earlier versions of Windows and MS-DOS. In addition, disk utilities that
were not designed explicitly for the FAT32 file system will not be able
to work with this disk. If you need to access this disk with other operating
systems or older disk utilities, do not enable large drive support.

Do you wish to enable large disk support (Y/N)..........? [Y]
```

**FIGURE 12.12**
Enabling large disk support causes any partitions you create to be FAT32 rather than FAT16.

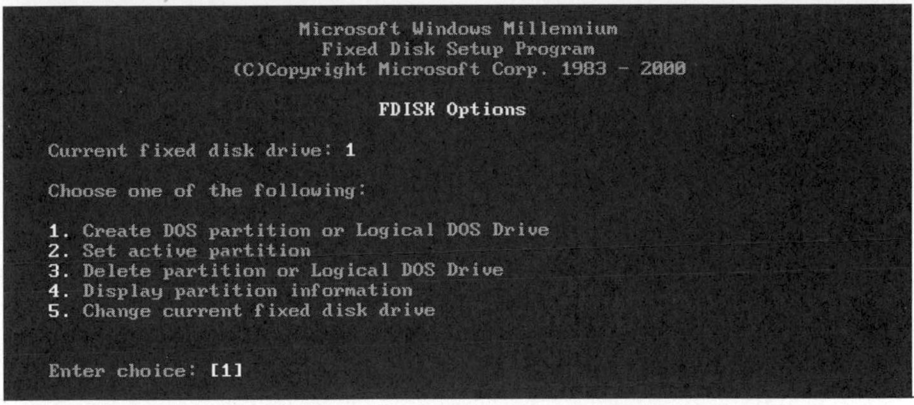

```
                    Microsoft Windows Millennium
                     Fixed Disk Setup Program
              (C)Copyright Microsoft Corp. 1983 - 2000

                           FDISK Options

  Current fixed disk drive: 1

  Choose one of the following:

  1. Create DOS partition or Logical DOS Drive
  2. Set active partition
  3. Delete partition or Logical DOS Drive
  4. Display partition information
  5. Change current fixed disk drive


  Enter choice: [1]
```

**FIGURE 12.13**
The FDISK Main Menu

- **Create DOS partition or Logical DOS Drive:** Use this option to create new partitions on a drive. If the drive is brand new, you will create a primary partition first, then optionally an extended partition.
- **Set active partition:** If there is more than one partition, you can choose which will be active (bootable) here. If you create a single primary partition that occupies all the disk space, it is automatically active; otherwise, you must manually activate a partition.
- **Delete partition or Logical DOS Drive:** Use this option to delete existing partitions, or to delete logical disk drives from the extended partition. (Remember, the extended partition can have more than one logical disk drive, whereas the primary partition can have only one.)
- **Display partition information:** Use this option to examine the current partitions without making any changes.
- **Change current fixed disk drive:** The partition information for all of the above options pertains to only one physical hard drive. If you have more than one physical hard drive, you can switch among them with this option. Otherwise, this option does not appear.

**FIGURE 12.14**
FDISK Main Menu Options

You can press Esc to back up a level in FDISK's menu system after choosing one of the above options. If you are already at the top-level main menu, Esc exits the program entirely.

To set up a disk's partition system, you would follow these steps. Each of these steps is explained in greater detail in the sections that follow.

1. If you have more than one physical hard drive, make sure that you are working with the desired one. Use the Display partition information and Change current fixed disk drive commands as needed.
2. If there are any existing partitions you want to delete, delete them. You would do this if the disk is already partitioned and you want to change how the space is allocated. For example, perhaps the disk is partitioned and formatted as FAT16 and you want FAT32. Or perhaps the entire disk is a single primary partition and you want to split it up into two or more logical drives.
3. If the disk does not have an existing primary partition, create one with the Create DOS partition or Logical DOS Drive command. You can make it take up the entire physical disk or only a portion of it.
4. If you did not assign all of the space to the primary partition, create an extended partition.
5. Create one or more logical drives within the extended partition.
6. If you have both a primary and an extended partition, make one of them active with Set active partition. This will be the partition from which the system attempts to boot, and when you install an operating system, it will be the partition on which the boot files are stored.
7. Exit from FDISK and reboot to allow the system to assign drive letters to the new partitions.

Use the above steps as your overall roadmap for the process, and refer to the following sections as needed to perform them.

**Displaying Partition Information.** Use this whenever you need to see the current partition assignments for the current physical disk drive.

1. From the FDISK main menu, key 4 and press Enter to select Display partition information. Information about the partitions appears, as shown in Figure 12.15.
2. When you are finished looking at the information, press Esc to return to the main menu.

```
                    Display Partition Information

Current fixed disk drive: 1

Partition  Status   Type    Volume Label  Mbytes   System   Usage
 C: 1              PRI DOS                 2000    UNKNOWN    49%
    2         A    EXT DOS                 2094               51%


Total disk space is  4095 Mbytes (1 Mbyte = 1048576 bytes)


The Extended DOS Partition contains Logical DOS Drives.
Do you want to display the logical drive information (Y/N)......?[Y]




Press Esc to return to FDISK Options
```

**FIGURE 12.15**
Displaying Partition Information

**Changing the Current Fixed Disk Drive.** If you do not have two or more physical hard drives installed, you will not see this option on the menu. If you do, however, make the following changes to the drives.

1. From the FDISK main menu, key 5 and press Enter to select Change current fixed disk drive.
2. A list of the drives appears. Key the number representing the drive you want and press Enter.
3. Press Esc to return to the main menu.
4. *Optional:* Display the partition information (see the preceding section) to confirm that you have chosen the desired physical drive. Then return to the main menu by pressing Esc.

**Deleting Partitions or Logical Disk Drives.** If the drive contains existing partitions, you may wish to delete them and create new ones. This is not necessary, but may be desirable to change partition sizes or to convert a drive from FAT16 to FAT32 (for example, if the drive was originally partitioned under DOS or Windows 95 but you have upgraded to Windows 98 or Me). You cannot resize a partition; you must delete it and re-create it.

Deletions must be done in the reverse order in which they are created. First, delete any logical drives on the extended partition; then delete the extended partition itself; finally, delete the primary partition.

To delete a logical drive on the extended partition:

1. From the FDISK main menu, key **3** to select Delete partition or Logical DOS Drive. Another menu appears.
2. Key **3** and press Enter to select Delete Logical DOS Drive(s) in the Extended DOS Partition. A list of the drives appears.
3. Key the letter of the drive you want to delete and press Enter.

4. A prompt appears asking you to key the volume label. Do so and press Enter. If there is none, just press Enter (see Figure 12.16).
5. An Are You Sure? prompt appears. Key **Y** and press Enter.
6. If there are any other logical drives to delete, repeat steps 3-5. Then press Esc to return to the main menu.

```
          Delete Logical DOS Drive(s) in the Extended DOS Partition

Drv Volume Label  Mbytes  System   Usage
D:                  2094  UNKNOWN   100%




    Total Extended DOS Partition size is  2094 Mbytes (1 MByte = 1048576 bytes)

    WARNING! Data in a deleted Logical DOS Drive will be lost.
    What drive do you want to delete..............................? [D]
    Enter Volume Label............................? [_          ]


    Press Esc to return to FDISK Options
```

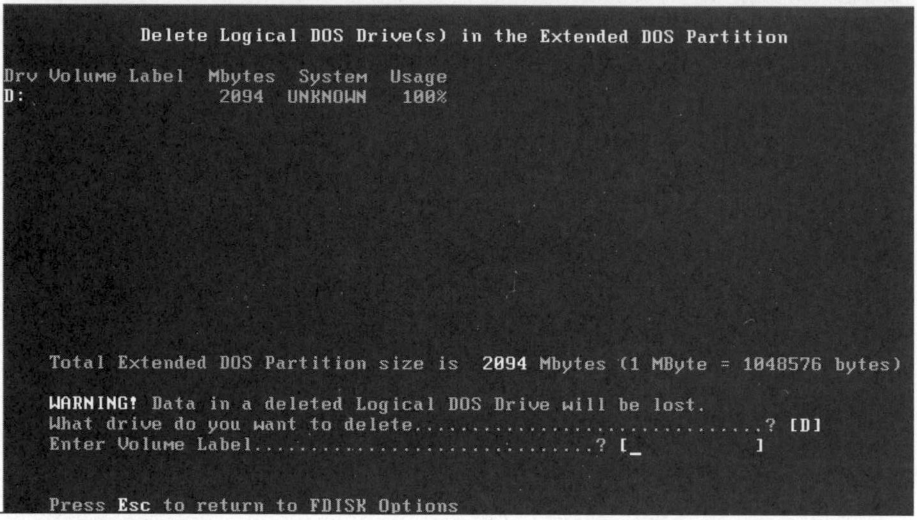

**FIGURE 12.16**
**Deleting a Logical DOS Drive on an Extended Partition**

After the extended partition has been emptied of logical drives, you can delete it. To do so, follow these steps:

1. From the FDISK main menu, key **3** to select Delete partition or Logical DOS Drive. Another menu appears.
2. Key **2** and press Enter to select Delete Extended DOS Partition.
3. A warning appears. Key **Y** and press Enter.
4. Press Esc to return to the main menu.

After the extended partition has been deleted, you can delete the primary partition. Follow these steps:

1. From the FDISK main menu, key **3** to select Delete partition or Logical DOS Drive. Another menu appears.
2. Key **1** and press Enter to select Delete Primary DOS Partition.
3. A warning appears. Key the partition number to delete (probably 1) and press Enter.
4. A prompt appears asking you to key the volume label. Do so and press Enter. If there is none, just press Enter.
5. An Are You Sure? prompt appears. Key **Y** and press Enter.
6. Press Esc to return to the main menu.

**Creating a Primary Partition.** With FDISK you can create only one primary partition; with third-party utilities you can create up to four. Focus on FDISK for the moment.

You can create a primary partition in FDISK only on a completely empty disk—that is, one that contains no other partitions. So first delete any other partitions, as previously described, and then do the following:

1. From the FDISK main menu, key **1** and press Enter to select Create DOS partition or Logical DOS Drive. The menu shown in Figure 12.17 appears.
2. Key **1** and press Enter to select Create Primary DOS Partition.

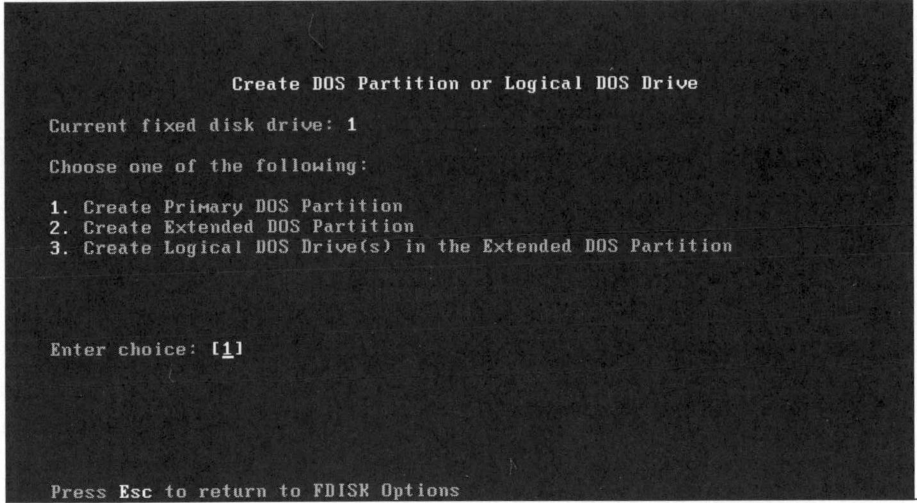


**FIGURE 12.17**
The FDISK Menu for Creating Partitions

3. A message appears about verifying the drive integrity, and it counts up to 100 percent. Then a message appears asking whether you want to use the maximum available size. If you do, key **Y** and press Enter to accept the full disk amount. A screen appears prompting you to press Esc to exit FDISK. Exit and then restart your PC—you are through partitioning.

   If you want an extended partition too, key **N** and press Enter. Then enter an amount of space in megabytes or a percentage (followed by the % symbol) and press Enter to describe the size you want for the primary partition (see Figure 12.18).

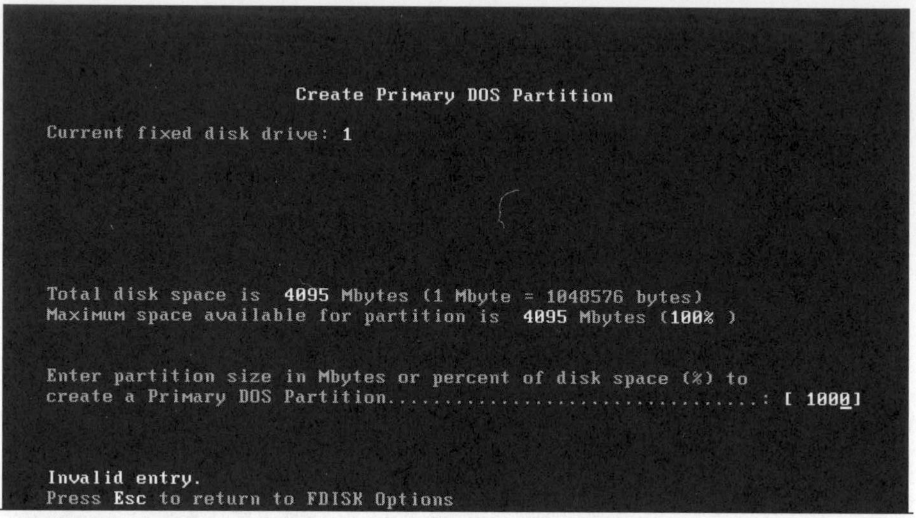

```
Create Primary DOS Partition

Current fixed disk drive: 1



Total disk space is  4095 Mbytes (1 Mbyte = 1048576 bytes)
Maximum space available for partition is  4095 Mbytes (100% )


Enter partition size in Mbytes or percent of disk space (%) to
create a Primary DOS Partition.................................: [ 1000]


Invalid entry.
Press Esc to return to FDISK Options
```

**FIGURE 12.18**
You can specify the size of the primary partition, up to the full size of the physical drive.

4. Press Esc to return to the main menu. Then create an extended partition as described in the following section.

**Creating an Extended Partition and Logical Drives.** If you have space left after creating the primary partition, you can either create an extended partition out of it now or leave it unpartitioned for the time being. You must partition the space if you want to use it for additional logical drives.

To create an extended partition, follow these steps:

1. From the FDISK main menu, key **1** and press Enter to select Create DOS partition or Logical DOS Drive.
2. Key **2** and press Enter to select Create Extended DOS Partition.
3. If you want to use all of the space for the extended DOS partition, press Enter to accept the default size. Otherwise, enter a smaller number for the size or a percentage (followed by the % symbol—see Figure 12.19). You can have several extended partitions on the disk, although there is little advantage in having separate extended partitions versus a single extended partition with multiple logical drives.

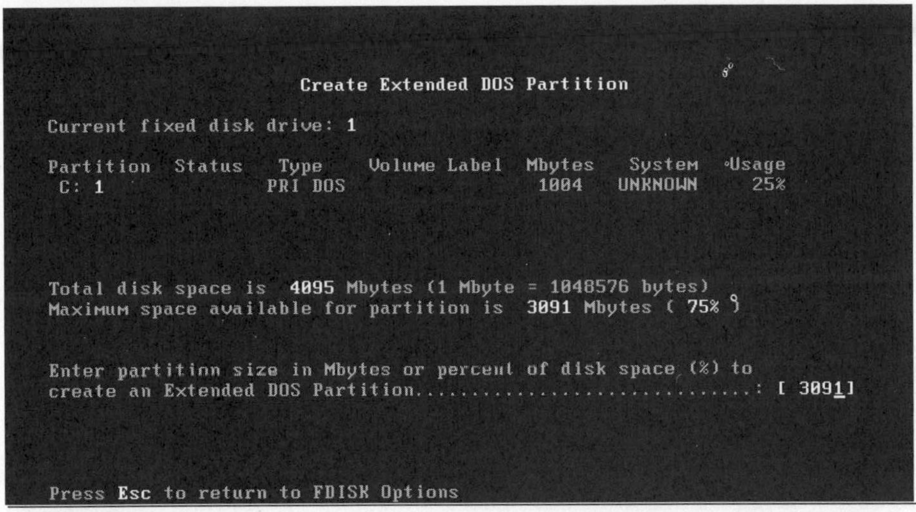

```
                    Create Extended DOS Partition

Current fixed disk drive: 1

Partition  Status   Type    Volume Label  Mbytes   System   Usage
 C: 1              PRI DOS                 1004    UNKNOWN    25%



Total disk space is  4095 Mbytes (1 Mbyte = 1048576 bytes)
Maximum space available for partition is  3091 Mbytes ( 75% )

Enter partition size in Mbytes or percent of disk space (%) to
create an Extended DOS Partition.............................: [ 3091]



Press Esc to return to FDISK Options
```

**FIGURE 12.19**
Creating an Extended Partition

4. Press Esc to continue. A screen appears offering to create the first logical drive on the extended partition. If you want to use the entire extended partition for it, press Enter to accept the maximum size. Otherwise, enter a smaller size or a percentage and press Enter.
5. If you did not use the full amount of space in step 4, the prompt reappears asking for the size of the next logical drive. Repeat step 4 until all of the space has been assigned. Then press Esc to return to the main menu.

**Setting the Active Partition.** If you created multiple partitions, none of them will be active, and a warning will appear to that effect on the FDISK main menu. You must set an active partition in order for the disk to be bootable. FDISK makes a partition active automatically only if it is a single primary partition that occupies the entire physical disk.

To choose a partition to be active, follow these steps:

1. From the FDISK main menu, key **2** and press Enter to select Set active partition.
2. A list of partitions appears. Key the number for the partition you want and press Enter (see Figure 12.20).

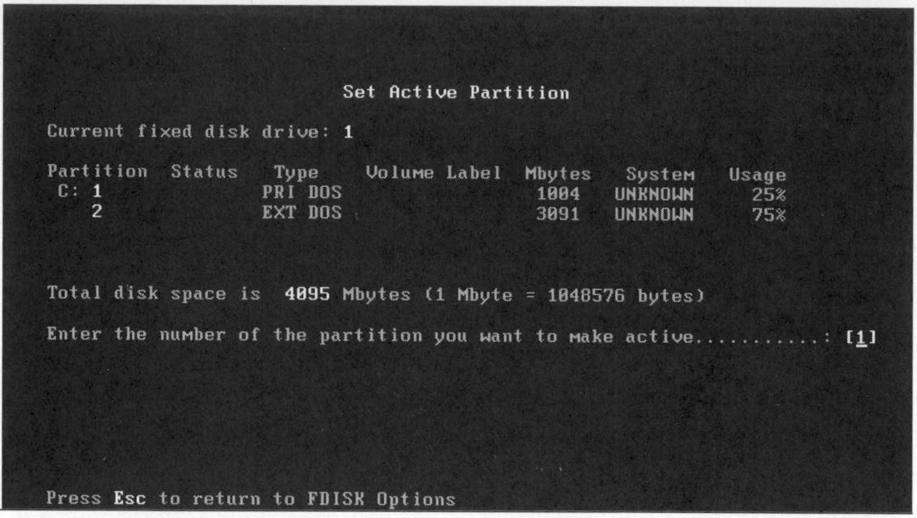

```
                         Set Active Partition

Current fixed disk drive: 1

Partition  Status   Type    Volume Label  Mbytes   System   Usage
 C: 1             PRI DOS                  1004   UNKNOWN    25%
    2             EXT DOS                  3091   UNKNOWN    75%


Total disk space is  4095 Mbytes (1 Mbyte = 1048576 bytes)

Enter the number of the partition you want to make active...........: [1]




Press Esc to return to FDISK Options
```

**FIGURE 12.20**
Setting the Active Partition

3. Press Esc to go back to the main menu.

After you have created all of the partitions you need, you must exit FDISK and reboot the computer. This is essential because when it reboots, it reassigns the drive letters to the new partitions. Only after you have rebooted can you proceed to the next step: high-level formatting.

## TRY IT!

Do this exercise only if you have an available empty hard disk (or one that contains nothing you need to keep). You will also need a Windows 95, 98, or Me startup floppy disk.

1. Boot from the startup floppy disk.
2. Use FDISK to delete all existing partitions on the drive.
3. Divide the disk into three equal-sized logical drives with FDISK.

### *Formatting*

Formatting is much simpler than partitioning because there are few options involved. Formatting a hard disk is a high-level format operation only; recall from Chapter 10 that hard disks are low-level formatted at the factory.

To format, use the FORMAT command at a command prompt. As with a floppy disk, the syntax is

**FORMAT *drive*:**

So, for example, to format the C drive you would key

**FORMAT C:**

Some OSes allow you to make the formatted hard disk bootable with the /S switch, as with a floppy. This copies the startup files IO.SYS,

MSDOS.SYS, and COMMAND.COM from the current disk to the named disk. To transfer the system files from the hard disk to a floppy, you would key

**FORMAT C: /S**

**WARNING**

The /S switch does not work on hard disks when using a command prompt from a Windows Me boot disk.

The FORMAT command checks each cluster as it formats to make sure it is readable, and isolates any that are not. You can bypass this checking on an already-formatted disk by adding the /Q switch (for Quick):

**FORMAT C: /Q**

To format a floppy, do the following:

1. Key **FORMAT**, press the spacebar once, then key the drive letter and a colon. Add any switches desired, then press Enter.
2. A warning appears about losing all of the data on the disk. Key **Y** to continue.
3. Wait for the format to complete. After the format has completed, the program will prompt you for a volume label.
4. Key a volume label and press Enter (11 characters maximum, no spaces) or just press Enter to skip it.

**TRY IT!**

If you did the preceding Try It! exercise, do this one as well:

1. Reboot from your startup floppy disk.
2. Use the FORMAT command at the prompt to format the logical drive on the primary partition of the physical drive you partitioned earlier.

## FORMATTING FROM MY COMPUTER

Partitioned logical drives show up in My Computer in Windows regardless of whether they have been formatted. Therefore, you can format them from there just like a floppy disk. To do so:

1. Right-click the drive icon in My Computer and choose Format from the shortcut menu. The Format dialog box opens, the same as with a floppy disk.
2. Choose any formatting options desired, such as doing a quick format or adding a label, then click Start (see Figure 12.21).

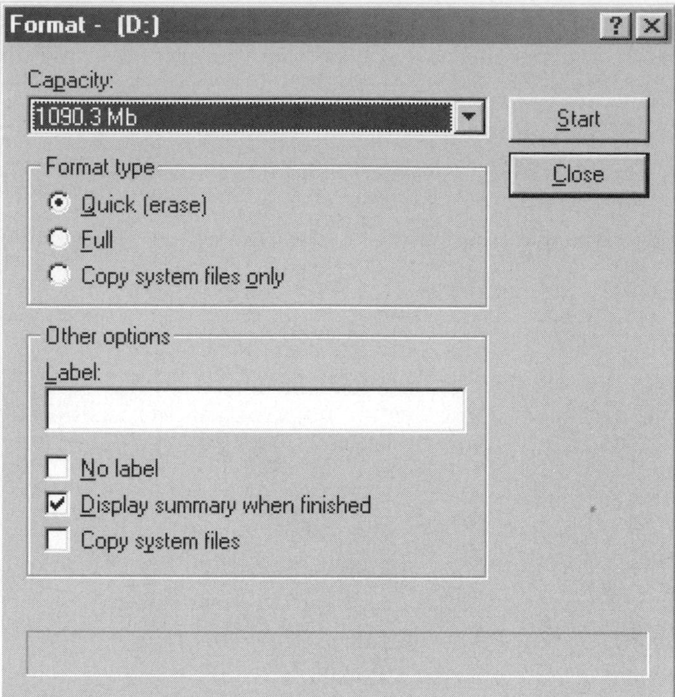


**FIGURE 12.21**
Formatting a Hard Drive from within Windows 98

3. A dialog box appears warning you that this is a hard disk, and that you will lose all data on it. Click OK to continue.
4. Wait for the formatting to finish. A Results box appears. Click Close to close it.
5. A box appears reminding you to check the disk for errors before using it. Click OK.
6. At this point, depending on the Windows version, a Help window may appear explaining how to check the drive for errors with Scandisk. Follow those instructions to check the disk. If you do not see such a window, run Scandisk manually by choosing it from the Programs/Accessories/System Tools menu.

Checking a hard disk after formatting is not strictly necessary, but it is a good idea. If you do check, make sure you choose a Thorough check, which checks the surface of the disk for errors. We will look at the Scandisk utility in more detail in Chapter 30.

## TRY IT!

If you have access to a working copy of Windows and also to a partitioned but not formatted blank hard drive in the same system, try formatting one of the logical drives through My Computer.

## Partitioning and Formatting during Windows 2000 Setup

The Windows 2000 Setup program has a disk partitioning and formatting utility built in. During the early part of the setup program you are asked whether you want to change the existing partitions and logical drives, and to specify on which one you want to install Windows 2000. For example, in Figure 12.22 the setup program has found no existing partitions but 4GB of unpartitioned space, and offers to create a new partition on it. If you want a single primary partition to be created out of the entire amount of space, you can simply press Enter to create such a partition. Alternatively, you can press C to specify the size you want for the primary partition.

Windows 2000 Professional Setup
The following list shows the existing partitions and unpartitioned space on this computer.
Use the UP and DOWN ARROW keys to select an item in the list.
• To set up Windows 2000 on the selected item, press ENTER.
• To create a partition in the unpartitioned space, press C.
• To delete the selected partition, press D.
4095 MB Disk 0 at Id 0 on bus 0 on buslogic
Unpartitioned space 4095 MB
ENTER=Install C=Create Partition F3=Quit

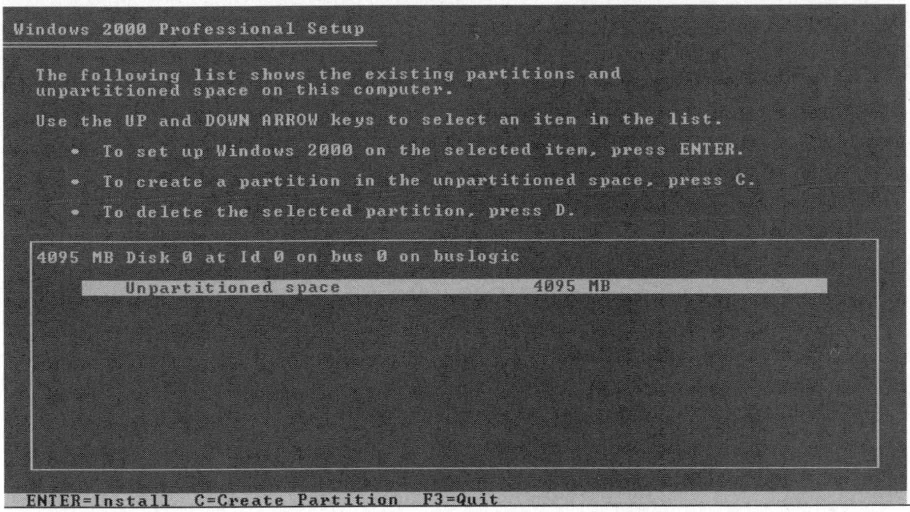

**FIGURE 12.22**
Create a partition from Windows 2000 setup.

After you have created the partition and specified that you want Windows to be installed on it, the setup program offers to format the partition for you. You can choose either NTFS or FAT. If you need compatibility with Windows 9x or DOS on a dual-booting system, choose FAT. Otherwise choose NTFS (see Figure 12.23).

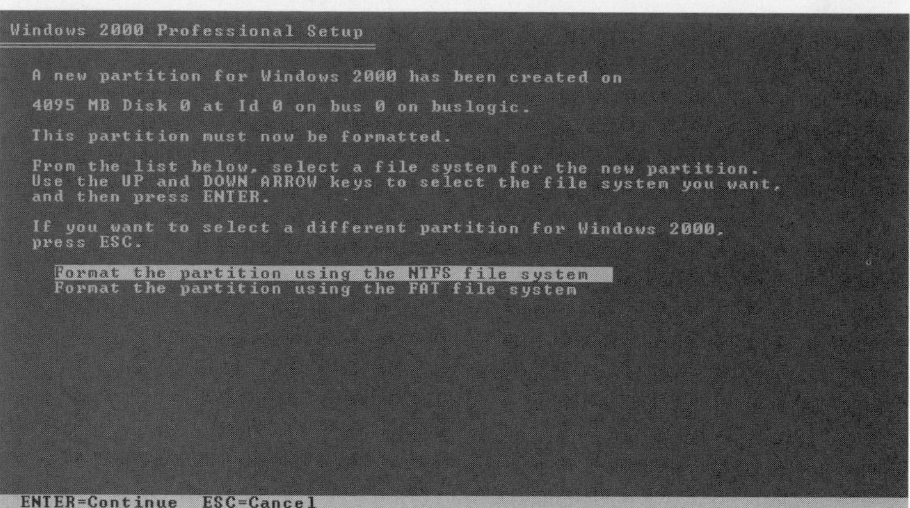

Windows 2000 Professional Setup
A new partition for Windows 2000 has been created on
4095 MB Disk 0 at Id 0 on bus 0 on buslogic.
This partition must now be formatted.
From the list below, select a file system for the new partition.
Use the UP and DOWN ARROW keys to select the file system you want,
and then press ENTER.
If you want to select a different partition for Windows 2000,
press ESC.
Format the partition using the NTFS file system
Format the partition using the FAT file system
ENTER=Continue ESC=Cancel


**FIGURE 12.23**
Format the partition as either FAT or NTFS.

It works the same way for Windows XP Setup, but Windows XP is not covered on the current A+ exam so you should focus on Windows 2000.

**TRY IT!**

For this exercise you need a Windows 2000 or XP Setup CD and an empty hard drive. Boot from the setup CD and start the setup program. Go through the setup program at least to the point where it partitions and formats the drive for you. Then you can either continue Windows Setup or abort it, depending on how much time you have. You will learn more about how to install Windows in a later chapter.

## From Windows 2000 Disk Management

Disk Management is an administrative tool in NT-based Windows versions (including 2000 and XP) that enables you to see all of the partitions and logical drives on the system, their sizes, their formatting, and their statuses. We will discuss it in that context later in the chapter, under "Windows Utilities." But for now we will focus on using it to create and format partitions.

To start Disk Management, do the following:

1. From the Control Panel, double-click Administrative Tools.
2. Double-click Computer Management.
3. On the folder tree at the left, double-click Disk Management. The Disk Management controls appear, as shown in Figure 12.24.

In Figure 12.24 there are three physical disk drives: two hard drives and one CD-ROM. The first physical hard drive is laid out as a single primary partition. The second physical hard disk has not yet been partitioned or formatted.

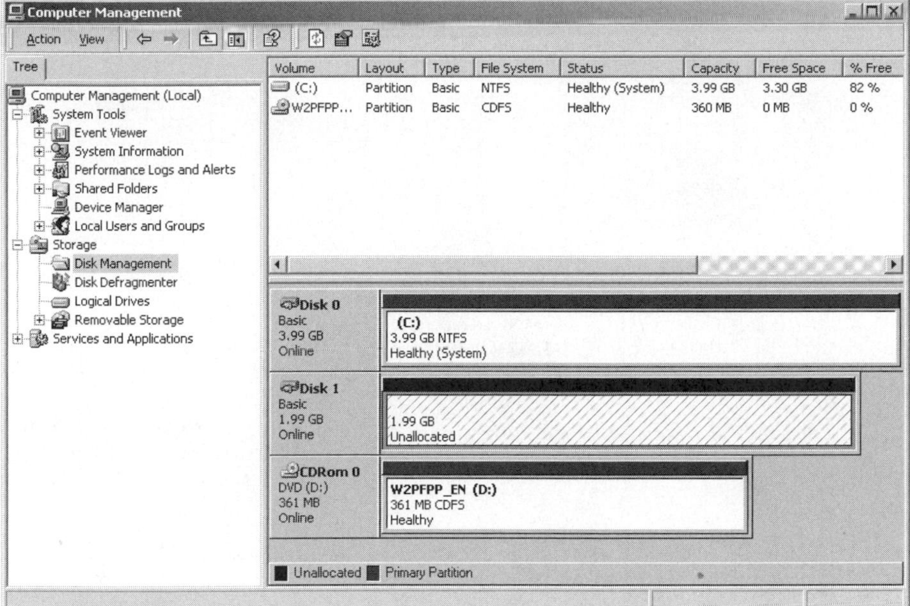


**FIGURE 12.24**
Manage partitions and formatting in Windows 2000 from Disk Management.

Disk Management works the same way in both Windows 2000 and Windows XP.

### *Creating a Partition*

To create a partition from Disk Management, do the following:

1. Right-click the unpartitioned space and choose Create Partition. The Create Partition Wizard will open. Click Next to begin it.
2. Select the type of partition you want: Primary or Extended (see Figure 12.25). Then click Next. (The rest of these steps assume that you chose Primary.)
3. Enter the amount of disk space to use for the partition, or leave it set at the default to use the maximum. Then click Next.
4. At the Assign a Drive Letter or Path screen, leave the Assign a Drive Letter option chosen and choose a drive letter from the drop-down list. Then click Next.
5. If you do not want to format the partition yet, choose Do not format this partition. Otherwise, leave the default option selected (Format this partition with the following settings), choose a file system (NTFS, FAT, or FAT32), and set any other formatting options desired (see Figure 12.26). Then click Next.
6. Click Finish. Windows partitions and formats the drive.

To delete a partition, right-click it and choose Delete Partition.

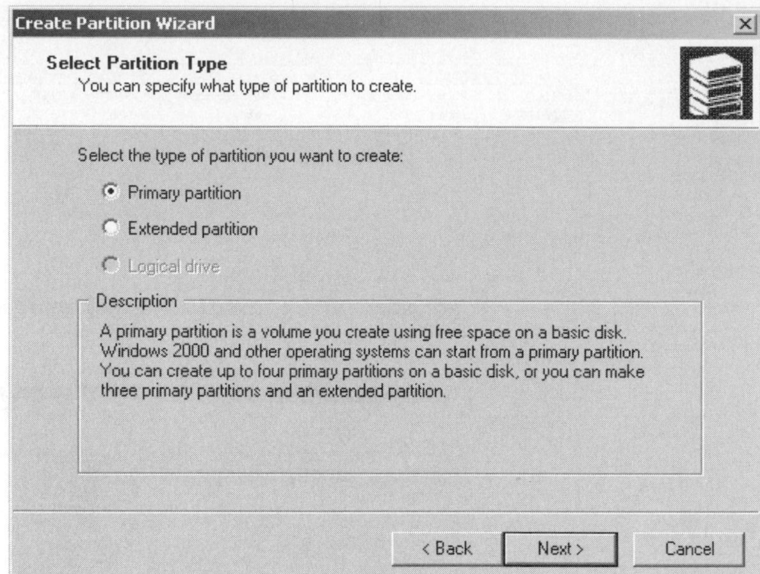


**FIGURE 12.25**
Use the Create Partition Wizard to create a new partition.

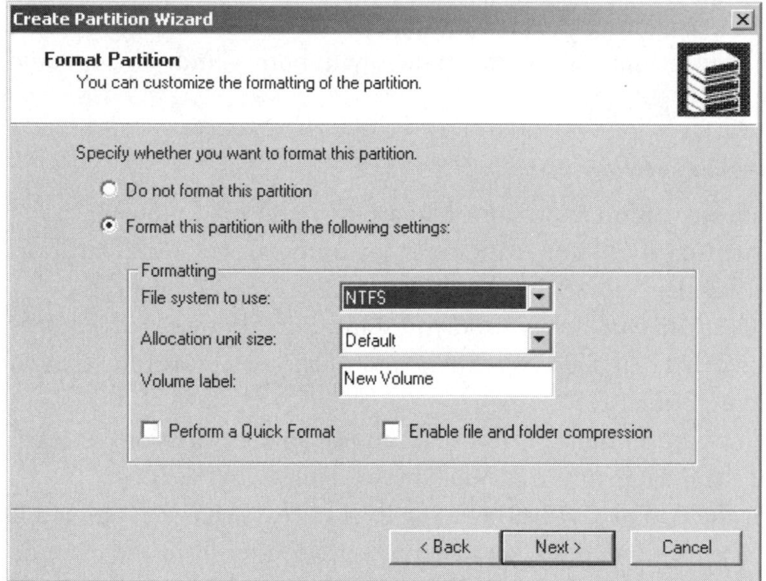


**FIGURE 12.26**
You can format a partition as part of the Create Partition Wizard.

### *Formatting a Partition*

If you did not format the partition when you created it in the preceding section, or if you want to reformat an already-formatted partition (perhaps using a different file system, for example), you can format it now by doing the following:

1. Right-click the partition in Disk Management and choose Format. A Format dialog box opens.

2. Enter a volume label if desired.
3. Choose a file system from the drop-down list.
4. Set any other formatting options desired, then click OK to format it (see Figure 12.27).
5. A warning appears; click OK.

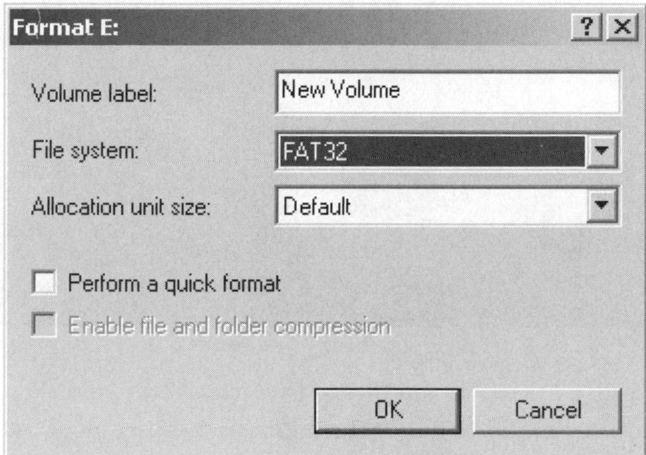


**FIGURE 12.27**
Formatting a Partition in Disk Management

**TRY IT!**

To do this exercise you need a working copy of Windows 2000 or XP and an extra physical hard drive installed (besides the one that contains Windows). In Disk Management, delete all of the partitions on the extra drive, and then re-create them and format them. Format some of them as FAT32 and others as NTFS.

# Examining Disk Properties in the OS

Each operating system version contains tools for examining a disk's properties. The following sections look at some of them.

## Command Prompt Utilities

MS-DOS and Windows contain several commands for finding the capacity, free space, and status of your disks. Some of them are available in both DOS and Windows; others were phased out after the first few Windows versions.

### *DIR*

DIR lists the contents of the current directory. It also tells you the total amount of space that the files in that directory occupy and the amount of available space left on the drive (see Figure 12.28).

```
 Volume Serial Number is 4C66-25E0

 Directory of D:\

01/17/2002  02:28 PM    <DIR>          AOL Instant Messenger
01/17/2002  02:28 PM    <DIR>          aolextras
04/24/2002  05:27 PM    <DIR>          Backups
04/24/2002  05:26 PM    <DIR>          books
08/14/2001  12:42 PM            61,440 cceditorialcalendar1.doc
01/22/2002  03:07 PM    <DIR>          Collage_Complete_2.0
04/03/2002  02:32 PM    <DIR>          Documents and Settings
04/15/2002  01:01 PM            32,768 Indianapolis.cx.doc
04/18/2002  02:45 PM            29,184 Indianapolis.cx2.doc
01/17/2002  02:28 PM    <DIR>          Install CompuServe2000
01/17/2002  02:28 PM    <DIR>          Install ICQ
01/17/2002  02:28 PM    <DIR>          Install Spinner
01/17/2002  02:28 PM    <DIR>          Install Winamp
01/10/2002  11:55 AM    <DIR>          My Music
01/06/2002  03:29 PM    <DIR>          Palm
04/24/2002  05:58 PM    <DIR>          Program Files
05/03/2002  12:04 PM            36,864 quote.doc
02/21/2002  12:52 AM            27,136 tammy.doc
02/27/2002  09:46 AM    <DIR>          Tax01
04/04/2002  01:21 PM            25,088 to-do list.doc
04/27/2002  03:54 PM    <DIR>          WINDOWS
04/15/2002  10:19 AM            26,624 zoning.doc
               7 File(s)        239,104 bytes
              15 Dir(s)   1,592,492,032 bytes free

D:\>
```

**FIGURE 12.28**
The DIR Command

DIR works all by itself, or you can add switches to it. Add /W to make a multicolumn listing, and/or add /P to display one screenful at a time.

**TRY IT!**

**Use the DIR command to find out how much available space is on your C drive.**

### *CHKDSK*

CHKDSK (which stands for Check Disk) is a precursor to the Scandisk utility. It still exists in Windows 9x, but you cannot use it for its original purpose, which was to check for FAT errors (with the /F switch). You can still use it to get information about the disk, however, as shown in Figure 12.29.

```
C:\>chkdsk

CHKDSK has NOT checked this drive for errors.
You must use SCANDISK to detect and fix errors on this drive.

Volume Serial Number is 2351-1103

4,285,165,568 bytes total disk space
3,437,182,976 bytes available on disk

        4,096 bytes in each allocation unit
    1,046,183 total allocation units on disk
      839,156 available allocation units on disk

      651,264 total bytes memory
      589,808 bytes free

C:\>_
```

**FIGURE 12.29**
The CHKDSK Command

## TRY IT!

Use CHKDSK to find the size of the allocation units (the number of sectors per cluster) on your hard drive.

### *MSD*

MSD (for Microsoft Diagnostics) is a very rich program, not just a simple command, that provides detailed information about all aspects of the system. Unfortunately it is not available in most Windows versions, but it comes with all versions of MS-DOS. (In Windows the System Information program performs much the same function.)

To start it, key **MSD** at a command prompt. Once inside the program (see Figure 12.30), you can use the mouse if a driver is loaded for it, or you can press the highlighted letter in a command's name to select it. For example, in Figure 12.30, to see disk drive information you would key D, and the information shown in Figure 12.31 would appear.

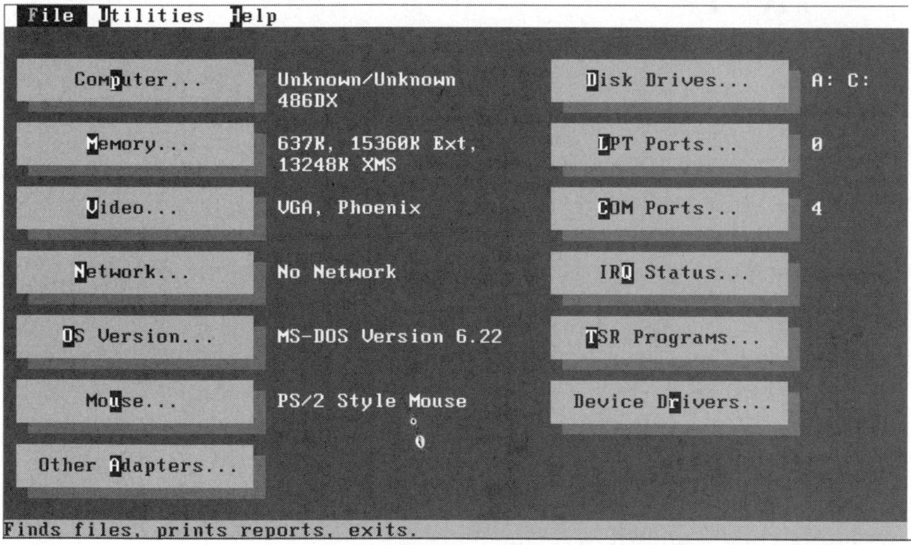

**FIGURE 12.30**
The MSD Main Screen

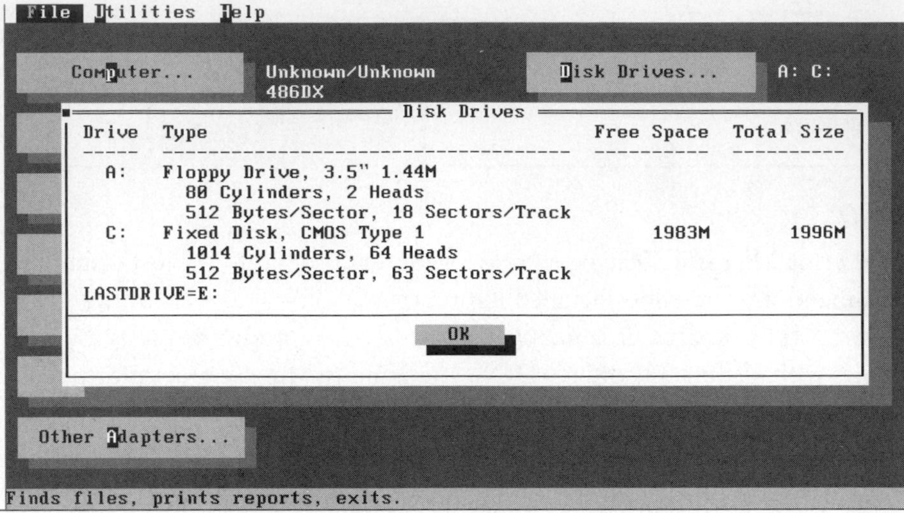


**FIGURE 12.31**
MSD provides disk drive information.

To access the menu system, press Alt and then press a highlighted letter in the menu name. To exit the program, press F3.

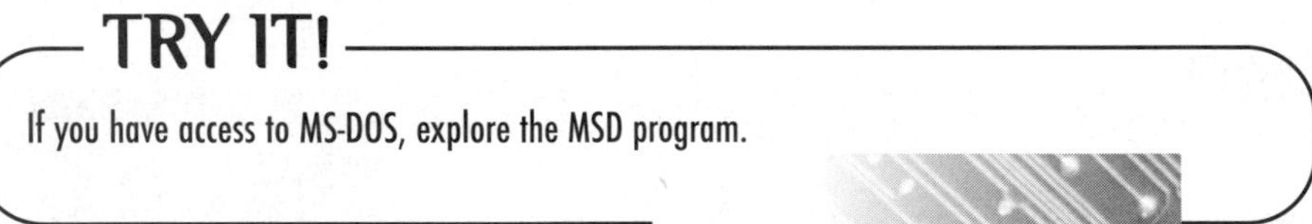

TRY IT!
If you have access to MS-DOS, explore the MSD program.


## Windows Utilities

Now look at the utilities in Windows that provide disk information.

### *My Computer*

The *My Computer* icon on the desktop opens a window containing icons for all of the drives on the system. To view a drive's properties from this window, right-click the drive and choose Properties. The Properties box that appears is a rich source of information about that drive (see Figure 12.32). The Properties box may vary in different Windows versions; Windows 2000 is shown in the figure.

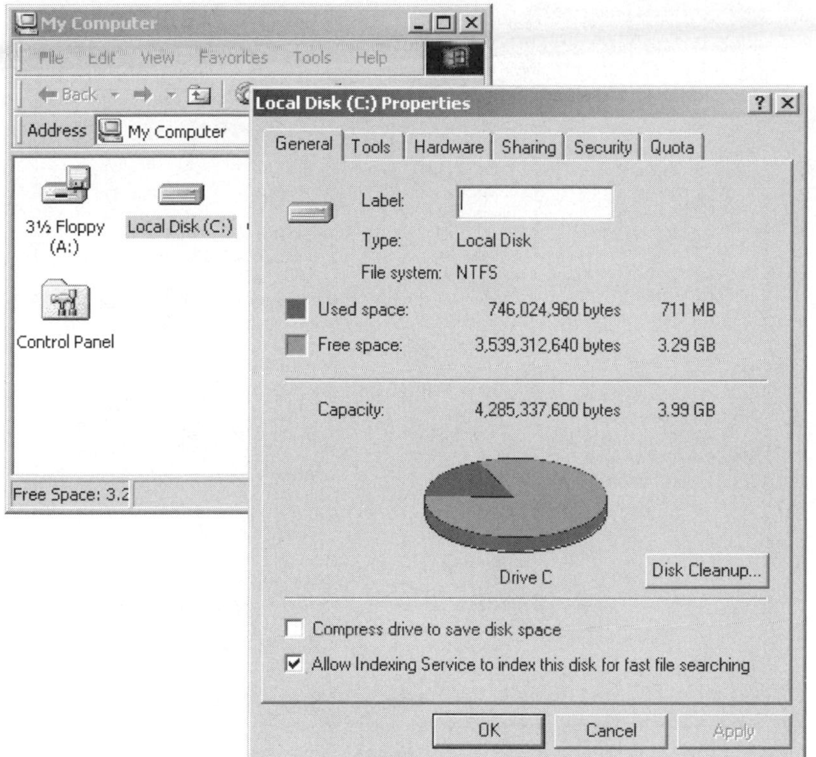


**FIGURE 12.32**
View a drive's properties through My Computer.

## TRY IT!

From the drive's properties in My Computer, determine which file system your C drive uses.

### *System Information*

System Information is the Windows equivalent of MSD in DOS. It provides detailed information about all aspects of the PC, including disks, video, CPU, memory, ports, and so on. To access it, choose Start, Programs, Accessories, System Tools, and System Information. It is slightly different in the various Windows versions; Figure 12.33 shows Windows 2000. The drive information is under the Components/Storage/Drives category. Navigate through the folder pane at the left to get to it.

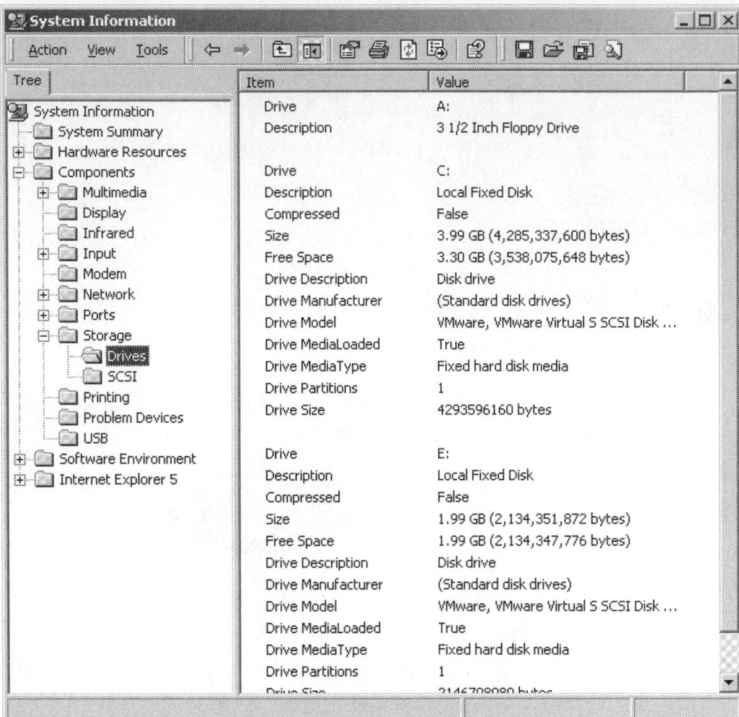


**FIGURE 12.33**
System Information provides information about the entire system.

## TRY IT!

**Using System Information, determine the total size of your C drive and the amount of free space remaining on it.**

### *Disk Management*

Disk Management is available only in NT-based Windows versions. It is an offshoot of a larger utility called Computer Management which we will cover in more detail in later chapters. To start Disk Management, select Administrative Tools on the Control Panel, double-click Computer Management, and then click Disk Management in the window's folder tree. Disk Management shows each logical drive on each partition and each physical drive, and tells its overall capacity, free space, and status (see Figure 12.34).

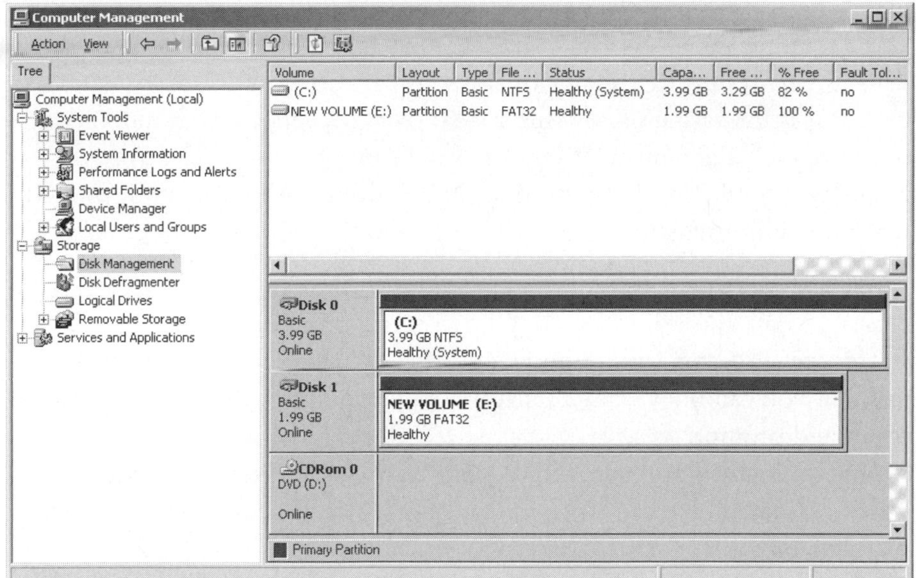


**FIGURE 12.34**
Disk Management provides basic information about each drive.

The Computer Management utility, as you can see in Figure 12.34, is a much more feature-rich program than is being covered here. You can access System Information from its folder tree, for example, rather than from the Start menu as already described. You might want to explore Computer Management on your own; we will be covering it in more detail later in the book.

**TRY IT!**

Using Disk Management, identify which drive is your System drive and which is your Boot drive. They may be the same, or they may be different. The System drive is the active partition that boots when the PC starts up. The Boot drive is the one where this version of Windows is installed.

# Troubleshooting Hard Disk Problems

The following sections describe some common problems users experience with hard disks and discuss some possible solutions.

## BIOS Sees Drive but Windows Does Not

If the BIOS sees the drive, the interface is working, so this is not an interface problem. It usually indicates that the drive has not yet been partitioned.

## Windows Sees Drive but Cannot Read It

This usually means that the drive has been partitioned but not formatted, or that it is formatted using a file system that this version of Windows does not recognize. Remember, Windows NT 4 cannot see FAT32 drives, and Windows 95, 98, and Me cannot see NTFS drives. Windows 2000 and XP recognize all formats.

## Not Bootable

In this scenario, you cannot boot MS-DOS or Windows 9x from the hard disk but you can boot from a startup floppy and access the hard disk from a command prompt.

This is usually a problem with one or more of the system files being missing. Remember that MS-DOS and Windows 9x require that IO.SYS, MSDOS.SYS, and COMMAND.COM all be present in the root directory of a bootable disk. The first two are hidden system files, but COMMAND.COM is not, and it can be accidentally deleted fairly easily.

You can manually copy COMMAND.COM from your startup floppy to the hard disk, but if IO.SYS and/or MSDOS.SYS are missing, they cannot be manually copied. The best way to transfer the system files is with the SYS command. To transfer from the A drive to the C drive, for example, you would make sure that the A drive contained a bootable disk created with the same OS version as the one you want on the hard disk, and then key this command from the A:\> command prompt:

**SYS C:**

For Windows NT/2000/XP, since you cannot boot to a command prompt, you cannot follow the above procedure. The best way to repair a nonbootable disk with one of these Windows versions is to boot from the setup CD for the OS and use the Repair Windows feature.

## Data Errors Reading or Writing Disk

The exact wording of this error message varies depending on the OS version. At a command prompt it will be *Data error reading drive {letter}:*. In Windows it might be *Cannot read from specified disk*. In either case it means that the drive's read/write head cannot read a specific physical spot on the disk because of damage.

In many cases, whatever file was stored in the damaged area is now unretrievable. However, sometimes you can manage a retrieval by running a disk repair utility such as Scandisk or Check Disk (or a third-party program such as Norton Disk Doctor). These programs typically have two modes:

Standard or Thorough. The Standard check looks only for logical errors, but what you want in this case is the Thorough check. It may take several hours to perform a full check. The utility looks at each physical sector on the disk and marks any unreadable ones as bad. Then it attempts to extract any data from the bad sectors and relocate it to a good sector. (This is not always possible; it depends on how bad the damage is.) In this way, the utility is sometimes able to restore access to an otherwise lost file.

**WARNING**

**Sometimes a file that is salvaged with a disk utility program turns out to be corrupted. This is because the utility will attempt to keep as much of the file as possible, even if it cannot reconstruct the whole thing. In a data file, that might mean the recovered file contains most of the pages of your document, but with some junk characters and missing text; in a binary file such as an executable program, it probably means that the program will not work at all.**

## Sector Not Found Errors

Whereas a data error means there is a problem with the physical surface of the disk, a sector not found error means there is a problem with the retrieval of data from the disk. This could be due to one of the following causes:

- faulty read/write head
- hard disk identified incorrectly to BIOS Setup with manual user settings
- damaged drive controller
- virus infection

No matter how you look at it, a sector not found error is problematic. Immediately copy as much data from the drive as you can. Then check in BIOS Setup to make sure its settings are appropriate. If they are, do some rigorous testing of the drive with a diagnostic utility program. If all tests come back positive for the physical operation of the drive, repartition and reformat it. Then use it cautiously for a while, and do not store your only copy of any important files on it.

## Loss of Partition Information or Accidental Formatting

The most common cause of the loss of partition information or the loss of the FAT is virus infection. Another is physical drive failure.

There are no mainstream utilities that can recover a lost partition table or FAT, but there are professional utility programs (rather high-priced) that offer this capability if the drive is still physically operable and BIOS Setup is able to see it. One of the best known is Easy Recovery by OnTrack International. See "For More Information" for this chapter on the Internet Resource Center for information about Easy Recovery and its competitors.

If the data on the disk is not critical, the best solution is simply to remove the virus (if there is one) by re-creating the master boot record (with FDISK /MBR at a command prompt or with the FIXMBR command in the Windows 2000 Recovery Console). See Chapter 27 for details about the Recovery Console and correcting errors that cause the PC not to boot.

## Wrong File System for OS

If a particular hard disk is inaccessible under a certain operating system, remember that not all OSes support all file systems. See Table 12.1 for a summary.

| OS | FAT16 | FAT32 | NTFS |
|---|---|---|---|
| MS-DOS | Yes | No | No |
| Windows 95 | Yes | No* | No |
| Windows NT 4 | Yes | No | Yes |
| Windows 98 | Yes | Yes | No |
| Windows 2000 | Yes | Yes | Yes |
| Windows Me | Yes | Yes | No |
| Windows XP | Yes | Yes | Yes |

*Windows 95 versions B and C do recognize FAT32.

**TABLE 12.1**
Supported File Systems by Operating System

## Nonhealthy Disks in Disk Management

In Disk Management, each partition should report a status of Healthy, as shown in Figure 12.34. If you see any other status, there is a problem. The first thing to try in solving the problem is the Reactivate Disk command. Right-click a failed partition and choose Reactivate Disk from the shortcut menu.

If only one partition on the drive reports a condition other than Healthy, and that condition persists after you try reactivating it, you should delete and re-create it. First, copy any data that you want to keep and then right-click the partition and choose Delete. Then re-create it through Disk Management as described earlier in this chapter.

If all of the partitions on the drive report a status other than Healthy, the drive may be defective. If you can still access the volumes or partitions from Windows Explorer, copy any files you want to keep and then replace the drive.

# STUDY GUIDE

Use the following summaries to review the key concepts of this chapter.

## UNDERSTANDING FILE STORAGE HIERARCHY

- The highest level of organization is the physical disk. Within the physical disk are partitions; within partitions are logical drives; within logical drives are directories, also called folders; and within directories are other directories, and also files.
- Directories are actually database files that list the names, properties, and locations of files. Files appear to be "in" a directory through the operating system interface.
- Operating systems support multiple layers of directories, so a file's location can potentially be many levels deep in the directory structure.

## FLOPPY DISK MANAGEMENT

- Standard floppy disks are 3.5-inch double-sided high-density, and hold 1.44MB of data. The earlier version of the 3.5-inch disk was double-density and held 720KB of data.
- Older style 5.25-inch disks can be either double-density and hold 360KB or high-density and hold 1.2MB.
- To write-protect a 3.5-inch floppy disk, slide the tab on the disk so the hole is exposed.
- To format a floppy disk use the FORMAT command at a command prompt or right-click the drive in My Computer in Windows and choose Format.
- Store floppy disks away from magnets. Keep them out of extreme heat and cold and avoid getting them wet.

## PARTITIONING A DRIVE

- For Windows 9x and DOS, use the FDISK program to create and manage partitions.
- With FDISK you can create a single primary partition containing a single logical drive, and an optional extended partition with one or more logical drives.
- The version of FDISK that comes with Windows 98 and higher includes FAT32 support. When you start up FDISK, answer Yes to the question about enabling large disk support to get FAT32 partitions.

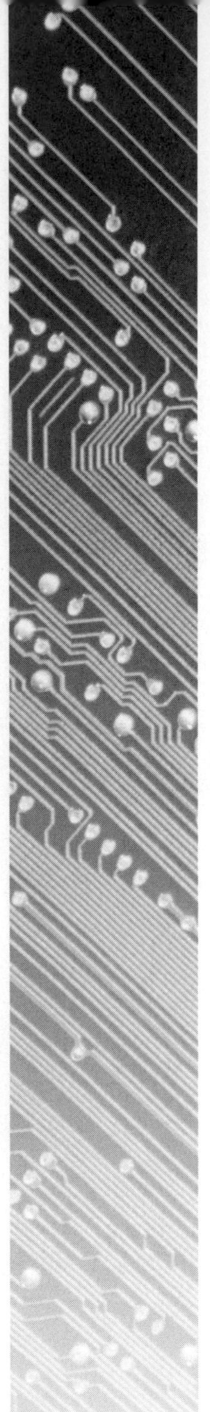

- First create the primary partition, then create the extended partition, and then create the logical drives on the extended partition.
- When deleting, work in the reverse order: first delete logical drives from the extended partition, then delete the extended partition, and then delete the primary partition.
- One partition must be made active in order to be bootable. Usually this is the primary partition.
- To format a hard drive use the FORMAT command at a command prompt, or right-click the drive in My Computer in Windows and choose Format.
- Windows NT, 2000, and XP require you to do your partitioning and formatting from within Windows (using the Disk Management utility) or from the Windows setup program.
- In Disk Management, right-click unpartitioned space on a drive and choose Create Partition.

## Examining Disk Properties

- The DIR command, keyed at a prompt, displays the content of the active directory, the amount of space the content occupies, and the available remaining space on the drive.
- The CHKDSK command, keyed at a prompt, displays information about disk size, usage, and allocation unit size.
- The MSD command, available only in MS-DOS, displays general system information, including information about the disks. It is the equivalent of System Information in Windows.
- View a drive's properties through My Computer in Windows by right-clicking and choosing Properties.
- System Information provides detailed system data, including drive information. Choose Start, Programs, Accessories, System Tools, and System Information.
- Disk Management is a subprogram within Computer Management, available only in NT-based Windows versions. It shows information about each disk, partition, and logical drive, and enables you to partition and format them.

## Troubleshooting Hard Disk Problems

- If the BIOS sees the drive, the interface is working. A drive that appears in BIOS Setup but not in Windows is probably not partitioned.

- If Windows sees a drive icon but cannot read the drive, the drive is probably not formatted or uses a file system that this version of Windows does not recognize.
- A hard disk that is not bootable has lost some of its essential boot or operating system files. For Windows 9x it needs IO.SYS, MSDOS.SYS, and COMMAND.COM.
- For Windows NT, 2000, or XP, boot from the Windows Setup CD and use the Repair Windows feature.
- Data errors indicate a physical problem with the surface of the disk. Check the disk for errors using Scandisk or Check Disk with the Thorough option turned on.
- A sector not found error message indicates bad BIOS description of the drive, a damaged controller or read/write head, or a virus infection.
- A drive that is unreadable due to FAT corruption probably has a virus.
- Professional data recovery services can retrieve data, or you can buy a professional utility program that can rebuild FATs and partition tables.
- Remember that not all Windows versions support all file systems. Refer to Table 12.1 for a sumary.

# PRACTICE TEST

On a blank sheet of paper, write the answers to the following multiple-choice questions and explain why each answer is correct.

1. Which of these can be stored in a directory?
   a. file
   b. directory
   c. partition
   d. both a and b

2. What is the relationship between folders and directories?
   a. A folder can be stored in a directory but not vice versa.
   b. A directory can be stored in a folder but not vice versa.
   c. Folders must be subordinate to directories in the hierarchy.
   d. They are the same thing.

3. If a command prompt appears as C:\Windows\System\Backup>, what is the active directory?
   a. Windows
   b. root directory
   c. Backup
   d. System

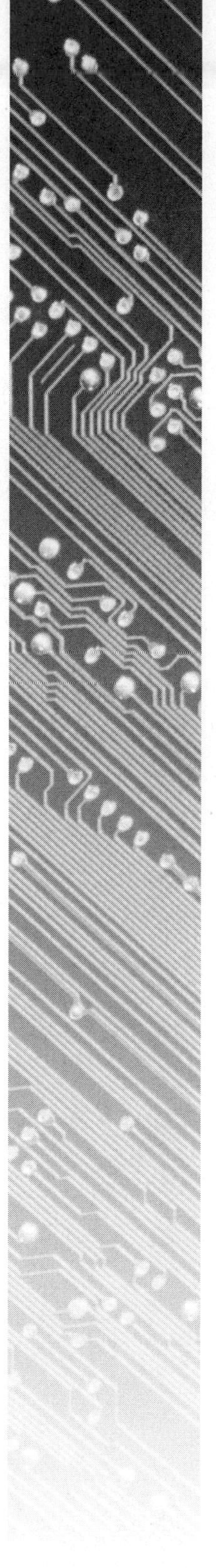

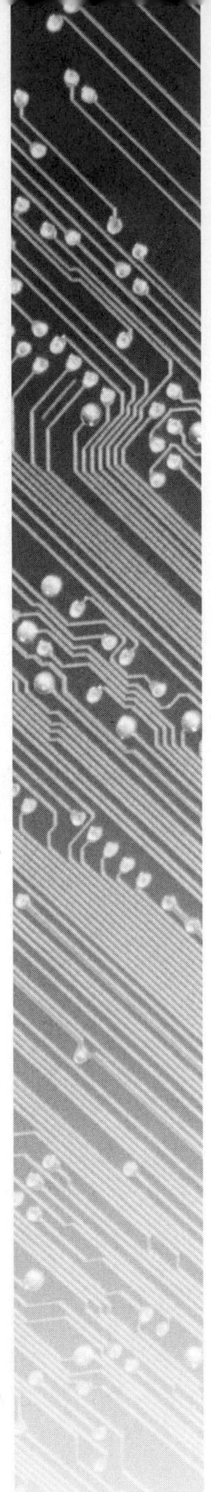

4. Which type of floppy disk has square holes in two of its corners, one of which is covered with a sliding tab?
   a. 3.5-inch high-density
   b. 3.5-inch double-density
   c. 5.25-inch high-density
   d. both a and b
5. On a 5.25-inch disk, the disk is write-protected when the notch in its side it is
   a. exposed.
   b. covered with a sticker.
   c. nonexistent.
   d. It does not matter; the notch has nothing to do with write-protection.
6. What command can you use to format the disk in drive A using quick formatting?
   a. FORMAT /Q A:
   b. FORMAT A: Q
   c. FORMAT A: /Q
   d. FORMAT C: A: /DEFAULT
7. What command starts FDISK?
   a. FDISK
   b. FDISK /Q
   c. FDISK E:
   d. FDISK /FMT
8. What does it mean if the Change current fixed disk drive option does not appear on FDISK's main menu?
   a. You are using an older version of FDISK.
   b. There is no extended partition defined.
   c. There is only one physical hard disk installed.
   d. It could be either b or c.
9. Under what circumstances does FDISK automatically make a partition active when it creates it?
   a. if it is the primary partition
   b. if it is a primary partition that occupies the entire physical disk
   c. if it is an extended partition
   d. if it is an extended partition with a single logical drive only

10. On a disk that contains an extended partition with several logical drives, what would you need to do to change the size of the extended partition through FDISK?
    a. delete the logical drives and then resize the partition
    b. delete the logical drives and then delete the extended partition and re-create it
    c. resize the partition; deleting the drives is not necessary
    d. delete the primary partition

11. When creating a partition of less than the maximum size with FDISK, you specify the size you want in
    a. megabytes.
    b. a percentage of the available space.
    c. sectors.
    d. either a or b

12. What does the /Q switch do when formatting a hard disk?
    a. It skips the low-level format.
    b. It skips checking of individual clusters for readability.
    c. It writes only one copy of the FAT.
    d. None of the above

13. Which is the way to open Disk Management in Windows 2000?
    a. Start, Programs, Accessories, System Tools, Disk Management
    b. Control Panel, Administrative Tools, Computer Management, Disk Management
    c. Control Panel, Computer Management, Disk Management
    d. a or b

14. What are your choices of file systems when formatting a hard disk through Disk Management?
    a. FAT or FAT32
    b. FAT32 or NTFS
    c. FAT or NTFS
    d. FAT, FAT32, or NTFS

15. Which command-line utility can tell you the allocation unit size of a hard disk?
    a. CHKDSK
    b. DIR
    c. SCANDISK
    d. SYSEDIT

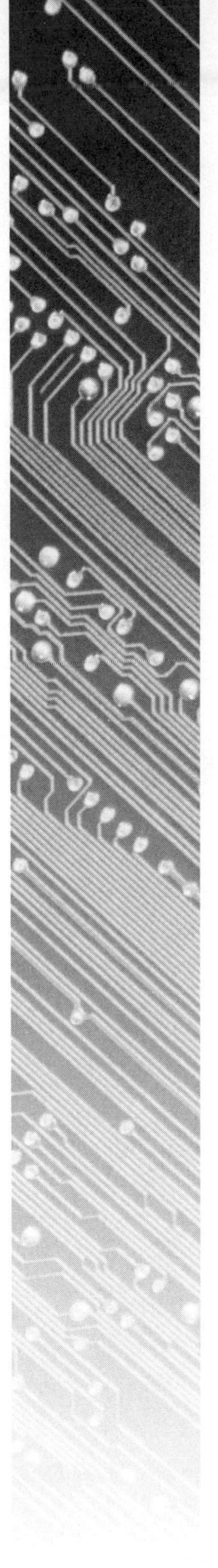

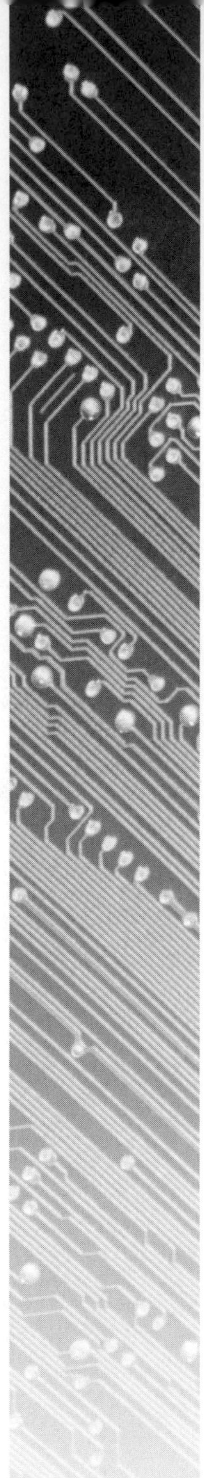

16. What is likely to be the problem with a hard disk visible in BIOS Setup but not in Windows?
    a. not formatted
    b. not partitioned
    c. master/slave jumpers not set correctly
    d. not connected to power supply

17. What is likely to be the problem with a logical drive that shows up as an icon in My Computer but cannot be read?
    a. not formatted
    b. not partitioned
    c. bad sectors
    d. set up improperly in BIOS Setup

18. What utility program can help correct a data error on a drive?
    a. System Information
    b. My Computer
    c. System Utility
    d. Scandisk

19. Which file systems are supported by Windows 95 (original release)?
    a. FAT and FAT32
    b. FAT32 and NTFS
    c. FAT, FAT32, and NTFS
    d. FAT only

20. Which file systems are supported by Windows NT 4?
    a. FAT and NTFS
    b. FAT32 and NTFS
    c. FAT, FAT32, and NTFS
    d. FAT only

# TROUBLESHOOTING

1. A client has mistreated a floppy disk, and now he is getting data error messages when he tries to read from it. What can you do that might help him retrieve the data?
2. A client has been playing around with FDISK and has accidentally deleted her primary partition. What questions will you ask, and what options will you recommend based on those answers?
3. You have just created a primary partition on a new hard disk and formatted it as FAT32 using a Windows 98 startup disk. Now you want to install Windows 95 on it, but the setup program does not see the drive. What is going on?

# CUSTOMER SERVICE

1. A client calls you complaining that she gets an Access Denied message when she tries to copy a file to a floppy disk. The disk is not full. What can you recommend that she check?
2. A client is having major system problems, and needs to reinstall Windows 2000. He has an old Windows 98 startup disk, and wonders whether he needs to reformat his drive with it first. What do you tell him?
3. A client who has just upgraded from MS-DOS to Windows Me complains that the CHKDSK /F command no longer works to repair FAT errors. What can you suggest as an alternative?

# FOR MORE INFORMATION

For links to Web sites that provide further information about the topics covered in this chapter, go to the EMC/Paradigm Internet Resource Center at www.emcp.com/College Division/Internet Resource Centers/PC Maintenance/For More Information.

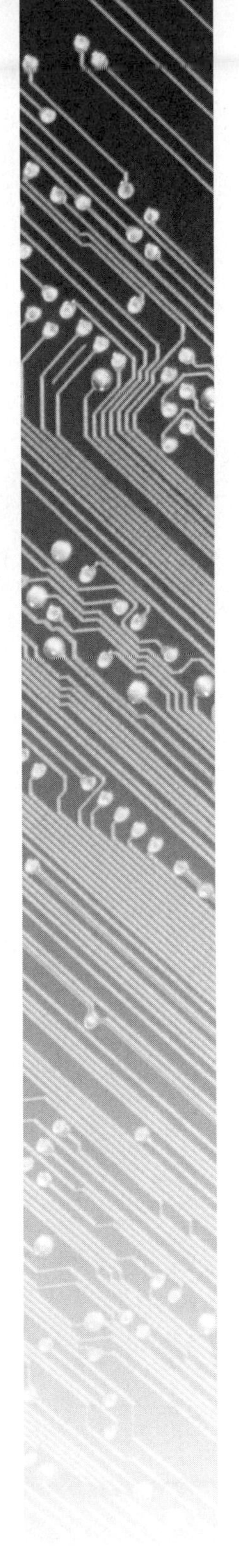

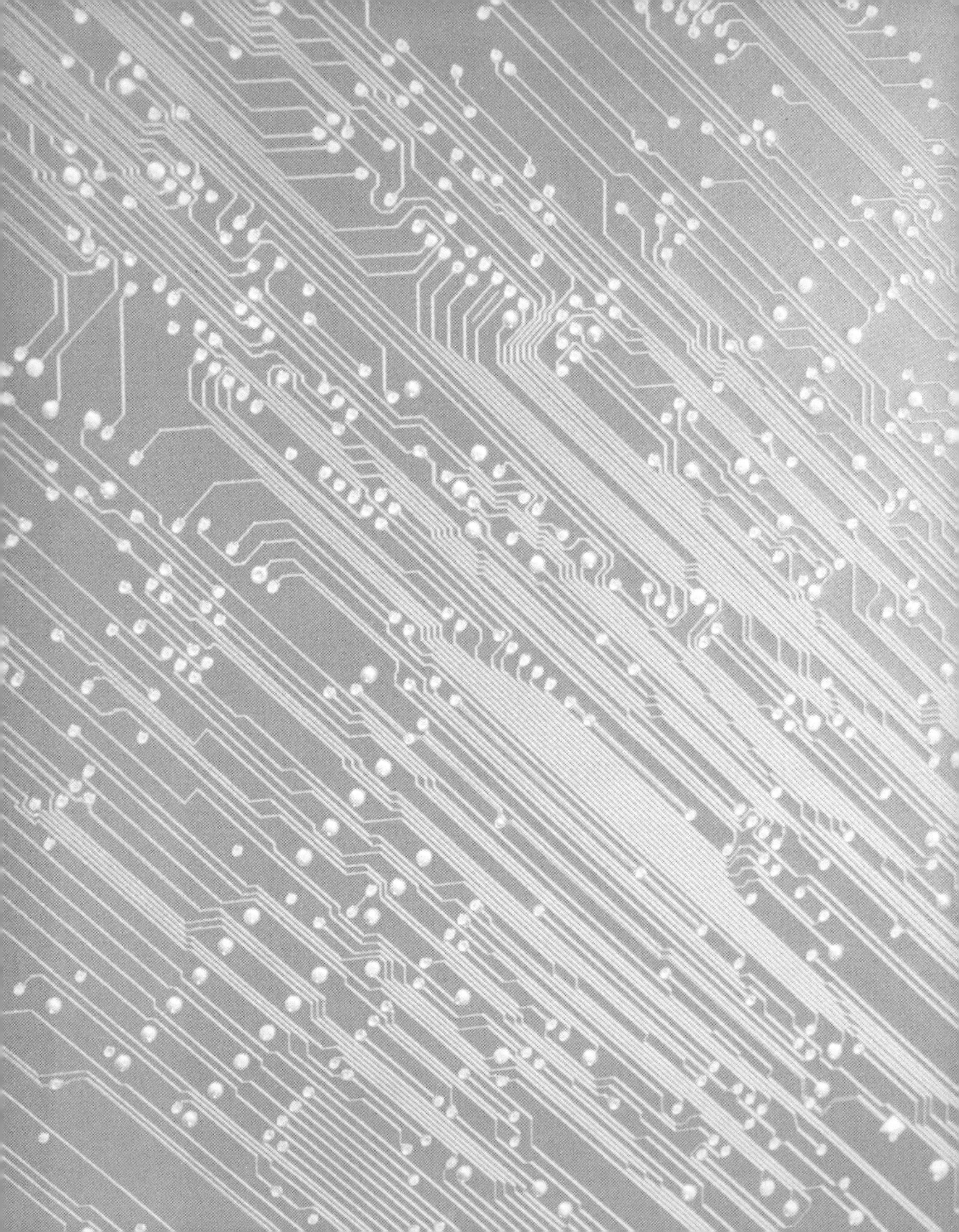

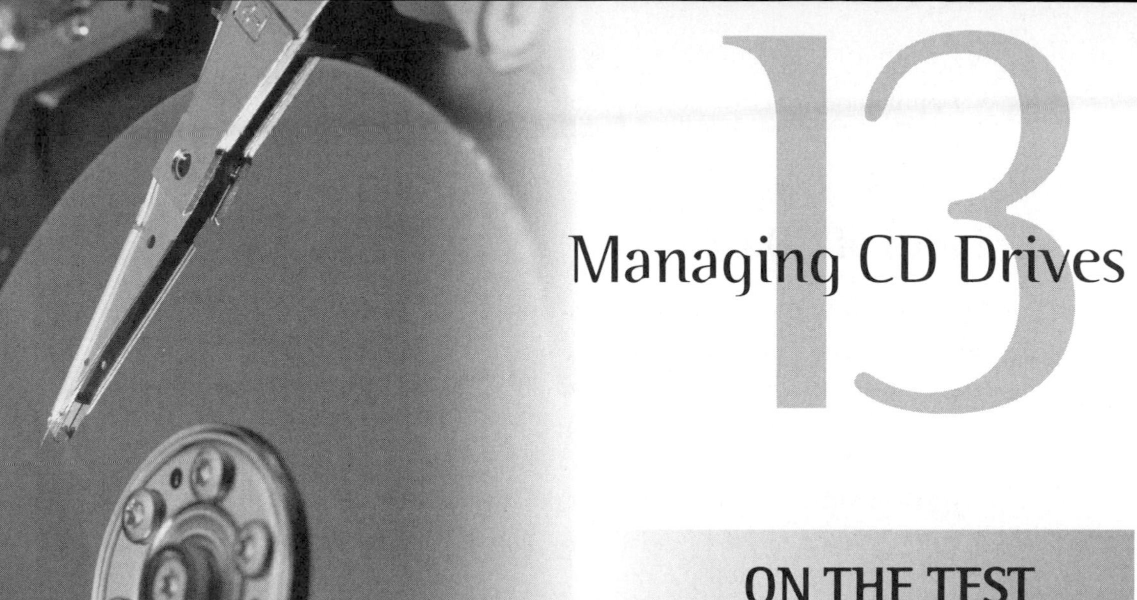

# 13 Managing CD Drives

## ON THE TEST

**A+ Core Hardware Technician Examination**

- **Objective 1.1:** Identify basic terms, concepts, and functions of system modules, including how each module should work during normal operation and during the boot process.
- **Objective 1.2:** Identify basic procedures for adding and removing field replaceable modules for both desktop and portable systems.
- **Objective 2.1:** Identify common symptoms and problems associated with each module and how to troubleshoot and isolate the problems.

**A+ Operating System Technologies Examination**

- **Objective 1.1:** Identify the operating system's functions, structure, and major system files to navigate the operating system and how to get to needed technical information.

## ON THE JOB

Almost every PC has at least one CD drive, so everyone knows how to use one—you just put in the disk. Fewer people actually understand how the CD drive works. As a PC technician you must understand the technology so you can separate major problems from minor ones and select and install the appropriate drives and discs for particular tasks.

Some of the real-world activities you might perform that pertain to this chapter include:

- choosing an appropriate CD drive for a client
- installing a CD-ROM drive
- installing a recordable CD drive
- selecting blank CDs for a writable drive
- installing a DVD drive

- troubleshooting drive access problems
- troubleshooting problems playing DVD movies
- creating a bootable CD

## Types of CD Drives

All CD drives look the same from the outside (except for the writing on them, of course), but inside there are several very different types of operation.

**Recordable CD (CD-R)**

A CD that can be written to once using a CD burning program.

**Rewritable CD (CD-RW)**

A CD that can be written and rewritten multiple times with a packet-writing CD writing program.

- A standard CD-ROM drive is a read-only drive that plays only regular CDs.
- A DVD drive plays both DVDs and regular CDs.
- A *recordable CD* drive (CD-R) is able to write to CD-R discs, to which you can write only once and cannot edit or erase.
- A *rewritable CD* drive (CD-RW) is able to write to CD-RW discs, which can be rewritten multiple times.

New technologies for recordable and rewritable DVDs are now emerging; there is no industry consensus as of this writing, and these are not covered on the A+ examination.

## CD Performance Factors

In the Chapter 10 section on optical storage, you learned that a CD-ROM stores data in patterns of pits (areas of less reflectivity) and land (areas of great reflectivity). A laser bounces off the CD surface and the amount of light bouncing back is measured by a sensor. When the sensor detects a transition, it sends a 1 bit to the drive controller. When it detects no transition, it sends nothing, which is interpreted as a 0 bit.

The performance of a CD drive, then, depends on the following factors. These factors are advertised in a CD drive's specifications, so you can use them when shopping for a drive.

### Speed (X)

**Data transfer rate**

The rate at which data can be read from a drive.

The *X* represents the drive's speed, the theoretical maximum *data transfer rate* for that drive. It also refers to the rotation speed of the disc, because the data transfer rate is determined by how fast the disc whizzes by the read head. (There is a little more to it than that, as we will discuss shortly.)

The original CD-ROM drives (1X) read 75 2,048-byte sectors of data per second, which comes out to 150Kbps. Drive speeds have advanced in multiples of 150Kbps. To determine a drive's maximum data transfer rate, multiply its X rating by 150Kbps. A 2X drive, for example, reads 150 2,048-byte sectors per second, for a rate of 300Kbps, while a 4X reads 300 sectors for a rate of 600Kbps.

Data transfer rate is only a theoretical measurement for a drive because no drive actually achieves its rated transfer rate in sustained performance. When a program calls for something to be read from the disc, it must start spinning and get up to speed, and the read head must move in and out to find the spot on the disc where the needed data resides. The actual speed when reading a certain spot on the disc also depends on whether the drive is CLV or CAV, to be discussed shortly.

## IN REAL LIFE

**A new technology is emerging called TrueX/Multibeam that uses several laser read heads to read more data at a time than on a normal CD-ROM. Since these drives read more data per rotation of the disc, their data transfer rate and their rotation speed are not the same.**

## ACCESS TIME

*Access time* is the amount of time that elapses between a PC's request for data from a CD drive and the drive's delivery of the first of that information. It is mostly a measure of the drive's mechanical ability to move the read head to the correct spot. Access time is not directly related to the drive's speed (X), although drives with faster speeds tend also to have superior mechanics inside that allow for better access time.

**Access time**

The delay between a request for data and the delivery of that data from a drive.

A 1X drive has a typical access time of around 400 milliseconds (ms). Today's best-performing drives have an access time of around 75ms.

## CLV VERSUS CAV

Two technologies are used for CD drives: *constant linear velocity* (CLV) and *constant angular velocity* (CAV). Generally speaking, CLV is found in older regular CD-ROM drives and in multipurpose drives such as CD-RW, while CAV is in newer regular CD-ROM drives.

**Constant linear velocity (CLV)**

A method of recording and reading data from a CD in which the amount of data read/written remains constant. The CD spins faster or slower as needed.

All CD data is recorded using CLV. No matter what spot is being recorded on the disc, it is recorded at the same area per second. When recording near the center of the disc, the drive must spin faster because there is less area to be covered there. As the recording reaches the outside of the disc, the drive must slow down. If you have a CD-R or CD-RW drive that also plays CDs, it plays them using CLV. A CLV drive has a single speed measurement, such as 8X, 16X, and so on, because the amount of data it reads per second does not vary. (The actual rotation of the disc—in revolutions per minute, or RPM—does vary.)

**Constant angular velocity (CAV)**

A method of reading data from a CD in which the CD's spin rate remains constant. The amount of data read changes depending on the area being read.

Most of the higher speed regular CD-ROM drives sold today play CDs at CAV, which means that the CD rotates at a constant speed or RPM, and the amount of data being read per second varies depending on the spot on the disc from which data is being read. Since these drives do not have a single data transfer rate, they cannot have a single, accurate X rating either, so you will often see them advertised with two X ratings, a minimum and a maximum, such as 28X/32X. The smaller number is the data transfer rate at the center of the disc; the larger number is the rate for the outside edge. Such drives almost never achieve their top speed, however, because data on a CD is written from the inside to the outside, and most CDs are blank at the outer edge.

CAV is typically found in drives 12X and above, and almost all 16X and above drives sold today are CAV. If you see a single speed rating for a drive above 16X, it probably refers to the highest speed for that drive, with the lower number omitted for marketing purposes. However, CLV drives are available up to 48X, though they are not common, so read the entire drive specification to be sure. High-speed CLV drives tend to be noisier and more expensive than comparable CAV drives.

## Other Performance Factors

Two major determinants of a drive's performance are its rotation speed (X) and its access time. In real-world use, however, several other factors play a part, as noted in Figure 13.1.

- **Drive Interface Type:** Traditionally SCSI interface has been considered superior to IDE for all types of drives, but recent advancements in IDE technology have helped level the playing field in drive performance. SCSI still has a slim advantage because of its decreased CPU utilization. There are various types of SCSI interfaces for CD, from the low-cost SCSI-3 to the top-of-the-line Ultra2 Wide. Low-end SCSI is appropriate for ordinary CD-ROM, while higher end SCSI would be advantageous for CD-R or CD-RW (see Chapter 11). Portable CD drives are also available with parallel or USB interfaces. Parallel is very slow; USB is very fast.
- **Competition for Interface Bandwidth:** If the CD drive shares an IDE subsystem (they are on the same cable) with another IDE device that gets heavy use, such as the main hard disk, you might experience performance problems with the CD drive, especially in time-critical applications like CD-R or playback of DVD movies. When feasible, place the CD drive on an IDE cable by itself for best performance.
- **Drive Cache:** The larger the size of the built-in cache (also called a buffer) in the CD drive, the less it needs to reread data from the disc when subsequent requests are made for the same data. A good drive should have at least a 512KB cache.

**FIGURE 13.1**
Factors Determining Drive Performance

*continued*

- **CPU Usage:** Drives vary as to how much of the computer's processing time they require to do their jobs (less is better). In very broad terms:
  - SCSI is better than IDE because SCSI operates more independently of the processor.
  - CLV is better than CAV because CLV uses a modest fixed amount of processor time while CAV varies widely from very little (at the center of the disc) to a great deal (at the outer part of the disc).
  - A large drive cache helps minimize CPU usage.
- DMA Usage: *Direct Memory Addressing* (DMA) is a method of drive access in which the drive communicates directly with the operating system, bypassing the processor whenever possible to improve performance. It requires a bus mastering IDE controller. Turning on DMA in the CD drive's properties in the operating system can enable it, but first make sure that the hardware is capable. Chapter 14 talks more about DMA and other device resources.

**Direct Memory Addressing (DMA)**

A drive access method that bypasses the CPU to improve performance between the device and RAM.

**FIGURE 13.1**
continued

## TRY IT!

Find out as much information about the CD drive(s) as you can. Read the outside labels and visit the manufacturer's Web site to get technical specs. For each drive, what is the data transfer rate? The access speed? Is it CLV or CAV?

# Installing a CD Drive

Installing an internal CD drive is similar to installing a hard drive (see Chapter 11). CD drives are IDE or SCSI, so their physical installation is the same as that for any drive. The following section presents a brief review. Look at Chapter 11 for more help if needed.

## Installing an IDE CD Drive

Most CD drives that you buy in retail stores are IDE. As mentioned, IDE devices are less expensive and do not require separate controller boards. To install an IDE CD drive, complete the following steps:

1. Remove the cover from the PC.
2. Prepare a drive bay to accept the drive. All CD drives use large external drive bays.
3. Select an IDE position for the drive from among the available options using these guidelines:
   a. If there is only one IDE device installed already (primary master only), make the new CD drive the secondary master.
   b. If there are already a primary master and secondary master, put the CD drive on the cable with the drive that gets less use.

c. If installing a writable or rewritable CD (CD-R or CD-RW), avoid placing it on the same cable as the primary hard drive or a CD drive from which you will be reading when copying CDs. If you move existing IDE devices around, make sure you remember to change their Master/Slave jumpers.

d. If all four IDE positions are already occupied, buy and install an IDE controller expansion board.

4. Set the Master/Slave jumper for the CD drive based on the position you chose in step 3.
5. Place the new drive in the drive bay but do not yet secure it with screws.
6. Attach the ribbon cable to the drive with the red stripe to Pin 1 (the end closest to the power supply plug on most drives).
7. If this is the first IDE device on this ribbon cable, connect the other end of the ribbon cable to the motherboard (or IDE expansion board).
8. Attach a Molex power connector to the drive from the power supply.
9. If audio CDs will be played on this CD drive, run an audio cable from the drive to the sound card (or to the motherboard if the sound card is built into it). You might need to buy an audio cable at a local computer or electronics store. Figure 13.2 shows the connectors on an audio cable and the spots where they plug into the drive and the sound card.

**FIGURE 13.2**
An audio cable makes it possible to play audio CDs through the sound card.

## In Real Life

There may be two connectors on the CD drive for audio cables, one for analog and one for digital audio, as shown in Figure 13.2. The analog connector has four pins. Not all sound cards support the use of the digital audio connector.

10. Adjust the drive in the bay so that its front aligns with the outside of the PC, and then attach screws to hold it in place.
11. Turn on the PC and enter BIOS Setup to check that it recognizes the new IDE device. If it does not, check the BIOS setting for the IDE position. Try setting it to Auto, or to CD-ROM or ATAPI. If the BIOS Setup has a Detect IDE command, run it.
12. After you get the CD drive recognized in BIOS, reboot and refer to the section "Controlling a CD Drive through the OS."

## TRY IT!

Install an IDE CD drive in your PC.

## Installing a SCSI CD Drive

SCSI CD drives are not as common as IDE CD drives, but they are good performers, especially for writable/rewritable operations. They require less CPU utilization and they share their interface better with other devices of the same type than IDE devices do.

To install a SCSI CD drive, complete the following steps:

1. Remove the cover from the PC.
2. Prepare a drive bay to accept the drive. All CD drives use large external drive bays.
3. If this is the first SCSI device you are installing, install a SCSI expansion board and attach a SCSI ribbon cable to it. Make sure the cable has the right type of connector to match the drive; install an adapter if needed.
4. Select an unused SCSI ID number and set the jumpers on the drive for that ID (see Chapter 11).
5. If this will be the last device on the SCSI chain, terminate it (again, refer to Chapter 11).
6. Place the new drive in the drive bay but do not yet secure it with screws.

7. Attach the ribbon cable to the drive with the red stripe to Pin 1 (the end closest to the power supply plug on most drives).
8. Attach a Molex power connector to the drive from the power supply.
9. If audio CDs will be played on this CD drive, run an audio cable from the drive to the sound card. (Check step 9 in the previous section for more details.)
10. Adjust the drive in the bay so that its front aligns with the outside of the PC, and then attach screws to hold it in place.
11. Turn on the PC and watch the screen for a message indicating that the SCSI controller sees the new drive.

### IN REAL LIFE

Some SCSI controller boards have their own BIOS Setup that you can enter by pressing whatever key is indicated in the on-screen message at startup. If this board has one, you can enter it and check the status of the CD drive from there.

12. See the next section to set up the CD drive in the OS.

### TRY IT!

Install a SCSI CD drive in your PC.

## Controlling a CD Drive through the OS

In order for the operating system to see and use a CD drive, a driver for the drive must be loaded into memory. In Windows 95 and higher, this driver loads automatically when Windows loads, so you do not need to worry about installing it. However, if you are working with MS-DOS, or are booting from a Windows 9x Startup floppy disk, a real-mode CD driver must be installed.

Windows 98 and Windows Me make startup disks that contain generic real-mode CD drivers for both IDE and SCSI drives, and when you boot from one of those startup disks, the drivers load automatically. However, a Windows 95 Startup disk does not contain these, so you must manually edit a Windows 95 Startup floppy to add them.

The reason the manual edit is needed is that when CD drives were first introduced, there was little standardization. Each CD drive came with a floppy disk containing its own real-mode driver file, and you could not interchange them. So when Windows 95 was introduced, it was assumed that the user would need to copy the driver file for the exact model of CD drive to the startup disk. But as the technology matured, standardization prevailed and generic drivers were able to work for almost all drives, so Microsoft decided to incorporate those generic drivers into the startup disks.

## Commands for Real-Mode CD Driver Installation

To enable the CD drive at a command prompt in MS-DOS or from a Windows 95 Startup floppy disk, you must add the following lines to the startup files:

- To CONFIG.SYS: **DEVICE={driver} /D:{name}**
- To AUTOEXEC.BAT: **MSCDEX.EXE /D:{name}**

The first line loads the real-mode driver for the CD drive, and assigns the drive a name specified in the {name} parameter. So, for example, it might look like this:

DEVICE=SSCDROM.SYS /D:SSCD000

The second line loads the Microsoft CD drive utility, called MSCDEX, and references the same name as was assigned in the first one, so it might look like this:

MSCDEX /D:SSCD000

Depending on the location of the CDROM.SYS and MSCDEX.EXE files, you might need to add the path information to the command lines to specify the drive and directory. For example, if the CDROM.SYS file was located in the *C:\DRIVERS* folder, the command would be:

DEVICE=C:\DRIVERS\SSCDROM.SYS /D:SSCD000

If the MSECDEX command was in the *C:\DOS* folder, the command would be:

C:\DOS\MSCDEX /D:SSCD000

There are other parameters and switches you can add to these commands, but you will not need them for normal operation.

One challenge is to find a real-mode CD driver for the drive. You can try visiting the drive manufacturer's Web site to see whether one is available for download. The drive might also have come with a floppy disk containing the driver.

If you have a setup program for the drive (such as on a floppy), running it will add the aforementioned lines to CONFIG.SYS and AUTOEXEC.BAT automatically so you do not have to edit those files yourself. See the next section if you need to do that editing manually. You will need to manually edit if you plan on adding CD support to a Windows 95 Startup disk, for example, because the setup program would assume you wanted the driver installed on your hard disk, but you would want to put it on the startup files on the floppy disk instead.

In the Chapter 6 section on examining and optimizing memory usage, you learned about using the Loadhigh or LH command before an AUTOEXEC.BAT line to load the program into high memory. You can do this with MSCDEX. You can use the DEVICEHIGH prefix in CONFIG.SYS with the CD driver to load it high as well. However, this would be an issue primarily on a system that loaded the real-mode CD driver as part of everyday operation (such as a MS-DOS system); most people would not bother with it on an emergency startup disk.

## Adding CD Support to a Windows 95 Startup Disk

To make a Windows 95 Startup disk load the real-mode CD driver, you must edit the CONFIG.SYS and AUTOEXEC.BAT files in a text editor program. MS-DOS comes with a program called EDIT that works for this purpose, and Windows 95 itself comes with Notepad. You can use either one.

To add a real-mode CD driver to a Windows 95 Startup disk, complete the following steps:

1. Locate and copy the MSCDEX.EXE file to the floppy disk. Use the Find command in Windows if needed to locate it. Two likely places to look for it are the *C:\Windows\Command* folder and the *C:\DOS* folder. Refer to Chapter 29 if you need help on how to locate and copy files.
2. Locate and copy a real-mode CD driver to the floppy disk. Check the drive manufacturer's Web site if needed. Make a note of the file name; you will need it in the next step.
3. Open the CONFIG.SYS file from the startup floppy disk in a text editing program, and add the following line to the bottom of the file:
   **DEVICE=A:*file* /D:*name***
   You can use any name you want for the *name*. For example, if the CD driver file is called SSCDROM.SYS, and you wanted to use SSCD000 for the name, the line you add would be:
   **DEVICE=A:\SSCDROM.SYS /D:SSCD000**
4. Save your changes to CONFIG.SYS, and open the AUTOEXEC.BAT file from the startup CD in the text editor program.
5. Add the following line to the bottom of the file:
   **A:\MSCDEX.EXE /D:*name***
   Use the same name that you used in step 3.

6. Save your changes and exit the text editor program.
7. Exit Windows and try booting from the floppy disk to make sure that it works.

## TRY IT!

1. Using Notepad in Windows, view the AUTOEXEC.BAT and CONFIG.SYS files on a startup floppy made in Windows 95. Then view the same files on a startup floppy made in Windows 98, and note the differences.
2. Locate a real-mode driver for the CD drive, and add it to the Windows 95 Startup floppy, along with MSCDEX.EXE.
3. Edit the AUTOEXEC.BAT and CONFIG.SYS files on the Windows 95 Startup disk to reference the driver and MSCDEX.EXE.
4. Boot from the Windows 95 Startup floppy and confirm that the CD drive is operational.

# Caring for CDs

Magnets, dirt, and water are the chief enemies of floppy disks, but the main reason a CD fails is because its surface gets scratched. Kits are available that can help minimize some scratches, but they do not remove all damage.

The best way to preserve the life of an important CD is to keep its surface away from nearly everything. Here are some tips on preserving CDs.

- Keep CDs in protective jewel cases or paper sleeves when not in use.
- Never set a CD face-down on anything except a CD drive tray.
- Touch a CD only by the edges or on the top (the side with the label), never on the underside.
- If a CD gets dusty, blow it off with compressed air. Wiping it off with a cloth will clean it, but is not the best method because the cloth might rub the dust particles across the surface and scratch it. If you must touch the surface with a cloth, make it the softest, most lint-free cloth you can find, and move the cloth around the circle rather than from center to edge.
- If a CD requires cleaning with liquid (for example, if you spill fruit juice on it or it falls into a mud puddle), wash it off with a lot of water and let the water carry away as much of the dirt as possible before you touch it with any kind of towel. You can use a mild dishwashing detergent if needed.

## TRY IT!

Check your CD collection to make sure all CDs are stored properly to avoid damage.

# DVD

**DVD**

A high-capacity optical CD used for storing large amounts of data or video movies.

*DVD* stands for Digital Versatile Disc (for data storage) or Digital Video Disc (for movies). The most popular use for a DVD is as a storage medium for movies, but data DVDs also exist and are becoming more common.

DVD is basically an enhanced version of CD, technologically speaking. CD data is stored in patterns of pitted and unpitted ("land") areas on a disc. DVD data is stored the same way, except the pits are much smaller and closer together. That is why CDs have a maximum of about 650–700MB of data, while DVDs can hold multiple gigabytes. Since the pits are more tightly written on a DVD, the mechanism in the drive for reading them has to be finer and more precise, which is the main reason why DVD drives cost more than CD drives. DVD drives can also read regular CD discs with no difficulty, since the difference is mostly in the spacing.

How much data does a DVD hold? With a single-sided, single-layer disc of the same thickness as a normal CD (120mm), it is 4.7GB of data or 135 minutes of video. (That is the DVD-5 standard.) If the disc is double-sided (DVD-10), that capacity can be doubled to 9.4GB or 270 minutes.

The DVD standard makers also have figured out another way to squeeze more data onto a disc—they record it in two layers. The top layer is semireflective, so the read laser can pass through it to read the second layer of data beneath it. This does not exactly double the amount of data, but it comes close: a two-layer disc (DVD-9) can hold 8.5GB. Combine the two methods in a double-sided, double-layer disc (DVD-14), and the capacity can go as high as 13.24GB.

What about the standards DVD-1 through DVD-4? Those were earlier standards that used a different thickness of disc (80mm as opposed to the normal 120mm). DVD-1 (single-sided, single-layer) held 1.4GB or a half-hour of video, while DVD-4 (double-sided, double-layer) held 5.3GB or 2.5 hours of video.

## DVD Drive Speeds

DVD drives spin the disc faster and read the data faster than a normal CD drive, so you cannot fairly compare the speeds using X ratings alone.

Earlier in the chapter we discussed how CD speed is measured in relation to the original 1X standard of 150Kbps data transfer rate. Because the data is stored on a CD at a fixed number of bits per area, you can determine the drive's raw speed at reading data from the speed at which the disc rotates. Therefore, a 2X drive would have to spin twice as fast as a 1X drive in order to double the data transfer rate to 300Kbps.

Since the data on a DVD disc is stored so much more compactly, a DVD drive spinning at 1X speed can transfer approximately 1.4Mbps, which makes it roughly equivalent to a regular 9X CD drive. The rates go up from there, with a 16X DVD drive transferring data at about 22Mbps, or faster than a 140X CD drive (if such a drive existed).

However, you cannot just look at DVD transfer rates when evaluating a DVD drive for a system because in reality it will probably be used mostly for regular CD discs, and with those the transfer rate drops back down. A 1X DVD drive spins about three times the speed of a 1X CD drive, so you can approximately triple the advertised X speed on a DVD drive to determine how it will perform with regular CDs. For example, a 16X DVD drive would be equivalent to a 48X CD drive when reading from regular CDs.

## DVD Drives and CD-R/CD-RW Media

A contemporary DVD drive can be used as a regular CD drive, but there are some minor issues with older models. For example, the earliest DVD drives could not read CD-R and CD-RW discs because of the difference in the light wavelength used for reading the discs. Regular CD-ROM drives use a wavelength of 780nm to read disks, the same wavelength required for CD-R and CD-RW discs. But DVD uses a different wavelength of 650nm. Regular mass-produced CD-ROMs are very reflective, and can be read at a variety of wavelengths, so the 650nm is not a problem for them. However, CD-R and CD-RW discs are not as powerfully reflective at other wavelengths, and a 650nm laser has trouble reading them.

Drive manufacturers struggled for a while to overcome this problem, and finally hit upon a two-laser system that blasts each disc with lasers at both 780 and 650nm at once. That way, no matter what type of disc it is, some data will bounce back from the laser that the drive can interpret. Such drives are designated *MultiRead;* almost all DVD drives manufactured today are MultiRead capable.

**MultiRead**

A technology that uses two read lasers with different wavelengths to ensure that the drive can read different types of CDs.

When different types of DVD became available (including writable), the standard underwent a revision, and the result was MultiRead2. A MultiRead2-capable drive can read not only all CD formats (including all writable CDs), but also all DVD formats, including DVD-ROM, DVD-Audio, DVD-Video, and DVD-RAM.

## DVD Drives and MPEG Decoders

**Motion Picture Experts Group (MPEG)**

A standards organization that creates specifications for video technology.

Many people are confused when they buy a DVD drive (or when one comes with their system) about whether a *Motion Picture Experts Group* (MPEG) decoder card is required. It all depends on what the drive will be used for.

If the DVD drive in a PC will be used to play DVD movies, you will need MPEG-2 (usually just called MPEG) decoding capability. If the DVD drive will be used only for data, you will not need that capability. MPEG decoding processes the audio and video data and allows it to play on the PC. When reading data from a DVD data disc, MPEG plays no role.

One type of MPEG decoder is a separate circuit card you install in the PC. Plug the monitor's Video Graphics Adapter (VGA) plug into it rather than into the video card, and then run a pass-through cable from the decoder card to the video card input. Some variants let you connect the monitor directly to the video card, but then an internal cable connects the video card to the MPEG decoder card. While this system takes up system resources (a PCI slot, an IRQ, and so on), it does result in good audio and video playback performance. It also takes most of the processing workload off the main system when playing movies.

An alternative to the separate MPEG decoder card is a video card with MPEG decoding built in. This is more convenient because a separate card (and separate resources) is not required, but the performance can lag behind that of a separate decoder card. In addition, more of the main system resources are consumed when playing a movie, and if it is not a fast system with lots of available RAM, playback performance can suffer.

Another alternative is to employ software-based MPEG decoding that uses a Windows program to simulate the existence of a real decoder card. However, unless the PC is very fast, performance problems can ensue with this solution.

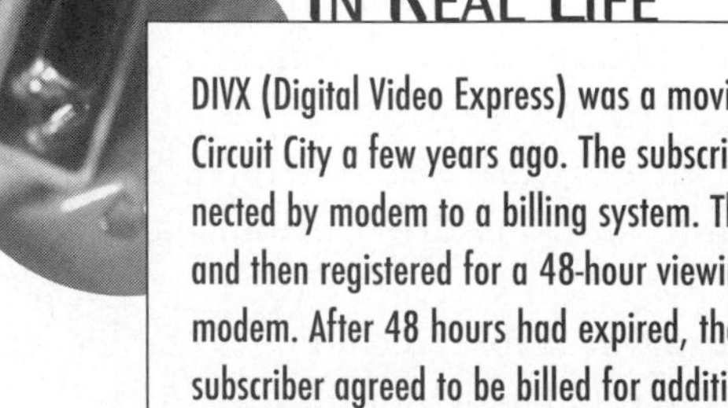

### In Real Life

DIVX (Digital Video Express) was a movie distribution format marketed mainly by Circuit City a few years ago. The subscriber had to buy a special player, which connected by modem to a billing system. The discs would be obtained from Circuit City and then registered for a 48-hour viewing period using the DIVX player and its modem. After 48 hours had expired, the disc would not play anymore unless the subscriber agreed to be billed for additional time or to buy the movie outright. DIVX movies are no longer being distributed; however, a DIVX player can still play regular DVD movies.

## Troubleshooting CD and DVD Drive Problems

Here are some of the most common issues with regular CD and DVD drives and some possible solutions.

### Not Accessible from Command Prompt

If the CD drive shows up in Windows but not when you boot from a DOS or Windows 95 Startup disk, it is because in the latter case the real-mode CD drivers are not being loaded. You learned how to add them to the startup files earlier in this chapter.

### CD Will Not Eject

If you press the Eject button on the drive and nothing happens, be patient. Sometimes an operation in the OS needs to complete before the disk can eject. If nothing happens after 60 seconds or so, the operating system may be locked up. Try Ctrl + Alt + Delete in Windows to see whether any programs are nonresponsive and can be shut down. If you still cannot get the CD to eject, try restarting the PC. If that does not work, the drive is probably having a physical problem.

To manually eject a drive's tray so you can retrieve a CD, straighten out a paper clip and poke the wire into the small hole on the front of the drive. The drive tray should pop out slightly, enough for you to grab it and pull it open the rest of the way. This works whether or not the drive is installed in a PC and whether or not it is receiving power (see Figure 13.3).

**FIGURE 13.3**
Manually Ejecting a CD from a CD Drive

## TRY IT!

With the PC's power off, manually eject the CD tray using a paper clip.

### Noisy Drive

A noisy CD drive (one that makes loud noises when a disc is spinning in it) usually indicates irreparable damage and the need for replacement.

### CD Drive Not Bootable

If you cannot boot from a CD drive, it is probably a BIOS Setup issue. Check in BIOS Setup to make sure that the CD is set to be one of the boot devices, and that it is set ahead of other boot devices that might intervene, like hard and floppy drives.

## Understanding CD-R

CD-ROMs are read-only, but there are two technologies for creating your own CDs: CD-R and CD-RW.

CD-R (for Compact Disc-Recordable) discs can be written to only once (except in the case of multisession writing, which will be covered later). The discs are inexpensive and work best when recording data that will not change. CD-RW (for Compact Disc-ReWritable) discs can be written to, erased, and reused many times, functioning somewhat like a hard disk or floppy. CD-RW is a good choice when you need to store small amounts of data over time, such as a daily backup of a few critical files. Early recordable CD drives were CD-R only, but many drives sold today support both CD-R and CD-RW writing.

## In Real Life

Some older CD drives cannot read CD-R and CD-RW, or cannot read them consistently. (A drive might be able to read one CD-R disc but not another that is seemingly identical, for example.) But most CD drives, including all of the drives manufactured in the last several years, treat a CD-R or CD-RW disc just like any other CD. Almost all audio-only CD players (as in a home stereo system) can read CD-R discs with no problem, so anyone can make personal music CDs and play them almost anywhere that regular CDs will play.

## How CD-R Works

PCs do not contain the manufacturing equipment to create the pitted aluminum layer that exists on a mass-produced CD; therefore, the recording process must be different.

The recording process for CD-R is made possible by the fact that CD readers do not actually touch the surface of the disc—they only look at it. As you just learned, a CD drive bounces light off the surface of the CD, and reads data depending on the amount of reflectivity it finds there. So a home-recorded CD need not actually have the pits and land areas of a normal CD, as long as it *appears* to have them.

Recordable CDs are physically different from mass-produced ones. They are coated with metal and then overlaid with photosensitive organic dye that reflects back to a CD drive just as a blank CD would (that is, all land). During the recording process a laser heats the metal and the dye layers in certain spots so that they change their reflectivity to resemble pits on an aluminum-pitted CD. When a drive reads the CD, the CD appears to have the normal pit and land areas of a commercially produced CD, even though there are not actually any pits.

## Multisession Recording

When data is written to a CD-R, the areas on which it is written are permanently changed. Many people found in the early days of CD-R, however, that they had far less than the 650MB limit to store on a CD, so much of the CD space was wasted. Because CD-R discs were then so expensive, *multisession recording* was devised to help take advantage of the available space.

**Multisession recording**

A method of rewriting to a CD-R after it has been written to previously by creating additional separate recording sessions.

Multisession-capable recording software allows the reuse of a partially used CD-R by creating a new session on the remaining blank space of the disc. In most cases only the last session on the disc can be read (although some software exists that allows access to multiple sessions). This might be useful for backing up a small number of files every day, especially if the previous day's backups are not needed. The same CD could be used several times, and the most recent session would always be accessible.

Since CD-R discs have become less expensive in recent years, the popularity of multisession recording has waned. Although most recording software supports it, few consumers go to the trouble.

## Speeds

A typical CD-RW drive has three speeds: CD-R writing, CD-RW writing, and reading. They are usually expressed as "X" numbers, separated by slashes; for example, 8x/4x/32x. The fastest number is the CD-ROM read speed (usually at the end). The next-fastest number (usually at the beginning) is the CD-R speed. The lowest number (usually in the middle) is the CD-RW speed. All CD-RW drives are CLV, so the reading speed measurement is constant.

## Selecting CD-R Media

The type of CD-R blanks to recommend to clients depends on what type of data they plan to burn, how much money they have to spend, how critical the data is, how tolerant they are of the occasional CD ruined by errors in the recording process, and how long they plan to keep the CDs.

Less expensive CD-R discs, such as generic or store brand, tend to exhibit more errors during recording. A person might spend $20 for a huge spindle of generic CDs, and then end up discarding 10 percent of them because of recording problems. These errors are usually caused by manufacturing defects in the CDs, inferior scratch-resistant coating, or scratches from being stored against other discs on the spindle. After figuring in lost time in waiting for the recordings, the low price is not much of a bargain.

If the PC has a high-speed recording drive, recommend discs that will support the desired recording speed. Almost any disc will record reliably at up to 4X, but for recording at higher speeds such as 6X or 8X, recommend discs that state clearly on the package that they are compatible with that speed. If the discs do not specifically indicate a speed limit on the packaging, assume that they can support no more than 4X.

Labeling discs is another consideration. When using a CD printer that accepts CD-R discs and prints directly onto them, make sure the discs have a blank face or only a minimal amount of text already printed on them. If a sticker is being applied to the disc, such as one created with a CD labeling kit, the writing on the face should make no difference.

If your clients do not need jewel cases for each CD, they can save some money by buying bulk CDs on a spindle. Some people experience problems with dust getting in between the stored discs and scratching them; keeping a dust cover on the spindle at all times will eliminate that problem.

Another consideration is disc capacity. Standard CD-Rs have a 650MB capacity (74 minutes of audio), but discs are also available that have a 700MB capacity (80 minutes of audio). These high-capacity discs are more expensive, and older CD-R drives might not be able to use them—or might not be able to utilize the extra capacity.

Different CD-R manufacturers have devised different combinations of metals and dyes. Any of them will work well for almost any task, but certain colors and combinations are especially advantageous for certain applications (see Figure 13.4). Unfortunately, it can be difficult to tell from the outside of the package what metal-dye combination a disc contains, since the same manufacturer may make several different kinds.

- **Green dye, gold metal:** This is the standard type of CD-R, and the first to be developed. It has a rated life span of 10 years, and uses cyanine dye, which can be more forgiving of disc-write and disc-read variations than some other dyes. This results in a CD that will likely play well in any CD player.
- **Gold dye, gold metal:** The gold dye used on this type of CD-R is phthalocyanine. It is a more sensitive CD with less tolerance for power variations and might be less likely to work in a wide variety of drives.
- **Blue dye, silver metal:** With a blue dye of azo, this combination has similar properties to the green-gold combination, but is rated to last much longer: 100 years. These discs are particularly well suited for long-term data storage.

**FIGURE 13.4**
Dye and Metal Color Combinations for CD-R Discs

## Troubleshooting CD-R Recording

Almost everyone who has ever experimented with CD-R recording has experienced the dreaded "buffer underrun" error, which means your recording has failed and the disc is ruined.

Because a CD-R disc can be written to only once, in a single pass (except in special cases like multisession and packet writing), recording success depends on the CD-R drive's being fed a steady, uninterrupted stream of data at exactly the right pace. The drive contains a small buffer (usually 512K or more) in which data from the PC waits to be recorded. If that buffer empties and no data is forthcoming from the PC, the writing laser is idle and a buffer underrun error occurs, ruining the disc.

Other problems can occur occasionally to ruin a disc, but the buffer underrun error is by far the most common. Figure 13.5 suggests ways to prevent buffer underrun from occurring, some of which you may want to share with your clients.

- Do not use the PC for anything else while recording, including checking e-mail. Do not play Solitaire. Do not even move the mouse.
- Turn off the screen saver before recording to prevent it from competing with the recorder for system resources.
- Disable all programs running in the background before recording, such as an antivirus program.
- Buy a CD-RW drive with a large buffer, such as 1MB or more.
- If the PC has an IDE CD drive, place it on its own IDE line (that is, a ribbon cable all by itself).
- When copying a CD from a CD drive to CD-R, and both are IDE, make sure each drive is on its own IDE line.
- If the writing software supports it, do a test write first.
- Use a lower recording speed than the maximum of which the drive is capable.
- Defragment the hard disk and run ScanDisk (or other disk-checking software) before making the CD (see Chapter 30 for details).
- If making a CD from data on the hard disk, turn off the power management feature for the hard disk before recording.
- If the writing software supports it, create a disc image first, and then create the CD from the image.

**FIGURE 13.5**
Ways to Prevent Buffer Underrun

**TRY IT!**

Use the CD burning software that came with your CD-R or CD-RW drive to make a CD containing some data from your hard drive, as a backup of the hard drive. If you encounter problems, use the techniques listed above to troubleshoot.

## Understanding CD-RW

The CD-RW medium is physically different from a CD-R disc. It is more complex and costs more to manufacture, which is why CD-RW discs are so much more expensive.

Earlier we discussed how data is burned into a CD-R by heating the dye and metal to change the disc's reflectivity in certain spots. That change is permanent, which is why you cannot make changes to the data on a CD-R. A CD-RW disc, in contrast, does not use dye-and-metal coating. Instead, it is coated with a metal alloy (containing silver, indium, antimony, and tellurium) with reflective properties that change depending on the temperature to which it is heated.

A CD-RW drive has a laser with three different power settings. The high write setting heats the alloy to around 1,112 degrees Fahrenheit (600 degrees Celsius), at which temperature it liquefies. When it solidifies again, it loses its reflective properties, simulating a pit. The same spot can be reheated by the low write setting to a lower temperature (around 392 degrees Fahrenheit [200 degrees Celsius]), causing it to revert to its original reflectivity, simulating a land area. That is how it rewrites an area. The lowest power setting is used to read the data without changing it.

CD-RW discs have less reflectivity contrast than regular discs, so older CD-ROM drives might not be able to read them reliably. However, almost all CD-ROM drives manufactured today, including all multiread drives, will have no trouble with them.

*Packet writing* is a software feature that enables you to transfer files to a CD-R or CD-RW disc individually, or a few at a time, rather than writing the entire disc at once. Most CD-RW drives come with packet-writing software; for example, with Roxio Easy CD Creator software, the program is called DirectCD. Packet-writing software enables a CD-RW disc to function more or less like a floppy or hard disk, with selective writing and erasing.

**Packet writing**

A scheme for writing data to CDs multiple times that creates a new table of contents with each rewriting.

Packet writing works by creating a *virtual allocation table* (VAT) each time data is written to the CD. It contains information about the files just written, plus all of the information from the previous VAT on the disc, forming a complete table of contents of the disc.

**Virtual allocation table (VAT)**

Like a FAT, except on a packet-written CD.

There are some limitations to packet-writing technology. Audio CDs cannot be packet written, and the CD-RW or CD-R drive must support packet writing. The resulting packet-written CDs require the computer on which they are read to have Universal Disk Format (UDF) reader software and a compatible operating system (such as a 32-bit version of Windows).

**TRY IT!**

**Insert a CD-RW disc in your CD-RW drive, and copy some files to it using drag and drop. If it does not work, check that the UDF reader software is installed. You might need to find the setup CD for your CD-burning software.**

## Creating a Bootable CD

If the PC has a CD-burning program that supports it, such as Roxio Easy CD Creator, you can make a bootable CD-R that starts the PC, just like the Windows Setup CD or other bootable CDs.

In order for a CD to be bootable, it must contain two files: BOOTCAT.BIN and BOOTIMG.BIN. BOOTCAT.BIN is a catalog file, and BOOTIMG.BIN is an image file containing a virtual floppy disk. The latter contains the needed startup files that one would normally expect to find on a bootable floppy disk.

When you browse the contents of a bootable CD in Windows or at a command prompt, you will not see any of the normal startup files that you would find on a bootable floppy because they are all stored within BOOTIMG.BIN. When you boot from the bootable CD, everything in BOOTIMG.BIN and BOOTCAT.BIN shows up as being on the A: drive, while everything else on the CD shows up on the regular CD drive letter.

To get started, you first create a bootable floppy containing the files that you want to use to boot from the CD. To create a bootable floppy (also referred to as a startup disk) in Windows 9x/Me, go to Add/Remove Programs in the Control Panel and create the disk from the Startup Disk tab.

Then, with that floppy in the drive, use a CD writing program (such as Easy CD Creator or Nero Burning) to start a new bootable CD layout, and specify the floppy as the source of the bootable content. The software copies all of the files from the floppy into the BOOTIMG.BIN file, and catalogs them in BOOTCAT.BIN. Then when you boot from the CD, it reads these files and treats the CD exactly as it would a floppy. (It even assigns the A drive letter to the content of BOOTIMG.BIN.)

The main purpose in creating a bootable CD is for emergency work—to boot a PC to a basic version of the operating system in case there is a problem starting normally. This works well for Windows 9x/Me users, but NT/2000 users are at a disadvantage because there is no such thing as a true "boot disk" in NT/2000/XP—at least not in the traditional sense as those used with MS-DOS and Windows 9x/Me. For Windows 9x/Me, you can create a startup disk that contains the files needed to start the PC and a command interpreter (Command.com), and essentially have a fully functional copy of an operating system that you can use to troubleshoot and repair the PC, with the help of some command-line utilities. This is not the case with Windows NT/2000. Therefore, making a bootable CD is a much more useful activity for someone with a Windows 9x/Me system.

## TRY IT!

1. Create a bootable Windows 98 startup floppy disk.
2. Create a bootable CD-R disc based on the floppy.
3. Boot your PC from the CD.
4. Remove the CD and reboot normally.

# STUDY GUIDE

Use the following summaries to review the key concepts of this chapter.

## Types of CD Drives

- A standard CD-ROM drive plays only normal CDs.
- A DVD drive plays both DVDs and normal CDs.
- A CD-R drive is able to write to CD-R disc, to which you can write only once and cannot edit or erase.
- A CD-RW drive is able to write to CD-RW disc, which can be rewritten multiple times.

## CD Performance Factors

- The X is the drive's speed—the theoretical maximum data transfer rate for that drive. It also refers to the rotation speed of the disc.
- A 1X CD drive can read 150Kbps. To determine a drive's maximum data transfer rate, multiply its X rating by 150Kbps.
- Two technologies are used for CD drives: constant linear velocity (CLV) and constant angular velocity (CAV).
- CLV keeps the area per second constant, so the drive spins faster when reading near the center of the disc. All CD data is written using CLV, so all CD-R and CD-RW drives are CLV.
- CAV keeps the rotational speed constant, so the drive reads different amounts of data per second depending on the spot on the disc being read. Most CD drives made today are CAV.
- SCSI is superior to IDE as a CD interface on a system with multiple drives that need to operate simultaneously.

## Installing a CD Drive

- Installing a CD drive is the same as installing a hard drive except you must connect an audio cable from the drive to the sound card to play audio CDs on it.
- CD drives come in both SCSI and IDE interface models.
- SCSI drives require a unique SCSI ID and termination; IDE models require a Master/Slave jumper setting.
- Both require a ribbon cable connection to a controller (expansion board or motherboard) and a power supply connection.

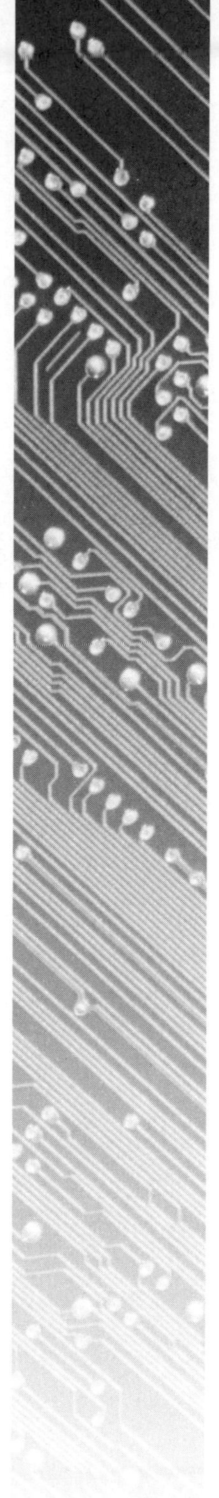

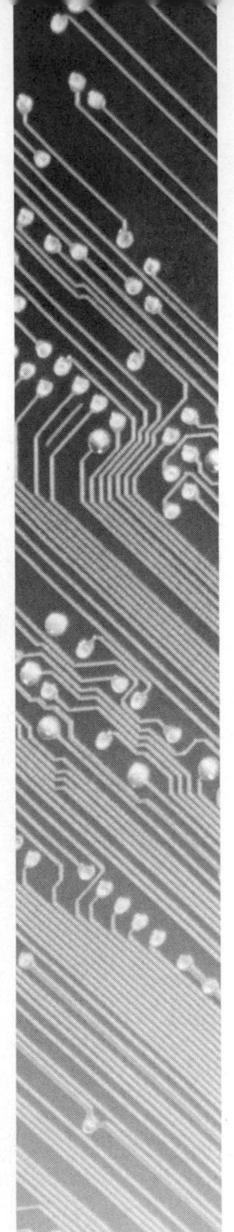

## Working with a CD Drive in the OS

- Windows 95 and higher automatically loads the needed driver for a CD drive.
- When working with MS-DOS, or from a startup floppy disk from Windows 9x/Me, real-mode CD drivers must be loaded.
- A setup program comes with most CD drives for setting up these drivers on an MS-DOS PC.
- You can manually edit the CONFIG.SYS and AUTOEXEC.BAT files to add the needed lines.
- Add a DEVICE= line to CONFIG.SYS that calls the CD driver file name. Add /D:name at the end of the command, where *name* represents a name you assign to the drive.
- Add MSCDEX.EXE to the AUTOEXEC.BAT file. Add the same /D: switch to the end that you used in CONFIG.SYS.

## Caring for CDs

- The primary danger to CDs is scratching them.
- Clean a CD with the minimum amount of surface-touching possible. Canned air works well.
- Keep CDs in protective cases when not in use.

## DVD

- DVD stands for Digital Versatile Disc or Digital Video Disc.
- Technologically, DVD is very similar to CD-ROM. Data is stored in pitted and unpitted areas on the disc.
- A DVD can hold multiple gigabytes of data, as opposed to only 650–700MB on a regular CD.
- A DVD's exact capacity depends on how many sides and layers it has and what standard it conforms to.
- DVD drive speeds cannot be fairly compared to the speeds of CD drives because they are technologically different.
- When reading DVD data, a 1X DVD drive transfers as much data as a 9X CD per second. When reading CD data, a 1X DVD transfers as much data as a 3X CD per second.
- Older DVD drives might not be able to read CD-R and CD-RW discs.
- To play DVD movies on a PC's DVD drive, the PC needs to have MPEG decoding capability.
- MPEG decoding is usually hardware (an expansion board or built into the video card).

## Troubleshooting CD and DVD Drive Problems

- If the CD drive appears in Windows but not at a command prompt, it needs real-mode drivers loaded.
- If the CD will not eject, you can use a pointed object such as a paper clip to push the manual eject button.
- A noisy CD drive is likely to fail in the near future.
- A CD drive that cannot be booted from is likely indicative of a BIOS Setup problem. Either the BIOS does not support CD booting or the boot order needs to be changed.

## Understanding CD-R

- CD-R works by burning photosensitive organic dye on the surface so that certain spots appear less reflective, simulating pits.
- CD-R is write-once, but a disc can be reused with multisession recording.
- Generic CD-R discs may seem a good bargain, but they can cause recording errors.
- High-speed drives require blanks that are designed for high-speed recording.
- Blanks come in two capacities: standard (650MB) or high (700MB). Older CD-R drives might not be able to use high-capacity discs.
- Different dye and metal color combinations are used on different types of CD-R discs. Any work well for most tasks.

## Troubleshooting CD-R Recording

- It is unfortunately common for buffer underrun errors to occur when writing CD-R discs. They happen because the PC cannot keep up with feeding the drive a steady stream of data to be written.
- To avoid buffer underrun errors, avoid using the PC for any other task while a CD is being created, and turn off any unnecessary background programs.
- Buffer underrun errors are less likely to occur on a SCSI interface, or an IDE interface where each drive is on its own IDE line.

## Understanding CD-RW

- CD-RW uses a metal alloy with reflective properties that change depending on the temperature to which it is heated. Its laser has two

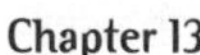

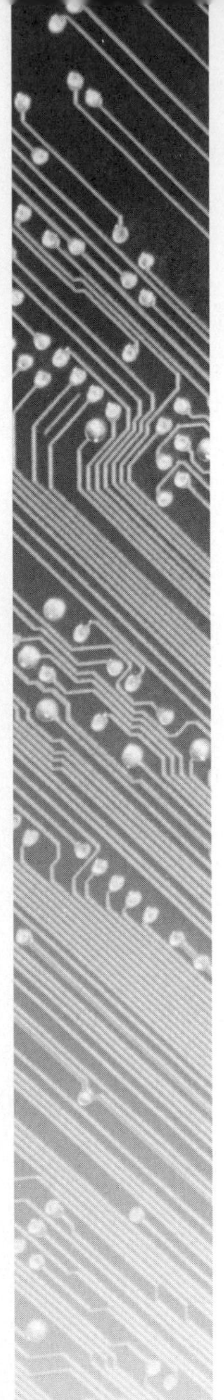

write settings: low and high. High setting removes reflectivity; low setting restores it.

- Packet writing is a software feature that enables you to transfer files individually to a CD-R or CD-RW disc rather than writing the entire disc at once.
- Packet writing works by creating a virtual allocation table (VAT) each time data is written to the CD.
- A packet-written CD can be read only on a PC that has Universal Disk Format (UDF) software installed.

### Creating a Bootable CD

- A bootable CD contains BOOTCAT.BIN and BOOTIMG.BIN files.
- BOOTCAT.BIN is a catalog file (like a directory).
- BOOTIMG.BIN is an image file containing a virtual floppy disk.
- The virtual floppy disk contains the startup files.
- When you boot from a bootable floppy, the system sees BOOTIMG.BIN as the A drive.
- To create a bootable CD, first create the startup floppy (Windows 9x/Me). Then use a CD-writing program to create the bootable CD.
- Creating a bootable CD is useful primarily for Windows 9x/Me systems because Windows NT/2000/XP does not start from a startup floppy.

## PRACTICE TEST

On a blank sheet of paper, write the answers to the following multiple-choice questions and explain why each answer is correct.

1. Which type of CD drive is rewritable?
   a. CD-ROM
   b. CD-RW
   c. CD-R
   d. CD-RE

2. Which of these would be a measurement of a CD drive's rotational speed?
   a. 150Mbps
   b. 2,048KB
   c. 24X
   d. CAV

3. CD-ROM access time is
   a. the rate at which data is retrieved from the disc.
   b. the speed at which the disc spins.
   c. the amount of time between the request for data and its delivery.
   d. None of the above

4. Which of these statements describes a constant linear velocity (CLV) CD drive?
   a The disc spins at the same speed no matter what data is being read; the data rate changes depending on the area being read.
   b. The disc spins at different speeds depending on the spot being read, so that the data can be read at a constant rate.
   c. The disc spins at a constant speed and the data is read at a constant rate.
   d. The disc spins at a variable speed and the data is read at a variable rate.

5. Which of these connections is necessary only on a CD drive, not on a hard drive?
   a. power
   b. ribbon cable
   c. video cable
   d. audio cable

6. Which type of CD drive must be terminated if it is the last device on the cable?
   a. SCSI
   b. IDE
   c. Zip
   d. external

7. Which type of CD drive has a jumper that must be set to MA, SL, or CS?
   a. SCSI
   b. IDE
   c. Zip
   d. external

8. Which Windows versions can make a startup floppy disk that automatically contains real-mode CD drivers?
   a. 95, 98, and Me
   b. 98 and Me
   c. 98, Me, 2000, and XP
   d. 95, 98, Me, 2000, and XP

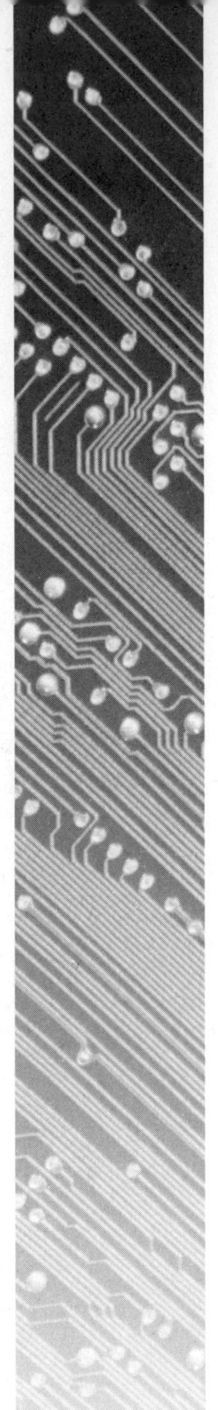

9. Which of these lines should be placed in CONFIG.SYS to enable a CD-ROM driver named CDROM.SYS located in the CD directory on the C drive?
   a. C:\CD\CDROM.SYS /D:CD001
   b. LOAD C:\CD\CDROM.SYS /D:CD001
   c. MSCDEX /D:CD001
   d. DEVICE=C:\CD\CDROM.SYS /D:CD001

10. Which of these lines should be placed in AUTOEXEC.BAT to enable a CD driver for the driver in question 9?
    a. C:\CD\CDROM.SYS /D:CD001
    b. LOAD C:\CD\CDROM.SYS /D:CD001
    c. C:\DOS\MSCDEX /D:CD001
    d. DEVICE=C:\CD\CDROM.SYS /D:CD001

11. Which of these poses a serious hazard to optical discs such as CDs?
    a. scratches and fingerprints
    b. water
    c. magnets
    d. These are all serious hazards.

12. *DVD* stands for
    a. Digital Versatile Disc.
    b. Digital Video Disc.
    c. Digital Variable Disc.
    d. either a or b depending on the type of content

13. Which of these is *not* a type of MPEG decoder?
    a. built into sound card
    b. built into video card
    c. separate add-on board
    d. These are all types of MPEG decoders.

14. How can you get a CD out of a CD drive that is not receiving power?
    a. Pry the tray open with a blunt blade such as a flathead screwdriver.
    b. Stick a pointed object in the manual eject hole in the front.
    c. Disassemble the drive by removing the four screws around the outer edge.
    d. None of the above; you cannot get a CD out unless the drive has power.

15. Multisession recording is an option when working with which type of disk recording?
    a. CD-ROM
    b. DVD
    c. CD-R
    d. CD-RW

16. For a CD-RW drive advertised as 16x/8x/40x, what is the CD-R writing speed?
    a. 16X
    b. 8X
    c. 40X
    d. 20X

17. Which of these is *not* a consideration when selecting CD-R media?
    a. recording speed rating
    b. capacity
    c. IBM versus Mac formatting
    d. These are all considerations.

18. What causes a buffer underrun error when writing to a CD?
    a. The CD drive is not fast enough to keep up with the hard disk.
    b. The PC is not delivering data to the CD drive for writing in a steady uninterrupted stream.
    c. The PC does not have enough memory.
    d. The CD drive is not configured correctly in Device Manager.

19. Each time data is written to the CD, packet writing creates a
    a. FAT.
    b. NTFS.
    c. VAT.
    d. CDFS.

20. Which files are necessary for a CD to be bootable?
    a. BOOTCAT.BIN and BOOTIMG.BIN
    b. BOOTLOG.BIN and BOOTIMG.BIN
    c. BOOTLOG.BIN and BOOTCAT.BIN
    d. BOOTLOG.BIN and BOOTLOG.TXT

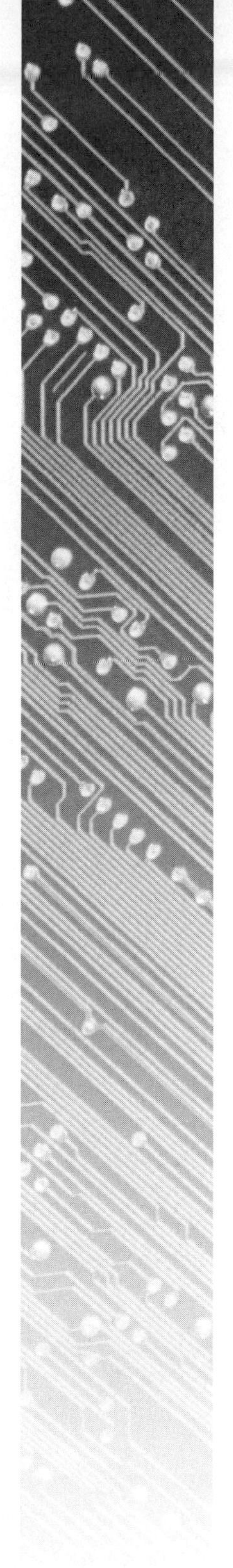

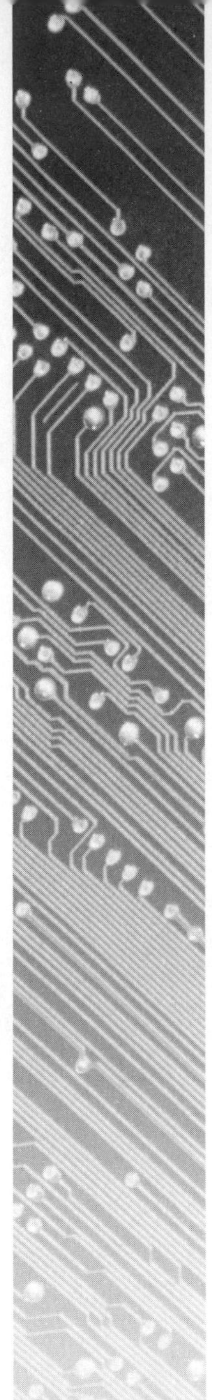

## TROUBLESHOOTING

1. A client's hard drive is unformatted and he wants to install Windows 95 on it. He has a floppy disk containing real-mode drivers for his CD-ROM drive, a Windows 95 CD-ROM, and a Windows 95 startup disk. You need to put the real-mode CD-ROM driver on the Windows 95 startup disk, and then edit its CONFIG.SYS and AUTOEXEC.BAT to point to them, but there is only one floppy drive in the PC and you cannot copy directly from one floppy disk to another. What can you do?
2. A client complains that she cannot play DVD movies on her PC, although data DVDs work fine. What might be the problem?
3. A client wants to boot from the Windows 2000 CD-ROM to install Windows 2000, but when he inserts the CD-ROM in the drive and tries to boot, the PC boots from the hard disk instead. What needs to be done to allow it to boot from the CD?

## CUSTOMER SERVICE

1. A client asks you to settle an argument he is having with a colleague. One claims that it is important to clean your CDs regularly with water and a soft cloth to get rid of the fingerprints; the other claims you should never unnecessarily touch a CD's surface. Describe the advice you would give.
2. A client is considering replacing her 32X CD-ROM drive with a DVD drive, but is concerned that the DVD drive's speed is only 20X—she does not want to downgrade in performance level. What would you tell her?
3. A customer received a CD-RW disc from his daughter, but his PC cannot read it. What do you think might be the problem and what would you suggest?

# Project Lab, Part 3
## Data Storage

In all of these projects, make sure that you do not delete any data from a hard drive that needs to be retained. For example, if an operating system is already installed on a drive, check with your instructor before you repartition and reformat that drive.

### Project #1: Installing a Floppy Drive

1. Prepare a drive bay for a floppy drive. What would you do if no small drive bays were available?
2. Install the floppy drive in the bay. Connect it to the power supply. Describe which type of power connector you would use.
3. Select an appropriate ribbon cable and connect the floppy drive to the floppy interface on the motherboard. Describe how you chose the ribbon cable, how you decided which orientation to use when connecting the plugs on both ends, and how you decided which connector to plug into each spot.
4. Start up the PC, enter BIOS Setup, and configure the new floppy drive.
5. Test the new floppy drive by formatting a floppy disk in it and then copying several files to it.

### Project #2: Installing an IDE CD-ROM Drive

1. Decide on which IDE channel you will install the drive, and set the drive's jumpers appropriately.
2. Install the drive in a drive bay and connect it to the power supply. Which type of connector will you use?
3. Select an appropriate ribbon cable and connect the drive to the IDE interface on the motherboard. Describe how you have chosen which connector to use in which plug and which direction to orient each connector.
4. Enter BIOS Setup and configure it to accept the new drive.
5. Set BIOS Setup to boot from the CD.

6. Insert a bootable CD in the drive (such as a Windows 2000 or Windows XP Setup disk) and boot from the CD. After confirming that you have successfully booted from the CD, turn off the PC.

## Project #3: Installing an IDE Hard Drive

1. Decide on which IDE channel you will install the drive, and set the drive's jumpers appropriately.
2. Install the drive in a drive bay and connect it to the power supply. Which type of connector will you use?
3. Select an appropriate ribbon cable and connect the drive to the IDE interface on the motherboard. Describe how you have chosen which connector to use in which plug and which direction to orient each connector.
4. Enter BIOS Setup and set the drive's IDE channel to Auto. Or, if the BIOS Setup has a Detect IDE utility, run it. Write down the drive's parameters (CHS and other settings) that the BIOS is using for this drive. Then exit BIOS Setup, saving changes.

## Project #4: Partitioning and Formatting a Drive with FAT32

Complete project #3 first, so you will have a newly installed hard drive to work with for this project.

1. Use a Windows 98 Startup disk (floppy) to start the PC. If you don't have one, make one using a PC that already has Windows 98 installed.
2. Using FDISK, partition half the hard disk as a primary partition and half as a secondary partition. Document the steps you take to do so.
3. Create a single logical drive on each partition. Make the primary partition active.
4. Format both logical drives, and make the C drive bootable. Document the steps you take to do so.
5. Reboot from the hard drive to a command prompt, and format a new, blank floppy disk using the command prompt.
6. Display a list of the files on the C drive. Write down the names of the files you find there.

## Project #5: Partitioning and Formatting a Drive with NTFS

This project requires a PC with Windows 2000 already installed.

1. On a PC with Windows 2000 installed, install a second hard drive (see Project #3). Write down the steps you take to do so, including the jumper setting you use for the drive.
2. Start up Windows 2000 and use Disk Management to partition and format the new drive as a single primary NTFS partition. Does this require two separate steps, or is it all part of the same wizard?
3. Delete the partition you just created, and re-create it at a smaller size, leaving about one-third of the drive as unpartitioned space. Do not format it; just partition it.
4. Create a second partition using the remaining unpartitioned space; again, do not format it.
5. Format the larger partition as NTFS, and format the smaller partition as FAT32. Why might you need to create FAT32 partitions in real life, even though NTFS is a superior file system?

## Project #6: (Challenge): Installing SCSI Drives

1. Install a SCSI adapter board. Write down what SCSI address the card is set to use. Can its ID be changed? If so, what are your choices for it?
2. Examine the SCSI drives you plan to install. What type are they? Will they work together on the same SCSI chain? Would performance be better if one or both were some other type?
3. Install the drives in the case and connect them to the power supply and the SCSI adapter. Set SCSI ID and termination as required. What type of termination are you using?
4. Using a Windows 98 startup disk, create a FAT16 primary partition on the hard drive and format it. Describe how you can get FAT16 instead of FAT32 using the Windows 98 version of FDISK. Which operating systems are incompatible with FAT32 partitions? What is the maximum size of a partition under FAT16? How much unpartitioned space remains on your drive?

## PROJECT #7 (CHALLENGE): TROUBLESHOOTING PRACTICE

1. Create problems with the hard drive installation on your PC. Do as many things to it as you can think of. For example, you might loosen cables, delete a partition (do this only on a hard drive that contains nothing you need to keep), disable the drive in BIOS Setup, change its IDE or SCSI jumpers, and so on.
2. Swap PCs with a classmate and restore the hard drive to working order, such that it is installed and properly partitioned and formatted for storing files. Document the steps you take to troubleshoot and repair.

# PART 4

# Input and Output Devices

# TEST OBJECTIVES IN PART 4

**A+ Core Hardware Service Technician Examination**

- **Objective 1.1:** Identify basic terms, concepts, and functions of system modules, including how each module should work during normal operation and during the boot process.
- **Objective 1.2:** Identify basic procedures for adding and removing field replaceable modules for both desktop and portable systems.
- **Objective 1.3:** Identify available IRQs, DMAs, and I/O addresses and procedures for device installation and configuration.
- **Objective 1.7:** Identify proper procedures for installing and configuring peripheral devices.
- **Objective 1.8:** Identify hardware methods of upgrading system performance, procedures for replacing basic subsystem components, unique components and when to use them.
- **Objective 2.1:** Identify common symptoms and problems associated with each module and how to troubleshoot and isolate the problems.
- **Objective 5.1:** Identify basic concepts, printer operations, and printer components.
- **Objective 5.2:** Identify care and service techniques and common problems with primary printer types.

**A+ Operating System Technologies Examination**

- **Objective 2.4:** Identify procedures for loading/adding and configuring application device drivers, and the necessary software for certain devices.
- **Objective 3.2:** Recognize common problems and determine how to resolve them.

# 14 Configuring Devices in Windows

## ON THE TEST

**A+ Core Hardware Service Technician Examination**

- **Objective 1.3:** Identify available IRQs, DMAs, and I/O addresses and procedures for device installation and configuration.

**A+ Operating System Technologies Examination**

- **Objective 2.4:** Identify procedures for loading/adding and configuring application device drivers, and the necessary software for certain devices.
- **Objective 3.2:** Recognize common problems and determine how to resolve them.

## ON THE JOB

When you install a new device and it does not work, it is probably not the device's fault, but rather a problem with the way the operating system interacts with the device. To operate successfully, a hardware device needs two things: a device driver, which translates between the language of the operating system and the language of the device, and device resources, which allocate communication pathways for the device's use. As a PC technician you will probably spend many hours troubleshooting issues with device drivers and resources. Your work in this area may include:

- installing Plug and Play (PnP) hardware
- manually assigning resources to non-PnP hardware
- checking device properties with Device Manager
- installing and updating device drivers
- resolving resource conflicts in Windows

# Device Resources

Device resources help devices such as drives and expansion boards communicate with the CPU and the operating system. There are four main types of resources a device can use. Not all devices use all four of these types.

**Interrupt Request (IRQ)**

A channel for a device to signal to the CPU that it is ready to begin a conversation.

- **Interrupt Requests (IRQs):** *Interrupt Requests* are lines of communication to the CPU. There are 16 of them in a PC, numbered 0 through 15, many of which are reserved for built-in system devices such as the keyboard and the IDE interfaces. They are necessary because the CPU must initiate all conversations with devices, but sometimes the devices need to signal the CPU to ask for a conversation to be initiated. They do so by sending a pulse on the interrupt request line, and the CPU responds by initiating a conversation.

**I/O address**

A memory address reserved for transferring data to and from a device.

- **I/O Addresses:** *I/O addresses* are memory addresses, expressed in hexadecimal. They define areas of memory reserved for transferring data to and from the device. They are usually written using only the last four digits of the full address, such as 03E8, and are usually expressed as a range of addresses: 03E8-03EF.
- **Memory Addresses:** Memory addresses define areas of memory reserved for the device's use. They are usually written with eight digits of hexadecimal, such as 00A0000, and are usually expressed as a range: 00A0000-00BFFFF.
- **Direct Memory Addressing (DMA) Channels:** These are pathways from a device directly into memory, bypassing the CPU. DMA is no longer popular because of advances in hardware technology, but it used to be employed by devices like the keyboard and the sound card to improve their reaction times.

Each built-in I/O port in a system has resources preassigned to it. For example, COM1 uses IRQ4 and I/O addresses 03F8 through 03FF. The port uses those resources whether or not anything is actually plugged into it (unless you disable it in the BIOS Setup program). This is true for both COM and LPT ports.

In contrast, the expansion slots in a motherboard do not have any resource assignments when they are empty. Instead the system waits until an expansion board is plugged into one of them, and then it assigns resources to that expansion board. For example, you might have four PCI expansion slots, one of them occupied by a modem. That modem uses an IRQ and an I/O address range, but the empty slots do not.

Of the four resource types listed here, the most critical are the IRQs because their number is limited and almost every device requires one. Older systems with multiple ISA devices would run out of IRQs and no more devices could be installed in them. One of the advantages of the PCI bus over ISA is that PCI devices can share IRQs; each PCI expansion board need not have a unique IRQ assigned to it.

Other interfaces also help devices share resources. Certain device types, such as SCSI, USB, and FireWire, work off a central controller that handles resource assignments for multiple devices. The controller requires an IRQ (and other resources as well), but the individual devices do not.

Originally there were only eight IRQs on a PC: 0 through 7. When the extra eight were added (8 through 15), there needed to be a way of connecting the two sets. To accomplish this, a link was established between IRQ 2 and IRQ 9; they are actually a single IRQ under two separate names. IRQ 2 exists only to create the link (called a cascade) between the two; IRQ 9 is available for device use.

## Default Resource Assignments

Many of the built-in system devices, such as the COM and LPT ports, the keyboard, and the IDE connectors, have default resource assignments. They can be set to use other resources if needed but they return to their defaults when not otherwise assigned.

These defaults are significant because some devices, such as ports, define themselves by their resource assignments. For example, if you assign IRQ 4 and the I/O address 3F8-3FF to a COM port, it will believe it is COM1; if you change that I/O address to 3F8-3EF, it will think it is COM3.

These defaults are also important because they are covered on the A+ exam; there will probably be at least one question asking you to name the resource that claims a certain IRQ by default. Table 14.1 lists the default IRQ assignments and, where applicable, the I/O addresses. Keep in mind that these are only the defaults; an individual system may be set up differently, either manually or through PnP assignments.

| IRQ | I/O Address | Device |
|---|---|---|
| 0 | 0040-005F | System timer |
| 1 | 0060-006F | Keyboard controller |
| 2 | 00A0-00AF | Cascade to IRQ 9 |
| 3 | 02F8-02FF | COM2 |
| 3 | 02E8-02EF | COM4 |
| 4 | 03F8-03FF | COM1 |
| 4 | 03E8-03EF | COM3 |
| 5 | 0278-027F | LPT2 or Sound card |
| 6 | 03F0-03F7 | Floppy drive controller |
| 7 | 0378-037F | LPT1 |
| 8 | 0070-007F | Real-time clock |
| 9 | | Cascade from IRQ 2 / Available |
| 10 | | Available |
| 11 | | SCSI expansion board or Available |
| 12 | | Mouse port or Available |
| 13 | | Math coprocessor |
| 14 | | Primary IDE |
| 15 | | Secondary IDE |

**TABLE 14.1**
Default IRQ Settings

## In Real Life

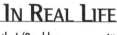

Frequently I/O addresses are written without the leading 0, so you might, for example, see COM2's I/O address written as 2F8-2FF. Sometimes an I/O address is expressed using only the starting address, so COM2's I/O address might be expressed simply as 2F8.

## How Device Resources Are Assigned

Built-in devices receive resources through BIOS Setup. The COM and LPT ports receive their assignments that way, and you can usually change them through the BIOS Setup program.

**Plug and Play (PnP)**

A technology for detecting hardware and installing drivers for it automatically.

Some expansion devices have jumpers on them that determine their IRQ and I/O address (more on that later); others are *Plug and Play* (PnP), a technology for detecting hardware and its resource and driver requirements and automatically assigning or installing them. It achieves full functionality only if all three pieces of the equation are PnP-compatible: the hardware device itself, the motherboard, and the operating system.

A PnP-capable motherboard (which includes all motherboards made in at least the last five years) can detect PnP-compatible expansion boards and assign resources to them, achieving partial PnP functionality no matter what operating system is installed. When you boot a PC and a list of devices appears that includes more than just drives, that is a signal that the motherboard is using PnP. For example, you might notice the sound card, modem, network card, or other expansion boards on the list, along with IRQ assignments. In this case the motherboard chipset itself handles resource assignments. (You will not see that information in BIOS Setup because the detection and assignment happens later in the boot process than the BIOS Setup operates.) When the boot process continues and Windows loads, Windows accepts the resource assignments that the motherboard established and adds any devices that it might have failed to detect. (Windows is more adept at PnP than are most motherboard chipsets.)

A PnP-capable motherboard usually has a setting in BIOS Setup where you can indicate whether or not a PnP operating system is installed. It is set to No by default, which allows the motherboard to handle all PnP resource assignments. If you are running Windows 95 or higher, however, you can set this to Yes, which turns off the motherboard's capability for PnP resource assignments and leaves all assignments up to Windows itself. This can be advantageous if you have many devices competing for resources because Windows is smarter about assignments than the motherboard and may be able to make everything fit when the motherboard could not. Most of the time, however, it makes little difference.

All versions of Windows (95 and higher) support PnP, but Windows NT 4.0 and MS-DOS do not. If the operating system does not support PnP, a setup program must be run for the device to assign resources and install the driver needed for the OS to recognize it. In Windows NT 4.0, for example, such a setup program writes data about the device to the Windows Registry. In MS-DOS, the setup program adds a line to CONFIG.SYS that calls a driver for the device. The A+ exam does not cover specifics about installing devices in non-PnP operating systems; all you need to know is which operating systems support PnP and which do not.

## Resource Assignments and ACPI

*Advanced Configuration and Power Interface* (ACPI) is a method of controlling all of the PC's PnP hardware at the operating system level rather than through the motherboard. For a system to use ACPI, it must have an ACPI-aware motherboard chipset and also an ACPI-capable operating system (Windows 98 and above). A chipset that does not support ACPI (but instead supports Advanced Power Management, or APM, an earlier power standard) can sometimes be upgraded to ACPI support through a BIOS update, as discussed in Chapter 9. ACPI makes Plug and Play work more reliably in Windows, resulting in fewer resource conflicts. It is enabled by default on systems that support it.

**Advanced Configuration and Power Interface (ACPI)**

A set of standards for controlling PnP hardware at the OS level and managing power conservation settings.

ACPI has two purposes: it manages PnP device resources and it enables power conservation utilities that shut off certain components after a specified period of inactivity. We will look at the power management aspects in Chapter 20.

One of the side effects of ACPI is that it makes automatic resource assignments mandatory for most devices; when you try to manually change a resource assignment (discussed in the next few sections), a message will usually appear telling you that it cannot be done. However, another side effect is that the resource assignments are much more adroitly handled, so there will be few—if any—conflicts that need resolving.

**IN REAL LIFE**

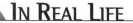

**If ACPI support is loaded and recognized in Windows, you will see an ACPI device in Device Manager under the Computer category. You can remove it, as you can remove any device, but when you reboot most of the devices will need to be redetected and reinstalled. You would then have increased control over the system resource assignments, but would lose ACPI support, so it is not recommended except to solve difficult resource allocation problems that cannot be resolved either way.**

## VIEWING RESOURCE ASSIGNMENTS IN WINDOWS

Windows provides two tools for viewing resource assignments: Device Manager and System Information. Most versions of Windows have these but they look and act a little different depending on the Windows version. Of the two, only Device Manager allows you to change the resource assignments; we will cover making those changes later in the chapter.

### *Viewing Resource Assignments in Windows 9x/Me*

Device Manager provides a look at the resource assignments. To access it, complete the following steps:

1. Right-click the *My Computer* icon on the desktop and choose Properties.
2. Select the Device Manager tab. A list of device categories appears (see Figure 14.1).
3. Click the plus sign next to a category to expand it.

Once Device Manager is displayed, there are two ways of looking at device resources. One is to see a complete list of all of the resource assignments. To do that, complete these steps:

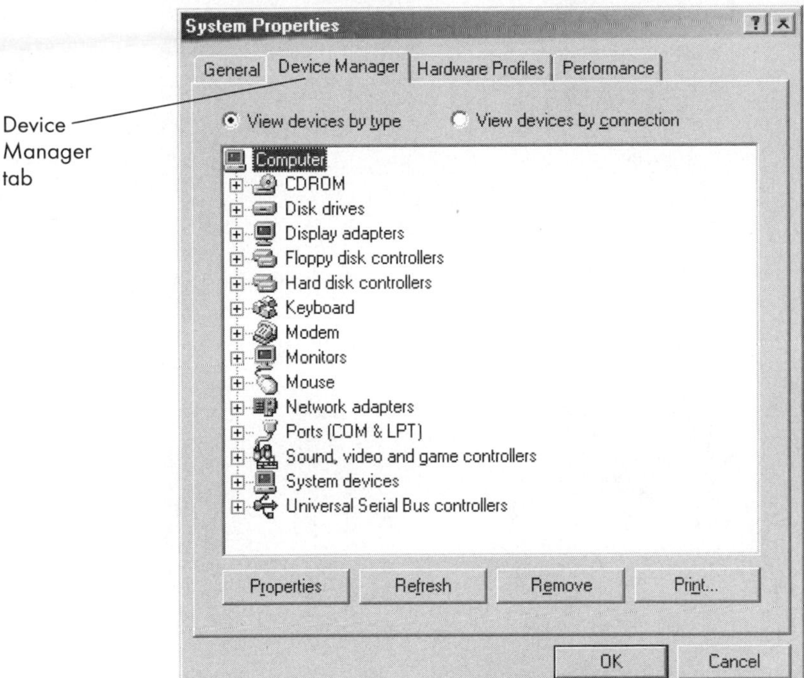


**FIGURE 14.1**
Device Manager in Windows 9x/Me is a tab on the System Properties dialog box.

1. Double-click *Computer* at the top of the list in Device Manager. The Computer Properties dialog box opens.
2. Click the option button for the resource type you want to see. For example, Figure 14.2 shows Interrupt request (IRQ) selected.

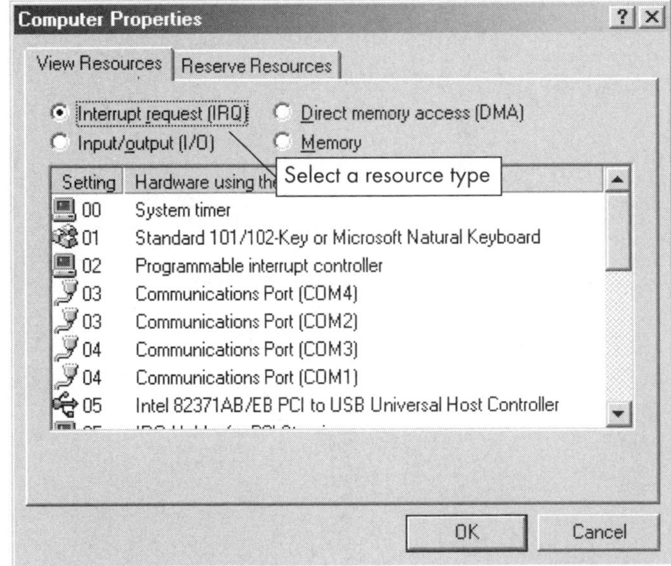


**FIGURE 14.2**
View a list of all assignments for a resource type from the Computer Properties dialog box.

Another method of viewing device resources is to check the resource assignments for individual devices. To do that, follow these steps:

1. Double-click on the device in Device Manager to open its Properties dialog box.
2. Select the Resources tab. The resource assignments for the device appear here, as shown in Figure 14.3. Notice that the network adapter is using IRQ 9, I/O address range FD000000 through FD00001F, and memory range 1080-109F.

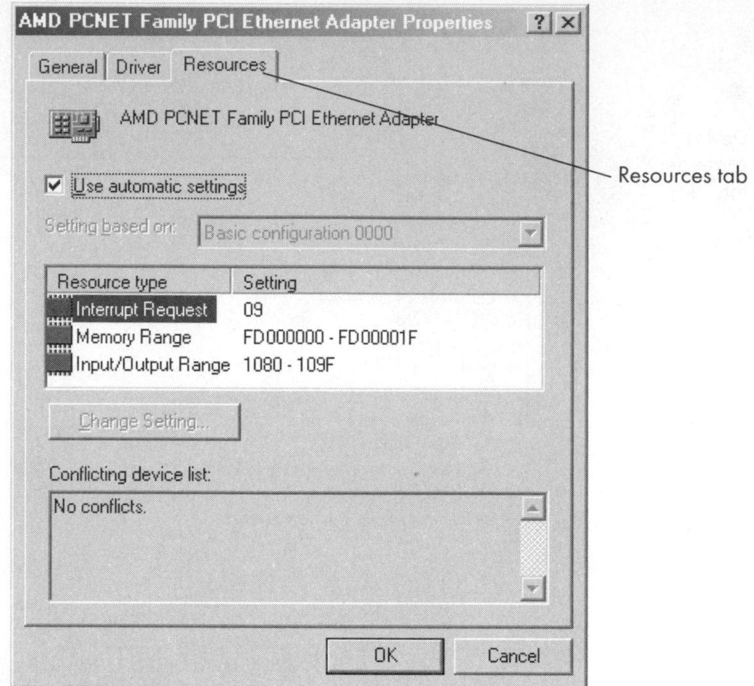


**FIGURE 14.3**
View all of the resource usage for a particular device from the Resources tab in its Properties dialog box.

Another tool for viewing resource assignments in Windows 98/Me is System Information. (It is not included in Windows 95.) To access resource assignments through it, do the following:

1. Choose Start/Programs/Accessories/System Tools/System Information. The System Information window opens. It looks a little different in Windows 98 versus Windows Me (the Me version appears in Figure 14.4).

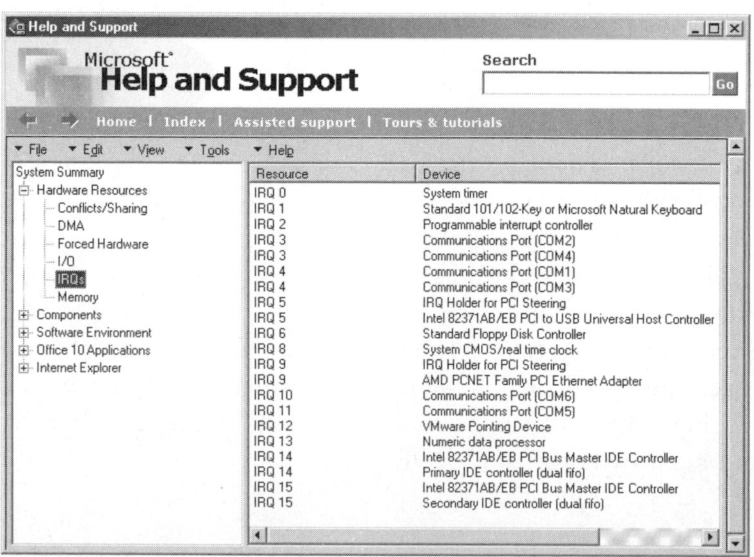


**FIGURE 14.4**
System Information provides a great deal of data, including system resource usage data.

2. Click the plus sign next to Hardware Resources, and then click the type of resource you want to view. For example, Figure 14.4 shows IRQ usage.

### *Viewing Resource Assignments in Windows 2000/XP*

Device Manager works basically the same way in Windows 2000/XP as it does in earlier versions, but opening it requires an extra step:

1. Right-click *My Computer* and choose Properties.
2. Select the Hardware tab.
3. Click the Device Manager button. A Device Manager window appears, as shown in Figure 14.5.

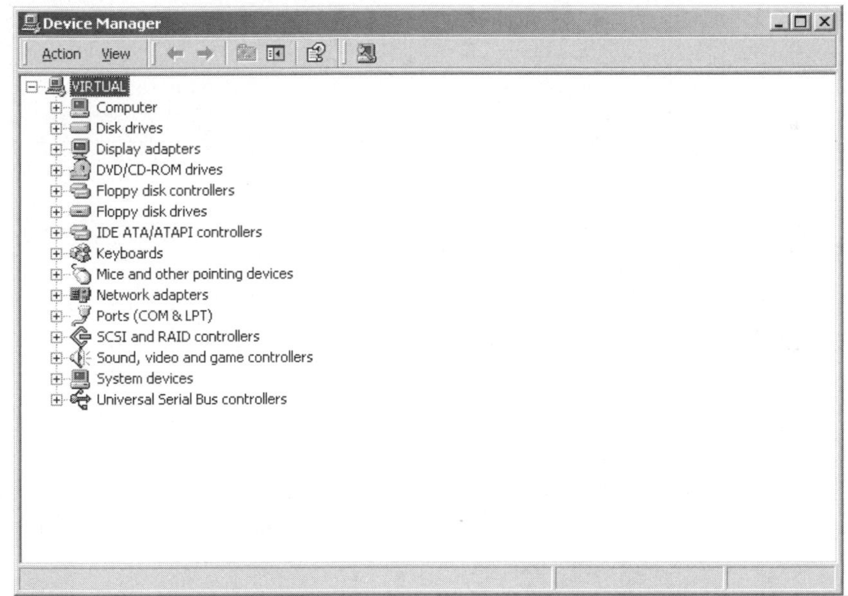


**FIGURE 14.5**
Device Manager in Windows 2000

To view all resources of a particular type, do the following:

1. Click the View menu in the Device Manager window and choose Resources by type.
2. Click the plus sign next to the resource you want to see, as shown in Figure 14.6.

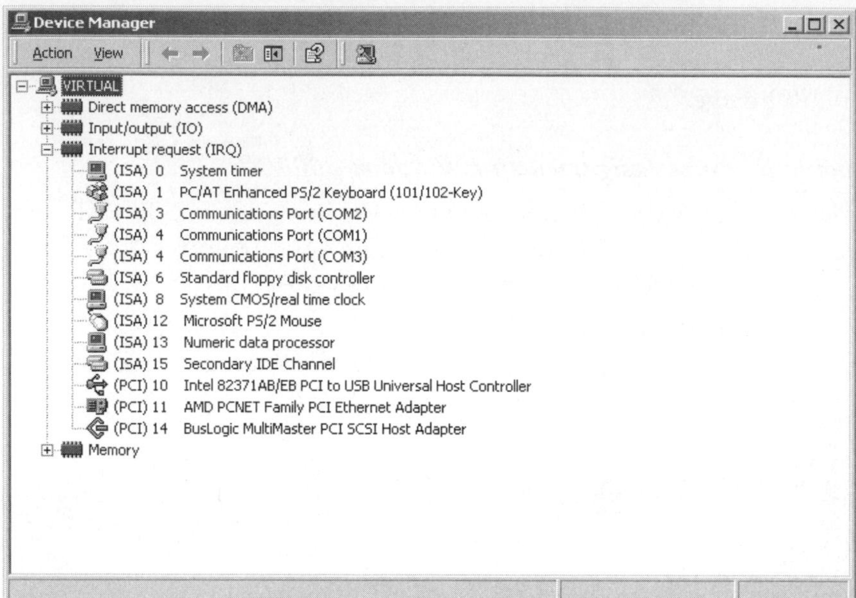


**FIGURE 14.6**
Viewing a Particular Resource Type in Windows 2000's Device Manager

3. When you are ready to go back to the default view, open the View menu and choose Devices by type.

Viewing resources for a specific device is the same in Windows 2000/XP as it is in Windows 9x/Me: just double-click the device to open its Properties dialog box. Windows 2000/XP also has its own System Information applet that provides the same kinds of detailed information. Use it the same way as in Windows 9x/Me:

1. Choose Start/Programs/Accessories/System Tools/System Information.
2. Click the plus sign next to Hardware Resources, then click the type of resource you want to view.

## TRY IT!

1. In Device Manager or System Information, jot down the IRQ assignments for your PC.
2. Reboot, enter BIOS Setup, and look for a setting for PnP Operating System.
3. Set it to the opposite setting (No if it is Yes, or Yes if it is No). Then exit BIOS Setup saving your changes.
4. Back in Windows, check the IRQ assignments again. Did any change?
5. If the setting is not currently Yes, reboot again, reenter BIOS Setup, and set it to Yes.

## Installing Plug and Play Devices

When you start Windows after physically installing a new piece of PnP-capable hardware, one of these things will happen:

- Windows detects the new device, assigns system resources to it, and installs a driver for it—all automatically. A message may briefly appear stating that this has happened.
- Windows detects the new device and assigns system resources to it, but cannot locate a suitable driver for it. It opens a New Hardware Wizard dialog box prompting you for the driver location; you can either supply the driver and complete the wizard or click Cancel to skip it if you do not have the driver file handy.
- Windows does not detect the new device. This may be because the device is not PnP-capable, because it is defective, or because it is not physically installed correctly.

The exact steps for working through the second option—the one in which Windows prompts you for a driver—depend on the Windows version and are fairly self-explanatory. Drivers and their installation are covered later in this chapter in more detail.

Later versions of Windows are much more adept at PnP than earlier ones, so the same device that would not install automatically under Windows 95 might install under Windows 98, Me, or XP. There are two reasons for this. One is that the hardware databases in the later Windows versions contain many more devices; the other is that PnP in general is improved.

Sometimes Windows installs a device with PnP and assigns resources to it but the device does not work afterward. This is often the result of a resource conflict—two or more devices claiming a resource such as an IRQ and being unable to share it peacefully. See the section "Resolving Resource Conflicts in Windows" later in this chapter for details. Resource conflicts are much more common in early Windows versions.

## Installing Non-Plug and Play Devices

A non-PnP device will have jumpers on it for setting the IRQ, and possibly the I/O address. Some PnP cards have such jumpers as well, for optional use. When all of the jumpers are off the card functions as PnP, but when the jumpers are on, it hard-wires certain resource assignments into it.

Figure 14.7 shows an expansion board with several jumpers on it. The bottom row, visible in the figure, is for the IRQ. Notice that there are many sets of pins, each one with a number; you put the jumper cap across the pin set that corresponds to the IRQ you want.

**FIGURE 14.7**
Jumpers on a Non-PnP Expansion Board for Setting the IRQ

Windows 95 and higher can detect a non-PnP device when specifically requested to do so (with Add New Hardware in the Control Panel) but cannot dynamically assign resources to it. Instead, it is forced to assign the resources that the device itself insists on having (by virtue of its jumper settings). If those resources are not available, a resource conflict occurs. You will learn about resolving resource conflicts later in this chapter.

To ask Windows to scan for non-PnP hardware, use the New Hardware Wizard:

1. From the Control Panel, double-click *Add New Hardware.*
2. Follow the prompts. The exact steps depend on the Windows version.

The above also works to ask Windows to detect new PnP hardware, although most PnP hardware is automatically detected.

## Removing Devices and Refreshing Assignments

Usually when you physically remove a piece of hardware, Windows detects its removal the next time you start up and removes it from Device Manager. However, sometimes an old device's name and information linger in Device Manager. It will probably not do any harm there, but if you experience problems (for example, with another device of the same type), you can remove it from there.

To remove a device from Device Manager:

1. Select the device.
2. Press the Delete key on the keyboard.
3. If a confirmation box appears, click Yes.

If you are having problems with a device, you can often fix the problem by removing it from Device Manager and having Device Manager redetect it and reassign resources. To redetect devices after a removal, click the Refresh button (in Windows 9x/Me) or the Scan for Hardware Changes button (in Windows 2000/XP).

**TRY IT!**

1. In Device Manager, check the resource assignments for one of the nonessential hardware devices, such as the sound card or modem.
2. Remove the device from Device Manager by selecting it and pressing Delete.
3. Use Refresh or Scan for Hardware Changes to have Windows redetect the device.
4. Check its resource assignments again. Are they still the same?

## Understanding Device Drivers

A *device driver* is a piece of software that acts as an interpreter between the operating system and the device. Since the operating system cannot possibly contain all of the specifics about every piece of hardware ever made, the device driver fills in the gaps by supplying Windows with information about how to interact with the device. It also translates messages between the two, and in many cases provides a Properties dialog box for the device in which the user can adjust how the device works.

**Device driver**

A file that acts as an intermediary between the operating system and the device, providing translation services and a description of the device's capabilities.

Some devices require only a single driver file; others require several different types of files. When you install a device driver, the needed files are registered in the Windows Registry and also copied into the Windows folder (or a subfolder within it). The information file that tells Windows which driver files it should install is a plain text file with an .inf extension.

**IN REAL LIFE**

A few devices, such as monitors, do not actually have any drivers. They do have INF files, however, which tell Windows the maximum settings they can accept. Windows uses this information to prevent unusable settings from appearing in the Properties dialog box for that device.

For best results, the device driver should be written specifically for the device and for the exact version of Windows. Sometimes a similar type device driver will work, but often such drivers cause system problems such as device failure or general Windows lockups.

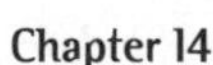

Most device manufacturers provide drivers for download at their Web sites, so you should be able to acquire a driver for almost any device and operating system combination. If that is not possible, try a driver for an earlier version of Windows in the same family as the current version. For example, if no Windows Me driver is available, try one for Windows 98 or 95. Or if no Windows XP driver is available, try one for Windows 2000 (or, as a last resort, Windows NT 4.0).

To determine what driver files a particular device uses, follow these steps:

1. Display the device's Properties dialog box from Device Manager.
2. Select the Driver tab.
3. Click the Driver Details button. A list of the driver files appears, as in Figure 14.8.
4. Click OK.

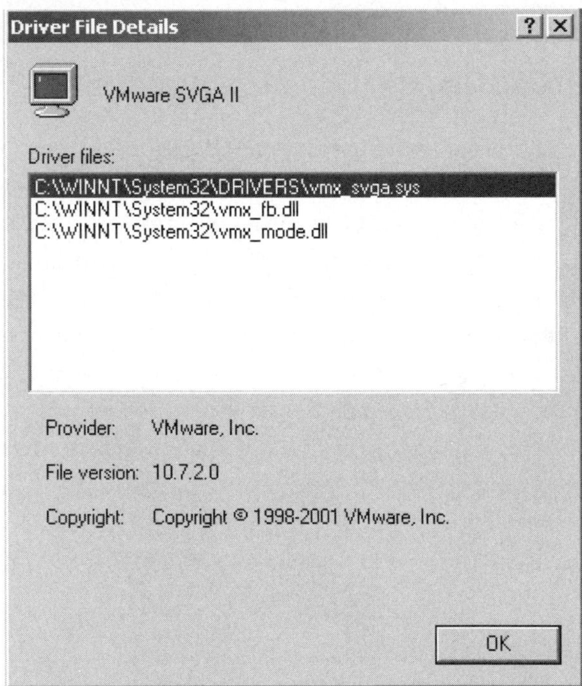


**FIGURE 14.8**
The Driver Files for a Video Card

## TRY IT!

Display the driver file details for several devices, and make a note of the names and paths. Locate a few of those files in Windows Explorer.

## Installing or Updating Device Drivers

When Windows detects a PnP device, in most cases it installs the driver for it at the same time that it assigns the resources. When Windows has not installed the driver, one of these things will occur in Device Manager:

- The device will appear with a yellow circle and exclamation point next to it. When you double-click the device, a message appears that the drivers for the device have not been loaded.
- The device does not appear. Instead, an unknown device appears in the Other Devices category. This indicates that Windows was unable to fully identify the device but is aware that a device of some sort is installed.

In either case, the solution is to install a driver for the device. The procedure for installing a driver initially and for replacing an existing driver is the same: run the Update Device Driver Wizard.

The wizard can operate in either of two ways. You can ask it to automatically locate a better driver than the one currently installed (if any), or you can manually specify a driver. The procedures are nearly the same in Windows 95, 98, Me, and 2000, with only minor differences.

### *Automatic Driver Discovery*

Sometimes Windows can find a better driver automatically. Try this first, before you try the less automated methods:

1. Display the device's Properties dialog box from Device Manager, and select the Driver tab.
2. Click the Update Driver button. The Update Device Driver Wizard runs.
3. Leave Automatic search for a better driver selected and click Next. (The wording varies depending on the Windows version. Windows 98 does not include the word "automatic"; in Windows 95 the wording is completely different; choose Yes.)
4. For Windows 98 only, click Next again to bypass the check boxes for locations to search, leaving them set at the defaults.
5. Finish working through the wizard, and allow it to install the driver it finds (if any). It may decide that the best driver is already installed.

### *Specifying the Driver Location*

If Windows has incorrectly detected the device model, or if the new driver is located somewhere that Windows does not automatically search, you will need to go the manual route. The manual method has two options. You can still have Windows search for a driver by telling it where to search, or you can tell it exactly what driver to use.

You might want to specify the locations for the search if you have downloaded a driver and placed it in a folder on your hard drive; you can point Windows to that folder.

The procedures for Windows 95 versus the other Windows versions diverge in this situation. For Windows 95, complete the following steps:

1. Complete steps 1–3 under "Automatic Driver Discovery." At the Finish screen, if the wizard does not find a driver, an Other Locations button appears; click it.
2. Type a path, or click the Browse button, select a location, and then click OK. Click OK to accept the location.
3. Continue through the wizard to install any drivers found in that location.

For all other Windows versions (98 through 2000), follow these steps:

1. Display the device's Properties dialog box from Device Manager, and select the Driver tab.
2. Click the Update Driver button. The Update Device Driver Wizard runs.
3. Click Specify the location of the driver and then click Next.
4. Leave the Search for a better driver… option selected (see Figure 14.9) and mark the check boxes for the locations you want it to search. If you want to browse for a location, click the Specify a location check box and then click the Browse button. In Windows 98 it works a little differently: the Search for a better driver… option and the check boxes are on two different screens, and you must click Next between them.

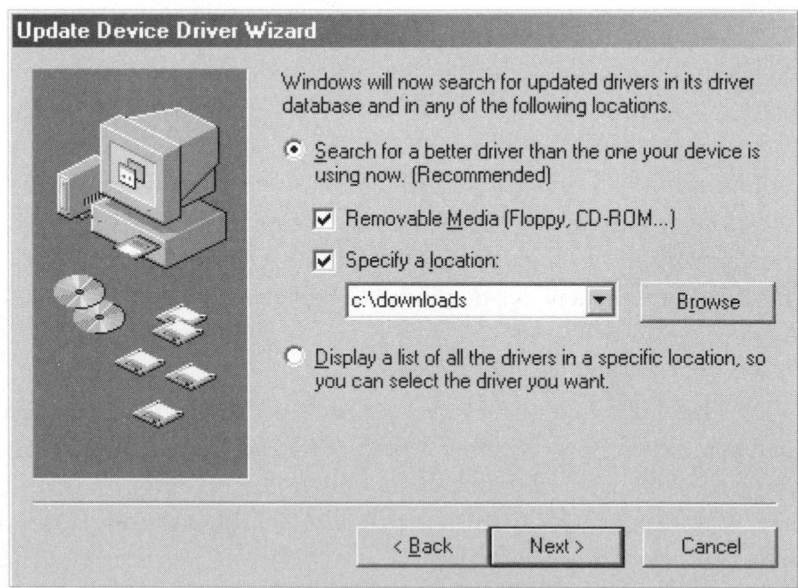


**FIGURE 14.9**
Select the locations where Windows should search for a driver.

5. Click Next and then finish working through the wizard to install the best driver Windows can find in the chosen locations. (Again, Windows may decide that the best driver is already installed.)

### *Manually Specifying a Driver*

If Windows has not correctly detected the hardware's model, or if there is a specific driver you want to use for some other reason, you will want to manually specify the exact driver you want. To do so, complete these steps:

1. Display the device's Properties dialog box from Device Manager, and select the Driver tab.
2. Click the Update Driver button. The Update Device Driver Wizard runs.
3. Click Specify the location of the driver and then click Next. (In Windows 95 the option is called No, Select Driver from List.)
4. Click Display a list of all the drivers in a specific location… and then click Next. (Skip this step for Windows 95.)
5. Do one of the following:
   a. Click the Have Disk button and then browse for the driver you want. (You are actually browsing for an INF file that will point to the driver.) Do this if you have acquired the driver yourself.
   b. Click the Show All Hardware option button and then select the make and model from the list provided, as in Figure 14.10. Do this if you do not have a driver you have acquired yourself.

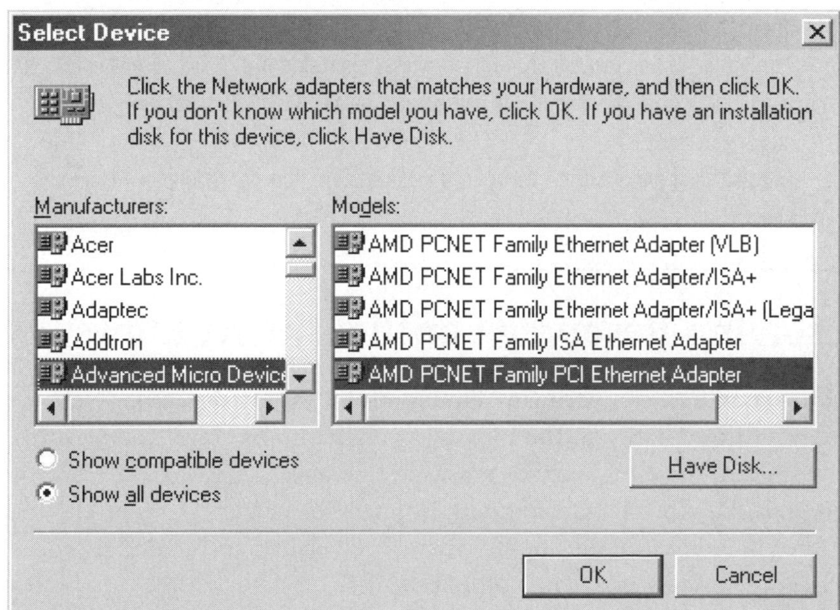


**FIGURE 14.10**
You can select one of the device models for which Windows has its own drivers.

6. Click Next and then complete the wizard and install the driver by continuing to follow the prompts.

### Windows XP and Signed Drivers

Windows XP is not covered on the 2001 version of the A+ exam, but you may need to know how to work with it on the job.

The steps for installing or updating a driver in Windows XP are virtually identical to those for other Windows versions. The main difference with Windows XP is the heavy reliance on *signed drivers,* which are drivers that have been certified by Microsoft to work with this version of Windows. Windows 2000 also uses signed drivers but does not insist on them as strongly. Signed drivers have digital signatures that verify that they have not been modified or corrupted since their creation. One of the reasons other versions of Windows crashed frequently was because of incompatibilities between drivers and the OS, so signed drivers are a way of making the system more stable by ensuring that the drivers do not cause problems. You can still use an unsigned driver in Windows XP, but dire warnings will appear on-screen when you try to install it. (You can ignore them if you have no choice but to use that driver.)

**Signed driver**

A driver that has been certified to work with a particular version of Windows and a device, containing a digital verification code tat shows it has not been altered since its certification.

**TRY IT!**

1. Turn off your PC and remove all of the nonessential devices such as modem, sound card, network card, or any USB, FireWire, or SCSI devices, and so on.
2. Turn on the PC again and remove any of the devices from Device Manager that still linger there after their physical removal.
3. Turn off the PC and reinstall one of the devices. Then restart the PC and allow Windows to redetect it. If it is not automatically redetected, manually install its driver using whatever means necessary.
4. Reinstall all of the rest of the devices and make sure they are all working in Windows again.

## Resolving Resource Conflicts in Windows

Resource conflicts can occur in Windows for a variety of reasons. If there are several ISA devices on the PC, there might simply not be enough IRQs to go around, since each device must have its own. Or if there are one or more non-PnP devices hard-set with jumpers for particular resources, the BIOS or Windows might not recognize those claims and might try to assign those resources to some other purpose.

Newer versions of Windows are much better than the older ones at managing system resources, so you are unlikely to run into resource problems on a Windows Me, 2000, or XP system. However, it is important to know how to resolve resource conflicts in all Windows versions, as they do still occur occasionally.

## Identifying a Resource Conflict

A device involved in a resource conflict usually does not work properly. Either it does not work at all or it works only sporadically, with the activation of some other device causing it to fail. For example, if the mouse and modem are in conflict, the mouse pointer might freeze up whenever you dial out. It is possible for a conflict to occur and show no definitive performance symptoms, however.

Most problems result in the affected devices showing a yellow circle with an exclamation point next to the device in Device Manager, as in Figure 14.11. When you double-click the device to display its properties, a message about a conflict appears in the Device status area. In Figure 14.12 the problem is that the system is simply out of IRQs. To solve this problem you would need to disable some other resource to free up an IRQ. For example, in Chapter 9 you learned how to disable built-in COM and LPT ports in BIOS Setup.

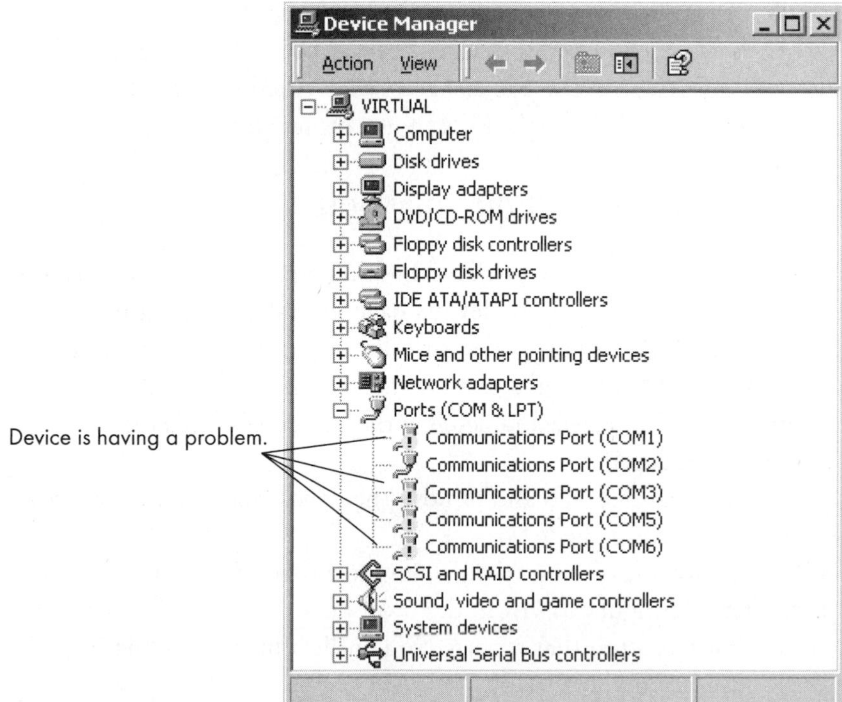


**FIGURE 14.11**
Problems appear in Device Manager as yellow circles with exclamation points.

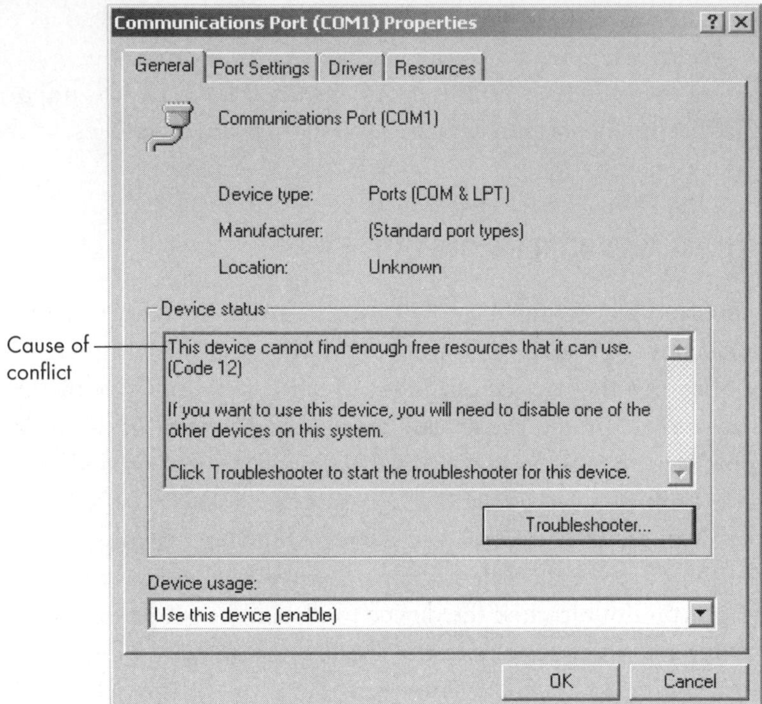


**FIGURE 14.12**
This status message reports that the system is out of available resources; you must disable some other device to enable this one.

In other cases there may be resources available, but for some reason two devices are claiming the same resource. When this happens, you will see a device listed on the Resources tab under Conflicting device list. This information is useful because if the current device cannot be changed, perhaps the other device in the conflict can change instead. A resource conflict can occur with any resource, although IRQs are the most common cause.

## Selecting an Alternate Configuration

The first course of action when troubleshooting a resource problem is to try an alternate configuration. Some devices have several configurations—combinations of IRQ, I/O addresses, or other resources—that they can accept. To check for these, and select one if possible, do the following:

1. From Device Manager, double-click the device to display its Properties dialog box.
2. Select the Resources tab and remove the check mark from the Use automatic settings check box.
3. Click the down-pointing triangle next to Setting based on and choose a different configuration from the drop-down list. Repeat until you find a configuration that reports No conflicts in the Conflicting device list (see Figure 14.13).

4. Click OK.

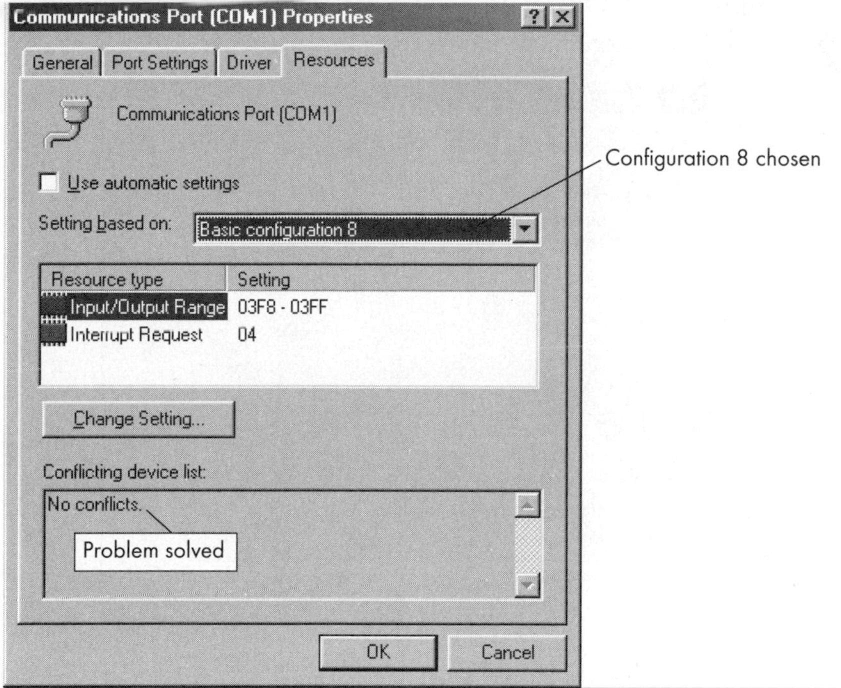


**FIGURE 14.13**
Find a configuration that results in no conflicts.

If there are no configurations on the list that resolve the conflict, see the following section.

## Manually Assigning a Resource

If none of the configurations worked in the preceding section, try choosing the exact setting for each resource that conflicts. For example, if only the IRQ is the problem, change only the IRQ. This works best in early versions of Windows such as Windows 95 (and sometimes 98); later versions of Windows do not allow you to make manual changes for most devices. You can always try; the worst thing that can happen is an error message letting you know you cannot do it.

To manually set a resource, complete these steps:

1. From Device Manager, double-click the device to display its Properties dialog box.
2. Select the Resources tab and remove the check mark from the Use automatic settings check box.
3. Click the resource you wish to change and then click the Change Setting button.

4. Change the setting in the dialog box that appears, as in Figure 14.14, and then click OK.
5. Click OK to accept the new setting for that device.

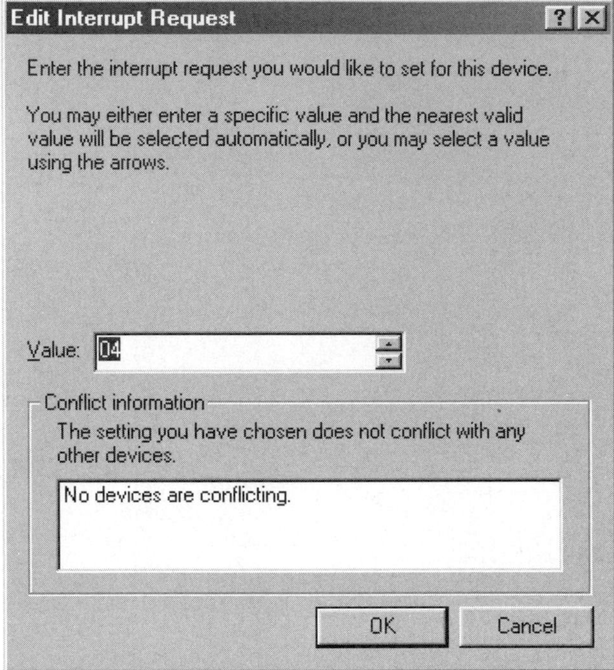


**FIGURE 14.14**
Find a configuration that results in no conflicts.

## TRY IT!

**Check your system for any resource conflicts, and resolve any that you find.**

## Disabling a Device

If you remove a PnP device entirely from Device Manager, Windows will usually redetect it each time you restart, and you will need to remove it again each time. To avoid this situation, you can disable the device rather than removing it. Disabling the device leaves it installed in Device Manager but turns off the resources for it. This can be especially useful when you want to disable a device that is not removable, such as a network interface card that is built into a notebook PC.

## In Real Life

In Chapter 20 you will learn about hardware profiles. One of the uses of a hardware profile is to set up different subsets of your hardware to be available at different times—especially convenient on a notebook PC. You create multiple profiles and then use the procedure described here for disabling a device driver to disable whatever hardware you will not want to appear in that profile.

To disable a device in Windows 2000 or XP, complete the following steps:

1. From Device Manager, click the device to select it.
2. Click the Disable Device button on the toolbar.
3. A warning appears; click Yes. An *X* appears through the device's icon (see Figure 14.15).

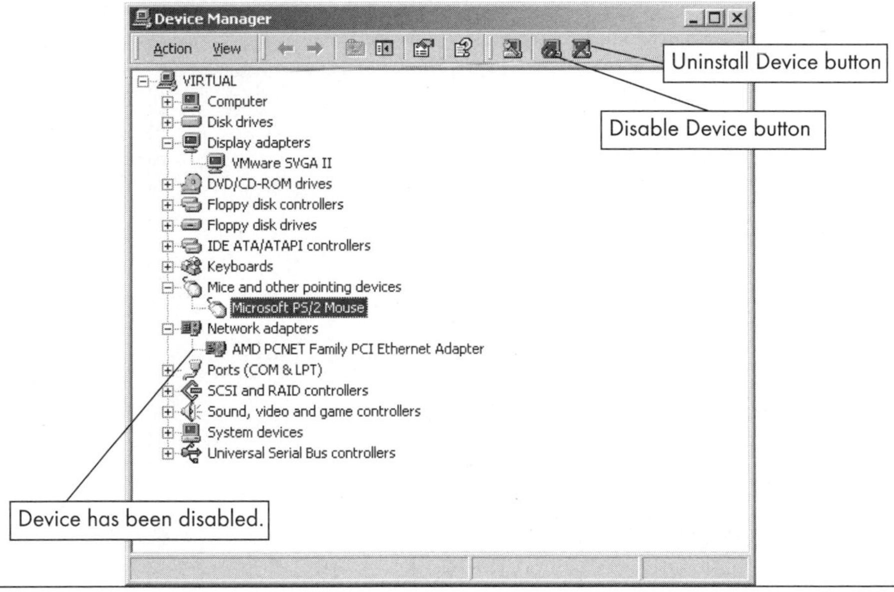


**FIGURE 14.15**
The network card has been disabled.

## WARNING

The Disable Device button is the one with the circle and line through the picture of the computer. It is the one that disables a device so that it appears in Device Manager with a red X through it. The Uninstall Device button removes it completely. Figure 14.15 points out both buttons.

To disable a device in Windows 95/98/Me, complete the following steps:

1. From the Device Manager, double-click the device to open its Properties dialog box.
2. On the General tab, click the Disable in this hardware profile check box to insert a check mark (see Figure 14.16).
3. Click OK.

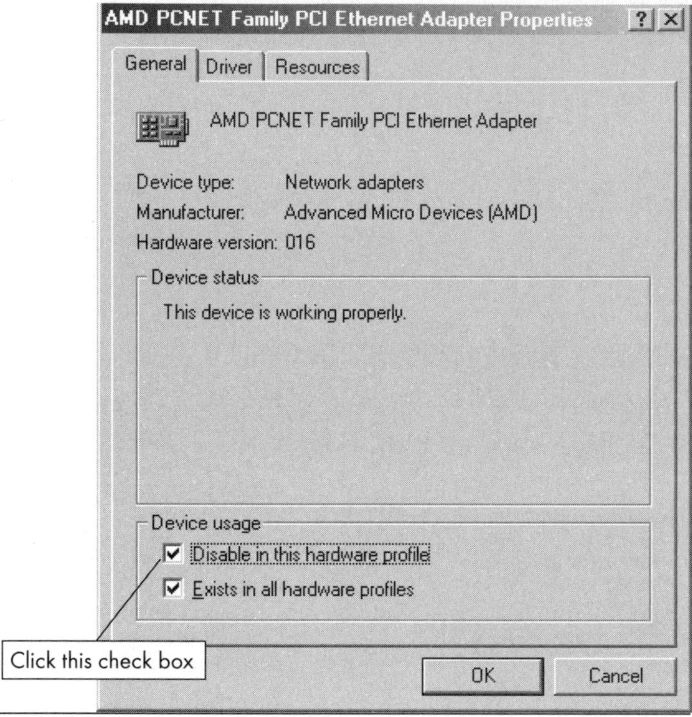


**FIGURE 14.16**
In Windows 9x/Me you disable a device from within its Properties dialog box.

## Disabling or Enabling PCI Bus IRQ Steering

**PCI bus IRQ steering**

A BIOS feature that allows PCI devices to share IRQs.

*PCI bus IRQ steering* is the feature that allows PCI devices to share an IRQ. When you look at the list of IRQ usage in Device Manager or System Information, some of the IRQs may be assigned to IRQ Holder for PCI Steering, as in Figure 14.17. This means that the PCI bus has taken control of those IRQs so it can dynamically assign them to whatever PCI devices might need them. Both the operating system and the motherboard chipset must support it in order for IRQ steering to work.

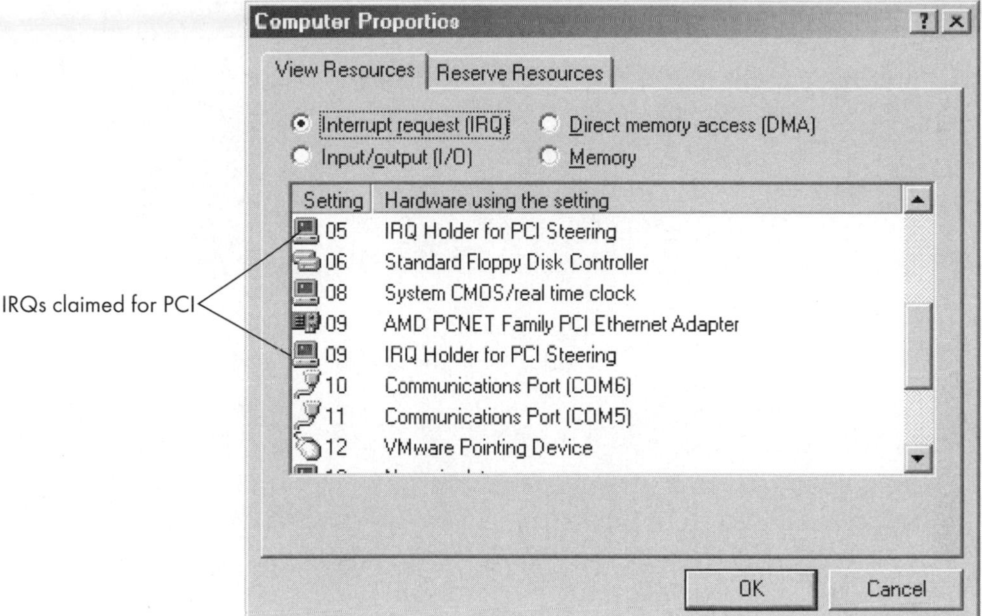


**FIGURE 14.17**
When PCI bus IRQ steering is enabled, some of the IRQs may be occupied by a PCI IRQ holder.

Most of the time you will want to leave PCI bus IRQ steering turned on because without it you are more likely to run out of IRQs. However, sometimes it causes problems such as masking a conflict between two PCI devices or assigning an IRQ to PCI that an ISA device is trying to use. The BIOS Setup program may have an option for turning it on/off there, and you can also enable or disable it in Windows.

To enable or disable PCI bus IRQ steering in Windows:

1. From Device Manager, click the plus sign next to System devices. (On some systems it is under Plug and Play BIOS rather than under System devices.)
2. Double-click *PCI Bus*. The PCI bus Properties dialog box opens.
3. On the IRQ Steering tab, click the Use IRQ Steering check box either to insert or to remove the check mark (see Figure 14.18).
4. Click OK to accept the change.

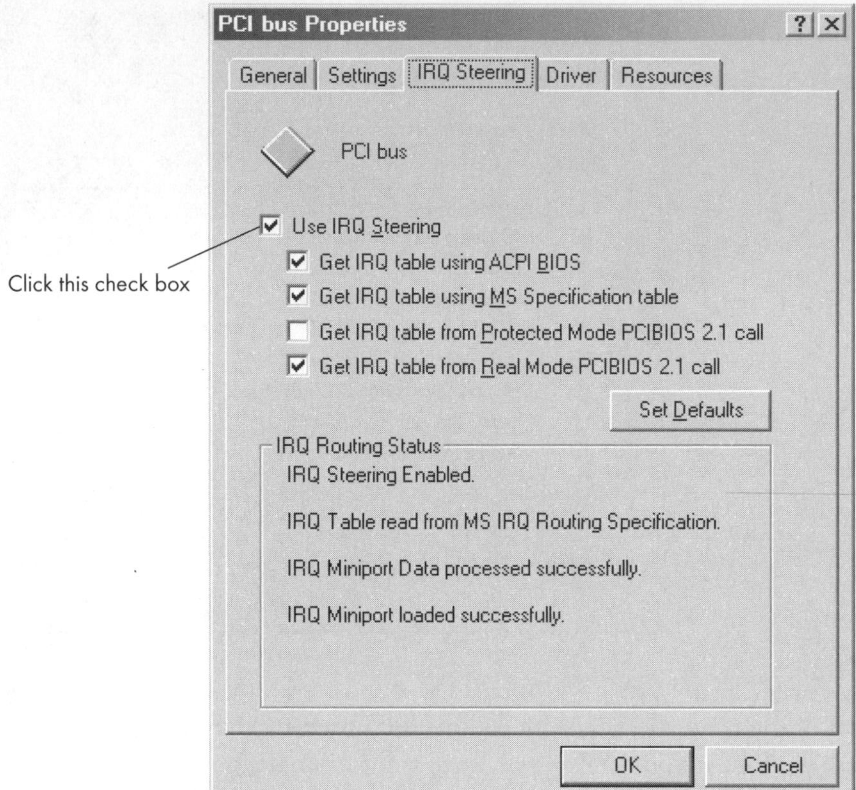


**FIGURE 14.18**
Enable or disable PCI bus IRQ steering from the PCI bus Properties dialog box.

## TRY IT!

1. Disable PCI bus IRQ sharing and then reboot, allowing Windows to reassign resources.
2. Did doing this create any resource conflicts? If so, resolve them.
3. Reenable PCI bus IRQ steering and restart again.
4. If you set any resources manually to resolve the conflicts, set these devices back to automatic assignments and restart again, so Windows can reinstitute PnP for these devices.

# STUDY GUIDE

Use the following summaries to review the key concepts of this chapter.

## DEVICE RESOURCES

- IRQs are lines of communication to the CPU. There are 16 of them in a PC, numbered 0 through 15.
- I/O addresses define areas of memory reserved for transferring data to and from the device. They are usually written using only the last four digits of the full address: 03E8.
- Memory addresses define areas of memory reserved for the device's use. They are usually written with eight digits of hexadecimal, such as 00A0000, and are usually expressed as a range: 00A0000-00BFFFF.
- Direct Memory Addressing (DMA) channels are pathways from a device directly into memory, bypassing the CPU.
- Each built-in I/O port has resources preassigned to it (COM and LPT ports).
- Expansion slots have no resources preassigned; they get resources only when something is plugged into them.
- Some interfaces such as SCSI, USB, and FireWire support multiple devices off the same set of resources.
- IRQs 2 and 9 are the same IRQ under two different names; they serve as a bridge between the lower 8 and upper 8 IRQs.
- You should memorize the default resource assignments as part of your study for the A+ exam; refer to Table 14.1 to review them.

## HOW DEVICE RESOURCES ARE ASSIGNED

- Built-in devices such as COM and LPT ports use whatever resources are assigned to them in BIOS Setup.
- Some expansion devices have jumpers that set their IRQ and I/O addresses; others are Plug and Play.
- Plug and Play (PnP) is a technology for detecting hardware and its resource and driver requirements and automatically assigning or installing them.
- PnP achieves full functionality only if all three pieces of the equation are PnP-compatible: the hardware device itself, the motherboard chipset, and the operating system.

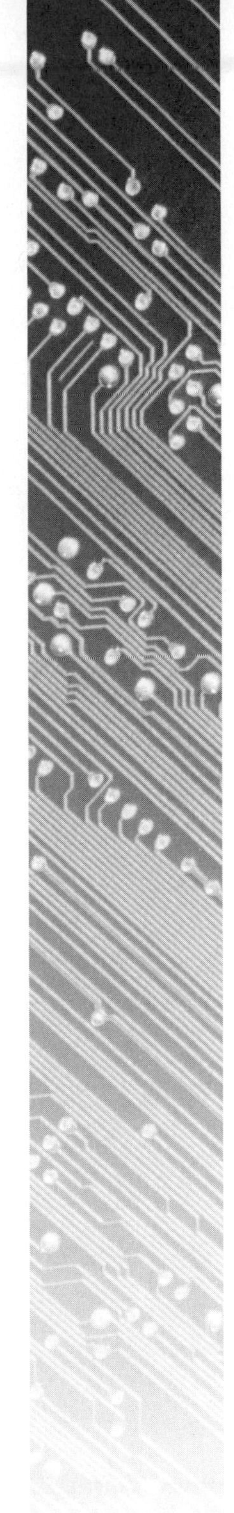

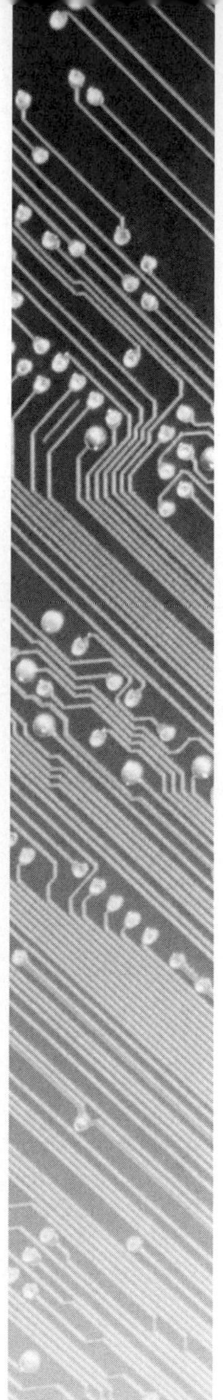

- A PnP-capable motherboard can detect PnP-compatible expansion boards and assign resources to them, achieving partial PnP functionality no matter what operating system is installed.
- Advanced Configuration and Power Interface (ACPI) is a method of controlling all of the PC's PnP hardware at the OS level. It also manages power savings settings.
- Windows 98 and above support ACPI. The motherboard must also support ACPI in order for it to be used.

## Viewing Resource Assignments in Windows

- There are two ways of viewing resources in Windows: Device Manager and System Information.
- To display Device Manager, right-click *My Computer* and choose Properties. In Windows 9x/Me, click the Device Manager tab; in Windows 2000/XP, click the Hardware tab and then the Device Manager button.
- Double-click a device to see its properties.
- Double-click *Computer* at the top of the tree in Windows 9x/Me to see a list of resources for the whole system. In Windows 2000/XP, choose View, Resources by type to see that list.

## Installing Plug and Play Devices

- Windows may automatically detect a PnP device, assign resources to it, and install a driver for it.
- Alternatively, Windows may detect and assign resources but not find a driver. In that case you will be prompted for one.
- If Windows does not detect a new PnP device, the device may be defective or improperly installed physically.

## Installing Non-Plug and Play Devices

- You might need to set jumpers on a non-PnP expansion board to set its IRQ and I/O addresses.
- Windows 95 and higher can detect a non-PnP device but cannot decide what resources it gets; it assigns the resources that the device asks for.
- If the resources the device requests are not available, a conflict results.
- To scan for new non-PnP hardware, use Add New Hardware in the Control Panel.

## Removing Devices from Device Manager

- Removing a device from Device Manager removes reference to its drivers from the Registry.
- To remove a device from Device Manager, select the device and press the Delete key.

## Understanding Device Drivers

- A device driver acts as an interpreter between the OS and the device.
- Some devices require only a single driver file; others require several.
- When you install a driver the needed files are registered in the Registry.
- The information file that tells Windows which driver files to install is a plain text file with an .inf extension.
- Windows works best with drivers written specifically for the exact hardware and exact Windows version.
- Most device manufacturers provide drivers for download at their Web sites.

## Installing or Updating Device Drivers

- A yellow circle with an exclamation point next to a device in Device Manager indicates that a driver is not installed or there is a conflict between devices.
- A device that Windows cannot completely identify may appear in an Other Devices category.
- To update or install a driver, find the device in Device Manager and double-click it, then click the Update Driver button on the Driver tab and complete the wizard that appears.
- The wizard lets you choose between automatic and manual driver location. The specific steps depend on the Windows version.
- Windows XP relies on driver signing to make sure a driver is appropriate for Windows XP and has not been altered. Windows 2000 also supports driver signing.

## Resolving Resource Conflicts in Windows

- Most conflicts result in one or both of the devices showing a yellow circle with an exclamation point next to the device in Device Manager.
- Information about the device status appears on the General tab of the device's Properties dialog box.
- If there is a resource conflict, look on the Resources tab to determine which other device is conflicting, and which resource.

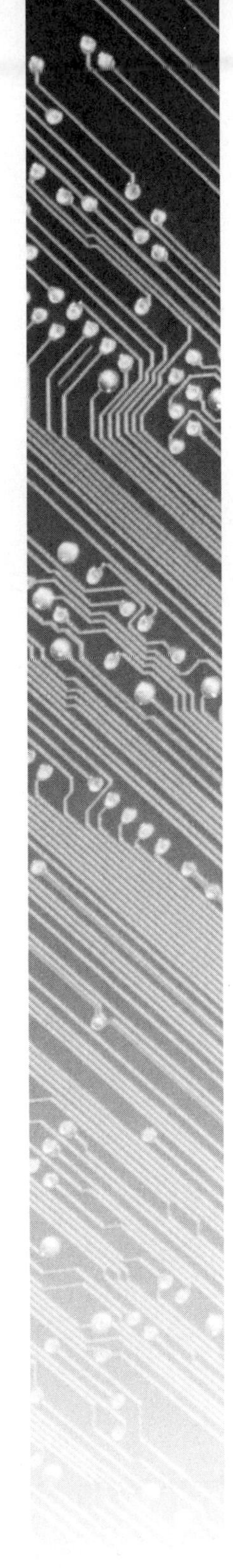

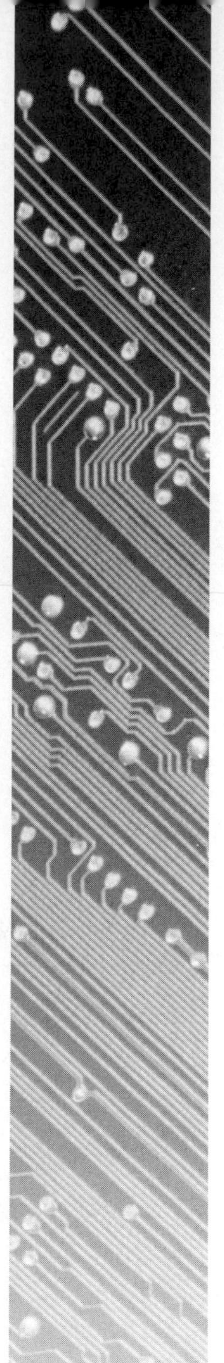

- To try a different configuration, clear the Use automatic settings check box and then select a different setting from the Setting based on list.
- In some cases you can change an individual resource by selecting it and then clicking Change Setting.

### PCI Bus IRQ Steering

- PCI bus IRQ steering is the feature that allows PCI devices to share an IRQ.
- In most cases it is enabled, both in BIOS Setup and in Windows.
- If you do not want PCI devices to share IRQs, you can turn it off in Windows.
- To turn it off, find PCI Bus on the System devices list (or on the Plug and Play BIOS list) in Device Manager and double-click to display its properties. Then on the IRQ Steering tab, clear the Use IRQ Steering check box by clicking in it.

## PRACTICE TEST

On a blank sheet of paper, write the answers to the following multiple-choice questions and explain why each answer is correct.

1. IRQ stands for
   a. Internal Request Query.
   b. Interrupt Request.
   c. Internal Recovery Query.
   d. Interrupt Question.

2. How many IRQs do today's PCs have?
   a. 8
   b. 9
   c. 12
   d. 16

3. What type of resource is expressed in a four-digit format like 03E8-03EF?
   a. IRQ
   b. I/O address
   c. memory address
   d. DMA

4. What type of resource is expressed in an eight-digit format like 00A0000-00BFFFF?
   a. IRQ
   b. I/O address
   c. memory address
   d. DMA

5. What is the purpose of a DMA channel?
   a. improve device response time by bypassing the CPU
   b. improve device response time by bypassing memory
   c. act as a buffer to decrease wait times
   d. None of the above

6. Which of these buses requires a separate IRQ for each device?
   a. PCI
   b. USB
   c. ISA
   d. FireWire

7. Which two IRQs cascade to one another?
   a. 1 and 8
   b. 2 and 9
   c. 0 and 9
   d. 15 and 16

8. Which COM port uses 3E8-3EF and IRQ 4?
   a. COM1
   b. COM2
   c. COM3
   d. COM4

9. Which IRQ does LPT1 use by default?
   a. IRQ 3
   b. IRQ 5
   c. IRQ 7
   d. IRQ 8

10. If there are four IDE devices in a system, how many IRQs do they require?
    a. 1
    b. 2
    c. 3
    d. 4

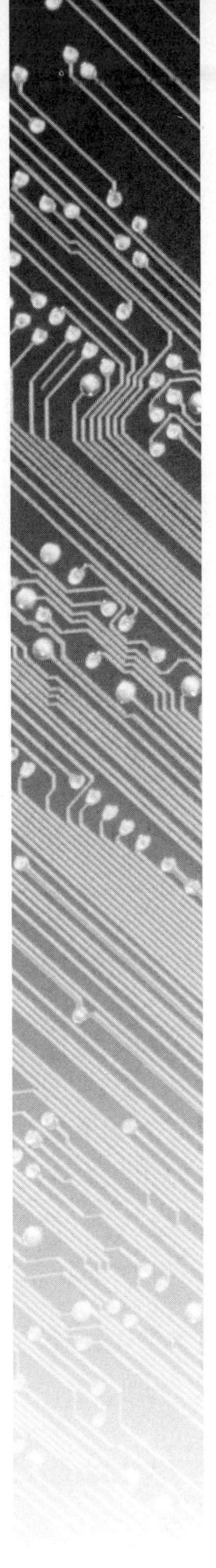

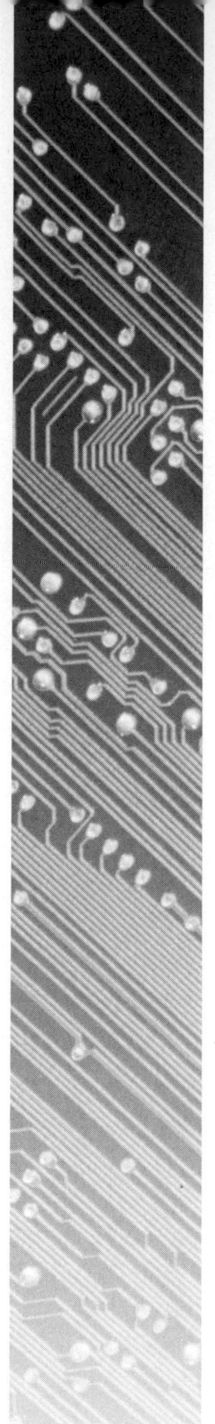

11. Which of these items does *not* affect whether the OS can set up an expansion board using Plug and Play?
    a. motherboard BIOS
    b. the OS version
    c. the device itself
    d. All of the above affect PnP capability.

12. If the PnP Operating System option is set to Yes in BIOS Setup, what is the effect on Plug and Play functionality?
    a. It allows the BIOS to assign system resources to devices.
    b. It prevents the BIOS from assigning system resources to devices.
    c. It changes BOOT.INI to load a PnP version of Windows if available.
    d. both b and c

13. Which of these was the first Windows version to support PnP?
    a. Windows NT 4.0
    b. Windows 3.1
    c. Windows 95
    d. Windows 98

14. Which of these Windows utilities enables you to both view and change device resource assignments?
    a. System Editor
    b. Device Manager
    c. System Information
    d. both b and c

15. What is the purpose of a device driver?
    a. It acts as a communicator between the device and the OS.
    b. It provides the communication pathway between the device and the CPU.
    c. It signals to the CPU that the device is ready to communicate.
    d. It supplies AC power to the device.

16. What is the purpose of an INF file?
    a. It is a device driver.
    b. It is a BIOS extension.
    c. It is a text file that tells Windows which driver files to install.
    d. It is a startup file loaded by CONFIG.SYS.

17. What resource causes a device resource conflict?
    a. DMA channel
    b. memory address
    c. IRQ
    d. Any of these

18. What is PCI bus IRQ steering?
    a. the feature that enables ISA and PCI devices to share a single bus
    b. the feature that enables PCI devices to share an IRQ
    c. the feature that enables PCI devices to select their own IRQs dynamically
    d. the feature that disables IRQ assignments in BIOS Setup so Windows handles them all

19. How many IRQs would you need for three USB devices plugged into a single USB hub?
    a. 1
    b. 2
    c. 3
    d. 6

20. What does it mean if Device Manager reports a device in the Other Devices category?
    a. It recognizes the device but cannot find a driver for it.
    b. It knows the device exists but does not know what type it is.
    c. It does not see the device at all.
    d. It is an ISA expansion card.

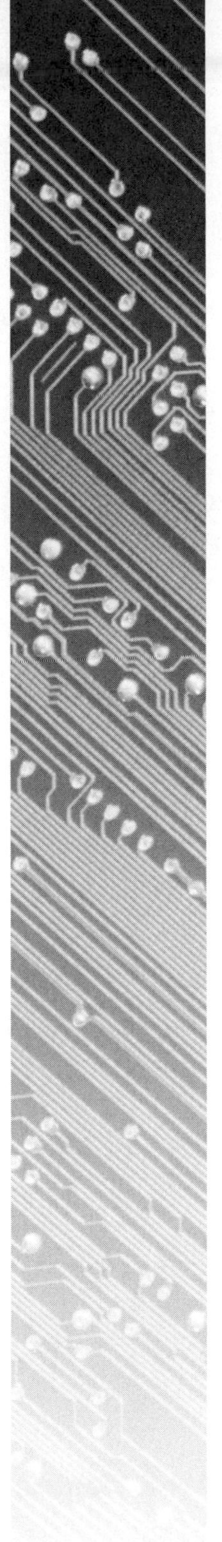

# TROUBLESHOOTING

1. The box for a sound card you are installing says that it is Plug and Play, but it has jumpers for IRQ and I/O address. How should you set the jumpers to use it as a Plug and Play device?
2. You are troubleshooting a problem with a possibly corrupt device driver, and you need to know the names and locations of the files that Windows is using for that device. How can you find this information?
3. No Windows XP driver is available for a multifunction printer device, but there are drivers for other operating systems, including Windows 98, Windows Me, and Windows 2000. Which would be the most likely one to try?

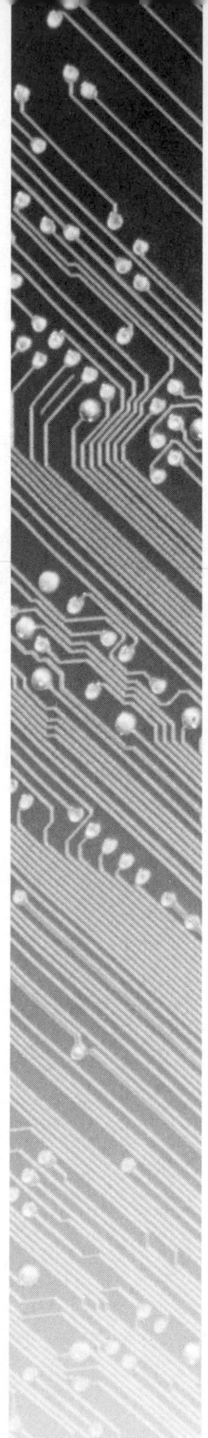

# CUSTOMER SERVICE

1. A client phones you saying he just installed a new internal modem but it does not work. Describe how you would check for device conflicts over the phone.
2. Another client is having a problem with a new external modem. Se has hooked it up to COM1, but in Device Manager there is no COM1, and the modem does not work. What can you suggest?
3. While in the BIOS Setup program a client notices the PnP Operating System setting and sees that it is set to No. He asks whether he should set it to Yes. What do you recommend?

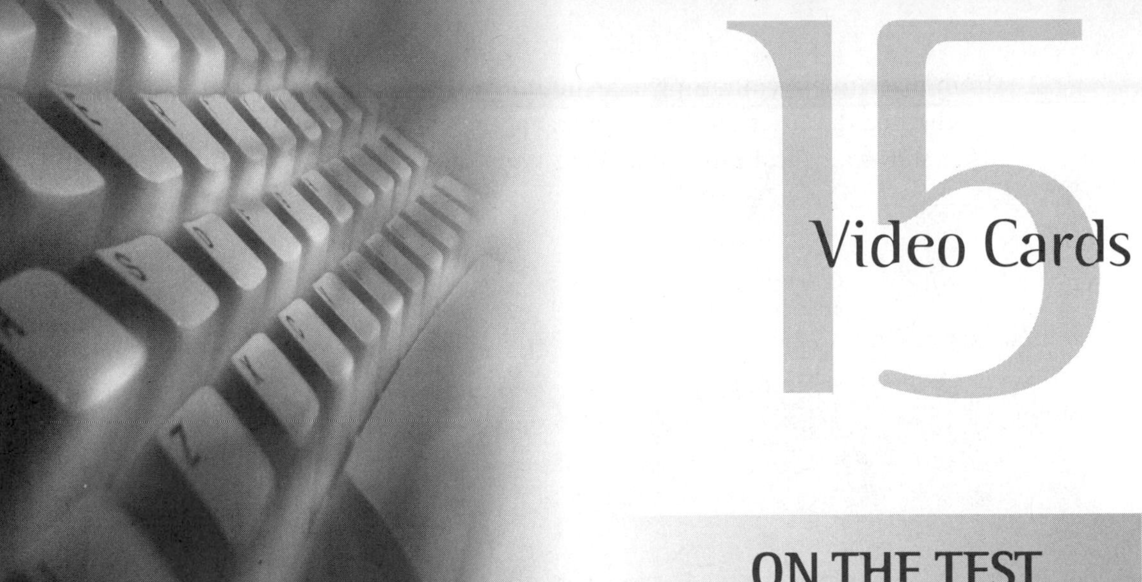

# 15 Video Cards

## ON THE TEST

**A+ Core Hardware Service Technician Examination**

- **Objective 1.7:** Identify proper procedures for installing and configuring peripheral devices.
- **Objective 2.1:** Identify common symptoms and problems associated with each module and how to troubleshoot and isolate the problems.

## ON THE JOB

The video card is part of the very important video subsystem. It translates instructions from the OS into directions for the monitor. When the video card malfunctions, or is not the right type for the job at hand, display performance suffers. It is therefore important to know both how to select a video card and how to install and troubleshoot it.

Skills you will learn in this chapter include:

- selecting an appropriate video card for a user's needs
- deciding how much video RAM is needed
- installing a video card
- troubleshooting display problems

## How a Video Card Works

A *video card* converts data from the OS into instructions to the monitor to light up certain areas of the screen with certain colors. It is typically an expansion board that fits into an AGP or PCI slot on a motherboard. If it is a separate board, the video card has its own RAM, chipset, and data bus (to carry data

**Video card**

An expansion board that provides an interface between the motherboard and the monitor.

from place to place on its own circuit board). If it is built into the motherboard, it uses the bus, chipset, and RAM of the motherboard. Figure 15.1 shows a typical expansion board-type video card.

**FIGURE 15.1**
A Typical Expansion Board-Type Video Card

The term "video card" is used to refer to the video capability in a PC, but, as mentioned earlier, it does not need to be a separate expansion board. Video capability can be built into the motherboard itself, as it is on many inexpensive PCs. In such cases a cable connects a 15-pin female connector from the motherboard to the back of the PC case.

> **WARNING**
>
> **On systems with built-in video support, the amount of RAM the PC has available for ordinary usage is decreased by the amount allocated to the video system. For example, if the PC has 64MB of RAM and 8MB of video support, the PC actually has only 56MB of RAM for running programs.**

**Pixel**

An individual dot in a particular display resolution.

The video card needs its own memory because it must hold all of the data needed to display the contents of the screen. For example, assume the individual *pixel* (dot) in the top left corner of the screen is supposed to be white. The video card must store the numeric code for white in its memory, and continually send messages to the monitor letting it know what color to display: "still white . . . still white . . . still white . . ." over and over, hundreds of times per second. When you do something in the OS that

causes the color of that pixel to change, the OS sends the message to the video card (for example, to change it to red), and the video card starts sending a new message to the video card: "change to red . . . still red . . . still red . . . ." Of course there are a great many more pixels than just that single one. The exact number of unique pixels that make up the display depends on the *resolution* at which you are running the operating system. A typical resolution is 800 x 600 (800 pixels across by 600 pixels high). The total number of pixels is determined by multiplying the vertical resolution by the horizontal resolution. The video card must send not only the code for the color, but also the code that tells which pixel it is describing. Figure 15.2 shows the path from the OS to the monitor.

**Resolution**

A display mode, expressed in the number of pixels across and the number of pixels down, such as 640 x 480 or 800 x 600.

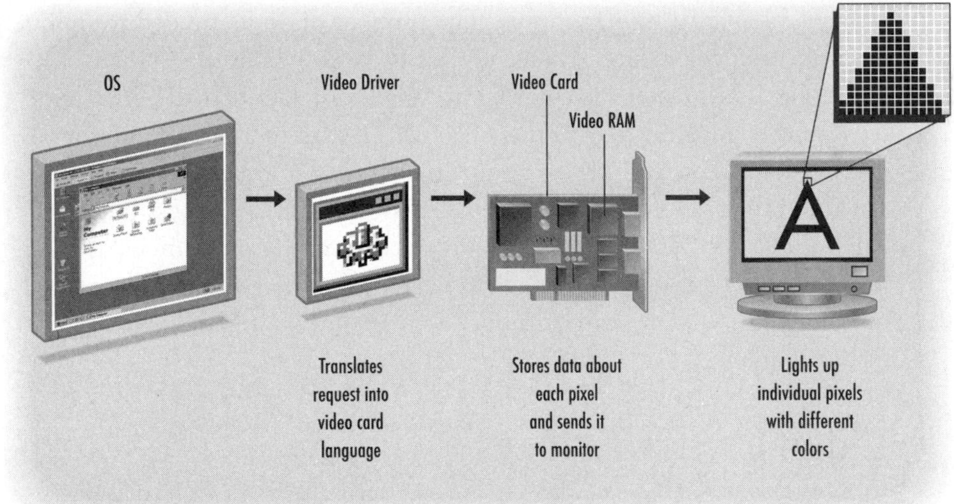


**FIGURE 15.2**
The Path of Display Data from the OS to the Monitor

Each monitor has a fixed number of tiny phosphors that make up its screen. Each of these phosphors can be individually lit up or not. They are arranged in groups of three called *triads*: one each of red, green, and blue. Any color can be displayed by various combinations of these three colors (see Figure 15.3). When a monitor is operating at its maximum resolution, the OS is sending data to the monitor about each of those triads individually. When a monitor operates at a resolution less than its maximum, multiple triads work together as a single pixel, sharing a single data instruction. You will learn more about monitors in Chapter 16.

**Triad**

A group of three colored phosphors on the monitor: red, green, and blue.

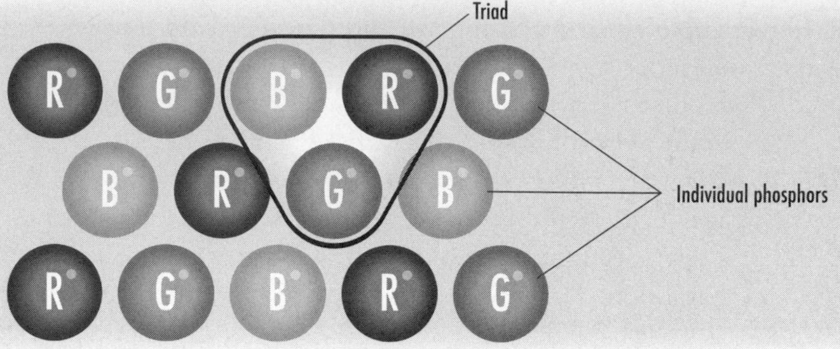


**FIGURE 15.3**
Groups of three different-colored phosphors make up a triad in a monitor.

**Color depth**

The number of bits needed to uniquely describe each color, and the resulting maximum number of colors produced by that number of bits.

Each color has a numeric value. The number of digits needed to uniquely describe each color depends on the *color depth* in which the OS is operating. The greater the color depth, the more data that the OS must send to the video card—and the video card must send to the monitor—every second. For example, in a four-digit binary number there are 16 possible values, so 4-bit color allows for 16 different color possibilities; 8-bit color allows for 256 colors; and so on. To determine the number of colors in a particular color depth, calculate 2 to the *X* power where *X* is the number of bits. There will be more about resolution and color depth later in the chapter.

## Video Card Interfaces

Since the video card acts as an interface between the motherboard and the monitor, it must have connectors for each. At the monitor end, almost all video cards have a standard VGA 15-pin female connector to which the monitor attaches, shown in Figure 15.4.

**FIGURE 15.4**
A VGA Connector to the Monitor

## In Real Life

**A few high-end video cards have three or four separate BNC connectors instead (or in addition); they connect to special-purpose, high-end monitors.**

At the motherboard end, a video card fits into either an Accelerated Graphics Port (AGP) or Peripheral Component Interface (PCI) slot. We covered these buses in earlier chapters, but let us briefly review them. AGP is a high-speed bus designed specifically for video cards, and a typical motherboard has only one of them. PCI is the general-purpose bus on modern motherboards. You can tell what type of slot a video card requires by reading the box, or by setting the card inside the PC and looking at where the edge connector lines up. An AGP card's edge connector is farther away from the metal backplate than the edge connector on a PCI. Figure 15.5 compares them.

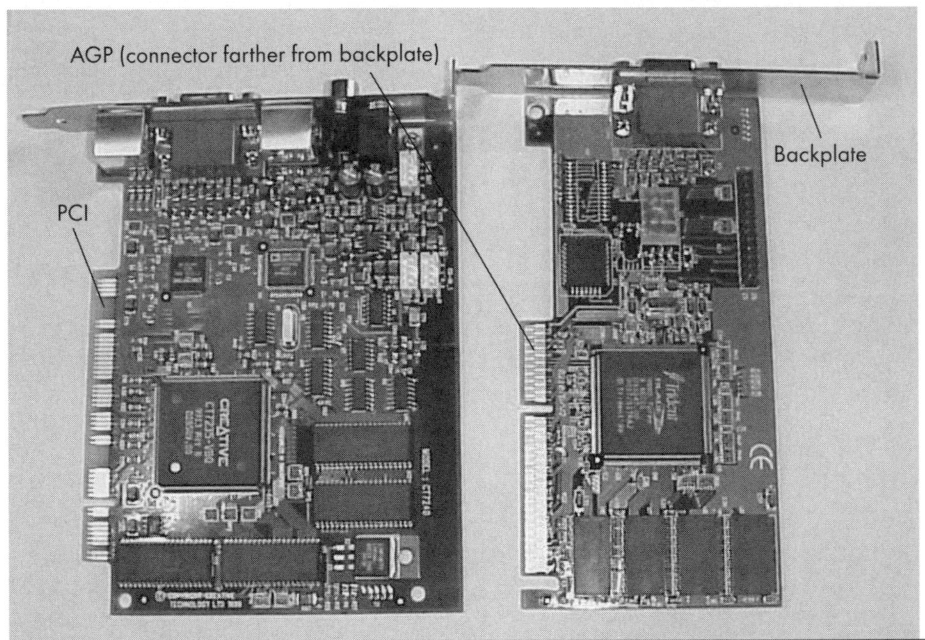


**FIGURE 15.5**
PCI versus AGP Video Card Interfaces

There are two other video card interfaces to the motherboard, but they are both obsolete. One is VESA local bus (VLB), a local-bus interface that predated PCI. The other is Industry-Standard Architecture (ISA), the general-purpose expansion board interface. Chapter 4 discussed all of these buses in detail, so you may want to review that information now. The key thing to remember is that AGP is the preferred bus for video if it is available; otherwise, PCI is the next preferable bus. ISA is the least desirable choice for video card bus because it is so slow and the bus itself becomes a bottleneck to video performance.

**TRY IT!**

**Identify the video card in your PC. What is its bus type?**

# Video RAM

The video card has its own RAM, separate from the RAM in the PC (except if the video card is built into the motherboard). It uses its RAM to keep track of what color each pixel should be displaying at any given moment. The operating system constantly updates the video RAM's information, and that information is constantly sent on to the monitor so it can update the on-screen image. The more video memory, the more data can be stored and relayed.

This RAM is different from the RAM in the PC both physically and in how it works. Video RAM is contained in chips mounted directly on the circuit board. On some older video cards the RAM is upgradeable (there are sockets where you can install more), but in most of the newer video cards the RAM is permanently soldered in place. Refer back to Figure 15.1 for RAM placement on a typical video card.

## Amount of Video RAM

Most video cards sold today have at least 8MB of RAM; some have up to 128MB. The amount of video RAM is important because more RAM enables higher resolution/color depth combinations. On some video cards, having more RAM can also result in better performance.

One way to determine the amount of video RAM on an installed card is to watch as the PC starts up. For a brief second or two at the very beginning, a message appears reporting the video card maker and model and the amount of video RAM. If you miss it, you can also find out from within Windows: open Display Properties, click the Settings tab, click the Advanced button, and then click the Adapter tab. Here you will find information about the video card, including the amount of video RAM available.

## TRY IT!

**Determine the amount of RAM your video card has available.**

The total number of pixels in a display resolution can be determined by multiplying the number across from the number down. For example, a display resolution of 800 x 600 has 480,000 pixels. If using 8-bit color depth (256 colors), it needs 8 bits (1 byte) to describe each pixel, so you nccd 480KB of video RAM to support the resolution. That is less than half a megabyte, and since the average video card has at least 8MB of RAM, all video cards should enable that combination. However, the required RAM begins to add up when you work with higher color depths and resolutions. Table 15.1 shows some examples of the amounts of memory required for some common color depth and resolution combinations.

| Resolution | Color Depth | Approximate Video Memory Required |
|---|---|---|
| 640 x 480 | 4-bit (16 colors) | 154KB |
| 800 x 600 | 8-bit (256 colors) | 480KB |
| 800 x 600 | 16-bit (65,536 colors) | 960KB |
| 1024 x 768 | 16-bit (65,536 colors) | 1.6MB |
| 1024 x 768 | 24-bit (16.7 million colors) | 2.4MB |
| 1280 x 1024 | 24-bit (16.7 million colors) | 3.9MB |
| 1280 x 1024 | 32-bit (4.3 billion colors) | 5.2MB |

**TABLE 15.1**
Example Video RAM Requirements for Display Modes

To summarize: To determine the RAM requirements of a particular video mode, multiply the height by the width of resolution, multiply that result by the number of bits of color depth, and then divide by 8.

As you can see in Table 15.1, even very high resolution and color depth combinations do not require as much as 8MB of RAM, so why do most video cards come with more than that? One reason is that some of the extra memory can serve as a *cache*, speeding up the video card's performance. A cache is a holding area for data that is waiting to exit or enter.

**Cache**

A holding area for data that is waiting to exit or enter.

Earlier in the chapter we talked about the bus that connects the video card to the motherboard—AGP or PCI, 32-bit or 64-bit. The video card itself has its own internal bus that carries data from its own internal chipset to its own RAM. This bus is usually 64- or 128-bit. On some cards, having more memory means a wider internal bus width can be used.

The main reason for all of the "excess" video memory is to support *3D video acceleration.* A video card with 3D is one that is optimized for running programs that have graphics with depth perspective, such as games

**3D video acceleration**

Additional features in a video card that process Application Programming Interface (API) commands from 3D-aware applications, helping relieve the processing burden on the CPU.

that enable a character to move through what seems like a three-dimensional space. It is like the difference between a drawing of a square and a drawing of a cube. In contrast, regular video operation that does not require 3D is known as 2D.

Operation in 3D requires additional RAM for three buffers that store video data and quickly transfer it in and out of the main video memory space to help improve the speed at which one graphic can morph into another. These buffers are the Front buffer, Back buffer, and Z buffer.

These buffers add quite a bit to the memory requirements. Table 15.2 shows some of the common resolutions and color depths used in 3D programs and the amount of video RAM required to run them. Suddenly 16MB no longer seems excessive.

| Resolution | Color Depth | Video Memory Required |
|---|---|---|
| 640 x 480 | 16-bit | 2.34MB |
| 640 x 480 | 24-bit | 3.52MB |
| 640 x 480 | 32-bit | 4.69MB |
| 800 x 600 | 16-bit | 3.66MB |
| 800 x 600 | 24-bit | 5.49MB |
| 800 x 600 | 32-bit | 7.32MB |
| 1024 x 768 | 16-bit | 5.49MB |
| 1024 x 768 | 24-bit | 9MB |
| 1024 x 768 | 32-bit | 12MB |
| 1280 x 1024 | 16-bit | 10MB |
| 1280 x 1024 | 24-bit | 15MB |
| 1280 x 1024 | 32-bit | 20MB |

**TABLE 15.2**
Example Video RAM Requirements for 3D Video Modes

## Types of Video RAM

There are many different types of RAM used on video cards. Some of these are basically the same as the RAM used in PCs (but in different external packaging); others are unique to video cards.

If you had shopped for video cards several years ago, you might have seen cards advertised with Video RAM (VRAM), Windows RAM (WRAM), or Multibank DRAM (MDRAM). These were all types of RAM made specifically for video cards that provided higher performance than the standard PC RAM. All are obsolete now. Figure 15.6 shows the types of RAM currently found on video cards.

- **SDRAM (synchronous synamic RAM):** The same type of RAM used in the PC's main memory (but packaged differently). Also called SDR (Single Data Rate) DRAM, it operates at the same speed as (that is, synchronous with) the motherboard's system bus.
- **DDR (Double Data Rate) SDRAM:** Alternative to regular SDRAM that can operate at up to twice the speed of regular SDRAM by performing two operations per cycle rather than one. It provides about a 20 percent actual performance boost from regular SDRAM but is less expensive to produce than SGRAM, making it an attractive mid-level choice.
- **SGRAM (synchronous graphics RAM):** High-end type RAM used in many of the highest quality video cards. It is one of the most expensive types of video RAM because it includes circuitry for performing block writes that can significantly increase the speed of graphics fill or 3D Z-buffer operations.

**FIGURE 15.6**
Types of Video RAM

It is difficult to tell which type of RAM a video card has by looking at the card; the best way to find out is to consult the manufacturer's specifications.

## Video RAMDAC

**Random access memory digital-to-analog converter (RAMDAC)**

The digital-to-analog converter on the video card.

The *random access memory digital-to-analog converter* (RAMDAC) on the video card takes the digital data from the PC and converts it to analog data that the monitor can display. Its speed is measured in megahertz; faster is better. A typical RAMDAC speed for today's video cards is 300 to 350MHz. The main benefit of faster RAMDAC is higher refresh rate capability. RAMDACs of 300MHz and higher allow 75Hz or higher refresh rates at resolutions of up to 1920 x 1200. That should be sufficient for almost any usage.

As with memory type, it is difficult to identify the RAMDAC by looking at the video card; consult the manufacturer's specifications to determine the RAMDAC speed.

## Video Chipset

There are hundreds of video card makers, but they all use chipsets obtained from the same few chipset makers and incorporate them into their video cards. The purpose of a video card chipset is similar to that of a motherboard chipset, which we discussed in Chapter 4. The chipset controls the movement of data within the video card, functioning as a traffic director, and more than any other card feature it determines the video card's overall performance capabilities. Therefore, when shopping for a video card one is mostly shopping for a chipset.

The most popular chipsets at this writing are made by ATI and NVIDIA. Both companies have their own branded line of video cards, but they also sell their chipsets to other video card makers. NVIDIA's line of GeForce chipsets currently dominates the mid-to-high-end market. The GeForce 3 and GeForce 4 chipsets are used in many of the best video cards sold today. Two other major players are ATI and Trident. By the time you read this, however, the information may be out of date, as new chipset manufacturers and chipsets come and go rapidly.

The chipset is usually the largest chip on the video card. For example, in Figure 15.1 the chip states that it is a Trident Blade chipset. That does not necessarily mean the video card is made by Trident Microsystems (it is not in this case), just that Trident Microsystems made the chipset and sold it to the video card manufacturer.

## Video Acceleration

As mentioned, some video cards support 3D acceleration. This means that they use a part of their RAM for multiple buffers that store data for quicker graphics handling in programs that have 3D graphics.

### Animation Support

To understand 3D animation in terms of the video card, think about an animated cartoon. In the past, each frame of the cartoon had to be drawn and colored by hand, so animation was very labor intensive. Computers have simplified the process in several ways. The computer can create some of the frames automatically with the use of *keyframes*. For example, you could move an object from point A to point B using computer animation by creating a still image of the object at point A and another one at point B; the computer would fill in all of the other frames between them (see Figure 15.7).

**Keyframe**

A frame of animation provided by the application rather than interpolated by the video card.

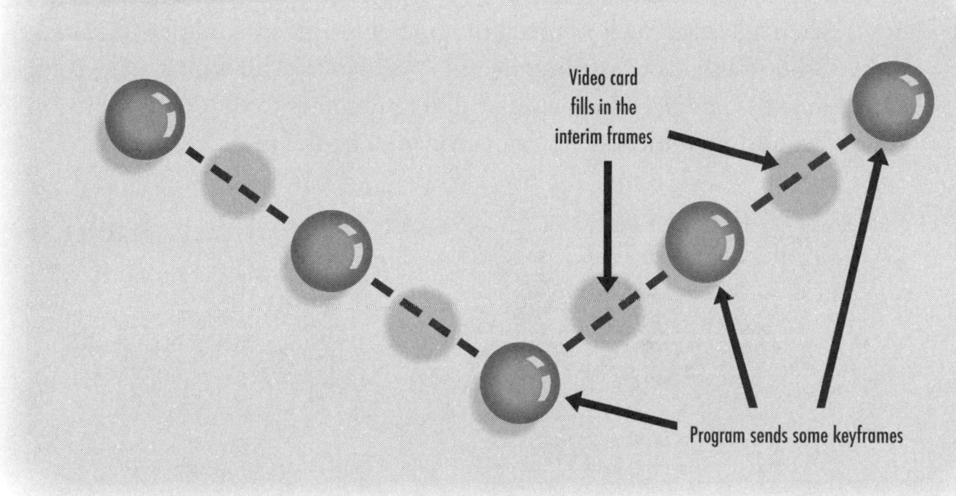
Video card
fills in the
interim frames
Program sends some keyframes

**FIGURE 15.7**
Keyframes cut down on CPU load by offloading some animation to the video card.

Many computer programs that contain a lot of animation employ keyframes so that the computer program does not have to send a staggering amount of data to the video card through its relatively slow connection. Instead the program sends only selected keyframes to the video card, and the video card uses its extra memory and processing capabilities to generate all of the other frames needed for the animation.

**Primitive**

An unfilled simple geometric shape.

In programs with 3D perspective, an object moving across the screen moves not just up (height) and across (width), but in the third dimension as well (depth). The location of an object in this 3D space is defined by the X, Y, and Z coordinates. These coordinates define simple geometric objects known as *primitives* that are used to create an object. As a simple example, three stacked spheres make a snowman; every object in every program is similarly made up of groups of primitives. Each primitive has its own position and animation.

## Texture/Shading Support

**Rasterization**

The process of filling in a primitive shape with texture or shading.

Almost any 3D video card can animate simple shapes, but today's sophisticated games and graphics applications require much more, such as shading and texture as the object moves across the screen. This process of filling in a primitive shape with appropriate texture and shading is known as *rasterization*. One of the ways that a computer application creates realistic-looking 3D objects is through *texture mapping*. The application includes textured patterns in the form of small graphic files that it tiles onto

**Texture mapping**

Filling in a 3D object with a two-dimensional repeating pattern.

**Flat shading**

Filling an object with a solid color.

**Gouraud shading**

Applying different colors to an object and then blending them.

the surface of the image, as shown in Figure 15.8. The application then modifies the appearance of each tile by applying perspective and shading to it, as when a surface such as metal or concrete is hit by sunlight, fog, or rain. Other methods of shading include *flat shading* (fill with a solid color) and *Gouraud shading*, which applies different colors to different points on an object and then blends the colors together in the middle.

**FIGURE 15.8**
**Texture mapping is one technique for creating realistic textured 3D images without placing undue burden on the CPU.**

Early 3D applications used software alone for rasterization, which slowed down the PC's CPU considerably. To help with this, video cards were developed that could accept some of the processing responsibility for rendering 3D images. Some of the functions that a good 3D video card can perform are listed in Figure 15.9.

- **Scan conversion:** Determining which pixels fall into the area delineated by a primitive.
- **Shading:** Applying color to a primitive shape using flat or Gouraud shading.
- **Texture mapping:** Filling primitives with images from 2D graphics files.
- **Visible surface determination:** Figuring out which primitives should obscure other primitives behind them in the display.
- **Antialiasing:** Smoothing the edges on objects to avoid jagged areas.
- **Fogging:** Simulating foggy weather conditions.
- **Alpha blending:** Creating translucent object fills that simulate see-through objects like glass and smoke.
- **Environment-based bump mapping:** Using lighting and texture effects to simulate rough textures such as bricks, ocean waves, and mountains. It combines three texture maps (color, size, and effects).
- **Stencil buffering:** Allowing part of the screen to display a fixed object, and using less overhead to do so, while other parts of the screen dynamically change. For example, a 3D action game might have a 2D player control panel on the side of the screen that remains the same while the rest of the screen shows a moving 3D image.
- **Z buffering:** Reducing overhead by allowing the details for a primitive that is nonvisible on-screen at the moment (because it is obscured by some other object) to not be constantly redrawn.

**FIGURE 15.9**
Functions of a 3D Video Card

There are many more functions of 3D video cards, but this gives a general idea. Some video cards use multiple passes to generate the display: one to lay down the basic primitives and another to shade and texture them. However, the best video cards these days use a single-pass method.

Just because a video card supports a particular operation does not mean it supports it well. The more effects the video card must process, the more time it takes for it to process each frame of the animation. Earlier we discussed refresh rate, measured in hertz, as the number of times per second that the video card updates the monitor display. The *frame rate* is analogous to that except it refers to the number of times per second that the video card alters what it sends to the monitor. When a video card is heavily taxed with operations to perform, its frame rate drops. Most people find that a frame rate of 20Hz is acceptable, but some notice choppiness at up to 40Hz. Therefore, some video cards do not support every 3D function possible to ensure that the card can maintain a decent frame rate.

**Frame rate**

The rate at which the video card alters what it sends to the monitor, measured in hertz.

## 3D API Support

The advanced features of a 3D video card are of use only if the application you are running happens to take advantage of these features. Therefore, it is essential that the video card you choose supports the same standards as the applications you want to run. Fortunately, most 3D video cards these days support most of the popular standards, as do most of the 3D applications.

The programmers who write 3D applications use industry-standard *Application Program Interfaces* (APIs) to create the lines of code that tell the video card what to do. This makes it possible for a program to work with many different video cards, rather than being written specifically for one model. The most popular APIs for graphics are shown in Figure 15.10.

**Application Program Interface (API)**

A set of standardized programming codes that application designers can use to create specific acceleration functions in a video card or other hardware.

- **OpenGL:** Supported by nearly all video cards. For many years OpenGL has been considered the superior API by most game programmers, and most 3D applications include an option for using it.
- **3Dfx Glide:** An enhanced version of OpenGL, found only on video cards that use 3Dfx chipsets. The company that made 3Dfx chipsets has withdrawn from the chip-making business, so this API is likely to become obsolete.
- **DirectX:** A collection of APIs, not just for video but also for sound. DirectX is a product of Microsoft, so all recent versions of Windows include good support for it.
- **Direct3D:** The subset of DirectX that deals specifically with video card graphics. Direct 3D was originally considered weaker than OpenGL by many programmers, but improvements have made it a strong competitor.

**FIGURE 15.10**
Video Card APIs

Any 3D video card on the market today should support both OpenGL and DirectX/Direct3D, as should any 3D application your client may want to run. Be sure to check the manufacturer's specifications.

## Other Video Card Features

Some video cards have extra features built in. If your client happens to need one of these features, the option can be valuable; if your client does not need them, there is no sense in paying extra for them.

### MPEG-2 Decoding

To play DVD movies on a PC, both a DVD drive (discussed in Chapter 13) and an MPEG-2 decoder card are needed. This functionality is built into some video cards, so an extra card is not needed.

### TV Out

Some video cards enable you to connect a television set to a PC and use it like a monitor. This can be convenient when a large screen is needed for a presentation, for example, but not for everyday use because the display quality is not as good as with a regular monitor.

### TV/Video Capture In

Some video cards have video inputs that allow a digital video camera or recorder to be connected and to transfer video data into a PC. Others have TV tuner cards built into them so TV can be watched on the monitor.

### Dual Monitor Output

Some video cards have more than one output plug so you can connect multiple monitors at once.

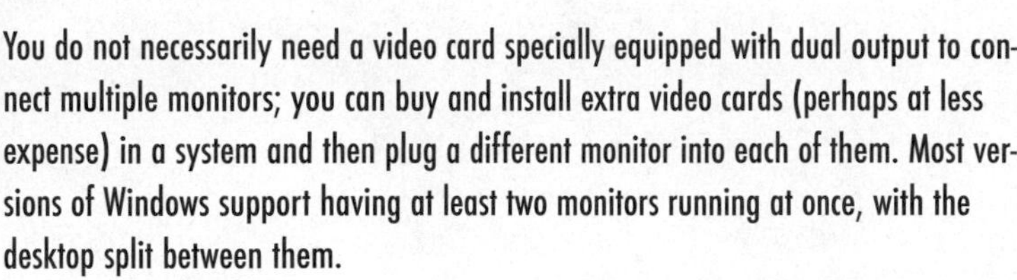

**IN REAL LIFE**

You do not necessarily need a video card specially equipped with dual output to connect multiple monitors; you can buy and install extra video cards (perhaps at less expense) in a system and then plug a different monitor into each of them. Most versions of Windows support having at least two monitors running at once, with the desktop split between them.

## Installing a Video Card

Chapter 8 discussed installing a video card. Let us briefly review.

1. If there is already a video card installed, remove it. To do so, remove the screw holding its backplate in place (see Figure 15.11) and then pull the card straight up, trying to hold it only by the edges and the backplate. If there is built-in video support in the motherboard, disable it through BIOS Setup.

**IN REAL LIFE**

Some motherboards with built-in video have a jumper on the motherboard that enables or disables on-board video rather than turning it on/off through BIOS Setup; check the motherboard manual.

2. Identify the slot in which you want to install the new video card, and if necessary remove the blank metal backplate from that slot.
3. Press the new video card firmly into the motherboard slot until it is completely seated (see Figure 15.12).
4. Secure it with the screw you removed in step 1 or 2.

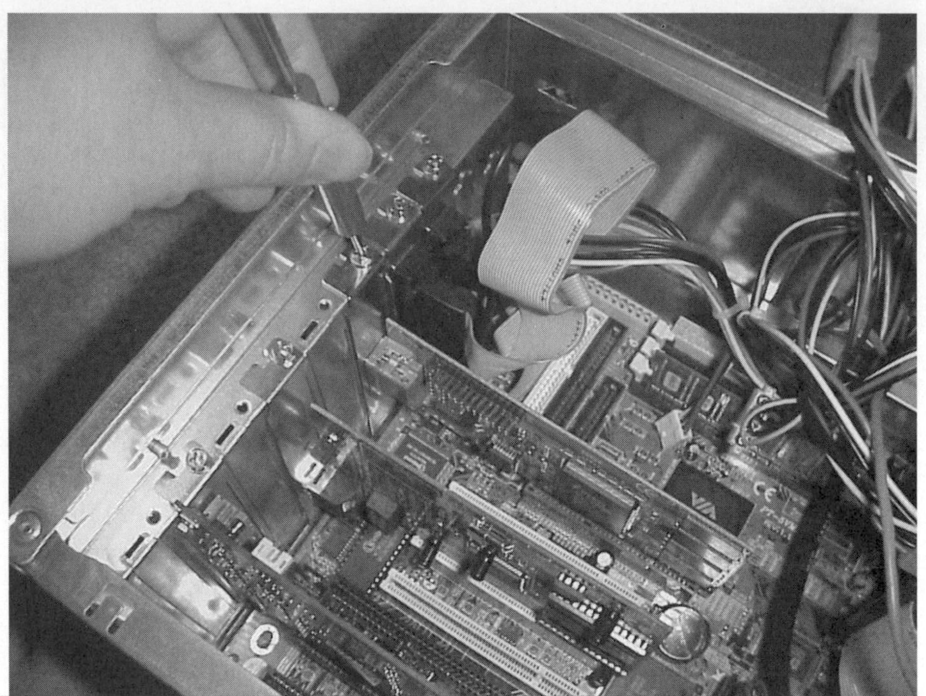

**FIGURE 15.11**
Remove the screw holding the old video card in place, and then pull the card out.

**FIGURE 15.12**
Insert the new video card into a slot.

5. Connect a monitor to the new video card, plug in the PC, and turn it on. If you see text on the screen (any text at all), the video card is installed correctly.
6. If Windows does not automatically detect the new video card, run the setup program that came with the video card or install a driver for it from a download from the manufacturer's Web site. See Chapter 14 for help.

**TRY IT!**

Remove and install your video card.

## Setting Display Properties in Windows

A typical video card can run in many different combinations of resolution and color depth, limited only by the video card's capabilities and the amount of RAM installed on it. Different users have different ideas of what constitutes optimal color depth and resolution. Some like to have the maximum number of colors at all times; others find that their system performs better at a lower color depth. Some like the crispness and detail of a high-resolution display mode while others prefer the larger text and graphic objects of a lower resolution.

### Installing the Driver

Before you can set display properties, you must install the correct driver for your video card. You learned about driver installation in Chapter 14. Usually the PC or the video card comes with a CD containing a setup program for the driver. If it does not, you can usually download a driver from the PC or video card maker's Web site.

If you cannot find a driver for the video card and the particular version of Windows anywhere—on disc, in Windows, from a Web site, or anywhere else you have tried—you have two choices. You can obtain a different video card, or you can try to get by with a driver that is not written specifically for the card or for that version of Windows.

Having a driver specifically for the video card is more important than having one for the Windows version. Generally, drivers for Windows 95, 98, and Me are all roughly compatible, so if a driver for one of these versions is available, you can try it with one of the other Windows versions. The same is true for Windows NT 4, Windows 2000, and Windows XP as a group. (You cannot, however, mix and match drivers between the two groups.)

If no driver is available for the video card for any Windows version, try a generic SuperVGA video driver if one is available in that Windows version. You might be able to choose SuperVGA from a list of standard display types, for example. Although this will not give great performance (no acceleration, for instance), it may at least allow for 256 colors and 800 x 600 resolution.

Somewhat riskier is choosing a driver specific to some other video card that you think may have a similar chipset. This may enable the video card's full capabilities, but it could also lock up the system. If Windows will not start normally after such a maneuver, go into Display Properties in Safe Mode and change to a generic VGA driver (or use the Roll Back Driver feature to go back to the previous driver).

## Changing the Color Depth

As mentioned at the beginning of this chapter, color depth is the number of possible colors in a particular display mode. Each dot on the screen is assigned a color, represented by a binary number. In a 4-digit binary number (0000 through 1111), for example, there are 16 possible combinations, so 4-bit color means 16 colors, 8-bit color is 256 colors, and so on. The highest color depth available in Windows is 32-bit.

The greater the color depth, the more vibrant and realistic photos and other graphics will look on-screen. High color depths make heavy demands on the video card, however, because it must handle many times more data per second than in the lower color depths. Eight-bit color (256 colors) is a good general-purpose mode for older video cards; higher modes such as 32-bit color are appropriate for the latest, fastest video cards.

To change the color depth, complete the following steps:

1. Open the Control Panel and double-click *Display*. Or, right-click the desktop and choose Properties.
2. In the Display Properties dialog box, select the Settings tab, shown in Figure 15.13 for Windows XP.
3. Click the down-pointing triangle below Color quality (called Colors in some Windows versions) and choose the color depth you want on the drop-down list.
4. Click OK. If a confirmation box appears, click Yes or OK to accept it.
5. Restart Windows if prompted to do so.

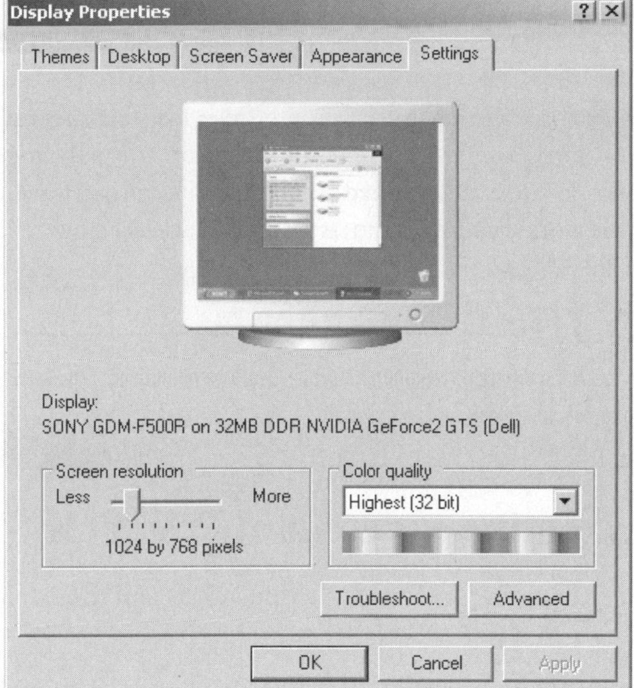


**FIGURE 15.13**
Setting Color Depth and Resolution in Windows XP

## CHANGING THE RESOLUTION

Recall that resolution is the number of unique dots that make up a display horizontally and vertically. Each monitor has a maximum resolution, which is the physical number of pixels it has. Each video card also has a maximum resolution. As a team they are limited by the lesser of the two maximums. Windows can run at any resolution from basic VGA (640 pixels across by 480 pixels up and down) to the monitor's maximum.

A high resolution makes everything appear smaller on-screen (except the Windows desktop, which expands to fill the area). Therefore, the highest resolution possible is not always the best choice. People with limited vision may find a more moderate resolution best for their needs. For small monitors (14- or 15-inch), 640 x 480 or 800 x 600 are typical resolutions; for a larger monitor (17-inch and up), most people prefer 1024 x 768.

To change the resolution, complete the following steps:

1. Open the Control Panel and double-click *Display*. Or, right-click the desktop and choose Properties.
2. In the Display Properties dialog box, select the Settings tab (see Figure 15.13).
3. Drag the Screen resolution (called Screen area in some Windows versions) slider to the left or right to decrease or increase the resolution.

4. Click OK. If a confirmation box appears, click Yes or OK to accept it. (Two boxes may appear: one before changing the resolution and one after.)

One other setting you can adjust is the refresh rate, but we will reserve that discussion for Chapter 16, where monitors are covered, since the maximum refresh rate is determined by the monitor. After learning about how a monitor works, you will understand much better how refresh rate fits into the picture.

**TRY IT!**

**Set Windows to several different resolution and color depth combinations. Experiment to find the highest combination your video card can produce.**

## Troubleshooting Video Card Problems

Here are some common problems with video cards and some solutions you can try.

**Nothing appears on-screen at all.** The video card may either be defective or not installed properly. Make sure the card is pushed all the way down into the slot, and that it is the right type of slot. Make sure the monitor cable is firmly connected to the video card and to the monitor, and that the monitor is turned on and its contrast and brightness turned up. This could also indicate a problem with some other component, such as the motherboard, CPU, RAM, or another expansion card, but if you just replaced the video card and did not change anything else, the video card is the prime suspect.

**Screen has a red, green, or blue tint.** This generally means that a pin is broken on the monitor or video card connector or that the connector is not snugly plugged in, so that one of the colors (red, green, or blue) is missing from the display. Check all connections for tightness, and check each connector for broken or bent pins. If all appears to be well, the video card or monitor is probably defective.

**Garbled Windows display.** If you see text clearly as the PC is booting but the Windows display is unreadable, there is a problem with the video card driver. Boot to safe mode (see Chapter 27), which uses the standard VGA video driver, and then update or reinstall the driver for your video card.

**Vertical stripes on Windows display.** This can indicate a corrupted video driver or a physical defect in the video card itself. It is not usually the monitor's fault. Try a different resolution and color depth; make sure all connectors are snug; update the video driver; and then try a new video card.

Some video problems are actually the fault of the monitor rather than the video card; see the troubleshooting section in Chapter 16 for information about monitor problems.

**Windows will not start except in safe mode.** This indicates a bad Windows video driver. Perhaps Windows detected the monitor incorrectly and used the wrong driver for it, or perhaps the driver file it used was corrupted. In such a case Windows will start in safe mode using a generic video driver but it will not start in normal mode. Try downloading and installing the newest video driver from the card manufacturer's Web site.

**Pictures and colors in Windows look bad.** In standard 16-color VGA mode, colors look washed out and pictures do not look real. If Windows starts in 16-color VGA mode after you install a new video card, it probably has detected it as a generic VGA card. You must install the correct driver for the card, as described in Chapter 14.

**Certain applications will not run.** If the problem is confined to a specific application, especially if it is a game, your problem is probably with the API. Recall from earlier in the chapter that game programmers use APIs to access the built-in 2D and 3D accelerator features in the video card. If the game uses a different API than the video card supports, or if the application has bugs in it that appear with certain video cards, problems can result. One solution is to download a patch for the game from the game manufacturer's Web site. Another possible solution is to make sure you have the latest version of DirectX installed in Windows. Remember that DirectX is a suite of APIs that Microsoft has released, of which Direct3D is a subset. Games that support DirectX usually come with a version of DirectX in their setup program, and it installs automatically if you do not already have that version or later. However, if it is an older game, an even newer version of DirectX may be available from Microsoft (see "For More Information" for this chapter on the Internet Resource Center).

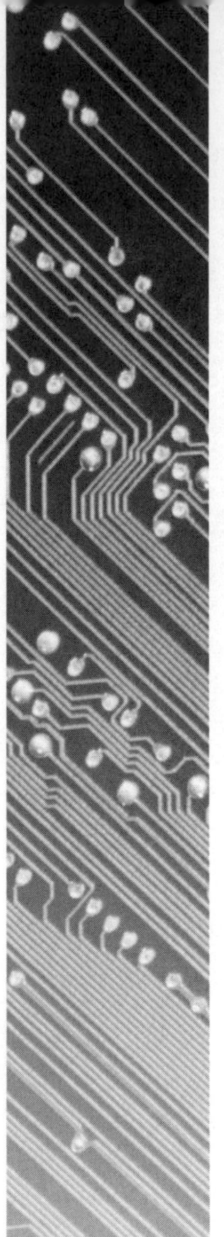

# STUDY GUIDE

Use the following summaries to review the key concepts of this chapter.

## How a Video Card Works

- A video card converts data from the OS into instructions to the monitor.
- A video card can be either an expansion board or built into the motherboard.
- If video support is built into the motherboard, it shares the RAM, chipset, and bus of the motherboard; if it is separate it has its own of these items.
- The video card needs memory to hold the data needed to display the screen content.
- Video card memory holds a numeric code representing the color that each dot on the monitor should be at any given moment.
- A unique dot in a particular screen resolution is a pixel.
- The resolution is the number of pixels across by the number of pixels down, such as 800 x 600.
- The monitor is made up of groups of three phosphors: red, green, and blue. Each of these groups is a triad.
- A pixel is comprised of one or more triads, depending on the display resolution that the operating system requests.
- The number of digits needed to represent a color is the color depth. The OS determines what color depth mode to use. The more digits, the more possible colors in that mode.

## Video Card Interfaces

- Almost all video cards have a 15-pin VGA connector to the monitor.
- The video card fits into either an AGP or PCI slot in the motherboard.
- The Accelerated Graphics Port (AGP) bus is designed specifically for video and offers the best performance.
- VESA local bus (VLB) and ISA are two obsolete video card interfaces.

## Video RAM

- When shopping for a video card there are two factors concerning video RAM to consider: the amount and the type.

- The amount of video RAM determines the maximum resolution and color depth combination that can be used. To determine the RAM requirements of a particular video mode, multiply the height by the width of resolution, multiply that result by the number of bits of color depth, and then divide by 8.
- RAM also serves as a cache to improve performance in graphic-intensive programs.
- Extra RAM is also useful in supporting 3D video acceleration. This requires additional RAM for three buffers that store video data and quickly transfer it in and out of the main video memory.
- Synchronous dynamic RAM (SDRAM) is the same as used in a PC. It operates at the same speed as the motherboard system bus.
- Double Data Rate (DDR) SDRAM is a double-speed version of SDRAM.
- Synchronous graphics RAM (SGRAM) is high-end RAM that includes circuitry for performing block writes that increase the speed of 3D operations.

## Video RAMDAC

- The RAMDAC is the digital-to-analog converter on the video card.
- Its speed is measured in megahertz. A typical speed is 300 to 350MHz.
- The main benefit of faster RAMDAC is higher refresh rate capability.

## Video Chipset

- A video card has a chipset, just like a motherboard. The chipset maker may be different from the video card maker.
- The chipset controls the movement of data within the video card, and determines the card's performance capabilities.
- Some popular chipset makers include ATI, NVIDIA, and Trident.

## Video Acceleration

- Video acceleration is the ability of a video card to support Application Program Interface (API) commands from programs that pass off some of the video processing to the video card, freeing up the CPU.
- One way a video card can help with animation is through keyframes. The application sends the video card certain object positions and the video card fills in the interim positions between them.

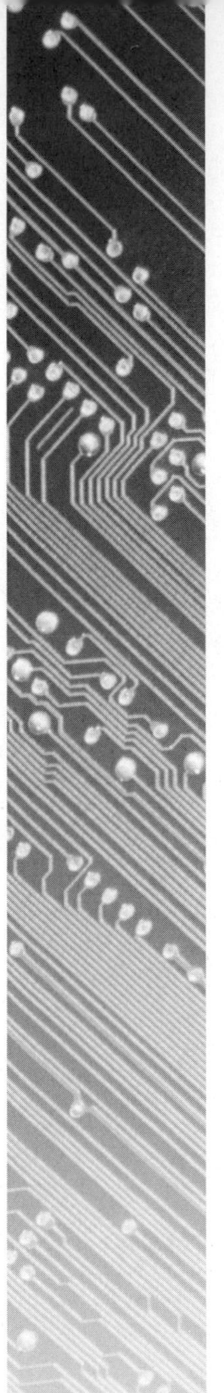

- An object's on-screen position in 3D perspective is defined by its X, Y, and Z coordinates.
- These coordinates define simple geometric shapes known as primitives that are used to create an object.
- To make an object look more realistic, it is filled in with texture or shading. This fill-in process is called rasterization.
- One method of rasterization is texture mapping, which tiles a small graphic file onto the surface of the object and then applies perspective and shading to it.
- Flat shading is filling an object with a solid color.
- Gouraud shading applies different colors to different points on the object and then blends them in the middle.
- Antialiasing is smoothing the edges on objects to avoid jagged areas.
- Z buffering reduces overhead by allowing the details for a primitive obscured by another object to not be constantly redrawn.
- The frame rate is the number of frames per second that the animation changes. Most people find a frame rate of 20Hz acceptable.
- For a video card to use its acceleration features with an application, the application and card must support a common API.
- The most popular APIs are OpenGL and Direct3D. Direct3D is part of a larger multimedia standard called DirectX.

## Other Video Card Features

- TV Out makes it possible to use a television as a monitor.
- TV/Video Capture In allows digital input to a PC from a video camera or a TV tuner.
- Dual monitor output allows more than one monitor to be connected at once to the same video card.

## Installing a Video Card

- A video card is a simple expansion board. Remove the old one if necessary, and then install the new one.
- To remove a video card, remove the screw holding its backplate and then pull the card out.
- To install a video card, prepare a slot for it by removing any empty backplate cover that is in place, and then press the new card into the slot and secure it with a screw.
- If replacing built-in video support with a real video card, disable the built-in video controller in BIOS Setup.

## Setting Display Properties in Windows

- Color depth in Windows can be from 4-bit (16 colors) to 32-bit. Higher color depths result in more realistic display of photographs but higher overhead.
- Resolution can be anywhere from 640 x 480 (standard VGA) up to the monitor's maximum. The higher the resolution, the smaller everything appears in Windows (text, icons, etc.).
- To change color depth and resolution, open Display Properties from the Control Panel or right-click the desktop and choose Properties.
- On the Settings tab, use the Color quality or Colors drop-down list to choose a color depth.
- Drag the Screen resolution or Screen area slider to choose a resolution.

## Troubleshooting Video Card Problems

- If nothing appears on-screen, the video card is defective or not installed properly, or there is a problem with the motherboard or some other component.
- A red, green, or blue tint to the screen may indicate a broken or bent pin or a loose connector.
- If the display is garbled in Windows but not at a command prompt, there is a problem with the video driver.
- Vertical stripes can indicate a bad video driver or a physical defect in the video card.

# PRACTICE TEST

On a blank sheet of paper, write the answers to the following multiple-choice questions and explain why each answer is correct.

1. A real video card (not just built-in video support in a motherboard) has its own separate
   a. CPU, memory, and system bus.
   b. chipset, memory, and data bus.
   c. drive controller and data bus.
   d. CPU and chipset.

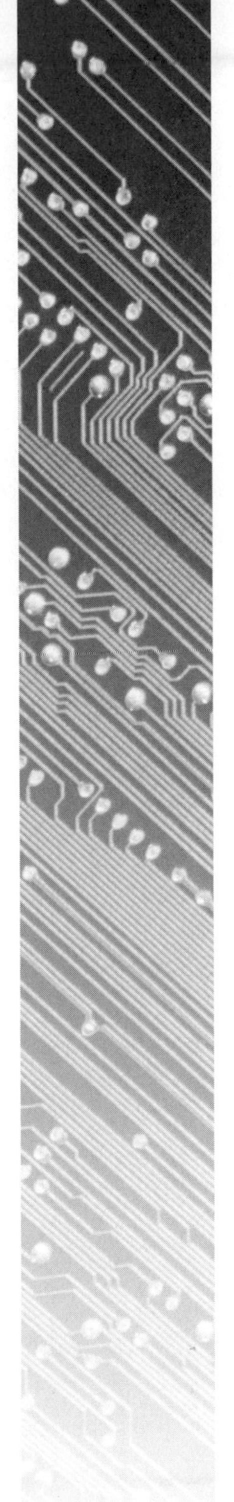

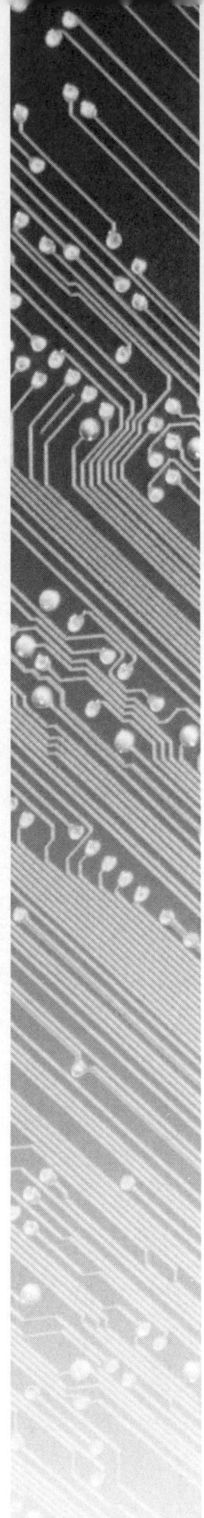

2. A system with 64MB of RAM on the motherboard and a 16MB separate video card will report how much system RAM in the operating system?
   a. 48
   b. 64
   c. 80
   d. 128

3. A system with 64MB of RAM on the motherboard and an 8MB video adapter built into the motherboard will report how much system RAM in the operating system?
   a. 56
   b. 64
   c. 72
   d. 76

4. A pixel is
   a. a single triad.
   b. a group of three triads.
   c. a group of nine triads.
   d. variable in size depending on the OS resolution.

5. How many pixels in a 640 x 480 display?
   a. 307,200
   b. 480,000
   c. 640,000
   d. It depends on the number of triads on the monitor.

6. Which colors comprise a triad?
   a. magenta, cyan, and yellow
   b. black and white
   c. red, green, and blue
   d. red, yellow, and blue

7. How would you determine the number of unique colors there could be in a 16-bit color depth display?
   a. multiply 2 by 16
   b. calculate 2 to the $16^{th}$ power
   c. multiply 16 by 16
   d. calculate 16 to the $2^{nd}$ power

8. How many pins on a standard VGA connector to the monitor?
   a. 9
   b. 15
   c. 16
   d. 25

9. Which of these statements about AGP is *not* true?
   a. It is only for video cards.
   b. It is faster than ISA.
   c. Another name for it is VLB.
   d. It is a local bus.

10. How much video RAM is needed for a 1024 x 768 resolution at 8-bit color depth?
    a. 786KB
    b. 432KB
    c. 629KB
    d. 6.29MB

11. Which of these is the best-performing and most expensive type of video RAM available on video cards today?
    a. SRAM
    b. SDRAM
    c. SGRAM
    d. SPRAM

12. A primitive is
    a. a texture used for shading 3D objects.
    b. a keyframe animation created by the video card.
    c. a simple geometric object located in 3D space.
    d. a vertex.

13. Which of these is *not* a type of rasterization?
    a. scan shading
    b. Gouraud shading
    c. flat shading
    d. texture mapping

14. What will happen if the video card frame rate drops below an acceptable level?
    a. The shading will become muddy looking.
    b. The animation will appear choppy.
    c. The wire frames will become visible for primitives.
    d. An out of memory error message will appear.

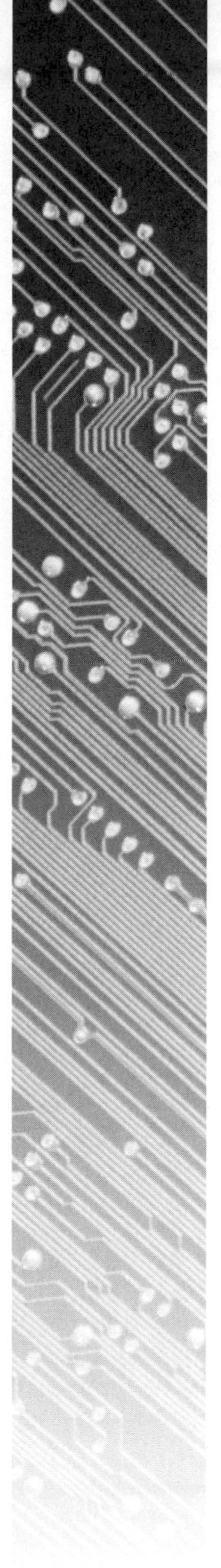

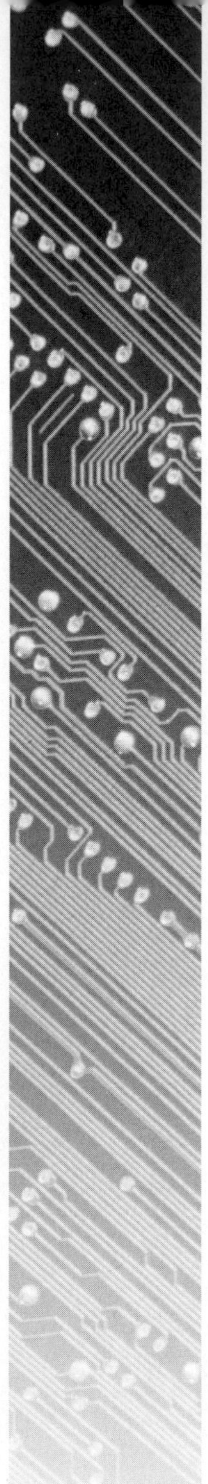

15. Which of these is not a popular API?
    a. Direct3D
    b. DirectX
    c. OpenGL
    d. 3D Now

16. When replacing built-in video with a separate video card, you must
    a. set jumpers on the new video card to indicate it should take over BIOS functionality.
    b. disable built-in video in BIOS Setup.
    c. install the new video card in an ISA slot so it does not conflict.
    d. buy a new video card with extra RAM on it.

17. On which tab in Display Properties do you control color depth and resolution?
    a. General
    b. Driver
    c. Settings
    d. Advanced

18. Which of these is not a standard Windows resolution?
    a. 640 x 480
    b. 768 x 520
    c. 800 x 600
    d. 1024 x 768

19. Which of these could *not* be the problem if video fails to appear on-screen?
    a. video card
    b. monitor
    c. motherboard
    d. They could all potentially be the problem.

20. If the display appears normally when the PC starts to boot but then becomes garbled, which of these is probably causing the problem?
    a. monitor
    b. video card
    c. video driver
    d. API

## TROUBLESHOOTING

1. After replacing a video card, the monitor has an odd blue tint to it and there does not seem to be any red in the display at all. What would you check?
2. A motherboard with built-in AGP video support displays no video when booted. Describe how you would determine whether the built-in video is the problem.
3. A client playing 3D video games complains that the video animation is choppy. What can you suggest to minimize the problem?

## CUSTOMER SERVICE

1. A client complains that every time she tries to increase the resolution in Windows, the color depth resets itself to a lower setting. What is happening and what do you recommend?
2. A client who is interested in playing 3D games wants your advice about the amount of video RAM he should look for when shopping for his next video card. What advice can you give?
3. A client is confused about the color depth settings in Windows; there are settings for 256 colors, 16-bit, and 32-bit color. Explain how the number of colors corresponds to the number of bits.

## FOR MORE INFORMATION

For links to Web sites that provide further information about the topics covered in this chapter, go to the EMC/Paradigm Internet Resource Center at www.emcp.com/College Division/Internet Resource Centers/PC Maintenance/For More Information.

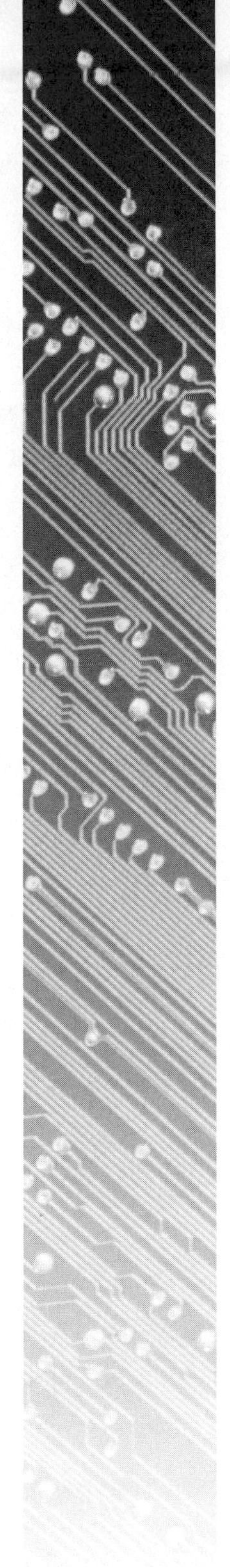

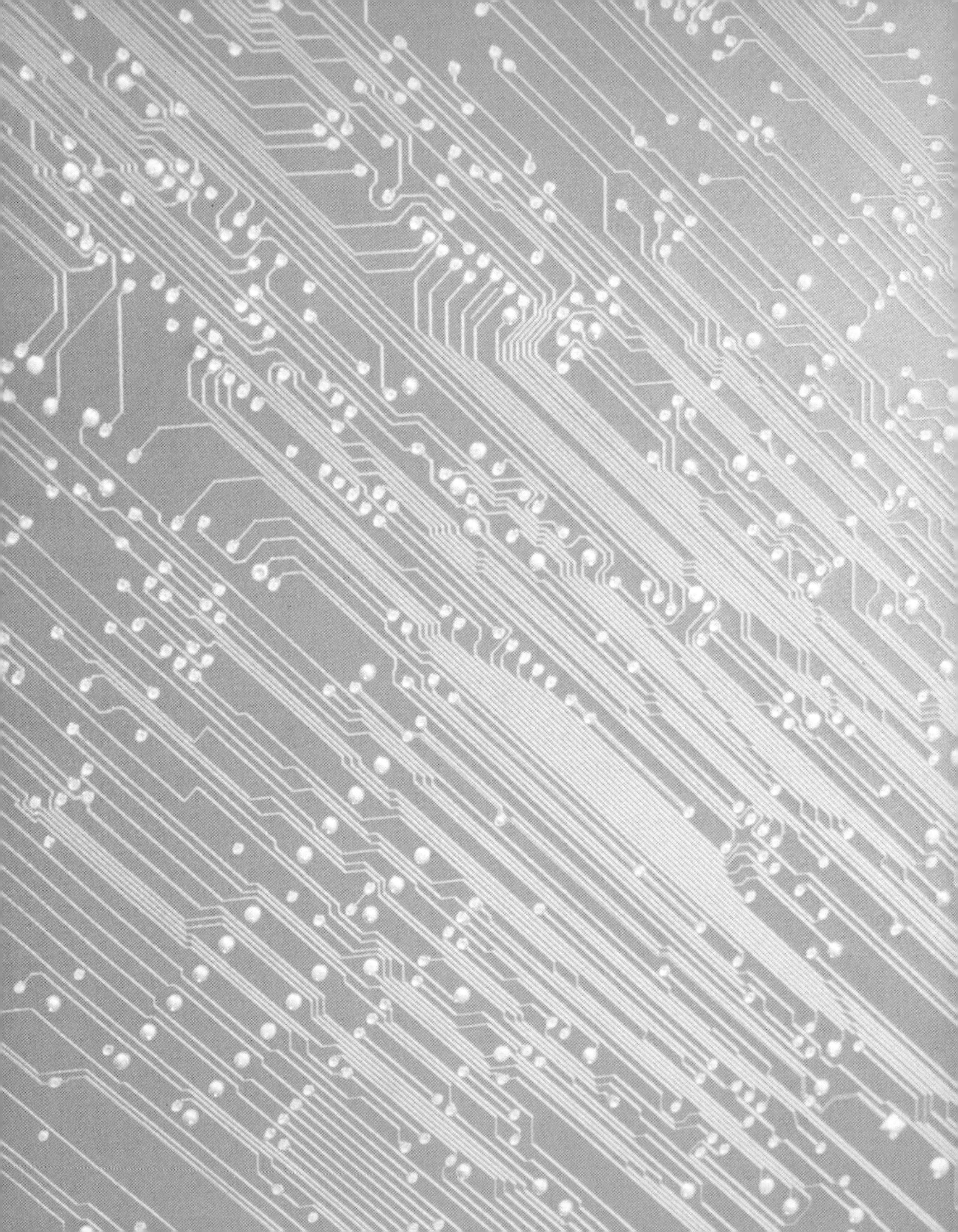

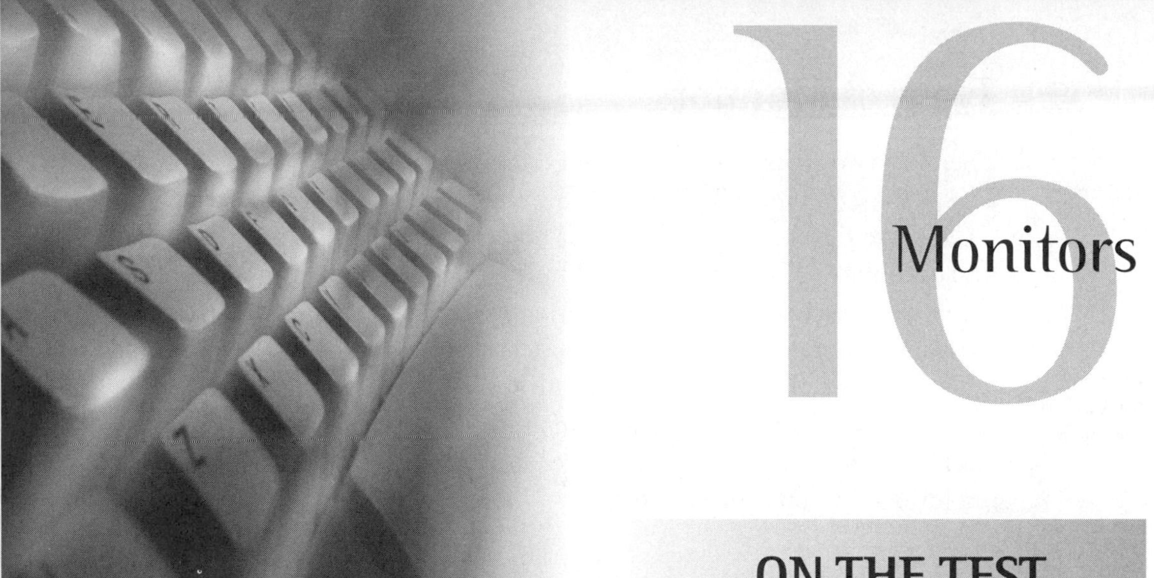

# 16 Monitors

## ON THE TEST

**A+ Core Hardware Service Technician Exam**

- **Objective 1.1:** Identify basic terms, concepts, and functions of system modules, including how each module should work during normal operation and during the boot process.
- **Objective 1.2:** Identify basic procedures for adding and removing field replaceable modules for both desktop and portable systems.
- **Objective 1.7:** Identify proper procedures for installing and configuring peripheral devices.
- **Objective 2.1:** Identify common symptoms and problems associated with each module and how to troubleshoot and isolate the problems.

## ON THE JOB

Whereas the video card is an integral part of the PC, the monitor is a separate unit designed to receive output. Technologically it is very different from the other components you have learned about so far. Because of the danger of electrocution, most technicians do not work on monitors, and there are very few questions on the A+ exam about monitors. When a monitor malfunctions, most technicians either take it to a monitor repair specialist or replace it.

Some of the real-life skills you will acquire from this chapter include:

- evaluating a monitor for purchase
- connecting a monitor to a PC
- testing a monitor for defects
- adjusting a monitor's settings

# Types of Monitors

**Cathode Ray Tube (CRT)**

A traditional box type of monitor that uses electrons hitting phosphors to create the display.

**Liquid Crystal Display (LCD)**

A flat-panel type of monitor that uses electricity passing through liquid crystals to create the display.

There are two types of monitors sold today: *Cathode Ray Tube* (CRT) and *Liquid Crystal Display* (LCD).

CRTs are the boxy type of monitor that most people think of when they hear "monitor." They are heavy and bulky, but they are inexpensive and they look good no matter what resolution you run them in. LCDs are the flat-panel monitors in notebook PC screens and the latest flat desktop units. They are lightweight and take up very little desktop space, and they display photos vibrantly. But they are much more costly than comparable CRTs and they tend toward fuzzy text display if you run them in a lower resolution than their maximum.

## How CRTs Work

A CRT is essentially a large vacuum tube. At the back of the CRT is a long, narrow neck containing a cathode, and at the front is a broad, rectangular surface with colored phosphors on it. When the cathode is heated, it emits negatively charged electrons. Those electrons are attracted to the positively charged front of the CRT, where they strike the phosphors and cause them to light up (see Figure 16.1).

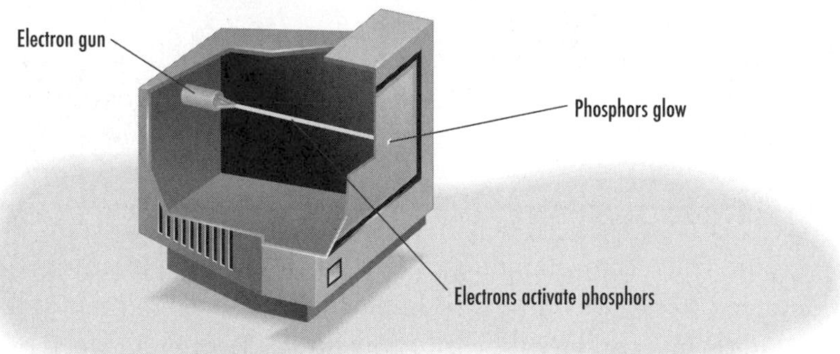
Electron gun
Phosphors glow
Electrons activate phosphors

**FIGURE 16.1**
**A CRT lights up phosphors by activating them with an electron gun.**

**Monochrome**

Consisting of only one color (plus black or white).

In a *monochrome* monitor there is only one electron gun, as in Figure 16.1; in a color CRT there are three guns, one each for red, blue, and green. The actual colors are created by the phosphors on the screen. For each pixel on the screen there are three phosphors—red, green, and blue—arranged in triads, as discussed in Chapter 15. Each electron gun works only on dots of a certain color. So, for example, if a certain pixel is supposed to be purple, the red and blue guns would fire at that triad, but the green gun would not, as in Figure 16.2.

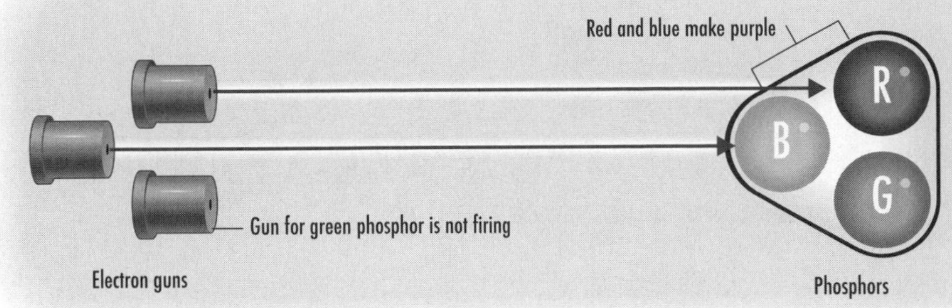


**FIGURE 16.2**
On a color monitor there are three electron guns, one for each color of phosphor. They fire at different phosphors to produce different colors.

The distance between one color in a triad and the same color in the adjacent triad is the *dot pitch* of the monitor, one measure of CRT quality (see Figure 16.3). A lower number means the dots are closer together, which makes for a better quality picture. LCD monitors (covered in the next section) are also evaluated in terms of dot pitch.

**Dot pitch**

The distance between two phosphors of the same color on a monitor.

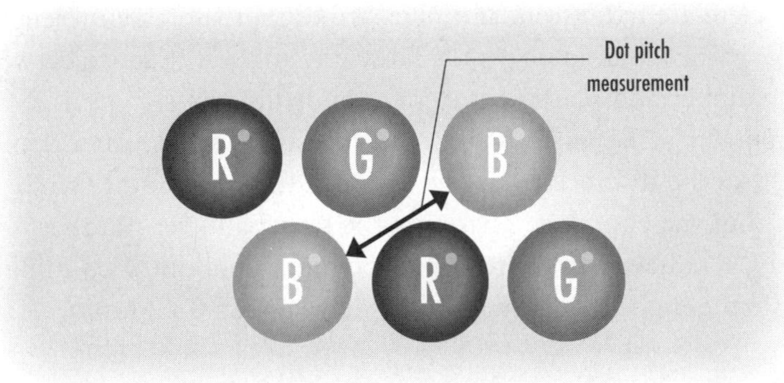

**FIGURE 16.3**
The distance between phosphors of the same color is the dot pitch.

As you can imagine, there is great potential for misalignment when you are dealing with such small phosphors. There are several technologies for keeping the electron beams properly aligned. The most common is a *shadow mask*, a thin sheet of perforated metal that sits between the guns and the phosphors. Each gun directs itself through the designated hole for a particular triad, masking any stray electrons (see Figure 16.4).

**Shadow mask**

A thin sheet of perforated metal that helps keep the electron beams aligned in a CRT.

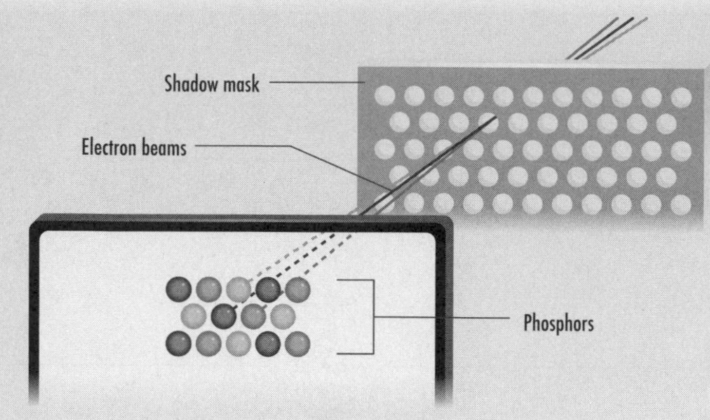


**FIGURE 16.4**
A shadow mask helps align the electron beams precisely.

**Aperture grille**

A system of vertical wires between electron guns and phosphors for keeping the electron beams aligned on a CRT.

**Slot mask**

A hybrid of aperture grille and shadow mask technologies for keeping electron beams aligned on CRTs.

Another technology for maintaining alignment is an *aperture grille*, made of vertical wires between the guns and the phosphors. A third method, *slot mask*, is a combination of the two technologies. In both aperture grille and slot mask, there are red, green, and blue stripes that run the full length of the monitor rather than interspersed dots. The main difference between the two is the number and placement of the stabilizing wires.

On an aperture grille or slot mask monitor, stripe pitch rather than dot pitch measures the distance from one colored stripe to another stripe of the same color, but the equation is basically the same: a lower number is better. Entry-level CRTs have a dot pitch or stripe pitch of about 0.28 millimeter (mm), while the highest quality monitors have about 0.22mm.

## In Real Life

**Aperture grille monitors have two thin lines running horizontally across the screen at roughly the one-third and two-thirds points. When you display a pure white screen, as with a word processing window, you may notice them, but most of the time they are not obvious. However, they do bother some people, and this is one reason that some users prefer a shadow mask monitor.**

## How LCDs Work

An LCD screen has two polarized filters, between which are liquid crystals. In order for light to appear on the display screen, it must pass through both filters and the crystals. The second filter, however, is at an angle to the first,

so by default nothing can pass through to the display. By applying current to a crystal, you can cause it to twist, which also twists the light passing through it. If the light twists so that it matches the angle of the second filter, it can pass through the filter and light up an area of the display (see Figure 16.5).

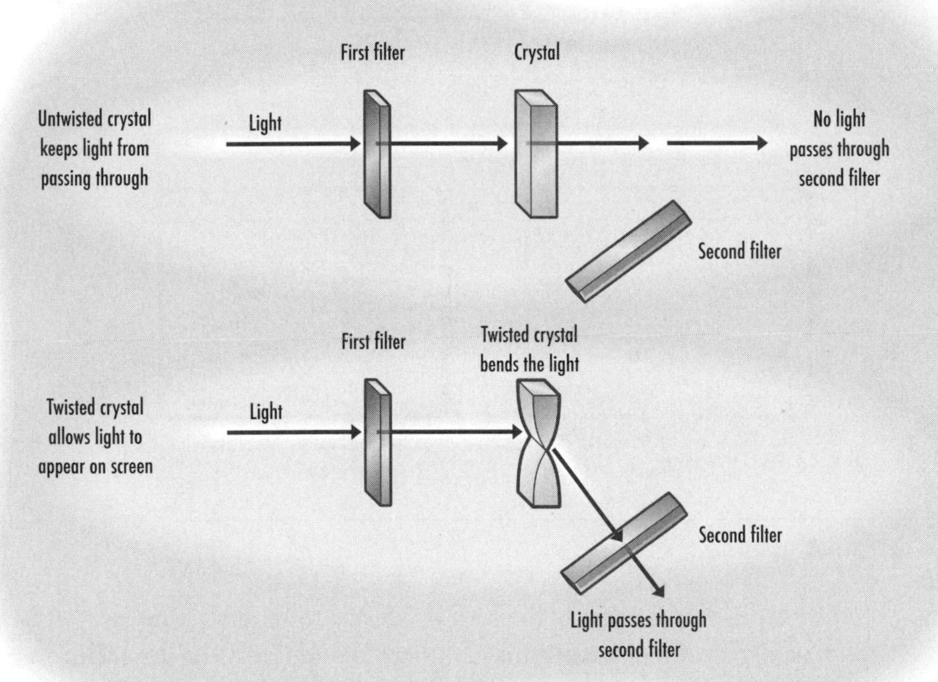


**FIGURE 16.5**
Liquid crystals twist when electricity is applied to them, enabling light to pass through them.

On a color LCD, there is an additional filter that splits the light into separate cells for red, green, and blue. Because there is no need for a mask to help direct electrons, there is no darkened area between pixels. That is what gives an LCD display that "saturated" appearance that most CRTs cannot fully duplicate, and makes photos look so good.

There are several different technologies for directing and controlling an LCD display. These differ primarily in the number of transistors controlling the cells. Figure 16.6 shows conceptual diagrams of transistors.

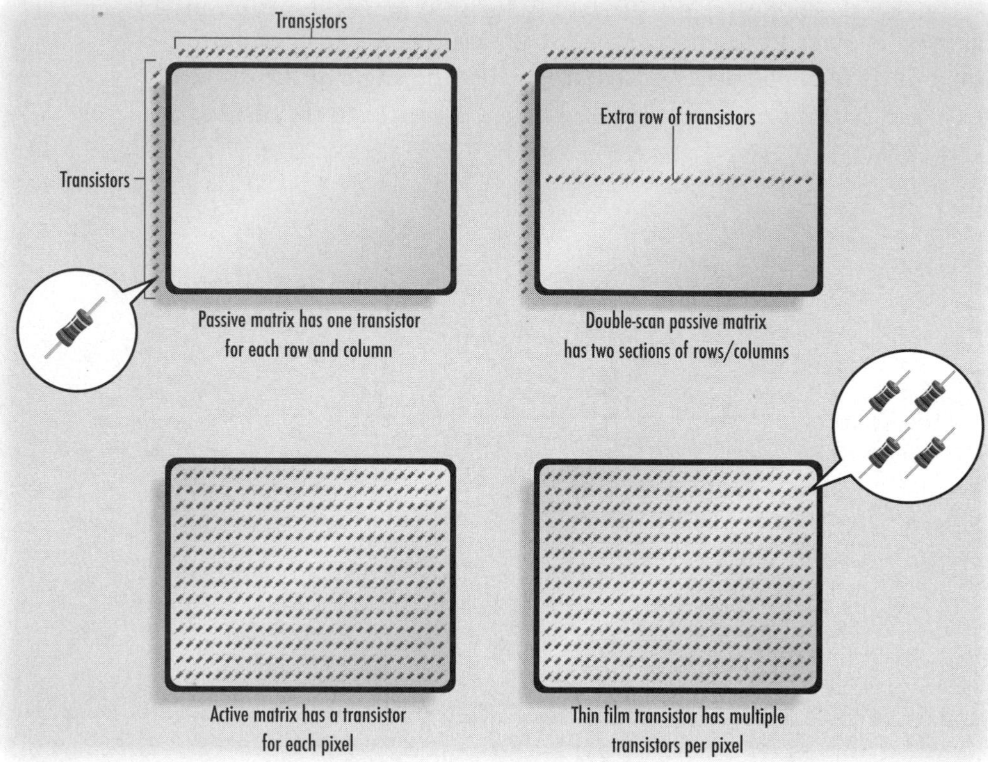
Transistors
Transistors
Passive matrix has one transistor for each row and column
Extra row of transistors
Double-scan passive matrix has two sections of rows/columns
Active matrix has a transistor for each pixel
Thin film transistor has multiple transistors per pixel

**FIGURE 16.6**
LCD screens differ in the number of transistors.

**Passive matrix**

A type of LCD screen that uses one transistor for each row and each column. The least expensive kind of LCD.

**Double-scan passive matrix (DSTN)**

A type of passive matrix LCD screen with an extra row of transistors for better performance.

The type of LCD that is the least expensive to manufacture is a *passive matrix* display. On a passive matrix, there is one transistor for each row and one transistor for each column, much like spreadsheet row numbers and column letters. (For example, a laptop with a maximum monitor resolution of 1024 x 768 has a total of 1,792 transistors.) The transistors emit pulsing charges, and the combination of charges from two sides twists the liquid crystals in that row/column intersection. Since a passive matrix relies on pulsing, each pixel has moments when it is receiving no signal, so passive matrix displays are not as bright as other types of LCD.

*Double-scan passive matrix* displays (also known as DSTN, for dual-scan twisted nematic technology) were developed to help improve the brightness of a passive matrix display without too great an increase in cost. These use the same technology as a normal passive display, but divide the screen into two sections with separate transistor rows/columns for each section. This allows the screen to be refreshed more rapidly.

WARNING

**One of the unfortunate qualities of any passive matrix screen is that it is difficult to view at an angle. Looking at the screen straight-on gives a fairly bright image, but if several people are trying to look at the monitor, only the person sitting directly in front of it will have a good view.**

In contrast, *active matrix* LCD provides a separate transistor for each pixel. Since pixels do not have to share, pulsing is not required and each cell can be constantly "on." This results in a much brighter display that is visible from any angle, but also one that uses a lot more power.

**Active matrix**

A type of LCD screen in which each pixel has its own transistor, resulting in better display than passive matrix.

The latest type of active matrix display, *thin film transistor* (TFT), uses multiple transistors for each pixel (up to four), resulting in very high refresh and redraw rates and even higher power consumption.

**Thin film transistor (TFT)**

A type of active matrix display that uses multiple transistors for each pixel.

# Measurements of Monitor Quality

The best way to choose a monitor is to see it in action, in the resolution and color depth that you plan on using. Stores that offer displays of various monitors all showing the same image at once can be of great help in deciding on a model. But subjective evaluation is not the only way of distinguishing one monitor from another. The following sections outline some more quantifiable monitor quality measurements.

## Maximum Resolution

The monitor has a maximum resolution, which is the physical number of pixels it can display across and down. Remember from Chapter 15 that the video card has a maximum resolution too, and you are limited to the resolution that the two can jointly agree upon. Therefore, it makes no sense to spend a lot of money for a monitor that can display an ultra-high resolution if the video card lacks that capability, and vice versa.

A low-end CRT might have a maximum resolution of 1280 x 1024. That means there are 1,280 pixels across and 1,024 pixels down, for a total of 1,310,720 pixels. More expensive monitors will usually have higher maximum resolutions, up into the 2,000s. LCD monitors usually have lower maximum resolutions than their CRT counterparts; a high-quality LCD might have a maximum resolution of only 1024 x 768.

Most monitors can operate in any of a range of resolutions by treating many triads together as an individual pixel. On a CRT this is routine, and in fact most people operate CRTs at a lower resolution than the maximum.

However, LCD monitors are less adept at simulating resolutions lower than their maximum, so an LCD monitor's display (especially text) can look fuzzy at lower resolutions. In such a case, a high-resolution LCD monitor operating lower than its maximum might give display results inferior to those of a less-expensive LCD monitor with a maximum resolution that matches the resolution at which it is being operated.

**WARNING**

**Not all LCD screens can operate in less than their maximum resolution. On some notebook PCs, if the resolution in Windows is changed to lower than the maximum, instead of everything's appearing larger on the screen, a big black ring appears around the outside. This is mostly an issue on older notebook PCs.**

Maximum resolution is not an important issue for most users because the maximum resolution is usually much higher than they would ever want to use. At high resolutions everything on-screen appears very small, and most people prefer a lower resolution to avoid eyestrain.

## Dot Pitch

Earlier in this chapter we briefly discussed dot pitch, stripe pitch, and slot pitch as measurements of monitor quality in CRTs. These all refer to how close together a phosphor of one color is to another phosphor of the same color. Lower numbers are better. A good baseline quality level would be 0.28mm. High-end monitors should have 0.25mm or less dot pitch. Dot pitch is a much more important factor than maximum resolution for a CRT because it affects the display's overall quality no matter what the resolution. Dot pitch is not an issue on LCD screens.

## Viewable Image Size

Screen size is often expressed in two numbers, such as 17-inch/15.9-inch. The larger number is the overall diagonal measurement of the monitor glass, including the part that is hidden behind the plastic bezel and is therefore unusable. The second number is the diagonal measurement of the real size of the viewable image. Viewable image size is significant because monitors differ in their bezel sizes. A 17-inch monitor might have a viewable image size ranging from 15.5 to 16.3 inches, which is almost an inch of difference.

## Maximum Refresh Rate

As soon as an electron hits a phosphor, it immediately begins to start decaying, so each triad in the display must be refreshed with the electron gun many hundreds of times per second. If pixels are not refreshed quickly enough, the display flickers, causing eyestrain. The measurement of how many times per second the display is refreshed is its *refresh rate.* The higher the refresh rate, the less flickering appears on the screen and the less likely it is to cause eyestrain. You will learn how to adjust refresh rate later in this chapter.

**Refresh rate**

The rate at which the electron guns in a monitor refresh each pixel of the display, expressed in hertz.

The higher the resolution used, the more challenging it is for the monitor to refresh it at top speeds because of the increased number of unique pixels involved. At a refresh rate of lower than 75Hz, a display flickers noticeably, so a high maximum refresh rate is an important feature in a monitor. The maximum refresh rate is typically not expressed as a single number, but rather as a separate number for each of several common resolutions. For example, a monitor might be capable of 120Hz refresh rate at 800 x 600 but only 85Hz at 1280 x 1024. Maximum refresh rate goes down as resolution goes up.

When recommending a monitor to a client, suggest one that offers a maximum refresh rate of at least 100Hz at the resolution that the client plans on using most often. That way the client will get a decent refresh rate at a slightly higher resolution as well, in case he or she ever wants to go higher.

Some older or less expensive monitors have electron guns that cannot keep up with the refreshing needs for displaying a quality picture. Rather than spending more money for better electron guns, the manufacturers sometimes use a technique called *interlacing.* Interlacing refreshes only every other line of the display with each pass, rather than every line. There is little reason to buy an interlaced monitor today—assuming you could even find one—because monitor technology has advanced over the last few years to the point where interlacing is seldom necessary.

**Interlacing**

Refreshing only every other line of a monitor display with each pass. Results in more screen flicker.

## Adjustments

Good quality monitors come with on-screen controls for adjusting the contrast, color tone, image size and positioning, and several other factors. You will learn about these later in the chapter.

### Interface

Almost all monitors sold today work with ordinary PC 15-pin VGA connectors, as discussed in Chapter 15. If the computer has an ordinary PC and video card, you do not need to be concerned about the interface.

If, however, the computer needs a nonstandard interface, recommend a monitor that supports it rather than trying to adapt a standard monitor to the nonstandard needs. For example, if the monitor will be used with a Macintosh PC, recommend a monitor that comes with a Macintosh video connector. Otherwise, there will be an additional cost of $10 or so for a converter.

Extremely high-end video cards do not use the normal VGA plug; instead they use four separate plugs for black, red, blue, and green. These typically use coaxial cable and BNC connectors. (BNC stands for British Naval Connector.) If the video card has BNC connectors rather than VGA, make sure the monitor also has connectors of that type. Some high-end monitors support both.

## Connecting/Disconnecting a Monitor

Connecting a monitor to a PC is a simple matter of plugging the 15-pin male connector on the monitor into the 15-pin female connector on the video card. Make sure the power to both monitor and PC are off before connecting or disconnecting them. The monitor also has its own power cord, which plugs into an ordinary AC outlet.

## Connecting Multiple Monitors to a Single PC

Some versions of Windows enable the use of multiple monitors with a single desktop so the user can open a different application on each screen. To set this up you need either a video card with dual output ports or multiple video cards. One of these video cards can be AGP if there is an AGP slot in the motherboard, but the rest of them must be PCI (or whatever bus slots are available). After connecting both video cards and monitors, you set up multimonitor Windows functionality through Display Properties.

### In Real Life

**If you do not have multiple monitors, the Settings tab buttons and settings mentioned here will not appear.**

If the computer has one video card with two ports, or it is a notebook PC with both an internal and external display, you use a feature called DualView in Windows. With DualView you cannot specify which is the primary monitor. On a notebook PC it is the built-in LCD screen; on a desktop PC it is the first video port labeled Primary on the dual-port card.

**WARNING**

**Not all notebook PCs support DualView, even in the latest version of Windows. Only certain brands of built-in notebook video adapters will work; check the Help file in Windows or the Microsoft Web site to find out if the PC is supported. For example, the very popular ATI Rage Mobility Pro does not support the feature in most Windows versions.**

However, if there are two or more separate video cards on a desktop PC, you can specify which monitor is the primary by clicking it on the Settings tab in the Display Properties dialog box and then clicking Use this device as the primary monitor.

By default, all monitors will show the same image in Windows. If you want to extend the desktop onto the nonprimary monitors, click the secondary monitor on the Settings tab and then click Extend my Windows desktop onto this monitor (see Figure 16.7).

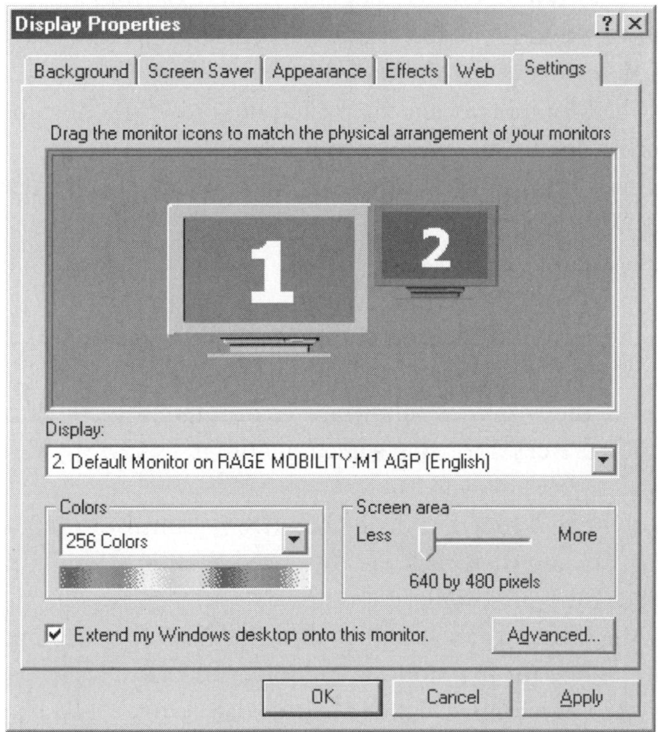


**FIGURE 16.7**
Multimonitor Support

Your physical arrangement of monitors may not match the Windows default. If it does not, click the Identify button on the Settings tab of the Display Properties box to see a graphic representation of the monitors with numbers on each one. Drag the graphics to make them match your physical arrangement.

## Installing a Monitor Driver

The monitor driver is not really a driver in the same sense as the driver for the video card. It is just an information file (with an *.inf* extension) that tells Windows what the monitor's maximum capabilities are (in terms of resolution and refresh rate) so it can eliminate any settings from the Display Properties dialog box that the monitor cannot support.

By default, Windows detects most monitors as Plug and Play Monitor. The problem is that the maximum settings for that driver are rather low. You can make better settings available in many cases by installing a driver for the exact monitor. It may have come on a floppy disk with the monitor, or it may have been downloaded from the monitor manufacturer's Web site. Here are steps for installing a monitor driver.

In Windows XP:

1. At the Display Properties dialog box (from Control Panel), select the Settings tab and then click the Advanced button. A Properties box for the video card and monitor appears.
2. Select the Monitor tab and then click the Properties button. A Properties box for the monitor appears.
3. Select the Driver tab and then click Update Driver. The Update Driver Wizard runs.
4. Choose Install from a list or specific location, and then click Next.
5. Click the Do not Search button, and then click Next.
6. Click the Have Disk button and browse to the location of the driver file.
7. Complete the wizard by following the prompts. If you see a warning about the driver's not being signed, ignore it.

In Windows 2000:

1. At the Display Properties dialog box (from Control Panel), select the Settings tab and then click the Advanced button. A Properties box for the video card and monitor appears.
2. Select the Monitor tab and then click the Properties button. A Properties box for the monitor appears.
3. Select the Driver tab and then click Update Driver. The Update Driver Wizard runs.

4. Click Next. Then click Display a list of the known drivers… and click Next again.
5. Click the Have Disk button and browse to the location of the driver file.
6. Complete the wizard by following the prompts.

In Windows 98:

1. At the Display Properties dialog box (from Control Panel), select the Settings tab and then click the Advanced button. A Properties box for the video card and monitor appears.
2. Select the Monitor tab and then click the Change button. A Select Device dialog box appears listing various makes and models of monitors.
3. Select the monitor from the list, or click Have Disk and then browse for the location of the driver file.
4. Complete the installation by following the prompts.

## Setting the Refresh Rate

The refresh rate is set through Windows, in the Display Properties dialog box. It is set either on the Adapter or Monitor tab, depending on the Windows version. Depending on the monitor and video card drivers, there may be a series of numeric values to choose from (probably between 60 and 100Hz) and/or Adapter Default and Optimal. Adapter Default sets the refresh rate to a "safe" setting that any monitor can support; Optimal sets it to the highest setting that the monitor and video card can mutually agree on.

Windows knows the monitor's capabilities only if it is a Plug and Play monitor or if there is a monitor driver installed (see the preceding section). Otherwise, it sees the monitor as a generic VGA model and does not assume that it can handle a high refresh rate. This is for its protection since a refresh rate that is too high can damage a monitor.

**WARNING**

**A refresh rate set too high can cause on-screen distortion, and can damage the monitor with continued use. If you have correctly identified the monitor to Windows, it will not let you set the refresh rate higher than the monitor can handle, but if you are using the wrong monitor driver, the wrong settings could be available.**

To adjust the refresh rate in Windows 2000/XP:

1. At the Display Properties dialog box (Control Panel), select the Settings tab and then click the Advanced button. A Properties box for the video card and monitor appears.

2. Select the Monitor tab.
3. Open the Screen refresh rate drop-down list and choose a refresh rate (see Figure 16.8).
4. Click OK to close all open dialog boxes.

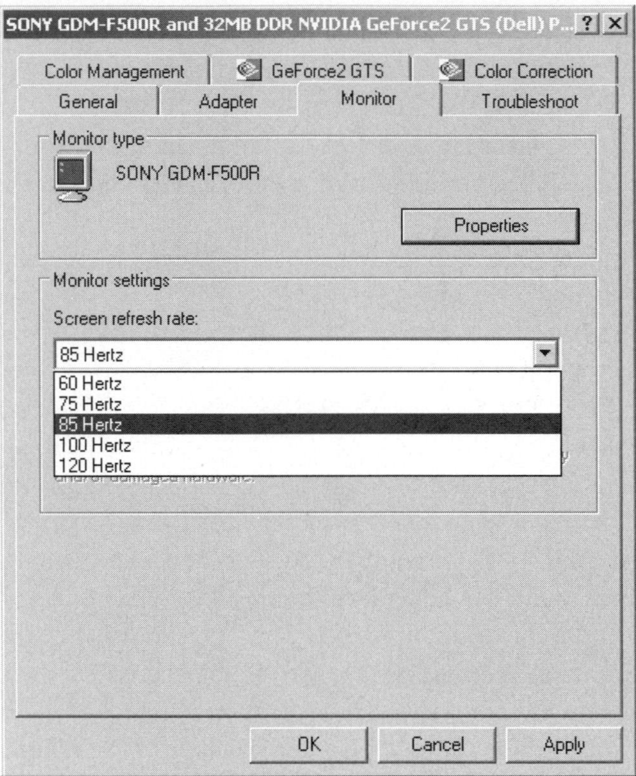


**FIGURE 16.8**
In Windows 2000 and XP you set the refresh rate on the Monitor tab (Windows XP shown here).

To adjust the refresh rate in Windows 9x/Me:

1. At the Display Properties dialog box (Control Panel), select the Settings tab and then click the Advanced button. A Properties box for the video card and monitor appears.
2. Select the Adapter tab.
3. Open the Refresh rate drop-down list and choose a refresh rate (see Figure 16.9).
4. Click OK to close all open dialog boxes.

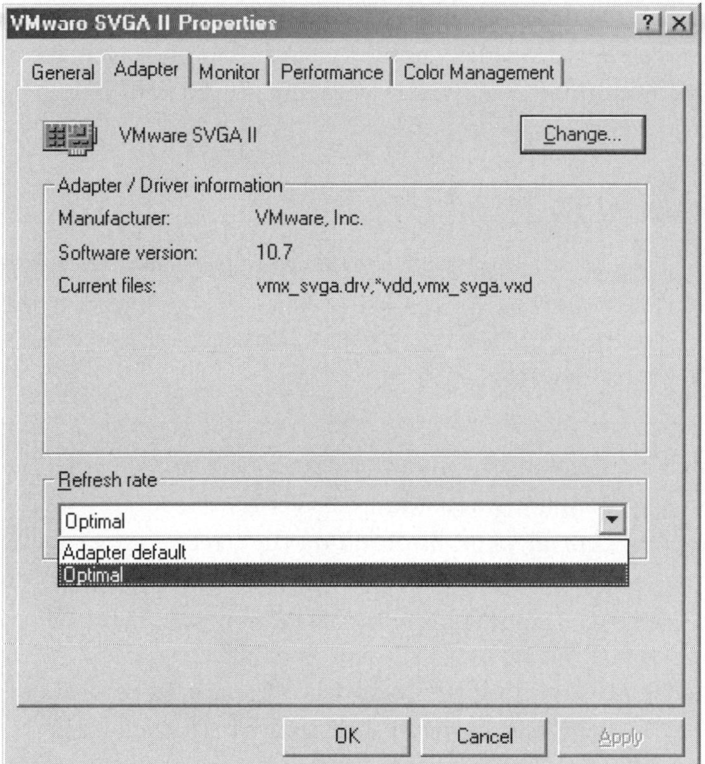


**FIGURE 16.9**
In Windows 9x and Me you set the refresh rate on the Adapter tab (Windows Me shown here).

# Testing and Troubleshooting a Monitor

When a client reports a problem with a monitor, you will need to run some tests on it to confirm that the problem is with the monitor itself rather than with the video card or some other component. To test a monitor, complete the following steps:

1. Turn on the monitor's power. Wait about five seconds, then turn on the PC.

> **WARNING**
>
> **Do not turn on the monitor and PC at the same time. They both draw more amps of power at startup than they need after they get going, especially the monitor, so turning them both on at once can cause a power sag.**

2. If you see text on the screen, the monitor is connected properly. Wait while Windows starts up. If you see no text, check the power light on the monitor. If it is not lit, the monitor is not receiving power, or is physically defective. If it is lit, the problem is probably the video card

or some other part of the PC rather than the monitor. On some monitors there are two lights: amber when the monitor is not receiving a signal from the PC and green when it is. If the light is amber, the PC is the problem.

### In Real Life

Some monitors have a test message that appears briefly when they are turned on, such as colored bars demonstrating that each of the electron guns is working. A message such as this offers definitive proof that the monitor is not at fault when no text appears at boot.

3. Install a driver for the monitor (as described earlier in the chapter) if Windows does not automatically detect it correctly.
4. If there are any areas of distortion on the screen, or overall fuzziness, try degaussing, or demagnetizing, the monitor. Degaussing discharges any magnetic buildup that might be causing distortion. There should be a degauss feature in the monitor's on-screen controls. When you select it the screen briefly turns itself off and back on again and the picture wavers for a moment, then comes back to normal.

### In Real Life

Magnetic buildup requiring degaussing can sometimes be generated by electrical storms or lightning strikes nearby.

### WARNING

Repeated degaussing can be hard on a monitor, so do not degauss very often. Do it only with a new monitor or when you notice display anomalies.

5. Use the monitor's on-screen controls to fine-tune the picture as described in the next section.

For more thorough testing of the monitor's performance, try the suggestions listed in Figure 16.10.

- Display an all-white screen (such as a blank word processing document) and look for areas that have a red, green, or blue tinge, indicating convergence problems. Some monitors have on-screen controls that enable you to correct convergence problems; other monitors must be serviced by a specialist.
- Try various combinations of color depths, resolutions, and refresh rates in Windows, and make sure that the monitor can correctly display them all. (You may be limited by the video card's capabilities.) The most challenging test of a monitor is to run it at the highest resolution, color depth, and refresh rate that it can support. If something is wrong, it will probably show up in that mode.
- Use a monitor testing program to run the monitor through its paces at a variety of screen resolutions, color depths, and refresh rates. Such programs are available for free download from various Internet sites, such as CNet (see "For More Information" for this chapter on the Internet Resource Center). These programs typically also include pure red, green, and blue screens that you can display to check for dead phosphors. One or two dead phosphors on a monitor under warranty should entitle your client to a new monitor.

**FIGURE 16.10**
More In-Depth Monitor Testing

## Adjusting a Monitor

When you change resolutions and refresh rates, the on-screen image might shift in one direction or become slightly larger or smaller than it was before. Most monitors have on-screen controls that adjust the image size, image position (also known as *phase* when referring to left-right positioning), contrast, brightness, and other factors. Check the monitor manual to figure out how the controls work; they are different for every model.

**Phase**

The left-right positioning of the image within the monitor.

Inexpensive or old monitors might have just a couple of thumbwheels or knobs; more sophisticated monitors will have complete menu systems of controls that pop up when you press a certain button. You then move through the menu system by pressing buttons or moving a joystick or wheel on the front of the monitor. Figure 16.11 shows the on-screen menu for a high-end Sony monitor, for example.

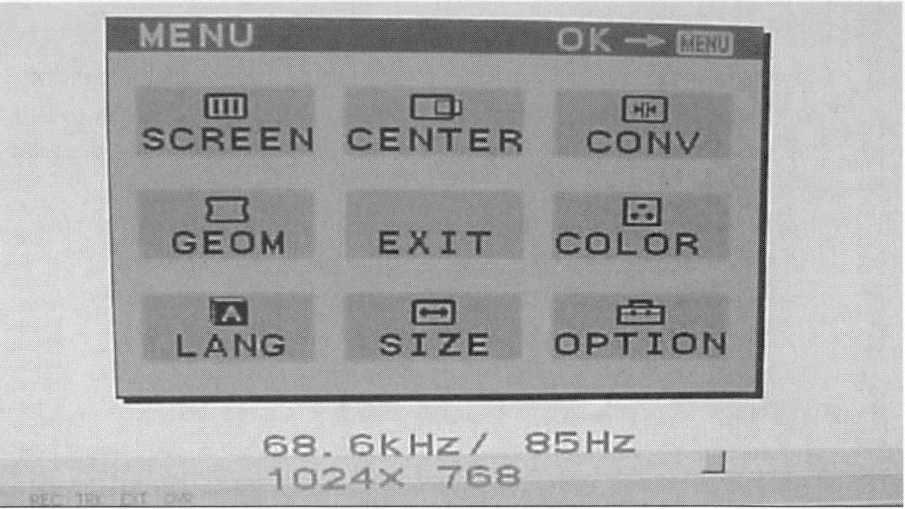


**FIGURE 16.11**
Some monitors have an on-screen menu system for making adjustments.

On a notebook PC's built-in monitor, adjustment controls may be more basic. You are likely to find certain keys on the keyboard with extra symbols in some contrasting color. Pressing these keys in combination with the Fn key activates that special function. For example, in Figure 16.12 notice that a key has a picture of the sun with an up arrow; that is the Increase Brightness function. Consult the notebook PC manual to learn various ways of adjusting the LCD display.

**FIGURE 16.12**
Display adjustments on a notebook PC are typically built into the keyboard.

Figure 16.13 lists the controls that may be available on a monitor.

- **Brightness:** Controls the amount of light in the display. Most people find that brighter is better, although too much brightness makes the black areas look gray.
- **Contrast:** Controls the difference between light and dark areas. Most people like a lot of contrast.
- **Geometry:** The tilt and shape of the picture on-screen. You can use it to tilt the picture slightly clockwise or counterclockwise, make the sides bow in or out slightly, or make the top or bottom of the display wider or narrower.
- **Size:** Makes the overall picture taller or shorter, wider or narrower.
- **Centering:** Moves the picture to the left, right, top, or bottom of the screen. This is also called phase (when referring to horizontal positioning) or position.
- **Convergence:** Describes the relationship of the red, green, and blue dots in the triads to one another. Adjust this if a pure white background shows a slight red, green, or blue tinge.
- **Color:** Adjustable on some monitors. On high-end monitors there may be very complex controls for this, including Bias and Gain settings for each color (red, green, and blue).

**FIGURE 16.13**
Typical Monitor Controls

## Servicing a Monitor

As stated earlier in the chapter, most PC technicians do not need to know how to service a monitor. Inside a monitor is a large electrical capacitor that can deliver a shock of thousands of volts, enough to kill a person, so the average technician is better off declining to work on monitors. Monitor servicing is not covered on the A+ exam except in a very cursory fashion.

The dangerous part of a CRT is the high-voltage anode. If you look at the back of a monitor with its cover off, you will see a suction cup with a wire running from it (see Figure 16.14). Underneath that suction cup is the anode.

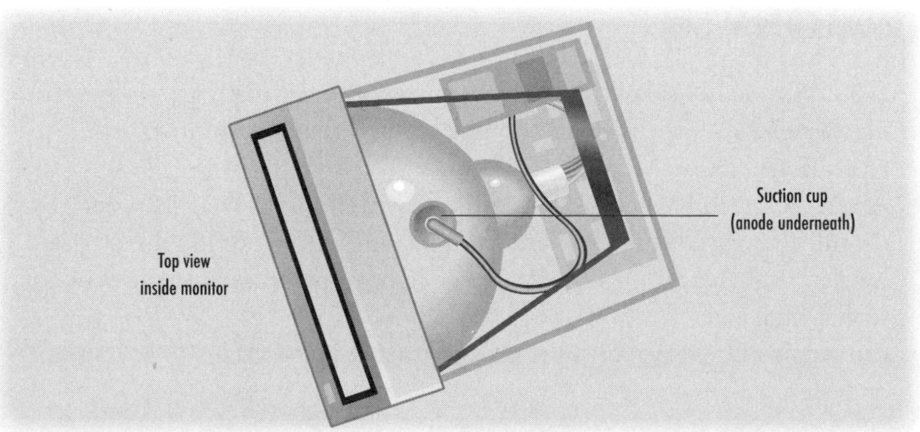


**FIGURE 16.14**
You should be able to identify the high-voltage anode inside a monitor, so you can stay away from it.

Before working on a monitor, a technician must discharge the electricity in the capacitor, allowing it to dissipate. Experienced monitor technicians do this routinely, but it should not be attempted by the inexperienced technician.

After all charge has been dissipated, the monitor technician can work on the adjustment controls that are inside the monitor. This is more trouble than it is worth for most people, which is why so few technicians work on monitors. It is usually cheaper to replace the monitor than to spend several hours trying to fix it.

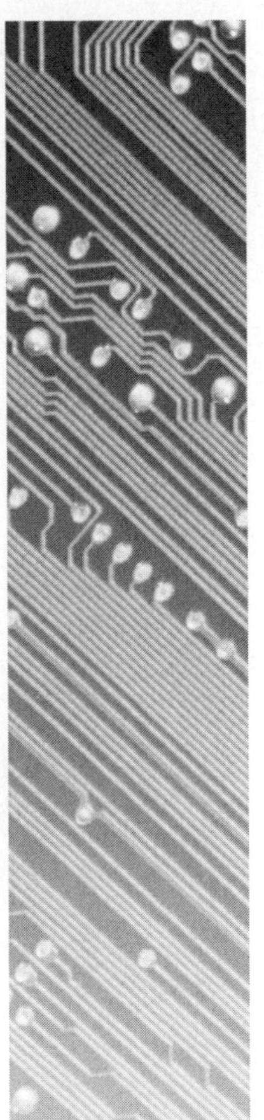

## STUDY GUIDE

Use the following summaries to review the key concepts of this chapter.

### How CRTs Work

- Cathode Ray Tube (CRT) monitors are the traditional box type. They are heavy, but they are inexpensive and work well.
- A CRT uses electron guns to light up red, green, and blue phosphors on-screen, arranged in groups of three called triads.
- The distance between two phosphors of the same color is dot pitch, a measurement of monitor quality.
- Shadow mask is one method of keeping the electron beams precisely aligned. It uses a perforated metal grid to direct the beams toward the phosphors.
- An alternative method, aperture grille, uses vertical wires between the guns and the phosphors.
- Slot mask is a combination of the two technologies.

### How LCDs Work

- Liquid Crystal Display (LCD) monitors are the flat panel type. They are lightweight but expensive and do not always look good in low resolutions.
- An LCD screen has two polarized filters with liquid crystals between. By default the crystals prevent light from passing through, but when twisted by electrical charge, the crystals enable light to pass, creating the on-screen image.
- On a color LCD, a filter splits the light into separate cells for red, green, and blue.

- A passive matrix display uses one transistor for each row and one transistor for each column, emitting pulses.
- Double-scan passive matrix displays (also called DSTN) have an extra row of transistors, so the display is brighter than traditional passive matrix.
- Active matrix displays have a transistor for each pixel, making for a brighter display viewable at any angle.
- Thin film transistor (TFT) displays have multiple transistors for each pixel, further improving active matrix technology.

## Measurements of Monitor Quality

- The monitor has a maximum resolution, just like the video card. A low-end CRT might have a maximum of 1280 x 1024, for example.
- LCD resolutions are usually lower than CRTs; an LCD might have a maximum resolution of 1024 x 768.
- CRTs can operate at any resolution by treating many triads as a single pixel. LCDs are less adept at this, but modern versions perform better than older ones.
- Dot pitch is an important measurement of CRT quality. A typical CRT has a dot pitch of between 0.25mm and 0.28mm. The lower number is better.
- Image size is expressed in two numbers such as 17-inch/15.9-inch. The first number is the overall dimension of the monitor glass, including the part hidden behind the plastic bezel; the second number is the viewable image size.
- The maximum refresh rate is the rate at which the electron guns in the monitor are physically able to refresh each pixel. It is measured in Hertz (Hz); 100Hz is a recommended measurement.
- Refresh rate is determined by the display settings in Windows (or other operating systems).
- Some bargain monitors use interlacing to keep up with the refresh function; it redraws every other line on the screen with each pass.
- Almost all monitors have a 15-pin VGA connector to the video card.

## Connecting Multiple Monitors to a Single PC

- To connect multiple monitors—and use them separately—you must have a video card with multiple output ports, two or more video cards, or a notebook PC with both a built-in display and an external monitor port.

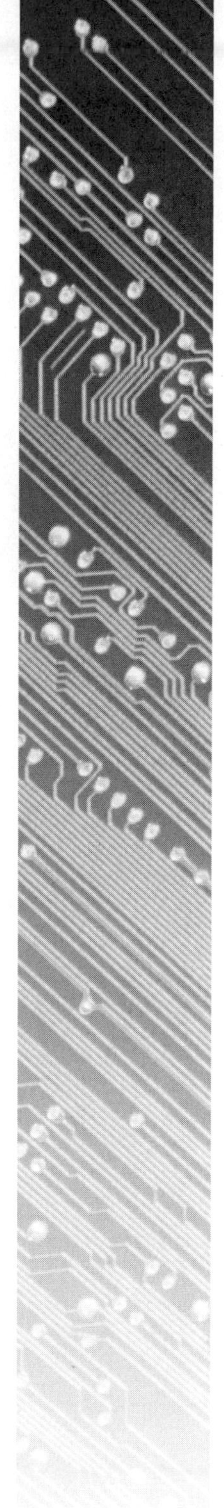

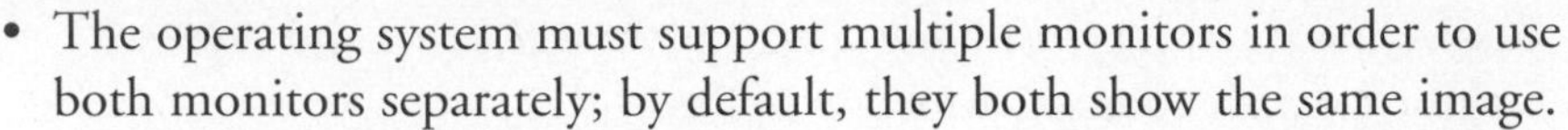

- The operating system must support multiple monitors in order to use both monitors separately; by default, they both show the same image.
- In Windows, set up multimonitor support on the Settings tab in the Display Properties dialog box.
- If you do not have multiple monitors installed, the controls for multiple monitors will not appear on the Settings tab.

## Installing a Monitor Driver

- A monitor driver is not really a driver; it is an information file (.inf) that tells Windows what the monitor's capabilities are.
- By default, Windows detects most monitors as Plug and Play Monitor. You can make better settings available by installing a driver for the exact monitor model.
- To install a monitor driver, use the Update Driver Wizard, as in Chapter 15. You can start it from Device Manager or from the Display Properties dialog box (Settings, Advanced).

## Setting the Refresh Rate

- Set the refresh rate in the Display Properties dialog box in Windows.
- Depending on the Windows version, you may be able to choose a specific numeric value for refresh rate or you may choose between Adapter Default and Optimal.
- In the Display Properties dialog box, click the Settings tab and then click Advanced. From there, the refresh rate controls are found on the Monitor tab in Windows 2000/XP or on the Adapter tab in Windows 9x/Me.

## Testing and Troubleshooting a Monitor

- If you see any text on the screen, the video card and monitor are both physically operational.
- For best results, install drivers for both video card and monitor in Windows.
- Degaussing can clear up fuzziness or distortion on-screen. Use the monitor's controls; check the monitor manual to find out how.
- Display an all-white screen and check for areas of red, green, or blue tint that might indicate convergence problems.
- Try out various combinations of color depths, resolutions, and refresh rates.
- Use a monitor testing program to run the monitor through its paces.

## Adjusting a Monitor

- Most monitors have on-screen controls. Use buttons on the front (or back) of the monitor to adjust.
- Brightness controls the amount of light in the display.
- Contrast controls the difference between light and dark areas.
- Geometry is the tilt and shape of the picture on-screen.
- Size controls the overall height and width of the picture.
- Centering moves the picture to the top, bottom, right, or left. It is also called phase or position.
- Convergence is the alignment of the red, green, and blue dots in the triads.
- Color changes the tint overall.

## Servicing a Monitor

- Servicing a monitor involves removing the cover and working inside, and is not recommended for the inexperienced because of the risk of serious electric shock.
- The suction cup inside the monitor covers the high-voltage anode, the dangerous part.
- Do not practice discharging a monitor, as it is dangerous. You do not need to practice this skill to pass the A+ exam.

# PRACTICE TEST

On a blank sheet of paper, write the answers to the following multiple-choice questions and explain why each answer is correct.

1. CRT stands for
   a. Centered Ring Tube.
   b. Cold Ray Technology.
   c. Cathode Ring Technology.
   d. Cathode Ray Tube.

2. LCD stands for
   a. Large Cathode Discharge.
   b. Liquid Cathode Display.
   c. Liquid Crystal Display.
   d. Large Crystal Diameter.

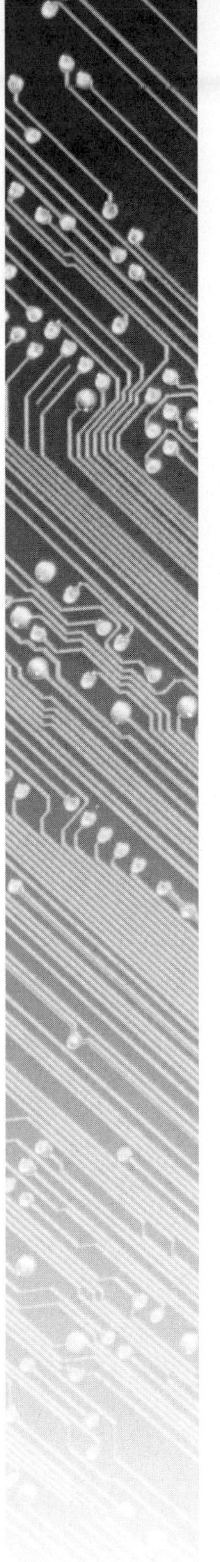

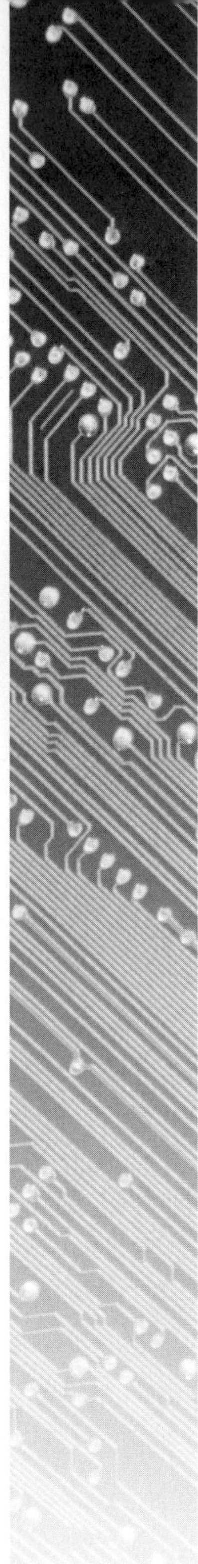

3. How many electron guns are there in a color CRT?
   a. 1
   b. 2
   c. 3
   d. 12

4. Dot pitch is a measurement of
   a. the distance between adjacent triads.
   b. the distance between phosphors of the same color in adjacent triads.
   c. the width of a pixel.
   d. the distance between adjacent pixels.

5. Which of these technologies uses vertical wires to align the electrons in a CRT?
   a. aperture grille
   b. dot pitch
   c. slot mask
   d. shadow mask

6. What is the difference between an active matrix and a passive matrix LCD screen?
   a. Passive matrix has more transistors.
   b. Active matrix has more transistors.
   c. Passive matrix is based on shadow mask technology; active is based on aperture grille.
   d. Passive matrix screens are slightly curved; active matrix are flat.

7. If the monitor has a maximum resolution of 1280 x 1024 and the video card has a maximum resolution of 1024 x 768, what will be the effective limit?
   a. 1280 x 1024
   b. 1024 x 768
   c. It depends on the color depth.
   d. It depends on the dot pitch.

8. Which of these would be a typical dot pitch measurement?
   a. 0.28mm
   b. 28mm
   c. 0.28cm
   d. 28cm

9. The viewable image size is
   a. the diagonal measurement of the monitor glass.
   b. the diagonal measurement of the externally visible portion of the screen.
   c. the number of square inches of the visible portion of the screen.
   d. None of the above

10. Which of these refresh rates would result in the best quality display (least flicker)?
    a. 60Hz
    b. 75Hz
    c. 85Hz
    d. It does not matter; refresh rate has no effect on flickering.

11. If a monitor's maximum refresh rate at 800 x 600 is 130Hz, what will be its maximum refresh rate at 1024 x 768?
    a. less than 130Hz
    b. more than 130Hz
    c. exactly 130Hz
    d. It depends on the color depth.

12. Interlacing compensates for poor refresh rate by
    a. using only half of the pixels; the others remain inactive.
    b. using only half of the phosphors; the others remain inactive.
    c. redrawing every other line vertically with each pass.
    d. redrawing every other line horizontally with each pass.

13. A Macintosh PC uses what type of connector for a monitor?
    a. a proprietary Macintosh video connector
    b. a standard 15-pin VGA connector
    c. a BNC connector
    d. a 50-pin SCSI connector

14. To enable multiple monitors in Windows where each monitor shows the same thing on-screen,
    a. do nothing; by default both monitors show the same thing.
    b. choose Extend my Windows desktop onto this monitor from the Settings tab of the Display Properties dialog box.
    c. choose DualView support from the Settings tab of the Display Properties dialog box.
    d. choose DualView from the Display Properties dialog box in Device Manager.

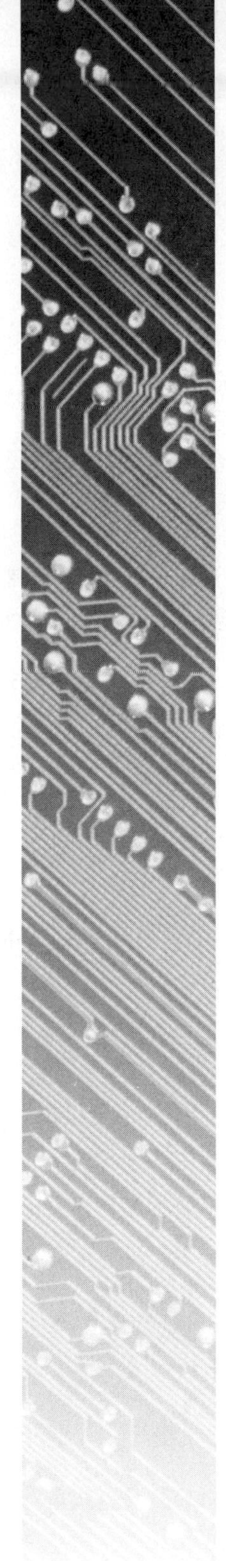

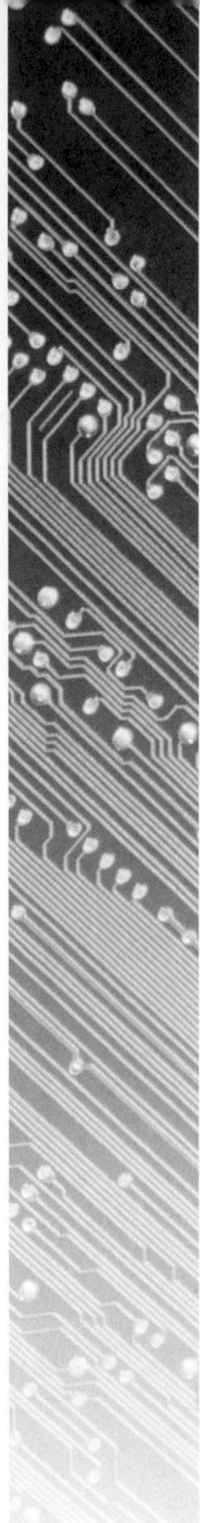

15. A monitor driver's .inf file
    a. tells which other driver files to install for the monitor.
    b. describes the monitor's maximum capabilities to the OS.
    c. specifies which video cards will work with the monitor.
    d. All of the above

16. What might happen if you use an INF file for a different monitor model?
    a. Refresh rates might be available that the monitor cannot support.
    b. Color depths might be available that the monitor cannot support.
    c. Nothing will happen provided the driver is signed.
    d. You will be limited to standard VGA resolution.

17. What does degaussing do?
    a. discharges static electricity
    b. discharges magnetic buildup
    c. discharges excess AC current
    d. None of these; it simply resets the monitor.

18. A white screen with a red tint to it indicates what type of problem?
    a. pincushioning
    b. phase
    c. convergence
    d. capacitance

19. What is a phase adjustment?
    a. same thing as convergence
    b. tilting the display
    c. changing the image position
    d. making the overall display image larger or smaller

20. Which part inside the monitor poses the most significant danger of electric shock?
    a. anode
    b. flyback transformer
    c. power supply
    d. phosphors

## TROUBLESHOOTING

1. A client complains that ever since the thunderstorm two days ago, his monitor has looked fuzzy. What can you recommend?
2. After changing refresh rates, the entire display looks like it has shifted about an inch to the left. There is a big black bar to the right of the Windows desktop, and the left side of it is cut off so you cannot see the Start button. What will fix the problem?
3. You see nothing on-screen. You know it is not the PC's fault because you have swapped monitors and another monitor works fine. The light on the monitor comes on, and it is green rather than amber, indicating that it is receiving a signal from the PC. What could you check before assuming the monitor is defective?

## CUSTOMER SERVICE

1. A client calls you to complain that he does not see anything on his monitor. Describe the questions you would ask him to help narrow down the problem.
2. A client wants to know how to adjust the brightness on her notebook PC. What can you suggest?
3. A client has dropped his monitor and now it does not work anymore. He asks whether you can fix it. Do you think you will be able to? Why or why not?

## FOR MORE INFORMATION

For links to Web sites that provide further information about the topics covered in this chapter, go to the EMC/Paradigm Internet Resource Center at www.emcp.com/College Division/Internet Resource Centers/PC Maintenance/For More Information.

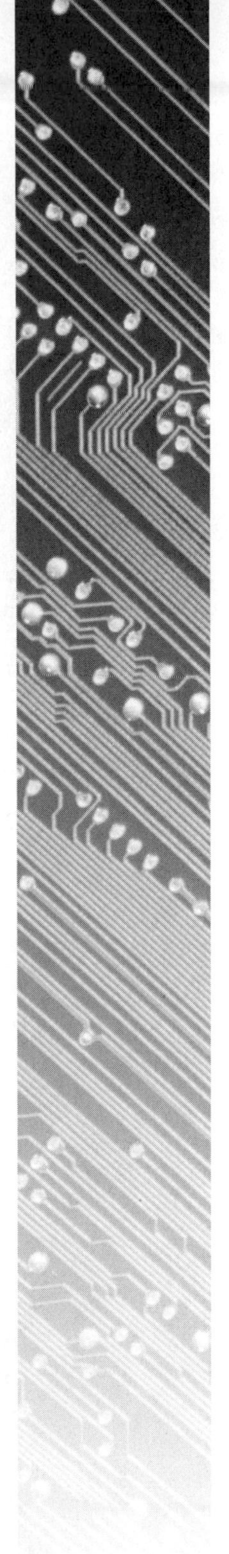

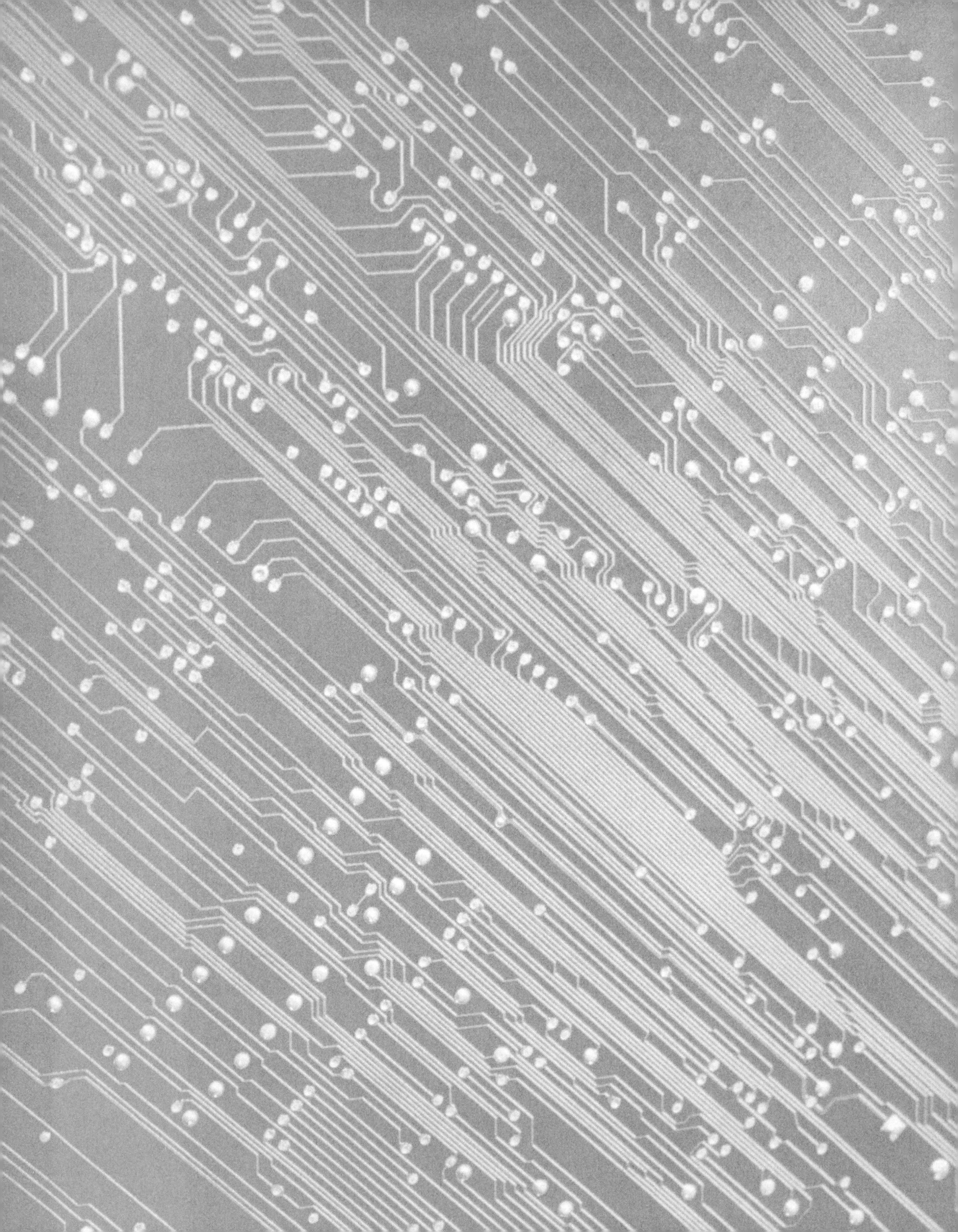

# 17 Keyboards and Mice

## ON THE TEST

**A+ Core Hardware Service Technician Examination**

- **Objective 1.2:** Identify basic procedures for adding and removing field replaceable modules for both desktop and portable systems.
- **Objective 2.1:** Identify common symptoms and problems associated with each module and how to troubleshoot and isolate the problems.

## ON THE JOB

In this chapter we will look at keyboards and mice, the two main methods of user input for a PC. Neither device is particularly complex or difficult to install or troubleshoot, but both cause a significant number of user problems because users interact with these devices almost constantly as they work with their PCs.

Some skills involved with this chapter's topics include:

- installing new keyboards and mice
- troubleshooting stuck or nonoperational keys
- troubleshooting mouse performance problems
- adjusting keyboard settings for user preference
- changing the mouse pointer size and appearance on-screen
- adjusting the mouse pointer speed and features
- setting up a mouse for a left-handed user

## Keyboards

Electronically, a keyboard is a grid of uncompleted circuits. When you press a number, letter, or symbol key, you lower a contact that completes the circuit and sends data to the PC. Different keys complete different circuits, resulting in different data being sent.

Some keys are modifiers; they trigger a circuit that changes any other values sent while they are pressed. The Shift key is the most common example; when you press Shift by itself, nothing happens. But when you hold down Shift and press the B key, a capital *B* is sent, a different value than when the B key is pressed by itself.

Other keys send function codes rather than letters or numbers. For example, the F1 key sends a code string to the PC that represents Function 1. What that entails depends on the operating system and/or the active application. For example, at a DOS prompt, pressing F1 has no effect, but within Windows (and in most operating systems and applications), pressing F1 opens the Help function. If an application is active that has a function assigned to the F1 key, it grabs that input and interprets it as its own command.

## Nonalphanumeric Keys

A typical keyboard has the standard letter and number keys as found on a typewriter; these are called *alphanumeric*. It also typically has the nonalphanumeric extra keys shown in Figure 17.1.

**Alphanumeric**

Derived from a combination of the words "alphabetic" and "numeric." Refers to all alphabet characters plus all number digits.

- **Function keys:** These are the "F" keys, usually across the top but perhaps along the left edge on an older keyboard. They perform preprogrammed functions in many applications, and in some applications and operating systems you can also program them yourself.
- **Esc:** Short for Escape, this key has different uses in various applications but it usually closes an active menu or window or goes back one level.
- **Ctrl** and **Alt:** These keys combine with the normal number and letter keys to perform special functions. For example, in most Windows programs Ctrl + S is a shortcut for issuing the Save command.
- **PrtScn/SysRq:** Short for Print Screen/System Request, pressing Shift + PrtScn in Windows takes a "picture" of the Windows screen and copies it to the Clipboard. You can then paste it into an application such as Word, Excel, or Paint.
- **Pause/Break:** A carryover from older days when it was used to pause or stop a running command-line program. Does not have much function in Windows.
- **NumLock:** Toggles the function of the numeric keypad at the right end of the keyboard between numbers and directional arrows.

**FIGURE 17.1**
Nonalphanumeric Keys on a Typical Keyboard

*continued*

- **Insert:** In many programs this toggles between Insert mode (in which existing text moves over when new text is keyed in front of it) and Overtype mode (in which existing text is deleted when new text is keyed in front of it).
- **Delete:** A shortcut for the Delete command in most applications, pressing the key deletes selected objects.
- **Home:** The purpose of this key varies depending on the application, but in Microsoft Word, for example, it moves the cursor to the beginning of the line. The Home key can also be combined with Shift, Ctrl, and Alt to move the cursor different places on-screen.
- **End:** The End key functions the same as the Home key except it moves to the end of a line (in Word).
- **Page Up and Page Down:** In a window that contains more than will fit on-screen at once, these keys scroll the display one screenful at a time.
- **Windows:** Only the most modern keyboards have this key. It has a picture of a flying windowpane on it (⊞) and it opens the Start menu in Windows.
- **Menu key:** Like the Windows key, this is found only on modern keyboards. It looks like a drop-down menu and opens the right-click shortcut menu for an object.

**FIGURE 17.1**
continued

## Keyboard Layouts

There have been many different keyboard layouts over the years, from many manufacturers. The original PC XT (8086 CPU) had a keyboard layout with about 83 keys. The IBM AT (80286 CPU) introduced the AT-style keyboard that is the basis for the keyboard we use currently. Today's keyboards have between 101 and 104 keys, depending on the model.

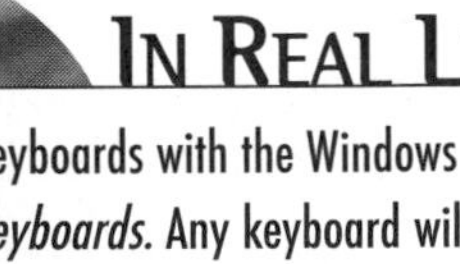

### In Real Life

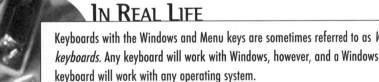

Keyboards with the Windows and Menu keys are sometimes referred to as *Windows keyboards.* Any keyboard will work with Windows, however, and a Windows keyboard will work with any operating system.

**Windows keyboard**

A keyboard containing special keys used only in Microsoft Windows, such as the Menu and Windows keys.

Figures 17.2 and 17.3 compare an old XT-style keyboard with a modern keyboard layout. Some of the differences include function key placement (left versus top), additional keys, and a set of arrow keys in addition to those on the numeric keypad.

**FIGURE 17.2**
An Old XT-Style Keyboard with 83 Keys

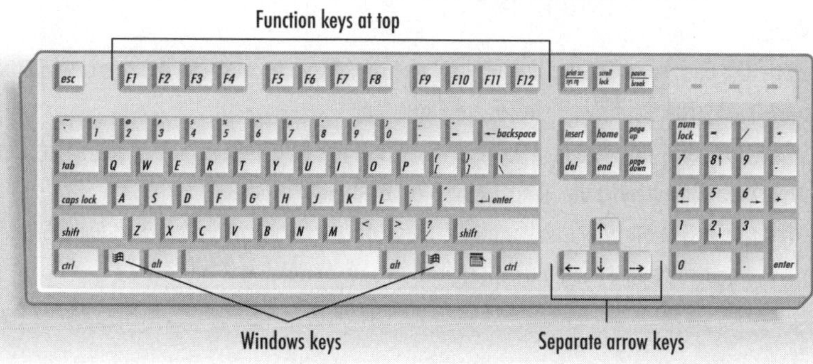


**FIGURE 17.3**
A Modern Keyboard with 104 Keys

**Dvorak keyboard**

A keyboard with a different arrangement of letters, designed for faster typing than with a traditional keyboard.

Although it is not widely used, there is also a completely different keyboard layout called Dvorak. It places the keys in different spots, and requires users to relearn touch typing. Many Dvorak keyboard users claim they can type even faster than on a traditional keyboard. Figure 17.4 shows a Dvorak keyboard layout.

**WARNING**

**If you use a Dvorak keyboard, you must make Windows aware of it so it can correctly interpret the data it receives. If the keyboard is not Plug and Play, you must load software that tells Windows about the different key arrangement; this software comes with the keyboard or you can download it from the keyboard manufacturer's Web site.**

FIGURE 17.4
The Dvorak Keyboard Layout

## Keyboard Connectors

Keyboards have traditionally had their own interface to the PC. As you saw in Chapter 4, AT motherboards have an AT-style keyboard connector, while ATX systems use the PS/2 style (see Figure 17.5).

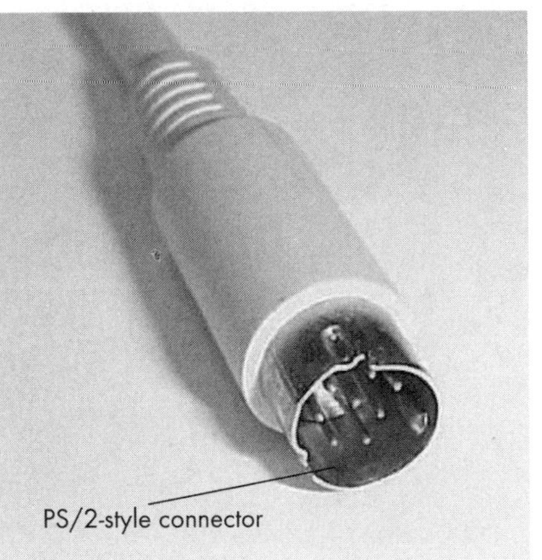


FIGURE 17.5
Traditional Types of Keyboard Connectors

Lately, however, more and more keyboards (and mice as well) use the USB interface, which we covered in Chapter 7. USB is increasingly the preferred interface for nearly all input devices. Remember, though, that to use USB devices the Windows version must support USB, and that does *not* include the non-Original Equipment Manufacturer (OEM) version of Windows 95.

**WARNING**

Some systems have problems with USB devices that need to start working before the OS fully loads, and a keyboard is one example of such a device. If the client uses a USB keyboard (or mouse), make sure that the Legacy USB Support option is turned on in BIOS Setup.

USB and the traditional keyboard interfaces are all serial connections, and therefore they are interchangeable with one another by using an inexpensive adapter plug found at any computer store. In addition, many USB keyboards have an extra PS/2 plug on the same cord so you can connect them either way.

## SELECTING A KEYBOARD

The type of keyboard interface is one of the primary considerations when selecting a keyboard. Some of the other considerations include:

- **Design:** Some keyboards are a standard rectangular block; others are split so that half of the keys point to the left and the other half to the right. This *ergonomic* design helps prevent wrist strain problems. Figure 17.6 shows a split keyboard.

**Ergonomic**

Designed to help the human body avoid unnecessary strain or stress.

**FIGURE 17.6**
A split keyboard, like this Microsoft Natural Keyboard, can help reduce wrist strain problems.

- **Extra keys:** Notice in Figure 17.6 that there is a row of small round buttons along the top of the keyboard, in addition to the regular square keys. These provide shortcuts for performing various functions, such as controlling the Web browser, the sound settings, and the CD player.

### IN REAL LIFE

On some keyboards the special keys do not work unless you install a keyboard utility program in Windows; others work directly with Windows with no special utility needed. Most keyboards come with a utility program, but try the keyboard first without loading the utility; it might work fine, and you can save the system overhead of having the program load every time the PC is turned on.

- **Wrist support:** The keyboard in Figure 17.6 also has a built-in wrist rest, to aid further in avoiding wrist strain. Conventional keyboards may or may not have this feature.
- **Cord:** Some keyboards are wireless, meaning they are not tethered to the PC by a cord. They communicate with the PC via radio waves or infrared. This can be convenient in situations in which the keyboard sits far away from the PC, but it also adds to the cost.

**TRY IT!**

**Identify the type of keyboard you have. How many keys does it have? What type of interface does it use? Are there any special features? If you were buying a keyboard, what other features would you want that you currently do not have?**

## Mice and Other Pointing Devices

A mouse is the most popular device for moving the on-screen pointer in a graphical operating system such as Windows. There are also several alternatives to the traditional mouse, however, such as trackballs, touchpads, and light pens.

A mouse works by translating the physical movement of the device into signal data to the PC. A traditional mouse has a ball inside it, as you saw when you took one apart for cleaning in Chapter 1. As you roll the ball on the desk, it rolls past sensors or wheels inside the mouse, and that movement triggers electrical pulses to be sent to the PC. Some modern versions do not have a ball, but instead have a single optical sensor. Figure 17.7 shows a disassembled mouse.

**FIGURE 17.7**
Bottom View of a Mouse with Ball Removed

## Mouse Connectors

Originally the mouse was a serial port device, connecting to the 9- or 25-pin serial port built into the PC. The IBM PS/2 computer, however, used a new type of mouse connector that plugged into a small round port. This port has become the PS/2 port standard of today. As discussed in the preceding section, ATX motherboards use the PS/2 connector type for the keyboard, and almost all modern motherboards include a PS/2 port for the mouse as well. Some mice available in stores today might also use the USB interface.

## Selecting a Mouse

As with a keyboard, the primary compatibility concern when selecting a mouse is an interface that the PC will support (serial, PS/2, or USB). Other criteria include:

- **Number of buttons:** Windows requires a mouse with at least two buttons. Some mice (especially those made by Logitech) have three buttons; the center button is programmable with the software included with the mouse but has no default functionality preassigned.

### In Real Life

Some mouse alternative devices, such as trackballs, might have four or six buttons. Usually, when there is an even number of buttons, all of the buttons on one side do the same thing by default (but can be programmed for different functions). That is for convenience, so the buttons will be located in the right place for a variety of usage styles.

- **Shape and comfort:** Some mice are curved to the right or left to accommodate a right-handed or left-handed person (lefties may need to special-order); some are larger or smaller than average.
- **Wheel:** Some two-button mice have a rubber wheel between the two buttons. This wheel performs special functions in Windows and in some Windows applications, such as scrolling. (Scrolling is its default function in Windows.) You can either roll the wheel or press it like a button.
- **Programmable functions:** Some mice come with software that programs extra features into the mouse, such as minimizing all windows or opening a favorite application. These special features are typically activated by the third button (if present) or by pressing both buttons simultaneously.

- **Cord:** As with keyboards, some mice are cordless and work with radio or infrared technology.
- **No ball:** As stated in Chapter 1, a mouse must be cleaned periodically because dirt gets inside the chamber where the ball sits. In some mice the ball has been replaced with a light sensor, so you never have to clean them. This style is called an optical mouse.

**TRY IT!**

**Identify the type of mouse you have. What kind of interface does it use? Does it have a ball? Any special functions? How many buttons? Does it have a wheel?**

## Mouse Variants

*Trackballs* are a very popular alternative to mice because they require less desktop space. With a traditional mouse, the ball is on the bottom and it moves when you move the mouse. With a trackball, the ball is on the top and you move the ball with your fingers while the base remains stationary. There are many types of trackballs available, some with radically different shapes and designs. Figure 17.8 shows one type.

**Trackball**

A stationary device with a rolling ball on top that functions as a mouse equivalent.

On notebook PCs, a popular mouse alternative is a *touchpad*. This is a small, rectangular, touch-sensitive pad; you glide your finger across to move the pointer, and then tap the pad to click. Buttons are also provided near the touchpad for manually clicking and right-clicking (see Figure 17.9). Although touchpads are most popular on portable PCs, they are also available as plug-in devices for desktop PCs.

**Touchpad**

A touch-sensitive rectangular pad that functions as a mouse alternative for moving an on-screen pointer.

**FIGURE 17.8**
A Trackball

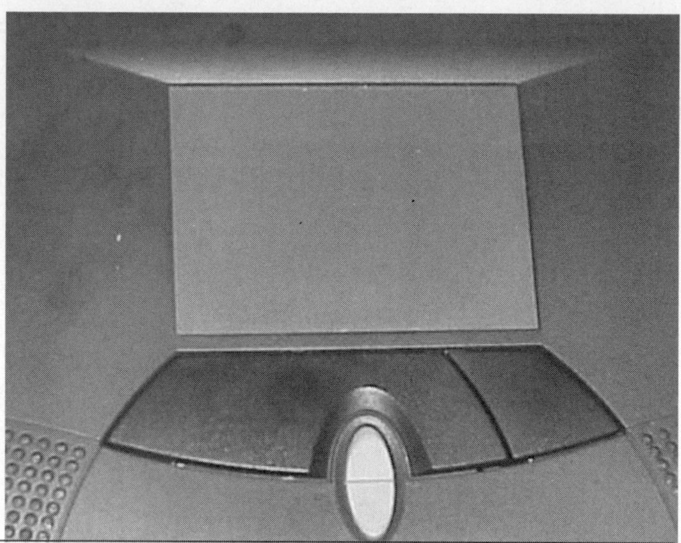

**FIGURE 17.9**
A Touchpad

## Connecting/Disconnecting Keyboards and Mice

The cable connections for keyboards and mice are simple—just plug them in. The real trick is in knowing when you can—and cannot—safely do so. The general rule is this: *Do not plug in or unplug a keyboard or mouse while the computer's power is on*. If you forget to attach one, turn off the PC before you attach it. The same goes for removal. This is especially important when attaching or removing from the keyboard connectors or the COM or LPT ports.

There are a couple of exceptions to the above rule:

- If you forget to connect a mouse before starting the computer, a warning appears when Windows boots about not detecting a mouse. At that point, you can connect a PS/2 mouse and press Enter without having to shut off the PC. However, if you need to connect a serial mouse, you must shut down first.
- You can connect or disconnect a USB input device at any time. However, before you disconnect a device ensure that it has finished transferring whatever data was involved in its last operation. You might want to stop the device first. See the section "Stopping a Removable Device" in Chapter 20 for more information.

### In Real Life

**If a keyboard or mouse accidentally gets unplugged while you are using the PC, go ahead and plug it back in as quickly as possible. If the PC does not work normally, restart Windows.**

## TRY IT!

Turn off your PC, and disconnect and reconnect the keyboard and mouse. If either is USB, try starting the system while it is disconnected. What happens? Then plug it in. Does the PC recognize it automatically when you plug it in?

## Adjusting Keyboard Settings in Windows

Depending on the Windows version, different keyboard properties may be available. From the Control Panel, double-click the *Keyboard* icon to open the Keyboard Properties dialog box. Figure 17.10 shows the Windows 2000 version for a standard keyboard. Figure 17. 11 shows the settings you may be able to adjust, depending on the keyboard and Windows version.

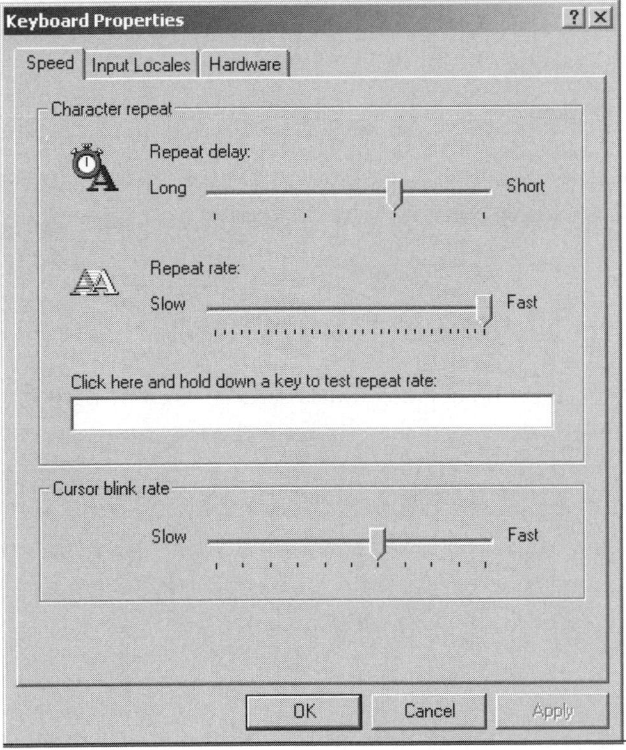


**FIGURE 17.10**
Keyboard Properties Dialog Box in Windows 2000

- **Repeat delay:** The delay between the time when you start holding down a key and when it starts repeating that character quickly on-screen. The feature is also called typematic delay.
- **Repeat rate:** The speed at which character repeat occurs once it starts. This is also called typematic rate.
- **Cursor blink rate:** The speed at which the vertical line cursor blinks off and on in a program that takes text input (such as a word processor).
- **Language or Input Locale:** If available, this option (on its own tab) lets you set up keyboard layouts for two or more languages so that certain keys produce the characters needed for foreign languages. You can switch back and forth between languages with shortcut keys you define.

**FIGURE 17.11**
Adjustable Keyboard Settings

The dialog box shown in Figure 17.10 includes a text box for testing purposes; click inside the text box and then key some text, or hold down a key, to test the settings.

## TRY IT!

Experiment with the keyboard settings available in your version of Windows. Try several different settings to find the ones most comfortable to you.

## Adjusting Mouse Settings in Windows

Many users find that the default mouse settings are not right for them in some way. Perhaps they need the pointer to be larger and more visible, or perhaps the pointer moves too slowly across the screen in connection with the mouse movement. The following sections outline some of the adjustments you can make. All of these adjustments start from the same place: the Mouse Properties dialog box. To open the dialog box, double-click the *Mouse* icon in the Control Panel.

### Buttons

By default the left mouse button is the primary button, and the right one is secondary. Left-handed users may prefer to place the mouse on the left, however, and switch the buttons. To do so, click the Left-handed option on the Buttons tab, as shown in Figure 17.12. In some versions the control is a little different; in Windows XP, for example, you click the Switch primary and secondary buttons check box to switch them.

You can also adjust the double-click speed from the Buttons tab. This controls how quickly the user must double-click in order for the action to be interpreted as a double click rather than two single clicks. Drag the slider to the left or right to change the setting; then double-click on the jack-in-the-box icon to test the setting.

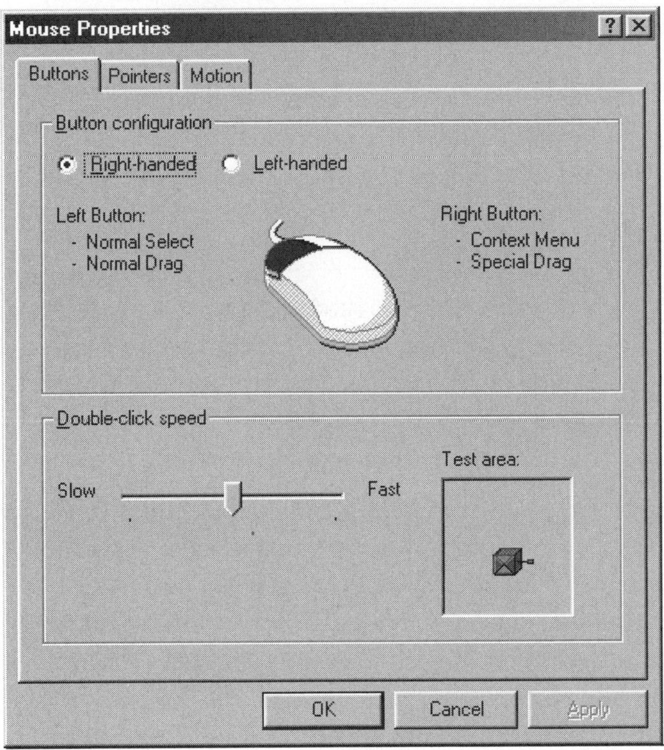


**FIGURE 17.12**
Mouse Button Properties (Windows 98 Shown)

In Windows 2000 there is also an option on the Buttons tab for choosing whether to use single-click or double-click operation for opening objects. The default in Windows is that you single-click to select and double-click to open, but you can set it to point to select and single-click to open, to make it more like a Web page. This same option is available in Windows XP, but it is not part of the Mouse Properties dialog box; instead it is a setting within the Folder Options (Tools, Folder Options from any file management window).

The Windows Me and Windows XP versions include a check box for turning on ClickLock, a feature that treats the mouse button as an on/off toggle so you do not have to hold it down to drag. You click once to set it, then click again to release it. This is useful for people with limited mobility.

## TRY IT!

**Try switching the left and right mouse buttons and using the mouse with the hand opposite to the one you normally use. Put it back to your usual setting when you are finished.**

### Pointer Appearance

The default mouse pointer appearance might not be suitable for all users. Some people may prefer a larger set of pointers, for example, or a black arrow rather than a white one.

## In Real Life

**If using a Windows version that includes Desktop Themes support (through the Control Panel), the user can also select a desktop theme that includes custom pointers; that setting will override any pointer choices made through the Mouse Properties dialog box.**

**Pointer scheme**

A group of mouse pointer graphics that are designed to work as a set.

There are actually many different graphics used for the mouse pointer, depending on the situation. The arrow pointer is the most common, but others include the Busy pointer (the hourglass) and the Text Select pointer (the curly capital *I*). You can select a different pointer graphic for any of these individually, or you can select a different *pointer scheme*.

To choose a different pointer scheme, open the Scheme drop-down list on the Pointers tab in the Mouse Properties dialog box and make your selection. The individual pointer graphics for that scheme will appear in the list box below, as shown in Figure 17.13.

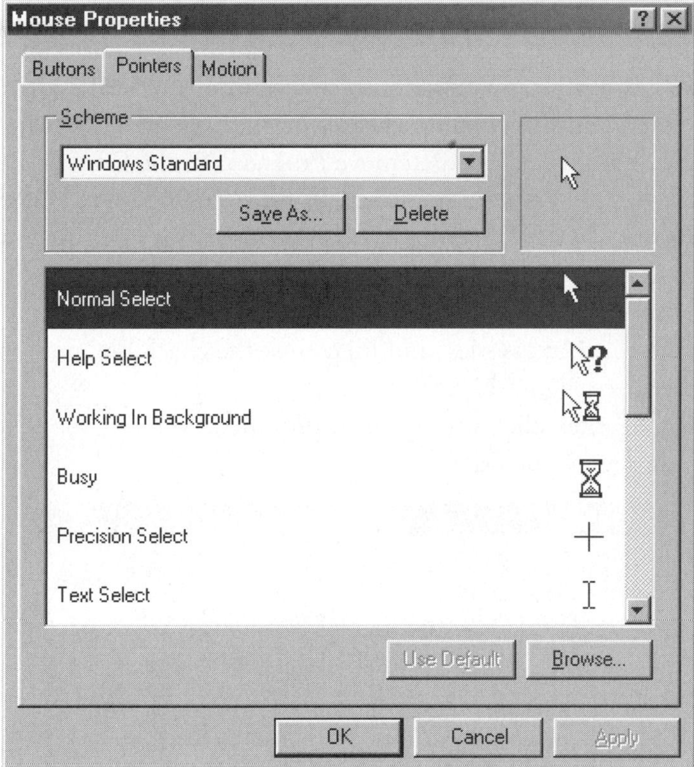


**FIGURE 17.13**
Select a set of pointers or choose pointer graphics individually.

To change an individual pointer, double-click it to open a Browse window. Then identify the graphic file you want to use instead of the current one. In most Windows versions you will find a selection of pointers in the *Windows\Cursors* folder (see Figure 17.14).

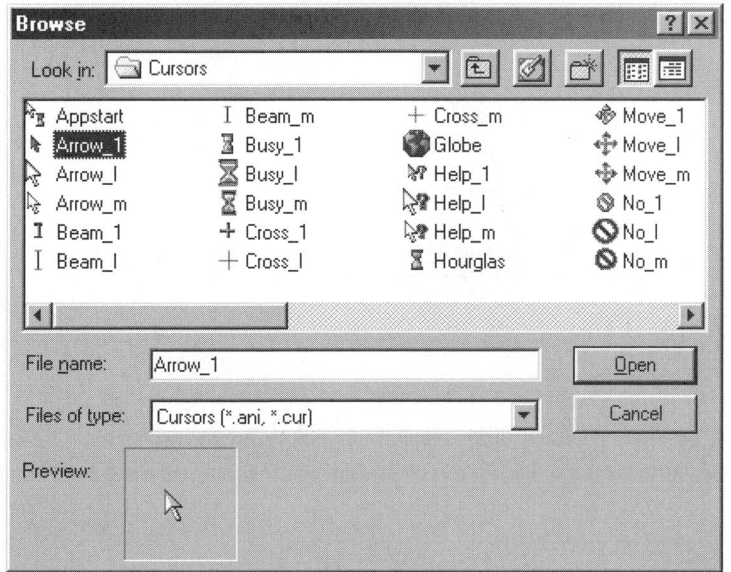


**FIGURE 17.14**
Browse for an individual pointer graphic.

In Windows 2000 and XP you can also enable or disable a pointer shadow from the Pointers tab by marking or clearing a check box.

If you do not have many graphics to choose from in the *Windows\Cursors* folder, or you do not have many schemes on the Scheme drop-down list, you can install more from Add/Remove Programs in the Control Panel. The additional pointers are an optional Windows component. In Windows 98, for example, do the following (with your instructor's permission):

1. From Control Panel, double-click the *Add/Remove Programs* icon. Then select the Windows Setup tab.
2. Double-click Accessories, and then click the check box next to Mouse Pointers (see Figure 17.15).
3. Click OK, then click OK again. If prompted to insert the Windows CD, do so and click OK.

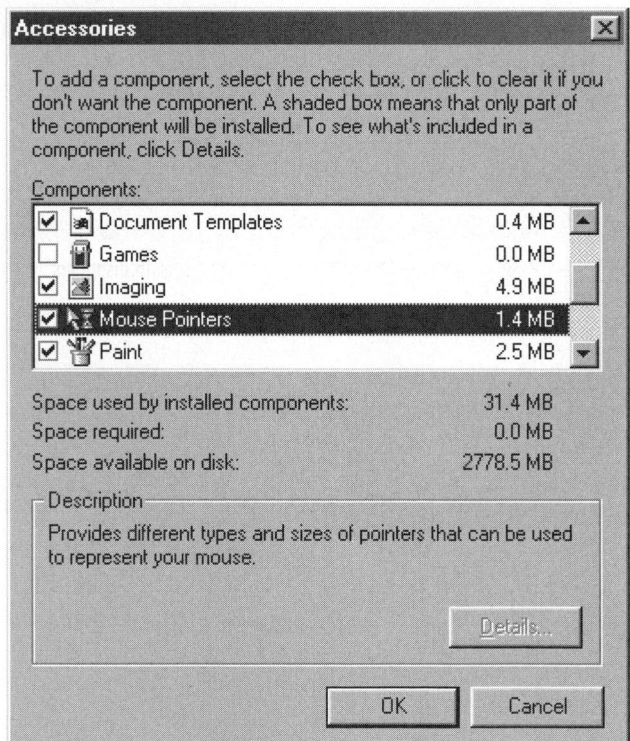


**FIGURE 17.15**
Install the additional pointer sets if they are not already installed.

## TRY IT!

Try several different pointer schemes. If the additional schemes are not installed yet, install them with Add/Remove Programs. Then go back to the default scheme and change only one of the individual pointers in it. Put the settings back as they were originally when you are finished.

## Pointer Movement

In all Windows versions you can adjust the mouse sensitivity—the relationship of mouse movement to screen cursor movement. To change mouse sensitivity, use the Motion tab in the Mouse Properties dialog box. (In some versions of Windows, notably Windows Me and XP, this tab is called Pointer Options.) Drag the Speed slider to the right or left. (In some Windows versions it is called Pointer speed.) Depending on the type of mouse and the Windows version, there may also be other motion settings you can adjust, as described in Figure 17.16.

- **Pointer trails:** If you turn on this feature, the pointer leaves a trail or residue behind as it moves on-screen, so people with limited vision can track it more easily. People with normal vision frequently find this annoying. (Available in Windows 95/98/Me only.)
- **Acceleration:** When this feature is enabled, the pointer moves slowly at first and then picks up speed. In Windows 2000, change the acceleration using a simple slider. In Windows Me, click the Accelerate button to open a separate dialog box for this setting.
- **Snap to or Snap to Default:** When this is enabled, the mouse pointer jumps automatically to the default button in a dialog box, such as the OK button. (Available in Windows 2000 and Me only.)
- **Hide pointer while typing:** An option that enables the pointer to disappear when you are typing text in a word processing program. It reappears when you move the mouse. (Available in Windows Me and XP only.)
- **Show location of pointer when you press the CTRL key:** An option that makes a little ripple of circles around the pointer when you press Ctrl, to help you find it. (Available in Windows Me only.)
- **Wheel:** If the mouse has a wheel, there may be a separate Wheel tab in Mouse Properties for setting it up.

**FIGURE 17.6**
Windows Pointer Adjustments

Figure 17.17 shows the Motion tab in Windows Me; Figure 17.18 shows the Pointer Options tab in Windows XP. The two tabs show the full gamut of available pointer movement settings.

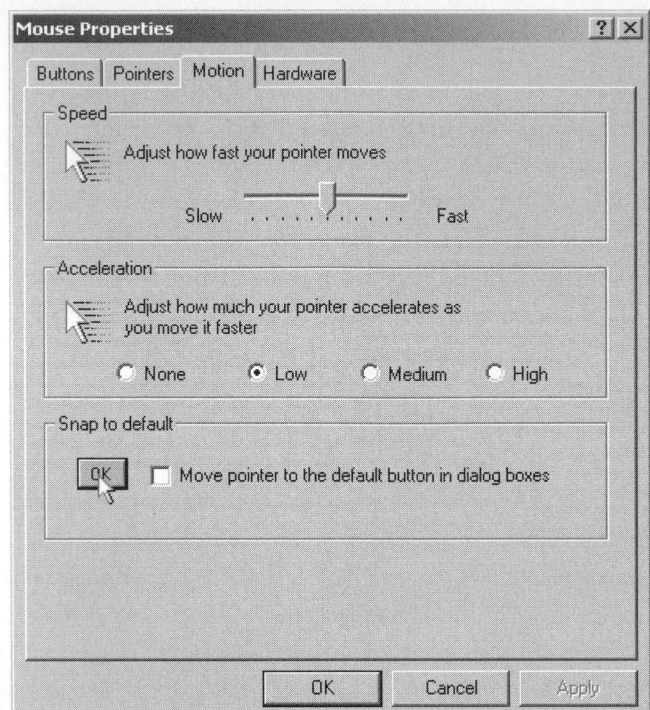


**FIGURE 17.17**
Windows Me Options for Pointer Movement

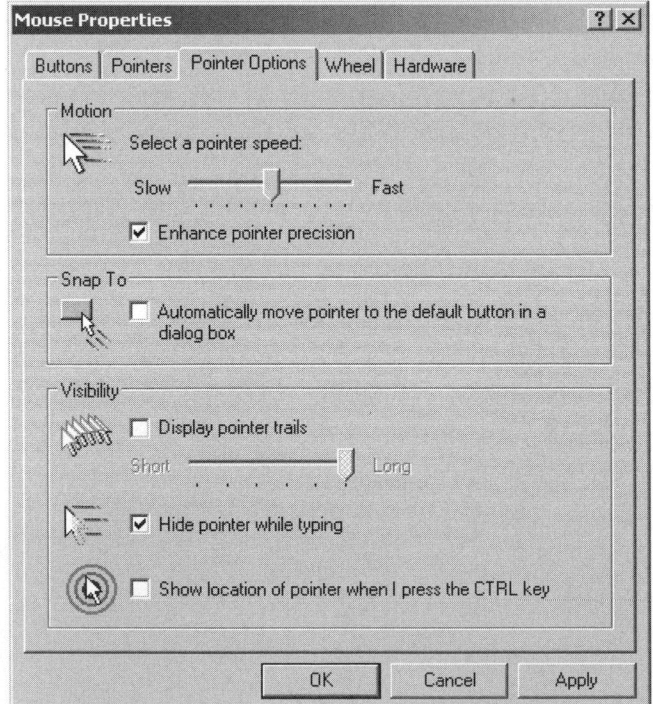


**FIGURE 17.18**
Windows XP Options for Pointer Movement

The settings described in this chapter pertain to the default mouse driver in Windows; if you install a driver that comes with a specific mouse model, the options will be different. The same basic capabilities will probably be available, as well as others, but the wording and placement may be different.

### TRY IT!

Experiment with the pointer settings available in your Windows version. Leave any nondefault settings enabled that are helpful to you.

## Making the Mouse Function as a Keyboard

Most versions of Windows contain an Accessibility feature called On-Screen Keyboard (see Figure 17.19). A keyboard layout appears in a window, and you can type by clicking on the letters. This is useful for someone with a motion-related disability who finds it difficult to use a keyboard but can operate a mouse.

To turn on the On-Screen Keyboard, first make sure the Accessibility tools are installed (through Add/Remove Programs in the Control Panel). Then choose Start/Programs/Accessories/Accessibility/On-Screen Keyboard. Then just click the key buttons as needed. Close the window when you are finished.

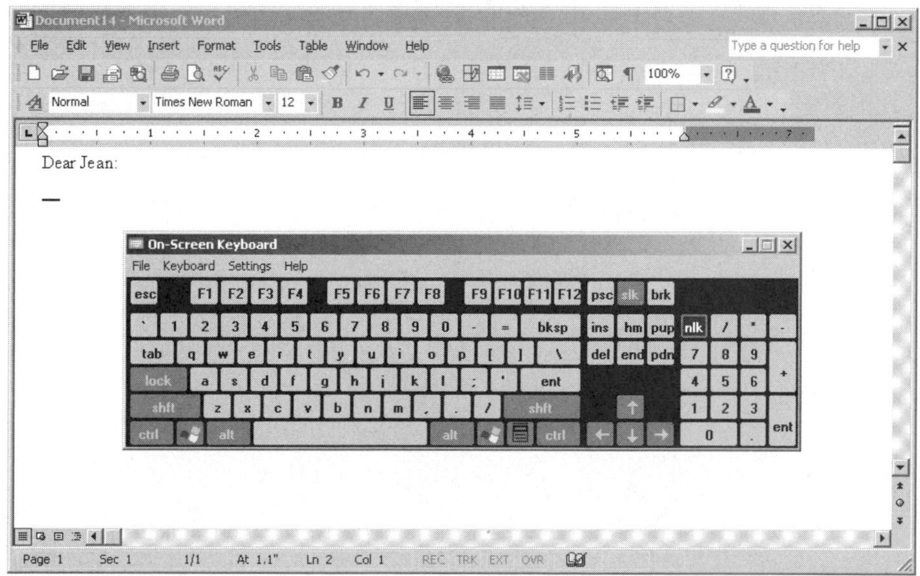


**FIGURE 17.19**
The On-Screen Keyboard utility makes the mouse function as a keyboard.

## TRY IT!

1. Open a word processing program such as WordPad.
2. Open the On-Screen Keyboard utility and key a few lines of text with it.
3. Close the On-Screen Keyboard.
4. Exit the word processing program, discarding your changes.

# Making the Keyboard Function as a Mouse

**MouseKeys**

A Windows feature that enables the keyboard's arrow keys to control the mouse pointer.

Most Windows versions also provide the opposite of the feature described in the preceding section: a keyboard that can be used as a mouse, with the mouse pointer controlled by the arrow keys. Again, this may be useful for someone who has difficulty using a mouse but who can use a keyboard. This feature is called *MouseKeys*.

To turn on MouseKeys, complete the following steps:

1. In the Control Panel, double-click the *Accessibility Options* icon.
2. On the Mouse tab at the Accessibility Properties or Accessibility Options dialog box, click the Use MouseKeys check box.
3. Click the Settings button to open the Settings for MouseKeys dialog box, shown in Figure 17.20.
4. Change any options desired here; then click OK. You can adjust the pointer speed and acceleration, for example.
5. Click OK to close the Accessibility dialog box.

After the feature has been turned on, you can enable it by pressing Alt + left Shift + Num Lock. A dialog box appears letting you know that you are turning on MouseKeys; click OK or press Enter to accept it.

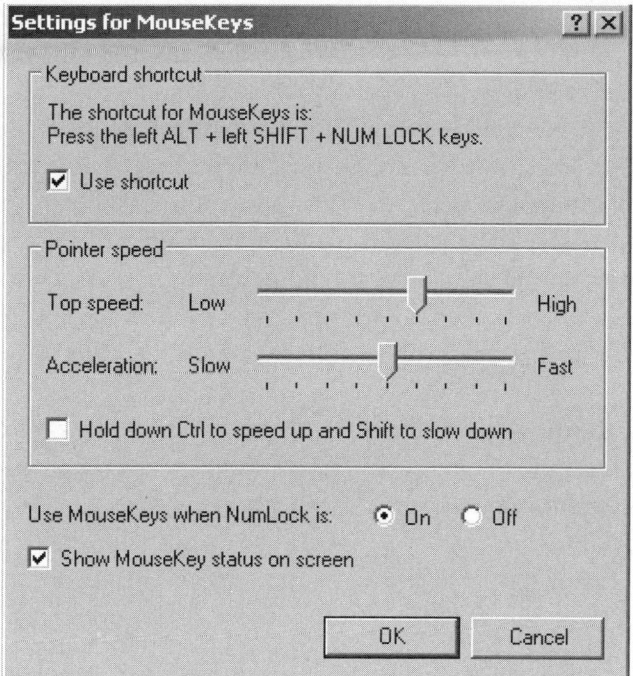


**FIGURE 17.20** Enable the MouseKeys feature at the Settings for MouseKeys dialog box.

**WARNING**

MouseKeys does not work when the mouse pointer is in text insert mode, such as in a word processing program. It works only when the pointer is an arrow.

**TRY IT!**

Enable MouseKeys and use it to move the mouse pointer around on the desktop.

## Troubleshooting Keyboard Problems

Here are some common keyboard problems and possible solutions.

**Keyboard not detected.** If no keyboard is detected, make sure it is firmly plugged in. If you are using an adapter to change from one type of keyboard interface to another, such as AT style to PS/2 style, make sure the connection is snug. Try a different keyboard if possible. If the problem is with the keyboard, you might be able to replace its cable to see if the cable was causing the trouble rather than the keyboard itself; however, keyboards are inexpensive and easy to replace, so this might not be the best use of your time.

**Stuck key message at startup.** The BIOS might detect a stuck key and display an error message if you are accidentally leaning on the keyboard, if you are holding down the F8 key too soon or too long, or if a key is actually stuck. If you believe a key is stuck, turn the keyboard upside down and shake it. If it is still stuck, try washing the keyboard in the dishwasher.

**Nonresponsive key.** If a certain key is not working, there is probably dirt on the contact inside the keyboard that is preventing it from completing the circuit. Shake it upside down to remove anything that might be blocking the contact, and/or blow out the space under the keys with compressed air. If that does not work, try washing the keyboard with soap and water.

**Key stuck down.** This has the same causes and fixes as a nonresponsive key (above).

**Wrong letters/numbers appear when keying.** Make sure the standard keyboard layout is chosen in Windows, not one of the unusual ones like Dvorak. Try removing the keyboard from Device Manager and having Windows redetect it with Plug and Play. Usually, however, this error is a result of a bad keyboard controller chip on the keyboard itself, and requires that the keyboard be replaced.

**Spilled liquid on keyboard.** If a liquid containing sugar is spilled on the keyboard, the keyboard needs to be thoroughly cleaned with soap and water, such as in a dishwasher. If the liquid contained no sugar, simply letting it dry thoroughly may be sufficient.

**WARNING**

**Do not operate a keyboard while it is wet because electrical short-circuiting can result.**

## Troubleshooting Mouse Problems

Here are some common mouse problems and possible solutions.

**Pointer does not move on-screen at all.** The mouse may have become disconnected; check its connector. Windows may be locked up; try rebooting. If the pointer is still unresponsive after a reboot, try a different mouse.

**Pointer moves in only one direction.** The mouse (or trackball) may be dirty and require cleaning. Blow out any debris with compressed air; if that does not help, disassemble the device and clean its rollers. If the problem persists, one of the directional sensors or rollers inside the mouse is probably physically broken; replace the device.

# Complete PC System

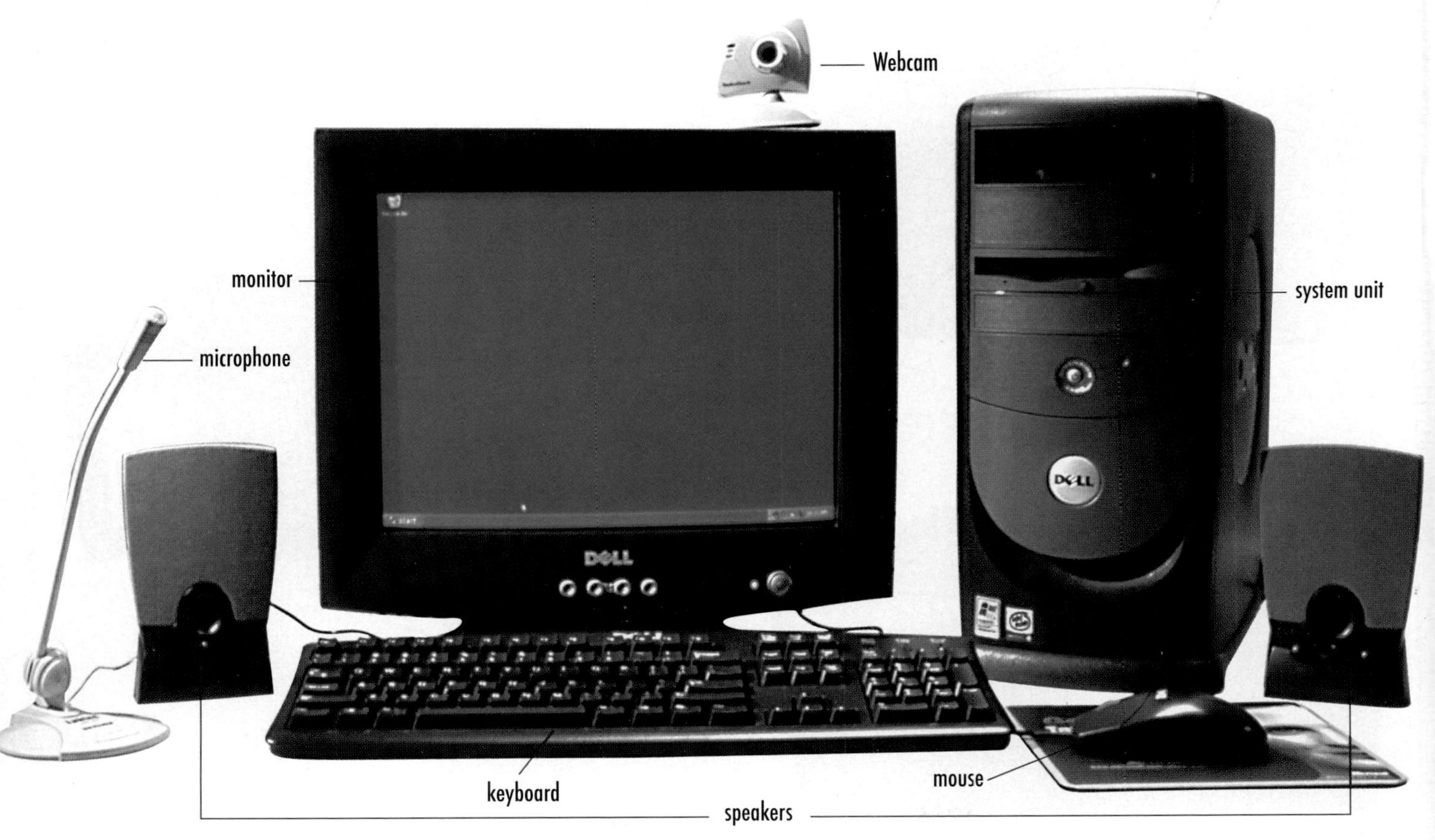

## System Unit (Front)

The system unit on the left is part of a workstation unit and includes a Zip® drive.

## System Unit (Back)

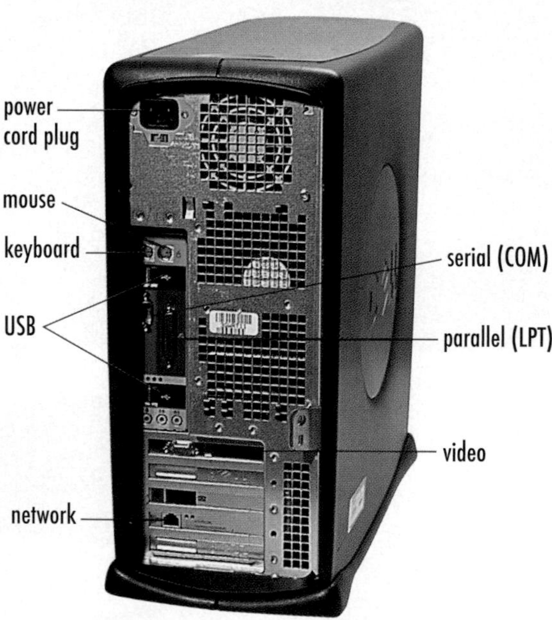


This is the rear view of the system unit shown at the right in the top photo. Ports for connecting various devices are identified. It opens in accordion fashion.

## Notebook Computer

LCD screen
touchpad
keyboard
mouse buttons

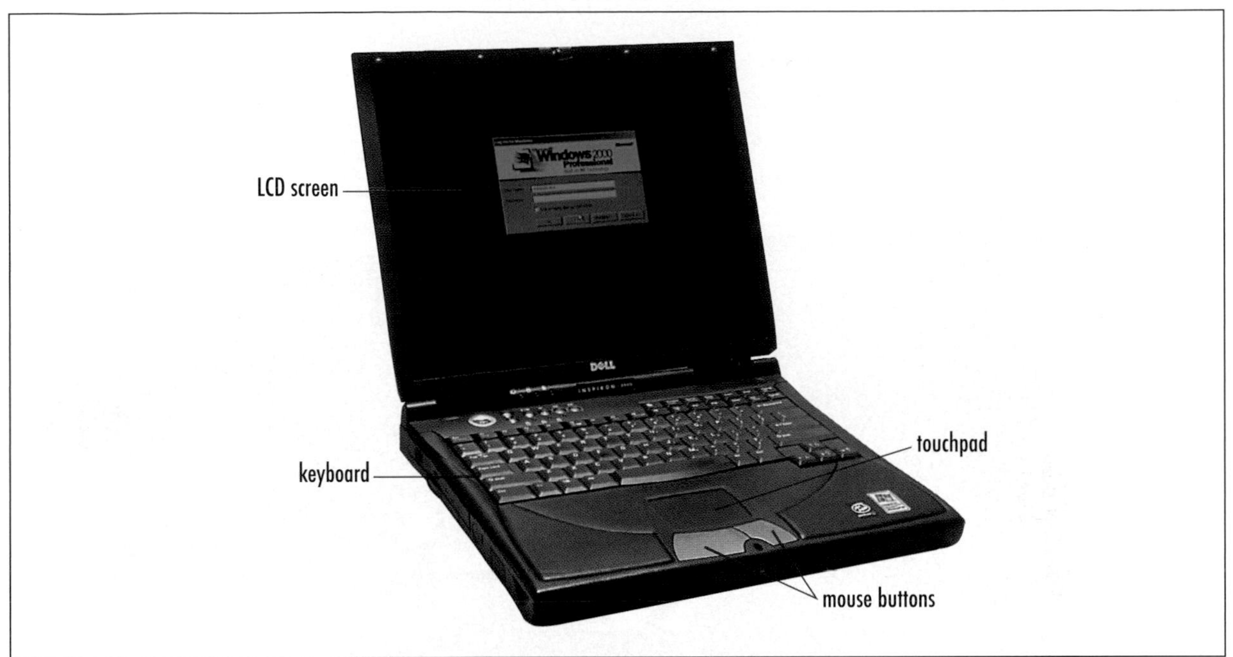

## Selected Notebook Components

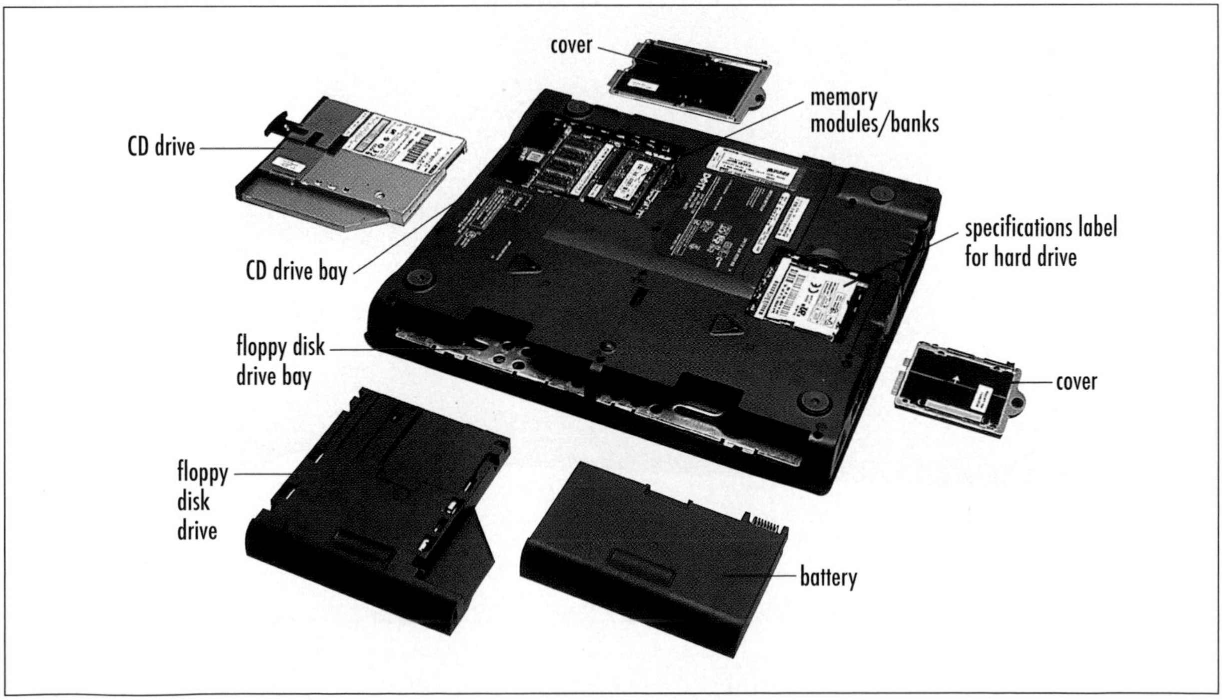

cover
memory modules/banks
CD drive
specifications label for hard drive
CD drive bay
floppy disk drive bay
cover
floppy disk drive
battery

# System Unit Interior

# Motherboard

floppy drive connector
hard drive connector
AGP video card
battery
PCI expansion slots
RAM
slots for additional RAM
CPU
onboard port for mouse
onboard port for keyboard
2 USB ports
NIC (network interface card)
BIOS chip
ISA expansion slots

## Motherboard and Components

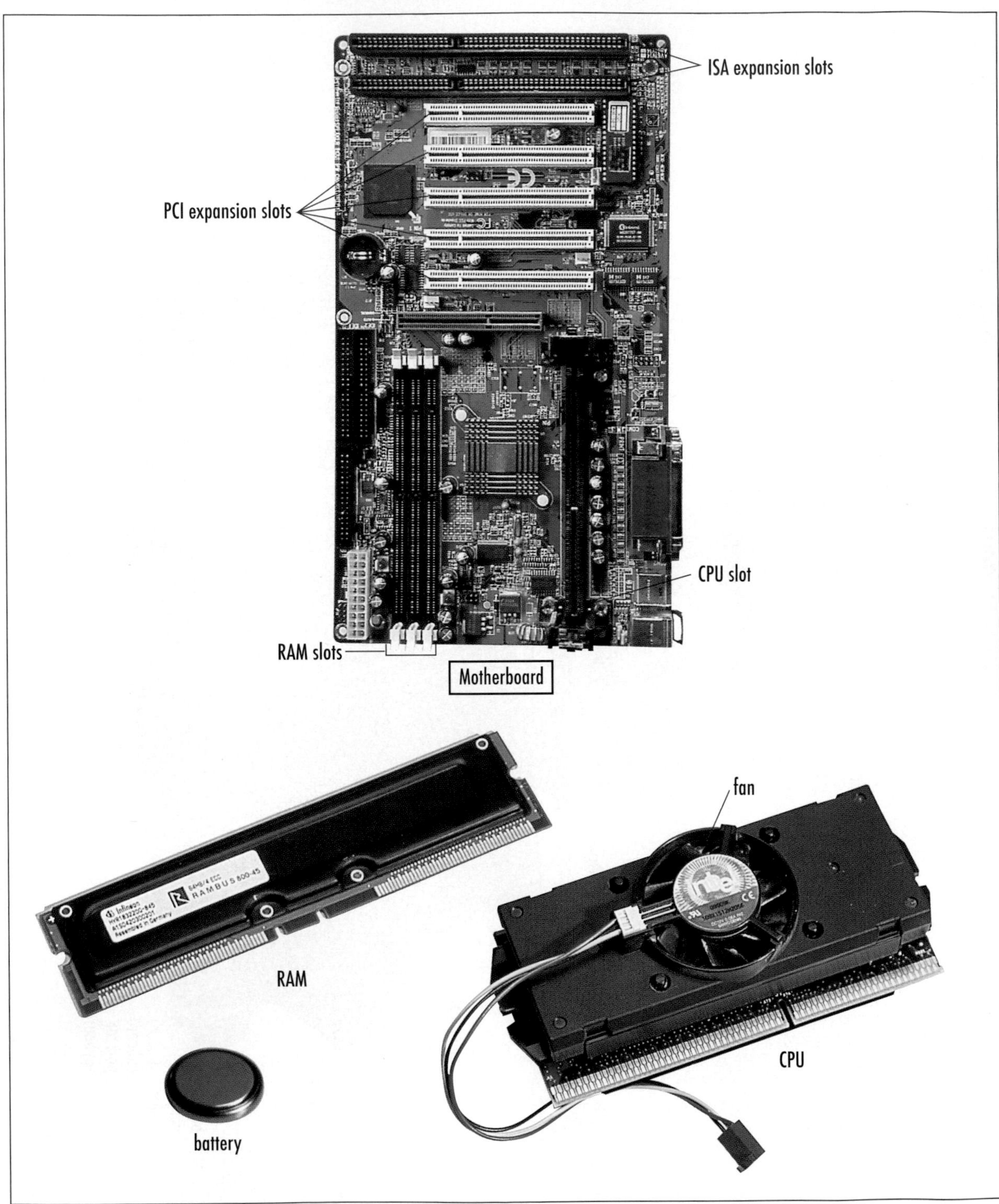

# Drives and Expansion Cards

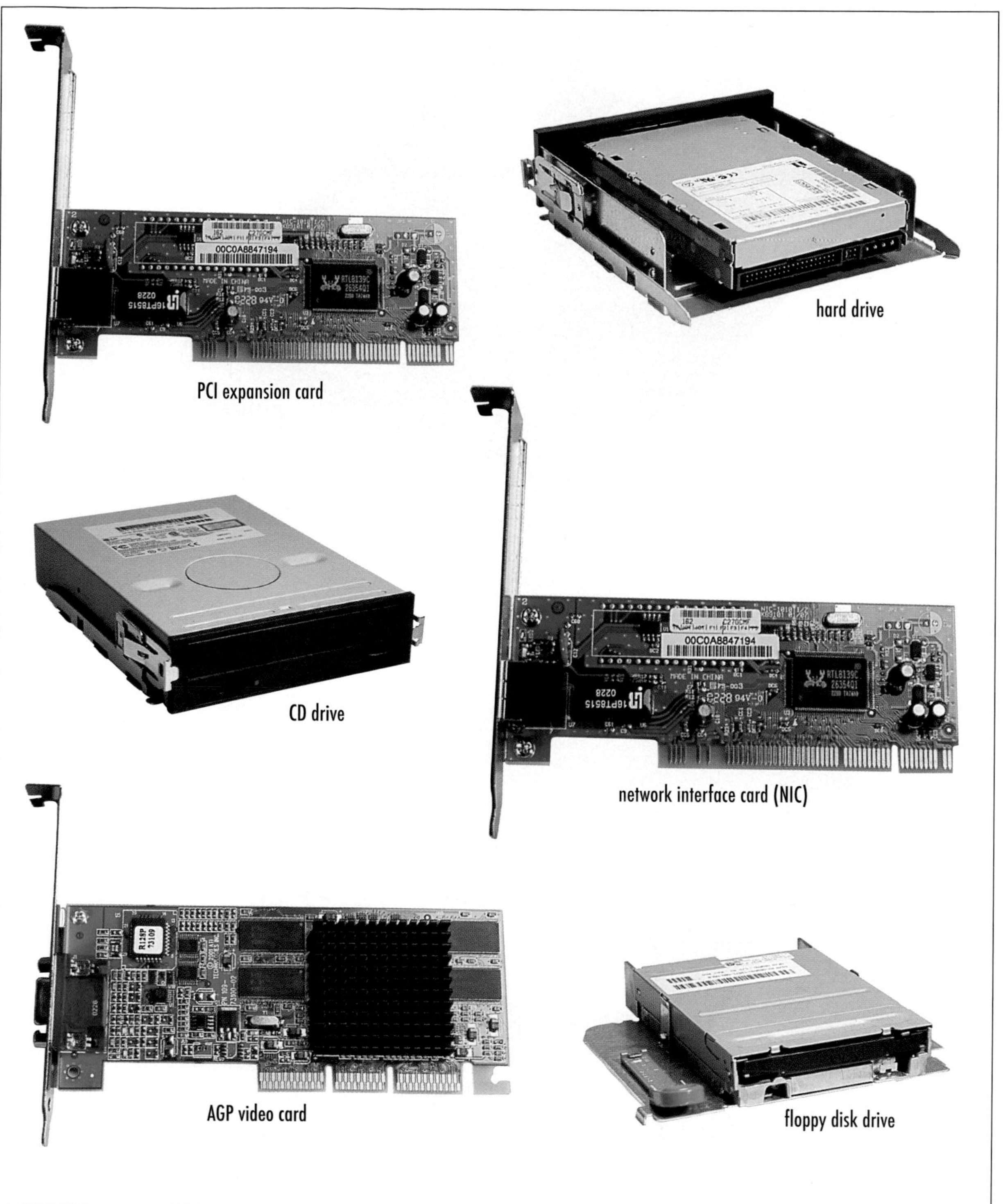


PCI expansion card

hard drive

CD drive

network interface card (NIC)

AGP video card

floppy disk drive

## IDE Drives

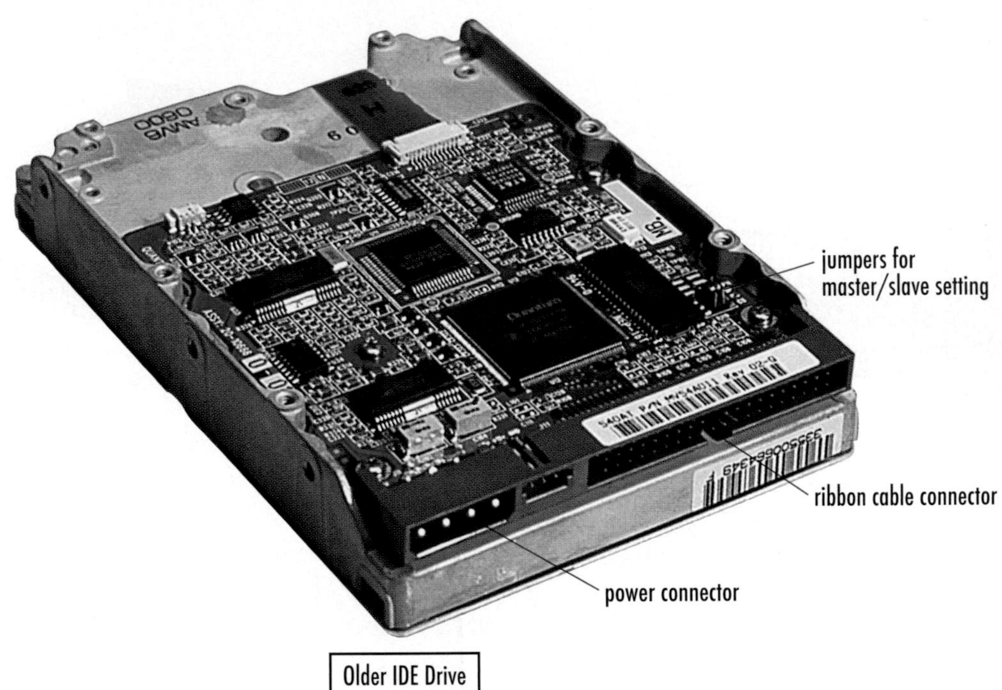


Older IDE Drive

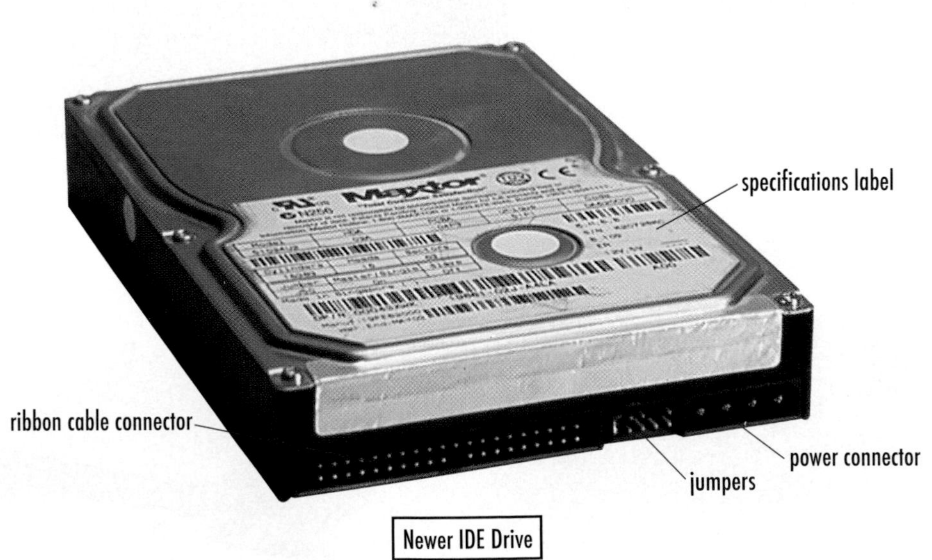


Newer IDE Drive

# SCSI Drives

Older SCSI Drive



Newer SCSI Drive

This view is from the top. Thus the specifications label, which is on the bottom, is not visible.

# PC Maintenance Toolkit

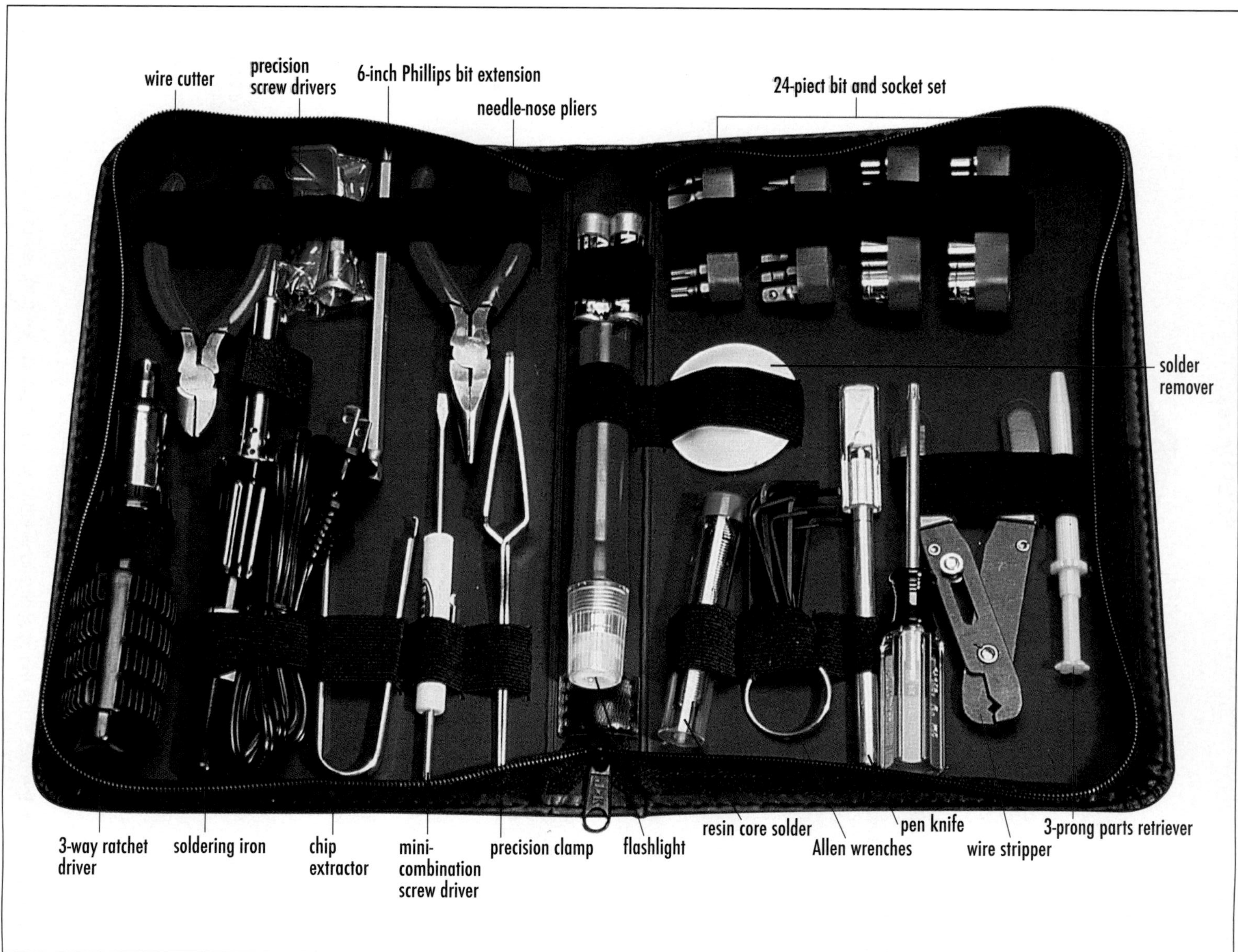
wire cutter
precision screw drivers
6-inch Phillips bit extension
needle-nose pliers
24-piect bit and socket set
solder remover
3-way ratchet driver
soldering iron
chip extractor
mini-combination screw driver
precision clamp
flashlight
resin core solder
Allen wrenches
pen knife
wire stripper
3-prong parts retriever

# Individual PC Maintenance Tools

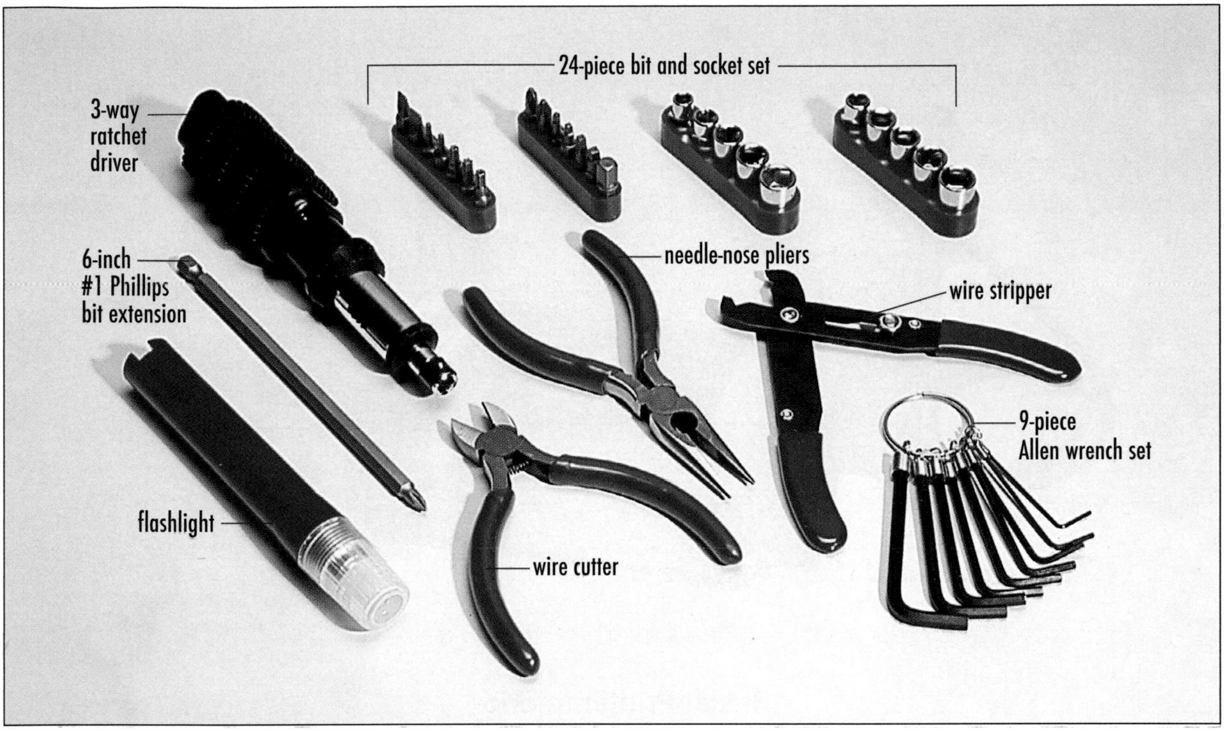

24-piece bit and socket set
3-way ratchet driver
6-inch #1 Phillips bit extension
needle-nose pliers
wire stripper
9-piece Allen wrench set
flashlight
wire cutter

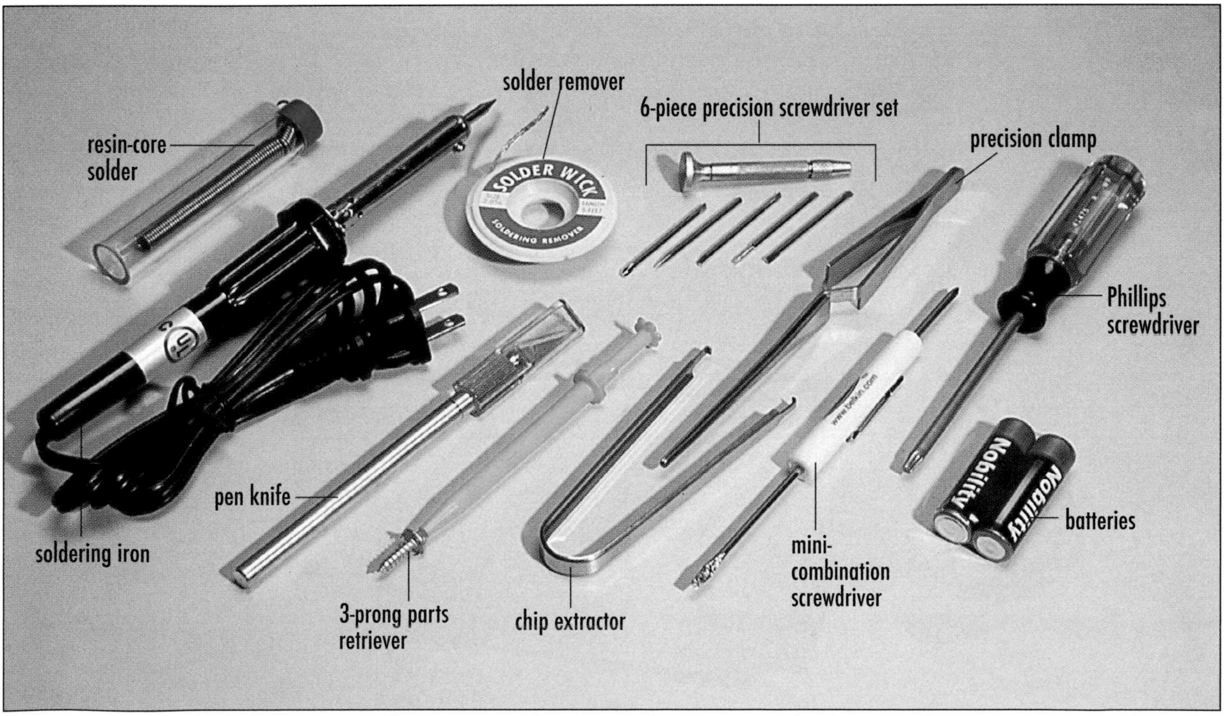

solder remover
6-piece precision screwdriver set
resin-core solder
precision clamp
Phillips screwdriver
pen knife
batteries
soldering iron
mini-combination screwdriver
3-prong parts retriever
chip extractor

## Color Inkjet Printer

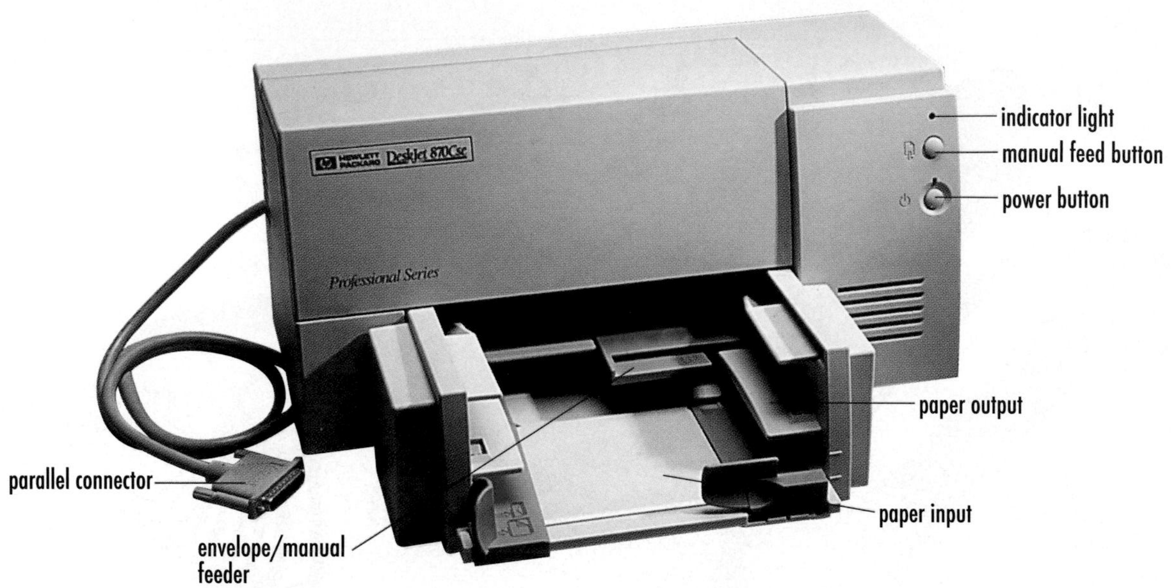


## Inkjet Printer Interior

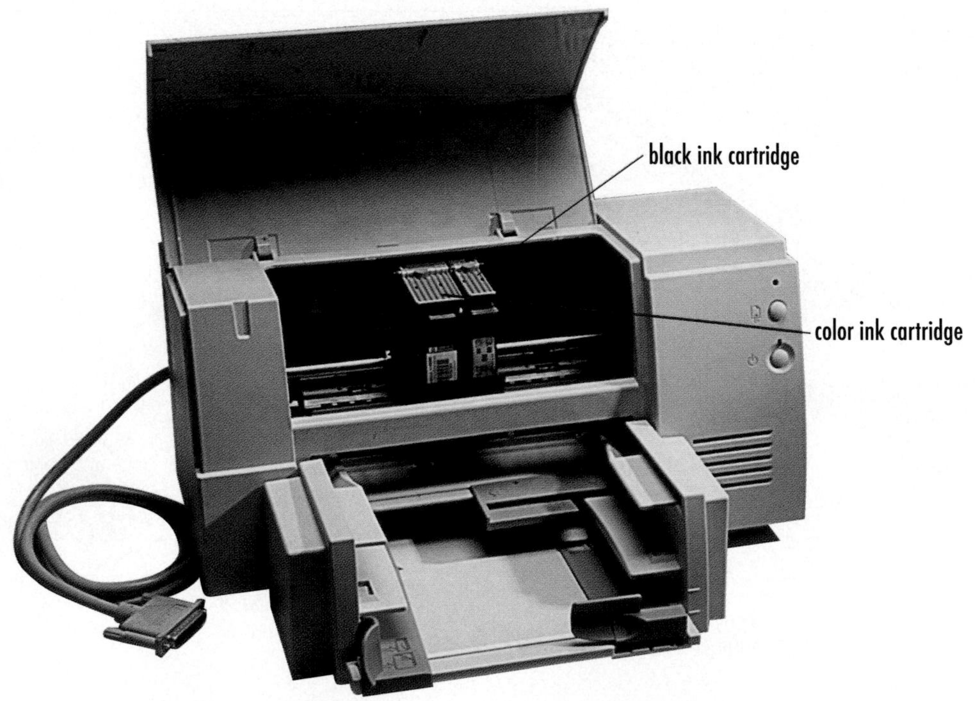

## Laser Printer

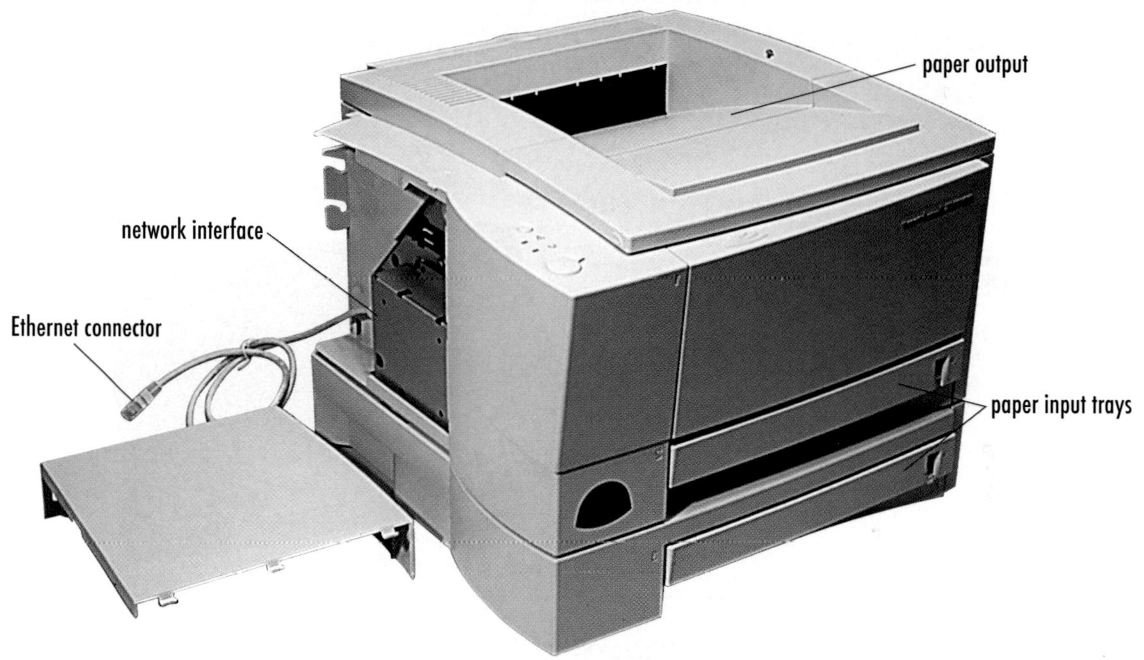


## Laser Printer Interior

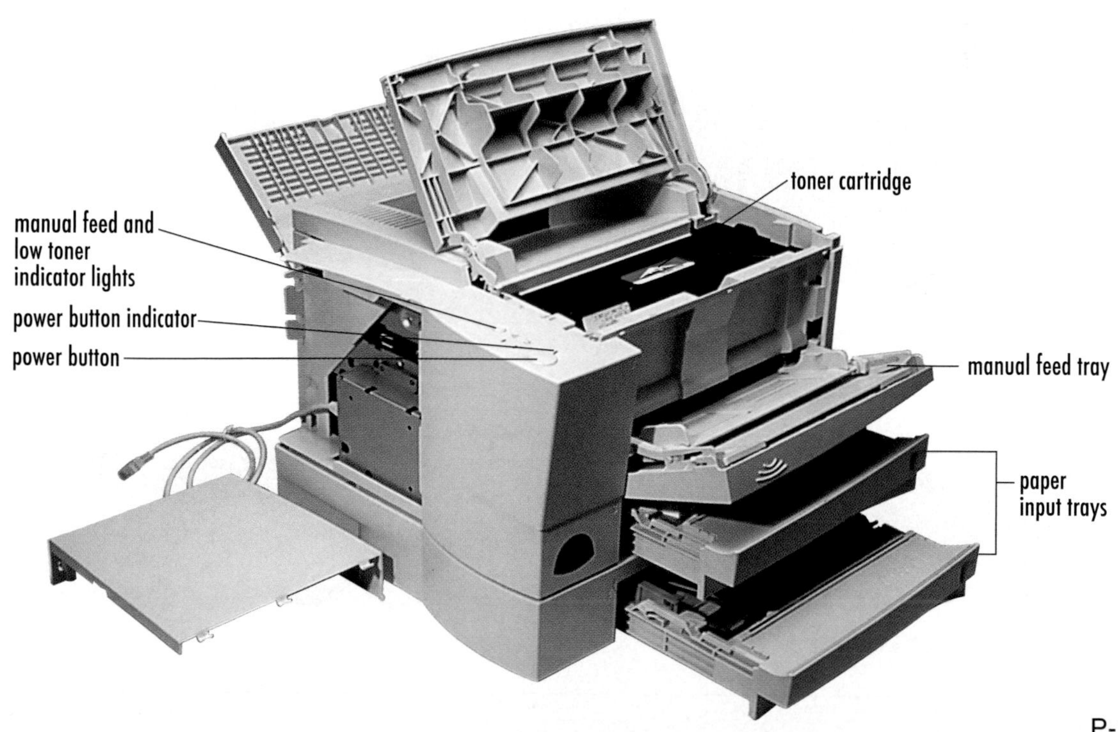

## Network Hub and Router

Cat5 cable
hub
RJ-45 connectors
indicator lights
router

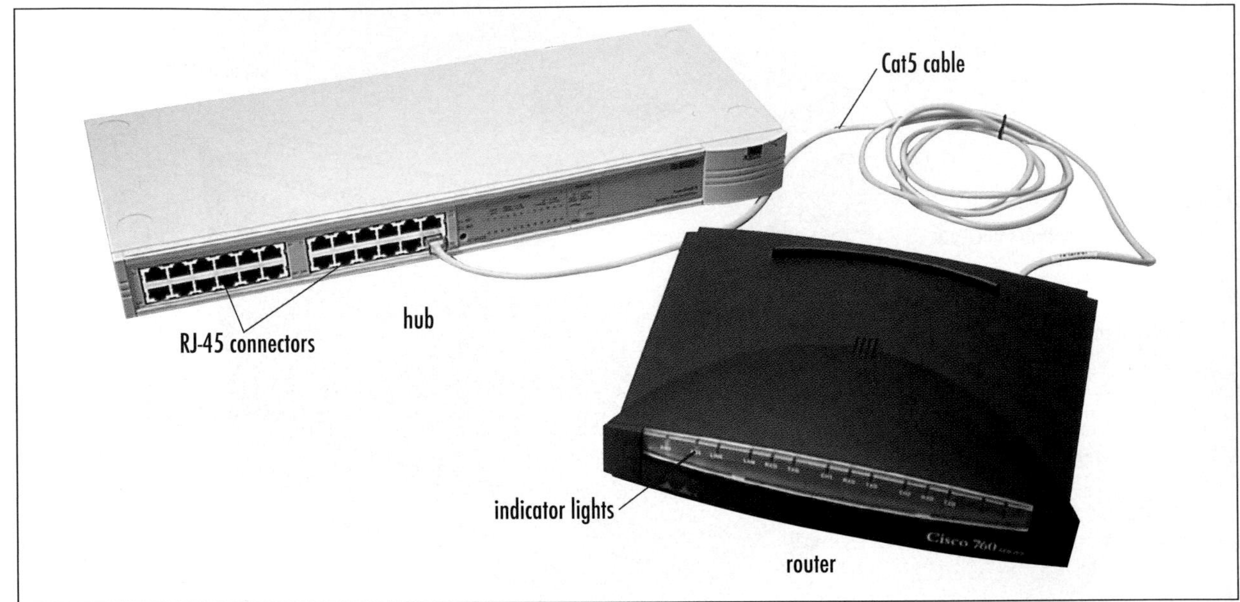

## Networking Cards

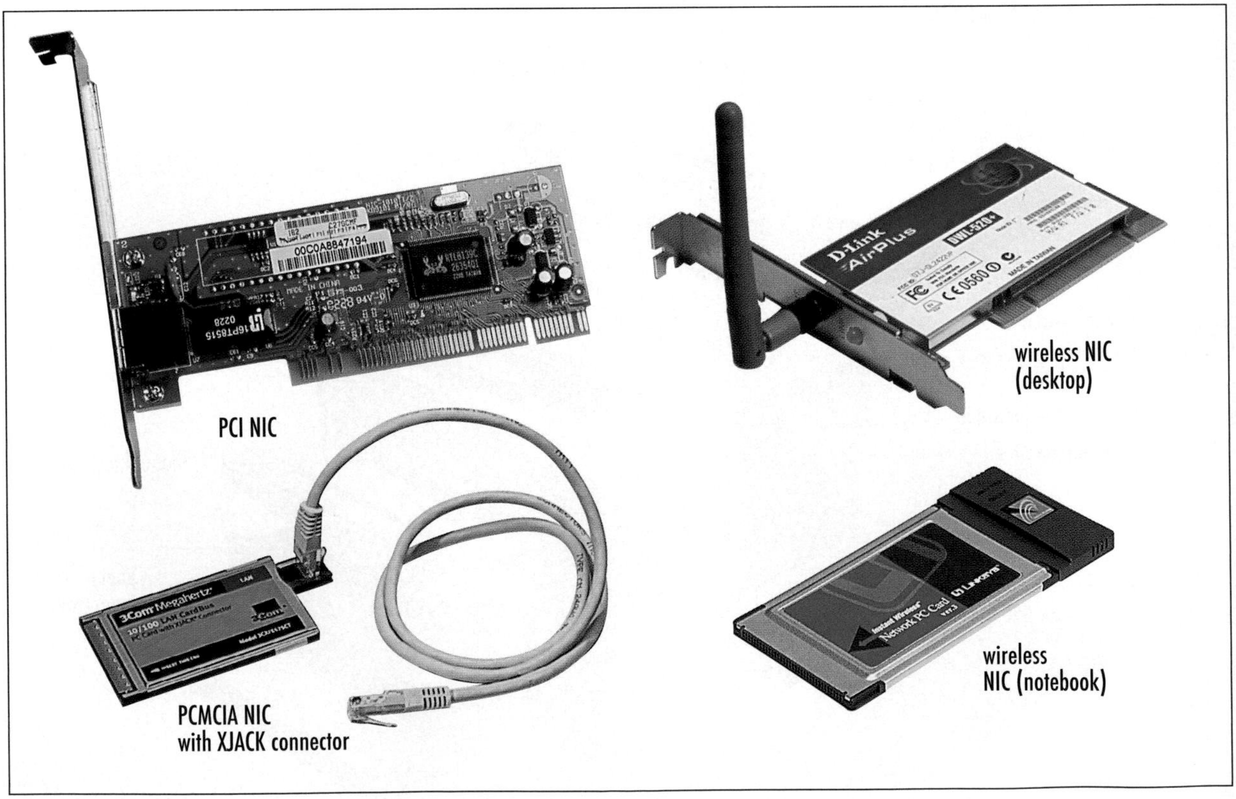

PCI NIC
wireless NIC (desktop)
PCMCIA NIC with XJACK connector
wireless NIC (notebook)

## Star Topology Network

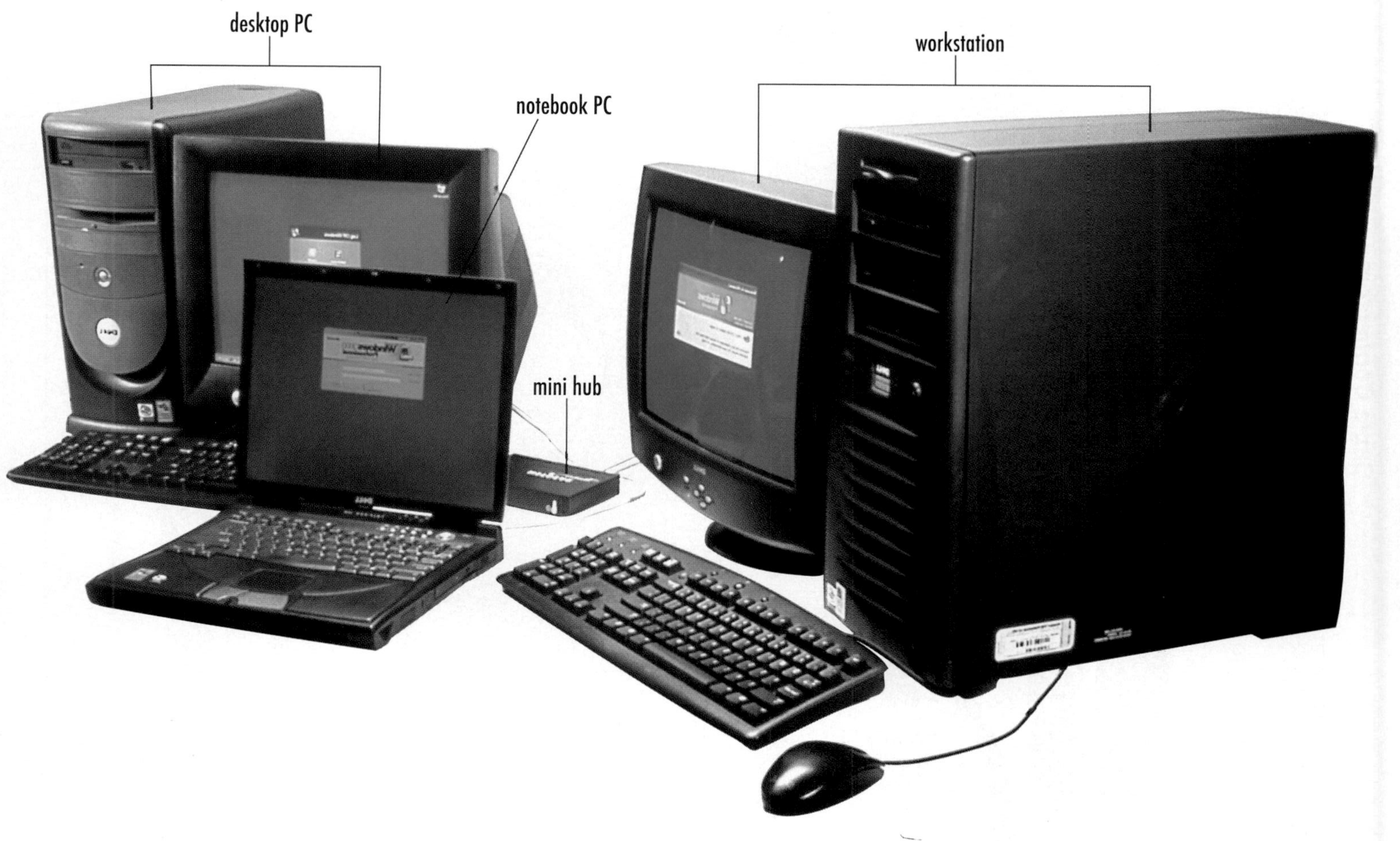

## Cable Connectors

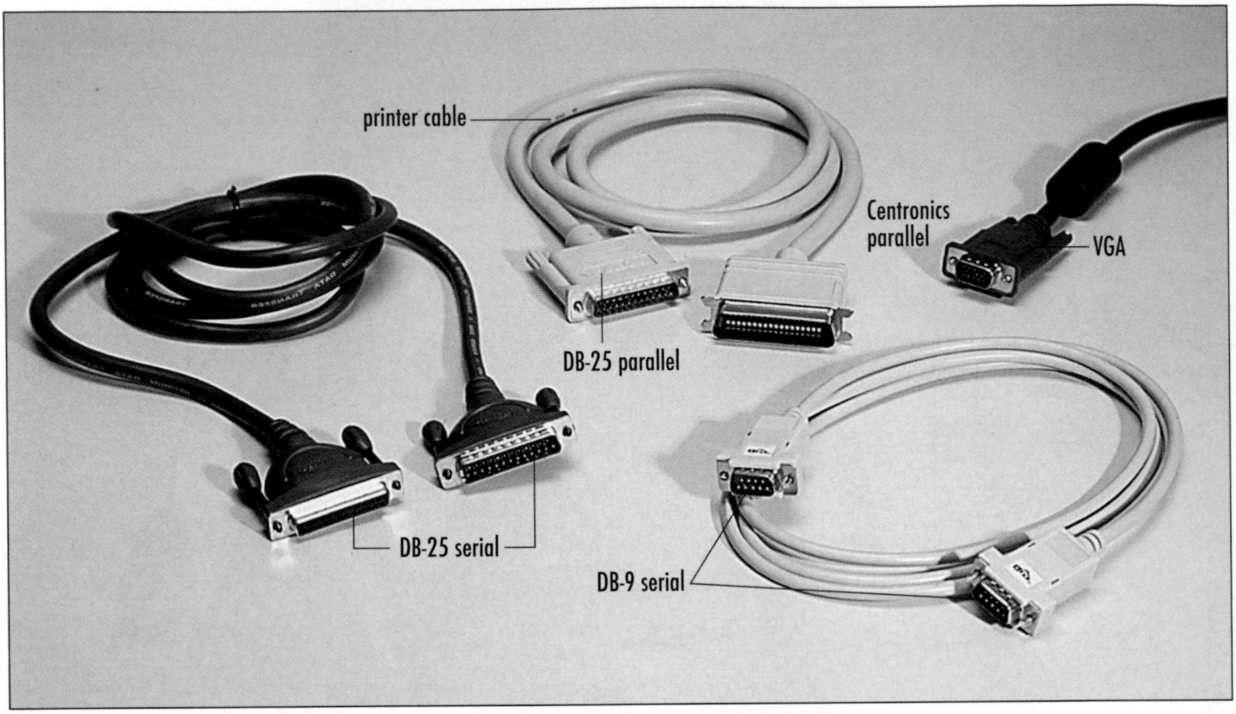

printer cable
Centronics parallel
VGA
DB-25 parallel
DB-25 serial
DB-9 serial

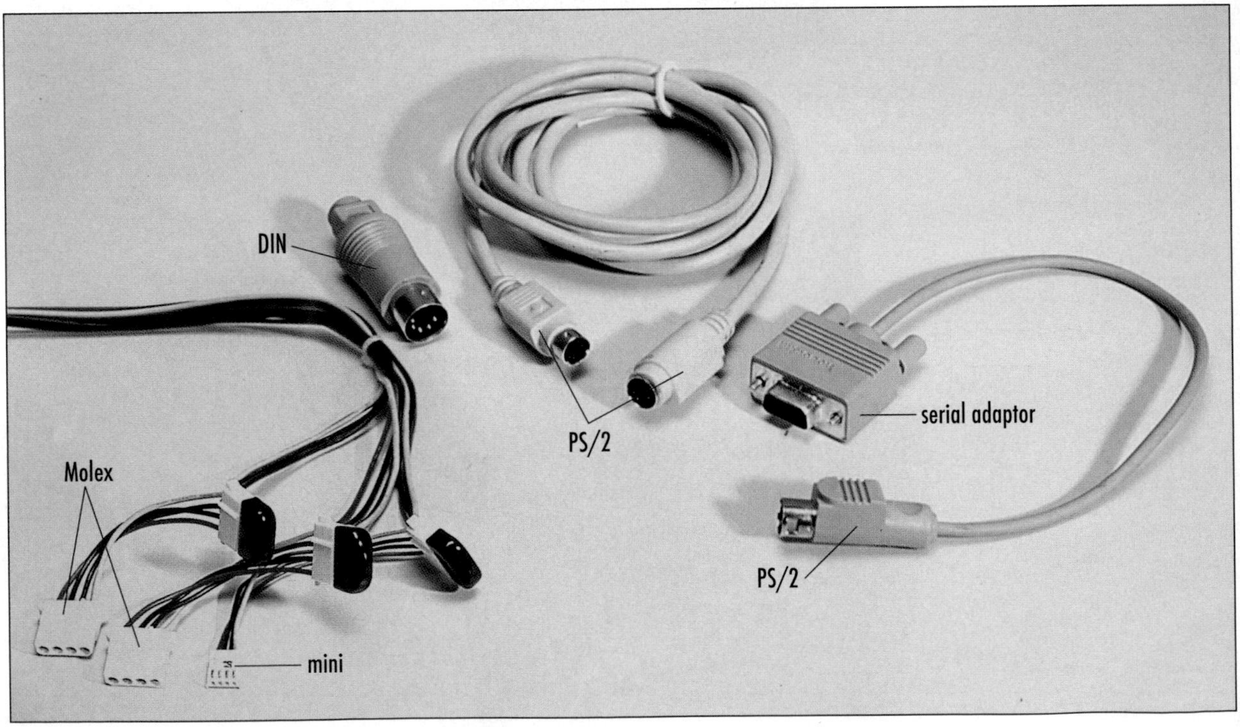

DIN
PS/2
serial adaptor
Molex
PS/2
mini

**Pointer jumps erratically all over the screen.** This can be the result of a dirty mouse, or it could be a bad or incompatible video driver. Try restarting Windows in Safe mode. If the problem persists, it is the mouse; if it clears up, it is the video driver.

**Extra buttons do not work.** The mouse may require a special driver or utility to utilize its advanced functions, such as extra buttons. Check the documentation that came with the mouse or the manufacturer's Web site.

**Touchpad does not click with tapping.** The touchpad is supposed to recognize tapping as clicking. If it does not, it needs a driver to be loaded to enable the feature.

# STUDY GUIDE

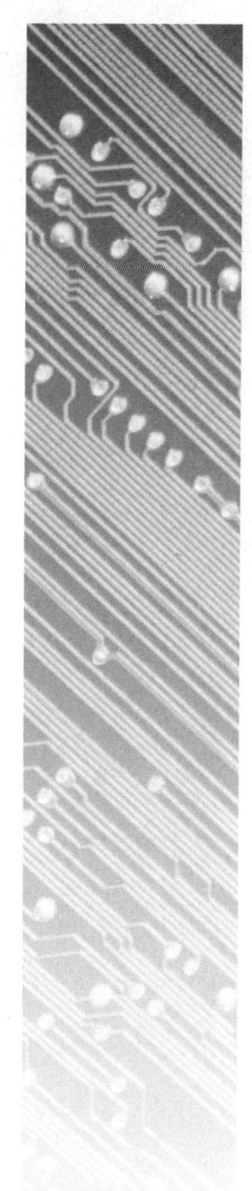

Use the following summaries to review the key concepts of this chapter.

## KEYBOARDS

- A keyboard is a grid of uncompleted circuits. When you press a key, you complete a circuit.
- Alphanumeric keys are keys with numbers and letters on them.
- Besides the alphanumeric and symbol keys, a keyboard has a variety of special-purpose keys such as function keys, Ctrl, Alt, Esc, and directional arrows.
- Windows keyboards have a Windows key and a Menu key.
- Old-style XT keyboards have approximately 83 keys. The numeric keypad doubles as an arrow keypad, and the function keys are along the left edge.
- Modern AT-style keyboards have more keys (between 101 and 104) and the function keys are on the top. There is a separate set of arrow keys.
- A Dvorak keyboard has different letter arrangement for faster typing but requires relearning touch typing.
- Keyboards can use AT-style keyboard connectors, PS/2 connectors, or USB connectors.
- Some keyboards have an ergonomic design to help prevent hand and wrist strain.
- Some keyboards have additional buttons for shortcuts for performing common PC operations.

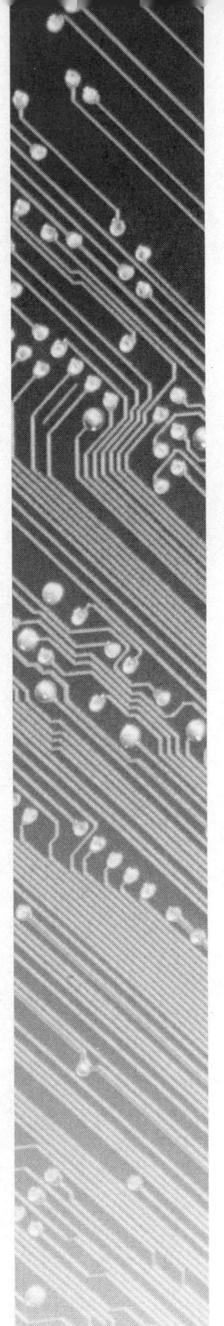

## Mice and Other Pointing Devices

- A mouse translates the physical movement of the device into signal data to the PC.
- A traditional mouse has a ball inside it that rolls past sensors to detect movement. Some modern versions have an optical sensor instead.
- A mouse can have a serial (COM port), PS/2, or USB interface.
- A mouse has either two or three buttons; the third, middle button is programmable if present—it has no default functionality in Windows.
- A trackball is a mouse variant with the mouse on top and a stationary base.
- A touchpad is a touch-sensitive rectangular pad; you glide your finger across to move the pointer on-screen, and tap it to click.

## Connecting/Disconnecting Keyboards and Mice

- As a general rule, do not plug in or unplug a keyboard or mouse with the power on.
- If no mouse is attached, Windows may display a message to that effect. You can attach a PS/2 mouse at that point and continue booting.
- USB devices can be connected or disconnected at any time, but you should make sure the device has finished its current operation before disconnecting it.

## Adjusting Keyboard Settings

- Use the Keyboard Properties dialog box, accessible from the Control Panel, to change keyboard settings.
- The available properties vary depending on the Windows version.
- Repeat delay is the delay between when you hold down a key and when it starts repeating on-screen. This is also called typematic delay.
- Repeat rate is the speed at which character repeat occurs once it starts. This is also called typematic rate.
- Cursor blink rate is the speed at which the vertical line cursor blinks in a program that takes text input.

## Adjusting Mouse Settings

- Use the Mouse Properties dialog box in the Control Panel to adjust the mouse settings.

- By default the left button is primary; switch the buttons on the Buttons tab in the Mouse Properties dialog box for left-handed use, if desired.
- Double-click speed is the speed at which one click must follow another to be considered a double click rather than two separate clicks.
- ClickLock is a feature that treats the mouse button as a toggle so you do not have to hold it down to drag.
- Pointer schemes are sets of mouse pointer graphics. You can choose a scheme or change an individual pointer from the Pointers tab.
- If few pointer choices are available, use Add/Remove Programs (Windows Setup tab) to install the extra pointers.
- Pointer trails leave a trail behind as the pointer moves on-screen to make it easier to track.
- Acceleration speeds up the pointer movement as it continues to move.
- Snap to jumps the pointer to the default button in a dialog box.

## Making the Mouse Function as a Keyboard

- The On-Screen Keyboard utility displays a keyboard in a window on-screen; you can click the key letters.
- This is useful for someone with a mobility impairment that hinders keyboard use but allows mouse use.
- Choose Start, Programs, Accessories, Accessibility, On-Screen Keyboard.
- If the program is not there, install Accessibility Tools through Add/Remove Programs (Windows Setup tab) in the Control Panel.

## Making the Keyboard Function as a Mouse

- MouseKeys is a feature that enables you to move the mouse pointer using the arrow keys on the keyboard.
- MouseKeys does not work in a program where the arrow keys move a text cursor, such as a word processing program.
- To turn on MouseKeys, double-click the *Accessibility Options* icon in the Control Panel and click the Use MouseKeys check box on the Mouse tab. To adjust the settings for MouseKeys, click the Settings button next to the check box.
- After the feature has been turned on, you can enable it by pressing Alt + left Shift + Num Lock. A dialog box appears letting you know the feature is being turned on; click OK or press Enter to accept it.

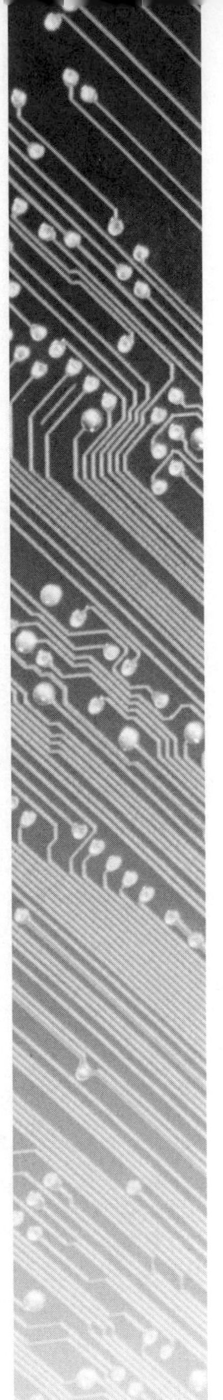

## Troubleshooting Keyboard Problems

- If the keyboard is not detected, check the connections. Try a different keyboard if possible.
- A stuck key error message can result from leaning on the keyboard or a keyboard's being dirty or defective.
- A nonresponsive key or a key that is stuck down probably has dirt or debris under it.
- Wrong characters appearing when keying usually means the keyboard's controller is bad and the whole keyboard must be replaced; it could also result from the wrong keyboard driver being loaded in Windows.
- If you spill a liquid containing sugar on the keyboard, you must wash it with soap and water, then let it dry completely.
- Other liquids can be left to dry without washing the keyboard.

## Troubleshooting Mouse Problems

- If the pointer does not move at all, the mouse may be disconnected or defective or Windows may be locked up because of software problems.
- If the pointer moves in only one direction, the mouse is either dirty or defective.
- If the pointer jumps erratically, the mouse may be dirty, or the video driver may be corrupt or incompatible.
- If extra mouse buttons do not work, special software may be required to enable them; check the documentation or the manufacturer's Web site.
- A touchpad that moves the pointer but does not recognize tapping as clicking requires a driver to enable the feature.

# PRACTICE TEST

On a blank sheet of paper, write the answers to the following multiple-choice questions and explain why each answer is correct.

1. When you press a key on the keyboard, it
   a. breaks a circuit, causing data to be sent to the PC.
   b. completes a circuit, causing data to be sent to the PC.
   c. completes a circuit, causing different data to be sent from other keypresses.
   d. Either b or c, depending on the type of key being pressed

2. What is the most common use of the F1 key?
   a. Search
   b. Help
   c. Shut Down
   d. Save

3. Which of the following is not an alphanumeric key?
   a. 7
   b. Y
   c. Esc
   d. 0

4. Which of these features differentiates a Windows keyboard from a regular one?
   a. ergonomic design
   b. Menu key
   c. cordless
   d. wrist rest

5. A keyboard with 101 keys can be assumed to be
   a. a Windows keyboard.
   b. ergonomic.
   c. PS/2.
   d. You cannot assume any of these things.

6. A keyboard with a PS/2-style connector will work with which type of motherboard with no adapter required?
   a. AT
   b. XT
   c. ATX
   d. a or b

7. How can a PS/2-style keyboard be modified to work with a PC that has no PS/2 keyboard port?
   a. Use an adapter that converts the PS/2 plug to a type of connector that the PC has, such as an AT-style plug.
   b. Remove the keyboard cord and replace it with a PS/2-style cord.
   c. It will not work; you must return the keyboard and get a PS/2 model.
   d. Use a splitter.

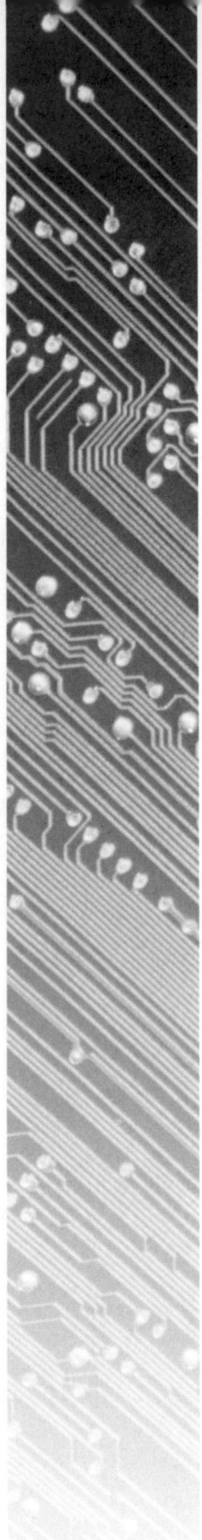

8. Which of these is an ergonomic feature in a keyboard?
   a. function keys at top rather than at left
   b. split design
   c. separate arrow keys
   d. b and c

9. What is a touchpad?
   a. a mouse alternative with a stationary base and a rolling ball on top
   b. a mouse alternative consisting of a small touch-sensitive rectangular pad
   c. a touch-sensitive LCD video monitor
   d. a membrane keyboard

10. Which of these is not a valid interface type for a mouse?
    a. USB
    b. serial
    c. parallel
    d. PS/2 mouse port

11. What is the default functionality in Windows of the middle button on a three-button mouse?
    a. opens shortcut menu
    b. selects the item
    c. scrolls the display
    d. It has no default functionality; it varies by manufacturer.

12. What is the default functionality in Windows of a rubber wheel between the left and right mouse buttons?
    a. opens shortcut menu
    b. selects the item
    c. scrolls the display
    d. It has no default functionality.

13. An optical mouse can be distinguished from a traditional mouse in what way?
    a. no ball
    b. stationary operation
    c. no cord
    d. None of the above

14. Which is the primary mouse button for a right-handed mouse user?
    a. left
    b. center
    c. right
    d. a or b

15. How do you turn on the On-Screen Keyboard?
    a. Start, Programs, Accessories, On-Screen Keyboard
    b. Start, Programs, Accessories, Accessibility, On-Screen Keyboard
    c. through the *Accessibility Options* icon in the Control Panel
    d. through the *Keyboard* icon in the Control Panel

16. What is the name of the feature that allows the mouse pointer to be controlled by the arrow keys on the keyboard?
    a. StickyKeys
    b. MouseArrows
    c. MouseKeys
    d. WinKeys

17. What is the name of the feature that allows the mouse button to act as an on/off toggle rather than needing to be held down to drag?
    a. StickyKeys
    b. MouseKeys
    c. ClickMouse
    d. ClickLock

18. Which of these would *not* be likely to help fix a single nonresponsive key on the keyboard?
    a. restarting Windows
    b. shaking the keyboard upside down
    c. blowing underneath the key with compressed air
    d. washing the keyboard in the dishwasher

19. If a trackball can move the pointer only to the left and right (not up and down), which of these might help?
    a. disassembling the device and cleaning the rollers inside
    b. updating the device driver in Windows
    c. blowing compressed air into the device to clear out any debris
    d. a or c

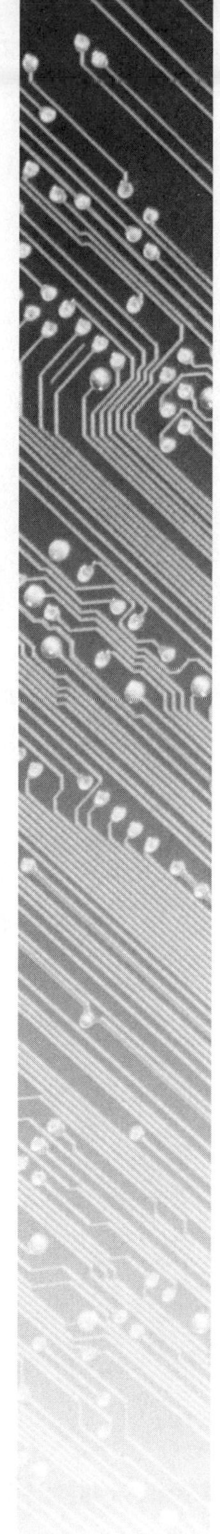

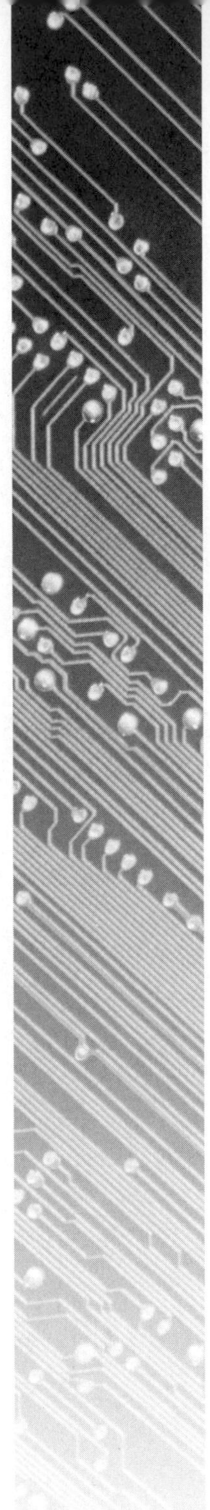

20. What type of damage do you risk if you do not let a washed keyboard dry thoroughly before using it?
    a. EMI
    b. ESD
    c. short-circuit
    d. All of the above

## TROUBLESHOOTING

1. A client buys a new USB keyboard and replaces her old one with it, but she gets a No Keyboard Installed error message at startup and cannot get into BIOS Setup. Describe the procedure for troubleshooting and fixing the problem.
2. A client installs a new keyboard with lots of extra buttons on it, including buttons that control the volume, open the Web browser, and so on, but these buttons do not appear to work. The keyboard itself is working properly. What can you suggest?
3. A client has downloaded a game from the Internet that has changed his default mouse pointer arrow to a picture of a gopher. He wants to change it back to the original mouse pointer. Explain how he can do this.

## CUSTOMER SERVICE

1. A client complains that he has to move his mouse too far on the mousepad to get it to move across the screen. What adjustment can you suggest?
2. A client with movement disability is having problems keying. She cannot release keys quickly enough, and the letters start repeating on-screen. What adjustment can you suggest for this client?
3. A client with a visual impairment is having trouble seeing the mouse pointer. Describe some of the mouse adjustments this client could make.

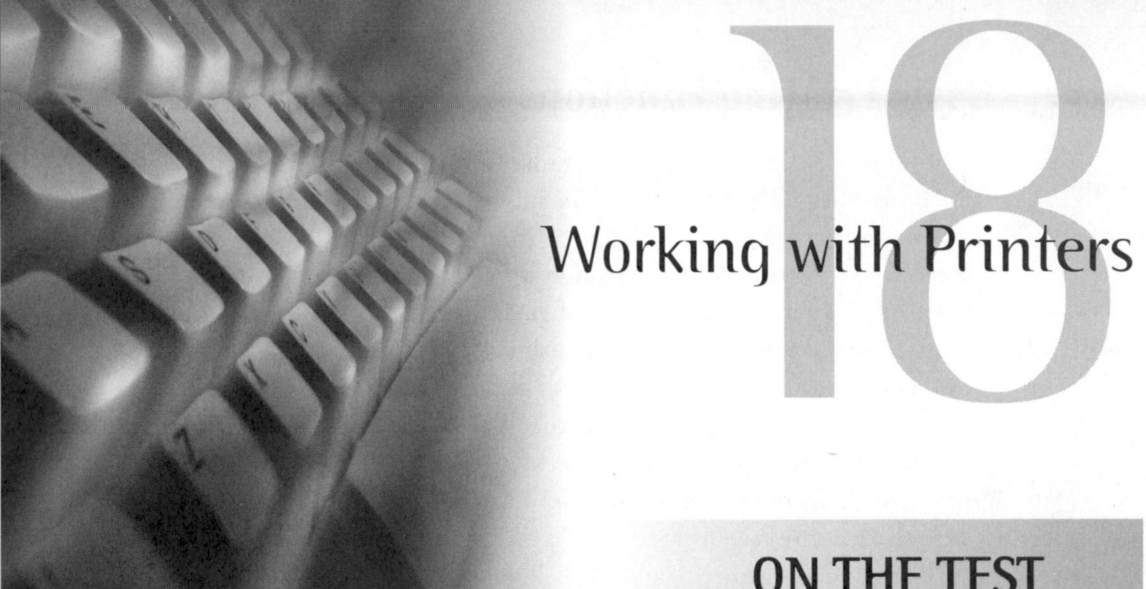

# 18 Working with Printers

## ON THE TEST

**A+ Core Hardware Service Technician Examination**

- **Objective 5.1:** Identify basic concepts, printer operations, and printer components.
- **Objective 5.2:** Identify care and service techniques and common problems with primary printer types.

## ON THE JOB

As a PC technician, you will select and install not only PCs, but also associated peripherals such as printers. This chapter prepares you to select the right printer for a job by familiarizing you with the various printer technologies on the market today and explaining what differentiates one printer from another. It also addresses printer driver installation and configuration, printer cleaning, and printer troubleshooting.

Real-world skills associated with this chapter include:

- selecting a type of printer to meet a client's needs
- choosing among several similar printer models
- deciding which printer interface best suits a particular situation
- connecting and disconnecting printers from PCs and networks
- installing a printer driver in Windows
- cleaning a printer
- troubleshooting print queue problems
- troubleshooting physical problems with a printer

# Basic Printing Functions

All printers perform the same basic function: they put an image onto paper. To do this, they all must have certain subsystems that perform these tasks. Here are the basic functions that any printer includes, regardless of type.

**Receive data from the PC through an I/O interface.** Each printer has at least one I/O interface, a means of getting data into the printer to be printed. This can be a parallel port, a serial port, USB, infrared, or network.

**Store the data in RAM.** The printer contains a small amount of RAM that holds the incoming data while it is waiting for the printer's physical print mechanism to print it. Printers that print one line at a time (*line printers*, such as inkjet and dot-matrix) have less memory than printers that compose an entire page before transferring it to paper (*page printers*, such as laser printers). Figures 18.1 and 18.2 illustrate the difference between a line printer and a page printer.

**Line printer**

A printer that receives data and transfers it to paper line-by-line.

**Page printer**

A printer that composes an entire page in memory before transferring it to paper.

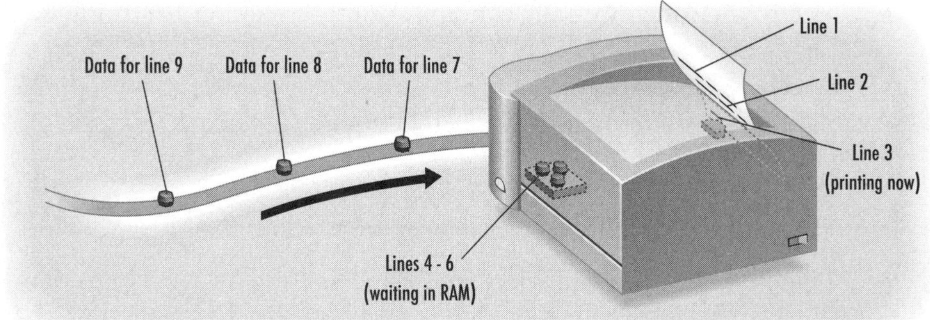


**FIGURE 18.1**
A line printer begins printing the first part of the page while the data for later parts of the page is still being received.

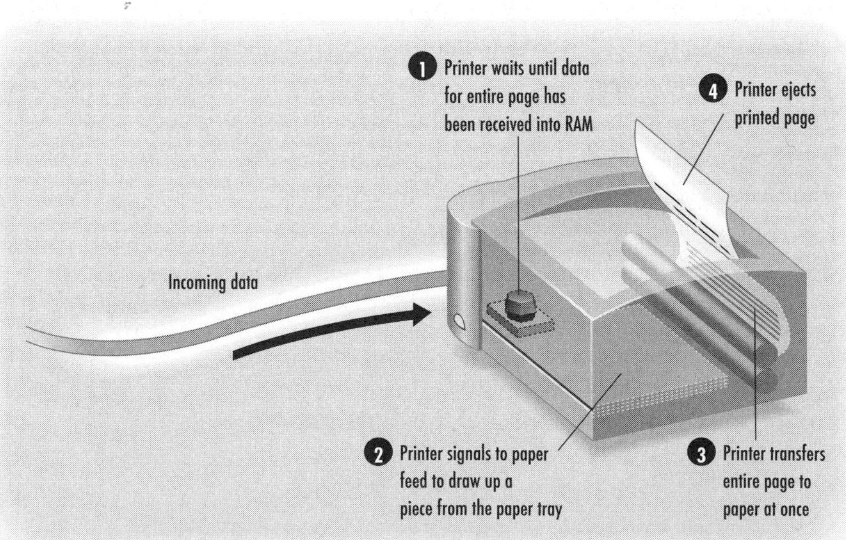


**FIGURE 18.2**
A page printer forms the entire page at once on the paper. It does not start until all data for that page has been received.

**Convert the data into print instructions.** Each printer has a motherboard and CPU inside that accept the data and convert it to instructions to the mechanical parts to transfer an image to paper. Just as with a PC, the CPU has a type and speed, and those factors partly determine the printer's overall printing speed. (The limitations of the mechanical components also determine the speed.)

**Feed the paper in and out.** Inside each printer is a series of gears, rollers, grabbers, and so on, that feed the paper through the printer. Depending on the type of printer, there could be a set of rollers that pull in single sheets at a time, or there could be a set of tractor-feed gears that pull through a continuous stream of paper. Most printers today are *sheet-fed,* which means they use individual precut sheets of paper. The exceptions are dot-matrix printers (uncommon these days but they do still exist); these are *tractor-fed* (also called continuous-fed). They use a continuous stream of paper and employ a system of gears and sprockets to pull the paper through by means of perforated holes on the sides. The user can feed individual precut sheets manually, but there is no paper tray for precut sheets (see Figure 18.3).

**Sheet-fed**

A printer that uses single sheets of paper, one sheet at a time.

**Tractor-fed**

A printer that uses continuous-feed paper by pulling it through with a series of gears and sprockets.

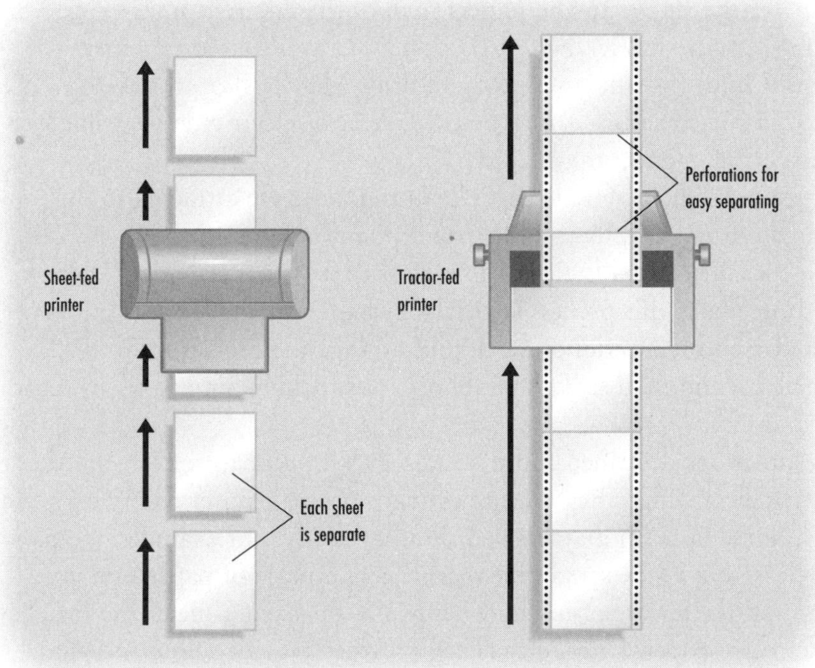


**FIGURE 18.3**
Sheet-Fed versus Tractor-Fed Paper Feed Mechanisms

**Store and dispense the ink or toner.** A printer needs some sort of colored material to create the image on the page. There are several different types of colored material; these are the most common ones:

- **Liquid ink:** Inkjet printers use liquid ink, stored in small plastic inkwells in the printer until it is needed. Different colors each have their own well.
- **Dry toner:** Laser printers transfer dry *toner* to a page. Toner is stored in a plastic cartridge inside the printer until it is needed.
- **Inked ribbon:** Dot-matrix printers use an inked ribbon, like on a typewriter. The ribbon is wound on a set of spools, and as the printer operates, the ribbon winds itself to a fresh spot.

**Toner**

A powdered blend of metal and plastic resin particles, used in laser printers to create an image on a page.

## In Real Life

There are also special-purpose printers that use colored wax, colored pencils, or film, but ordinary end users do not normally utilize them because they are expensive and designed for specific industries. For example, architectural firms might use a color plotter that employs colored pencils.

**Transfer the image to the paper.** Each of the different image creators mentioned above has its own method of being transferred to paper:

- **Liquid ink:** The ink is squirted out of nozzles (jets) onto the page. The force that drives the jets may be either heat or electricity; we will cover the specifics later in the chapter.
- **Dry toner:** The magnetic particles in the toner are attracted to the charged drum, and then to the paper; then they pass through a heating unit that melts the plastic particles so they stick to the paper. There will be more about this process later in the chapter as well.
- **Inked ribbon:** A series of metal pins arrange themselves to form characters and then strike the ribbon, thus making a mark on the page behind it.

The functions described above do not always occur in the listed order; the actual order in which they execute depends on the printer technology and model. Some of them may happen simultaneously. For example, the printer may release ink at the same time that it feeds a piece of paper into its rollers, and the release of ink may happen at the same time as the image is transferred to paper. Later in the chapter, when we talk about individual printer technologies, we will review the step-by-step processes for some of these technologies.

## Measures of Printer Performance

Selecting the right printer for a job involves finding the best balance among cost, output quality, output speed, and options. A printer with the correct balance of these features will be appropriate for a job regardless of the technology it uses. Therefore, before examining the specifics of various printer technologies, we will look briefly at how each of those four factors may be evaluated.

### Cost

The initial price tag on a printer is only part of its total *cost of ownership*. When evaluating a printer's cost, you should also factor in these items:

- **Ink or toner:** Laser printers, although they have a higher initial cost, use toner rather than ink. Toner is less expensive per page than inkjet ink, so if your client prints a lot of pages, the cost of owning a laser printer may be less than the cost of owning an inkjet.
- **Paper:** Some printers require special paper that is more expensive than normal paper. For example, thermal wax transfer printers (an uncommon kind of high-quality color printer) use very expensive paper, and printing high-quality photographs on an inkjet printer requires shiny photo paper.
- **Routine maintenance:** Some printers, especially laser printers, require regular maintenance at certain intervals, usually involving a "maintenance kit" of replacement parts. Figure in the cost of the kit and the cost of having an authorized representative service the printer.

**Cost of ownership**

The total cost of an item including the costs for supplies and maintenance over its lifetime.

### Quality

Print quality refers to the crispness and realism of the printed output. There are quantifiable measurements of print quality, but the best way to evaluate quality is to see a sample for yourself.

One measure of print quality is the resolution—how many different-shaded dots there are in a certain area of the printout. Resolution is measured in *dots per inch* (dpi). A printer with a higher dpi will produce text with crisper edges and more realistic-looking graphics. For example, in Figure 18.4 notice the difference in this magnified look at the edge of some text.

**Dots per inch (dpi)**

A measurement of printer resolution.

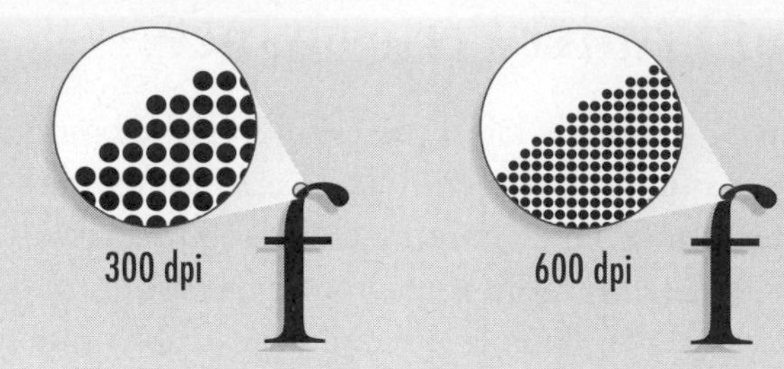


**FIGURE 18.4**
Higher resolution means more, smaller dots per inch on the paper.

The minimum resolution for a laser printer is 300 x 300 (horizontal by vertical). A resolution of 600 x 600 is most common these days. Laser printers have the same horizontal and vertical resolutions. Inkjet printers, however, may have different maximum horizontal and vertical resolutions. For example, an inkjet printer might have a resolution of 1440 x 720.

For a line printer such as an inkjet, more dots per inch means that the inkjet dispenses smaller dots of ink and the head makes more passes across each sheet of paper. This does not require any extra RAM. However, on a page printer such as a laser, the entire page full of dots must be composed in RAM before transferring to the paper, so a printer with a higher maximum resolution must have more RAM than a lesser quality model. Most laser printers can be operated in a variety of resolutions, so if there is not very much RAM in a laser printer and out-of-memory messages appear when printing a complex page, you can set its resolution lower and possibly be able to print the page.

Another measurement of print quality is the ability to print color photographs realistically. This is primarily an issue on inkjet printers, since they are the most affordable type of color printer. Color quality can be an elusive thing to measure. Some printers are advertised as "photo quality," but you really need to see the output from the printer to judge it.

Color accuracy is still another factor. A picture could look good on the printout but not necessarily match the colors you saw on the screen. Some printers have color correction capability built into their driver in Windows, so that you can compare a printout to the monitor display and then make adjustments.

**Print engine**

The part of the printer that calculates the instructions for the print mechanism and sends instructions for moving the paper and creating the print image.

## SPEED

All other factors being equal, a printer that prints faster is better than a slower one. A printer's speed is determined not only by its physical mechanical limitations, but also by the speed and calculating power of its CPU and motherboard (also called its *print engine*).

Printer speed is measured in pages per minute (ppm). Printers that print in both black-and-white and color typically have two separate ratings. For example, a color inkjet printer might print 10ppm for black-and-white or 3ppm for color.

A printer's rated ppm is a theoretical maximum, and will seldom be achieved in real-life use. It is merely a way of comparing two printers' specifications on paper.

Earlier printers, such as daisywheel and dot-matrix, have speeds measured in characters per second (cps) rather than ppm.

## Options

In addition to the factors already discussed, one printer may be differentiated from another by the extra features or options it offers. Some of these features might include:

- **Paper tray:** A paper input tray that holds 100+ sheets makes for less reloading. Room for numerous sheets in the paper output area is a plus as well, because it reduces the possibility of pages spilling over and falling behind the printer if the printer is not frequently monitored.
- **Extra RAM:** A laser printer with a lot of RAM can handle complex pages at high resolutions. Extra RAM is not a major issue for line printers, although extra RAM could be used as a buffer to hold incoming print jobs so that the PC's involvement ends sooner.
- **Interfaces:** We will cover interfaces later in the chapter, but extra flexibility of multiple interfaces on a printer can be handy; for example, a printer with both a parallel and a USB interface, and possibly a network interface as well, can adapt to input from a variety of sources.
- **PostScript compatibility:** PostScript is an alternative set of printer commands that has some benefits, especially for the desktop publishing professional. There will be more about it later in the chapter, but for now just know that it adds extra costs.

### TRY IT!

**Research several models of laser printers on the Internet and compare their quality, speed, and options. Which one offers the best overall value for the price?**

# Types of Printer Technology

There are several questions on the A+ exam about how various printer technologies work. The following sections outline each technology and explain how each one takes the data from the PC and converts it to printed output.

There are two major categories of printers: impact and nonimpact. An impact printer strikes an inked ribbon to produce an imprint on paper behind it. A nonimpact printer squirts or fuses colored material onto the paper. Almost all printers today are nonimpact, but we will start by discussing a couple of old-technology impact printers: daisywheel and dot-matrix.

## Daisywheel Printers

**Daisywheel**

A disk with plastic spikes radiating from its center, with a different character at the end of each spike. In a daisywheel printer, a hammer strikes a spike, causing its letter to be pressed into an inked ribbon.

Daisywheel printers are similar to automated electric typewriters. The heart of a daisywheel printer is the *daisywheel* itself, so named because it resembles the head of a daisy. It is a small round disk with spikes radiating from its center. At the end of each spike is a raised letter, like the raised letters on a typewriter (see Figure 18.5). In response to input from the computer, the daisywheel rotates until the desired letter is at the top of the wheel, and then it strikes the letter, pressing into an inked ribbon in front of a piece of paper.

The advantage of a daisywheel printer is that it produces output that looks just like it came from a typewriter. (In the early days of computing, this was a big selling point.)

Daisywheel printers use continuous-feed paper—that is, each sheet is joined to the next at the top and bottom, and each sheet has a perforated strip of holes along each side that align with sprockets that feed the paper through. Many models can also accept individual sheets of plain paper or envelopes, but you must feed each sheet individually. There typically is no paper tray for single sheets.

Daisywheel printers have several disadvantages. One is that you cannot change typeface or size in the middle of a document. You can change typefaces by changing daisywheels, but this requires stopping the printer and making the switch manually. They do not print graphics—only text, like a typewriter. They are also very noisy and very slow (fewer than 20 characters per second on the average). When daisywheel printers were popular, many offices kept the printers in soundproof enclosures to help muffle the racket.

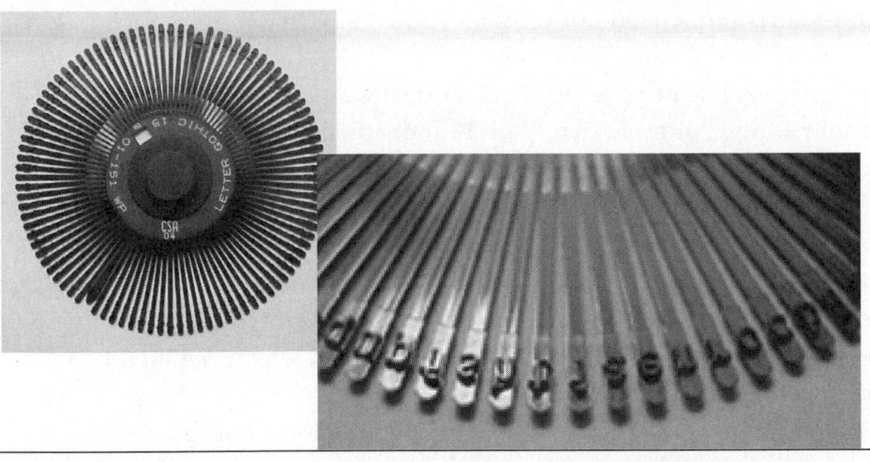

FIGURE 18.5
A Daisywheel

## Dot-Matrix Printers

Like a daisywheel, a *dot-matrix printer* is an impact printer, but it uses tiny metal pins that can change their arrangement on-the-fly to form each character rather than relying on a fixed representation of each letter or number.

**Dot-matrix printer**

A printer that forms characters on the page by pushing in/out a set of metal pins and then hitting them against an inked ribbon.

A dot-matrix printer is a line printer that gets its name from the print head, which is made up of 9 or 24 metal pins that stick out or retract as commanded by the print engine to form the shape of whatever character needs to be printed. Each character is formed by a matrix of these pins, or dots, that strike an inked ribbon. Behind the ribbon sits the paper, and behind that is a rigid *platen* that absorbs the impact. It is similar to the action of a typewriter, except that each character is created on-the-fly by rearranging the pins (see Figure 18.6).

**Platen**

The hard rubber roller behind the paper that absorbs the impact of the print head striking the ribbon and paper.

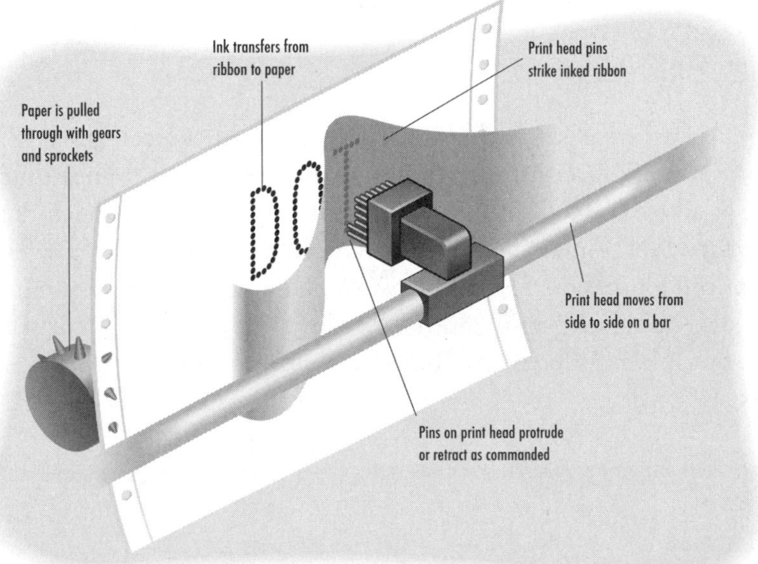
Ink transfers from ribbon to paper
Print head pins strike inked ribbon
Paper is pulled through with gears and sprockets
Print head moves from side to side on a bar
Pins on print head protrude or retract as commanded

FIGURE 18.6
On a dot-matrix printer, pins arrange themselves to form characters on the page.

Dot-matrix printers do not print an entire character at once; each pass of the 9 or 24 pins produces only a part of each line. It takes several passes to complete each line of printing. This means that a single character is generally formed of more than 9 or 24 individual dots, making it possible to reproduce a variety of type sizes and fonts.

**Letter quality (LQ)**

The best quality output from a 24-pin dot-matrix printer.

**Near letter quality (NLQ)**

The best quality output from a 9-pin dot-matrix printer.

The traditional dpi measurement is not used when speaking of the quality of a dot-matrix printer's output. Instead, print quality is expressed as *letter quality* (LQ), *near letter quality* (NLQ), or draft quality. A 9-pin head can print only NLQ; a 24-pin head can print either LQ or NLQ depending on the print mode used. All can print in draft quality, which is a high-speed mode designed for rough drafts.

Dot-matrix printers do not print in multiple colors. You can install a different color of ribbon, such as red or blue, but then you will not be able to print in black.

Like daisywheel printers, dot-matrix printers use continuous-feed paper. Single sheets may be fed by hand, but there is no paper tray for them.

## In Real Life

**You may have a client who is attached to one of these outmoded types of printers, or you may need a source for replacement parts. Look online to see which models of dot-matrix and daisywheel printers are still being sold. Also check stores that sell new printers and auction sites such as eBay that sell used ones. See "For More Information" for this chapter in the Internet Resource Center for some possible Web sites.**

## Inkjet Printers

**Inkjet printer**

A nonimpact sheet-fed printer that prints by forcing ink out of nozzles and onto the paper.

*Inkjet printers* are printers that squirt ink onto paper (see Figure 18.7). Inkjet is a nonimpact print technology; the print heads do not touch the paper at all (so it does not print multipart carbon copies, which dot-matrix and daisywheel printers do). There are between 21 and 256 nozzles for each of the four colors (cyan, yellow, magenta, and black) in the print head, depending on brand and model; the print engine tells the jets to squirt out ink in different combinations and proportions to form whatever colors are needed.

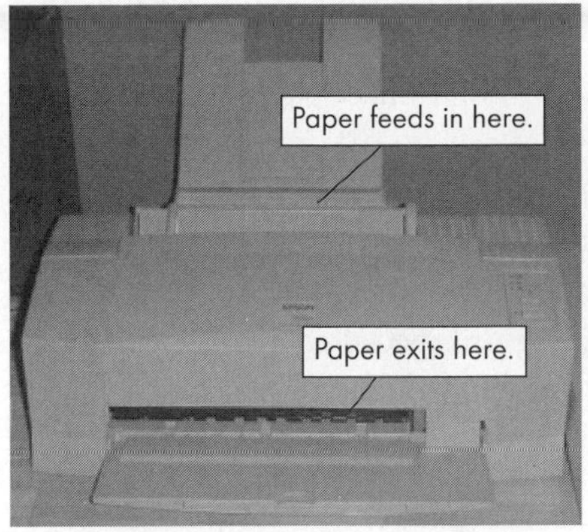
Paper feeds in here.
Paper exits here.
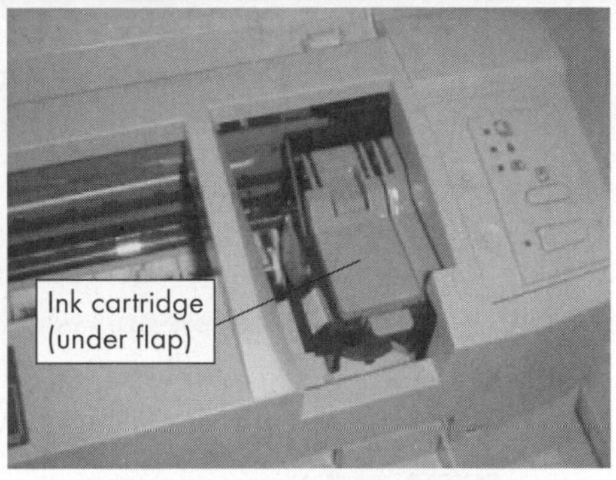
Ink cartridge
(under flap)

**FIGURE 18.7**
An Inkjet Printer

There are two technologies for forcing the ink out of the nozzles: thermal and piezoelectric.

**Thermal inkjet**
An inkjet printer that uses heat to create vapor bubbles that force ink onto a page.

*Thermal inkjet* heats the ink to about 400 degrees Fahrenheit (204 degrees Celsius), which creates vapor bubbles that force out the ink. This creates a vacuum inside the cartridge, which in turn draws more ink into the nozzles. This technology is also called *bubble jet*. Most inkjet printers made by Hewlett-Packard and Canon use this technology. Since the heat tends to degrade the print heads over time, ink replacement cartridges for these models often include replacement print heads as well. Recommend that your clients avoid home-refilling inkjet kits because by simply refilling the ink, they will not get a new print head.

**Piezoelectric inkjet**
An inkjet printer that uses electricity to force ink onto a page.

In contrast, *piezoelectric inkjet,* or piezo, moves the ink with electricity instead of heat. The nozzles contain piezoelectric crystals, which change their shape when electricity is applied to them and force out the ink. Piezo technology is newer and is used in most of the inkjet printers sold today by Epson and Lexmark. It is easier on the printer because the printer does not need to contain a heating element, and it is better for the output because the ink used is less prone to smearing.

Even inexpensive models of inkjet printers can produce good-quality color results because the technology for transferring the ink onto the page is the same regardless of the color of ink used. To make the color inkjet from the original one-color model, manufacturers simply added a few more ink cartridges to the design and added the ability to mix those colors on-the-fly.

Inkjet printers, like dot-matrix and daisywheel, are line printers. They print the document in a series of horizontal passes, as the paper moves vertically past the print head. Like any line printer, an inkjet requires only a limited amount of RAM—just enough to hold a few fonts and a few lines' worth of incoming data to be printed. Most inkjet printers do not even advertise the amount of RAM they contain.

Unlike impact printers, inkjet printers use single-sheet pages, rather than continuous-feed. Most have a paper tray that accepts 50 or more sheets of paper at a time.

The maximum resolution of many inkjet printers today exceeds 1440 x 720dpi, but most are capable of operating in lower dpi modes as well for increased speed. The highest dpis usually require special coated paper. Printing speeds range from 1 to 2 ppm for a high-quality full-page color graphic to 10 ppm or more for low-resolution one-color printing.

**TRY IT!**

**Research several models and brands of inkjet printers on the Internet. Which ones offer the best resolution? Speed? Which ones use thermal versus piezoelectric technology?**

## Laser Printers

A laser printer works much like a photocopier. The main difference is that a photocopier scans a document to produce an image, while the laser printer receives digitized data from a computer. Typically, a laser printer looks like a big square box, with the paper tray inside. Printed pages are fed into an output tray on the top or at the back of the printer (see Figure 18.8).

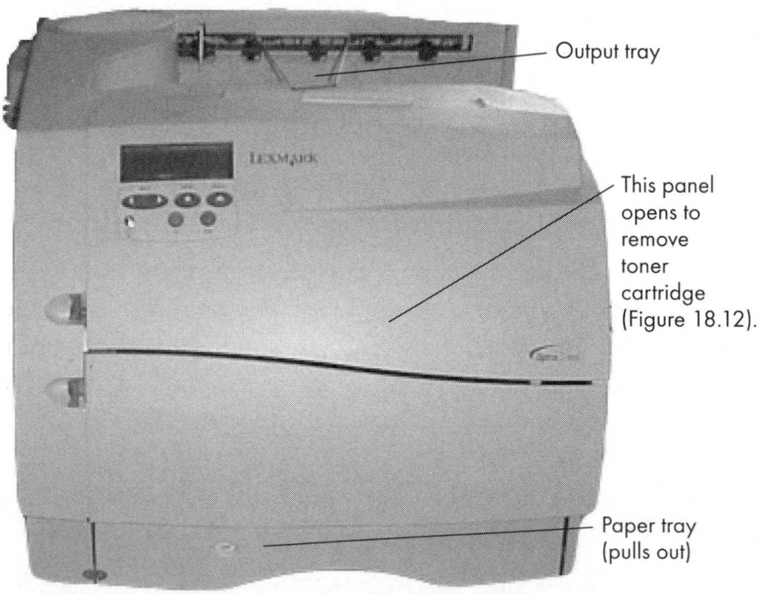


**FIGURE 18.8**
A Laser Printer

A laser printer contains a large cylinder, known as a *drum*, which carries a high negative electrical charge. The printer directs a laser beam to partially neutralize the charge in certain areas of the drum. When the drum rotates past a toner reservoir, the toner clings to the areas of lesser charge, and the page image is formed on the drum. Then the drum rotates past positively charged paper, and the toner jumps off onto the paper. The paper then passes through a *fuser* that melts the plastic particles of the toner so that it sticks to the paper.

**Drum**

The large cylinder in a laser printer to which the page image is written before being transferred to paper.

**Fuser**

A heater in a laser printer that melts the toner so it sticks to the paper.

There are six steps in creating a laser-printed page: cleaning, charging, writing, developing, transferring, and fusing. You should know these steps—and their correct order—for the A+ exam.

**Cleaning.** Before a page is printed, all remnants of the previous print job must be purged from the drum. The cleaning process consists of scraping leftover toner from the drum with a cleaning blade and removing any residual electrical charge from the drum either electrostatically or with LEDs.

**Charging (or Conditioning).** The *primary corona wire* applies a uniform negative charge of -600 volts (v) to the drum's surface. The wire itself has -6,000v, but only 10 percent of that gets transferred to the drum (see Figure 18.9).

**Primary corona wire**

The wire in a laser printer that applies a uniform negative charge to the drum, preparing it to accept the page image.

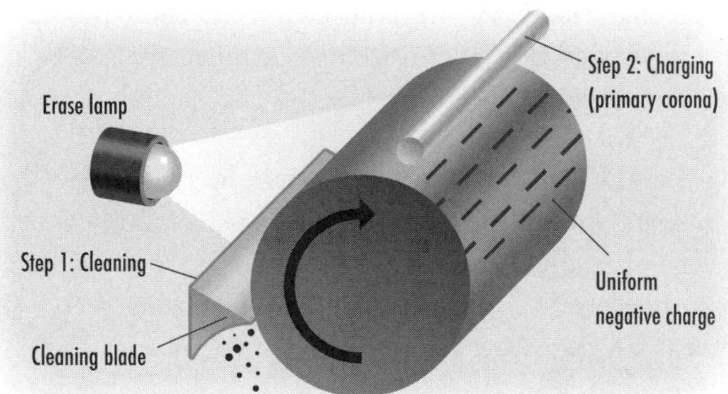


**FIGURE 18.9**
Steps 1 and 2 in the Laser Printing Process

**Writing.** The laser sweeps across the drum's surface, turning itself on and off at precise moments. Wherever the laser is on, the drum surface charge is reduced to about -100v. The mirror image of the entire page is written to the drum this way, with electrical charges. The on/off status of the laser can be changed a certain number of times per inch; this is the printer's maximum dpi setting. For early lasers it was 300dpi; for today's lasers it is 600 to 1200dpi or more.

**Developing.** The drum rotates past toner (a mix of iron oxide and plastic resin) on a developing cylinder, which has the same -600v charge as the unlasered portions of the drum (see Figure 18.10). The areas of lesser negative charge on the drum attract the toner, which jumps onto the drum and sticks to it at those spots, but the toner and the drum ignore one another in the spots where the charge is the same. Now the mirror image of the page exists on the drum in toner.

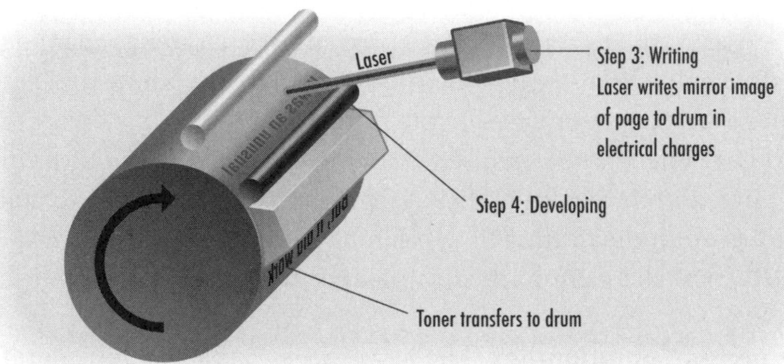


**FIGURE 18.10**
Steps 3 and 4 in the Laser Printing Process

**Transferring.** The *transfer corona wire* applies a +600v positive charge to the incoming paper. When the paper passes by the drum, the -100v toner particles on the drum jump off onto the paper because its positive charge, at 600v, is greater than the drum's negative charge at -100v. Before exiting the printer, the paper runs past a static charge eliminator, a row of metal teeth with a negative charge that neutralizes the paper's high positive charge.

**Transfer corona wire**

The wire in a laser printer that applies a positive charge to the paper so that the negatively charged toner will be attracted to it.

**Fusing.** After the transfer step, the toner is held on the paper by gravity and weak electrostatic forces. The fuser applies pressure and heat to the paper, melting the plastic resin particles in the toner so that they stick to the paper and form a positive image of the page. The paper then ejects from the printer (see Figure 18.11).

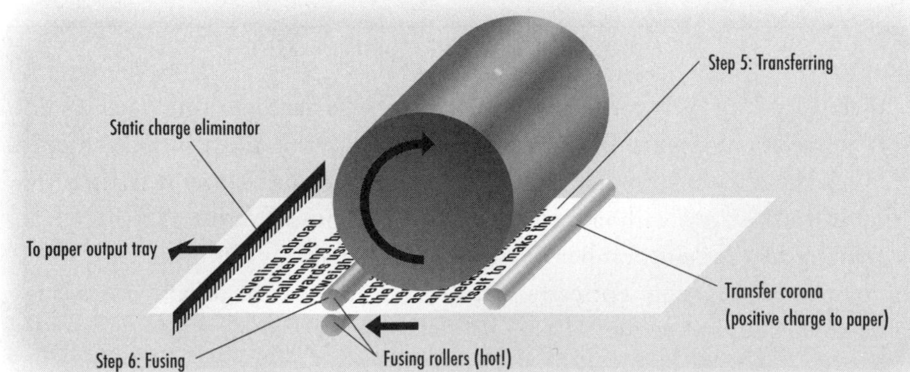


**FIGURE 18.11**
Steps 5 and 6 in the Laser Printing Process

## In Real Life

To remember the laser printing process for the exam, you can memorize the steps by the first initials of each phase, CCWDTF, and then assign a logical group of words to represent the initials. One example might be *CompTIA Certification Will Do Things Faster.*

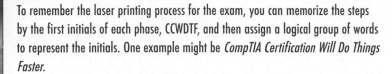

In some models the drum is inside the toner cartridge; when you replace the toner, you replace the drum too (see Figure 18.12). In other models the drum and toner are separate and so you replace them separately.

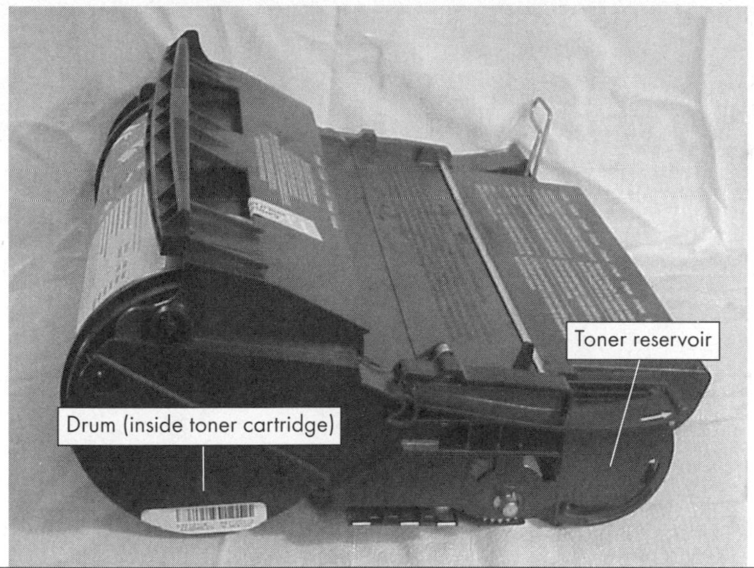


**FIGURE 18.12**
This toner cartridge has the drum built in.

Color laser printers are typically much more expensive than one-color laser printers because the laser printing technology does not lend itself readily to multicolor printing. To print in color, a laser printer must make four passes across the same page, laying down a different color each time (cyan, magenta, yellow, and black). However, a color laser printer may be less expensive than an inkjet in the long run if your client plans on printing a large number of copies because color inkjet cartridges are much more expensive than color toner for a color laser. A color laser also produces better-looking output than most color inkjet printers.

## LED Page Printers

An LED page printer is similar to a laser printer, but it uses light-emitting diodes (LEDs) instead of a laser to place the image on the drum. This technology was originally developed by Okidata as a low-cost laser printer substitute; some Panasonic and Lexmark models also use the technology. The price is lower, but the output quality is not quite as good; LED page printers are limited to around 800dpi.

In the color models, the LED page printer has a speed advantage over the laser. It can print faster than a color laser because it needs to make only one pass; a color laser must make four passes.

## Dye Sublimation Printers

This is a specialty type of printer used mostly in high-end graphic arts and photography. The heating element in the printer converts a solid ink into a gas that is then applied to the paper. Color is applied in a continuous tone, rather than with individual dots, and colors are applied one at a time (yellow, magenta, cyan, and black). The ink comes on film rolls. The paper required for this type of printer is very expensive, and you cannot use regular paper with it. Printing speeds are very low—less than one page per minute.

## Solid Ink Printers

There is one final type of printer to consider: one that uses a solid, waxlike ink. These printers produce stunning color printouts at about the same initial cost as a color laser (about $2,500), with lower ink cost than any other type of color printer. At present, Tektronix is the only company that manufactures printers of this type, so they are not widely available in stores.

These printers use chunks of colored wax as the ink. The printer melts the wax and sprays it onto the page, much like an inkjet printer. Then it cools the wax to fuse it to the paper. The wax is much cheaper per page than inkjet ink, and gives a much higher quality printout, at up to 1200dpi. The print quality is as good as or better than a color laser, and the printing speed is significantly faster since it needs only one pass. Some models require a special thermal paper that is rather expensive.

## Types of Printer Interface

The following sections look at ways that a printer can connect to a computer.

### Parallel

The most common printer interface is the PC's built-in parallel port. The standard for this interface is IEEE 1284. As you learned in Chapter 7, IEEE is a standards organization that defines the protocols for various types of communication ports. The IEEE 1284 standard dictates how the various parallel port modes will operate. The modes are reviewed in Figure 18.13.

- **SPP (Standard Parallel Port):** The original parallel port mode, designed primarily for output. It has 8-bit output at 150Kbps and 4-bit input at 50Kbps.
- **Bidirectional:** An improved version of SPP that uses 8 bits for both input and output. Other names for it are PS/2 or Extended. It transfers data at 150Kbps in both directions.
- **8-bit data at up to 2Mbps.** It was developed to support nonprinter parallel devices such as tape backup drives and external disk drives, but also works with printers.
- **Enhanced Capabilities Port (ECP):** Another fast standard, the same as EPP in speed and bit width but designed primarily for printers and scanners rather than external drives. It requires a DMA channel in addition to an IRQ (which all modes require).

**FIGURE 18.13**
Review of Parallel Ports

You set the parallel port mode in BIOS Setup. Most of the time you can simply connect a printer to a parallel port and it will work with the default setting, but if the printer requires special communication capabilities with the PC or if there is a shared parallel port between a printer and a scanner with a pass-through connector, one of the other modes might provide better performance; experimentation will help you find the best one for the situation.

To connect a printer via parallel port, use a parallel printer cable. Such a cable can be distinguished from other cables because it has a male 25-pin D-sub connector at one end (for the PC) and a Centronics connector at the other (for the printer). See Chapter 7 if you need a reminder about connector types.

## In Real Life

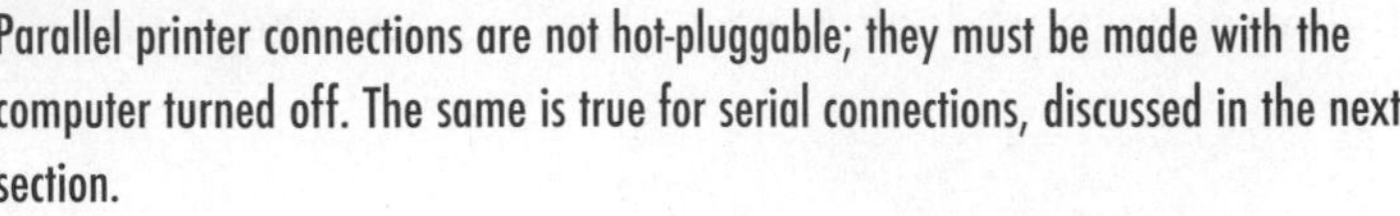

Parallel printer connections are not hot-pluggable; they must be made with the computer turned off. The same is true for serial connections, discussed in the next section.

## TRY IT!

Turn off your PC, disconnect the printer cable from both ends, and then reconnect it.

### Serial

At one time the legacy serial port on PCs was used for printer connection. Serial printers were never as popular as parallel because the connection was slower, but having a serial printer enabled a user to connect two different printers directly to one computer at the same time (since there is only one parallel port on the average computer). It is difficult to find printers with a serial connector today, and no simple adapter exists that will enable conversion from another connection type.

## In Real Life

Some MS-DOS-based programs might not recognize a COM port as a valid printer port. You can redirect output from a parallel port (LPT) to a serial port (COM) by keying the following command: MODE LPTx=COMx (the x's are the port numbers). For example, to make any data sent to LPT1 come out through COM1, key MODE LPT1=COM1 at the command prompt before entering the application. You might even put this line in the Autoexec.bat file so that it executes automatically at startup.

To connect a serial printer, run a standard serial cable from PC to printer. It needs to have a 25-pin serial connector at each end. A 9-pin will not do, and a 9-to-25 adapter will not help. If there is not a 25-pin serial port on the computer, you will not be able to hook up a serial printer. The female end of the cable connects to the male serial cable at the PC and the male end of the cable connects to the printer.

WARNING

Do not confuse the 25-pin serial connector on the PC with the 25-pin parallel connector. On the PC, the male one is serial and the female one is parallel.

TRY IT!

Check the back of your PC. Do you have a 25-pin serial port? If there are other PCs in your lab, check them as well.

## USB

USB is becoming increasingly popular as a printer connection because of its high speed and relatively trouble-free setup. Refer to Chapter 7 for details about USB connectivity. With USB you can connect as many printers as you like; you are not limited to a single printer as with the parallel interface. (You can connect a parallel printer *and* several USB printers if necessary, depending on your client's needs.) USB is hot-pluggable, so you can connect or disconnect a USB printer while the PC is running or not—your choice.

TRY IT!

Check your PC. Do you have a USB port available for connecting a USB-based printer?

### NETWORK

Any printer can be shared on a network, without its being a real "network connection." You can attach a printer to a PC and then allow that PC to share the printer as a resource on the network. The method by which the printer is attached to the PC is invisible to other network users.

However, there is also a separate type of network connectivity for a printer, in which the printer is connected directly to the network independent of any particular PC. To do this, the printer must have a network interface card built in. Some printer models have an "N" at the ends of their names; this usually signifies networkability.

The advantage of connecting a printer directly to the network is that the print jobs do not place a processing burden on a host PC. The printer handles job queuing by itself. It is wise to add extra RAM to a network-capable printer, however, so it will have plenty of RAM for storing the waiting print jobs.

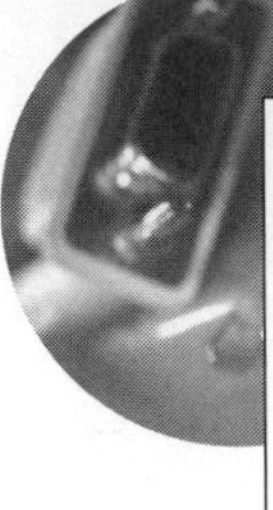

## In Real Life

To set the properties for a printer that is not associated with a PC, you would configure a router or other non-PC network device with the Web browser and the device's IP address. You enter the device's network IP address in the Web browser, just as you would enter a Web site address, and a Web page appears allowing you to configure the printer.

### Infrared

**Infrared**

A standard for transmission of data via infrared signal. Also called infrared data, or IrDA.

*Infrared* (also called *infrared data* or *IrDA* [for Infrared Data Association]) promised at one time to become a popular technology. The general idea was that a printer and a computer could be placed close to one another (in the same room, for example), and they would automatically work together without cables. Few computers and printers are infrared-capable, however. Notebook PCs are more likely than desktop PCs to include infrared capability. The infrared port is seen as a type of serial port, and on a notebook PC it is enabled and disabled in BIOS Setup.

One reason that the demand for infrared is no longer high is that IEEE 802.11b (and recently 802.11a) "WiFi" wireless Ethernet has become popular. It is a wireless networking technology through radio signal that extends an Ethernet network throughout an entire house or business department, and its range and speed are superior to infrared.

## Printer Drivers

**Printer driver**

A file or group of files that take instructions from the operating system and relay them to the printer.

**Page description language (PDL)**

The language used for communication between a printer driver and a printer.

As we have discussed in earlier chapters, hardware devices (such as printers) and the operating system speak different languages. For them to work together, a translator must be employed. A *printer driver* serves as this translator. The language that a driver speaks is known as the *page description language (PDL)*. There are many different PDLs.

In MS-DOS there was no OS-wide printer driver. A separate printer driver was required for each application you wanted to use—one for the word processor, one for the spreadsheet, and so on. To make matters worse, each brand of printer (and in many cases each model) required a different PDL; there was little standardization. A company releasing a program, such as a word processor or database, had to include dozens or even hundreds of printer drivers with the program. To help resolve these difficulties, many manufacturers of lower-price printers began using the same PDLs as the more popular printer models. This trend toward *emulation* made it possible for an end user to buy an inexpensive printer and use it with programs that did not directly support that make and model.

One of the most popular PDLs for laser printers to emulate is Hewlett-Packard's *Printer Control Language* (PCL). The original LaserJet printer used PCL 3. There have been many versions of PCL over the years, but nearly every laser printer made today is capable of emulating some version of PCL.

Another popular PDL that many laser printers emulate is Adobe's *PostScript*. PostScript is a high-end PDL that includes many beneficial features, including the ability to use PostScript fonts (covered later in this chapter). However, PostScript requires special hardware in the printer, so most entry-level laser printers do not include it. There are three versions of PostScript: Level 1, Level 2, and PostScript 3. Level 2 PostScript, released in 1992, provides improved support for color printing. PostScript 3, released in 1997, supports more fonts, handles graphics better, and includes several features to speed the PostScript printing process.

Microsoft Windows makes print driver management much easier than DOS because Windows handles all printing activity for all Windows-based programs. Rather than each program's having its own printer drivers, the programs simply send each print job to Windows, which then sends the job to the printer. Therefore you need only one print driver that lets Windows and the printer communicate. Since the critical connection now is between Windows and the printer, rather than between the printer and a particular program, the responsibility for providing a printer driver has shifted to the printer manufacturer. The printer manufacturer provides a Windows driver with the printer and/or makes one available for download from the company's Web site. You install that driver in Windows and all programs can automatically print to that printer.

Some printers can speak more than one PDL. For example, a laser printer might have two operating modes: PCL 6 and PostScript. Such printers come with two separate drivers. You can install either driver in Windows, or you can install both of them as separate "printers" and choose either printer on a job-by-job basis.

**Emulation**

A device or driver that functions the same way as another brand or model, for compatibility purposes.

**Printer Control Language (PCL)**

A PDL developed by Hewlett-Packard for laser printers and widely emulated by other manufacturers.

**PostScript**

A PDL developed by Adobe for use with certain high-end laser printers; designed for professional desktop publishing.

### In Real Life

**Windows refers to a printer driver as a "printer," but Windows does not actually work with printers–only drivers. You can have multiple drivers for the same physical printer attached to a single printer port, and Windows will think it is two separate printers, each with its own queue and settings.**

Whenever you experience data-related problems with a printer, it is almost always the printer driver's fault. If you use the wrong printer driver—either one for a different model of printer or one for a different version of Windows—you might experience problems. The printer might not work at all, or it might print garbage, or it might print normally but with some odd quirks, such as using the wrong fonts in certain places.

## Installing a Printer Driver in Windows

Some printers (particularly USB printers) are truly Plug and Play. You connect them, and Windows instantly notices and prompts you for a driver disk. You insert that disk (which came with the printer), click OK, and seconds later you are ready to print.

Other printers come with a full-blown setup program on a CD-ROM. If Windows detects the printer, you can allow it to look for the needed driver on the CD-ROM, or you can click Cancel and then run the setup program. Inkjet printers often work better if you run the full setup program for them because they often have their own print *spooler* software. A spooler is a program that holds print jobs in a queue while they are waiting to be printed.

**Spool**

A holding tank for print jobs waiting to be sent to the printer. Using a print spool frees up the application from which you are printing more quickly to continue working on other things.

If there is no setup program for the printer, and Windows does not detect it automatically, the next preferable method is to use the Add Printer (or Add New Printer) utility in the *Printers* folder (Control Panel). This wizard walks you through the process of installing a driver. This is what you will need to do if you want to install more than one driver for the same printer, or if you want to set up Windows to use a printer that is not physically connected to the PC (that is, a network printer).

The exact steps involved in the Add Printer Wizard vary depending on the Windows version and depending on whether or not you allow the wizard to detect the printer's settings.

### *Windows 2000*

To set up a local printer (directly attached to the PC, not accessed through the network) in Windows 2000 on LPT1, complete the following steps:

1. Open the Control Panel and double-click the *Printers* icon.
2. Double-click the *Add Printer* icon in the *Printers* folder.
3. Click Local printer.
4. If you want Windows to detect the printer, click the Automatically detect and install my Plug and Play printer check box. (Let us assume that you are *not* doing this.)

5. Click Next.
6. Select the port to which the printer is connected (see Figure 18.14). Then click Next.

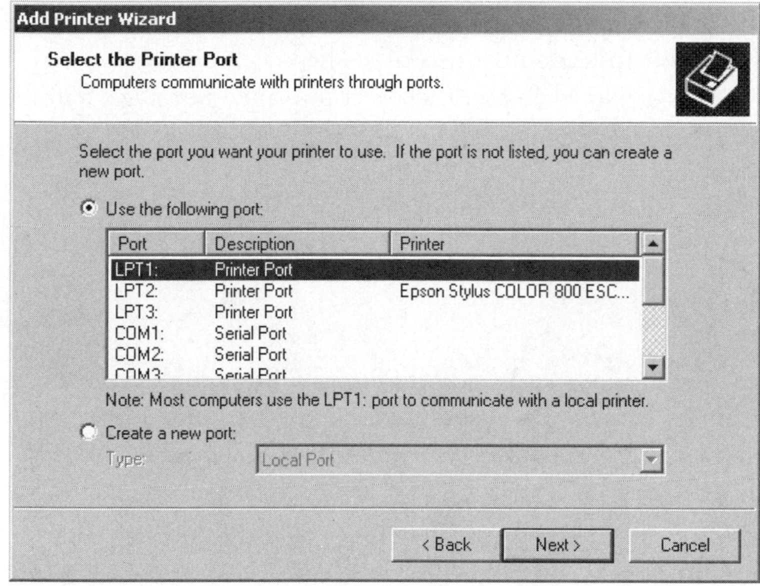


**FIGURE 18.14**
Choose the port in the Add Printer Wizard.

7. Select the printer manufacturer and model (see Figure 18.15), or click the Have Disk button if you have a disk containing the driver or have downloaded a newer version than the one that came with Windows. Then click Next.

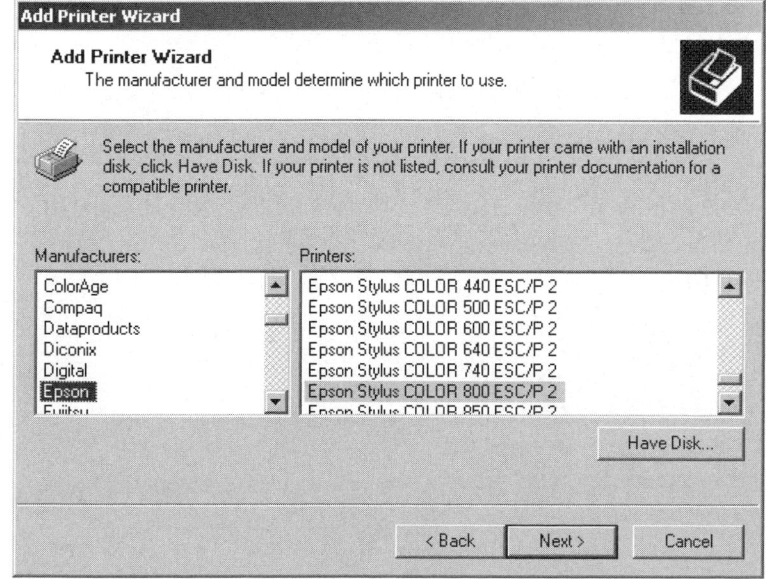


**FIGURE 18.15**
This list shows printer makes and models for which drivers came with Windows.

8. Key a name for the printer, or leave the default name.
9. Choose Yes or No when asked whether to set this printer as the default. Then click Next.
10. If you want to share the printer, mark the Share As option and then enter a share name for the printer. This is the name by which the printer will appear on the network. Then click Next.
11. Click Yes or No when asked whether to print a test page, and then click Next.
12. Click Finish.
13. Wait for the files to be copied. If prompted, insert the Windows 2000 CD-ROM.

### *Windows 98*

To set up a local printer in Windows 98 on LPT1, complete these steps:

1. Open the Control Panel and double-click the *Printers* icon.
2. Double-click the *Add Printer* icon in the *Printers* folder.
3. Click Next.
4. Select the printer manufacturer and model from the list, or click Have Disk if you have one containing a driver or have downloaded one. Then click Next.
5. Click the port to which the printer is connected, and then click Next.
6. Edit the printer name if desired. Then click Next.
7. Choose Yes or No when asked whether to print a test page.
8. Click Finish.
9. Wait for the files to be copied. If prompted, insert the Windows 98 CD-ROM.

## Removing a Printer Driver

To remove a printer driver, select the printer's icon in the *Printers* folder and press the Delete key. A confirmation appears; click Yes to accept it (see Figure 18.16).

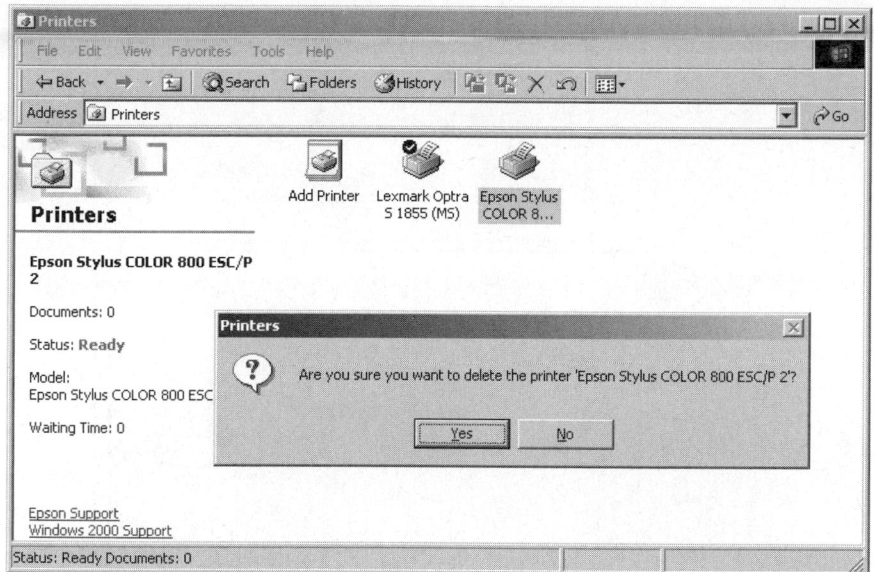


**FIGURE 18.16**
Removing a Printer Driver

## TRY IT!

In Windows, if there are any printer icons in the *Printers* folder, delete them. Then re-create them by using the Add Printer Wizard to reinstall each printer.

## Choosing the Default Printer Driver

The first printer driver that you install is the default. Clicking the Print button in applications that have a "quick print" feature that bypasses the Print dialog box activates the default settings.

When you install another printer driver, the wizard asks whether you want it to be the default. You can change which printer is the default at any time by doing the following:

1. Right-click the printer driver icon.
2. Choose Set as Default. The previous default will be unselected.

## Changing Printer Driver Properties

Each printer driver has its own set of options that you can configure. To access them, right-click the printer icon and choose Properties. Figure 18.17 shows a Properties dialog box for a Lexmark printer in Windows XP (other Windows versions will appear similar).

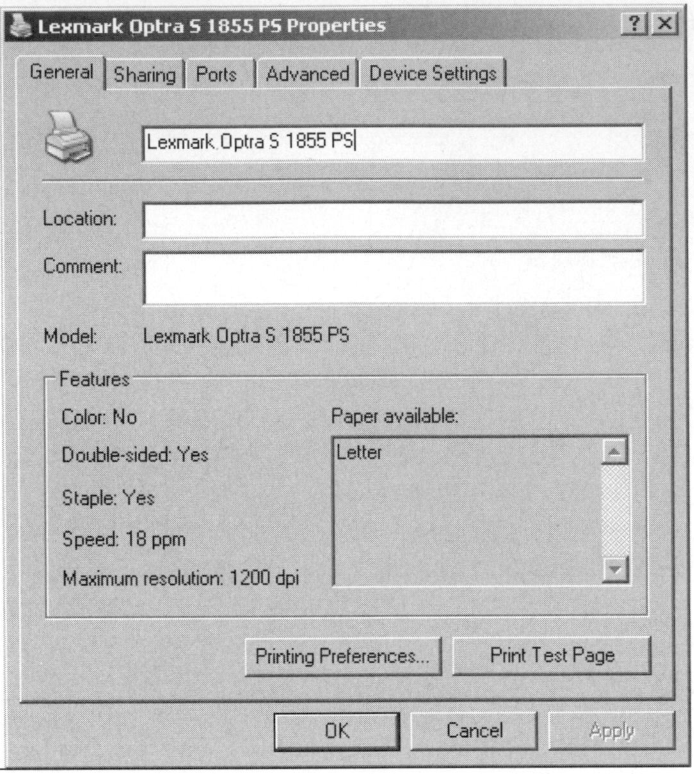

**FIGURE 18.17**
A Properties Dialog Box for a Laser Printer (shown in Windows XP)

The exact options and tabs in the Properties dialog box depend on the printer, but they all have certain things in common, such as:

- **General:** The General tab enables you to change the name of the driver (that is, the name that appears beneath the icon in the *Printers* folder), and to enter a location and comment, as in Figure 18.17. It also contains a Print Test Page button and a Printing Preferences button.
- **Printing Preferences:** The Printing Preferences button opens another dialog box in which you can set layout options such as *portrait* versus *landscape*, number of copies, page order, and default paper tray (see Figure 18.18 for an example that includes some of these options).

**Portrait**

A page orientation wherein the text runs parallel to the narrow edge of the paper.

**Landscape**

A page orientation wherein the text runs parallel to the wide edge of the paper.

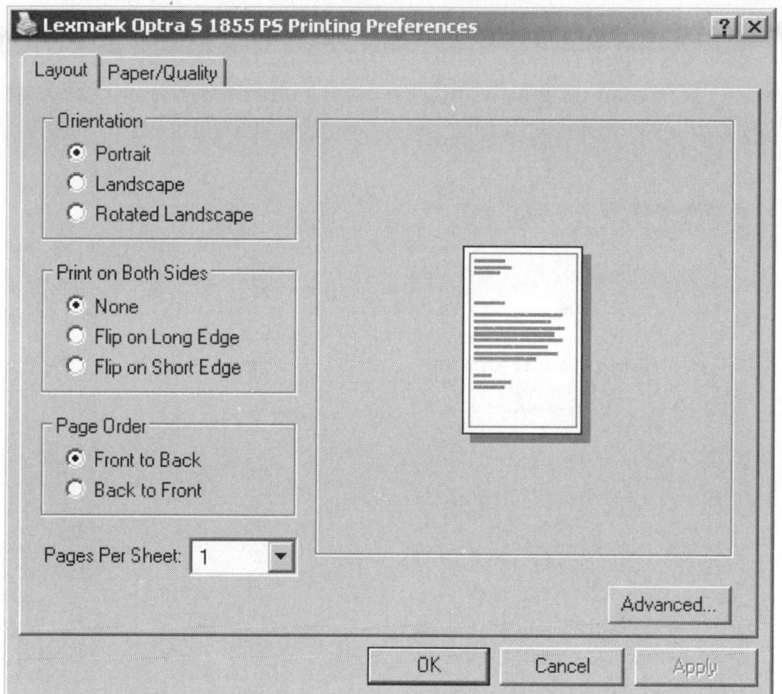


**FIGURE 18.18**
The Printing Preferences for a printer control many of the most common user settings.

**WARNING**

The number of copies setting in the Printing Preferences will be combined with any number of copies settings you specify in an application. For example, if you set the Printing Preferences to print two copies of everything, and then in the word processor you specify that you want two copies of a particular document, you will get four copies. To avoid this confusion, most people set the number of copies only in an application, and not in the general properties for the printer.

- **Sharing:** The Sharing tab controls whether or not the printer will be shared with other users on the network. We will discuss that further in Chapter 23.
- **Ports:** This tab lets you specify which port is associated with the printer. It can be useful if you need to move the printer to a different port but do not want to completely uninstall and reinstall it.
- **Advanced:** This tab has a variety of settings, useful mostly for the shared network printer in an office, including setting time-of-day restrictions on the printer's usage, setting spooling options, and choosing whether or not to separate each print job with a separator page.

- **Device Settings:** This tab's content is completely dependent on the printer type. The options that appear here are defined by the printer driver. There may be many options, as in Figure 18.19, or very few. In general, laser printers will have more options than inkjet.

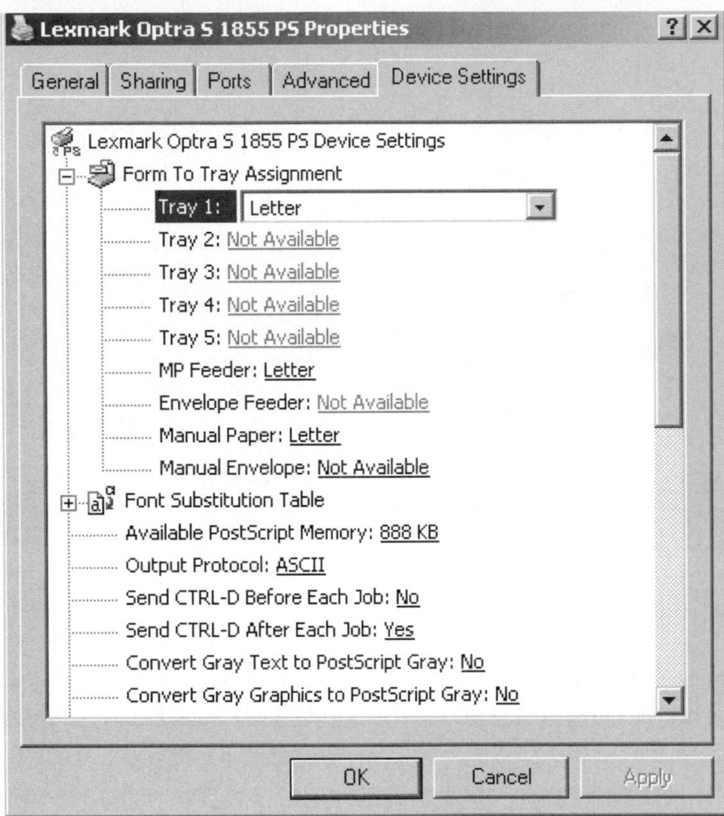


**FIGURE 18.19**
The Device Settings tab displays options unique to the specific printer.

**Resident font**

A font that is built into the printer, so it is always available.

**Soft font**

A font that is contained in a computer file and sent to the printer whenever a document requiring that font must be printed.

# Fonts and Typefaces

Printers use fonts to generate the text in printouts. These fonts may either be built into the printer *(resident fonts)* or downloaded from the PC to the printer as needed *(soft fonts)*.

What is the difference between a *font* and a *typeface*? The terms have become synonymous, but it was not always so. In earlier days of PC computing, "font" referred to a specific typeface at a specific size with certain attributes; for example, Times Roman 12-point was a different font from Times Roman 10-point, and Times Roman 10-point Italic was yet another font. When a printer advertised that it had 70 or more built-in fonts, you might expect only three or four typefaces, each in an assortment of sizes and attributes (regular, bold, italic, and bold italic).

**Font**

A specific typeface at a specific size with certain attributes such as bold or italic. Used as a synonym for typeface.

**Typeface**

A style of lettering, not tied to any specific size of text.

If you wanted to use a font that was not resident in the printer, you had to download it to the printer through the application you were using. For example, Ventura Publisher was a popular desktop publishing program. When you installed it, you could choose to generate font files in various typeface/size/attribute combinations. Each of these font files took up hard disk space, so it was advantageous to limit yourself to the ones you thought you would actually use. Then, when you printed a document, the application would send the needed font files to the printer along with the print job itself. If you had two printers, you had to have two completely separate sets of files. The term "font" referred to these individual files, each of which contained a unique description of a typeface/size/attribute for a specific printer.

With this type of font, each character in each typeface/size/attribute combination is a stored graphic. To print the document, the printer pulls the needed graphics from the font files. This is known as a raster or *bitmap font*.

**Bitmap font**

A font in which each letter at each size is an individual graphic stored in the font file(s).

During this time (1980s), PostScript printers were available that had 35 built-in typefaces (not fonts) that were fully *scalable* (they could be used to produce characters in varying sizes). That meant you could print documents using any of those typefaces, in virtually any combination of size/attributes, without having a single font file stored on your hard disk, and without the application's having to send any font files to the printer. This feature was the main reason why PostScript printers were so popular for a while. PostScript fonts are *outline fonts*. They contain a description of the shape of each character in the typeface as an outline; then they size that outline as needed and fill in the center with black to form the letter.

**Scalable**

Resizable to any size.

**Outline font**

A font file that contains an outline of each letter that can be scaled to any size and then filled in to create the characters.

Then Windows 3.1 was introduced, and with it came *TrueType fonts*. TrueType fonts were soft fonts that got downloaded to the printer as needed, but they were outline fonts (and as such, were scalable), so you needed only a single file to represent all sizes. Some of them included the various attributes built into the same file; others provided separate files for bold versus italic versus regular. TrueType fonts made it practical for users

**TrueType fonts**

Scalable soft fonts in Windows and the Macintosh that work with all applications in the operating system and that can be displayed and printed at any size.

who did not want to spend $1,000 or so for a PostScript printer to use many different typefaces without filling up their hard disk with font files.

## In Real Life

The newest versions of Windows and Microsoft Office come with a new type of font called *OpenType*. Although the name is different, the concept is the same; OpenType is simply an improved version of TrueType.

**OpenType fonts**

An improved version of TrueType.

Since files were no longer needed to store individual typeface/size combinations, the meaning of the term "font" gradually shifted to mean the TrueType files, which represented typefaces. Over time, font and typeface have come to be synonymous.

**Vector fonts**

Fonts consisting of mathematical equations that draw lines to create the characters.

There is one more type of font that you need to know about: *vector*. These scalable fonts are created with mathematical equations that draw lines (think geometry) and are designed for use with plotters (which are printers that create line drawings). Windows 2000 includes three of these fonts: Roman, Modern, and Script.

## Serif versus Sans-Serif Fonts

There are thousands of fonts, but all fall into one of two categories: serif or sans-serif. A serif is a little extra piece or "tail" on a letter that makes it easier to read. Examples include Times New Roman and Courier. A sans-serif font does not have serifs (see Figure 18.20).

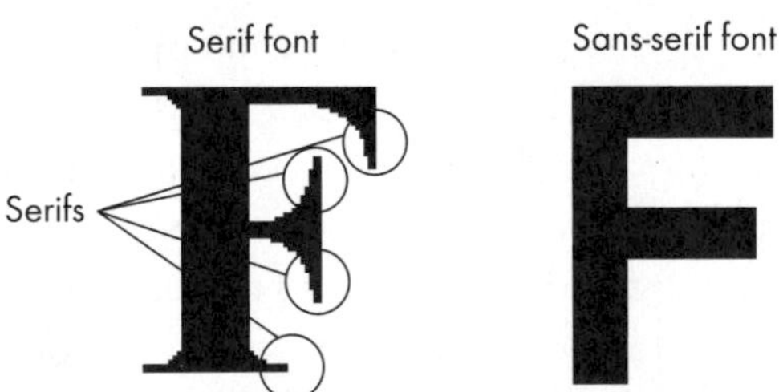


**FIGURE 18.20**
Serif versus Sans-Serif Fonts

## Viewing Installed Fonts in Windows

To see what fonts are installed, open the Fonts window from the Windows Control Panel (see Figure 18.21).

## WARNING

In Windows XP, if you use the Control Panel in Category View, it may be difficult to locate the Fonts applet since it is not assigned to any of the categories. Switch to Classic View first; then double-click the *Fonts* icon.

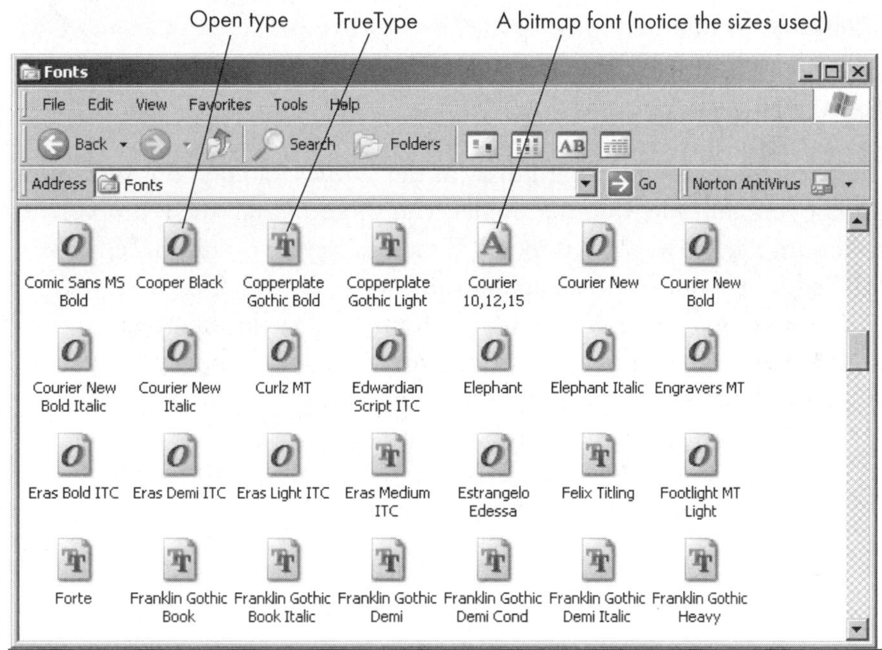


**FIGURE 18.21**
Installed Fonts in Windows

Notice the different icons for the fonts. The *O* icons are for OpenType fonts, an improved version of TrueType that comes with Microsoft Office XP and Microsoft Windows XP. The *TT* icons are for TrueType fonts, and the *A* icons are for fonts that are neither OpenType nor TrueType. Such fonts are usually not scalable; they have only a few sizes available. In Figure 18.21, notice that the Courier font lists its sizes: 10, 12, and 15. You can see a sample of a font by double-clicking it.

## TRY IT!

To preview a font or fonts, follow these steps:

1. Open the *Fonts* folder.
2. Double-click on a font to see a preview of it.
3. Click Print to print that preview.
4. Close the window for the font.
5. Preview several other fonts.

One convenient feature in the Fonts window is the ability to sort fonts by their similarity to other fonts. To do so, choose View/List Fonts By Similarity, and then choose the baseline font from the List fonts by similarity to drop-down list. The fonts that are most similar to that font will appear first on the list. This can be useful when you want to delete fonts that are essentially duplicates of one another, to cut down on the overall number of fonts installed without compromising the desktop publishing capabilities.

## Installing Fonts in Windows

The *Fonts* folder is on the hard disk, in the *Windows* folder. But instead of just copying font files into that folder, you should install them properly to make sure they are registered in the Windows Registry. This makes the installed fonts available to all applications.

You (or your client) can acquire new fonts by downloading them from the Internet or purchasing CDs with fonts. A CD with fonts usually comes with an installer program, or you can follow this procedure:

1. In the Fonts window, choose File/Install New Font.
2. Navigate to the drive and folder containing the font(s) to install.
3. Select the font(s) to install (see Figure 18.22).
4. Click OK to install the fonts.

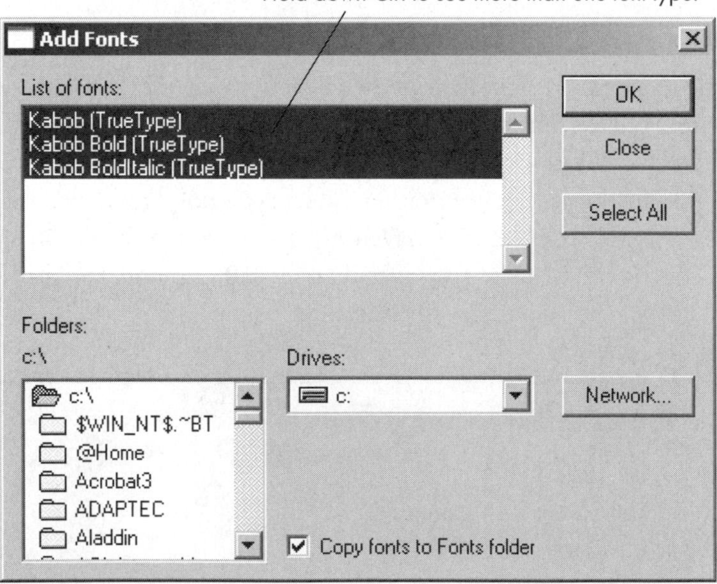


**FIGURE 18.22**
Installed Fonts in Windows

# Routine Printer Maintenance

Some printers, particularly high-volume lasers, require periodic servicing by a trained professional, and require certain parts to be replaced. You may need to buy maintenance kits containing the needed parts, and have the printer(s) serviced by someone who has been trained on that specific model. A general PC technician can learn to perform this service on the models in his or her organization, but it is usually more cost effective to have it done professionally.

However, there are many routine maintenance tasks that you as a general technician can perform on printers, and some of these can even be delegated to end users after some training.

## Laser Printers

Here are some of the maintenance and service adjustments you can perform on a laser printer.

### *Cleaning a Laser Printer*

All printers tend to accumulate paper particles and dust inside, and periodically must be cleaned. The best tool for this job is a soft cloth. Do not use a regular vacuum because the toner particles can get through the vacuum filter and circulate in the air, where people could breathe them in and get sick. Conventional vacuums can also generate static electricity. There are special low-static or nonstatic vacuums available for working around computers; if you must have a vacuum for the job, use one of those.

You will want to wipe down the outside of the printer casing as well, if only for cosmetic reasons, and make sure no dust balls are accumulating near the vents.

Some printers have specific cleaning routines or features. For example, some Hewlett-Packard laser printers have a cleaning procedure that involves running a sheet of paper through the printer so that a uniform layer of black toner is printed on it, and then running the same sheet back through again. This removes excess paper and toner particles from the fusing assembly. Follow the instructions in the owner's manual.

Print quality problems, such as white or black streaks on the page of a laser printer's output, are often caused by dirty corona wires. (There will be more about troubleshooting later in the chapter.) As discussed earlier, the primary corona applies the negative charge to the drum and the transfer corona applies the positive charge to the paper. The primary corona is usually inside the toner cartridge; the transfer corona is somewhere near where the paper enters. One, both, or neither may be accessible, depending on the model. (In some newer models the corona wires have been eliminated and their functions have been taken over by other technology; check the manual.) If a corona wire is accessible, you can clean it either with a special cleaning tool or with an alcohol-dipped cotton swab. Be very careful; too much pressure will cause these wires to break.

## TRY IT!

Consult the manual for your laser printer, and then clean the printer in accordance with its instructions.

### *Adjusting the Toner Delivery*

As the drum ages it transfers the image less efficiently, so you may notice the printouts getting lighter. Most laser printers have a Darkness or Contrast adjustment knob to compensate for drum wear. If you turn it too high, the entire printout will have a grayish cast to it, even the white areas. If you turn it too low, the print will not be a crisp, dark black. Check the printer manual to find the location of this setting.

## TRY IT!

Experiment with different Darkness settings for your laser printer until you find the optimal setting.

### *Changing the Toner Cartridge*

Some printer drivers will notify you when you are out of toner; a message will appear on the screen, or an area in the printer's Properties dialog box may report the toner status. On other models an Out of Toner message may appear on the printer's own LED panel. Printout symptoms of low toner include faint or splotchy printing.

## In Real Life

Some printers have an optional utility program that talks to the printer and reports back about the number of pages printed, the amount of toner left, and so on.

Before installing a new toner cartridge, you can sometimes wring a few extra pages out of the old one by some of these methods:

- Take out the toner cartridge and gently shake it from side to side (never up and down, or toner could spill out) to redistribute the remaining toner evenly.
- Temporarily turn up the Darkness or Contrast setting (see the preceding section). Do not forget to turn it back down again when you install the new toner cartridge.

To install a new toner cartridge, follow the instructions that came with it, or the instructions in the printer's manual. Here is a general outline:

1. Remove the new cartridge from its protective bag. Toner cartridges usually ship in metallic-coated plastic bags.
2. Remove any pieces of tape on the new cartridge. Several areas may be taped down for shipping. Some cartridges also have a plastic strip on a tab that you must pull out.
3. Open the printer and pull out the old cartridge, noting exactly where it is inserted and in what orientation.
4. Insert the new cartridge the same way that the old cartridge came out.
5. Close the printer and run any self-tests or cleaning routines recommended in the printer's manual.
6. If the new cartridge came with a felt pad (see the following section), find the old pad on the printer (again see the manual) and replace it with the new one.

**TRY IT!**

**Remove the toner cartridge from your laser printer and then reinsert it. Or, if it is empty, replace it with a new one.**

Old toner cartridges may be sent back to the manufacturer for recycling, or sold to a company that recycles them. Do not simply throw a toner cartridge in the trash; if nothing else, take it to your local hazardous waste disposal site.

Toner cartridges may be refilled, but the refilling industry is not regulated and there is a wide variety in the quality of suppliers. Using a carelessly remanufactured cartridge can ruin your printer. On most laser printers, using anything other than brand-new toner cartridges voids the warranty.

### *Changing the Cleaning Pad*

Some laser printers have a removable felt pad on a plastic mounting that you must change every time you change the toner cartridge. (For such printers the felt pad comes with the new toner, so you do not have to buy the pad separately.)

The location of the pad varies from printer to printer, so the best way to find it is to look in the printer's manual for a diagram. For example, on the Lexmark Optra S laser printer, the pad is located on top of the printer under a removable plastic panel (see Figure 18.23).

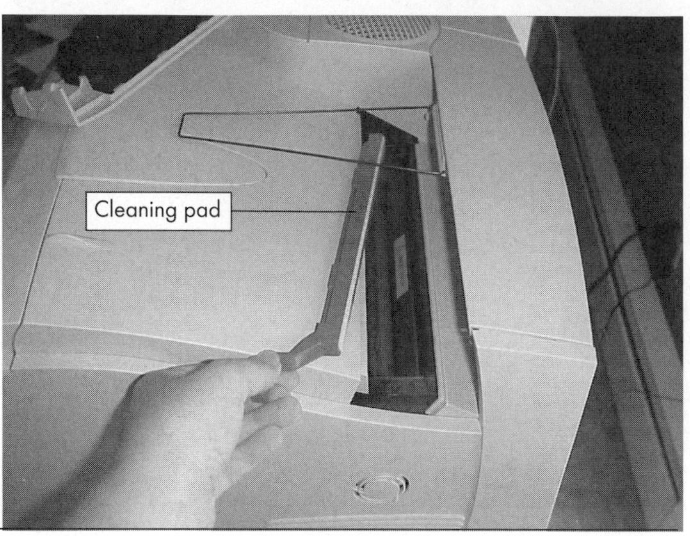


**FIGURE 18.23**
Removable Felt Cleaning Pad Mounted on a Plastic Bracket

### *Replacing the Drum*

Depending on the model, the drum may be built into the toner cartridge in the laser printer, or it may be a separate unit. If it is separate, in time the drum will need to be replaced. The owner's manual for the printer should tell how many copies a drum can print before it needs replacement. It should also tell how to remove the old drum and reinstall the new one. If the drum is built into the toner cartridge, you get a new drum whenever you replace the cartridge.

## IN REAL LIFE

How can you gauge the number of pages a printer has printed since the last drum or toner cartridge replacement? Most printers have a variety of self-test and information sheets that print out when you press certain buttons on their LED panel. Check the printer owner's manual to find out how to print a sheet that tells the number of pages printed.

If the drum must be changed, you will probably want to do it yourself rather than delegate the job to an end user. That is because the drum is very susceptible to being scratched, and a scratched drum can cause a cosmetic flaw on every printout it generates.

## Inkjet Printers

Inkjet printers typically are not used in a high-volume business setting. They are designed primarily for personal use, not heavy-duty output. Therefore, they do not usually require professional servicing. When one wears out, you simply get another. Inkjet printers generally wear out before they become out-of-date, and they are so inexpensive that buying a new one every three to five years is a reasonable expectation.

### *Changing Ink Cartridges*

Inkjet printers go through ink very quickly. You will want to train your end users to change their own ink cartridges, but that means you will need to learn to do it yourself for each inkjet model that you support.

The printer driver in Windows may tell you that a particular color of ink is empty, or you might simply notice that color missing from a printout. If in doubt, clean the ink jets using the printer's self-cleaning utility, and then print a test pattern. This will show you whether all of the colors are printing.

If a certain color is printing in some areas of the test pattern but not others, or if you are getting stripes on the printouts of color photos, it could be that the ink for one of the colors is nearly empty, but it is more likely that one or more of the ink jets are clogged; rerun the cleaning utility multiple times as needed to break the clog. See the next section for details.

Most inkjet printers have cartridge-changing instructions written on the inside of the printer. If not, look in the owner's manual. Here is a general overview:

1. Remove the new ink cartridge from its protective wrapping. It is usually transported in a metallic plastic bag.
2. Look on the new cartridge for a plastic seal that you need to remove. Do not remove all of the plastic labeling from the cartridge—just the one little strip that the instructions say to remove.

3. Press buttons on the printer to move the old cartridge into reach. The button sequence depends on the printer; read the manual or look for instructions inside the printer itself.
4. Open the flap holding the old cartridge in place, and lift it out. Drop in the new cartridge, holding it at the same position and orientation as the old one.
5. Close the flap, pushing the new cartridge into place. If the flap does not snap or click when it closes, it might not be completely shut.

**WARNING**

**All sorts of problems can result from not inserting the ink cartridge properly. Some printers will not work at all; others might create such oddities as the entire page printing at one edge of the paper, the document printing at the wrong size, or one or more colors not showing up. When troubleshooting a problem with an inkjet printer that started right after changing an ink cartridge, always suspect improper cartridge insertion.**

### *Cleaning Ink Jets*

Inkjet printers periodically must have their ink jets cleaned to ensure smooth operation. If some of the jets are clogged, certain colors may not appear or the entire printout might have a striped appearance. This happens particularly in printers that sit idle for a long time because the ink in the jets tends to dry and create clogs.

In the printer's manual there should be instructions for running a cleaning utility by pressing certain buttons on the printer in a certain order. You can also initiate the cleaning from Windows through the Properties dialog box for the printer driver. Inkjet printers typically have a Utilities tab in the Properties dialog box, and on that Utilities tab there should be a cleaning button you can click (see Figure 18.24).

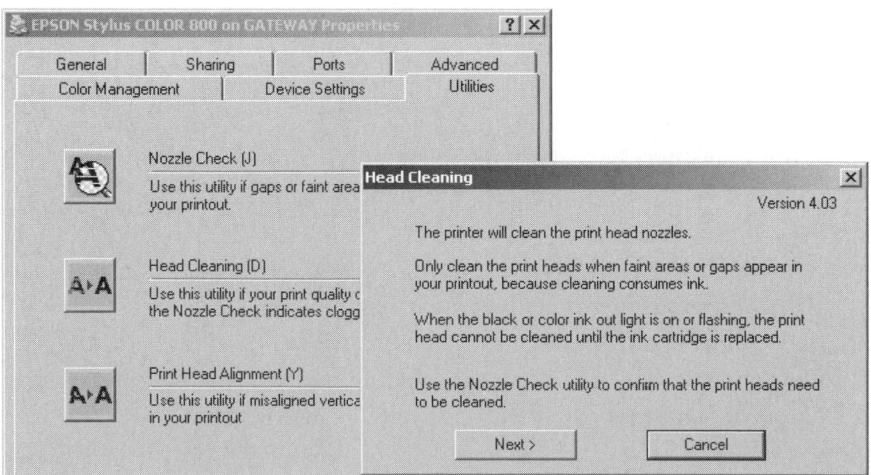


**FIGURE 18.24**
The cleaning process can be initiated from the printer driver in Windows.

# Managing a Print Queue

Each printer driver has its own *print queue* in Windows. When you print from an application, the document goes first to the print queue, then to the printer. This frees the application to continue working while the document prints. The print queue then spools (sends) the print job to the printer as quickly as the printer can accept it. For this reason, the print queue is also called the print spooler.

**Print queue**

A holding area for print jobs waiting to be sent to the printer.

## VIEWING THE PRINT QUEUE

To view the print queue for a printer driver, double-click its icon in the *Printers* folder. A list of the jobs waiting to be printed on that printer appears (see Figure 18.25). If no print jobs are waiting to be printed, nothing appears in the box.

### IN REAL LIFE

Print jobs disappear from the list as soon as they finish printing. Therefore, if you print a short document and then open the print queue, the document may have already finished spooling to the printer. If you want to see the print job in the print queue, as in Figure 18.25, pause the printer first. (See the next section to learn how to pause and otherwise control the print queue.)

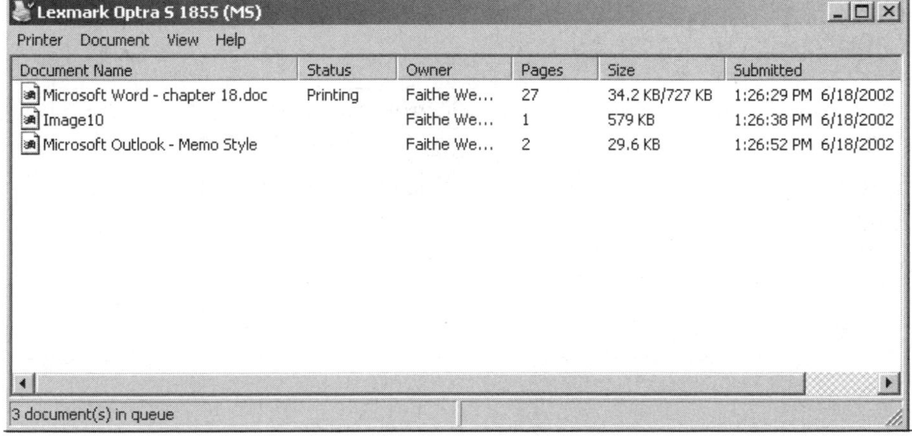


**FIGURE 18.25**
The print queue shows the documents waiting to be printed.

## Controlling the Print Queue

The print queue as a whole can be either paused or cleared. Pausing it simply places it in a "hold" mode but retains all print jobs that are waiting. This might be useful when you need to adjust something on the printer, such as changing the type of paper loaded in it. Clearing the print queue deletes all waiting print jobs.

- To pause the print queue, double-click the printer's icon in the *Printers* folder, click Printer, and then choose Pause Printing to insert a check mark. To resume, follow the same steps to remove the check mark next to Pause Printing.
- To clear the print queue, double-click the printer's icon in the *Printers* folder, click Printer, and then choose Cancel All Documents.

## Controlling Individual Print Jobs

Individual print jobs may also be paused or cleared. You might pause a print job to allow another print job to go ahead of it in line, for example, or you might clear a print job if you accidentally printed a large document and do not want to waste the paper.

- To pause a print job, click it in the print queue and then choose Document, Pause. To resume that document, choose Document, Resume.
- To cancel a print job, click it in the print queue and then choose Document, Cancel, or press the Delete key.

## Disabling the Print Queue

You can turn off the print queue for a printer driver on the Advanced tab in its Properties dialog box by choosing the Print Directly to the Printer option (see Figure 18.26). This will enable applications to send print jobs directly to the printer, bypassing the queue. In most cases, however, you will want to leave the print queue enabled.

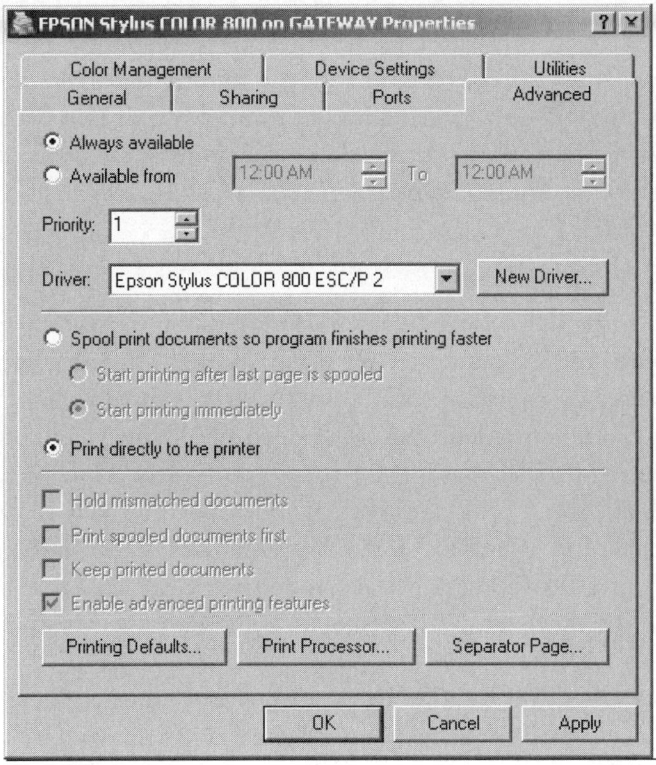

**FIGURE 18.26**
Turn off the print queue for a printer driver on the Advanced tab of its Properties dialog box.

# Troubleshooting Printing Problems

Here are some things that can go wrong with printers, along with some suggestions for fixing them.

## Stalled Print Queue

If a printer is not printing, check its print queue. It might report an error condition for one of the print jobs, and this error might cause the print queue to stall. Try pausing and resuming the queue after deleting the job with the error.

## Junk Characters in Printout

The printer may go temporarily haywire, spitting out pages of junk characters. If this happens just occasionally, it is not a serious problem—the slightest data transfer error can cause such actions. But if it happens regularly, make sure the right driver is installed for the printer and that it has not been corrupted and does not need updating for the OS version.

## Illegal Operation or General Protection Fault (GPF)

If an error occurs that causes the print queue to terminate, try opening it from the Printers window, pausing it, and resuming it. If that does not work, restart the computer. If this error occurs continually, remove and reinstall the printer driver. Chapter 28 explains application error messages in more detail.

## Paper Jams

Because laser printers run at faster speeds than other printers, a great many errors are caused by paper jams. Other printer types can also have jams.

A lot of paper jam problems can be avoided simply by using the right type of paper. Any paper that is extra-heavy (more than 24 lb.) or extra-light (less than 16 lb.), or is torn, curled, or wrinkled is likely to cause a jam. So is paper that is heavily textured or embossed. Paper jams can also be the result of a buildup of paper and toner particles inside the printer, so clean the printer thoroughly as a first step. See the printer's manual for instructions.

Sometimes when the humidity is high, the paper can stick together in the paper tray, feeding multiple sheets and causing jams. To avoid this, take out the paper and fan it.

If the printer is still jamming, check to see whether it has a control that specifies thickness of paper. If this adjustment does not match the actual paper in use, jams can result.

If none of these suggestions solve the problem, and the printer is old, perhaps the paper feed rollers are getting worn and too smooth. Try roughening them up slightly with a kitchen pot-scrubber or fine-grain sandpaper. This helps the paper advance through the feed mechanism.

## Laser Quality Problems

Here are some common problems with laser output.

**Printout faint in some spots.** This can happen when the toner in the cartridge starts running out. Take out the toner cartridge and shake it from side to side several times (never up and down, or it could spill). It should be good for another 100 pages or so. Faint printing can also be the result of the drum's reaching the end of its useful life. On printers in which the drum and toner are separate, the drum has a longer life but must eventually be changed. Such printers usually have a print density control that adjusts the amount of toner used for each page. When the drum is new, this setting should be on Low, but as the drum ages, you might need to turn it up gradually to compensate for the drum's growing ineffectiveness. Faint printing can also indicate a dirty transfer corona. Remember, the transfer corona charges the paper so that the toner on the drum will be attracted to it. If the transfer corona is dirty, the paper does not receive the full charge and the toner is insufficiently attracted.

**Loose or smeared toner.** A tiny bit of loose toner now and then might simply mean the printer is dirty inside and needs to be cleaned. However, if the toner is consistently loose and the image suffers, the fuser is probably not heating well enough to melt the plastic resin in the toner.

**Vertical white streaks.** These can indicate dirty corona wires. Clean the wires if possible.

**Gray mist.** If the whole page looks as if it has been airbrush-painted with a fine mist of toner, the corona wires probably need to be cleaned. It could also be the result of the print density control's being turned up too high, or the drum's not holding a strong enough charge.

**Horizontal black lines.** These usually result from a dirty or damaged roller. You can measure the distance between the black lines to determine which roller is the problem, but the rollers on different models are different sizes so you must consult the printer manufacturer for help.

**Regularly spaced splotches.** Splotches typically indicate a scratched or dirty drum.

**All-white page.** The transfer corona may be broken, or the printer is out of toner.

**All-black page.** The primary corona may be broken. If the drum is not charged enough, the toner will jump off indiscriminately onto the drum, resulting in a full page of toner.

## Inkjet Quality Problems

Quality problems with inkjets are usually the result of empty or dried-up ink cartridges or clogged print heads. This could manifest itself as total lack of one color, as odd discolorations, or as colored stripes on the printout.

If the printer has a self-test, run it and see which color(s) are missing, either entirely or in spots. Then check the ink to make sure there is plenty of ink of that color in the printer.

If lack of ink is not the problem, try running the head-cleaning utility, and then run the self-test again. If you see a little improvement after the cleaning, clean again. Keep cleaning until you see no more improvement or until print quality is acceptable.

### Dot-Matrix Quality Problems

If the quality on a dot-matrix printer starts to suffer, here are some suggestions:

- **Flecks and smudges:** The ribbon is probably too tight. Look in the printer's manual to find out how to loosen it.
- **Faint printing overall:** The ribbon needs to be replaced.
- **Faint printing on one side of the page:** The platen is misaligned.
- **Missing sections of letters:** One or more of the pins on the head may be damaged.

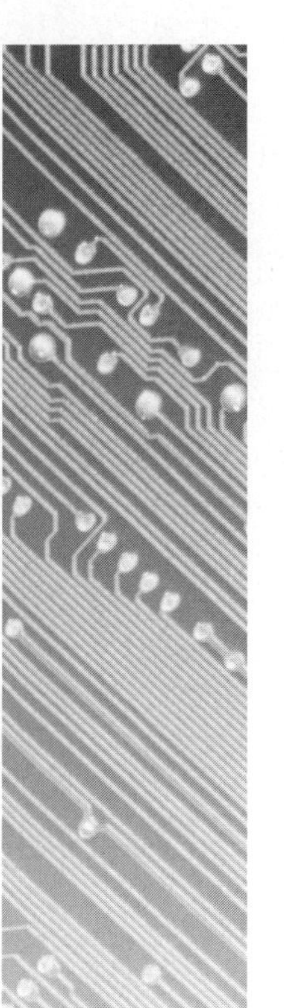

## STUDY GUIDE

Use the following summaries to review the key concepts of this chapter.

### Basic Printing Functions

All printers perform the same basic functions. These include:

- Receiving data from the PC
- Storing data in RAM
- Converting the data into print instructions
- Feeding the paper in and out
- Storing and dispensing the ink or toner
- Transferring the image to the paper

### Measures of Printer Performance

- When figuring the cost of a printer, calculate the total cost of ownership including selling price, paper, ink/toner, and maintenance.
- Print quality is measured in dots per inch (dpi). An average dpi for a laser printer is 600 x 600; for an inkjet it is 1440 x 720.
- A line printer prints one line at a time. It requires less memory than a page printer.
- A page printer forms the entire page in memory and then transfers it to paper all at once.
- Color quality and accuracy are printer performance issues but are not easily quantifiable.
- The printer's speed depends on the power of its internal processor (print engine) and on the physical limits of the mechanical parts.

- Printer speed is measured on most of today's printers in pages per minute (ppm). On older impact-style printers it is measured in characters per second (cps).
- Printers may also be evaluated according to their features. You might expect to pay more for a large paper tray, a variety of interfaces, network connectivity, and/or PostScript compatibility, for example.

## Daisywheel Printers

- A daisywheel printer is an obsolete technology. It is much like an automated typewriter. You may occasionally encounter one in your work as a PC technician.
- The daisywheel is a hub with spikes radiating from the center. On each spike is a letter. The wheel rotates to place the desired letter at the top and then a hammer hits it into an inked ribbon (impact printing).
- Daisywheel printers typically use continuous-feed paper with perforated strips of holes along the sides.
- Daisywheel printers are slow and very noisy, and the font can be changed only by changing the wheel.

## Dot-Matrix Printers

- A dot-matrix printer uses tiny metal pins that can change their arrangement on-the-fly to form each character rather than relying on a fixed picture of each letter or number.
- The metal pins strike an inked ribbon with paper behind it (impact printing). Behind the paper is a rigid platen, a hard rubber cylinder that absorbs the impact and keeps the paper in place.
- A 9-pin dot-matrix printer is an older model. Its output is called near letter quality (NLQ).
- A 24-pin dot-matrix printer is a newer model. Its output is called letter quality (LQ).
- Dot-matrix printers typically use continuous-feed paper with perforated strips of holes along the sides.

## Inkjet Printers

- Inkjet printers squirt ink onto paper through tiny nozzles. The print heads do not touch the paper; it is nonimpact printing.
- There are two technologies: thermal and piezoelectric.

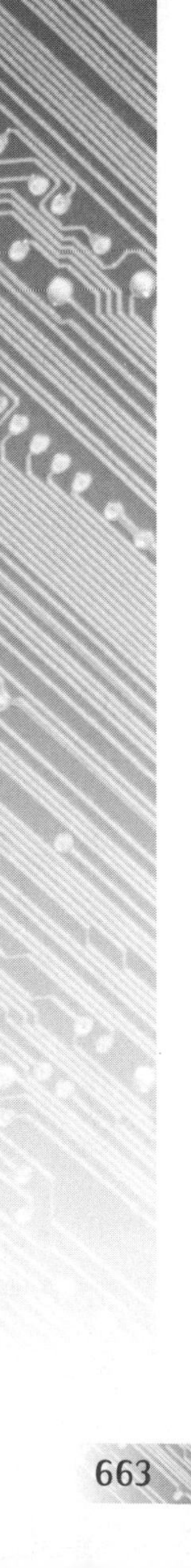

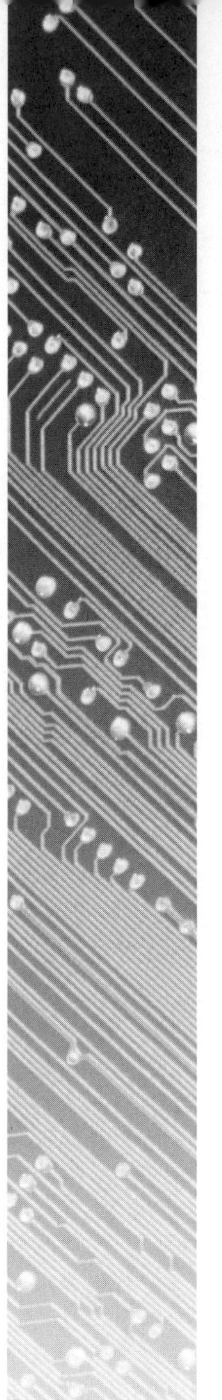

- Thermal inkjet heats the ink to about 400 degrees Fahrenheit (204 degrees Celsius), creating vapor bubbles that force out the ink.
- Piezoelectric inkjet moves ink with electricity instead of heat.
- Inkjet printers are line printers that produce one line at a time, so they do not need much RAM.
- Inkjet printers are sheet-fed, feeding a single sheet of paper at a time out of a paper tray.

## Laser Printers

- A laser printer works much like a photocopier.
- It contains a large cylinder known as a drum. The drum is charged with a high negative electrical charge. The printer directs a laser beam to partially neutralize the charge in certain areas.
- When the drum rotates past the toner, the toner clings to the areas of lesser charge. Then the drum rotates past positively charged paper, and the toner jumps off onto the paper.
- The paper then passes through a fuser that melts the plastic particles of the toner so that it sticks to the paper.
- There are six steps in creating a laser-printed page: cleaning, charging, writing, developing, transferring, and fusing. You need to know these, in that order, for the A+ exam.
- During the charging phase, the primary corona wire applies a uniform negative charge of -600v to the drum's surface.
- The number of times the laser can be turned on/off per inch is the printer's maximum dpi.
- During the transferring phase, the transfer corona wire applies a +600v positive charge to the paper to attract the toner on the drum to it.
- An LED page printer is like a laser but it uses light-emitting diodes (LEDs) instead of a laser.

## Printer Interfaces

- Parallel is the most common printer interface. The standard governing parallel printer ports is IEEE 1284.
- You set the parallel port mode in BIOS Setup. The modes typically available are:
  - SPP (Standard Parallel Port): 8-bit output at 150Kbps and 4-bit input at 50Kbps.
  - Bidirectional: 8-bit input and output at 150Kbps.
  - EPP (Enhanced Parallel Port): 8-bit I/O at 2Mbps.

- ECP (Enhanced Capabilities Port): Same as EPP, but designed primarily for printers and scanners. Requires a DMA channel.

- The legacy serial port on a PC was at one time a popular way of connecting a printer, but is obsolete for that usage today. Connection requires a 25-pin serial port on the PC.
- USB is a popular way of connecting printers today. Refer to Chapter 7 for details about USB.
- A printer with its own network interface can exist directly on the network without having to be shared by any specific PC.
- Infrared was at one point a promising new technology for printer connectivity, but is rarely used today.

## Printer Drivers

- A printer driver translates instructions from the PC into a language the printer will understand.
- The language that a driver speaks is a page description language (PDL).
- Emulation allows different printer brands and models to work with the same driver.
- One of the most popular, widely emulated PDLs for laser printers is Hewlett-Packard's Printer Control Language (PCL).
- PostScript is a high-end PDL used in professional desktop publishing.
- Microsoft Windows makes printer driver management easy because a single driver can be shared by all Windows applications.
- To install a printer driver in Windows, open the *Printers* folder from the Control Panel and double-click *Add Printer*.
- To remove a printer driver, select its icon and press Delete.
- To change a printer's properties, right-click its icon and choose Properties.

## Fonts and Typefaces

- A typeface is a style of lettering. Examples include Arial and Courier.
- The term "font" used to refer to a specific typeface at a specific size, but since most fonts are scalable to any size within Windows, "font" has become synonymous with "typeface."
- A bitmap font stores each character at each size as a graphic.
- An outline font stores an outline of each character which it resizes as needed. PostScript and TrueType fonts are outline fonts.
- A vector font is a scalable font created with math equations, designed for use with plotters.

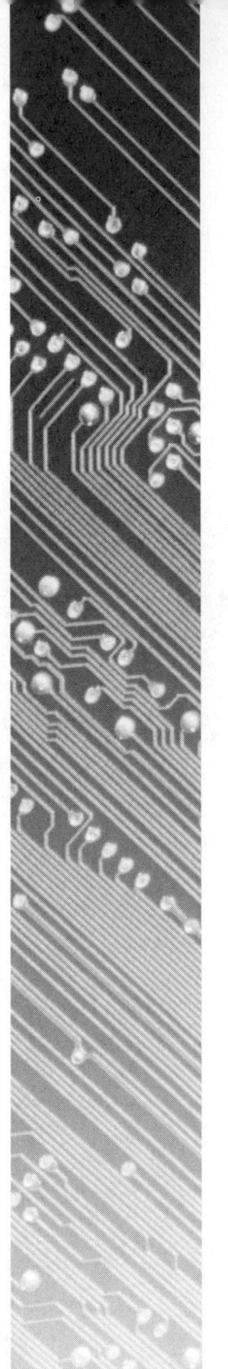

- A serif font has little tails on the letters; a sans-serif font does not.
- To view fonts in Windows, open the *Fonts* folder from the Control Panel. Double-click a font to see a preview of it.
- To install new fonts, from the *Fonts* folder choose File/Install New Font.

## Laser Printer Maintenance

- To clean loose toner on the inside of a laser printer, wipe it with a soft cloth.
- Do not use a regular vacuum cleaner. If you must vacuum, use a special low-static or nonstatic vacuum designed for computer cleaning.
- Some printers have specific internal cleaning routines or features; follow the instructions in the printer's manual.
- Some print quality problems are caused by dirty corona wires. If the printer has corona wires that you can access, clean them with an alcohol-dipped cotton swab.
- Some printers have an adjustment knob controlling the amount of toner dispensed. Turn it up higher as the drum ages.
- You can sometimes get a few extra pages out of an old toner cartridge by shaking it from side to side to redistribute the remaining toner.
- Some laser printers have a felt cleaning pad. If one comes with the new toner cartridge, find the old one and switch them.
- Some printers have a drum unit that is separate from the toner cartridge. Check the manual to see when to replace it.

## Inkjet Printer Maintenance

- When a printer is running out of a certain color of ink, that color may be entirely missing from the printout, or there may be stripes on the printout.
- If there are stripes but the ink level appears to be okay, try cleaning the inkjets with the printer's self-cleaning utility.
- The procedure for changing an inkjet ink cartridge varies depending on the printer model; follow the instructions in the manual.
- Most ink cartridges come in a metallic bag, and most have a plastic seal that you must peel off before installing them.
- Inkjet printers must have their jets cleaned periodically to remove any dried-up ink that may be clogging them. This is done through the printer's own cleaning utility.
- You can activate the cleaning utility from the Windows driver or by pressing a certain sequence of buttons on the printer itself.

## Managing a Print Queue

- Each printer driver has its own print queue. To view it, double-click the printer icon in the *Printers* folder.
- To pause or clear the entire queue, open the Printer menu and choose Pause Printing or Cancel All Documents.
- To pause or delete an individual print job, open the Document menu and choose Pause or Delete. To resume a paused job, choose Document, Resume.
- You can disable the entire print queue from the Advanced tab in the printer driver's Properties dialog box.

## Troubleshooting Printer Problems

- Check a printer's queue if it is not outputting; perhaps one of the jobs has an error. You can delete the error-causing job by clicking it and pressing Delete.
- A printout may occasionally display junk characters for no apparent reason. If this happens frequently, try reinstalling the printer driver.
- High humidity and extra-heavy or extra-light paper can cause paper jams.
- Fan paper before putting it in the paper tray to help minimize jams.
- Some printers have a thickness adjustment that can help reduce jamming.

## Laser Quality Problems

- If the printout is faint in spots, check the toner level. The drum may also be wearing out or the transfer corona might be dirty.
- Loose or smeared toner can mean the fuser is malfunctioning.
- Vertical white streaks indicate a dirty corona wire.
- A gray mist indicates dirty corona wires, the print density (darkness) set too high, or the drum wearing out.
- Horizontal black lines indicate dirty or damaged rollers.
- Regularly spaced blotches indicate a scratched or dirty drum.
- An all-white page comes from a broken corona wire or an empty toner cartridge.
- An all-black page is caused by a broken primary corona wire.

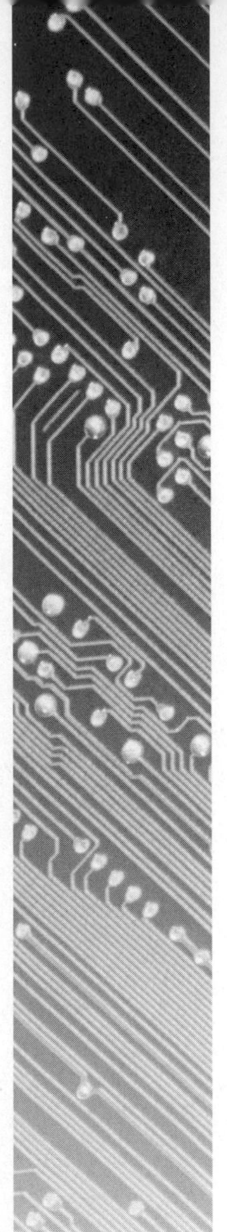

### Inkjet Quality Problems

- Inkjet quality problems are usually caused by empty or dried-up ink cartridges or clogged print heads.
- Run the printer's self-test and run its inkjet cleaning utility (multiple times if needed).

### Dot-Matrix Quality Problems

- Flecks and smudges mean the ribbon is too tight.
- Faint printing overall means the ribbon needs replacing.
- Faint printing on one side means the platen is misaligned.
- Missing sections of letters indicates that one or more pins on the head may be damaged.

## PRACTICE TEST

On a blank sheet of paper, write the answers to the following multiple-choice questions and explain why each answer is correct.

1. Which type of printer must have the greatest amount of RAM?
   a. page printer
   b. line printer
   c. impact printer
   d. nonimpact printer

2. Which of the following is *not* true about tractor-fed printers?
   a. They use continuous-feed paper.
   b. They have no paper tray for precut sheets.
   c. They will not print on precut sheets.
   d. They are usually impact printers.

3. Which type of colored material does a laser printer use to produce the image on the paper?
   a. powdered toner
   b. liquid ink
   c. colored wax
   d. inked ribbon

4. What is dpi a measurement of?
   a. the maximum theoretical print speed
   b. the actual average print speed
   c. the color quality
   d. the print resolution

5. If you see a printer's resolution expressed with two numbers such as 1440 x 720, what type of printer can you assume it to be?
   a. PostScript
   b. laser
   c. inkjet
   d. thermal

6. Which type of printer measures its speed in cps?
   a. laser
   b. dot-matrix
   c. inkjet
   d. both dot-matrix and inkjet

7. Which of the following would *not* be possible with a daisywheel printer?
   a. printing multipart forms with carbon paper between each part
   b. printing invoices on continuous-feed paper
   c. printing mailing labels for shipping
   d. printing a customer newsletter that includes graphics

8. Which of the following would *not* be possible with a dot-matrix printer?
   a. printing multipart forms with carbon paper between each part
   b. printing a document that uses multiple sizes of fonts
   c. printing a high-quality color photo
   d. All of these are possible with a dot-matrix printer.

9. What is NLQ?
   a. the best output quality from a 24-pin dot-matrix printer
   b. the best output quality from a 9-pin dot-matrix printer
   c. the output quality from a daisywheel printer
   d. the output quality from a laser printer

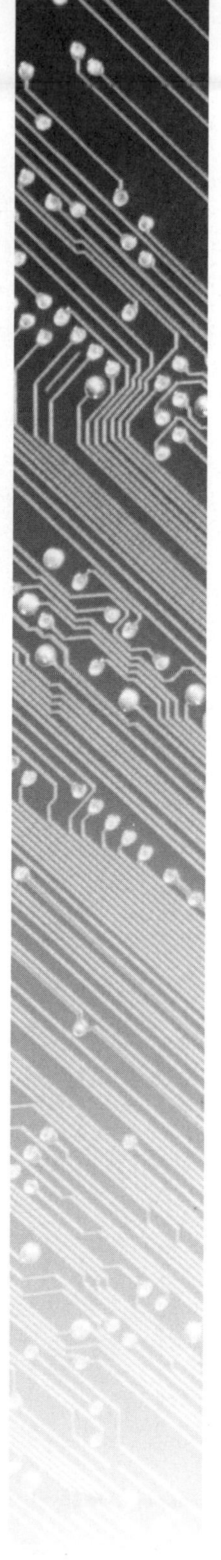

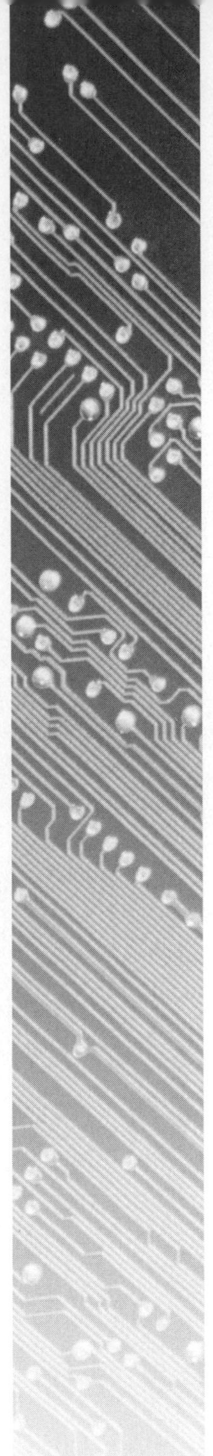

10. Which of the following would *not* be possible with an inkjet printer?
    a. printing on multipart forms with carbon paper between each part
    b. printing a color photo
    c. printing a document that uses multiple sizes of fonts
    d. All of these are possible with an inkjet printer.

11. What are the four colors of ink used in a color inkjet printer?
    a. black, red, blue, and green
    b. black, red, blue, and yellow
    c. black, cyan, magenta, and yellow
    d. black, cyan, red, and blue

12. Which type of inkjet printer contains a heating element?
    a. bubble jet
    b. piezoelectric
    c. Both
    d. Neither

13. The large cylinder inside a laser printer is the
    a. fuser.
    b. primary roller.
    c. transfer corona.
    d. drum.

14. What type of charge does the primary corona apply?
    a. positive charge to the paper
    b. positive charge to the drum
    c. negative charge to the paper
    d. negative charge to the drum

15. Which is the correct order for the laser printing process?
    a. charging, writing, transferring, developing, fusing, cleaning
    b. charging, cleaning, transferring, writing, developing, fusing
    c. cleaning, charging, writing, developing, transferring, fusing
    d. cleaning, writing, transferring, developing, charging, fusing

16. Which of these parallel port modes requires a DMA channel?
    a. SPP
    b. Bidirectional
    c. EPP
    d. ECP

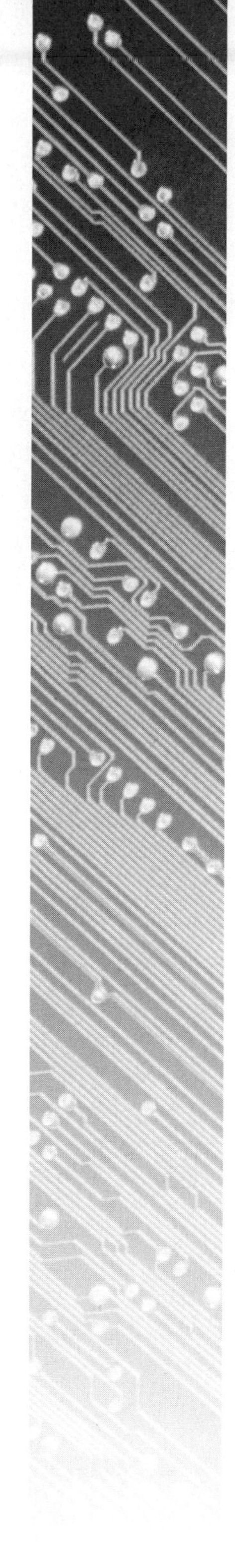

17. What is PDL?
    a. It is a generic term referring to the language that the printer driver speaks to the printer.
    b. It is a specific language developed by Hewlett-Packard for communicating with laser printers.
    c. It is a communication protocol used for parallel and serial ports that have a printer connected to them.
    d. It is an IEEE 1284 standard for parallel ports.
18. Which applet in the Control Panel do you open to add a new printer?
    a. Add/Remove Hardware
    b. Add/Remove Programs
    c. Printers
    d. System
19. Which of these is *not* applicable to a TrueType font?
    a. scalable
    b. outline
    c. soft
    d. printer-resident
20. Which is the command to delete an individual print job from the print queue?
    a. Printer, Clear
    b. Document, Cancel
    c. Document, Clear
    d. File, Delete

# TROUBLESHOOTING

1. A client has an old, off-brand laser printer that he wants to use in Windows XP, but Windows XP does not have a driver for it. He has a manual for the printer that states that it has PCL 5 emulation. How might you get it to work?
2. One of the users you support accidentally tilted and shook a toner cartridge while removing it from her printer, and now the inside of the printer is covered with toner. How would you go about cleaning it up?
3. A client has an inkjet printer that seemed to be working well until he installed a parallel port scanner on the same port, with a pass-through to the printer. Now neither one works. How would you troubleshoot this?

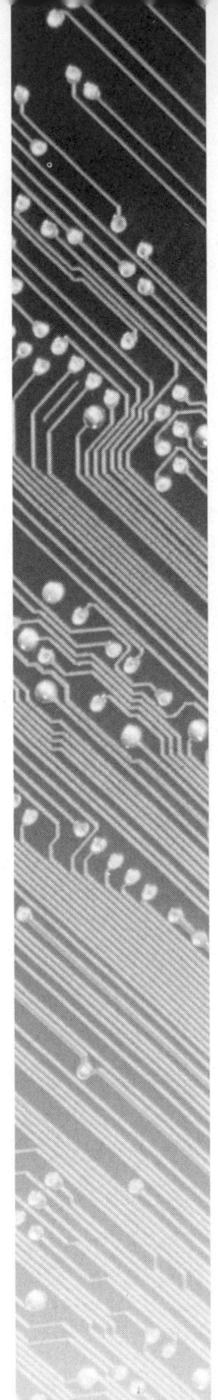

## CUSTOMER SERVICE

1. A client wants your advice on selecting a color printer. He is looking at two models: a $1,000 color laser printer and a $400 inkjet printer. What factors would you point out to him when helping him decide?
2. A client cleaning out an old office supply cabinet finds a 72-in-1 font cartridge for a LaserJet II printer. She wants to know whether it is worth keeping. What is your opinion, and why?
3. A client has bought a CD-ROM with 1,000 different fonts on it, and has installed all of them in Windows. Now he is upset because Windows takes longer to load and he has to scroll down through dozens of pages of fonts in the Font drop-down list in his word processor. How would you go about helping him get rid of some of them?

## FOR MORE INFORMATION

For links to Web sites that provide further information about the topics covered in this chapter, go to the EMC/Paradigm Internet Resource Center at www.emcp.com/College Division/Internet Resource Centers/PC Maintenance/For More Information.

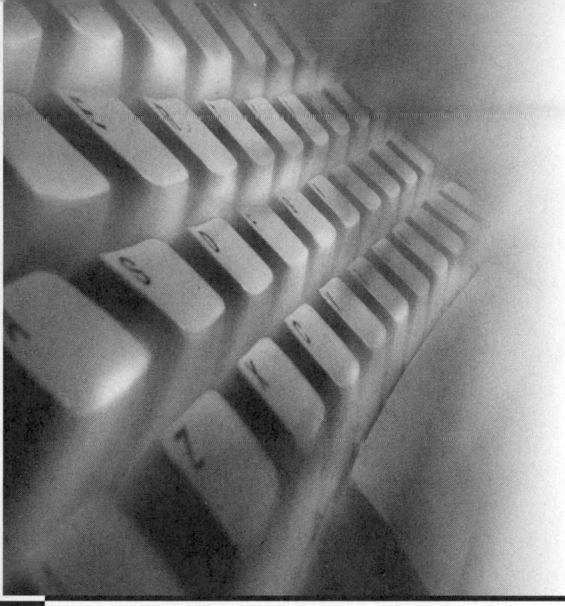

# 19 Imaging and Sound Devices

## ON THE TEST

**A+ Core Hardware Service Technician Examination**

- **Objective 1.2:** Identify basic procedures for adding and removing field replaceable modules for both desktop and portable systems.

## ON THE JOB

Ten years ago, imaging and sound devices were found only on high-end PCs owned by music enthusiasts and graphic arts professionals. Today, however, the prices are so low that anyone can enjoy them, and most home and office PCs include them. As a PC technician you will often be called upon to recommend models for purchase, to set up new devices, and to troubleshoot problems with them.

Some real-life activities that pertain to this chapter include:

- choosing among different models of scanners to buy
- troubleshooting problems with scanners
- selecting a digital camera
- transferring images from a camera to a PC
- selecting a sound card for a game enthusiast
- selecting a sound card for a musician
- troubleshooting sound problems on end user PCs
- setting up sound options for people with disabilities

# Scanners

**Digitize**

To convert to digital (number-based) format, such as converting a picture to a binary file on a computer.

A scanner *digitizes* a hard-copy page, converting it into a graphic file on the PC. Scanners can be black-and-white or color (although most are color these days), and can use any of several technologies. Scanners work primarily with flat paper items; if you need to digitize three-dimensional items, use a digital camera instead.

Although the A+ examination does not include detailed questions about the inner workings of scanners, this chapter discusses scanner technology because it may be helpful in your work as a PC technician; for example, you may need to evaluate various scanner models for purchase.

## Scanner Technology

For this discussion let us assume we are talking about a flatbed scanner—the kind that looks like a small photocopier. You place the original on the glass and close the lid, and then either press a button on the scanner or issue a command in an application that starts the scan. There are specialty types, such as handheld or 35mm slide, but flatbed is the overwhelming favorite.

**Charge-coupled device (CCD)**

A grid of photosensitive cells that records light levels and converts it to electrical charge, which is then processed as data by a computer.

Inside the scanner is a fixed linear array called a *charge-coupled device* (CCD). It is composed of an array of photosensitive cells, similar to the eye of an insect, that converts light to electrical charge. A light bar moves across the object being scanned, and a system of mirrors reflects the light to a lens, and then into the CCD. Some scanners have two mirrors; others have three. The mirrors are slightly curved, to compact the image as it reflects (see Figure 19.1).

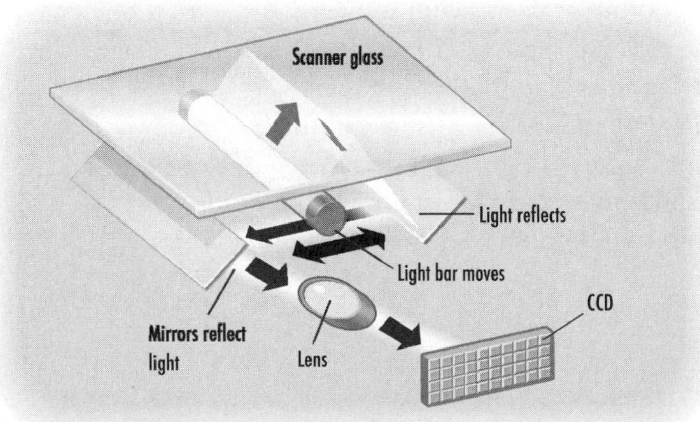


**FIGURE 19.1**
How a Typical Scanner Digitizes a Picture

Each of the photosensitive cells produces an electrical signal proportional to the strength of the reflected light that hits it, and that signal is converted to a binary number and sent to the computer. Dark areas have lower numbers; light ones have higher (this is for a black-and-white scanner; we will talk about color scanners shortly).

The CCD receives data for one line of the image at a time, sends it on to the computer, and then tells the stepper motor to advance the lamp to the next line. The CCD does not have to have a number of cells equivalent to the number of pixels in the entire page—only the number of pixels in a single row. On a scanner that can accept an 8.5-inch sheet, at 300 dots per inch (dpi), that is about 2,600 cells. Scanners with a higher dpi have more CCD cells—for example, about 10,400 in a 1,200dpi model. This is the scanner's horizontal dpi or horizontal resolution (also called the *x*-direction sampling rate).

Many scanners also report a vertical dpi or vertical resolution in their specifications (also called *y*-direction sampling rate). This is the number of separate lines per inch that are recorded as the light moves down the page. It is technologically easier for a scanner manufacturer to make a light that moves in more precise increments than it is to include a CCD with more cells, so you will often see scanners advertised with a lower horizontal than vertical resolution, such as 600 x 1200dpi. When you see two numbers like that, the first one is always the horizontal.

**Interpolation**

A method of creating extra bits of data between two ordinary bits by averaging them. Useful for increasing the resolution of pictures, for example.

Some scanners' specifications report very high resolutions, such as 4800 x 4800. When you see a high resolution, you should be skeptical. The reported resolution is probably not the hardware resolution but the resolution of the scanner itself. The numbers probably refer to a software-enhanced resolution. One method of software enhancement is called *interpolation*. Interpolation invents extra pixels between the actual scanned ones, and uses a mathematical formula to determine their value (see Figure 19.2). For example, if one pixel has a value of 10 and the next one is 20, interpolation would insert a pixel between them with the value of 15. (Regular base 10 numbers are used here for the sake of discussion, but in a real scanning situation the numbers would be binary values.)

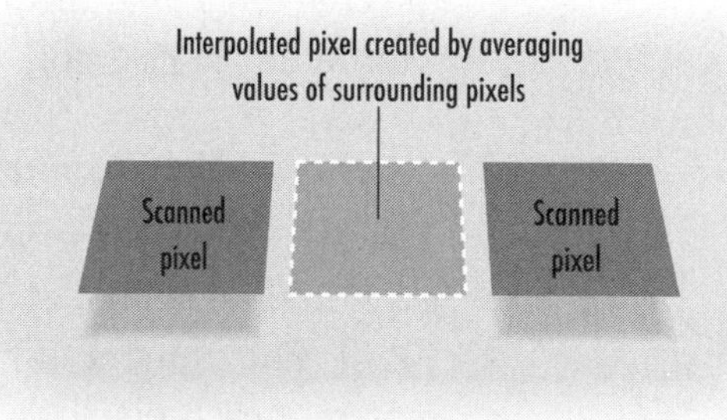


**FIGURE 19.2**
Interpolation produces higher resolution images from a scanner than it is physically capable of producing.

Some inexpensive scanners do not have a CCD and mirror/lamp/lens system, but instead a *contact image sensor* (CIS) consisting of rows of red, green, and blue LEDs. The image sensor mechanism, consisting of 300 to 600 sensors spanning the width of the scan area, sits very close to the glass.

**Contact image sensor (CIS)**

A low-end scanner technology that uses rows of LEDs to illuminate the image and capture the light reflecting from it.

When the image is scanned, the LEDs combine to provide white light and the illuminated image is then captured by the row of sensors. CIS scanners are less expensive, lighter, and thinner, but do not provide the same level of quality and resolution found in most CCD scanners.

### *Color Scanners*

In black-and-white or grayscale scanners, a single light bar and mirror system transmits grayscale data to the CCD. In a color scanner, however, there must be three separate evaluations of each pixel in the image: amount of red, amount of blue, and amount of green. There are several methods of gathering this data during the scanning process.

Early color scanners made three passes across the image, gathering the color data separately. This worked well with the limited technology available, but was very slow. A slightly newer method is to use three different colored lights, all moving down the page together. Each light has its own mirror system, or a single mirror system has three filters so that it can separately accept each color's data.

**Registration**

The precision with which colors align on a scanner or a printout to produce a true image.

On any system that gathers data for each color separately, there is the potential for misalignment. The accuracy of a scanner's color alignment is known as *registration*. When evaluating a used scanner, it is a good idea to scan a complex color image and check the results for registration problems.

The most modern method employs three separate CCDs (or a single CCD with three stripes), each one collecting data about a single color. This is the most common method in scanners sold today. Among scanners that have separate CCD areas for each color, there is one further differentiation. Some use a beam splitter, in which the single image coming from the mirror is split into the three colors, each of which is read by a different CCD. Others coat each CCD with a film so that it can read only one of the colors from an unsplit beam. Beam splitting often produces a better scan result, but is more expensive.

### *Understanding Scanner Color Depth*

The original scanners were 1-bit. They were black-and-white only (no grayscale, no color), and transmitted a single bit of data for each cell in the CCD. The number of bits is the number of binary digits required to represent each pixel's value. In a 1-bit system, each pixel is either 0 or 1: off or on. Then came 4-bit scanners (16 unique values), and then 8-bit (256).

## In Real Life

> To determine the number of unique values in a certain number of bits, take 2 to the nth power where n is the number of bits. For example, 4-bit is 24, or 16, and 8-bit is 28, or 256. This works for the color depth in display modes as well as in scanning.

Today, all scanners support at least 24-bit scanning. This is known as "true color," and it uses a 24-digit binary code to represent each pixel. That amount of color depth provides 16.7 million colors to choose from, which is more than the human eye can detect, so in theory 24-bit color depth is the most you would ever need in a scanner. However, many scanners today advertise 36-bit support or more, even though the best that most monitors can display (and most printers can print) is 24-bit.

The reason for the 36-bit support is that a 24-bit scanner offers an 8-bit range (256 levels) for each primary color (8 + 8 + 8 = 24), but a few of the least significant bits are lost in noise, and any postscanning tonal corrections reduce the range still further. Therefore, you want the scanner driver to make any brightness and color corrections before making the final scan. If the scanner starts with a 36-bit depth, it has a wider range to begin with, so it can make tonal corrections and still end up with 24 bits at the end. Using the scanner driver through the OS, you can control which 24 of those 36 bits are kept and which ones are discarded by changing the Gamma Curve setting.

### *Scanner Light Types*

When desktop scanners were first introduced, many manufacturers used fluorescent bulbs as light sources. However, fluorescent bulbs cannot emit consistent white light, and they produce heat that can distort the other optical components. Therefore, most manufacturers moved to cold-cathode bulbs as soon as was practical. Cold-cathode bulbs resemble fluorescent bulbs, but they have no filament and thus they operate at much lower temperatures and are more reliable. Most scanner manufacturers have recently switched to xenon bulbs, which produce a stable, full-spectrum light source, although they use slightly more power than do the fluorescent and cold-cathode bulbs.

### *Dynamic Range*

**Dynamic range**

The ability of a scanner to distinguish between light and dark.

A specification related to color depth is *dynamic range*. Not all scanners advertise their dynamic range, but if you can find that data, it can be extremely helpful in comparing scanners without actually seeing their output.

Dynamic range is a measure of the scanner's ability to distinguish between light and dark. The scale runs from 0 to 4, and most inexpensive desktop scanners rate about 2.4. Higher end scanners might have a rating of 2.8 to 3.2. More expensive professional quality scanners can approach 3.8 in their dynamic range.

### *Scanning Speed*

Speed refers to the amount of time the scanner takes to scan. This is a difficult factor to evaluate, because the actual speed varies so much depending on what you are scanning (full page versus smaller item), at what resolution you are scanning (150dpi, 300dpi, etc.), whether you are scanning in grayscale or color (most color scanners can do either), and whether you are using Optical Character Recognition (OCR) software to import scanned text.

An extremely fast speed rating, such as 9 to 20 seconds, probably refers to the raw capability of the scanning head to move from the top to the bottom of the glass at its top speed. It is a quick way to compare one scanner to another in terms of hardware, but does not take into account many factors that will affect the actual mileage, such as the scanner software, the PC operating system, and the image size and resolution.

A slower speed rating, such as 45 to 60 seconds, probably refers to the time for a typical scan. This number is not very meaningful, however, unless the specification also tells the exact resolution and image size. For example, a scanner might take 60 seconds to scan a 4 x 6-inch color photo or a full-page black-and-white drawing, 90 seconds to scan an OCR page of text into a word processor, and 150 seconds to scan an 8.5 x 11-inch color photo.

### *Scanner Interface*

Speed is also affected by the interface with which the scanner connects to the computer. In the past, most low-end scanners used a parallel interface (IEEE 1284). Since most PCs have only one parallel port, parallel scanners typically come with some sort of pass-through that allows the scanner and printer to share a single parallel port. However, parallel pass-throughs do not always work very well. In particular, inkjet printers seem to have difficulty sharing a parallel port. You can sometimes make system-setting adjustments in BIOS to work out a compromise between the two devices, as discussed in Chapter 18, or you can unhook the scanner and hook up the printer every time you want to print, but this sharing is less than an ideal arrangement. Parallel is also the slowest scanning interface, resulting in overall slower performance for the scanner than other interfaces.

Most high-end scanners, in contrast, have traditionally used a SCSI interface. Since most computers do not already have a SCSI interface, it is an extra expense to add a SCSI card (see Chapter 11). SCSI has many advantages, such as high speed and the ability to chain several devices in sequence to use a single SCSI port. SCSI scanners are not common in local computer and office supply stores these days, so you will probably need to special-order a SCSI scanner if you need one.

In today's consumer-level scanner market, USB has become the interface of choice. It is fast and it can chain together several devices on a single port, like SCSI, and most computers already have a USB port, as they have a parallel port.

### *Choosing a Scanner*

Figure 19.3 summarizes the major factors that determine a scanner's quality.

- **CCD versus CIS:** CCD is the traditional scanning technology, and produces better results; CIS is cheaper and lighter, but limited to 300 to 600dpi.
- **Resolution:** The higher the hardware resolution, the costlier the scanner. Do not confuse hardware resolution with software-enhanced resolution achieved via interpolation. If there are two numbers advertised, the first one is the horizontal resolution, and it is the more important measure of scanner quality.
- **Light type:** If power consumption is not a critical issue, choose a scanner with xenon bulb(s), for more consistent light and less heat build-up.
- **Color depth:** 24-bit is sufficient for casual use, but you are unlikely to find a scanner that is less than 30-bit these days. Therefore, color depth is not an important factor unless you are buying a high-end model for professional graphics use. In that case, look for 36-bit models.
- **Dynamic range:** This is the scanner's ability to recognize light and dark, and is a fairly good measurement of the overall quality of the scanner. For casual use a rating of 2.4 is acceptable; for the highest quality professional scans look for a rating in the high 3s.
- **Speed:** There are many ways of reporting a scanner's speed. Make sure you are comparing apples to apples when comparing the speeds of two or more scanners. The most accurate way to compare is raw capability–the amount of time needed for the scan head to move from top to bottom. If comparing average scan times, make sure the type and size of image being scanned are the same in each rating.
- **Interface:** For commercial and professional use, SCSI is still preferred, but USB is a less expensive and viable alternative for personal or small office use. Avoid parallel interface when possible because of speed and sharing issues.

**FIGURE 19.3**
Scanner Feature Comparisons

## TRY IT!

Using the Internet, research the current offerings from several scanner manufacturers. See "For More Information" for this chapter on the Internet Resource Center for Web site addresses. Make notes about various model numbers, their resolutions, their scanning speeds, their color depths, their interfaces, and other facts.

## INSTALLING A SCANNER

Installing a scanner is usually very straightforward because a scanner is an external device. To install a scanner, complete the following steps:

1. Unpack the new scanner and remove any tape seals that held it during shipping.
2. Check the scanner's manual to find out whether the scanner has a locking mechanism for transport. This locking switch prevents the light bar from moving around, and the scanner will not be able to operate if it is left in locked position. Find it and unlock it. Figure 19.4 shows a locking switch at the bottom of a scanner.

**WARNING**

If you operate a scanner while it is locked, you will hear a grinding sound. That is the scanner's light bar trying to move while it is locked in place. Turn off the scanner (by unplugging it), unlock it, and try again.

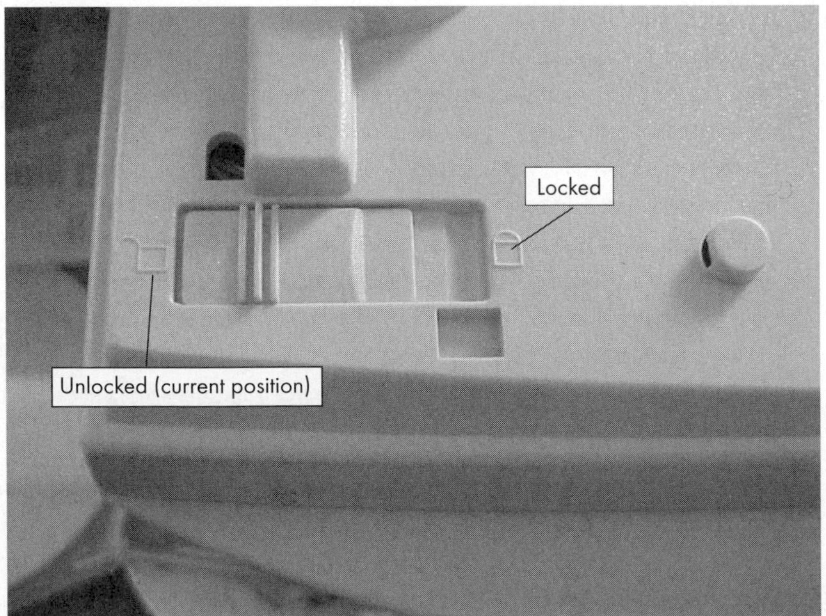


**FIGURE 19.4**
Unlock the scanner before using it.

3. With the PC off, connect the scanner to the PC using whatever interface is appropriate (USB, SCSI, or parallel). If you are installing a parallel scanner, disconnect the parallel printer from the PC (if applicable) and connect the scanner directly to the PC, then connect the printer to the scanner (see Figure 19.5).

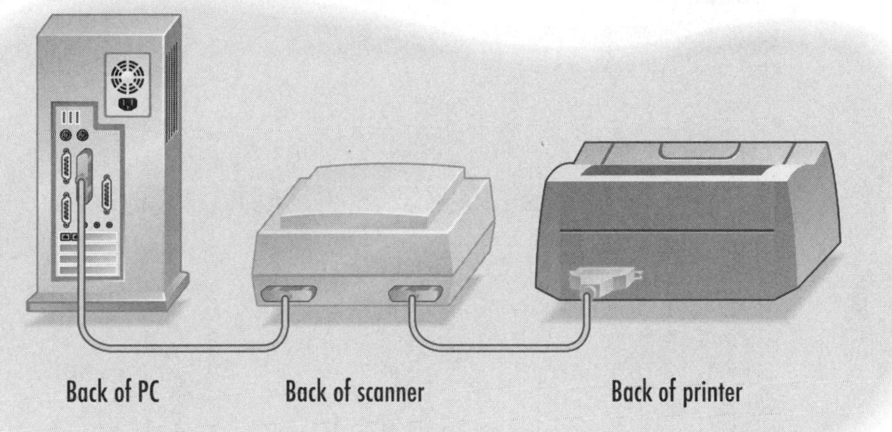


**FIGURE 19.5**
Cabling for a Scanner with a Parallel Pass-Through and a Parallel Printer

4. Connect the scanner's power supply to a wall outlet and to the scanner itself.
5. Turn on the scanner if it has a separate on/off switch. (Most do not; they are on when they are plugged in.)
6. Turn on the PC. Windows may automatically detect the new scanner with Plug and Play. If not, run the setup program that came with the scanner. See the next section for more about how Windows interacts with scanners.

## Windows Versions and Scanners

Windows 95, 98, and 2000 do not include any native support for scanners. To set up a scanner in these Windows versions, you must run the setup program that comes with the scanner. This program installs a driver for the scanner and also installs TWAIN support. TWAIN is a scanner interface standard—a protocol for delivering graphical images—that many applications support, so you can run the scanner from within an application (such as a word processor or desktop publishing program). For example, in Figure 19.6 a TWAIN-based scanner is being called from within a graphics program.

## In Real Life

TWAIN is not an acronym. It comes from the Kipling phrase "and never the twain shall meet." It is sometimes disparagingly said to stand for "Technology Without an Interesting Name."

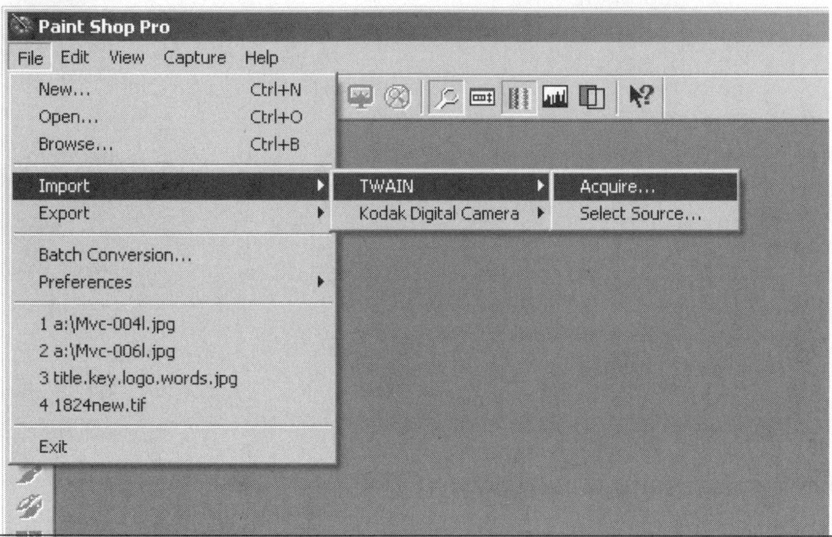


**FIGURE 19.6**
TWAIN compatibility ensures that a scanner installed in Windows will work with a variety of Windows-based applications.

Windows Me and XP include built-in support for many popular scanners. (For a list of supported scanners in each Windows version go to the Hardware Compatibility List [HCL] at www.microsoft.com/hcl.) If the scanner is supported, Windows will detect it automatically when you hook it up and will not require any third-party software in order for it to work. The scanner will appear in the Control Panel in the Scanners and Cameras section (see Figure 19.7), and also in Device Manager. Windows XP supports many more scanners than does Windows Me.

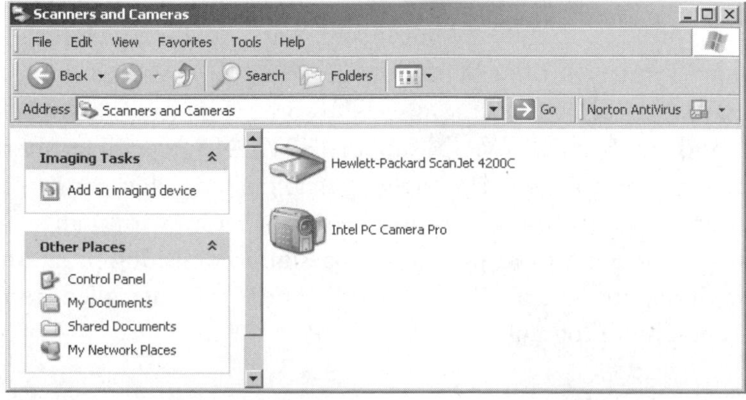


**FIGURE 19.7**
A Supported Scanner in Windows XP

If the scanner is recognized hardware in Windows, the Scanner and Camera Wizard will also work with it as a scanner interface; you do not need to install separate scanning software that came with the scanner. When you activate the scanner through an application, as in Figure 19.6, the Windows interface for the scanner will appear.

With a supported scanner you can also scan using the Scanner and Camera Wizard independently of any application. This is useful because you do not need any applications installed that support scanning; you can scan and save directly to files on the hard drive.

The following steps show how to run the Scanner and Camera Wizard to scan a picture in Windows XP; Windows Me steps are similar.

1. Choose Start/(All) Programs/Accessories/Scanner and Camera Wizard.
2. If you have more than one scanner and/or camera, a box appears in which you select the one to work with; click OK after making your selection.
3. Click Next.
4. Place the image to be scanned on the scanner glass and then click the Preview button. A preview of the image appears (see Figure 19.8).
5. Click the type of saved image you want: Color, Grayscale picture, or Custom. If you choose Custom, click the Custom settings button to define the settings.

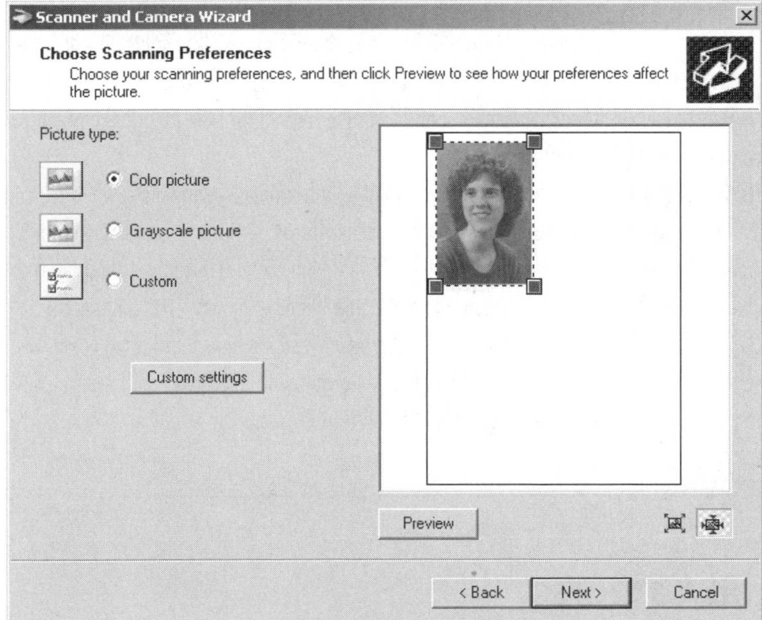


**FIGURE 19.8** Scanning with the Scanner and Camera Wizard in Windows XP

6. Click Next.

7. Type a name for the scan, choose a file type, and select a location to save in (just fill in the boxes provided for that information). Then click Next.
8. Wait for the picture to be scanned and saved.
9. Click Next and then click Finish. The scanned picture appears in a preview window. You can work with it the same as any other graphic in Windows (a topic covered later in this chapter).

**TRY IT!**

1. Connect a scanner to your PC using the interface applicable to the scanner you will use.
2. Turn on the PC and see whether Windows detects the scanner.
3. If it does not, run the setup software that came with the scanner.
4. Scan a picture using the scanner and save it to your hard disk.

### TROUBLESHOOTING SCANNER PROBLEMS

Figure 19.9 lists some things to check if a scanner does not work.

- Is the scanner receiving power? On most scanners there is an LED that lights up when the scanner is plugged in, regardless of its hookup to a PC.
- Is the scanner unlocked? Remember that the scanner cannot function in locked position, which is how it ships from the factory.
- Is the interface to which the scanner is attached fully functional? Many times when Windows cannot see a scanner, it is because the port is disabled. This is particularly common with USB ports; remember that USB works only in Windows 98 and higher and USB support must be enabled in BIOS Setup. Check in Device Manager to make sure Windows knows it has USB ports.
- Is it a parallel scanner sharing a port with a printer? If so, perhaps the sharing is not working out. Try hooking up the scanner without the printer to see if that makes a difference. If it does, try different parallel port settings in BIOS Setup (see Chapter 18).

**FIGURE 19.9**
Scanner Troubleshooting Checklist

## Digital Cameras

A digital camera is like a scanner except that it works "standing up." Rather than scanning a flat, two-dimensional image, it projects its vision out into the 3D world and creates an image based on what it sees.

## How Digital Cameras Work

How does a digital camera compare to a traditional camera? Technologically they are very similar. They both have lenses that "see" the image, and they both have focusing controls for that lens and usually a built-in flash for improving the lighting when needed. The main difference is that a traditional camera's lens sends its data to film, whereas a digital camera sends it data to a data storage cartridge or floppy disk.

The preceding sections explained how scanners work; digital cameras have many of the same internal components as scanners. The camera lens sends its data to a CCD, as in a scanner, which measures the amount of light received in each cell and conveys an electrical charge to the camera's processor in proportion to the amount of light in a particular spot. As with a scanner, a color filter must be applied to the CCD to enable color photography. This data passes through an analog-to-digital converter, which turns those electrical charges into binary computer data.

The data from the CCD passes through a digital signal processor that cleans it up and makes some corrections that improve the image quality, and then the data is stored inside the camera until it can be transferred to a computer. So, a camera differs from a scanner in that it has an internal storage area for pictures. For most cameras it is a flash ROM cartridge (CompactFlash and SmartMedia are the two most popular types), but a few cameras (notably the Sony Mavica) use floppy disks instead of cartridges. Figure 19.10 shows the general process for taking a digital photo.

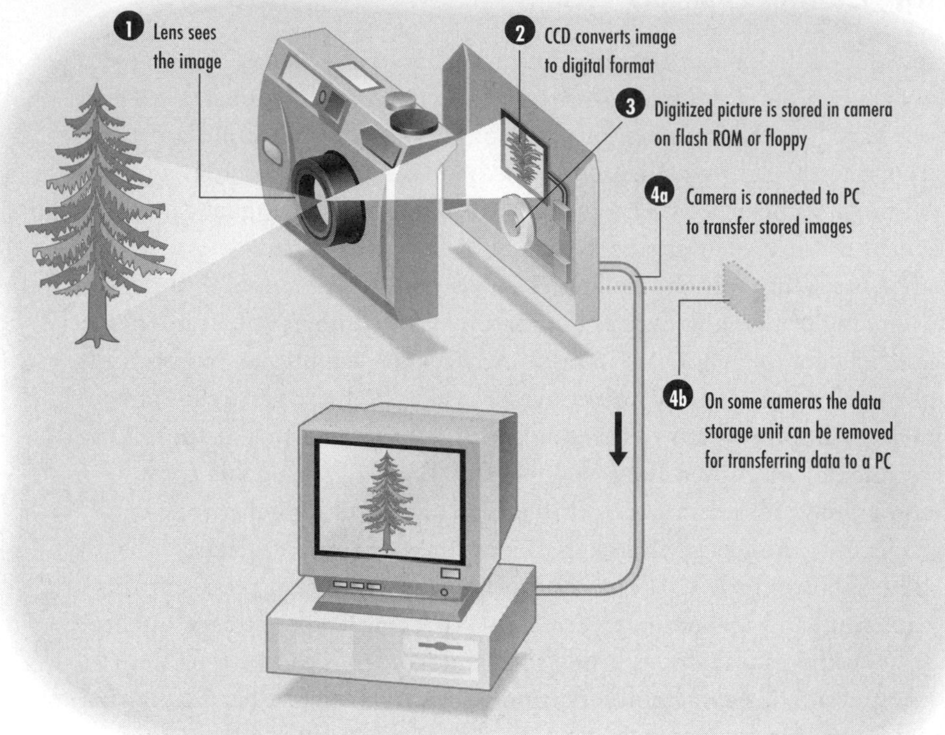
1 Lens sees the image
2 CCD converts image to digital format
3 Digitized picture is stored in camera on flash ROM or floppy
4a Camera is connected to PC to transfer stored images
4b On some cameras the data storage unit can be removed for transferring data to a PC

**FIGURE 19.10**
How a Digital Camera Digitizes a Picture

## Digital Camera Features

The following sections outline some of the features and capabilities that make one digital camera better than another. You will need this information to competently advise end users who are interested in buying a digital camera.

### *Camera Size*

Some of the latest digital cameras are truly pocket models, fitting easily into a shirt pocket. Others are much bigger and bulkier. Generally the larger cameras are more feature-rich and a better choice for professionals while the smaller models are more automatic and convenient for the casual user. Figure 19.11 shows a typical compact model.

**Megapixel**

A million pixels.

**Pixel**

An individual dot in a display or print image.

**FIGURE 19.11**
A Typical Compact Digital Camera Suitable for Everyday Consumer Use

### *Resolution*

Just as with scanner output and monitor display, a digital camera picture has a resolution. Today's digital cameras describe their output in terms of *megapixels*, which means millions of *pixels*. For example, a camera with a maximum resolution of 1280 x 1024 produces about 1.3 million pixels in total, so it might be described as a 1.3 megapixel camera.

Generally speaking, more pixels are better, especially if you plan to print the images in large sizes. Table 19.1 lists some typical photo print sizes and the minimum resolution recommended for quality prints.

**Compression algorithm**

A mathematical formula that makes a file smaller by removing certain bits. These removed bits may be added later when the file is opened in a program that understands the compression algorithm in use, or may be lost forever, depending on the algorithm.

| Print Size | Resolution Recommended |
|---|---|
| 4 x 6 inches | 640 x 480 |
| 5 x 7 inches | 1024 x 768 (less than 1 megapixel) |
| 8 x 10 inches | 1600 x 1200 (2 megapixels) |
| Larger than 8 x 10 inches | 2048 x 1536 or more (3 megapixels) |

**TABLE 19.1**
Digital Camera Picture Resolution for Print Output

The highest resolution is not always appropriate for every photo, however. The higher the resolution, the larger the resulting file size. Large file sizes mean that you need a larger storage area inside the camera for the pictures, and that fewer photos will fit into it. The alternative is to allow the camera to apply a *compression algorithm* to the photos to make them smaller, but this can result in loss of quality that is worse than simply taking the pictures at a lower resolution to begin with.

### *Zoom*

**Optical zoom**

A real zoom lens with adjustable focal length.

**Digital zoom**

A simulated zoom created by interpolation.

A zoom lens does just what it sounds like—it zooms in, magnifying whatever you are photographing. There are two types. An *optical zoom* uses a real multi-focal-length lens. A *digital zoom* does not actually utilize a zoom lens; it just simulates zooming in by interpolating the picture. A digital zoom is not as good because the interpolated pixels are not totally accurate and can cause the image to look fuzzy.

### *Storage Medium*

Very inexpensive digital cameras do not have removable storage; the flash ROM they use to store the pictures is permanently built into the camera. You must always hook up the camera to the PC to transfer the pictures.

Most Sony Mavica cameras use floppy disks to store the images. You can swap floppies quickly, filling up many disks before taking them back to the PC. However, because of the 1.44MB limitation of floppy disks, such cameras are limited in the resolution they can provide.

The vast majority of digital cameras today store the pictures on removable flash ROM cartridges, of which there are two major types: CompactFlash and SmartMedia.

CompactFlash cards come in sizes exceeding 380MB, whereas SmartMedia's largest cartridge is 128MB and is slightly smaller physically. Kodak, Panasonic, Canon, Nikon, and Epson (except for their low-end models) use CompactFlash, while Olympus, FujiFilm, Ricoh, and Minolta all use SmartMedia.

Most new cameras come with a 16MB card, but it is advantageous to buy a larger capacity card for taking more pictures between visits to the PC. You can fit more pictures on a card by enabling compression, but that negates the benefit of megapixel resolution.

Some cameras have been released recently that use other technologies for storage, such as a 120MB SuperDisk (which can be read by an LS-120 floppy drive in a PC), a 340MB IBM MicroDrive, or a 3-inch mini writable CD.

### *PC Interface*

Closely related to the storage medium is the method used for retrieving the pictures from that storage. Here are the most common ways of getting pictures into the PC from the camera:

- **Cable connection:** Most cameras have a USB, parallel, serial, or FireWire (IEEE 1394) connector. You can connect the camera to the PC using this interface and transfer the pictures either through the camera's proprietary software or through Windows itself (provided Windows supports the camera model directly).

- **Floppy disk:** If the camera uses floppy disks to store the pictures, just remove the floppy from the camera and put it in the PC's floppy drive, and then access the floppy drive normally through Windows.
- **Card reader:** This is a fairly inexpensive add-on option for cameras that store pictures on removable CompactFlash or SmartMedia flash ROM cartridges. A card reader allows you to remove the cartridge from the camera and transfer the pictures directly to the PC (see Figure 19.12). This is useful for taking a number of pictures (multiple cartridges full of them) before stopping to transfer them to the PC. Card readers come in SCSI, USB, PC Card, and parallel models. Some card readers are for either CompactFlash or SmartMedia only; others can read both.

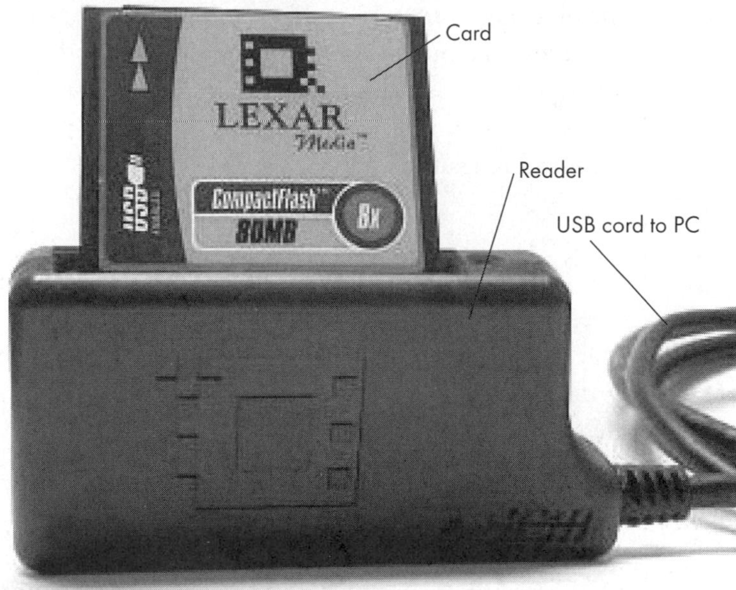


**FIGURE 19.12**
A card reader makes it possible to transfer images from cartridges without the camera.

- **FlashPath adapter:** With a SmartMedia-compatible camera, the SmartMedia card can be put into a FlashPath adapter (an add-on option) and then the adapter put into the floppy drive to transfer up to 16MB of files without a card reader.

### *Manual Adjustments*

Most digital cameras are fully automatic. Experienced 35mm camera users might want a model with more manual options, however. Some of the typical manual adjustments that might be available on high-end models include:

- **Aperture:** Changes the amount of light entering the camera. Manual aperture adjustment can be used to accentuate certain details by under- or overexposure.
- **Exposure compensation:** Allows minor adjustments to the automatic exposure settings, such as lightening or darkening.
- **Focus:** Focuses the lens, bringing spots at different distances from the lens into or out of sharpness.
- **Shutter:** Sets the speed at which the shutter opens and closes. Faster shutter speeds are useful for action photos, slower ones for special effects or low-light conditions.
- **White balance:** Lets you set a white point for the picture so that the camera's sensor does not make incorrect color adjustments.

### *Delay between Pictures*

Cameras vary in the quickness with which they can fire off rapid shots. Higher end cameras record the pictures more quickly, enabling the camera to take another picture sooner. Cameras that write to floppy disk can be especially slow in recording an image; you might have to wait up to 10 seconds before the camera is again ready.

### *Flash*

**Hot shoe**

A metal bracket with a connector on it for attaching an external flash to a camera.

Most digital cameras have a built-in flash. (Avoid very inexpensive cameras that do not have one.) Some high-end cameras may also have a *hot shoe* for attaching an external flash. As with regular 35mm cameras, some flashes have more features than others. Some might have a strobe, for example, that helps eliminate red eye.

### *Special Features*

Digital cameras come with a variety of special features. Some of them play MP3s, record short video clips, or record photos in special modes such as negative, black-and-white, or sepia. Some also have remote operation and/or a time delay.

## TRY IT!

**Using the Web sites for digital camera manufacturers listed under "For More Information" for this chapter on the Internet Resource Center, research several brands and models of cameras. Make notes about maximum resolution and other features, and decide which one would represent the best value if you were buying one for your personal use. Prepare a speech to the class outlining your findings and explaining the reasons for your choice.**

## DIGITAL VIDEO CAMERAS

We have been talking about digital cameras that take the place of traditional 35mm cameras to photograph still images. Also available are digital video cameras that can capture motion video clip (see Figure 19.13). These are not covered on the A+ exam, but it is useful to know a little about them.

Digital video cameras record on small digital cartridges that resemble the small tape units used in PC tape backup drives. Different models may use different cartridge types. They typically record both sound and video, and connect to a PC with a FireWire (IEEE 1394) interface.

Programs such as Windows Movie Maker (free with Windows Me and Windows XP), as well as higher end video editing programs, accept input directly from digital video cameras and store it on the hard drive. Digital video clips can be very large, however, so the user should be selective about which clips are kept unless there is hard drive space to spare.

**FIGURE 19.13**
A digital video camera looks like a regular camcorder but records on digital media.

### IN REAL LIFE

**The user with a regular (nondigital) camcorder might still be able to transfer video footage to the PC. A special interface will be needed that has an analog-to-digital converter in it.**

## WEBCAMS

There is one final category of camera known as a *webcam*, shown in Figure 19.14. Webcams are digital video cameras that do not stand alone; they connect to the PC via parallel, serial, or USB port (usually USB these days) and draw power and instructions from the PC. They are essentially just a lens on a cord; the PC and the driver for the device handle all of the image capture and recording.

**Webcam**

A digital video camera that connects to the PC and operates only while it is connected.

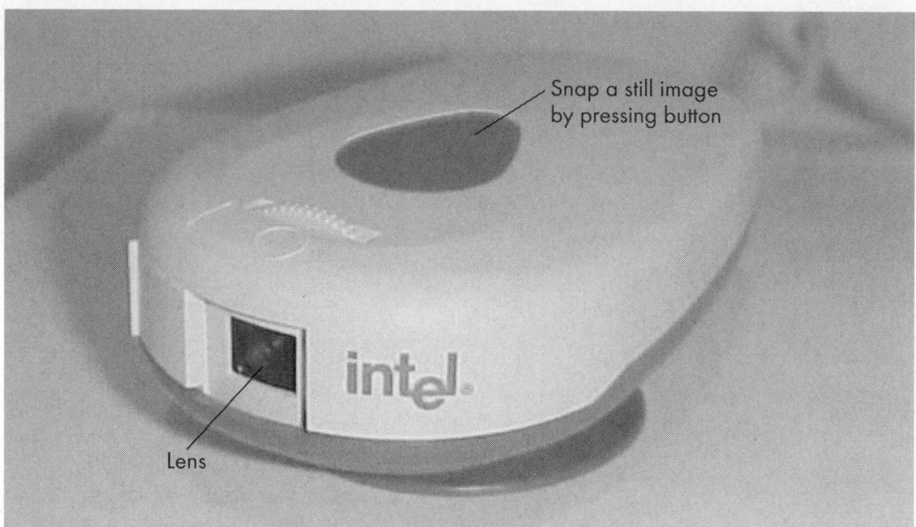


**FIGURE 19.14**
A webcam is a low-end digital video camera that works only when connected to the PC.

## TRY IT!

Research digital video cameras, either on the Internet or by visiting your local consumer electronics store. Look at both digital camcorders and webcams. What are the price ranges of each type that you find? What are the extra features that the high-end models have that the lower priced ones lack? Based on your findings, recommend to a fellow student the device best suited to her or his requirements.

## Digital Camera Support in Windows

As with scanners, digital camera support varies greatly depending on the version of Windows and on whether that version supports the particular model of camera. You might need to install and use the software that came with the camera for image transfer, or you might be able to access the camera directly from Windows.

One way to transfer pictures to the PC, as discussed earlier, is to connect the camera to the PC via USB, parallel, serial, or some other interface. When you do that with a supported camera in Windows Me or Windows XP, the camera shows up in the Scanners and Cameras applet in the Control Panel (see Figure 19.7).

To transfer the pictures from the camera using the Scanner and Camera Wizard, complete these steps:

1. Choose Start/(All) Programs/Accessories/Scanner and Camera Wizard.

2. If there is more than one scanner and/or camera, a box appears in which you select the one to work with; click OK after making your selection.
3. The pictures stored in the camera appear with a check mark beside each one. Clear the check box for any that you do not want to transfer (see Figure 19.15). Then click Next.

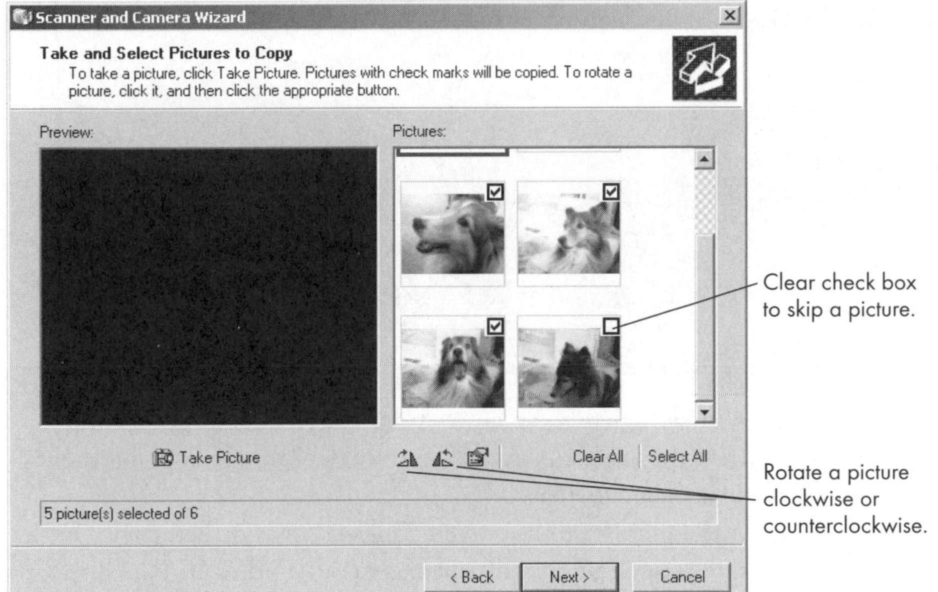


**FIGURE 19.15**
Transferring Pictures from a Digital Camera to the PC

4. Key a name for the group of pictures you are transferring. The pictures will all have the name you keyed as a prefix (followed by a number), and will be stored in a subfolder with that name within the *My Pictures* folder.
5. If you want to change the save location, edit the location in the Choose a place to save this group of pictures text box (see Figure 19.16).

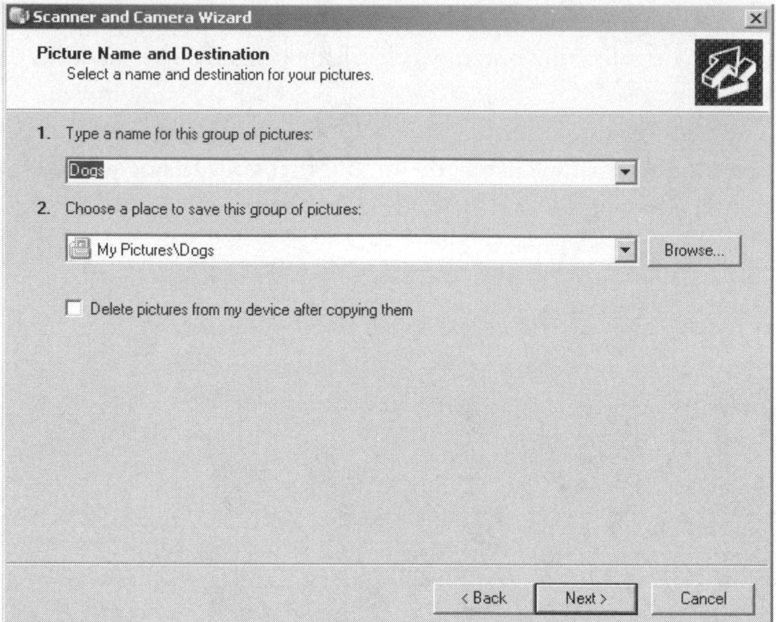


**FIGURE 19.16**
Select a name and location for the pictures.

6. If you want to delete the pictures from the camera after copying them, click the Delete pictures from my device after copying them check box, then click Next.
7. Wait for the pictures to be copied. Click Next and then click Finish. The pictures open up in a file management window in Filmstrip view. For more information about this window see "Working with Images in Windows" later in this chapter.

**TRY IT!**

1. Take some pictures with a digital camera.
2. Connect the camera to your PC and transfer the images to your hard drive.
3. Erase the images from the camera.

## Troubleshooting Digital Camera Problems

Many of the problems with digital camera operation have to do with the cameras themselves and therefore are not covered on the A+ exam; most technicians refer their clients to camera technical support staff. If your organization uses a particular brand of digital camera extensively, keep the technical support toll-free number handy for your clients.

For PCs using Windows Me or XP, check Microsoft's Hardware Compatibility List at www.microsoft.com to make sure the version of Windows supports that camera model. If it does not, you will need to install the software that came with the camera in order for Windows to recognize it.

If Windows does not see the camera even with its software installed, check the following:

- Make sure the camera is firmly connected to the PC using a recognized interface. For example, if it is a USB interface, make sure that Windows has USB support enabled.
- Turn on the camera. With some cameras it makes a difference.
- Some cameras have a switch that changes between picture-taking mode and transfer mode. Make sure it is in the right position for the PC to see it. Check the camera documentation for help if needed.
- Find the toll-free support number for the camera manufacturer and ask the support staff for help.

When a webcam does not work in Windows, it is usually a software- or driver-related issue. Not all software that uses webcams supports every model. For example, the Yahoo! Messenger chat program supports only certain cameras, as does Microsoft's NetMeeting. Sometimes updating the driver for the camera can correct the problem of its not being seen in certain applications; another possibility is updating the application itself to a newer version.

## Working with Images in Windows

Whether images are acquired from a scanner, from a digital camera, or from some other source, you can work with them the same way in Windows. Windows treats graphic files like any other file; you can move, copy, rename, and delete them freely. Chapter 29 covers those activities in detail. The interface is slightly different in various Windows versions.

### Image Management in Windows XP

Figure 19.17 shows a folder containing some images in Windows XP. Windows XP contains a view option called Filmstrip that allows you to preview images in a larger size than the standard thumbnail. To change a folder to this view, choose View, Filmstrip. Windows XP also has a Thumbnails view for browsing several pictures at once.

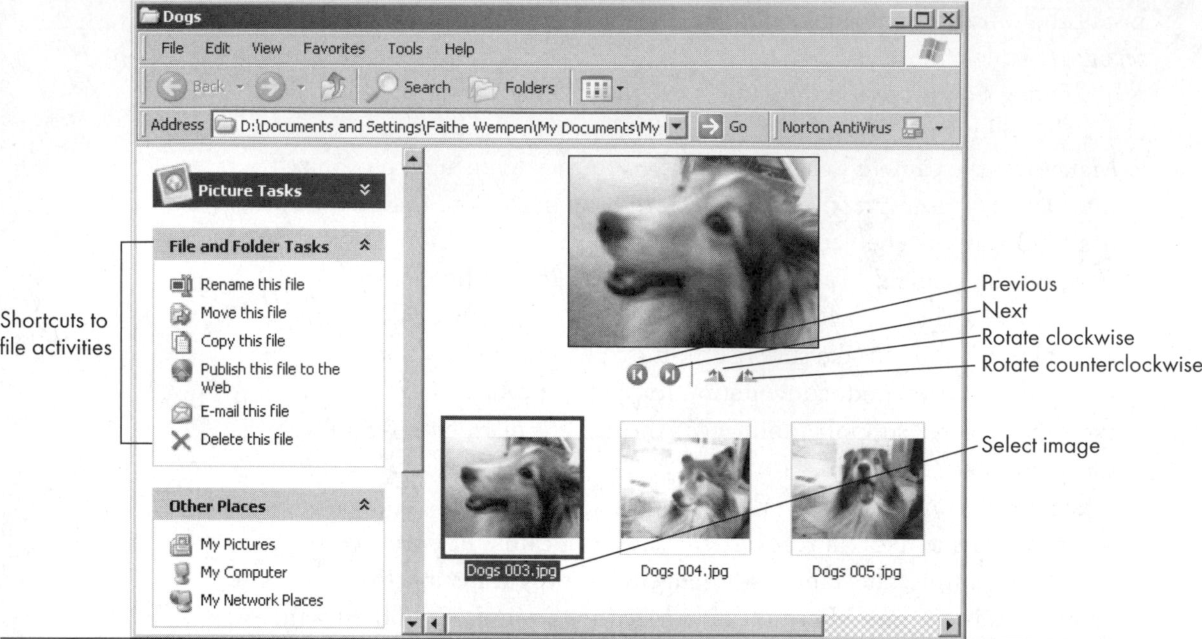


**FIGURE 19.17**
Pictures transferred from the camera appear in a window so you can browse and work with them.

Not all folders have Filmstrip view available—only folders that have been designated as containing pictures. That includes the *My Pictures* folder and any subfolders within it. You can also manually designate a folder as having graphic content by following these steps:

1. Open the folder.
2. Choose View/Customize This Folder.
3. Open the Use This Folder Type as a Template list and choose Photo Album.
4. Click OK.

Now when you open the View menu for this folder, the Filmstrip option will be included.

## Image Management in Windows 2000

Windows 2000 also has a special graphics viewing mode, like Windows XP, but it looks different and is set up differently. Figure 19.18 shows a folder that is set up to use Image Preview.

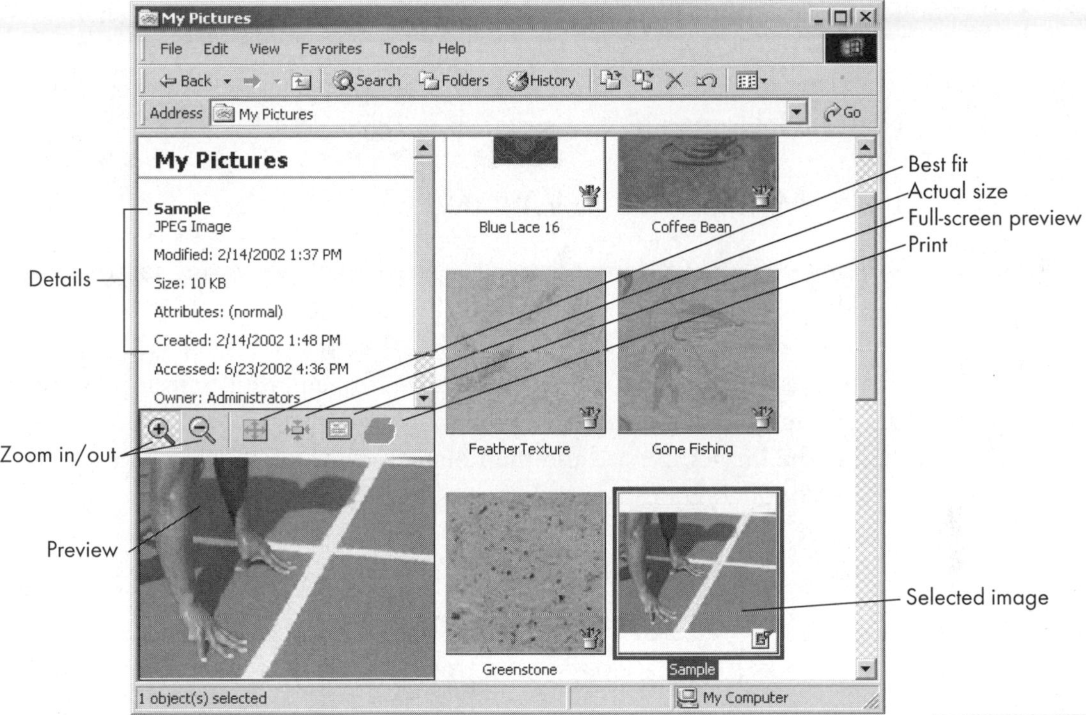


**FIGURE 19.18**
The Image Preview pane appears in Windows 2000 when the folder is set up to use the Image Preview template.

To set up a folder for Image Preview:

1. Open the folder.
2. Choose View/Customize This Folder.
3. The Customize This Folder Wizard starts. Click Next.
4. Click the Choose or edit an HTML template for this folder check box, and clear all other check boxes (see Figure 19.19). Then click Next.

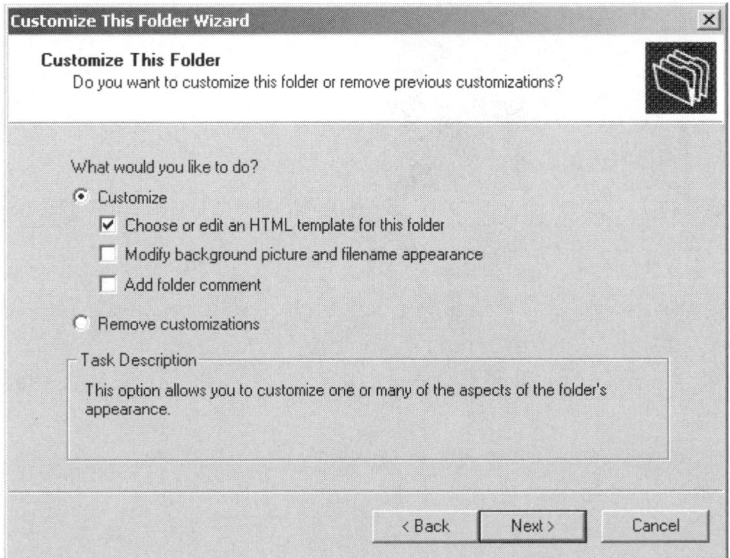


**FIGURE 19.19**
Image Preview is an HTML template you apply in Windows 2000.

5. Click Image Preview from the Choose a Template list; then click Next.
6. Click Finish.

Now this folder uses Image Preview, as in Figure 19.19.

## Image Management in Windows Me

Windows 95 and 98 do not have any special graphics viewing modes. Windows Me's graphics viewing mode is similar to that of Windows 2000, but has a few extra features. In Figure 19.20 notice that there is a View pictures as slideshow hyperlink; clicking on it opens a full-screen preview of the first image, with navigation buttons in the top right corner for moving among the images. Notice also the Rotate button, which was not available in the Windows 2000 version.

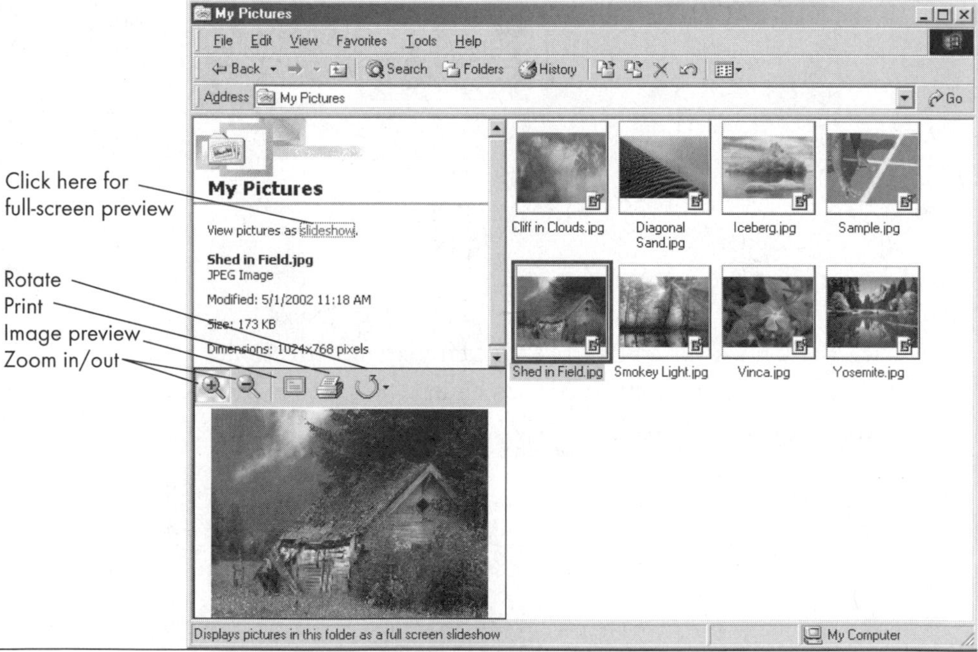


**FIGURE 19.20**
Windows Me offers its own version of an Image Preview view.

Setting up a folder for Image Preview is the same in Windows Me as in Windows 2000; follow the steps in the preceding section.

## TRY IT!

1. In a Windows file management window, display a folder that contains some graphics. This could be the folder in which you stored the images you transferred from the digital camera or some other folder. (The *Windows* folder has some graphics in it, so you can use it if you do not have any other appropriate folder.).
2. Display the folder in a view that gives you a preview of the pictures. The view you get and the steps for setting it up will vary depending on your Windows version.
3. Preview each picture.

# Sound Cards

The subject of sound support can be rather complex. The A+ exam covers it thoroughly, so it is important to have a good basic understanding of how Windows handles incoming and outgoing sounds and music through its sound subsystem.

## Understanding the Sound Subsystem

The sound subsystem's primary component is the sound card. It is an expansion board with its own chipset and circuitry that converts analog sound—from a microphone—to digital input, and converts digital sound—like from a CD or a game—to analog output to the speakers.

The other components of the sound subsystem are shown in Figure 19.21.

- **Motherboard:** The sound card plugs into an expansion slot on the motherboard, and the type of slot it uses determines the speed at which the sound card and the motherboard's chipset can communicate. Some motherboards have built-in sound support, meaning that the functionality of a sound card is integrated so that you do not need a separate sound card.
- **Speakers:** Speakers plug into the sound card. Depending on the sound card there might be one or two speaker jacks; each is a stereophonic jack that supports two separate speakers hooked together.
- **Microphone:** The microphone plugs into the sound card. Most sound cards have a port specifically designated Mic; others have a generic Input jack for microphones and other devices.
- **MIDI instruments:** A variety of musical instruments, such as keyboards and the like, have a Musical Instrument Digital Interface (MIDI) jack, and can be connected to a sound card for recording music. On some sound cards the 15-pin connector on the sound card doubles as both a MIDI port and a joystick port.

**FIGURE 19.21**
Sound Subsystem Components

## Digital Audio and MIDI Sounds

**Waveform**

A digital sound clip recorded from an analog source.

A sound card can play two types of sound files: digital audio (sometimes called *waveform* or just wave) and MIDI. They are technologically different, and they use two different functions of the sound card. Some sound cards are better at one function than the other, and the types of activities performed with the PC determine which is more important when selecting a sound card.

A digital audio file is one that was originally an analog sound (that is, a real sound generated by something) but has been digitally recorded. Examples include an audio CD by a favorite singer, a sound recorded with a microphone, the "You've Got Mail!" voice that AOL users hear, and all of the sound effects clips that Windows uses to generate its system sounds. The .wav extension is one of the most popular for digital audio files, but far from the only one; others include .wma, .mp3, .cda, and .au.

A MIDI file has been computer-generated from its inception—it never existed as an analog sound. For example, when you hook up a digital keyboard to a PC and record a tune, that music is purely digital. Most MIDI files have a .mid extension.

**FM synthesis**

A sound card method of playing MIDI music by simulating the sounds made by real instruments.

There are two ways that a sound card can generate the music for MIDI. *FM synthesis* is a method of simulating the sound of a real instrument such as a piano, a flute, a clarinet, and so on. The MIDI file contains instructions that tell the sound card to play a certain note on a certain "instrument" and the sound card does its best to make it sound real. It does not sound very real, however; it sounds like a computer emitting synthetically generated sounds.

**Wavetable synthesis**

A sound card method of playing MIDI music by playing back recorded clips of instruments playing the specified notes.

A more sophisticated and realistic method of generating MIDI music is called *wavetable synthesis*. Sound cards that support this method have stored on them actual analog-recorded clips of various instruments playing all of the different notes. For example, when a MIDI clip calls for a piano playing middle C, the sound card retrieves that sound clip from its archive and plays it, resulting in music that does not sound "computerish." Almost all sound cards today are wavetable synthesis cards, but there are varying degrees of support for it (different numbers of instruments and different maximum numbers of instrument sounds that can play simultaneously). We will look at these differences later in the chapter.

## TRY IT!

1. Using the Search (or Find) command on the Start menu in Windows, locate a file with a .wav extension.
2. Double-click that file to play it through your speakers. If you do not hear anything, check to make sure you have a sound card and that speakers are connected to it.
3. Locate a file with a .mid extension.
4. Double-click the file to play it.

## SELECTING A SOUND CARD

Browsing some online computer hardware vendor sites will reveal a dramatic price range for sound cards, from $20 to over $200. What are the differences? Which are worth it?

No matter what are your client's other priorities, be sure to meet the minimum requirements listed in Figure 19.22.

- **Plug and Play:** All sound cards made today are Plug and Play compatible, allowing Windows to detect them automatically and assign resources to them.
- **Windows version compatibility:** Make sure the sound card you select comes with drivers specifically written for whatever Windows version your client has.
- **PCI interface:** Unless there are no PCI expansion slots available, make sure you use a PCI card rather than an ISA.
- **MPU 401 UART:** A UART is a controller chip; serial ports have UARTs too, as discussed earlier in this textbook. All sound cards should have an MPU 401 UART, but it is always a good idea to make sure.
- **MPC3-compatible:** *MPC* stands for multimedia personal computer, and the 3 represents version 3. This is a standard for PCs to make sure they conform to minimum requirements needed for certain programs. All sound cards sold today should be MPC3-compatible.

**FIGURE 19.22**
Sound Card Minimum Requirements

### *MIDI Features*

MIDI is not only a type of sound file, but also a standard for hooking up musical instruments to a PC and recording music from them. On most sound cards the 15-pin port doubles as both a joystick and a MIDI instrument connector.

The most important feature that a sound card can have for processing MIDI is wavetable synthesis, discussed earlier. Nearly all sound cards these days support wavetable synthesis, but not in equal degrees of quality and complexity. Figure 19.23 shows the MIDI features that differentiate one sound card from another.

- **New instrument capability:** For music composition, use a sound card that enables downloading and incorporating new instrument clips.
- **Polyphony:** Enables many MIDI "voices" to play simultaneously. That is, does the sound card simulate a 64-piece orchestra, or just a 4-piece string quartet? More is better. Most good-quality sound cards support 64 voices.
- **ROM size:** Some sound cards have Read-Only Memory (ROM) for holding clips; others rely on system RAM for this. A card that has ROM might have 1MB or so of it.
- **RAM size:** This is how much memory can be allocated to working with sound. A card with ROM might have some RAM on it, perhaps between 4 and 24MB. On cards that use system RAM, the usable amount depends on the available system RAM, but a sound card will have a theoretical maximum. A midrange card might support up to 32MB; a higher end card up to 1GB.
- **Synthesizer effects:** Some sound cards include built-in effects such as Reverb, Chorus, Flanger, Pitch Shift, and Distortion. Having these effects built in is superior to having such effects created by software when composing or playing music. Low-end sound cards do not typically have synthesizer effects built in.
- **MIDI channels:** This determines the maximum number of channels of data for MIDI recording and playback. Sixteen would be typical of a low-end card; 48 would be typical of a midrange to high-end card.
- **Effects engine:** Some higher end sound cards have one of these for generating special effects; most midrange and low-end cards do not.
- **Recording depth:** This refers to the number of bits of data that can be recorded simultaneously; 16-bit is typical.
- **Maximum recording rate:** This is a measurement of the number of sounds per second (called samples) the card can record. A maximum of 48KHz is typical.
- **Playback depth:** This is the number of bits of data that can be played back simultaneously. A low-end or midrange card might have 16-bit, a high-end card 24-bit.

*continued*

**FIGURE 19.23**
MIDI Features

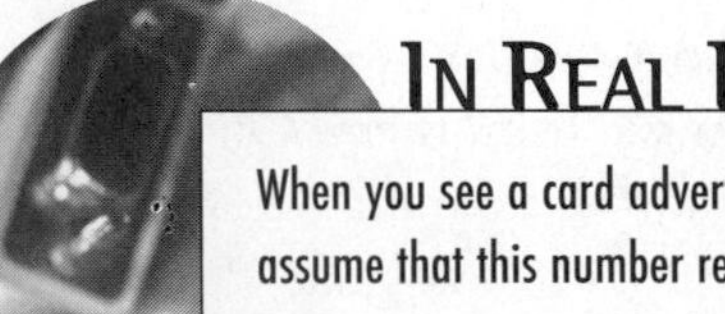

## In Real Life

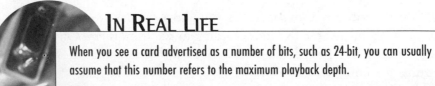

When you see a card advertised as a number of bits, such as 24-bit, you can usually assume that this number refers to the maximum playback depth.

- **Maximum playback rate:** This is the number of sounds per second the card can play back. It might range from 48 to 96KHz, depending on the card quality.
- **Signal-to-noise ratio (SNR):** This measures the amount of distortion (noise) in proportion to the amount of sound produced. Higher is better. Cards might range from between 80 and 100db (decibels).

FIGURE 19.23
continued

### *Digital Audio Features*

Recall from an earlier discussion that digital audio refers to the card's ability to play back recorded sounds in non-MIDI digital format. Gamers will want sound cards that are strong in the digital audio area. Many of the latest games conform to certain Application Program Interfaces (APIs). An API is a standard that programmers use to hook into the features of a piece of hardware such as a sound or video card. By looking for a sound card that supports the latest APIs, you ensure that the latest games and other programs will work to their full potential.

Figure 19.24 describes some digital audio features.

- **Built-in amplifier:** Usually you do not need this because the speakers contain their own amplification, but some sound cards have it anyway. It enables you to get decent volume from the system using inexpensive, unamplified speakers.
- **Sound Blaster compatibility:** If your client plans on using the sound card only in Windows, where a driver written specifically for that sound card will be available, compatibility is not an issue. However, if he or she plans on playing sound in older MS-DOS programs, each of which must provide its own sound driver, compatibility with an established sound card type is useful. Sound Blaster is the most popular sound card standard, and almost all MS-DOS programs that include sound come with a Sound Blaster driver.
- **Microsoft DirectSound and DirectSound 3D support:** This is the dominant standard for 3D sound support. There will be more about 3D sound later in this chapter.
- **EAX support:** EAX is another API for rendering 3D sound support. If the sound card supports it, programs (mostly games) that include EAX API programming calls will sound better. EAX is a proprietary standard developed by Creative Labs, and as of this writing is found only on cards manufactured by that company.
- **Dolby Digital 5.1 decoding:** Dolby Digital 5.1 is a standard for digital sound playback when watching DVD movies (actually it is only one standard; DTS is the other); a sound card that supports it will play back audio recorded in Dolby Digital 5.1 more clearly, including supporting Surround Sound.
- **Separate speaker and woofer adjustments:** If there are more than two speakers, look for a sound card that supports more of them–up to six–and allows you to adjust the balance and volume of each speaker separately, in addition to the woofer (if there is one separate from the speakers).

FIGURE 19.24
Digital Audio Features

## In Real Life

There is software available that can make some cards work with three sets of speakers for Surround Sound output even if your sound card supports only one set; it maps the front speakers to the regular speaker port, the rear speakers to the Line In port, and the subwoofer speakers to the Mic port. This is called 5.1 Channel Audio Effects.

### *External Ports*

Figure 19.25 shows the external ports on a typical sound card. It has five round plugs and one 15-pin MIDI connector, and is typical of a midpriced card. Other cards have more or fewer ports. Figure 19.26 lists some of the external ports you might encounter on a sound card.

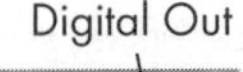

**FIGURE 19.25**
External Sound Card Ports

- **MIDI:** Most sound cards have a 15-pin D-shaped MIDI connector that doubles as a joystick connector. Sound cards designed primarily for MIDI might have two DIN connectors (the same type of connector used for an AT-style keyboard), one for MIDI in and one for MIDI out.
- **Line Out:** Use this type of port to export audio from the PC to an analog device such as a cassette recorder. It can also be used for speakers, and in fact on some systems the speaker plug is color-coded for this port.
- **Line In:** With this type of port you can connect a stereo or other analog audio device and record its sounds into files on the PC. You could retrieve audio from a portable CD or cassette player, for example.
- **Microphone:** This is like the Line Out port except it is just for a microphone. The two (Line Out and Mic) can be interchanged, as long as you remember when adjusting recording volume in Windows and change the appropriate setting.

**FIGURE 19.26**
External Ports Commonly Found on a Sound Card

*continued*

- **Speaker:** This output port sends analog data to speakers. Usually this is stereo data. One speaker is the primary; it connects directly to the sound card. The secondary speaker connects only to the primary speaker, and receives its data from it. Some sound cards have more than one Speaker output port (Speaker 1 and Speaker 2, perhaps) for connecting multiple sets of speakers. Other cards let you connect multiple sets of speakers off a single plug. This usually works by connecting a subwoofer to the sound card and then connecting the rest of the speakers to the subwoofer.
- **Digital Out:** This output port lets you transfer data from the PC to an external digital device without converting it to analog (sound wave).
- **Headphones:** A few sound cards have a headphone jack separate from the speaker jack(s).
- **Optical Out:** This port might be used for exporting to a mini-disc player.
- **Optical In:** This port might be used to accept input from a set-top DVD player or a gaming system, to allow it to use the PC's speakers.

**FIGURE 19.26**
continued

Notice that in Figure 19.25 the ports are not labeled with text (except for Digital Out), but with cryptic pictures. It can be difficult to tell what a picture stands for. Fortunately, the most common plugs are also color-coded on most sound cards made today. Table 19.2 lists the colors and their default purposes.

| Port | Color |
|---|---|
| Line Out | Green |
| Speaker Out | Black |
| Microphone | Red |
| Line In | Blue |
| Digital Out | Yellow |

**TABLE 19.2**
Color Assignments for Sound Ports

## TRY IT!

Look at the external ports on your sound card. Which of the ports listed in Table 19.2 do you have?

### *Internal Ports*

The internal ports on a sound card are pin-based connectors on the circuit board that enable you to attach internal cables running from one device to another inside the PC. For example, you might run a cable from an internal modem to the Telephone Answering Device (TAD) internal connector on a sound card to enable the modem to be used as an answering machine (with the right software).

Figure 19.27 shows the internal ports on a typical sound card. Figure 19.28 lists some of the more common internal ports used today.

**FIGURE 19.27**
Internal Sound Card Ports

- **Telephone Answering Device (TAD):** Run a cable between an internal modem and this port to be able to hear messages from an answering machine through the PC speakers.
- **CD IN (Audio In):** Run a cable from the CD-ROM drive to this port to be able to hear audio CDs play through the PC speakers.
- **Sony/Philips Digital Interface (S/PDIF):** An internal S/PDIF interface typically would connect via cable to an extra backplate with several S/PDIF external ports on it. An S/PDIF output port might be useful for exporting sound to a portable digital audio (MP3) player, for example.
- **TV Tuner:** If there is a TV tuner card installed in the PC, connect it to the sound card via this port so you can hear the TV's sound through the speakers.
- **Mic Con:** If there is an internal microphone, connect it to the sound card here. Most microphones are external, however.
- **AUX IN:** This is an all-purpose input port; use it for a second CD drive or some other internal device that generates sound that you want to be able to play through the PC speakers.

**FIGURE 19.28**
Internal Ports Commonly Found on a Sound Card

## TRY IT!

Open the PC case and locate the sound card. What internal ports does it have? If you need to remove the sound card to get a good look at it, do so; replace it when you are finished.

### *3D Sound*

*3D sound* is similar to Surround Sound in a movie theater; the sounds seem to be coming at you from all sides, with realistic effects. For example, if you are playing a game in which a monster is creeping up behind you, you would hear it from the rear speakers (if you have multiple sets of speakers). But 3D sound is more than just positional audio; in some games it can be extremely sophisticated. For example, suppose the monster is to your character's left in the game, and the character moves so that a brick wall is between himself and the monster. The monster will now make the muffled sound of someone behind a brick wall.

**3D sound**

Sounds and music in a game that seem to come from all sides and seem to change depending on the position of the game character.

In order for 3D sound to work, the programmers who wrote the game must have included commands that use an API that the sound card supports. For example, if the sound card supports Microsoft's DirectSound 3D, and the game has DirectSound 3D API commands embedded in it, you will get the 3D sound effects; otherwise the sound will be rather ordinary. Because the feature will not work unless both the hardware and the software support it, serious gamers should look for sound cards that support as many different APIs as possible.

The 3D standards to look for are shown in Figure 19.29.

- **A3D:** Developed by Aureal Semiconductor, A3D 2.0 is found in the Vortex 2 audio accelerator chip. It is a very sophisticated audio engine that supports the A3D 2.0 API. One benefit of A3D is that it produces fairly good 3D sound with a single pair of speakers; you do not need multiple speaker sets (true Surround Sound) to enjoy some 3D effects. However, this company has been bought by Creative Labs, and no further support or development for this standard is anticipated.
- **EAX:** This is an API standard developed by Creative Labs, the makers of the venerable Sound Blaster line of sound cards. It is currently in version 3.0, which competes fairly well with A3D in its capabilities. EAX is much better with four speakers than with two, however, and Creative Labs sells four-speaker kits to take advantage of that.
- **Sensaura:** This API uses some very sophisticated modeling techniques to accurately reproduce sounds as they would be heard by a human ear. Sensaura is popular with programmers because they do not have to learn a new API to program Sensaura support into a game; it is layered beneath Microsoft DirectSound 3D. Sound cards that use the Yamaha Waveforce and ESS Maestro 2 chips include Sensaura support.
- **DirectSound3D:** This is the common denominator, the baseline for 3D sound support. Nearly all sound cards and all games support it. It is not as sophisticated as the other technologies mentioned, but it does provide some basic 3D functionality.

**FIGURE 19.29**
3D Sound Standards

## TRY IT!

**Check the documentation for a favorite game to see which APIs it supports.**

### *Other Sound Card Features*

**Sound font**

An effect applied to regular sound that modifies it without changing its essential character, much like a text font changes basic lettering.

At the high end of sound card functionality you can find various distinctive features. Some sound cards have add-on devices that work with them, such as drives that store MIDI clips or *sound fonts*. A sound font applies effects that are the rough equivalent of a text font. For example, if you apply a different font to some text in a word processing program, it may look different but it will say the same thing. If you apply a distortion filter to a sound clip, it will sound different but it will still contain the same basic material. That is a sound font.

Another recent development in sound cards is an external sound card. It is not a "card" per se; it is an add-on appliance that you connect to the PC via USB port that functions as a sound card, processing the ins and outs of all sound-related data. One of the limitations of a traditional sound card is that the backplate is only so big; it can accommodate a limited number of ports. But this large external box can have many different ports on it, including multiple jacks for speaker sets. The most popular of these models is the Sound Blaster Extigy by Creative Labs. It includes nearly all of the external I/O ports listed in Figure 19.26, plus three sets of speaker connectors (for Dolby Digital 5.1 Surround Sound) and just about every other connector type.

## TRY IT!

**Check the specifications for several brands and models of sound cards on the Internet. Use the sound card manufacturer addresses listed in "For More Information" for this chapter on the Internet Resource Center. Compare the sound cards based on the criteria you learned about in the preceding sections, including MIDI features, digital audio features, APIs supported, and so on.**

## INSTALLING A SOUND CARD

Installing a sound card is much like installing any other expansion board. On some systems you might need to disable internal sound support on the motherboard before installing a "real" sound card. (You do not need to disable it, strictly speaking. You can have two sound devices in the same system, but they use up system resources unnecessarily in most cases.) You can usually disable built-in sound support either in BIOS Setup or with a jumper on the motherboard. See the motherboard manual, or check BIOS Setup or the motherboard to find the setting. Depending on the motherboard style, the ports for built-in sound support might be on a backplate mounted to the case and attached to the motherboard with a ribbon cable (as with the AT system shown in Figure 19.30), or they might be built directly into the motherboard side like the parallel and serial ports (as with the ATX system shown in Figure 19.31).

**FIGURE 19.30**
Sound support built into an AT-style motherboard uses ports that attach to the motherboard via small ribbon cables.

**FIGURE 19.31**
Sound support built into an ATX-style motherboard typically has the ports built directly into the side of the motherboard.

After disabling any built-in sound support, do the following to install a new sound card:

1. Open the case.
2. If you are replacing an old sound card, remove it.
3. Select an expansion slot. The new sound card may or may not use the same type of slot as the old one.
4. Remove the backplate for the new slot and insert the card in the slot. If you removed an old sound card from a different slot, cover the old slot's hole with the backplate you just removed.
5. Attach the card to the case with the screw from the backplate you removed.
6. Run any internal cables as needed to connect the sound card to the CD drive, modem, and so on. (Review the section on internal ports earlier in this chapter.) In most PCs the audio cable from the sound card to the CD drive will be the only connection you need to make.
7. Close the case.
8. Turn on the PC. If Windows does not automatically detect the sound card, see the following section.

## Setting Up the Sound Card in Windows

When you start up Windows after installing the new sound card, one of these things will happen:

- It will see the new sound card immediately and automatically install the needed drivers.
- It will see the new sound card but will not be able to detect it completely; you will need to run the setup software that came with the sound card to complete the installation.
- It will not see the new sound card at all. Running the setup software may force it to recognize the card. If it does not, the sound card may be defective or improperly installed physically.

If you hear sound right away, it means that the version of Windows and the sound card understand each other. You do not have to load the software that came with the sound card unless you want to. There might be some useful utility programs there, but much of the software that comes with a typical sound card is of little use, or merely duplicates the functionality of programs you probably already have.

If you do not immediately hear any sound, check to see whether the new sound card shows up in Device Manager. Open Device Manager and click the plus sign next to the Sound, video and game controllers category if it is not already open. If you see the sound card there, Windows sees it too (see Figure 19.32).

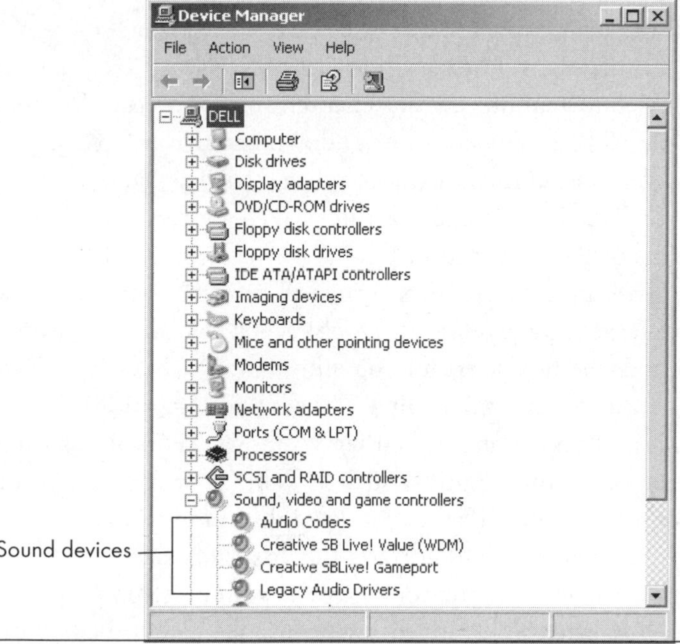


**FIGURE 19.32**
Look for the sound card and its associated devices (joystick port, etc.) in Device Manager.

If the sound card is not there, look in the Other Devices (or Unknown Devices) category. If it is there—or if some mysterious new entry is there—then Windows has detected that there is something new but does not know what it is. If this is your situation, run the setup software that came with the sound card. (If you do not have any software, download it from the card manufacturer's Web site.)

If there is no sign of Windows detecting anything about the new sound card, check its physical installation. Run the setup software that came with it. If it still does not work, call the toll-free tech support number for the sound card and get a technician to help you.

## TRY IT!

1. Remove your current sound card and replace it with a different one. Or, if you do not have a different card, put the same one back in.
2. Start Windows, and note whether the new sound card is automatically detected. Use Device Manager to check for its proper installation.
3. Run the setup software that came with the sound card if it is not already set up properly in Windows.

## Updating Sound Drivers

For best results you should have sound drivers for the exact version of Windows and the exact model of sound card. If you do not, try downloading the drivers from the card maker's Web site.

See "For More Information" for this chapter on the Internet Resource Center for some Web sites where you can download drivers. If your manufacturer is not listed there, use a search site such as Yahoo! (www.yahoo.com) to find the manufacturer's Web address, and then look for a Downloads or Support section.

The sound driver updates you download will probably be contained in a single executable file (.exe extension). Double-click that file to start a setup program that updates the drivers for you automatically.

**ZIP file**

A file or group of files that has been compressed using the ZIP compression algorithm and has a .zip extension.

In some cases the drivers may be in a *ZIP file* (.zip extension) instead of an .exe. If that is the case, you need either Windows XP (which has built-in ZIP support) or an unzipping utility such as WinZip (www.winzip.com). Extract the contents of the ZIP file to a new folder, and in that new folder there should be a *Setup.exe* file that starts the driver install.

Very rarely you might encounter sound drivers with no setup program—just a group of .drv, .sys, and .dll files. If that happens, place all of the files in a new folder and then use the Update Driver Wizard from Device Manager.

1. From Device Manager, double-click the sound card to open its Properties dialog box.
2. On the Driver tab, click the Update Driver button.
3. Work through the Update Driver Wizard, pointing it to the folder containing the drivers when prompted.

**TRY IT!**

**Visit the Web site of your sound card's manufacturer and download the latest driver for your sound card. Then install it.**

## Troubleshooting Sound Problems

The following sections will look at possible corrections for some of the problems that can occur with a sound card.

### *Windows Does Not See the Sound Card*

If your sound card does not show up at all in Windows, it is either broken or there are no drivers installed for it. See the section "Setting Up the Sound Card in Windows" earlier in the chapter.

***Card Is Recognized in Windows but No Sound Is Heard***

If the sound card shows up in Device Manager, the drivers are probably correctly loaded. If you still are not hearing any sound from it, check the following:

- Are speakers plugged into the Speaker jack on the sound card? Are the speakers plugged in, turned on, and turned up?
- Is the volume control in Windows muted? Double-click the speaker icon in the notification area (by the clock) to display the Volume Control (or Play Control; see Figure 19.33), or get to it from the Accessories/Entertainment submenu on the Start menu. The speaker icon will not appear in the notification area if Windows fails to detect the sound card.

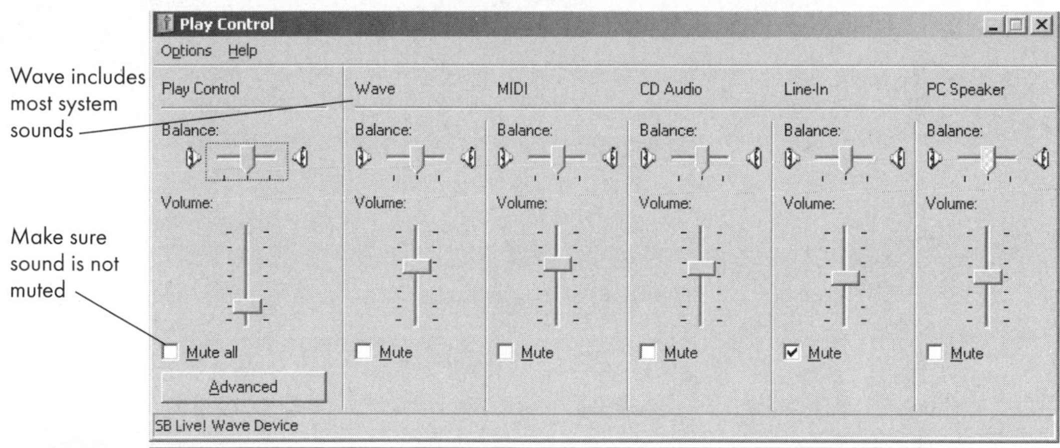


**FIGURE 19.33**
Check that the volume is not muted.

## IN REAL LIFE

**Many keyboards these days have a host of extra function buttons across the top and on the sides, one of which is for muting the system sound. An inexperienced user can easily press this button accidentally and then wonder why the sound does not work.**

- Is it just audio CDs that will not play? If you hear system sounds but not audio CDs, the cable that connects the sound card to the CD drive may be missing. Check inside. Also make sure that CD Audio is not muted (see Figure 19.33).

## In Real Life

Turtle Beach, a sound card manufacturer, offers a free sound card testing utility called Sound Check, which you can download. See "For More Information" for this chapter on the Internet Resource Center for the Web site address.

- In Control Panel, open the Sounds applet, which goes by slightly different names depending on the Windows version. In Windows XP, for example, it is Sounds and Audio Devices. Click the Sounds tab, and then click on one of the sounds (for example, Asterisk) and click the Play button (which looks like a right-pointing triangle; see Figure 19.34). If you hear the sound, all is well. If not, keep troubleshooting. We will look at the Sounds applet in more detail later in the chapter.
- Make sure the speaker cable is plugged into the correct jack on the sound card, and that the speakers are turned on and turned up.

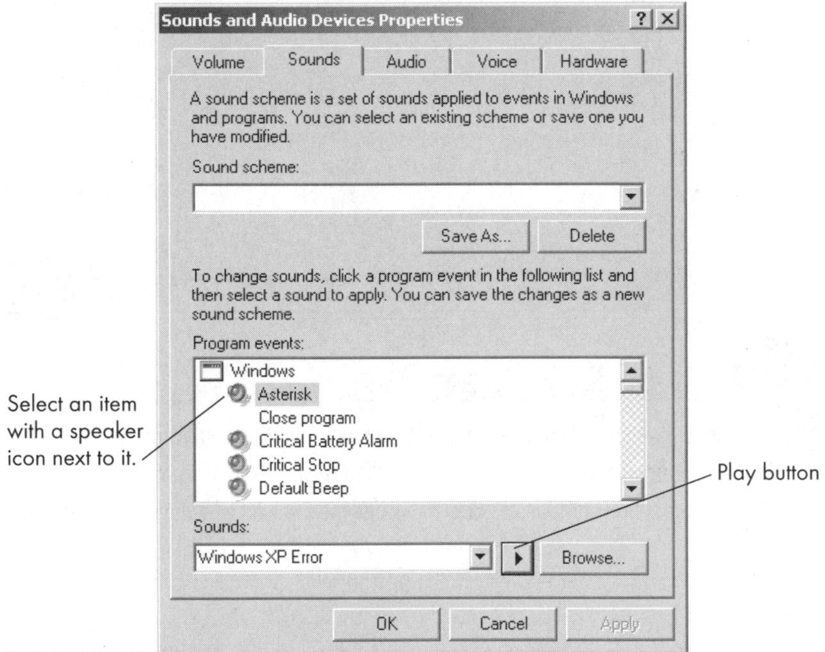


**FIGURE 19.34**
Try playing one of the system sounds to test the sound card and speakers.

### *Microphone Problems*

If you can hear sounds but not record them, make sure the microphone is plugged into the Mic port on the sound card, and that the on/off switch, if it has one, is turned on. Also check the Recording properties in Volume Control to make sure the Mic port has not been muted. If you are hearing crackling noises from the speaker, go into the Volume Control and do the opposite—mute the Mic port. To do either one:

1. Double-click the speaker icon in the notification area, near the clock.
2. Choose Options, Properties, and then choose Recording in the Properties dialog box that appears.
3. Click OK. Now you see the controls for recording devices (see Figure 19.35). Mark or clear the Select check box for the Microphone, then close the dialog box.

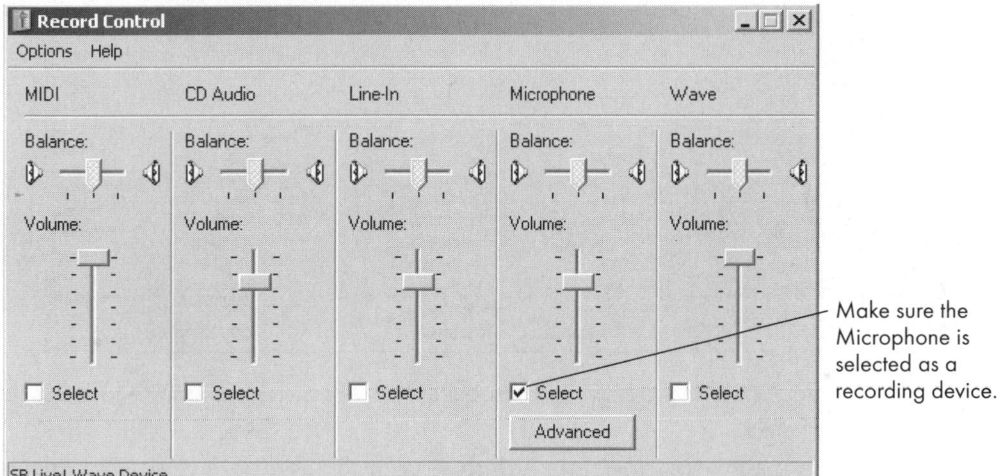


**FIGURE 19.35**
Switch to Recording controls to check the volume on the microphone.

Notice in Figure 19.35 that when you are dealing with recording volumes rather than play volumes, the check box beneath each item is Select, not Mute, and that you mark the check box, not clear it, to enable the device.

## TRY IT!

**Plug in a microphone to your sound card and use the Sound Recorder applet in Windows to record your voice. Troubleshoot as needed if it does not work.**

### *Sound Quality Problems*

Problems with crackling sounds or poor quality playback in a certain program (usually a game) may be a problem with the sound API for that game. Use the DirectX Troubleshooter to check for sound problems involving DirectX:

1. Choose Start, Run. Key **DXDIAG** and click OK.
2. In the DirectX Diagnostic Tool that appears, select the Sound tab (see Figure 19.36).
3. Click the Test DirectSound button.
4. Follow the on-screen prompts. The program will play sounds using various modes and then ask whether you heard them.

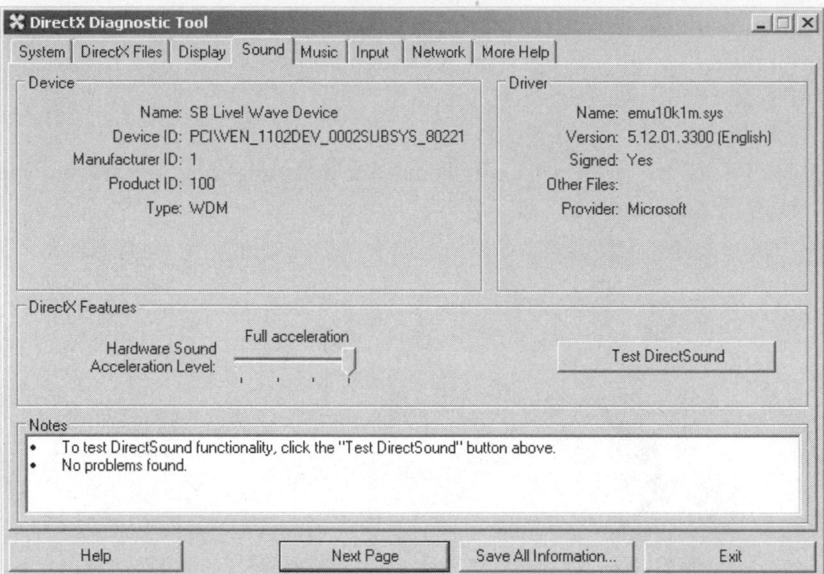


**FIGURE 19.36**
Use the DirectX Diagnostic Tool to make sure that DirectSound support is working.

5. Select the Music tab and then click Test DirectMusic and follow the prompts.
6. Select the More Help tab and then click the Sound button. This opens the Sound Troubleshooter in Windows Help. Follow the prompts.

If there are no problems found with DirectSound, try running the game in DirectX mode rather than one of the other API modes. Notice also in Figure 19.36 that there is a Hardware Sound Acceleration Level slider; you can try setting it to a lesser acceleration level to troubleshoot sound problems.

Sometimes such problems can be solved by downloading a patch or update for the specific application that is experiencing the problem.

# Selecting and Installing PC Speakers

The following sections outline some tips for choosing PC speakers and for setting them up.

## Amplification

Amplification is almost a given for speakers—or should be. Any speakers should be amplified, and most of them are. (Stereo speakers designed for the home stereo system are not amplified, in contrast, because they are hooked up to a separate amplifier/tuner that does that job.) Amplification does just what the name says: it amplifies the sound coming from the sound card so humans can easily hear it. If there is no amplification in the speakers, you might have problems getting the sound loud enough. Amplification is achieved through electricity, so to be amplified, speakers must either have batteries or (better yet) an AC adapter. Some have both.

What does the speaker do with this electricity it receives from battery or wall outlet? It creates watts of amplification. The subwoofer will have its own watts (more is better), as will each of the satellite speakers. An average wattage for a subwoofer is around 18; for each satellite speaker it might be around 6.

Wattage is determined using the following measurements:

- **Root Mean Squared (RMS):** This is a standard measurement of the amount of wattage a speaker can reliably handle in a sustained manner.
- **RMS Maximum:** This is the wattage that the speaker can handle in short bursts; it will be higher than the regular RMS.
- **PMPO:** This is the absolute maximum that the speaker can handle for a split second, just before it dies from wattage overload. It is not a realistic measurement of the speaker's capabilities. Manufacturers of inexpensive speakers often advertise wattage in PMPO, but you cannot fairly compare that claim to speakers that advertise wattage in RMS.

## Shielding

Shielding is also important but, as with amplification, it is nearly a given, provided the speakers are designed specifically for use with computers. Speakers have magnets in them, and placing them too close to the monitor or other components can result in electromagnetic interference (EMI). Speakers with shielding have a protective barrier that minimizes the amount of EMI that leaks out of the speakers, so you can set them next to just about anything without any problems.

## Number of Speakers

The main decision to make when purchasing PC speakers is how many are needed. Most PCs come with two speakers, designed for stereo operation. One speaker connects to the PC, the other connects to the first speaker. This is known as a 2.0 configuration.

The alternative is a setup that includes a *subwoofer*. In a two-speaker stereo system with no subwoofer, each speaker has its own subwoofer that handles bass (although not as well as a dedicated subwoofer). One of the following configurations might be considered:

**Subwoofer**

A speaker that is dedicated to handling the bass range; having one enhances that thump-thump effect and makes sound effects in the lower range (below 150Hz) much more dramatic.

- **Two speakers plus a subwoofer:** This is known as Dolby Digital 2.1. It is a midlevel setup that enhances the stereo performance by adding increased bass.

- **Four speakers plus a subwoofer:** This is Dolby Digital 4.1. Two speakers are for the front (right and left) and two for the rear. For this setup you will need a sound card that has two speaker jacks and supports 4-channel operation.
- **Five speakers plus a subwoofer:** This is 5.1, or Surround Sound. It has the same four speakers (front/rear, right/left) as 4.1, but adds a single center speaker as well. This is useful primarily for playing DVD movies; not many games support it. For this you will need a sound card that supports Dolby Digital 5.1.

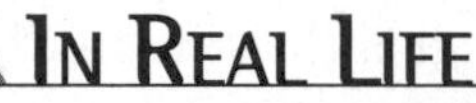

**In Real Life**

There is a new 7.1 standard that uses seven speakers, but it is very high end and not common on PCs. It is used primarily in home entertainment systems.

## Frequency Range

**Frequency range**

The range of sound wavelengths, measured in hertz (Hz), that a speaker can reproduce.

Speaker systems with a very wide *frequency range* will reproduce sounds much more accurately. Look for a frequency range of at least 50 to 10,000Hz.

## Analog versus Digital Speakers

Most speakers are analog. The Speaker connector on a sound card sends analog data to the speaker, and the speaker broadcasts it. However, digital speakers are also available, and hardcore audiophiles claim that they are better—less background noise and hiss at high volumes. Most people will not notice a difference. To use digital speakers there must be a Digital Out port on the sound card to which they can be connected.

## Installing Speakers

Speakers can be difficult to install because there is so much cable and so many connectors. What plugs into what? Consult the installation diagram that came with the speaker set.

Generally speaking, you must make the following connections:

- **Speaker to sound card:** At least one of the speakers (or the subwoofer) must connect to the sound card.
- **Speaker to speaker:** Each of the other speakers must plug into the speaker or subwoofer that is connected to the sound card. Usually they all plug into one central location, such as the subwoofer, but occasionally a set might chain them.

- **Speaker to power:** Assuming the speakers have amplification, they must receive power. There may be an AC adapter that plugs into each speaker, or perhaps the adapter plugs only into the main speaker or subwoofer and all other speakers draw their power from it.

Figures 19.37 and 19.38 show the typical cabling for two different speaker setups.

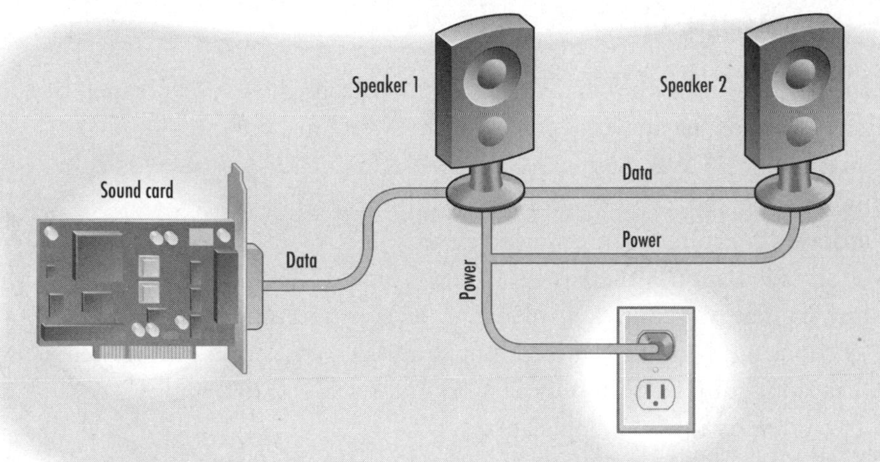


**FIGURE 19.37**
Simple stereo speakers with no subwoofer may each get their own AC power, as shown here, or one may draw power from the other through the data cable.

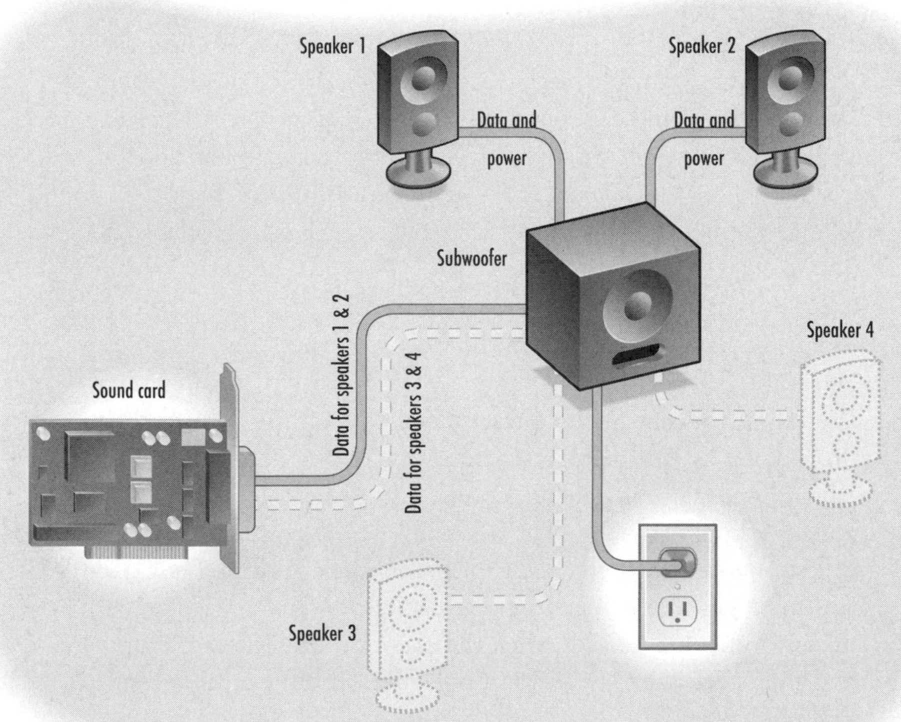


**FIGURE 19.38**
When a subwoofer is present, it typically feeds both data and power to the speakers. If there are four speakers, there is usually an additional cable from sound card to subwoofer for the data.

## TRY IT!

**If you already have speakers attached, examine how your speakers are plugged into your PC. If speakers are not already attached, connect them. Report on the kinds of connections you had to make.**

# Sound Support in Windows

The Sound properties in Windows are accessed from the Control Panel, but the exact name of the applet depends on the Windows version:

- Windows 95, 98: Sounds
- Windows Me and 2000: Sounds and Multimedia
- Windows XP: Sounds and Audio Devices

In Windows 95 and 98, there is a separate Control Panel applet called Multimedia that is used to control system-level properties involving sound, such as choosing the preferred recording and playback sound card if there is more than one sound card installed. In Windows Me, 2000, and XP, the two are combined into the single applet.

## System Sounds

System sounds are the beeps, clicks, and announcements you hear as you operate Windows. Examples might include the beep that accompanies an error message, the sound that plays when the e-mail program receives a new message, and the tunes that play when Windows starts up and shuts down.

There are two ways to change the system sounds. One is to apply a sound scheme, a set of predefined sounds for various occasions. Another is to manually select the sound for each event.

To select sounds, complete the following steps:

1. Open the Sounds applet from the Control Panel.
2. Select the Sounds tab.
3. If you want to start with a preset scheme, open the Sound scheme drop-down list and select a scheme.
4. If you have made any changes previously to sounds, a message will appear letting you know that you will lose the current sound scheme unless you save it. If you want to save it, click Yes and a box will appear to give it a name. To discard it, click No.
5. To test individual sounds, click the event on the Program events list and then click the Play button (looks like a right-pointing triangle; see Figure 19.39).

6. To change an individual sound, click the event and then do one of the following:
   a. Open the Sounds list and choose a sound.
   b. Click the Browse button and locate the sound file you want to use.
7. Repeat steps 5 and 6 as needed until you are satisfied with the sounds.
8. *Optional:* To save the new sound collection as a scheme, click Save As, enter a name for it, and click OK.
9. Click OK to close the Properties dialog box.

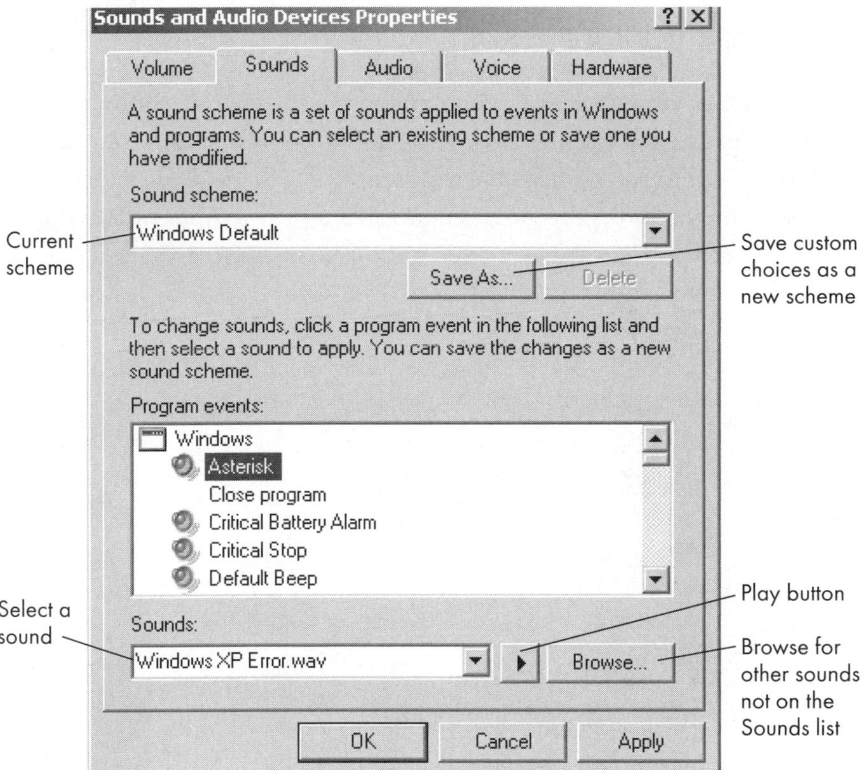


**FIGURE 19.39**
Choose an existing sound scheme or create your own custom scheme.

## In Real Life

**Additional sound schemes are available as optional Windows components. Use Add/Remove Programs to install them. See "Adding and Removing Windows Components" in Chapter 28 for details.**

## TRY IT!

1. Using Add/Remove Programs in Windows, install any additional sound schemes that are not already installed.
2. Apply one of the newly installed sound schemes.
3. Customize the sound scheme by changing one of the sounds.
4. Save the revised scheme as a new sound scheme.

### Hardware Controls

Most Windows versions enable you to choose which input and output devices should be the default for sounds. In Windows 95 and 98, these controls are under Multimedia in the Control Panel; in all later versions they are in the Sounds properties. Figure 19.40 shows them in Windows XP on the Audio tab. This is an issue only if there is more than one sound card and/or sound input device.

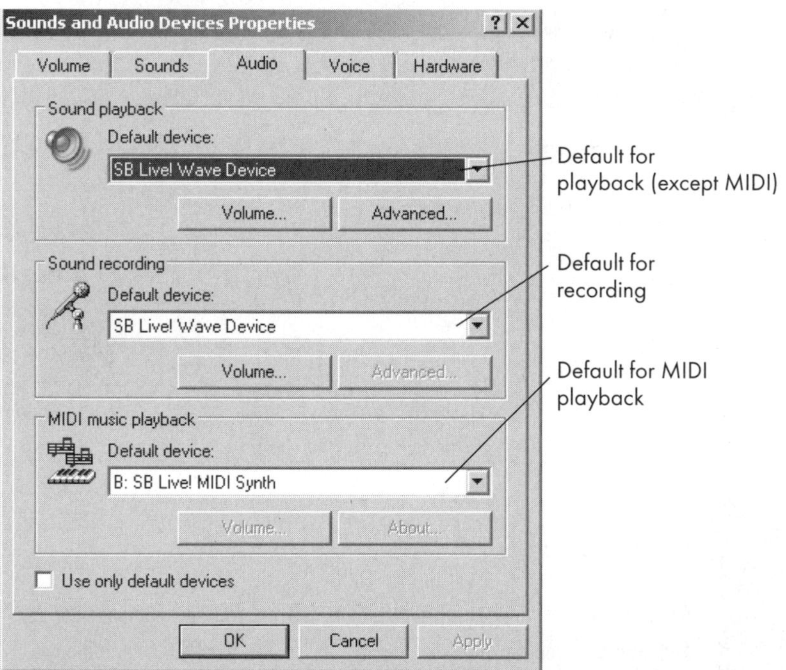


**FIGURE 19.40**
Select the default devices for sound input and output operations.

## Sound Options for People with Disabilities

Many Windows versions come with sound-related utilities that can help people with disabilities use Windows more effectively. The following sections describe some of them. Except for Narrator, these utilities are available in all Windows versions from 98 on.

## Narrator

This utility comes only with Windows XP. When enabled, it reads the text of every dialog box that appears, as well as the text in some applications that support the feature. This can be helpful for people with visual impairments who find it difficult to read the text on-screen even in low-resolution, high-contract display modes.

To run Narrator, choose Start, All Programs, Accessories, Accessibility Options, Narrator (see Figure 19.41).

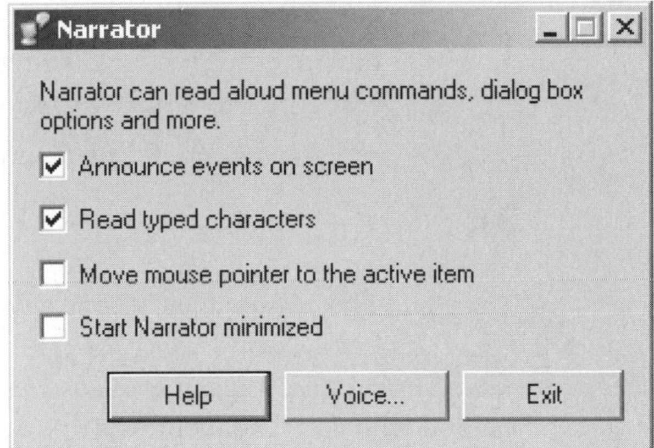


**FIGURE 19.41**
Narrator helps users with visual impairment by reading the text that appears on-screen.

**TRY IT!**

If you have Windows XP, turn on Narrator and experiment with it. Turn it off by closing its box when you are finished.

## SoundSentry

This feature provides a visual cue whenever Windows generates a system sound. It is useful for people with hearing impairments who cannot hear the system sounds. It might also be useful for someone who has a sound card but no speakers.

To turn on SoundSentry:

1. From the Control Panel, double-click Accessibility Options.
2. Select the Sound tab.
3. Click the Use SoundSentry check box to select it.
4. Open the Choose the visual warning drop-down list and choose the visual cue you want (see Figure 19.42).
5. Click OK.

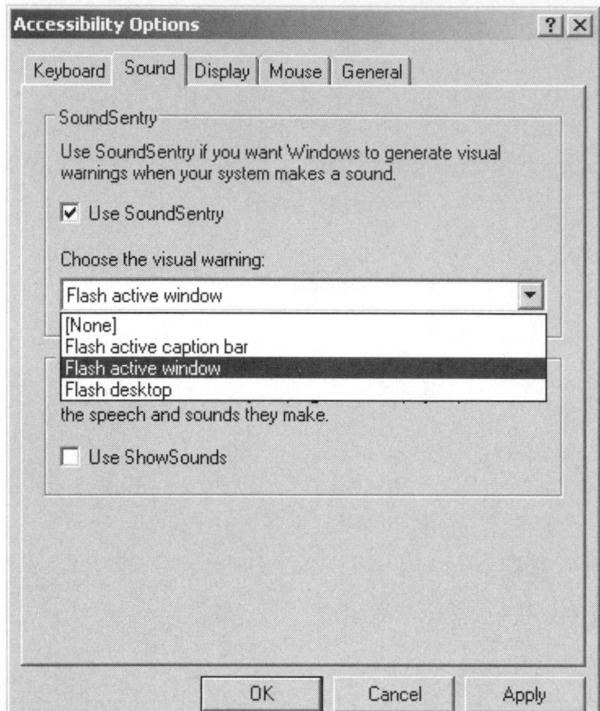


**FIGURE 19.42**
SoundSentry makes a visual cue correspond to system sounds, for anyone who cannot hear them.

## ShowSounds

This feature turns on captioning for any applications that support it. If a program supports captioning, a dialog box appears whenever an event sound or speech message plays in the program. Again, this is useful for anyone who cannot hear such sounds normally.

ShowSounds turns on/off in the same place as SoundSentry (described in the preceding section): on the Sound tab of the Accessibility Options dialog box (see Figure 19.42).

## ToggleKeys

This feature plays a tone whenever Caps Lock, Num Lock, or Scroll Lock is pressed. ToggleKeys is useful for someone who is able to hear and who accidentally presses one of those keys and then gets unexpected results. The accident can be due to a mobility impairment or just poor keying. To turn on this feature:

1. From the Control Panel, double-click Accessibility Options.
2. Select the Keyboard tab.
3. Click the Use ToggleKeys check box to select it.
4. Click OK.

To turn ToggleKeys on or off after it has been enabled, press and hold the Num Lock key for five seconds. If you forget which key to press and hold, you can get a reminder by clicking the Settings button next to the Use ToggleKeys check box. A dialog box appears enabling you to turn that shortcut on or off, and reminding you what it is.

### TRY IT!

**Enable SoundSentry, ShowSounds, and ToggleKeys, and experiment with each one. Disable them again when finished.**

# STUDY GUIDE

Use the following summaries to review the key concepts of this chapter.

## Scanner Technology

- A scanner digitizes an image, converting it from a hard copy to a file on the computer.
- The heart of a scanner is the charge-coupled device (CCD), an array of photosensitive cells.
- Scanner resolution is measured in dots per inch (dpi).
- The number of cells in the CCD is the horizontal resolution of the scanner (for example, 600dpi).
- The number of unique positions at which the CCD takes readings as it moves down the page is the vertical resolution for the scanner, also measured in dpi.
- Some scanners use interpolation to simulate higher resolutions. This invents extra pixels between the actual scanned ones using a math formula.
- Some inexpensive scanners use a contact image sensor (CIS) rather than a CCD.
- The alignment of the three colors on a color scanner is called registration.
- Scanner color depth is measured in bits, just like display color depth.
- A 24-bit color picture is the functional limit, but extra bit depth on scanners can be useful for making color corrections during the scan.
- Dynamic range is the ability of a scanner to distinguish between light and dark (0 to 4).
- Scanners can use parallel, USB, or SCSI interfaces.

## Installing and Supporting Scanners

- When installing a new scanner, remove any tape holding it for shipping, and set its locking switch to Unlocked position.
- Most scanners do not have an on/off switch; they are off when unplugged.
- Windows 95, 98, and 2000 require that you load the scanner software that comes with the scanner. Windows Me and XP might automatically be able to use the scanner without it.
- TWAIN is a scanner interface that many applications support; the driver that comes with the scanner is based on TWAIN.

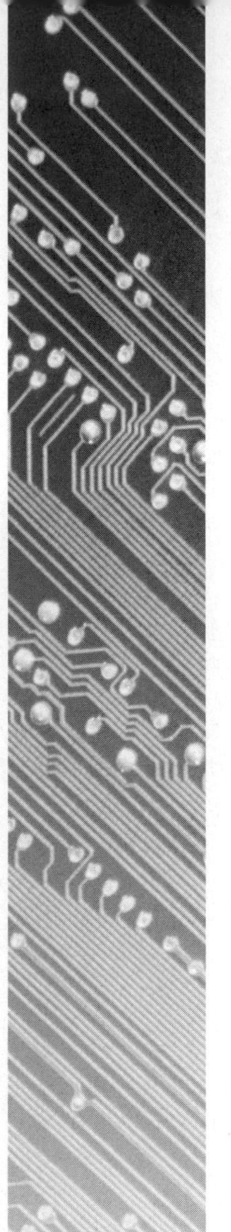

- If your scanner is supported by Windows Me or XP, you can scan using the Scanner and Camera Wizard rather than having to run the scanner through an application.
- When troubleshooting a scanner, check that it is physically powered up and unlocked, that it is connected to the PC, and that the PC recognizes the port to which it is connected.
- Sharing conflicts between parallel scanners and printers may be resolved by adjusting the settings for the port in BIOS Setup.

## Digital Camera Technology

- A digital camera uses a CCD, like a scanner, but in 3D rather than on a flat sheet of paper.
- Digital cameras sold today describe their maximum resolution in megapixels (1 million pixels), derived by multiplying the horizontal by the vertical number of pixels in the maximum resolution.
- Some cameras store pictures on floppies, but most use removable cartridges, either CompactFlash or SmartMedia.
- These cartridges hold up to hundreds of megabytes of data, allowing the cameras to take multiple high-resolution pictures.
- To transfer the pictures to the PC, most cameras have a cable connection (usually USB).
- An optional card reader can read pictures from a cartridge without the camera.
- A FlashPath adapter allows cartridges to be inserted into a normal floppy drive.
- Digital video cameras (camcorders) work like conventional video cameras but save to digital cartridges.
- A nondigital camcorder can save its data on a PC using a special interface with an analog-to-digital converter.
- A webcam is a digital video camera that remains attached to the PC at all times.

## Supporting Digital Cameras

- The Scanner and Camera Wizard in Windows XP and Me helps transfer pictures to the PC.
- All other Windows versions, and unsupported cameras, must use the software that comes with the camera to do the transfer.

- If Windows does not detect the camera, make sure it is on Microsoft's Hardware Compatibility List. Also check that the cable is firmly connected and that Windows supports the port you are using.
- Some cameras have a switch between picture-taking mode and transfer mode.
- Some cameras will transfer data only when powered on.

## Working with Images in Windows

- Some versions of Windows have a special view useful for viewing pictures. Windows XP has both Filmstrip and Thumbnails views.
- Not all folders can by default use all graphics viewing modes. Use the View, Customize This Folder command to set it up as a graphics folder.

## Sound Card Technology

- Waveform sound files are sounds recorded originally from analog source. Common extensions include .wav, .wma, .mp3, .cda, and .au.
- MIDI sound files are sounds created digitally with digital instruments and music software. Most have a .mid extension.
- Some sound cards simulate MIDI instrument sounds with FM synthesis. Others play back actual clips of instruments (wavetable synthesis).
- Some features of a good sound card include Plug and Play, PCI interface, MPU 401 UART, and MPC3 compatibility.
- For users who plan on recording MIDI music, a sound card strong in this area is appropriate, including new instrument capability, 64-voice polyphony, ample ROM and RAM, synthesizer effects, and a large number of MIDI channels.
- For users who plan on using the sound card for game playing, a card strong in digital audio features is appropriate. These may include Sound Blaster compatibility, support for various APIs such as EAX and DirectSound 3D, and Dolby Digital 5.1 decoding.
- The most common external I/O ports on a sound card are MIDI, Line Out, Mic, and Speaker. Slightly less common are Line In and Digital Out.
- Internal I/O ports include CD In, TAD, S/PDIF, TV Tuner, Mic Con, and Aux In.
- 3D sound is like surround sound in a movie theater; it is also called positional audio. It works best with more than two speakers.
- Games include support for APIs (application programming interfaces) that take advantage of 3D sound, but the sound card and the game must both support the same API for it to work.

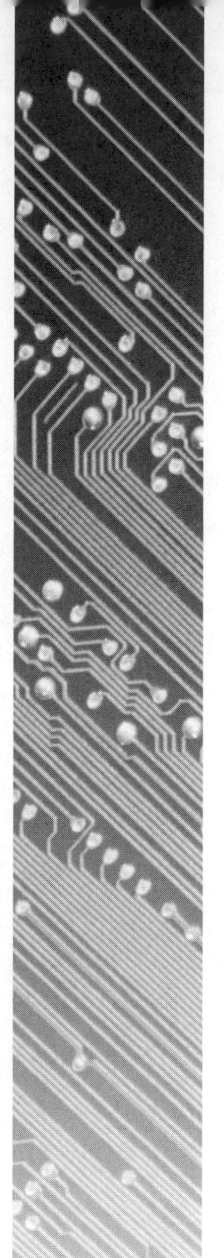

- Popular game APIs for sound include A3D, EAX, Sensaura, and Microsoft DirectSound 3D (part of DirectX).

## Installing and Supporting Sound Cards

- If you are replacing built-in sound with a sound card, disable the built-in sound support via BIOS Setup or a motherboard jumper, depending on the system.
- Sound cards are typical expansion boards that fit into motherboard slots (usually PCI these days, but older ones may be ISA).
- If the system has a CD drive that plays audio CDs, run a cable between the sound card's CD internal I/O connector and the CD drive.
- If Windows does not automatically detect the new sound card at startup, run the setup software that came with the card.
- Download updated drivers for the sound card from the manufacturer if needed (that is, if the drivers you have do not work or create errors).
- If Windows sees the sound card but you do not hear any sound, the problem is probably the volume control or the speakers.
- Test the sound by playing a system sound on the Sounds tab of the Sounds applet in the Control Panel.
- If a recording device such as a microphone does not work, make sure it is enabled in Volume Control. Choose Options, Properties, and then choose Recording to see the recording devices.
- Use the DirectX Diagnostic tool to troubleshoot problems with game sound involving DirectSound. Choose Start, Run, key **DXDIAG**, and then click OK.

## Selecting and Installing PC Speakers

- Amplification is standard on almost all speakers. It requires some sort of power, either battery or AC current (preferred).
- Amplification is measured in watts.
- There are several ways of measuring wattage. One of the most common is RMS (Root Mean Squared). RMS Maximum and PMPO are two alternative measures that will show higher numbers for the same quality of speaker.
- Speakers designed for use near computers will include EMI shielding.
- A standard set of speakers is two. Add a subwoofer for extra bass, and it is known as Dolby Digital 2.1.
- Dolby Digital 4.1 uses four speakers plus a subwoofer. Dolby Digital 5.1 uses five speakers plus a subwoofer, and is also called Surround Sound.

- The frequency range of a speaker is the range of sound wavelengths it can reproduce. An average range is 50–10,000Hz.
- A pair of ordinary stereo speakers connect to the sound card via a single plug. One speaker connects to the sound card; the other connects to the first speaker.
- Speaker systems involving a subwoofer connect the subwoofer to the sound card and all other speakers to the subwoofer.

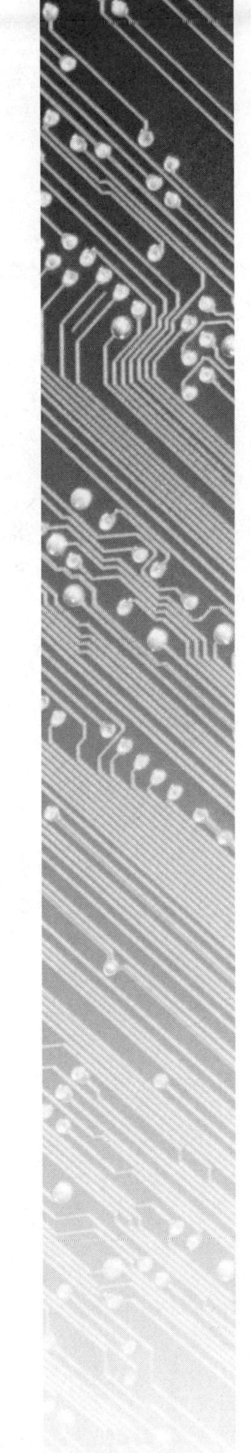

### Sound Support in Windows

- The applet for sounds in the Control Panel depends on the Windows version. In Windows 95 and 98, it is called Sounds. In Windows Me and 2000, it is Sounds and Multimedia. In Windows XP, it is Sounds and Audio Devices.
- System sounds may be assigned event-by-event or as part of a complete sound scheme on the Sounds tab in the Sound Properties dialog box.

### Sound Options for People with Disabilities

- Narrator is a utility in Windows XP that reads the text of every dialog box that appears as well as text in some applications that support it. Run it from the Accessories/Accessibility Options submenu of the Start menu.
- SoundSentry provides a visual cue whenever Windows generates a system sound. Turn it on from the Accessibility Options applet in the Control Panel.
- ShowSounds turns on captioning for any applications that support it.
- ToggleKeys plays a tone whenever Caps Lock, Num Lock, or Scroll Lock is pressed.

## PRACTICE TEST

On a blank sheet of paper, write the answers to the following multiple-choice questions and explain why each answer is correct.

1. What happens when you digitize something?
   a. You convert it to digital format.
   b. You count and record the number of digits contained in it.
   c. You convert hexadecimal numbers to binary digits.
   d. You convert decimal numbers (base 10) to binary digits.

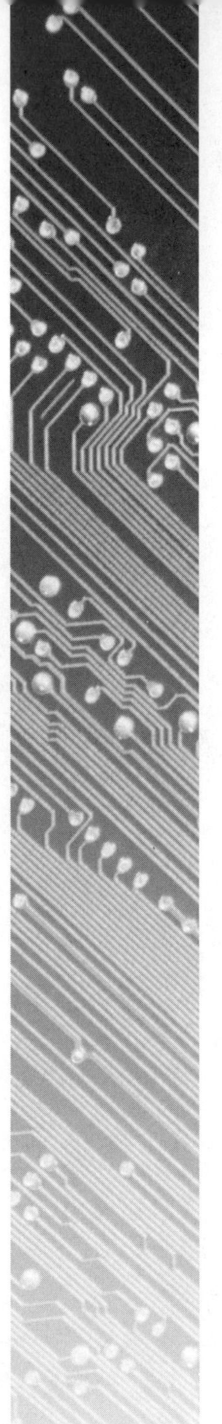

2. What is a CCD?
   a. a halogen light bar that illuminates an image to be scanned
   b. an algorithm for interpolation at the hardware level
   c. a stepper motor that advances the scanner lamp to the next line
   d. an array of photosensitive cells that convert light to electrical charge

3. Which of these statements is *not* true of interpolation?
   a. It increases the resolution of the scanned image file.
   b. It uses mathematical formulas to determine values for extra pixels between actual scanned ones.
   c. It decreases the size of the scanned image file through compression.
   d. A scan with an interpolated resolution of 1200 x 1200 is inferior in quality to a scan with a hardware resolution of 1200 x 1200.

4. What is the minimum color depth required to produce a 16.7 million color scanned image?
   a. 16-bit
   b. 24-bit
   c. 32-bit
   d. 36-bit

5. Why are scanners produced in bit depth higher than is required to produce a 16.7 million color image?
   a. The extra bits allow the scanner to perform color and brightness correction.
   b. The extra bits produce a higher color depth image, resulting in greater printout quality.
   c. The extra bit quality is noticeable on high-resolution monitors.
   d. both b and c

6. Which of these is *not* a common interface for a scanner?
   a. IEEE 1284
   b. IEEE 1394
   c. USB
   d. SCSI

7. How do you unlock a new, fresh-out-of-the-box scanner?
   a. through the scanner driver
   b. by a physical switch on the scanner itself
   c. by a key
   d. through the proprietary software that came with the scanner

8. In order to use the Scanner and Camera Wizard in Windows, what must be true?
   a. You must have a version of Windows that includes the wizard.
   b. You must have a scanner or camera on the HCL for the Windows version.
   c. You must have at least one free USB port.
   d. both a and b

9. Which of these resolutions is approximately 3.1 megapixels?
   a. 1024 x 768
   b. 1280 x 800
   c. 1600 x 1200
   d. 2048 x 1536

10. Which is the best type of zoom lens to have on a digital camera?
    a. digital
    b. optical
    c. vector
    d. megapixel

11. What is a CompactFlash?
    a. an add-on flash (lighting) that works with multiple models of digital cameras
    b. the built-in flash (lighting) in a digital camera
    c. a flash ROM cartridge for storing photos taken with a compatible camera
    d. a card reader that makes it possible to transfer pictures from a SmartMedia cartridge without the camera being present

12. What is a webcam?
    a. a video camera that works only on the Web
    b. a video camera that works only when connected to the PC
    c. a camcorder that records on digital cartridges rather than film
    d. None of the above

13. What type of sound file is a digitized version of an originally analog sound?
    a. waveform
    b. MIDI
    c. JPEG
    d. wavetable synthesized

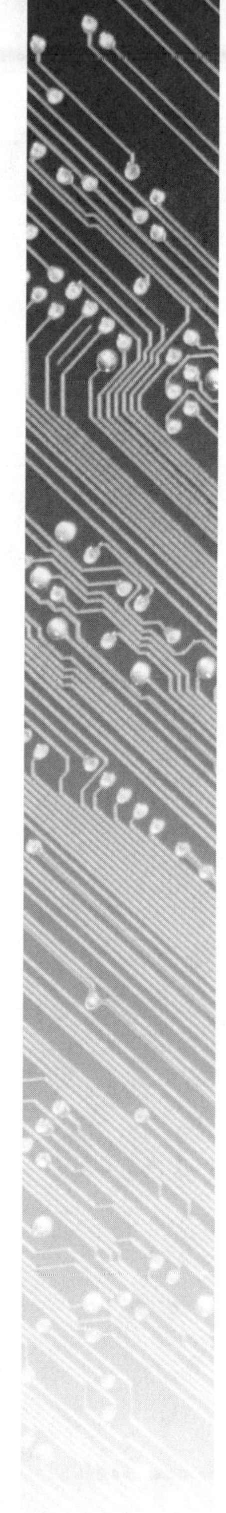

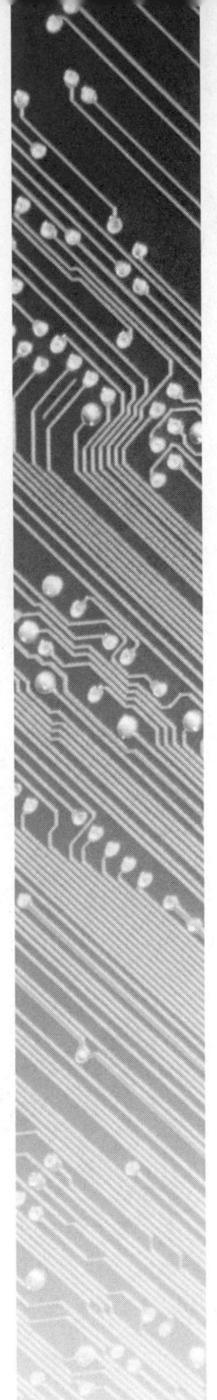

14. A sound card that relies exclusively on FM synthesis for MIDI playback
    a. lacks wavetable synthesis support.
    b. lacks the ability to record MIDI input.
    c. has no built-in amplification.
    d. supports only one pair of speakers.

15. Which of these specifications would be most important when selecting a sound card for someone who wanted to use it primarily to play games?
    a. MIDI channels
    b. recording depth
    c. support for popular APIs
    d. ROM size

16. Which I/O port has a red plug on a sound card with color-coded plugs?
    a. Line out
    b. Line in
    c. Speaker out
    d. Microphone

17. Which is the most common sound API, the one that nearly every game supports?
    a. DirectSound
    b. A3D
    c. EAX
    d. Sound Blaster

18. A Surround Sound speaker system that includes five speakers and a woofer is also known as
    a. Dolby Digital 2.1.
    b. Dolby Digital 4.1.
    c. Dolby Digital 5.1.
    d. Dolby Digital 7.1.

19. In Windows 98, sounds are assigned to system events through which Control Panel applet?
    a. Multimedia
    b. Sound
    c. System
    d. Events

20. Which accessibility feature in Windows provides a visual cue whenever Windows generates a system sound?
    a. SoundSentry
    b. ShowSounds
    c. ToggleSounds
    d. Narrator

# TROUBLESHOOTING

1. A client has a brand-new scanner, and Windows recognizes it. However, when he tries to use the scanner, it makes a horrible grinding noise and will not work. What could be the problem?
2. A client is trying to transfer images from her digital camera to her PC, and she claims that she has successfully done so before with this PC and this camera. Now, however, it is not working. What can you suggest that she try?
3. A client has just reinstalled Windows, and her system is almost back to normal, but she no longer hears system sounds. What could be the problem?

# CUSTOMER SERVICE

1. A client calls asking you whether he should spend extra money to get a 3-megapixel camera instead of a 2-megapixel. What questions would you ask him about his intended usage in order to advise him well?
2. A client with a five-year-old PC running Windows 95 asks what type of scanner interface she should shop for. What will you advise?
3. One of your friends who formerly had no sound support in his computer has recently bought and installed a sound card. It works fine, he reports, except he cannot hear audio CDs he plays in his CD drive. What can you recommend?

# FOR MORE INFORMATION

For links to Web sites that provide further information about the topics covered in this chapter, go to the EMC/Paradigm Internet Resource Center at www.emcp.com/College Division/Internet Resource Centers/PC Maintenance/For More Information.

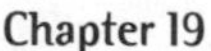

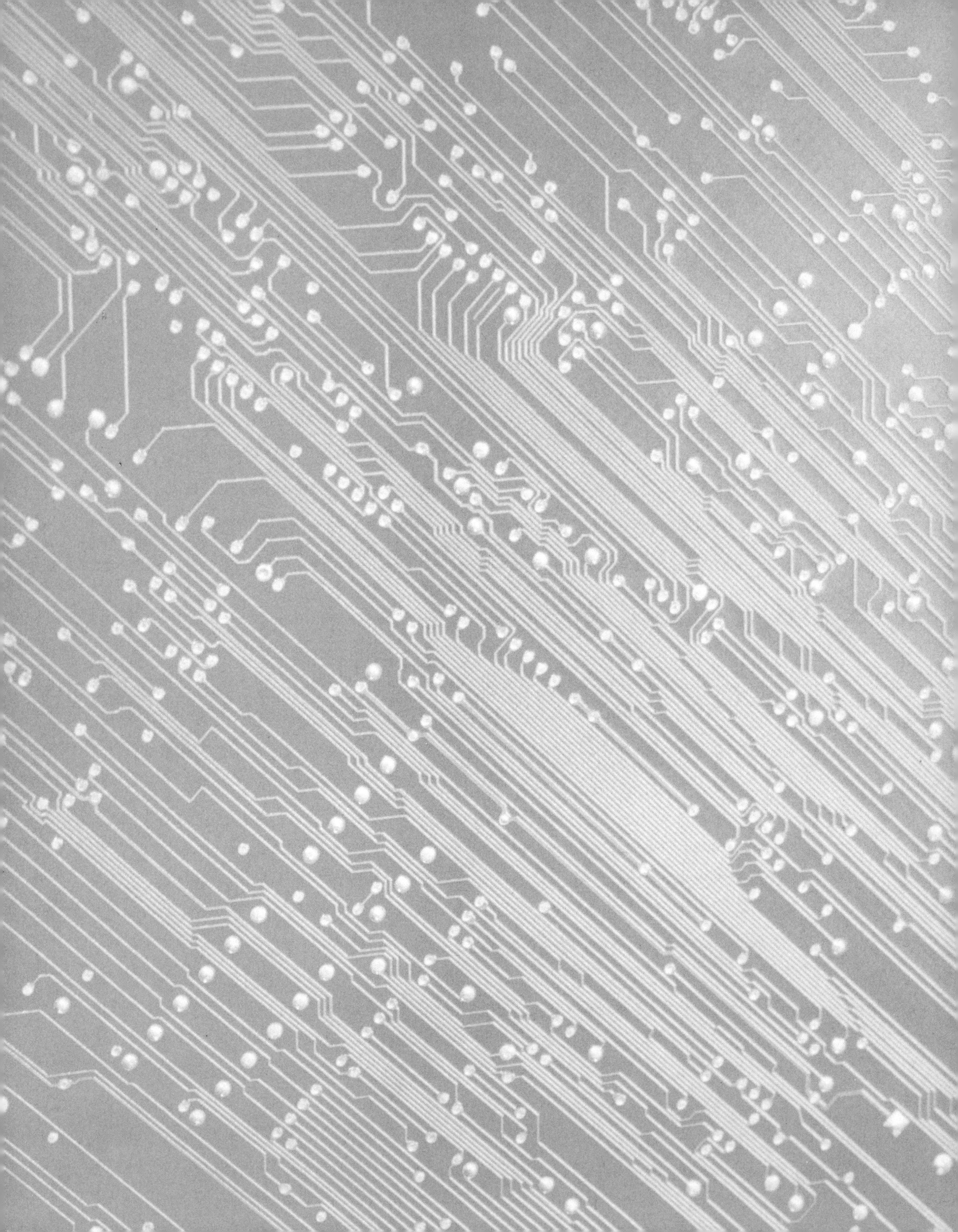

# 20 Portable PCs

## ON THE TEST

**A+ Core Hardware Service Technician Examination**

- **Objective 1.1:** Identify basic terms, concepts, and functions of system modules, including how each module should work during normal operation and during the boot process.
- **Objective 1.2:** Identify basic procedures for adding and removing field replaceable modules for both desktop and portable systems.
- **Objective 1.3:** Identify available IRQs, DMAs, and I/O addresses and procedures for device installation and configuration.
- **Objective 1.7:** Identify proper procedures for installing and configuring peripheral devices.
- **Objective 1.8:** Identify hardware methods of upgrading system performance, procedures for replacing basic subsystem components, unique components and when to use them.

## ON THE JOB

Portable PCs are no longer the exotic luxury item they once were; they are a staple of business users everywhere. Therefore, as a PC technician working in a business environment, many of the PCs you support will be portables. Some of the tasks you might need to perform include:

- educating users about the features of their notebook computers
- teaching users how to select and use PC Card devices
- teaching users how to use external drives
- setting up notebook PCs to work with docking stations
- purchasing and installing notebook batteries
- enabling infrared ports

- setting up power management
- creating hardware profiles
- troubleshooting problems with LCD displays
- troubleshooting standby and hibernation issues
- installing new software on PDAs

## Types of Portable Computers

The definition of "portable" is a bit difficult to pin down, but generally it refers to any computer with a built-in monitor that is easily carried from one location to another. The original portable computers back in the late 1980s would not be considered portable today; they were as large and heavy as a suitcase. In fact, they were often called "luggables" rather than portables for that reason.

**Notebook PC**

A portable PC that folds up into a unit the approximate size and shape of a thick writing notebook. Also called laptop.

**Subnotebook PC**

A portable PC that is smaller than a conventional notebook PC.

**Laptop PC**

Any notebook or subnotebook PC.

As technology has continued to advance, portables have become much smaller. Most of the portables sold today are *notebook PCs*, which means they are approximately the size and shape of a paper notebook (although somewhat thicker). PCs that are slightly smaller than regular notebooks are called *subnotebooks*. There is no objective division between notebooks and subnotebooks; the PCs that we call subnotebooks today might be considered ordinary notebooks five years from now, or there might be an entirely different naming scheme for classifying the various sizes of portables. *Laptop* is sometimes used as a generic term to refer to a notebook or subnotebook. Figure 20.1 shows a typical notebook computer.

**FIGURE 20.1**
A Typical Notebook PC

## In Real Life

The terms *notebook, portable,* and *laptop* are often used generically and interchangeably.

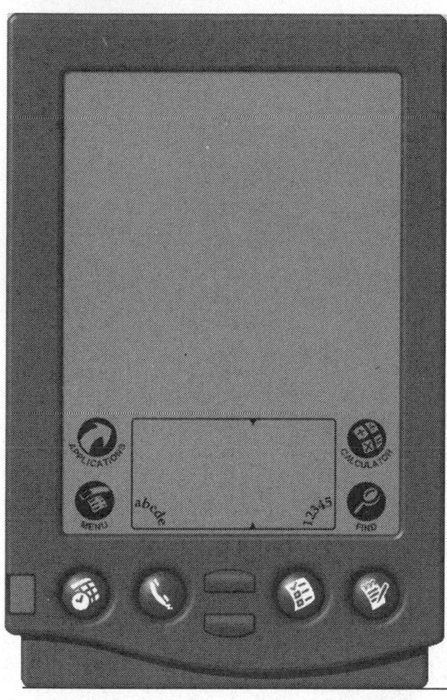


There are even smaller computers called *personal digital assistants* (PDAs) or handhelds. Examples include the PocketPC, the Palm, and the Handspring Visor. These handhelds are characterized by a touch-sensitive screen, a *stylus* for writing and selecting, and (usually) a lack of a keyboard capable of touch typing, although some of them have external keyboard options you can purchase separately. We will look at some basic operations of handhelds later in the chapter, but they are not covered in any detail on the A+ exams. Figure 20.2 shows a typical PDA.

**Personal digital assistant (PDA)**

A handheld computer, usually with a touch-sensitive screen and a writing stylus.

**Stylus**

A pointing device, resembling a leadless pencil, with which you write or tap on a touch-sensitive screen.

**FIGURE 20.2**
A Typical PDA

# Features of Notebook Computers

Notebook computers are functionally the same as desktop PCs, and they run the same operating systems (Windows 9x, Windows 2000, Windows XP, and so on). Most versions of Windows include special features that appear only when Windows is installed in a notebook, such as a battery power indicator and a PC Card manager. The newer the Windows version, the more special features it will have for notebook PCs, some of which will be covered later in the chapter.

The following sections describe some aspects of notebook computers that are not usually found on desktop PCs.

## LCD Screen

One of the reasons that notebook computers have traditionally been more expensive than their desktop counterparts is that a Liquid Crystal Display

(LCD) screen is more expensive to manufacture than a CRT. You learned about LCD technology in Chapter 16. A notebook PC has an LCD monitor built into the inside of the lid of the computer, so that when the lid is closed, the monitor is protected.

## Fn Key

Notebook computers require several additional keyboard functions that a normal computer would not need. For example, they need keys that adjust the brightness and contrast of the built-in LCD monitor, and they need a key that toggles between the LCD monitor and an external monitor port. Rather than add more physical keys to the keyboard, many notebook computers simply add an additional function key, the Fn key, and then assign additional duties to existing keys when they are pressed in combination with Fn. Figure 20.3 shows a notebook keyboard; notice that some keys have some extra symbols on them (in a different color). Those represent the functions of the Fn key. The Fn key itself is usually located in the bottom left corner of the keyboard.

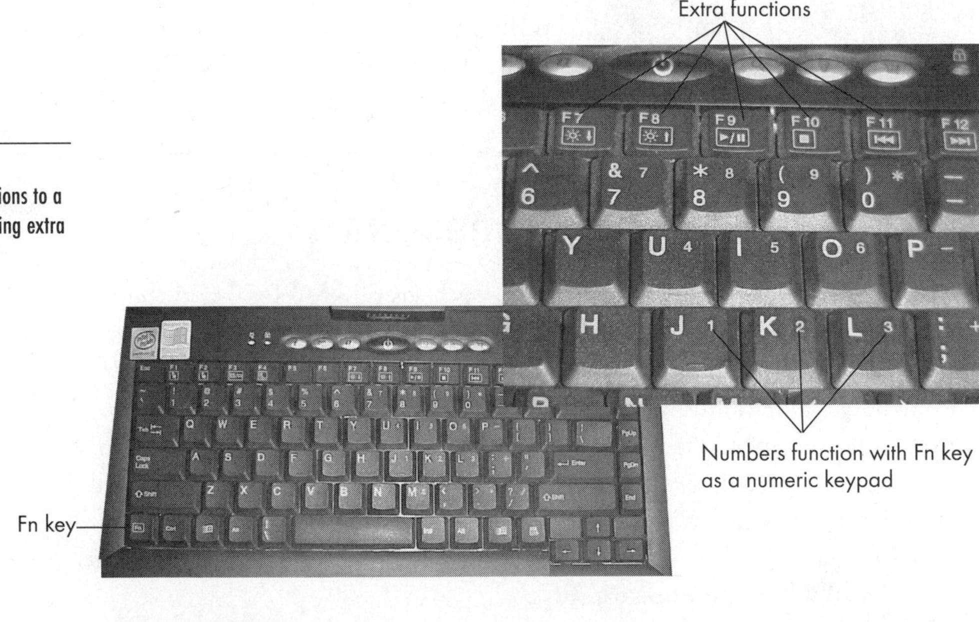


**FIGURE 20.3**
The Fn key adds functions to a keyboard without adding extra keys.

### TRY IT!

Identify the Fn functions available on your notebook computer and try them out. For example, you might be able to adjust the display with them, or use regular keys as directional arrow keys for moving the cursor.

## PC Card Slots

*PC Card* is a standard for connecting add-on devices to a notebook PC. PC cards fit into a slot in the side of the notebook PC. Another name for PC Card is *PCMCIA*.

**PC Card**

A cartridge approximately the size and shape of a credit card (but thicker) that adds functionality such as modem or NIC to a notebook PC.

**PCMCIA**

The standards organization that developed the PC Card standard. Stands for Personal Computer Memory Card International Association.

There are three sizes of PC Card devices:

- **Type I:** Up to 3.3mm thick; used mostly for adding more memory. These are no longer common since most notebook computers have plenty of RAM and a special RAM upgrade socket.
- **Type II:** Up to 5.5mm thick; the most popular size of PC Card, and the type that most people visualize when they hear the term "PC Card." Type II is used to add devices that would be expansion cards if they were in a regular desktop PC. This might include modems, network cards, and so on. Figure 20.4 shows a typical Type II PC Card (which happens to be a wireless Ethernet card).

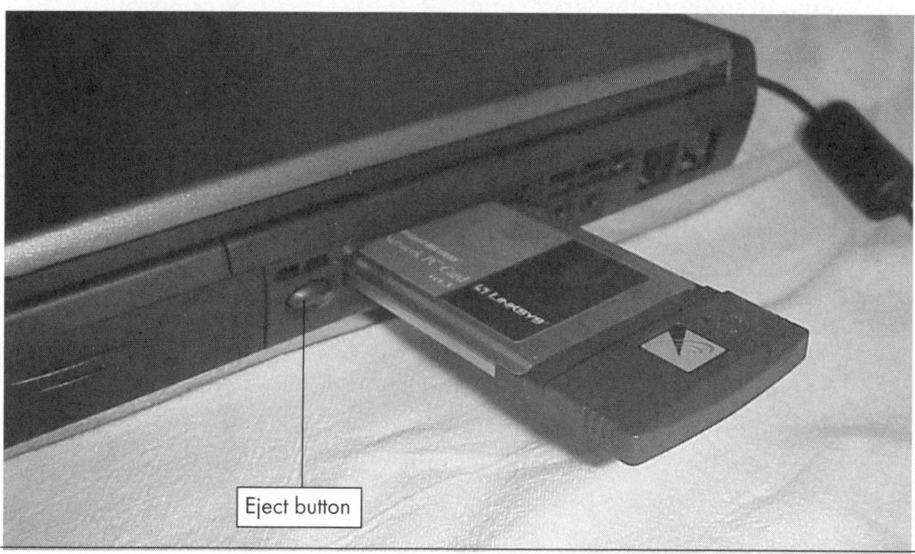


**FIGURE 20.4**
A Type II PC Card

- **Type III:** Up to 10.5mm thick; used as tiny hard drive. Like Type I, Type III is not widely employed; users have less need these days for a small removable hard drive because notebook PCs have adequate hard disk space.

Most notebook computers have a PC Card slot that can accommodate two Type I or Type II cards or a single Type III card.

The PC Card standard has recently been updated to a new version called *CardBus*. It is backward-compatible with the PC Card standard but has improved speed and bus width as well as support for lower voltage cards. When you locate a PCMCIA controller in Device Manager, it usually has

**CardBus**

A recent update to the PC Card standard that provides speed, bus, and voltage improvements.

**Dots per inch (dpi)**

A measurement of printer resolution.

the word "CardBus" in its name, indicating that it conforms to the CardBus standard.

You can insert and remove PC Card devices while the PC is running. See the section "Managing PC Cards in Windows" later in this chapter for more details about how Windows interacts with a PC Card.

To insert a PC Card:

1. Locate the PC Card slot.
2. Push the card into the slot, making sure to align it with the guides inside the slot so that it goes in straight. Push until it will not go in any further.

To remove a PC Card:

1. Locate and press the release button for that slot. It is usually a button or tab that sticks out of the corner of the slot whenever something is inserted in it (see Figure 20.4).
2. The card pops out of the slot an inch or so; pull it the rest of the way out and store it somewhere safe.

## TRY IT!

1. **With Windows running, insert a PC Card device. Watch Windows detect it.**
2. **Open Device Manager and locate the device.**
3. **Remove the device (physically) and watch it disappear from Device Manager. If it does not immediately disappear, press F5 to refresh.**

For several reasons, storing PC Cards in cases can be a useful precaution. They are not particularly fragile, but they are expensive; some have jacks (such as a phone jack on a modem) that stick out and can be broken off with rough handling. Some PC cards come with their own storage cases; cases can also be purchased as separate items.

## INTERNAL AND EXTERNAL DRIVES

Most notebook PCs have floppy and CD drives built in, as in Figure 20.5. This is very convenient, but makes the computer somewhat heavier overall.

FIGURE 20.5
Built-In Drives

Earlier models typically had one drive built in and the other as an external unit that plugged in whenever it was needed. Some notebook PCs had swappable internal drives, such that you could use only one drive at a time (floppy or CD).

Subnotebooks, in which small size and light weight are important features, may still allow for optional external drives. In Figure 20.6, which shows an external floppy drive, notice that the drive fits into an outer plastic sheath; this gives added flexibility for removing the drive from the sheath and installing it at some time as an internal floppy drive.

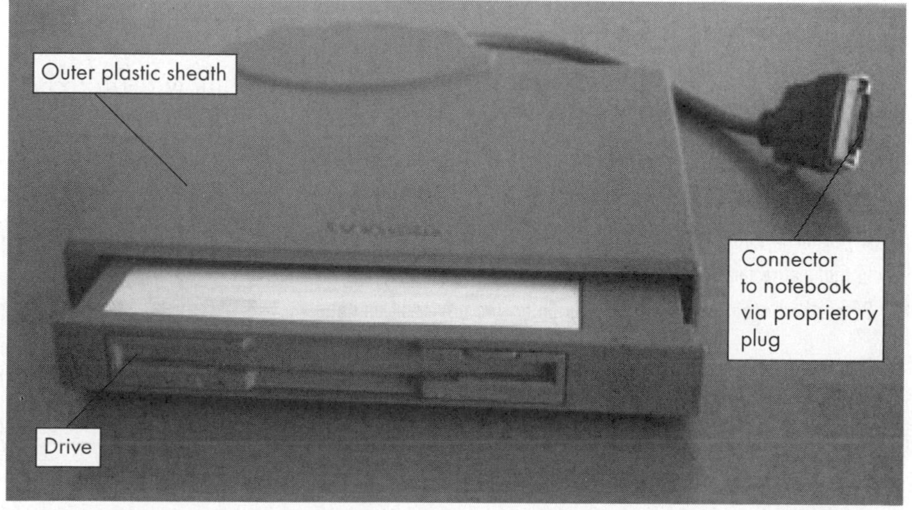


FIGURE 20.6
Some notebook PC drives may be external to keep down the overall weight of the base unit.

Another way that some subnotebooks manage the balance between weight and performance is to include an optional section that contains the floppy and/or CD drives and can be removed and left behind if desired (see Figure 20.7). This type of removable drive base is sometimes called a "slice," and can be used as a port replicator/docking station (described in the next section).

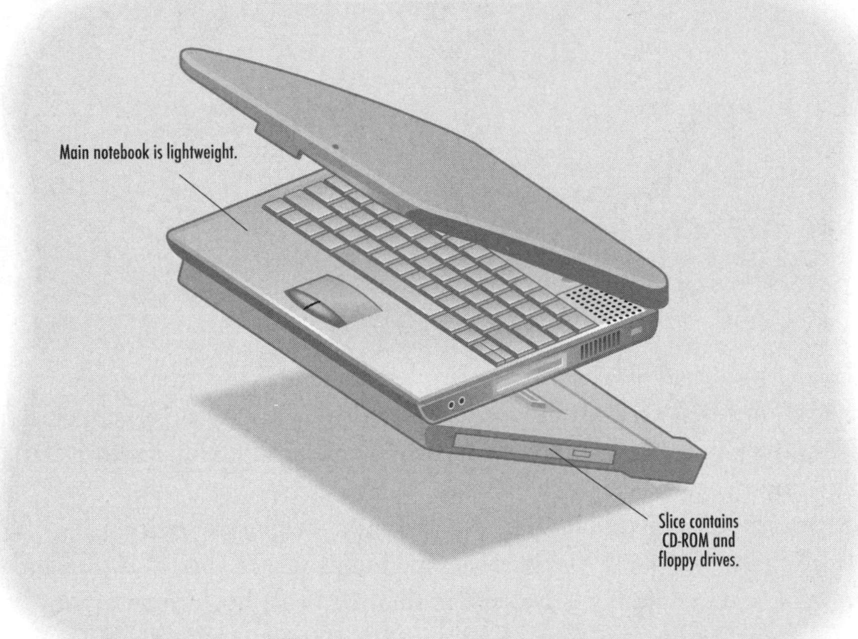
Main notebook is lightweight.
Slice contains CD-ROM and floppy drives.

**FIGURE 20.7**
Some notebook PCs have an optional "slice" containing some of the drives that can be removed to make the base unit lighter.

Different models of computers have different procedures for removing and connecting external drives. Make sure you read the instructions carefully because some models require the PC to be off before disconnecting or connecting external drives, while others allow them to be *hot-swapped*.

**Hot-swapping**

Connecting or disconnecting a device while the PC is running. Also called hot-plugging.

## TRY IT!

If you have a notebook PC that has an external drive, connect it and then turn on the PC. Check to make sure the drive is visible in My Computer, then shut down and remove the drive. Turn the PC back on again and check My Computer; the drive will be gone.

If you have a notebook PC with swappable drives, turn on the PC and see which drives appear in My Computer; then shut down, swap in the other drive, turn it on again, and check My Computer to confirm that the other drive appears there.

## Docking Stations

A *docking station* is an external unit that attaches to a notebook or subnotebook PC and gives it extra capabilities, such as additional ports or drives. It is similar in concept to the removable "slice" discussed in the preceding section but somewhat larger and more complex, and is designed to remain at a fixed location rather than transported with the notebook PC (see Figure 20.8).

**Docking station**

A stationary unit to which a notebook PC attaches to gain extra capabilities while in a fixed location.

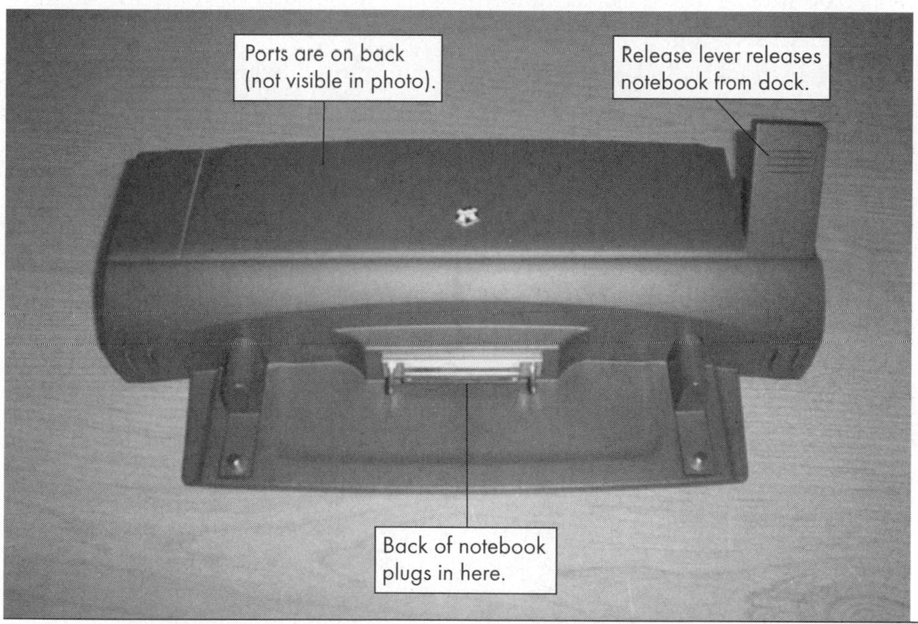
Ports are on back (not visible in photo).
Release lever releases notebook from dock.
Back of notebook plugs in here.

**FIGURE 20.8**
**A Docking Station for a Notebook PC**

A docking station has two purposes. One is to make extra ports available; the other is to make it easier to connect to and disconnect from other stationary devices. For example, a typical notebook PC has a connector for an external VGA monitor; you do not need a docking station to connect an external monitor. However, connecting and disconnecting from a monitor many times a day can become inconvenient. A docking station might provide an external VGA port, but may also offer simple connect/disconnect with the notebook to eliminate having to screw and unscrew the monitor plug over and over again.

Older docking stations are rather large; some take as much space as a desktop PC, and provide extra drives. The newer models are generally smaller and more compact. An especially small docking station, particularly one that contains only ports and no drives, is sometimes referred to as a *port replicator*. There is no objective distinction between docking stations and port replicators; different manufacturers use different names.

**Port replicator**

A small docking station that exists primarily to provide easy connect/disconnect access to external ports such as external mouse, keyboard, and monitor.

## MOUSE ALTERNATIVES

When notebook computers were first introduced, manufacturers were not sure about the best way to integrate mouse functionality. Early models had clip-on trackballs that hung off the side of the keyboard; later models have had various types of pointing devices built in. Some of these include:

- **Pointing stick:** A little nub the size and shape of a pencil eraser sticks up in the middle of the keyboard, and you push it in the direction you want the pointer to move. Separate buttons below the keyboard are for clicking and right-clicking.
- **Built-in trackball:** A small roller ball is mounted below the keyboard, with buttons at its top. You roll the ball with a finger to move the pointer.
- **Touchpad:** This is the most popular mouse alternative used today in notebook PCs (see Figure 20.9). It is a touch-sensitive rectangular pad; you slide your finger across it to move the pointer or tap it to click. There are also buttons above or below it that function as mouse buttons (for example, when you need to right-click or if you are not comfortable tapping to click).

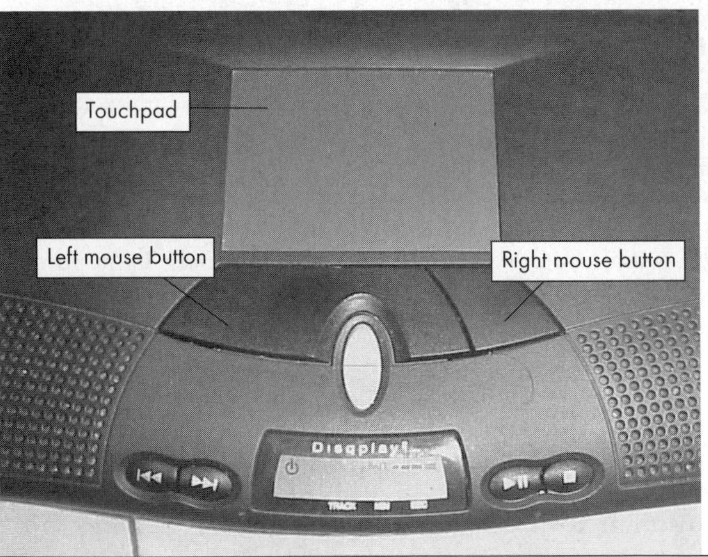


**FIGURE 20.9**
A notebook PC's touchpad serves as a mouse equivalent.

## AC ADAPTER AND BATTERIES

As you learned in Chapter 3, computers take in AC power and convert it to DC power for the use of the motherboard and the other components. A notebook PC can run off AC power, and comes with its own power cord.

However, it also includes a battery that charges whenever the notebook is plugged into an AC outlet, and that battery (which supplies DC current, like all batteries) can also run the PC.

Windows is rather smart about working with notebook batteries and detecting when AC power is present; you will learn about Windows features involving power later in this chapter. The following sections look at how the battery and AC adapter work physically.

There is not much to the AC adapter. It typically contains a transformer block, which takes the place of a desktop PC's power supply in stepping down the current to a usable level for the PC. The battery is a monolith-style cartridge that fits into a large slot in the PC. There is usually a cover over it to ensure that it does not get bumped or removed accidentally.

### *Types of Batteries*

The most common substances used in computer battery packs are Nickel Cadmium (NiCad), Nickel-Metal Hydride (NiMH), and Lithium Ion (LIon).

**Nickel Cadmium (NiCad) batteries** can provide considerable power, but you must recharge them every 3 to 4 hours. A full recharge can take as long as 12 hours, but some batteries can be recharged in less time.

> **WARNING**
>
> NiCad batteries work best when they are allowed to run down completely before being recharged. If you leave a NiCad-powered laptop plugged in all of the time, letting its battery run down only a little and only occasionally, in time the battery loses its ability to retain a full charge. Even with full drainage, all batteries can be recharged only a limited number of times. The maximum for most NiCad batteries is about 1,000 recharges.

**Nickel-Metal Hydride (NiMH) batteries** do not use heavy metals that can have toxic effects, so in that way they are superior to NiCad. In addition, NiMH batteries can store up to 50 percent more power than NiCad batteries, and do not suffer loss of functionality from partial draining and recharging.

**Lithium Ion (LIon) batteries** are composed of lithium, the lightest metal and the one with the highest electrochemical potential. Lithium, however, is an unstable metal, so LIon batteries are made with lithium ions from chemicals. LIon is considered the superior battery choice for notebooks today because of its light weight and long life. In addition, LIon batteries are not affected by partial draining and recharging, and do not use poisonous metals such as lead, mercury, or cadmium. Their only disadvantage is that they are more expensive than NiCad and NiMH batteries.

### *Battery Safety Precautions*

Use the same care with a notebook battery that you would with regular alkaline batteries. Keep it away from extreme heat and cold, do not get it wet, and if you ever notice that it is leaking any fluids, avoid touching the discharge and discard it immediately at your local hazardous waste disposal facility.

### *Charging a Battery*

To charge a battery, put it in the PC and plug the PC's AC cord into a wall outlet. A battery may take 4 hours or longer to charge fully. You can also buy external battery chargers for some types of batteries.

### *Removing and Replacing a Battery*

Most notebook batteries are hidden behind a panel or cover. On some models you can simply pull out the battery; on others you must release a latch that causes the whole keyboard to lift up for battery access. Check the manual that came with the notebook PC to be sure, or check the manufacturer's Web site. Figure 20.10 shows a battery being removed from a Compaq Presario notebook.

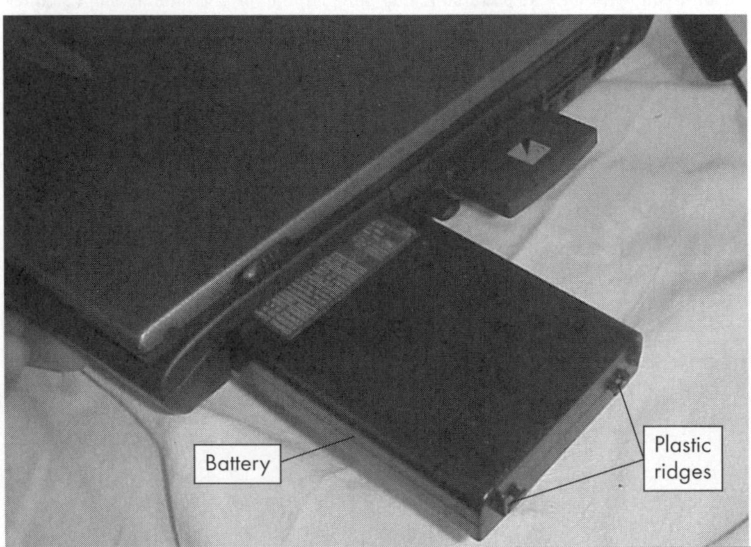


**FIGURE 20.10**
Remove the battery according to manufacturer's instructions.

## IN REAL LIFE

**Some batteries are difficult to remove because there is no handle on the battery, so there is no good way of getting a grip on it. Sometimes you have to improvise. For example, the battery in Figure 20.10 has some little plastic ridges on the outside; to pull it out as shown, grab one of the ridges with a pair of pliers.**

## INFRARED PORTS

Infrared technology provides a way of exchanging data wirelessly between devices in close range of one another. Infrared is an invisible band of radiation at the lower end of the electromagnetic spectrum, between the middle of the microwave spectrum and the beginning of visible light. Data can be sent via infrared, but it requires an unobstructed line of sight between the transmitter and the receiver. It is most widely used in remote controls for home electronics such as TVs.

Some notebook PCs have a built-in infrared port that the operating system treats as a serial port. One of the most common uses for an infrared port is to synchronize data between a notebook PC and a Windows CE-based PDA.

The standard for infrared communication is defined by an organization called the *Infrared Data Association* (IrDA). The standard itself is commonly referred to as IrDA as well (much like the PC Card standard being referred to as PCMCIA because PCMCIA is the standards board that developed the specifications). The operating system must have an IrDA driver in order for the notebook to support an infrared port. The current standard for IrDA communications allows data transfer at up to 4Mbps at a 180-degree range of up to 10 meters between devices.

**Infrared Data Association (IrDA)**

The standards board that developed the industry standard for infrared communication ports between notebook PCs, desktop PCs, PDAs, and other electronics.

## IN REAL LIFE

**Windows 98 and higher include an IrDA driver. You can download an IrDA driver for Windows 95 from the Microsoft Web site.**

On notebooks that have an IrDA port, it is usually an option that you enable/disable in the BIOS Setup, and the operating system sees the port as serial. When another device with IrDA support comes into its range, the OS signals to the user that a connection is possible (for example, by flashing an icon in the notification area in Windows). You can buy add-ons for desktop PCs that provide IrDA support, although it is not a common practice because there are other, more appealing choices for networking desktop PCs wirelessly, such as IEEE 802.11a and 802.11b (both of which will be discussed in Chapter 21).

## Managing PC Cards in Windows

Early versions of Windows (notably Windows 3.x and Windows NT 4) did not have built-in support for PC Cards, so you had to load a PC Card manager application to use them. All versions of Windows 95 and higher support PC Cards natively, however, so you do not need any special driver. When you insert a PC Card device, Windows automatically detects it and installs it with Plug and Play, just like any other device you might install.

To display the properties for PC Card devices, find the individual device in Device Manager and work with it as discussed in Chapter 14. If you want to manage the properties of the PC Card slot itself, do the following:

1. From the Control Panel, double-click the *PC Card (PCMCIA)* icon. This icon appears in the Control Panel only on PCs that have a PC Card slot. The PC Card (PCMCIA) Properties dialog box opens (see Figure 20.11).

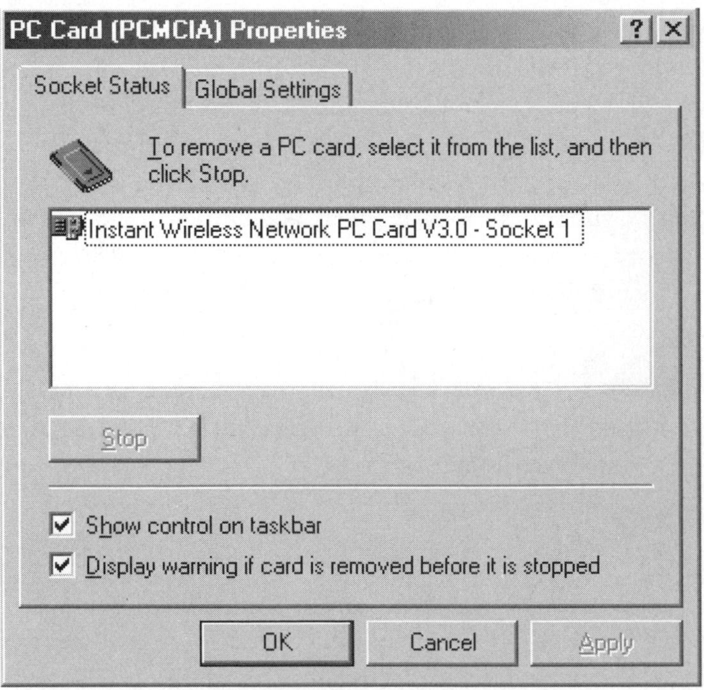


**FIGURE 20.11**
Access PC Card settings from the Control Panel's PC Card (PCMCIA) Properties dialog box.

2. On the Socket Status tab, mark or clear either of these check boxes:
    a. Show control on taskbar: This displays/hides a shortcut icon in the notification area of the Taskbar when a PC Card device is inserted.
    b. Display warning if card is removed before it is stopped: This turns on/off a dialog box warning message about stopping a card before you remove it. (More on this in the next section.)
3. Select the Global Settings tab (see Figure 20.12).

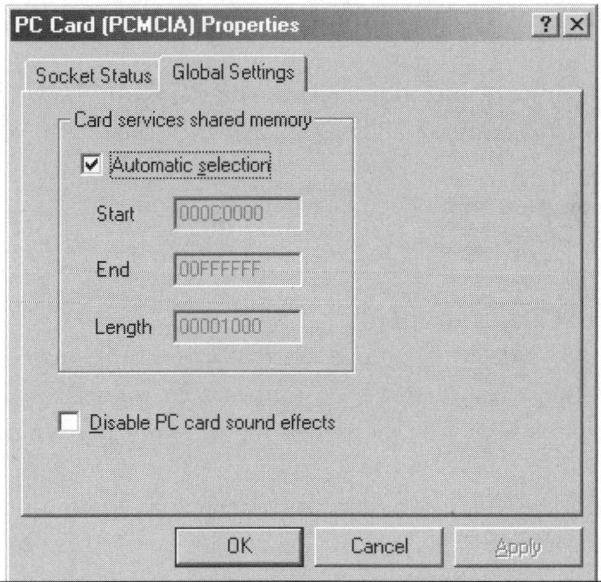


**FIGURE 20.12**
Adjust the memory address range for the PC Card slots and turn on/off sound effects.

4. Mark or clear either of these check boxes:
    a. Automatic selection: When this is marked, Windows automatically assigns system resources to the PC Card slots. This is usually the best setting. When this is cleared, you can manually enter a memory address range.
    b. Disable PC card sound effects: When this is selected, you hear a sound when a PC Card is inserted or removed.
5. Click OK when finished to close the dialog box.

## Stopping a Removable Device

PC Cards are the most common type of removable device on a notebook PC. USB is another common type (both on desktop and notebook). "Removable" is another way of saying hot-swappable; you can connect and disconnect the devices without powering off the PC.

You might have noticed in Figure 20.11 that the PC Card (PCMCIA) Properties dialog box enables you to stop a connected PC Card device. When Windows stops a device, it completes any pending operations for that card and then disables it so it cannot accept any new instructions until it is removed and reinserted (or until Windows restarts). The purpose of stopping a device before removing it is to ensure that no Windows activities are interrupted by the physical removal. For example, suppose you want to remove a PC Card modem; stopping it would disconnect any dial-up connections using that modem.

One way to stop a PC Card is through the properties from the Control Panel:

1. From the Control Panel, double-click the *PC Card (PCMCIA)* icon.
2. On the Socket Status tab (Figure 20.11), click the device you want to stop.
3. Click the Stop button.
4. A dialog box appears telling you that you may safely remove this device. Click OK.
5. Remove the device physically.

You can also stop a device from the shortcut icon in the notification area of the Taskbar (unless you turned it off in the preceding section). The dialog box associated with that shortcut is for all removable devices, not just PC Card. To do this:

1. Double-click the Unplug or Eject Hardware button in the notification area. The Unplug or Eject Hardware dialog box appears (see Figure 20.13).

**FIGURE 20.13**
Stop a device (PC Card or other removable device) from the Unplug or Eject Hardware dialog box.

2. Click the Stop button. The Stop a Hardware Device dialog box opens.
3. Click the device you want to stop and then click OK.
4. A message appears that the device can now be safely removed. Click OK.
5. Remove the device physically.

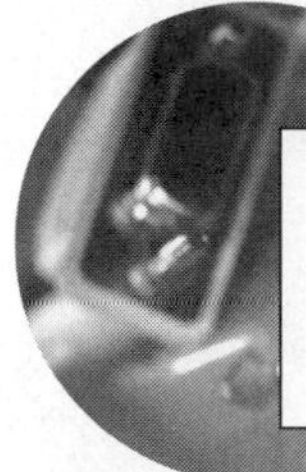

### In Real Life

Stopping a device before removing it is a good safety measure, but nothing bad is likely to happen if you forget to do it, especially if the device you are removing has not been used in several minutes.

## Power Management for Notebook PCs

There are two *power management* standards—for all PCs, not just notebooks—and almost all PC BIOSes support one or the other:

- **Advanced Power Management (APM):** The older of the two standards. It deals mainly with the monitor and the hard drives powering down during periods of inactivity.
- **Advanced Configuration and Power Interface (ACPI):** The newer standard. It is more comprehensive, dealing not only with the monitor and hard drive, but also the CPU and peripheral devices.

It is advantageous to have ACPI support rather than APM because the ACPI support offers more features and is less prone to problems and conflicts. Some BIOSes that support APM can be updated to a revision that supports ACPI; see Chapter 9 for information about BIOS updates.

**Power management**

Features that help the PC extend its battery life or conserve electricity.

### Power Management Options in BIOS Setup

Most BIOSes that support APM or ACPI include BIOS-based power management utilities, in case your client is using an operating system that has no power management utilities of its own. These utilities can be useful, but Windows versions 95 and higher have their own power management utilities, and they often conflict with the BIOS-based utilities. Most problems involving a computer that will not wake up after being placed in a low power consumption mode turn out to be conflicts between a BIOS power management utility and a Windows power management utility. Therefore it is a good idea to turn off the BIOS-based utilities if your client is running Windows 95 or higher. Figure 20.14 shows some typical BIOS-based power management utility settings for a notebook PC with PhoenixBIOS.

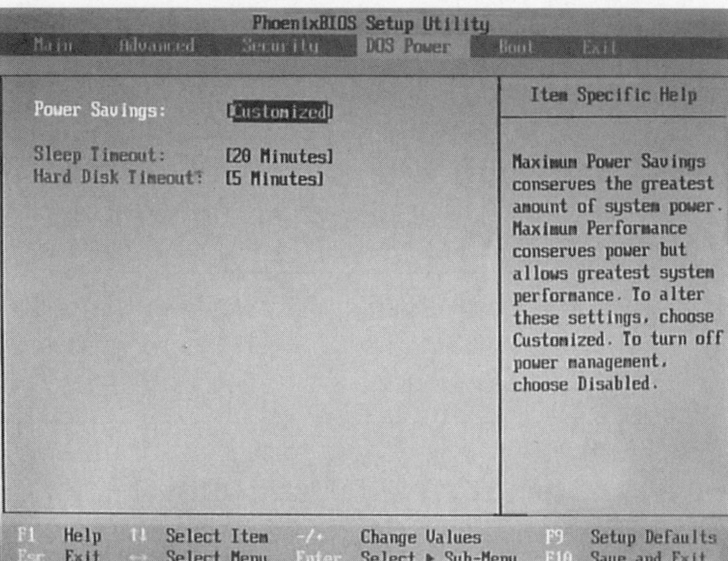


**FIGURE 20.14**
BIOS Settings Governing Power Management

## In Real Life

**Turning off BIOS-based power management utilities will not completely disable APM or ACPI; Windows will still be able to take advantage of APM or ACPI compatibility in the BIOS to run its own power management utilities.**

**Sleep**

A power management mode for a PC that shuts off many of the components but keeps memory supplied with power so the OS remains loaded.

**Save to Disk**

A BIOS-based feature that copies RAM content to the hard disk and then shuts down the PC completely.

**SpeedStep Technology**

A feature of some CPUs designed for notebook PCs that allows the BIOS to direct the CPU to run at a slower speed and use less power when the PC is running on batteries.

In Figure 20.14 there are two settings you can adjust. *Sleep* is a low-power-consumption operating mode that shuts off the display and other components but retains the contents of memory so the PC can wake back up again more quickly than if you had to restart from scratch. The hard disk timeout allows the hard disk(s) to stop spinning after a specified period, further conserving power.

Some notebook PCs also have a *Save to Disk* feature built-in. It uses a small hidden partition on the hard drive to save the contents of RAM before shutting down completely. Then when you turn on the PC again, it reads the RAM content from the hard drive and restores it so you do not have to go through a full startup.

## SpeedStep Technology

Some notebook PCs have CPUs with a feature called *SpeedStep Technology*. It allows the CPU to run at two different speeds—a faster one when plugged into AC power and a slower one (using less power) when running on batteries. This enables the user to preserve battery life by accepting slightly degraded performance. The feature is enabled/disabled through BIOS Setup, as shown in Figure 20.15.

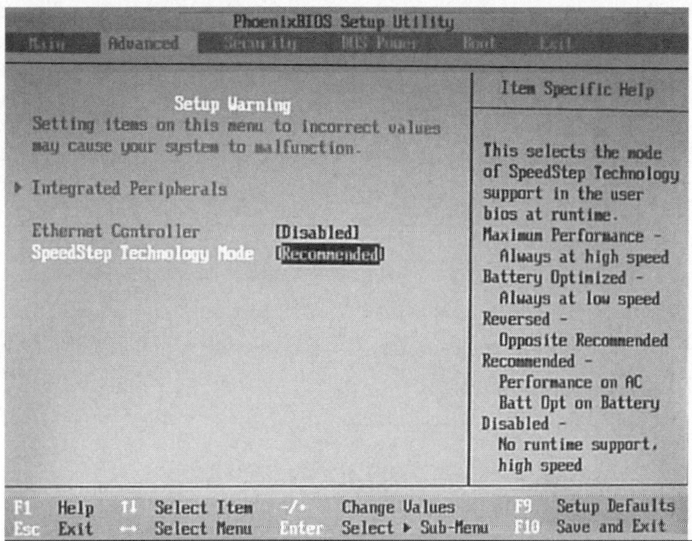


**FIGURE 20.15**

Turn SpeedStep on/off in BIOS Setup if the CPU supports it. It is found only on notebook computers.

You can also enable/disable SpeedStep in Windows, provided it is enabled in BIOS Setup. If it is enabled in the BIOS, a tab for SpeedStep will appear in the Power Options Properties dialog box in Windows (most versions):

1. From the Control Panel, double-click the *Power Options* icon.
2. Select the Intel® SpeedStep™ technology tab (see Figure 20.16).

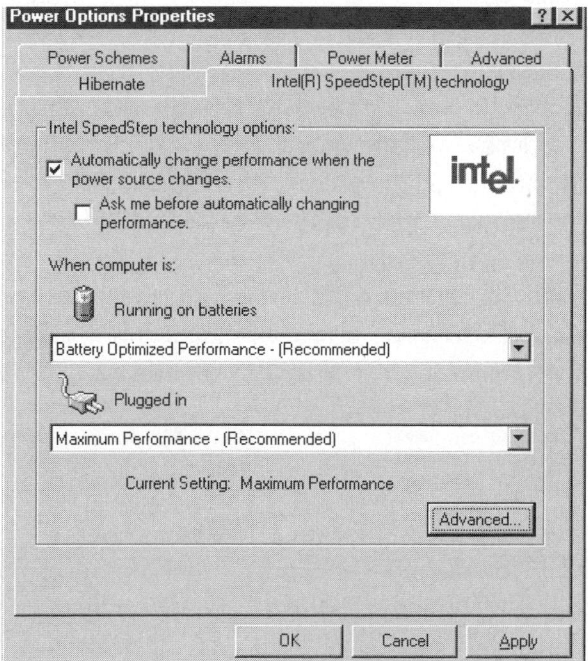


**FIGURE 20.16**

You can control SpeedStep settings from within most versions of Windows.

3. To enable the feature, make sure that the Automatically change performance when the power source changes check box is marked.
4. *Optional:* Change any other settings desired for SpeedStep. For example, you can choose to be notified when the power source changes, choose what the speed should be with each power source, and control other fine-tuning options.
5. Click OK to close the Power Options Properties dialog box when finished.

## TRY IT!

1. Enter BIOS Setup for your notebook PC and see what power management settings are available. Is there a Sleep feature? Save to Disk? SpeedStep technology?
2. Set all power management features except SpeedStep technology to Disabled.
3. Exit BIOS Setup, saving your changes.

## Power Management Options in Windows

Figure 20.17 describes the power management features available in most versions of Windows.

**Standby**

A power management feature of Windows that enables the computer to place itself in a low-power-consumption mode, keeping RAM content.

**Hibernate**

A power management feature of Windows that enables the computer to copy RAM contents to the hard disk and then shut down completely. Restarting is quicker than a full startup.

- **Turn off monitor:** Turns off the power to the monitor after a specified period of inactivity. Pressing a key or moving the mouse turns the monitor back on.
- **Turn off hard disks:** Tells the hard disk to stop spinning after a specified period of inactivity. Pressing a key or moving the mouse, or a background activity that requests reading or writing to the disk, makes it spin up again.
- ***Standby:*** Places the computer in a low-power-consumption mode whereby almost everything is powered off, but the power to the RAM remains so that it retains its content. Pressing a specified key on the keyboard or performing some other specified action (which will be discussed shortly) wakes everything. This is roughly equivalent to the Sleep utility in BIOS-based power management.
- ***Hibernate:*** Copies the contents of RAM to the hard disk and then shuts down completely. Pressing a specified key (usually the Power button) starts up the PC and copies the saved RAM contents back into RAM, avoiding a full restart. This is roughly equivalent to the Save to Disk utility in BIOS-based power management.

**FIGURE 20.17**
Windows Power Management Features

Some versions of Windows use the BIOS support of APM or ACPI to accomplish the activities in Figure 20.17; others do not. For example, the Hibernate feature of Windows 2000/XP is independent and does not require anything from the BIOS.

### *Power Schemes*

A power scheme tells Windows what you want it to do when you have not used the PC in a certain number of minutes (that is, no mouse or keyboard action). A power scheme can involve any or all of the four features listed in Figure 20.17.

Power schemes are set up in the Power Options Properties dialog box from the Control Panel. For a notebook computer there will be two columns on the Power Schemes tab: one for Plugged in and one for Running on batteries (see Figure 20.18). You can enter settings for each situation separately. (For a desktop PC there will be only one column, since there is no battery to account for.)

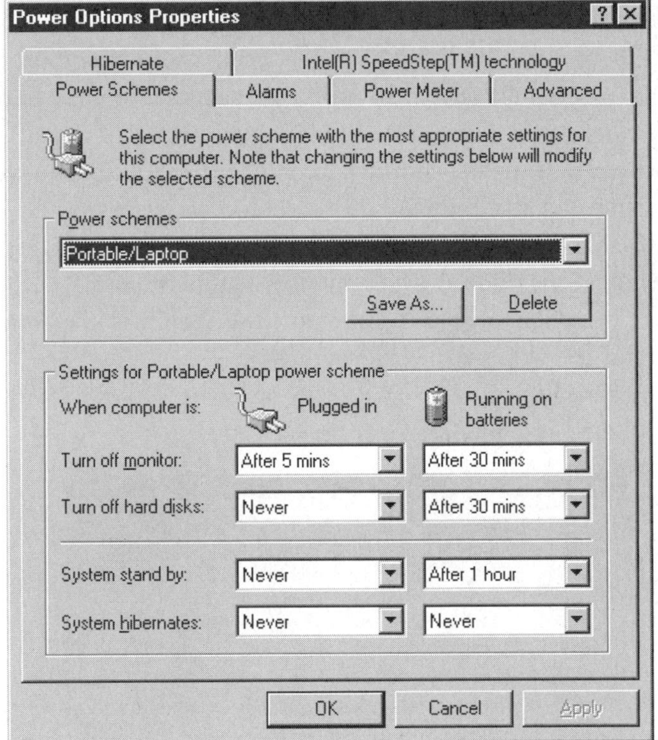


**FIGURE 20.18**
Power schemes for a notebook computer include columns for both AC power and battery power.

You will probably want to set the time delays from short to long, starting with the least extreme power savings tools. For example, you might set the Turn off monitor and Turn off hard disks features to a relatively short delay, like 5 minutes, but set the System stand by or System hibernates settings to a longer interval, like 15 minutes or more. When considering the times to use, think about how much inconvenience your client is willing to deal with (such as waiting for the PC to resume from standby or hibernation) versus how much power needs to be conserved.

To set up or change a power scheme complete the following steps:

1. From the Control Panel, double-click the *Power Options* icon. The Power Options Properties dialog box opens.
2. Select the Power Schemes tab.
3. Open the Power schemes drop-down list and choose the power scheme you want to modify. (If you want to create a new scheme, choose the one that is closest to the settings you want.)
4. Open the drop-down lists for each row and column and make your selections of time delays before the various features are activated (see Figure 20.18).
5. *Optional:* To save your settings as a new scheme, click the Save As button. Key a name in the Save Scheme dialog box that appears and then click OK.
6. Click OK to close the Power Options Properties dialog box.

There are more settings related to power management behavior on the Advanced tab, shown in Figure 20.19. Here you can:

- Choose whether to show a shortcut icon for power options in the notification area of the Taskbar.
- Choose whether to prompt for a password (the screen saver password) when the computer resumes after standby or hibernation.
- Choose the behavior to occur when you close the lid of the computer (None, Stand By, Hibernate, or Power Off).
- Choose the behavior to occur when you press the Power button on the computer (Stand By, Hibernate, or Power Off).

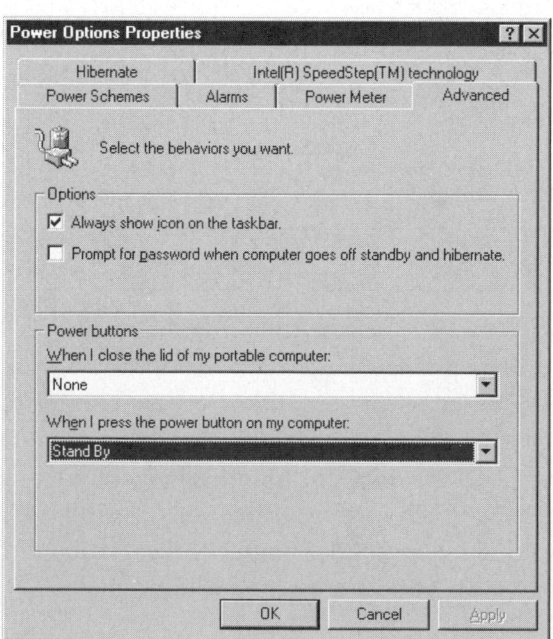


**FIGURE 20.19**
More power management options are available on the Advanced tab.

Not all computers support hibernation. If your computer does not, or if the feature is not supported in the current version of Windows, the Hibernate tab will not appear in the Power Options Properties dialog box. If it does appear, you can turn hibernation on or off (see Figure 20.20).

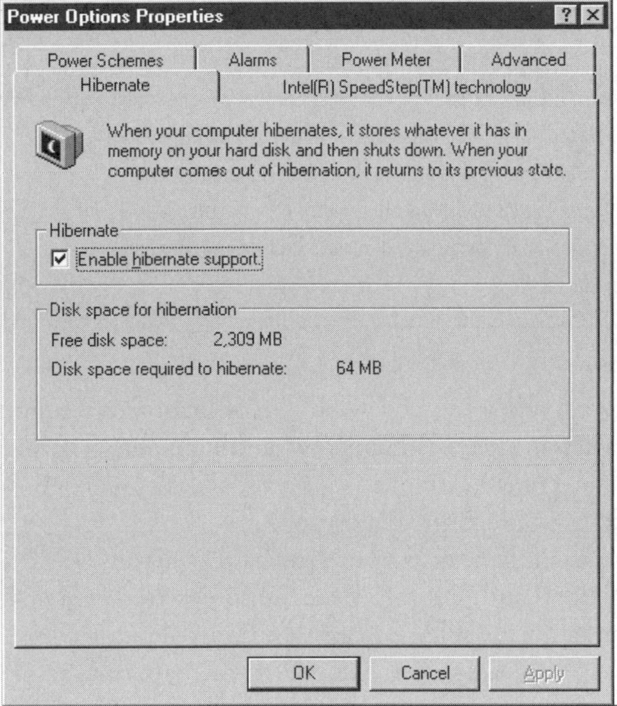


**FIGURE 20.20**
Hibernation, if supported, usually appears on its own tab (although it could be a check box on some other tab, depending on the model of computer).

## In Real Life

If the computer tries to go into hibernate mode and fails either to go into it or to wake up from it, a message will appear asking whether you want to disable hibernation support on the PC. If you answer Yes, you will not see any mention of Hibernate anywhere in the Power Options Properties dialog box. Should you ever change your mind and want to try hibernation again, the best way to get back the option of using it is to delete APM or ACPI support from the System category of Device Manager and then let Windows go through the lengthy process (including several restarts) of redetecting most of the hardware.

You can also manually place the computer into Standby or Hibernate modes through the Start menu's Shut Down command. The process varies depending on the Windows version, but in Windows Me the procedure is as follows:

1. Choose Start, Shut Down. The Shut Down Windows dialog box opens.
2. Open the drop-down list and choose Stand By or Hibernate. Then click OK.

After placing the PC in Standby, you can wake it up by moving the mouse or pressing a key. After placing it in Hibernate mode, you can wake it up by pressing the Power button.

## TRY IT!

1. Set your notebook PC to hibernate when the Power button is pressed.
2. Press the Power button and watch the PC go into Hibernate mode.
3. Press the Power button again to wake it out of hibernation.
4. Place the PC in Standby mode with the Start, Shut Down command.
5. Wake it up again.

### *Power Alarms*

Power alarms help the computer warn you of low-battery conditions. You can specify what you want to happen when the battery gets low, such as go into Standby or Hibernate mode. Set power alarms on the Alarms tab of the Power Options Properties dialog box.

There are two alarms you can set: Low battery alarm and Critical battery alarm. What "low" and "critical" mean are subjective—you define the battery percentage thresholds for each. For example, in Figure 20.21, Low is set to 10% and Critical is set to 3%. When the battery's charge falls below those levels, the alarm events will be triggered.

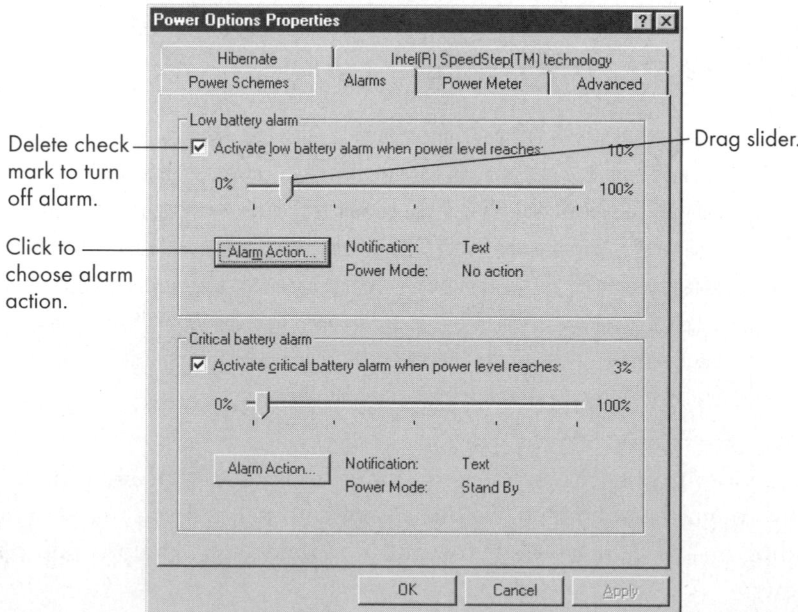


**FIGURE 20.21**
Set alarm thresholds to warn of battery rundown.

To set or change an alarm:

1. From the Control Panel, double-click the *Power Options* icon.
2. Select the Alarms tab.
3. For the alarm you want to set (Low battery or Critical battery), drag the slider to adjust the percentage of battery life that will trigger the alarm (see Figure 20.21).
4. Click the Alarm Action button. The Alarm Actions dialog box for that alarm appears. Figure 20.22 shows the Low Battery dialog box.

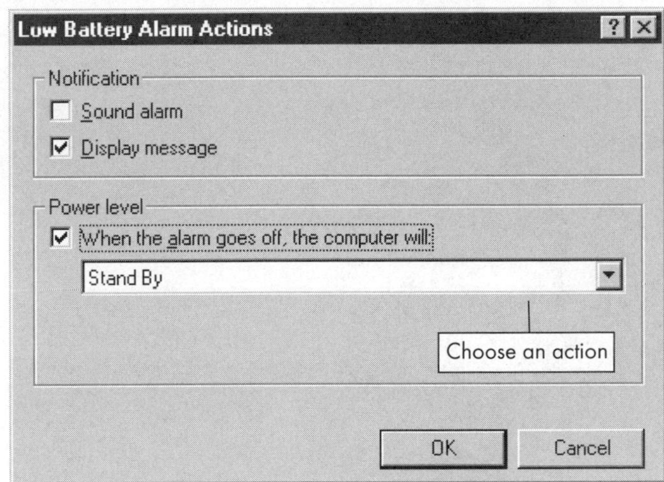


**FIGURE 20.22**
Specify what will happen when the alarm is triggered.

5. In the Notification area of the dialog box, mark or clear the check boxes to hear an alarm and/or display a message.
6. In the Power level area, if you want an action to occur when the alarm is triggered, mark the check box to select it and then open the drop-down list and select the action (Stand By, Hibernate, or Power Off).
7. Click OK to return to the Power Options Properties dialog box.
8. Repeat steps 3–7 for the other alarm if desired.
9. Click OK to close the Power Options Properties dialog box.

### *Power Meter*

The *Power Meter* icon sits in the notification area of the Taskbar and shows how much battery power remains. It can be useful for notebook users who operate frequently on battery power.

When the PC is plugged in, the *Power Meter* icon looks like an electrical plug; when the PC is running on battery power, it looks like a battery. When the battery is fully charged the battery icon is solid blue; as the battery runs down the icon turns partially white and then almost completely white. Figure 20.23 shows the battery icon with a nearly full charge and the dialog box that appears when you double-click on the icon. Similar options are available on the Power Meter tab in the Power Options Properties dialog box.

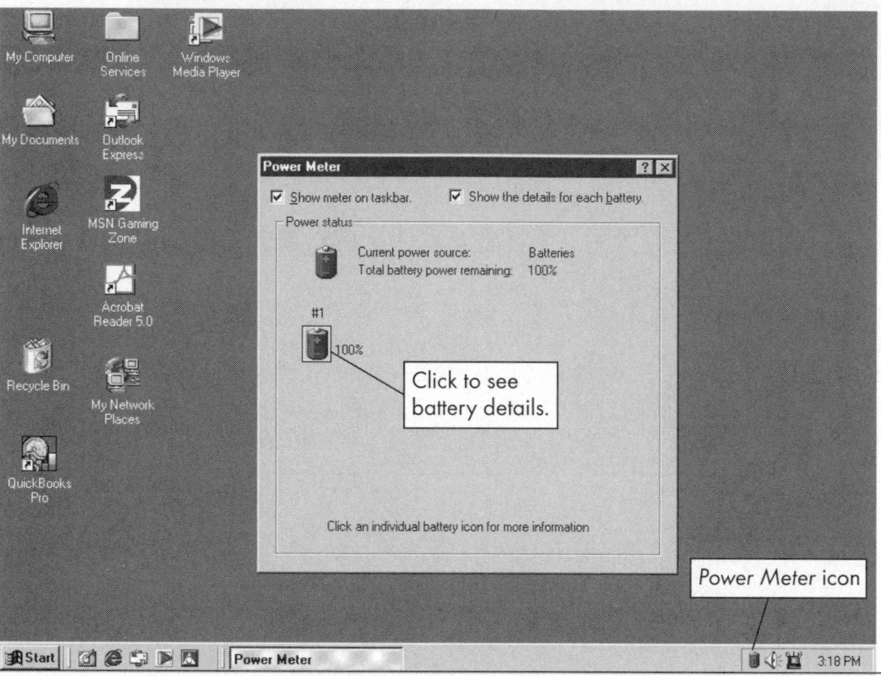


**FIGURE 20.23**
The *Power Meter* icon in the system tray provides a shortcut to battery properties.

Most notebook PCs have only one battery, but if there are multiple batteries connected, each will have its own icon in the dialog box. You can click on a battery icon to get more information about that specific battery (as in Figure 20.24).

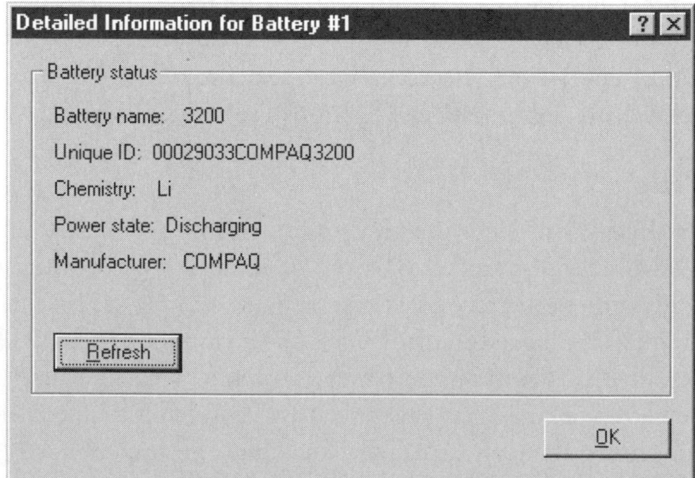


**FIGURE 20.24**
View the properties pertaining to individual batteries.

## Hardware Profiles

A *hardware profile* is a group of settings that tell Windows what hardware is installed. All PCs have at least one hardware profile, called Original Configuration in Windows 9x/Me or Profile 1 in Windows 2000/XP. By default it is the only profile, and all changes you make to the hardware configuration apply to it. Such changes could include disabling or uninstalling a device, adding a device, or using a different driver for a device.

**Hardware profile**

The Device Manager settings that describe a particular hardware configuration.

**WARNING**

**Hardware profiles do not have anything to do with user profiles. A user profile is for a specific user of the PC, and can contain custom settings for such matters as desktop colors, installed applications, and security settings. Hardware profiles, in contrast, pertain only to hardware devices.**

Creating additional hardware profiles is useful when the hardware for a PC can be configured in more than one way. The most common example is a notebook PC that has a docking station. It needs to have two hardware configurations: one for when it is connected to the docking station and one for when it is not connected. Another example might be a notebook PC with a built-in NIC. When the user is working at the office, he or she wants the NIC to be available, but when working on the road, he or she does not need it and in fact would prefer that it not be there (because it slows down Windows startup as Windows searches for a network that is not there).

### Creating a New Hardware Profile

To create a new hardware profile, first you copy an existing one. When you start out there is only one existing hardware profile: Original Configuration (or Profile 1, depending on the Windows version). However, after you create the first copy, you can then copy either of them to make additional profiles.

To create a new hardware profile in Windows 95/98/Me, complete the following steps:

1. From the Control Panel, double-click the *System* icon.
2. Select the Hardware Profiles tab, and then choose the profile you want to copy.
3. Click the Copy button. Key a name for the new profile and click OK (see Figure 20.25).
4. Click OK to close the System Properties dialog box.

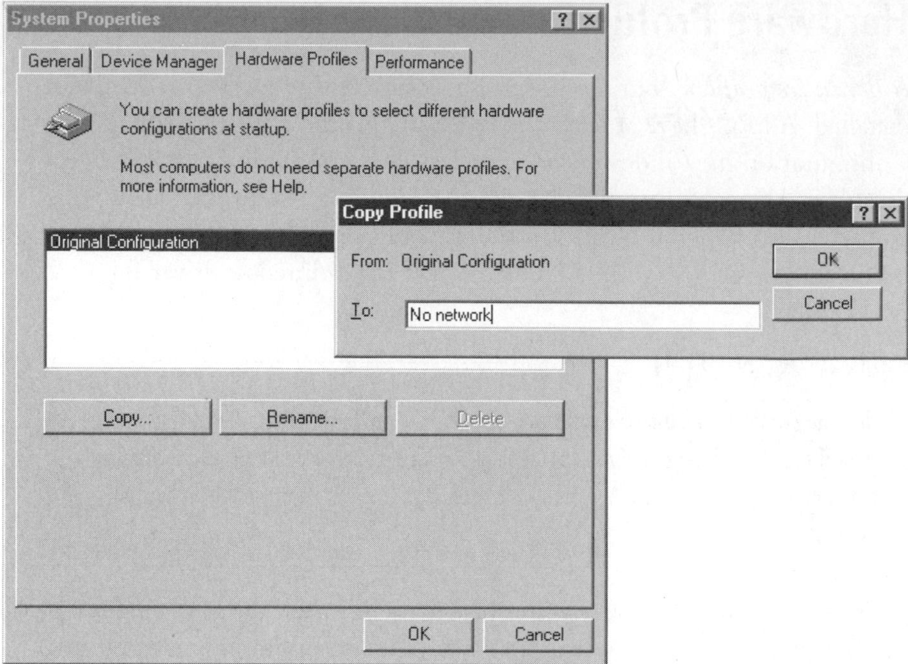


**FIGURE 20.25**
Creating a New Hardware Profile

To create a new profile in Windows 2000/XP, complete these steps:

1. From the Control Panel, double-click the *System* icon.
2. Select the Hardware Profiles tab and then click the Hardware Profiles button.
3. Select the profile you want to copy and click the Copy button. Key a name for the new profile and click OK.
4. *Optional:* Change the setting in the Hardware profiles selection area if desired (see Figure 20.26). Your choices are:
   a. Wait until I select a hardware profile: When Windows starts, a menu of hardware profiles will appear and will remain on-screen until you make your selection.
   b. Select the first profile listed if I don't select a profile in [] seconds: When Windows starts, it will wait the specified number of seconds and then use the first profile on the list.

## In Real Life

**The option described in step 4 is not available in Windows 95/98/Me; those operating systems wait until you choose a profile without timing out.**

5. Click OK to close the Hardware Profiles dialog box and then click OK again to close the System Properties dialog box.

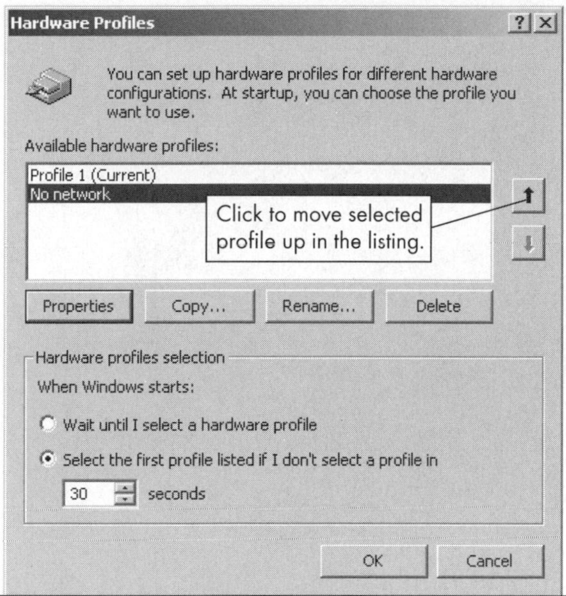


**FIGURE 20.26** In Windows 2000/XP you can choose how Windows addresses hardware profiles at startup.

## Customizing a Hardware Profile

You have created an additional profile, but it is identical to the original profile. To make it different, do the following.

To customize a hardware profile in Windows 95/98/Me:

1. Restart Windows. A dialog box or menu appears asking which hardware profile you want to use. Select the profile you want and press Enter.

### In Real Life

**Windows Me is the only Windows version to use a dialog box in step 1; most Windows versions use a plain text menu.**

2. To exclude a device from the profile, do the following:
   a. Open System Properties and display the Device Manager tab.
   b. Double-click the device to open its Properties dialog box.
   c. On the General tab, mark the Disable in this hardware profile check box (see Figure 20.27).
   d. Click OK. A red *X* appears on the device's icon in Device Manager, indicating it is disabled.

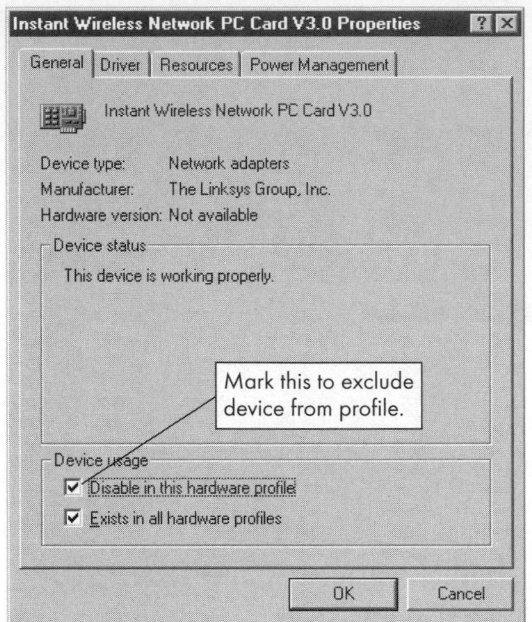


**FIGURE 20.27**
Disabling a Device in the Current Profile in Windows 95/98/Me

The Exists in all hardware profiles check box is marked by default for each device. If you remove a device from Device Manager, that device will continue to be installed in all other hardware profiles when this check box is marked. Clear it to allow each hardware profile to have its own set of hardware. This might be useful in a docking station situation, for example, where some of the devices are not just disabled when the PC is undocked but actually do not exist.

To customize a hardware profile in Windows 2000/XP (steps will vary slightly in the two systems):

1. Restart Windows. A menu appears asking which hardware profile you want to use. Select the profile you want and press Enter.
2. To exclude a device from the profile, do the following:
   a. Open the System Properties dialog box and display the Hardware tab.
   b. Click the Device Manager button.
   c. Double-click the device to open its Properties dialog box.
   d. On the General tab, open the Device usage drop-down list and choose Do not use this device in the current hardware profile (see Figure 20.28).

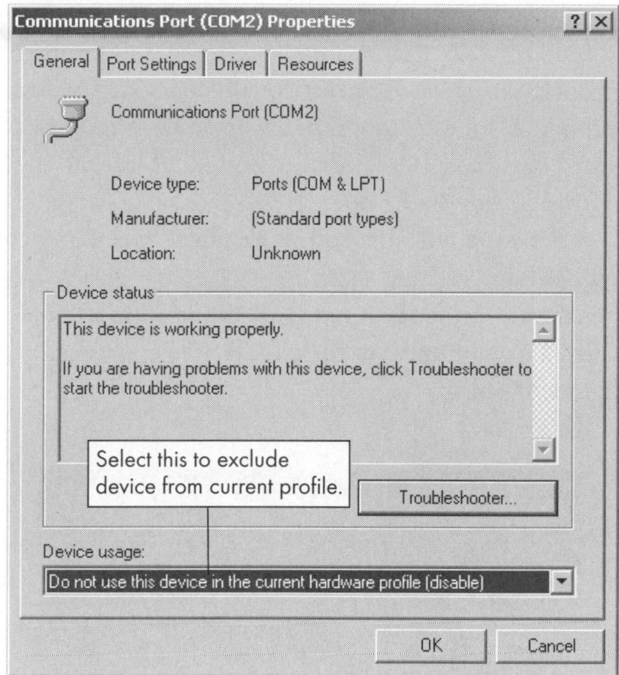
Communications Port (COM2) Properties
General
Port Settings
Driver
Resources
Communications Port (COM2)
Device type:
Ports (COM & LPT)
Manufacturer:
(Standard port types)
Location:
Unknown
Device status
This device is working properly.
If you are having problems with this device, click Troubleshooter to start the troubleshooter.
Select this to exclude device from current profile.
Troubleshooter...
Device usage:
Do not use this device in the current hardware profile (disable)
OK
Cancel

**FIGURE 20.28**
Disabling a Device in the Current Profile in Windows 2000/XP

## SWITCHING BETWEEN HARDWARE PROFILES

To switch profiles you must restart Windows. Whenever more than one profile exists, a menu will appear at startup asking you to choose which one you want, as in Figure 20.29.

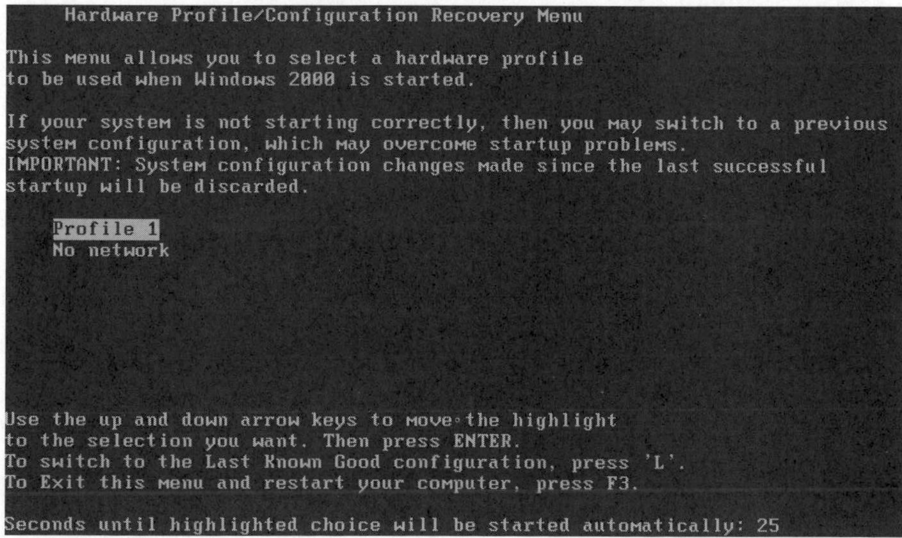
Hardware Profile/Configuration Recovery Menu
This menu allows you to select a hardware profile
to be used when Windows 2000 is started.
If your system is not starting correctly, then you may switch to a previous
system configuration, which may overcome startup problems.
IMPORTANT: System configuration changes made since the last successful
startup will be discarded.
Profile 1
No network
Use the up and down arrow keys to move the highlight
to the selection you want. Then press ENTER.
To switch to the Last Known Good configuration, press 'L'.
To Exit this menu and restart your computer, press F3.
Seconds until highlighted choice will be started automatically: 25

**FIGURE 20.29**
Windows prompts you to choose the profile you want at startup. The Windows 2000 version is shown here.

Windows 2000 and XP are able to automatically detect docked/undocked status and choose between two profiles that represent a notebook PC with or without a docking station. In order for this to work, you must define the profiles as either docked or undocked. To do so in Windows 2000 or XP:

1. From the Hardware Profiles dialog box, double-click the profile to open its Properties dialog box.
2. Mark the This is a portable computer check box if it is not already marked.
3. Choose an option that best represents the profile: The docking state is unknown, The computer is docked, or The computer is undocked (see Figure 20.30).
4. Click OK.

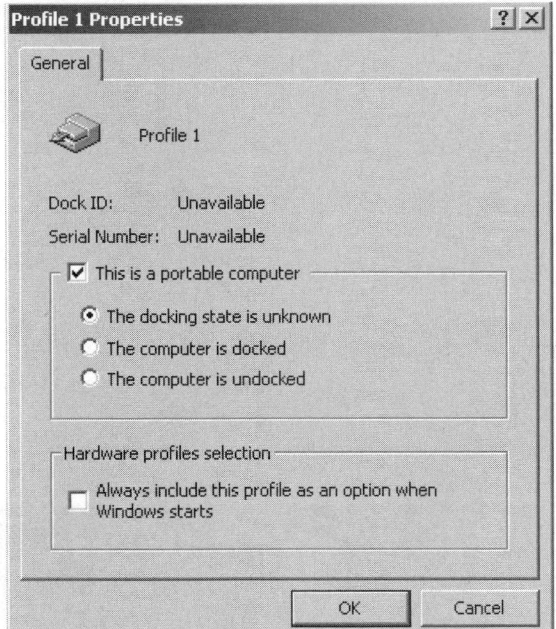


**FIGURE 20.30**
Defining the Current Profile as Docked or Undocked in Windows 2000/XP

## TRY IT!

1. Create a new hardware profile and call it Plain.
2. Boot to the new hardware profile, and in Device Manager, disable all nonessential devices, such as sound card, modem, NIC (unless you need it for basic operation in your classroom), and so on.
3. Boot to the original hardware profile, and look in Device Manager to confirm that the disabled devices are still enabled there.
4. Delete the Plain profile, and reboot. Notice that the menu for selecting a hardware profile no longer appears at startup.

# Upgrading a Notebook PC

Notebook PCs are harder to work on than desktop PCs, mainly because they have more proprietary parts and the case of every model opens differently. Because of this, there are only a few activities that the average PC technician will want to undertake when upgrading or repairing notebook hardware. The most common ones are adding RAM and replacing a hard drive.

## Adding RAM to a Notebook PC

Most notebook PCs have two RAM banks. One of them is built into the motherboard and cannot be removed; this is the notebook's base amount of RAM. The other is an optional socket (usually proprietary) into which you insert a small circuit board containing additional RAM. If this computer socket is not already full, you can install more RAM. If it is already full, you can remove the existing board and install one of a higher RAM capacity.

On most models you remove a screw, remove the plate, and then insert a small RAM circuit board into the socket beneath. Different models look and work differently; Figure 20.31 shows an example of RAM installed.

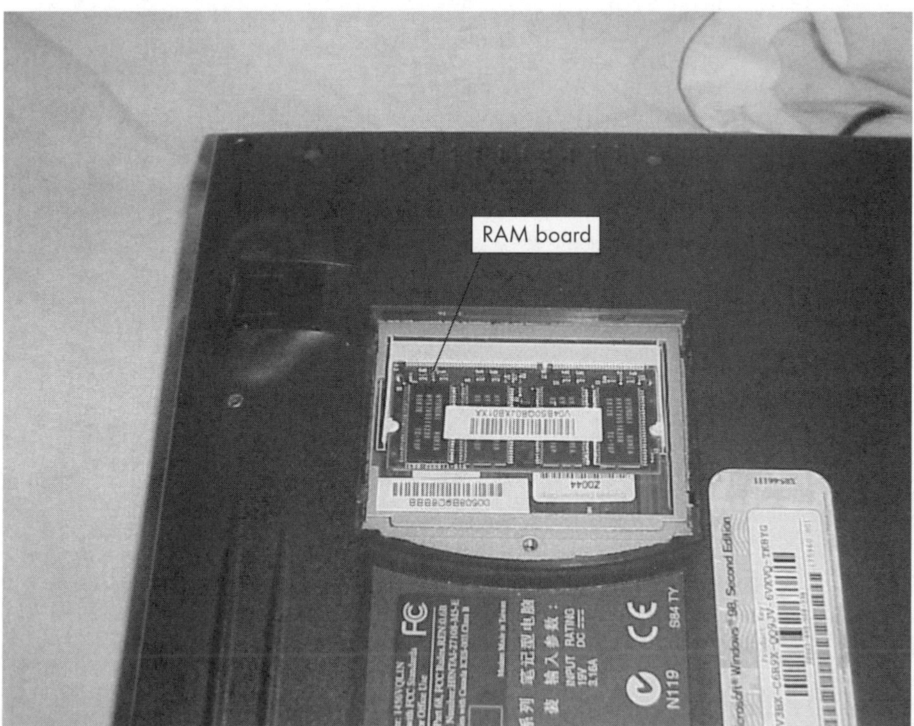


**FIGURE 20.31**
Most notebook computers have a compartment on the bottom where you can insert more RAM .

## Replacing a Notebook Hard Drive

The main problem with replacing a notebook's hard drive is getting physical access to it. There are many different notebook case designs, and each one comes apart differently. Your best option is to look online for documentation about the particular model. Consumer-level documentation may not be adequate; what you really want is a service manual designed for PC professionals. Notebook manufacturers usually discourage ordinary consumers from attempting any activities that involve disassembling the computer because it can be challenging to put back together again.

Here is a general overview of the process:

1. Unplug the notebook PC and remove the battery.
2. Buy a new hard drive designed specifically for notebook computers. A regular hard disk for desktop PCs will not work.
3. Find out by reading documentation which screws must be removed to get access to the hard drive. Then remove them, setting aside the screws for later reassembly.

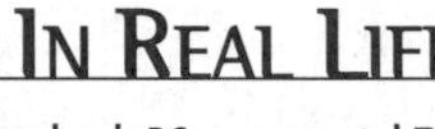

### In Real Life

**Many notebook PCs use special Torx screws (usually T-8 size), for which you must have a special screwdriver. Some models sink the screws down into deep holes, so you cannot use a Torx bit on a multibit screwdriver; you must have a real Torx screwdriver with a long, thin body. Torx screwdrivers are usually available at any discount store.**

4. Open the case and locate the hard drive. In Figure 20.32, for example, the hard drive is under the keyboard, on the left side.

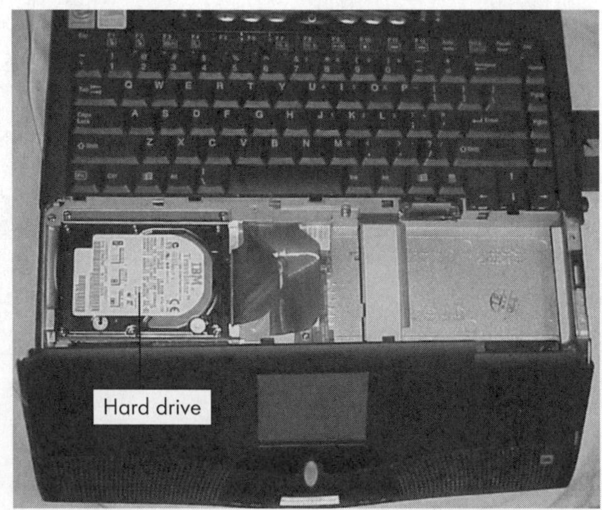


**FIGURE 20.32**
Locate the existing hard drive.

5. Disconnect the data cable from the existing hard drive. The cable connecting the hard drive to the rest of the notebook is a flexible piece of plastic with wires inside it. It is rather fragile, so do not pull on it directly. Instead look for a plastic loop, as shown in Figure 20.33, and pull on the loop to disengage the connector.

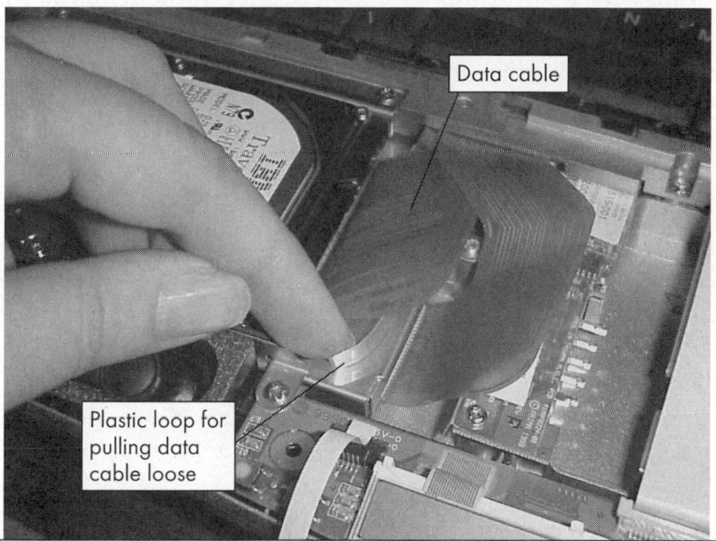


**FIGURE 20.33**
Find a plastic loop to pull on to disconnect the connector.

6. Locate and remove the screws holding the existing drive in place; then lift it out of the notebook.
7. Insert the new hard drive and attach it with the same screws you removed in step 6.
8. Attach the data cable.
9. Close the notebook and secure it with the screws you removed in step 3.

After physically replacing a notebook hard drive, you must partition it and format it as described in Chapter 12.

# Troubleshooting Notebook PC Problems

Many of the problems with notebook PCs are general problems that could occur on any computer, not just a notebook. The following sections outline some problems that are specific to notebooks.

## Display Problems

Although a number of typical notebook display problems are not fixable, it is useful to understand why they are happening.

### *Thick Black Ring around Picture*

The ring results from running an older LCD screen in a lower resolution than its maximum. Some of these old-style LCD monitors will fill the screen only in their top resolution. When you use lower resolutions, rather than expanding the desktop to fill the available space (as with a conventional monitor), they create the lower resolution display in the center of the physical screen with a big black ring around the outside. There is nothing you can do about this other than switch to a higher resolution.

### *Dead Pixels*

Many LCD screens have one or two pixels that do not work. These are known as dead pixels, and there is nothing you can do about them. A brand-new PC should not have any; if the PC is still under warranty, advise your client to exchange it.

### *Fuzzy Text*

In resolutions lower than an LCD monitor's maximum, text may appear fuzzy. (Pictures will usually look fine in any resolution.) This is an issue with older or lower priced LCD screens, and there is not much you can do about it.

Windows XP comes with a font-smoothing feature called ClearType that you can turn on to help minimize text fuzziness on an LCD monitor. To try it out (Windows XP only):

1. Right-click the desktop and choose Properties.
2. Click the Appearance tab, and then the Effects button.
3. Mark the Use the following method to smooth edges of screen fonts check box.
4. Open the drop-down list and choose *ClearType* (see Figure 20.34).
5. Click OK twice to close the dialog boxes.

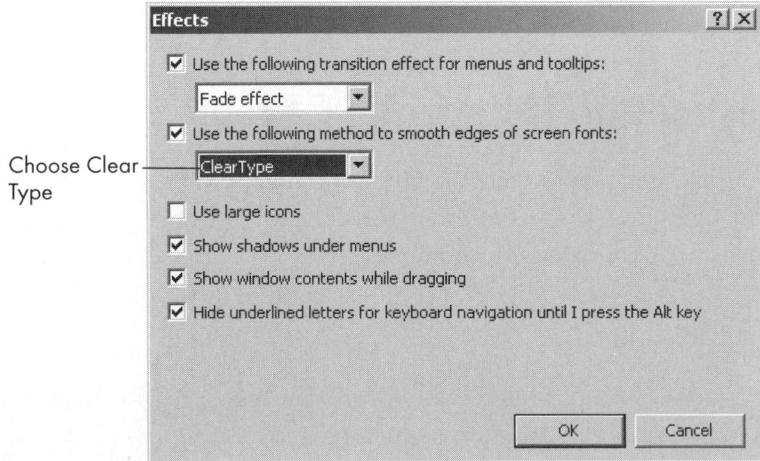


**FIGURE 20.34**
Turn on ClearType font smoothing for an LCD monitor with fuzzy text display

## Power Problems

The vast majority of problems with notebook computers involve power management settings. Either the notebook will not enter a low-power mode or it will not resume properly from one. The following sections provide some help.

### *Will Not Go into Standby or Hibernation*

If the computer will not go into standby or hibernation after the time period specified in the Power Options Properties dialog box, perhaps it is because an OpenGL-type screen saver is in use. Such screen savers make the computer think that it is in use, so the inactivity never times out. Try using a different screen saver, or turning off the screen saver feature altogether.

**In Real Life**

**Some Windows versions indicate which screen savers are OpenGL (a programming API) in the list of screen savers in the Display Properties dialog box; other Windows versions indicate which are OpenGL by preceding them with "3D."**

Another possible reason for not being able to use these features is the video driver. The standard VGA video driver that comes with Windows does not support power management; the video driver you have installed must be compatible with power management features.

If Windows will not enter Standby and you see an error message about a driver or program not permitting it, try closing all running programs. If it persists, perhaps you have an outdated device driver that is not ACPI compliant.

If you have trouble determining which program is causing the situation, try the Windows Power Management Troubleshooter, available for free download from Microsoft. See "For More Information" for this chapter on the Internet Resource Center for the Web site address. It is written specifically for Windows 98, but may be of some use in other versions as well. Also look for a file called Nohiber.txt in the *Windows* folder; if present, it will give you clues about what device is preventing Hibernate or Standby.

You can also try looking for the errant device on your own. For example, some models of Epson USB printers have been known to prevent a PC from entering Standby, as have several models of multifunction devices, particularly those that listen for incoming faxes. Try disconnecting all USB devices and removing all PC cards as part of your troubleshooting process.

If that does not work, try disabling all USB devices in Device Manager if they do not automatically disappear from Device Manager when disconnected.

Also investigate whether you have any built-in device disabled; this can sometimes cause Standby problems. For example, there are known issues with Intel network cards interfering with Standby when they have been disabled in Device Manager.

A few devices have no workaround, and cannot coexist with Standby or Hibernate. Some versions of the Tseng Labs ET-4000 video adapter under Windows 2000 are like that. On such computers you cannot use Windows-based Standby or Hibernate; you might try the OS-independent BIOS power management if available.

Although it is seldom an issue on laptops, the use of Internet Connection Sharing (ICS) in Windows 98/Me can also prevent a computer from going into Standby or Hibernate. This behavior is deliberate, to prevent the computer that is serving the Internet connection from disconnecting others in the workgroup who might be using the connection. The Turn Off Monitor and Turn Off Hard Disks power management options also do not work on the host Internet sharing computer, for the same reason.

### *Will Not Wake Up from Standby or Hibernation*

When a PC will not wake up, it can be alarming for the user because it seems as if the PC is completely dead. It is not, of course. It is just stuck in Standby or Hibernate mode. In the short term, here are some ways to regain control of the PC:

- Be patient. Some PCs take up to 30 seconds to wake up.
- Look for a Suspend or Hibernate key. Some laptops have special keys or buttons for one or both, but the user might not have noticed them if he or she normally uses some other wakeup method.
- Try pressing and holding the PC's Power button for 5 seconds or more. On a PC that is configured to suspend or hibernate with a press of the Power button, holding down the button will usually reset and reboot.
- Look in the PC's documentation for a key combination that might wake it up. Most laptops have an Fn key that you can press in conjunction with other keys to control laptop-specific features.
- As a last resort, remove all batteries, wait a few minutes, and then replace the batteries.

After you successfully restart the PC, you need to look for the underlying problem, which is generally a disagreement either between the power management features of the BIOS and those of your Windows version or between power management and the video card.

To begin troubleshooting, first make sure you have the most recent version of the video driver installed. Download the latest from the manufacturer's Web site and install it. Outdated video drivers have been known to cause power management problems in some systems.

Next, look on the hard disk for a Nohiber.txt file. If such a file exists, it may contain information about why Windows will not hibernate.

A conflict between the BIOS power management and Windows power management is the most common cause of wakeup failure. Experiment with different settings in the BIOS to see if any can solve the problem. For example, one scenario under which a PC might not wake up is if APM is enabled in the Power Options Properties dialog box in the Control Panel and the BIOS is configured to suspend the computer with a time-out value less than the value configured in Windows. To correct this, you would set the BIOS time-out higher than the Windows time-out.

**WARNING**

**Microsoft recommends that all BIOS-based power management be disabled on PCs running Windows NT 4.0.**

If tweaking the BIOS and Windows power settings does not help, try visiting the PC manufacturer's Web site to see whether a BIOS update might be available. The failure of some PCs to resume from Standby can often be corrected by updating the BIOS. A BIOS upgrade can add ACPI support to the computer, and can potentially clear up compatibility problems between APM and the hardware or OS. If you cannot upgrade from APM to ACPI in the BIOS, and you continue having wakeup problems, try disabling APM entirely in the BIOS.

**IN REAL LIFE**

**There is an APM diagnosis tool, apmstat.exe, on the Windows 2000 CD-ROM in the *Support/Tools* folder. Use the -v switch for Verbose to get more data.**

If you cannot solve the problem from the BIOS, try it from the Windows side. Experiment with Windows power management settings to see whether any of them make a difference.

Remember also that you do not necessarily have to use the Windows interface for Standby or Hibernate if the BIOS has direct support for it. It is possible that the client will have to forego the Windows power management and use the Hibernate feature built into the BIOS.

The generic VGA video driver that comes with the OS with a PCI or AGP video card does not support hibernation. You might also see this error with other video drivers, especially on inexpensive laptops that use off-brand video drivers not supporting APM or ACPI. With some Windows versions it is also an issue with older video drivers not written specifically for that version. For example, using a Windows NT version of a video driver in Windows 2000 could cause a black screen on wakeup or no wakeup at all.

If possible, switch to a newer video driver or one designed specifically for the video card. If not, you will not be able to use Hibernate on this PC; go into Power Options in the Control Panel and turn off hibernation support.

#### *Standby Is Not on the Shutdown Menu*

If Standby locks up the computer two times in a row, a message appears asking whether you want to disable the feature. If you answer Yes to that message, Standby will no longer be a choice at shutdown. Standby will also be missing if the PC is not APM or ACPI compatible.

If Standby is off but you think the PC is actually capable of using it, you can turn it back on. To do so, remove APM or ACPI support from Device Manager (in the System category) and then restart the PC and let it redetect it. It might restart several times before it redetects all devices.

If that does not work, try removing the floppy disk controller from Device Manager and letting Windows redetect it upon restart. When it redetects it, it will reset the SuspendFlag entry in the Registry.

## PDAs

There are many different personal digital assistants (PDAs), or handheld computers, available today, and all are physically different—that is, they have different buttons arranged in different ways. However, they all perform the same basic functions.

### Physical Characteristics

Figure 20.35 shows a simulation of a Palm PDA and points out some of its features. Figure 20.36 describes some of the physical characteristics of a PDA.

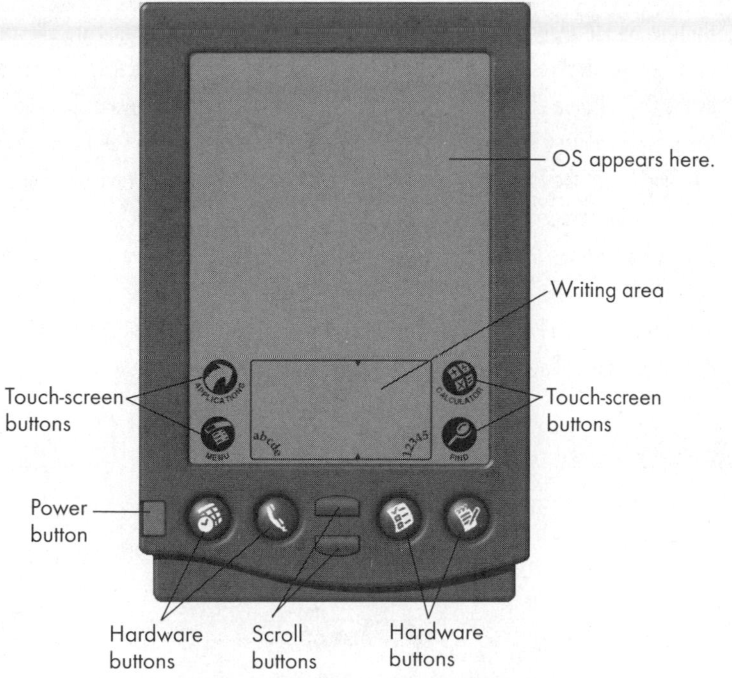


**FIGURE 20.35**
A Palm PDA

- **Touch-sensitive screen:** Since a PDA has no keyboard, a touch-sensitive screen is the primary interface. You can point-and-click by tapping on icons on the screen with the stylus, and you can "type" either by writing with the stylus (using a special handwriting-recognition alphabet) or by bringing up an on-screen keyboard and tapping the stylus on the keys to "press" (see Figure 20.37).
- **Handwriting recognition:** Tapping on an on-screen keyboard can be rather slow, so most PDA users quickly learn how to use the handwriting recognition system. There are different alphabets for different PDA operating systems, but they are similar. Some of the characters are the same as in regular block lettering; others are slightly modified. For example, in the Palm language, an A is written as an upside-down V. A chart comes with the PDA to help you learn them. Figure 20.35 points out the writing area; any stylus activity in that area is assumed to be text entry, whereas any stylus activity outside of that area is assumed to be graphical icon and menu selection.
- **Hardware buttons:** Various models of PDAs have different physical buttons. On the PDA shown in Figure 20.35 there are four. From left to right they are Calendar, Address Book, To Do List, and Memo Pad. They function as shortcuts for choosing those applications' icons in the operating system.

*continued*

**FIGURE 20.36**
Physical Characteristics of a PDA

- **Buttons on touch-sensitive screen:** Palm PDAs have several buttons that are silk-screened onto the touch-sensitive screen. They are not really software buttons because they are not generated by the OS. In Figure 20.35 they are Applications (returns to the main menu of applications); Menu (opens a menu in the current application); Calculator (opens the Calculator application); and Find (opens the Find utility). PDAs that are Pocket PCs (based on Windows CE operating system) may not have such buttons.
- **Power button:** All PDAs can be turned on and off; in Figure 20.35, the on/off button is at the bottom left of the unit.
- **Scroll buttons:** The PDA in Figure 20.35 has two scroll buttons: up and down. On some other PDAs there may be four directional buttons (up, down, right, and left).

**FIGURE 20.36**
continued

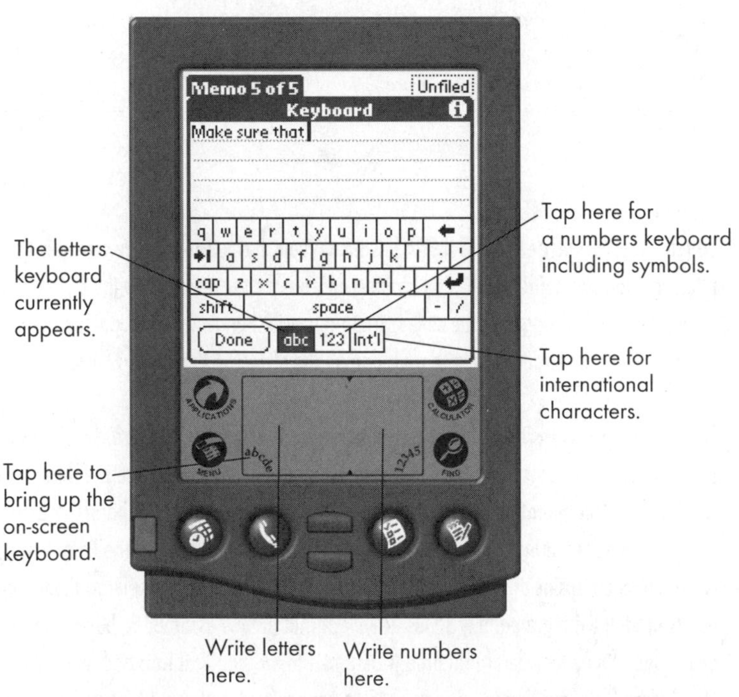

Memo 5 of 5
Unfiled
Keyboard
Make sure that
Done
abc
123
Int'l
The letters keyboard currently appears.
Tap here for a numbers keyboard including symbols.
Tap here for international characters.
Tap here to bring up the on-screen keyboard.
Write letters here.
Write numbers here.

**FIGURE 20.37**
You can tap on an on-screen keyboard or write directly with the stylus.

## PDA Operating Systems

There are two popular operating systems for handheld computers. One is the Palm OS (see Figure 20.38), which is used on all Palm products including the Palm V, Palm VII, and so on, and also on the Handspring Visor. The other is Windows CE, which runs on a variety of Pocket PC devices made by various manufacturers including Hewlett-Packard, Casio, and Sony.

Notice in Figure 20.38 that the Palm OS interface is icon-based, like Windows. Instead of clicking on an icon, you tap it with the stylus. For example, in Figure 20.38 you would tap *Address* to open a list of stored addresses.

**FIGURE 20.38**
The Palm OS Interface

Some PDAs have rechargeable batteries that get refueled whenever the device is in its docking cradle. Other PDAs use regular alkaline batteries, the same kind of batteries used in a calculator, TV remote control, and photo flash units.

Part of the benefit of using a PDA is that it can be synchronized with the program on the PC that is used to keep addresses, a calendar, and a to-do list. A PDA may come with its own proprietary program (for example, the Palm comes with a program called Palm Desktop), but it can also be set to synchronize with programs such as Outlook, Lotus Notes, and ACT! You can initiate a synchronization action either from the PDA's docking cradle (by pressing a button on it) or from within Windows.

### In Real Life

**Which PDA OS is better? It depends on what you want to use it for. For integration with Microsoft Office applications, Pocket PC/Windows CE models are preferable. For quickness and ease of use, Palm is superior.**

## Installing New Programs on a PDA

You need a PC to install new programs on a PDA. Place the programs you want to install in a specified folder on the hard drive, and then tell the PDA's synching software where that folder is and that you want to install whatever it finds there. The next time you synch, the software is installed on the PDA. Figure 20.39 shows the Install utility on the desktop PC that installs programs onto the PDA.

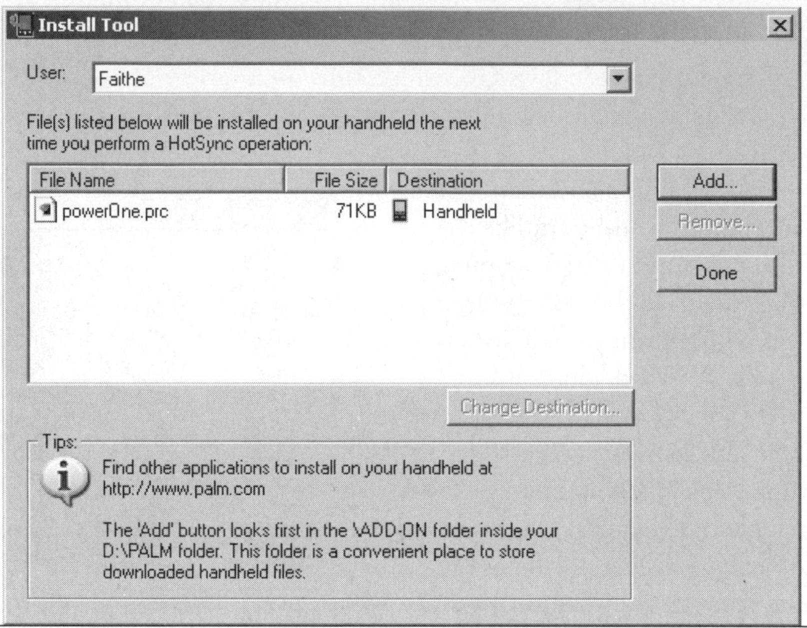


**FIGURE 20.39**
Install programs on a PDA through an Install utility on the desktop PC.

To remove an installed program, work directly from the PDA itself. Check the PDA's operating system manual for specifics.

**TRY IT!**

Download a new application (perhaps a game) from a Web site that has applications for your type of PDA. See "For More Information" for this chapter on the Internet Resource Center for some Web sites. Then install it on your PDA.

## Troubleshooting Common Problems with PDAs

Here are some common problems with PDAs and some possible fixes:

- **Blank screen:** Check the Contrast (probably a wheel or button on the back). Make sure the batteries are not dead.
- **Locked up:** Reset the device. Check the manual to find out how. For example, on a Palm there is a little hole on the back, as in Figure 20.40; insert the tip of a paper clip into it, then release to reset. This type of reset retains all of the data stored on the PDA and is known as a soft reset.

**FIGURE 20.40**
Palm PDAs have a recessed Reset button on the back.

- **Still locked up, or locks up every time it starts:** If resetting does not help, try a hard reset. Again, check the manual to find out how. You should avoid this procedure if possible because it will cause you to lose all of the data stored in the PDA. (If you synched with the PC, the data will still be in the PC and will transfer back to the PDA the next time you synch.) To perform a hard reset on a Palm, press down the Up scroll button while you reset.
- **Will not run a certain program:** Check the OS requirements for the program. It might require a higher version of the PDA's OS. If that is the case you can probably download and install a BIOS update for the PDA from the manufacturer's Web site.

## TRY IT!

Installing an incompatible OS version can disable a PDA. Make sure that the OS update you download is compatible with the exact PDA model.

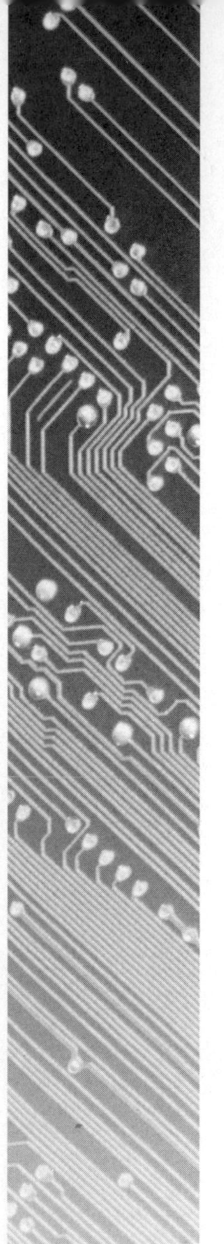

# STUDY GUIDE

Use the following summaries to review the key concepts of this chapter.

## TYPES OF PORTABLE COMPUTERS

- A notebook PC is the most common type of portable PC today. It is approximately the size and shape of a thick notebook of paper.
- A subnotebook is a smaller PC than a notebook, but still has a keyboard large enough for touch typing. There are no standardized criteria for distinguishing a notebook from a subnotebook.
- A personal digital assistant (PDA) is a handheld computer with a touch-sensitive screen, a writing stylus, and no keyboard (or a tiny keyboard not usable for touch typing).

## FEATURES OF NOTEBOOK COMPUTERS

- Notebook PCs have a built-in LCD screen. Most also have an external VGA port for connecting another monitor if desired.
- The Fn key is an extra key found on many notebook computers that performs special commands or functions when combined with other keys, much like the Ctrl and Alt keys.
- PC Card is a standard for connecting add-on devices to a notebook PC. It is also called PCMCIA, for the standards organization that defined it.
- CardBus is the current standard for PC Card devices. It improves the speed and supports lower voltage cards but is otherwise backward-compatible with earlier PC Card devices.
- There are three sizes of PC Card devices. Type I is up to 3.3mm thick, used primarily for memory. Type II is up to 5.5mm thick and is the most popular size; it is used for expansion card-type devices like modems. Type III is up to 10.5mm thick and is used for small drives.
- PC Cards can be removed and inserted while the PC is running (hot-swapped).
- You should stop a PC Card through Windows before removing it to ensure no data is lost.
- A docking station is a larger shell into which a notebook PC fits; it adds extra ports, drives, or other capabilities. A port replicator is a smaller version of the same thing, usually with no extra drives.
- Mouse alternatives for notebooks include built-in or clip-on trackball, pointing stick, and touchpad.

- Notebook computers have batteries. Nickel Cadmium (NiCad) is the older type; it is subject to losing its ability to charge if it is not fully drained each time before recharging.
- Nickel-Metal Hydride (NiMH) batteries are not subject to losing their charge when not fully drained, and have 50 percent more power than NiCad.
- Lithium Ion (LIon) batteries are light and deliver a lot of power, but are more expensive than the other two types.
- Some notebook computers have an infrared (IrDA) port as one of their serial ports.

## Managing PC Cards in Windows

- Use the PC Card applet in the Control Panel to display information about connected PC Cards and to stop them before removing them.
- There may also be a *PC Card* icon in the notification area of the Taskbar that you can double-click to open a dialog box for managing the PC Cards.

## Power Management for Notebook PCs

- There are two power management standards: APM and ACPI.
- Advanced Power Management (APM) is the older standard. Advanced Configuration and Power Interface (ACPI) is newer, more comprehensive, and less problem prone.
- A PC supports one or the other, depending on what is built into its BIOS. A BIOS update can switch a PC from APM to ACPI.
- Many BIOS Setup programs include some power management features that you can turn on and off. These may conflict with Windows power management features.
- SpeedStep Technology is a feature in Intel-brand CPUs for portable PCs that enables the CPU to run slower and use less power when the PC is running on batteries.
- Standby is a Windows mode for power savings that shuts down the monitor, hard drives, and other nonessential components to save power after a specified period of inactivity.
- Hibernate is a Windows power-savings feature that copies the contents of RAM to the hard disk and then shuts down. When you turn the PC back on, the RAM content is copied back into RAM, so a full restart is not required.

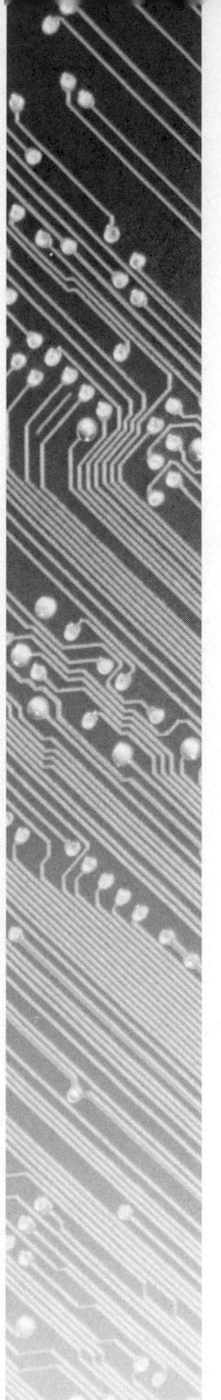

- A power scheme is a group of settings in Windows that dictate the length of the inactivity before power savings features take effect.
- A power alarm is a Windows feature that displays a dialog box or performs an action such as shutting down the PC when the remaining battery power falls below a certain threshold.
- The *Power Meter* icon sits in the notification area of the Taskbar and shows how much battery power remains.

## Hardware Profiles

- A hardware profile is a group of settings that tell Windows what hardware is installed.
- When only one hardware profile exists, the PC boots normally. When there are multiple profiles, Windows tries to detect which one to use. If it cannot, it displays a menu at startup asking which profile to use.
- You might create different hardware profiles to exclude a certain device from having resources assigned to it.
- Hardware profiles are set up through the System applet in the Control Panel.

## Upgrading a Notebook PC

- Notebook PCs are not as easy to work on as regular PCs because of their proprietary designs. They often use Torx screws, for which not everyone has a screwdriver.
- To add RAM to a notebook PC, look for a cover on the bottom that you can remove to expose a RAM slot. Notebook PCs use different RAM than the SIMMs and DIMMs in normal PCs.
- To replace the hard disk in a notebook, read the instructions for disassembly in the manual that came with the PC or in a service manual for that model. Use care when disconnecting the data cable from the hard drive, as the cable is delicate.

## Troubleshooting Notebook Problems

- Most display problems in notebooks are the result of older hardware, and are not fixable.
- Windows XP has a feature called ClearType that can improve fuzzy text on an LCD screen.

- Power management is the main problem with notebook PCs. Either the PC will not go into a low-power mode like Standby or Hibernate, or will not come back out of it.
- Some screen savers can prevent a PC from entering Standby or Hibernate.
- Other reasons a PC might not go into Standby or Hibernate include older, non-ACPI-compliant device drivers.
- When a PC will not wake up from Standby or Hibernate, it is usually a problem with the video driver or a conflict between the BIOS Setup program's power management utilities and those in Windows.
- To wake up a nonresponsive computer, try holding down the Power button for 5 seconds. As a last resort, unplug the PC and remove the battery.

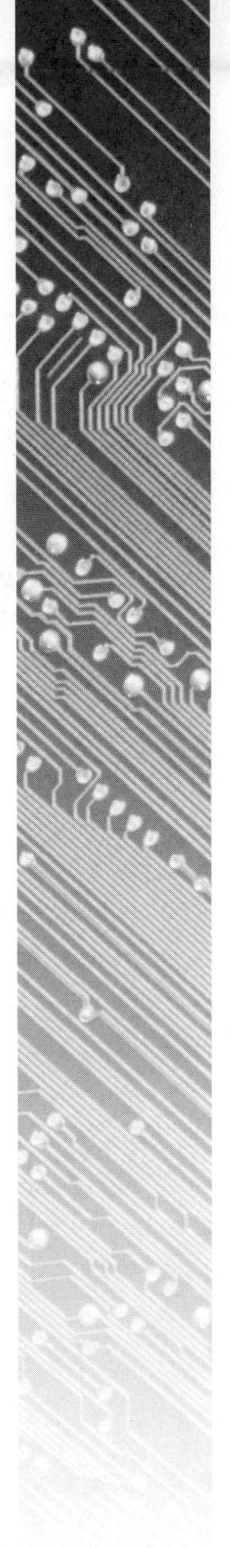

## PDAs

- Most PDAs have a touch-sensitive screen, handwriting recognition, and a graphical user interface based on icons.
- There are two main operating systems: Palm and Windows CE. Windows CE devices are called Pocket PCs and are made by several different hardware companies. Palm devices are made by Palm Computing and by Handspring.
- To install new programs on a PDA, you must use a computer with a PDA installer program set up to interface with your PDA through its docking cradle.
- To reset a PDA, look for a reset button (consult its documentation). On Palm PDAs there is a recessed Reset switch on the back that you press with a pointed object.

# PRACTICE TEST

On a blank sheet of paper, write the answers to the following multiple-choice questions and explain why each answer is correct.

1. Which of these types of PCs uses a stylus and handwriting recognition?
   a. subnotebook
   b. pocket PC
   c. Palm
   d. b and c

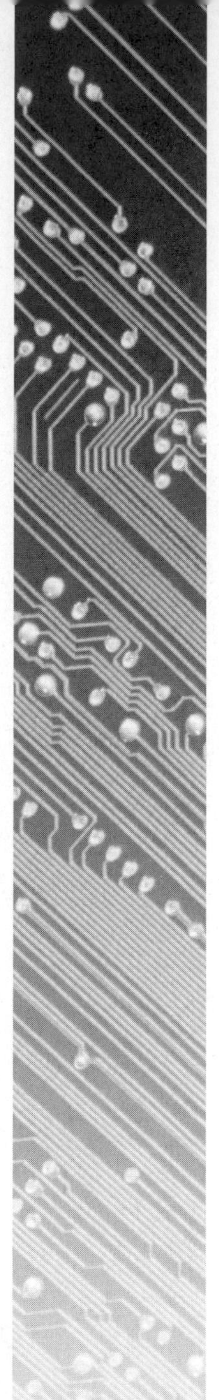

2 Which of these is *not* a feature of a typical notebook PC?
   a. touch-sensitive screen
   b. built-in monitor
   c. Fn key
   d. PC Card slots

3. Which of the following is *not* a type of PC Card?
   a. CardBus
   b. RamBus
   b. Type I
   c. Type III

4. What does hot-swapping allow you to do?
   a. safely remove or connect a device without shutting down the PC
   b. safely remove a PC Card of any type without stopping it first in Windows
   c. connect or disconnect an external monitor while Windows is running
   d. All of the above

5. A docking station could add which of these features to a notebook PC that it could not get with a port replicator?
   a. USB
   b. infrared
   c. drive
   d. FireWire

6. Which type of notebook battery is prone to having problems retaining a full charge if it is not run down fully before recharging?
   a. NiMH
   b. NiCAD
   c. LIon
   d. alkaline

7. Which of these is a characteristic of IrDA?
   a. transmits data at up to 100Mbps
   b. connects a PDA to an Ethernet network
   c. transmits data at a range of up to 100 meters
   d. does not work when the devices are on different floors of a building

8. Why is it advantageous to stop a PC Card device before removing it?
    a. to make sure that Windows removes it from Device Manager
    b. to free up its resources
    c. to make sure that all operations involving the device complete normally
    d. to avoid physical damage to the PC

9. Which power management standard is the most comprehensive and up-to-date?
    a. ACM
    b. APM
    c. ACPM
    d. ACPI

10. What does SpeedStep do?
    a. changes the CPU speed depending on the amount of power the PC Card slots are drawing
    b. decreases the CPU speed when the PC is on battery power
    c. increases the CPU speed when using an external monitor
    d. allows multiple hardware profiles to be created with different CPU speeds

11. What component remains powered on in Standby mode?
    a. RAM
    b. hard disk
    c. floppy disk
    d. None of the above

12. What component remains powered on in Hibernate mode?
    a. RAM
    b. hard disk
    c. floppy disk
    d. None of the above

13. For which component does a power scheme enable you to set an amount of idle time that must occur before it shuts off?
    a. hard drive
    b. video card
    c. CPU
    d. All of the above

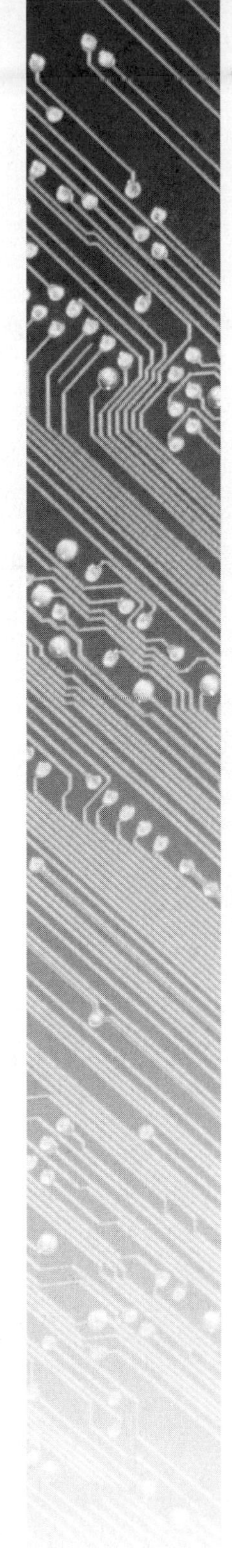

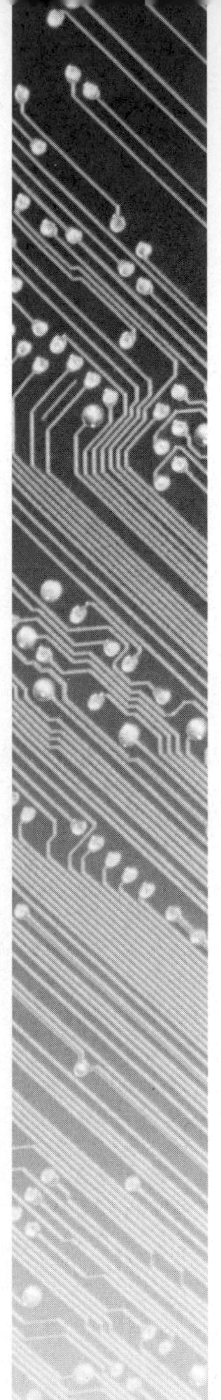

14. How can you manually place the PC in Standby mode without waiting for it to time out due to inactivity?
    a. Use the Start, Shut Down command.
    b. Activate the screen saver.
    c. Move the mouse pointer to the lower left corner of the screen.
    d. Any of the above will work.

15. After creating an additional hardware profile, how can you customize it?
    a. Select it in the User Profiles in the Control Panel and click Properties.
    b. Select it from the Hardware Profiles list in the System applet and click Customize.
    c. Boot the computer into the new profile and disable/enable devices in Device Manager.
    d. Either b or c

16. What is ClearType?
    a. a type of font similar to TrueType
    b. a method of smoothing screen fonts to make more readable text
    c. an LCD screen font
    d. None of the above

17. Which of the following could potentially cause a PC to *not* be able to hibernate?
    a. Internet Connection Sharing
    b. non-ACPI device driver
    c. standard VGA video driver
    d. All of the above

18. Which of the following will force a PC that is stuck in Standby to reboot?
    a. unplugging it and booting using the battery
    b. pressing the Esc key for 5 seconds
    c. pressing the Power button for 5 seconds
    d. holding down the F8 key until it restarts

19. What text file contains information about why a PC cannot hibernate?
    a. Nohiber.txt
    b. Hiber.txt
    c. Apmstat.txt
    d. There is no such file.

20. What is a hard reset on a PDA?
    a. a reset that turns the power off and then on again
    b. a reset that wipes out any data stored on the PDA
    c. a reset that retains any data stored on the PDA
    d. a reset caused by removing the batteries

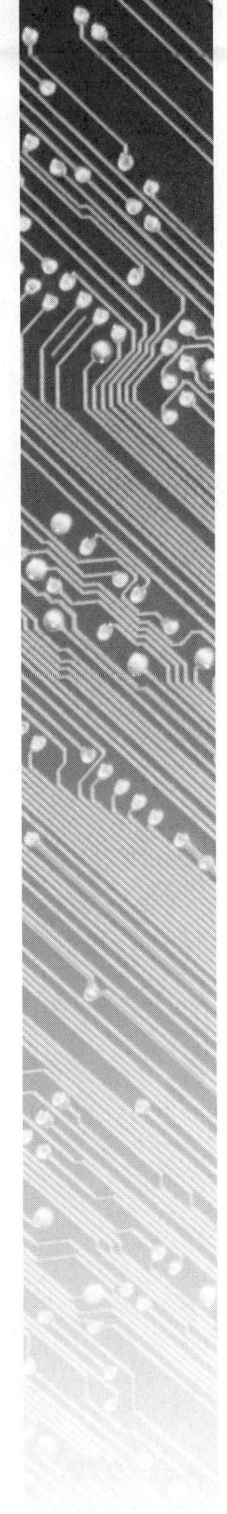

## TROUBLESHOOTING

1. A client complains that the LCD monitor on her notebook PC is not very bright. Where can you recommend that she look for a contrast or brightness adjustment?
2. A client reports that the battery in his notebook PC will not hold a charge, even though he leaves it plugged in almost all of the time. What does he need to do?
3. A client with a brand-new computer calls you, alarmed. She walked away from her computer for a few minutes when it was running on batteries, and when she came back it was dead, and pressing the Power button or tapping the keyboard has no effect. What can you suggest?

## CUSTOMER SERVICE

1. A client wants a computer on which he can run normal applications, like Word and Excel, but that is lightweight and easy to transport. What can you recommend?
2. A client complains that every time she brings her notebook PC into work, she must spend several minutes connecting it to her external monitor and keyboard. Further, she does not like that she can use only an external keyboard or an external mouse—not both at once. What can you recommend?
3. After a BIOS update, a client reports that her notebook computer's screen goes blank after only a couple of minutes of inactivity. What is going on, and how can you help her adjust it?

## FOR MORE INFORMATION

For links to Web sites that provide further information about the topics covered in this chapter, go to the EMC/Paradigm Internet Resource Center at www.emcp.com/College Division/Internet Resource Centers/PC Maintenance/For More Information.

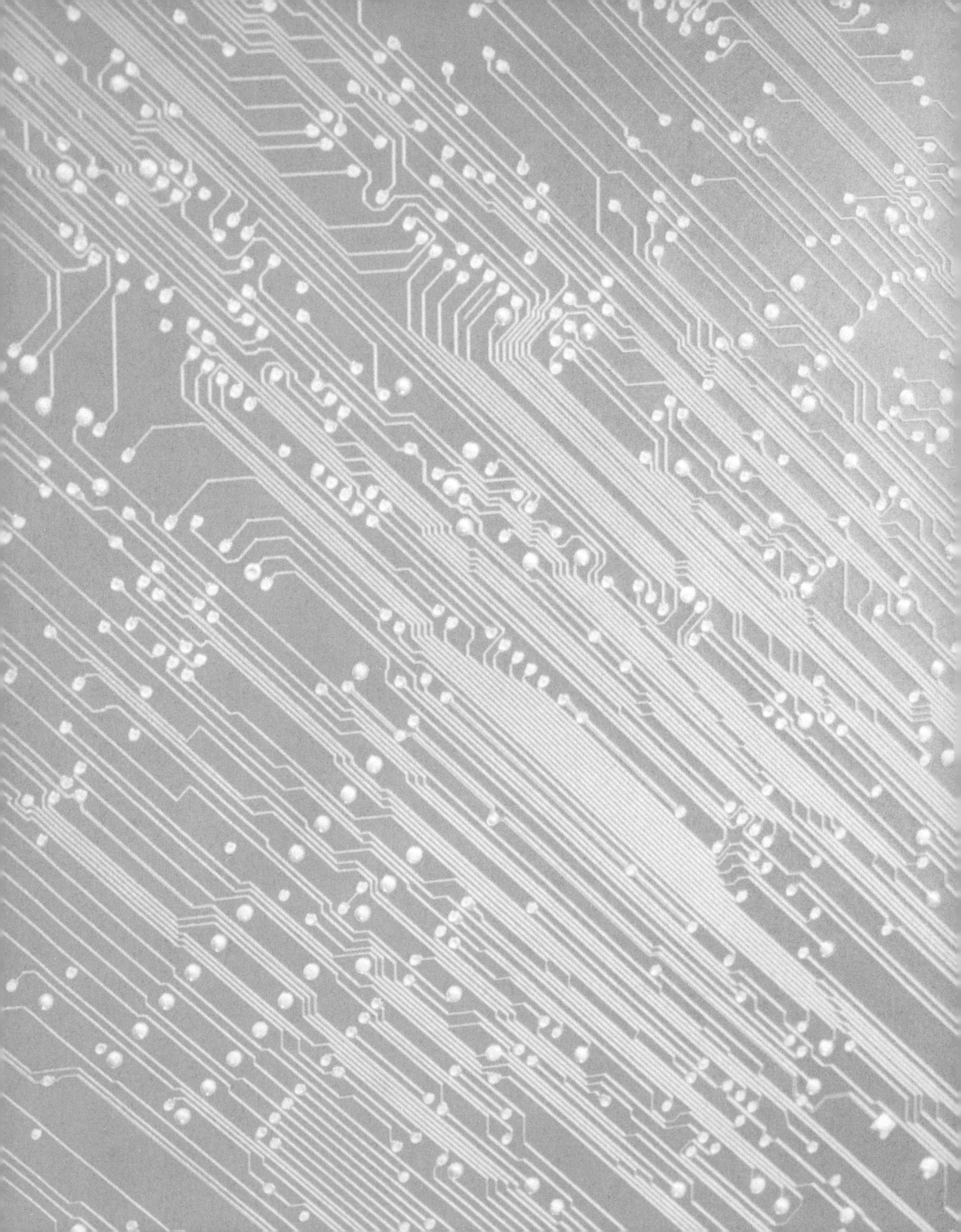

# Project Lab, Part 4
## Input and Output Devices

These projects require a PC with Windows 95 or higher already installed.

### Project #1: Working with Device Resources

1. Enter BIOS Setup and make sure that all legacy COM and LPT ports are enabled.
2. In Windows, print out a list of the IRQ assignments in use on your computer. What are the IRQ assignments for your legacy COM ports?
3. Disable COM1 in BIOS Setup. What resources did you free up by doing so?
4. Install an internal modem (ISA or PCI) and force it to be COM1 if it is not automatically detected as COM1.
5. In BIOS Setup, reenable the legacy COM1 port. Then reenter Windows and observe the resource assignment for the modem. What has changed, if anything? Are there any conflicts? If so, resolve them.
6. Compare notes with your classmates. Did everyone have the same experience? Were there differences based on Windows version? Based on whether the modem was ISA or PCI? Based on whether the modem chose COM1 freely or was forced into it? What conclusions can you draw?

### Project #2: Selecting a Video Card

1. Go to Amazon.com on the Internet (http://www.amazon.com) and find out what is the top-selling Action game for the PC at the moment. What is the top game?
2. What are the game's video requirements? If it does not specify on Amazon.com, visit the game manufacturer's Web site to find out.
3. Recommend video cards from three different card manufacturers that would all meet or exceed the video requirements for this game.

## Project #3: Changing Video Settings

1. In Windows, try to set the graphics mode to 1024 x 768 resolution with a color depth of 16-bit. If your PC is not capable of one of these settings, make a note of it. What is the maximum refresh rate for your monitor in this mode?
2. What monitor does Windows report that you have? If it is not correct, go to the Web site for your monitor's manufacturer and download a Windows .inf file for your monitor for your Windows version. Install it in Windows, replacing the current monitor driver.
3. What is the current refresh rate setting? Change it to the highest setting available in the current video mode. What is that new setting?
4. Adjust your monitor so that there is no black ring around the screen, so that the screen image is centered in the monitor, and so that the screen image is perfectly rectangular with no tilting or bowing. Document what settings you adjusted.

## Project #4: Working with a Printer Driver and Queue

1. If you have any existing local printers installed, remove them from Windows.
2. Connect a printer to the PC and have Windows detect it with Plug and Play and install a driver for it.
3. Install a second copy of the driver for that printer without Plug and Play (by selecting it from a list). If your printer is PostScript capable, there are probably two drivers available for it: one with PostScript and one with PCL. If that is the case, install the version that did not install in step 2.
4. Go to the printer manufacturer's Web site and download a newer driver for the printer for your OS if one is available. If it is, install it manually as a third copy of that printer in Windows and make it the default printer.
5. View the properties for all three drivers, and write down what differences you see among them, if any.
6. Print a test page for the default printer driver.
7. Pause the print queue for the default printer, and then print a document from a text editing program such as Word or Notepad. View the print queue. What information can you determine about the document being printed?
8. Delete the print job without allowing it to print.

## Project #5: Sound Cards and Speakers

1. Install a sound card in the PC, and install any drivers needed for it. If you do not have the needed drivers, how could you get them? Where in Windows could you check to make sure the sound card is correctly installed?
2. Connect speakers to the sound card, and confirm that they are working. How can you make Windows play a sound so you can test the speakers?
3. Try playing an audio CD. If it does not play, troubleshoot until it does. What are some reasons why an audio CD might not play even though the sound card and speakers are working?
4. Install a microphone and use it to record your voice with Sound Recorder. If it does not record, troubleshoot until it does. What are some reasons the microphone might not record on an otherwise working sound card?

## Project #6 (Challenge): Dual Monitor Support

1. Hook up a second monitor to your notebook computer, and switch the video display so that only the external monitor operates.
2. Switch the video display back so that both monitors operate, and then set them up as a dual monitor system so that the desktop is extended across both of them (that is, they do not simply show identical copies of one another). If this doesn't work, research on the Internet to find out why. Is there a known issue with your video adapter? Is there an updated driver that will allow the feature to work? If so, download and install it.
3. Install a second video card in your desktop PC, and hook up a second monitor to it. Then enable dual monitor support in Windows and extend the desktop over both monitors. Describe any problems you encountered, if any, and any differences between that and the notebook PC's dual monitor setup.
4. If you have the equipment available, try adding a third video card and monitor. Does it work? If not, why?

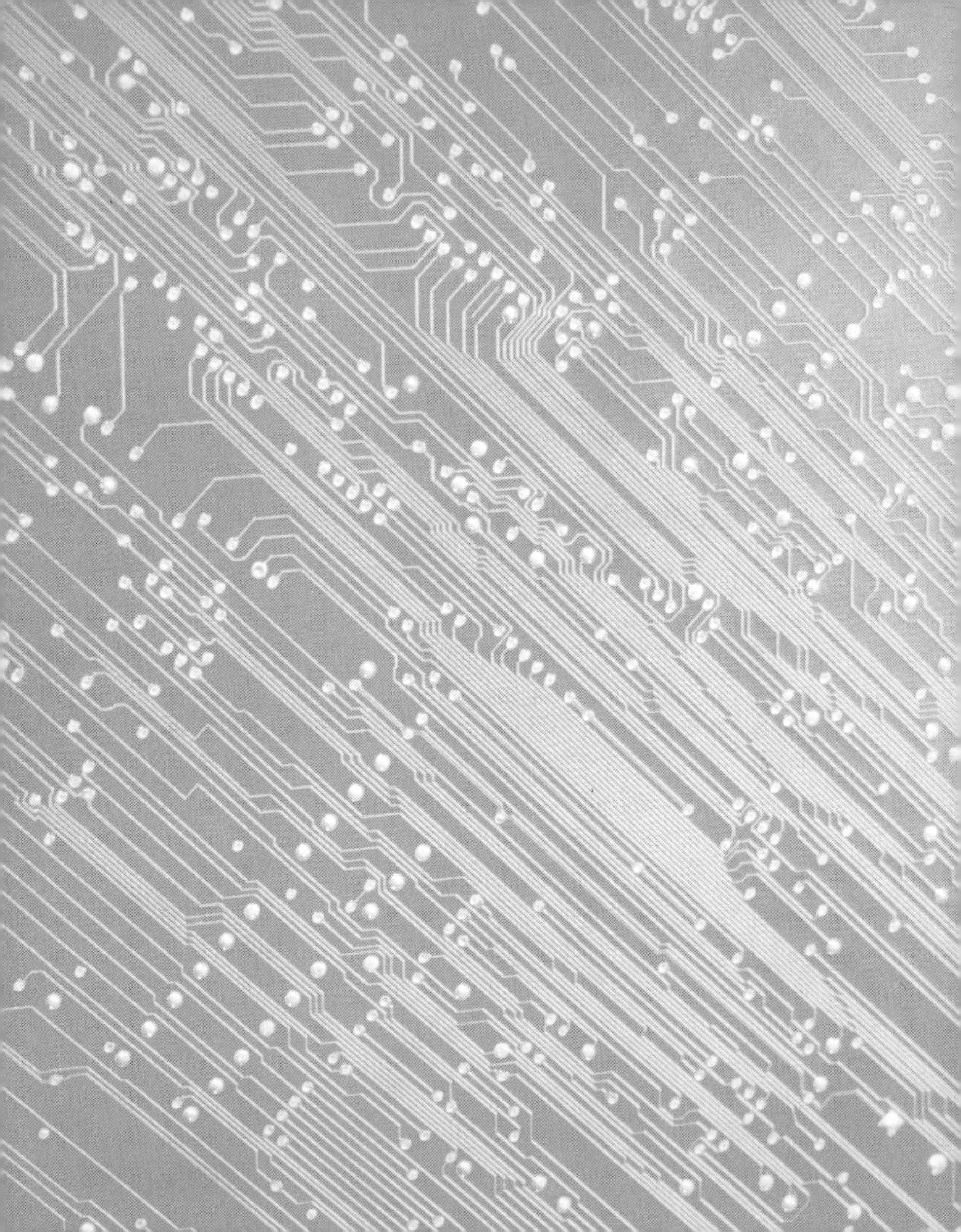

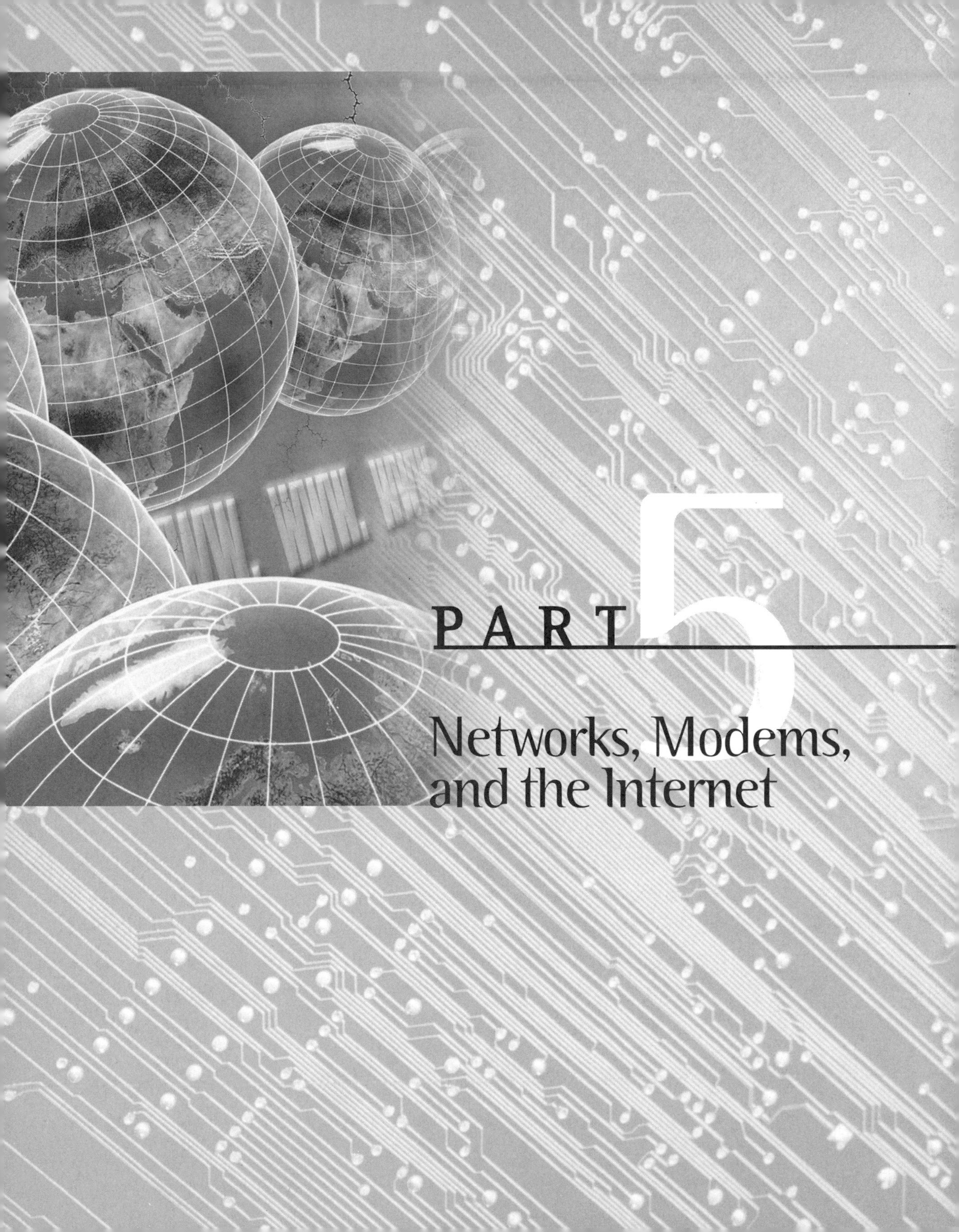

# PART 5

# Networks, Modems, and the Internet

# TEST OBJECTIVES IN PART 5

## A+ Core Hardware Service Technician Examination

- **Objective 1.1:** Identify basic terms, concepts, and functions of system modules, including how each module should work during normal operation and during the boot process.
- **Objective 1.2:** Identify basic procedures for adding and removing field replaceable modules for both desktop and portable systems.
- **Objective 1.7:** Identify proper procedures for installing and configuring peripheral devices.
- **Objective 2.1:** Identify common symptoms and problems associated with each module and how to troubleshoot and isolate the problems.
- **Objective 6.1:** Identify basic networking concepts, including how a network works and the ramifications of repairs on the network.

## A+ Operating System Technologies Examination

- **Objective 1.2:** Identify basic concepts and procedures for creating, viewing and managing files, directories and disks. This includes procedures for changing file attributes and the ramifications of those changes (for example, security issues).
- **Objective 2.4:** Identify procedures for loading/adding and configuring application device drivers, and the necessary software for certain devices.
- **Objective 3.2:** Recognize common problems and determine how to resolve them.
- **Objective 4.1:** Identify the networking capabilities of Windows including procedures for connecting to the network.
- **Objective 4.2:** Identify concepts and capabilities relating to the Internet and basic procedures for setting up a system for Internet access.

# 21 Networking Hardware Concepts

## ON THE TEST

**A+ Core Hardware Service Technician Examination**

- **Objective 6.1:** Identify basic networking concepts, including how a network works and the ramifications of repairs on the network.

## ON THE JOB

Networking can be an intimidating topic for most beginning PC technicians because there are so many different types of networks. There are several ways to categorize various network types—by physical connectivity, by the type of interface card and cabling, or by the software used to run the network. Before you start setting up any networks (in later chapters), you need to know what hardware is available and how it fits together.

Skills connected to this chapter's material include:

- helping managers and end users choose between peer-to-peer and client/server networking
- knowing when a group of users has grown past the practical limit of a peer-to-peer network and needs to add a server to its network
- deciding what network technology, speed, cabling, and physical arrangement are appropriate when setting up a new network
- selecting and purchasing networking hardware that will work together
- deciding whether wireless networking will work in a certain environment

# Network Basics

**Network**

Two or more computers that are connected in order to share data and resources.

The term *network* is generic. A network can be as simple as two computers connected together to share data and resources, or as complex as the entire Internet. Each computer on the network is known as a *node*. (A printer that is directly connected to the network can be a node, too.) Whenever a node has access to another node, a network exists.

**Node**

An individually addressable computer or printer connected directly to the network.

## LAN versus WAN

**Local-area network (LAN)**

A network in which the connected nodes are located within a limited area, such as a single building.

When all of the connected nodes in the network are located within a limited area, it is called a *local-area network*, or LAN. For example, all of the PCs at a company's corporate headquarters are located together in a LAN. When not all of the nodes are at the same location, it is called a *wide-area network*, or WAN. For example, if a company has 12 locations all over the world, the total network including all of the connections between locations would be the WAN. The Internet is also a WAN.

**Wide-area network (WAN)**

A network in which the connected nodes are spread out over a wide geographical area, such as in different cities.

## Client/Server versus Peer to Peer

There are two basic models for network operation: client/server and peer-to-peer. Client/server is the type used in most business networks.

A *server* is a PC that exists only to route network traffic and to provide access to shared files and printers. It manages the connections between the *client* PCs and serves as a storage repository for files that users want to make available to others. A server can be physically just an ordinary PC, but it has a special server OS installed (such as Microsoft Windows 2000 Server, for example) that enables it to provide network services. A *client/server* network includes one or more servers and one or more clients (see Figure 21.1).

**Server**

A PC that exists to route network traffic and provide access to shared network resources.

**Client**

A PC that an end user employs to run applications, with no special network management duties.

**Client/server**

A network that includes at least one PC dedicated for use as a server.

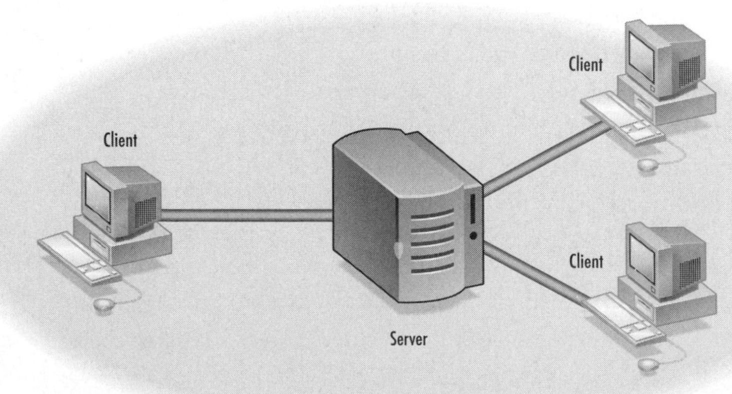


**FIGURE 21.1**
A Client/Server Network

Client/server is the network model used for almost all business networks because the presence of the server takes the networking burden off the clients. The clients do not experience performance problems caused by the network, even when network traffic is high. The main drawback to a client/server network is that there must be a PC dedicated to functioning as a server, and not every company can spare the extra PC. Another drawback is that the server PC must have a special server operating system, such as Microsoft Windows 2000 Server, which costs more than a regular version of the OS.

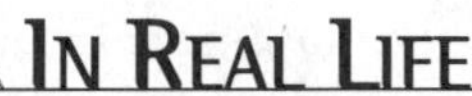

### In Real Life

Windows 2000 Server has all of the features of the "normal" version of Windows 2000 (Windows 2000 Professional) in addition to its extra server functionality, so in a pinch it can be used as the operating system on an end user PC. This almost never happens, however, because of the high price of the server version and because activity as a server degrades the performance of any client applications running on the PC.

### TRY IT!

If you are not sure what version of Windows is installed on a PC (that is, whether it is a client or a server version), do the following to find out:

1. Open My Computer.
2. Choose Help, About Windows. A box will appear with version information.

Large networks often have many servers, each with a specific function. For example, one might be a file server, one might be a print server, and one might provide Internet service. Many large networks even have multiple servers for each function—several file servers, several print servers, a mail server, an application server, and so on.

### In Real Life

The servers and clients need to be connected, but their physical configuration can take a number of forms. The diagram in Figure 21.1 shows the server in the center, but in reality the PCs could be physically connected in a straight line, in a star with a hub in the center, or in a ring. The physical way in which a network is laid out with cabling or wireless connections is called its topology; we will cover that later in the chapter. The topology of a network is not related to whether or not it has a server.

Having a server does not preclude individual client PCs from sharing their resources directly with other clients. For example, there might be a central file server, and a user could copy some files to that file server for sharing with others, but he could also make those files available from his own hard drive, and grant permission for other users to access them from there. Similarly, a printer could be shared by connecting it to a print server, or it could be shared from an individual *local* PC to which it is connected. However, one of the main advantages of a client/server network is that it relieves the sharing burden from the client PCs, and when a client PC shares a resource locally rather than giving it to the server to share, the network loses some of that benefit and becomes more like a peer-to-peer network, discussed below.

**Local**

Connected directly to the individual client PC.

Small networks (10 PCs or fewer) can be configured as peer-to-peer instead of client/server. A *peer-to-peer* network has no central server; each of the client PCs takes on a portion of the burden of maintaining the network. For example, instead of a server managing the traffic, all of the PCs in the network listen for traffic and grab any messages that are addressed to them. Instead of a server storing shared files, the shared files remain on the client hard disks. Whenever someone wants to access them, the client hard disk reads the file and the OS sends it down the network pipeline. Figure 21.2 shows a diagram of a peer-to-peer network. Another name for a peer-to-peer network is a *workgroup*.

**Peer-to-peer**

A type of network that lacks a server; each of the client PCs is equally responsible for sharing the networking burden.

**Workgroup**

A peer-to-peer network.

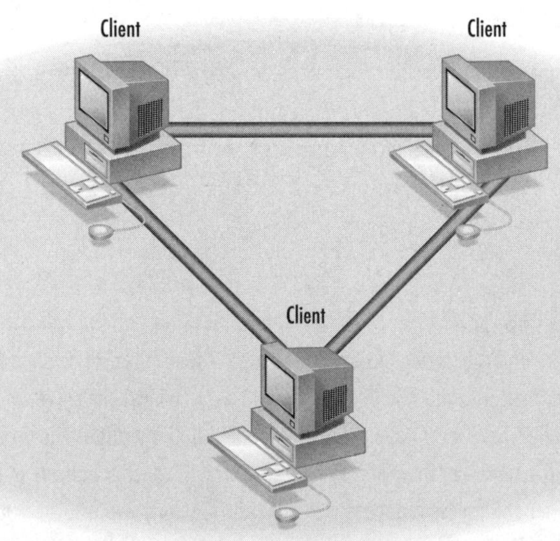


**FIGURE 21.2**
A Peer-to-Peer Network

Peer-to-peer networks are advantageous for small businesses and for home networks because they do not require a PC to be dedicated for use as a server and they do not require a server operating system. Their main drawback is that the network traffic causes a performance drain on the PCs in the network. The more PCs and the more traffic between them, the more noticeable this drain becomes. At 5 PCs, a performance difference begins to become noticeable; at around 10 PCs the performance drain is significant enough to make peer-to-peer networking undesirable. Another drawback is that peer-to-peer networks have weaker security capabilities.

## Resources Shared on a Network

The most common resource shared on a network is hard disk space. One PC can access a hard disk on another PC through the network; for example, one user might make a word processing document available to all other users in her workgroup, or might copy that document to a file server. The Internet's main functionality also involves file sharing; whenever you access a Web site, you are reading a file from a *remote* hard drive.

**Remote**

Not physically connected to the PC, accessible only through networking.

The second most commonly shared resource is printer access. One user on a network can send print jobs to a printer attached to someone else's PC, or attached directly to the network itself. There are several ways to make a printer available on a network. A printer can be attached to an individual client PC and shared; it can be attached to a server and shared; or it can be attached directly to the network itself as a separate entity. (The latter requires the printer to be network-capable, that is, to have a built-in network interface card inside it.)

A network can also serve as a conduit to other resources, such as Internet access. For example, you can share an Internet connection over a network, so that all of the PCs in the network can take advantage of the same single high-speed connection. There are different ways to configure Internet sharing: an individual PC can use Internet Connection Sharing in Windows (Windows 98 Second Edition and higher) to share its local Internet connection; or an incoming high-speed cable, DSL, or dedicated line connection (such as a T1 line) can be connected to a network router and its connection shared among all PCs on the network. Other local hardware, such as scanners, modems (except for a specific Internet connection using a modem), and sound cards, cannot be easily shared over a network.

# Physical Topologies

**Topology**

The physical arrangement or connectivity of a network.

A network's *topology* is the physical way in which the computers and other network resources are connected to one another. The diagrams in Figures 21.1 and 21.2 dealt with the network model, the concept behind network communication. They were not intended to represent the physical connections between the PCs. That physical connectivity—the way the cables are strung together—is discussed in the following sections.

## Bus Topology

**Bus**

A network topology that arranges the PCs in a single-file chain.

*Bus* is the oldest topology. It consists of a single networking line running from one PC to another, as in Figure 21.3. On the ends are terminators (much like on a SCSI chain) that signal the ends. Bus is used in 10Base-5 Ethernet networking, an old type of Ethernet that might still be in use in some businesses. You will learn more about 10Base-5 later in this chapter.

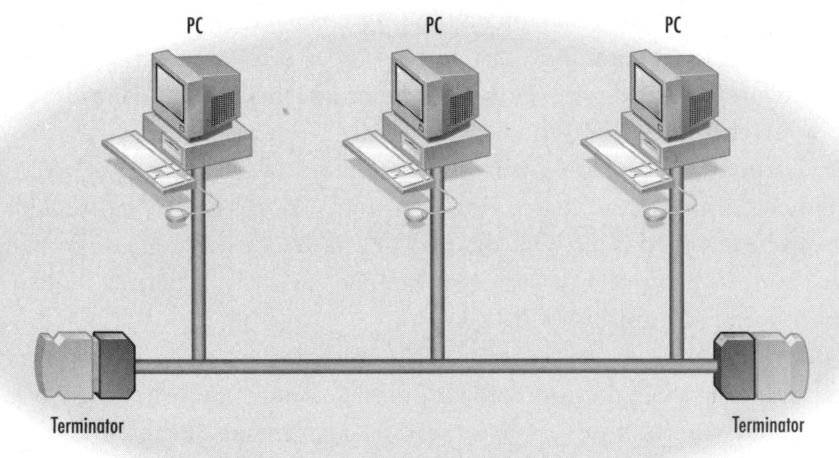


**FIGURE 21.3**
Bus Network Topology

> **WARNING**
>
> Notice that in Figure 21.3 (and the next few figures as well), each device is labeled generically as "PC." That is to remind you that topology has nothing to do with whether a given PC is a client or a server. In these diagrams all PCs are equal. A client or server's physical position in the network topology is not significant (unless the network includes a router, discussed later).

The main drawback to a bus topology is that a break anywhere in the line of PCs cuts off all of the PCs.

## RING TOPOLOGY

Rather than arranging the PCs in a single line, the *ring* topology (Figure 21.4) arranges them in a closed loop. This minimizes the impact when a break occurs in the connectivity. Traffic stops at the break point, of course, but traffic that does not need to pass by that break point can still flow in some cases. In addition, some variants of the ring topology (notably FDDI, which will be discussed later) have two rings, each going in a different direction. If traffic cannot get through on the main ring, it switches to the secondary ring and goes around the other way.

**Ring**

A network topology in which the PCs are physically connected in a closed loop.

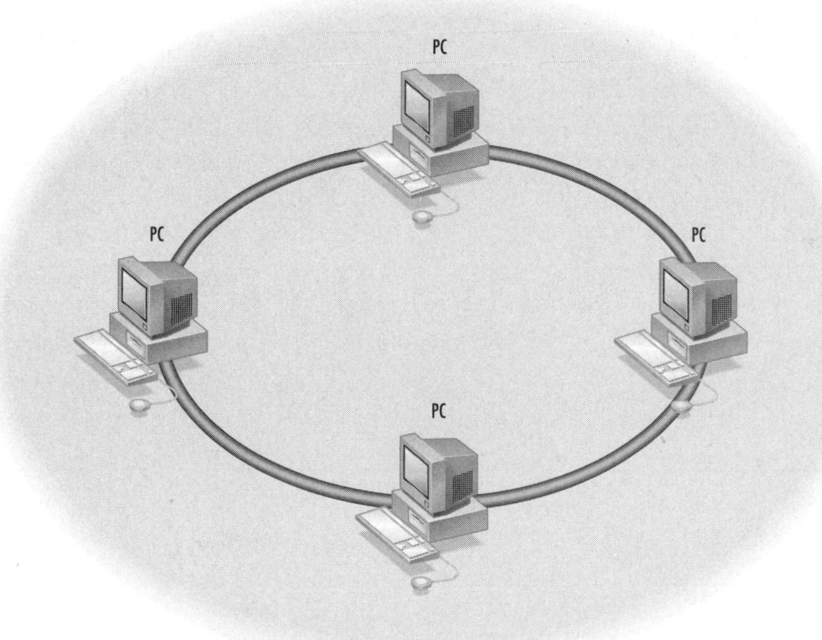


**FIGURE 21.4**
Ring Network Topology

## Star Topology

A star topology (Figure 21.5) connects all computers to a central gathering point, such as a hub or switch. The hub then manages all of the traffic among them. In this topology, failure of one PC does not cause failure of any others; however, if the hub fails, all of the computers connected to it lose networking capability.

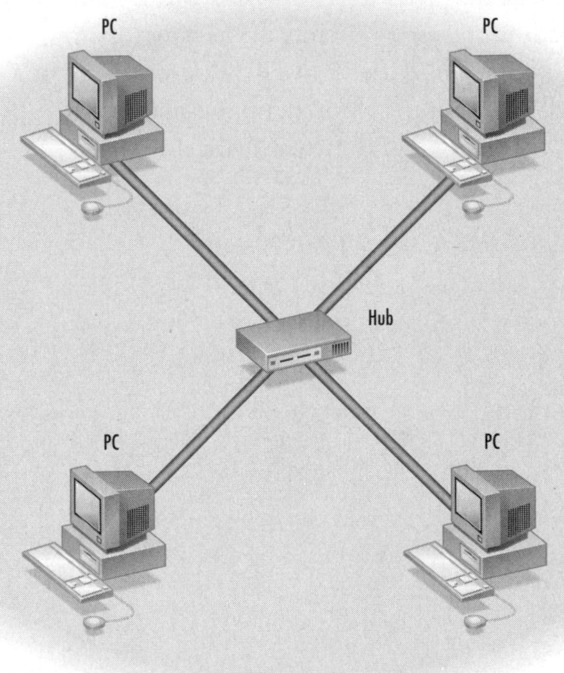


**FIGURE 21.5**
Star Network Topology

## Mesh Topology

**Mesh**

A network topology in which all computers are directly connected to every other computer to ensure reliability.

A *mesh* topology (Figure 21.6) connects every computer to every other computer by separate cables. This redundancy ensures reliability; if one cable fails, another can carry the traffic. The redundancy is also its drawback; it requires a lot of cable and several hours of labor to set up and maintain. This topology is seldom used except in mission-critical situations, and is not covered on the A+ exam.

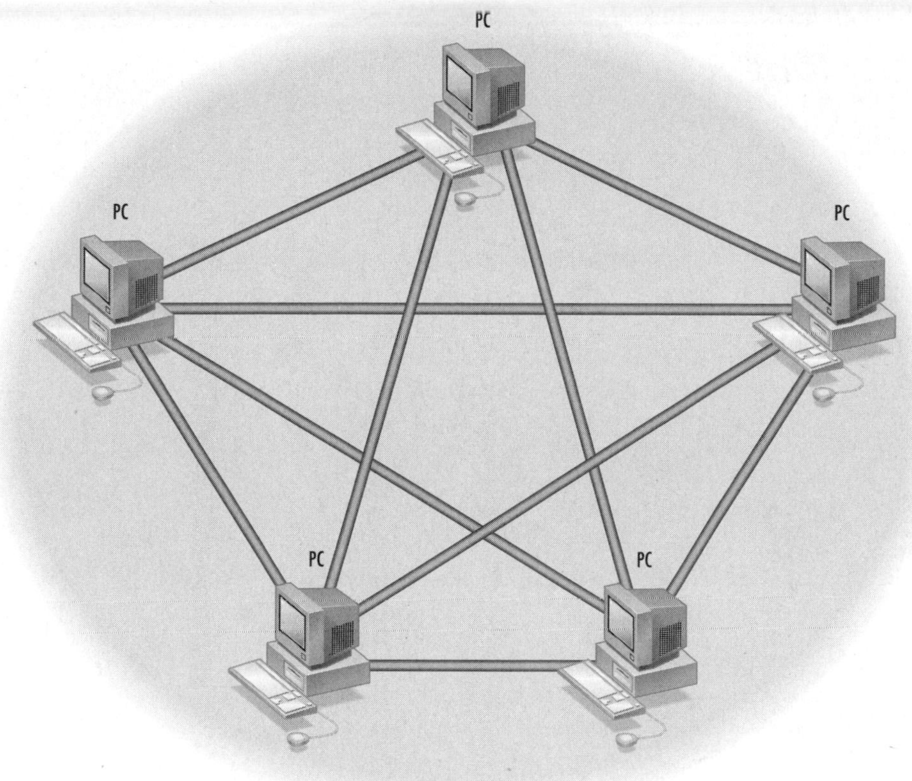


**FIGURE 21.6**
Mesh Network Topology

## COMBINATIONS OF PHYSICAL TOPOLOGIES

An actual network will probably be much more physically complex than the models shown in Figures 21.3 through 21.6. A network might include several different topologies and/or several instances of different physical topologies. Figure 21.7 shows a combination of star and bus topologies. The main *backbone* of the network is a bus, and there are satellite stars radiating out from it.

**Backbone**

The central part of the network, through which traffic flows between remote segments.

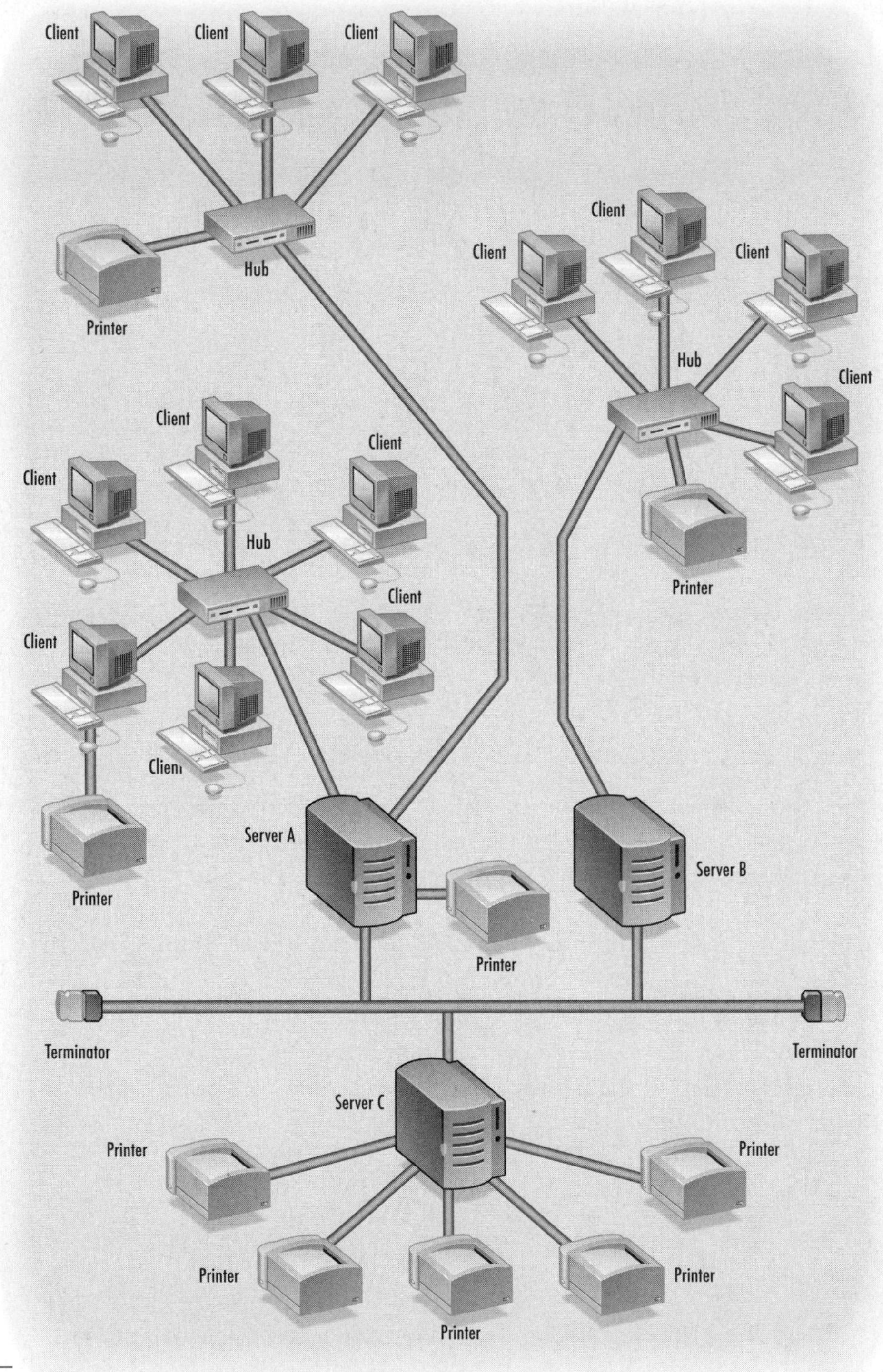


**FIGURE 21.7**
A Star-Bus Physical Topology

## Logical Topologies

One of the things that makes networking potentially confusing to beginners is that "topology" can mean two different things. On one hand, it refers to the physical arrangement of the PCs, as discussed in the preceding section. On the other hand, it refers to the way the data travels through the physical connections, or its logical arrangement. For example, workstations might be physically connected to a central hub, forming a star, but might pass data from PC to PC in a circular fashion, forming a logical ring.

There are two primary logical topologies: bus and ring. The main difference between them is in the way that they avoid *collisions* in network traffic.

**Collision**

A network traffic snarl that occurs when two PCs try to send data at the same time.

In a logical bus topology, the network is like a telephone party line. A computer that wants to send some data listens to make sure no other PC is sending data, and then it sends. If another PC does the same thing simultaneously, a collision occurs. When there is a collision, all of the PCs involved must retry their send operation after a random amount of time. (The random retry interval ensures that all of the PCs do not try to resend at the same time.) In Figure 21.8, two PCs have tried to send data at the same time, and a collision has occurred. One PC decides to retry after 2 seconds; the other retries after 4 seconds. This time there is no collision. The version of collision detection used in Ethernet networks is called *CSMA/CD*, which stands for Carrier Sense Multiple Access/Collision Detection.

**CSMA/CD (Carrier Sense Multiple Access/Collision Detection**

The method used on logical bus network topologies for detecting collisions and retrying transmission.

It is important to distinguish between a physical bus and a logical bus topology, because a network does not have to be physically arranged as a bus in order to use the bus method of collision avoidance. For example, all Ethernet networks are logically a bus even though most of them are physically set up as star or star-bus.

The other logical topology a network can use is a ring. A logical ring topology uses a *token* system to prevent collisions. There is only one token in the ring, and only the PC in possession of it may send data. PCs do not monitor the network to see whether the line is free; instead they wait until they receive the token. When no PCs need to send anything, the token passes continually among them. When a PC has data to send, it waits for the token, sends the data, and then releases the token again. Figure 21.9 shows data being passed via token in a logical ring topology.

**Token**

A permission file that is passed around a ring network. The computer that has the token is allowed to send data on the network; all others must wait until it is their turn to have the token.

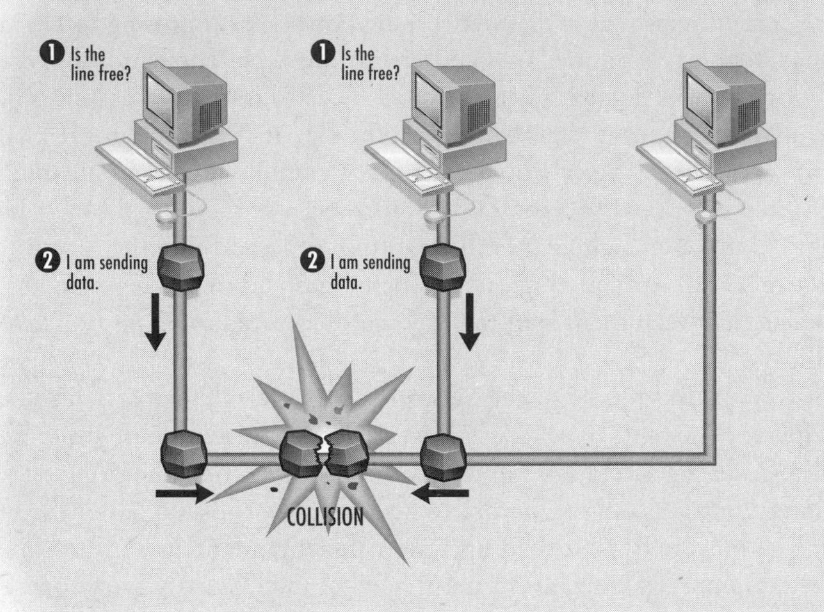


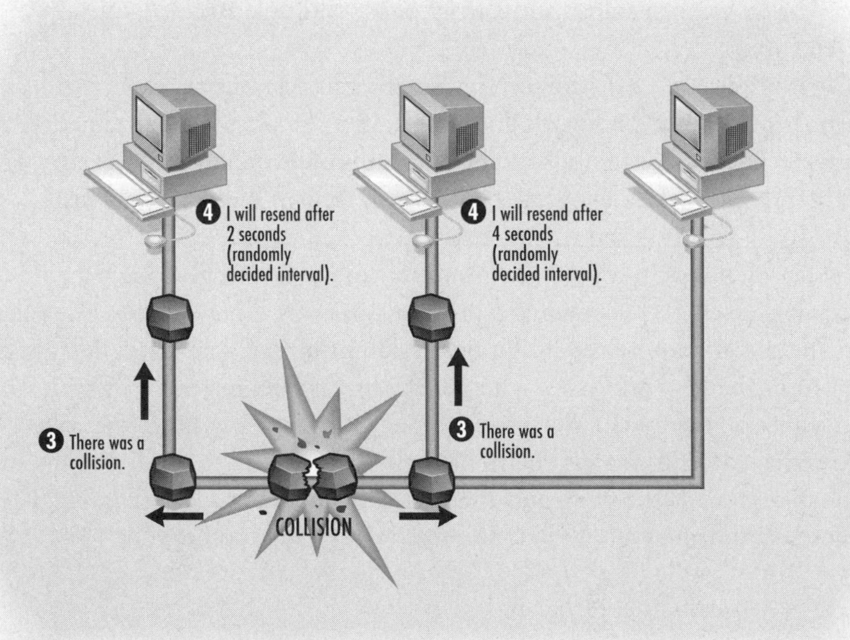


**FIGURE 21.8**
Collision Avoidance in a Logical Bus Topology

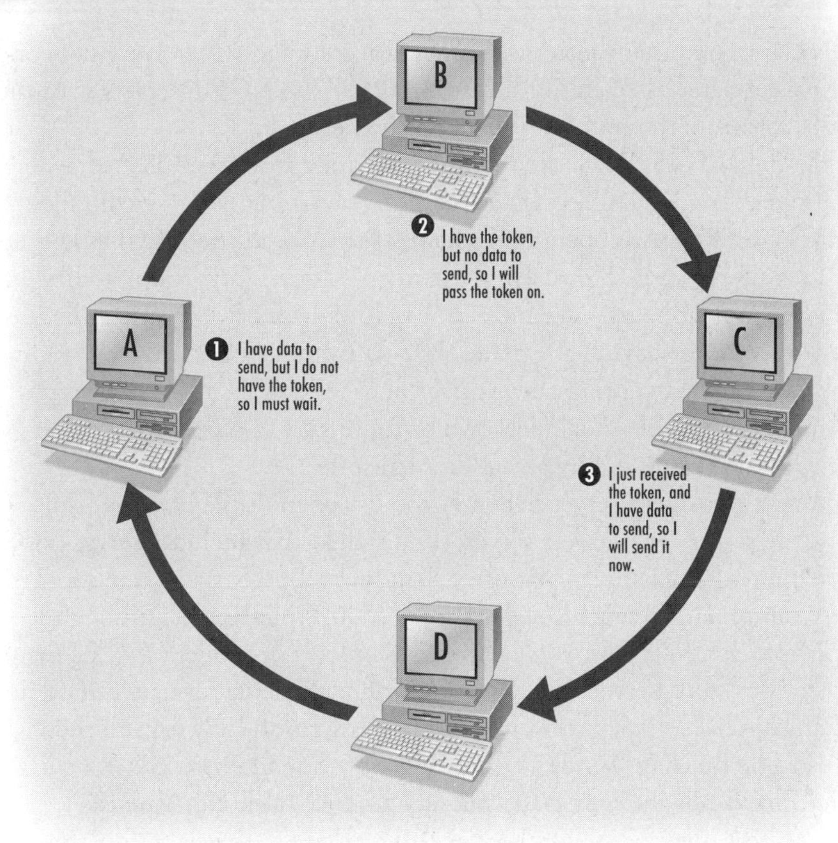
B
2 I have the token, but no data to send, so I will pass the token on.
A
1 I have data to send, but I do not have the token, so I must wait.
C
3 I just received the token, and I have data to send, so I will send it now.
D

**FIGURE 21.9**
A logical ring topology relies on a token to make the networked PCs take turns sending data.

> **WARNING**
>
> There is a specific networking technology called Token Ring, but not all networks that are physically or logically in a ring arrangement conform to its standard. You will learn more about Token Ring technology later in the chapter.

Some ring networks have two rings—an inner one and an outer one, which run in opposite directions.

As with the bus topology, a network that uses a ring topology logically is not necessarily physically configured as a ring. For example, a token-ring network might be arranged physically either as a ring or as a star.

## Network Operating System (NOS)

Just as every computer must have an operating system (OS), every network must have a network operating system (NOS). The NOS interacts with the OS to coordinate the transfer of data on the network.

In the days of MS-DOS, the NOS was separate from the OS. You would load drivers for your NOS, such as Novell NetWare, in your startup files in MS-DOS, and the two operating systems (the OS and the NOS) would do their jobs side-by-side. However, Windows 3.11 for Workgroups and higher have NOS functionality built in, so a Windows-based PC can be a client on a network without having any extra NOS software installed, just by loading the appropriate networking client driver in Windows' Network properties. This makes it possible to connect two or more PCs in a peer-to-peer network without having to buy any additional software.

However, in a client/server network, the PC or multiple PCs that function as the server must have a server OS installed that includes server NOS functionality. For example, Microsoft Windows 2000 Server is the standard server counterpart to Microsoft Windows 2000 Professional. Although it can be used as a fully functional copy of Windows on a client PC, its main purpose is to run a server PC. Client PCs on a client/server network do not need any special software to participate in a Microsoft network; all they need is to be running Windows 95 or higher as the OS.

Microsoft is not the only NOS manufacturer; Novell NetWare is a popular alternative that might be installed on the PC that is to function as the server. Most versions of Windows include a Client for Novell NetWare driver, but may require additional drivers for full participation in a NetWare network. UNIX is an alternative operating system that also functions as a popular NOS for Web servers on the Internet. Linux is a free variant of UNIX that is admired by high-end networking enthusiasts and anti-Microsoft activists; it can also act as a network server as well as a stand-alone operating system. However, none of these are covered on the A+ exam, so this textbook will not discuss them. If you decide to take the Network+ exam, you will study network operating systems in greater detail.

# Network Technologies

There is one more way to categorize a network: by its technology. "Technology" can be a generic term, but in this case it means the system of rules and customs by which the hardware agrees to play. Another way to think about network technology is network "brand." For example, hardware devices that share a common network technology know how to communicate with one another.

Networking hardware is designed for use with a particular technology. Therefore the networking technology you choose determines the type of hardware needed—the network interface card, the cabling, and the connection devices such as hubs, routers, and so on. The three network technologies you need to know about are Ethernet, Token Ring, and Fiber Distributed Data Interface (FDDI). There are other technologies, but they are specialized and are not covered on the A+ exam.

Networking technology has no direct relationship to the physical or logical topology or to the NOS, but some technologies work with only certain topologies and OSes. Table 21.1 summarizes their requirements for physical and logical topologies.

| | Ethernet | Token Ring | FDDI |
|---|---|---|---|
| Physical topology | Star or bus | Ring or star | Ring |
| Logical topology | Bus | Ring | Ring |

**TABLE 21.1**
Physical and Logical Topologies Used with the Most Common Network Technologies

## Ethernet

The most popular network technology is Ethernet. Nearly all of the networking hardware available in computer superstores is Ethernet, and it is the primary networking technology that you need to know about for the A+ exam. Ethernet networks use a physical bus or star topology, or a combination of the two.

There have been several versions of Ethernet developed over the years. Each uses a different type of cable and different networking hardware, and has a different maximum data transfer speed.

### *10Base-5 (Thicknet)*

The oldest type of Ethernet system is *10Base-5*. It uses a very thick coaxial cable, about 0.5 inch in diameter. As discussed in Chapter 7, coaxial cable is the type used for cable TV and satellite TV. However, there are many different grades of coaxial cable, and the type used for TV will not work for computer networks. Coaxial cable has a center wire core covered by

**10Base-5**

An old style of bus topology Ethernet that uses 0.5-inch coaxial cable (also called thicknet).

insulation and then wrapped in a wire-mesh outer casing that acts as an EMI shield.

A 10Base-5 network uses a physical bus topology. Its cable is one long, single piece that stretches out over the entire network segment (up to 545 yards [500 meters]). The cable has marks on it to indicate where devices should connect; pay attention to these markings because they establish the minimum amount of spacing required between devices. Individual PCs attach to it with a vampire connector, a transceiver that pierces the cable to tie into it. The transceiver is a box, and attached to the box is a cable with a female DB-15 connector that attaches to the network interface card in the PC (see Figure 21.10). A 10Base-5 network can send and receive data at up to 10Mbps.

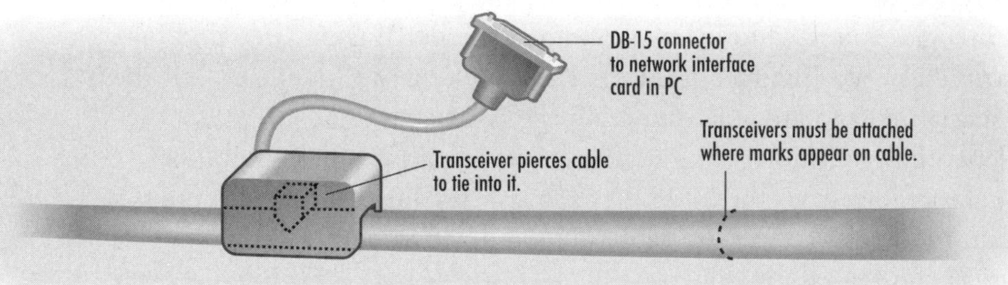


**FIGURE 21.10**
10Base-5 Network Technology

### *10Base-2 (Thinnet)*

**10Base-2**

A style of bus topology Ethernet that uses coaxial cable and connects individual segments of cable and PC network interface cards with T-style connectors.

A more modern version of 10Base-5 is *10Base-2*. It is physically a bus topology, but improves on the method for connecting PCs to the cable. Instead of one long piece of cable, 10Base-2 allows you to connect segments of cable together with a T-shaped connector. The main flow of the network goes into and out of the top of the T, and individual PCs connect through the bottom of the T, as shown in Figure 21.11. You can easily connect and disconnect PCs with regular coaxial cable BNC connectors. The maximum segment length is 607 feet (185 meters), and it uses a thinner, easier-to-handle cable than 10Base-5.

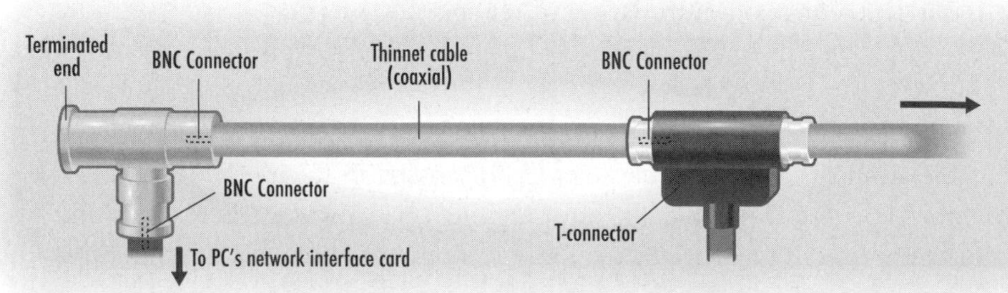


**FIGURE 21.11**
10Base-2 Network Technology

### *10Base-T and 100Base-T*

These two Ethernet types are the same in most respects; the main difference is that *10Base-T* tops out at a speed of 10Mbps while *100Base-T* (also known as Fast Ethernet) goes up to 100Mbps. Most networking hardware today is sold as 10/100Base-T, which means it will work at either speed. Other than the speed, the hardware for the two types is identical.

These Ethernet types use a physical star topology, wherein each PC or other device (such as a network-aware printer) runs individually into a hub or other network manager device (Figure 21.12). The device helps manage the network traffic, so most collisions are avoided. They use unshielded twisted pair (UTP) cable, which you learned about in Chapter 7, and connect using RJ-45 connectors.

**10Base-T**

A modern style of Ethernet hardware that uses UTP cable with RJ-45 connectors and a physical star topology, and transfers data at up to 10Mbps.

**100Base-T**

Also called Fast Ethernet, a modern style of Ethernet hardware that uses UTP or STP cable with RJ-45 connectors and a physical star topology and transfers data at up to 100Mbps.

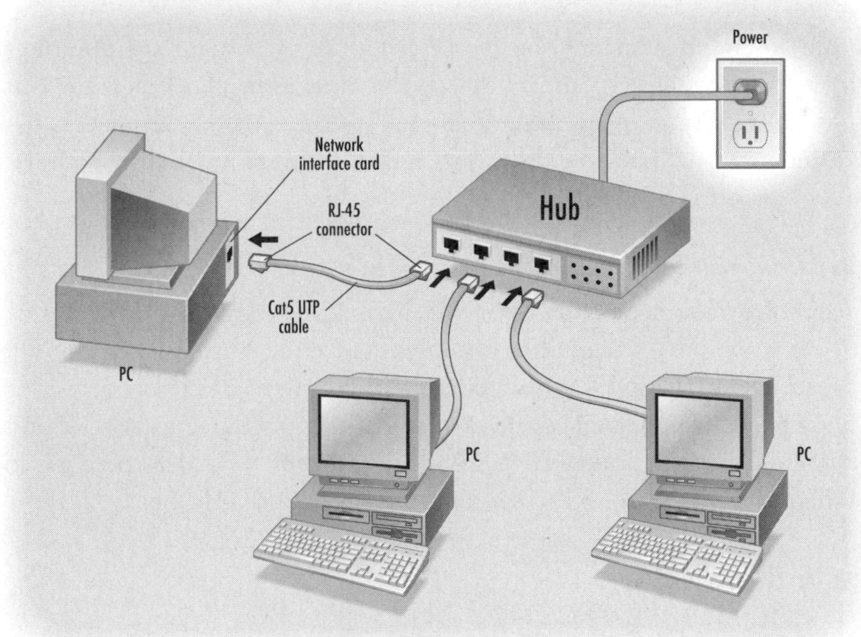


**FIGURE 21.12**
10/100Base-T Network Technology

There is an even faster version of Ethernet, Gigabit Ethernet, that takes Ethernet up to 1Gbps. It is new and expensive at this writing, but expect it to become more popular in the next few years. A new technology has also recently been introduced for 10Gbps Ethernet.

### *Wireless Ethernet*

Wireless Ethernet technology (also known as WiFi) is exploding in popularity these days, so you will almost certainly encounter it in your work as a PC technician. However, it was not yet popular when the A+ exam was last revised in early 2001, so there is little about it on the exam. The following information is more important for your career preparation than for the exam.

The current popular standards for wireless Ethernet are IEEE 802.11a and IEEE 802.11b. (The "b" version is older and less expensive.) As mentioned in earlier chapters, IEEE is a standards board that defines the rules by which various communication technologies operate. The 802.11b standard allows wireless network interface cards (NICs) to communicate with a *wireless access point* (which is the equivalent of a hub) at up to 11Mbps at a range of up to 250 feet (76 meters). The newer standard, IEEE 802.11a, allows for faster speeds (around 22Mbps) and longer distances, but it is just now becoming popular and is incompatible with IEEE 802.11b devices.

**Wireless access point**

A hub that directs the traffic between wireless Ethernet devices.

From an end user's standpoint (and from a PC technician's standpoint as well), wireless Ethernet is almost exactly the same as regular Ethernet; you can easily combine wireless and regular 10/100Base-T Ethernet devices in the same network. The only difference is the hardware involved, which we will look at later in the chapter.

### *Other Ethernet Types*

As technology advances, other types of Ethernet become available. They are not covered on the A+ exam, but you might encounter them on the job. The 10Base-FL and 10Base-FX types are fiber-optic versions of Ethernet technology. Fiber-optic cable carries data using light pulses rather than electrical pulses and can transmit data at 10Mbps or 100Mbps. The high-speed version of Ethernet called Gigabit Ethernet transmits data at up to 1Gbps.

## Token Ring

Token Ring technology, developed by IBM, used to be a very popular network technology, but has taken a back seat to Ethernet in recent years because it does not work with Windows Server and so is not suitable for corporate networks based on Microsoft servers.

Token Ring uses a logical ring topology, but the actual physical technology is likely to be a star. The data flows in a ring from PC to PC, but physically a central controlled access unit (CAU) or multistation access unit (MSAU or MAU) manages the connections. Figure 21.13 shows how the data flows into and out of each device. You can connect MSAUs together with cables (connect the Ring Out port of one to the Ring In port of the other) to expand the network.

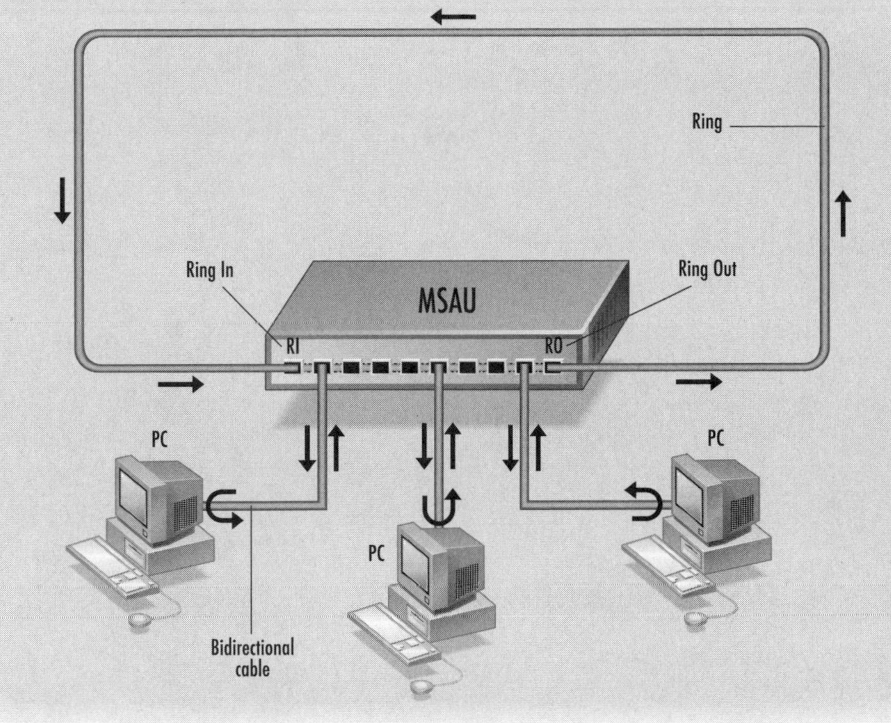


**FIGURE 21.13**
Token Ring technology uses a physical star arrangement, but data flows in a ring.

As you would expect from the name, a Token Ring network uses a token to control the permission to send data (Figure 21.14). The token arrives at a PC from its nearest active upstream neighbor (NAUN) and, if the PC has data to send, it attaches its data to the token and sends it on. The next PC (the nearest active downstream neighbor, or NADN) receives the token and the data, and reads the data. If the data is addressed to it, the PC takes the data and changes 2 bits to indicate the data has been successfully delivered; otherwise it just passes the token on to the next PC, and the token continues, with data attached, down the line until it comes to its destination. When the original sending PC receives word that the data has been delivered, it releases the token. The fact that the token release does not occur until the delivery has been confirmed is significant because it differs from the behavior with FDDI, which is discussed next.

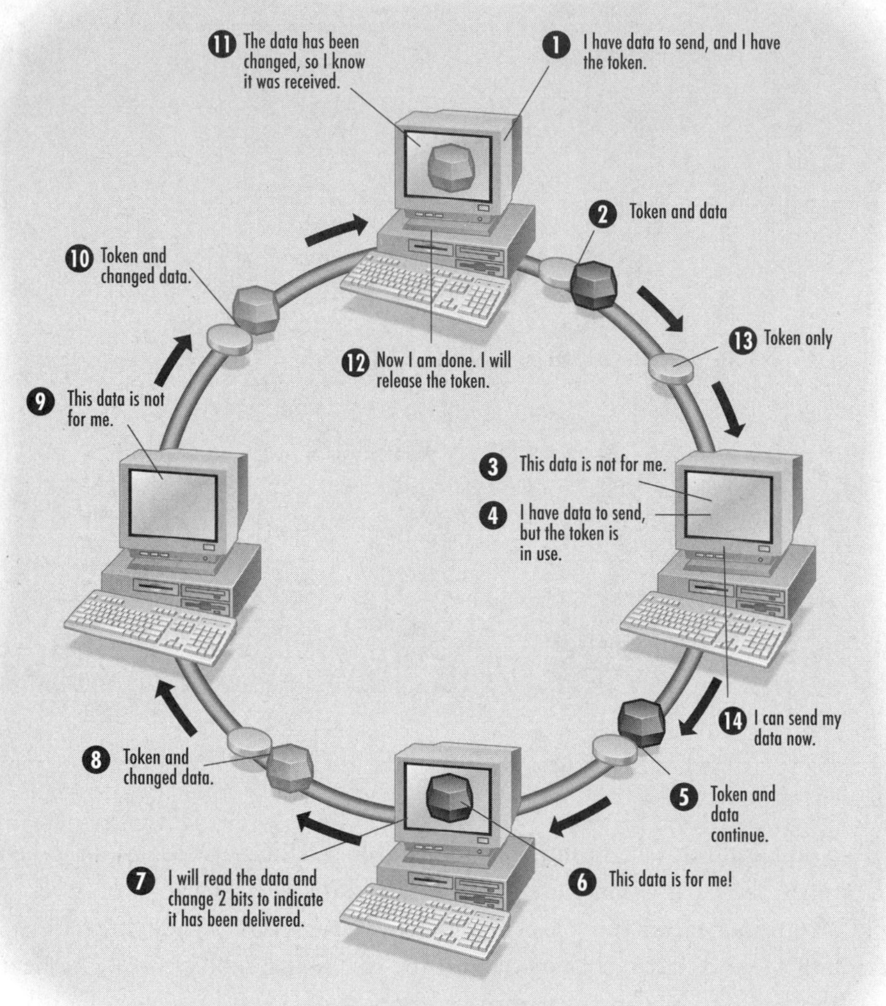


**FIGURE 21.14**
The Process for Sending Data on a Token Ring Network

## FDDI

Fiber Distributed Data Interface (FDDI) is a fiber-optic, high-speed version of Token Ring. Its speed is between 155 and 622Mbps, and the workstations can be as far as 1.6 miles apart. Normally an entire network is not comprised of FDDI; instead, FDDI is used for the network backbone, or to connect two remote locations to one another. The fiber-optic cable makes it more expensive than ordinary networking, but the high speed helps prevent network delays in heavy traffic paths.

One main differentiating feature of FDDI as opposed to Token Ring is that there are two rings, each going in opposite directions (Figure 21.15).

The primary ring carries most of the data, but a secondary ring exists as an alternate route for data in the event that the primary ring becomes unable to carry it. This built-in redundancy makes FDDI more fault-tolerant and reliable than Token Ring or Ethernet.

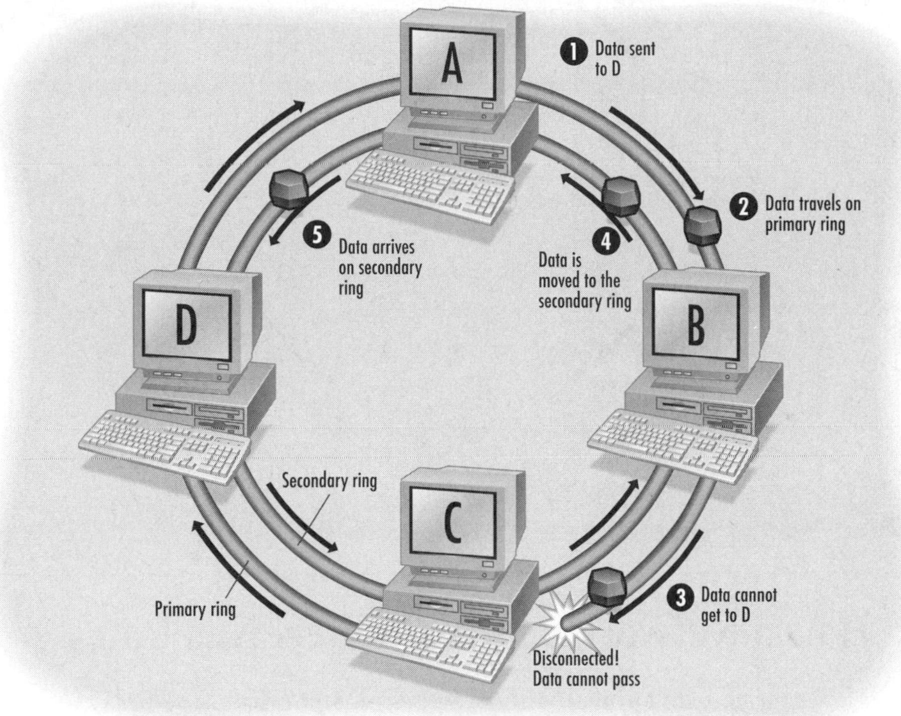


**FIGURE 21.15**
An FDDI network has two rings going in opposite directions.

The other important difference is that the token is released earlier with FDDI than with Token Ring. As mentioned, a Token Ring network waits for the token to come back with a confirmation to the sending PC before any other PC can use it to send data. With an FDDI network, a PC captures the token and then sends all of the data it needs to send without sending the token itself. It might send multiple packets of data in succession, all without the token (see Figure 21.16). When it is finished it releases the token to the next PC in the ring, which is then free to start sending its own data regardless of whether the first PC's data has been received at its destination yet.

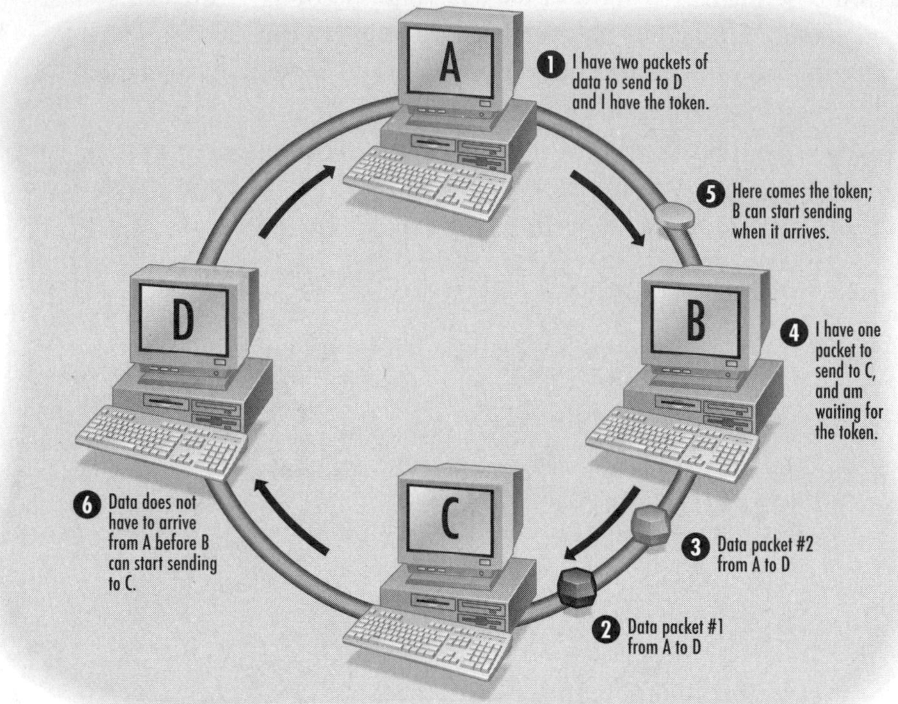
A
B
C
D
1 I have two packets of data to send to D and I have the token.
5 Here comes the token; B can start sending when it arrives.
4 I have one packet to send to C, and am waiting for the token.
3 Data packet #2 from A to D
2 Data packet #1 from A to D
6 Data does not have to arrive from A before B can start sending to C.

**FIGURE 21.16**
FDDI does not send the token with the data and does not require confirmation of receipt before the token can be passed to the next PC.

# How a Network Sends and Receives Data

Now that you are familiar with the types of networks in use today in most businesses and homes, take a moment to deal with networking in general. How does it work? How does the data move from one PC to another across those wires? The following sections explain those concepts.

## Data Packets

**Packet**

A logical container file for sending data over a network, containing the data itself plus a header and a footer.

**Frame**

The header and footer that accompany data when it is sent as a packet over a network.

When you send a letter to a friend via the postal mail system, you place it in an envelope, include both the recipient's address and your own on the envelope, and place the envelope in a mailbox. That is roughly what happens when data is sent on a network. The data is divided up into chunks and placed in packets. A *packet* is like an envelope; it contains the data itself plus an identifying header and footer. The header and footer together (minus the data) are known as a *frame*.

The *header* is like the address on a mailing label. It tells the destination, and it specifies the *protocols* used in the transmission. The *footer* contains error-checking information that ensures the data is accurately delivered. When the receiving PC gets the packet, it strips off the "envelope" (in this case the header and footer) and reads the data.

The size of a packet is determined by the NOS, so many times a file must be broken into multiple packets for transmission. When that happens the data is reassembled at the receiving end into a contiguous file.

**Header**

The address portion of a data packet sent on a network, which precedes the data.

**Footer**

The error-checking portion of a data packet sent on a network, which follows the data.

**Protocol**

The language or set of rules governing a data transmission.

## OSI Layers

From a user perspective, networking is fairly simple. You connect a couple of computers and they start sending data between them via network cables. But underneath is a very complex system involving multiple layers of functionality. This system is called the *Open Systems Interconnection (OSI) reference model*, and it provides a basis for networking standardization. Ethernet, token ring, and FDDI all conform to the OSI model.

**Open Systems Interconnection (OSI) reference model**

The model that describes the various layers of activity involved in sending a packet of data from one PC to another on a network.

As a PC technician you will probably never do anything with the OSI model directly, but there are three reasons why you should learn something about it:

1. It helps you understand how networking really works at a base level.
2. It can be helpful when troubleshooting network problems to know at what point a transmission is breaking down.
3. If you plan to take the Network+ exam or become MCSA or MCSE certified, you will need to know it for those tests.

As data passes from one PC to another, it gets handed off from one piece of hardware or software to another. There is a seven-layer chain it passes through, from 7 to 1 on its way out and from 1 to 7 on its way in. These seven layers are the OSI layers. Figure 21.17 shows how the data passes through each of the layers on both the sending and the receiving PC.

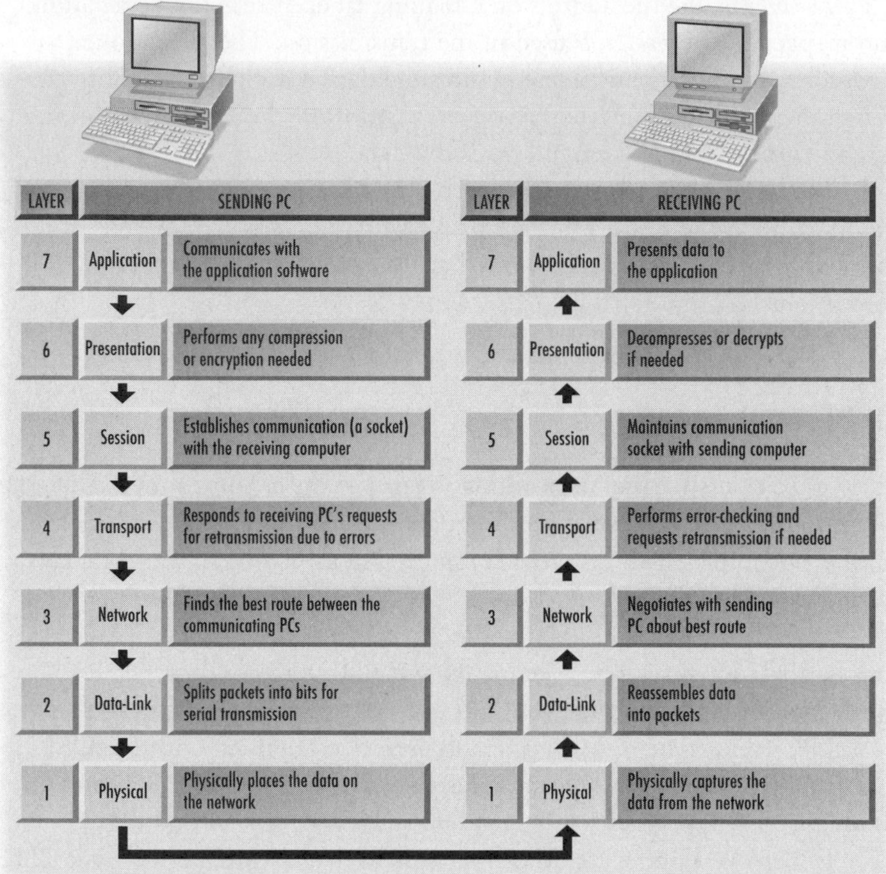

LAYER
SENDING PC
7
Application
Communicates with the application software
6
Presentation
Performs any compression or encryption needed
5
Session
Establishes communication (a socket) with the receiving computer
4
Transport
Responds to receiving PC's requests for retransmission due to errors
3
Network
Finds the best route between the communicating PCs
2
Data-Link
Splits packets into bits for serial transmission
1
Physical
Physically places the data on the network
LAYER
RECEIVING PC
7
Application
Presents data to the application
6
Presentation
Decompresses or decrypts if needed
5
Session
Maintains communication socket with sending computer
4
Transport
Performs error-checking and requests retransmission if needed
3
Network
Negotiates with sending PC about best route
2
Data-Link
Reassembles data into packets
1
Physical
Physically captures the data from the network


**FIGURE 21.17**
Data travels through the OSI model from the application layer on the sending PC to the application layer on the receiving PC by traveling through all of the other layers.

## Network Protocols

The term "protocol" was briefly introduced earlier in the chapter. A protocol is an agreed-upon format or language for transmitting data between devices. The protocol determines things like the type of error-checking method, how the sending and receiving devices let each other know that they have finished, and what data compression method should be used, if any. The protocol operates at the Network and Transport levels of the OSI model (levels 3 and 4).

The most common protocol in Windows-based networking as well as on the Internet is TCP/IP. However, there are many other networking protocols, which will be covered in Chapter 22 when we discuss installing protocols in Windows.

When you work with the Internet, you encounter additional protocols. These are protocols in the sense that they are languages for exchanging data over a network, but they do not work directly with the network hardware and do not require drivers to be installed for them. They include FTP, HTTP, PPP, POP, IMAP, and SMTP, and you will learn about them in Chapter 25.

## TRY IT!

Try the following to see what networking protocols are installed on your PC in Windows:

1. Open the Control Panel and double-click the *Network* or *Network Connections* icon.
2. If working with Windows 2000 or XP, right-click the icon for your network connection and choose Properties. You do not have to do this step in Windows 9x/Me.
3. A list of drivers appears. Find TCP/IP and notice the icon next to it, which stands for a protocol. Different icons stand for other types of network devices, services, and clients.
4. Make a note of other protocols that are on the list.
5. Close all open dialog boxes without making any changes.

# Network Hardware

As a PC technician you might be responsible for selecting hardware to work with an existing network or to set up a brand-new network yourself. The following sections describe the various kinds of hardware involved.

## Network Interface Cards (NICs)

Each PC must have a network interface card (NIC) (Figure 21.18). In a desktop PC, this is usually an expansion board with a port on its backplate for connecting a network cable. On a notebook PC the NIC may be built in, or it may be a PC Card.

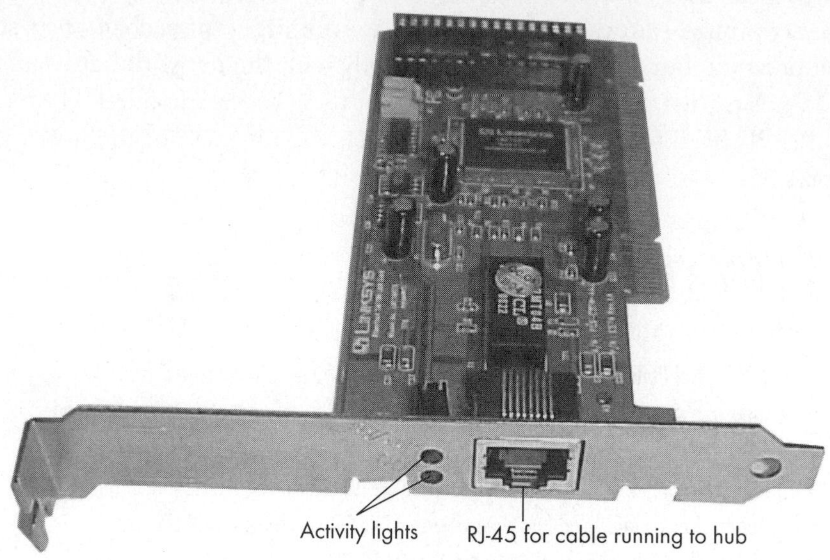


**FIGURE 21.18**
A PCI NIC for a Desktop PC

The most important consideration when selecting a NIC is to match it to the network technology of the rest of the network. For example, if the rest of the network is Ethernet, so must the NIC be. If you are not sure of the network technology of the rest of the network, look at the NICs in existing PCs, or ask the person in charge of the network.

If you are installing an Ethernet card, you must also consider the Ethernet type because the connectors are different. Recall from an earlier discussion that 10Base-5 uses a 15-pin D-sub connector, 10Base-2 uses a BNC connector, and 10/100Base-T uses an RJ-45 connector. Some Ethernet cards have more than one connector type, especially older cards, but most of the new cards will have only the RJ-45 connector.

One final concern is the expansion bus used. As with the other components discussed in earlier chapters, PCI is better than ISA, so select a PCI NIC whenever possible.

The NIC takes data from the PCI or ISA bus, which comes to it via a parallel bus (16 or 32 bits wide), and converts it to the electrical or light pulses that will travel in serial fashion (that is, one bit at a time) through the network cable. The converter between parallel and serial is called a transceiver. Cards that have multiple connectors (such as for 10Base-2 and 10Base-5) have multiple transceivers.

Each Ethernet or Token Ring NIC has a unique hard-coded serial number called its Media Access Control (MAC) address. This address is a

6-byte hexadecimal number assigned during manufacturing; no two NICs in the world have the same number. The MAC address is used during network communication to uniquely identify each NIC.

## TRY IT!

To find out the MAC address of your NICs:

1. Open a command prompt window from within Windows (Start/Programs/Accessories/Command Prompt).
2. Key **IPCONFIG/ALL** and press Enter. After a few seconds information about each NIC appears, including the MAC address.
3. Close the command prompt window.

In Windows 95, IPCONFIG is not available. In Windows XP, the GETMAC command is available as an alternative for retrieving MAC adresses.

## TRY IT!

If you have the hardware available, hook up a simple 10Base-2, 10Base-5, and/or 10Base-T network and try them all. If not, try whichever ones you can. Remember:

- With 10Base-5, attach the connectors to the cable only at the areas marked on the cable to ensure proper spacing.
- With 10Base-2, do not forget the T-connectors; you cannot hook the cable directly to the NIC, and both ends must be terminated.
- With 10Base-T, every device must connect to a hub; you cannot connect the devices in a chain.

## Network-Capable Printers

Any printer can be shared on a network by accessing it from the individual PC to which it is attached. However, some printers, referred to as network-ready or network-capable, have built-in NICs (usually Ethernet) and can function as separate nodes all by themselves. This is useful because it does place a drain on a host PC when other users print to it.

## In Real Life

When shopping for a network-ready printer, look for a printer with the letter N in its model number. This indicates that it has a built-in NIC.

## TRY IT!

If you have Internet access, try shopping for network-capable laser printers.

1. Go to Hewlett-Packard's Web site, http://www.hp.com, and browse through the laser printer section.
2. After you have identified a network-capable printer, find an equivalent model that lacks this capability.
3. Find a good price for each model at http://shopper.cnet.com. What is the difference between the prices for a network-capable versus non-network-capable model?

## Network Cabling

Chapter 7 was devoted to cables, so you already know a lot about network cabling. A quick review follows:

- Thick Ethernet cable for 10Base-5 Ethernet is coaxial and about 0.5 inch in diameter. Transponders hook into it and then connect to the NIC with a D-sub 15-pin connector, so the cable has no direct connection to the NIC.
- Thin Ethernet cable for 10Base-2 Ethernet is also coaxial, but it is of a smaller thickness. It connects to a T-connector, and that T-connector hooks into the NIC via a BNC connection.

**WARNING**

Although a thin Ethernet cable will physically connect to the BNC connector on a 10Base-2 NIC, it will not function that way because, as you may recall from an earlier discussion, this type of network requires a T-connector to let the network cable pass through. The bottom of the T connects to the NIC and the top of the T passes the network through.

- 10Base-T and 100Base-T use Category 5 or Category 6 unshielded twisted pair (UTP) cable with RJ-45 connectors.
- Token Ring networks use shielded twisted pair (STP) cable with a hermaphroditic connector on the network end and a DB-9 connector to the NIC.
- FDDI networks use fiber-optic cable.

## Hubs

Hubs are an essential part of any network that is physically configured as a star (and that includes 10/100Base-T Ethernet networks). Each node plugs into the hub. In larger networks, hubs then connect to one another, forming larger star formations like snowflakes, or they plug into a bus.

Hubs vary in the number of plugs they have for connecting nodes. A small hub might have only 5 connectors, as in Figure 21.19; a large hub might have 20 or more connectors.

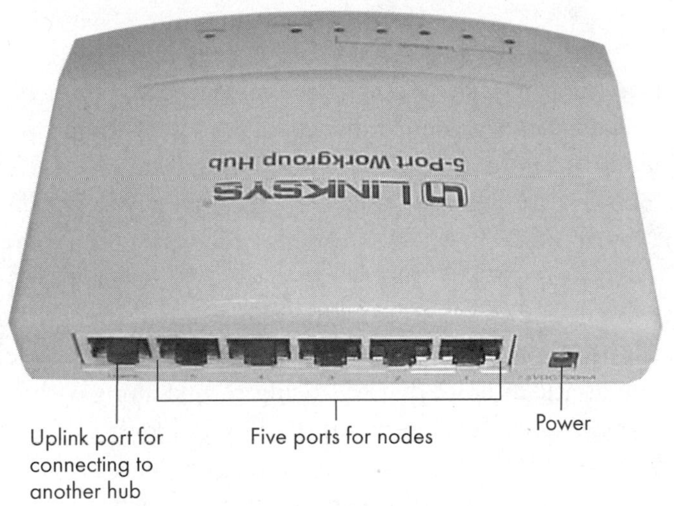


**FIGURE 21.19**
A Small Hub for a 100Base-T Network

Some hubs have different types of Ethernet connectors, such as 10Base-2, 10Base-5, and 10/100Base-T. This is useful for connecting different network segments together so they can communicate. For example, suppose the Marketing department has an existing 10Base-2 network, and the Sales department was just set up with 100Base-T. You can connect the two departments by connecting the end of the 10Base-2 bus to the 100Base-2 hub. Since it is all Ethernet, no special translation is required.

## MSAU

We stated earlier that a Token Ring network is physically a star but logically a ring. That means it cannot use an ordinary Ethernet hub; instead it must use a multistation access unit (MSAU), which looks like a hub but actually routes the network signal into and out of each node in a loop. A typical MSAU has eight connectors for nodes plus a Ring In and a Ring Out plug, for a total of ten connectors.

## Other Expansion Devices

In addition to the basic components just described that form the basis of any network, there are several optional components that a network might employ as it grows.

### *Repeater*

**Signal**

The data being sent on a network.

**Attenuation**

Loss of signal power in a cable carrying data, usually because the data has to travel too far.

**Repeater**

A network device that accepts and rebroadcasts a data signal to compensate for signal weakening caused by traveling long distances.

**Signal regeneration**

The rebroadcasting of a network signal in order to improve its strength and quality.

**Bridge**

A network device that directs traffic between network segments, screening out any traffic that is not addressed to a node within a particular segment.

All network technologies have a maximum cable length; if you exceed that cable length, the *signal* degrades so that the data transmission is not reliable. For example, the maximum cable length for a 10/100Base-T Ethernet network is 328 feet (100 meters). This loss of signal power is called *attenuation*. Signal noise interference can also occur when the signal is weak.

A *repeater* is a device that accepts an incoming signal, strengthens it, and sends it on. It does not just amplify the original signal; it rebroadcasts it, eliminating any static or noise that was being carried along with it. This is called *signal regeneration*. It functions at the Physical layer of the OSI model. It does not perform any error-checking or repackaging of the original signal, so if the signal was corrupt before it reached the repeater, the repeater would not notice or fix it.

**WARNING**

**The recommended limit for signal regeneration from point A to point B is five repeating devices. If the path between the points stretches out longer than that, problems begin to occur because of the time lag in reporting a collision.**

### *Bridges and Switches*

A repeater just passes on whatever data it receives; it does not evaluate it. *Bridges* and switches are smarter devices. They are able to read the MAC address in the header to determine where data is going, and based on that header information they can decide whether or not to allow the data to go down a certain path.

The primary purpose of a bridge or switch is to reduce the overall amount of traffic in individual network "neighborhoods." When some data comes to the bridge or switch, it decides whether that data is addressed to a node within a certain network segment. If it is, that data is allowed to pass through to that segment. If it is not, the bridge or switch prevents it from passing. Only the traffic addressed to PCs in a particular segment is allowed to flow through to that segment, thus greatly reducing the amount of traffic on that segment.

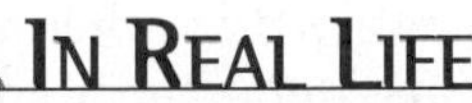

## In Real Life

Bridges and switches are frequently referred to collectively because they accomplish almost exactly the same purpose. Behind the scenes they operate in slightly different ways, but this is transparent to users. Switches are slightly newer technology, and offer better collision avoidance. Bridges are usually employed to divide a LAN into a few segments, while switches usually are used to create many segments. Bridges usually have only a few ports; a switch can have up to hundreds of ports.

### *Router*

A *router* does basically what its name implies: it finds the best route from point A to point B. The Internet is full of routers, and those routers direct the messages you send to the recipient's address. When you send e-mail to a friend, you do not have to specify the names of all of the servers to pass through on the way there—routers handle that task. You simply specify the end address, and routers plan and execute the journey.

**Router**

A more sophisticated version of a bridge, the router screens out traffic not addressed to a particular segment and also plans and executes the best route to deliver a packet to the address destination.

A router works at the Network level of the OSI model, but is essentially similar in functionality to a bridge, in that it is able to screen out traffic that is not destined for a particular segment.

### *Gateway*

A *gateway* is a translator between dissimilar network types. A gateway might be used to connect an IBM mainframe computer to a LAN, for example, or to connect an Apple network to an Ethernet network. Gateways are unique in that they can function on any level of the OSI model—whatever is necessary to bring together the dissimilar networks.

**Gateway**

A network device that creates compatibility and connectivity between dissimilar network types.

Gateways are not generic. When you buy a gateway, it is with a certain connection in mind—that is, it connects a specific type of network to another specific type. You might buy a gateway that would connect Ethernet to Token Ring, for example.

Whereas the other devices in this section (repeaters, routers, and bridges) are usually external boxes, a gateway can be either an internal expansion board for a server PC or an external stand-alone box.

## Wireless Networking Hardware

Since Ethernet is the dominant technology in networking today, the networks you create will almost certainly be Ethernet-based. But within Ethernet there are two classes of hardware: wired and wireless.

When we talk about wired Ethernet, we mean standard Ethernet that uses cables to connect each node to the hub and each hub to other hubs and expansion devices. Wireless Ethernet components use the same Ethernet protocols and standards, but instead of cables they send the packets via radio waves. The equipment is more expensive than wired Ethernet (at this writing about three times the cost), but frees up users to move their PCs around without worrying about network connectivity.

One advantage of wireless Ethernet is that it allows mobility. Any PC that is relocated within a building can greatly benefit from wireless Ethernet. For example, suppose a company has three wireless access points (WAPs), each located on a different floor. When a manager goes to a meeting on one of these floors and takes her notebook PC, the PC automatically detects the WAP on the new floor and uses it to keep connected to the corporate LAN.

A second advantage of wireless Ethernet is that a network can be constructed with no need to drill holes or run cables through walls or alter the building in any way.

Wireless Ethernet does have drawbacks, however. One is range. The practical limit of a single WAP is about 250 feet with a clear shot between the points (for example, outdoors, or in a large building with no walls) or about 100 feet if there are walls and floors to go through. After that, the signal becomes unreliable. In a large building, multiple WAPs might be required.

Another drawback is security. Most WAPs today come with security encryption features, but they are not enabled by default, and unless proper security is implemented, anybody driving by the building with a notebook PC can potentially have access to the network. In contrast, a wired Ethernet network with no special encryption in place is more secure because someone would have to make a physical connection in order to access it.

Wireless hardware looks very much like conventional hardware. Figure 21.20 shows a wireless router and access point. Notice that it has several regular RJ-45 connectors, for hooking into a wired section of the Ethernet network; this allows wired and wireless components to coexist in the same network. Notice that it also has two antennas for broadcasting the radio waves.

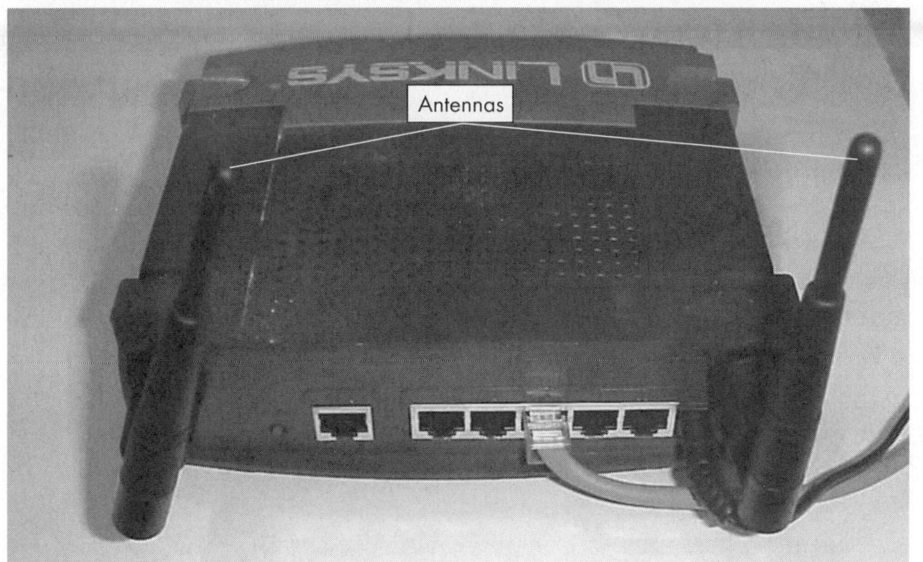


**FIGURE 21.20**
A Wireless Router/Access Point

A wireless NIC expansion board looks like a regular NIC except, instead of an RJ-45 connector, it has a small antenna sticking up out of it. A wireless PC Card NIC looks like a regular PC Card except, again, there is no connector. Some have antennas; others simply have a thick area on the outside that serves as an antenna, as in Figure 21.21.

**FIGURE 21.21**
A Wireless PC Card NIC

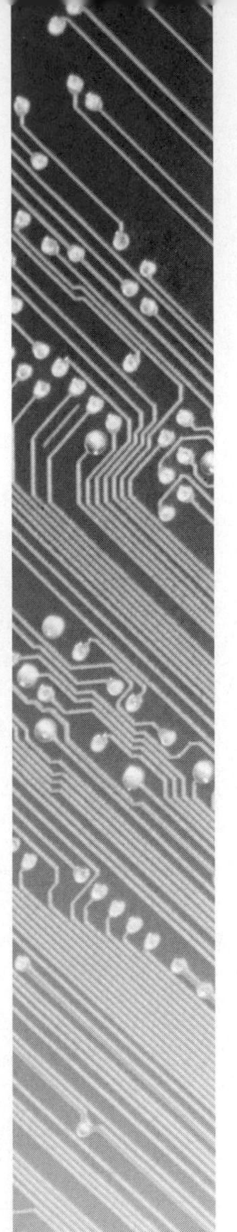

# STUDY GUIDE

Use the following summaries to review the key concepts of this chapter.

## Network Basics

- A network is any two or more computers connected together to share data and resources.
- A node is a computer or printer on the network.
- A local-area network (LAN) is a network in which all of the nodes are physically near one another.
- A wide-area network (WAN) is a network in which some of the nodes are separated physically, such as in another part of town or in another city.
- A client is a computer or printer that uses the network as an end user. A server is a computer that exists on the network to help the clients communicate.
- A client/server network is a network that has at least one server. The server takes the network processing load off the clients so being on the network does not slow them down.
- Having a server requires a dedicated PC and a special version of the operating system. A large network might have many servers.
- A peer-to-peer network is a network with no servers, in which all of the clients share the burden of keeping the network running. Peer-to-peer becomes impractical when there are more than 10 computers.
- Having a server does not preclude individual clients from sharing their resources directly with other clients.
- Resources that can be shared on a network include hard disk space, printing, and Internet access.

## Network Topologies

- A physical topology is the physical way in which the nodes are connected to one another. A logical topology is the way that data flows between the nodes.
- A bus topology is a single networking line connecting one node to another, with terminators on each end. A physical bus is used in 10Base-5 or 10Base-2 Ethernet. All Ethernet networks use the logical bus topology.

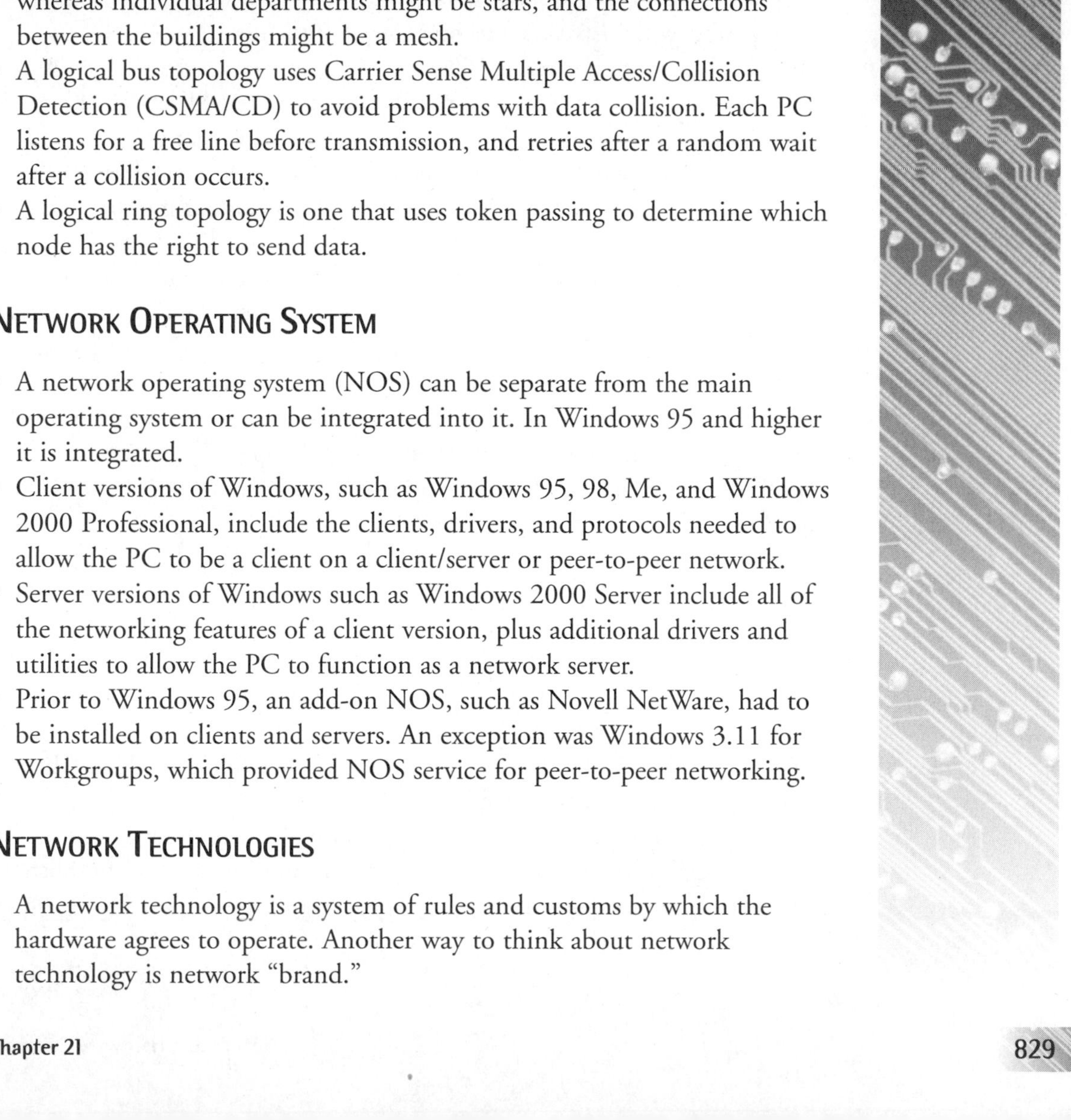

- A ring topology is a closed loop running from one node to another. Early versions of Token Ring network technology used a physical ring, but current Token Ring networks are physically stars but logically rings.
- A star topology is a central hub or connecting point to which each node connects individually. Both 10/100Base-T Ethernet and Token Ring networks use a physical star arrangement, but neither one is logically a star. The Ethernet is logically a bus, and the token ring is logically a ring.
- A mesh topology is uncommon because of the high overhead it entails. It physically connects every node to every other node. It is used only in applications requiring the greatest amount of stability.
- Several physical topologies may be combined in a single network. For example, the backbone of a network within a building might be a bus whereas individual departments might be stars, and the connections between the buildings might be a mesh.
- A logical bus topology uses Carrier Sense Multiple Access/Collision Detection (CSMA/CD) to avoid problems with data collision. Each PC listens for a free line before transmission, and retries after a random wait after a collision occurs.
- A logical ring topology is one that uses token passing to determine which node has the right to send data.

## Network Operating System

- A network operating system (NOS) can be separate from the main operating system or can be integrated into it. In Windows 95 and higher it is integrated.
- Client versions of Windows, such as Windows 95, 98, Me, and Windows 2000 Professional, include the clients, drivers, and protocols needed to allow the PC to be a client on a client/server or peer-to-peer network.
- Server versions of Windows such as Windows 2000 Server include all of the networking features of a client version, plus additional drivers and utilities to allow the PC to function as a network server.
- Prior to Windows 95, an add-on NOS, such as Novell NetWare, had to be installed on clients and servers. An exception was Windows 3.11 for Workgroups, which provided NOS service for peer-to-peer networking.

## Network Technologies

- A network technology is a system of rules and customs by which the hardware agrees to operate. Another way to think about network technology is network "brand."

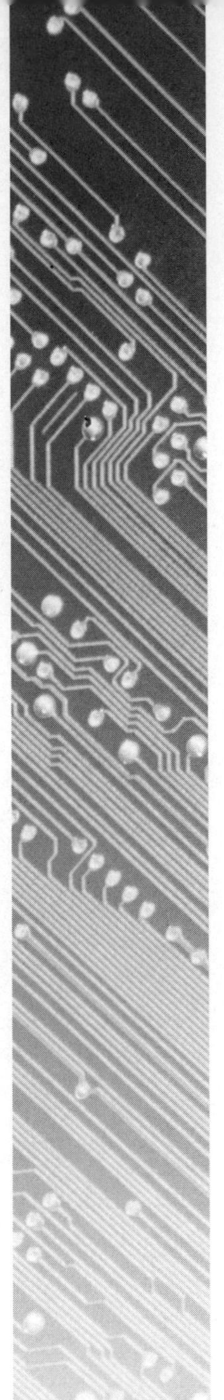

- Networking technology has no direct relationship to the physical or logical topology or to the NOS, but some technologies work with only certain topologies and OSes.
- The most popular network technology is Ethernet. Token Ring and Fiber Distributed Data Interface (FDDI) are two alternatives.
- Within Ethernet, there are several variations. The oldest is 10Base-5, also called thicknet. It uses a thick coaxial cable and a bus topology. Its maximum speed is 10Mbps.
- 10Base-2 is a modernized version of 10Base-5. It uses thinner cable and T-shaped metal joints with BNC connectors to attach nodes to the central bus. Its maximum speed is 10Mbps.
- 10Base-T uses Cat5 UTP cable. Its maximum speed is 11Mbps and its maximum range is 250 feet. A faster version, 100Base-T, is physically compatible with 10Base-T but operates at 100Mbps.
- Gigabit Ethernet operates at 1Gbps.
- Wireless Ethernet, also known as WiFi, operates at 10Mbps (IEEE 802.11b standard) and is compatible with other Ethernet types.
- Token Ring technology is no longer very popular. Developed by IBM, it uses a physical star but a logical ring, and uses token passing to avoid collisions.
- Rather than using a hub, a Token Ring network uses a multistation access unit (MSAU or MAU) to connect each node. The ring passes into and out of each node through the MSAU.
- FDDI is a fiber-optic version of Token Ring. It is very high speed (between 155 and 622Mbps) and workstations can be as far as 1.6 miles apart. It is commonly used for a network backbone.
- FDDI has two rings running in opposite directions, so traffic can continue if a break occurs in the primary ring.

## How a Network Sends and Receives Data

- Network data is sent in data packets. A packet consists of a header containing the address, the data itself, and a footer containing error correction codes.
- The nondata part of a data packet is a frame. The frame is added when the packet is sent and removed when it is received.
- OSI stands for Open Systems Interconnection; it is a reference model describing how the various layers of hardware and software accomplish a network data transmission.

- There are seven layers in the OSI model. Data travels from the top (7) to the bottom (1) when leaving the sending computer and from the bottom (1) to the top (7) when coming into the receiving computer.
- The seven layers, from bottom (1) to top (7), are: Physical, Data Link, Network, Transport, Session, Presentation, and Application. Figure 21.17 shows what each layer does.
- A protocol is an agreed-upon format or language for transmitting data between two devices.
- The most common protocol in Windows-based networking is TCP/IP. It is also the dominant protocol on the Internet, but there are many other protocols as well.

## Network Hardware

- Each node must have a network interface card (NIC). It can be an expansion board in a desktop PC, or a PC Card device in a notebook. Some PCs have built-in NICs on the motherboard.
- Some printers have built-in NICs that make them able to function as stand-alone nodes on the network.
- Modern Ethernet networking (10/100Base-T) uses Cat5 UTP cable with RJ-45 connectors.
- Earlier Ethernet networking used thick Ethernet cable (thicknet) for 10Base-5 and thin Ethernet cable (thinnet) for 10Base-2.
- Token Ring networks use shielded twisted pair (STP) cable.
- FDDI uses fiber-optic cable.
- A hub is an essential part of an Ethernet network because it forms the center of the physical star. Hubs can connect to one another to form larger networks.
- Token Ring networks use a central box that looks like a hub, but is actually a multistation access unit, that routes the data in a ring rather than on a bus.
- A repeater cleans up and strengthens a network signal, preventing data loss due to distance (attenuation).
- A bridge or switch helps route data in a network based on the MAC address.
- A router routes data in a network based on its IP address; it is a more sophisticated and powerful version of a switch.
- A gateway translates between dissimilar network types.
- Wireless hardware includes wireless access points (WAPs) that serve as hubs, wireless routers, and wireless NICs.

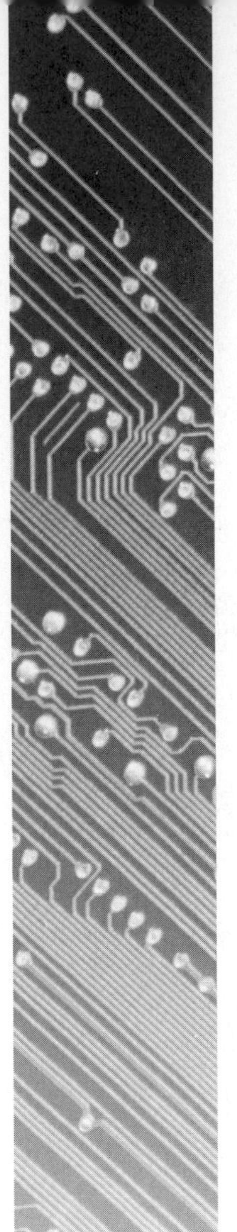

# PRACTICE TEST

On a blank sheet of paper, write the answers to the following multiple-choice questions and explain why each answer is correct.

1. Which of these is *not* a network node?
   a. a client PC on a client/server network
   b. a client PC on a peer-to-peer network
   c. a local printer shared by a client PC on a client/server network
   d. a network-capable printer connected directly to the network

2. What is the difference between a LAN and a WAN?
   a. physical location
   b. logical topology
   c. physical topology
   d. All of the above

3. What differentiates a client/server network from a peer-to-peer network?
   a. A client/server is a WAN and a peer-to-peer network is a LAN.
   b. A client/server network contains at least one server.
   c. A peer-to-peer network requires a special version of the OS.
   d. both b and c

4. Which of these resources *cannot* be shared over a network?
   a. disk drive
   b. Internet connection
   c. scanner
   d. printer

5. Which physical topology uses terminators?
   a. bus
   b. star
   c. ring
   d. mesh

6. Which logical topology uses a token?
   a. bus
   b. star
   c. ring
   d. mesh

7. Which logical topology avoids collisions via CSMA/CD?
   a. bus
   b. star
   c. ring
   d. mesh

8. Which of these OSes does *not* have networking client capabilities built in, such that you would have to install a separate NOS?
   a. MS-DOS
   b. Windows 3.11
   c. Windows 95
   d. both a and b

9. Which of these is *not* a type of Ethernet?
   a. 10Base-2
   b. 100Base-5
   c. 10Base-T
   d. 100Base-T

10. Which type of Ethernet uses a T-shaped connector to tap into the bus at each node?
    a. 10Base-2
    b. 10Base-5
    c. 10Base-T
    d. Gigabit Ethernet

11. What is the maximum speed on a 100Base-T network?
    a. 100Kbps
    b. 1Mbps
    c. 10Mbps
    d. 100Mbps

12. Which of these is known as Fast Ethernet?
    a. 10Base-T
    b. 100Base-T
    c. Gigabit Ethernet
    d. 10Base-2

13. Which type of Ethernet uses Cat5 UTP cable?
    a. 10Base-T
    b. 100Base-T
    c. 10Base-2
    d. both a and b

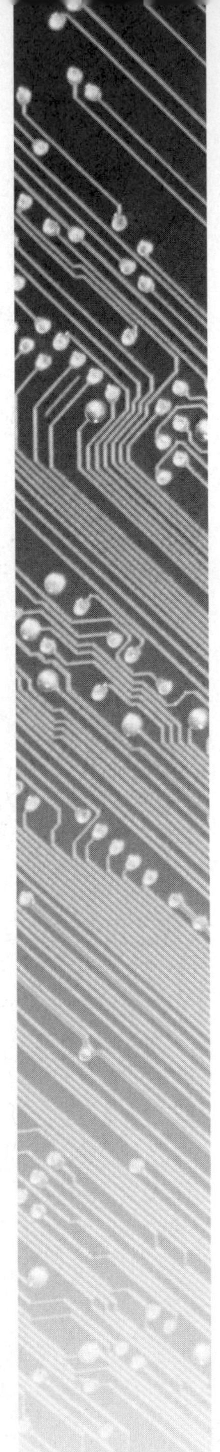

14. What is the standard for wireless Ethernet called?
    a. IEEE 1394
    b. IEEE 1284
    c. IEEE 802.11b
    d. IEEE 1394.11b

15. A wireless access point is the functional equivalent of a
    a. hub.
    b. router.
    c. bridge.
    d. gateway.

16. Which of these is true of an FDDI network?
    a. It uses a double Token Ring logical topology.
    b. It uses a high-speed logical bus topology.
    c. It uses Cat5 UTP cable, like Ethernet.
    d. both a and c

17. What does a packet consist of?
    a. data, a header, and a footer
    b. a header and a footer
    c. data and a header
    d. data and a footer

18. When a PC sends data, how does that data move through the OSI model on its way to the network?
    a from level 7 (Physical) to level 1 (Application)
    b. from level 1 (Physical) to level 7 (Application)
    c. from level 7 (Application) to level 1 (Physical)
    d. from level 1 (Application) to level 7 (Physical)

19. A NIC with a BNC connector on it is designed for which type of network?
    a. 10Base-5
    b. 10Base-2
    c. 10Base-T
    d. Token Ring

20. Which network device reduces attenuation?
    a. hub
    b. router
    c. repeater
    d. bridge

# TROUBLESHOOTING

1. A client has a built-in 100Base-T Ethernet card in his laptop, but he needs to connect to a Token Ring network. What does he need to do?
2. A client has a 10Base-2 network with three PCs. At one end she has a terminator, and in the middle she has a T-connector that the bus passes through and that is connected to the middle PC's NIC. At the far end she has the third PC, with the BNC connector plugging directly into the NIC. What has she done wrong?
3. A client has a Token Ring MSAU with three PCs plugged into it; there are five empty slots for extra PCs, and the Ring In and Ring Out ports are both free as well. What has he done wrong?

# CUSTOMER SERVICE

1. A client wants to create a small network in her home consisting of three desktop PCs and one notebook PC. She asks whether she should look at regular Ethernet or wireless. What questions will you ask her in order to formulate your recommendation?
2. The owner of a small business with nine PCs has asked you to help the company get a network set up. She does not know whether she wants a client/server network or peer-to-peer. What questions will you ask in order to help her make the decision?
3. A small business client already has an Ethernet network with about 35 PCs, grouped around four hubs. Each hub is connected to the other hubs, and there are two servers. Lately network access has seemed very slow, and employees are complaining. What can you recommend?

# FOR MORE INFORMATION

For links to Web sites that provide further information about the topics covered in this chapter, go to the EMC/Paradigm Internet Resource Center at www.emcp.com/College Division/Internet Resource Centers/PC Maintenance/For More Information.

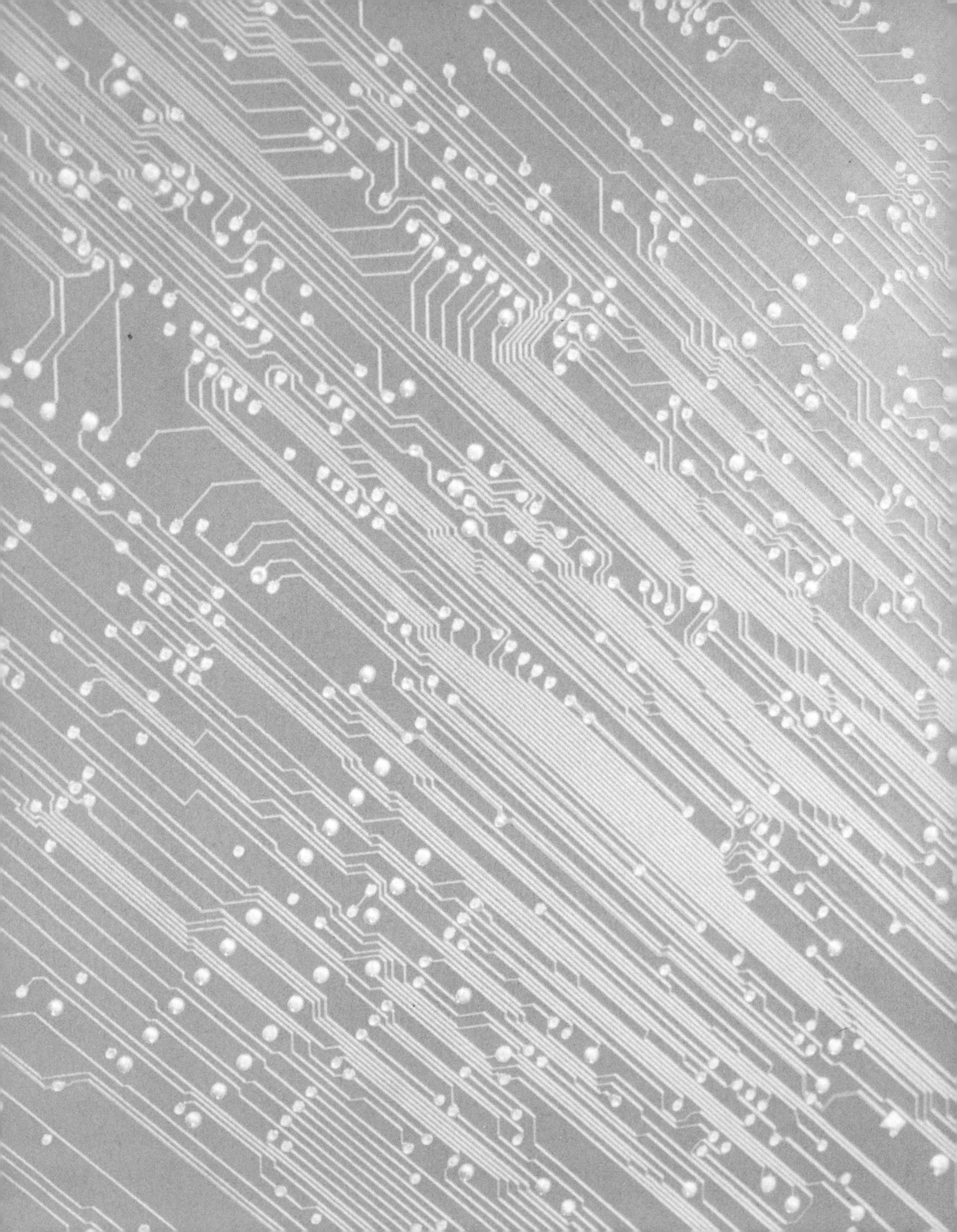

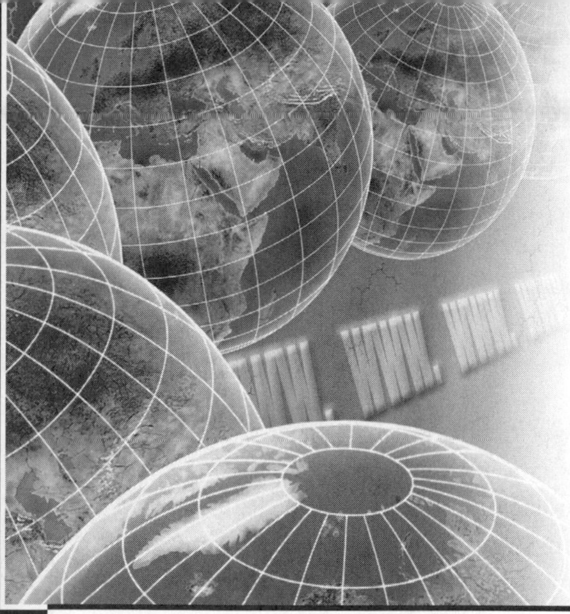

# 22 Setting Up a Windows Network

## ON THE TEST

**A+ Core Hardware Service Technician Examination**

- **Objective 1.2:** Identify basic procedures for adding and removing field replaceable modules for both desktop and portable systems.
- **Objective 6.1:** Identify basic networking concepts, including how a network works and the ramifications of repairs on the network.

**A+ Operating System Technologies Examination**

- **Objective 4.1:** Identify the networking capabilities of Windows including procedures for connecting to the network.
- **Objective 4.2:** Identify concepts and capabilities relating to the Internet and basic procedures for setting up a system for Internet access.

## ON THE JOB

The concepts you learned in the preceding chapter will serve you well when selecting networking hardware and planning networks, but in reality you will probably spend more time with hands-on network installation and setup. This chapter explains how to install and configure networking equipment and how to set up a network in Windows.

Skills you will learn include the following:

- installing a Network Interface Card (NIC) in a PC
- setting up a peer-to-peer Ethernet network
- installing communication clients, protocols, and services in Windows to prepare a PC for network use
- explaining TCP/IP settings to end users

# Installing Network Hardware

As you learned in Chapter 21, network hardware consists of a network interface card (NIC) for each PC, one or more hubs, switches, routers, or other connecting devices, and cables that run between them. Most of this hardware is very easy to set up physically.

## Installing a NIC

A NIC or other network adapter is required for every PC that will participate in the network. On a desktop PC the NIC will be an internal expansion board (ISA or PCI); on a notebook PC it will be a PC Card device or built in to the PC itself. In addition, external USB network adapters are now available, but these hook up with a simple USB connection, so are not covered here. There are two parts to the installation process for a network adapter: the physical installation and the setup in Windows.

### *Physical Installation*

You learned to install expansion boards in earlier chapters, but the following steps review the procedure with NICs specifically in mind. The procedure is the same for both wired and wireless NICs.

> **WARNING**
>
> **As with any other computer installation or repair activity, turn off the PC and unplug it before starting the NIC installation. In addition, take steps to avoid electrostatic discharge as much as possible, which may include putting on an antistatic wrist strap.**

1. Remove the cover from the PC and locate the slot in which you want to insert the NIC. A NIC may be either an ISA or PCI expansion board.
2. Remove the NIC from its protective plastic bag and examine it. If there are any jumpers, consult the documentation to determine how to set them. The default settings are probably correct, but it is a good idea to check them.
3. Remove the backplate from the slot and set it aside. Keep the screw handy.
4. Insert the circuit board in the expansion slot, being careful to handle it only by the edges. Press it firmly into the slot.
5. Attach the screw to hold the circuit board in place, then replace the cover on the PC.

Physically installing a PC Card NIC is even easier—just insert it in the PC Card slot in a notebook PC. Refer to Chapter 20 for help with notebook PC components as needed.

### *Setting Up a NIC in Windows*

Nearly all NICs are Plug and Play; Windows generally recognizes them immediately when you turn on the PC after installing them physically. Depending on the NIC and the Windows version, if Windows cannot automatically load a driver, you might be prompted for a setup disk (which came with the NIC). If Windows does not detect the NIC at all, it may be non-PnP, physically defective, or not firmly seated in its slot. If it is a non-PnP card, run the setup disk or, if you do not have a setup disk, try the Add New Hardware applet in the Control Panel. Non-PnP NICs might not work in Windows 2000 or XP.

The NIC does not need to be connected to a network for Windows to detect it, so you can check it right away, before going any further with the network setup. To make sure the NIC is set up in Windows, do the following:

1. Open Device Manager.
2. Click the plus sign next to Network Adapters. If you see the NIC listed there, and there are no special symbols next to it, such as an exclamation point, it is installed correctly (see Figure 22.1, for example).

If there is an exclamation point next to the icon, there is probably a resource conflict or a problem with the driver. Refer to Chapter 14 to fix it.

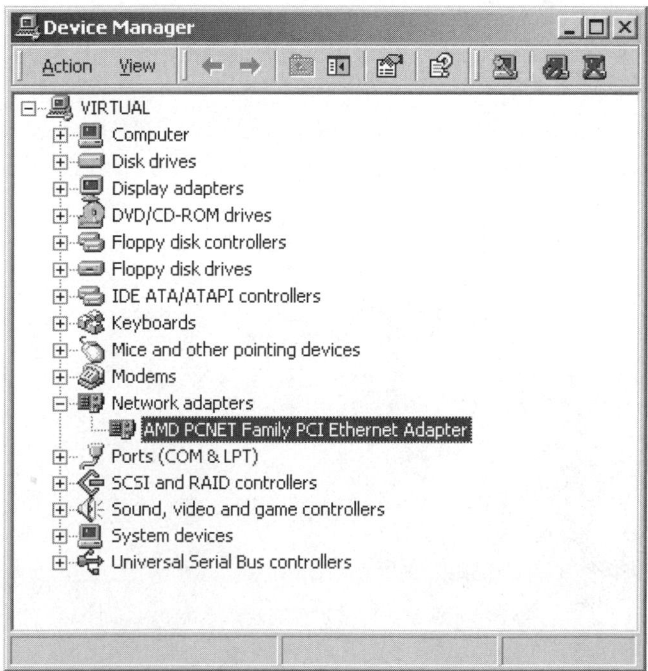


**FIGURE 22.1**
The NIC appears in Device Manager, indicating it is ready for use.

## TRY IT!

1. Install a NIC in your PC.
2. Start Windows, and make sure the NIC appears in Device Manager. If it does not, install a driver for it.
3. Repeat for a second PC (unless you are in a classroom setting where other students have also installed NICs), so you will have at least two PCs to connect in a later activity.

## Setting Up a Hub or Wireless Access Point

Each PC in an Ethernet network must be connected to a hub via cable. If it is a wireless network, instead of a hub there is a wireless access point (WAP), and each PC may connect to it via either cable or wireless connection.

Hubs are simple to set up because they are not very smart; you just plug them in and they start working. A WAP functions much like a hub, but may have some additional settings you can configure for security encryption. The default settings almost always work right out of the box, so changing a WAP's settings is optional. The instructions that come with the WAP will tell you how to change the settings. The procedure usually involves using a Web browser program on a connected PC to open a setup page for the device.

To set up a hub or WAP, complete the following steps:

1. Connect the AC power cord to the device and plug it into a wall outlet. At least one light should illuminate on the hub, indicating it is receiving power.
2. Connect network cables (usually Cat5 UTP with RJ-45 connectors) from one of the ports on the hub to the NIC in each of the PCs (unless, of course, the PC has a wireless NIC and the hub is a WAP). These connect just like telephone cables (see Figure 22.2).

**FIGURE 22.2**
Connecting Cables to a Hub

3. Turn on the PC and let Windows start.

The following sections describe the software that Windows requires for networking.

**TRY IT!**

1. Set up a wired Ethernet hub.
2. Connect at least two PCs to it with Cat5 cable.

## Networking Software and the OSI Model

In Chapter 21 you learned about the OSI reference model governing network communications and the seven layers through which data passes in a network. Different pieces of software work at different layers. A review of those layers, summarized in Figure 22.3, will provide an overview of the software involved in networking.

The Physical and Data Link layers are the bottom layers (1 and 2), which interact directly with the hardware. These are the levels at which the network itself operates (Ethernet, Token Ring, or FDDI, as discussed in Chapter 21, or PPP for dial-up networking, which will be introduced in Chapter 25). You do not have to install any special software in Windows to support these levels; Windows recognizes and supports them automatically.

The Network and Transport layers (3 and 4) deal with the communication *protocols* by which the communication traffic is controlled. By far the most common protocol at this level is TCP/IP; the other two most popular are IPX/SPX and NetBEUI. These protocols must be installed in the Network dialog box in Windows, but TCP/IP is installed by default in all versions of Windows 98 and higher so it is probably already set up. The next section explains how to install them.

**Protocol**

The language or set of rules governing a data transmission.

The Session layer (5) is where the higher level protocols run that govern the individual activities users perform within applications. On a LAN, the protocols at this level are NFS (file sharing), LPR (print sharing), FTP (File Transfer Protocol), and terminal emulation. On an Internet connection, the protocols are HTTP for Web pages, IRC for chatting, POP, SMTP, and IMAP for e-mail receiving and sending, FTP for file transfer, and so on. We will talk more about those in Chapter 25. You do not have to install anything in Windows for these protocols to be recognized; they are built into Windows itself or into the applications that support them.

In the Presentation and Application layers (6 and 7), the programs run that use the higher level protocols. In some cases they have a one-to-one relationship with those protocols, such as an FTP program and the FTP protocol; in other cases a single program uses multiple protocols, such as an e-mail program that can send and receive mail using POP, SMTP, or IMAP protocols.

Figure 22.3 summarizes this information for network and Internet connectivity. This chapter focuses mainly on LANs; Internet is covered in more detail in Chapter 25.

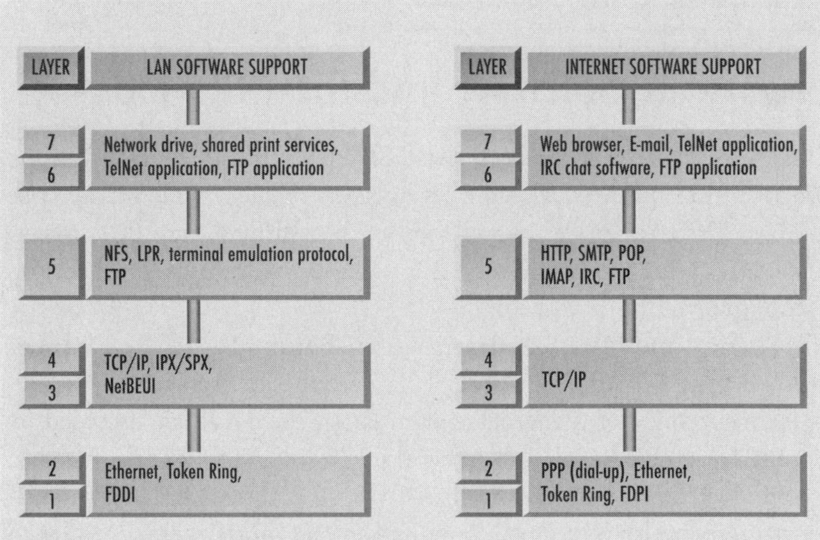


**FIGURE 22.3**
Software at Work at the Various OSI Levels for LAN and Internet

## Setting Up Networking in Windows

Many versions of Windows, especially the newest ones, automatically install the needed protocols and other software when you set up networking hardware. If you have a network physically set up when installing Windows, Windows not only detects the hardware and installs a driver for it, but also installs the Windows Networking client (explained shortly) and at least one protocol (usually TCP/IP). However, automatic setup will not always work flawlessly, so the following sections explain how to perform manual installations.

### Understanding Windows Version Differences in Networking

There are many versions of Windows, but only two basic classes: the Windows 95/98/Me family is one class, and the Windows 2000/XP family is the other. The Windows 95/98/Me family handles networking rather simply; there is a single set of properties for all networking as a whole. Each installed NIC or other network adapter appears as an entry in the list on the Configuration tab of the Network dialog box, as shown in Figure 22.4.

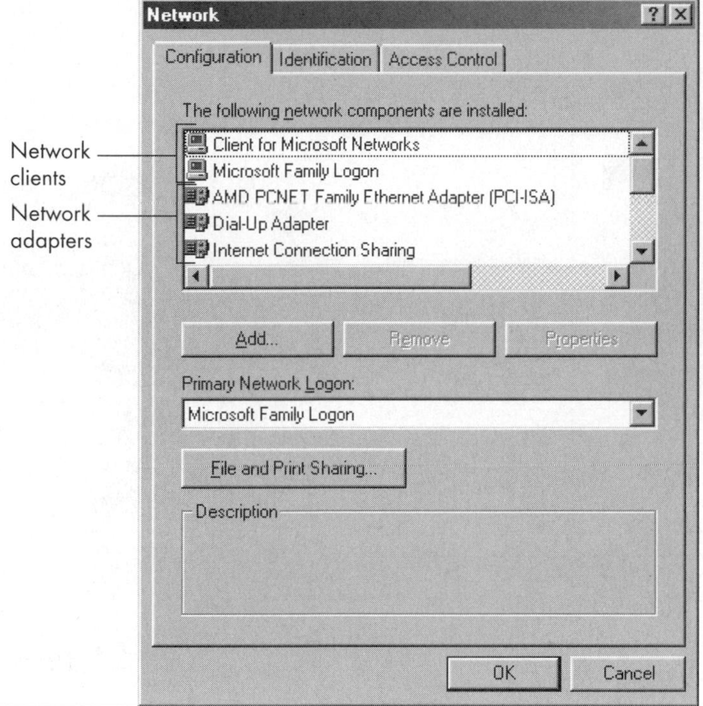


**FIGURE 22.4**
The network properties in Windows 95/98/Me refer as a whole to all network connections.

In Windows 2000/XP, there is no single set of properties; instead each networking connection has separate properties. When you open the Network Connections or Network and Dial-Up Connections applet in the Control Panel, a list of the NICs and dial-up connections appears. You can then display the properties for each of them separately (right-click one and choose Properties). Figure 22.5 shows the properties for two different connections in Windows XP.

The main thing to notice in Figure 22.5 is that there is a separately configurable list of protocols, clients, and services for each NIC. In Figure 22.4, in contrast, a single set of clients, services, and protocols serves for all NICs together.

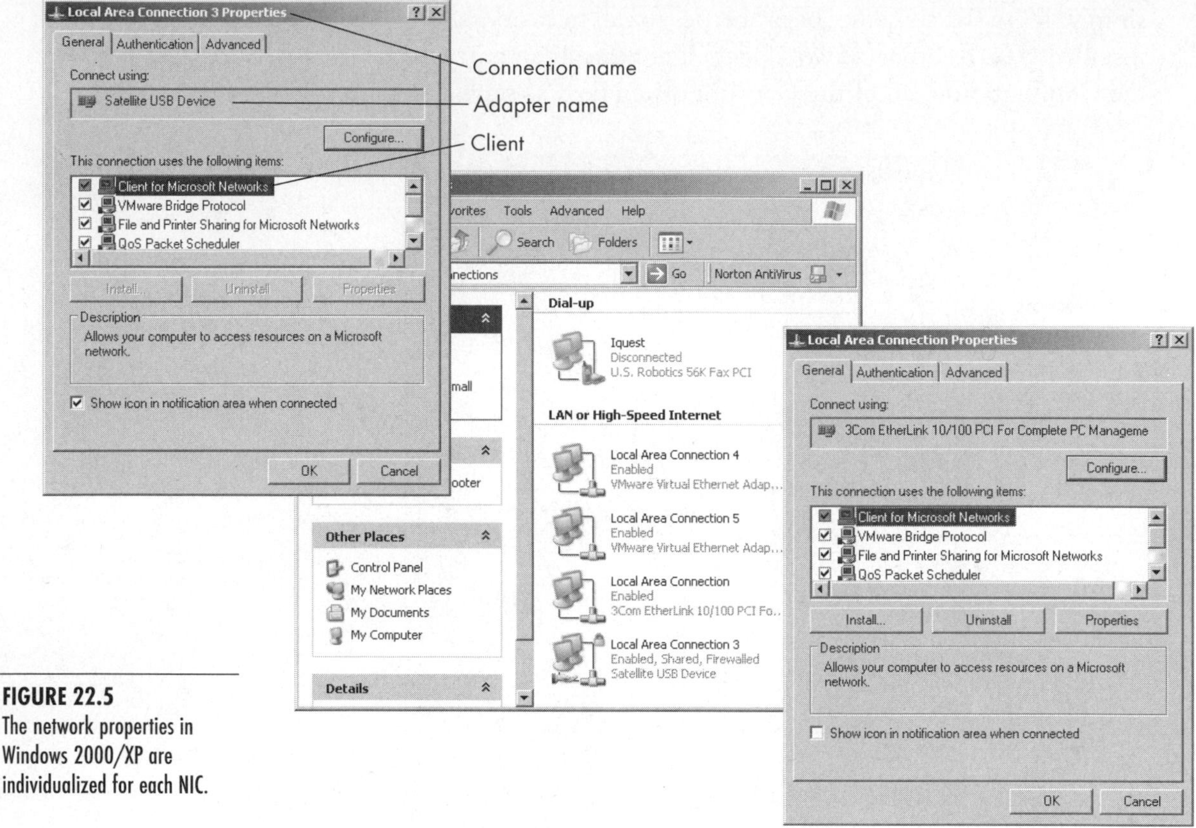


**FIGURE 22.5**
The network properties in Windows 2000/XP are individualized for each NIC.

## Installing Adapters

**Network adapter**

A piece of hardware that Windows recognizes as capable of connecting to a network or the Internet, or a piece of software that simulates network hardware.

A *network adapter* is a piece of hardware that Windows recognizes as capable of connecting to a network or the Internet, or a piece of software (such as Dial-Up Networking) that simulates network hardware. Most of the time a network adapter is a network interface card (NIC), but occasionally a network device may be something different. For example, it could be a USB terminal adapter for connecting to the Internet via satellite, cable, or DSL. If such devices connect via network cable to a NIC, Windows sees only the NIC, but if they connect via USB, Windows sees the actual terminal adapter. For example, in Figure 22.5, Local Area Connection 3 is a Satellite USB Device rather than a real NIC.

## In Real Life

Some other items may appear to be adapters in Windows even though they are not physical devices. For example, Dial-Up Adapter is software that enables you to establish network connections via dial-up networking, and Internet Connection Sharing is software that makes it possible for Windows 98 Second Edition or Windows Me to share its Internet connection with other PCs on the network. One or both of these may appear in the network properties in Windows 95/98/Me, as they do in Figure 22.4. (You will learn more about them in Chapter 25.)

Adapters appear in the network properties in Windows 95/98/Me. To view the installed adapters in one of those OSes, follow these steps:

1. From the Control Panel, double-click the *Network* icon. The Network dialog box appears.
2. Look on the component list on the Configuration tab for the installed adapters (see Figure 22.4). Each adapter has an icon next to it that looks like a tiny circuit board.
3. To see an adapter's properties, double-click it. When finished, click OK.

In Windows 2000/XP, you view the properties for an adapter as follows:

1. From the Control Panel, double-click the *Network Connections* icon (Windows XP) or the *Network and Dial-Up Connections* icon (Windows 2000). A list of the installed network adapters and connections appears. This list loosely represents the network adapters, but it individually includes each dial-up networking connection instead of having one generic entry for Dial-Up Networking as in Windows 95/98/Me (see Figure 22.5).
2. To see the properties for an adapter, right-click it and choose Properties. When finished, click OK.

If the desired network adapter does not appear, you probably do not have a driver installed for it yet. See the section "Setting Up a NIC in Windows" earlier in the chapter.

## Installing Clients

For Windows to act as an NOS as well as a regular OS, it must have networking client software installed. Windows calls this a *client,* but the term has a different meaning than you have seen so far in this book. In this case, it means networking software for a client PC.

**Client**

Networking software for a client PC.

Most versions of Windows automatically install Client for Microsoft Networks when they detect a network adapter during Windows Setup. As an alternative, you can install Client for NetWare Networks if the PC will be connecting to a NetWare client/server network rather than one that is Windows-driven. ("Windows-driven" refers to a network that uses Windows as both the OS and the NOS; a NetWare network could conceivably use Windows as the OS but NetWare as the NOS.)

### *Checking for Installed Clients*

To check for the client driver, open the Properties dialog box for networking (Windows 95/98/Me) or for an individual adapter (Windows 2000/XP) and look for a client on the list that appears. "Client" will be the first word in the name and it will have a computer icon next to it (see Figures 22.4 or 22.5, depending on the OS version).

### *Adding a Client*

If the client you want to use for the network does not appear, you can add it. It is somewhat like adding a device driver, which was explained in Chapter 14.

In Windows 95/98/Me:

1. Open the Network dialog box and click the Add button on the Configuration tab. The Select Network Component Type dialog box opens.
2. Click Client, and then click Add. The Select Network Client dialog box opens.
3. Click the client manufacturer name, then click the client on the list from that manufacturer (see Figure 22.6).

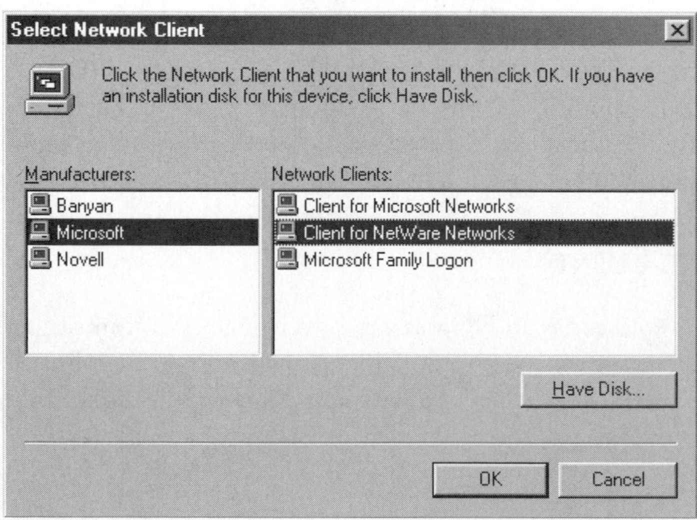


**FIGURE 22.6**
Select the manufacturer and model of the client you want.

### In Real Life

Windows 95/98 come with NetWare-compatable Novell NetWare clients (not just the Microsoft Client for NetWare Networks), under the Novell manufacturer name. Later versions of Windows do not come with this. However, you can still get the client from Novell and install it from disk by clicking the Have Disk button (see Figure 22.6).

4. Click OK. The new client appears on the list.

In Windows 2000/XP there are fewer choices. Client for Microsoft Networks is always automatically installed in Windows 2000/XP, and there is only one client that comes with the OS: Client Service for NetWare. To install it:

1. From the Control Panel, open Network Connections (Windows XP) or Network and Dial-Up Connections (Windows 2000).
2. Right-click the adapter you want and click Properties to open the Properties dialog box.
3. Click Install. The Select Network Component Type dialog box opens.
4. Click Client, and then click Add. The Select Network Client dialog box opens. There is only one choice: Client Services for NetWare.
5. Click Client Services for NetWare and then click OK.
6. The Select NetWare Logon dialog box may appear; if it does, select the preferred server or enter a default Tree and Context. If you are not sure what to enter, leave the preferred server set to None and click OK to move on; you can check with a NetWare administrator in your company later.
7. If a message appears that you must restart, click Yes to do so.

#### *Removing a Client*

You will probably not want to remove Client for Microsoft Networks. However, if you have added the NetWare client, you might want to remove it if the NetWare network is no longer being used. To remove a client:

1. Display the list of installed components.
2. Click the client you want to remove.
3. Click Uninstall. A warning box appears.
4. Click Yes. If you are prompted to restart, click Yes again to restart.

## INSTALLING PROTOCOLS

We have already talked about protocols in this and the preceding chapter; a protocol is a language spoken between two devices or two points in a process. Various protocols operate at different levels of the OSI model, but in this section we will deal specifically about the protocols that operate at the Network and Transport layers (3 and 4).

All versions of Windows install at least one protocol automatically when they detect a network adapter during Windows Setup. Windows 95 installs NetBEUI and IPX/SPX; all other versions of Windows install TCP/IP. The following sections briefly explain these three protocols and their primary abilities, so you will be able to decide which protocols you want to install.

### *TCP/IP*

**Transmission Control Protocol/Internet Protocol (TCP/IP)**

The standard networking protocol for the Internet and for most Microsoft-based networks.

*TCP/IP* is the protocol around which the entire Internet is structured, so it is an important one to install if your client plans on using the Internet (either dial-up or through a broadband connection). It is also the default protocol for all versions of Windows (98 and higher). Nearly every PC should have TCP/IP installed. A special section on TCP/IP at the end of this chapter covers the technical details behind it.

### *NetBEUI*

**NetBIOS Extended User Interface (NetBEUI)**

An older networking protocol with compact packets that is incompatible with router usage.

*NetBEUI* is an older, compact, very efficient protocol that results in fast network transmission on a small network. It is compact because the header and footer are small, resulting in smaller packets overall that carry the same amount of data as a larger packet in another network protocol. NetBEUI is limited, however, in that it cannot go across a router, so it can be used only on routerless networks—and these days that means only very small networks. It is not available in Windows XP.

### *IPX/SPX-Compatible*

Internetwork Packet Exchange/Sequenced Packet Exchange (IPX/SPX) is a protocol used in NetWare networks. Microsoft provides a compatible protocol for IPX/SPX, which should be installed on any PCs that are using Client for NetWare Networks or Client Service for NetWare. (Note that because of trademark restrictions Microsoft's product is not the actual IPX/SPX protocol, but only something compatible.)

### *Installing a Protocol*

Protocols are like human languages—communication occurs not because of the words themselves but because of the shared understanding of their meaning. As long as all of the PCs in the network have the same protocol installed, they can communicate, regardless of which protocol it is.

For a small workgroup, any protocol will work. However, TCP/IP is the recommended protocol because it is needed for Internet access and because it is a versatile protocol that has no problems with routers and other network equipment. Installing a protocol is much like installing a client. Complete the following steps.

For Windows 95/98/Me:

1. On the Configuration tab of the Network dialog box, click Add. The Select Network Component Type dialog box opens.
2. Click Protocol and then click Add. A list of manufacturers and models appears.
3. Click the manufacturer you want, and then the model. All of the standard protocols are found under Microsoft as the manufacturer. (In Windows Me, Microsoft is the only manufacturer listed.)
4. Click OK. The protocol appears on the list.
5. Click OK again. If prompted to insert the Windows CD, do so and click OK.
6. If prompted to restart, click Yes.

For Windows 2000/XP:

1. From the Control Panel, open Network Connections (Windows XP) or Network and Dial-Up Connections (Windows 2000).
2. Right-click the adapter you want and click Properties to open the Properties dialog box.
3. Click Install. The Select Network Component Type dialog box opens.
4. Click Protocol, and then click Add. The Select Network Protocol dialog box opens.
5. Select the protocol to install. Notice in Figure 22.7 that in Windows 2000/XP, the IPX/SPX-compatible protocol is not a stand-alone item; it is integrated in a combination protocol: NWLink IPX/SPX/NetBIOS Compatible Transport Protocol.
6. Click OK. The protocol is added to the list. Click Close to close the dialog box.
7. If prompted to insert the Windows CD and/or to restart, click OK or Yes to do so. You may not be prompted for these, depending on the protocol and on the Windows version.

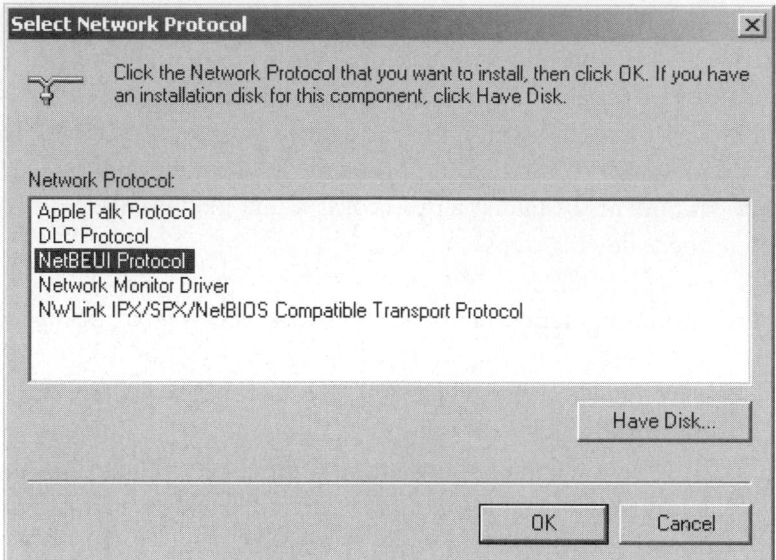


**FIGURE 22.7**
Select a protocol to install in Windows 2000/XP.

### *Removing a Protocol*

In theory, having many different protocols installed should not cause a problem. However, in practice, having several protocols to choose from for communication can result in transmission problems. If you are having communication problems in a workgroup, such as file transfers aborting in the middle of transfer with an error message that the network is not available, try removing all of the protocols except TCP/IP.

Uninstalling a protocol is similar to uninstalling a client. To uninstall, complete the following steps:

1. Select the protocol to uninstall, either from the network properties as a whole (Windows 95/98/Me) or from the properties for a specific network connection (Windows 2000/XP).
2. Click the Uninstall button. A warning appears.
3. Click Yes. If prompted to restart, click Yes to do so.

## Installing Services

Services are drivers that support specific networking tasks. Examples of services include File and Printer Sharing for Microsoft Networks, QoS Packet Scheduler, and Service for NetWare Directory Services.

The most common service for most client PCs is File and Printer Sharing for Microsoft Networks. This service is required in order to share local files and printers with other network users. It might or might not be installed by default, depending on the Windows version. One way to install it is to add it as a service; Chapter 23 shows another way to install it.

Services install exactly the same way as clients and protocols—through the network properties. The steps are the same as in the preceding sections, except you choose Services instead of Clients or Protocols in the Select Network Component Type dialog box.

**TRY IT!**

1. In Windows, make sure the following are installed for the network adapter you use for your LAN; install them if they are not:
   Client for Microsoft Networks
   TCP/IP
   File and Printer Sharing for Microsoft Networks.
2. Install NetBEUI (unless you have Windows XP, in which case it is not available; install some other protocol instead.)
3. Remove the protocol you installed in step 2.

## Binding and Unbinding Protocols

In Windows 95/98/Me, because there is only a single Network dialog box for all adapters, there needs to be a way of tying a protocol to a particular adapter. In Windows 2000/XP this is not an issue because the properties for each adapter are separate.

Windows 95/98/Me handles this by allowing you to bind or unbind items to protocols. When you look at the component list in Windows 98, for example, you may notice some protocols appearing more than once, with -> symbols and the name of a particular network adapter, as in Figure 22.8. This notation indicates that those items are bound, so they can work together.

By default, everything is bound to everything else, but if you do not need a particular binding you can unbind the items. This can streamline the network software and avoid potential problems resulting from extra protocols or services that are not needed for a specific usage. For example, suppose you have two NICs installed in a PC. One of them is

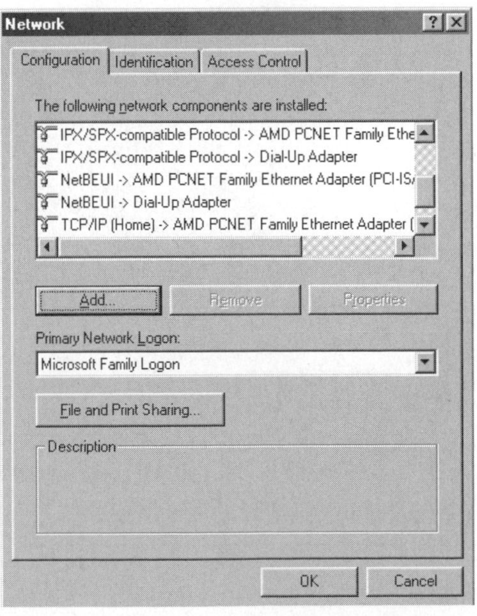


**FIGURE 22.8**
In Windows 95/98/Me, protocols can be bound or unbound to adapters through the Network dialog box.

for the LAN and the other is for a DSL terminal adapter for Internet connectivity. The LAN uses NetBEUI as the protocol, while the DSL connection uses TCP/IP. You could unbind NetBEUI from the NIC used by the DSL connection, keeping it bound to the other NIC.

To change binding, do the following:

1. Open the Network dialog box from the Control Panel.
2. On the Configuration tab, double-click the adapter that you want to bind or unbind to a certain protocol. (You work with bindings from the adapter's properties, not the protocol's properties.)
3. Select the Bindings tab on the adapter's Properties dialog box. All of the installed protocols appear there.
4. Deselect the check box for any protocol you do not want to be bound to this adapter (see Figure 22.9).
5. Click OK.

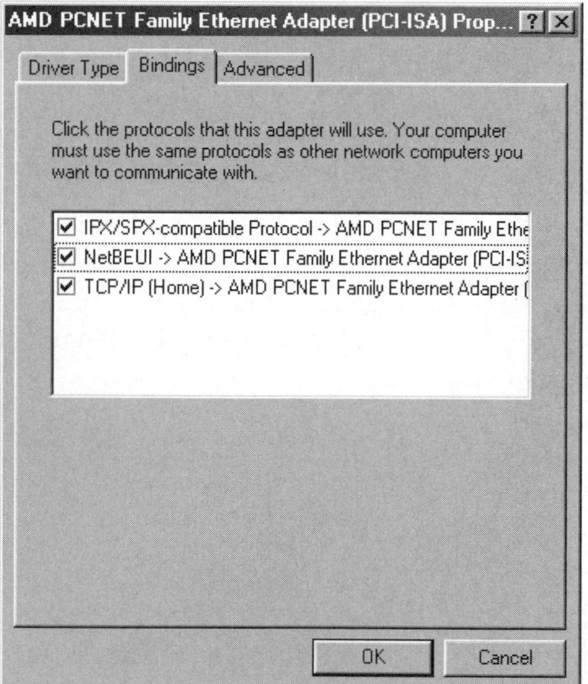


**FIGURE 22.9**
Deselect any protocols that do not need to be bound to the adapter.

## TRY IT!

1. In Windows 95/98/Me, add the NetBEUI protocol if it is not already installed.
2. Unbind it from the NIC that you use to connect to your LAN.

## Checking for Network Connectivity

After you have installed the networking components in Windows, check for network connectivity by doing the following.

In Windows 95/98/Me or Windows 2000:

1. Double-click the *My Network Places* icon (Windows 2000/Me) or *Network Neighborhood* icon (Windows 95/98) on the desktop.
2. Look for icons for other computers, or for the computer on which you are working. If you see any, the network is working. Figure 22.10 shows a network with only the local PC itself, because no other PCs have been set up yet in its workgroup.

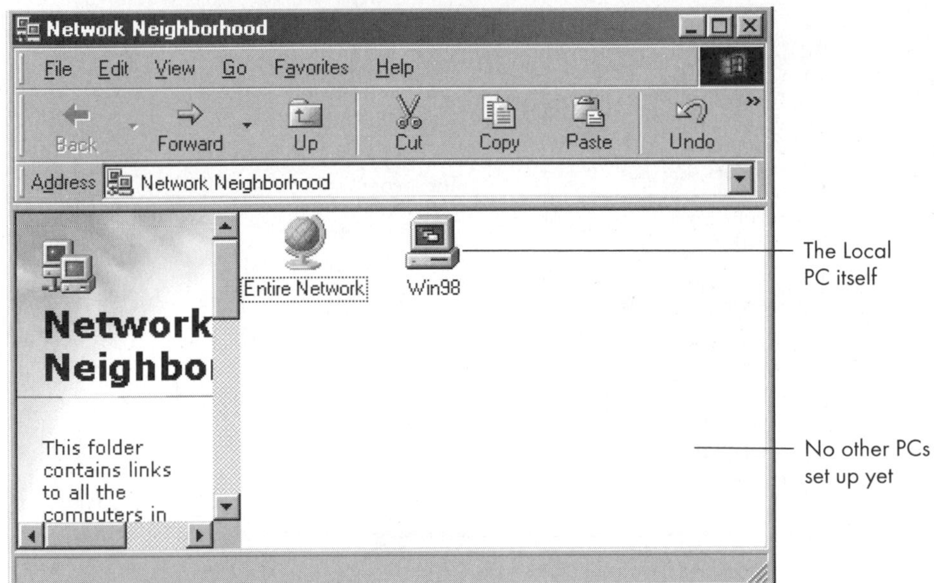


**FIGURE 22.10**
A Windows 98 Workgroup, Containing Only the Local PC

3. Do an additional search for icons:
   a. Icons for computers might be in the window you opened in step 1.
   b. The window might contain a Computers Near Me icon (Windows 2000); if so, double-click it to see the icons for the computers.
   c. The window might contain an icon for a workgroup such as WORKGROUP or MSHOME; if so, double-click it to see the icons for the computers.
4. If you were unable to find icons for any computers in step 2, double-click the *Entire Network* icon. If you then see icons for other computers, the network is working. If you instead see an error message about being unable to browse the network, it is not working.

In Windows XP:

1. Choose Start, My Network Places.
2. Click *View workgroup computers.* If you see icons for the other computers in the workgroup, the network is working (see Figure 22.11). If you see an icon only for the PC on which you are working, the network is working but no other PCs have been set up on it yet.

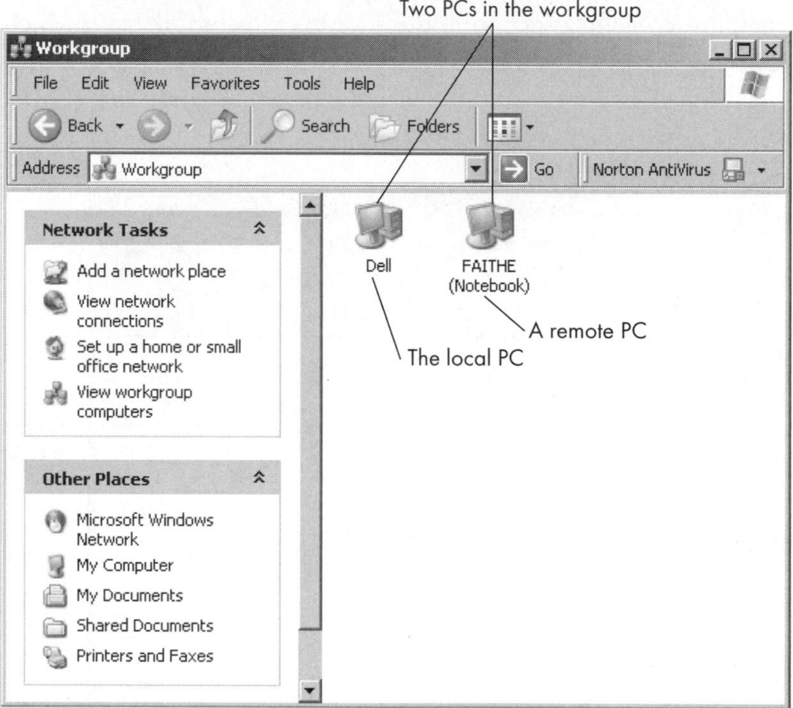


**FIGURE 22.11**
A Windows XP Workgroup Up and Running

## TRY IT!

**Check all of the PCs that are physically connected together in the workgroup to see whether each can see the others in Network Neighborhood or My Network Places. Make notes of which ones work and which ones do not.**

## Changing the Computer Name and Workgroup Name

If you do not see any computers when you browse the network—not even the PC you are working on—then the computer may not be set up with a valid, unique name. Each computer in a workgroup needs a name by which other computers will know it. A default name is assigned automatically based on the user name with which you are logged in, but this can result in duplication if you have set up more than one computer with the same user name.

If you see only your own PC when you browse the network but other PCs have been set up and should be visible, you are probably not using the same workgroup name for all of them. WORKGROUP is the default name in some versions of Windows; MSHOME is the default in others. If you are constructing a workgroup that includes PCs using different versions of Windows, you will have to change the default name on some of the PCs so that they all match. To change the computer name and/or workgroup name, complete the following steps.

In Windows 95/98/Me:

1. Open the Network dialog box from the Control Panel and select the Identification tab.
2. Change the name in the Computer name text box. The name can be up to 15 characters and cannot include spaces (see Figure 22.12).

**WARNING**

**If the PC has cable or DSL Internet access through one NIC and participates in a LAN workgroup with another NIC, you may run into a problem if you change the computer name. Some cable or DSL providers require the PC to have a certain unique name for their network (usually a long string of characters); if you change it, the Internet connection will not work anymore. If that is the case, you are stuck with that name.**

3. Change the workgroup name if needed. It does not matter what you use, but it must match on all PCs in the workgroup.
4. Click OK. A prompt appears to restart the PC. Click Yes.

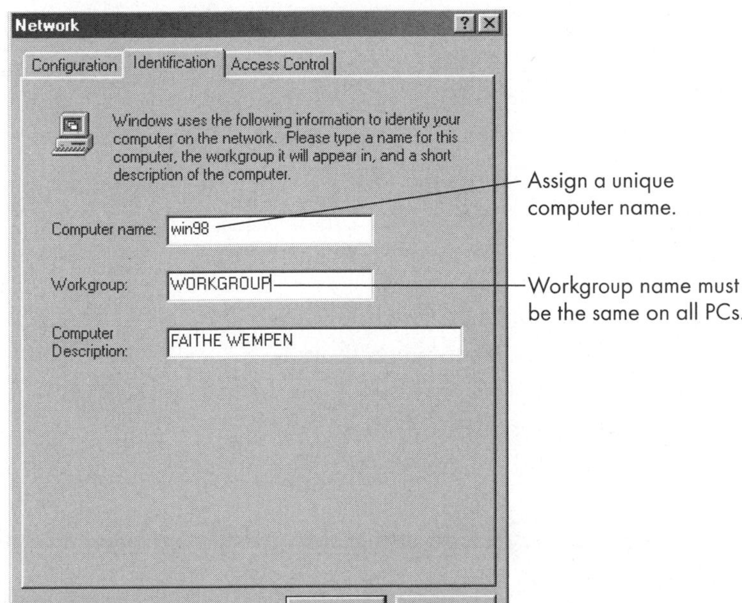


**FIGURE 22.12**
**Changing the computer name and/or workgroup name can sometimes help the computer participate in the local workgroup.**

5. After Windows restarts, try reopening Network Neighborhood or My Network Places. If you now see an icon for the PC you are working on, and for other PCs if they should be there, you have fixed the problem. If not, there is more troubleshooting help available in Chapter 23.

In Windows 2000:

1. Open the Control Panel and double-click the *System* icon.
2. Select the Network Identification tab in the System Properties dialog box.
3. Click the Properties button. The Identification Changes dialog box opens (see Figure 22.13).

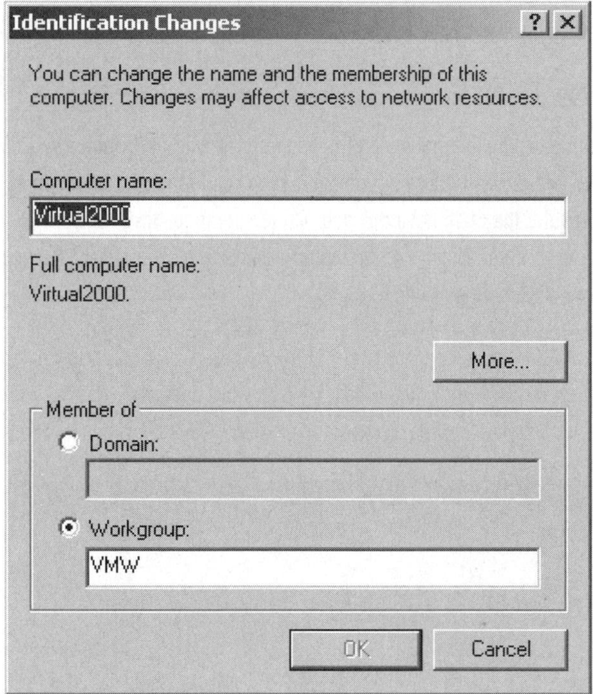


**FIGURE 22.13**
Change the computer's name and workgroup in the Identification Changes dialog box.

4. Change the computer name if desired.
5. Change the workgroup name if desired.
6. Click OK. (The OK button will not be available if you made no changes; if that is the case, click Cancel.)
7. If you changed the workgroup, a Welcome box appears for that workgroup; click OK.
8. If you made any changes, a message appears telling you to reboot; click OK.

9. Click OK to close the System Properties dialog box. A message appears asking if you want to restart now; click Yes.

In Windows XP:

1. Open the Control Panel and double-click the *System* icon.
2. Select the Computer Name tab in the System Properties dialog box.
3. Click the Change button. The Computer Name Changes dialog box opens.
4. Change the computer name if desired.
5. Change the workgroup name if desired.
6. Click OK. A message appears that you must restart for the change to take effect; click OK.
7. Click OK to close the System Properties dialog box. A message appears asking if you want to restart now; click Yes.

**TRY IT!**

1. If any of the computers on the network cannot see any PCs in the network, even themselves, check their connections and change their computer names.
2. Change the workgroup name on one PC in the workgroup to PARADIGM.
3. Using Network Neighborhood or My Network Places, browse the network to find that computer from another computer that uses a different workgroup name.
4. Browse to find the second computer from the first one.
5. Change the second computer's workgroup to PARADIGM.
6. Try again to find each computer from the other. How is it different? Were you able to find them at all with different workgroup names, or was it just harder to do so?

## Setting Up Networking with Wizards

In the preceding sections you have learned the "hard" way of setting up networking because a PC technician should know how things work and how to set them up manually—and because manual setup is the only choice in Windows 95, 98, and 2000, which are the Windows versions explicitly covered on the current A+ exams. (Windows 2000 is good at automatically detecting settings, so most of the needed configuration in that OS will occur without user intervention.)

However, in Windows Me and Windows XP, networking can be configured using a *wizard*, bypassing some of the manual installation of clients, protocols, and services. The following sections address the automated setup wizards in various Windows versions.

**Wizard**

A step-by-step series of dialog boxes that walk a user through a setup, configuration, or troubleshooting process.

## Using the Home Networking Wizard in Windows Me

The Home Networking Wizard sets up a PC to participate in a workgroup (peer-to-peer) network by installing the appropriate clients, protocols, and services and configuring the network settings. This wizard also sets up your Internet connection, which you will learn more about in Chapter 25.

To use the Home Networking Wizard, complete the following steps:

1. Choose Start/Programs/Accessories/Communications/Home Networking Wizard. The wizard opens.
2. Click Next to begin. A box appears asking about your Internet connection.
3. Choose the Internet connection description that is most applicable to this PC, as in Figure 22.14, and then click Next.

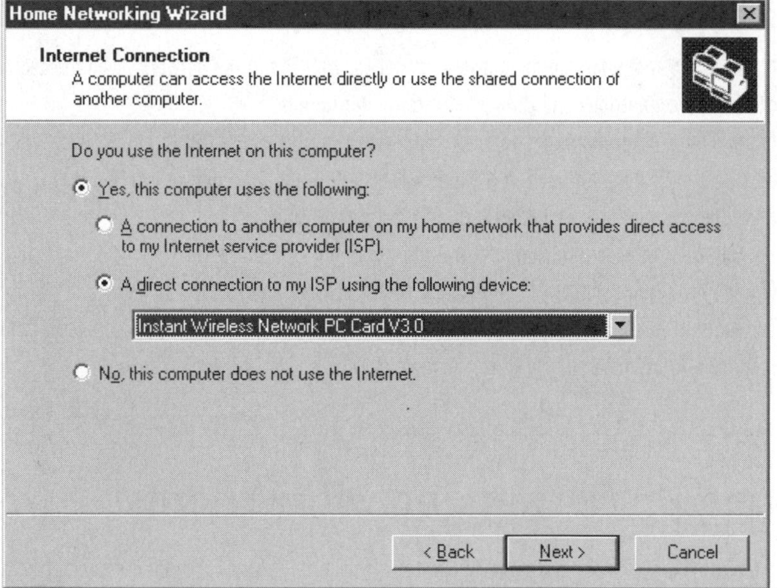


**FIGURE 22.14**
Select the description that most closely matches how this computer connects to the Internet.

4. Enter a computer name and workgroup name to use, as in Figure 22.15, and then click Next.
5. If you want to share the *My Documents* folder on the network, click the My Documents folder check box to select it. You can manually set up other folders to share later, as will be described in Chapter 23.
6. If you want to share any of the local printers, select them from the list of printers provided. If there are no printers listed, there are no local printers. Then click Next.

7. Next the wizard asks about creating a network setup disk. If there are other computers in the workgroup that run Windows 95 or 98, create the setup disk; otherwise, it is not needed. Choose Yes, Create a Home Networking Setup Disk and then click Next. Or, choose No, Do Not Create a Home Networking Setup Disk, click Next, and skip to step 10.
8. Insert a blank floppy disk and click Next. Then wait for the setup disk to be created.
9. Remove the floppy disk from the drive and label it Windows Me Network Setup. Then click Next to continue.
10. Click Finish to complete the wizard. You are prompted to restart; click Yes.
11. After the restart, a Congratulations box appears; click OK.

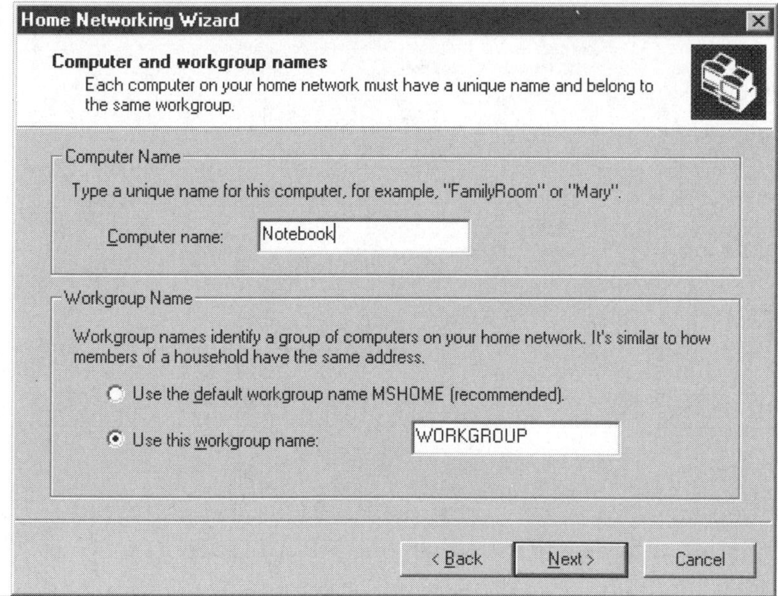


**FIGURE 22.15**
Specify a computer name and workgroup name.

If there are Windows 95 or 98 PCs in the workgroup and they have not already been set up manually to use the network, you can run the network setup utility on them from the floppy.

## Using the Network Setup Wizard in Windows XP

Windows XP is very effective at detecting settings automatically, so you might not need to use the wizard at all—things might simply begin to work when you install the NIC. If you run into any connectivity problems, the

Network Setup Wizard is a good place to start. It walks you through the setup process and makes sure that all of the needed components are installed.

To run the Network Setup Wizard in Windows XP:

1. Choose Start/All Programs/Accessories/Communications/Network Setup Wizard. Click Next to begin.
2. Read the information about network setup; then click Next.
3. Select the statement that best describes this computer's Internet connectivity (see Figure 22.16). Then click Next.

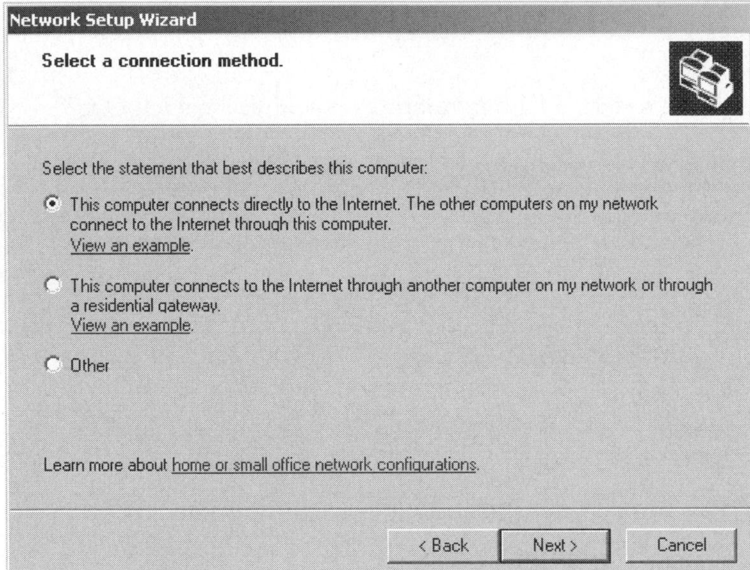


**FIGURE 22.16**
Choose the Internet connectivity for this PC.

4. If you indicated in step 3 that the PC connects directly to the Internet, and there is more than one NIC, a list appears asking which one is for the Internet connection. Select it and click Next.
5. If there is more than one connection on the computer, a message appears asking whether you want to bridge them. Leave the default setting marked (Determine the appropriate connections for me) and click Next.
6. Enter or change the computer description and name. Remember, the description is just for informational purposes and has no special restrictions; the name must be 15 or fewer characters with no spaces and must be unique to the network (see Figure 22.17). Then click Next.

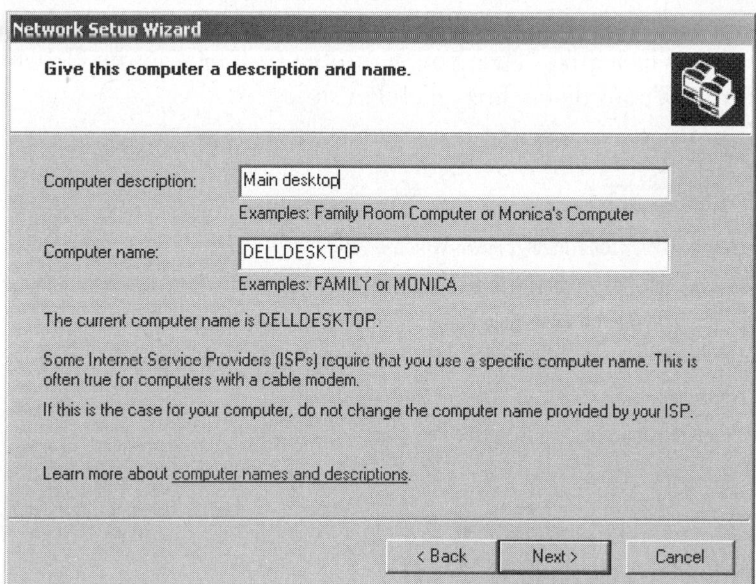


**FIGURE 22.17** Specify the computer's name and description.

7. Enter or change the workgroup name. Remember that all PCs in the workgroup must use the same workgroup name. Then click Next.
8. Check the settings that appear on the summary, and then click Next to apply them.
9. A prompt appears telling you that you need to run the Network Setup Wizard on all of the other PCs in the network. You have several options for doing so, as shown in Figure 22.18. Select the option you plan on using, and then click Next.

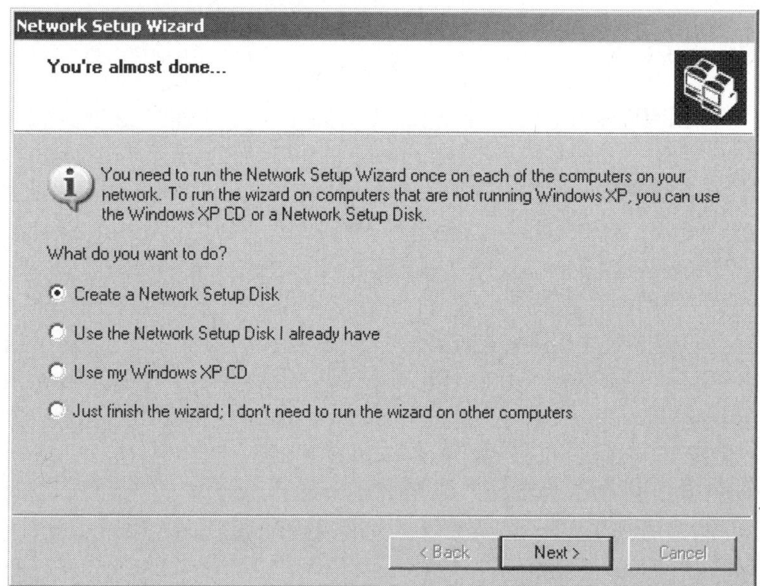


**FIGURE 22.18** Specify how you will set up the other PCs in the workgroup.

10. Read the instructions and follow the prompts for the option you selected in step 9. When you get to the Completing the Network Setup Wizard dialog box, click Finish.
11. If prompted to restart the computer, click Yes to do so.

**TRY IT!**

**This exercise is only for Windows Me or Windows XP.**

1. **Run the Home Networking Wizard (Me) or the Network Setup Wizard (XP) and configure the workgroup to use the workgroup name *TESTING*.**
2. **Create a network setup disk, and use it to set up another PC on the network using the same workgroup name.**
3. **Confirm that the PCs can see each other in My Network Places.**

## Understanding TCP/IP

TCP/IP is the most important protocol, both in Ethernet networking and in the Internet. TCP/IP is not a single protocol, but rather a suite of interconnected protocols that act at the Network and Transport levels of the OSI model. Every PC technician should have a basic understanding of it because so many other things are based upon it. The following sections provide a brief overview; if you decide to study for the Network+ exam, you will want a much more comprehensive understanding of TCP/IP and will probably want to study reference books that deal specifically with the subject.

### IP Addresses

**IP address**

A number that uniquely identifies a device on a network. It consists of a string of four three-digit numbers separated by periods.

The IP in TCP/IP stands for Internet Protocol. IP operates at the Network level of the OSI model. IP addresses are a way of assigning a unique numeric address to a particular PC or network resource so that other PCs can access it from anywhere in the network. An *IP address* appears as a string of four numbers of up to 3 digits each, separated by periods; 207.150.192.12 is an example. Each number does not necessarily have to be a full three digits; leading zeros are assumed (i.e., 012 is the same as 12).

An IP address is actually a 32-digit binary number, broken up into four 8-digit binary numbers to make it easier to work with. For example, 207.150.192.12 is 11001111.10010110.11000000.00001100 in binary. Such long numbers are difficult to key accurately, however, so IP addresses are normally converted to decimal to make them easier to read and remember.

## TRY IT!

To use Windows Calculator to convert the IP address 192.168.3.2 to binary, complete the following steps:

1. Open Calculator.
2. Choose View/Scientific.
3. Click the Dec button. Key the decimal-based number (without the periods and with the leading zeroes where needed) and then click the Bin button. The binary equivalent appears.

### *Static versus Dynamic IP Addressing*

When you set up a network connection on a PC, there are two ways to handle IP addressing. One is to enter a *static IP address* for it. Such an address would be assigned by the ISP or LAN administrator. Network administrators at large companies spend a lot of time and energy developing complex systems of IP addressing, so you should never guess at the IP address—always ask. The same goes for the IP address assigned by an ISP to a broadband connection to the Internet.

**Static IP address**

An IP address that is assigned to a network device for its exclusive use, and that it retains even after disconnecting and reconnecting.

The other way is to allow a DHCP server to dynamically assign IP addresses. This is how large corporate networks generally do it. They set up a server with *Dynamic Host Configuration Protocol* (DHCP), and every time a computer logs on, it asks the DHCP server "What is my IP address?" and it is assigned one immediately. This system is advantageous because it eliminates the possibility of duplicate addresses.

**Dynamic Host Configuration Protocol (DHCP)**

A server utility that dynamically assigns IP addresses to client PCs that request them.

Most dial-up Internet connections use a *dynamic IP address* assigned by the ISP's server every time the connection is established. The main reason for this is financial. An ISP buys a block of IP addresses that its customers are allowed to use on the Internet, and the ISP typically buys fewer of them than it has dial-up customers because it assumes that not all customers will be connected at the same time. So when a PC connects to the ISP via dial-up networking, it receives a dynamic IP address—that is, a random assignment from the pool of available addresses.

**Dynamic IP address**

An IP address that is assigned to a device when it connects to the network. It retains that address for the duration of the connection and then releases it back into the pool when it logs off.

### *Automatic Private IP Addressing*

Since a small workgroup does not have a DHCP server and you did not enter static IP addresses when you set up a workgroup earlier in the chapter, how can the PCs in the workgroup be connected without either of those helpers? The answer is *automatic private IP addressing*. This is a system whereby Windows automatically assigns IP addresses within a certain range of reserved addresses whenever it cannot locate a DHCP server and no static address has been supplied. The range of addresses for autoamtic private addressing begin with 192.168, as in 192.168.1.1.

**Automatic private IP addressing**

A range of reserved IP addresses (192.168.0.1 through 192.168.255.255) that Windows automatically assigns to network devices whenever it cannot find a DHCP server and does not have a static IP address assigned.

Figure 22.19 shows the differences among static, dynamic, and automatic private addresses. The real negotiations are more complex, but this conveys the general idea.

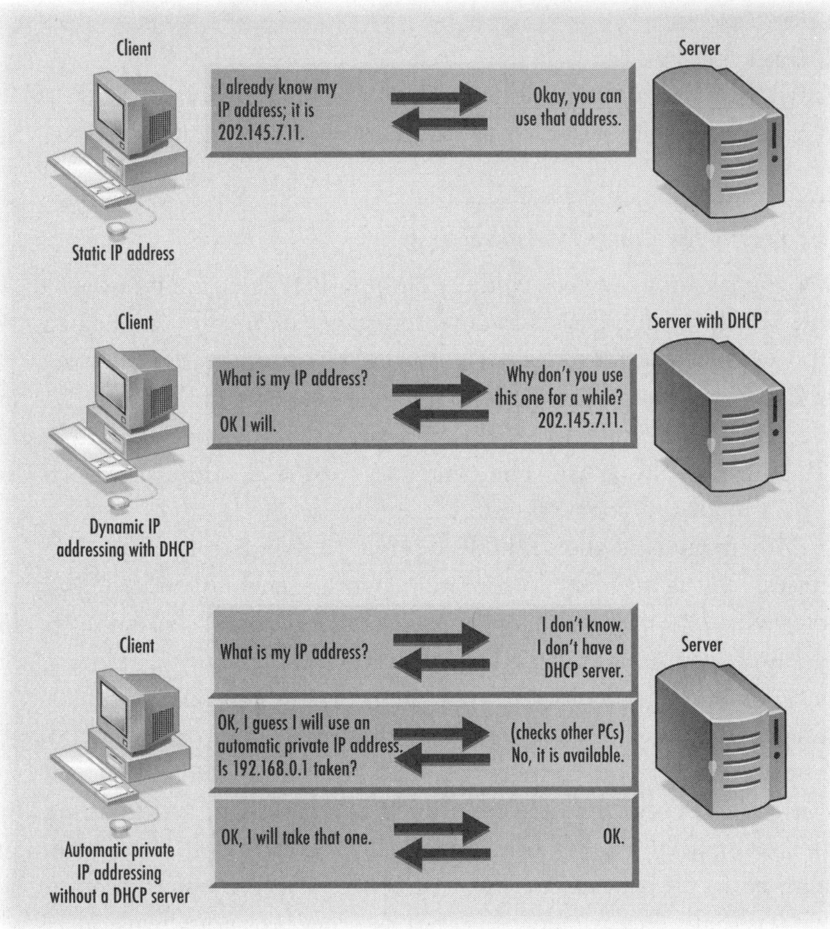
Client
Server
I already know my IP address; it is 202.145.7.11.
Okay, you can use that address.
Static IP address
Client
Server with DHCP
What is my IP address?
OK I will.
Why don't you use this one for a while? 202.145.7.11.
Dynamic IP addressing with DHCP
Client
Server
What is my IP address?
I don't know. I don't have a DHCP server.
OK, I guess I will use an automatic private IP address. Is 192.168.0.1 taken?
(checks other PCs) No, it is available.
OK, I will take that one.
OK.
Automatic private IP addressing without a DHCP server

**FIGURE 22.19**
How IP Addresses Are Assigned with a Static, Dynamic, or Automatic Private Addressing Method

## SUBNET MASKS

When you set up a static IP address, you also have the opportunity to enter a subnet mask. This usually involves 255s and 0s; for example, 255.255.255.0. The simplest approach is just to enter what the network administrator or ISP tech support department tells you. However, a good PC technician should understand the basics of subnet masks in case a subnet mask ever gets changed or erased.

**Network address**

The portion of an IP address that refers to the network segment to which the node belongs.

In a TCP/IP network, each IP address can be broken down into two parts. The first part is the *network address;* it tells what network segment (subnet) the PC belongs to. The second part, the *host address,* is the unique identifier of that device within that network segment. The address breakdown is similar to the use of area codes and prefixes in a telephone number, except in that case there are three levels of division rather than two. The network address is like the area code, and the host address is like the phone number. Multiple devices can have the same host address as long as they have different network addresses, just as multiple households in different area codes can have the same phone number.

The dividing line between the first and second parts of the IP address is not a fixed point; it can vary depending on the way the network is set up. This is beneficial for people designing networks because it gives them maximum flexibility. You could have several domains with a few addresses each, or a few domains with several addresses each, or anything in between. The *subnet mask* defines where the separator line should be placed. In simplistic terms, the separator comes at the point where the 0s begin. So, for example, in 255.255.255.0, the separator comes after the third group of digits.

In actual use, the process becomes more complicated because an IP address is actually a 32-digit binary number, not decimal. Each number between the periods is an 8-digit binary. So the address 255.255.255.0 is actually 11111111111111111111111100000000. The breaking point between 1 and 0 is actually after the 24th digit. It does not need to break on an even 8, so you could potentially have a subnet mask such as 255.255.248.0, which would break after the 21st digit. The more 1s in the subnet mask, the more possible domains there can be and the fewer nodes within each domain.

IP addresses are sometimes referred to as Class A, Class B, or Class C addresses. The difference among these classes of addresses is in the subnet mask. A Class A address has a subnet mask of 255.0.0.0, which means that 8 digits refer to the domain and the remaining 24 refer to individual nodes within the domain. In such a domain there can be about 16 million unique IP addresses. A Class B address has a subnet mask of 255.255.0.0, and a Class C address has a subnet mask of 255.255.255.0.

Subnet mask is important because two identical IP addresses with different subnet masks refer to two completely different network addresses. For example, in an IP address of 203.211.14.1, if the subnet mask is 255.255.0.0, then the network address is 203.211.0.0, but if the subnet mask is 255.255.255.0, the network address is 203.211.14.0. The zeros are added to the end of the network address to make four full sets of numbers, just for consistency.

**Host address**

The portion of an IP address that refers to the individual network device, not the network segment on which it resides.

**Subnet mask**

A numeric code that specifies what portion of the IP address refers to the domain and what part refers to the individual node within the domain.

If you ever take a course on networking, or study for the Network+ exam, you will spend time learning how to calculate subnet masks. But for our purposes in this chapter, all you need to know is how to key one into a dialog box.

## Default Gateway

When multiple subnets are connected together, the IP addressing is different for each subnet. For example, if you are using Class C addresses (255.255.255.0 subnet mask), you might have two network subnets. On one subnet all of the IP addresses might begin with 202.158.1, and on the other they might all begin with 202.158.2. When a PC sends data to another PC within the same subnet, the data stays within that subnet. However, when the data has to travel to the other subnet, it needs a pathway to get out of its local subnet, into the router to which both subnets are attached, and into the other subnet. The IP address for this pathway out is the *default gateway*. It is usually the IP address of a port in the router or gateway to which the subnet is connected (see Figure 22.20).

**Default gateway**

The IP address of the pathway that leads out of the local subnet.

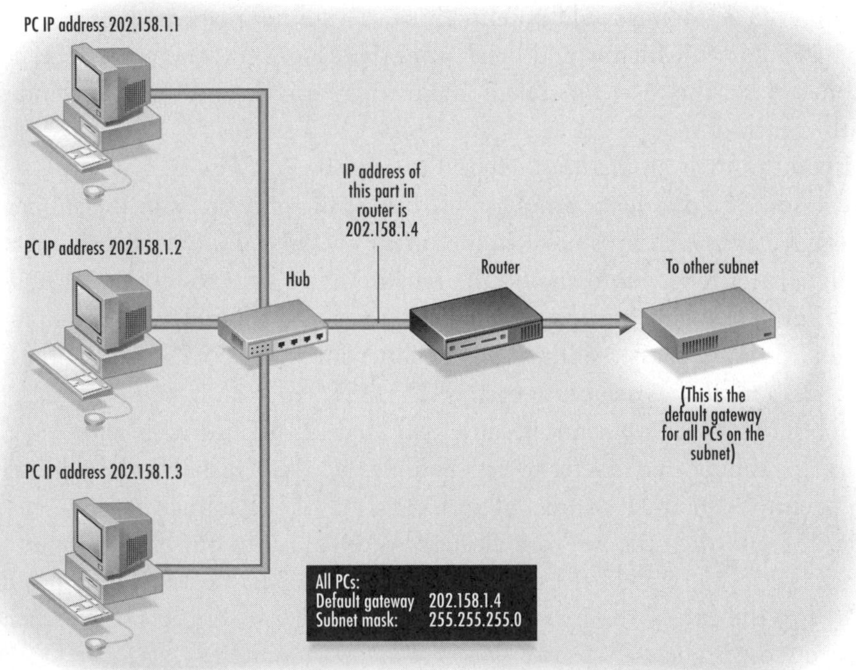


**FIGURE 22.20**
A default gateway tells PCs in a subnet where to send requests for addresses that are outside the subnet.

## DNS Server Address

Even with the decimal numbering system and the separators, IP addresses are not exactly catchy, and it can be difficult to remember them. A *Domain Name System (*DNS) server, therefore, is used to translate IP addresses into text-based addresses—*domain names*—that contain familiar words that people can remember. One use for a DNS server is on the Internet, to translate the *Uniform Resource Locator* (URL) addresses entered in a Web browser to IP addresses that point to specific Web servers storing Web content. For example, when you key **http://www.microsoft.com** into a Web browser, it queries a DNS server, finds out the IP address for Microsoft's server, and then requests the content at that address, all invisibly to you as the end user.

There are DNS servers all over the world. These specialized servers have the job of translating each address that a client requests in URL form into an IP address and sending that IP address back to the client for its use. All of the DNS servers share information with one another, so they all contain the same data (although sometimes when there is a change it takes a day or so for that change to filter out to all of the DNS servers worldwide).

For example, suppose the client keys **www.sycamoreknoll.com**. The DNS server comes back with the information that this address translates to 207.150.192.12, and the Web browser software uses that information to connect to the Web site. This is called *DNS lookup*. If you ever see a DNS Lookup Error in a Web browser, it means the DNS server has failed to provide a translation for the address you entered. It could be because there is no information available or because the DNS server is not working.

**Domain Name System (DNS)**

A server application that keeps track of the relationships between IP addresses and text names and provides translation services to PCs that request them.

**Domain name**

The text-based name of a network server or other network location.

## Checking a PC's IP Address and Other TCP/IP Settings

If you ever need to troubleshoot a problem with a network connection, as you will learn to do in Chapter 23, you will need to determine the PC's IP address and other TCP/IP settings such as subnet mask, default gateway, and DNS server address.

In Windows XP or Windows 2000:

1. From the Control Panel, double-click the *Network Connections* icon (XP) or *Network and Dial-Up Connections* (2000).
2. Right-click the adapter you want to check and choose Properties.
3. Double-click TCP/IP on the list of installed components. A Properties dialog box for TCP/IP appears.

**Uniform Resource Locator (URL)**

A Web address consisting of a domain name such as microsoft.com, plus the address of an individual Web page or other file within that domain; for example, www.microsoft.com/games/combatfs1/drivers.htm.

**DNS lookup**

The process of looking up a domain name in a DNS server's database and sending the equivalent IP address back to the requester.

4. Check the IP address. If it is set to Obtain an IP address automatically, the IP address is coming either from a DHCP server or from automatic private IP addressing. If it is set to Use the following IP address, the address has been manually entered. Figure 22.21 shows a manually entered IP address, subnet mask, and default gateway.
5. Close all open dialog boxes without making any changes.

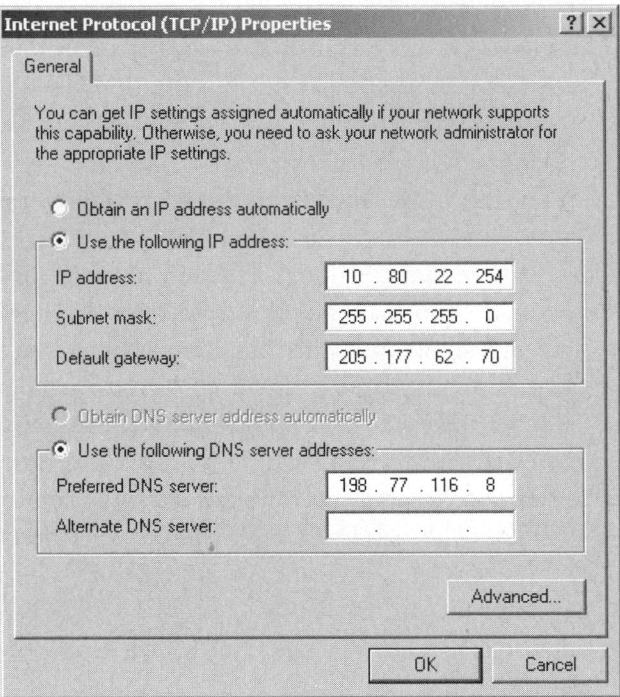


**FIGURE 22.21**
On this PC, an IP address has been entered manually

In Windows 95/98/Me:

1. From the Control Panel, double-click *Network*.
2. Double-click TCP/IP. A Properties dialog box for TCP/IP appears.
3. On the IP Address tab, check the IP address. If it is set to Obtain an IP address automatically, the IP address either came from a DHCP server or it is a an automatic private IP address (192.168, etc.). If it has been manually entered, there will be an IP address and a subnet mask (see Figure 22.22).

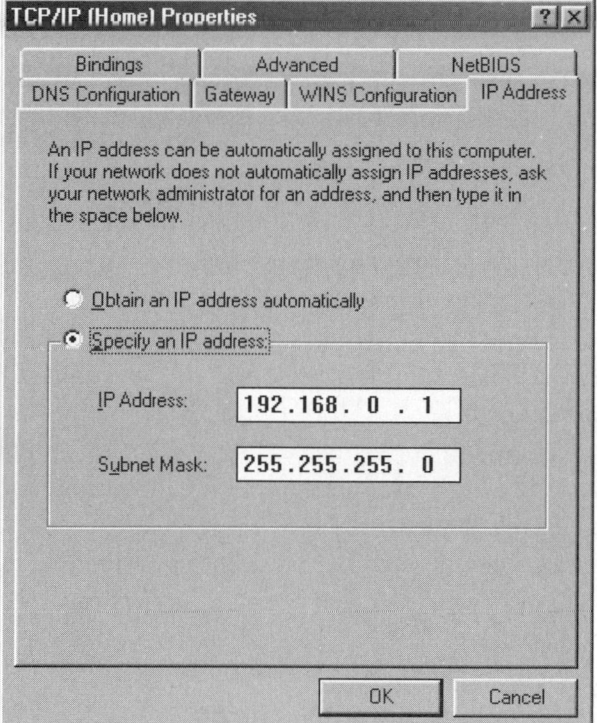


**FIGURE 22.22**
Manual IP settings in Windows 98; notice that in this OS version DNS and default gateway are on separate tabs.

4. *Optional:* If you need to set a default gateway, select the Gateway tab and enter it there.
5. *Optional:* If you need to specify a DNS server, select the DNS Configuration tab. Click Enable DNS and then enter the DNS server's address.
6. Click OK to close the dialog box, then click OK to close the Network dialog box.

## TRY IT!

Display the TCP/IP settings for your computer, and write down the IP address, subnet mask, default gateway, and DNS server that you find there. If there is no entry for one or more of them, make a note of that.

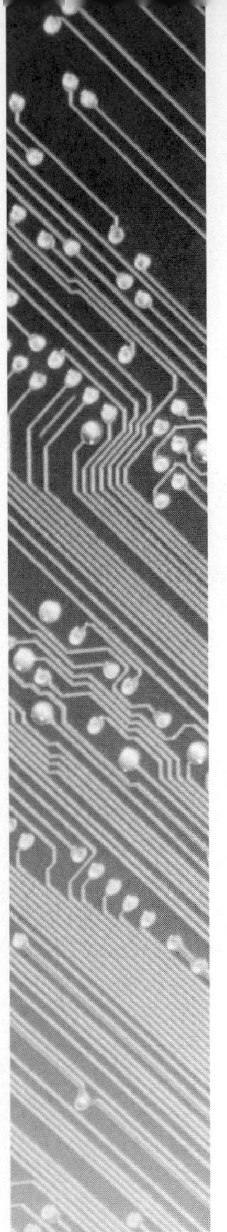

# STUDY GUIDE

Use the following summaries to review the key concepts of this chapter.

## Installing Network Hardware

- A network interface card (NIC) or other network adapter is required for each PC that will participate in the network.
- A NIC is usually a circuit board that fits in a motherboard expansion slot. It could also be a PC Card or an external USB device.
- A circuit board NIC can be either PCI or ISA; it installs just like any other expansion card.
- Windows might automatically detect the new NIC with Plug and Play; if not, use the Add New Hardware applet in the Control Panel or run the setup program that came with the NIC.
- In an Ethernet network, each PC must be connected to a hub or switch (or have access to a wireless access point). Connect each NIC to the hub with Cat5 UTP cable.

## Setting Up Networking in Windows

- There are two families of Windows versions, each of which operate networking similarly: Windows 95/98/Me and Windows 2000/XP.
- In Windows 95/98/Me, networking settings for all network adapters collectively are set in the network properties. You can bind or unbind protocols from individual adapters.
- In Windows 2000/XP, each network connection has its own properties that can have clients, protocols, and services installed.
- Setting up a network in Windows requires installing certain software drivers, including clients, protocols, and services.
- A network adapter can be a NIC, a PC Card, an external USB device, or a software-based adapter such as Dial-Up Networking.
- A client is software that tells Windows what type of network you have. The most popular client for Windows is Client for Microsoft Networks; an alternative is Client for NetWare Networks.
- A protocol is a language or set of rules governing data transmission.
- TCP/IP (Transmission Control Protocol/Internet Protocol) is the default protocol for Windows networking and for the Internet. It should almost always be installed.
- NetBEUI is an older protocol that was the default in Windows 95. It has compact, efficient packets but cannot go across a router.

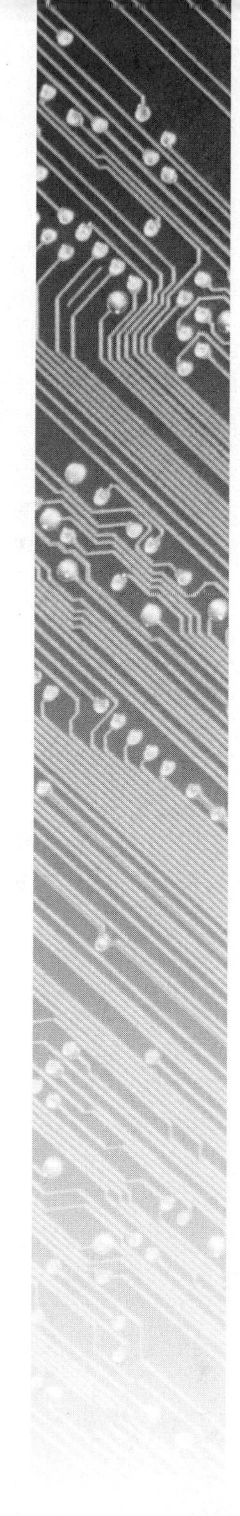

- IPX/SPX-compatible is a protocol for compatibility with NetWare networks.
- In Windows 95/98/Me, protocols are bound to all network adapters by default; you can unbind a protocol from an adapter from the adapter's Properties dialog box (Bindings tab).
- A service is a specialized driver that enables a certain activity. The most popular service is File and Printer Sharing for Microsoft Networks.
- To install a client, protocol, or service, view the properties for the network (95/98/Me) or for the connection (2000/XP) and then click Install or Add (depending on the OS version).
- A good way to check network connectivity is to try to browse the network through Network Neighborhood (Windows 95/98) or My Network Places (Windows Me/2000/XP).
- Each computer must have a unique name on the network and must have the same workgroup name as every other computer in the same workgroup.
- In Windows 95/98/Me, set the computer and workgroup name from the Identification tab in the Network dialog box.
- In Windows 2000, set the computer and workgroup name from the Network Identification tab in the System Properties dialog box.
- In Windows XP, set the computer and workgroup name from the Computer Name tab in the System Properties dialog box.

## Setting Up Networking with Wizards

- Windows Me and Windows XP come with wizards for setting up a network.
- Windows Me provides a Home Networking Wizard on the Programs/Accessories/Communications menu.
- Windows XP has a Network Setup Wizard on the All Programs/Accessories/Communications menu.
- Both wizards enable you to create a network setup disk that can be taken to other PCs that are running earlier Windows versions in order to set them up with the wizard.

## Understanding TCP/IP

- TCP/IP is the most important protocol in networking today. It is actually a suite of related protocols that operate at the Network and Transport levels of the OSI model.

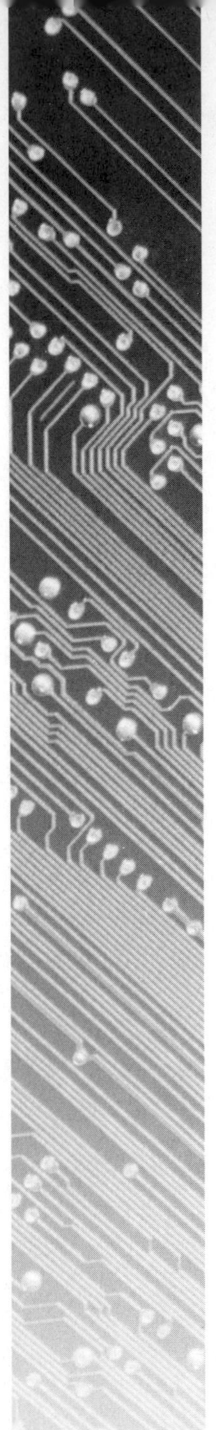

- IP addresses assign unique numeric addresses to a particular resource so that other PCs can access it from any other location.
- An IP address is a string of four three-digit numbers separated by periods. Each of these three-digit numbers translates to an eight-digit binary number.
- Static IP addressing manually assigns a certain IP address to a network adapter.
- Dynamic IP addressing uses a DHCP (Dynamic Host Configuration Protocol) server to assign IP addresses.
- Automatic private IP addressing uses an address from a pool of reserved IP addresses for local networking only (no Internet) when a DHCP server is not available; the most common use for this is in a small workgroup with no server.
- An IP address consists of a network address (like an area code) followed by a host address (like a phone number). The breaking point between the two address parts varies depending on the subnet mask. All computers with the same network address are said to be in the same subnet.
- The subnet mask is a 32-digit binary number with 1s at the beginning and 0s at the end. The breaking point where 1s change to 0s defines the breaking point of network versus host address in the IP address with which it is associated.
- The default gateway is the address of the exit port from a subnet to the larger network (such as through a router).
- A DNS (Domain Name System) server translates IP addresses into text-based addresses such as Internet URLs. A DNS server has its own IP address to which a network adapter can refer.
- To check a PC's TCP/IP settings, view the properties for TCP/IP.
- In Windows 2000 or XP, right-click the network adapter and choose Properties, then double-click TCP/IP.
- In Windows 95/98/Me, display the Network properties and double-click TCP/IP.

# PRACTICE TEST

On a blank sheet of paper, write the answers to the following multiple-choice questions and explain why each answer is correct.

1. Which of these is *not* a physical form that a network adapter might take?
   a. built-in chip on the motherboard
   b. PCI expansion board
   c. AGP expansion board
   d. PC Card device

2. If Windows detects new hardware at startup after installing a NIC but is unable to locate a driver for it, what is likely to be the problem?
   a. The NIC is not firmly seated in the motherboard slot.
   b. The NIC is not connected to the hub.
   c. There is an IRQ conflict.
   d. The installed version of Windows does not come with a driver for the NIC.

3. Where in Windows could you check to make sure the NIC's driver was correctly installed?
   a. Device Manager
   b. My Network Places or Network Neighborhood
   c. Communication Properties
   d. Internet Connection Wizard

4. Which of these protocols does *not* need to be installed in Windows networking properties (or the properties for a specific network adapter) in order to be used for networking?
   a. SMTP
   b. TCP/IP
   c. NetBEUI
   d. IPX/SPX-compatible

5. Which Windows versions have a single Network properties dialog box listing all installed network adapters, and allow you to bind or unbind installed protocols to individual adapters through the adapter properties?
   a. Windows 95/98/Me
   b. Windows 2000/XP
   c. Windows 95 and 98 only
   d. Windows Me and XP only

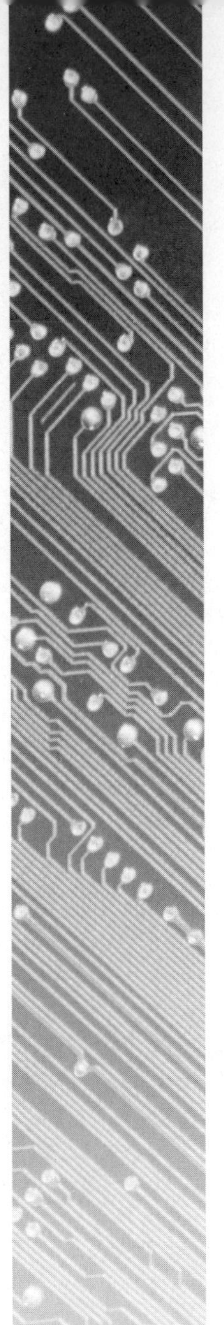

6. Why is it necessary to have Client for Microsoft Networks installed for a Windows peer-to-peer network?
   a. It provides a common protocol by which PCs can communicate.
   b. It installs file and printer sharing services.
   c. It provides the NOS, enabling the PC to act as a workgroup client.
   d. All of the above

7. How could you find out whether Client for NetWare Networks was installed in Windows 98?
   a. Open the System Properties dialog box and look for it on the Device Manager tab.
   b. Open the Network dialog box and look for it on the Configuration tab.
   c. View the Network and Dial-Up Connections and right-click the network adapter.
   d. Any of the above would work

8. For what type of network would NetBEUI be suitable?
   a. communication between PCs in a stand-alone workgroup
   b. workgroup that also connects to a larger LAN via a router
   c. LAN connection to the Internet
   d. Windows XP computer connecting to a NetWare network

9. How would you remove a protocol from Windows 2000?
   a. from Device Manager
   b. from the overall network properties
   c. from the properties for a specific network connection
   d. from the System Properties dialog box

10. Which of these is a service?
    a. Client for NetWare Networks
    b. File and Printer Sharing for Microsoft Networks
    c. TCP/IP
    d. HTTP

11. In Windows 95/98, by default
    a. all installed protocols are bound to all adapters.
    b. all installed protocols are unbound.
    c. each protocol is bound to the primary adapter only.
    d. there is no standard; it depends on the protocol.

12. In configuring a peer-to-peer network, the correct name to use as the workgroup name is:
    a. WORKGROUP.
    b. MSHOME.
    c. PEER.
    d. It does not matter as long it is the same on all computers.

13. Which of these is the correct format for an IP address?
    a. 192.168.3
    b. 192.168.3122.17
    c. 192.168.202.155
    d. both b and c

14. What is the purpose of a DHCP server?
    a. translates IP addresses to text names such as URLs
    b. assigns IP addresses to network nodes
    c. translates URLs to IP addresses
    d. both a and c

15. What can you assume about this address: 192.168.3.2?
    a. It is a static address.
    b. It was dynamically assigned with DHCP.
    c. It is an automatic private IP address.
    d. either b or c

16. What type of address is 255.255.0.0 likely to be?
    a. It is a subnet mask.
    b. It is a fixed IP address.
    c. It is a virtual private IP address.
    d. It is a default gateway.

17. Which of these subnet masks would be used with a Class C IP address?
    a. 255.0.0.0
    b. 255.255.255.0
    c. 255.255.0.0
    d. 255.255.255.255

18. What is the purpose of a DNS server?
    a. translate IP addresses into domain names
    b. assign dynamic IP addresses to clients
    c. support DHCP services
    d. host a Web site

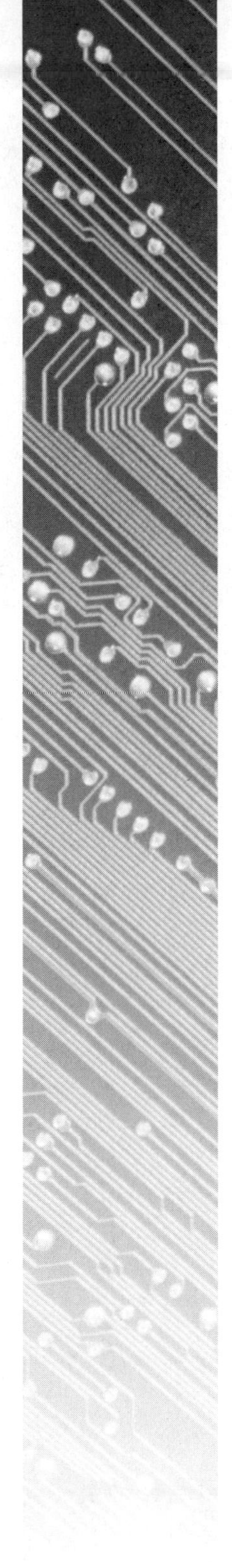

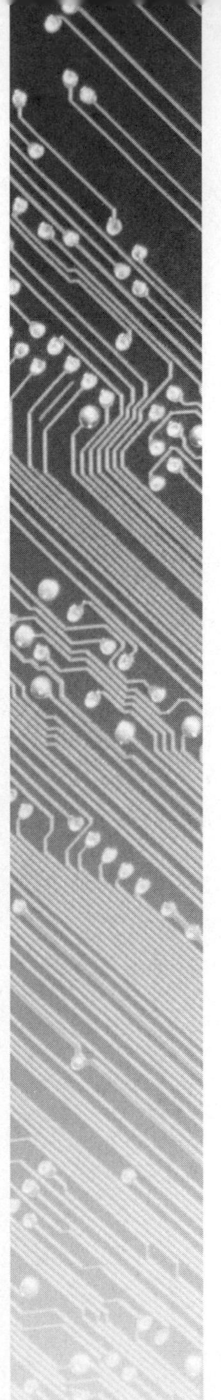

19. If a PC is set to obtain an IP address automatically, and there is no DHCP server available, which of these addresses would it be likely to use?
    a. 204.255.0.1
    b. 255.255.255.0
    c. 197.162.5.1
    d. 192.168.1.2

20. What is dial-up networking in Windows?
    a. a client
    b. a network adapter
    c. a service
    d. a protocol

# TROUBLESHOOTING

1. At a client site you have set up a workgroup consisting of three PCs, one each running Windows 95, Windows 98, and Windows XP. You have installed all of the needed hardware and connected each NIC to a common hub, but the PCs do not see each other in Network Neighborhood (or My Network Places). How would you troubleshoot this?
2. You have replaced the NIC in a PC because it stopped working, but the new NIC does not work either. Windows does not see the NIC at all in Device Manager, and Add New Hardware fails to detect it. What could you try next?
3. If a PC can see itself in My Network Places but it cannot see any other PCs in the workgroup, what can you assume is working correctly? What do you need to check as potential causes?

# CUSTOMER SERVICE

1. A client wants to buy a NIC for a recently acquired PC and is going to try to install it himself. What recommendations would you make?
2. A client would like to use NetBEUI as the primary protocol for her workgroup. What potential problems or limitations would you warn her about?
3. A client wants to assign fixed IP addresses to the four PCs in her workgroup. There are no other PCs in the network—just those four. She is going to use 192.168.1.1, 192.168.1.2, 192.168.1.3, and 192.168.1.4. What subnet mask should she use, and what default gateway?

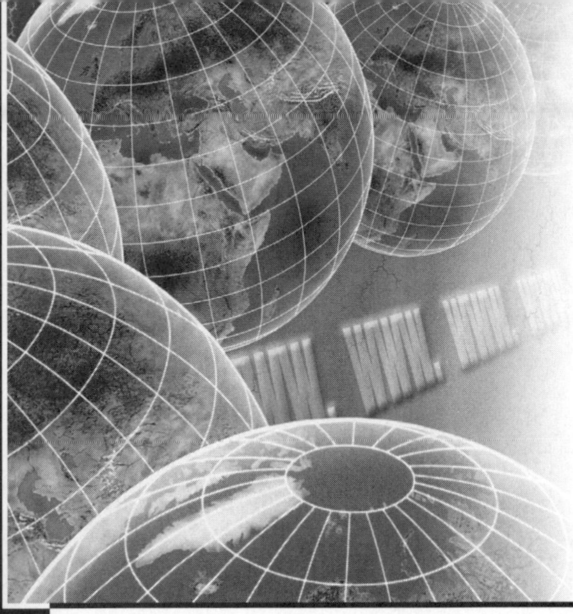

# 23 Using a Windows Network

## ON THE TEST

**A+ Core Hardware Service Technician Examination**

- **Objective 2.1:** Identify common symptoms and problems associated with each module and how to troubleshoot and isolate the problems.
- **Objective 6.1:** Identify basic networking concepts, including how a network works and the ramifications of repairs on the network.

**A+ Operating System Technologies Examination**

- **Objective 2.4:** Identify procedures for loading/adding and configuring application device drivers, and the necessary software for certain devices.
- **Objective 3.2:** Recognize common problems and determine how to resolve them.
- **Objective 4.1:** Identify the networking capabilities of Windows including procedures for connecting to the network.

## ON THE JOB

This chapter deals with the everyday usage and troubleshooting of a network, focusing on the skills that a PC technician is likely to need to support workgroup and client/server networking. Many of the skills covered here are file and printer management skills that a technician may need to teach to end users.

This chapter will help you be able to:

- browse a network for shared drives and folders
- map a network folder to a drive letter
- install file and printer sharing
- share a folder or drive

- share a printer
- install drivers for a shared printer for users with different Windows versions
- set permissions to determine which network users have access to a resource
- troubleshoot network problems

## Logging On and Off a Network

Windows can be set up so that the user logs on to the network automatically at startup with a specified user name and password, or Windows prompts each time for that information.

There are two kinds of logons: logging on to the local PC and logging on to the network. They are the same on PCs in a peer-to-peer network because a peer-to-peer network does not require separate logon. However on a client/server network they are different.

A peer-to-peer network handles network IDs and permissions individually on each PC. Each PC maintains its own settings, and is in charge of granting or denying users permission to its own shared resources. On a client/server network, users log on to the network and are validated by the network server's list of allowed user names and passwords. Then the server specifies that the user has permission to participate in the network. Note, however, that just logging onto the network does not grant permission to use any resources; those are assigned through file- and printer-sharing permissions for the individual resources.

### Windows 95/98/Me Logon

Versions of Windows designed for home use (95/98/Me) have very simple logon capabilities (see Figure 23.1). You can bypass the logon screen (in the Enter Network Password dialog box) by clicking Cancel. This starts up the PC without connecting to the network.

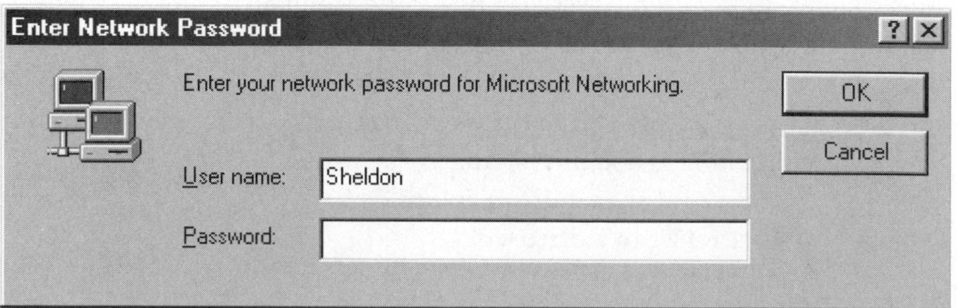


**FIGURE 23.1**
Logging On in Windows 98

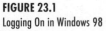

### *Selecting the Primary Logon*

In Windows 95/98/Me, you can select a primary logon in the Network dialog box. It makes no difference what you pick for a peer-to-peer network but, for a client/server network, if you do not pick Client for Microsoft Networks you will not be able to connect to the network.

To make sure that Client for Microsoft Networks is the primary logon:

1. In the Control Panel, double-click the *Network* icon.
2. In the Network dialog box with the Configuration tab selected, open the Primary Network Logon drop-down list and select *Client for Microsoft Networks* (see Figure 23.2).
3. Click OK.

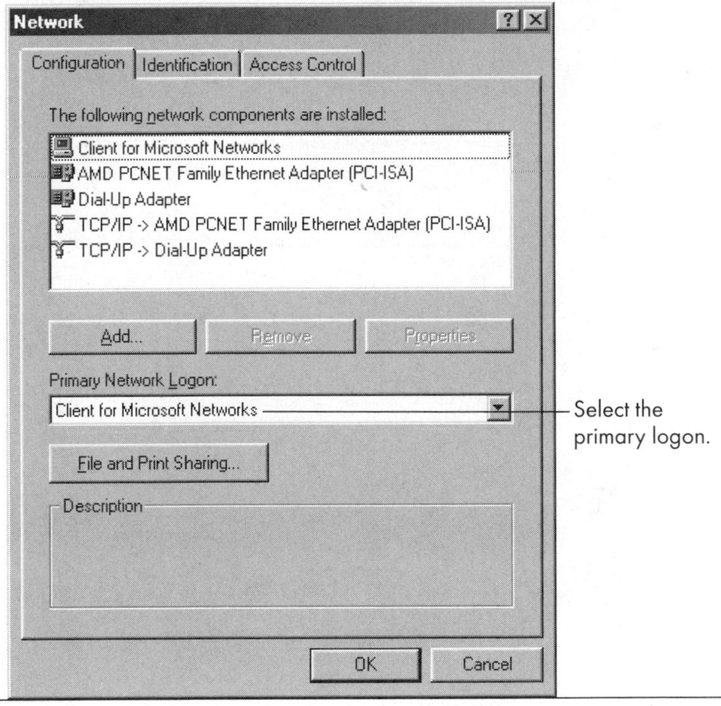


**FIGURE 23.2**
Choosing a Primary Logon

With these versions of Windows, if you do not enter a password the first time Windows prompts you to log on, it does not show the logon box at startup each time; it simply assumes that the default user is logging on. If a different user wants to log on, you must log off first.

### *Connecting to a Domain*

**Domain**

A client/server network controlled by a server that provides addressing services to the connected clients, such as assigning IP addresses.

These versions of Windows assume that you want to be a part of a peer-to-peer workgroup rather than a *domain*. If you need to make one of these PCs a part of a domain, do the following:

1. From the Control Panel, open the Network dialog box.
2. On the Configuration tab, double-click *Client for Microsoft Networks* in the Primary Network Logon list box.
3. Enter a check mark in the Log on to Windows NT domain check box, and enter the domain name in the Windows NT domain text box (see Figure 23.3).
4. Click OK twice. When prompted to restart, click Yes.

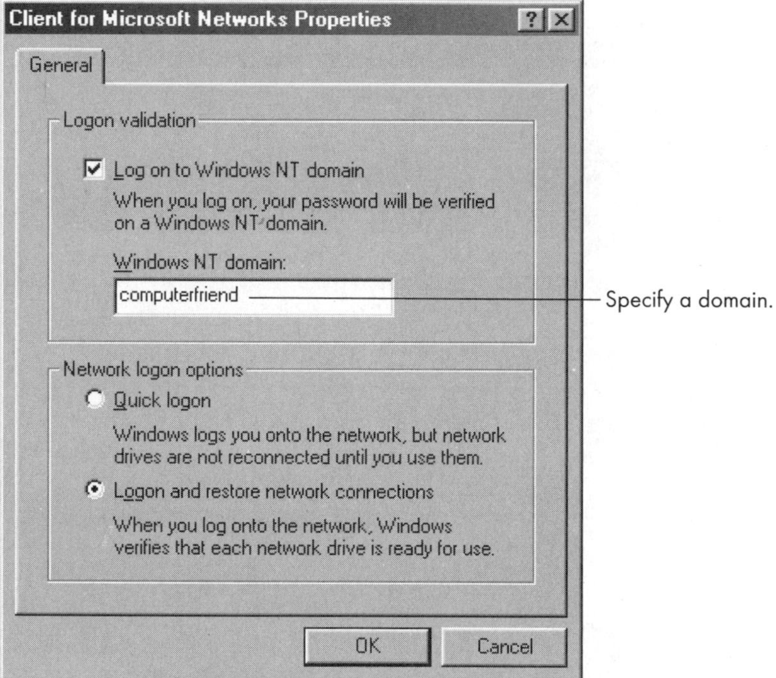


**FIGURE 23.3**
You can set a Windows 95/98/Me PC to log on to a domain rather than a workgroup.

After you have set up the PC to log on to a domain, an extra text box for the domain name appears in the Enter Network Password dialog box at startup. The default domain name is already filled in. Just enter the user name and password normally and click OK to log on.

### *Logging Off and On*

To log off, choose Start, Log Off, and then click Yes. This reopens the Enter Network Password dialog box so another user can log on.

## TRY IT!

1. Log off and then on again. When you log on, key a different user name than you used before. Does Windows allow you to create a new user?
2. If a client/server network is available, set up the PC to be part of that domain. Log off, and then on again, and this time log on to the domain.
3. Log off again, and this time log on to the local PC.

## WINDOWS 2000 LOGON

If a logon box appears in Windows 2000, it cannot be bypassed by clicking Cancel (as it can in 95/98/Me); the user must enter a valid user name and password. This gives Windows 2000 better security than Windows 95/98/Me since nobody except an authorized user can access the computer.

### *Specifying Whether Logon Is Required*

If only one person uses the PC, and local security is not an issue (for example, in a home), you might not want to bother with a logon screen each time the PC starts up. You can choose whether or not you want Windows to prompt for a user name and password at startup by doing the following:

1. From the Control Panel, double-click *Users and Passwords.*
2. On the Users tab, mark or clear the Users must enter a user name and password to use this computer check box (see Figure 23.4).
3. Click OK.

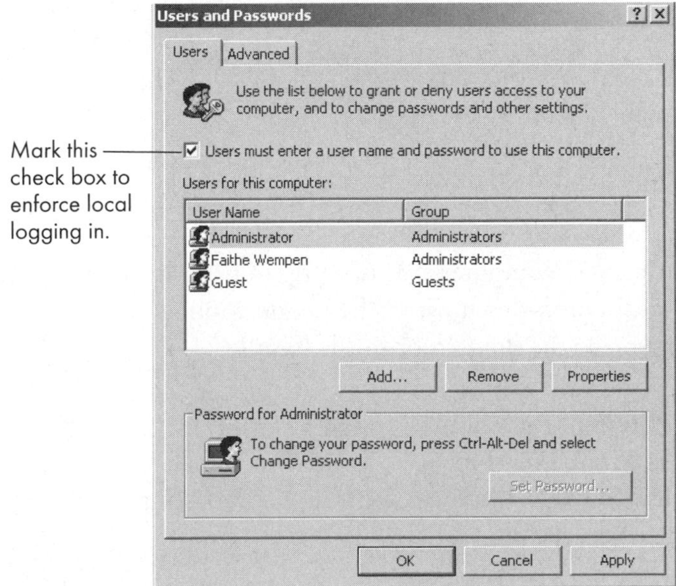


**FIGURE 23.4**
Specify whether or not Windows 2000 should use a logon screen.

These steps are for stand-alone or workgroup-networked PCs, for securing logon access to the computer itself. They do not pertain to logging on to a client/server domain.

### *Connecting to a Domain*

To set up a Windows 2000 PC to be part of a client/server domain, do the following:

1. From the Control Panel, double-click the *System* icon.
2. Select the Network Identification tab in the System Properties dialog box.
3. Click the Properties button.
4. Click the Domain option button to select it, and then key the domain name in the text box (see Figure 23.5).
5. Click OK.

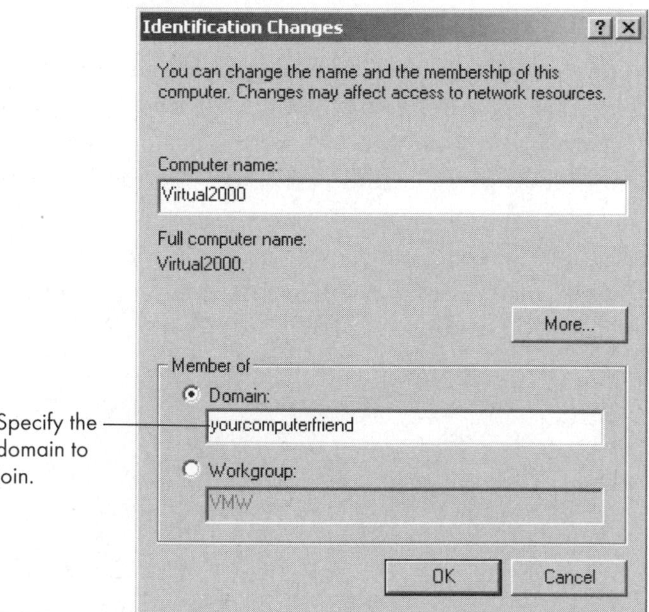


**FIGURE 23.5**
Set up the PC to participate in a domain instead of being a peer-to-peer workstation.

When you log on to a computer that is set up to participate in a domain, there will be an extra drop-down list in the Logon window that gives you a choice of logging on to the domain or to the local PC.

### *Logging Off and On*

Unlike Windows 95/98/Me, there is no Log Off command on the Start menu in Windows 2000. Instead you must do the following:

1. Press Ctrl + Alt + Delete.

2. Click Log Off. This reopens the Enter Network Password dialog box, preparing the PC for some other user to log on.

## TRY IT!

1. Log off and then on again. Try making up a new user name when you log on; does Windows allow it?
2. If a client/server network is available, set up the PC to be part of that domain. Log off and then on again, and this time log on to the domain.
3. Log off again, and this time log on to the local PC.

### *Managing the List of Allowed Local Users*

Only valid user names set up for that domain can be used to log on to a domain network. If logging on to the computer itself, or on to a workgroup network, the allowed user names are specified on the local PC's settings.

Windows 95/98/Me also allow you to manage the list of local users, but since those OS versions allow you to bypass the logon, the list of local users is not nearly as significant.

To manage the allowed users for the local PC in Windows 2000, do the following:

1. From the Control Panel, double-click *Users and Passwords.*
2. If the Users must enter a user name and password to use this computer check box is not already selected, click it. This makes the user list active.

From here you can perform the following activities:

- **Change passwords:** To change a password for an existing user, select that user on the User Name list and click the Set Password button. In the Set Password dialog box that appears, key and then rekey the new password and click OK (see Figure 23.6).
- **Add users:** To add a user, click the Add button. Then complete the Add New User Wizard that appears. When working through the wizard, you are asked what type of user you are setting up. Your choice places the user in a specific user group, from which the user inherits permissions (see Figure 23.7).

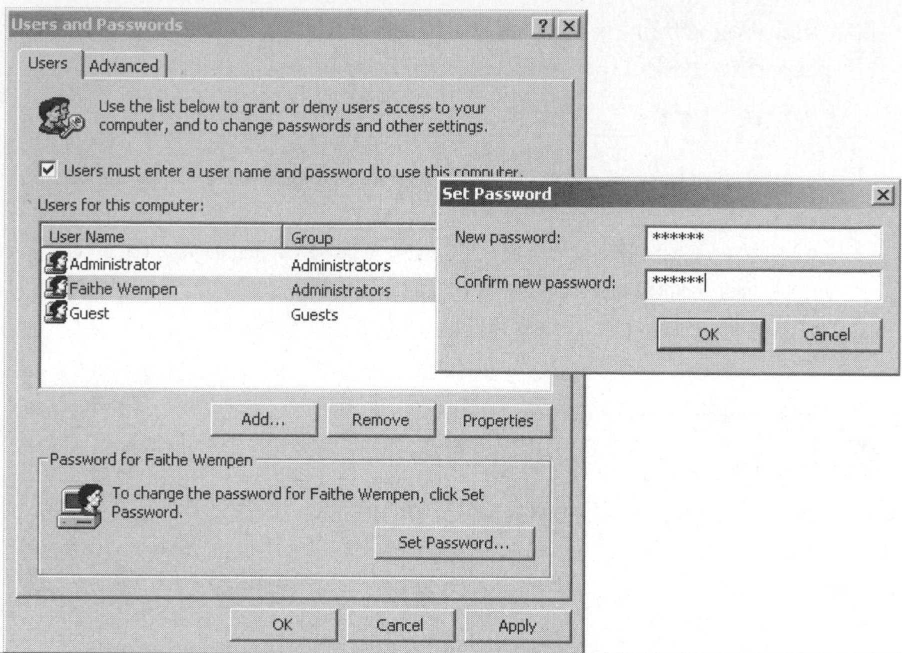


**FIGURE 23.6**
Change the password for an existing user of this PC.

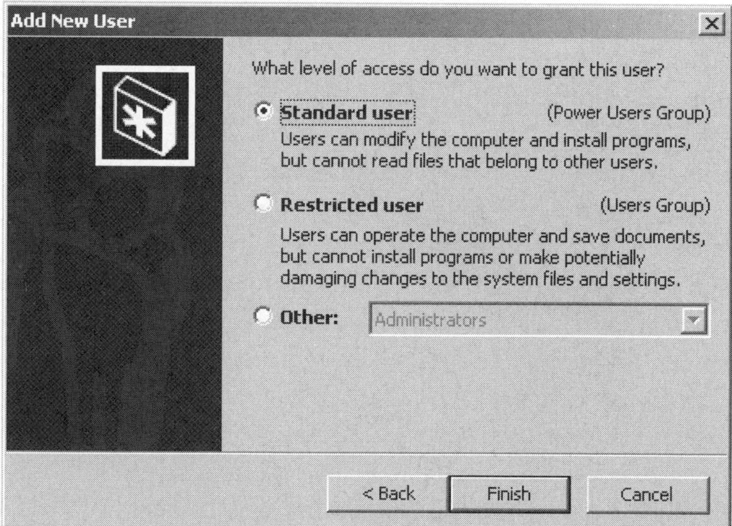


**FIGURE 23.7**
Add a user and place that user in a specific user group.

**WARNING**

Assigning a user to the Administrators group gives that user complete power to change everything, including passwords for other users.

- **Modify a user:** To change the name, description, or group membership for a user, select the user, click Properties, and then make the changes in the dialog box that appears.
- **Delete a user:** To remove a user, select the user and click Remove. At the confirmation box, click Yes.

**TRY IT!**

1. Create a new user and assign that user to the Users group (restricted).
2. Log on as that user, and come back to the Users and Passwords dialog box. What activities are disallowed?
3. Log on as yourself again, and change the new user to the Power Users group.
4. Log on as that user, and come back to the Users and Passwords dialog box. What activities are disallowed now?
5. Log on as yourself again, and delete the new user.

## Windows XP Logon

Windows XP is not covered on the current (2001) version of the A+ exam, but you will need to know how it works for your on-the-job work as a PC technician.

### *Selecting a Logon Screen Type*

Windows XP has two types of logon screens: the Welcome screen and the traditional logon screen, shown in Figures 23.8 and 23.9. You can switch between them by doing the following:

1. From the Control Panel, double-click *User Accounts.*
2. Click Change the way users log on or off.
3. If you do not want the Welcome screen, clear the Use the Welcome screen check box.
4. If you do use the Welcome screen, enable Fast User Switching if desired. This enables you to switch users without the first user's logging off, so the first user can leave programs open while another user checks e-mail, makes a quick printout, or does whatever is needed.
5. Click Apply Options.

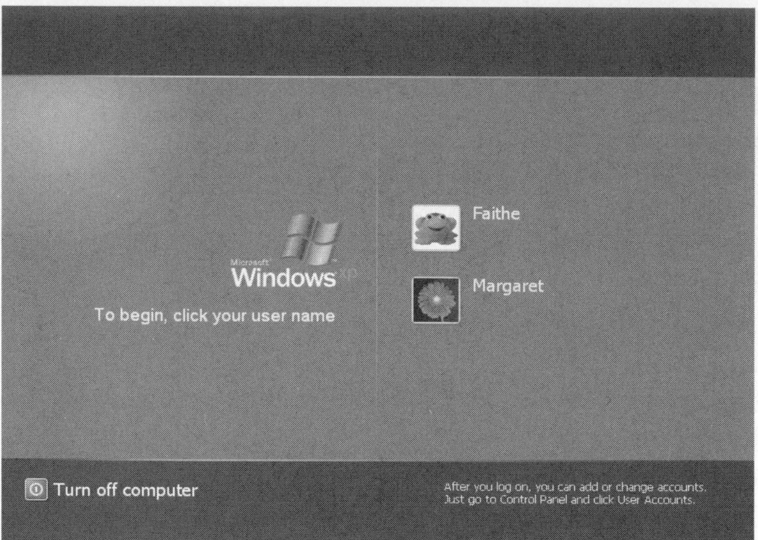


**FIGURE 23.8**
The Windows XP Welcome Screen

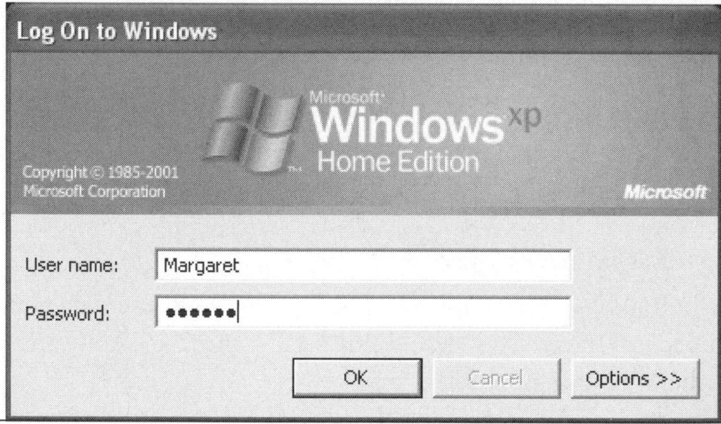


**FIGURE 23.9**
The Traditional Windows Logon Screen in Windows XP

Users can be set up to require a password or not, but with the traditional logon screen the user name must be keyed as well, whereas in the Welcome screen the user name is selected from the icons provided.

### *Connecting to a Domain*

The procedure for connecting to a domain is the same for Windows XP as it is for Windows 2000 except the name of the tab in the System Properties dialog box is different.

1. In the Control Panel, double-click the *System* icon.
2. Select the Computer Name tab in the System Properties dialog box.
3. Click the Change button to open the Computer Name Changes dialog box, which is very similar to the Identification Changes dialog box shown in Figure 23.5.

4. Click the Domain option button, and then key the domain in the text box.
5. Click OK.

### *Logging Off and On*

To log off Windows XP, do the following:

1. Choose Start, Log Off.
2. A confirmation box appears; click Log Off.

That basic procedure will always work, but there are many variations based on which logon screen you have set up.

If you are using the Welcome screen with Fast User Switching enabled, the confirmation box in step 2 appears with three choices: Log Off, Switch User, and Cancel. If you are using the Welcome screen without Fast User Switching, or if you are not using the Welcome screen at all, the confirmation box has only Log Off and Cancel as the options.

There are alternative ways of logging off based on which logon screen you have chosen. Recall that in Windows 2000 you press Ctrl + Alt + Delete and then click Log Off to log off; when you press Ctrl + Alt + Delete in Windows XP, one of the following happens:

- If you are using the Welcome screen, the Windows Task Manager opens. Open the Shut Down menu and choose Log Off [user name] (see Figure 23.10).

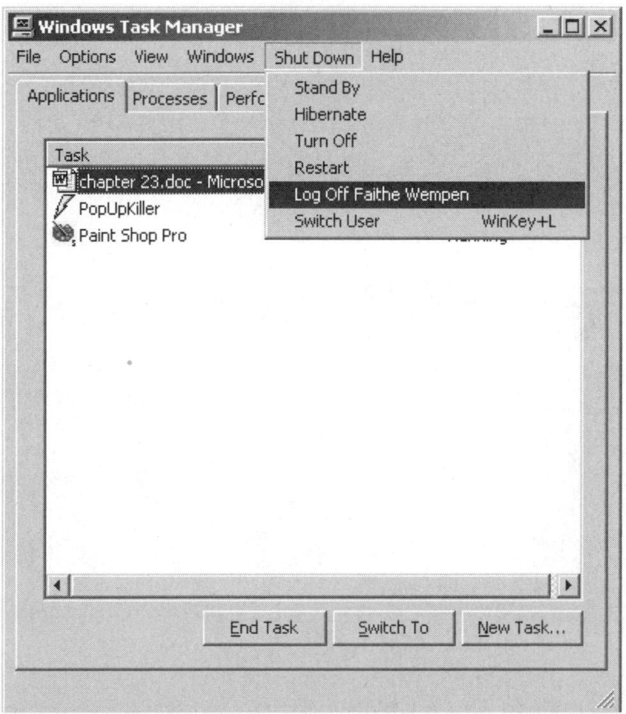


**FIGURE 23.10** The Windows Task Manager opens with Ctrl + Alt + Delete when the Welcome screen is the logon screen.

- If you are not using the Welcome screen, the Windows Security dialog box appears. From here you can click the Log Off button (see Figure 23.11).

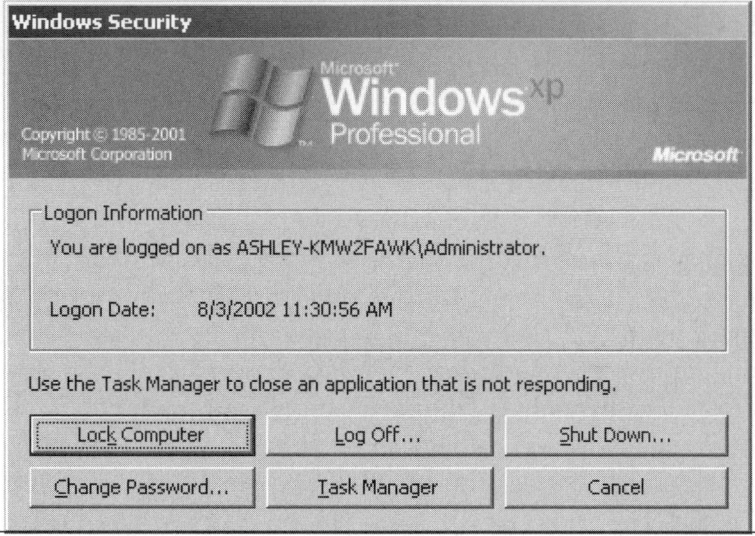


**FIGURE 23.11**
Pressing Ctrl + Alt + Delete when the Welcome screen is disabled opens a Windows Security dialog box similar to the one in Windows 2000.

### *Managing the List of Allowed Local Users*

As in Windows 2000, only specifically allowed users may log on to the local PC. However, when you use the Welcome screen and do not assign passwords to user IDs, anyone may log on to the computer simply by choosing one of the allowed user names.

To create and manage users, complete the following steps:

1. From the Control Panel, double-click *User Accounts*.
2. To change an existing account, click Change an Account. Then click the account you want to change, and a list of hyperlinks appears for activities you can perform on that account (see Figure 23.12).

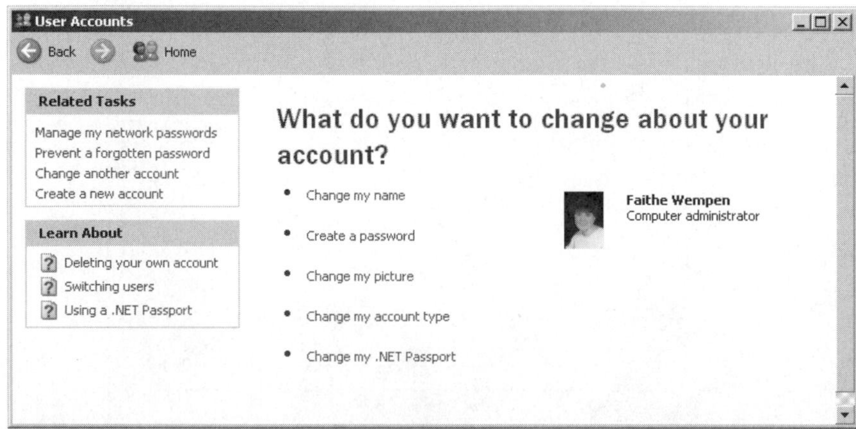


**FIGURE 23.12**
Change user account properties here.

3. To create a new account, click Create a new account and work through the steps presented.

## Accessing Remote Computers on the Network

File sharing is one of the main benefits of networking. When two or more PCs are connected on a network, one PC can access files on the other PC's hard drive.

**WARNING**

**By default, nothing is shared on a PC. You must turn on sharing for the folders or drives that you want to share. This is for your own protection. You will learn how to share later in the chapter.**

Network file sharing occurs at the folder or drive level. You cannot share individual files. Either an entire folder (or an entire drive) is shared, or it is not shared. Only shared folders and shared drives show up when you browse the network, or when you set up a shortcut to point to a folder or drive.

### Browsing the Network

The most straightforward way of accessing a file on the network is to browse for it in My Network Places (Network Neighborhood in Windows 95/98). It acts just like My Computer, allowing you to browse in progressively more detail until you find what you want.

The basic process for browsing is the same in all Windows versions and with all types of networks, but the details vary. You saw this in Chapter 22 when you were testing the network you set up by checking whether the PC could see any other PCs.

#### *Browsing the Network in Windows 95/98*

In these OS versions, network browsing is straightforward. Just start with Network Neighborhood and browse through the levels to find what you want.

To browse the network in Windows 95/98:

1. Double-click the *Network Neighborhood* icon on the desktop.
2. If an icon appears for the computer you want to browse, double-click it; otherwise double-click the *Entire Network* icon and then locate the computer you want.

### *Browsing the Network in Windows 2000 or Windows Me*

Windows 2000 and Windows Me let you create Network Places shortcuts (the procedure is described later in this chapter). These are special icons that refer to network locations, and they appear at the top level for easy access when you are browsing the network. When you open the *My Network Places* folder, you can choose to browse the network or you can jump immediately to a location represented by one of the Network Places shortcuts.

To browse the network in Windows 2000 or Me:

1. Double-click the *My Network Places* icon on the desktop. A window appears with any existing shortcuts. If a shortcut appears for the network location you want, double-click to view it directly. Otherwise, go on to step 2.
2. If there is a *Computers Near Me* icon in the window, double-click it to see the computers in the local workgroup (see Figure 23.13). If not, double-click the *Entire Network* icon to browse the whole network.
3. In Windows Me, a mostly blank window might appear at this point. If it does, click the *View the entire contents of this folder* hyperlink at the left to display icons for the workgroups or domains.
4. Continue double-clicking icons to find the computer, then the drive or folder you want. When you see the file you want, you can open it, delete it, copy it, or perform any other operation upon it that you could perform with a locally stored file.

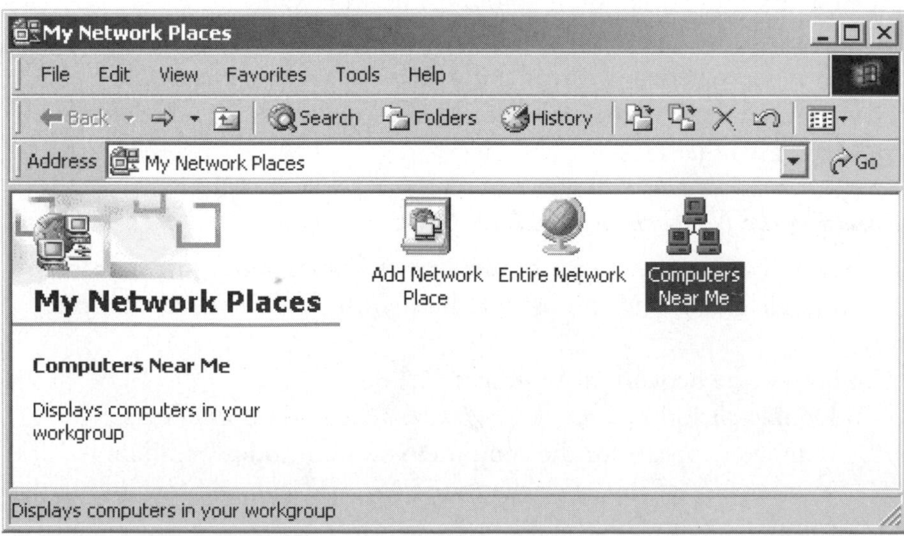


**FIGURE 23.13**
In Windows 2000 you might have a choice of the local workgroup or the larger network.

### *Browsing the Network in Windows XP*

The following steps show how to browse a workgroup in Windows XP. If there is a client/server network instead of a workgroup, you will be able to browse computers in a domain, but the principles are similar.

To browse the network in Windows XP:

1. Choose Start/My Network Places, or double-click the *My Network Places* icon on the desktop. A window appears with any existing shortcuts (called network places) that have been set up (see Figure 23.14). If a shortcut appears for the network location you want, double-click it to view it directly. Otherwise, go on to step 2.

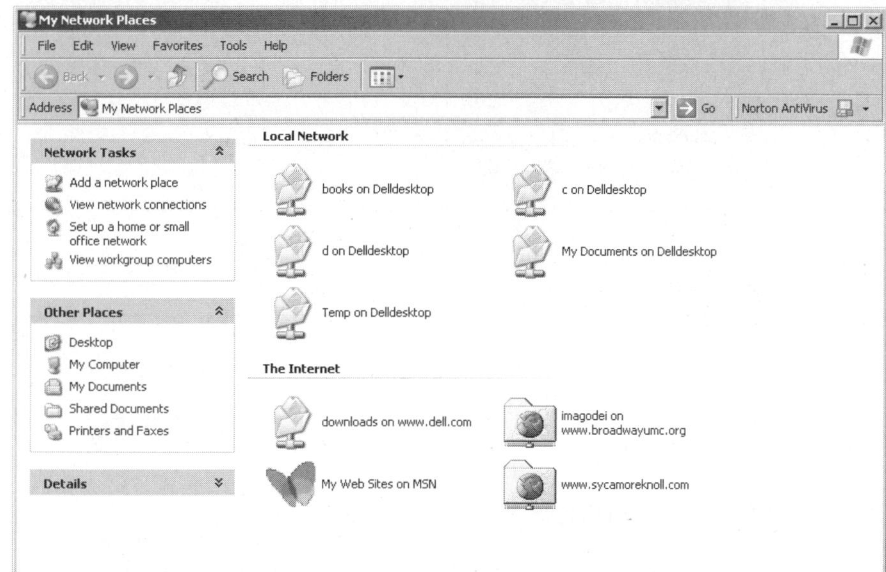


**FIGURE 23.14**
The My Network Places Window in Windows XP

2. Click View workgroup computers on the Network Tasks bar to the left of the main window. A window appears containing icons for each of the PCs in the workgroup.
3. Double-click the computer you want to browse. Icons appear for any drives that contain any shared folders, or that are shared in entirety. For example, in Figure 23.15 there are two shared items: the entire C drive and the *My Documents* folder.
4. Double-click the drive or folder you want, and keep going until you see the file you want. From there you can open it, delete it, copy it, or perform any other operation upon it that you could perform with a locally stored file (provided, of course, that you have permission to do so; permissions are discussed later in this chapter).

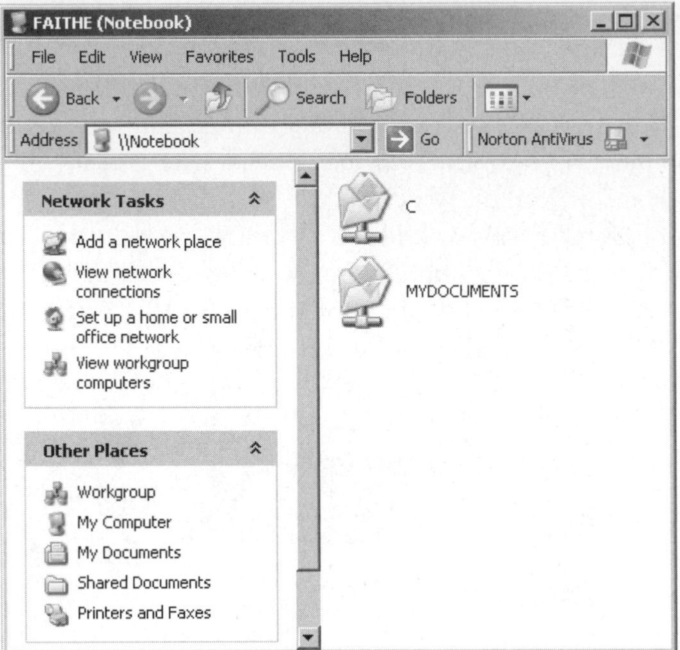


**FIGURE 23.15**
Shared drives or folders appear for the selected computer.

## TRY IT!

**Using whatever version of Windows is available, browse the shared folders on the network.**

## Setting Up a Network Shortcut

Browsing the network to find the desired resources can take a long time, as you saw in the preceding sections, so if your clients use a particular network file or folder regularly you will probably want to create a shortcut for it.

**Network place**

A shortcut to a folder or drive that does not reside on the local PC, usually set up through My Network Places in Windows.

In Windows Me, 2000, and XP you can create a shortcut called a *network place*. Network place shortcuts appear in the *My Network Places* folder, as you saw in Figure 23.13. You can also place copies of them on the desktop or anywhere else that a normal shortcut can go.

In Windows 95 and 98 you can create shortcuts to network resources just like any other shortcuts, but they are not "special"—that is, Windows does not treat them any differently from local shortcuts—and they do not appear as a group in the *Network Neighborhood* folder.

### *Creating a Network Shortcut in Windows 95/98*

There is no wizard in these OS versions, so you must create the shortcut manually.

To set up additional shortcuts in Windows 95/98:

1. Open the folder into which you want to place the shortcut. You can also choose to place the shortcut directly on the desktop if you prefer.
2. Double-click the *Network Neighborhood* icon on the desktop.
3. Browse to locate the folder or drive for which you want to create the shortcut, and select it.
4. Drag the folder or drive to the desktop or to the folder location where you want it. If you drag anywhere except to the desktop, a box appears saying that you cannot move or copy, and asking whether you want to create a shortcut; click Yes. If you drag to the desktop, the shortcut is simply created.

### *Creating a Network Place Shortcut in Windows 2000 or Me*

Both of these OSes can be set up to automatically recognize some shared locations as shortcuts. Whenever a certain drive or folder is explicitly shared on another computer (not just its parent drive or folder, but that drive or folder specifically), it appears as a Network Places shortcut.

To set up additional shortcuts in Windows 2000 or Me:

1. Double-click the *My Network Places* icon on the desktop.
2. Double-click the *Add Network Place* icon. The Add Network Place Wizard opens.
3. Key the path to the network location to which you want the shortcut to refer, or click the Browse button to locate it. If you use Browse, a Browse For Folder dialog box appears, as in Figure 23.16. Click a plus sign next to a resource to see what is available on it, then make your selection and click OK. Click Next.
4. Key a name for the Network Place. This will be the text that appears with its icon. Click Finish.

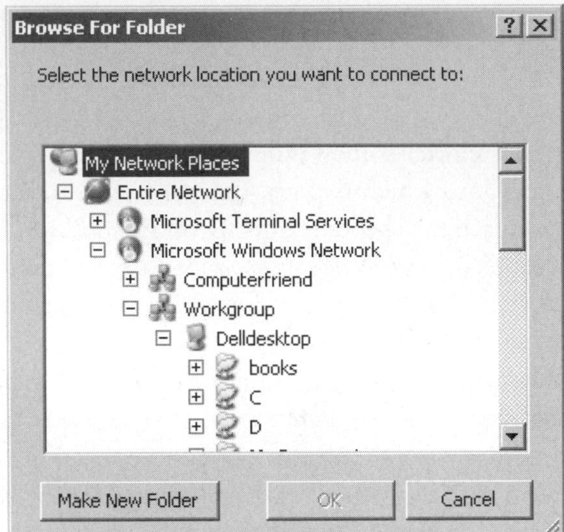


**FIGURE 23.16**
Select the drive or folder for the shortcut.

### *Creating a Network Place Shortcut in Windows XP*

Like Windows 2000 and Me, Windows XP also sets up some shortcuts automatically.

To set up additional shortcuts in Windows XP:

1. Choose Start/My Network Places.
2. Click Add a network place. The Add Network Place Wizard opens.
3. Click Next to begin the wizard. A list of service providers appears after a brief wait. Click Choose another network location and then click Next.
4. Key the path to the network location to which you want the shortcut to refer, or click the Browse button to locate it. It can be a Web location or an FTP site, but it will most likely be a folder or drive on the LAN. If you use Browse, a Browse For Folder dialog box appears, as in Figure 23.16. Click a plus sign next to a resource to see what is available on it, then make your selection and click OK. Click Next.
5. Key a name for the network place. This will be the text that appears with its icon. Click Next.
6. Click Finish. The wizard closes and the chosen location (folder or drive) opens in a new window.

**TRY IT!**

**Using any available version of Windows, create several shortcuts to network folders.**

## MAPPING A NETWORK DRIVE

Windows 95 and higher make it fairly easy to browse network resources and set up shortcuts, as you have seen in this chapter. However, it was not so easy in the past. In the days of MS-DOS and Windows 3.x, in order to use a network drive it was necessary to create a link between it and a drive letter on the local PC so that the PC would be tricked into thinking that the network location was one of its own drives. This is still necessary in most 16-bit applications (such as Windows programs designed to work under Windows 3.x). The process of linking a network location to a local drive letter is known as *mapping* a network drive.

**Mapping**

Creating a link between a name and a location. For example, mapping a network drive makes a network drive or folder appear as a local drive letter on a client PC.

Even though most 32-bit applications are network-aware, mapping a network drive still has its benefits. In a client/server network where the file server has a complex system of file storage involving very long paths, it can be much easier for a client PC to see a particular shared folder as a drive rather than as that folder's real name. For example, it is much easier to tell an employee to "look on the K drive for it" than "look in the *C:\Shared files\marketing\current\letters\clients* folder."

When you map a network drive, you can choose whether or not to have the mapped connection reestablished each time the PC starts up. If you choose not to, the mapping goes away when the client PC restarts or logs off the network.

The procedure is basically the same in all Windows versions.

1. Double-click the *Network Neighborhood* or *My Network Places* icon on the desktop.
2. Browse to the drive or folder you want to map, and select its icon.
3. Choose File/Map Network Drive. (In Windows XP the command is on the Tools menu; see the information that follows these steps.) The Map Network Drive dialog box opens. Figure 23.17 shows the dialog box for Windows 98. It looks slightly different in other versions, but has the same options.

Map Network Drive

Drive: E:

Path: \\DELLDESKTOP\books

Reconnect at logon

OK

Cancel

**FIGURE 23.17**
Mapping a Network Drive in Windows 95/98/Me

4. Select the drive letter you want to use from the Drive drop-down list.
5. If you want the mapping to persist each time you restart, mark the Reconnect at logon check box.
6. Click OK. A window for that location opens.

In Windows Me and 2000, the Map Network Drive command also appears on the Tools menu; you can select it from either place. In Windows XP, it appears *only* on the Tools menu.

There is a subtle difference between selecting the command from the File menu versus the Tools menu in Windows Me and 2000. The command on the File menu is available only if you have selected the icon for something that is mappable (that is, a drive or folder). The command on the Tools menu is available all of the time, and when you use it, the Folder text box is available in the Map Network Drive dialog box, so you can change the network path to which the shortcut refers if you want. (It is grayed out when you run the command from the File menu.)

To disconnect (unmap) a network drive, choose Tools, Disconnect Network Drive.

## Sharing Local Folders and Printers

By default, all PCs start out with nothing shared, and then each PC user must explicitly share any resources desired. Sharing is not automatically reciprocal; one PC can share its files with other computers without those others sharing anything in return.

### Installing File and Printer Sharing

In order for a PC to share anything (files or printers), the File and Printer Sharing for Microsoft Networks service must be installed. Some versions of Windows install it automatically; others do not.

To check to see whether it is installed, right-click a folder and look for a Sharing command on the shortcut menu. If it appears, File and Printer Sharing for Microsoft Networks is installed. If it does not appear, install the service as you learned in Chapter 22.

In Windows 95/98/Me only, there is a shortcut for installing the service:

1. At the Network dialog box, click the File and Print Sharing button on the Configuration tab. A dialog box appears with two check boxes, as shown in Figure 23.18.
2. Select both check boxes and click OK.
3. If prompted for the Windows CD, insert it and click OK.
4. If prompted to restart the computer, click Yes. When you restart, the service will have been installed.

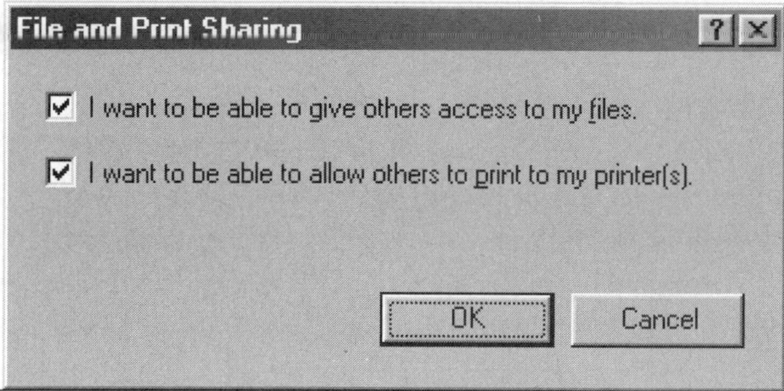


**FIGURE 23.18**
Enable file and printer sharing here in Windows 95/98/Me.

In Windows 2000 or XP, if File and Printer Sharing is not already installed, do the following:

1. At the Network Connections window, right-click the connection for the LAN and choose Properties.
2. If File and Printer Sharing for Microsoft Networks does not appear on the General tab's list of components, click Add and add it as you learned in Chapter 22.

## SHARING A FOLDER

Sharing a folder makes it available to other network users. You can also share an entire drive, but in most cases it is a better security decision to share only the specific folders that others need to access.

The procedure for sharing a folder is nearly the same in all Windows versions, with a few variations as outlined in the following sections. In each version you turn on sharing for the folder, specify a *share name* for it, and indicate whether other users should be able to make changes to the contents of the shared folder.

**Share name**

The name by which remote users of a shared resource will know it. This can be the same as the local name for the item or it can be different.

**WARNING**

If PCs running operating systems that do not support long file names (e.g., MS-DOS or Windows 3.x) might be using the shared folder, limit the share name to eight characters with no spaces.

**WARNING**

Security experts recommend not sharing an entire hard drive, especially the one on which Windows is installed or the one from which you boot. That is because such sharing opens the possibility of others making changes to the drive content that will prevent the PC from booting. Share only the folders that need to be shared.

### *Sharing a Folder in Windows 95/98/Me*

1. From My Computer, right-click the icon for the folder or drive you want to share and choose Sharing. The Properties dialog box for that folder opens with the Sharing tab selected.
2. Click the Shared As option button.
3. If you want the share name to be different from the actual folder name, change the name in the Share Name text box (see Figure 23.19).
4. In the Access Type section, choose whether you want others to be able to make changes (Full) or not (Read-Only). If you want to grant password-based full access, choose Depends on Password.
5. In the Passwords section, enter any passwords you want to assign. If you do not assign a password, everyone will have that level of access.

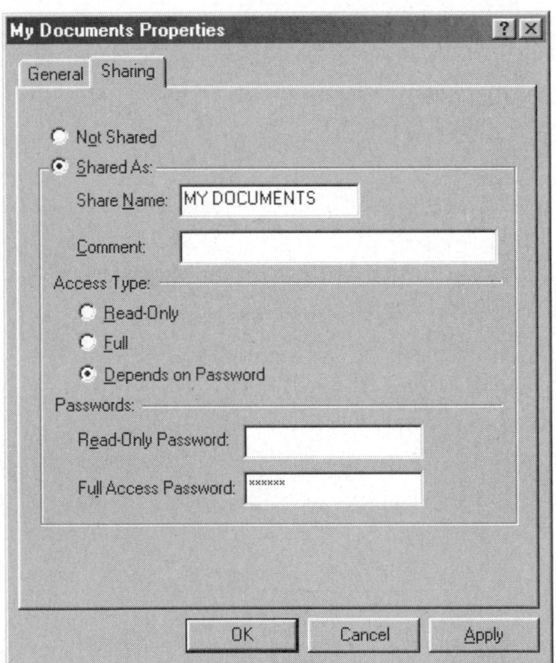


**FIGURE 23.19**
Sharing a Folder in Windows 98

## IN REAL LIFE

If you use Depends on Password in step 4, you might want to leave the Read-Only Password blank in step 5 and set a password only for Full Access.

6. Click OK. A confirmation box appears for the passwords.
7. Rekey them and click OK. The folder's icon changes to show a hand underneath it, indicating that it is now shared.

### *Sharing a Folder in Windows 2000*

1. From My Computer, right-click the icon for the folder or drive you want to share and choose Sharing. The Properties dialog box for that folder opens with the Sharing tab selected.
2. Click the Share this folder option button (see Figure 23.20).

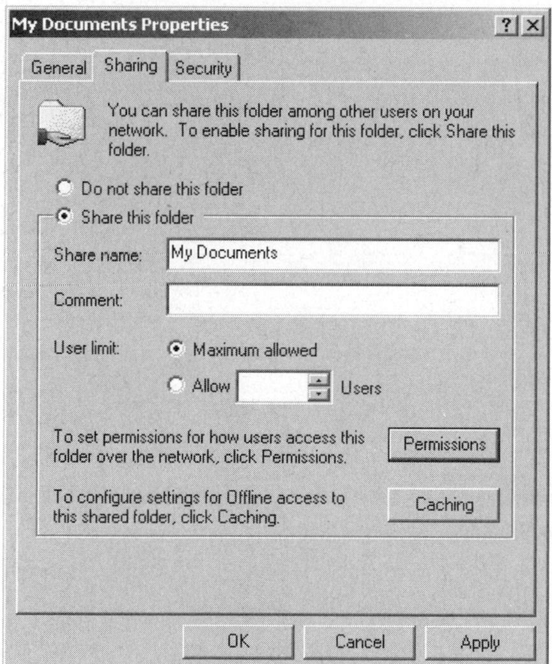


**FIGURE 23.20**
Sharing a Folder in Windows 2000

3. If you want the share name to be different from the actual folder name, change the name in the Share name text box.
4. If you want to set a limit for the maximum number of simultaneous users for the folder, enter it in the Allow ____ Users text box.
5. By default the folder is shared with full permission for everyone. To change that, click the Permissions button and assign different permissions to different groups and individuals, as in Figure 23.21. There will be more details on this later in the chapter.
6. Click OK. A hand appears beneath the icon indicating that it is shared.

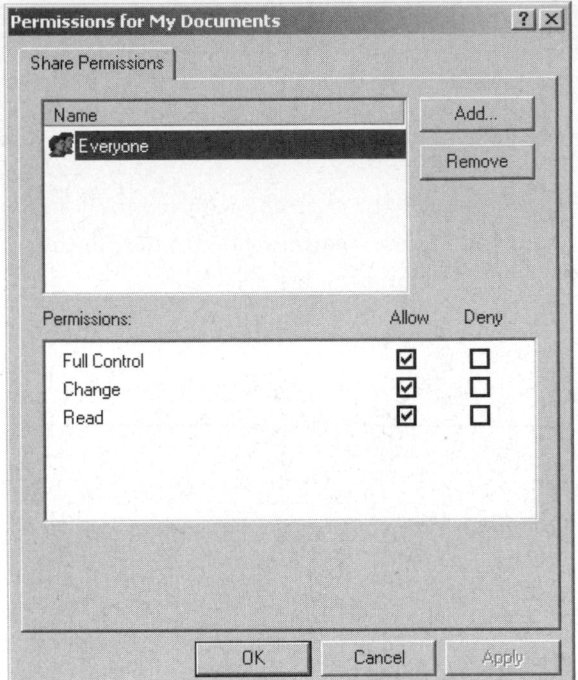


**FIGURE 23.21**
By default, everyone has full permission for the shared folder.

> **WARNING**
>
> When removing permissions, deselect the Allow check box rather than selecting Deny. Deny overrides Allow, so if you have nested levels of permissions (covered later in the chapter), and you forget that you have set a certain folder to Deny, you could spend hours trying to track down why a particular user cannot access that resource.

### *Sharing a Folder in Windows XP*

Windows XP has two settings for file sharing: simple and normal. Simple is enabled by default. It provides only very basic file sharing settings, and is suitable for beginning end users because it is not confusing. To share a folder when simple file sharing is on, do the following:

1. From My Computer, right-click the icon for the folder or drive you want to share and choose Sharing and Security. The Properties dialog box for that folder opens with the Sharing tab selected (see Figure 23.22). If your screen does not look like Figure 23.22, simple file sharing is probably turned off; see the next set of steps.
2. Select the Share this folder on the network check box.

3. *Optional:* If you want to grant full access, mark the Allow network users to change my files check box.
4. Click OK.

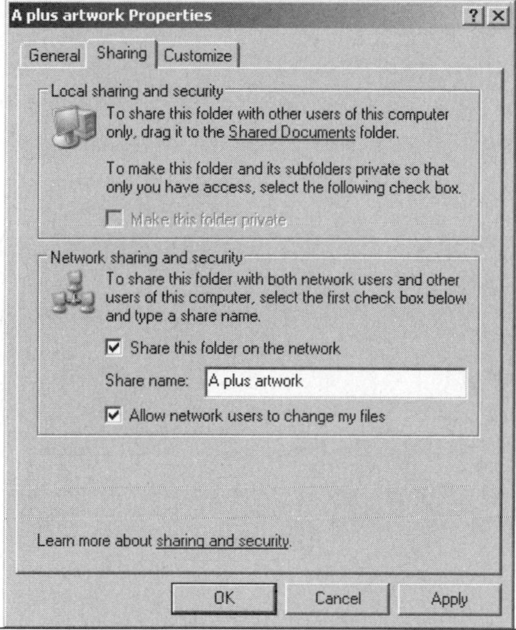


**FIGURE 23.22**
Sharing a Folder in Windows XP with Simple File Sharing Enabled

The disadvantage of simple file sharing is that you cannot specify which users get full versus read-only access to the shared folder, nor can you establish a sharing password. To get that capability, you must turn off simple file sharing.

To change the simple file sharing setting:

1. From My Computer, choose Tools/Options.
2. Select the View tab.
3. Scroll down to the bottom of the Advanced Settings list and deselect the Use simple file sharing check box.
4. Click OK.

After you turn off simple file sharing, the steps for sharing a folder are the same as those for Windows 2000 (except the command name on the right-click menu in step 1 is Sharing and Security, rather than Sharing).

## Sharing a Printer

Sharing a printer in any of the Windows versions involves the same basic process as sharing a folder except you start with the printer's properties (from the *Printers* folder) rather than from the Control Panel.

1. Choose Start/Settings/Printers (or Printers and Faxes in Windows XP).
2. Right-click the printer and choose Sharing. The printer's Properties dialog box opens with the Sharing tab selected (see Figure 23.23).
3. Choose Shared as (or Share this printer in Windows XP).
4. Change the share name if desired.
5. Set any other sharing options desired, as with folders.
6. Click OK. The printer's icon appears with a hand under it, indicating it is shared.

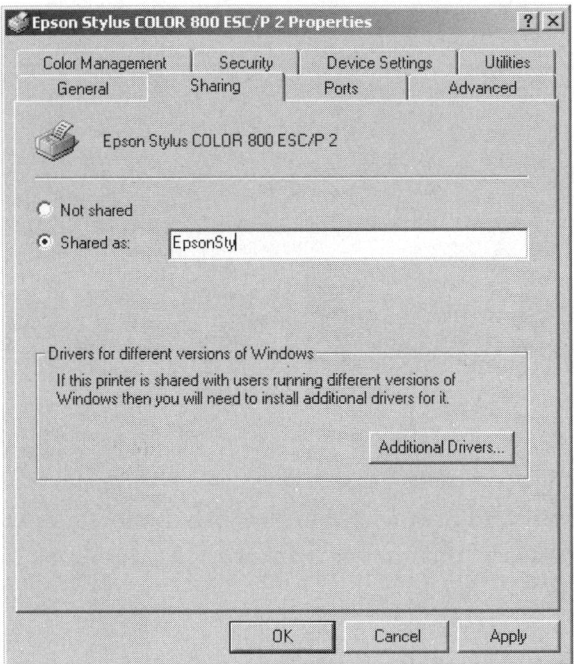


**FIGURE 23.23**
Sharing a Printer (Windows 2000 Shown Here)

Windows 2000 and XP have some additional sharing options on the Advanced tab of the printer's Properties dialog box. For example, you can limit the time of day during which the printer should be shared, and you can set up a *separator page*.

**Separator page**

A page that prints before a print job reporting the user and computer that initiated the job. Used on network-shared printers to organize the printouts from multiple users.

## Loading Additional Printer Drivers for Sharing

In Windows 2000 and XP, an Additional Drivers button appears in the printer's Properties dialog box, as in Figure 23.23. This feature enables you to load drivers for the printer for other Windows versions. Suppose, for example, one PC runs Windows 2000 and there are two other users in the workgroup—one with Windows 2000 and one with Windows 98. Both want to set up the shared printer as a network printer. Any printer must have a driver installed for it, so each of those users will need to have either the driver disk that came with the printer or a copy of the driver from the initial PC. The Windows 2000 user has no problem—when she installs the network printer on her PC, her PC copies the driver from the initial PC automatically. However, the Windows 98 user cannot do that because the driver needed is not the driver on the initial PC. Therefore, he must use the setup disk for the printer. If that disk is not available, he cannot set up the printer. By installing additional drivers through the printer properties, you make additional drivers available automatically through the network to other users who need them, so you do not have to use the setup disk.

When you click the Additional Drivers button, a dialog box appears listing the available drivers for that printer. Mark the ones you want to install and click OK (see Figure 23.24).

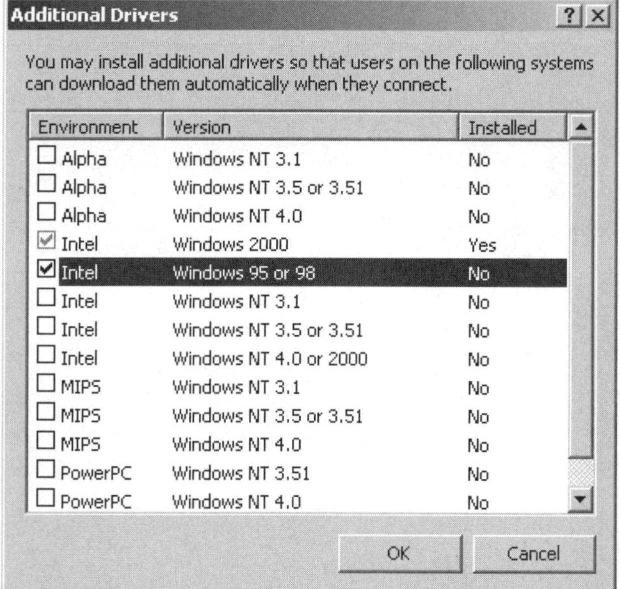


**FIGURE 23.24**
You can make additional drivers available for other operating systems.

## TRY IT!

1. Share your default printer.
2. Make the Windows 95/98 drivers for your default printer available to other networked PCs.

## Using a Network Printer

If you want to set up a client PC to use a printer that another PC is sharing, you can do it through the Add Printer Wizard, the same as a local printer (see Chapter 18), except you specify that it is a network printer.

When you install a network printer, an icon for the printer appears in the *Printers* folder with a bar under it indicating it is a network printer. It shows up in the Print dialog box in any applications that allow you to select a printer.

To use a network printer in Windows 95/98/Me:

1. Open the *Printers* folder (Start/Settings/Printers) and double-click the *Add Printer* icon. The Add Printer Wizard runs.
2. Click Next to begin. Click Network Printer and then click Next.
3. Click the Browse button to locate the printer. In the Browse for Printer dialog box, click the plus signs to find the shared printer, and then select it (see Figure 23.25). Click OK.

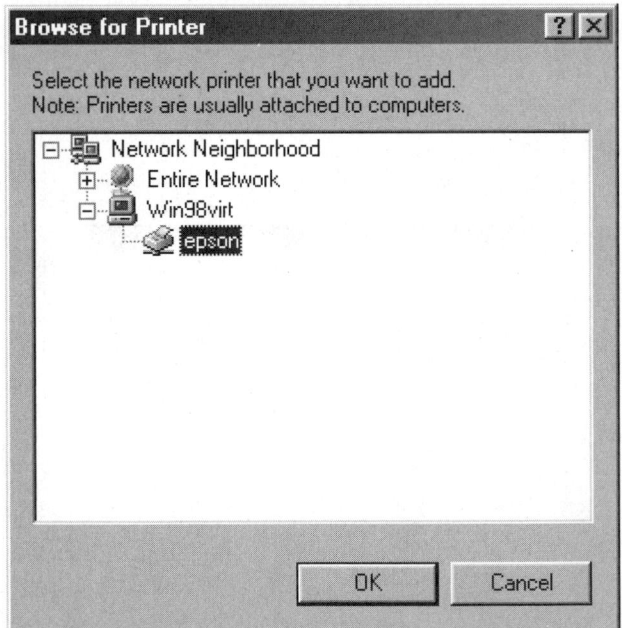


**FIGURE 23.25**
Browse for the network printer from which you want to print on the local PC.

4. Choose Yes or No to be able to print from MS-DOS programs, then click Next.
5. Confirm the printer name and specify whether it should be the default printer. (This is the same as setting up a local printer, discussed in Chapter 18). Click Next.
6. Click Yes or No to print a test page, then click Finish.

To use a network printer in Windows 2000:

1. Open the *Printers* folder (Start/Settings/Printers) and double-click the *Add Printer* icon. The Add Printer Wizard runs.
2. Click Next to begin. Click Network Printer and then click Next.
3. If you know the name and network path of the printer, key it; otherwise click Next to browse for it. If you choose to browse for it, click it on the Shared printers list that appears and then click Next (see Figure 23.26).

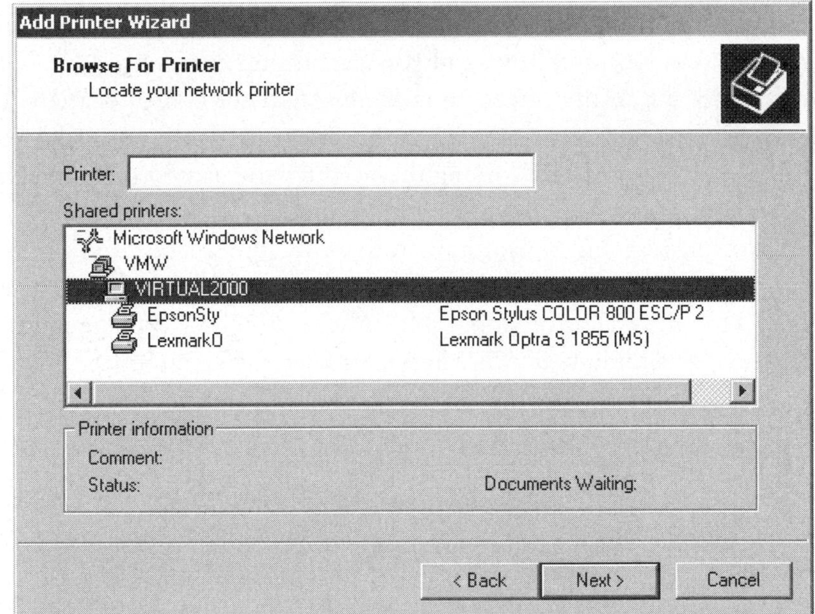


**FIGURE 23.26**
The Add Printer Wizard in Windows 2000 presents the available shared printers in a list.

4. Choose Yes or No to set the printer as the default printer, and then click Next.
5. Click Finish.

To use a network printer in Windows XP:

1. Open the *Printers and Faxes* folder (Start/Printers and Faxes) and click the *Add a Printer* hyperlink. The Add Printer Wizard runs.
2. Leave the Browse for a printer option selected and click Next.
3. Click the printer you want to share (the box is similar to that shown in Figure 23.26) and then click Next.
4. Click Yes or No to set the printer as the default printer, and then click Next.
5. Click Finish.

## Network Permissions and Security Settings

Windows 95, 98, and Me have very simple sharing permissions, which you saw earlier in the chapter when you learned about sharing folders. You can specify read-only or full access to a folder, and you can assign passwords for one or both types of access. Access to the local computer itself is not restricted, as you saw at the beginning of the chapter; anyone can click Cancel at the Logon screen to bypass it. Access to shared resources is based on passwords, rather than user logon.

However, Windows 2000 and XP have much more sophisticated permission and security settings. You can prevent unauthorized users from logging on to the local machine, and you can assign permissions for network folder and printer access to individual users or groups of users. Access to network resources is based on the user name and password under which the user is logged in, avoiding the need for the user to remember a separate password for accessing a network resource.

The following sections explain how to fine-tune the permissions assigned for sharing certain resources so that different users can have different levels of access. This information is applicable only to Windows 2000 and Windows XP, as Windows 95/98/Me do not have this capability.

### How Permissions Are Administered

In a workgroup network environment, each PC is responsible for maintaining its own list of variations in user access. All permissions—whether permission to log on to the network or to access the folders through the network—are stored on the individual client PC.

In a client/server domain, the permission to log on to the network is based on user names stored in the user directory on the server, and the individual PC has no control over that directory. However, the individual PC still maintains a list of allowed users for logging in to the local PC. The individual PC also maintains the permissions for using its own shared resources, such as local folders and printers, but when granting a new user permission it is able to pull names from the server's directory.

### Assigning Permissions to a Resource

You can assign permissions to a resource for a user or a group. However, except in the smallest of workgroup networks, you should assign permissions to resources in Windows 2000/XP based on groups rather than on individuals, thereby making it much easier to make changes.

Windows already has several groups set up for you, including Administrators, Power Users, and Users. You saw these groups earlier in the chapter (Figure 23.7) when you added users to a Windows 2000/XP system for logging in. When you create a user, you assign him or her to at least one group. Each user is also a member of the Everyone group.

By default, the Everyone group has access to each shared resource (folder, drive, or printer). You can modify the permissions for a resource so that the Everyone group has less than full permission, and/or you can add other groups to the list and assign different permissions to those groups.

### *Changing the Permissions for the Everyone Group*

If you do not want everyone to have full permission to a shared resource, change the permission settings for the Everyone group. The Everyone group refers to all users, so you modify it whenever the changes you want to make are not user specific.

1. Right-click the resource's icon and choose Sharing (or Sharing and Security in Windows XP).
2. Click the Permissions button. The Permissions dialog box for that resource opens.
3. Clear one or more of the check boxes for the permissions available for that resource. In Figure 23.27, for example, the Everyone group is permitted only read access to the folder.
4. Click OK.

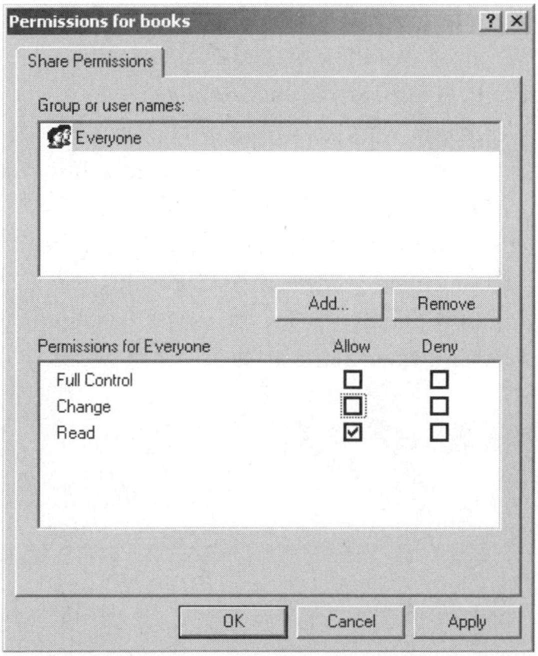

**FIGURE 23.27**
Change permission for the Everyone group to control overall permission for the shared resource, regardless of the user.

**WARNING**

Except in very rare circumstances, do not use the Deny check box column. If you want to remove a permission, simply remove the check mark from the Allow column. Subfolders inherit permissions from main folders, and Deny overrides Allow, so permission conflicts can result if you forget that you have set a particular permission to Deny.

### *Adding a Permission to a Resource*

To give different permission to a particular group, add that group to the permissions for the resource and then make its settings different from those of the Everyone group.

The overall result is the same in Windows 2000 and XP, but the procedure varies slightly because of different ways of viewing and selecting existing groups. The procedure will also vary a bit for a client/server domain that maintains lists of users and groups; the figures in this chapter show a workgroup.

To add a permission in Windows 2000:

1. Right-click the resource's icon and choose Sharing.
2. Click the Permissions button. The Permissions dialog box for that resource opens.
3. Click the Add button. A box appears for selecting the users or groups you want.
4. Open the Look in drop-down list and choose where you want to look for the users and groups. To look on the local PC (for a workgroup), choose the local PC; to look on the domain controller for a client/server network, choose the domain.
5. Select the group you want to add, and click the Add button. The group names all in caps are system-generated groups; scroll down the list to find other groups (see Figure 23.28).
6. Add more groups if desired (or add individual users, although this is not usually recommended) and then click OK.
7. In the Permissions dialog box for the resource (Figure 23.27), select the new group and then mark or clear check boxes to define its permissions.
8. Click OK.

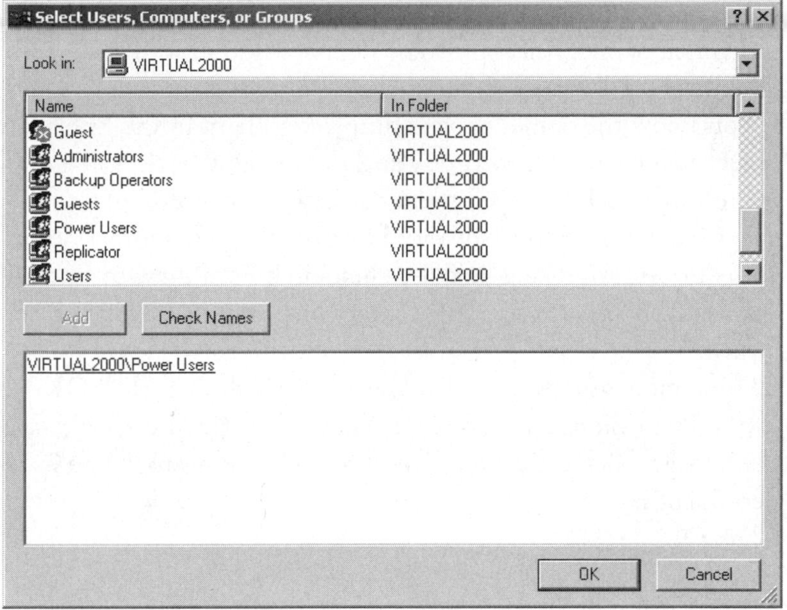


**FIGURE 23.28**
Adding More Groups to the Permissions for a Resource in Windows 2000

To add a permission in Windows XP:

1. Right-click the resource's icon and choose Sharing.
2. Click the Permissions button. The Permissions dialog box for that resource opens.
3. Click the Add button. A box appears for selecting the users or groups you want (see Figure 23.29).

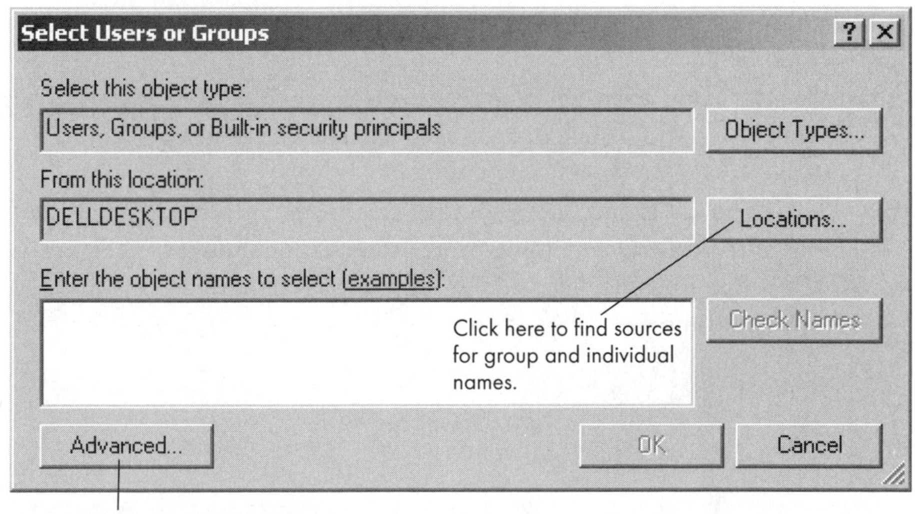


**FIGURE 23.29**
Adding Groups to a Resource's Permissions in Windows XP

4. Click the Locations button to open a list of sources for group and individual names. Select the local PC (workgroup) or the domain (client/server domain) and then click OK to return.
5. If you know the names of the groups, key them in the Enter the object names to select text box and then click Check Names to make sure you have keyed them correctly. If you do not know the group names, click the Advanced button to open another Select Users or Groups dialog box and then click Find Now to find all of the available users and groups. Select one and then click OK to return.
6. Choose more groups (or individuals) if desired, then click OK.
7. In the Permissions dialog box for the resource (Figure 23.27), select the new group and then mark or clear check boxes to define its permissions.
8. Click OK.

### *Removing a Group or Individual Permission*

To remove a permission from a resource, select the user or group name in its Permissions dialog box and click Remove. You can remove any group, even the Everyone group, from a resource.

## Managing Local Group Membership

Groups that are defined by the domain controller cannot be changed at the local level; you must ask the network administrator to add or remove a user from a group. However, the local users and groups on the individual PC may be modified at any time.

To access the Local Users and Groups controls:

1. From the Control Panel, double-click *Administrative Tools.*
2. Double-click *Computer Management.*
3. Click Local Users and Groups on the folder tree.
4. Double-click the *Groups* folder to see the existing groups (see Figure 23.30). From here you can add groups, add or remove users from groups, and more.

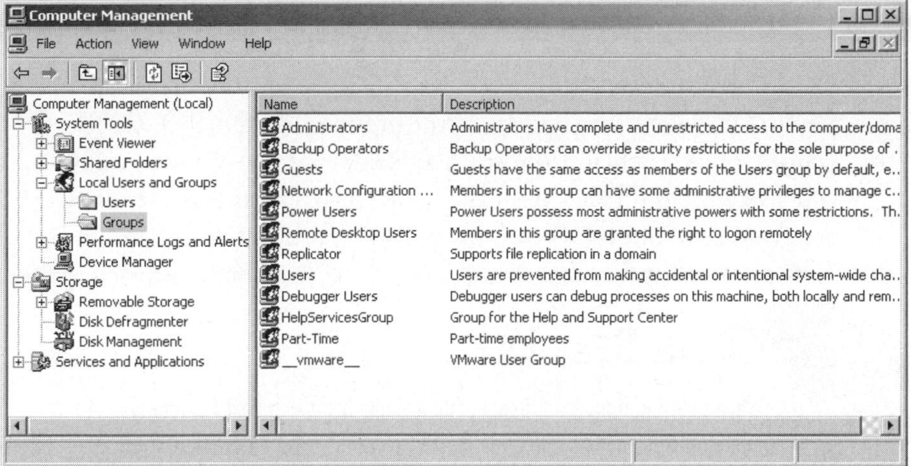


**FIGURE 23.30**
Manage local users and groups here.

### *Creating a New Group*

Create a new group whenever the existing ones do not let you differentiate adequately between users based on a needed criterion. For example, you might want to create new groups to represent such organizational divisions in a company as Sales, Marketing, Accounting, and so on, and then use those groups to assign permissions to certain folders on a file server.

To create a new group:

1. Start in the *Groups* folder in Local Users and Groups (see the preceding set of steps).
2. Choose Action/New Group. The New Group dialog box opens.
3. Key a name and description for the group in the text boxes provided (see Figure 23.31).

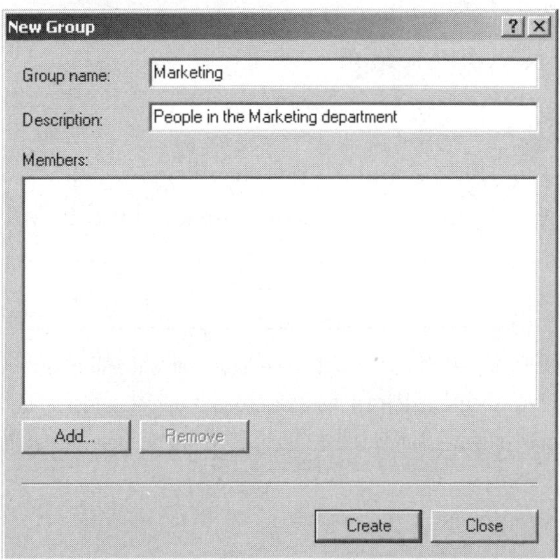


**FIGURE 23.31**
Creating a New Group

4. Click the Add button. The dialog box opens for selecting users or groups, just as you saw in Figure 23.28 for Windows 2000 or Figure 23.29 for Windows XP.
5. Key the user names to be part of the group and then click Check Names, or select them from the list. Remember, in Windows 2000 you select them directly from the list in the top pane of the dialog box, but in Windows XP you must click Advanced and then Find Now to see a list.

**IN REAL LIFE**

**When selecting from a list, names with a single head icon next to them are individuals and names with a multihead icon are groups. You can have groups within groups, but it can make changes unnecessarily complicated, so it is not recommended in most cases.**

6. When you are finished adding users to the group, click OK. Click Create to finish creating the group, and then click Close to close the New Group dialog box.

### *Changing the Membership of a Group*

To modify the membership of a group, double-click it to open its Properties dialog box, which is very similar to the dialog box you worked with when initially creating the group (Figure 23.31). The only difference is that you cannot change the group name. From here you can:

- Change the group description
- Remove a user by selecting the name and clicking Remove
- Add a user by clicking Add and then selecting the user(s) as you did in the steps in the preceding section

### *Creating a New User*

You can create new local users to be a part of the groups for permission assignments. These new users will exist only on the local PC; they will not be a part of any domain-based user directory on the server.

**TRY IT!**

**If you are using Windows XP and you want to create a local user who will physically sit down and log on to this PC, you should do it from the User Accounts applet in the Control Panel. If, on the other hand, the user you are creating will access the PC only through the network, you can use the following procedure.**

1. From Local Users and Groups, click the *Users* folder on the tree to open it.
2. Choose Action/New User. The New User dialog box opens.
3. Key the information for the new user, including user name, description, and password (if desired) (see Figure 23.32).
4. Mark any of the check box options desired. For example, you might want to force the user to change his password the next time he logs on, or you might want to start out with the account disabled (if you are setting it up for future use).
5. Click OK. The new user is created.
6. Click Close to close the New User dialog box.
7. To assign the new user to groups, double-click the new user's name on the list of users.
8. Select the Member Of tab, and then click Add.
9. Select the group(s) to which the user should belong. This is the same interface as selecting groups for permissions to resources (Figure 23.28 for Windows 2000 or Figure 23.29 for Windows XP).
10. Click OK to close the dialog box.

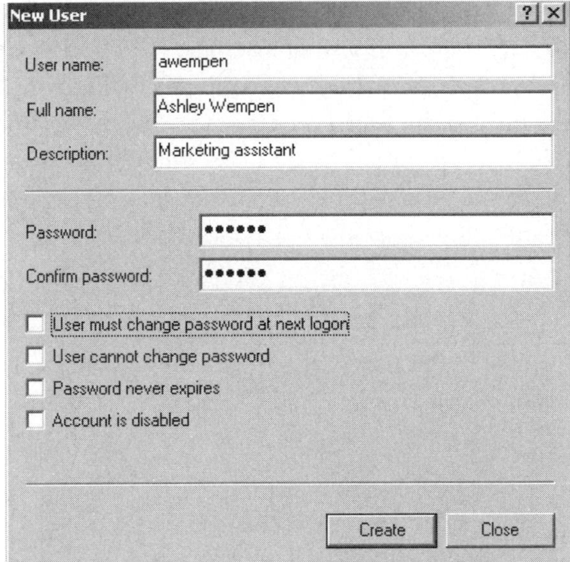


**FIGURE 23.32**
Creating a New User

## TRY IT!

1. Create two new users.
2. Create a Marketing group, and assign both of those users to that group.
3. Grant full permission for a folder on your hard drive to the Marketing group.

## NTFS Permissions

**NTFS permission**

Security permission that allows different users logging on to the same local PC to view one another's files.

If you use Windows 2000 or XP and the drive uses the NTFS file system, there is an additional type of permission you can set—*NTFS permission.* These permissions apply to local access too, not just network access, and are based on Windows 2000/XP's ability to control who logs on to the local PC.

For example, suppose Jane and Jim share a PC, and each has a separate local user name and password. When Jane is logged on, she can set the NTFS permissions for a folder where she keeps her private documents such that those documents are accessible only when she is logged on. When Jim logs on, he will not be able to access them.

**WARNING**

**Beginners often get network sharing permissions and NTFS permissions confused. Network sharing permissions, which we have been talking about up to this point, are applicable only when the PC is accessed via network. NTFS permissions are applicable only at the local level—that is, someone physically logging on to the local PC.**

NTFS permissions are not covered on the A+ exams, but here is a brief description of how they work. If a drive uses the NTFS file system, there will be an extra tab in a drive or folder's Properties dialog box: Security. You set NTFS permissions for the folder on this tab. You can restrict general access (the Everyone group) or access by a specific user or group in basically the same way you restrict access for network file sharing (see Figure 23.33).

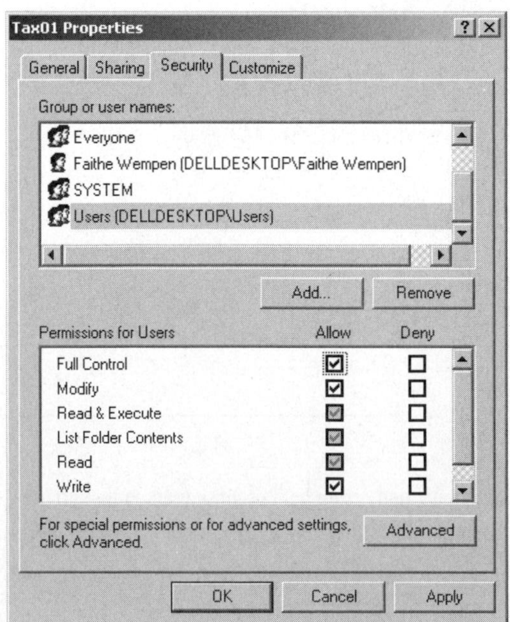


**FIGURE 23.33**
Setting NTFS Security Permission for a Resource

Notice in Figure 23.33 that some of the check boxes are gray, meaning their settings cannot be changed. These represent permissions inherited from a higher level folder or from the permissions for the drive itself. Because permissions can be inherited (or not) from higher level folders, you can set up fairly complex systems of NTFS permissions in a drive's file system. This is beyond the scope of this course, but you might want to experiment with it on your own.

**TRY IT!**

1. Set the NTFS permission for a folder to read-only for everyone.
2. Log on as a different user and try to access that folder. What happens?
3. Log on as yourself again and restore the permissions for that folder for everyone.
4. Log on as a different user and try to access that folder. Can you access it now?

## Troubleshooting Network Problems

When one computer cannot see another in a network, sometimes tracking down the problem can be a challenge because of all of the different layers of utilities, drivers, and hardware that must work for a successful connection to occur.

Here is a general troubleshooting procedure that works in most cases.

1. Confirm that the driver for the NIC is installed and recognized in Windows. (Check in Device Manager.)
2. Confirm that a common protocol is installed on both PCs that are trying to communicate, and that Client for Microsoft Networks is installed.
3. Confirm that the PC that you are trying to access via network has some resources set up to be shared (a drive, a folder, or a printer).
4. Determine the PC's IP address. To do so:
   a. In Windows 95/98/Me, choose Start, Run, key **winipcfg**, and press Enter. A Windows-based IP configuration window opens. Open the drop-down list at the top and select the appropriate Ethernet adapter, and its configuration information appears (see Figure 23.34). Close the utility when finished.

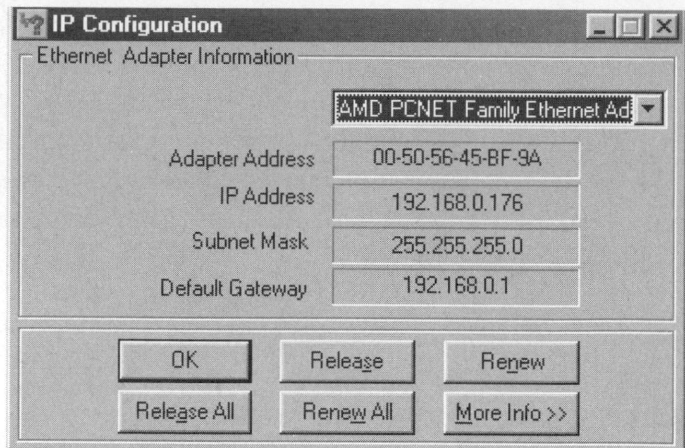


**FIGURE 23.34**
Use winipcfg in Windows 95/98/Me to see the IP address for the NIC.

b. In Windows 2000/XP, display a command prompt (Start, Programs/All Programs, Accessories, Command Prompt), key **ipconfig**, and press Enter. A command line utility reports the IP address, as in Figure 23.35. Close the window when finished.

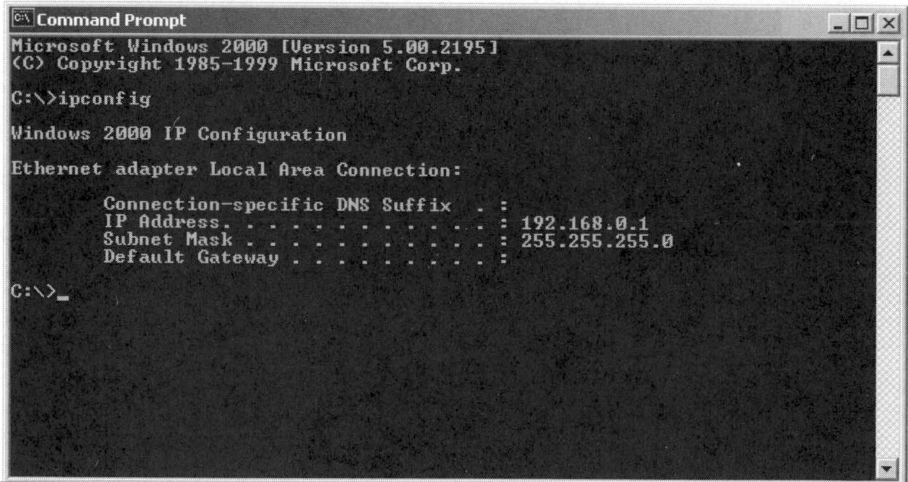


**FIGURE 23.35**
Use ipconfig in Windows 2000/XP to see the IP address for the NIC.

5. Display a command prompt and try a loopback test. To do so, key **ping 127.0.0.1**. This address refers to the initial PC. If a reply comes back, as in Figure 23.36, TCP/IP is working.

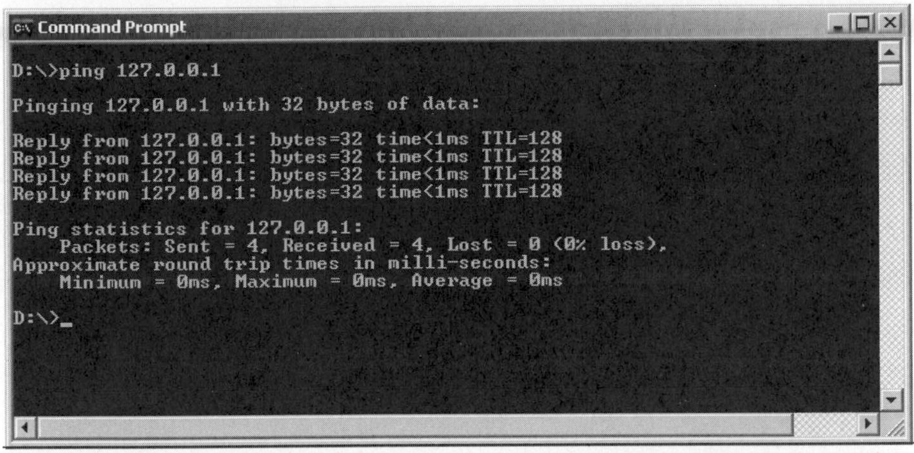

```
D:\>ping 127.0.0.1

Pinging 127.0.0.1 with 32 bytes of data:

Reply from 127.0.0.1: bytes=32 time<1ms TTL=128
Reply from 127.0.0.1: bytes=32 time<1ms TTL=128
Reply from 127.0.0.1: bytes=32 time<1ms TTL=128
Reply from 127.0.0.1: bytes=32 time<1ms TTL=128

Ping statistics for 127.0.0.1:
    Packets: Sent = 4, Received = 4, Lost = 0 (0% loss),
Approximate round trip times in milli-seconds:
    Minimum = 0ms, Maximum = 0ms, Average = 0ms

D:\>_
```

**FIGURE 23.36**
Ping the loopback address to check TCP/IP operation.

6. Ping the initial PC's IP address. Key **ping**, followed by the IP address you determined in step 4. If you get a reply, the PC is set up correctly for networking and the problem is somewhere else on the network (perhaps a physical connection or a problem with another PC's configuration).
7. If there is a default gateway (remember, that is the port that leads out of the local subnet), ping it. If you get a reply, the problem is outside of the local subnet.
8. Find out the IP address of the computer you are trying to reach, and ping it. If it replies, you should be able to access it via My Network Places. If it does not reply, the problem lies somewhere in between; check cables, routers, and anything else that is physically in the path.

## TRY IT!

1. Use winipcfg or ipconfig (depending on your Windows version) to determine your PC's IP address and subnet mask.
2. Ping the address you got in step 1. What reply do you get?
3. Swap IP address information with a classmate and ping each other's PC. What reply do you get?

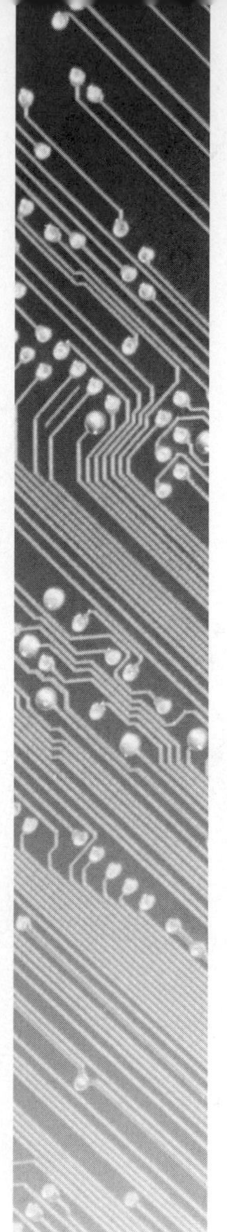

# STUDY GUIDE

Use the following summaries to review the key concepts of this chapter.

## Logging On and Off a Network

- There are two kinds of logons—logging on to the local PC and logging on to the network.
- In Windows 95/98/Me, anyone may log on to the local PC. At the logon box, click Cancel to bypass it. In Windows 2000/XP, only authorized users may log on.
- In a peer-to-peer network each PC manages its own list of users. In a client/server domain network the server maintains the list.
- In Windows 95/98/Me you can select a primary logon in the Network dialog box: Windows Logon or Client for Microsoft Networks.
- To make a Windows 95/98/Me PC part of a domain, open the Network dialog box and double-click *Client for Microsoft Networks.* Select the Log on to Windows NT domain check box and enter the domain name.
- To log off Windows 95/98/Me, choose Start, Log Off.
- To specify whether logon is required in Windows 2000, open Users and Passwords from the Control Panel and, on the Users tab, select or clear the Users must enter a user name and password to use this computer check box.
- To join a domain in Windows 2000, open the System Properties dialog box from the Control Panel, click Network Identification, click Properties, click Domain, and key the domain name.
- After setting up a PC to be part of a domain, an extra box appears on the Logon screen, so you can choose whether to log on to the local PC or to the domain.
- In Windows 2000 you log off by pressing Ctrl + Alt + Delete and clicking Log Off.
- To manage the allowed users for the local PC in Windows 2000, open Users and Passwords from the Control Panel and add or delete users or change passwords.
- Windows XP has a Welcome screen for logging on, from which you can click the user to log on. You can disable the Welcome screen to make Windows XP behave more like Windows 2000.
- To join a domain in Windows XP, open the System Properties dialog box, click Computer Name, click Properties, click Domain, and key the domain name.

- To log off in Windows XP, choose Start/Log Off, and then click Log Off.
- To create and manage users in Windows XP, choose User Accounts from the Control Panel.

## Accessing Remote Computers on the Network

- Network file sharing occurs at the folder or drive level. You cannot share individual files.
- In Windows 95/98, Network Neighborhood is the gateway to shared folders and drives on the LAN. In Windows Me/2000/XP it is called My Network Places.
- The details vary by Windows version and by network type, but generally you can browse the network by double-clicking on icons to arrive at the desired location, just as in My Computer for local drives.
- Windows Me, 2000, and XP let you create Network Places shortcuts, special shortcut icons that refer to network locations. They appear at the top level when browsing the network.
- You can also create normal shortcuts on the desktop for any network location in any Windows version.
- To create a shortcut from Windows 95/98, drag an icon from a network folder to the desktop or to a local folder.
- To create a Network Place in Windows Me/2000/XP, double-click the *Add Network Place* icon in Network Neighborhood.
- Mapping a network drive involves setting up a drive letter alias for a shared network folder. It is useful when the actual network path to a resource is long or when working with 16-bit Windows applications that are not network aware.
- To map a network drive, choose File/Map Network Drive.
- In some Windows versions there is also a Tools/Map Network Drive command. It is virtually identical to the one on the File menu except you are able to change the network path to which the drive letter will refer.

## Sharing Local Folders and Printers

- If you right-click a folder and there is no Sharing command, File and Printer Sharing for Microsoft Networks has not been installed.
- You can install it as a service in the Network properties (Windows 95/98/Me) or in the properties for the LAN connection (Windows 2000/XP).
- In Windows 95/98/Me, to install file and printer sharing, you can click the File and Print Sharing button in the Network dialog box and then select both check boxes in the dialog box that appears.

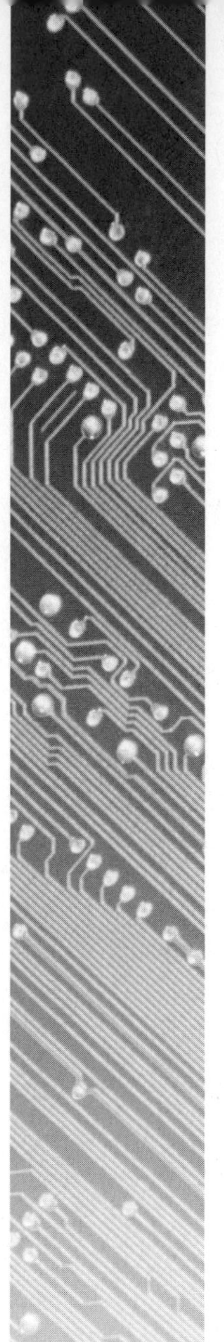

- To share a folder, right-click it and choose Sharing, and then choose Shared As (Windows 95/98/Me) or Share this folder (Windows 2000) or Share this folder on the network (Windows XP).
- In Windows XP, by default simple file sharing is enabled, which provides only minimal permission settings. To turn off simple file sharing, choose Tools/Options, select the View tab, and deselect the Use simple file sharing check box.
- To share a printer, right-click its icon in the *Printers* folder and choose Sharing, and then share it as you would a folder.
- In Windows 2000 and XP you can install additional drivers for a shared printer to allow PCs that run Windows 95/98/Me to connect to it and use it via the network. Click the Additional Drivers button on the Sharing tab for the printer.
- To set up a workstation to use a network-shared printer, run the Add Printer Wizard just as you would for a local printer, but choose Network rather than Local for the printer location. Then browse for and select the network-shared printer.

## Network Permissions and Security Settings

- In a workgroup, each PC maintains its own list of which users are allowed to log on. In a client/server domain, the server maintains the user directory.
- Each PC maintains its own permissions for allowed users for sharing local resources.
- Windows 2000/XP allow you to specify permissions for shared access based on users and groups. Windows 95/98/Me do not have this capability.
- By default the Everyone group has access to each shared resource. You can modify the permissions for a resource so that the Everyone group has less than full permission, and you can add other groups and assign different permissions to those groups.
- To give different permission to a particular group, create the group and add that group to the permissions for the resource, and then make its settings different from those of the Everyone group.
- Permissions are set by clicking the Permissions button on the Sharing tab for the resource.

- To remove a permission from a resource, select the user or group in the Permissions dialog box and click Remove.
- You can manage the list of users and groups from the Local Users and Groups utility. From the Control Panel, double-click *Administrative Tools,* double-click *Computer Management,* and click *Local Users and Groups* on the folder tree.
- From Local Users and Groups you can create a new user or group on the Action menu.
- To change the membership of a group, double-click the group name in Local Users and Groups and then add or remove from there.
- NTFS permissions are totally separate from network sharing permissions, and are available only on drives that use the NTFS file system. They dictate permissions for local users logging on to the local PC.
- To set NTFS permissions, use the Security tab in the resource's Properties dialog box.

## Troubleshooting Network Problems

- Trace network connectivity problems starting with the local PC and working your way out to the network toward the resource that cannot be contacted.
- Start by making sure that the NIC's driver is installed and that there is a common protocol installed as well as Client for Microsoft Networks.
- Check the local PC's IP address with winipfcg (Windows 95/98/Me) or ipconfig (Windows 2000/XP).
- To ping, open a command prompt and key **ping** and then the address to ping.
- Ping the loopback address, 127.0.0.1, to make sure TCP/IP is functional.
- Ping the local PC's IP address to make sure that the PC is network-ready. If it is, then the problem must exist somewhere else on the network.
- Ping the default gateway out of the subnet (if appropriate). If it replies, the problem is outside the local subnet.

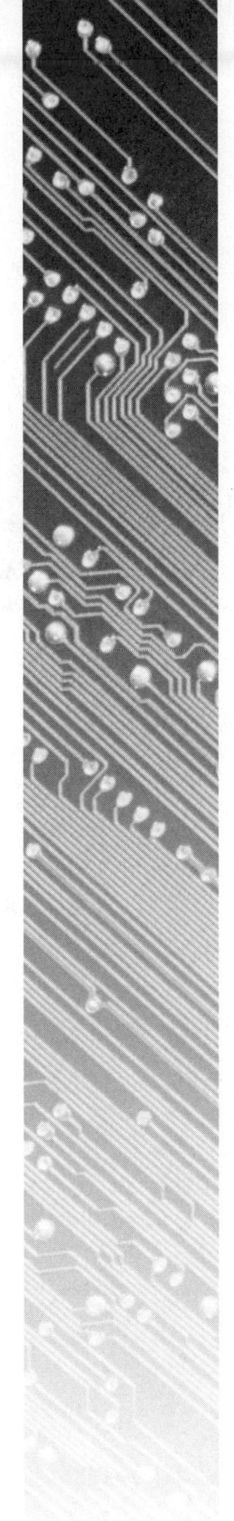

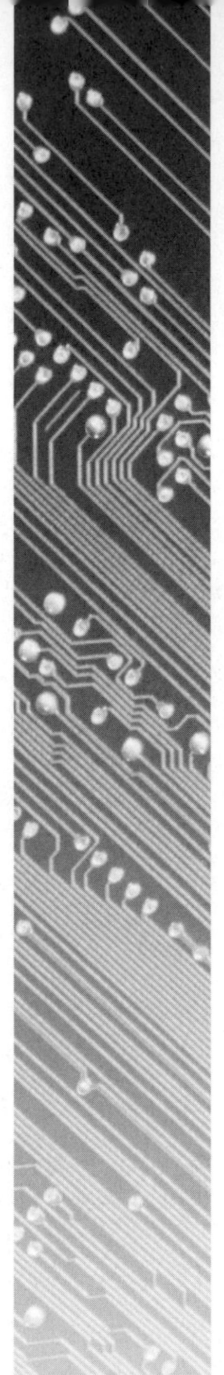

# PRACTICE TEST

On a blank sheet of paper, write the answers to the following multiple-choice questions and explain why each answer is correct.

1. Where are network logon names and passwords stored in a peer-to-peer workgroup network?
   a. on the server
   b. in Active Directory
   c. on a single client for the entire workgroup
   d. on each individual client PC

2. Where in Windows 98 do you select a primary logon?
   a. System Properties
   b. Network
   c. Client for Microsoft Networks Properties
   d. TCP/IP Properties

3. Where in Windows 98 do you specify a domain to which to connect?
   a. System Properties
   b. Users and Groups Manager
   c. Client for Microsoft Networks Properties
   d. TCP/IP Properties

4. How do you log off in Windows 2000?
   a. Press Ctrl + Alt + Delete and click Log Off.
   b. Choose Start, Log Off.
   c. Choose Start, Switch User.
   d. Either a or b will work.

5. Which versions of Windows allow you to use the local PC without logging on by clicking Cancel at the logon screen?
   a. Windows 95 and 98
   b. Windows 95, 98, and Me
   c. Windows 95
   d. Windows 95, 98, and 2000

6. Where in Windows 2000 do you set up a domain to which to connect?
   a. System Properties
   b. Network
   c. Client for Microsoft Networks Properties
   d. TCP/IP Properties

7. Which operating systems use My Network Places to browse the network and allow you set up Network Places shortcuts?
    a. Windows 95, 98, and Me
    b. Windows 2000 and XP
    c. Windows Me, 2000, and XP
    d. Windows Me and XP

8. What does mapping a network drive do?
    a. creates a directory of its content
    b. creates a Network Place shortcut
    c. places a shortcut for the drive on the local desktop
    d. assigns a drive letter to a network location

9. Why is mapping a network drive useful?
    a. It gives users a simpler path to the network resource.
    b. It allows network use in 16-bit Windows programs.
    c. It makes logging on to the network quicker.
    d. both a and b

10. What is File and Printer Sharing for Microsoft Networks?
    a. a client
    b. a service
    c. a protocol
    d. an adapter

11. How do you share a folder on the local PC with others on the network?
    a. from Network
    b. from My Network Places
    c. from the folder's Properties dialog box
    d. Any of the above will work.

12. What does a hand beneath a folder icon indicate?
    a. that it is shared
    b. that it is a shortcut to a folder on the network, not a local folder
    c. that it is shared with full access for everyone
    d. that it has been mapped to a network drive letter

13. How do you share a local printer with others on the network?
    a. from the print queue
    b. from the printer's Properties dialog box
    c. from My Network Places (or Network Neighborhood)
    d. with the Add Printer Wizard

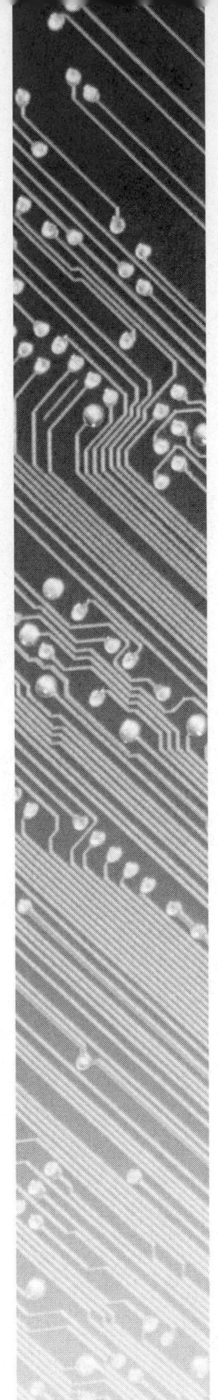

14. Where do you set up the local PC to be able to print to a network printer?
    a. from the print queue
    b. from the printer's Properties dialog box
    c. from My Network Places (or Network Neighborhood)
    d. with the Add Printer Wizard
15. In Windows 2000 how do you assign different permissions for a folder to different user groups?
    a. Click the Permissions button on the Sharing tab in the folder's Properties dialog box.
    b. Choose groups in Local Users and Groups through Computer Management.
    c. Right-click the folder in My Network Places and choose Permissions.
    d. Use the Permission Wizard.
16. In Windows 2000/XP, what does the Security tab control in a folder's Properties dialog box?
    a. network sharing permissions
    b. NTFS encryption
    c. NTFS local user permissions
    d. All of the above
17. What can you assume if there is no Security tab in a folder's properties?
    a. The drive does not use the NTFS file system.
    b. The drive uses the NTFS file system.
    c. The folder is not shared on the network.
    d. File and Printer Sharing for Microsoft Networks is not installed.
18. What utility in Windows 95/98/Me reports the IP address of the local PC?
    a. winipcfg
    b. ipconfig
    c. nslookup
    d. ping
19. What utility do you use in Windows 2000/XP to get the IP address of the local PC?
    a. winipcfg
    b. ipconfig
    c. nslookup
    d. ping

20. What utility do you use at a command prompt for an IP address loopback test?
    a. winipcfg
    b. ipconfig
    c. nslookup
    d. ping

# TROUBLESHOOTING

1. A client has set up a shortcut on his desktop to the *Sales* folder on a coworker's PC. The shortcut no longer works—an error message appears when he double-clicks it. However, the client can still browse all of the computers in his workgroup, including that coworker's PC, through Network Neighborhood. What do you think is the root problem, and what do you suggest as a fix?
2. Yesterday while working on-site for a client, you mapped the *Sales\Group1\Documents\Active* folder to drive letter S for that client and set up a shortcut to S on her desktop. Today she phones you saying that she gets an error message when she double-clicks that shortcut. What went wrong, and how can you talk her through fixing it over the phone?
3. A client is trying to limit network sharing access to a folder on his Windows 2000 PC. He has removed all permissions from the Security tab of the folder's properties except for the Everyone group, and has set that group to have only Read permission. However, other users are still able to make changes to the folder's contents over the network. What is he doing wrong?

# CUSTOMER SERVICE

1. A client has recently upgraded from Windows 98 to Windows 2000 in his small business. In Windows 98 he could enter new users at the logon screen anytime he wanted, but now when he tries to enter a new user there, he gets an error message. What can you tell him that would help him?
2. A small business has a network consisting of three computers. Computer A has a printer connected directly to it, and Computers B and C can print to it through the network. The owner has decided that he wants to move the printer to Computer C since it is seldom used. Describe the process you would use for making the needed

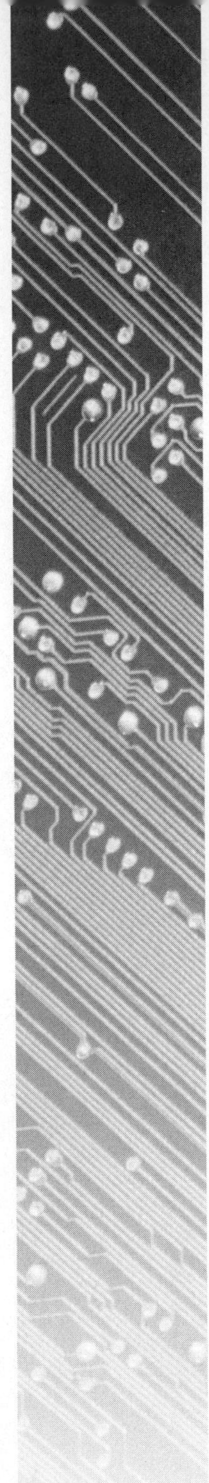

changes in Windows so that all PCs can continue to print from this printer.

3. A medium-sized business has a client/server network of 50 PCs, including several servers. The owner has just bought a high-speed laser printer (just a regular one, not one with a built-in NIC) and wants all users to be able to share its use. The PCs in the organization run a variety of different Windows versions, from Windows 95 through Windows XP. He asks you if it matters which PC the printer is connected to. What can you tell him?

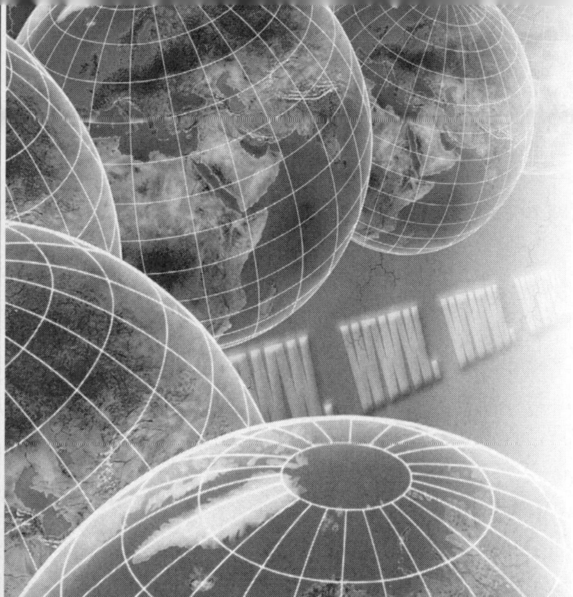

# 24 Modems

## ON THE TEST

**A+ Core Hardware Service Technician Examination**

- **Objective 1.1:** Identify basic terms, concepts, and functions of system modules, including how each module should work during normal operation and during the boot process.
- **Objective 1.7:** Identify proper procedures for installing and configuring peripheral devices.
- **Objective 2.1:** Identify common symptoms and problems associated with each module and how to troubleshoot and isolate the problems.
- **Objective 6.1:** Identify basic networking concepts, including how a network works and the ramifications of repairs on the network.

**A+ Operating System Technologies Examination**

- **Objective 1.2:** Identify basic concepts and procedures for creating, viewing, and managing files, directories and disks. This includes procedures for changing file attributes and the ramifications of those changes (for example, security issues).

## ON THE JOB

Until the recent explosion in popularity of broadband Internet, most connections to the Internet used a modem and a dial-up connection, and most PC service jobs will continue to include modem work for years to come.

Clients with modems will need your help with some of the following issues that you will learn about in this chapter:

- selecting a new or replacement modem
- setting up a modem in Windows

- troubleshooting problems with modem connectivity
- creating dial-up networking connections to Internet service providers
- using Terminal software for direct dial-in to a LAN
- issuing AT (Hayes) commands to a modem

## How Modems Work

The word "modem" is an amalgamation of two terms: **mo**dulate and **dem**odulate. Modems enable computers to communicate with one another through analog telephone lines by converting the digital data of the PC to analog waveform (sound) and then back again at the receiving end.

Some broadband devices call themselves modems, but they are not really modems because they do not convert between digital and analog. They simply send digital data through digital lines. Examples include ISDN modems and cable modems. These devices are more properly called terminal adapters.

### Baud Rate and Bps

A modem sends data in an analog signal, as in Figure 24.1. The basic carrier frequency at which the modem transmits and receives is a certain number of cycles per second, or a certain *baud rate.* A 2,400-baud modem modulates at 2,400 cycles per second.

**Baud rate**

The cycles per second of a modem transmission.

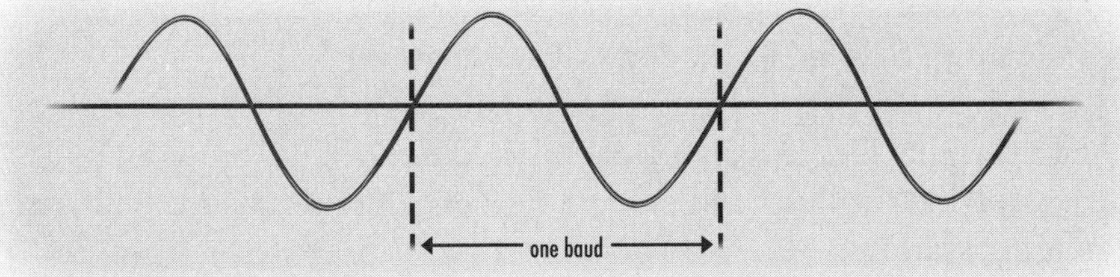


**FIGURE 24.1**
One baud is one complete up/down cycle in the waveform.

On old modems (2,400 baud and below), one bit of data was transmitted with each baud, such that the baud rate and the *bits per second* (bps) were the same. However, modern modems can modulate multiple bits in each cycle, so the bps is a multiple of the basic baud rate. For example, a bps of 9,600 carries four bits per 2,400-baud cycle.

**Bits per second (bps)**

The rate at which data is carried during a modem transmission.

## UARTs

Modems are serial devices, but they must interact with parallel devices in the system such as the CPU and system bus. Therefore an internal modem contains a *Universal Asynchronous Receiver/Transmitter* (UART) chip. A UART converts serial data to parallel data so the rest of the system can use it. An external modem does not need a UART chip because it uses the UART in the serial port by which it attaches to the PC.

**Universal Asynchronous Receiver/Transmitter (UART)**

A chip that converts serial data to parallel data so the CPU can use it.

The standard UART chip in most motherboards today is the 16550A, which operates at up to 115,200bps. Earlier motherboards may have older chips, such as the 16550, the 16450, and the 8250, 8250A, and 8250B. The 16550A UART is advantageous because it has 16 built-in first-in-first-out (FIFO) registers for receiving and transmitting data. In the modem's Properties dialog box in Windows you can enable or disable FIFO usage for 16550A and higher UARTs. Higher UARTs, such as 16650 and 16750, are available but not widely used. You might find them in high-performance I/O expansion boards that add high-speed COM ports to a system (useful for high-speed external serial connections, but less widely used since USB has become popular).

To find out what UART a motherboard has in Windows 95/98/Me, complete the following steps:

1. From the Control Panel, double-click *Modems.*
2. Select the Diagnostics tab.
3. Click the port to which the modem is attached, and then click More Info. The More Info dialog box that appears will list the UART.

Although there is no good way of determining the exact UART in Windows 2000/XP, you can assume that any system capable of running Windows 2000 or Windows XP is recent enough to have a 16550A UART for the built-in COM port(s).

For the A+ exam, the main fact you need to know is that the 16550A UART is necessary to enable FIFO buffers and is the current standard for legacy COM ports.

## Modem Communication Settings

In the last several chapters you have learned about networking and how networks place data into packets for transmittal. Each packet contains a header and footer for identification and error correction, and also the data itself. In modem transmission the process is similar: the modem packages the outgoing data so that the receiving modem can understand how to reassemble it at the other end.

The packets involved in modem transfer are much simpler than those for a network. Since a modem connection is point-to-point, for example, there does not need to be a destination address in each packet. The destination is always the single PC with which the connection was established at the start of the conversation.

### *Data Bits, Start Bits, and Stop Bits*

**Start bit**

The leading 0 at the beginning of a packet in modem data transfer.

**Stop bit:**

The trailing 0 at the end of a packet in modem data transfer.

Each packet contains either seven or eight data bits. At the beginning is a *start bit*, which is always 0, and at the end is a *stop bit*, which is also always 0 (see Figure 24.2). The stop bit is optional and can be eliminated from the transmission via modem settings, but it is usually used.

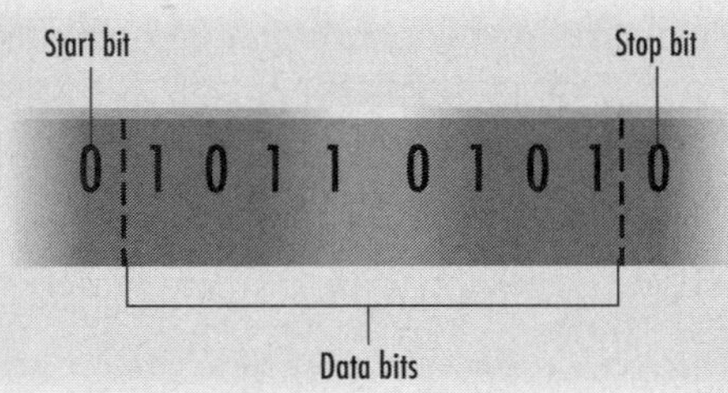


**FIGURE 24.2**
**A Typical Packet for Modem Transfer Containing a Start Bit and a Stop Bit**

### *Parity Bits*

**Parity bit**

A bit included in a packet in modem data transfer that helps the receiving PC determine whether it has correctly received the packet by counting the number of 1s in the overall packet and determining whether it is an odd or even number.

Data is divided up into packets rather than sent as a steady stream to aid in error correction. If one packet does not transmit correctly, the modem can retransmit that packet only rather than starting the entire transmission again. The sending and receiving modems agree on an error detection and correction strategy at the beginning of the communication. One of these error detection strategies is to include a *parity bit* in each packet. The two modems negotiate at the beginning whether parity should be even or odd. Parity bit usage is optional, and is no longer common since modem technology is now good enough that almost all packets are sent successfully.

With even parity, the sending computer makes the total number of 1s in a packet even. It counts the number of 1s in the data, and if the number is already even, the parity bit is set to 0. If the number is odd, it makes the parity bit 1. If the receiving modem gets a packet with an odd number of 1s, it knows something is wrong and asks for that packet to be resent.

The opposite occurs with odd parity. The sending computer once again counts the number of 1s. If the number is even, it sets the parity bit to 1; if the number is odd, it sets the parity bit to 0, thereby creating an odd number of 1s in the packet. Then the receiving modem expects each packet to have an odd number of 1s, and asks for a resend if the number is even.

Figure 24.3 shows a typical packet that uses even parity. Notice that because there was an odd number of 1s in the data (five of them), the parity bit is a 1. If there had been an even number of 1s, the parity bit would have been 0. Packets do not necessarily have to use parity; the two modems can agree to use No parity as the parity setting and eliminate the parity bit from the packets altogether. When writing communication settings, parity is represented in the communication settings by *N* for No parity, *O* for Odd parity, or *E* for Even parity.

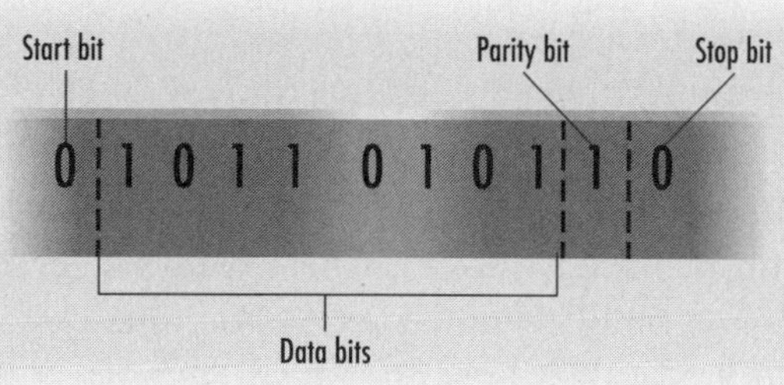


**FIGURE 24.3**
A Packet That Uses Even Parity

### *Flow Control*

Each modem has a way of signaling to the other when it is done sending, so that the two do not try to send at the same time. This flow control signaling goes on behind the scenes, and there are no options users can set for it.

There is another type of flow control associated with a modem, however: the flow between the modem and the COM port. This is mostly an issue with external modems, because an internal modem is a COM port in itself.

This flow control between the modem and the COM port can either be hardware-based or software-based. On almost all modems these days it is hardware-based—that is, built into the modem hardware. Hardware-based flow operates through extra wires in the serial connection between the modem and the COM port. These wires are Ready to Send (RTS) and Clear to Send (CTS). Another name for hardware-based flow control is RTS/CTS.

**RTS/CTS**

A hardware-based flow control scheme between the COM port and the modem.

The alternative is software-based flow control. It uses a special character, XON, to signal the start of the data stream, and another character, XOFF, to signal the end, so this flow control is commonly known as *XON/XOFF*. It is slower and less dependable than hardware flow control.

**XON/XOFF**

A software-based flow control scheme between the COM port and the modem.

### *Hardware-Based Error Detection and Compression*

Most modems have hardware-based error detection and data compression built in, and their use is enabled by default. You can disable it through the modem's properties in Windows, but there is little reason to do so in most cases.

### *Changing Communication Settings in Windows*

Most users will never need to change the communication settings for a modem because the typical TCP/IP dial-up connections to the Internet assume the defaults. However, it is useful to know that they exist as exam preparation and also in case you ever need to change them for a direct connection between two PCs.

The communication settings for a connection are often abbreviated as parity-data bits-stop bit. For example, a connection might have settings of N-8-1, which means no parity bit, eight data bits, and one stop bit. Another connection might have E-7-1, which would be even parity, seven data bits, and one stop bit. This notation is sometimes written with the data bits first, as in 8-N-1 or 7-E-1.

When you are using a terminal program such as HyperTerminal or Procomm, you can set the communication settings for each session individually before you connect it. The settings must be the same on both ends, so you must agree on them beforehand with the owner of the remote modem. Almost all connections these days use 8-N-1 as the settings, so use those if in doubt.

You can also establish default communication settings for the modem in its Properties dialog box in Windows.

In Windows 95, 98, and Me, complete the following steps:

1. From the Control Panel, double-click *Modems*.
2. Click the modem name and then click Properties.
3. Select the Connection tab in the modem's Properties dialog box and specify the settings in the Connection preferences area (see Figure 24.4).

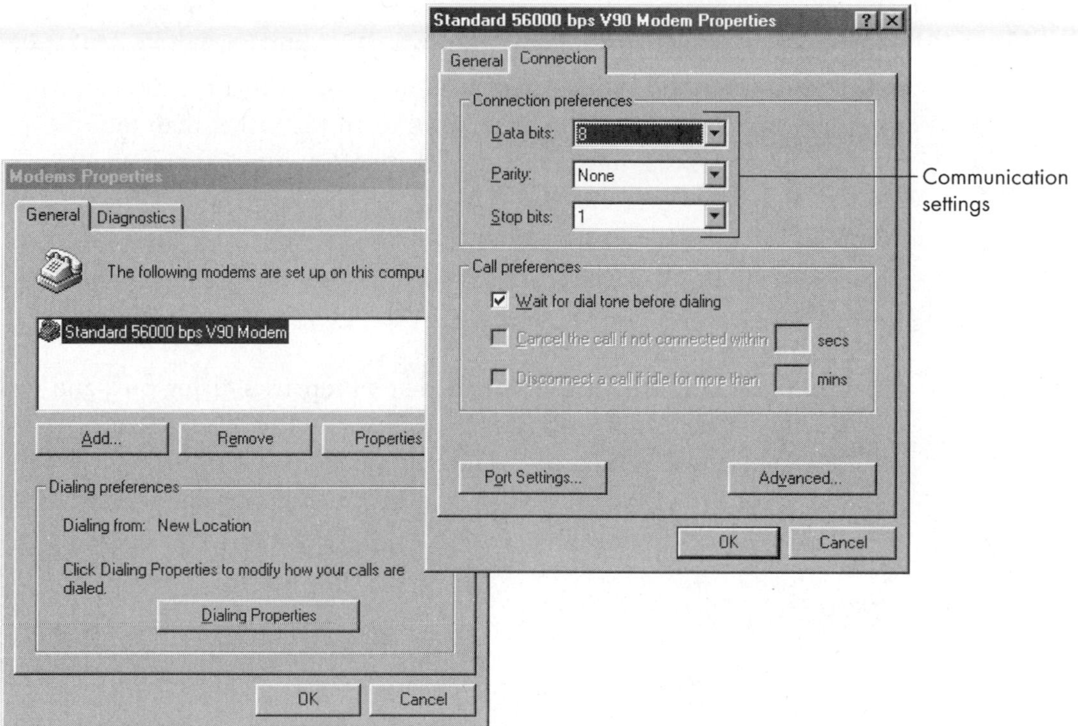


**FIGURE 24.4**
Specifying the Data Bits, Parity, and Stop Bits in Windows 95/98/Me

4. Click the Advanced button. The Advanced Connection Settings dialog box opens.
5. Specify hardware- or software-based flow control, and enable or disable hardware-based error correction and data compression (see Figure 24.5). (These latter two options will be unavailable if the modem does not support them.) Then click OK.

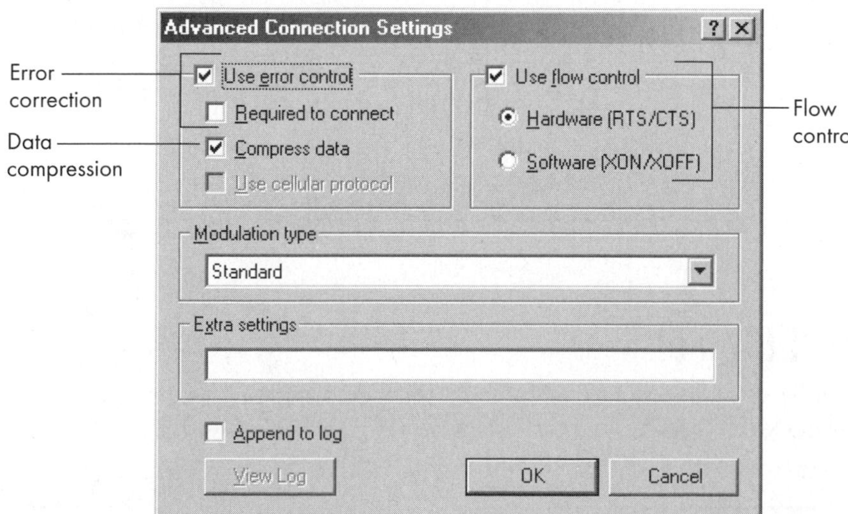


**FIGURE 24.5**
Specifying Hardware or Software Flow Control

6. Click OK.

In Windows 2000 and XP the settings are more difficult to access, mainly because it is assumed in these later Windows versions that the modem will be used primarily for Internet connections to an ISP rather than for terminal programs that might require different data bits, parity, and stop bits settings.

In Windows 2000/XP, complete these steps:

1. From the Control Panel, double-click *Phone and Modem Options.*
2. Select the Modems tab. Click the modem name and then click Properties (see Figure 24.6).
3. Select the Advanced tab in the modem's Properties dialog box, and then click the Change Default Preferences button. The Default Preferences dialog box for the modem opens.
4. Select the Advanced tab and then change the settings in the Hardware Settings area as needed.

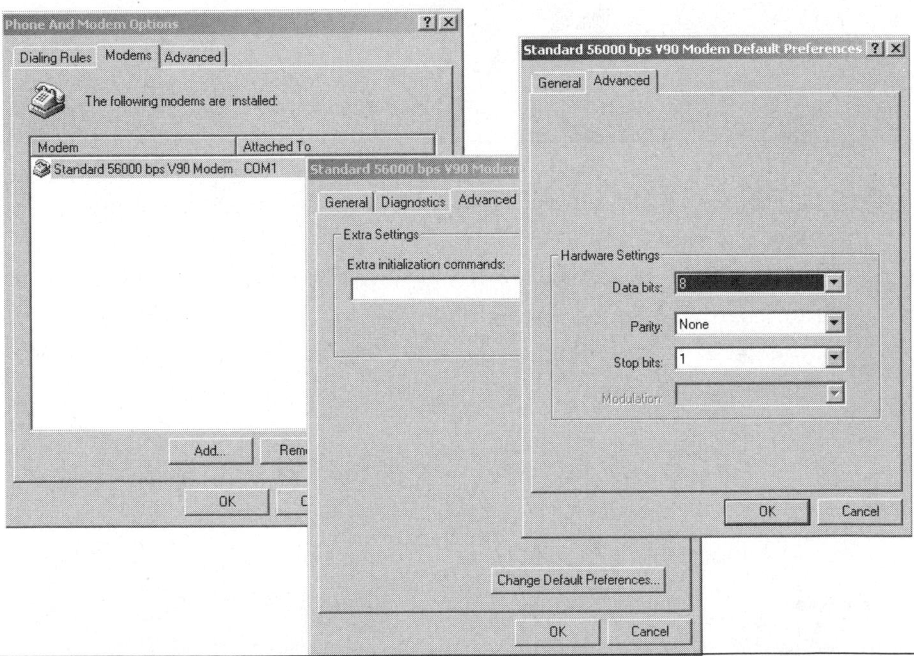


**FIGURE 24.6**
Specifying the Data Bits, Parity, and Stop Bits in Windows 2000/XP

## TRY IT!

Check the settings for your modem. What are the communication settings for data bits, parity, and stop bits? What type of flow control is being used? What COM port is assigned to the modem?

# Types of Modems

When shopping for modems, it is helpful to understand the basic ways in which one modem differs from another. There are three main differentiating factors: the standards to which the modem conforms, whether the modem is hardware-controlled or software-controlled, and whether it is internal or external. In addition, some modems have extra capabilities such as the ability to send and receive faxes (very common) and/or the ability to work as a telephone answering device (less common, called "voice modems").

## V.92 and Other Standards

Just like networking components, modems must meet agreed-upon standards in order to send and receive data. These standards include rules for maximum speed, for compressing data, and for performing error correction. Modem standards are set forth by the International Telecommunications Union (ITU), so the full name of each standard begins with "ITU" although it is not always spelled out in everyday usage.

The most recent modem standard is ITU V.92, but let us look at the modem's history to understand how the modem-making industry eventually arrived at V.92.

### *V.34*

An early modem standard that endured for several years was called V.34. It transferred data at up to 28.8Kbps. Its speed was eventually ramped up to 33.6Kbps, which is the physical limit of an analog telephone line.

The analog telephone is limited to 33.6Kbps under normal circumstances because at that point it reaches a *signal-to-noise ratio* that inhibits effective communication. In other words, at higher speeds the static and interference from the line, because of its analog nature, become so great that data cannot be transmitted reliably.

**Signal-to-noise ratio**

The ratio of usable data signal to static interference in a transmission.

### *56KFlex, X2, and V.90*

Traditional modem standards like V.34 assume that both ends of a modem connection have an analog connection to the telephone network. Data signals are converted from digital to analog and back again, limiting transmission speeds to 33.6Kbps with V.34 modems. This limitation assumes that all of the transfers that the data makes from the end-user PC to the end destination (such as the Internet) are analog transmissions. However, today most ISPs and corporations have a digital connection to the Internet

**T1 line**

A high-speed, high-bandwidth digital telephone line connection for data networks that is always on (not dial-up).

through a high-speed line from the phone company, such as a *T1* line. Therefore, the limitation of 33.6Kbps may not be functionally applicable to all transmissions. Put simply, since a portion of the journey is being made over digital lines, the journey can potentially be speeded up somewhat.

By viewing the phone network as a digital network, a 56Kbps modem can accelerate data being transmitted downstream from the Internet to your computer to up to 56Kbps. These standards are different from the earlier modem standards because the modem digitally encodes downstream data instead of modulating it as analog modems do. The data transfer is asymmetrical: Upstream transmissions (keystroke and mouse commands from your computer) continue to be analog transmissions using the V.34 standard (33.6Kbps); only the downstream transfer uses 56Kbps.

**56KFlex**

One of two early competing standards for 56Kbps modem data transfer, developed and supported by Rockwell and Lucent.

**X2**

One of two early competing standards for 56Kbps modem data transfer, developed and supported by U.S. Robotics.

For a 56Kbps connection to work, the modems at both ends have to use the same standards, but two competing, incompatible standards arose concurrently with the development of 56Kbps modem technology, each with major corporations and a lot of financial support behind them: *56KFlex* (supported by Rockwell and Lucent) and *X2* (supported by U.S. Robotics). A 56KFlex modem communicating with an X2 modem (and vice versa) was limited to 33.6Kbps speed. Online services like America Online (AOL) had to maintain separate dial-up numbers for use with 56KFlex and X2 modems.

## In Real Life

**The FCC has imposed an arbitrary limitation of 53Kbps on modem transfer rates, so 56Kbps modems never actually operate at the full 56Kbps.**

**V.90**

A standard for 56Kbps modem data transfer developed to bridge the two earlier competing standards of 56KFlex and X2.

Eventually the two competing 56Kbps standards were rolled together into a new standard called *V.90* which bridges the two earlier technologies; it is backward-compatible with both.

You will not get the fastest connection speed in all cases. The actual top speed that is negotiated between the two modems at the beginning of the call depends on the quality of the copper phone lines and the proximity of the modem to a digital-to-analog converter. An average V.90 actual speed is around 40Kbps. If an application reports a speed of higher than 56Kbps for your modem, such as 57,600 or 115,200bps, it is reporting the Data Terminal Equipment (DTE) speed, which is the speed between the computer and the modem, rather than the Data Communications Equipment (DCE) speed, which is the speed between the two modems through the phone lines.

## In Real Life

Some 56KFlex and X2 modems can be updated to support V.90 with a BIOS update. You can download it from the manufacturer's Web site and install it by running a Windows-based setup program.

### *V.92*

V.92 is a revision to the V.90 standard that operates using the same basic principles and at the same speeds, but adds three new features: QuickConnect, PCM Upstream, and Modem-on-Hold. All of these features work even when the modem is operating in V.34 mode rather than V.90 mode.

QuickConnect shortens the time it takes to make a connection by remembering the phone line characteristics and storing them for later usage. Typically, the modem handshake (all that noise you hear) takes from 25 to 27 seconds. QuickConnect can cut the modem handshake time in half for repeat calls.

PCM Upstream boosts the upstream data rates between the user and ISP to reduce upload times for large files and e-mail attachments. A maximum of 48Kbps upstream rate is supported, rather than the traditional 33.6Kbps. PCM Upstream is especially helpful when using webcams, which upload much more than they download.

Modem-on-Hold allows users to receive an incoming call with Call Waiting and stay connected to the Internet while taking the call. It also works in reverse; you can initiate a voice call while connected and maintain the modem connection.

### *V.42bis and V.44*

V.42bis and V.44 are both standards for compressing the data being sent via modem, and then decompressing it at the other end. They work alongside V.90 or V.92, performing different functions in the same data transfer. V.44 is the newer standard and results in higher data compression ratios, and therefore higher overall data throughput, typically between 20 and 60 percent higher than V.42bis.

## Hardware versus Software Controlled

Originally all modems had an on-board controller that was independent of the operating system. Today such modems are called *hardware modems.* They will work with any operating system: Windows, DOS, UNIX, Linux,

**Hardware modem**

A modem with an on-board controller, usable in any operating system.

and so on. They also do their own processing, so they do not place a performance drain on the PC.

To cut down on manufacturing costs, modem manufacturers have been moving toward modems that lack an on-board controller. The controller functions are handled by Windows-based software. These work only in Windows (or perhaps in Linux too, depending on the modem), and are known as Winmodems or *software modems.* The processing burden they place on the PC can slow down other applications, making them inferior to true hardware modems. However, the industry trend has been toward software modems in the last several years, to the point where it is becoming difficult to find hardware modems in consumer retail stores.

**Software modem**

A modem without an on-board controller, relying on Windows software for control functions. Also called Winmodem.

One way to determine whether an internal modem is hardware controlled is to look on the circuit board for a BIOS chip. This may look like the BIOS on a motherboard; only hardware-controlled modems have one. External modems are always hardware-controlled; the BIOS chip is usually a removable chip in a socket.

## In Real Life

**Hardware and software modems are equivalent in function in almost all applications, but occasionally you may encounter an application that will accept only a hardware modem. For example, the setup utility for two-way satellite Internet service requires a hardware modem to download the permission/configuration file needed to complete its setup.**

## Internal versus External

Internal modems are circuit boards that fit into expansion slots in the PC. External modems are separate boxes with their own power supplies that connect to the PC via a serial port. Internal modems are less expensive to manufacture, and thus are more common in consumer-grade PCs. They have the advantage of not requiring an AC outlet or any space on the desk. However, they require resource assignment in Windows (usually automatically through Plug and Play) and designation as a COM port. In a system in which remaining IRQs are scarce, resource conflicts may occur (covered in Chapter 14) when installing an internal modem. An internal modem has its own UART and functions as a new COM port in the system.

In contrast, an external modem plugs into an existing legacy COM port, so that it does not require any resources in addition to those already assigned to the port. Some new external modems use the USB interface instead of a COM port, which also requires no resources other than those already assigned to the USB hub.

### Fax and Voice Capabilities

Almost every modem sold today is a facsimile (fax) modem, which means that it is capable of sending and receiving faxes (with software help) in addition to functioning as a data modem.

When a modem faxes, it uses a different transmission mode. Rather than sending packets of data, it sends single bits that are assembled into a black-and-white bitmap image at the receiving end. A faxing application converts the data file you want to fax into a bitmap graphic, which is exactly what a printer driver does. That is why a fax driver typically shows up as a printer driver in the *Printers* folder. Once a fax driver has been installed, any program can "print" to it as if it were a printer, sending the program's data to the fax software for faxing.

There have been several standards for faxing. The first two, Group 1 and Group 2, were standards for 300bps modems and are now obsolete. The current standard, Group 3, supports up to 14,400bps. The Group 3 standard has had several revisions, classifiable with ITU version numbers: V.27 (4,800bps), V.29 (9,600bps), and V.17 (14,400bps). All fax modems sold today support V.17.

Modems advertised as "voice modems" are able to work with software that functions as a telephone answering device. With them you can use a microphone to record a greeting and then have the modem automatically answer the telephone after a certain number of rings and record the caller messages as sound files on the PC.

**TRY IT!**

**Determine as much information as you can about your modem. Is it internal or external? Hardware-controlled or software-controlled? At what speed does it operate? What standards does it support? Find these answers by looking at its documentation, looking at the board physically, checking the modem's properties in Windows, and/or running diagnostic tests on it (as described later in this chapter).**

## Installing a Modem

After the complex installations you have performed in some earlier chapters, a modem will seem easy. An internal modem is a circuit board that fits into an expansion slot. Install as you would any other circuit board. An external modem plugs into an AC outlet and connects to the PC's COM port via serial cable.

## Installing an Internal Modem

Before physically installing an internal modem, check its documentation to make sure it is a Plug and Play model (nearly all made in the last several years are). If it is not Plug and Play, you will need to set jumpers on the board to indicate what resources it should use. For example, in Figure 24.7 you can set a jumper for the IRQ; it is currently set for IRQ 4.

**FIGURE 24.7**
Non-Plug and Play modems have jumpers for IRQ, and sometimes also for COM port or I/O address.

If you must set resources via jumper on the modem, it is helpful to know what resources are not already taken on your system. To determine what is available, consult Device Manager in Windows. See Chapter 14 for help with device resources.

If the PC has no free IRQs before modem installation, a Plug and Play PCI-based modem is a good choice because it is likely to be able to share an IRQ with some other PCI device. You might also be able to disable one of the legacy COM ports in BIOS Setup to free up its IRQ for use.

### In Real Life

Some modems come with instructions telling you that you must run a setup program before physically installing the modem. In some cases this is necessary because the Setup utility scans your current IRQ assignments to determine which it will assign to the modem. In others cases it is a waste of your time because the preinstallation "setup" simply consists of some installation instructions displayed on-screen. Experience working with different brands will tell you the best course of action.

To physically install a modem, follow these steps:

1. Turn off the PC, take off the cover, and select a slot.
2. Remove the backplate cover from behind that slot. Keep the screw handy.
3. Insert the modem in the slot, as in Figure 24.8.
4. Fasten the modem's backplate to the case with the screw you removed.
5. Attach a telephone line from the wall outlet to the Line port on the modem. It may be labeled "Line" or it may show a picture of a phone jack.
6. *Optional:* Attach a telephone line from the telephone to the Phone port on the modem. It may be labeled "Phone" or it may show a picture of a telephone receiver.
7. Start Windows, and run the setup program that came with the modem. A hardware modem might not require the setup program because Windows might be able to install its driver automatically with Plug and Play. A software modem will always require the setup program, even if Windows detects it, because that software plays a vital role in modem functionality.

If the modem does not work, see the section "Testing and Troubleshooting Modems" later in this chapter.

**FIGURE 24.8**
Installing an Internal Modem

## TRY IT!

**Install an internal modem. If one is already installed, remove it, including its driver, from Windows and then reinstall it.**

## INSTALLING AN EXTERNAL MODEM

An external modem does not require any system resources because it uses the resources of the legacy COM port to which it attaches, or, in the case of a USB external modem, it uses the USB hub's resources.

To install a traditional COM-port type of external modem like the one shown in Figure 24.9, complete the following steps:

1. Turn off the PC.
2. Connect the modem's AC power cord to the modem and to an AC wall outlet.
3. Connect the modem to the PC via serial cable (9-pin or 25-pin legacy COM port).
4. Turn on the modem if it has a separate power switch.
5. Start Windows and run the setup software that came with the modem.

If the modem does not work, see the following section, "Testing and Troubleshooting Modems."

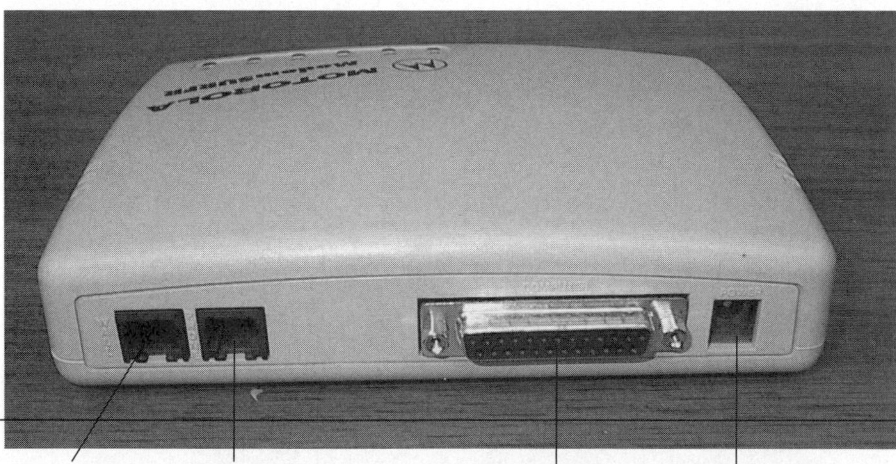


**FIGURE 24.9**
The Ports on the Back of an External Modem

To install an external USB modem, follow these steps (you do not need to turn off the PC):

1. Connect the modem's AC power cord to the modem and to an AC wall outlet.

2. Connect the modem to the PC, or to an external USB hub, with a USB cable.
3. Wait a few seconds for Windows to detect the new modem. You may or may not need to install the software that came with the modem.

## Testing and Troubleshooting Modems

If you are not sure whether the newly installed modem is working, use the following testing and troubleshooting procedures.

### Testing a Modem in Windows

All versions of Windows (95 and higher) include a modem diagnostic test. This test does not require a telephone line to be connected, so you can perform it anywhere. If the modem fails the diagnostic test, it may be defective, installed incorrectly, or have a resource conflict.

To test a modem in Windows 95/98/Me:

1. From the Control Panel, double-click *Modems.*
2. Select the Diagnostics tab.
3. Click the COM port for the modem, and then click More Info. After a few seconds the test results appear (see Figure 24.10).

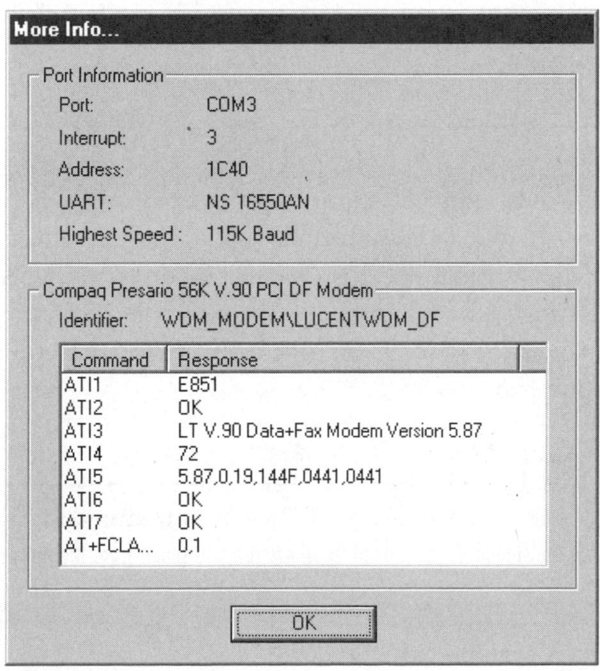


**FIGURE 24.10**
Testing a Modem in Windows 95/98/Me

To test a modem in Windows 2000/XP:

1. From the Control Panel, double-click *Phone and Modem Options.*
2. Select the Modems tab.
3. Click the modem and then click Properties.
4. Select the Diagnostics tab and then click the Query Modem button. After a few seconds the test results appear (see Figure 24.11).

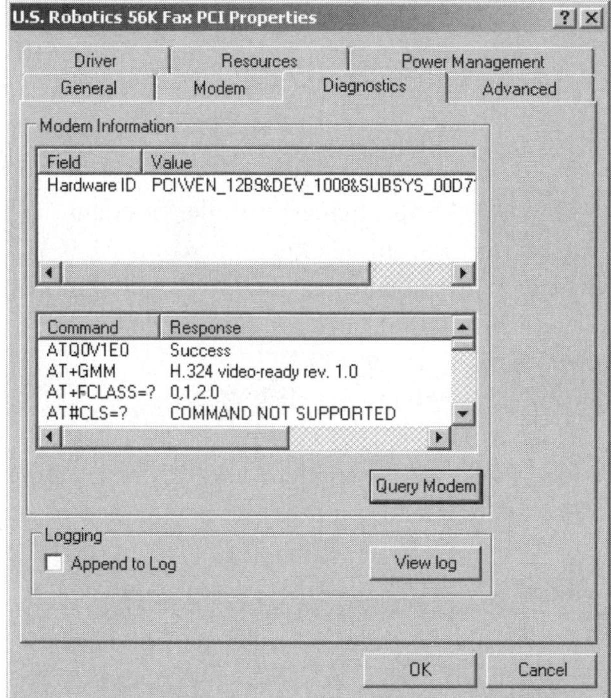


**FIGURE 24.11**
Testing a Modem in Windows 2000/XP

The specifics of the results do not matter (except in very specific technical troubleshooting situations); if at least one line of the test reports Success, OK, or some other affirmative statement, the modem is installed correctly and communicating with Windows. If an error is reported, such as Could Not Open Port, Port Already Open, or Modem Failed to Respond, the modem has a problem.

## TRY IT!

**Test your modem. Which lines report Success or OK? Are there any errors reported? What information about the standards the modem supports can you glean from the test results?**

## TROUBLESHOOTING MODEM PROBLEMS WITH DEVICE MANAGER

If the modem fails the test described in the preceding section, it may be defective, but the failure more likely indicates a problem with resources or with the driver. Device Manager is the appropriate starting place for troubleshooting all types of modem problems. You learned to use it in Chapter 14, so this will be a review aimed specifically at modems.

Recall from Chapter 14 that opening Device Manager is different for Windows 95/98/Me versus Windows 2000/XP. In 95/98/Me Device Manager is a tab in the System Properties dialog box, while in 2000/XP you select the Hardware tab in the System Properties dialog box and then click the Device Manager button.

After opening Device Manager, complete these steps to determine the source of a problem:

1. Is the Modems category present? If so, Windows at least knows that there is some sort of modem device installed. If the modem does not appear in that location, look in the Other Devices category. If something appears there (probably the modem), running the setup program that came with the modem should complete the installation. If the modem does not show up in Device Manager at all, check that it is physically installed correctly.
2. Click the plus sign next to the Modems category if one appears there. This shows the modems in the category if they did not already appear (see Figure 24.12). The category will already be open if Windows recognizes that there is a problem with the modem.

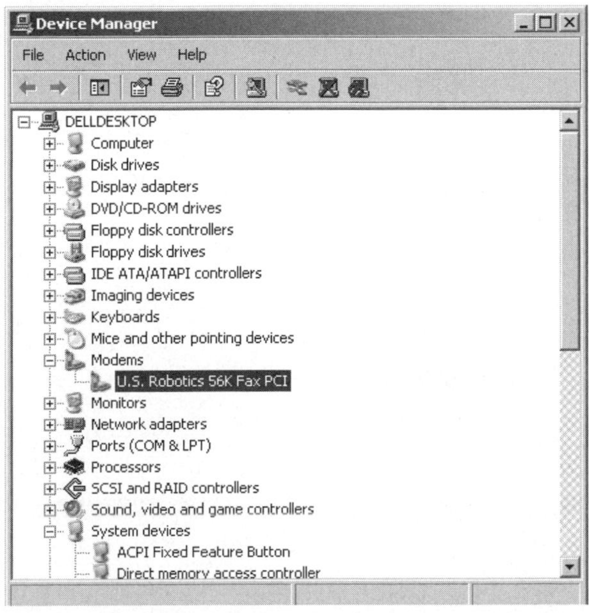


**FIGURE 24.12**
Click the plus sign next to Modems to display a list of modems in the category.

3. Is there a yellow circle and exclamation point next to the modem's name? If so, there is a problem with its driver installation.
4. Double-click the modem to open its properties dialog box, and check the device status. If it says "This device is working properly," as in Figure 24.13, then the modem is installed correctly. If a message appears about a resource conflict, see the following section, "Resource Allocation Problems." If a message appears about the driver's not being installed, or the driver's being corrupted or missing, see "Problems with Lack of Usable Driver."

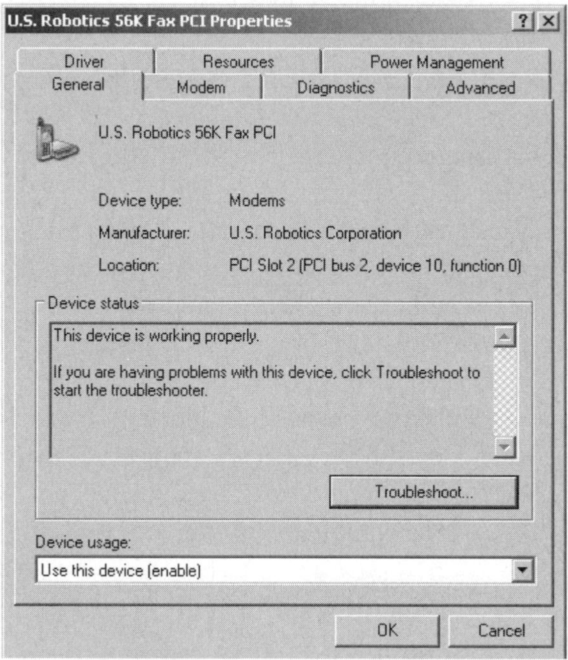


**FIGURE 24.13**
Locate the modem in Device Manager and display its properties to check its status.

## TRY IT!

**Locate your modem in Device Manager. What is its status?**

### *Resource Allocation Problems*

Resource conflicts occur because the modem is not fully Plug and Play, because there are not enough resources to go around, or because the modem or some other device has had resources set manually that conflict. To troubleshoot resource conflicts, see Chapter 14.

### *Problems with Lack of Usable Driver*

Resource conflicts become less likely with newer versions of Windows, but another problem persists across many Windows versions: that of not having an appropriate driver available.

New modems come with setup software that installs the needed drivers, so a lack of driver should not be an issue. This problem is more likely to occur when you reinstall Windows on an existing system. When Windows comes preinstalled on a consumer PC, all of the drivers are preinstalled too, but when you reinstall Windows the driver might not be included with Windows. On such a system you will need to find the driver disk for the modem that came with the PC, or download a driver from the manufacturer's Web site.

## Setting Modem Properties in Windows

If the modem passes the diagnostic test and appears in Device Manager without problems, it is ready for use. Its default properties will work well in most cases. However, a good technician should know about the modem properties available for adjustment, for the exceptional situations.

The exact tabs of the Modem Properties dialog box on which the various options appear depend on the Windows version. Figure 24.14 shows some of the settings you might be able to control.

- **Speaker volume:** This is usually a slider between Off and High.
- **Maximum port speed:** This refers to the speed between the modem and the COM port, not the speed of the modem itself. It should be set to a higher value than the modem's speed (usually 115,200bps).
- **Extra initialization commands (or Extra settings):** This is a text box into which you can key modem commands directly. See "Using AT Commands" later in this chapter for details.
- **Advanced port settings:** This button opens a dialog box where you can enable or disable FIFO buffers, assuming you have at least a 16550A UART.
- **Power management:** The wording varies, but most versions of Windows have a check box that enables the modem answering a call to wake up the computer from Standby. This feature, also called Wake on Ring, works only on systems that have ATX motherboards with BIOS that supports it.

**FIGURE 24.14**
Modem Settings Available for Adjustment

## TRY IT!

Change the modem speaker's volume in the modem properties.

# Setting TAPI Properties

**Telephony Application Programmers Interface (TAPI)**

A set of codes that programmers can use to access programming libraries for working with the modem. Nearly all programs that use the modem work with the TAPI interface.

**Dynamic Link Library (DLL)**

A file containing programming codes that help applications communicate with hardware.

*Telephony Application Programmers Interface* (TAPI) is a set of codes developed by Microsoft that allow application programmers to hook into consistent programming libraries (*Dynamic Link Libraries,* or DLLs) for modem and phone usage so that each application does not have to "reinvent the wheel." TAPI allows programs to perform basic modem activities such as picking up the line, identifying a dial tone, and dialing a number.

Windows has TAPI settings you can configure that pertain to the basic phone functionality involved in modem use. These properties include the default area code, the rules for dialing or omitting area codes, whether to disable call waiting, whether a number must be dialed for an outside line, and so on.

Windows allows you to set up multiple dialing locations and have separate TAPI settings for each location. This permits portable computers, for example, to have preconfigured settings for connecting from different cities or from buildings with different types of phone systems (such as a PBX system at work and a residential phone line at home).

The location from which these TAPI properties are configured depends on the Windows version.

In Windows 95/98/Me, complete the following steps:

1. From the Control Panel in Windows 95, double-click *Modems*, then click the Dialing Properties button.
   OR
   From the Control Panel in Windows 98/Me, double-click the *Telephony* icon.
2. If you want to have different settings for different dialing locations, click the New button on the My Locations tab in the Dialing Properties dialog box to create a new dialing location. Key a name for the new location.
3. Open the I am dialing from list and select the dialing location for which you want to set the properties.
4. Change any of the dialing settings as needed (see Figure 24.15). If you need to set up a calling card, click the Calling Card button. If you need to configure area code rules, click the Area Code Rules button.

5. If you need to change the settings for another dialing location, go back to step 3; otherwise, click OK.

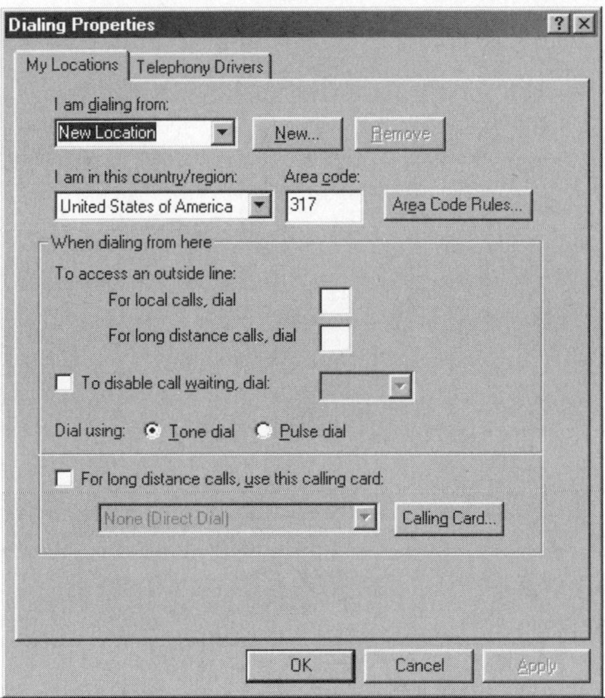


**FIGURE 24.15**
Configuring TAPI Settings in Windows 95/98/Me

In Windows 2000/XP, complete these steps:

1. From the Control Panel, double-click *Phone and Modem Options*.
2. Click the Dialing Rules tab in the Phone and Modem Options dialog box. A list of locations appears. To edit a current location, double-click it. To create a new location, click New.
3. At the Edit Location or New Location dialog box with the General tab selected, set any dialing properties desired (see Figure 24.16). If you need to set up area codes or calling cards, click the appropriate tab to view those controls.
4. Click OK.

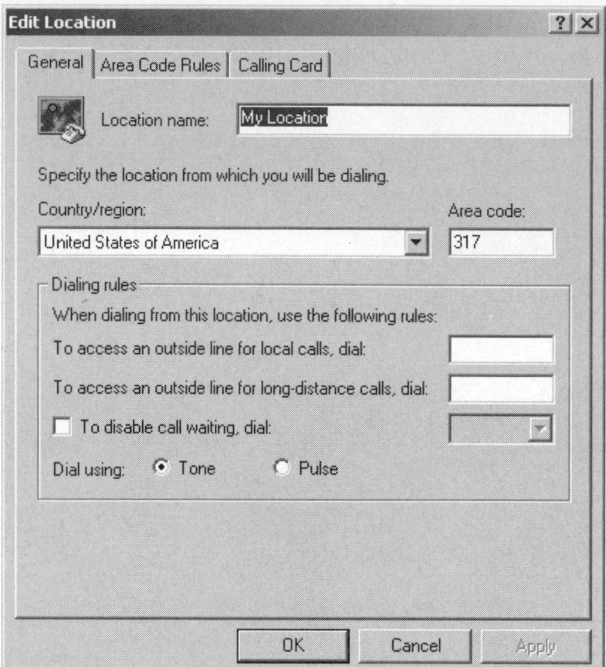


**FIGURE 24.16**
Configuring TAPI Settings in Windows 2000/XP (2000 Shown Here)

## TRY IT!

Create a new dialing location called Classroom, and set up the telephony settings as appropriate for getting an outside line and dialing a local call from the classroom. If you do not have a phone line connected to your modem, set it up as if you did.

# Setting Up a Dial-Up Networking Connection

Windows sees the modem as a type of network adapter. When you dial up a connection, you create a network between a PC and another remote one. Dial-Up Networking (DUN) is the Windows standard for establishing such connections.

The most common type of DUN connection is one that connects a PC to an Internet service provider. To establish the connection it uses a protocol called *Point-to-Point Protocol* (PPP), designed specifically for Internet and Windows-to-Windows connections. The PPP is the default protocol for all DUN connections, but you can change to other protocols for special-purpose DUN connections as needed. It uses TCP/IP by default for the communication itself (except in Windows 95, where TCP/IP is not installed by default, as you learned in Chapter 22). The alternative to PPP

**Point-to-Point Protocol (PPP)**

A Windows-based streaming protocol used by default for Dial-Up Networking connections.

is *Serial Line Internet Protocol* (SLIP), which is used to connect to some UNIX-based servers.

**Serial Line Internet Protocol (SLIP)**

A UNIX-based protocol for communicating with some UNIX-based dial-up servers.

Whatever type of DUN connection you want, you create it through the New Connection Wizard and then edit its properties later to select any nondefault settings. The following sections describe the minor differences in the process in various Windows versions.

## Creating a DUN Connection in Windows 95/98/Me

Dial-Up Networking might not be already installed in Windows 95. To check, open My Computer. If there is a *Dial-Up Networking* folder there, it is installed. If not, add it through Add/Remove Programs in the Control Panel (Windows Setup tab, Communications category). You will learn more about adding and removing Windows components in Chapter 28.

For an Internet connection, TCP/IP will need to be installed as a protocol in network properties. It is installed by default in Windows 98/Me, but not in Windows 95. You learned how to do this in Chapter 22, so refer to it if you need to install TCP/IP.

One final element: the Dial-Up Adapter must be installed in the network properties. This is separate from Dial-Up Networking. It is considered a Microsoft adapter, and is installed like any other adapter, as discussed in Chapter 22. If you do not do this, the first time you create a DUN connection, as in the following steps, Windows will offer to install it for you automatically at the end of the process.

To create a new DUN connection:

1. In Windows 95/98, open the My Computer window and double-click *Dial-Up Networking*. In Windows Me, instead choose Start/Settings/Dial-Up Networking. If the Make New Connection Wizard immediately runs, skip to step 3; otherwise, go on to step 2.
2. In the Dial-Up Networking window, double-click *Make New Connection*. The Make New Connection Wizard starts.
3. Key a name for the new connection.
4. Choose the modem you want to use for the connection (if you have more than one), then click Next (see Figure 24.17).

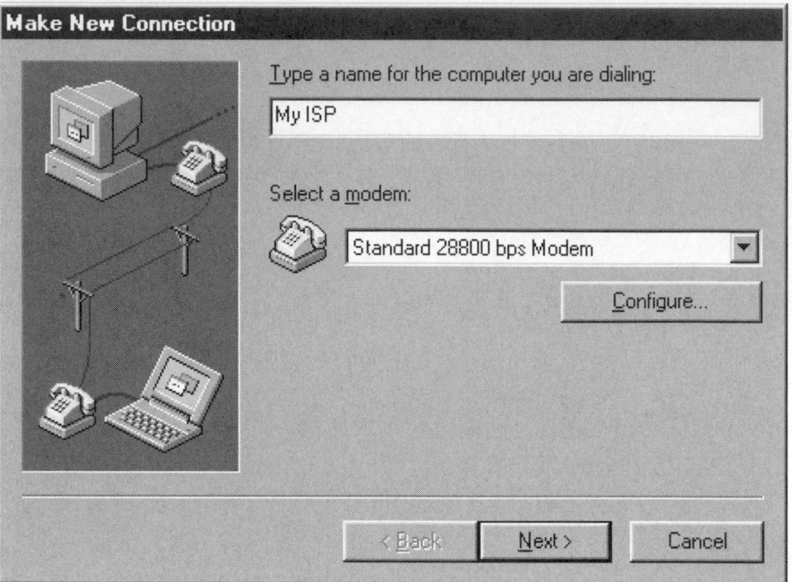


**FIGURE 24.17**
Creating a DUN Connection in Windows 95/98

5. Key the phone number to dial for the connection. Select a different country code if needed, then click Next.
6. Click Finish.
7. At this point, if the Dial-Up Adapter has not yet been installed, a dialog box appears to that effect. Click OK to install it.

The icon for the connection appears in the Dial-Up Networking window. From here you can double-click it to establish the connection, drag it to the desktop to create a shortcut there, or do anything else that you can do with a shortcut.

In Windows 98 and Me, there is also an Internet Connection Wizard that you can use to create new DUN connections specifically for Internet access.

This wizard also directs users toward a list of Microsoft-partnered ISPs in case the user does not already have an ISP account. For our purposes here, however, we will assume that the ISP account has already been established.

To run the Internet Connection Wizard:

1. In Windows 98, choose Start/Programs/Accessories/Internet Tools/Internet Connection Wizard; in Windows Me, choose Start/Programs/Accessories/Communications/Internet Connection Wizard.
2. Choose I want to set up my Internet connection manually… and then click Next.
3. Choose I connect through a phone line and modem and then click Next.

4. Key the phone number to dial. If you do not need to dial the area code, clear the Dial using the area code and country code check box (see Figure 24.18).
5. If you need to specify any nondefault settings for the connection, such as entering a static IP address, click the Advanced button. (You can make these changes later as well, from the DUN connection's Properties dialog box.) Otherwise, just click Next.
6. Enter the user name and password for connecting, and then click Next.
7. Key a name for the connection, and then click Next.
8. When asked if you want to set up a mail account, choose No and then click Next. (You will learn about mail accounts in Chapter 25.)
9. Click Finish. The new DUN connection's icon appears in the *Dial-Up Networking* folder and Windows starts dialing the connection immediately to test it.

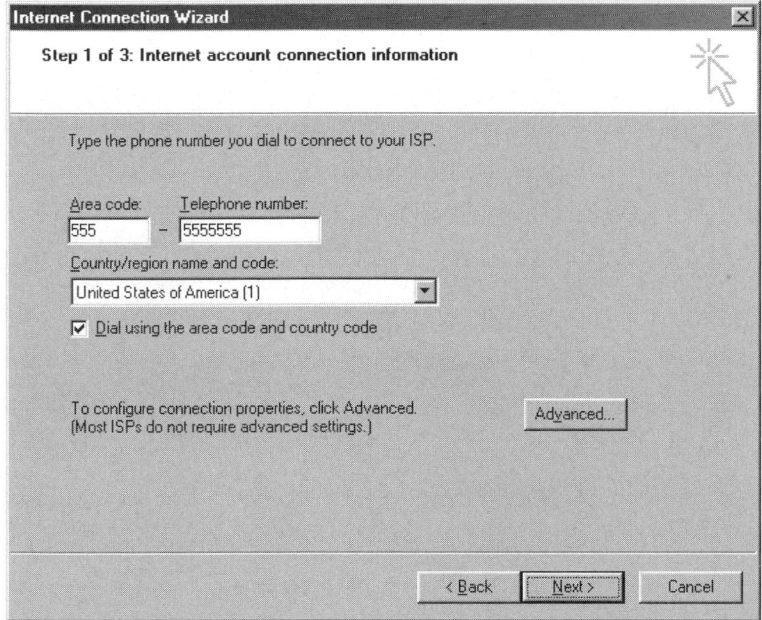


**FIGURE 24.18**
Setting Up a DUN Connection to an ISP with the Internet Connection Wizard in Windows 98/Me

## CREATING A DUN CONNECTION IN WINDOWS 2000

Windows 2000 has two wizards from which you can start a new DUN connection: the Network Connection Wizard and the Internet Connection Wizard. The Network Connection Wizard offers either a private DUN connection or an Internet connection; if you choose the Internet, it closes itself and opens the Internet Connection Wizard. Therefore, if your goal is an Internet connection, it is easier simply to start with the Internet Connection Wizard.

### *Setting Up an Internet DUN Connection*

Use the Internet Connection Wizard to set up an Internet DUN connection. The steps are exactly the same as for Windows Me, covered in the preceding section.

### *Setting Up a Private DUN Connection*

A private DUN connection might be a connection to a corporate or university server on which you are authorized. Most companies and schools these days provide access through the Web or through a virtual private network via the Internet, so a true private DUN connection is rare. However, you might occasionally need to set one up.

1. From the Control Panel, double-click *Network and Dial-Up Connections*.
2. Double-click *Make New Connection*. The Network Connection Wizard runs. Click Next to begin.
3. A list of networking types appears, as in Figure 24.19. Choose Dial-up to private network, and then click Next.
4. Key the phone number for the server to dial, then click Next.
5. Specify whether you want the connection to be available to all users of this PC or only the currently logged-in user name. Click Next.
6. Key a name for the connection. Click Finish to create it.

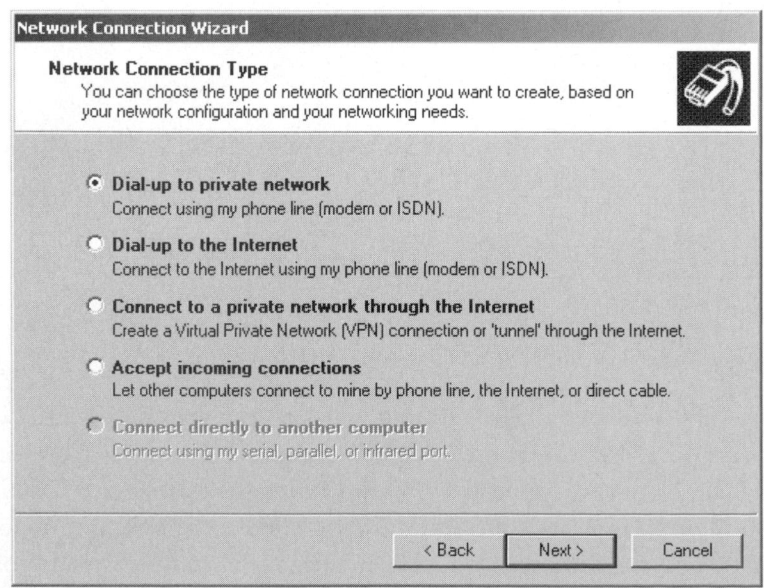


**FIGURE 24.19**
In Windows 2000 the Network Connection Wizard lets you choose the type of DUN connection you want.

## Creating a DUN Connection in Windows XP

Windows XP works similarly to Windows 2000 with a few minor differences. First, the Internet Connection Wizard does not appear as a stand-alone item; it is integrated into a single wizard called the New Connection Wizard. Windows XP is not covered on the current version of the A+ exam, but is useful to become familiar with it for on-the-job use.

### *Setting Up an Internet DUN Connection*

To create an Internet DUN connection in Windows XP:

1. Choose Start/All Programs/Accessories/Communications/New Connection Wizard. Click Next to begin.
2. Choose Connect to the Internet and then click Next.
3. Choose Set up my connection manually and click Next.
4. Choose Connect using a dial-up modem and click Next.
5. Key the ISP name (for your own use only) and click Next.
6. Key the phone number to dial, including a 1 and an area code if needed, and click Next.
7. Key your user name and password (and repeat the password in the Confirm Password box), and mark or clear as appropriate any of the check box options provided (see Figure 24.20). Click Next.
8. Click Finish. The connection is created.

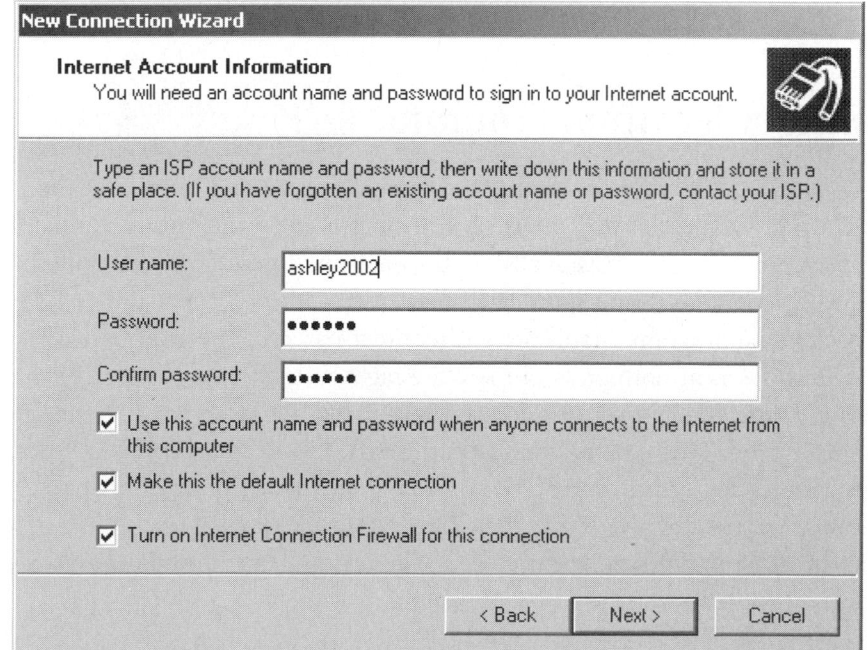


**FIGURE 24.20**
Setting Up an Internet DUN Connection in Windows XP

### *Setting Up a Private DUN Connection*

To create a non-Internet private DUN connection in Windows XP:

1. Choose Start/All Programs/Accessories/Communications/New Connection Wizard. Click Next to begin.
2. Choose Connect to the network at my workplace and then click Next.
3. Choose Dial-Up connection and click Next.
4. Key the company name (for your own use only) and click Next.
5. Key the phone number to dial, including a 1 and an area code if needed, and click Next.
6. Click Finish. The connection is created.

**TRY IT!**

**Create a DUN connection to your local ISP, if you have one. If you do not, create a dummy connection using your own phone number.**

## Changing DUN Connection Properties

After setting up a DUN connection, you might want to change something about the way it works. For example, you might change the phone number that it dials, specify a different number of redial attempts when the line is busy, specify whether you are calling a PPP or SLIP server, and so on. To work with a connection's properties, right-click its icon and choose Properties.

# Using a Terminal Program

**Terminal program**

Communication software that establishes a direct dial-up connection between two PCs in which users at each end can key messages to one another and transfer files between them.

The *terminal program* is becoming a thing of the past, a reminder of the days when simple dial-up bulletin board systems were the online standard. However, you might occasionally need to use one to connect to a Bulletin Board System (BBS) or a specialized network.

A terminal program establishes a direct text-based connection between two PCs. Users at both ends can key messages to each other, or one of the PCs can function as a server and send text-based menus to the live user at the other end. This type of connection uses ASCII as the main communication protocol. ASCII, you may remember from earlier chapters, is the set of numbers, letters, and symbols used for text-based communications. When one user keys, the text appears on the other user's screen as well.

## HyperTerminal

Windows comes with a terminal program called HyperTerminal, located on the Accessories/Communications menu in most Windows versions. You can use it to create and establish connections to remote servers that use direct connection rather than Dial-Up Networking. Figure 24.21 shows an example of a connection established in HyperTerminal.

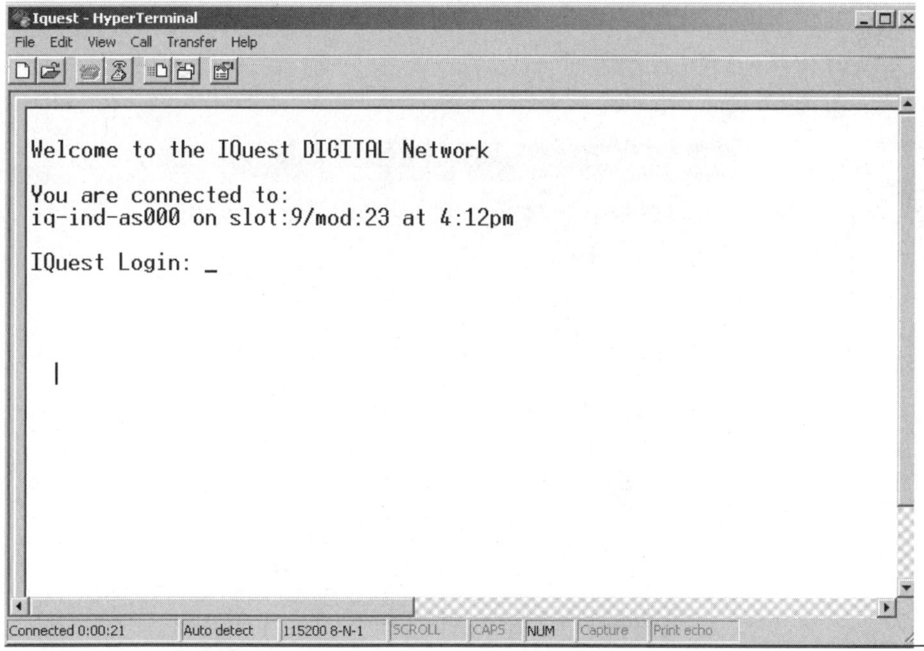


**FIGURE 24.21**
HyperTerminal Connecting to a Terminal-Based Server

When you start HyperTerminal, a wizard walks you through the process of creating the new connection by prompting you for its name and phone number. Fill in the blanks as prompted, and then it dials the connection automatically. For future connections to the same site, you can simply double-click the icon for that site in the *HyperTerminal* folder.

## Half Duplex and Full Duplex

When exchanging messages with another user via a terminal program, you might run into a duplex problem. *Duplex* (also called full duplex) is the ability to transmit and receive on the same channel at the same time. When you connect to a server with a terminal program, it probably supports duplex. When you connect directly to another personal computer with a terminal program, it probably does not. If you are keying and you do not

**Duplex**

The ability to transmit and receive on the same channel at the same time. Duplex settings in most terminal programs are full duplex and half duplex.

see what you are keying, switch the terminal program's settings to half duplex; if you see two of everything, switch it to full duplex.

Not all programs call half duplex and full duplex by that terminology. In HyperTerminal, for example, half duplex is represented by a setting called Echo typed characters locally. To set it in HyperTerminal, do the following:

1. Choose File/Properties.
2. Select the Settings tab and then click the ASCII Setup button.
3. Check or clear the Echo typed characters locally check box. When it is checked, half duplex is in effect; when it is cleared, full duplex is turned on (see Figure 24.21).
4. Click OK, then click OK again to close the open dialog boxes.

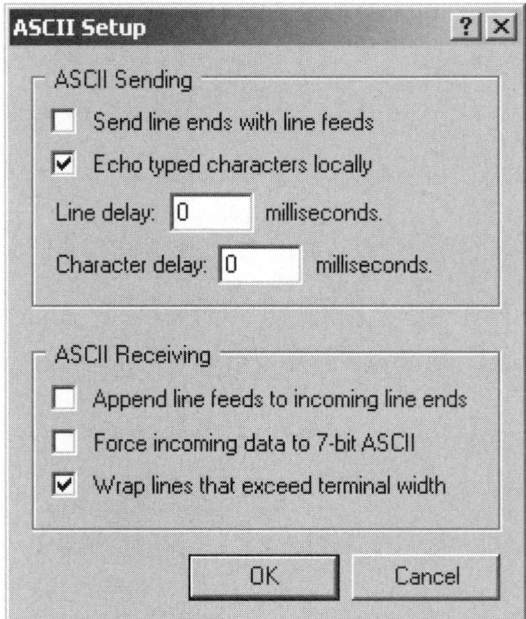


**FIGURE 24.22**
In HyperTerminal, duplex is controlled by the Echo typed characters locally setting.

Another way of selecting these same settings is through an AT command, which will be discussed later in this chapter. The command ATE1 turns on the local echo, and ATE0 turns it off.

## Binary File Transfer in a Terminal Program

When a terminal program sends and receives binary files, it must use a protocol different from that used for exchanging ordinary text-based messages. Various transfer protocols have been developed over the years for terminal-based file transfer, each with its own error-detection strategy and some with compression as well. These include KERMIT, XMODEM, YMODEM, and ZMODEM. You do not need to know the differences among them for the A+ exam. If you are ever called upon to choose one to use, ZMODEM is the best choice because it includes all of the features of XMODEM and YMODEM, plus extra benefits such as crash recovery and automatic downloading.

## Using AT Commands

Almost all modems understand a common set of configuration commands known as the *AT command set*. AT is short for "attention," and the name is derived from the fact that each command string begins with the letters AT to signal the modem that a command will follow. Another name for the AT command set is Hayes commands, because they were originally developed by Hayes, an early leading modem manufacturer. In Windows, the modem driver takes over most of the command-issuing functions, so that end users no longer need to know the AT commands. However, a good PC technician should be familiar with at least a few of the most basic AT commands.

**AT command set**

A set of codes that tell the modem what mode to operate in and what to do.

For example, you might issue the command ATDT5552311 to tell the modem the following:

| | |
|---|---|
| AT | Attention, the following is a command |
| DT | Dial the following number using Tone dialing |
| 5552311 | This is the number to dial |

To reset the modem, you might issue the command ATZ:

| | |
|---|---|
| AT: | Attention, the following is a command |
| Z: | Reset yourself |

Some terminal programs require that you enter a command mode before issuing commands to the modem. Most start out in command mode, however, so you can dial the required number and switch to communication mode (for keying back and forth with the remote computer) only after the connection has been established.

### Setting Up HyperTerminal for Command Line Entry

HyperTerminal is designed to operate through dialog boxes that set up and establish connections; it accepts AT commands only as an afterthought. However, you can still use it to issue AT commands to the modem should you ever need to do so.

To issue an AT command to the modem through HyperTerminal, complete the following steps:

1. Start HyperTerminal. A Connection Description dialog box appears for you to create a new connection.

2. Click Cancel. The box disappears and you see a blank white screen.
3. Key **ATE1** and press Enter. You will not see what you key. The modem will send back an OK message. The E1 command you just issued is for full duplex, and it resets the duplex setting so that any subsequent commands you key will be visible.
4. Issue whatever AT commands you need to issue to the modem. See the following section for some sample commands.

## Some Common AT Commands You Can Issue

Many of the AT commands have Windows dialog box equivalents, especially through the modem's Properties dialog box. Therefore, in on-the-job usage you will probably have little reason to use AT commands. However, it is useful to be familiar with them just in case. Table 24.1 lists some of the most common commands. Each one starts with AT for "Attention."

| Command | Purpose |
|---|---|
| ATM0 | Turns off the modem speaker |
| ATM1 | Turns on the modem speaker |
| ATE0 | Turns off local echo of commands you key (use this if everything you key appears double) |
| ATE1 | Turns on local echo (use this if what you key does not appear on-screen) |
| ATDT[number] | Dials a number using Tone dialing |
| ATDP[number] | Dials a number using Pulse dialing |
| ATH1 | Takes the phone off the hook; not necessary before using a dialing command (such as ATDT or ATDP) because those commands assume that you want it |
| ATH0 or ATH | Hangs up the phone, terminating any connection |
| ATQ0 | Turns on verbal responses; this is helpful when troubleshooting |
| ATQ1 | Turns off verbal responses |
| ATZ | Resets the modem; some people issue this command preceding any other commands as a matter of habit, to clear any other codes or settings from the modem |
| (comma) | Pauses for one second; this is useful if you want the modem to pause before checking for a dial tone, for example |

**TABLE 24.1**
Common AT Commands

### TRY IT!

1. Start HyperTerminal, and click Cancel to get to a blank screen.
2. Key **AT** and press Enter. What happens? Do you see the text you keyed?
3. Key **ATE1** and press Enter, then key AT and press Enter again. This time did you see it?
4. Key **ATE0** and press Enter, then key AT and press Enter again. What did you see this time?
5. Key **ATM1** and press Enter to make sure the modem speaker is on.
6. Key **ATH1** and press Enter. What do you hear?
7. Key **ATH0** and press Enter. Now what do you hear?
8. Key **ATDT5555555** and press Enter. The modem begins to dial. Press Esc to stop it before it finishes dialing.
9. Close HyperTerminal.

## Other Uses for AT Commands

Entering AT commands through a terminal program is only one method of entering them. Windows enables you to enter AT command strings in other places as well. For example, in the modem's Properties dialog box in Windows 95/98/Me (on the Connection tab, click Advanced), you will find an Extra Settings text box where you can enter a setup string to execute each time a program uses the modem. In Windows 2000 and XP the text box is on the Advanced tab of the modem's Properties dialog box, and it is called Extra initialization commands (see Figure 24.23). If the modem manufacturer indicates that you should issue certain setup commands before running an application, this would be the place to enter them.

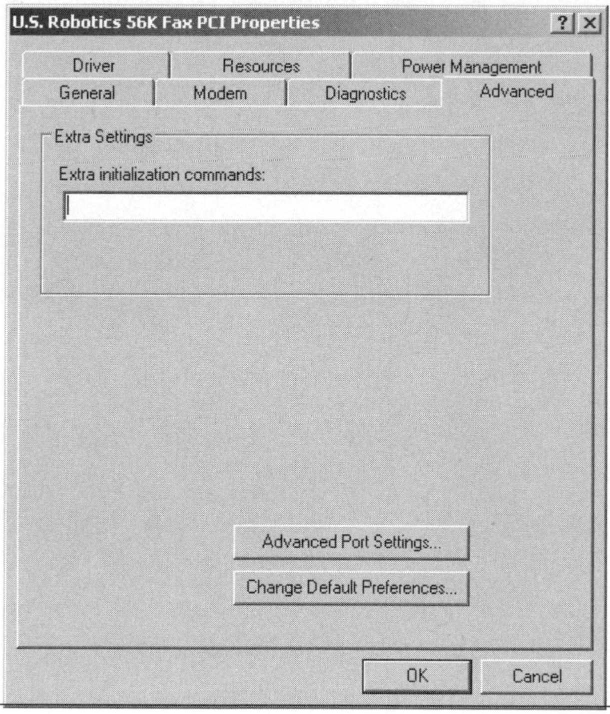

**FIGURE 24.23** Enter AT commands manually in the modem's Properties dialog box (Windows 2000 shown).

Another place where you might need to enter a string of AT commands is in the software that connects you to an online service such as AOL. The software supports many different modem brands and types, but if your particular modem is not listed, you might be able to make it work with the service by manually entering a setup string, as directed by the documentation that came with the modem. Alternatively, you might tweak the existing setup string for the modem if directed by the support staff for the online service when troubleshooting a problem. Figure 24.24 shows the setup string for a modem in AOL 7.0.

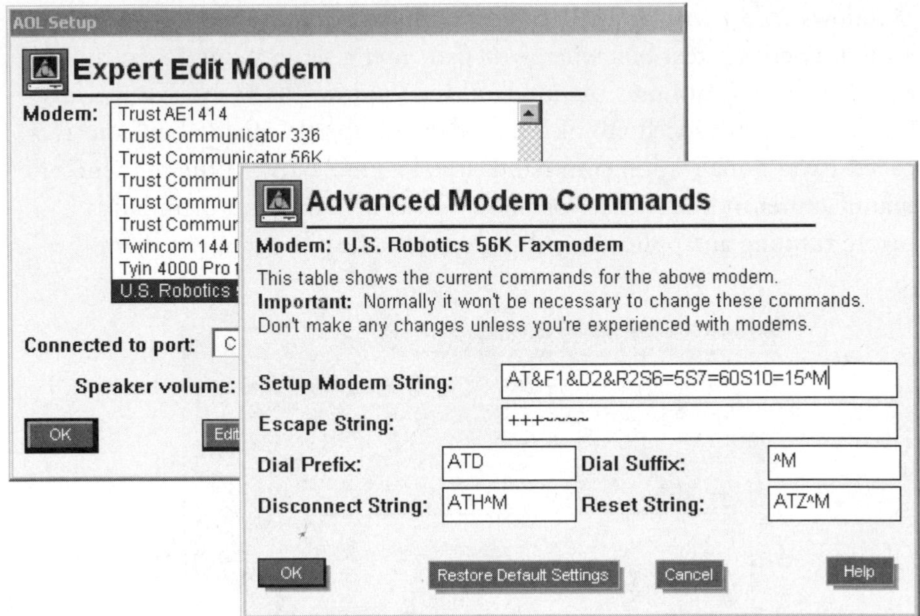


**FIGURE 24.24**
Based on the modem make and model, programs like AOL provide their own setup strings to the modem, which you can edit if needed.

# STUDY GUIDE

Use the following summaries to review the key concepts of this chapter.

## How Modems Work

- The word "modem" is a combination of **mo**dulate and **dem**odulate.
- Modems convert between digital (computer) data and analog sounds that can be transmitted via phone lines.
- The basic carrier frequency at which a modem transmits and receives is its baud rate. Early modems transmitted one bit of data per cycle.
- Today's modems transmit multiple bits per cycle, such that the bits per second (bps) is a multiple of the baud rate.
- A UART (Universal Asynchronous Receiver/Transmitter) is a converter between parallel and serial. An internal modem has a UART built in; an external serial-port modem uses the one of the COM port to which it is attached.
- The standard UART chip in most motherboards is the 16550A, which operates at up to 115,200bps. It has 16 built-in first-in-first-out (FIFO) registers for receiving and transmitting data.
- Modems transmit data in packets of either seven or eight data bits. At the beginning of each packet is a start bit (0) and at the end is a stop bit (0), which is optional.
- Modem communication can include a parity bit, which checks to make sure the packet has been received correctly by adding up the number of 1s in the packet and checking whether it is odd (odd parity) or even (even parity).
- The most common settings for modems today are N (no parity) 8 (eight data bits) 1 (one stop bit). These settings are assumed in almost all cases.
- A modem can use either hardware or software flow control. Hardware flow control, also called RTS/CTS (Ready to Send/Clear to Send), is preferable. Software flow control is also called XON/XOFF.
- Most modems have hardware-based error detection and data compression built in, enabled by default.

## Types of Modems

- V.34 is an early modem standard. It communicates at up to 33.6Kbps and most modems today support it as a backup to their primary communication standard.

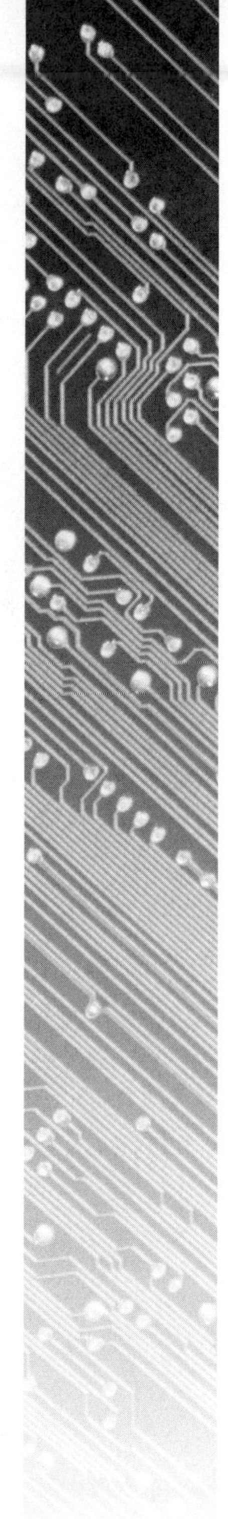

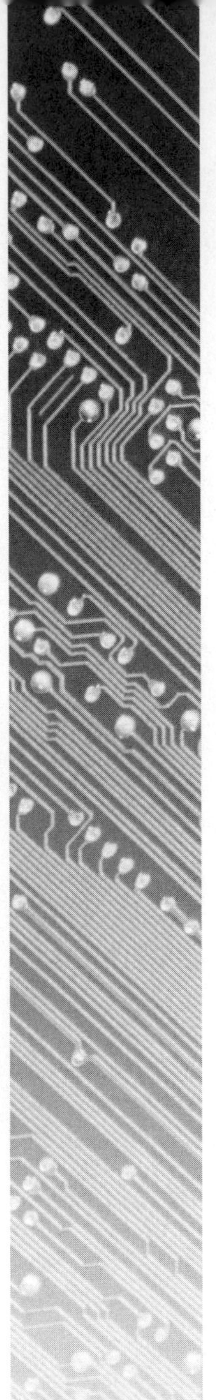

- 56KFlex and X2 were two early standards for 56Kbps modem communication. They were incompatible with one another and were eventually merged into a common standard called V.90.
- The current standard is V.92, which is just like V.90 except for three new features: QuickConnect, Modem-on-Hold, and PCM Upstream.
- V.42bis and V.44 are standards for compressing data being sent via modem. V.44 is the newer standard and results in higher compression ratios than V.42bis.
- Modems with an on-board controller are called hardware modems. They will work with any operating system.
- Modems that rely on Windows software for some of the functions of a controller are called software modems or Winmodems. They work only with Windows, and are less desirable but cheaper than hardware modems.
- Modems can be internal (circuit boards) or external (separate devices that connect via COM port or USB port).
- Almost all modems are fax modems, which means they have faxing capabilities. Some modems are also voice modems, which means they work with telephone answering software.
- The standards for faxing are Group 1, Group 2, and Group 3. Group 3 is the current standard, and any modem you buy should support it. Within Group 3 are several revisions: V.27 (4,800bps), V.29 (9,600bps), and V.17 (14,400bps).

## Installing a Modem

- Internal modems fit into motherboard expansion slots, the same as any other expansion board.
- Non-Plug and Play internal modems have jumpers for setting the IRQ and possibly also the COM port number or the I/O address.
- PCI internal modems are preferable to ISA modems because of their IRQ-sharing capabilities.
- External modems connect either to a legacy COM port or to a USB port, and have separate power adapters of their own.
- A modem has two phone jacks on it—one for Line (may be labeled Line, In, Telco, Jack, or Wall) and one for Phone (may be labeled Phone, Extension, or Ext).

## Testing and Troubleshooting Modems

- To test a modem in Windows 95/98/Me, open its Properties dialog box and click the Diagnostics tab. Click the COM port for the modem and then click More Info.
- To test a modem in Windows 2000/XP, open its Properties dialog box, click the Diagnostics tab, and then click Query Modem.
- If the modem fails the test, check its status in Device Manager, as in Chapter 14, and troubleshoot any resource conflicts found.
- If the modem's driver is not installed, install it from the disk that came with the modem or download a driver from the manufacturer's Web site.

## Setting Modem Properties in Windows

- The Properties dialog box for the modem enables you to specify some basic settings and preferences for the modem.
- The exact options vary depending on the Windows version and on the modem type, but will include speaker volume, maximum port speed, advanced port settings, and power management.

## Setting TAPI Properties

- TAPI is a set of programming codes consistent across almost all applications that use the modem.
- User-selectable TAPI settings include area codes, calling card numbers, dialing locations, and codes that disable call waiting or produce an outside line.
- Windows allows you to set up multiple dialing locations, each with separate TAPI settings.
- In Windows 95, access TAPI settings by opening Modems in the Control Panel and clicking the Dialing Properties button.
- In Windows 95/Me, access TAPI settings by opening Telephony from the Control Panel.
- In Windows 2000/XP, access TAPI settings by opening Phone and Modem Options from the Control Panel and selecting the Dialing Rules tab.

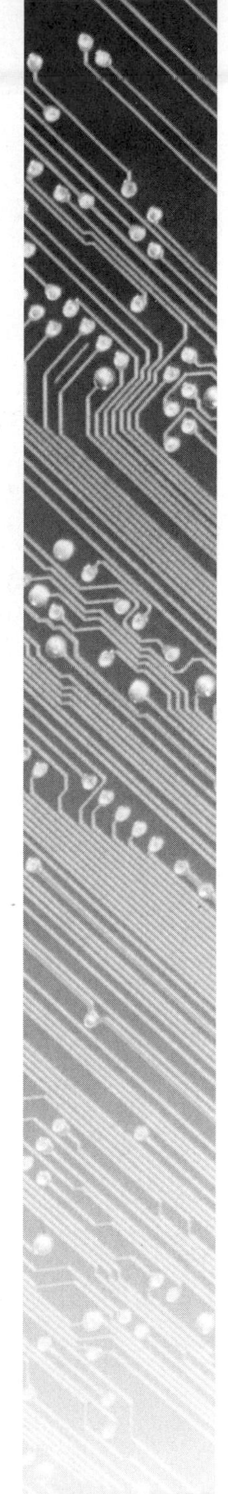

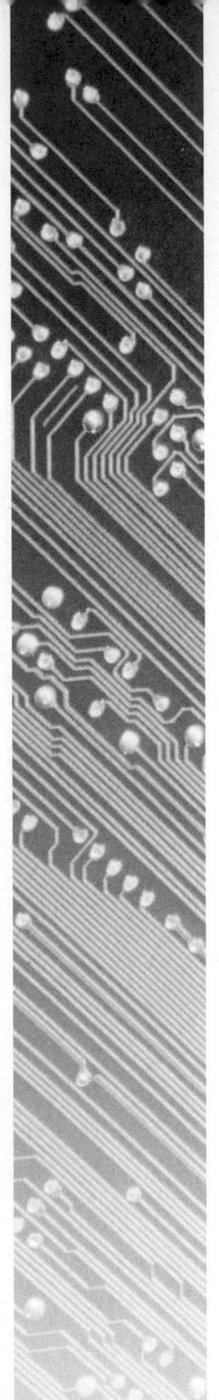

## Setting Up a Dial-Up Networking Connection

- The most common type of Dial-Up Networking (DUN) connection is one that connects to an Internet ISP.
- In Windows 95/98/Me, you can use the Make New Connection Wizard from the *Dial-Up Networking* folder to create a new DUN connection.
- In Windows 98 and higher you can use the Internet Connection Wizard instead if you prefer to create a DUN connection specifically for Internet access.
- Windows XP does not have the Internet Connection Wizard per se, but all of its features are included in the New Connection Wizard.
- After creating a DUN connection, you can right-click its icon and choose Properties to alter its settings.

## Using a Terminal Program

- Terminal programs are no longer very popular because nearly everyone uses the Internet. However, there are still some specialized uses for them.
- A terminal program establishes a point-to-point connection between two computers, which communicate via ASCII text and transfer files using special binary protocols such as ZMODEM.
- Windows comes with a program called HyperTerminal that functions as a terminal. It is on the Accessories/Communications menu.
- If the text you key in a terminal program appears double, set the program to full duplex. You can do this through a dialog box in the program or by keying **ATE0**. If the text you key does not appear at all, set the program to half duplex, either through a dialog box or by keying **ATE1**.
- Some of the protocols that terminal programs use for binary transfers include KERMIT, XMODEM, YMODEM, and ZMODEM. Of these, ZMODEM is the best choice in most cases.

## Using AT Commands

- Almost all modems understand a common set of configuration commands known as the AT command set. AT is short for "Attention," and the letters AT precede each command.
- Some terminal programs require that you enter a command mode before issuing AT commands. Most start out in command mode, however.
- In HyperTerminal, you can enter AT commands by starting the program and then clicking Cancel to clear the opening dialog box.

- If you do not see your commands, key **ATE1** and press Enter. If you see double commands, key **ATE0** and press Enter.
- To dial a number, key **ATDT** and then the number. For pulse dialing, key **ATDP** instead.
- ATM0 turns off the modem speaker; ATM1 turns it on.
- You can enter AT commands to be issued each time the modem is used in the Modem Properties dialog box. In Windows 95/98/Me, click the Advanced button on the Connection tab and then enter the setup commands in the Extra Settings text box.
- In Windows 2000/XP, enter the setup commands in the Extra initialization commands text box on the Advanced tab.
- Some programs have their own area for entering modem initialization commands. America Online is one example.

# PRACTICE TEST

On a blank sheet of paper, write the answers to the following multiple-choice questions and explain why each answer is correct.

1. A modem's primary purpose is to
   a. convert between binary and decimal.
   b. convert between synchronous and asynchronous communication.
   c. convert between parallel and serial transfer.
   d. convert between analog and digital data.

2 What is the relationship between bps and baud rate in a modem?
   a. They are always the same.
   b. The bps can be either the same as the baud rate or a multiple of it.
   c. The baud rate can be either the same as the bps or a multiple of it.
   d. The baud rate is always higher than the bps.

3. A UART's primary purpose is to
   a. convert between binary and decimal.
   b. convert between synchronous and asynchronous communication.
   c. convert between parallel and serial transfer.
   d. convert between analog and digital data.

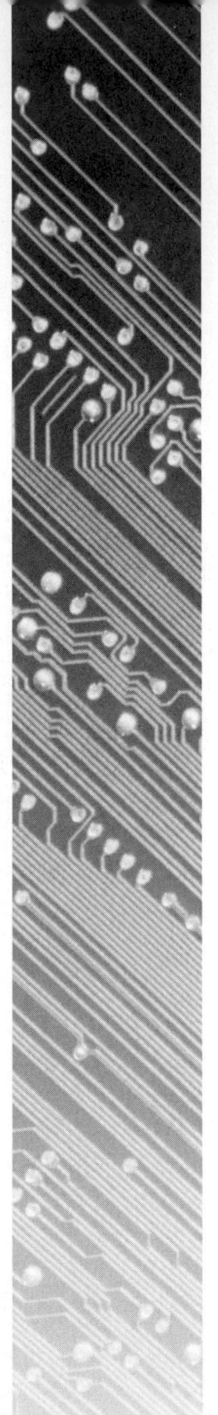

4. Which UART is the most common for legacy COM ports in modern motherboards, and supports FIFO buffer usage?
   a. 16650
   b. 16550
   c. 16770
   d. None of the above
5. What does the 7 represent in the communication settings E-7-1?
   a. parity setting
   b. stop bit
   c. data bits
   d. None of the above
6. What does the N represent in the communication settings N-8-1?
   a. parity setting
   b. stop bit
   c. data bits
   d. None of the above
7. What type of flow control uses RTS/CTS?
   a. hardware
   b. software
   c. binary
   d. analog
8. Which modem standard supports 56Kbps modem operation?
   a. V.90
   b. X2
   c. 56KFlex
   d. All of the above
9. Which of these statements is true of almost any 33.6Kbps modem?
   a. It supports the V.90 standard.
   b. It supports the V.34 standard.
   c. It supports the X2 standard.
   d. It supports only software-based error correction.
10. What is the difference between V.90 and V.92?
    a. V.92 includes extra features like QuickConnect and Modem-on-Hold.
    b. V.92 supports up to 115,200bps, while V.90 is limited to 56Kbps.
    c. Both a and b
    d. Neither a nor b

11. Which compression standard results in greater compression ratios, resulting in higher overall data throughput?
    a. V.42
    b. V.42bis
    c. V.44
    d. V.90

12. What is the difference between a hardware modem and a software modem?
    a. The software modem has an on-board controller, which interacts with the BIOS software; the hardware modem does not.
    b. The software modem works only in Windows (or possibly Linux); the hardware modem works in any operating system.
    c. The hardware modem works only in Windows; the software modem works in any operating system.
    d. Both a and b

13. Why does an internal modem need a UART chip but an external modem connected to a legacy COM port does not?
    a. because it functions as a COM port on its own, while an external modem uses an existing COM port
    b. because an external modem is a parallel device and does not need a parallel-to-serial converter, which is what a UART is
    c. because an internal modem is a Winmodem, while an external modem is a hardware modem
    d. None of the above—an external modem does have its own UART.

14. To which standard would you expect a new fax modem to conform?
    a. Group 4
    b. Class C
    c. V.17
    d. V.34

15. What should be the IRQ jumper setting on the modem when connecting an external modem to COM2 if the modem is not Plug and Play?
    a. IRQ 3
    b. IRQ 4
    c. IRQ 2
    d. None of the above

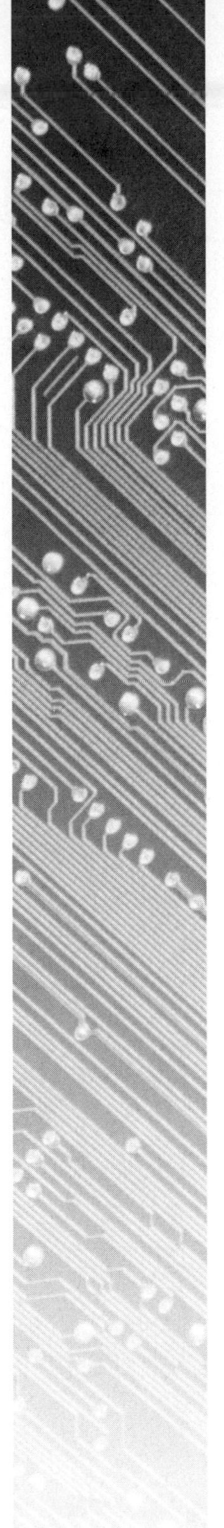

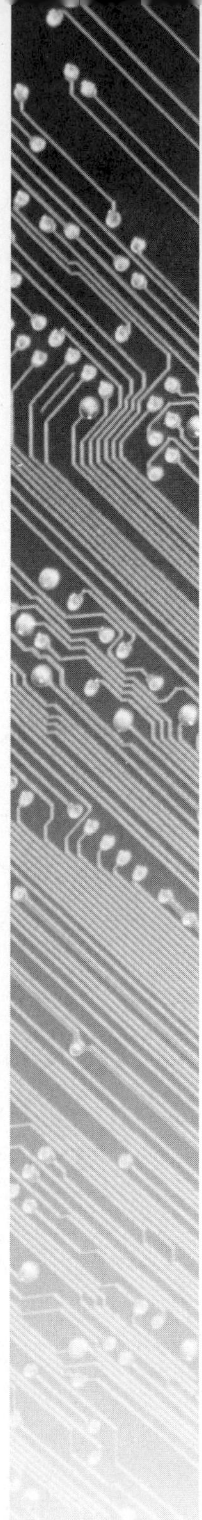

16. From which Control Panel applet do you start when you want to run a diagnostic test on a modem in Windows 98?
    a. Modems
    b. Networks
    c. System
    d. Dial-Up Networking
17. Which of these settings would you configure in the TAPI (Telephony) properties?
    a. phone number to dial for your ISP connection
    b. type of Dial-Up Networking server (PPP or SLIP)
    c. modem speaker volume
    d. number to dial to get an outside line
18. Which of these protocols is associated with binary transfer in terminal programs?
    a. SLIP
    b. PPP
    c. TCP/IP
    d. ZMODEM
19. If you are keying AT commands in a terminal program and the text you key does not show up on-screen, what command should you key?
    a. ATE1
    b. ATM0
    c. ATDT
    d. ATE0
20. What AT command turns off the modem speaker?
    a. ATM1
    b. ATM0
    c. ATE1
    d. ATE0

## TROUBLESHOOTING

1. A client is trying to dial up his ISP, but he gets an error message "Could Not Open Port" when he double-clicks the DUN connection icon. How will you troubleshoot this?
2. Windows automatically detects your client's new voice modem, and it works correctly as a modem, but the telephone answering software does not work. When you look in Device Manager, there is an item in the Sound, Video, and Game Controllers category called Wave Device for Voice Modem with a yellow circle and exclamation point next to it. How will you troubleshoot this?
3. A Windows 95 user has created a DUN connection, and it makes connection sounds when it connects to the ISP but will not stay connected; it hangs up after about 30 seconds each time. What would you check?

## CUSTOMER SERVICE

1. A client complains that his modem makes too much noise when dialing. What can you suggest?
2. A client just got a new computer, and needs to transfer her Internet connection settings to the new PC. Her old PC runs Windows 98, and her new one runs Windows 2000. Explain how to look up the settings for the old DUN connection in Windows 98 and how to reproduce them in Windows 2000.
3. A novice computer user wants to buy a modem and install it himself. What type of modem do you suggest, and why?

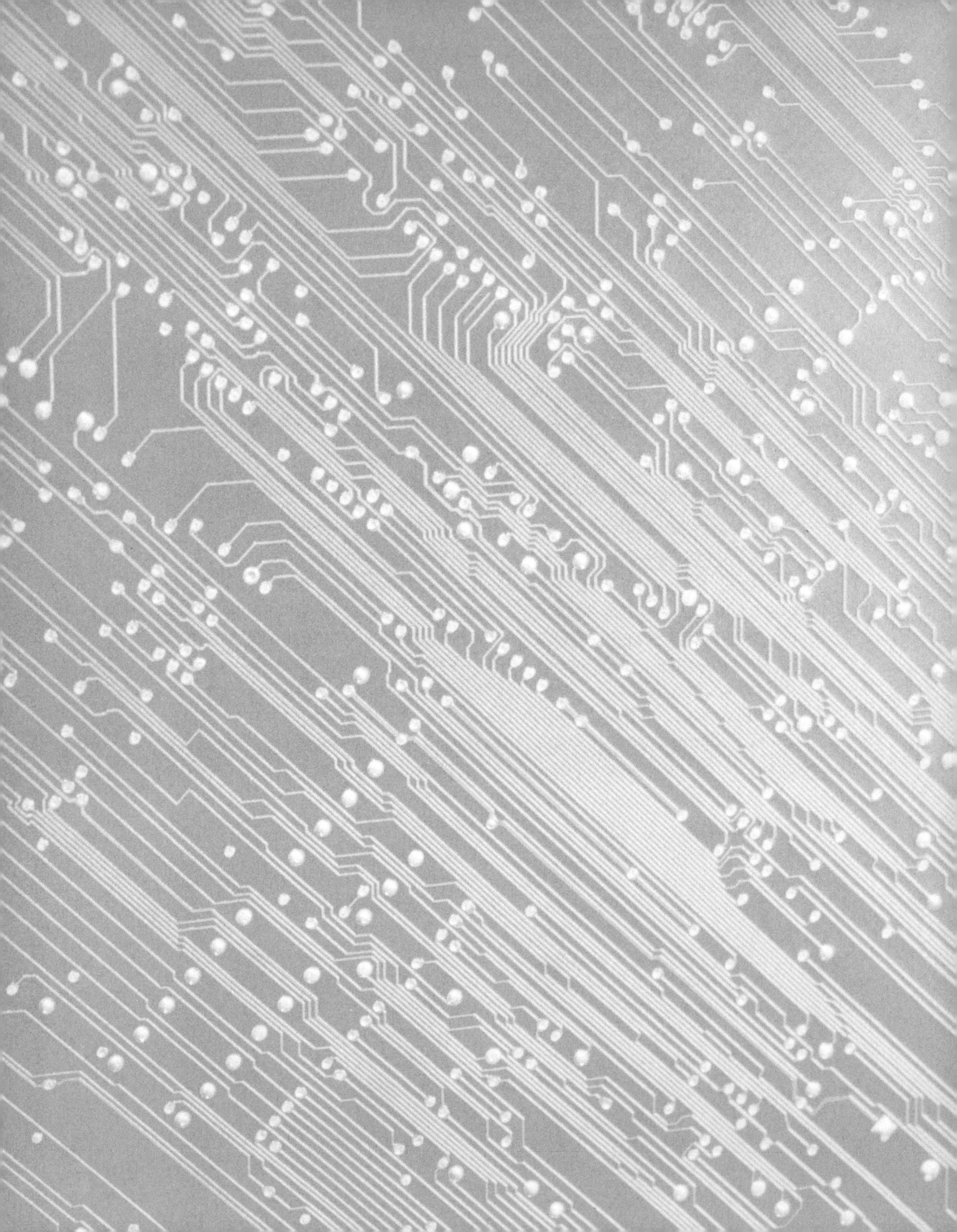

# 25 The Internet

## ON THE TEST

**A+ Operating System Technologies Examination**

- **Objective 4.1:** Identify the networking capabilities of Windows including procedures for connecting to the network.
- **Objective 4.2:** Identify concepts and capabilities relating to the Internet and basic procedures for setting up a system for Internet access.

## ON THE JOB

Almost everyone knows how to use the Internet to do simple Web searches and send e-mail, but a PC technician must have more than just end user knowledge on the subject. Technicians must know how the Internet actually functions behind the scenes and how to set up and change Internet access on PCs that connect to it in various ways.

Some on-the-job activities related to this chapter's content include:

- selecting an appropriate Internet connection method for a client
- configuring TCP/IP settings to use a static or dynamic Internet IP address
- explaining Internet protocols such as HTML, FTP, and POP to end users
- changing Internet configuration settings in Windows
- setting up an e-mail account in e-mail software such as Outlook Express
- sharing an Internet connection on a LAN
- adjusting Internet security and privacy settings for individual users
- troubleshooting Internet connectivity problems

## What Is the Internet?

**Internet**

A global, decentralized, publicly accessible TCP/IP-based network

The *Internet* is a huge public network of interconnected networks all over the world. It is held together by a common protocol set—Transmission Control Protocol/Internet Protocol (TCP/IP)—that all of the computers agree to use for communications among them.

TCP/IP was developed in 1969 by the U.S. Department of Defense to use on its Advanced Research Project Agency network (ARPANET). A key feature of ARPANET, and of the Internet today, is decentralization. Each server is in charge of only a tiny piece of the whole network, so the failure of a single server or router cannot harm the whole. Another key feature is path redundancy. There are many possible paths between every point A and point B, so if one path is not available the data can simply take another route. As with corporate networks, routers are employed to direct the traffic. In Chapter 22 you learned about the various network topologies; one of them was a mesh, in which every computer is connected to every other computer. The Internet achieves redundancy by a modified form of a mesh, in which each router is connected to several others (see Figure 25.1).

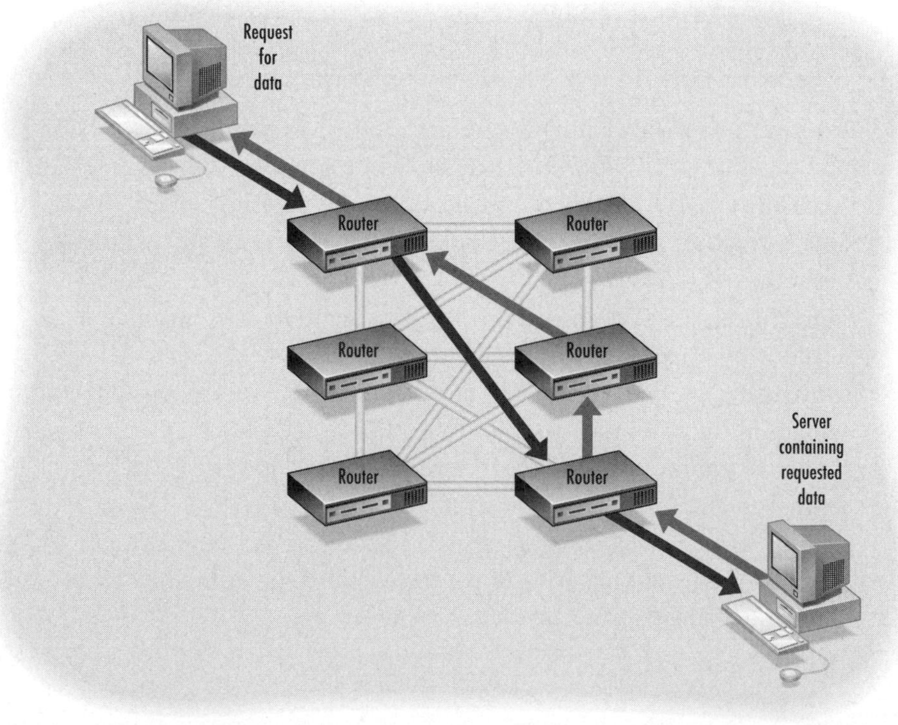


**FIGURE 25.1**
Data can take any of many different paths from one point to another on the Internet.

As discussed in Chapter 22, TCP/IP works at the Network and Transport levels of the OSI model (levels 3 and 4). Even though all of the computers on the Internet share TCP/IP in common, there are many different operations going on at higher and lower levels. For example, at the lowest OSI layers (Data-Link and Physical) could be any number of different network types, including Ethernet, Token Ring, or Dial-Up Networking with PPP. At higher levels (Session, Presentation, and Application), various activities could be taking place, such as Web browsing, e-mail sending and retrieving, or terminal emulation (see Figure 25.2). Later in this chapter we will look at those higher level Internet activities with the focus on supporting end users.

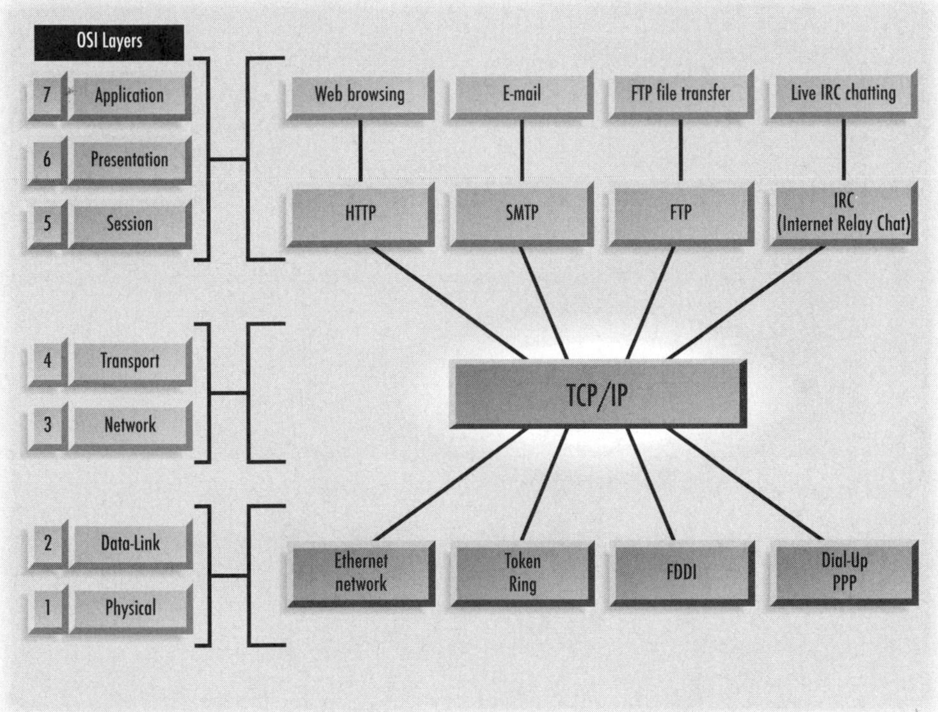


**FIGURE 25.2**
The Internet's only common denominator is the TCP/IP protocol.

## Ways to Connect to the Internet

Large companies typically have their own Internet-connected servers that connect their employees to the Internet via the corporate LAN (local-area network). The company leases a dedicated line from the phone company that connects full-time into the Internet, and all of the PCs on the company's LAN share that single on-ramp. Individual Internet users do not

**Internet Service Provider (ISP)**

A company that sells Internet access to the public.

have access to such an on-ramp, so they contract with *Internet Service Providers* (ISPs) to lease access to an on-ramp. Different ISPs offer different types of connections, including dial-up, cable, or DSL. Along with providing Internet access, the ISP also typically provides e-mail service and a limited amount of file storage space for posting Web pages. An ISP provides a connection from its central server to each customer location, through cable, through DSL via the phone company, or through Dial-Up Networking with a modem (see Figure 25.3).

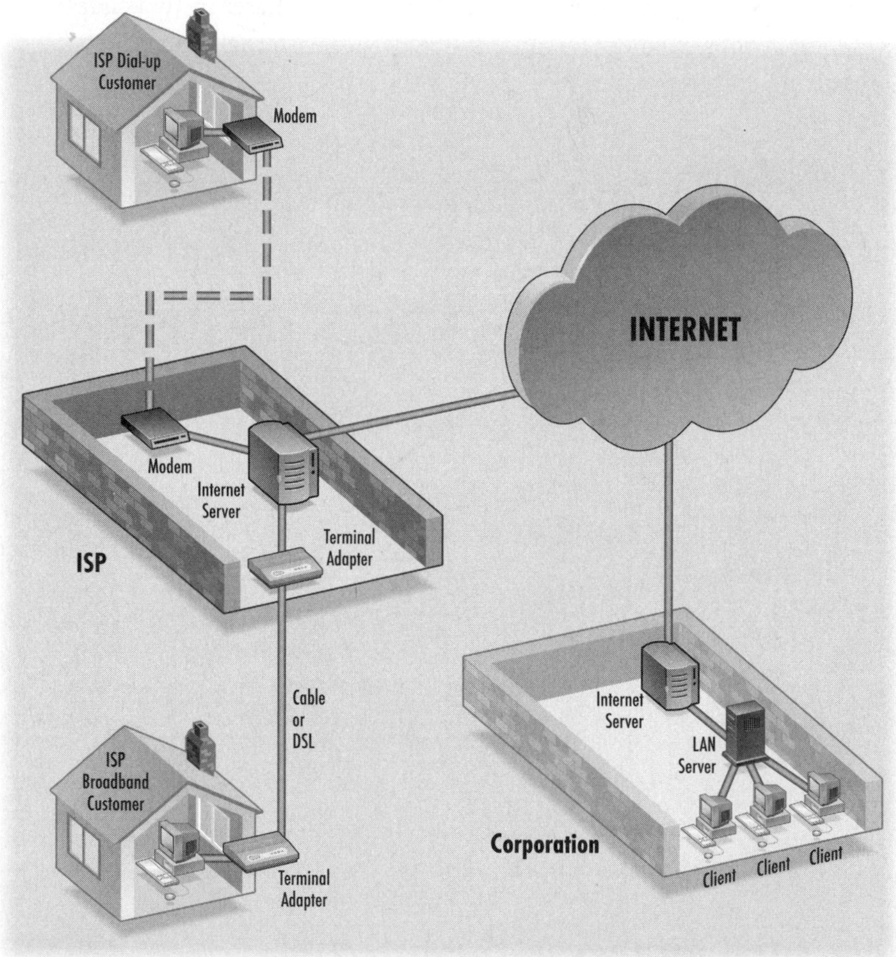


**FIGURE 25.3**
Some companies have their own Internet server; small businesses and individuals lease access to an Internet server from an ISP.

## Modem

Until the last few years, modem access to an ISP through Dial-Up Networking (DUN) was the primary way that home users connected to the Internet. It is still very popular. Chapter 24 covered how to install a modem and how to create a DUN connection to an ISP or private network.

Modem access requires a compatible modem at each end and a telephone line between them. The modems convert the digital data from the sending PC to an analog signal, and then convert the analog signal back to digital at the receiving end.

## ISDN

*Integrated Services Digital Network* (ISDN) is a digital line from the telephone company. Before the other broadband Internet options were widely available—such as cable and Digital Subscriber Line (DSL)—ISDN provided a way to increase Internet connection speed in homes and small offices without spending hundreds of dollars a month.

**Integrated Services Digital Network (ISDN)**

A type of digital telephone line with two 56Kbps data channels for Internet connection and a voice channel.

An ISDN connection to an ISP uses two 56Kbps channels simultaneously, for a combined speed of approximately 112Kbps. In addition to the two data channels, it also has a separate voice channel, so you can place and receive regular phone calls on the same line while connected to the Internet. ISDN is dial-up based, so you use a DUN connection to connect to the ISP and hang up the connection when finished. ISDN uses a terminal adapter, which is similar to a modem except, since the data is sent and received in digital format, it does not translate between analog and digital.

ISDN is no longer popular because it is rather expensive, and because there are higher-speed alternatives in the same price range. The special ISDN phone line costs $50 or more a month, and most ISPs charge more for ISDN access than for regular dial-up access. ISDN also can be tricky to set up in Windows, depending on the brand and model of the terminal adapter.

**WARNING**

**Residential telephone customers can have an ISDN phone line installed, but it will not work with the existing telephone wiring in the home, so no existing phone jacks can be used for that line.**

## DSL

*Digital Subscriber Line* (DSL) is a service that must be provided and supported by the local telephone company. It is suitable for both businesses and residences.

**Digital Subscriber Line (DSL)**

A broadband Internet connection type that operates through normal telephone lines.

**Asynchronous DSL (ADSL)**

A type of DSL service in which upload speed is slower than download speed.

**Synchronous DSL (SDSL)**

A type of DSL service in which upload and download speeds are the same.

There are two kinds of DSL: *ADSL* (Asynchronous DSL) and *SDSL* (Synchronous DSL). Asynchronous and Synchronous refer to the speed difference between downloading and uploading. ADSL is the most common type, and it allows faster downloads than uploads. SDSL is the more expensive, less common type, and it has the same speed for both uploading and downloading. The speed of DSL varies depending on the service type, but it can range from 256Kbps to over 2Mbps, usually in the 1Mbps range.

Even though DSL service comes through the phone line, it is not a dial-up service and does not tie up the telephone line. It works using unused portions of the phone line, so users can receive and place regular calls while it is running.

Instead of a modem, DSL uses a terminal adapter (usually an external box) that connects to the PC and manages the connection. Windows then sees the connection as a LAN connection to the Internet. Monthly fees vary, but are usually in the $40 to $50 range for basic ADSL residential service.

## Cable

Cable Internet service comes from the local cable TV company, and is available only in residential areas where the cable TV system has been updated to "digital cable" using a fiber-optic backbone. The cable carries both the TV signal and the Internet (two-way). An external terminal adapter connects to a NIC (network interface card) in the computer, and the computer sees the Internet connection as an ordinary LAN connection through which Internet flows. It provides a full-time, always-on Internet connection with no dial-up. Since it has nothing to do with the telephone, no phone line is needed.

Unlike DSL, cable bandwidth is shared with others in the neighborhood, so users might experience slightly slower service during periods of high usage if many people in the area have cable Internet access. The speed of cable access varies between 512Kbps and 2Mbps, usually hovering around 1Mbps, so it is more or less equivalent to DSL speed. As with DSL, monthly prices vary, but are typically in the $30 to $50 range.

## One-Way Satellite

One-way satellite works with a satellite dish like the one for satellite TV service. An ordinary satellite dish will not work for Internet access, however; it must be a dish specifically designed for satellite Internet use.

DirecWay, from the makers of DirecTV, is the most popular kind. The DirecWay dish will also work with DirecTV television programming, so users can have a single dish for both. Users can watch TV and use the Internet simultaneously because the features function separately (through separate cables off the common dish).

One-way satellite service is less than ideal; it broadcasts data to the user PC, but it does not accept input; requests for data, as well as uploads, must be sent via a separate modem. Therefore, all of the drawbacks of a dial-up modem connection apply to a one-way satellite connection, including tying up a phone line, having to dial-up to connect, and creeping along at only 56Kbps. The only advantage that one-way satellite offers is superior download speeds, up to 512Kbps.

### Two-Way Satellite

Two-way satellite uses the same technology as one-way satellite for downloading, but for uploading it has its own transmitter, so users do not need to rely on a phone line. As with the one-way service, the most popular provider is DirecWay.

Adding the transmitter to the mix solves most of the problems with the one-way satellite. The connection is always on, you do not need a phone line for it, and it does not tie up the phone. Upload and download speeds are reasonably good—between 100 and 512Kbps. The drawbacks are the expense of buying the hardware (nearly $700 to get started) and the substantial monthly fee for service (around $70 as of this writing). Other minor annoyances include the chance of temporarily losing the Internet connection in heavy rain, and the need for a hardware modem (that is, not a Winmodem) to get the service set up initially.

## IP Addresses on the Internet

As you learned in Chapter 22, an IP address is a number string that uniquely identifies each network device to all other network devices (such as client PCs, servers, routers, network-enabled printers, and so on). Chapter 22 covered TCP/IP addresses in detail from a Windows configuration perspective, so review that information if needed for clarification of terms like IP address, default gateway, or subnet mask.

On a LAN, the network administrator can assign IP addresses to each PC, and assign subnet masks to differentiate one group of computers from another. It does not matter what IP addresses are used on an internal LAN as long as no two devices have the same assignment. As mentioned earlier, IP addresses can be assigned manually by configuring each PC's TCP/IP properties, or can be assigned automatically through a DHCP (Dynamic Host Configuration Protocol) server. Multiple networks can have duplicate IP addresses as long as the networks are completely separate; if you connect them, any duplicate addresses must be changed.

The Internet is considered a single large network, so there can be no IP address duplication on it. To avoid potential duplication problems, a central IP address assignment authority assigns IP addresses to ISPs and corporations that want to connect servers directly to the Internet. An ISP or corporation will typically lease a block of addresses, from dozens to thousands depending on its needs.

## Network Address Translation (NAT)

If a LAN administrator in a corporation sets up an entire network using IP address assignments of his own choosing, and then is asked to connect his LAN to the Internet, how does he avoid conflicts? He installs a Network Address Translation (NAT) service on his Internet server. When a PC on the LAN requests a Web page, for example, that PC sends the request, along with its internal IP address, to the company's Internet server. The Internet server then changes the IP address on the request to an allowed IP address from the pool of valid Internet IP addresses it has been given to work with. When the information comes back from the Internet, the server removes the external IP address and replaces it with the requesting PC's original LAN IP address; then it places the data back on the local network for retrieval by the requesting PC. This process is illustrated in Figure 25.4.

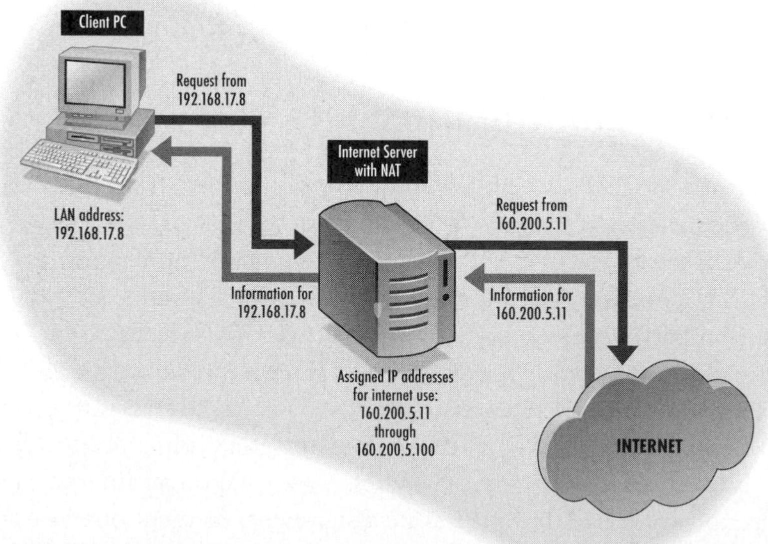


**FIGURE 25.4**
Network Address Translation converts a LAN's internal IP addresses to IP addresses allowed on the Internet.

## Static and Dynamic Internet IP Addresses

There are more Internet users in the world today than there are IP addresses. Therefore, not every device can have a permanent, full-time IP address assignment. An ISP typically will have a block of IP addresses, and dynamically assign them to dial-up customers each time they connect. In other words, each time a dial-up Internet user connects to the ISP, she gets a randomly assigned dynamic IP address from the available pool. When she disconnects, that IP address is released back into the ISP's pool. An ISP needs significantly fewer IP addresses than it has clients because not all clients will be connected simultaneously. Dynamic IP addressing is appropriate for end user PCs because the PCs are not hosting anything, so they do not need a consistent address in order for other PCs to find them. Using a dynamic IP address is like borrowing a different cell phone each time you make a telephone call.

Servers that are connected full-time to the Internet have *static IP addresses*—that is, more or less permanent assignments. Why "more or less"? Because an IP address is assigned to a particular device much as a phone number is assigned to a residence. The fact that the number stays constant on a day-to-day basis makes it possible for others to contact the owners. Static IP addresses are appropriate for servers that provide content on the Internet. A static IP address makes it easier for other PCs to find them and access that content. Using a static IP address is like having a regular telephone line installed in a building and having its number published in the phonebook.

**Static IP address**

An IP address that is assigned to a network device for its exclusive use, which it retains even after disconnecting and reconnecting.

The advantage of having a static IP address is that it allows you to host a Web site directly on your computer. This requires a static IP address because that IP address must be referenced on DNS servers as linked to your domain name. The disadvantage of a static IP address is that it is easier for hackers to find you and try to break into your system.

### In Real Life

**Most broadband Internet ISPs that use dynamic addressing have their systems set up so that when it comes time to renew an IP address assignment, each PC automatically is renewed with the same IP address it had before unless otherwise specified. It may thus appear that a PC's IP address remains the same for months or even years on end, even though it is officially a "dynamic" IP address.**

### INTERNET DNS SERVERS

Recall from Chapter 22 that a Domain Name System (DNS) server converts between domain names, such as Microsoft.com, and IP addresses. There are public DNS servers all over the Internet that store domain name/IP address translation tables and look up whatever translations are needed when a request comes through.

For example, suppose a user wants to view the Web site for Sycamore Knoll Bed and Breakfast. He knows that the domain name is sycamoreknoll.com, so he keys **http://www.sycamoreknoll.com** into his Web browser. The Web browser conveys the request to the nearest Web server. The server has no idea where sycamoreknoll.com is, so it consults a DNS server. The DNS server determines that the IP address for the site is 207.150.192.12, and it sends that information back to the server. The server adds that to its own information banks, and whenever a client PC requests sycamoreknoll.com, the server is able to translate the request to the equivalent IP address without having to query the DNS server again.

All DNS servers on the Internet share information with each other, so when a change is made at one location, it eventually filters out to all of the other DNS servers in the world. It sometimes takes a few days, however, and during that time users may get different results when accessing certain domain names depending on which DNS server answers the request.

When reading a domain name, the order of domains moves from right to left, with the top-level domains at the end. For example, in the domain name sycamoreknoll.com, the "com" portion is the top-level domain and the "sycamoreknoll.com" portion is the second level. An organization called Internic administers the top-level domain names, and maintains DNS servers that direct requests to secondary DNS servers to process them. The request for sycamoreknoll.com would go to the Internic server in charge of "com." That server, in turn, maintains a list of all of the .com domain names in the world, but has no information about any domain names that end with any other suffix.

## TCP/IP Communications Protocols

IP addressing occurs at the Network layer (Layer 3) of the OSI model, and the Transmission Control Protocol (TCP) portion occurs at the Transport level (Layer 4). All TCP/IP connections have those protocols in common. As you saw in Figure 25.2, however, at the Session and Presentation layers (5 and 6) a variety of different communications protocols can be active.

These different high-level protocols are necessary because of the different uses people make of the Internet.

When an application requests information from the Internet, the address is usually preceded by the code for the communication protocol, to avoid confusion. For example, most people are familiar with http as a prefix to Web addresses. The Web address http://www.sycamoreknoll.com opens the default page at the specified Web site. In contrast, the address ftp://ftp.sycamoreknoll.com opens the FTP site for that domain. The full address of a file on the Internet, including the protocol prefix, is its *Uniform Resource Locator* (URL). A URL is the standard notation by which people refer to retrievable files across all the various Internet protocols.

The following sections outline some of the most popular Internet communication protocols, and explain what types of applications (Application layer, Layer 7) commonly work with them.

**Uniform Resource Locator (URL)**

The complete address of a file available on the Internet, including a prefix such as http or ftp that indicates the communication protocol with which to retrieve it.

## HTTP

*Hypertext Transfer Protocol* (http://) is the protocol used for the Web. The most common application that uses it is a Web browser, but other programs might also have HTTP capability. For example, some Microsoft Office applications support HTTP, as do most Web site design applications.

*Hypertext Markup Language* (HTML) is the programming language in which Web content is written. For years it was the only language supported by Web browsers, but today other programming types are available that also create Web content, such as Java and CGI. HTML files are plain text files with encoding that creates formatting and integrates external graphics files. For example, the string would format the text as Bold and then insert a paragraph break:

<B>This is great!</B></P>

HTML code-writing is not covered on the A+ exam, but a well-rounded PC technician should be familiar with its basic structure and with at least a basic set of simple HTML codes. (For more information on HTML, see *HTML Essentials* by Steve Callihan [St. Paul: EMC/Paradigm]).

**Hypertext Transfer Protocol (HTTP)**

The protocol used by Web browsers to request and receive Web page content.

**Hypertext Markup Language (HTML)**

The programming language used to create formatted Web pages. Consists of formatting codes enclosed in angle brackets in plain text strings.

### TRY IT!

**Open a Web page in Internet Explorer, and then choose View/Source to see the HTML codes behind that page.**

## FTP

File Transfer Protocol (FTP://) is the protocol used for uploading and downloading files. FTP applications are the most common use of FTP, but most Web browsers also support FTP in at least a limited way. For example, you can key a URL beginning with FTP:// in a Web browser to open a list of files in a certain Internet location, and some links on Web pages download files via FTP.

## TELNET

Telnet (TELNET://) is an old communications protocol that is seldom used today. It was designed for terminal emulation in the days when logging on to a mainframe or server via direct modem connection was common. Telnet emulates the text-only dial-in of a terminal program such as HyperTerminal, but does it over the Internet. There are telnet applications available, but most people utilize telnet through a Web browser.

## E-MAIL PROTOCOLS

There are several e-mail protocols. The most common is POP (Post Office Protocol); it is used for receiving e-mail via a mail server. With POP, the messages are transferred from the mail server to the local PC and read from there, so it is most suitable for people who work from only one local PC.

An alternative to POP is IMAP (Internet Message Access Protocol). IMAP is advantageous because it allows mail to be accessed from multiple locations. People who sometimes want to be able to send and receive mail from a local PC but also want to access mail via a Web interface while traveling will find IMAP preferable to POP.

For sending mail, the dominant protocol is SMTP (Simple Mail Transfer Protocol). It is necessary because both POP and IMAP are receive-only protocols; they do not send.

The traditional use for e-mail protocols is through an e-mail program such as Microsoft Outlook Express, Microsoft Outlook, or Eudora. You configure an e-mail account in one of these programs, using an SMTP server to send mail and a POP or IMAP server to receive it. Many ISPs also offer Web-based e-mail access, enabling users to retrieve their e-mail from any location via IMAP or POP.

There is also an entire class of Web-based e-mail that uses the HTTP protocol to send and receive. This type of e-mail account is typically provided by a major Web portal such as MSN, Yahoo, or Hotmail, and is generally offered free of charge.

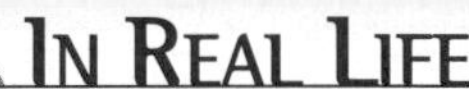

## In Real Life

Your ISP or domain hosting company might allow you to specify whether e-mail addresses use POP or IMAP. If you plan on accessing the mail primarily from the Web, choose IMAP because of its more feature-rich Web interface capabilities.

# Using and Configuring Internet Explorer

The Web is the most popular component of the Internet, and Internet Explorer is the most popular Web browser application. It comes free with all versions of Windows except some earlier versions of Windows 95. You can download a free copy of Internet Explorer from Microsoft's Web site to install on such PCs.

This book shows Internet Explorer 6.0, but the version you are working with might be older or newer. The program's basic functionality is the same across all versions; later versions simply have more options. You can download a free update to the latest version of Internet Explorer at any time from Microsoft at http://www.microsoft.com/ie.

## Using Internet Explorer to Access Web Content

You probably already know how to use a Web browser, therefore this course will not spend time teaching basic Web browser functionality. Figure 25.5 shows the basics.

- **To access a particular URL:** Key it in the Address bar and press Enter or click Go (see Figure 25.6).
- **To search the Web:** Go to a major search site such as www.msn.com or www.google.com, enter the keywords you are searching for, and then press Enter. You can also click the Search button on the toolbar to open a search pane to the left of the main window.
- **To reload (refresh) a page:** Click the Refresh button, press F5, or choose View/Refresh.
- **To stop a page from loading:** Click the Stop button, press Esc, or choose View/Stop.
- **To return to the previous page:** Click the Back button (left-pointing arrow) or press the Backspace key or Alt + Left Arrow. To move forward after using Back, click the Forward button (right-pointing arrow) or press Alt + Right Arrow. Click the drop-down arrow on the Back or Forward button to go back or forward multiple steps at once.
- **To return to the home page** (the page the browser opens by default each time you start it): Click the Home button, press Alt + Home, or choose View/Go To/Home Page.
- **To change the browser home page:** Choose Tools/Internet Options and enter the desired URL in the Address text box on the General tab.

**FIGURE 25.5**
Web Browser Basics

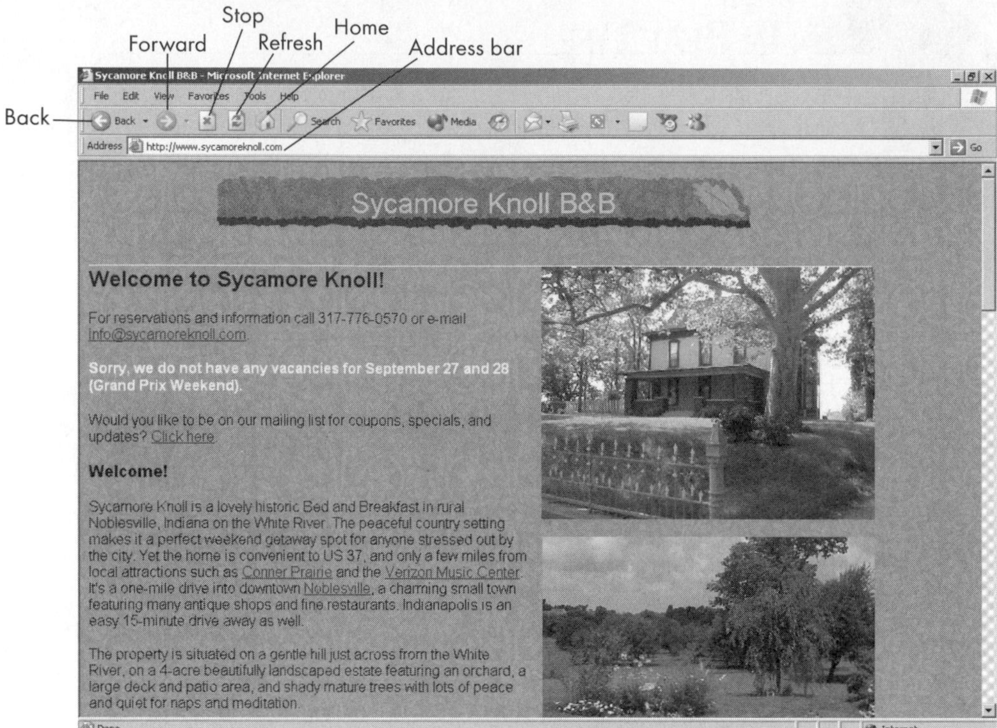


**FIGURE 25.6**
Internet Explorer, the most popular Web browser software, comes with Windows.

## TRY IT!

1. Open http://www.emcp.com in Internet Explorer.
2. Click a hyperlink to move to another page; from there click yet another hyperlink.
3. Open the drop-down list on the Back button and jump back to the initial page.
4. Click the Forward button twice to move forward again.
5. Click the Home button to return to the home page for your Web browser.

## Working with Favorites

You can save a URL to a Favorites list in Internet Explorer for easy return. To do so, follow these steps:

1. Display the page and then choose Favorites/Add to Favorites. The Add Favorite dialog box opens.
2. *Optional:* Change the name if desired. The default name is the page title.

3. *Optional:* Choose a folder in which to place the URL if desired. The default is to place the URL directly on the top-level Favorites menu. You can create new folders with New Folder. If the list of folders does not appear, click the Create in button to open it up (see Figure 25.7).
4. Click OK. The item is added to the Favorites menu.

To return to any URL on the Favorites list, choose it from the Favorites menu, or open the Favorites list in the Explorer bar (see the next section) and click it from there.

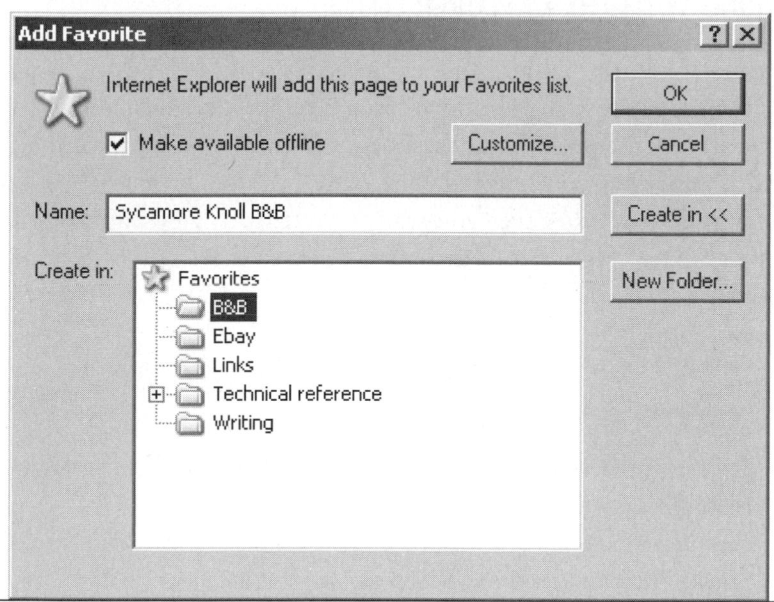


**FIGURE 25.7**
Adding a URL to the Favorites List

The Make available offline check box in Figure 25.7 saves the Web page to the hard drive so that it will continue to be viewable even when there is no Internet connection. This consumes disk space but can be useful on a PC with dial-up access. It is not necessary for PCs with broadband always-on connections. There is an Offline Favorite Wizard that fine-tunes the settings for offline saving, available when you click the Customize button in Figure 25.7. This wizard allows you to specify how many levels deep you want the Web materials to be saved offline. For example, if you specify two levels deep, it will save not only the current page offline, but also every page that it links to, and every page that those pages link to. You would not want to specify many levels deep for a Web page with a lot of links because of the amount of disk space it would consume.

## TRY IT!

Make http://www.emcp.com a favorite on your Favorites list. Make it offline, with content saved one level deep.

After saving a page offline, you can synchronize (update) your offline copy by choosing Tools/Synchronize.

### Working with the Explorer Bar

In Internet Explorer 6.0 and higher, an Explorer bar pane appears to the left of the main browsing window when you click certain toolbar buttons or issue certain menu commands. The content of that pane changes depending on what you selected. The pane has its own Close (*X*) button, so you can close it whenever you want to return to viewing the full-width Web page. Figure 25.8 describes some of the types of Explorer bar panes.

- **Search:** Displays text boxes and controls for searching the Web. The exact controls depend on the Windows version.
- **Favorites:** Displays your Favorites list in a separate pane. This is the same list as on the Favorites menu, but it remains visible until you close the pane.
- **Media:** Displays a media player panel for controlling the playback of video or sound clips you find on the Web. Appears automatically when you click a link that points to such a clip.
- **History:** Displays a list of the Web sites that this Web browser has recently visited. Useful for returning to a site when you do not remember its URL or for checking to see what sites someone else has visited on this PC. Figure 25.9 shows the History list in the Explorer bar. You can clear the history list from the Internet Options dialog box (Tools/Internet Options) on the General tab.

**FIGURE 25.8**
Internet Explorer Bar Panes

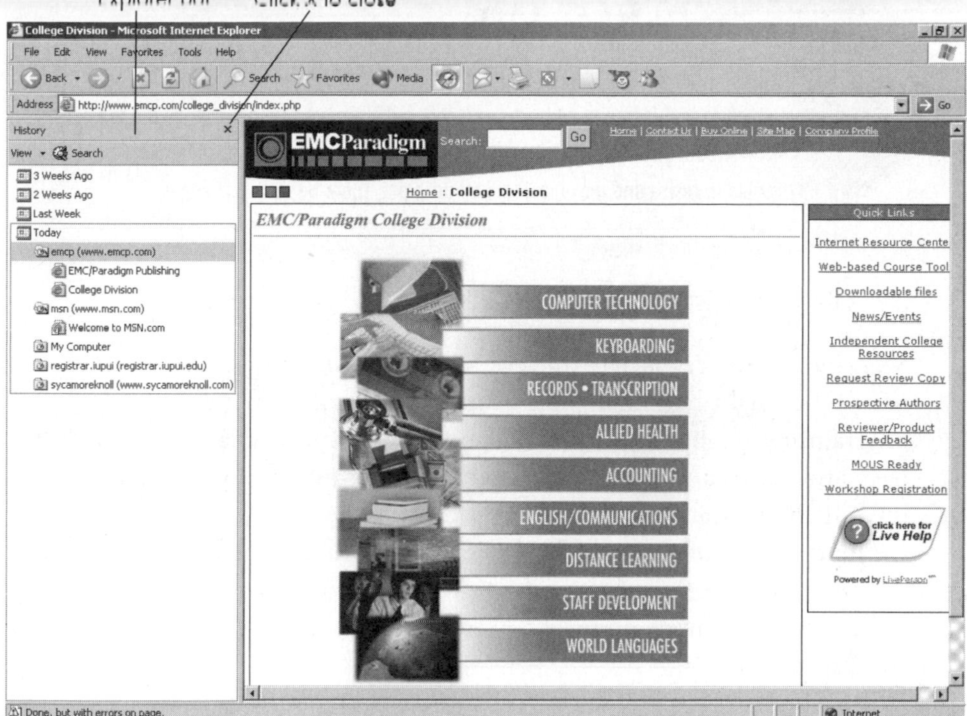


**FIGURE 25.9**
The Explorer bar can show the History list, as it does here, or the Media, Favorites, or Search pane.

## Changing Internet Explorer Viewing Preferences

Knowing about the viewing options in Internet Explorer not only helps you configure your own copy, but also assists you in helping end users when they make changes and are unable to remember how to reverse them. Here are some of the key settings:

- **Toolbars and Status Bar:** Turn these on/off from the View menu. There are several toolbars. One is the Address bar, in which you type the URL to which you want to go.
- **Text Size:** Choose a smaller or larger text size on the View/Text Size menu. This changes the text size of any text that is not coded in HTML for a specific fixed size.
- **Full Screen:** Choosing View/Full Screen or pressing F11 removes all toolbars, menus, and so on, for maximum browser space. F11 or the Maximize button brings everything back.

## In Real Life

In Internet Explorer 6.0 and higher there is a View/Toolbars/Lock the Toolbars feature that is turned on by default. When it is on, you cannot change the toolbars on-screen; you can only turn them on or off. Turn off that feature and you will be able to resize and move toolbars by dragging them by their left edges.

## Setting Security Preferences

Security preferences specify the level of protection desired against other users who might hack or exploit a PC via Web access. For example, a programmer might write a Java or ActiveX application that runs on a Web page and shows a video or plays a game, but also opens up a security hole in your PC that allows him to hack into it.

The trade-off on security settings is that if you set them too high, you are not able to enjoy much of the legitimate content on the Web. Therefore, most users prefer the Medium or Medium-Low setting as a compromise.

To change the security setting for Internet Explorer 6.0:

1. Choose Tools/Internet Options and select the Security tab.
2. Click the *Internet* icon (see Figure 25.10).
3. Drag the slider to change the security level for the Internet zone. (If you do not see the slider, click the Default Level button to make it appear.) This zone includes all Web sites that are not marked otherwise. If you have specific settings in mind, click the Custom Level button to access the Security Settings dialog box.
4. *Optional:* If there is a corporate intranet to which you have access, repeat step 3 for the *Local intranet* icon.
5. Click the *Trusted sites* icon, and then drag the slider to change the security setting for trusted sites (that is, sites that you know and trust). Then click the Sites button to open a dialog box where you can edit the list of trusted URLs.
6. Repeat step 5 for the *Restricted sites* icon.
7. Click OK to close the Internet Options dialog box.

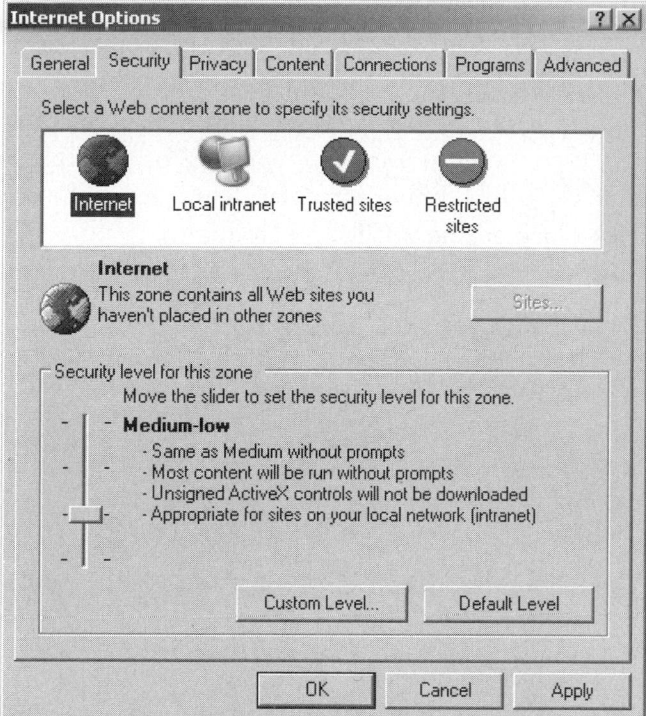


**FIGURE 25.10**
Set the security level for the Internet in general, for trusted sites, and for restricted sites.

## Setting Privacy Preferences

Privacy preferences specify how much information a Web site owner can collect from you when you visit the site. Web browsing is no longer automatically an anonymous activity, because applications that run behind the scenes on the Web server can collect data such as the number of times you visited a certain page, the pages you looked at on the site, and the searches you performed at that site. The higher you set your privacy settings, the more anonymous you will be.

However, some features on the Web site might not work if your privacy settings are too high. Many Web sites use *cookies* to identify returning users and restore their preferences. A cookie is a small text file stored on your own hard drive that conveys information to the Web site each time you visit it. Embedded in that Web page's HTML code is a directive to check the hard disk for a cookie. If it finds one, it loads the data from the cookie along with the rest of the page content. You can turn off or restrict cookie usage, but you might be unable to shop online at some shopping sites.

**Cookie**

A small text file stored on the hard drive that remembers settings for a particular Web site and reloads them each time you revisit that site.

To configure privacy settings in Internet Explorer 6.0:

1. Choose Tools/Internet Options and select the Privacy tab (see Figure 25.11).
2. Drag the slider up or down to increase or decrease the privacy setting.
3. *Optional:* If you want to override the normal privacy rules for certain Web sites, click the Edit button, enter the names of the sites, and then click Block or Allow. Click OK to return.
4. Click OK.

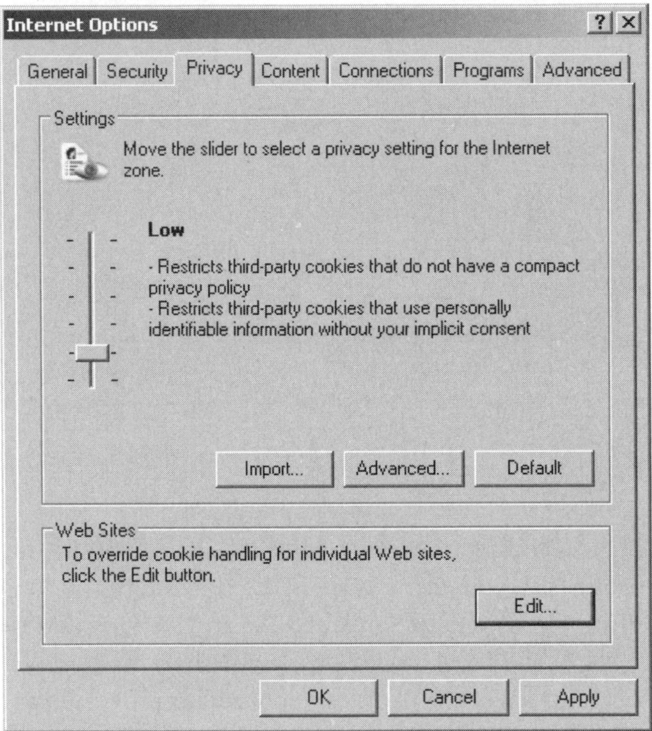


**FIGURE 25.11**
Configure privacy settings in Internet Explorer, allowing or blocking cookies as a whole or from certain sites.

There are a few other areas in Internet Explorer 6.0 where you can specify whether sensitive information should be stored locally. Many users are concerned about their privacy being protected, so that someone sitting down locally at their PC will not be able to tell what Web sites they have visited. Figure 25.12 lists some other areas in Internet Options (Tools/Internet Options) in which this information can be cleared or set up so as not to be recorded at all.

- **Clear Cookies:** On the General tab, click the Delete Cookies button to erase all current cookies.
- **Clear Offline Files:** On the General tab, click the Delete Files button to delete all offline files (which you might have if you set up one or more Favorites for offline viewing).
- **Clear AutoComplete:** When AutoComplete is on, and you start keying in a text box, it will attempt to fill in the text based on your previous entries. To turn this off, click the AutoComplete button on the Content tab to open the AutoComplete Settings dialog box (see Figure 25.13). Then deselect all of the check boxes to turn off all forms of AutoComplete and click the Clear Forms and Clear Passwords buttons to eliminate the current AutoComplete listings.

**FIGURE 25.12**
Explorer 6.0 Internet Options Settings

**FIGURE 25.13**
Turn off AutoComplete and clear existing AutoComplete entries for more local privacy.

## TRY IT!

1. Set Security and Privacy settings in Internet Explorer to the highest levels. Make note of the current settings before you change them.
2. Visit several Web sites, including sites that sell things. Make notes on any activities that are not possible because of the security or privacy settings.
3. Return the Security and Privacy settings to their previous levels.

# Using and Configuring Outlook Express

Outlook Express is a popular e-mail program because it comes free with Windows 98 and higher. (Windows 95 came with a similar program called Internet Mail.) The A+ exams do not focus on any particular e-mail program, but Outlook Express is an excellent example to work with because its features and operations are typical and because technicians are likely to encounter it frequently on the job.

As with Internet Explorer, this book assumes that you already have a passing familiarity with e-mail and e-mail software. We will briefly review the basic features, but the majority of this section will focus on configuring Outlook Express.

## Basic Program Features

To start Outlook Express, select it from the Start menu or click its icon on the Quick Launch toolbar.

Outlook Express is based on a system of folders. By default you start out in the top-level folder, but most people prefer to start in the *Inbox* folder. When the top-level folder is displayed, insert a check mark in the When Outlook Express starts, go directly to my Inbox check box, and from then on it will start up in the *Inbox* folder.

To check for new mail (assuming a mail account has been set up; see the next section if it has not), click the Send/Recv button on the toolbar. New messages appear in bold. Messages with attachments appear with a paper clip icon next to them (see Figure 25.14).

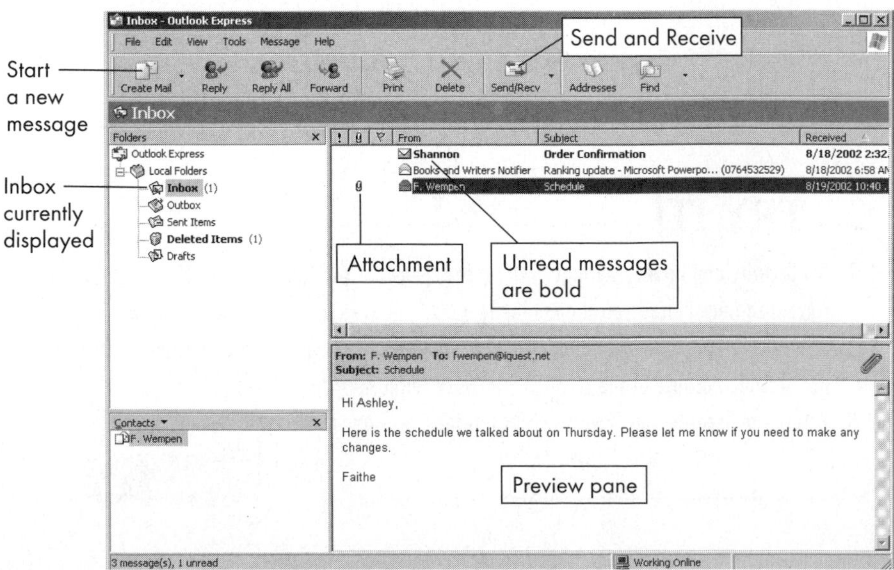


**FIGURE 25.14**
The Outlook Express *Inbox* folder lists incoming e-mail messages.

To preview a message in the lower right pane, click it once. To open the message in its own window, double-click it. To reply to it or forward it, click the Reply or Forward buttons, respectively.

## Setting Up E-Mail Accounts

The first time you start Outlook Express, if no e-mail accounts have been set up a wizard runs to help you set one up. You can also run this wizard at any time from within the program by doing the following:

1. Choose Tools/Accounts.
2. Click the Add button, and then click Mail. The Internet Connection Wizard runs, starting with the section where you set up a mail account.

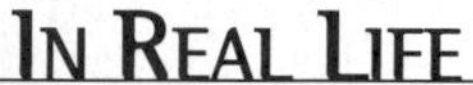

### In Real Life

**The Internet Connection Wizard that appears in step 2 is the same wizard that you might have used to create a DUN connection in Chapter 24. The wizard asks whether you want to create an e-mail account now; in Chapter 24 you were directed to answer No to that question. If you had answered Yes, you would have ended up exactly where you are now, at step 2.**

3. Key the name for the account. This can be any name that you want to appear in the *From* field when people receive e-mails from you. It does not need to be the same as your e-mail address. Click Next.
4. Key your e-mail address and click Next.
5. Select the mail account type from the My incoming mail server is a drop-down list; this is usually POP, but might be IMAP. You can also set up Outlook Express for a Web-based mail account, but that is less common.
6. Enter the addresses of your incoming and outgoing mail servers in the boxes provided (see Figure 25.15). Click Next.

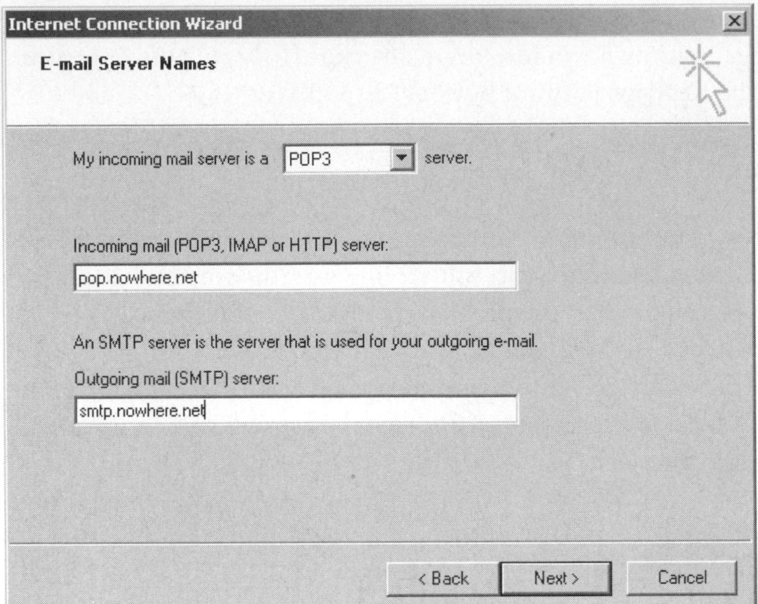


**FIGURE 25.15**
Enter the information for the mail servers from which you send and receive e-mail for this account.

## In Real Life

If you do not know the names of the mail servers, you might be able to guess them. The POP server is often *pop* followed by the domain name—for example, if your e-mail address is tom@nowhere.net, the POP server might be pop.nowhere.net. The SMTP server is often *smtp* followed by the domain name.

7. Enter the account name and password in the boxes provided; then click Next.
8. Click Finish. The mail account is now set up, and you can receive mail from it by clicking the Send/Recv button.

## TRY IT!

Set up Outlook Express for a POP e-mail account. If you have one of your own, use it; otherwise, ask your instructor for the settings for a practice account, or just create an account if there is no practice account available.

## Filtering Out Junk Mail

Different e-mail programs have different mechanisms for mail filtering. Outlook Express has a Message Rules feature that sorts incoming e-mail based on criteria you specify and delivers it to a different folder or simply deletes it altogether.

To create a rule, do the following:

1. With Outlook Express open, choose Tools/Message Rules/Mail. If no other rules have yet been created, the New Mail Rule dialog box opens. Otherwise the Message Rules dialog box appears; click New to get to the New Mail Rule dialog box.
2. Set up the rule by specifying the Conditions, Actions, and Rule Description, as shown in Figure 25.16.
3. Key a rule name by which to identify this rule, and then click OK.

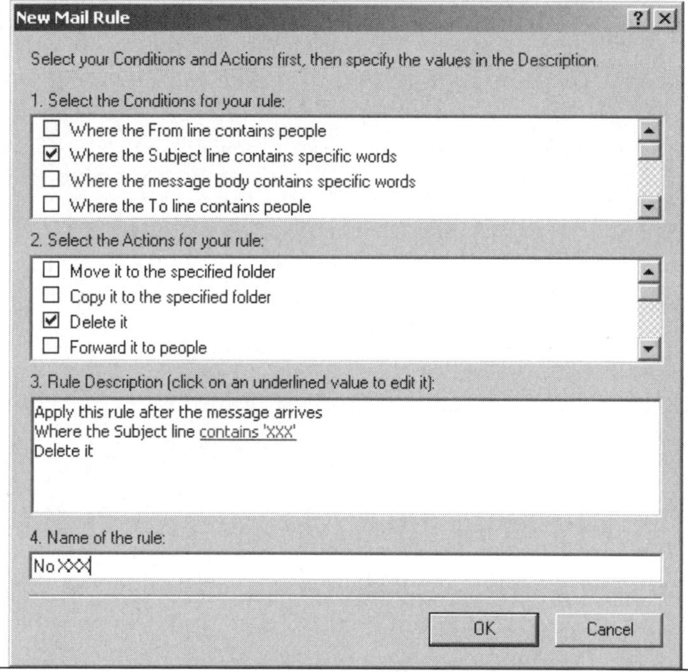


**FIGURE 25.16**
Filter out junk mail by subject with a mail rule.

You can also set up a Blocked Senders List to prevent certain people from sending you e-mail. This is useful if you keep getting junk mail from a specific sender even after asking to be removed. To add someone to the Blocked Senders List, right-click the sender's name on a received e-mail message and choose Add to Blocked Senders List.

### SETTING OUTLOOK EXPRESS CONFIGURATION OPTIONS

Choose Tools/Options in Outlook Express to open a dialog box containing tabs full of options you can set (see Figure 25.17). Virtually every aspect of the program's operation is configurable, from how often to check for new messages to how to quote text from the original when replying to a message. Explore these on your own.

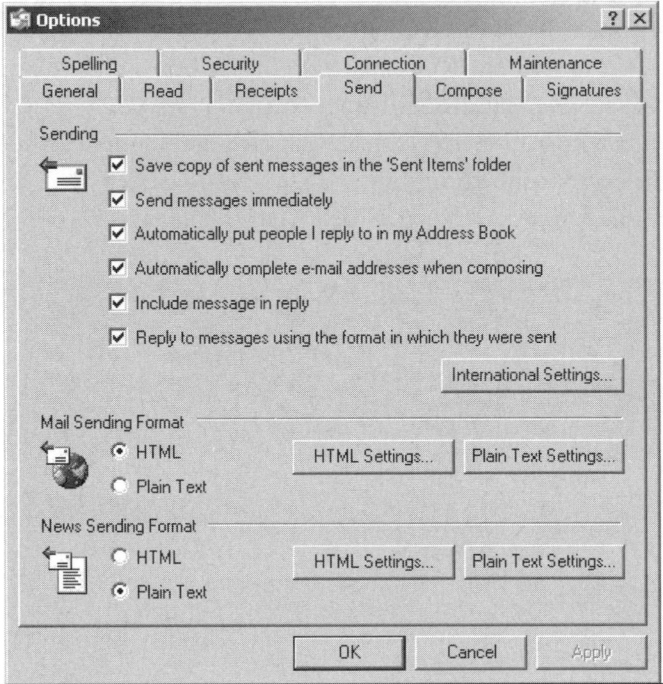


**FIGURE 25.17**
Outlook Express is fully customizable through the Options dialog box.

## Transferring Files with FTP

The FTP protocol provides an efficient way of uploading and downloading files between computers. Files can be transferred using other protocols, such as HTTP, but FTP results in faster transmission because it is designed specifically for that purpose.

**Anonymous FTP**

An FTP download that is available to all Internet users without their having to identify themselves.

In addition to maintaining a Web server, many companies also maintain an FTP server from which users can download files. Access may be through *anonymous FTP*, as with a public shareware archive, or may require a user name and password, as with a corporate document library.

When you log in as "anonymous" at an FTP server, you can enter any password you like; it does not matter. However, when a server offers anonymous FTP access, it is a great public service. As a courtesy, it is considered polite to include your e-mail address as the password when logging in using the anonymous user ID.

## SELECTING AN FTP PROGRAM

Most Web browsers, including Internet Explorer, support FTP in at least a limited way. By entering a URL that begins with ftp:// you can access a file listing of an FTP server. Figure 25.18 shows Internet Explorer being used in this way. It looks very much like a local or LAN file management window. To download a file, simply drag its icon to the desktop or to a local folder. To upload (if allowed), drag a local file into the folder.

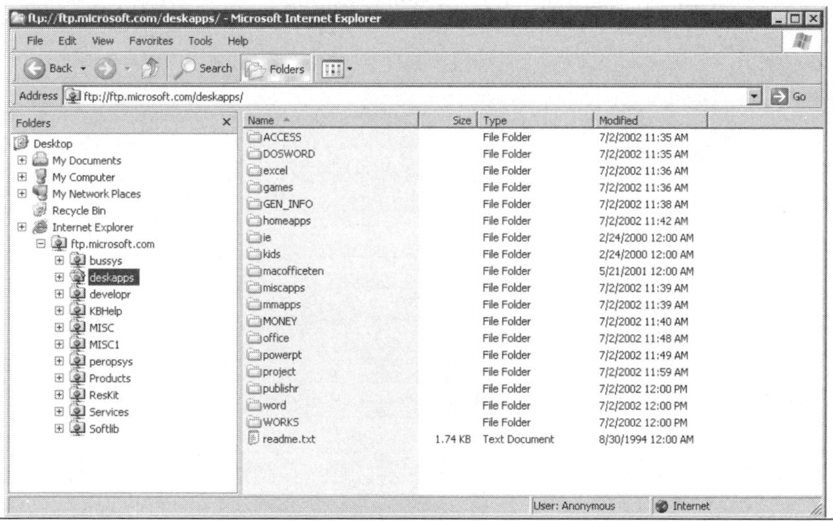


**FIGURE 25.18**
Internet Explorer can be used for FTP download.

For more FTP options, you might want a full-featured FTP program. One of the most popular is WS_FTP. The following section shows how to download it via Web FTP access, how to install it, and how to use it. There are many other FTP programs available, most of which are *shareware* or *freeware*.

**Shareware**

Software that is distributed to the public on the honor system, with the expectation that anyone who likes and continues using the program will pay for it.

## INSTALLING AND USING WS_FTP

WS_FTP is a commercial program, but there is a Limited Edition version that is free for personal use and for student/academic use. The manufacturer operates an FTP site that can be accessed via the Web; the

**Freeware**

Software that is distributed to the public without cost or obligation.

following steps show how to download and install WS_FTP Limited Edition (LE):

1. Open Internet Explorer and key the following in the Address text box: **ftp://ftp1.ipswitch.com/pub/win32**. Click Go or press Enter.
2. Find the *WS_FTPLE.exe* icon and drag it to the desktop. (Resize the Internet Explorer window if needed so the desktop is visible.)
3. When the file transfer has completed, close Internet Explorer and double-click the *WS_FTPLE.exe* icon to install the program.
4. Run the WS_FTP program from the Start menu after it is installed. A Session Properties dialog box opens.
5. Open the Profile Name drop-down list and choose an FTP site to connect to. You can set up other FTP sites on your own by clicking the New button, but for now choose an existing one, such as CDROM.com.
6. Insert a check mark in the Anonymous check box if it is not already marked, and enter your e-mail address in the Password text box. This is not essential, but it is considered courteous in the FTP community to indicate your e-mail address when logging in anonymously (see Figure 25.19).

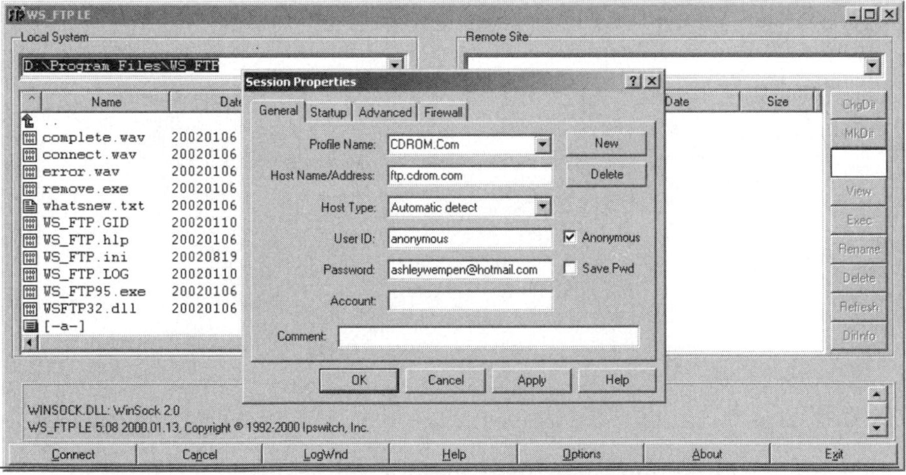


**FIGURE 15.19**
WS_FTP is a full-featured FTP program.

7. Click OK. The connection is established. The FTP server's folder structure appears at the right, and the structure of your own local drives at the left.
8. To upload, select a file or folder on the left (local drives) and click the right-pointing arrow. To download, select a file or folder on the right (FTP server) and click the left-pointing arrow.
9 When you are finished, click Exit.

## TRY IT!

1. Download and install WS_FTP Limited Edition using a Web-based FTP connection to ftp://ftp1.ipswitch.com/pub/win32.
2. Use WS_FTP to connect to CDROM.com.
3. In the *Pub\Gutenberg\etext00* folder, find and download the file 00ww110.txt to your Windows desktop.
4. Open that file in Notepad after downloading it. What is the first line of text in that file?
5. Exit WS_FTP and delete the downloaded file from your desktop.

## Command-Line FTP Access

You can also perform FTP from a command line, although this method is not frequently used because of the ease with which FTP works in Internet Explorer.

1. To enter the FTP command line program, key **ftp** at a command prompt and press Enter. The prompt changes to ftp>.
2. To open a session with an FTP server, key **OPEN** and then key its IP address or domain name.
3. A User prompt appears. Key the user name and press Enter. If you want anonymous access, key **Anonymous** as the user name.
4. A Password prompt appears. Key the password and press Enter. Nothing appears as you key. If you used Anonymous as the user name in step 3, key your e-mail address as the password.
5. Key **DIR** and press Enter to see a list of folders. Change to the folder you want by keying **CD** ***/foldername***.
6. When you find the file you want to download, key **GET** ***filename*** and press Enter. Or, if you want to upload a file, use the PUT command along with the path on your local PC. For example, to upload C:\books\sample.txt, key **PUT C:\books\sample.txt**.
7. When you are finished, terminate the connection by keying **BYE** and pressing Enter.

Figure 25.20 shows a typical command line FTP session.

```
D:\>ftp
ftp> open ftp.cdrom.com
Connected to cdrom.wip.digitalriver.com.
220 drftp.digitalriver.com NcFTPd Server (licensed copy) ready.
User (cdrom.wip.digitalriver.com:(none)): anonymous
331 Guest login ok, send your complete e-mail address as password.
Password: myemail@nowhere.net
230-You are user #56 of 500 simultaneous users allowed.
230-
230-Welcome to ftp.cdrom.com, a service of Digital River, Inc.
230-There are currently 56 users out of 500 possible.
230-
230 Logged in anonymously.
ftp> dir
200 PORT command successful.
150 Opening ASCII mode data connection for /bin/ls.
drwx—x--    4 ftpuser  ftpusers       512 Mar 14 09:33 locked
drwxr-xr-x   4 ftpuser  ftpusers        512 Aug 14 16:57 pub
drwxr-x--    2 ftpuser  ftpusers        512 Jul 22 13:30 trend
226 Listing completed.
ftp: 188 bytes received in 0.06Seconds 3.13Kbytes/sec.
ftp> cd /pub
250 "/pub" is new cwd.
ftp> dir
200 PORT command successful.
150 Opening ASCII mode data connection for /bin/ls.
lrwxrwxrwx   1 ftpuser  ftpusers         15 Jul 22 09:40 gutenberg -> ../.1/gutenberg
lrwxrwxrwx   1 ftpuser  ftpusers         14 Jul 22 22:27 imsifree -> ../.1/imsifree
drwxr-x--    2 ftpuser  ftpusers        512 Jul 29 12:56 intelligentapps
lrwxrwxrwx   1 ftpuser  ftpusers         13 Jul 22 22:27 malcolm -> ../.1/malcolm
lrwxrwxrwx   1 ftpuser  ftpusers         16 Jul 22 22:27 micrografx -> ../.2/micrografx
226 Listing completed.
ftp: 1763 bytes received in 0.00Seconds 1763000.00Kbytes/sec.
ftp> cd gutenberg
250 "/.1/gutenberg" is new cwd.
ftp> dir
200 PORT command successful.
150 Opening ASCII mode data connection for /bin/ls.
-r—r—r—   1 ftpuser  ftpusers     57197 Aug 16 16:00 GUTINDEX.00
-r—r—r—   1 ftpuser  ftpusers     67742 Aug 16 16:00 GUTINDEX.01
-r—r—r—   1 ftpuser  ftpusers     64462 Aug 16 16:00 GUTINDEX.02
-r—r—r—   1 ftpuser  ftpusers    120262 Aug 16 16:00 GUTINDEX.03
-r—r—r—   1 ftpuser  ftpusers    117843 Aug 16 16:00 GUTINDEX.04
-r—r—r—   1 ftpuser  ftpusers    592151 Aug 16 16:00 GUTINDEX.ALL
-r—r—r—   1 ftpuser  ftpusers      6026 May 18 03:52 donate-howto.txt
drwxr-xr-x   2 ftpuser  ftpusers      23040 Aug  5 01:02 etext00
drwxr-xr-x   2 ftpuser  ftpusers      33280 Aug 19 01:01 etext01
drwxr-xr-x   2 ftpuser  ftpusers      36864 Aug 11 01:00 etext02
drwxr-xr-x   2 ftpuser  ftpusers      58368 Aug 19 01:01 etext03
drwxr-xr-x   2 ftpuser  ftpusers      46080 Aug 19 01:02 etext04
drwxr-xr-x   2 ftpuser  ftpusers       2560 Mar 18 02:59 etext90

226 Listing completed.
ftp: 2471 bytes received in 0.07Seconds 35.30Kbytes/sec.
ftp> get donate-howto.txt
200 PORT command successful.
150 Opening ASCII mode data connection for donate-howto.txt (6026 bytes).
226 Transfer completed.
ftp: 6191 bytes received in 0.12Seconds 51.59Kbytes/sec.
ftp> bye
221 Goodbye.
D:\>
```

**FIGURE 25.20**
A typical FTP session at a command line (truncated for example purposes).

## Sharing an Internet Connection on a LAN

Many people are interested in sharing the Internet connection of one PC with other PCs in their home or small-office network. With Windows 98 Second Edition and higher, this is fairly simple. Broadband connections naturally lend themselves to sharing, but you can share a regular dial-up modem connection if needed.

To use *Internet Connection Sharing* (ICS), the PCs must first be networked. The PC with the connection to be shared must have Windows 98 Second Edition or higher, but the other PCs—the ones that will use the shared connection—can be running any version of Windows.

**Internet Connection Sharing (ICS)**

A feature in Windows 98 Second Edition and higher that enables a network client to share its local Internet connection with other PCs on the LAN.

Internet Connection Sharing must be installed manually in Windows 98 Second Edition and Windows Me; it is preinstalled in Windows 2000 and XP, and you configure it when you set up the Internet connection.

### Installing ICS in Windows 98 Second Edition

ICS is not installed by default in Windows 98 SE, so you must add it with Add/Remove Programs. You install ICS on the PC containing the Internet connection to be shared. To install ICS, complete the following steps:

1. From the Control Panel, double-click *Add/Remove Programs.*
2. Select the Windows Setup tab, and then double-click Internet Tools.
3. Insert a check mark next to Internet Connection Sharing.
4. Click OK until you have closed all open dialog boxes. If prompted, insert the Windows CD and click OK.
5. When the Internet Connection Sharing Wizard starts, click Next to begin.
6. If you see a list of adapters, select the adapter for the shared connection. For a modem, it is Dial-Up Adapter.
7. If asked what type of connection you have (dial-up or high-speed), click the appropriate button and then click Next.
8. If prompted, select the connection from a list provided. You will not see this prompt unless you have chosen high-speed and the wizard cannot determine which connection is for Internet. Click Next.
9. When you see a message that the wizard will create a client configuration disk, click Next. When prompted, place a blank disk in the floppy drive and click OK.
10. When prompted, remove the disk from the drive and click OK. Click Finish. When prompted to restart, click Yes.

That disk that is created can be used to set up PCs running other versions of Windows to use the shared connection. To run it on one of those PCs, insert it in the floppy drive, display the floppy drive content in My Computer, and double-click the *Icslet* icon. Then just follow the prompts.

The setup disk will not work with Windows NT/2000/XP PCs, but these should work automatically with the shared connection without any special setup. If the Internet connection does not work automatically, run the Internet Connection Wizard and instruct Internet Explorer to connect through a LAN.

## Installing ICS in Windows Me

As with Windows 98 Second Edition, ICS is not installed by default with Windows Me. The Windows Me version is more sophisticated, and its setup process asks a few more questions than the 98 version. To install it:

1. From the Control Panel, double-click *Add/Remove Programs.*
2. Select the Windows Setup tab, and then double-click Communications.
3. Place a check mark next to Internet Connection Sharing.
4. Click OK until you have closed all open dialog boxes. If prompted, insert the Windows CD and click OK.
5. When the Home Networking Wizard starts, click Next to begin.
6. Choose Yes, this computer uses the following. Then choose A direct connection to my ISP using the following device.
7. Open the drop-down list and choose the Internet connection. It is a dial-up networking connection if you use a modem; it is a network card or USB device if you have an always-on connection. Click Next.
8. When asked whether you want to share your connection, click Yes. Open the drop-down list and select the network card to use for the sharing. This is the network card for your local network. Click Next.
9. You are then prompted to create a setup disk. If you have PCs on the network that do not use Windows Me or higher, choose Yes; otherwise, choose No and skip to step 11.
10. When prompted, place a blank disk in the floppy drive and click OK. When prompted, remove it and click OK again.
11. Click Finish. When prompted to restart the computer, click Yes.
12. After restarting, a box appears that Home Networking has been set up. Click OK.

You can use the setup disk to set up the PCs that will share the connection; just insert the floppy and run the setup utility on the disk. As with Windows 98, the setup disk will not work with Windows NT/2000/XP PCs, but these should work automatically with the shared connection without any special setup.

## Sharing an Internet Connection in Windows 2000

To share an existing Internet connection in Windows 2000, do the following:

1. Choose Start/Settings/Network and Dial-Up Connections.
2. Right-click the connection to share and choose Properties.
3. Select the Sharing tab and then insert a check mark in the Enable Internet connection sharing for this connection check box.
4. Click OK.

## Sharing an Internet Connection in Windows XP

When you create an Internet connection in Windows XP, the wizard may ask you if you want to share the connection. If so, and if you indicate you do, it may already be set up for you. If not, or if you are not sure, do the following:

1. Choose Start/Connect To/Show all connections.
2. Right-click the connection you want to share and choose Properties.
3. Select the Advanced tab.
4. In the Internet Connection Sharing section, insert a check mark in the Allow other network users to connect through this computer's Internet connection check box.
5. Click OK.

## Setting Up Other PCs to Use the Shared Connection

The Windows 98 Second Edition and Windows Me ICS wizards enable you to create a setup disk to set up other PCs for Internet sharing access. Using this disk prepares PCs with earlier Windows versions for connection sharing.

You can also manually change a PC's settings, doing essentially the same thing that the ICS setup disk would do. To do so:

1. From IE, choose Tools/Internet Options.
2. Select the Connection tab.
3. Make sure Never Dial a Connection is selected.

4. Click the LAN Settings button.
5. Make sure Automatically Detect Settings is selected.
6. Click OK twice.

**TRY IT!**

**Connect several PCs in a small peer-to-peer network, and then share the Internet connection on one of them with all of the others. Confirm that each PC can open a Web page from the Internet using the shared connection.**

## Troubleshooting Internet Connection Problems

For dial-up Internet connections, problems with the Internet may actually be problems with the modem or with Dial-Up Networking. See Chapter 24 for troubleshooting suggestions. However, if you have network or broadband access, or if you have already eliminated DUN and the modem as sources of the problem, see the following sections for help.

### No Web, No E-Mail

If you are not getting any Web or e-mail access, look at the lights on the front of the broadband Internet terminal adapter. If it has been working in the past, you probably know what the lights look like when everything is functioning. If the lights do not look like that now, the terminal adapter either is not getting a signal from the ISP or needs to be reset. Steady lights usually mean it is working and flashing lights mean problems, but it all depends on the model.

Sometimes resetting the terminal adapter and restarting the PC will solve the problem. To reset the terminal adapter, turn it off, wait 10 seconds, and turn it back on. If there is no on/off switch, unplug it. If you are using a router to share the connection with multiple PCs, you can try resetting the router. You can also experiment with the following two utilities as part of your troubleshooting.

#### *Ping*

As you learned earlier in the book, ping is a handy command-line utility that works for both network and Internet connections. It queries a specified IP address and lets you know whether that IP address responded. The syntax is ping *ip_address*, as in ping 192.168.0.1.

(The word "ping" is not case-sensitive.) You can also ping domain names, such as www.microsoft.com, and a DNS server will translate the domain address to an IP address (that is, if a DNS server is reachable).

The first thing to ping is the loopback address: 127.0.0.1. If a response comes back, as in Figure 25.21, you know that the local PC is set up correctly for networking. Then ping the server, if you are on a LAN, to make sure that the LAN is operational. Finally, ping a well-known Web site, such as Microsoft: **ping microsoft.com**. If a response comes back, the Web connection is working. If you get a message that the request timed out, try some other, less busy Web site.

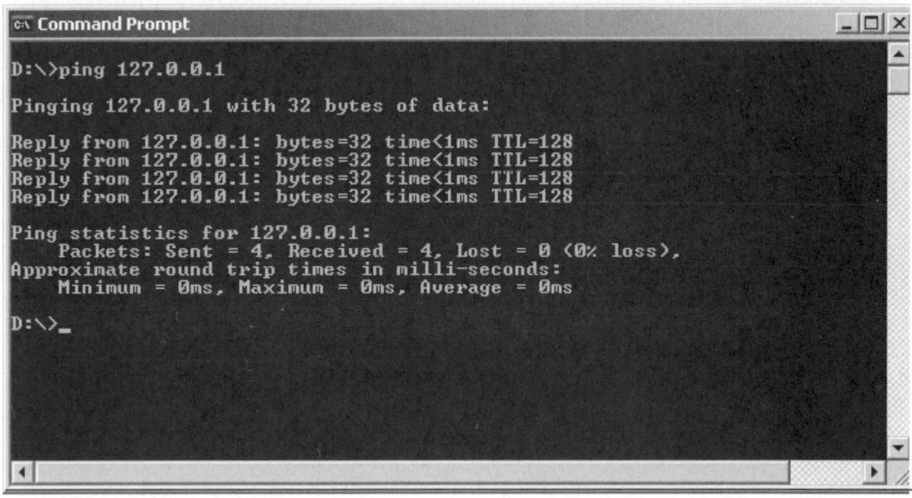

```
Command Prompt

D:\>ping 127.0.0.1

Pinging 127.0.0.1 with 32 bytes of data:

Reply from 127.0.0.1: bytes=32 time<1ms TTL=128
Reply from 127.0.0.1: bytes=32 time<1ms TTL=128
Reply from 127.0.0.1: bytes=32 time<1ms TTL=128
Reply from 127.0.0.1: bytes=32 time<1ms TTL=128

Ping statistics for 127.0.0.1:
    Packets: Sent = 4, Received = 4, Lost = 0 (0% loss),
Approximate round trip times in milli-seconds:
    Minimum = 0ms, Maximum = 0ms, Average = 0ms

D:\>_
```

**FIGURE 25.21**
Use ping to check for TCP/IP connectivity between the local PC and a specific IP address or domain.

### *Nslookup*

Nslookup is a command-line utility that looks up the IP addresses of domain names. Nslookup also reports the local PC's IP address, which can be helpful if the IP address is dynamically assigned and changes each time the user connects.

Here is a simple example. Suppose you want to find out the IP address of EMC Paradigm, the publisher of this textbook. To get it, go to a command prompt and key **nslookup emcp.com**. It reports your IP address first, and then the requested IP address, as in Figure 25.22.

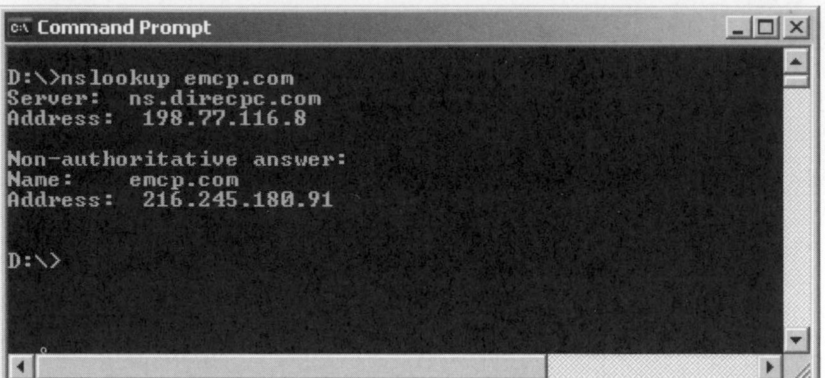


**FIGURE 25.22**
Use nslookup for a report of your local PC's IP address, and to look up the IP address of a specific domain.

Nslookup is a very complex, robust tool for gathering DNS information, not only on the Internet but in LANs and WANs. However, most of its features and subcommands are beyond the scope of this book, and useful primarily for a network administrator.

## Web but No E-Mail

If the Web works but e-mail does not, the e-mail account is probably not set up correctly in the e-mail program. Check the settings. In Outlook Express, choose Tools/Options, select the Mail tab, and double-click the account to see its settings. If nothing has changed since it stopped working, the settings are probably correct; the ISP's mail server is probably down temporarily for maintenance. Wait an hour or so and try again, or call the ISP's tech support to find out if there is a problem.

## E-Mail but No Web

**Proxy server**

A server maintained by an ISP or corporation through which all Web content requests pass. The proxy server caches the most commonly accessed Web content, speeding up access for its clients.

This error is fairly uncommon, and happens only with broadband connections. Some broadband services configure the Web browser to use a *proxy server* to speed up access. A proxy server sits between the real Web and the computer; if you call for any pages that it happens to have stored, it provides them more quickly than it could retrieve them from the Internet at large. DirecWay Satellite Internet service uses a proxy server, for example, as do some cable and DSL providers.

If you can send and receive e-mail but cannot get to the Web, maybe the proxy server is down, or maybe someone has changed the proxy server settings in the Web browser program. To check, open Internet Options from Internet Explorer (Tools/Internet Options), select the Connections tab, and click the LAN Settings button. Try deselecting the Use a proxy server check box. Or click the Advanced button and check the proxy server address against the information given to you by the ISP or network administrator.

## No Access to Specific Web Site

If the connection is basically working but one particular Web site will not display, that Web site is probably down for repairs. Try again in an hour or so, and you might find it working.

If one PC cannot access a certain Web site but another PC can, perhaps there is no route available from the PC to that site's server. A request from one point to another goes through a process somewhat like running a maze; when it hits a dead end, it backs up to the previous junction and tries another route. Even though the Internet has a mesh of interconnected routers, if multiple routers or paths fail at the same time it is possible to have a temporary situation in which you simply "can't get there from here." To check for routing, use the tracert command-line utility. It traces the route from the local PC to the destination, reporting the pathways it took to get there. Figure 25.23 shows tracert being used to check for a valid route from the local PC to the EMC Paradigm Web server.

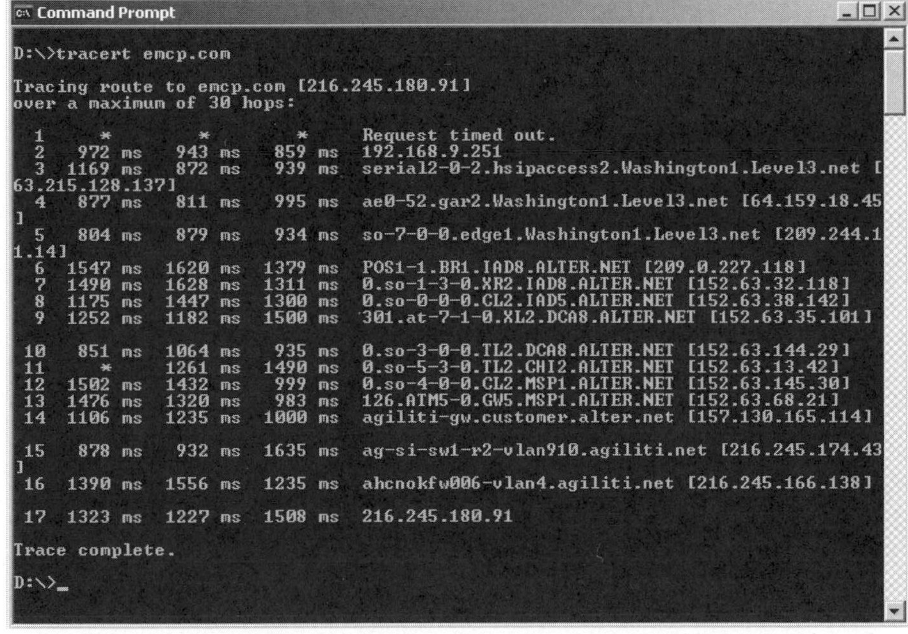


**FIGURE 25.23**
Tracert can be useful in tracing the path between the local PC and a certain site to make sure a path to it exists.

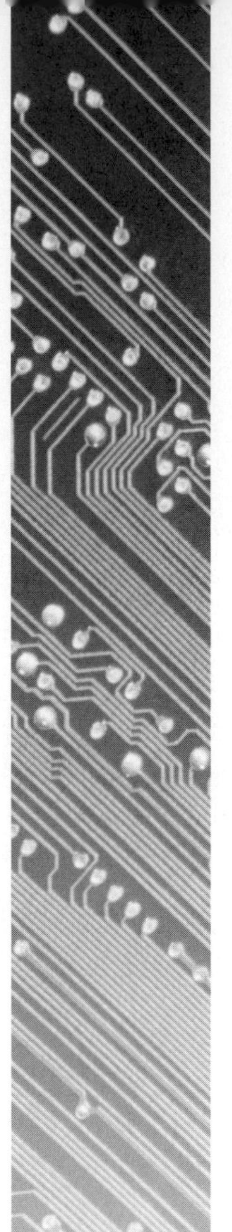

# STUDY GUIDE

Use the following summaries to review the key concepts of this chapter.

## WHAT IS THE INTERNET?

- The Internet is a huge public network of interconnected computers all over the world.
- The Internet is held together by TCP/IP as the common protocol set.
- The Internet's topology is a type of mesh, with multiple paths available between points; this ensures that the failure of an individual path or router will not cut off any segment.

## WAYS TO CONNECT TO THE INTERNET

- Large companies have their own Internet-connected servers that provide Internet access to their employees.
- Small companies and individuals contract with Internet Service Providers (ISPs) to provide them with dial-up or broadband Internet connectivity.
- An ISP may also offer e-mail, Web hosting, or other services, either included in the monthly service fee or at additional change.
- The slowest, oldest method of connecting to an ISP is via modem; see Chapter 24.
- ISDN is a digital line from the telephone company. Like a modem, it provides dial-up access. It connects at up to 112Kbps through dual-channel 56Kbps access.
- DSL stands for Digital Subscriber Line. There are two types: ADSL (Asynchronous) and SDSL (Synchronous). ADSL is the less expensive and more common type.
- DSL speed varies, but can range from 256Kbps to over 2Mbps.
- DSL uses regular copper phone lines, but does not interfere with normal telephone operations. It uses always-on, not dial-up, connections.
- Cable Internet service is available only in residential areas where service has been upgraded to digital cable.
- Cable Internet uses cable TV, not telephone, so you do not need telephone service for it. It is an always-on connection that the PC sees as a LAN connection.
- One-way satellite uses a satellite dish for receiving data and a modem for sending data. It is a dial-up connection that requires an ISP.
- Two-way satellite connection uses the satellite for both sending and receiving, and requires no telephone line.

## IP Addresses on the Internet

- An IP address is a string of numbers that uniquely identifies each network device to all other network devices.
- Each device on the Internet must have a unique IP address. Because some corporate networks have their own IP addressing schemes, Network Address Translation (NAT) is used to temporarily assign Internet IP addresses to LAN devices when they need to use the Internet.
- Some devices on the Internet have static IP addresses that are permanently assigned. This is typical of Web servers. Other devices have dynamic IP addresses that change (or can potentially change) with each logon. This is typical of ISP clients.
- DNS servers on the Internet provide translation services between domain names and IP addresses.
- DNS servers work at a specific level. A top-level DNS server deals only with the final extensions on domain names, such as .com, .org, and .net. They then pass requests to second-level servers that contain information for specific top-level domains.

## TCP/IP Communications Protocols

- At the Session and Presentation layers, a variety of different communications protocols can be active. This is necessary because people make different uses of the Internet.
- When an application requests information from the Internet, the address is usually preceded by a code for the communication protocol to use. One example is http://.
- The full address of a file on the Internet, including the protocol prefix, is its Uniform Resource Locator (URL). For example, http://www.sycamoreknoll.com/index.htm.
- HTTP is Hypertext Transfer Protocol, the protocol used for Web pages. It can be used through a Web browser or through some other application that supports HTML display, such as some Office applications.
- HTML is Hypertext Markup Language, the programming language used for coding Web pages. It is a plain text language that uses angle-bracketed codes to specify formatting and alignment.
- FTP is File Transfer Protocol, the protocol used for file transfers. It can be used through a special FTP application or through a Web browser.
- Telnet is an old communications protocol that is seldom used today. It was designed for terminal emulation.

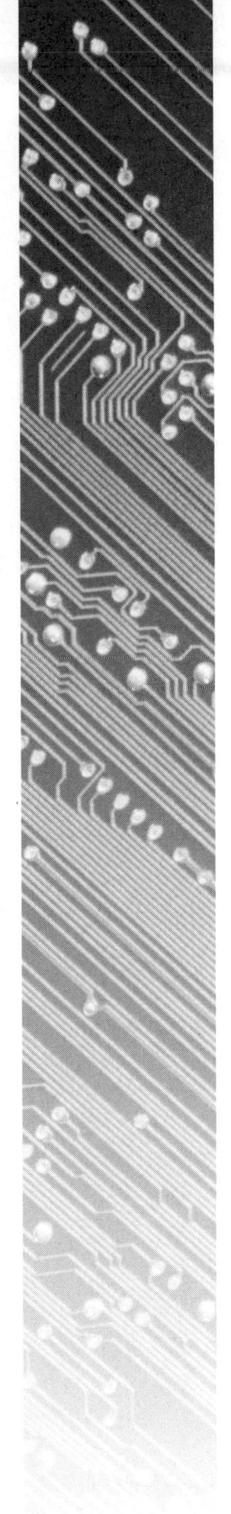

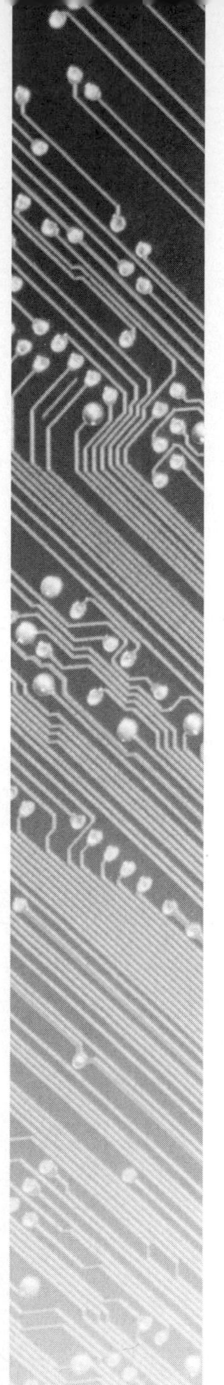

- There are several e-mail protocols. The most common is Post Office Protocol (POP), for receiving e-mail. An alternative is Internet Message Access Protocol (IMAP), also for receiving mail.
- For sending mail, the dominant protocol is Simple Mail Transfer Protocol (SMTP).
- There is also an entire class of Web-based e-mail that uses the HTTP protocol to send and receive.

## Using and Configuring Internet Explorer

- Internet Explorer is the most popular Web browser application. It comes free with all versions of Windows except 95, and is available for free download for 95.
- To access a URL, key it in the Address bar.
- To refresh a page, click Refresh or press F5.
- Use the Back and Forward buttons to navigate between the current page and pages you have already visited.
- The Favorites list can be accessed either through the Favorites menu or by clicking the Favorites button to open the list on the Explorer bar.
- To add an item to the Favorites list, choose Favorites/Add to Favorites.
- The Explorer bar, in Internet Explorer 6.0 and higher, is a separate pane to the left of the main window that can display Search, Favorites, Media, or History. Open it by clicking one of those buttons on the toolbar.
- To change viewing preferences, use the View menu. To change Internet and Web options in general, choose Tools/Internet Options.
- The Security tab in the Internet Options dialog box lets you set a security level for browsing. A high security level may prevent some Web content from being displayed.
- The Privacy tab lets you configure how cookies will be accepted. A cookie is a text file identifier saved on the local hard drive that a Web page uses to reload past settings.

## Using and Configuring Outlook Express

- Outlook Express is an e-mail reading and sending program that comes with Windows 98 and higher. Windows 95 came with a similar program called Internet Mail.
- Outlook Express is based on a system of folders; it has a folder tree in the left pane. The *Inbox* folder contains incoming mail.
- To set up new accounts in Outlook Express, choose Tools/Accounts. Click Add, and then click Mail. Then complete the wizard.

- To filter junk mail, create message rules. Choose Tools/Message Rules/Mail.
- Choose Tools/Options to open a dialog box for Outlook Express configuration options.

## Transferring Files with FTP

- FTP applications transfer files between computers. FTP may be anonymous (that is, open to the public) or may require a user name and password.
- It is considered courteous in the FTP community to supply your e-mail address as the password when connecting with the user name "anonymous."
- Windows has a command-line FTP utility available. From a command prompt key **ftp** and press Enter.
- To open a session with an FTP server, key **OPEN** and then its IP address or domain name.
- The DIR command displays a list of the current folder's content. Key **CD *foldername*** to change folders.
- To download, key **GET *filename***. To upload, key **PUT *filename***. To exit, key **BYE**.

## Sharing an Internet Connection on a LAN

- Internet Connection Sharing (ICS), available in Windows 98 Second Edition and higher, allows a network client to share its local Internet connection with other PCs on the LAN.
- ICS is not installed by default in Windows 98 or Me; add it with Add/Remove Programs. It is in the Internet Tools category in Windows 98, and in the Communications category in Windows Me.
- When you install ICS, a wizard for its configuration runs automatically.
- In Windows 2000 and XP, Internet connection sharing is available by default.
- To enable ICS in Windows 2000, display the Properties dialog box for the connection, and on the Sharing tab insert a check mark in the Enable Internet Connection Sharing for this connection check box.
- To enable ICS in Windows XP, display the Properties dialog box for the connection, and on the Advanced tab insert a check mark in the Allow other network users to connect through this computer's Internet connection check box.

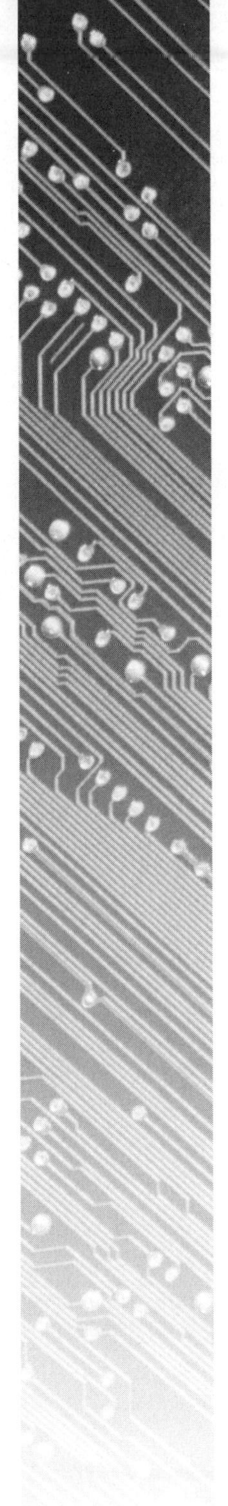

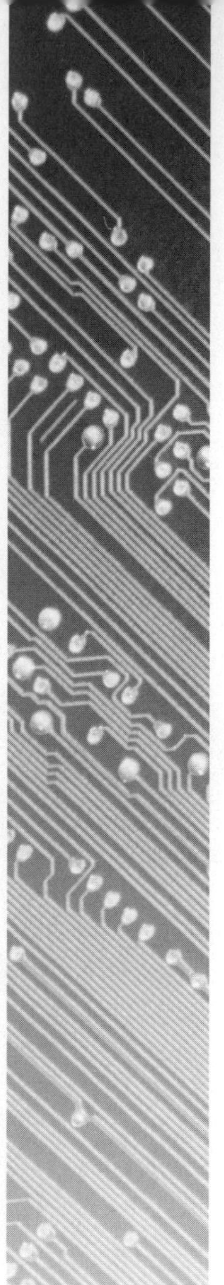

### Troubleshooting Internet Connection Problems

- For DUN troubleshooting, see Chapter 24.
- For connectivity problems with broadband, try resetting the terminal adapter and rebooting the PC. If a router is used to share the connection, reset the router.
- Ping is a command-line utility that checks whether an IP address is reachable. You can ping an IP address or a domain name, as in *ping microsoft.com*.
- Nslookup looks up the IP addresses of domain names and reports the local PC's IP address. Key **nslookup** followed by the domain you want to look up.
- If Web access is available but e-mail is not, the mail server is probably down; try again later. If it still does not work, check the settings in the e-mail application.
- If e-mail is available but Web is not, a proxy server problem is likely to be the reason.
- If a specific Web site cannot be reached, its server is probably down. Try tracert if you want to see where the route to the site breaks down.

# PRACTICE TEST

On a blank sheet of paper, write the answers to the following multiple-choice questions and explain why each answer is correct.

1. Which network topology does the Internet most resemble?
   a. ring
   b. star
   c. bus
   d. mesh

2. What is the primary function of an ISP?
   a. connects users to the Internet
   b. hosts Web sites
   c. acts as a firewall
   d. provides Web-based FTP services

3. What is ISDN?
   a. a dual-channel 56Kbps connection over regular copper phone lines
   b. a digital dial-up connection over digital phone lines
   c. an always-on connection over digital phone lines
   d. an always-on connection via satellite

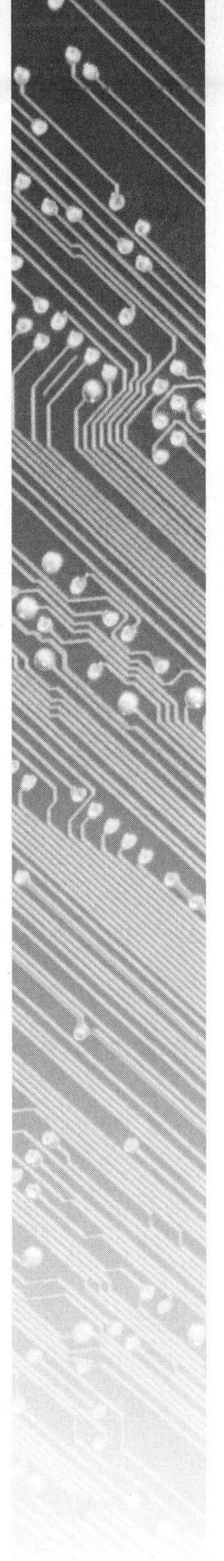

4. What differentiates ADSL from SDSL?
   a. ADSL is faster.
   b. ADSL has different speeds for uploading and downloading.
   c. SDSL is for residential use only.
   d. All of the above

5. What differentiates cable from DSL broadband service?
   a. DSL requires a phone line; cable does not.
   b. DSL ties up the phone line while the connection is on; cable does not.
   c. DSL is a dial-up connection and cable is an always-on connection.
   d. DSL requires a digital phone line; cable requires an analog line.

6. Which of these computers would require a static IP address on the Internet?
   a. a computer connecting to an ISP via DUN
   b. a computer connecting to an ISP via ADSL
   c. a computer that frequently uploads Web content to an ISP's server
   d. a server on which an ISP hosts Web sites

7. Which of these is *not* a URL?
   a. http://www.microsoft.com
   b. http://www.emcp.com/students/folders/test_questions.htm
   c. ftp://ftp.cnet.com
   d. They are all URLs.

8. What protocol is associated with files written in Hypertext Markup Language files?
   a. FTP
   b. telnet
   c. HTTP
   d. HTML

9. Which of these is a protocol for sending e-mail?
   a. POP
   b. SMTP
   c. IMAP
   d. They are all protocols for sending e-mail.

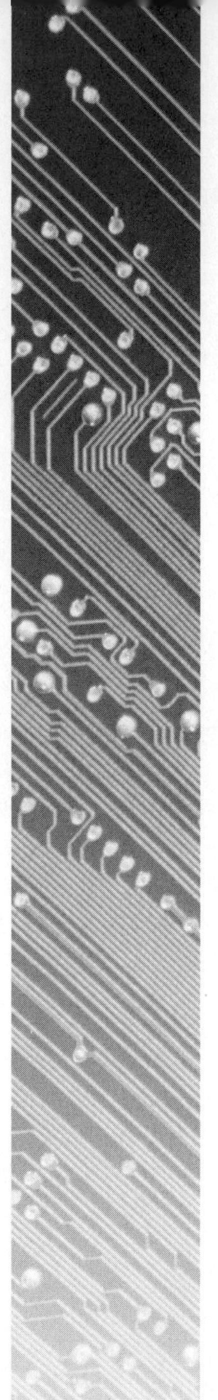

10. How can you change the start page in Internet Explorer?
    a. Right-click a Web page and choose Set as Home Page.
    b. Choose Tools/Internet Options and key the URL in the Address text box.
    c. Add it to your Offline Favorites list with the Set as Home Page check box marked.
    d. Any of these methods will work.

11. What key toggles Internet Explorer into and out of Full Screen view?
    a. F6
    b. F9
    c. F11
    d. F12

12. What is a cookie?
    a. a database record stored on a Web server
    b. an executable file stored on the local PC
    c. a text file stored on the local PC
    d. a virus

13. Which IE configuration option uses lists of Trusted sites and Restricted sites to determine how IE will interact with the Web pages?
    a. Security
    b. Privacy
    c. Content Advisor
    d. Temporary Internet Files

14. Which of these is most likely to be the address of an outgoing mail server?
    a. pop.nowhere.net
    b. smtp.nowhere.net
    c. imap.nowhere.net
    d. www.nowhere.net

15. When transferring files via anonymous FTP, what should be entered as the user name and password?
    a. Username: leave blank; Password: anonymous
    b. Username: your e-mail address; Password: leave blank
    c. Username: your e-mail address; Password: anonymous
    d. Username: anonymous; Password: your e-mail address

16. Which of these versions of Windows does not include Internet Connection Sharing (ICS)?
    a. Windows 95
    b. Windows 98 (Original)
    c. Windows 98 Second Edition
    d. Both a and b
17. How do you share an Internet connection on a Windows 2000 PC?
    a. through the Properties dialog box for the connection
    b. by running the Internet Connection Sharing Wizard
    c. by running IPCONFIG
    d. in the Internet Options dialog box within Internet Explorer
18. Which of these can nslookup do?
    a. request a new IP address for the local PC through DHCP
    b. confirm that a route exists between one IP address and another
    c. report the IP address of a domain name
    d. determine whether an IP address is static or dynamic
19. What is the purpose of a proxy server?
    a. caches frequently accessed pages to speed up Web access
    b. backs up e-mail server, to ensure e-mail access is always available
    c. backs up Web server, to ensure Web access is always available
    d. filters Web content to screen out objectionable material
20. What does tracert do?
    a. certifies URLs, indicating which ones are working or nonworking
    b. tracks security breaches for an Internet-connected server
    c. traces the route that a request takes from the local PC to the destination
    d. None of the above

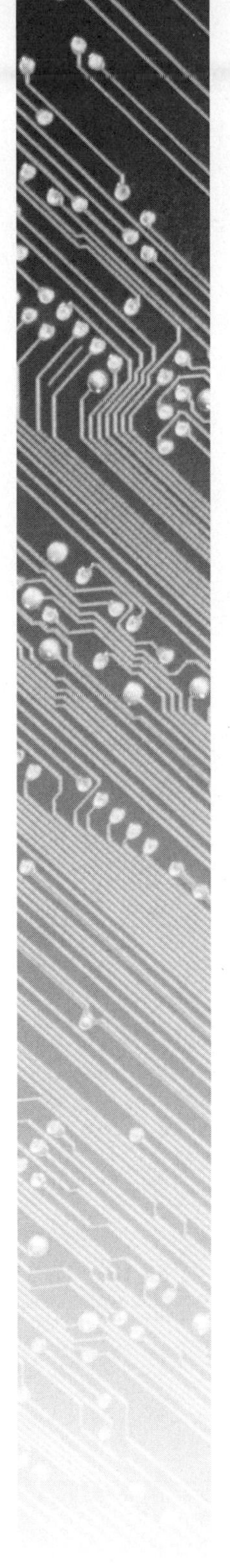

# TROUBLESHOOTING

1. A client can send and receive e-mail through his Internet connection, but cannot view any Web pages. What would you check first?
2. A client calls you and says that she gets an error message every time she tries to send or receive e-mail. The problem has been going on for about 15 minutes. She swears she did not change any settings and it worked fine earlier in the day. What do you suggest?

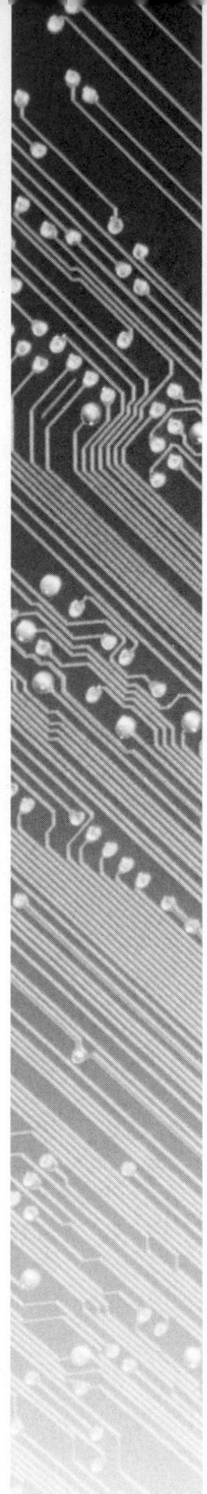

3. A client with Windows Me wants to set up Internet Connection Sharing on a small peer-to-peer network. He has installed ICS, but other network PCs are not able to access the Internet (either Web or e-mail). How would you troubleshoot this?

## CUSTOMER SERVICE

1. A rural client wants to get Internet access, but cable and DSL are not available to her. What options would you review with her, and what would be the pros and cons of each?
2. A client wants to share her home computer's DSL Internet connection with her husband's computer in another room of the house. What are the options she has, and what would you recommend?
3. A client complains that his e-mail is filled with junk, and he wonders whether there is anything he can do about it. He uses Outlook Express as his mail program. What do you suggest?

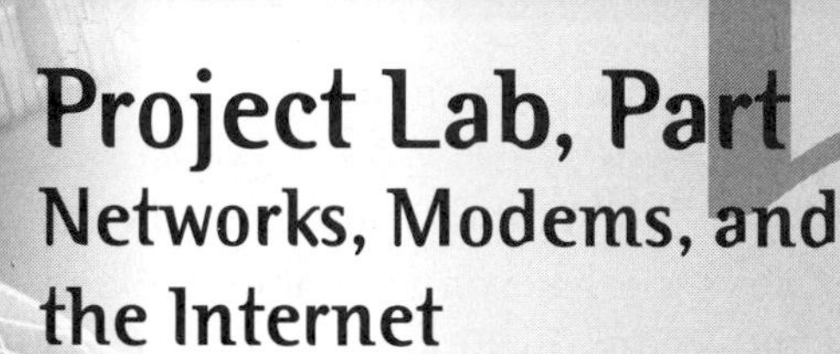

# Project Lab, Part 5
## Networks, Modems, and the Internet

## Project #1: Configuring a Peer-to-Peer Ethernet Network

For this project you will need at least three PCs with Windows 95 or higher installed, a 4-port (or greater) hub, and three 10/100BaseT NICs. For the best practice, use three different Windows versions and three different NIC models.

1. Install the NICs in the PCs, and install drivers for them in Windows if they do not install automatically with Plug and Play. Did you observe any differences with different versions of Windows or different models of NICs?
2. Confirm that the TCP/IP protocol is installed on all three PCs. On which OS is it most likely *not* to be installed by default?
3. Check for Client for Microsoft Networks on each PC, and install it if it is not there.
4. Connect each of the NICs to the hub, and plug in/turn on the hub. What lights are lit on the hub? What do they indicate?
5. Try browsing other PCs through My Network Places or Network Neighborhood on each PC. What do you observe?
6. Enable file and printer sharing on each PC. Now what do you observe when browsing the network?
7. Share a folder and a printer on each PC. Now what do you observe when you browse the network?
8. If all PCs are not seeing other PCs' shared resources, troubleshoot as needed. Document the steps you took and the results you got. If you are having permission problems accessing a Windows 2000 or XP PC, add the users from the other PCs to the Windows 2000/XP's list of Allowed Local Users.

## Project #2: Changing the Workgroup Name

Start with a functioning peer-to-peer network, as at the end of the preceding project.

1. Change the workgroup name on one of the PCs to TEST. What effect does this have on your ability to browse the network from each of the PCs? Document any changes you observe.
2. Change the workgroup name on the remaining PCs to TEST. What changes do you now observe in browsing the network?
3. From this exercise, what can you conclude about workgroup naming?

## Project #3: Static versus Dynamic IP Addresses

Start with a functioning peer-to-peer network, as at the end of Project #1.

1. Check the current IP address assignments for each PC. What are they? Use a command-line utility to determine them if they do not appear in a Windows dialog box. Are any of them static already? If so, which ones, and how did they get that way?
2. Set the IP addresses for each of the PCs to the following static addresses, with a 255.255.255.0 subnet mask:
   192.168.1.5
   192.168.1.6
   192.168.1.7
3. Browse the network from each of the PCs. Do they see one another? Why or why not?
4. Set two of the PCs to the same IP address: 192.168.1.0. Then try browsing again. Which PCs are still browsable? Which are not?
5. Return each PC to its original IP addressing. What can you conclude about IP addressing from this exercise?

## Project #4: Sharing an Internet Connection

For this project start with a working network, as at the end of Project #1. One of the PCs must have Windows 98 Second Edition, Windows Millennium Edition, or Windows XP and a working Internet connection.

1. Confirm that the Internet connection works.
2. Set up the Internet connection to be shared. The method is different for each Windows version; document the method you used for yours.
3. Try to access the Internet using one of the other PCs. If it does not work, troubleshoot the problem and document the steps you take.

## Project #5: Installing and Configuring an Internal Modem

For this project start with a PC with Windows 95 or higher installed.

1. Physically install the modem in the PC, in an ISA or PCI slot.
2. Set up the modem in Windows so that the modem appears in the Device Manager with no problems reported. Troubleshoot as needed if you run into any problems, and document the process.
3. Run a diagnostic test on the modem through Windows. Document the results you get.
4. Connect a phone line to the modem.
5. Create a dial-up networking connection to your local ISP, or if you do not have a local ISP dial-up number, create one to your own phone number for practice.
6. Dial the connection and confirm that it works. If you are dialing your own phone number, an error message will appear instead of the connection being established.

## Project #6 (Challenge): Configuring a Client/Server Network

For this project you need the same hardware as in Project #1, but one of the PCs should have a server version of Windows 2000 installed (Windows 2000 Server/Advanced Server).

1. Start with the NICs installed and configured in all PCs and with TCP/IP installed, as in the preceding project.
2. On the server PC, use the Set Up Your Server utility to promote it to a domain controller. Create a domain and install Active Directory using the wizards that appear.
3. Configure the remaining PCs to be a part of that domain rather than part of a workgroup.

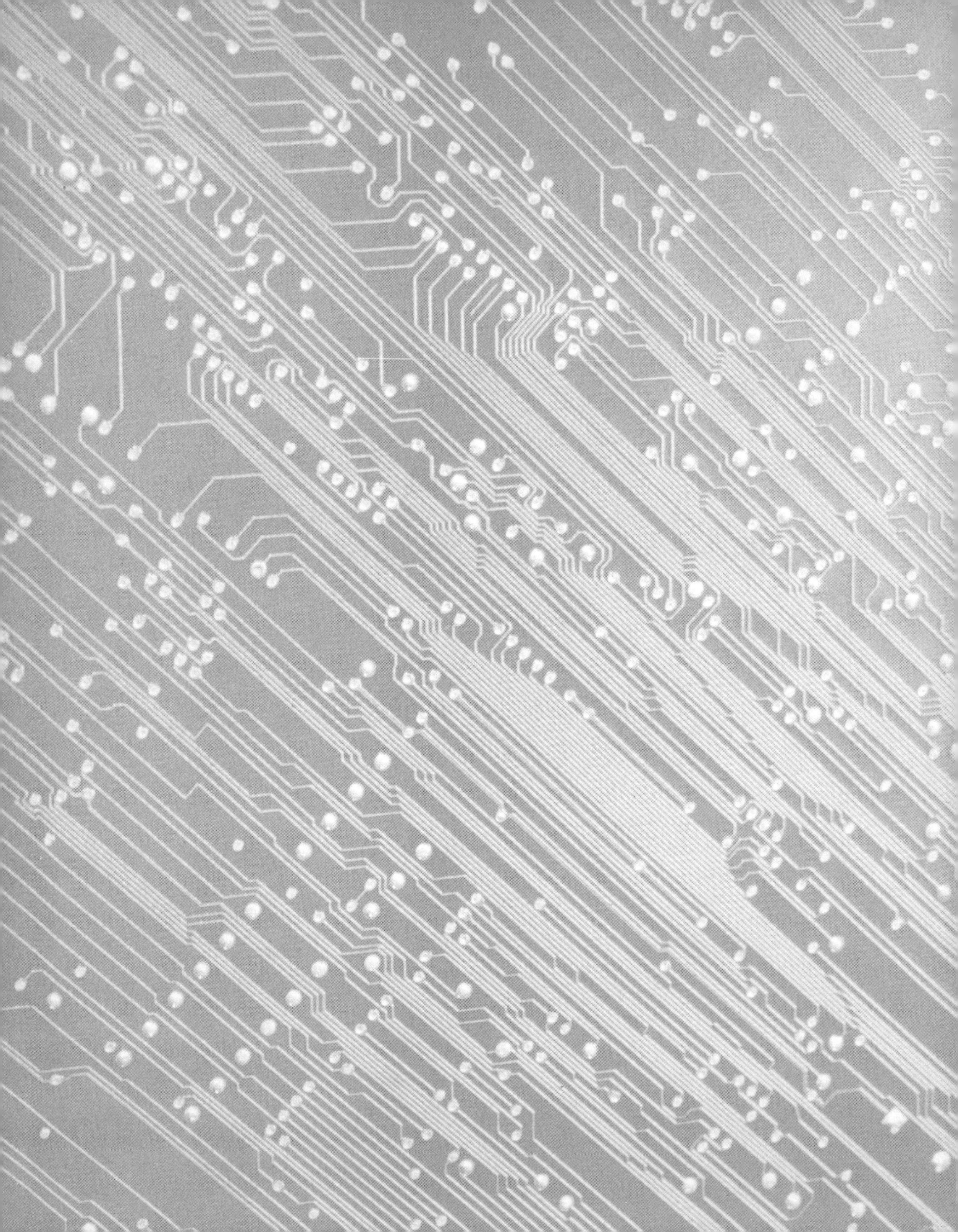

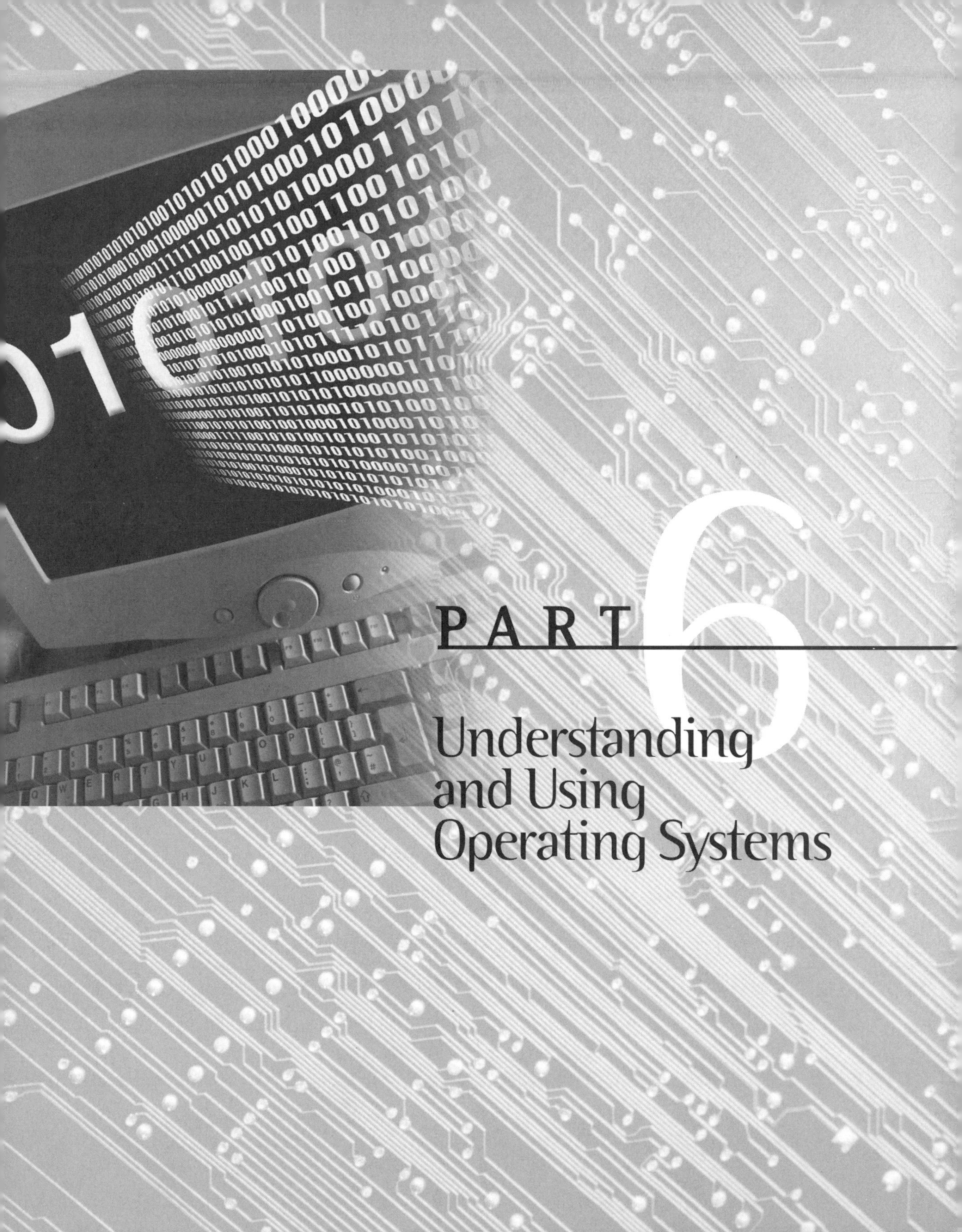

# PART 6

# Understanding and Using Operating Systems

# TEST OBJECTIVES IN PART 6

## A+ CORE HARDWARE SERVICE TECHNICIAN EXAMINATION

- **Objective 2.2:** Identify basic troubleshooting procedures and how to elicit problem symptoms from customers.

## A+ OPERATING SYSTEM TECHNOLOGIES EXAMINATION

- **Objective 1.1:** Identify the operating system's functions, structure, and major system files to navigate the operating system and how to get to needed technical information.
- **Objective 1.2:** Identify basic concepts and procedures for creating, viewing and managing files, directories and disks. This includes procedures for changing file attributes and the ramifications of those changes (for example, security issues).
- **Objective 2.1:** Identify the procedures for installing Windows 9x, and Windows 2000 for bringing the software to a basic operational level.
- **Objective 2.2:** Identify steps to perform an operating system upgrade.
- **Objective 2.3:** Identify the basic system boot sequences and boot methods, including the steps to create an emergency boot disk with utilities installed for Windows 9x, Windows NT, and Windows 2000.
- **Objective 2.4:** Identify procedures for loading/adding and configuring application device drivers, and the necessary software for certain devices.
- **Objective 3.1:** Recognize and interpret the meaning of common error codes and startup messages from the boot sequence, and identify steps to correct the problems.
- **Objective 3.2:** Recognize common problems and determine how to resolve them.

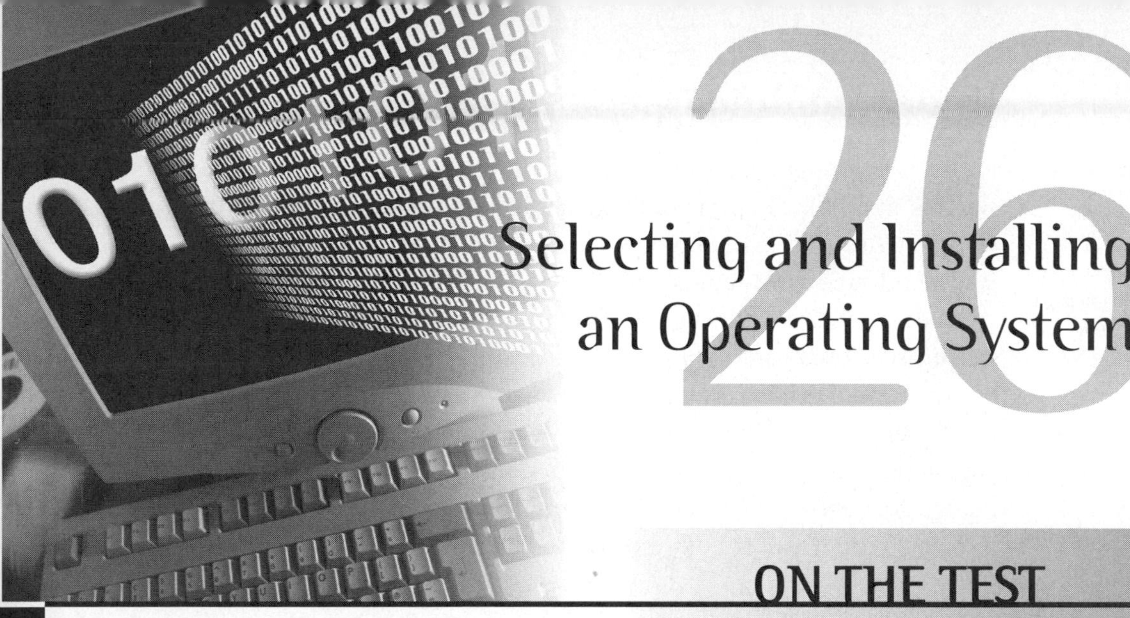

# 26 Selecting and Installing an Operating System

## ON THE TEST

**A+ Operating System Technologies Examination**

- **Objective 1.1:** Identify the operating system's functions, structure, and major system files to navigate the operating system and how to get to needed technical information.
- **Objective 2.1:** Identify the procedures for installing Windows 9x, and Windows 2000 for bringing the software to a basic operational level.
- **Objective 2.2:** Identify steps to perform an operating system upgrade.

## ON THE JOB

In an ideal world for support technicians, every PC would run the same operating system. However, on the job you are likely to encounter many different OSes, including MS-DOS, all of the many versions of Windows, UNIX, Linux, and the Macintosh OS. A good technician should have a basic understanding of all of those operating systems.

Some of the job skills you will acquire in this chapter include:

- determining what operating system is currently installed
- selecting an appropriate OS for a PC
- installing an OS on an empty hard disk
- performing an OS upgrade
- troubleshooting problems relating to OS installation

## Understanding Operating Systems

**Operating system**

Software that performs housekeeping tasks that keep the PC running and provides an interface between the end user and the hardware.

An *operating system* is software that handles the administrative/support systems in a PC. These can include managing memory, directing drives to read or write, and maintaining an interface through which users can issue commands and view results.

When a PC first starts up, the BIOS on the motherboard processes its startup sequence, and then passes off control to the OS. From that point on, the OS controls nearly every aspect of the system, from helping devices talk to the CPU to showing users messages and results on the monitor. Any applications that run do so with the permission and assistance of the OS. Figure 26.1 shows the OS's place in the hierarchy of computing activity. It interacts with the user both directly and through applications.

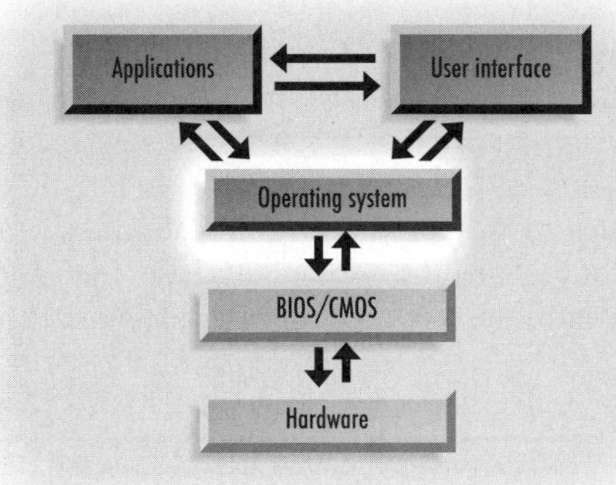


**FIGURE 26.1**
**The operating system keeps interfaces between the hardware/firmware and applications.**

There are many operating systems, and entire books are devoted to each individual version. Since this book's primary purpose is A+ certification preparation, however, it focuses mainly on the handful of OSes covered on the exam: Windows 95, Windows 98, Windows NT 4.0 Workstation, and Windows 2000 Professional.

MS-DOS and Windows 3.1 are not covered on the exam specifically, but it is useful to understand their basic underpinnings because many of the features of Windows 9x arose from them. Therefore, this chapter will look at MS-DOS and Windows 3.1 briefly as well. Similarly, even though Windows Me and Windows XP are too new to be covered on the exam (which was last revised in early 2001), it is useful to know something about them because you will find them in use at many client sites.

There are two types of operating systems: *command line* and *graphical user interface* (GUI, pronounced "gooey"). A command-line OS provides a command prompt at which the user keys commands. The best-known example of this is MS-DOS. In order to use MS-DOS, the user had to memorize the commands and their syntax. For example, to see a file listing, the user had to remember that the DIR command displays a listing.

A GUI operating system provides a graphical way for the user to interface with the computer, usually by clicking on icons with the mouse. All versions of Windows have GUIs. A GUI OS does not require any memorization because all commands appear on menus or in dialog boxes.

**Command line**

A user interface based on keying text-based commands at a prompt. MS-DOS is one example. Also can refer to the command prompt itself.

**Graphical user interface (GUI)**

A user interface based on icons and on pointing and clicking with a mouse. Windows is one example.

## Checking the Current OS Version

If a command prompt appears when the PC starts up, the operating system is probably some version of MS-DOS (or a competitor such as PC-DOS). To determine the OS version, key **VER** and press Enter (see Figure 26.2).

If a GUI interface appears when the PC starts up, look for clues during startup as to the version number. For example, you might see the opening screen (called a splash screen) that reports that this is Windows 95. Another way to get this same information is to choose Help/About Windows from any file management window; the result is shown in Figure 26.3.

```
C:\>ver

MS-DOS Version 6.22

C:\>_
```

**FIGURE 26.2**
Key VER at a command prompt to see the OS version number.

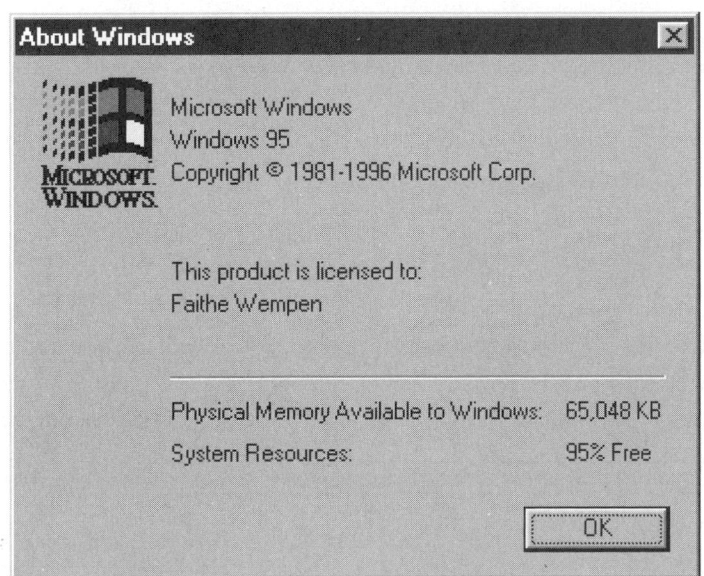


**FIGURE 26.3**
The About Windows box lists the version number.

The above methods provide only the general version number. To get more specific information, do the following:

1. From the Control Panel, double-click *System*.
2. On the General tab of the System Properties dialog box, read the version number listed. For example, in Figure 26.4, the version number is Windows 95 4.00.950 B, also known as "Windows 95 Version B."

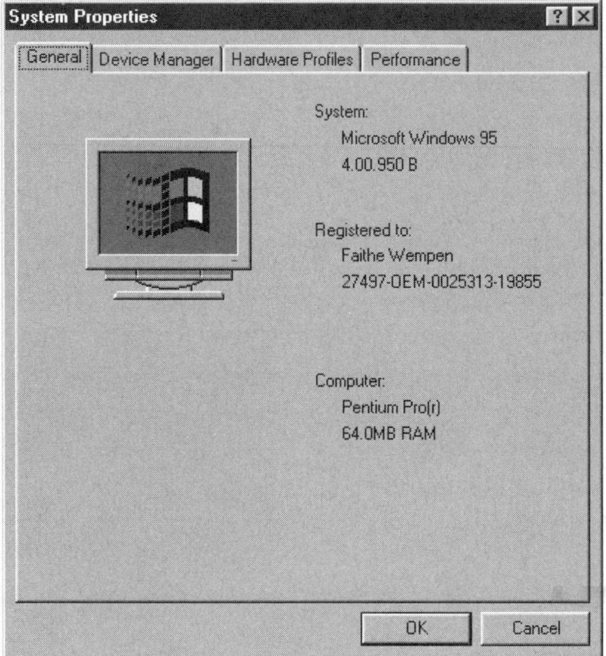


**FIGURE 26.4**
Find the exact version number from the System Properties dialog box.

The preceding steps are especially useful when working with an operating system for which there were several versions, and in which different versions had different features. For example, the original Windows 95 did not support USB, but Windows 95C did.

## TRY IT!

Check the MS-DOS or Windows version numbers on all of the PCs in your lab. Make a list of the available versions you have to work with. This will determine which other exercises you can do in this chapter.

# Understanding MS-DOS

MS-DOS 1.0 was the original operating system for the IBM PC, the personal computer that started the boom in home and business personal computing that continues today. There have been many versions of MS-DOS, up to 6.22, which was the last commercially available version.

MS-DOS is no longer covered on the A+ exam per se, but many of the basic skills for working with MS-DOS are still included. For example, the exam does cover issuing commands at a command prompt, and knowing a core set of MS-DOS commands to use there for such activities as running programs, managing files, identifying system components, and running maintenance and repair utilities.

## User Interface

The MS-DOS user interface is based on a command prompt. Users key commands at the prompt, and then press Enter to execute them. Some commands perform file management tasks or configure MS-DOS in a certain way; others run applications that open their own program screen, possibly with graphics and mouse support. The MS-DOS operating system itself, however, does not include graphics or mouse usage. Figure 26.5 shows a typical MS-DOS user interface.

```
D:\>dir *.
 Volume in drive D has no label.
 Volume Serial Number is 4C66-25E0

 Directory of D:\

06/08/2002  12:57 PM    <DIR>          Documents and Settings
01/10/2002  11:55 AM    <DIR>          My Music
08/01/2002  03:04 PM    <DIR>          Palm
08/20/2002  02:24 PM    <DIR>          Program Files
06/08/2002  12:58 PM    <DIR>          Tax01
08/23/2002  09:04 AM    <DIR>          WINDOWS
               0 File(s)              0 bytes
               6 Dir(s)   1,714,147,328 bytes free

D:\>mem


    655360 bytes total conventional memory
    655360 bytes available to MS-DOS
    598800 largest executable program size

   1048576 bytes total contiguous extended memory
         0 bytes available contiguous extended memory
    941056 bytes available XMS memory
           MS-DOS resident in High Memory Area

D:\>
```

**FIGURE 26.5**
The MS-DOS Command-line Interface

There are two types of commands: internal and external. Internal commands are built into the MS-DOS command interpreter (COMMAND.COM), which loads automatically at startup and which manages the command prompt. Such commands do not require any files on disk in order to run. Examples include DEL (delete), DIR (directory listing), and COPY (copy). External commands are executable program files that come with MS-DOS and reside in the DOS directory on the hard disk. Whenever a user issues one of these commands, it runs from that directory. Examples include FORMAT, FDISK, and EDIT. The Chapter 29 section "Working with a Command Prompt" explains command-line activities in more detail.

## TRY IT!

On an MS-DOS PC, key the following commands, pressing Enter after each one, and document what happens with each.

1. CD \DOS
2. DIR
3. DIR /W
4. DIR *.COM
5. MEM
6. CHKDSK

## Major System Files

MS-DOS has three system files. IO.SYS is the interface between the hardware and the operating system, and MSDOS.SYS is the interface between the user and applications and the operating system. The third file, COMMAND.COM, is the command interpreter that provides the command prompt, interprets the commands that the user keys, and passes them along to the hardware and the OS as appropriate. For an MS-DOS disk to be bootable, those three files must be present.

## In Real Life

IO.SYS and MSDOS.SYS are hidden files, so they do not appear in a normal file listing. You can check whether they are there with the ATTRIB command, which lists files with attributes such as hidden, read-only, and system. To check for their presence, first key **CD** and press Enter to change to the root directory on the drive. Then key **ATTRIB*.SYS** and press Enter. This shows all files with the .sys extension, along with their attributes. You will learn more about issuing commands at a command prompt in Chapter 29.

In addition, MS-DOS has two configuration files: CONFIG.SYS and AUTOEXEC.BAT. Both execute automatically at startup, and are plain-text files containing listings of items to be loaded or applications to be executed. Both can be edited using any text editor program, such as EDIT (which comes with MS-DOS).

CONFIG.SYS can be executed only at startup. It contains a list of drivers to be loaded, such as the drivers for running the CD-ROM drive or the mouse, and memory management utilities such as HIMEM.SYS and EMM386.EXE (covered in Chapter 6). Figure 26.6 shows a typical CONFIG.SYS file for MS-DOS, open in the EDIT text editing program.

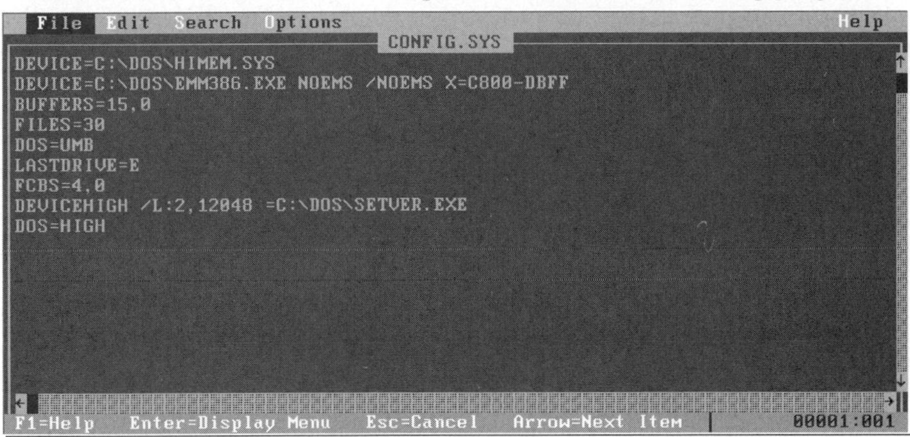


**FIGURE 26.6**
The Contents of a Typical CONFIG.SYS File

AUTOEXEC.BAT contains a list of commands to be executed at startup. These might include lines that start programs that run in the background. Such programs are known as *terminate-and-stay-resident* (TSR) programs. The user can press a certain key sequence to activate the program when it is needed. An example might be a screen capture program.

**Terminate-and-stay-resident (TSR)**

A type of program that runs in the background, either constantly providing a service or ready to be activated with a certain key combination.

AUTOEXEC.BAT, like all batch files (note the *.bat* extension), can be run at any time, not just at startup, by keying its name at the command prompt. Figure 26.7 shows a typical AUTOEXEC.BAT.

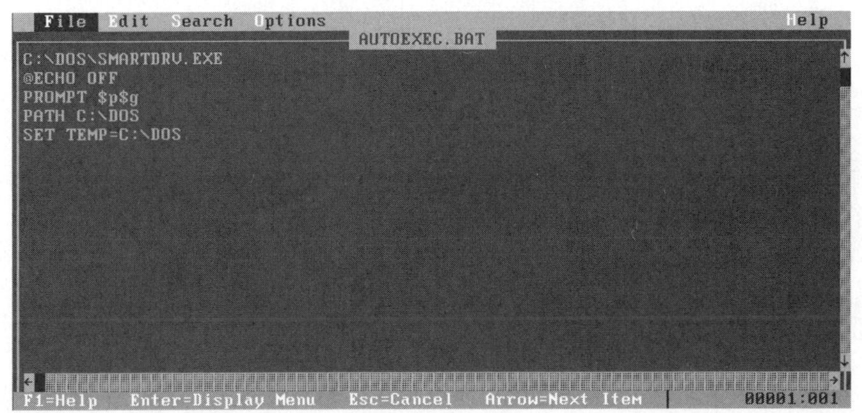


**FIGURE 26.7**
The Contents of a Typical AUTOEXEC.BAT File

In Chapter 6 you learned about DOS-based memory management, and two key files to that management are HIMEM.SYS and EMM386.EXE. The HIMEM.SYS file is an extended memory manager that provides programs with access to extended memory when operating in protected mode; EMM386.EXE allocates extended memory to be used as XMS or EMS memory as needed. In a typical MS-DOS system both of those utilities are loaded in CONFIG.SYS. Refer to Chapter 6 for more information about memory management utilities.

Another system file common on MS-DOS systems is SMARTDRV.EXE. It is typically loaded in CONFIG.SYS, and is a real-mode disk caching utility. It is not necessary, but it makes the PC run more efficiently.

Table 26.1 summarizes the major system files in MS-DOS.

| File | Purpose |
|---|---|
| IO.SYS | Interacts with hardware and BIOS |
| MSDOS.SYS | Interacts with applications |
| COMMAND.COM | Command interpreter; interacts with user |
| CONFIG.SYS | Startup configuration file that loads device drivers and system settings |
| AUTOEXEC.BAT | Startup configuration file that loads applications and user settings |
| HIMEM.SYS | Extended memory manager |
| EMM386.EXE | Expanded memory manager |
| SMARTDRV | Disk caching utility |

**TABLE 26.1**
System Files in MS-DOS

## TRY IT!

From the MS-DOS command prompt, enter the following commands, pressing Enter after each command.

1. Key **C:** to change the prompt to the main hard drive if needed.
2. Key **CD** \ to change to the root directory of the drive if needed.
3. Key **DIR**. Why do IO.SYS and MSDOS.SYS not appear in the directory listing, when this is the location they are supposed to be in? Why does COMMAND.COM appear?
4. Key **ATTRIB**. Do you now see IO.SYS and MSDOS.SYS? Why?

## FEATURES

MS-DOS is a real-mode operating system. As discussed in Chapter 6, in real mode the system can address only 1MB of RAM. The first 640KB is conventional memory, for application usage. The last 360KB is upper memory, reserved for system use. MS-DOS can run only one program at once in real mode; it cannot multitask. Chapter 6 covered how certain memory management utilities could access extended memory for MS-DOS applications, circumventing the normal MS-DOS limitations. Nevertheless, MS-DOS remains a limited operating system, and is no longer in widespread use except on very old computers that cannot run anything else.

## Understanding Windows 3.1

**Operating environment**

A shell that runs on top of an operating system, providing a different user interface than the operating system itself provides.

Early versions of Microsoft Windows were not true operating systems, but rather graphical *operating environments* that ran on top of MS-DOS. These versions of Windows, ranging from Windows 1.0 to Windows 3.11 for Workgroups, were 16-bit operating environments that could run either 16-bit Windows applications or 8- or 16-bit MS-DOS applications. Since Windows was just an environment, most users exited from Windows whenever they wanted to run an MS-DOS application, freeing up memory for the application's use.

Although there were many early 16-bit Windows versions, the only versions that technicians are likely to encounter are Windows 3.1, Windows 3.11, and Windows 3.11 for Workgroups. They are virtually identical except that the last supports peer-to-peer networking. This chapter refers to them generically as Windows 3.1.

Students preparing for the A+ exam do not need to remember every detail about Windows 3.1. However, many of the conventions and practices established in Windows 3.1 have carried over into later Windows versions, so understanding it will greatly help students in understanding later versions.

### User Interface

The Windows 3.1 interface is a GUI, involving icons, a mouse, and framed areas called windows. Each window can be opened, closed, minimized, or maximized. The main window is the Program Manager. All other windows exist within it. Behind the Program Manager window is the desktop. In Windows 3.1, nothing can sit directly on the desktop; it is always blank (see Figure 26.8).

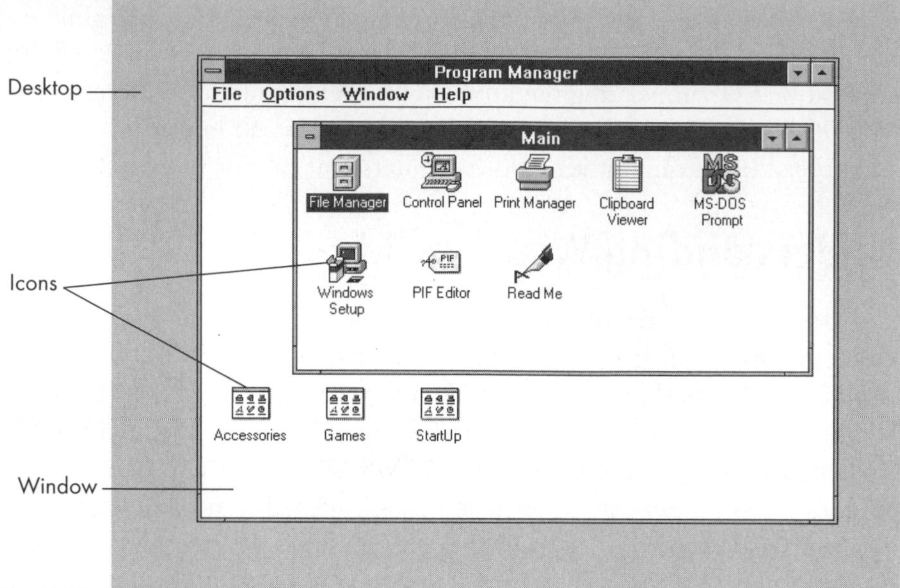


**FIGURE 26.8**
Windows 3.1 has a desktop, windows, icons, and a mouse pointer, much like modern Windows versions.

**TRY IT!**

**If you have access to a Windows 3.1 PC, open the File Manager applet from the Main program group. Which Windows 9x tool does it most resemble?**

## Major System Files

Since Windows 3.1 runs on top of MS-DOS, the system files are the same: IO.SYS, MSDOS.SYS, and COMMAND.COM. In addition, since Windows 3.1 is itself a 16-bit protected-mode program, it requires HIMEM.SYS to be loaded in the CONFIG.SYS file. It does not need EMM386.EXE because Windows manages extended memory automatically, supplying it in either EMS or XMS form to whatever programs running within Windows that need it.

The file that starts up Windows 3.1 is WIN.COM. To enter Windows, key **WIN** and press Enter at the command prompt. Once up and running, Windows 3.1 relies on three core files:

GDI.EXE manages the graphical user interface.
KRNL386.EXE manages the memory allocation to applications.
USER.EXE manages user input and output.

There is also a KRNL286.EXE file, but it is not used unless Windows is run in Standard mode. Windows 3.1 automatically starts in Standard mode if run on a 286 PC; it automatically starts in 386 Enhanced mode on 386 and higher PCs. Standard mode lacks some of the multitasking and memory management benefits described in the "Features" section on page 1037.

Windows 3.1 has its own initialization files that execute each time Windows starts up. They are SYSTEM.INI and WIN.INI. The SYSTEM.INI file contains information about the drivers that should load when Windows starts, and WIN.INI contains information about the TSR programs and user settings that should load. These are plain-text files that can be edited in any text editor, such as Notepad or EDIT. Figure 26.9 shows part of WIN.INI, for example. In later Windows versions these two files' functionality is replaced by the Windows Registry, but later versions retain the ability to read and execute WIN.INI and SYSTEM.INI files at startup for backward compatibility.

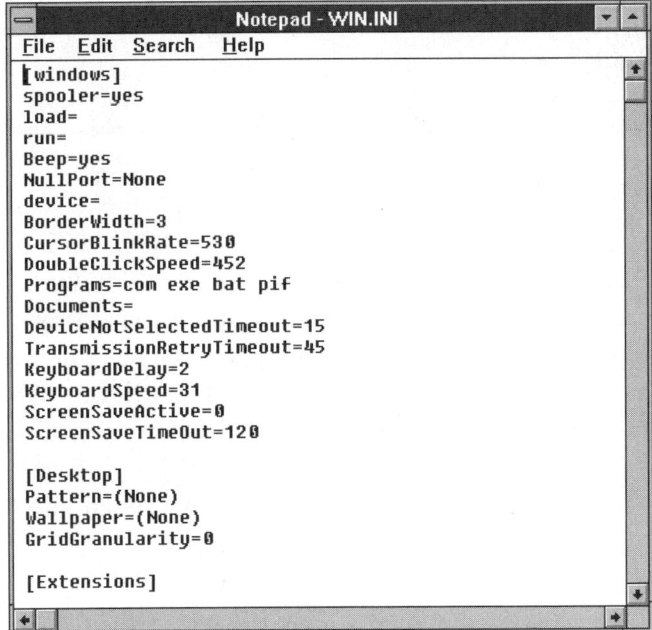


**FIGURE 26.9**
WIN.INI is one of two configuration files used by Windows 3.1. The other is SYSTEM.INI.

In addition to this basic set of system files, Windows 3.1 relies on a set of *dynamic-link library* (DLL) files, which are libraries of programming routines that applications can call upon to execute certain standardized functions as they run. Some DLLs come with Windows; others come with specific applications that the user installs. DLLs remain the cornerstone of modern application interactivity with Windows today.

**Dynamic-link library (DLL)**

A file containing a set of programming routines on which an application can call as it runs.

Individual applications and devices in Windows each have their own initialization (INI) files. These are plain-text files that list the preferred startup settings for the application or device. They can be edited through the device or application's setup program, or directly using Notepad. Figure 26.10 shows an example of an INI file.

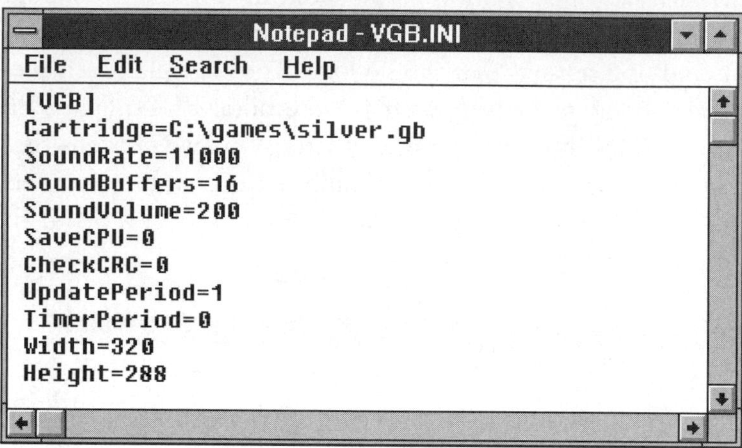


**FIGURE 26.10**
Each application and device has its own INI file governing its startup settings in Windows.

SMARTDRV, the disk caching utility from MS-DOS, continues to be used under Windows 3.1. However, the last release of the Windows 3.1 family (Windows 3.11 for Workgroups) introduced a new, protected-mode disk caching program called VCACHE that takes the place of SMARTDRV in Windows 3.11 and in every subsequent Windows release. Windows 95 and higher automatically use VCACHE with no user configuration required.

Windows 3.11 for Workgroups has two additional system files that can be enabled/disabled through the Control Panel: 32-bit disk access (FASTDISK) and 32-bit file access (VFAT). FASTDISK is an early form of BIOS bypass for hard disks, somewhat like the modern UltraDMA; it allows Windows and the hard drive to communicate directly. VFAT allows Windows to update the FAT on the hard disk directly without going through DOS. Both features are integrated into later versions of Windows and are invisible to the user.

To summarize, since Windows 3.1 runs on top of MS-DOS, it has all of the same system files at its core. In addition, it has the Windows-specific system files listed in Table 26.2.

| File | Purpose |
|---|---|
| WIN.COM | The program file for Windows |
| KRNL386.EXE | 16-bit memory manager |
| USER.EXE | 16-bit user I/O manager |
| GDI.EXE | 16-bit graphical interface manager |
| SYSTEM.INI | Initialization file that loads device drivers and system settings |
| WIN.INI | Initialization file that loads application settings and user settings |
| VCACHE | Disk caching utility, a protected-mode version of SMARTDRV (Windows 3.11 for Workgroups only) |
| FASTDISK | 32-bit disk access manager (Windows 3.11 for Workgroups only) |
| VFAT | 32-bit file access manager (Windows 3.11 for Workgroups only) |

**TABLE 26.2**
System Files in Windows 3.1

## FEATURES

Windows 3.1 exists in order to run 16-bit Windows applications. These applications are better than their MS-DOS equivalents because they can take advantage of the common Windows interface and drivers. For example, an MS-DOS-based desktop publishing program must provide its own fonts and printer drivers, but a Windows-based desktop publishing program can use the common fonts and printer drivers in Windows, sharing them with any other 16-bit Windows programs that also need access to fonts and printing. Some of the key benefits of Windows 3.1 over MS-DOS are noted below.

**Memory allocation.** Windows 3.1, being a protected-mode application, is able to access all of the extended memory in the PC and make it available to Windows-based applications as needed.

**TrueType fonts.** Windows 3.1 supports scalable TrueType fonts, which work in any Windows application and with any printer. The same TrueType font format is used in all future Windows versions, so TrueType fonts can be shared among all of the Windows versions. (Windows XP has an improved type called OpenType, but it also accepts the traditional TrueType.)

**Common device drivers.** All Windows programs share the same drivers for printers, mouse, display, and other hardware devices, relieving individual programs of the burden of providing the drivers.

**Virtual memory.** When the system runs low on physical RAM, it can simulate additional memory by using part of the hard drive to swap data into and out of physical RAM. This is called virtual memory, or a swap file. See Chapter 6 for more information.

**Virtual machines.** Windows 3.1 can run either in Standard mode (on 80286s) or Enhanced mode (on 80386s and higher). In Enhanced mode, it can run more than one program at once by creating *virtual machines*. A

**Virtual machine**

A simulated 8086 CPU operating in its own separate address space.

virtual machine is a simulated 8086 CPU operating in its own separate address space. An 8086 CPU can execute only one task at once, but multiple virtual machines running at once results in multiple programs being able to run at once.

**Data sharing.** The Windows Clipboard in Windows 3.1 uses a technology called Dynamic Data Exchange (DDE) that enables users to cut-and-paste data from one application to another. However, it cannot create dynamic links between documents (as can OLE, the data-sharing mechanism in later Windows versions).

**Cooperative multitasking.** When multiple applications are running, they must share the CPU by taking turns. One program runs for a while, and then takes a break so that another program can run. The amount of time a program runs is called its timeslice, and this system of each program's voluntarily pausing so another program can run is *cooperative multitasking.*

**Cooperative multitasking**

An early system of CPU time sharing wherein each application is in charge of pausing itself so another application can run.

**TRY IT!**

**Explore the Windows 3.1 user interface. Make a list of features that are different from Windows 9x, and discuss them in class.**

## Understanding Windows 95, 98, and Me

Windows 95 is partly a 16-bit and partly a 32-bit operating system. It can run the 16-bit Windows programs designed for Windows 3.1, and it can also run 32-bit Windows programs that work only with 95 and higher.

Windows 95, 98, and Me are similar enough to be referred to generically as "Windows 9x." Even though Windows Me does not have a "9" in its name, it is the same basic operating system as 95 and 98, and so is included in the group.

Windows 98 is nearly the same as Windows 95 in all of the important system-level ways. It offers a few improvements, such as support for the FAT32 file system, for USB devices, and for power management. It also has a few extra utilities, and includes Internet Explorer and Outlook Express. Windows 98 Second Edition adds support for more new hardware and provides Internet Connection Sharing and greater stability.

Windows Me (Millennium Edition) provides a minor update to Windows 98 Second Edition. It offers some new utilities and home/small business user features, and provides wizards that make it easier to perform some complex tasks, like setting up a home network. It is not covered on the A+ examinations.

## User Interface

You are probably already familiar with the Windows 9x interface, as it has become the standard on most desktop PCs. It features a Start button that opens a menu system, and icons that sit directly on the desktop (unlike Windows 3.1). Instead of File Manager, it uses My Computer and Windows Explorer for file management (see Figure 26.11).

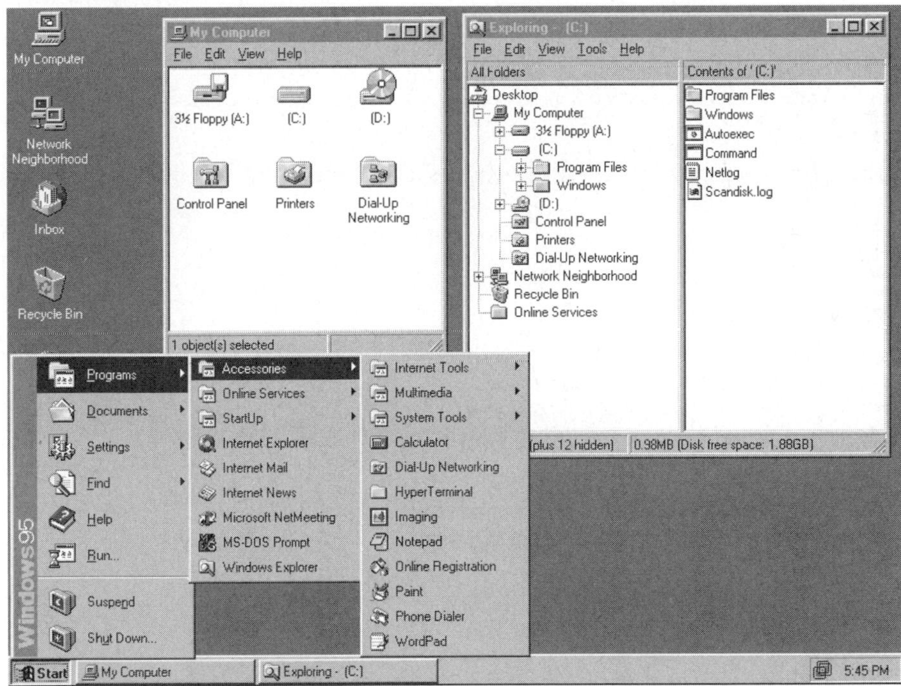


**FIGURE 26.11**
The Windows 95 interface established the standard for all other releases of Windows that came after it.

## Major System Files

Windows 9x is not just an add-on to MS-DOS; it is an operating system in its own right. However, some of its system files are very similar to those of MS-DOS. IO.SYS is still present in Windows 9x, and so is MSDOS.SYS. In Windows 9x, however, MSDOS.SYS is just a text-based configuration file; IO.SYS takes on all of the functionality that was previously assigned to both files.

Windows 9x can read and process CONFIG.SYS and AUTOEXEC.BAT, but it does not require them. Windows 9x requires HIMEM.SYS to be loaded, and that usually happens through CONFIG.SYS, but if no CONFIG.SYS is present Windows 9x will load HIMEM.SYS itself as it starts up.

**Registry**

The configuration database that defines Windows startup configuration settings in Windows 95 and higher.

The startup configuration files of Windows 3.1 (WIN.INI and SYSTEM.INI) are replaced in Windows 9x with USER.DAT and SYSTEM.DAT, which together form the Windows *Registry*. It tells the main Windows program (WIN.COM) about the configuration settings to use, including what hardware is installed, what applications are installed, and what user preferences have been defined.

Once it is up and running, Windows 9x uses the same three key system files as Windows 3.1: Krnl386, User, and GDI. However, it uses separate files for the 16- and 32-bit functions. The 32-bit versions are DLLs: KERNEL32.DLL, USER32.DLL, and GDI32.DLL. One other system file that Windows 9x uses is VMM386.VXD, which loads the 32-bit device drivers.

Table 26.3 summarizes the important system files in Windows 9x.

| File | Purpose |
|---|---|
| IO.SYS | Interacts with hardware, BIOS, and applications |
| MSDOS.SYS | Text-only configuration file |
| COMMAND.COM | Command interpreter; interacts with user at command prompt |
| WIN.COM | Program file for Windows |
| HIMEM.SYS | Extended memory manager |
| KERNEL32.DLL | 32-bit memory manager |
| USER32.DLL | 32-bit user I/O manager |
| GDI32.DLL | 32-bit graphical interface manager |
| KRNL386.EXE | 16-bit memory manager |
| USER.EXE | 16-bit user I/O manager |
| GDI.EXE | 16-bit graphical interface manager |
| VCACHE | Disk caching utility |
| VMM386.VXD | 32-bit device driver manager |
| SYSTEM.DAT | Contains Registry settings for the system and the hardware |
| USER.DAT | Contains Registry settings for users and applications |
| SYSTEM.INI | Initialization file for backward compatibility with 16-bit applications |
| WIN.INI | Initialization file for backward compatibility with 16-bit applications |
| CONFIG.SYS | Initialization file for backward compatibility with MS-DOS |
| AUTOEXEC.BAT | Initialization file for backward compatibility with MS-DOS |

**TABLE 26.3**
System Files in Windows 9x

## Features

Windows 9x and higher can run both 16-bit and 32-bit applications. As you know from earlier chapters, a 32-bit application deals with the CPU in 32-bit chunks, so it runs more efficiently than a 16-bit application. It also has several other benefits because of the way Windows 9x handles 32-bit applications, such as the ability to create dynamic links between data in different applications and to access network drives without having to map them. Here are some of the key benefits of Windows 9x:

**Plug and Play.** With *Plug and Play*, Windows 95 can "talk" to new hardware you install, determine its specifications, and install a driver for it automatically. The actual success rate of the feature has improved in later Windows versions.

**Plug and Play**

A technology for detecting hardware and installing drivers for it automatically.

**Windows virtual machines.** Windows 9x greatly improves on the virtual machine (VM) concept. Windows 3.1 segmented each running program in a separate VM, but Windows 95 runs multiple Windows programs in a single VM, so they can exchange data between them more easily.

**Preemptive multitasking.** Windows 9x offers *preemptive multitasking*, which is superior to cooperative multitasking because Windows controls the timeslices that each program can use. This prevents a rogue program from failing to share CPU time with other applications.

**Preemptive multitasking**

A feature of Windows 9x and higher that allows Windows to control the sharing of CPU time between applications, ensuring that no one program monopolizes the CPU at the expense of all others.

**Object linking and embedding (OLE).** Windows 9x greatly improves on the Clipboard in Windows 3.1 by adding *object linking and embedding* (OLE) support. Not only can you move and copy data, but you also can create dynamic links between applications so that when data changes in one, it also changes in another.

**Object linking and embedding (OLE)**

A technology for sharing information between Windows applications that allows dynamic links between files.

**Safe mode.** Windows 9x offers a startup mode that avoids all nonessential drivers and startup routines, enabling you to start the system for troubleshooting after a problem has occurred, such as a bad video driver's being loaded.

**Long file names.** MS-DOS and Windows 3.1 are limited to file names of no longer than 8 characters with a single 3-character extension. With Windows 9x you can have file names of up to 255 characters, and the names can include spaces.

## Windows 9x Versions

As you have seen throughout this book, sometimes different sub-versions of Windows have different features. For example, USB support is available in some Windows 95 versions but not in others.

Table 26.4 lists the Windows 95, 98, and Me version numbers and explains the differences among them. After the initial retail release of each Windows version, Microsoft continued to make improvements to the OS, and provided those improvements to PC makers for copies of Windows to be preinstalled on new PCs. These versions are designated OEM, for *Original Equipment Manufacturer*. SP stands for Service Pack, which is a bug fix that can be added to existing copies via download or included in new copies. SR stands for Service Release, which is a new version with new features, not generally available for patching existing versions.

**Original Equipment Manufacturer (OEM)**

A version of hardware or software provided by a PC maker rather than bought at retail. It sometimes is slightly different from the retail version.

## In Real Life

In some cases you can distinguish an OEM version from a retail version by looking at the product key for installation. A retail version will have a 25-digit product key, broken into five chunks, like this: xxxxx-xxxxx-xxxxx-xxxxx-xxxxx. An OEM version might be a 20-digit code with OEM as the sixth through eighth characters: xxxxx-OEM-xxxxxxx-xxxxx.

| Version | Number | Distribution | Added Features |
|---|---|---|---|
| Windows 95 | 4.00.950 | Retail, OEM | n/a |
| Windows 95 SP1 | 4.00.950A | Retail, OEM, Patch | Bug fix only |
| Windows 95 SR2 | 4.00.1111 | OEM only | FAT32, Internet Explorer, NetMeeting, DirectX |
| Windows 95 SR2.1 | 4.03.1212-1214 | OEM only | USB |
| Windows 95 SR2.5 | 4.03.1214 | OEM only | Outlook Express, Internet Connection Wizard |
| Windows 98 | 4.10.1998 | Retail, OEM | Disk Cleanup, System Information, Drive Converter, Maintenance Wizard |
| Windows 98 SE | 4.10.2222A | Retail, OEM | Internet Connection Sharing |
| Windows Me | 4.90.3000 | Retail, OEM | System Restore, Home Networking Wizard, Windows Movie Maker |

**TABLE 26.4**
Windows 95, 98, and Me Versions

As you can see in Table 26.4, even though major releases of Windows touted new features, in many cases Microsoft introduced a feature in an interim release of a previous version. For example, even though we talk about USB as being first available in Windows 98, it was actually added in Windows 95 SR2.1. The SR releases were not available to the general public, so Windows 98 was the first retail version to have USB. See "Checking the Current OS Version" at the beginning of this chapter to determine an installed copy's version number.

The features noted in Table 26.4 and described below are not comprehensive by any means. There were many minor improvements and features introduced in each version update. However, these lists should serve to familiarize you with the most important features from an end user's standpoint.

### *Windows 98 Improvements*

These are some of the major benefits of Windows 98 over Windows 95 (original version).

**FAT32.** Support of the FAT32 file system allows larger partitions with smaller, more efficient cluster sizes. Windows 98 comes with a Drive Converter utility that can convert FAT16 to FAT32 partitions without reformatting.

**Internet Explorer.** Having a Web browser built into the operating system makes for tighter integration between Web and local content. Microsoft has been continually striving to make Windows more like the Web with each new version.

**Outlook Express.** Windows 95 included an e-mail program called Internet Mail, and a separate newsreader program called Internet News. Outlook Express combines both into a single, more feature-rich program.

**System Information.** This information window provides detailed information about Windows. We will look at it more closely in Chapter 30.

**Windows Update.** Starting with Windows 98, Windows became able to update itself by downloading patches from Microsoft's Web site.

**Disk Cleanup.** This utility helps users who are running out of disk space by identifying files that could safely be deleted. It is covered in more detail in Chapter 30.

**Active Desktop.** Among other things, this feature allows users to use Web pages as the wallpaper on the desktop, with the hyperlinks active on the page.

**Better startup disk.** The startup disk you create in Windows 98 (through Add/Remove Programs in the Control Panel) contains real-mode CD-ROM drivers; the one in Windows 95 does not. See Chapter 13 for more information about adding real-mode CD-ROM drivers to a Windows 95 startup disk.

One important new feature in Windows 98 Second Edition is Internet Connection Sharing, which was discussed in Chapter 25. It allows a PC on a peer-to-peer network to share its Internet connection with other PCs through network address translation.

### *Windows Me Improvements*

Here are some of the new features of Windows Me.

**System Restore.** This feature saves a snapshot of the Registry and some other essential system files, so that you can restore to that point if you do something (such as installing a poorly written application) that corrupts the Registry or causes the PC to malfunction.

**Home Networking Wizard.** This wizard helps configure a peer-to-peer network. The Internet Connection Sharing Wizard from Windows 98 Second Edition is built into it.

**Windows Movie Maker.** This video editing program enables users to combine still photos, video clips, narration, and soundtracks to create their own movie files.

# Understanding Windows NT, 2000, and XP

Windows NT 4.0, Windows 2000, and Windows XP are all built on a common foundation, often called the "NT platform." Because they all use the same basic set of system files and the same user interface, we can address them as a group as well as look at their individual differences.

The original Windows NT, called Windows NT 3.1, was an attempt to make a version of Windows 3.1 that was tailored for corporate networking and less crash-prone than the standard Windows product. A later revision, Windows NT Workstation 3.51, was the first version to be commercially popular. Its interface was very similar to that of Windows 3.1.

Windows NT Workstation 4.0 was the corporate version of Windows 95. Its development actually predates Windows 95, and the user interfaces are similar. However, it lacks a few of the Windows 95 features, most importantly Plug and Play. Windows NT 4.0 comes in two versions: Workstation and Server.

Windows 2000 offers users the best of both Windows NT 4.0 and Windows 9x. Windows 2000 is based on Windows NT, so it shares the enhanced security and stability benefits of that OS. In addition, it incorporates most of the user-friendly features of Windows 9x that are lacking in Windows NT Workstation 4.0, including Plug and Play hardware installation and many useful utilities. It also supports all three major file systems included with earlier versions—FAT16, FAT32, and NTFS 4.0. Its version of NTFS is NTFS 5.0, and it converts NTFS 4.0 drives to 5.0 upon upgrade.

Windows 2000 comes in several versions. Windows 2000 Professional is the desktop client version, and the one covered in this book. There are also several server versions, including Windows 2000 Server, Windows 2000 Advanced Server, and Windows 2000 Datacenter Server.

Windows XP is the current version as of this writing. It comes in two versions, Professional and Home, both of which are based on Windows NT. The Windows 9x platform is being phased out. A server version of Windows XP called Windows.NET should be available by the time you read this book. Windows XP is not covered on the current A+ exam, but it will be covered briefly in this chapter because most technicians will encounter it in their work.

## USER INTERFACE

The Windows NT Workstation 4.0 and Windows 2000 user interfaces are similar to that of Windows 9x. NT 4.0 is more like Windows 95, while 2000 is more like Windows 98.

In Windows NT Workstation 4.0, some of the icons are slightly different from later versions, and several of the applets in the Control Panel are different as well, as shown in Figure 26.12. Notice, for example, that there is no *Add New Hardware* icon. Instead, there are icons for various types of hardware such as Multimedia and Modems from which you can install those individual device types. There are some extra icons in the Control Panel that you will not find in a Windows version that supports Plug and Play, such as Tape Devices and SCSI Adapters. Figure 26.13 shows Windows 2000, for comparison.

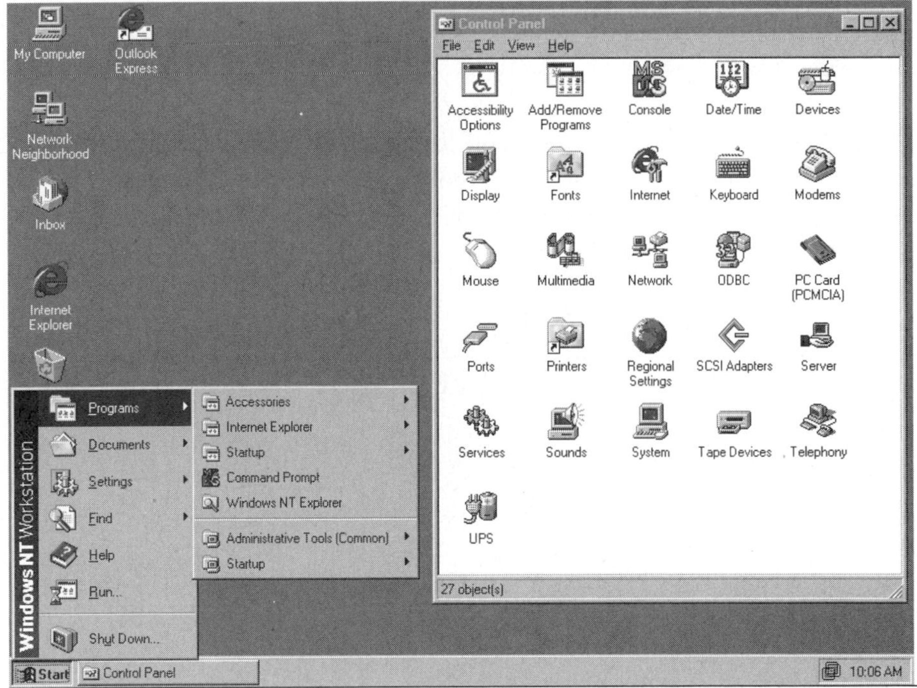


**FIGURE 26.12**
The Windows NT Workstation 4.0 Interface

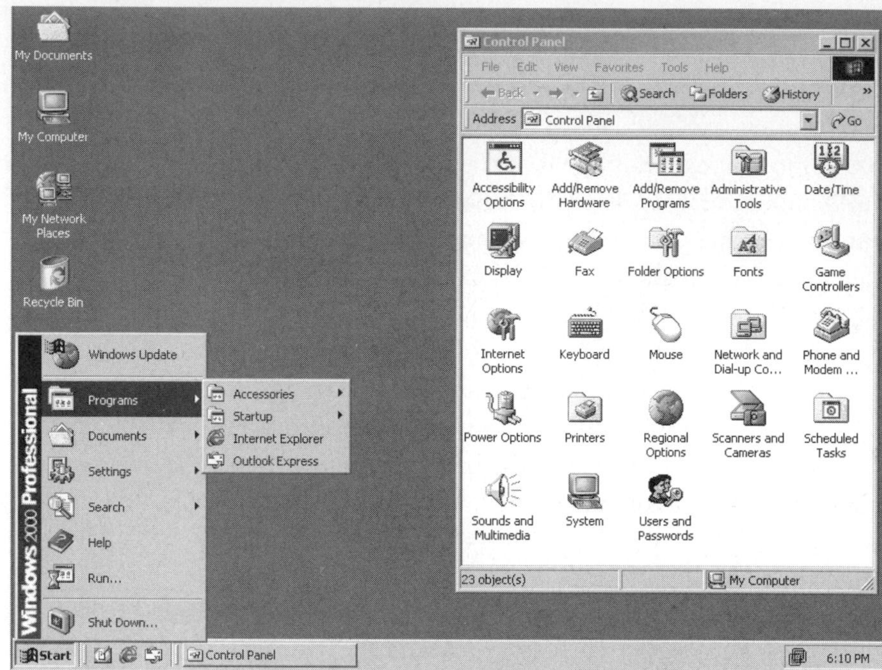


**FIGURE 26.13**
The Windows 2000 user interface is very similar to that of Windows 9x and Windows NT 4.0.

Windows XP has a default look and feel different from the others, but it can be customized to resemble them more closely if the end user is uncomfortable with the difference. The most striking difference in Windows XP is the two-column Start menu, as shown in Figure 26.14.

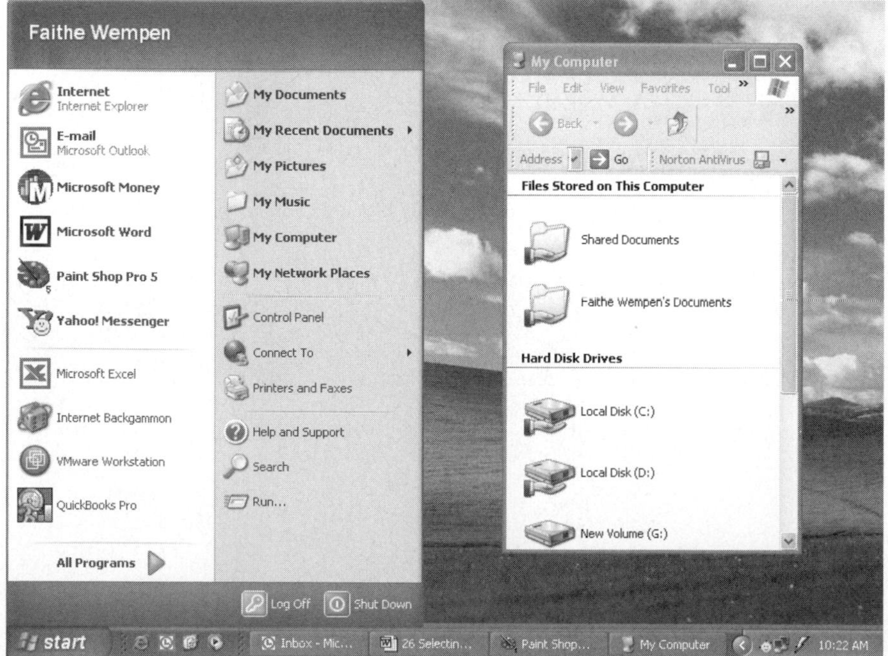


**FIGURE 26.14**
Windows XP's interface is a modification of the design in the previous versions.

## Major System Files

Recall from the earlier discussion of Windows 9x that the primary startup file for that class of OS is IO.SYS. (MSDOS.SYS plays a secondary role, supplying only a few text-based settings.) The equivalent file in Windows NT/2000/XP is called NTLDR, which is short for NT Loader. It takes control of the system at startup and loads the operating system. Some other files involved in the boot-up process are NTDETECT.COM (which checks the hardware) and BOOT.INI (which is an initialization file similar to MSDOS.SYS under Windows 9x). Chapter 27 discusses the boot process in greater detail.

The main program file for Windows NT/2000/XP is WINNT32.EXE. One of the last startup steps that NTLDR takes is to start WINNT32, which then takes over loading the operating system. Some other files required to run Windows NT/2000/XP include NTOSKRNL.EXE (short for NT OS Kernel, the equivalent of Krnl386.exe in earlier Windows versions) and HAL.DLL (short for Hardware Abstraction Layer, a dynamic-link library that helps communicate between the hardware and the OS).

Like Windows 9x, Windows NT/2000/XP use a Registry to maintain system settings. However, instead of storing Registry content in System.dat and User.dat, the Registry in these Windows versions stores its data in five files: Sam, Security, System, Software, and Default, known as *registry hives*. Each of these files has no extension, and there are corresponding log files (*.log*) and backup files (*.sav*) for each. They are all stored in the *\Winnt\System32\Config* folder for Windows NT/2000 and in *\Windows\System32\Config* for Windows XP (see Figure 26.15).

**Registry hive**

A physical file containing some of the registry settings in Windows NT/2000/XP, which combines with other hives under the Registry Editor in a single interface.

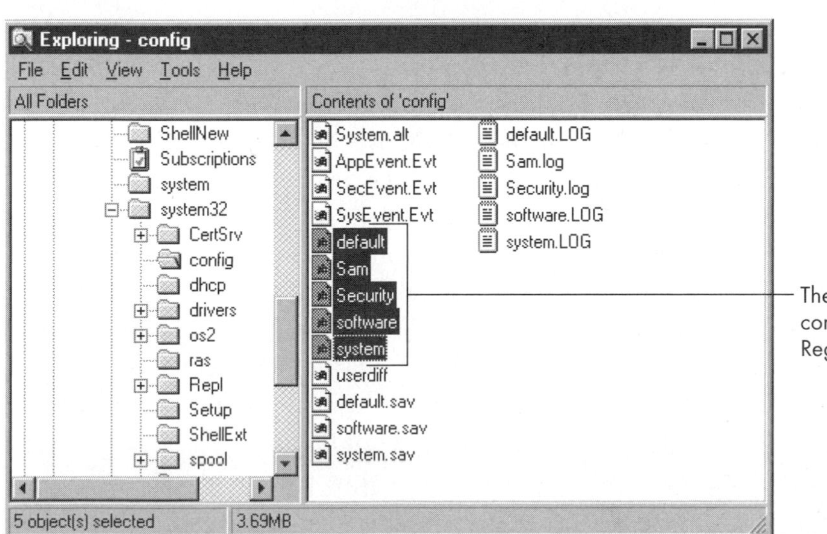


**FIGURE 26.15**
The Winnt\System32\Config folder holds the hive files that comprise the Windows NT Workstation 4.0 Registry.

There is one additional file included in the Registry—Ntuser.dat. A different copy of it is stored for each user who logs on to the PC, in the *\Winnt\Profiles\username* folder, where *username* is the name of the user, or in *\Windows\Profiles\username* in Windows XP.

When you open the Registry Editor (regedit.exe or regedt32.exe), the files appear to be a single unit. Appendix D covers Registry editing.

Table 26.5 summarizes the main system files in Windows NT 4.0, 2000, and XP.

| File | Purpose |
|---|---|
| NTLDR.EXE | Loads Windows NT at startup |
| NTDETECT.COM | Detects hardware at startup |
| BOOT.INI | Initialization file for booting |
| WINNT32.EXE | Main program file for Windows NT |
| NTBOOTDD.SYS | Boot loader for SCSI devices (if present) |
| HAL.DLL | Interface between hardware and OS |
| NTOSKRNL.EXE | Memory manager |
| GDI.EXE | GUI manager |
| USER.EXE | I/O manager |
| SAM | Stores Registry settings |
| SECURITY | Stores Registry settings |
| SOFTWARE | Stores Registry settings |
| SYSTEM | Stores Registry settings |
| DEFAULT | Stores Registry settings |
| NTUSER.DAT | Stores Registry settings for the current user |
| SYSTEM.INI | Initialization file for backward compatibility with 16-bit applications |
| WIN.INI | Initialization file for backward compatibility with 16-bit applications |

**TABLE 26.5**
System Files in Windows NT 4.0, 2000, and XP

## Features

Whereas Windows 9x focused on being backward-compatible with MS-DOS and 16-bit Windows applications, and suffered from some stability and reliability problems because of it, Windows NT/2000/XP do not promise universal backward compatibility, and are therefore able to provide a more crash-proof OS.

These Windows versions are fully 32-bit protected-mode operating systems, with no MS-DOS behind them. Because of this, you cannot bypass the GUI to boot to a command prompt at startup, and you cannot make a startup floppy disk in these OSes. (You can, however, boot to a Recovery Console utility, which is a type of command prompt. In Windows XP it *is* possible to make a plain MS-DOS boot floppy.)

Does that mean MS-DOS and 16-bit Windows programs will not run under Windows NT/2000/XP? Not necessarily. Any applications that do not attempt to access resources directly can run in a virtual machine (VM) within NT, much as they do under Windows 9x. Windows XP in particular can run MS-DOS programs very well.

### *Features of Windows NT Workstation 4.0*

Almost all of the benefits of Windows NT Workstation 4.0 over Windows 9x also apply to Windows 2000 and XP, so we will start with the NT 4.0 items and move toward the later versions.

**NTFS file system.** Windows NT Workstation 4.0 supports NTFS 4.0, a superior file system to FAT which allows for much larger logical drives. This feature is especially useful in a corporate environment where the half-gigabyte limitation imposed by FAT16 did not permit logical drives large enough to hold large databases. It can also support FAT16 partitions, for compatibility with MS-DOS and Windows 9x.

#### In Real Life

**Windows NT Workstation 4.0 was updated through a series of Service Packs over the years, and some of these Service Packs added major new features, such as Internet Explorer. It is necessary to install the Service Packs in order for Windows NT Workstation 4.0 to be Y2K-compatible.**

**Improved networking.** Windows 9x had some networking capabilities, but it was designed primarily for the home and small office where networking was not yet pervasive. In contrast, Windows NT Workstation 4.0 was developed specifically for network clients, so it has more effective networking features for connecting to both peer-to-peer and client/server networks, including much better network and local logon security than Windows 9x.

**Better security.** Windows NT forces users to have valid user names and passwords in order to gain access to the local PC, and allows multiple users to log on to the same PC at different times and maintain separate settings and private documents.

**Server version.** Windows NT 4.0 was the first Windows release to offer two separate versions: Workstation and Server.

**Multiple CPU support.** Windows NT supports up to two CPUs on the same motherboard. (Some high-end systems in the mid- to late 1990s had two CPUs.)

**Support for non-PC hardware.** Windows NT can be installed on other types of hardware besides Intel-based PCs. For example, it runs on R4x00 and DEC Alpha workstations.

Windows NT 4.0 lacks one important feature of Windows 9x: Plug and Play support. Since Windows NT 4.0 cannot automatically identify new hardware, users must run setup programs for the hardware being installed, and in some cases set jumpers or switches on the hardware itself to configure resource settings.

### *Features of Windows 2000*

Windows 2000 combines the best features of Windows 9x with the solid NT-based platform of Windows NT Workstation 4.0.

**Plug and Play.** The most significant improvement for most users is the addition of Plug and Play capabilities.

**Hardware support.** Windows 2000 adds support for many new types of hardware that had been introduced since Windows NT 4.0's inception, including UltraDMA drives and USB ports.

**NTFS 5 and other file system support.** Windows 2000 supports many different file systems, including FAT16, FAT32, and its own new file system, NTFS 5.0, offering several new benefits such as the capability to encrypt and compress files and to establish space usage quotas on an NTFS drive. We will discuss these features in Chapter 29.

**Dynamic disks**

A disk organization type in Windows 2000 and XP that discards the traditional paradigm of partitioning to create volumes that can be resized, combined, mirrored, or striped.

**Dynamic disks.** Windows 2000 supports *dynamic disks*, a totally new way of organizing disk space. It discards the concepts of partitioning and master boot records and instead creates volumes. These volumes have a number of benefits over traditional partitions, such as the ability to be resized, to be combined (spanning), and to create disk mirroring, *Redundant Array of Inexpensive Disks* (RAID), and striping. See Chapter 29 for more information.

**Redundant Array of Inexpensive Disks (RAID)**

A method of creating a single logical disk out of multiple physical disks to protect the data from loss in the event of the failure of a single drive.

**Active Directory.** From a networking standpoint, *Active Directory* is a very important new feature in Windows 2000. Active Directory allows for a single point of administration for network resources, regardless of their type. A single directory of printers, shared drives and folders, user names, computer names, and so on, is maintained, and multiple domain controller servers can share it and keep it constantly updated. Active Directory is not covered on the A+ exams, but if you work in a company that has a Windows 2000 or .net network, you are likely to encounter it.

**Active Directory**

A resource management system for client/server networks based on Windows 2000 or XP servers that enables multiple domain controllers to share and constantly update a central directory.

**Internet Printing Protocol.** Windows 2000 introduces the Internet Printing Protocol, a tool for sending to a printer via a TCP/IP address. This can be used to send print jobs to printers that have their own TCP/IP Web addresses anywhere on the Internet.

**Microsoft Management Console.** Windows 2000 is the first version to contain the Microsoft Management Console (MMC). It is a generic utility window from which technicians can install *snap-ins* for working with almost all of the Windows 2000 configuration and management utilities. This has several benefits, which will be covered in Chapter 30.

**Snap-in**

A utility module that you can add to the Microsoft Management Console to make a particular tool available, such as Computer Management or Event Viewer.

**Administrative Tools.** Many of the components you can add to the MMC are also available in the *Administrative Tools* folder in the Control Panel.

### *Features of Windows XP*

Windows XP is basically Windows 2000 with a more user-friendly appearance. The two are quite similar in terms of system files, but Windows XP adds features useful to nonexpert users such as additional wizards and walkthroughs and an expanded Help system. In addition, Windows XP offers the following advantages.

**Utilities from Windows Me.** Many of the most popular consumer features and utilities that were introduced in Windows Me are also in Windows XP, including an improved Windows Media Player, Windows Movie Maker, System Restore, and the Scanner and Camera Wizard.

**Friendlier logon.** To accommodate less-experienced users, Windows XP has an option (turned on by default) that allows a Welcome screen to appear for logon rather than the austere Logon prompt from Windows NT/2000. The user can simply click on his or her name to log on.

**Fast User Switching.** This feature enables a second person to work on the computer without the first person's logging off. The first person's open files remain open while the second person does his or her work, and then the first one can switch back again.

**Driver signing and roll back.** To help users avoid problems with poorly written drivers and DLLs, Windows XP prefers not to install unsigned drivers. A driver is "signed" with a digital code that certifies that it has been tested to work with Windows XP and that it has not been modified or tampered with since its creation. If you try to install an unsigned driver, a dire-sounding warning will appear. Expert users can bypass the warning as needed. Driver updates can also be rolled back to the earlier driver if the new one is found to cause problems.

**Internet Connection Firewall.** Along with providing Internet Explorer 6.0, Windows XP also includes a built-in *firewall* for both dial-up and network connections.

**Firewall**

Software that helps prevent hackers from breaking into a computer via its network or Internet connection.

**Wireless access.** Windows XP supports wireless networking (802.11b) much better than any earlier version did.

**Remote desktop.** This feature, in the Professional version only, enables you to take control of your local Windows desktop remotely.

The workstation version of Windows XP is available in two models: Professional and Home. Home is a stripped-down, less expensive version of Professional. These are the features that are only in the Professional version:

- Multiple CPU support
- 64-bit CPU support
- Advanced security features
- Support for file encryption
- Support for setting up a personal Web server through Internet Information Services (IIS)
- Remote desktop connection
- Membership in a domain on a client/server network
- Ability to work with dynamic disks

# Preparing to Install an Operating System

The actual installation of a Windows version is relatively simple. You insert the CD, you start the Setup.exe application, and you follow the prompts. The steps you must take before that installation, however, are somewhat more complex.

## Checking System Requirements

Each version of Windows has different system requirements, such as a minimum CPU speed, minimum amount of RAM, minimum amount of free hard disk space, and so on. Most versions have both a minimum and a recommended amount; you will likely find that the OS's performance is unsatisfactory if the PC does not meet or exceed the recommended amounts in each category.

Table 26.6 lists the requirements for each of the Windows versions covered on the A+ examination. In addition to the requirements shown here, each version also requires a VGA monitor, a CD drive or network access (for the installation), and a mouse.

| Version | CPU | Memory | Hard Disk | Other |
|---|---|---|---|---|
| Windows NT Workstation 4 | Pentium | 16MB (32MB recommended) | 110MB | |
| Windows 95 | 386DX (486 recommended) | 4MB (8MB recommended) | 50-55MB | |
| Windows 98 | 486DX 66 (Pentium recommended) | 16MB (24 MB recommended) | 165-355MB | |
| Windows 2000 Professional | 133MHz Pentium | 64MB (more improves performance) | 2GB with at least 650MB free | |
| Windows Me | Pentium 150 | 32MB | 480-645MB | |
| Windows XP | 233MHz (300 MHz recommended) | 64MB (128MB recommended) | 1.5GB | Super VGA (800 x 600) |

**TABLE 26.6**
Windows System Requirements

A computer that does not exceed the requirements will likely run Windows very slowly; in all cases a faster CPU and more memory will improve performance substantially.

Office supply and computer stores stock copies of the most recent Windows version. However, if an older OS is the right choice for a particular PC, you might find a copy on eBay (www.ebay.com) or at a store that sells overstock computer components. Make sure that the copy you buy is genuine (not bootleg) and make sure that it comes with the installation key code, usually a 25-digit combination of numbers and letters (OEM copies may have different numbers) that you must enter when you install the product.

In addition, if you buy a copy of Windows XP, make sure that the copy has never been activated. *Product activation* locks the installation key code to the hardware on which it was originally installed, so you cannot install it on another PC.

**Product activation**

An anticopyright-infringement feature of Windows XP and Office XP that locks that copy of the software to a particular hardware configuration.

## TRY IT!

**Check the system configuration for your current PC. Which of the Windows versions listed in Table 26.6 would run well on it?**

## Planning How You Will Start the Setup Program

You will need a plan for starting up the PC and starting the setup program on the Windows CD-ROM. The plan will differ depending on what Windows version you are going to install and whether it will be an upgrade or an install to a blank drive.

### *Starting from a Startup Floppy (Windows 9x)*

The Windows 95 CD is non-bootable, as are some copies of Windows 98 and Me. Therefore if you are installing one of these copies on an empty hard drive, you will need command-line access to the CD drive to start the setup program. To get this, you can boot from a startup floppy created in Windows 98 or Me, or from a startup floppy from Windows 95 that has been modified to contain the needed real-mode CD driver (see Chapter 13).

When you boot from the startup floppy, you can immediately change to the CD-ROM drive (by keying its letter and a colon and pressing Enter) and key **Setup**.

Some technicians like to copy the Windows 9x setup files to the hard drive before running the setup program. That way, whenever the user tries to access a feature of Windows that would normally require reinserting the Windows CD-ROM (such as adding Windows components), it can read the needed data from the hard disk so the CD is not required. It also makes the setup go faster because the hard disk is faster than the CD drive, and it eliminates the potential for errors in reading from the CD during the setup process. However, it does take up between 200 and 300MB of space on the hard disk.

To copy the setup files to the hard drive, you must first partition and format the hard disk (see Chapter 12 for a reminder of how to do that). After partitioning and formatting, if needed, do the following:

1. Boot from the startup floppy to a command prompt.
2. Create a new folder on the hard drive to hold the Windows setup files. You can call it anything you like. Winsetup is a good name, for example. To create a new folder at a command prompt, key **MD** followed by the folder name, as in *MD WINSETUP*. (It is not case-sensitive.)

**IN REAL LIFE**

Many technicians use the popular convention of storing CABs (cabinet files, explained on page 1068) in Windows\Options\CABs, but you can store them anywhere.

3. Copy the contents of the *Win95*, *Win98*, or *Win9x* folder on the CD (depending on the Windows version) to the new folder you just created. For example, to copy from the Windows 98 CD where D was the CD drive, you would key **COPY D:\WIN98 C:\WINSETUP**.

4. Start the Setup.exe program from the new folder. To do so, change to the new folder (*CD WINSETUP,* for example) and then key **SETUP** and press Enter.

***Booting from the Windows Setup CD (Windows NT/2000/XP)***

NT-based Windows versions (NT 4.0, 2000, and XP) come on bootable CD-ROM discs, as do some copies of Windows 98 and Me, so if the BIOS allows for booting from the CD, you can start the setup program by doing so. Chapter 9 covers configuring the BIOS to boot from the CD, if you need help. Since there are no bootable partitions and no existing system files on an empty hard drive, it should boot from the CD without having to change the order of boot preference in BIOS. The CD will likely be the only bootable disc available. When you boot from the CD, the setup program starts automatically.

## Planning an Upgrade

If you are upgrading from a previous Windows version, starting the setup program is easy. From within the existing Windows version you simply insert the CD; a window opens automatically inviting you to start the setup program. If AutoInsert Notification is turned off for the CD-ROM drive, you can double-click it from My Computer.

Before upgrading, you should plan for any issues that may arise as a result of the upgrade. For example:

- Is all the hardware on the Hardware Compatibility List (HCL)? Check the list at the Microsoft Web site.
- Are you crossing over from a 9x version of Windows to an NT-based version? If so, the drivers for many of your hardware devices will probably need to be replaced. If you do not already have drivers (perhaps stored on disk) for the new OS for each device, download them from the manufacturers' Web sites.
- Does the PC meet the system requirements for the new OS? A PC that runs Windows 95 very well, for example, might have trouble with Windows Me if it does not have enough memory or a fast enough CPU.
- To which partition will you install? If you want to replace the old version of Windows, plan to install the new one to the same location. If you want to keep the old version and dual-boot, plan to install the new one to a different partition.
- Might you want to install a fresh copy of the new OS, rather than upgrading the old one? You will get a fresh start, getting rid of outdated or extraneous files associated with the old copy. However, you will have to reinstall all of your applications.

## Planning for Multi-Booting

**Multi-boot**

The capability of installing more than one operating system on a PC and then selecting which OS you want each time the PC starts up. Also called dual-boot.

Windows NT 4, 2000, and XP are all fully *multi-boot* capable. In other words, they come with everything you need to set up a system that can boot to your choice of operating system. Every time you start the PC, a menu appears allowing you to select which operating system you want. This function is controlled by the system file BOOT.INI, which is a text file containing the menu that appears and some other settings that make it work.

Windows 9x and MS-DOS are not multi-boot capable in themselves, but they can be dual-booted either in conjunction with an NT-based version of Windows or by using a third-party utility.

If you want to multi-boot, you should have a separate logical drive for each operating system. You can partition a single hard drive for multiple logical drives, as you learned in Chapter 12, or you can install two or more different physical hard drives, each with one or more partitions.

If one of the OSes you plan to multi-boot with is not multi-boot-aware (MS-DOS or Windows 9x), you should install that OS first, on the primary partition. Then when you run the setup program for the other OS, the one that is multi-boot-aware (Windows NT, 2000, or XP), it will automatically notice that there is already an OS installed; if you specify a different partition as the target for the installation, it will set up multi-booting automatically.

For example, suppose you want to multi-boot between Windows 98 and Windows 2000. You would first install Windows 98, and then install Windows 2000 on a different logical drive. Windows 2000 would configure the multi-booting. If you want to multi-boot between two OSes that are both multi-boot-aware, install the older one first. If you want to multi-boot between two OSes and neither of them supports multi-booting, you will need to buy a utility program to allow it, such as Norton System Commander.

If you are installing two different NT versions of Windows (for example, 2000 and XP) in a multi-boot configuration, install the older one first.

**WARNING**

**If you install Windows 2000 or XP to multi-boot with Windows NT Workstation 4.0, you must install Service Pack 4 in Windows NT in order for Windows NT to be able to read drives that use NTFS 5 (the native version of NTFS for 2000 and XP).**

According to Microsoft, you cannot have a multi-boot system with two different 9x versions of Windows. They will both try to use the same startup files, since neither is multi-boot-aware. There may be ways around this by using a third-party OS manager, however.

### SPECIAL UPGRADING ISSUES FOR SPECIFIC OSES

Here are some special upgrading situations of which you should be aware.

#### *MS-DOS to Windows 9x*

Many MS-DOS utilities can interfere with Windows 9x setup. Examine CONFIG.SYS and AUTOEXEC.BAT and disable any third-party memory management programs, such as QEMM, and any disk caching and antivirus programs.

#### *Windows NT/2000/XP to Windows 9x*

You cannot directly upgrade an NT-based version of Windows to a 9x version. If you make this switch you will lose all of your Windows settings and application installations, and you will start with a fresh Windows 9x copy into which you will need to reinstall everything.

#### *Windows 9x to Windows NT/2000/XP*

You can upgrade from any 9x platform to a workstation version that is NT-based with a minimum of effort; the setup program supports it directly. Problems might occur with individual pieces of hardware or software that might not be compatible with the new Windows version, however; you might have to get driver updates or software patches from the manufacturers. You cannot upgrade from a 9x version to a server OS.

## Installing Windows 9x

After the preceding discussion, you probably already know how to start installing Windows 9x:

- If you have a copy on bootable CD, boot from it.
- From a command prompt, change to the CD drive and key **Setup**.

- If you want the Windows setup files on the hard disk, partition and format it, then create a folder for them and copy the content of the *Win95*, *Win98*, or *Win9x* folder from the CD to the folder. Run Setup.exe from there.
- From within an earlier Windows 9x version, insert the CD. If it does not automatically offer to install the new version, double-click the CD-ROM drive icon in My Computer. The setup program may start at that point. If a file listing appears, double-click Setup.

The next steps depend on the Windows version and upon whether you are doing an upgrade or a clean install. Just follow the prompts.

## Product Key

**Product key**

A string of numbers and letters used to identify your copy of a product for installation.

At some point during the setup, you will be prompted for the *product key*. This is usually a 25-digit combination of numbers and letters, broken into five 5-digit segments such as: xxxxx-xxxxx-xxxxx-xxxxx-xxxxx. On an OEM version of Windows it could be a 20-digit code with OEM as the sixth through eighth digits: xxxxx-OEM-xxxxxxx-xxxxx. A CD that comes in a jewel case typically has the product key on a sticker on the back of the case. Some copies may have the product key imprinted directly on the CD itself, or may include it on a Certificate of Authenticity in the package, along with the documentation.

If you ever need to know the product key for a previously installed copy of Windows, you can find it in the Registry. Enter the Registry Editor (described in Appendix D) and look in the section HKEY_LOCAL_MACHINE\Software\Microsoft\Windows\CurrentVersion. For Windows 98 there will be two separate values: ProductID and ProductKey. For Windows 95 they are the same thing, under ProductID.

## Example: Installing Windows 98

This book does not go through every Windows version's setup in detail, but as an example, it covers the procedure for a clean install of Windows 98.

Complete the following steps to install Windows 98:

1. Partition and format the drive if needed.
2. Start the setup program. A message appears that it is going to perform a routine check on your system. Press Enter to allow that.
3. A DOS-based version of ScanDisk runs (see Figure 26.16). Wait until it is finished and then click the Exit button or, if your mouse is not working, key **X** (the bold letter in the word *Exit*).

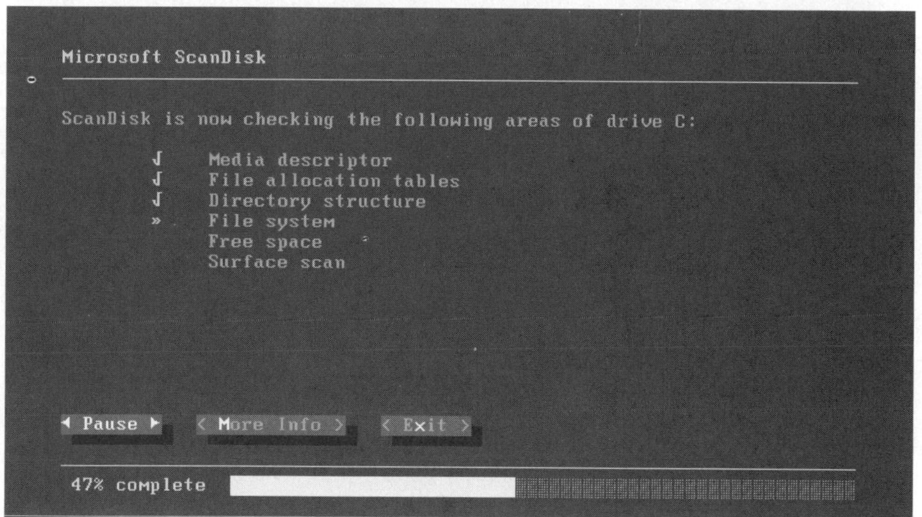


**FIGURE 26.16**
ScanDisk checks the disk for errors before installing Windows.

4. A Windows 98 Setup introductory window appears. Click Continue.
5. A license agreement appears. Click I Accept the Agreement and then click Next.
6. A prompt for the product key appears. Supply it, and then click Next.
7. A prompt appears asking where you want to install Windows: in C:\Windows or in some other location. In most cases C:\Windows is the best choice. Make your selection and click Next. If you chose Other Directory, an additional prompt appears for you to key that path; do so and click Next.
8. Wait a few minutes for some files to be copied to the hard disk. Then a Setup Options menu appears, as in Figure 26.17. Choose a file set to install (Typical is usually the best choice) and click Next.

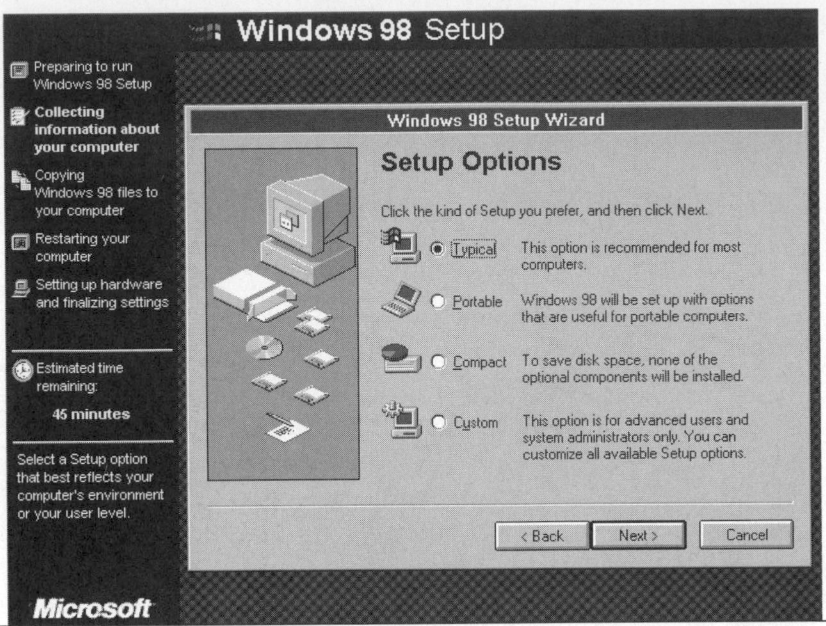


**FIGURE 26.17**
Specify the type of installation you want.

9. A User Information screen appears. Enter your name and company (if applicable), then click Next. Name is required; company is not.
10. A Windows Components prompt appears. You can choose to install the most common components or choose which ones you want.
11. An Identification window appears. Fill in the user name, workgroup, and computer description to use on the network, and then click Next. If this computer is not going to be on a network, leave the defaults.
12. An Establishing Your Location window appears. Select your country and click Next. This setting determines features such as the default currency symbol and the date format.
13. A Startup Disk window appears. Click Next, then insert a blank floppy and click OK to copy startup files to it. This creates an extra copy of a boot disk in case you need one later. If you do not want to create the startup disk, click Cancel.
14. A prompt appears to remove the disk and click OK. Do so.
15. At the Start Copying Files window, click Next. Then wait while the setup program copies Windows files to the hard drive. This takes between 20 and 45 minutes. A File copy progress bar shows what percent is finished and how much time is remaining (see Figure 26.18).

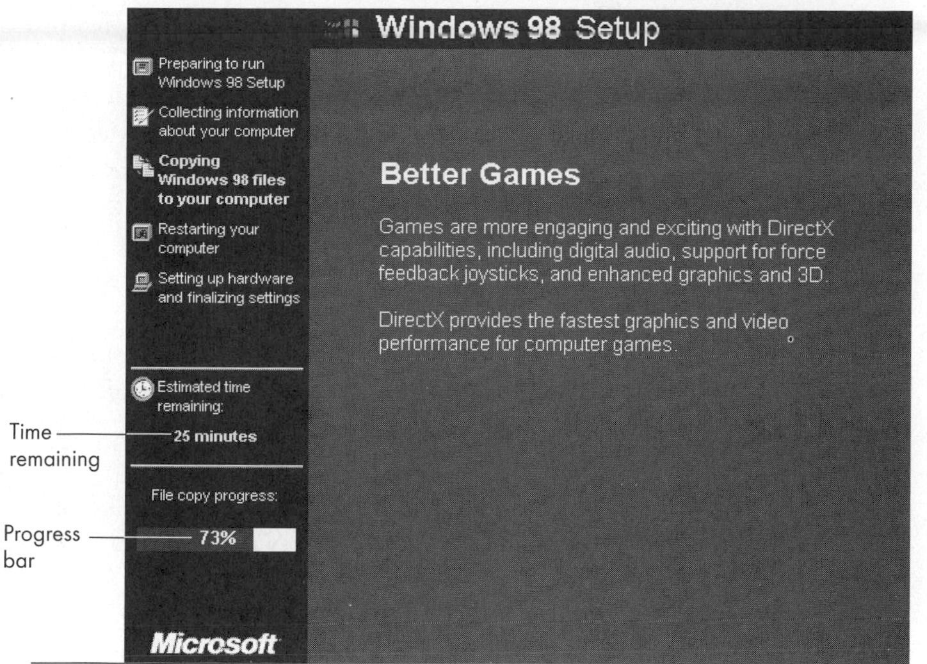


**FIGURE 26.18**
Wait as Windows is installed.

16. A message box appears stating that Windows needs to restart your computer. Click Restart Now. If you do not click it within 15 seconds, it restarts automatically (useful for unattended setups).
17. A Hardware Detection dialog box appears. Wait while Windows searches for Plug and Play devices. It takes several minutes.
18. A Date/Time Properties dialog box appears. Choose your time zone and correct the date and time if needed; click Close (or click Apply and then OK).
19. Wait for Windows to finish its setup and to restart. (Again you will see a Restart Now button, but it will restart automatically after 15 seconds if you do not click it.)
20. An Enter Network Password dialog box appears. Change the user name if you want to use some name other than the one you entered in step 9.

Windows 98 is now fully installed.

## TRY IT!

**Install Windows 95 on an empty hard disk. How is the procedure different from the one for Windows 98 described above?**

## Installing Windows NT, 2000, or XP

All of these versions come on bootable CDs, so to install them on a new hard drive, set up the BIOS to prefer the CD drive as the boot device; when you turn on the PC with the CD inserted, the setup program will start automatically.

### Setup Boot Disks

If you are installing Windows NT or 2000 on a PC that does not support booting from CD, you can use Setup Boot Disks. These are a set of floppies; you boot from the first one and then feed in the others as prompted to start the setup program.

Windows NT 4 comes with the Setup Boot Disks, a set of three floppies; insert the first one in the PC's floppy drive, and the NT CD in the CD drive, and turn on the computer.

Windows 2000 does not come with the Setup Boot Disks, but you can make a set by taking the CD to a working PC and running a utility program from the CD to create them. You will need four blank floppy disks to do so. Either from a command prompt or with the Start/Run command in Windows, run the following (where x: is your CD-ROM drive letter): **x:\bootdisk\makeboot a:**. Then just follow the prompts.

Windows XP does not come with the capability for making Setup Boot Disks because it is assumed that any PC that meets XP's system requirements will be capable of booting from a CD.

### Example: Installing Windows 2000

As another example, let us look at the procedure for Windows 2000 Setup on a blank hard disk, to see how it differs from that of Windows 98. One difference is that you do not need to partition and format the drive first; the setup program will help you with that task, as shown below.

1. With the Windows 2000 Professional CD in the drive, start the computer. Wait for the setup program to examine the system and load itself. It takes several minutes. (Early in the examination you will see a message prompting you to press F6 if you need to load a third-party driver. This might be necessary if you are installing Windows on a hard drive attached to an I/O controller that is too new for Windows 2000 to recognize, for example. If that were the case, you would download a Windows 2000 driver for the controller from the manufacturer's Web site and have it ready on a floppy disk for this

install, then press F6 when prompted and follow the instructions.)

2. A Welcome to Setup screen appears. Press Enter to start the setup.
3. If the hard disk is not partitioned or formatted, a message appears that the hard disk either has been erased or is new. Key **C** to continue setting it up.
4. A license agreement appears. Press F8 to accept it.
5. A list of the existing partitions and unpartitioned space appears, as in Figure 26.19. Do one of the following:
   a. If you want the entire unpartitioned space to be devoted to Windows 2000, select it.
   b. If you want to create a partition out of the space for Windows, and to leave part of the disk unpartitioned for now, key **C**, enter the amount of space for the partition, and press Enter.
   c. To delete an existing partition, select it and press D.

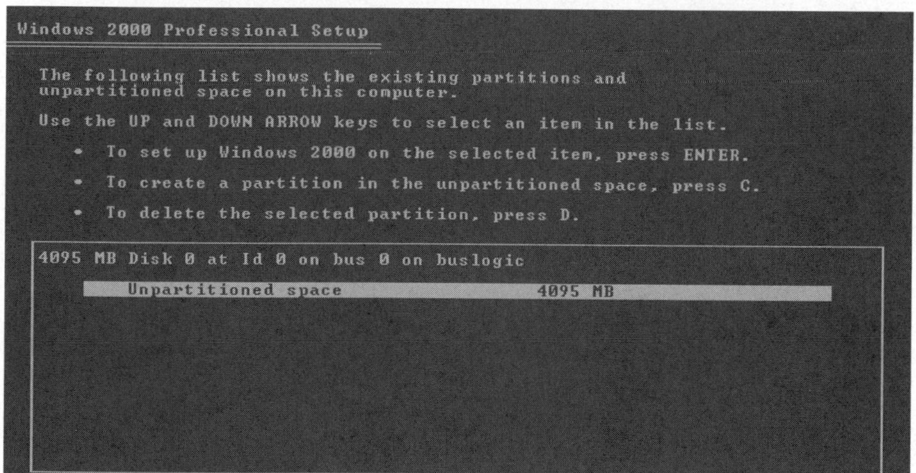
Windows 2000 Professional Setup
The following list shows the existing partitions and unpartitioned space on this computer.
Use the UP and DOWN ARROW keys to select an item in the list.
• To set up Windows 2000 on the selected item, press ENTER.
• To create a partition in the unpartitioned space, press C.
• To delete the selected partition, press D.
4095 MB Disk 0 at Id 0 on bus 0 on buslogic
Unpartitioned space 4095 MB

**FIGURE 26.19**
Install Windows 2000 on the unpartitioned space (Windows will create a partition automatically) or create partitions manually by keying C.

6. If you created a partition, a prompt appears asking which file system you want: FAT or NTFS. Choose NTFS unless you will need the logical drive to be readable under Windows 9x. Then wait while the partition is formatted.
7. Wait while the setup program checks the disk and copies the setup files to the hard disk. This process takes several minutes.
8. The PC restarts and a Windows-based screen appears welcoming you to Windows Setup. Click Next to go on.
9. Wait while Setup detects the basic hardware, including keyboard and mouse. A Regional Settings dialog box appears. If the language and region are not correct, click Customize to change them; otherwise click Next.

10. Key your name and company name in the boxes provided, and then click Next.
11. Enter the product key for the CD. It is a 25-digit string of numbers and letters, probably on a sticker on the dust jacket that the CD came in. Click Next.
12. A Computer Name and Administrator Password dialog box appears (see Figure 26.20). Change the assigned Computer name if desired, and key and rekey an Administrator password. Click Next.

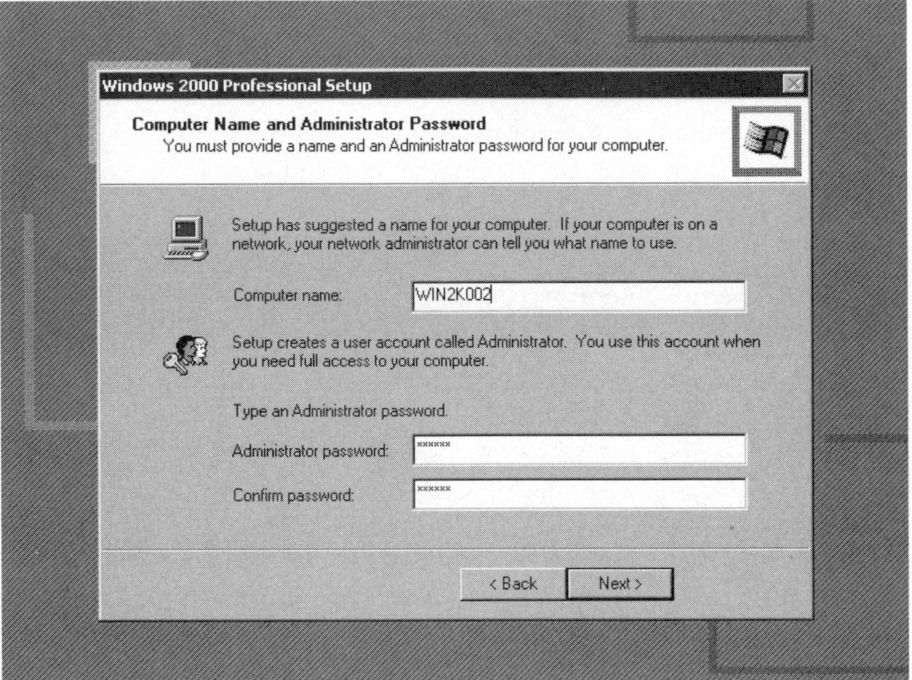


**FIGURE 26.20**
Assign Computer name and Administrator password.

13. A Date and Time Settings dialog box appears. Change the Date, Time, and Time Zone if any are incorrect, and then click Next.
14. At the Networking Settings dialog box, leave Typical Settings selected and click Next.
15. A message box asks whether the computer is part of a workgroup or domain. Choose No if it is a workgroup or Yes if it is a domain; then enter the workgroup or domain name in the text box provided (see Figure 26.21). Click Next.

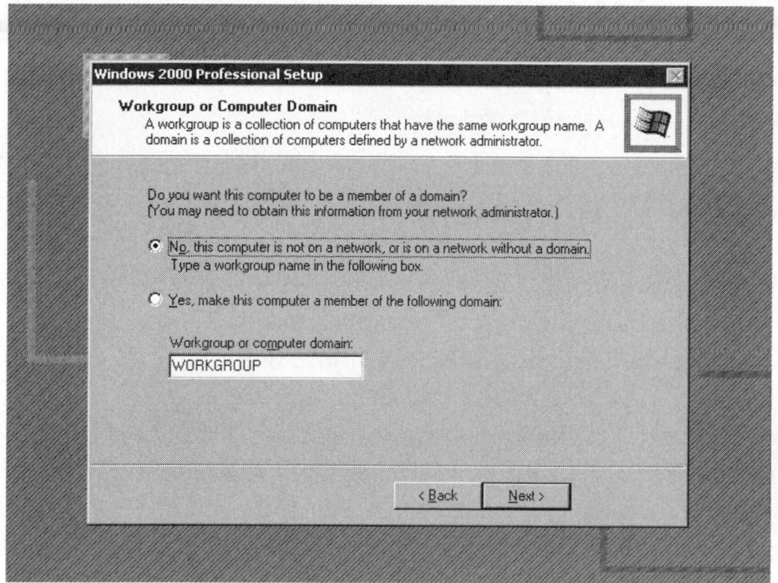


**FIGURE 26.21**
Specify the workgroup or domain.

16. Wait for Setup to finish copying files. It takes another several minutes. At the Completing the Windows 2000 Setup Wizard screen, click Finish. Windows restarts.
17. After the restart, if the PC is on a network, the Network Identification Wizard may run. Click Next at its opening screen.
18. At the Users of This Computer dialog box, specify whether Windows should assume that a certain user is logging on every time, or whether the traditional logon box requiring a user name and password should appear (see Figure 26.22). Click Next, and then click Finish.

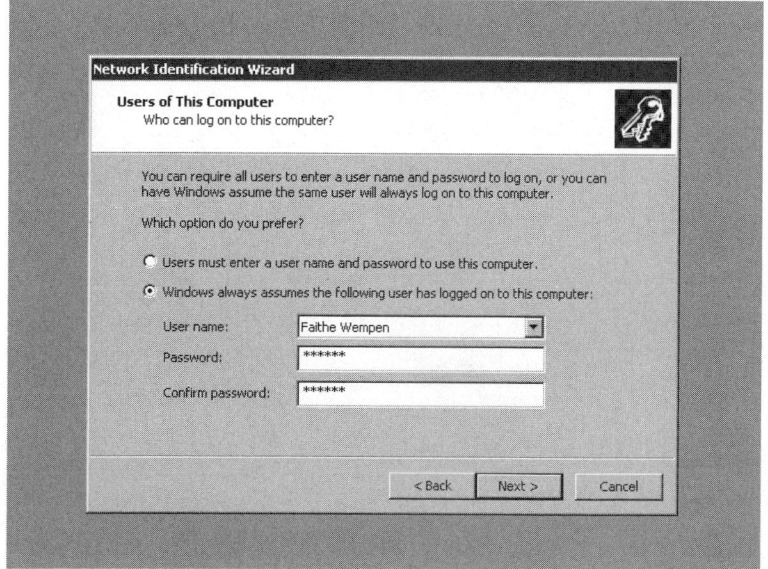


**FIGURE 26.22**
Specify whether or not Windows should log you on automatically at startup.

## TRY IT!

Install Windows NT 4.0 or Windows XP Professional on an empty hard disk. How is it different from the steps described above for Windows 2000?

# Managing Multi-Boot Settings

As discussed earlier, when you install an NT-type version of Windows on a system that already has another Windows version on it, and you put it on a different partition, it automatically sets up multi-booting. The settings are contained in a file called BOOT.INI in the root directory of the boot drive (usually C). BOOT.INI does not exist on systems that have only Windows 9x version(s) installed because they are not multi-boot-aware.

BOOT.INI provides the text for the menu that appears each time the PC starts up, from which you select the operating system you want. Therefore, if you ever need to change the content of that menu (perhaps because you have removed an operating system that still shows up on that menu, for example), you can edit it using any text-editing program, such as Notepad.

There is an easier and safer way to edit BOOT.INI, however: through System Properties in the Control Panel:

1. In the Control Panel, open the System Properties dialog box and then click the Advanced tab.
2. Click the Settings button in the Startup and Recovery section. The Startup and Recovery dialog box appears.
3. In the System startup section, make changes to the boot settings as desired (see Figure 26.23). Then click OK.

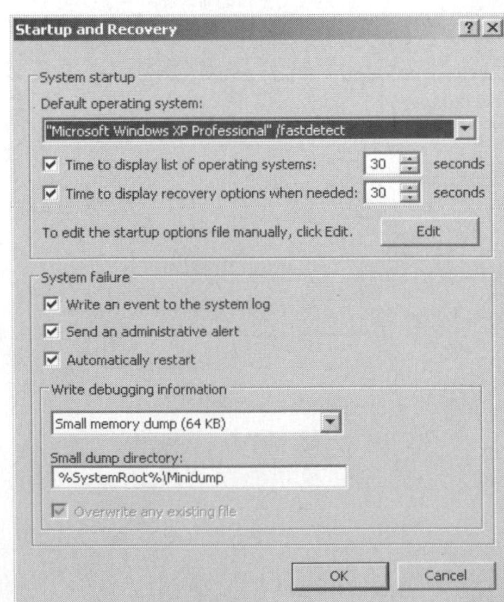


**FIGURE 26.23**
BOOT.INI settings are accessible through the Control Panel, so you do not usually have to edit BOOT.INI manually.

## Troubleshooting Installation Problems

The following sections address some of the most common setup problems.

### Hardware Incompatibilities

The most common reasons that a clean install of Windows fails are hardware incompatibilities. These include not only drives and circuit boards, but also the BIOS. In many cases firmware updates are available that can make devices more compatible with later Windows versions.

The most common symptom of a hardware-incompatibility problem is for Windows Setup to terminate with an error message saying that it cannot complete, or the appearance of a blue screen with a STOP error. When this occurs, use this troubleshooting procedure:

1. Check the Hardware Compatibility List (www.microsoft.com/hcl) to make sure that all of the remaining hardware is compatible with the Windows version you are installing. If it is not, try replacing the noncompatible device temporarily with one on the list.
2. Remove all nonessential hardware from the computer. Leave only the hard disk, the CD drive, the keyboard, the mouse, and the video card installed.
3. Check the manufacturer's Web site to see whether an update is available for the motherboard's BIOS. If so, download and install it.
4. Try reinstalling Windows.

### Cannot Get Past ScanDisk

Windows runs ScanDisk at the beginning of the setup process. If it will not run for some reason, the Windows 9x versions of Setup will not continue. If you run into this situation, add the /is switch to the Setup command at the command prompt by keying **setup /is**.

### Errors Reading from CD

If you get an error message during setup about not being able to read a certain file from the CD, here are some things to try:

- Remove the CD, rotate it a quarter turn, and put it back in the drive. (Microsoft suggests this in its setup documentation.)
- Clean the dirt and fingerprints off the CD with a soft, dry cloth.

- If possible, copy the setup files from the CD to a hard drive and install from there instead. You do not have to copy the entire CD—just the *Win95*, *Win98*, or *Win9x* folder for Windows 95, 98, or Me, respectively, or the *i386* folder for Windows 2000 or XP.
- If you have more than one CD drive, abort Setup and retry using the other drive.

## Stops Recognizing CD Drive (98)

Sometimes during a Windows 98 Second Edition install when you are upgrading from Windows 95, the setup program will lose access to the CD drive. If this happens, Microsoft recommends doing the following:

1. Restart and boot directly to a command prompt, either from a startup disk or by pressing F8 and then choosing Command Prompt Only when you see the Starting Windows message on-screen.
2. Use EDIT to edit Autoexec.bat. Remove the text "Rem by Windows 98 Setup" from in front of the *mscdex.exe* line of text.
3. Exit from EDIT, saving your changes, and reboot. If Setup does not restart and continue on its own, rerun Setup, choosing Safe Recovery if prompted.

## File Is Missing after Installing

In rare cases the Windows Setup does not install a needed file. Windows might not start because this file is missing, or you might see an error message when you attempt to access a certain feature. This can also occur if Windows does install everything correctly, but then an important system file later gets corrupted or deleted.

One way to correct such a problem is to rerun Windows Setup, but that is a very extreme, time-consuming solution. An easier method might be to copy the needed file from the Windows CD.

**Cabinet (CAB) files**

Compressed archives containing files needed for Windows Setup.

Most of the files on the Windows CD are compressed in *cabinet (CAB) files*, so you cannot do a simple copy operation to retrieve one. Instead you must use the Extract utility to extract and decompress the needed file. To do so from a command prompt, use the following syntax:

**EXTRACT *x:\path\cabinetfile x:\path\filename***

In this example, *cabinetfile* is the name of the CAB file containing the file you want and *filename* is the name of the file to be extracted.

Usually, however, you will not know which CAB file contains the particular compressed file you want. You can search all of the CAB files in a certain location (such as the Windows CD) with the /A switch:

**EXTRACT /A *x:\path\cabinetfile x:\path\filename***

In the above command, the cabinet file you specify is the one to start looking in, but it will look in all of them in the current location.

## IN REAL LIFE

Windows XP lets you open CAB files as if they were folders in an Explorer window, so you can drag-and-drop them out of the CABs without having to use EXTRACT.

The full syntax for the EXTRACT command looks like this (the parts in brackets are optional):

**EXTRACT [/Y] [/A] [/D | /E] [/L dir] cabinetfile [filename]**

| | |
|---|---|
| /Y | Does not prompt before overwriting an existing copy. |
| /A | Searches all CAB files in the specified location, starting with the one specified by the *cabinetfile* variable. |
| /D | Displays the cabinet directory. If you use this switch along with using a file name, it will display the list only, and will not extract anything. |
| /E | Extract all. You can use this instead of *.* for the name to extract all files. |
| /L dir | Location to place the extracted files. The default is the current directory. |
| *cabinetfile* | The name of the cabinet file, either the only one or the one to start with depending on whether you have used the /A switch. |
| *filename* | The name of the file you want to extract. You can use multiple files separated by spaces, or you can use wildcards * or ?. This is optional; if you leave it out it will extract all of the files in the specified cabinet file. |

You can also use EXTRACT to decompress a single compressed file. These are not CABs; instead they are individual files that can be distinguished from the uncompressed versions by the underscore in their extension, such as mfc42._ll. The syntax for using EXTRACT with them is as follows:

**EXTRACT [/Y] source [newname]**
**EXTRACT [/Y] /C source destination**

| | |
|---|---|
| source | The compressed file name. This is different from a CAB in that it contains only one file. |

| | |
|---|---|
| newname | This is optional. The default is to give it the original name under which the file was compressed. |
| /C source destination | Copies the specified source file to the specified destination. |

EXPAND is an alternative command that does much the same thing as EXTRACT, but has a somewhat different syntax. It is not covered on the A+ exams. To learn about EXPAND's syntax, key **EXPAND /?** at a command prompt.

**TRY IT!**

Extract the file mwclw32.dll from the Windows 2000 Setup CD, and place it in a temporary directory you create for the exercise. Or, if you do not have Windows 2000 to work with, extract the file checkos.exe from the Windows 98 or 98 Second Edition CD.

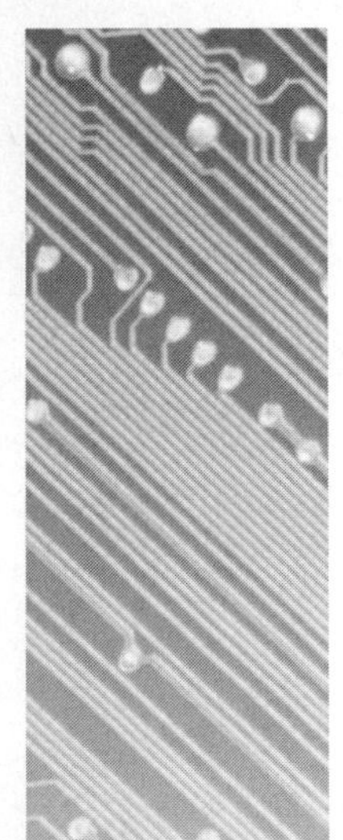

# STUDY GUIDE

Use the following summaries to review the key concepts of this chapter.

## UNDERSTANDING OPERATING SYSTEMS

- An operating system is software that handles the PC's administrative/support systems in a PC, including managing memory, telling drives to read or write, and maintaining the user interface.
- The operating systems covered on the A+ exam are Windows 95, Windows 98, and Windows 2000 Professional. Windows NT Workstation 4.0 is also covered, but less extensively.
- A command-line OS requires users to issue text commands at a prompt. MS-DOS is an example.
- A graphical user interface (GUI) OS interacts with the user via icons, menus, and a mouse. Windows is an example.

## CHECKING THE CURRENT OS VERSION

- At a command prompt, key **VER** and press Enter to see the version number.
- In Windows, open System Properties and look on the General tab.

## Understanding MS-DOS

- MS-DOS was the original operating system for IBM PCs.
- It is a command-line operating system, and in its native mode (real mode) it runs only one program at a time and supplies only 640KB of memory to the running program.
- In DOS protected mode, additional memory can be addressed and there can be a limited type of switching between tasks.
- Internal commands are those built into the command interpreter (COMMAND.COM). They do not require additional files to run. Examples include DIR and DEL.
- External commands are programs included with DOS that must be present (usually in the DOS directory) in order to run. Examples include FDISK and FORMAT.
- The major system files involved with DOS are IO.SYS (manages devices), MSDOS.SYS (manages the OS and applications), and COMMAND.COM (communicates between the user and the OS).
- CONFIG.SYS and AUTOEXEC.BAT run automatically at startup if they are present. CONFIG.SYS loads device drivers and system settings; AUTOEXEC.BAT processes commands and loads programs that run in the background.
- A terminate-and-stay-resident (TSR) program loads at startup and remains loaded while the computer operates.
- HIMEM.SYS, EMM386.EXE, and SMARTDRV are optional memory management utilities commonly loaded in CONFIG.SYS under MS-DOS.

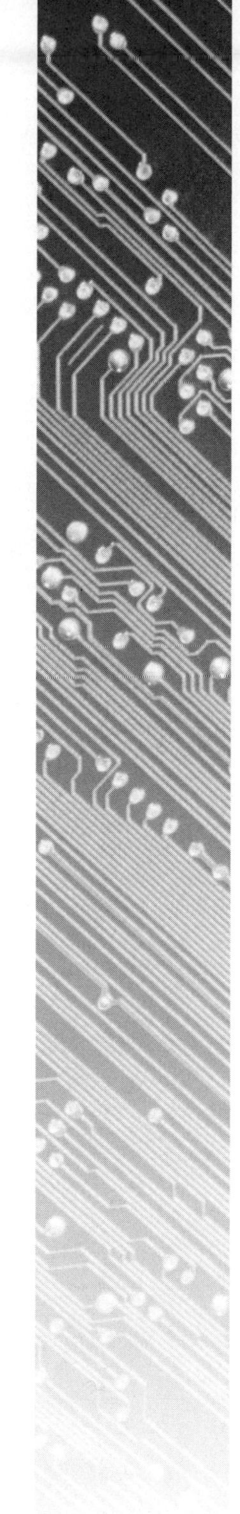

## Understanding Windows 3.1

- Windows versions prior to 95 were not really operating systems, but operating environments that ran on top of MS-DOS. Windows 3.1 was the last major version prior to Windows 95.
- A minor release, Windows 3.11 for Workgroups, added peer-to-peer networking and a few other minor improvements.
- Since Windows 3.1 is a protected-mode program it requires HIMEM.SYS to be loaded into CONFIG.SYS.
- The file that starts Windows 3.1 is WIN.COM, keyed at the command prompt.
- The three main files that run Windows 3.1 are KRNL386.EXE, USER.EXE, and GDI.EXE.

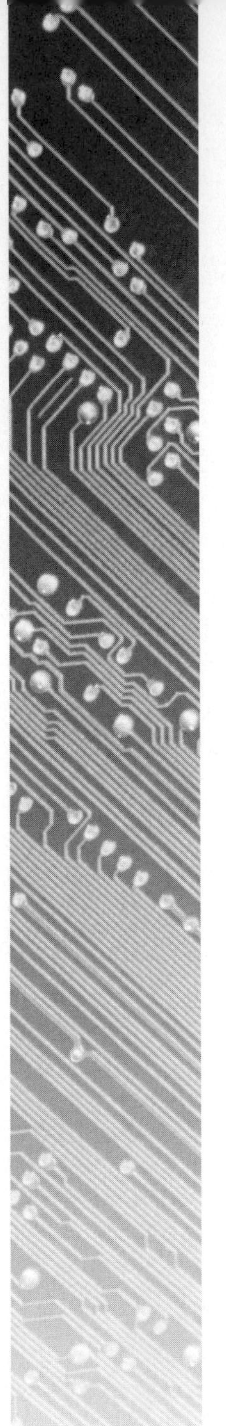

- SYSTEM.INI and WIN.INI are initialization files that execute at startup.
- Individual applications and devices have their own INI files.
- Dynamic-link library (DLL) files contain standard programming routines that applications can call upon as they run.
- Virtual machines are simulated 8086 CPUs operating in their own address spaces.
- Windows 3.1 has a clipboard that shares data via Dynamic Data Exchange (DDE), which can cut, copy, and paste, but cannot create dynamic links.
- Multitasking in Windows 3.1 is cooperative multitasking, in which the programs themselves voluntarily pause to allow other programs to run.

## Understanding Windows 95, 98, and Me

- Windows 95 runs 32-bit applications, but retains some 16-bit underpinnings for backward compatibility with MS-DOS and Windows 3.1.
- Windows 95, 98, and Me are very similar, and are all based on the same system files. Windows Me is not on the A+ exam.
- IO.SYS and MSDOS.SYS exist in Windows 9x, but IO.SYS takes on all of the functionality that they shared in MS-DOS. MSDOS.SYS is just a text-based configuration file.
- Windows 9x can read and process CONFIG.SYS and AUTOEXEC.BAT if they are present but it does not require them.
- The startup configuration files are USER.DAT and SYSTEM.DAT, which together form the Registry.
- Windows 9x uses the same three system files for 16-bit applications: Krnl386, User, and GDI. For 32-bit applications it uses Kernel32.dll, User32.dll, and GDI32.dll.
- VMM386.vxd loads the 32-bit device drivers.
- Windows 9x introduces Plug and Play for automatically detecting hardware.
- Preemptive multitasking, featured in all 32-bit versions of Windows, allows Windows to dictate when each program takes its turn (in time slices), so a rogue program cannot consume all of the resources.
- Windows 9x and higher use object linking and embedding (OLE) for clipboard-based data sharing and to create dynamic links between data files and applications.
- Windows 9x and higher allow file names up to 255 characters, including spaces.

- There were many minor revisions of Windows 95 that introduced new features, most notably FAT32 (in Windows 95 SR2) and support for USB (in Windows 95 SR2.1).

## Understanding Windows NT, 2000, and XP

- Windows NT Workstation 4.0 predates Windows 95. It is a fully 32-bit version of Windows, but lacks Plug and Play. It supports only FAT16 and NTFS 4.0 file systems.
- Windows 2000 includes Plug and Play as well as most of the other consumer-friendly features from Windows 95 and 98. It supports FAT16, FAT32, and NTFS 5.0.
- Windows NT 4 came in two versions: Workstation and Server. Windows 2000 comes in four versions: Professional, Server, Advanced Server, and Datacenter Server.
- Windows XP is the current version as of this writing. It comes in two workstation versions: Home and Professional. The server version is called Windows.NET.
- NT-based versions of Windows do not use IO.SYS, MSDOS.SYS, or COMMAND.COM.
- NTLDR, which is short for NT Loader, is the equivalent of IO.SYS.
- BOOT.INI describes how booting should occur (especially multi-boot); its rough equivalent in Windows 9x would be MSDOS.SYS.
- WINNT32.EXE is the main program file.
- NTOSKRNL.EXE takes the place of Krnl386.exe or Kernel32.dll.
- The Registry consists of five files: Sam, Security, System, Software, and Default. These are known as registry hives. A sixth file, Ntuser.dat, stores information about users and integrates with the Registry.
- The NTFS file system is incompatible with Windows 9x, but offers performance improvements.
- Windows 2000 introduced NTFS 5.0, with additional enhancements to NTFS such as file encryption and compression.
- Other new features with Windows 2000 include Active Directory, Internet Printing Protocol, and Dynamic Disks.

## Preparing to Install an Operating System

- Check the system requirements of the OS version before attempting to install it.

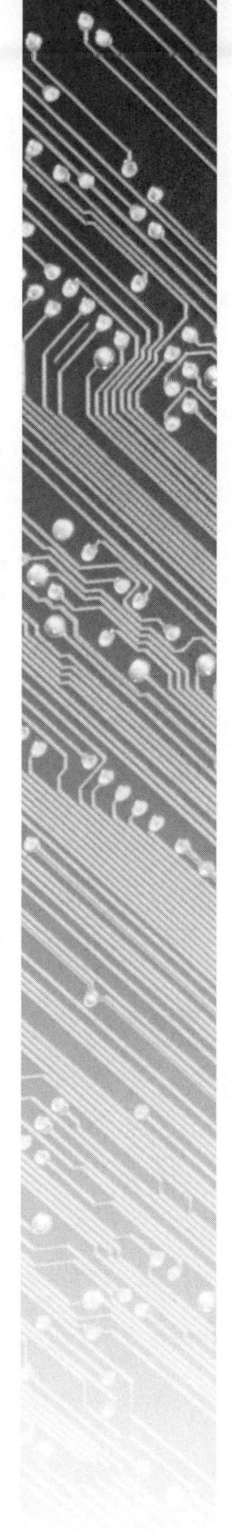

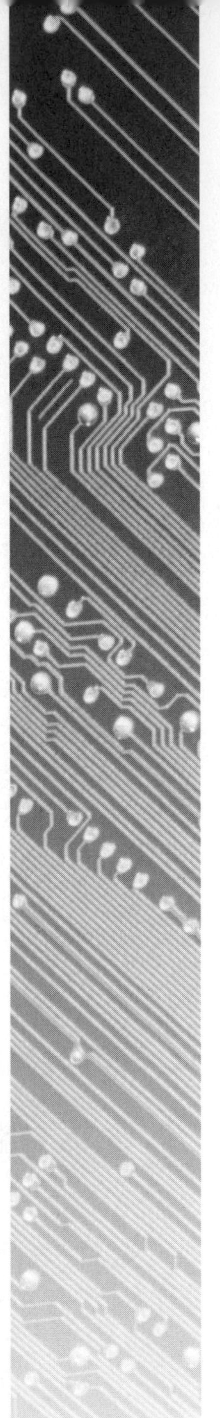

- Windows NT Workstation 4 requires a Pentium CPU and 16MB of RAM.
- Windows 95 requires a 386DX and 4MB of RAM.
- Windows 98 requires a 486DX66 and 16MB of RAM.
- Windows 2000 requires a 133MHz Pentium and 64MB of RAM.
- Windows Me requires a Pentium 150MHz CPU with 32MB of RAM.
- Windows XP requires a 233MHz CPU and 64MB of RAM.
- Windows 9x setup can be run from within Windows or from a command prompt by keying **Setup**.
- The Windows 98 CD has a utility called FAT32EBD that creates a bootable floppy disk.
- Copying the contents of the *Win95*, *Win98*, or *Win9x* folder from the CD to the hard disk before running Setup enables all future setup to be done without reinserting the CD.
- Windows NT, 2000, and XP CDs are bootable, so you can start the setup from there without using a startup disk.
- 9x versions of Windows can be upgraded to an NT version, but not vice versa.
- Multi-booting allows several OSes to exist on different partitions of the same system. It is controlled by the BOOT.INI file.
- NT-based versions of Windows are multi-boot-aware; install the 9x version first and then the NT-based version to set up a multi-boot system.
- Two different 9x versions cannot be multi-booted without a third-party utility.
- Two different NT versions, or an NT and a 9x version, can be multi-booted with no extra software required.

## Installing Windows 9x

- To start Windows 9x installation from a command prompt, change to the CD drive and key **Setup**.
- From within an earlier 9x version, insert the CD and run the setup program from within Windows.
- The product key may be a 25-digit number or a 20-digit code with OEM as the sixth through eighth characters.
- After you start the setup program, simply follow the prompts.

### Installing Windows NT, 2000, or XP

- Windows NT 4 comes with setup boot floppies that can start the PC. Windows 2000 does not come with them, but provides a utility (makeboot) for making such disks.
- To upgrade from a previous Windows version, start Setup.exe from the CD from within Windows.
- NT-based versions of Windows can partition and format drives from within the setup program.

### Managing Multi-Boot Settings

- The BOOT.INI file controls the boot menu that appears at startup, listing the available OSes.
- You can edit BOOT.INI manually, or you can change its settings through System Properties in the Control Panel (on the Advanced tab).

### Troubleshooting Installation Problems

- The most common reason for problems to occur in Windows Setup is hardware incompatibility. Not all Windows versions support all hardware.
- Consult the Microsoft Hardware Compatibility List (www.microsoft.com/hcl) to determine hardware compatibility if in doubt.
- If Windows will not install, try removing all nonessential hardware and installing the latest available BIOS update for the motherboard.
- To run Setup without running ScanDisk, start Setup with the /is switch.
- If there are problems reading the CD, clean it, reinsert it, or try copying its content to a hard disk and installing from there.
- You can extract any missing Windows files from the Setup CD with the EXTRACT command-line utility.

## PRACTICE TEST

On a blank sheet of paper, write the answers to the following multiple-choice questions and explain why each answer is correct.

1. Which of these does not have a GUI?
   a. Windows NT 4.0
   b. Windows 3.1
   c. MS-DOS
   d. Windows 95

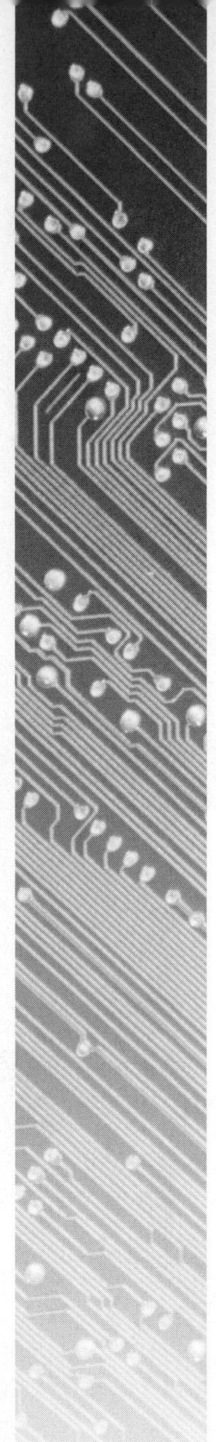

2. What command shows the version number at a command prompt?
   a. SETVER
   b. VER
   c. Help/About
   d. HELP VER

3. What is required to execute an internal command under MS-DOS?
   a. an executable file
   b. a DLL
   c. CONFIG.SYS
   d. Command.com

4. TSRs are loaded on an MS-DOS system using which file?
   a. Command.com
   b. IO.SYS
   c. Config.sys
   d. Autoexec.bat

5. What is the purpose of SYSTEM.INI in Windows 95?
   a. backward compatibility with 16-bit Windows applications
   b. with WIN.INI, it forms the Registry
   c. controls multi-booting
   d. All of the above

6. Which of these OSes does not support Plug and Play?
   a. Windows 3.1
   b. Windows NT 4.0
   c. Windows 95
   d. both a and b

7. Why is preemptive multitasking preferable to cooperative?
   a. It supports object linking and embedding.
   b. It supports Dynamic Data Exchange.
   c. Windows controls multitasking, so programs cannot take more than their assigned share of CPU time.
   d. Each application controls its own multitasking, freeing up Windows resources for other tasks.

8. What was the first retail version of Windows to support USB?
   a. Windows 95 SR2
   b. Windows 95 SP1
   c. Windows 98
   d. Windows 98 Second Edition

9. Which of these files is *not* needed for Windows 2000?
   a. NTLDR
   b. NTDETECT
   c. NTOSKRNL
   d. They are all required for Windows 2000.

10. Which of these files is *not* part of the Windows 2000 Registry?
    a. System.dat
    b. User.dat
    c. Security
    d. both a and b

11. Because Windows 2000 is not based on the MS-DOS kernel, it does not allow you to
    a. use the first 640KB of RAM (conventional memory).
    b boot to a command prompt.
    c. run 16-bit applications.
    d. run MS-DOS applications.

12. What is a reason to prefer NTFS 4 over FAT16?
    a. encryption
    b. disk quotas
    c. larger maximum logical drive size
    d. All of the above

13. What is the recommended minimum amount of RAM needed for Windows 2000?
    a. 32MB
    b. 64MB
    c. 96MB
    d. 128MB

14. Which version of Windows contains a boot disk-making utility called FAT32EBD on its Setup CD?
    a. Windows 95
    b. Windows 98
    c. Windows 2000
    d. Windows XP

15. What is the advantage of copying the Windows 9x setup files to the hard disk before installing Windows?
    a. Setup completes faster.
    b. The CD need not be reinserted later when adding Windows components.

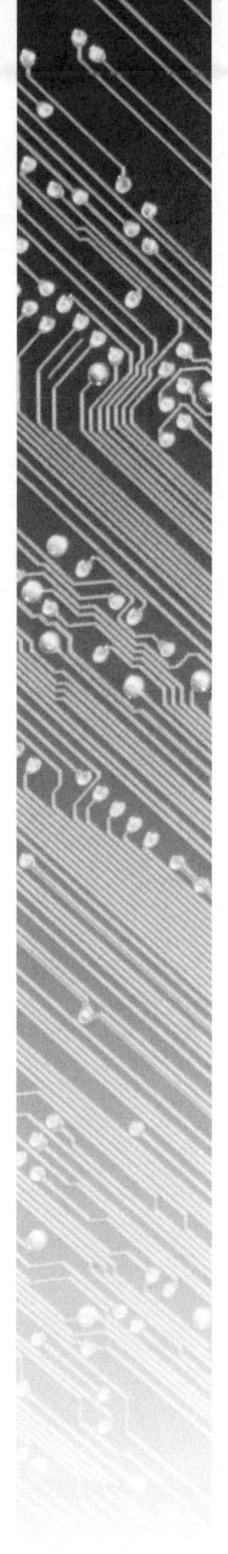

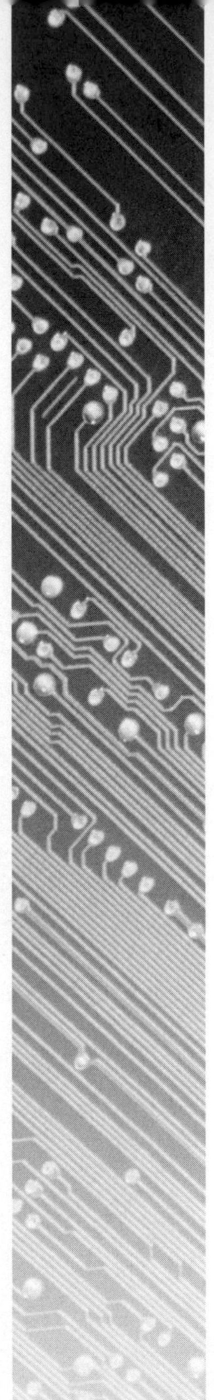

c. It eliminates the potential for errors reading from the CD during setup.
d. All of the above

16. Which of these Windows versions can be upgraded to Windows 98 Second Edition?
    a. Windows 95
    b. Windows 2000
    c. Windows Me
    d. both a and b

17. If you want to multi-boot Windows 98, Windows 2000, and Windows XP on the same computer, in what order would you install them?
    a. XP, 2000, 98
    b. 98, 2000, XP
    c. The order does not matter.
    d. None of the above; these three cannot coexist on the same system.

18. Which of these is a valid product key format for Windows 95 (assuming the *X*s were replaced by numbers or letters)?
    a. xxxx-xxxxxx-xxx-xxxxxxx-xxxxx-xxxx
    b. xxxxx.xxxxx.xxxxx.xxxxx.xxxxx
    c. xxxxx-OEM-xxxxxxx-xxxxx
    d. either b or c

19. What is the function of the makeboot utility on the Windows 2000 CD?
    a. It creates a set of four floppy disks that start Windows Setup, for systems that cannot boot from the CD.
    b. It creates a startup disk similar to the one in Windows 9x, from which you can boot to a command prompt.
    c. It can do either a or b, depending on the command syntax.
    d. It creates a bootable backup of the Registry.

20. Which text file do you edit to control multi-boot settings on a system that contains Windows 95 and Windows 98 on separate partitions?
    a. C:\BOOT.INI
    b. MSDOS.SYS
    c. D:\BOOT.INI
    d. None of the above; those operating systems are not multi-boot-aware.

# TROUBLESHOOTING

1. A client wants you to install Windows XP on a dozen PCs in his office, but none of them have CD drives. They all currently have Windows NT 4.0 installed, and they have 1.44MB floppy drives and 100MB Zip drives. What are your options?
2. You are trying to install Windows 2000 on a PC but the setup program keeps aborting with a blue-screen STOP error. Describe how you will troubleshoot.
3. A client wants you to wipe out everything on her hard disk and start fresh, reloading all her software including Windows. She has her original Windows CD, but she has misplaced the product key. How can you find the product key?

# CUSTOMER SERVICE

1. A client has just acquired a secondhand computer with no operating system installed. It is a Pentium 120MHz with 32MB of RAM and a 500MB hard drive, which is empty. What operating system do you recommend?
2. A client has a custom-written MS-DOS application for her business that runs on some very old computers (286, 386, and 486 models), and she worries that if she upgrades her office PCs to Windows 2000, the application will not run anymore. What advice can you give?
3. You are building a PC for a client who wants Windows XP installed, but he also wants to retain the flexibility of dual-booting with Windows Me if he later decides to install it too. You have installed a single 40GB hard drive. How would you partition and format it while installing Windows XP?

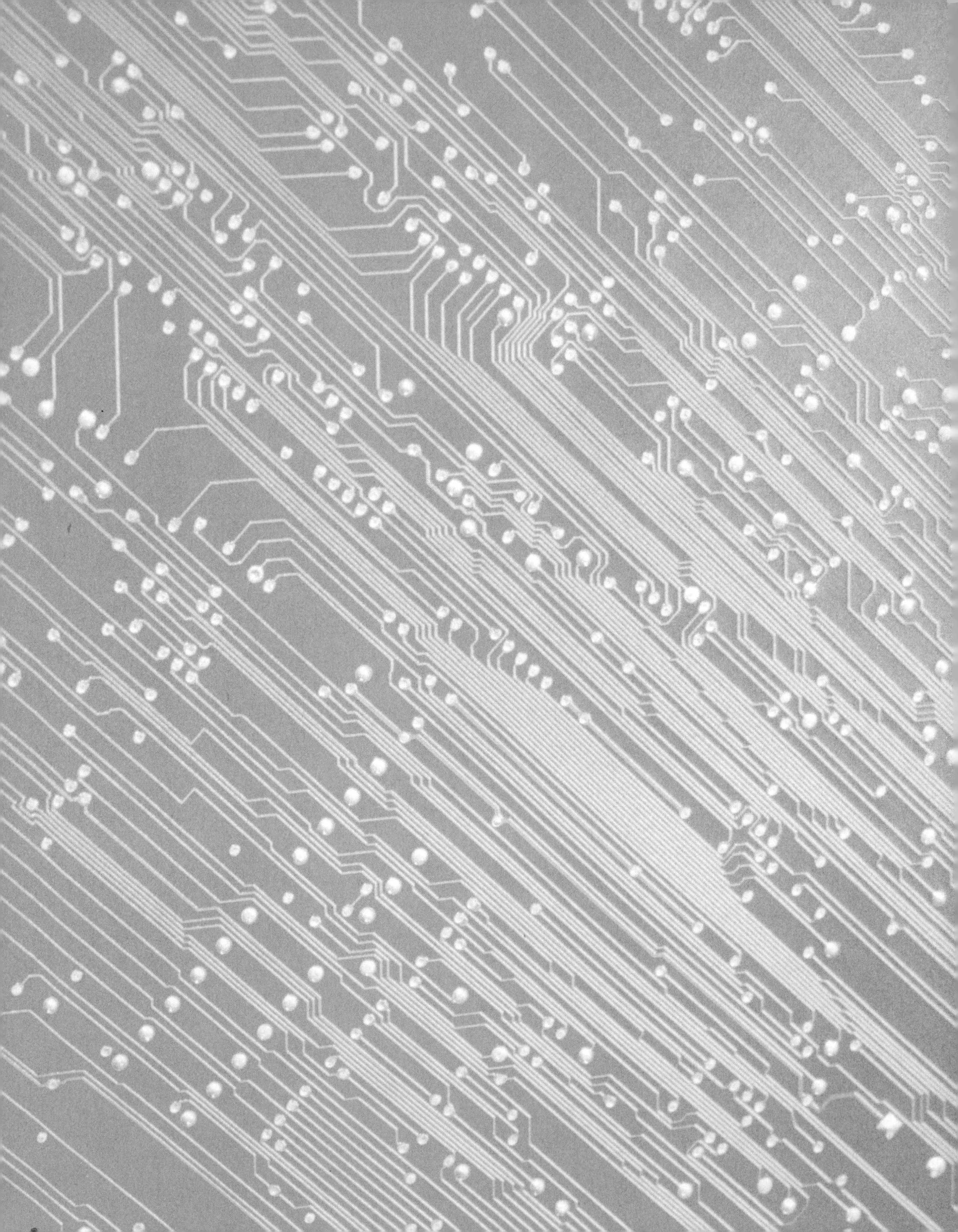

# 27 The Boot Process

## ON THE TEST

**A+ Operating System Technologies Examination**

- **Objective 1.1:** Identify the operating system's functions, structure, and major system files to navigate the operating system and how to get to needed technical information.
- **Objective 1.2:** Identify basic concepts and procedures for creating, viewing and managing files, directories and disks. This includes procedures for changing file attributes and the ramifications of those changes (for example, security issues).
- **Objective 2.1:** Identify the procedures for installing Windows 9x, and Windows 2000 for bringing the software to a basic operational level.
- **Objective 2.3:** Identify the basic system boot sequences and boot methods, including the steps to create an emergency boot disk with utilities installed for Windows 9x, Windows NT, and Windows 2000.
- **Objective 3.1:** Recognize and interpret the meaning of common error codes and startup messages from the boot sequence, and identify steps to correct the problems.

## ON THE JOB

When a PC will not boot up, end users are at a productivity standstill until it gets fixed. That usually means a PC technician will be making a trip to the workstation to see what is wrong. This chapter explains how different operating systems boot up, what makes them fail to boot, and what you can do to improve a situation in which the PC will not boot normally.

Some of the skills you will learn include:

- editing startup files
- using alternative Windows boot modes
- booting using a startup floppy
- booting to the Windows 2000/XP Recovery Console
- creating and using an Emergency Repair Disk (ERD)
- using safe mode
- eliminating startup error messages

## What Constitutes a Bootable Disk?

**Bootable disk**

A disk that contains the OS startup files needed to bring an operating system and its associated user interface up to operational level.

A *bootable disk* is one that can be used to bring the PC to a functional level, with the OS ready to accept user commands. That could be a command-line OS, like MS-DOS, or a GUI (graphical user interface) OS, like Windows.

MS-DOS, being a command-line OS, requires only three files for a bootable disk: IO.SYS, MSDOS.SYS, and COMMAND.COM. You learned about these in Chapter 26. The first two boot the OS, and are hidden system files. COMMAND.COM provides the user interface (the command prompt).

The native mode of Windows 9x is a GUI interface, but since it has an underlying MS-DOS core it can also boot to a command prompt, as with a startup floppy. Therefore, there are two separate sets of requirements for a bootable disk under Windows 9x. If you just want to boot to a Windows 9x command prompt, you need the same three files as with MS-DOS: IO.SYS, MSDOS.SYS, and COMMAND.COM. If you want to boot into the GUI, you also need the startup files for Windows, including WIN.COM. We will look at the complete list later in the chapter.

NT-based versions of Windows (NT 4.0, 2000, and XP) are not based on MS-DOS, and do not have any of the traditional DOS startup files. They cannot boot to a command prompt as an alternative startup. However, you can boot to a prompt-style Recovery Console for troubleshooting. To start a Windows NT/2000/XP system you need a hard disk on which the full OS has been installed, or you need a bootable CD containing the setup program for the OS.

You can start up an NT-based system using the startup floppy from a Windows 9x system, but unless the disk uses FAT16 or FAT32 you cannot browse its contents. (Most NT-based systems use NTFS as the file system, which Windows 9x startup disks cannot read.)

As you learned in Chapter 13, a bootable CD does not directly contain boot files for the OS. Instead it contains two container files: BOOTCAT.BIN and BOOTIMG.BIN. BOOTCAT.BIN is a catalog file and BOOTIMG.BIN contains an image of a bootable floppy disk. When a PC tries to boot from CD, it looks for those two files, and it mounts the contents of BOOTIMG.BIN as a virtual floppy. If the correct files for booting the OS are contained in BOOTIMG.BIN, the OS can start, exactly as if those files had been contained on a floppy disk in the A drive.

## Startup Configuration Files

Every operating system has a set of startup configuration files that run or load automatically each time the OS starts up. These configuration files store user preferences, device driver locations, installed programs, and other environment variables, and reload those settings with each startup.

In MS-DOS, those startup configuration files are AUTOEXEC.BAT and CONFIG.SYS. In Windows 3.1 they are WIN.INI and SYSTEM.INI. In Windows 95 and higher they are the files that comprise the Registry. (See Chapter 26 for details on those files.) Each version includes backward compatibility with the startup configuration files of earlier versions, so when Windows 95 starts up, it also looks for and processes CONFIG.SYS, AUTOEXEC.BAT, SYSTEM.INI, and WIN.INI.

### CONFIG.SYS

CONFIG.SYS is a plain-text file that lists environment variables and device drivers that should be loaded. It is the primary method of device setup under MS-DOS. You need to know about it even if you never work on DOS or Windows 3.1 systems. When a user upgrades from one of those OSes to Windows 9x or NT/2000/XP, sometimes drivers and other settings are left behind in CONFIG.SYS, and you need to be able to open CONFIG.SYS, understand the settings there, and disable any that may be causing problems.

CONFIG.SYS can be edited using any text editor, including EDIT (MS-DOS) or Notepad (Windows). Each command must be on a separate line, and must include the full path to any files that are referenced. Figure 27.1 shows a typical CONFIG.SYS file for MS-DOS.

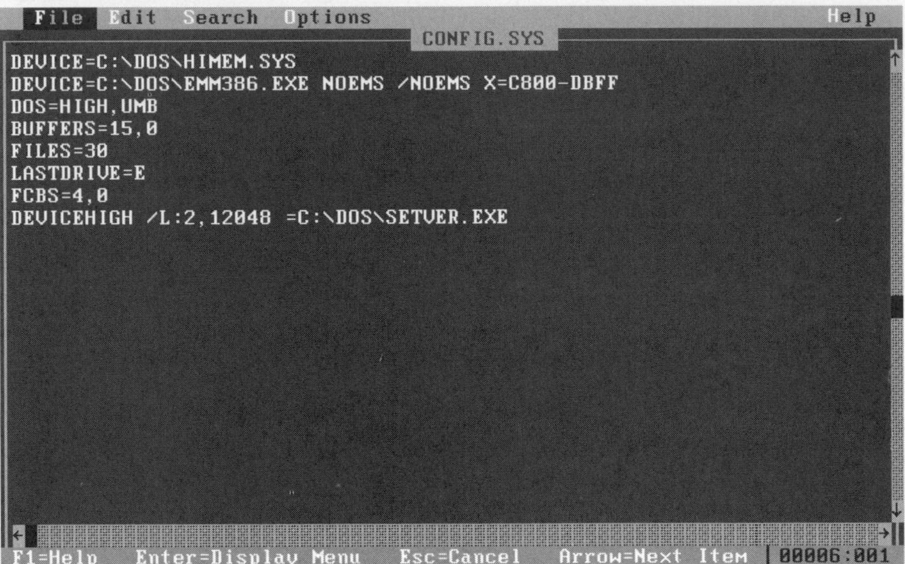


**FIGURE 27.1**
A typical CONFIG.SYS file for MS-DOS will probably have fewer commands, or be completely empty, under Windows 9x.

It is not necessary to know what all of the lines in Figure 27.1 do, because they are mostly for MS-DOS, which is not covered on the A+ exam. However, Figure 27.2 shows a few of the highlights.

- HIMEM.SYS: The extended memory manager, covered in Chapter 6.
- EMM386.EXE: The expanded memory manager, also covered in Chapter 6
- DOS=HIGH,UMB: Loads the DOS kernel into high memory and enables upper memory blocks. See Chapter 6.
- BUFFERS: Sets aside a certain amount of memory to serve as a buffer (a type of cache) for application use.
- FILES: Specifies the maximum number of files that can be open at once.
- LASTDRIVE: Specifies the last drive letter for which the system should set aside memory to allocate for usage.
- DEVICEHIGH=: A substitute for DEVICE= that allows the driver to load into high memory.
- SETVER.EXE: Loads a utility that tricks programs into thinking a different version of the OS is installed, so they will run.

**FIGURE 27.2**
Commands in a CONFIG.SYS File

Windows 9x can read and process CONFIG.SYS if it is present. However, hardware drivers that load through CONFIG.SYS are real-mode drivers, and Windows 9x is a protected-mode operating system. This can cause Windows 9x to be forced to run in DOS compatibility mode, slowing down its performance considerably. When you upgrade a PC from

Windows 3.1 or MS-DOS to Windows 9x, the setup program automatically removes any real-mode drivers for supported hardware from CONFIG.SYS and adds them to the Registry instead. However, if there is an unsupported driver, it remains in CONFIG.SYS, and Windows starts in DOS compatibility mode. You can check for DOS compatibility mode by doing the following:

1. Right-click My Computer and choose Properties.
2. Select the Performance tab. The status should read *Your system is configured for optimal performance* as in Figure 27.3. If it indicates instead that it is running in MS-DOS compatibility mode, open up CONFIG.SYS and see what may be causing this.

**WARNING**

**The most likely cause is a DOS-based memory or hard disk enhancement driver that has no Windows 9x equivalent. If this is the case you might need to abandon that utility program in order to get maximum Windows performance. Beware, however, of disabling a hard disk utility program that might cause you to lose the data on your hard drive, such as an old disk-doubling program like Stacker.**

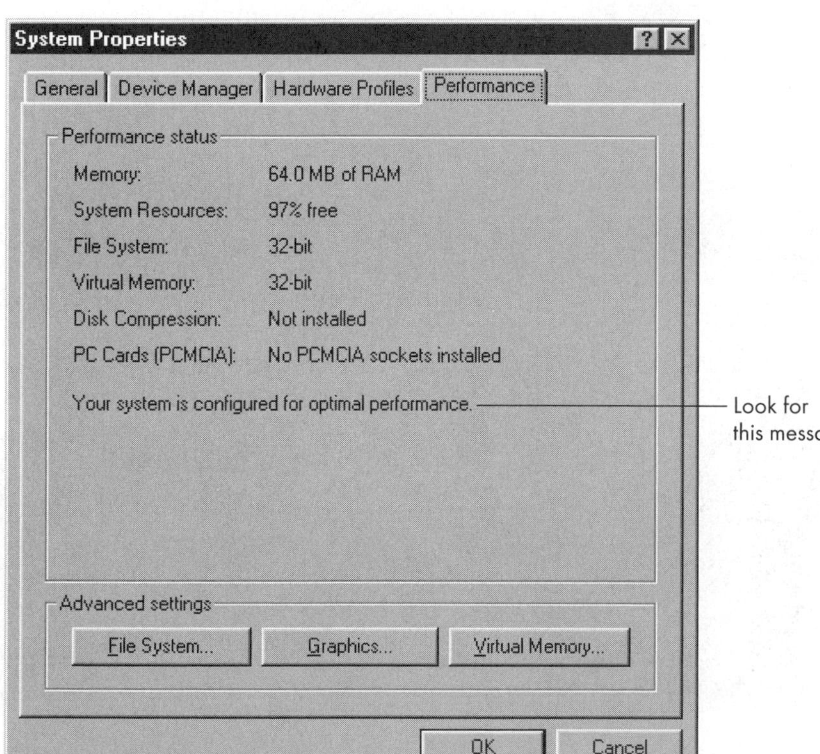


**FIGURE 27.3**
Check the System Properties dialog box to make sure that a real-mode driver from CONFIG.SYS is not forcing Windows 9x to run in MS-DOS compatibility mode.

It is good practice to disable lines in CONFIG.SYS rather than deleting them entirely, in case you should ever have to restore them. The standard way of disabling a line without deleting it is to add the letters *REM* to the beginning of the file. This is called "remming out," as in "I remmed out the line that was loading the real-mode mouse driver." Another way is to add a semicolon in front of the line. (This is typically done in WIN.INI and SYSTEM.INI.)

## AUTOEXEC.BAT

AUTOEXEC.BAT is also a plain-text file, and it also can be edited in EDIT or Notepad (or any other text editor). As with CONFIG.SYS, you need to know about AUTOEXEC.BAT so you can troubleshoot any leftover problems on systems that have been upgraded from MS-DOS or Windows 3.1 to later OS versions.

What is the difference between the two? Whereas CONFIG.SYS contains drivers that can load only at startup and can execute automatically only as part of the OS's startup routine, AUTOEXEC.BAT is a *batch file.* It runs at startup, but it can also be rerun at any time simply by keying **AUTOEXEC.BAT** at the command prompt. The individual commands within AUTOEXEC.BAT can also be reentered at any time. Figure 27.4 shows a typical AUTOEXEC.BAT file for MS-DOS.

**Batch file**

A text file containing a list of commands to be executed, in the order listed, as a group or batch.

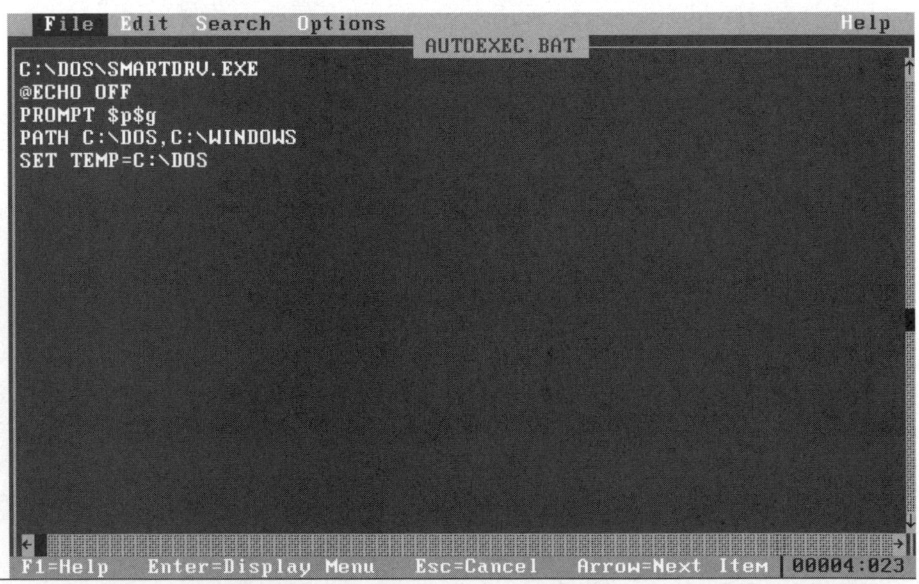


**FIGURE 27.4**
A Typical AUTOEXEC.BAT File

As with CONFIG.SYS, it is not important to know what all of the commands in Figure 27.4 do, but Figure 27.5 lists them.

- SMARTDRV: A disk caching program for Windows 3.1, covered in Chapter 26.
- @ECHO OFF: Turns off the display of the commands that follow it. The @ sign also turns off the display of the ECHO OFF line itself.
- PROMPT $P$G: Dictates that the command-line prompt should contain the current folder name ($P) and a > sign ($G). There are many other choices; $P and $G are just the traditional ones. Key **PROMPT /?** at a command prompt to see a full list.
- PATH: Specifies the folders in which the OS should look for a command if it is not in the current folder. For example, suppose you key **SETUP** at the C:\> command prompt. There is no SETUP file in that folder, so it next looks in C:\DOS because that is the first location listed in the PATH statement. It then looks in the next location (C:\WINDOWS). If it cannot find the file in any of the path locations, it displays an error message.
- SET: Used to set environment variables. In Figure 27.4 it is being used to set the TEMP variable to C:\DOS. This provides the DOS directory as the default folder in which applications store the temporary files they create as they operate.

**FIGURE 27.5**
Commands in an AUTOEXEC.BAT File

Windows 9x can also process AUTOEXEC.BAT automatically if it is present. Items loaded in AUTOEXEC.BAT usually do not force Windows 9x into MS-DOS compatibility mode, but they do occupy space in RAM, so you might want to examine the AUTOEXEC.BAT file after upgrading from MS-DOS/Windows 3.1 to Windows 9x to see whether any items could be removed. If you are not sure about a line, rem it out and try booting without it. You might even encounter lines that have been automatically remmed out by a setup program. For example, if you upgrade from MS-DOS to Windows 95 you might see the following line in AUTOEXEC.BAT:

rem - by Windows Setup - C:\DOS\MSCDEX.EXE /D:MSCD001

## TRY IT!

View the CONFIG.SYS and AUTOEXEC.BAT files on as many different systems as possible, with many different operating systems, and document the differences you find.

## SYSTEM.INI

SYSTEM.INI is an initialization file that serves the same function for Windows 3.1 as CONFIG.SYS does for MS-DOS. It loads system settings and device drivers for Windows 3.1. It also is included in Windows 9x and higher for compatibility with 16-bit Windows programs, but 32-bit Windows programs do not write to it. Figure 27.6 shows part of a typical SYSTEM.INI file. Even though the A+ exam does not cover Windows 3.1, you need to know about SYSTEM.INI and WIN.INI because they remain a part of later Windows versions; when you install 16-bit Windows programs in a 32-bit Windows OS, they write their settings to those files.

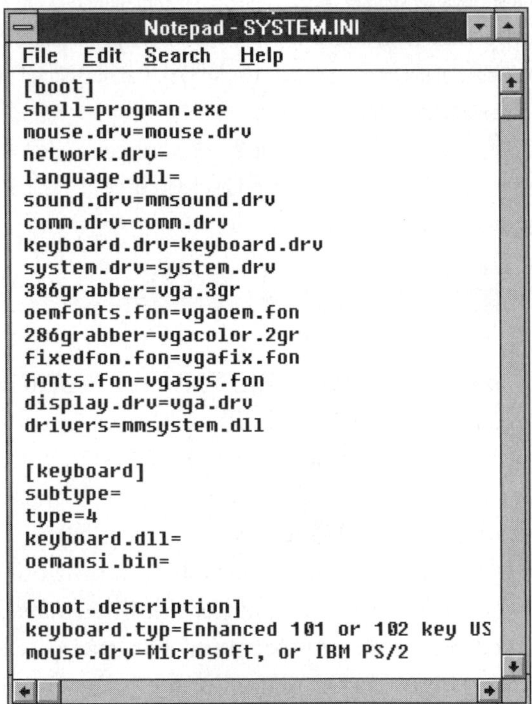


**FIGURE 27.6**
A Typical SYSTEM.INI File in Windows 3.1

The sections in SYSTEM.INI (and also WIN.INI) are delineated by headings in square brackets, such as [boot]. Within each section are lines of commands that execute at Windows startup. Almost all are in the format *setting=value*. For example, in Figure 27.6 the first command is *shell=progman.exe*. That means the user interface comes from the file progman.exe (the Program Manager). Notice that some of the lines in Figure 27.6 have no value, such as *network.drv=*. That means that no components of that type have been installed. SYSTEM.INI includes placeholders for all supported hardware types and settings.

## WIN.INI

WIN.INI is the Windows 3.1 equivalent of AUTOEXEC.BAT. It loads application-level settings and user preferences, and starts programs that should load at startup. It is structured just like SYSTEM.INI, and edited the same way (through Notepad). Figure 27.7 shows an example.

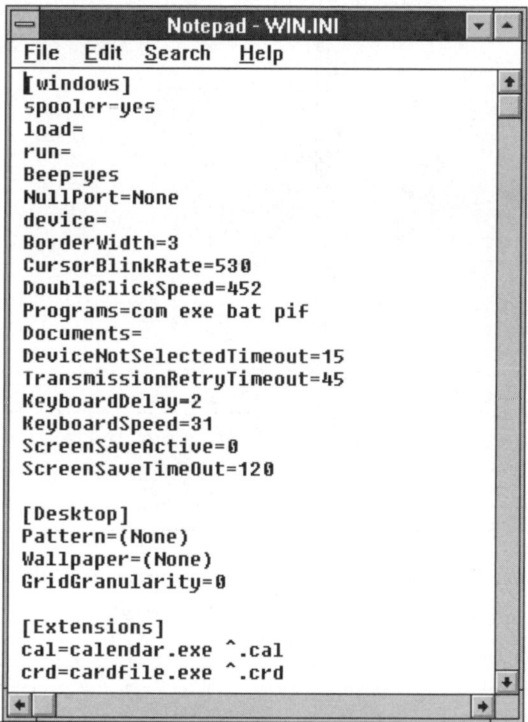


**FIGURE 27.7**
A Typical WIN.INI File in Windows 3.1

Notice in Figure 27.7 the *load=* and *run=* lines. They are blank, but if you wanted a certain program to load at startup you could add the executable file there using the following command: *load=c:\utilities\calendar.exe*. *Load* starts up the program minimized; *run* starts it up in an open window. Most of the lines in WIN.INI correspond to user settings in the Control Panel, such as desktop wallpaper, border width, keyboard delay, screen saver timeout, and so on.

## REGISTRY

The Registry, as discussed earlier, is the way that 32-bit versions of Windows store and restore system settings. In Windows 9x the Registry consists of two files: SYSTEM.DAT and USER.DAT; in NT-based Windows versions there are registry hive files (Sam, Security, System,

Software, and Default). In all 32-bit versions these files are accessed through the Registry Editor (regedit.exe or regedt32.exe), and appear as if they are a single settings database with multiple sections. Figure 27.8 shows the Registry open for editing; see Appendix D for more information about how to do so.

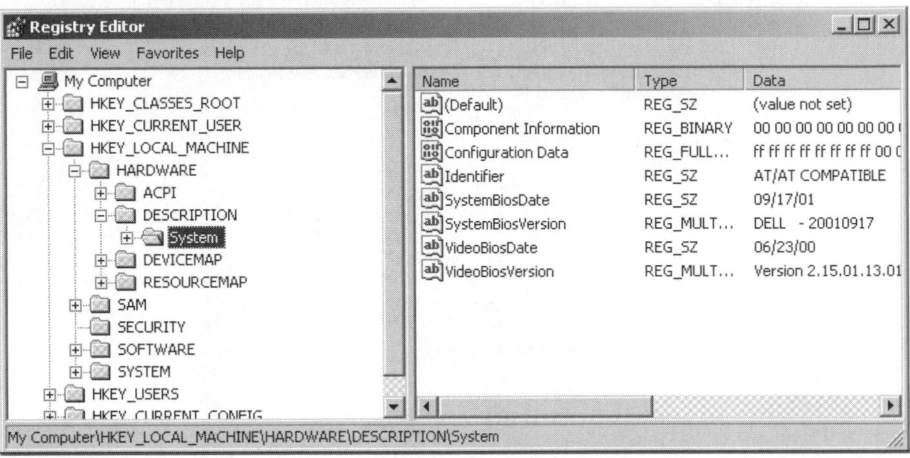


**FIGURE 27.8**
The Registry is the central repository for startup settings in all 32-bit versions of Windows.

## TRY IT!

**Examine WIN.INI and SYSTEM.INI on a Windows 3.1 system if one is available. Then examine them on a Windows 9x PC; how are they different? Do Windows 2000 or XP have them at all? If so, what do they contain?**

# MS-DOS Boot Process

MS-DOS is very simple to boot up compared with Windows and other OSes. Its boot sequence is as follows:

**Power-on self test (POST)**

The hardware check that the BIOS performs on the major hardware components prior to passing control to the OS at startup.

1. The BIOS performs a power-on self test (POST).
2. The BIOS searches the drives for a master boot record (MBR). The MBR contains data about the partitions, including which partition is active, as you learned in Chapter 12.
3. The MBR takes control and locates IO.SYS.
4. IO.SYS takes control. It identifies the installed hardware. It looks for CONFIG.SYS and, if it finds it, executes its instructions.
5. MSDOS.SYS takes control. It loads MS-DOS (the operating system kernel) into memory, and looks for AUTOEXEC.BAT. If it finds it, it executes its instructions.

6. COMMAND.COM displays a command prompt, indicating it is ready to accept user commands.

If the system being booted contains a CONFIG.SYS and/or AUTOEXEC.BAT file, you will not be prompted for the date and time at startup. Otherwise, the first thing you will see after startup is an *Enter current date* prompt.

# Windows 9x/Me Boot Process

There are two parts to Windows 9x: a graphical user interface (GUI) and a *DOS protected-mode interface* (DPMI). You can boot to either of them and it is still Windows 9x. However, ordinary users almost never use the DPMI; they boot directly into the graphical interface that has become synonymous with Windows 9x.

**DOS protected-mode interface (DPMI)**

A command-line interface designed for use with 32-bit OSes that use protected mode for memory handling.

The sequence for Windows 9x booting is as follows:

1. The BIOS performs a POST.
2. The BIOS searches the drives for the MBR.
3. The MBR takes control and locates IO.SYS.
4. IO.SYS takes control. It looks for MSDOS.SYS and processes its instructions. In Windows 9x, all of the functions of the MS-DOS IO.SYS and MSDOS.SYS have been combined into IO.SYS. The MSDOS.SYS file is just a passive list of settings that IO.SYS works with.
5. IO.SYS looks for a LOGO.SYS file, which is a graphic file that contains the Windows *splash screen*, and displays it. You can press Esc while the splash screen displays to clear it away so you can watch startup commands being executed at the command prompt.
6. IO.SYS looks for the Registry files, SYSTEM.DAT and USER.DAT, and checks them. Then it loads SYSTEM.DAT.
7. IO.SYS looks for CONFIG.SYS and AUTOEXEC.BAT, and executes them if found. They are not integral to Windows 9x, but might exist for backward compatibility.
8. IO.SYS loads HIMEM.SYS if it was not already loaded in CONFIG.SYS. (Remember from Chapter 6 that HIMEM.SYS enables the use of extended memory.)
9. IO.SYS loads WIN.COM, which is the main Windows program, and then hands off control to it.
10. WIN.COM loads the virtual memory manager, VMM386.VXD.
11. VMM386.VXD loads the 32-bit device drivers into memory.
12. WIN.COM reads SYSTEM.INI if present and executes its instructions.

**Splash screen**

A graphic that appears briefly as an application or OS loads, usually displaying the name of the product.

13. WIN.COM loads the GUI by loading three files: KRNL32.DLL, GDI.EXE, and USER.EXE.
14. WIN.COM reads and executes any commands from WIN.INI if present.
15. WIN.COM checks the content of the *StartUp* folder on the Start menu, and executes any programs that have shortcuts there.

Knowing the functions of all of these files can help greatly in troubleshooting Windows problems. For example, suppose you see an error message involving VMM386.VXD. You know that this is the virtual memory manager, so you know there is likely to be a problem with the virtual memory paging file. Without knowing what VMM386.VXD is, you would have no idea where to start.

## Alternative Boot Modes

Windows 9x versions offer several alternative boot modes that may be useful for troubleshooting. They include several variants of a command-line interface and several types of *safe mode*.

**Safe mode**

A way of starting up the GUI without loading nonessential drivers and applications, useful when a driver or program is preventing Windows from starting.

When Windows 9x is starting up, you see a message briefly on the screen: *Starting Windows 95* (or *98*, or *Me*). It roughly corresponds to the single beep from the PC speaker. If you press F8 before that message disappears (typically you have about 3 seconds), the Windows Startup menu appears, and from that menu you can select an alternative boot mode.

Windows 95 has eight choices on its Startup menu (see Figure 27.9), Windows 98 has six, and Windows Me has four. Table 27.1 summarizes these options by version number.

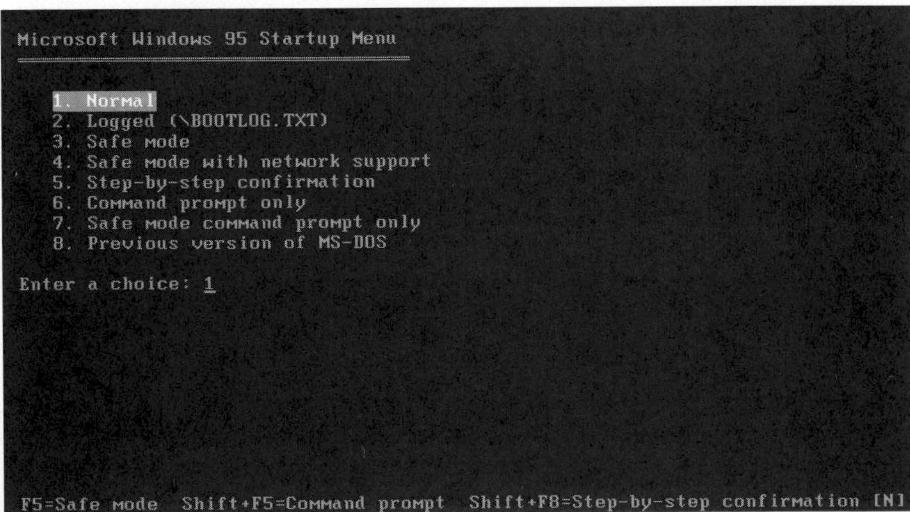


**FIGURE 27.9**
The Windows 95 Startup Menu

| Startup Mode | Description | Win95 | Win98 | WinMe |
|---|---|---|---|---|
| Normal | Normal Windows boot | Yes | Yes | Yes |
| Logged (\BOOTLOG.TXT) | Logs each step of startup for troubleshooting purposes | Yes | Yes | Yes |
| Safe Mode | Starts with minimal set of drivers | Yes | Yes | Yes |
| Safe Mode with Network Support | Same as safe mode but includes networking | Yes | No | No |
| Step-by-Step Confirmation | Steps through startup line-by-line | Yes | Yes | Yes |
| Command Prompt Only | Boots to DPMI command prompt | Yes | Yes | No |
| Safe Mode Command Prompt Only | Boots to command prompt and bypasses all startup files | Yes | Yes | No |
| Previous Version of MS-DOS | Boots to old DOS version (if you upgraded); if it cannot find your old files it boots as Normal | Yes | No | No |

**TABLE 27.1**
Startup Menu Options for Windows 95, 98, and Me

The next sections describe some of these startup modes and their uses.

### *Safe Mode*

Safe mode starts the GUI with a minimal set of drivers, including a standard VGA video driver in 16-color 640 x 480 video mode. It does not load any programs that are set to load at startup, and does not load the drivers for any nonessential hardware (such as CD drives, sound cards, modems, and so on). When in safe mode, the words *Safe mode* appear in the corners of the screen and, depending on the Windows version, a dialog box may appear letting you know you are in safe mode. Figure 27.10 shows safe mode for Windows 98.

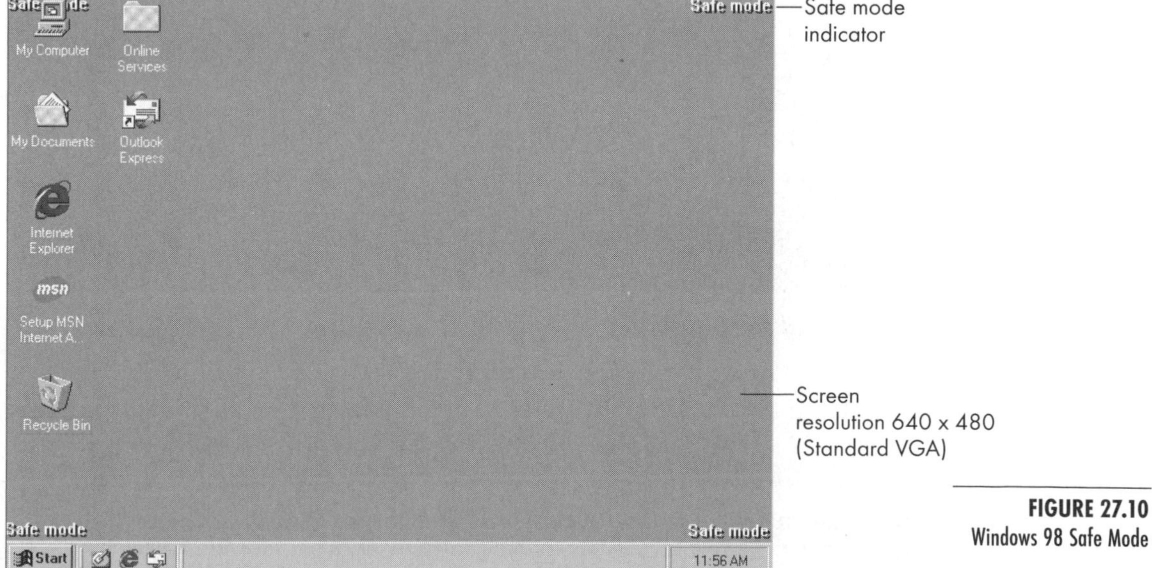


**FIGURE 27.10**
Windows 98 Safe Mode

Safe mode is useful when Windows will not start normally and you suspect that the reason is a bad driver or a bad application trying to load at startup. You can boot into safe mode, correct the problem, and then boot normally again. Safe mode is not suitable for normal use because so many of Windows' capabilities are disabled in safe mode. For example, you cannot access the CD drives or most expansion devices.

### *Step-by-Step Confirmation*

Step-by-step confirmation allows the user to confirm or reject each individual step of the startup process by keying **Y** or **N**. This is useful when you are unsure which startup item is causing the PC not to boot. To troubleshoot using step-by-step confirmation, key **Y** to confirm each startup action. When the computer locks up, check the screen to see the last item that you confirmed; it is probably what is causing the problem (see Figure 27.11). Then use the System Configuration Utility (MSCONFIG) to disable that line from starting. See "Controlling What Loads at Startup" later in this chapter for details.

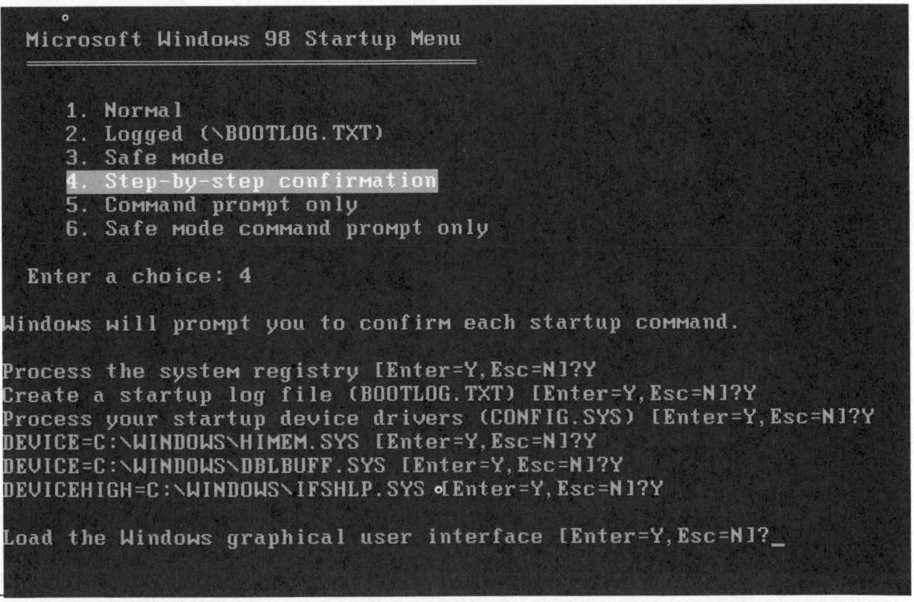

```
 Microsoft Windows 98 Startup Menu
 ══════════════════════════════════

    1. Normal
    2. Logged (\BOOTLOG.TXT)
    3. Safe mode
    4. Step-by-step confirmation
    5. Command prompt only
    6. Safe mode command prompt only

 Enter a choice: 4

Windows will prompt you to confirm each startup command.

Process the system registry [Enter=Y,Esc=N]?Y
Create a startup log file (BOOTLOG.TXT) [Enter=Y,Esc=N]?Y
Process your startup device drivers (CONFIG.SYS) [Enter=Y,Esc=N]?Y
DEVICE=C:\WINDOWS\HIMEM.SYS [Enter=Y,Esc=N]?Y
DEVICE=C:\WINDOWS\DBLBUFF.SYS [Enter=Y,Esc=N]?Y
DEVICEHIGH=C:\WINDOWS\IFSHLP.SYS [Enter=Y,Esc=N]?Y

Load the Windows graphical user interface [Enter=Y,Esc=N]?_
```

**FIGURE 27.11**
Step-by-Step Startup Confirmation

### *Command Prompt Only*

Command prompt only is useful for quick access to a command prompt on a system that will not boot Windows at all. For example, perhaps you know that the Windows installation has failed and you just want to get to a command prompt to copy a few essential documents onto a floppy before reformatting and starting over. Command prompt only would get you there.

In Windows 95 and 98 there is also a Safe mode command prompt only option on the startup menu. The difference is that it bypasses the commands in CONFIG.SYS and AUTOEXEC.BAT, whereas the regular Command prompt only choice does not.

**TRY IT!**

Try all of the available boot modes on your version of Windows 9x, and note the differences.

## MS-DOS Mode

MS-DOS mode is an operating mode for Windows 95 and 98 that enables you to reboot the PC into a plain, DOS-like command prompt environment rather than to the GUI. You could then run MS-DOS based applications that do not run correctly from within Windows. This is not available in Windows Me or in any of the NT-based Windows versions.

You cannot boot the PC directly into MS-DOS mode; you must call for it from within Windows. To enter MS-DOS mode, complete the following steps:

1. Choose Start/Shut Down.
2. Choose Restart in MS-DOS mode.
3. Click OK. A command prompt appears.
4. Run the DOS applications as needed.
5. When you are finished, key **Exit** and press Enter to return to Windows.

**TRY IT!**

1. Reboot into MS-DOS mode and use the *MEM /C | MORE* command to see what is loaded into memory.
2. Reboot and use the Startup menu to start up using the Command prompt only option, and check memory again.
3. Reboot and use the Safe mode command prompt only option, and check memory again. What are the differences?

## Examining the Boot Log

Option 2 on the Startup menu (Figure 27.9) logs the entire startup process in a text file called BOOTLOG.TXT. You can find this file in the root directory of the boot drive (usually C:\). It is a hidden file, so it will not appear in Windows file listings unless you turn on the display of hidden files (in the Folder Options dialog box, on the View tab).

Figure 27.12 shows the contents of a typical BOOTLOG.TXT file in Wordpad. (It may be too large for Notepad to open.) As you scan its contents, look for LoadFailed lines that indicate problems loading specific items; these can be the key to determining why Windows is having startup problems.

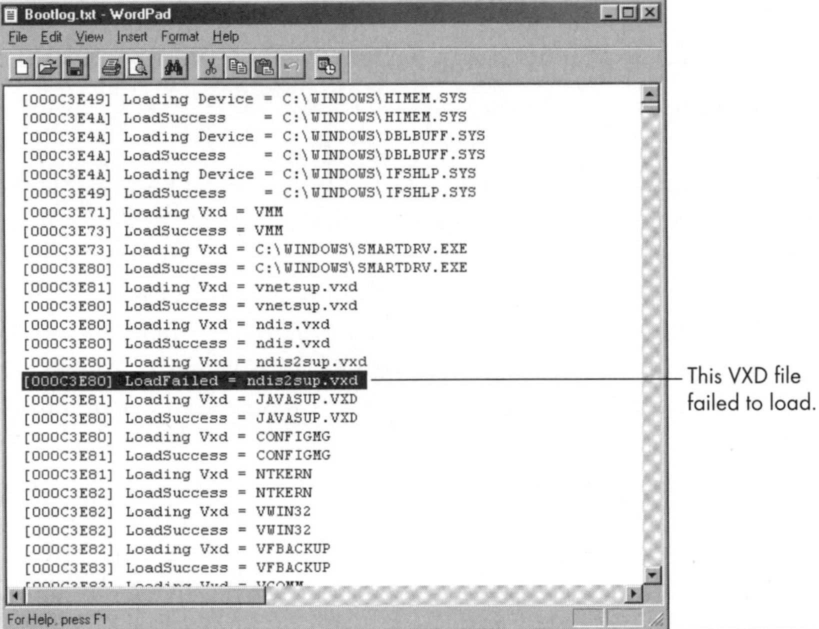


**FIGURE 27.12**
Check the boot log for startup error messages.

## In Real Life

BOOTLOG.TXT is useful mostly for troubleshooting systems that fail boot to Windows, so most of the time when you work with it, Notepad would not be available for viewing it. You can open it using EDIT from a command prompt, but since it is a hidden file you will need to turn off its hidden attribute first with this command: *ATTRIB -H C:\BOOTLOG.TXT.*

## TRY IT!

Start up the computer and enable boot logging through the Startup menu. Then view BOOTLOG.TXT using a text editor.

# Windows NT, 2000, and XP Boot Process

Windows NT versions start up very differently from Windows 9x. All three versions (NT 4, 2000, and XP) are virtually identical in their startup sequence:

1. The BIOS performs a POST.
2. The BIOS searches the drives for the MBR.
3. The MBR takes control and locates NTLDR (which stands for NT Loader).
4. NTLDR switches the CPU into 32-bit protected mode.
5. NTLDR finds and reads BOOT.INI, the file that controls the menu for dual-booting. If there are multiple operating systems, it displays a menu for user choice. If the user chooses Windows 2000, or if there are no other operating systems, it continues the Windows 2000 boot process. Otherwise, the other chosen OS takes over.
6. NTLDR runs NTDETECT.COM, which detects the installed hardware and sends the information to the Registry.
7. NTLDR reads NTOSKRNL.EXE into memory. This is the equivalent of the DOS kernel loaded in MS-DOS by MSDOS.SYS.
8. NTLDR locates the drivers for the hardware that the Registry reports is installed (but does not install them yet).
9. NTLDR hands over control to NTOSKRNL.EXE.
10. NTOSKRNL.EXE loads the device drivers and the GUI.

To prepare for the A+ exam, make sure that you know the order in which NTLDR, NTDETECT, and NTOKSRNL execute at startup. Also make sure you know which file interacts with BOOT.INI (NTLDR does).

One thing to note about the Windows NT/2000/XP startup process is that each of the major startup files interacts with the hardware in its own way: NTDETECT detects the installed hardware and reports its findings to the Registry (step 6); NTLDR locates the drivers for the hardware reported in the Registry (step 8); and NTOSKRNL loads the device drivers (step 10).

## Alternative Boot Modes

The different NT-based versions of Windows have different alternative boot mode choices, so the following sections look at them individually.

### *Windows NT 4 Alternative Boot Modes*

Windows NT Workstation 4.0 has only one boot alternative: you can boot to VGA mode rather than the standard graphics mode. This is useful for bypassing an improperly installed video driver that is causing a startup problem.

Each time you start the PC, the OS Loader menu appears, as in Figure 27.13. From it you can choose to start normally or in VGA mode. If you set up the system for multi-booting, other OSes may appear on this list as well.

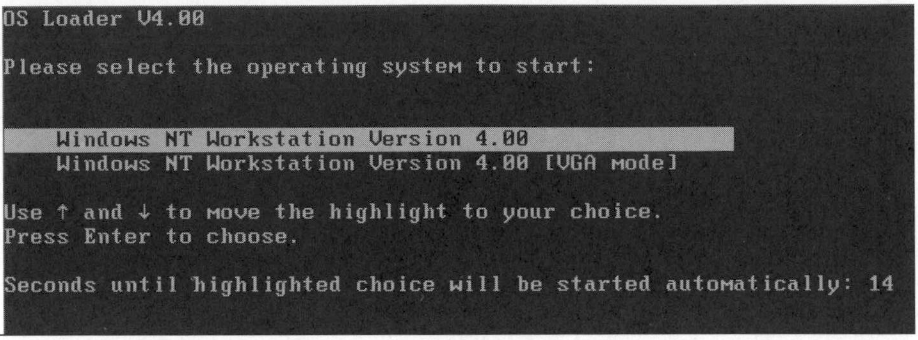

```
OS Loader V4.00

Please select the operating system to start:


   Windows NT Workstation Version 4.00
   Windows NT Workstation Version 4.00 [VGA mode]

Use ↑ and ↓ to move the highlight to your choice.
Press Enter to choose.

Seconds until highlighted choice will be started automatically: 14
```

**FIGURE 27.13**
The OS Loader menu in Windows NT 4 lets you boot Windows in VGA mode to troubleshoot a video adapter problem.

If some other change to the system has rendered Windows NT unbootable, you can revert to the last known good version of the Registry by pressing the spacebar when indicated during the boot process. This opportunity occurs immediately after the screen shown in Figure 27.13. This is made possible by the fact that every time the system boots successfully, it copies the Registry files to backup versions.

When you press the spacebar, the menu shown in Figure 27.14 appears. From here, key **L** to select the last known good configuration and then press Enter to boot from it.

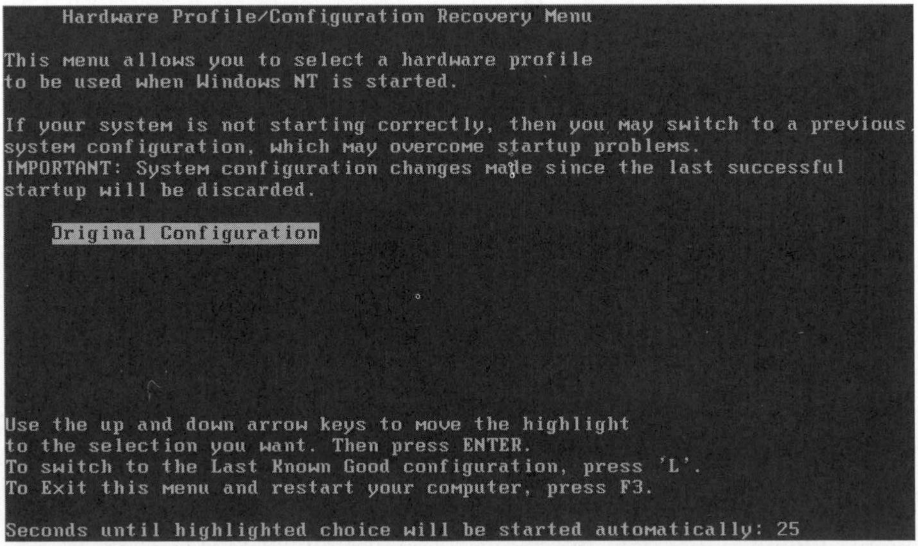

```
    Hardware Profile/Configuration Recovery Menu

This menu allows you to select a hardware profile
to be used when Windows NT is started.

If your system is not starting correctly, then you may switch to a previous
system configuration, which may overcome startup problems.
IMPORTANT: System configuration changes made since the last successful
startup will be discarded.

   Original Configuration

Use the up and down arrow keys to move the highlight
to the selection you want. Then press ENTER.
To switch to the Last Known Good configuration, press 'L'.
To Exit this menu and restart your computer, press F3.

Seconds until highlighted choice will be started automatically: 25
```

**FIGURE 27.14**
You have the opportunity to revert the Registry to the last known good configuration during startup.

### *Windows 2000 and XP Alternative Boot Modes*

In Windows 2000 and XP there are actually two different menus that can appear at startup. One of these is the multi-boot menu, from which you select which OS you want if more than one is installed. (Technically the menu that appears in Figure 27.13, for Windows NT 4.0, is such a menu, even though both items on the list refer to the same version of Windows. That is just NT's way of providing the VGA boot option.) Such a menu is shown in Figure 27.15. It also appears every time if the Windows Recovery Console has been installed on the hard disk (covered later in this chapter).

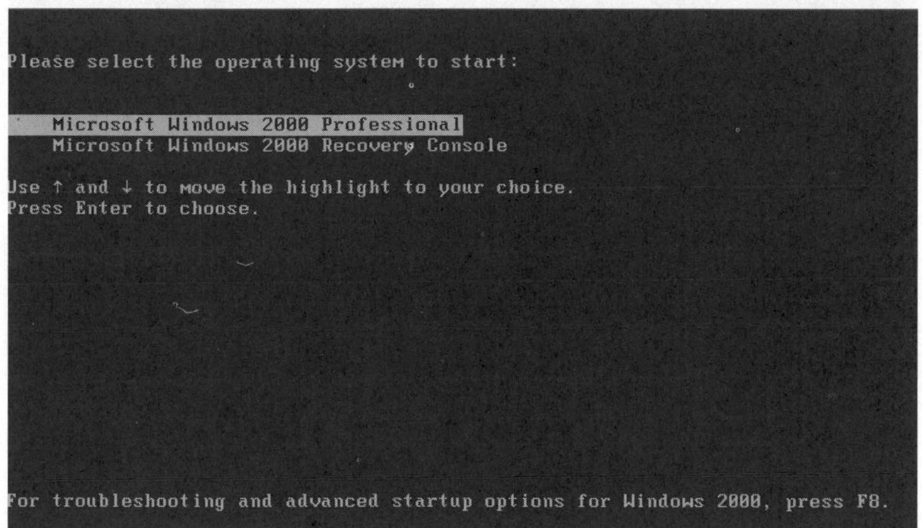
Please select the operating system to start:
Microsoft Windows 2000 Professional
Microsoft Windows 2000 Recovery Console
Use ↑ and ↓ to move the highlight to your choice.
Press Enter to choose.
For troubleshooting and advanced startup options for Windows 2000, press F8.

**FIGURE 27.15**
If more than one OS is installed, or an OS and the Recovery Console, this menu appears at startup.

The other menu that can appear at startup in Windows 2000 and XP is the Advanced Options menu, from which you can choose alternative boot modes. It does not appear automatically unless you have set up the system to display it or unless Windows failed to boot the last time you started the PC (see Figure 27.16). To display the Advanced Options menu, you must press F8 when you hear the speaker's beep, or when the multi-boot menu (Figure 27.15) appears on-screen. Table 27.2 explains these modes.

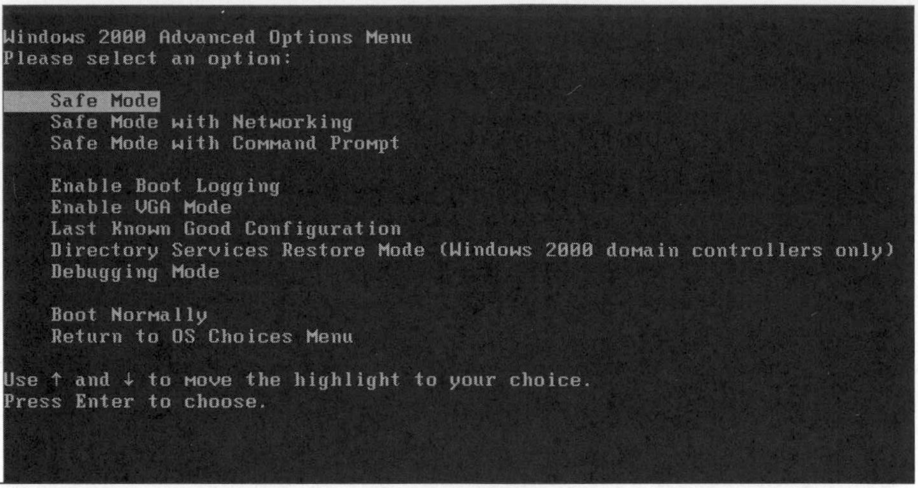

```
Windows 2000 Advanced Options Menu
Please select an option:

    Safe Mode
    Safe Mode with Networking
    Safe Mode with Command Prompt

    Enable Boot Logging
    Enable VGA Mode
    Last Known Good Configuration
    Directory Services Restore Mode (Windows 2000 domain controllers only)
    Debugging Mode

    Boot Normally
    Return to OS Choices Menu

Use ↑ and ↓ to move the highlight to your choice.
Press Enter to choose.
```

**FIGURE 27.16**
The Advanced Options menu enables Windows 2000 users to select a startup mode.

**TABLE 27.2**
Boot Options in Windows 2000/XP

| Mode | Description |
|---|---|
| Safe Mode | Starts without any nonessential drivers and programs |
| Safe Mode with Networking | Same as safe mode except includes network drivers and protocols |
| Safe Mode with Command Prompt | Same as safe mode except a command prompt window opens within safe mode |
| Enable Boot Logging | Logs startup information in NTBTLOG.TXT |
| Enable VGA Mode | Starts normally except uses the plain VGA video driver |
| Last Known Good Configuration | Copies the last good copy of the Registry over the current Registry files, reversing the most recent Registry edits |
| Directory Services Restore Mode | For domain controllers only; not used for workstations |
| Debugging Mode | For programmers' use only; not useful for ordinary PC troubleshooting |

# Troubleshooting Startup Problems

This section of the chapter focuses on features and techniques that help you get Windows started when it will not start normally or when errors occur during the startup process.

## Common Windows 9x Startup Issues

Here are some common problems that prevent Windows 9x systems from starting up properly.

### *No Operating System Found*

This message appears if there is no bootable disk available. It can happen if the PC does not see its hard drive, if the hard drive is not formatted, or if no operating system has been installed on it.

If the computer previously booted but suddenly has stopped, it is probably a loose connection to the hard disk, a physical malfunction of the drive, or a virus infection.

If IO.SYS or MSDOS.SYS are missing or corrupted, insert the startup floppy and from the A:\> prompt key the command **SYS C:** to restore the files so it will boot again.

### *Error in CONFIG.SYS Line xx*

This usually occurs on an MS-DOS system, and indicates that a particular driver called for in CONFIG.SYS is missing or corrupted. You might not see it unless you use step-by-step confirmation because it might scroll by too fast.

This error can safely be ignored in most cases unless Windows is not booting because of the error. You can prevent the error from appearing by disabling the line in CONFIG.SYS that is causing the problem.

### *Bad or Missing COMMAND.COM*

This message occurs on a DOS or Windows 9x system when IO.SYS and MSDOS.SYS are present but COMMAND.COM is not. This could occur if you accidentally leave in the drive a floppy disk that has at some point been a boot disk but from which you have deleted all of the files. When you delete all files, COMMAND.COM goes away because it is not protected but IO.SYS and MSDOS.SYS remain because they are hidden and read-only. Copy COMMAND.COM back to the C drive from the startup floppy by using the SYS C: command at the A:\> prompt.

### *Missing, Corrupt, or Unloaded HIMEM.SYS*

One way or another, HIMEM.SYS must load in order for Windows 9x to work. It can be loaded from CONFIG.SYS, or Windows can load it itself. But if HIMEM.SYS is missing or corrupted, this message will appear. Replace HIMEM.SYS from the startup floppy if needed, or use EXTRACT to recopy it from the Windows CD (see Chapter 26).

Sometimes a hard reboot (power off/on) will correct a problem with a missing HIMEM.SYS, so try that first before you go to the trouble of recopying the file.

### *Stuck at Windows Splash Screen*

The splash screen hides what is really going on behind the scenes. You can press Esc when it appears to see the command-prompt commands executing behind it.

When the boot process gets stuck at the splash screen, it is usually a problem with a corrupted paging file. To re-create it:

1. Boot in safe mode.
2. Open the System Properties dialog box, select the Performance tab, and click Virtual Memory.
3. Choose Let me specify my own virtual memory settings, and then mark the Disable Virtual Memory check box.
4. Click OK, then reboot. If Windows starts normally (but slowly), repeat steps 2 and 3 and clear the Disable Virtual Memory check box, then choose Let Windows Manage My Virtual Memory Settings.
5. Click OK and reboot again.

### *Windows Protection Error*

A Windows protection error occurs when a virtual device driver (a file with a .vdx extension) encounters a problem. VXDs are used to support legacy devices, as a substitute for installing real-mode drivers for them in CONFIG.SYS. When a Windows protection error appears, boot into safe mode and check CONFIG.SYS for the presence of a real-mode driver for the device causing the problem. Rem it out if it exists. If that does not help, try removing and reinstalling the device in Device Manager. Check for any resource conflicts in Device Manager.

### *Device Referenced in SYSTEM.INI or WIN.INI Not Found*

Unless you are running Windows 3.1, SYSTEM.INI and WIN.INI exist only for backward compatibility, so it is not critical if there is an error in their execution. You can get rid of the error by disabling the line in the file that is causing the error, either by deleting it or by placing a semicolon at the beginning of the line.

### *General Protection Fault (GPF)*

This error occurs when two programs try to use the same memory space. It may happen at startup if a program that is set to load automatically at startup has a problem. These errors are much less common in later versions of Windows than in earlier ones. When a GPF occurs, make note of the name of the file that caused the error and restart the computer. The problem may not recur. If it does recur repeatedly and it is the same file every time, try reinstalling the associated program or using the EXTRACT command to reinstall the file from the Windows CD if it is a Windows file.

### *Noncritical Driver Loading Problems*

During the text phase of startup, you might get a message that a particular file is not found or cannot be loaded, followed by a prompt to press any key to continue. Do so, and Windows continues loading normally. Such errors are an annoyance, but are not critical.

These errors typically appear because you have removed a piece of hardware but failed to completely remove all traces of its software from Windows. For example, perhaps your scanner is broken so you have removed it from Windows, but for some reason the line in the Registry that loads its driver has not been removed. Every time you restart, Windows searches for that driver. It cannot find it, so the error appears. To troubleshoot this error, see the section "Controlling What Loads at Startup" on page 1104.

### *Errors with Programs Loading at Startup*

Sometimes problems occur with programs that are supposed to load automatically each time Windows starts. For example, the program may have been removed but the line in the Registry that starts the program still exists, or the program may have gotten corrupted so it no longer starts properly. An error will appear in the GUI phase of startup, but will not prevent Windows from working. Troubleshooting these errors is similar to troubleshooting drivers that should not be loading; see "Controlling What Loads at Startup" below for help.

## Common Windows 2000/XP Startup Issues

Windows 2000 and XP have fewer startup problems than Windows 9x because these OS versions do not have to contend with MS-DOS compatibility issues like CONFIG.SYS and SYSTEM.INI.

If Windows will not start normally, try safe mode, and see whether you can determine what driver or application is causing the problem. As you saw in Figure 27.16, NT versions of Windows do not include a Step-by-step confirmation option for startup. However, if you can start in safe mode but not normally, a driver or application loading at startup is almost certainly at fault. In addition, as with Windows 9x, you may occasionally encounter noncritical startup errors involving drivers or applications that try to load but cannot. For both of these types of errors, see "Controlling What Loads at Startup."

If Windows will not start at all, try recovering the system using an Emergency Repair Disk (ERD), described later in the chapter. If that does not work, you can try the Recovery Console (also covered later in the chapter), or you can simply rerun Windows Setup from the bootable CD.

One of the most common startup errors for NT-based versions of Windows is the STOP error. It consists of a string of text in a small font displayed on a bright blue background, reporting a STOP error along with a certain code or file name. This is usually the result of a problem with a piece of hardware—either an incompatible piece of hardware (unlikely if Windows has started properly in the past) or a corrupted driver. The best way to troubleshoot such an error is by using an ERD to repair Windows; reinstalling Windows completely will also work.

## Controlling What Loads at Startup

Many Windows startup errors are caused by problems with a particular driver or program trying to load at startup but having a problem because of missing hardware, missing files, or file corruption. If you can at least boot into safe mode, you can troubleshoot by systematically disabling the optional startup items one-by-one until you find which one has been causing the problem.

If you have upgraded this PC from MS-DOS or Windows 3.1, there may be problems with incompatible lines in WIN.INI, SYSTEM.INI, CONFIG.SYS, or AUTOEXEC.BAT. You can edit these files in Notepad, looking for suspicious lines (that is, lines with file names that correspond to names listed in the error message you have seen). You can also edit all four of them at once in a Notepad-like window by running the System Configuration Editor (SYSEDIT) with the *Run* command (see Figure 27.17).

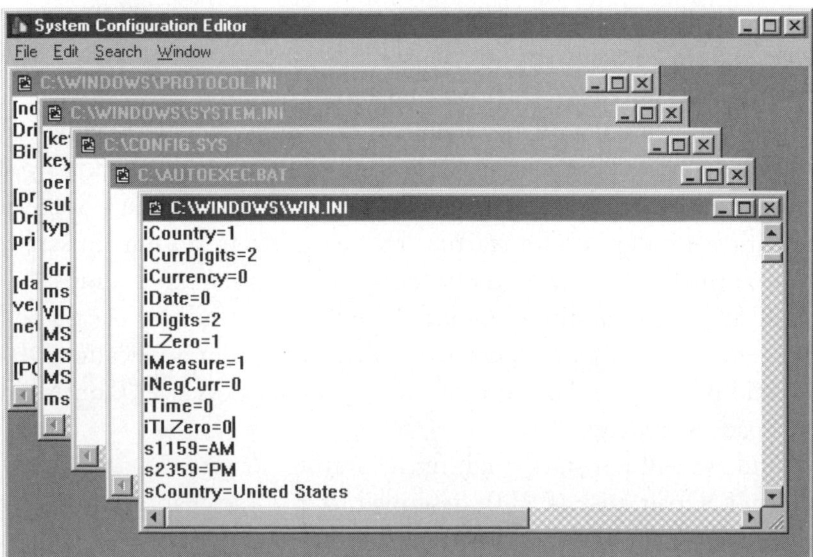


**FIGURE 27.17**
System Configuration Editor (SYSEDIT) is a Notepad interface that automatically opens several important legacy configuration files.

The next place to look for items loading at startup is in the *StartUp* folder on the Start menu. If you find an item on that submenu that you do not want to load at startup, right-click its shortcut there and choose Delete, as shown in Figure 27.18.

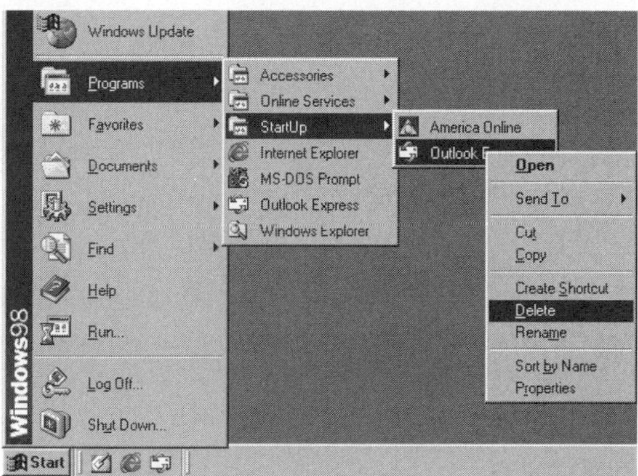


**FIGURE 27.18**
Right-click a shortcut on the StartUp submenu and choose Delete to prevent that item from loading at startup.

You can also use the System Configuration Utility to turn off a particular driver. To do so, choose Start/Run and key **MSCONFIG**. Select the Startup tab and clear the check box for anything that you do not want to load (see Figure 27.19). You can use this same utility to disable lines in the other startup files (listed on the other tabs in the System Configuration Utility dialog box). If you are not sure what is causing the problem, disable items one at a time, attempting to reboot in normal mode after each one. If it still will not boot, reboot into safe mode, disable another item, and keep going until you find the one causing the problem.

System Configuration Utility

File View Help

General | Config.sys | Autoexec.bat | System.ini | Win.ini | Startup

Select the check box to enable a startup item, or clear the check box to disable a startup item.

| | | |
|---|---|---|
| ☑ | ScanRegistry | C:\WINDOWS\scanregw.exe /autorun |
| ☑ | TaskMonitor | C:\WINDOWS\taskmon.exe |
| ☑ | SystemTray | SysTray.Exe |
| ☑ | LoadPowerProfile | Rundll32.exe powrprof.dll,LoadCurrentPwrScheme |
| ☐ | VMware Tools | C:\Program Files\VMware\VMwareTray.exe |
| ☐ | VMware Tools Service | C:\PROGRAM FILES\VMWARE\VMWARESERVICE.EXE |
| ☑ | LoadPowerProfile | Rundll32.exe powrprof.dll,LoadCurrentPwrScheme |
| ☑ | SchedulingAgent | C:\WINDOWS\SYSTEM\mstask.exe |
| ☑ | VMware Tools Service | C:\PROGRAM FILES\VMWARE\VMWARESERVICE.EXE |
| ☑ | America Online | C:\PROGRA~1\ONLINE~1\AOL\AOLSETUP.EXE |
| ☑ | Outlook Express | C:\PROGRA~1\OUTLOO~1\MSIMN.EXE |

OK Cancel Apply

**FIGURE 27.19**
System Configuration Utility (MSCONFIG) allows you to enable or disable individual startup file lines interactively.

As a last resort, you can manually edit the Registry, as described in Appendix D. This is not the best method, however, because of the risk of introducing unwanted changes into the Registry that might cause more problems with Windows than the ones you are trying to fix.

## Using a Windows 9x Startup Disk

As mentioned previously, the Windows 9x startup disk is a bootable floppy disk created under Windows 95, 98, or Me from which you can start a computer if it does not start normally. Besides containing the files needed to get to a command prompt, it also contains some important command-prompt utilities for troubleshooting, partitioning, and formatting a drive.

There are more utilities than will fit on the startup disk, so some of them are compressed. When you start the PC using the startup disk, it creates a *RAM disk* and decompresses the compressed archive file onto that RAM disk. Therefore, when you boot from a startup floppy you have an extra drive letter. For example, suppose the hard disk is C and the CD-ROM is normally D. When you boot from a startup disk you will also have a drive E available, and it will contain the utilities that were decompressed from the floppy (see Figure 27.20). See the section "Startup Disk Utilities and Commands" later in this chapter for details about the utilities available.

**RAM disk**

A virtual disk created out of RAM, used to temporarily store files. The RAM disk exists only as long as the PC remains on.

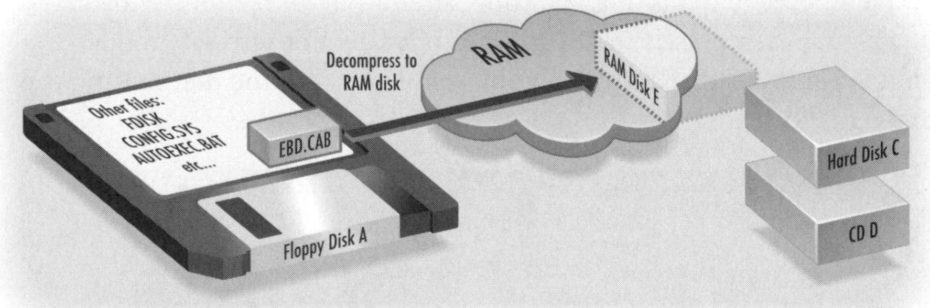


**FIGURE 27.20**
A RAM disk is created to hold the extra compressed utilities.

### *Creating a Startup Disk*

When you install Windows 9x, the setup program offers to help you create a startup disk. To create one through Add/Remove Programs in the Control Panel, complete the following steps:

1. From the Control Panel, double-click *Add/Remove Programs* and then select the Startup Disk tab.
2. Click the Create Disk button. If a prompt appears to insert the Windows CD, do so and click OK.

3. A prompt appears to insert a disk. Place a blank floppy disk (or one that contains nothing you want to keep) into the floppy drive, then click OK.
4. Wait for the startup disk to be created. Then click OK to close the dialog box.

### *Startup Disk Utilities and Commands*

The startup disk contains the three files needed to start the PC: IO.SYS, MSDOS.SYS, and COMMAND.COM. It also contains the items described in Figure 27.21.

- DRVSPACE.BIN: Provides support for hard disks that have been compressed with DriveSpace.
- CD-ROM drivers: There are a variety of real-mode drivers for various CD drives. These are the files that have .sys extensions, such as OAKCDROM.SYS and ASPI2DOS.SYS.
- EBD.CAB: The compressed archive file containing the extra utilities that would not fit normally on the disk.
- AUTOEXEC.BAT and CONFIG.SYS: Same as their normal uses; CONFIG.SYS loads the aforementioned CD drivers and AUTOEXEC.BAT issues the commands that set up the RAM disk and extract the compressed files from EBD.CAB to it.
- FINDRAMD.EXE: Sweeps all of the drive letters to locate the RAM disk. The Setup disk runs it through AUTOEXEC.BAT to find the RAM disk so it can extract the compressed files to it.
- EXTRACT.EXE: Extracts files from compressed archive CAB files such as those on the Windows CD (see Chapter 26). The Setup disk runs it through AUTOEXEC.BAT to extract the compressed files onto the RAM disk.
- FDISK.EXE: Partitions disks, as discussed in Chapter 12.
- README.TXT: A text file containing basic information about the startup disk and its contents.

**FIGURE 27.21**
Items on Windows 9x Startup Disk

After you have booted using the Setup disk, you will have a RAM disk containing the utilities listed in Table 27.3. To get the syntax for a command, key it at a command prompt followed by **/?**.

| Command | Purpose |
|---|---|
| ATTRIB.EXE | Views and changes file attributes: Read-Only, Hidden, and System. Useful for turning off the Read-Only attribute on a system file so you can modify or delete it. |
| CHKDSK.EXE | An old disk-checking utility predating ScanDisk. |
| DEBUG.EXE | Enters a debugging mode for a program. Useful primarily to programmers. |
| EDIT.COM | A text editor. Useful for editing text files such as AUTOEXEC.BAT and CONFIG.SYS. |
| EXT.EXE | Microsoft Extract. Similar to EXTRACT; most people do not use this. |
| FORMAT.COM | Formats floppy and hard disks. |
| HELP.BAT | Opens a Help file in the EDIT text editor. |
| MSCDEX.EXE | The Microsoft utility for enabling the CD drive at a command prompt. |
| RESTART.COM | Restarts the PC. |
| SCANDISK.EXE | Checks the disk for file system errors and corrects them. |
| SCANDISK.INI | An initialization file for SCANDISK.EXE. |
| SYS.COM | Transfers the startup files between disks. For example, SYS C: transfers the boot files from the current drive to the C drive. |

**TABLE 27.3**
Command Prompt Utilities Placed on the RAM Disk When Booting from a Windows 9x Startup Floppy

### *Other Useful Command-Prompt Commands*

Besides the external commands described in the preceding section, you may also need to use some of the internal commands built into COMMAND.COM, such as those listed in Table 27.4. We will look at the syntax of some of these in Chapter 29; you can also see the syntax for any of them by keying the command name followed by **/?**.

| Command | Purpose |
|---|---|
| COPY | Copies files from one location to another. Useful for copying files between folders on a hard disk or from a floppy to a hard disk or vice versa. |
| DEL | Deletes files. |
| DIR | Displays a listing of the current directory (folder). |
| CD | Changes to a different directory. |
| MD | Makes a new directory. |
| RD | Removes a directory. |

**TABLE 27.4**
Commonly Used Internal Commands in COMMAND.COM

### *Using a Startup Disk to Repair a System*

The last few sections have provided general information about using a startup disk. The following steps explain how to actually use the disk to troubleshoot and repair an ailing PC.

1. Try booting from the hard disk. If it will not boot, go to step 2.
2. Boot from the startup floppy, and try changing to the hard disk by keying **C:** and pressing Enter.
3. If you cannot get to a C:\> prompt, the partition is gone. Use FDISK to examine the partition information as in Chapter 12, and repartition/reformat as needed.
   OR

If you can get a C:\> prompt, try keying **DIR** and pressing Enter to see whether you can get a listing of its contents.

a. If you can get a DIR listing, then perhaps the disk just needs to have the system files retransferred to it. Key **SYS C:** and press Enter, then try rebooting. If the system still does not boot, go on to step 5.

b. If a message appears about invalid media type, the hard disk's formatting has been erased. Make sure you cannot get a file listing for C, and then key **FORMAT C:** to reformat it. You can add the /S switch if desired to transfer the system files to it so it will be bootable.

4. Check the disk for file system errors with ScanDisk. Correct any errors found.
5. Remove the floppy and reboot. If you can boot from the hard disk to a command prompt, you are ready to reinstall Windows.

## Using a Windows 2000/XP Emergency Repair Disk (ERD)

An Emergency Repair Disk (ERD) in the NT-based versions of Windows is a floppy disk containing backups of certain system settings that are useful to the Windows setup program when it is attempting to repair a damaged Windows installation. It is *not* a bootable disk, and it is *not* the same thing as a startup disk under Windows 9x. An ERD is not required for the setup program to attempt to repair Windows, but it increases the quality level of the recovery. For example, using an ERD for recovery prevents you from having to reinstall service pack updates after repairing a Windows installation.

### *Creating an ERD*

To create an ERD, you use the Backup utility, as follows:

1. Start Backup (Start/Programs/Accessories/System Tools/Backup).
2. Click the Emergency Repair Disk button. A dialog box appears.
3. *Optional:* If you want to back up the Registry too, mark the check box shown in Figure 27.22. This backs up the Registry to the *Repair* folder on the hard drive. (It does not copy it to the floppy; the Registry is too large for that.) This might be useful if the hard disk is still readable but the Windows installation has a problem.
4. Insert a blank formatted floppy disk in the drive and click OK.
5. Wait for the data to be copied. When a message appears that it is done, click OK.

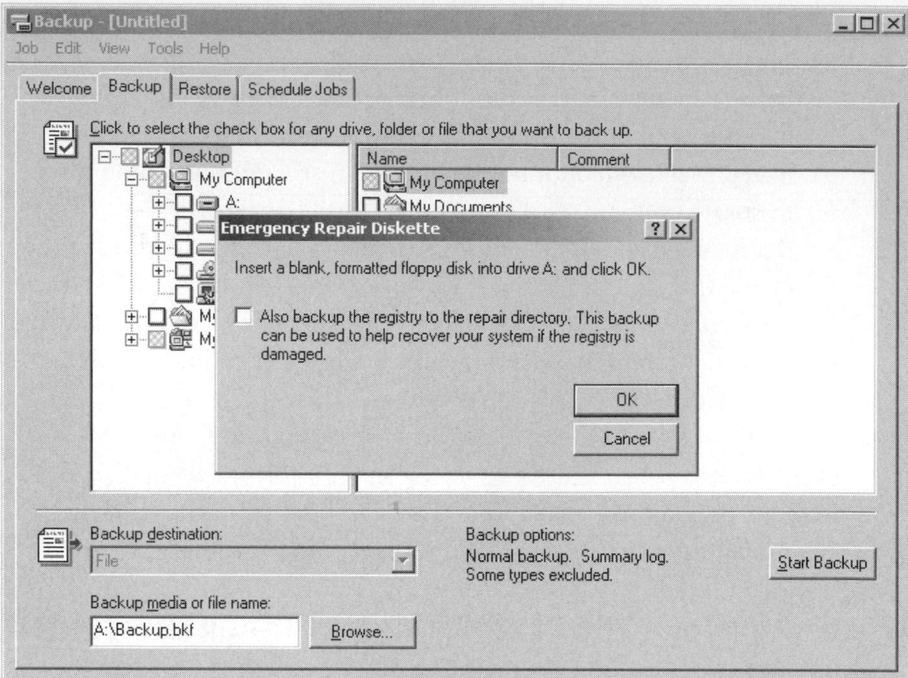


**FIGURE 27.22**
Creating an ERD through the Windows 2000 Backup Program

### *Using an ERD to Repair a Windows Installation*

If Windows will not boot normally, do the following to attempt to repair it through the Windows setup program:

1. Set up the BIOS to boot first from the CD. Restart the PC and allow the setup program to start from the CD.
2. At the setup program's opening screen, key **R** to select Repair.
3. Key **R** to start the emergency repair process.
4. Key **F** to select Fast Repair.
5. At the prompt, press Enter to indicate that you have an ERD available.
6. Insert the ERD and press Enter.
7. Follow the prompts to allow the setup program to repair your Windows installation.

## Using the Recovery Console in Windows 2000/XP

The Recovery Console is another way to repair a damaged Windows installation, or to retrieve important files from the drive before reformatting it. It provides a command-line interface, somewhat similar to booting from a Windows 9x startup disk. Using the Recovery Console you can copy files from a floppy or CD to the hard disk, repair the MBR, or enable or disable services.

Extensive Recovery Console familiarity is not required for A+ certification; you should simply know what it is, how to get into and out of it, and how to issue basic commands through its interface.

### *Booting to the Recovery Console*

By default, the Recovery Console exists only on the Windows CD-ROM. To use it from there, do the following:

1. Boot from the Windows CD. The Windows setup program starts.
2. At the Welcome to Setup screen, key **R** to select Repair, and then key **C** to choose Recovery Console.
3. Key **1** and press Enter to select the first Windows installation on the system.
4. If prompted for the Administrator password, key it and press Enter.

You are now at a c:\WINNT command prompt. From here you can issue commands to work with the hard disk content. See "Recovery Console Commands" below for details.

### *Installing the Recovery Console Files on the Hard Disk*

You can also install the Recovery Console program on the hard disk, so you will not need the CD if you should ever require the Recovery Console. To do so:

1. While Windows is running normally, insert the Windows CD in the drive. If a window opens automatically for the CD, close it.
2. Choose Start/Run. Key **x:\i386\winnt32 /cmdcons** (where *x* is the drive letter of the CD) and click OK.
3. A confirmation message appears. Click Yes.
4. After the installation, another confirmation appears. Click OK.

One of the side effects of installing the Recovery Console on the hard disk is that the multi-boot menu will appear automatically each time you start Windows, as if you had multiple operating systems installed. You can choose the Recovery Console from there.

### *Recovery Console Commands*

To see a list of the available commands in the Recovery Console, key **HELP** and press Enter. Some of the commands are the same as with a Windows 9x startup disk. These include ATTRIB, CD, MD, COPY, DEL, CHKDSK, DIR, EXIT, EXPAND, FORMAT, MD, RD, and REN. Table 27.5 lists a few extra commands that are unique to the Windows Recovery Console.

| Command | Purpose |
|---|---|
| BATCH | Executes batch commands in a specified text file. |
| DISABLE | Disables a particular Windows service or driver. |
| DISKPART | Manages hard disk partitions; roughly equivalent to FDISK. |
| ENABLE | Enables a particular Windows service or driver. |
| FIXBOOT | Writes a new boot sector on the boot partition. |
| FIXMBR | Repairs the master boot record on the disk. |
| LISTSYS | Lists all available drivers, services, and startup types. |

**TABLE 27.5**
Windows Recovery Console Commands

# Common Shutdown Problems

Any computer can be shut down, of course—just unplug it or press its Power button. But that is not a good way of doing it because any unsaved changes will be lost. In addition, shutting down abruptly can sometimes create file system errors. That is why ScanDisk runs automatically in Windows 9x versions when the computer starts up after an improper shutdown.

The proper way to shut down Windows is to choose Start/Shut Down and then select Shut Down from the list of options. The following sections provide some help in case that does not work.

## Does Not Shut Off Automatically

On systems with ATX motherboards, the Shut Down command turns off the system altogether. This is a feature of ACPI (Advanced Configuration and Power Interface), which almost all ATX motherboards support.

On systems with AT motherboards, a message is displayed (orange text on a black background) that says *It is now safe to turn off your computer*, and then you must press the Power button manually to finish shutting it down.

If an ATX system will not shut down automatically (that is, if it acts like an AT), check the following:

- Is ACPI enabled in BIOS setup?
- Is ACPI enabled in Windows?
- Are all of the necessary case wires connected to the motherboard?
- Is a BIOS update available for the motherboard?

## Application Not Responding

In order to shut down in an orderly way, Windows must shut down each running application and process. If one of them is not responding, you might get an error message.

The box that appears usually asks whether you want to wait for a program to begin responding again or end the task. End Task is almost always the right choice. This will enable Windows to continue shutting itself down.

If you see the same Application Not Responding box every time you shut down Windows, you know that you have a problem with one of the programs that is running in the background in Windows. Check the System Configuration Utility (MSCONFIG) to see what is loading at startup. Perhaps you can reinstall the one that is having the problem, or remove it entirely.

## Will Not Shut Down with Power Button

When Windows locks up "hard," to the point where a normal shutdown will not work, you might have to press the Power button to shut it down. But on ATX systems, the Power button is controlled through the motherboard, so severe problems will prevent it from functioning normally.

The override for the Power button is to press and hold it for five seconds. This turns off the computer even with the worst system problems going on. This is not an issue on AT systems because the power switch is wired directly to the power supply (see Chapter 4).

## Windows 98 Shutdown Issues

It is widely known that Windows 98 Second Edition does not always shut down properly on some systems. A patch is available from Microsoft's Web site that will correct this.

If the patch does not help, the system may be experiencing a problem with the Fast Shutdown feature. Normally Windows 98 turns off all of the device drivers as it shuts down, ensuring that each device has finished. To make Windows 98 shut down faster you can enable Fast Shutdown, which bypasses this device-by-device shutdown routine. However, this feature can cause some PCs to not shut down properly.

To check whether Fast Shutdown is enabled, and to change its setting, use the System Configuration Utility (MSCONFIG):

1. Choose Start/Run, key **MSCONFIG**, and then press Enter.
2. On the General tab, click the Advanced button. The Advanced Troubleshooting Settings dialog box appears (see Figure 27.23).
3. Mark or clear the Disable fast shutdown check box, then click OK.
4. Close the System Configuration Utility window.

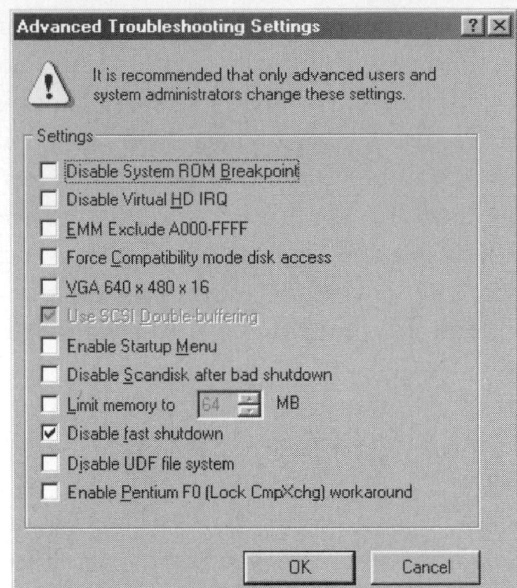


**FIGURE 27.23**
Enable or disable Fast Shutdown at the Advanced Troubleshooting Settings dialog box.

## Shutdown Sound Problem

If the sound file assigned to the Exit Windows system event is corrupted, the system will lock up when it tries to shut down. Use the Sound applet in the Control Panel to set the Exit Windows sound to None.

# STUDY GUIDE

Use the following summaries to review the key concepts of this chapter.

## What Constitutes a Bootable Disk?

- A bootable disk is one that can be used to bring the PC to a functional level.
- MS-DOS (and Windows 9x startup disks) require IO.SYS, MSDOS.SYS, and COMMAND.COM on a bootable disk.
- NT-based Windows versions cannot boot from a startup floppy. They must boot either from a hard disk on which Windows is installed or from a Windows Setup CD.
- A bootable CD contains BOOTCAT.BIN and BOOTIMG.BIN, which work together to simulate a bootable floppy disk in the A drive.

## Startup Configuration Files

- In MS-DOS, the startup files are AUTOEXEC.BAT and CONFIG.SYS.
- In Windows 3.1 they are WIN.INI and SYSTEM.INI.
- In Windows 95 and higher they are the Registry.
- CONFIG.SYS is a plain-text file that lists device drivers to load at startup.
- AUTOEXEC.BAT is a plain-text file that lists applications and settings to load at startup. It is a batch file, processing a list of commands.
- SYSTEM.INI is an initialization file for Windows 3.1 that serves the same function that CONFIG.SYS does for MS-DOS.
- WIN.INI is the Windows 3.1 equivalent of AUTOEXEC.BAT.
- Later versions of OSes recognize the configuration files of earlier versions for backward compatibility. For example, Windows 9x recognizes CONFIG.SYS, AUTOEXEC.BAT, WIN.INI, and SYSTEM.INI.
- The Registry stores startup settings for Windows 95 and higher. It was covered in detail in Chapter 26.

## MS-DOS Boot Process

- The process for MS-DOS boot is as follows:
  1. After the power-on self test (POST) through BIOS, the BIOS searches for a master boot record (MBR) containing data about the partitions.
  2. The MBR locates IO.SYS and passes control to it. IO.SYS identifies the installed hardware and processes CONFIG.SYS.
  3. MSDOS.SYS takes control, loads the MS-DOS kernel into memory, and processes AUTOEXEC.BAT.
  4. COMMAND.COM then displays a command prompt.

## Windows 9x/Me Boot Process

- Windows 9x consists of a GUI and a DOS protected-mode interface (DPMI). You can boot to either and it is still Windows 9x. The GUI is the default, however.
- The process for booting to Windows 9x/Me is as follows:
  1. The BIOS performs a POST and then searches for the MBR.
  2. The MBR locates IO.SYS, which processes instructions from MSDOS.SYS.
  3. IO.SYS loads the graphic in LOGO.SYS (the splash screen).

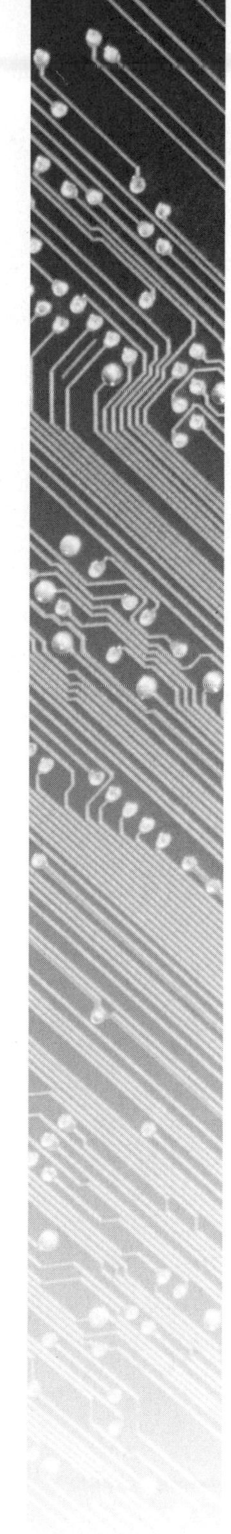

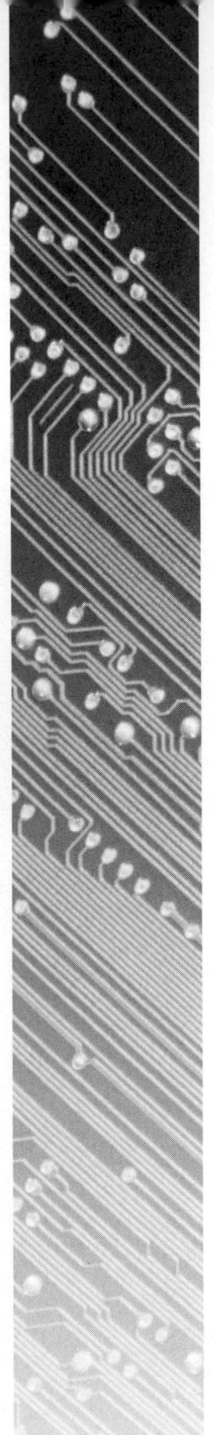

4. IO.SYS locates SYSTEM.DAT and USER.DAT, and then loads SYSTEM.DAT.
5. IO.SYS processes CONFIG.SYS and AUTOEXEC.BAT if present.
6. IO.SYS loads HIMEM.SYS if it is not already loaded.
7. IO.SYS loads WIN.COM, the main Windows program.
8. WIN.COM loads the virtual memory manager, VMM386.VXD.
9. VMM386.VXD loads 32-bit device drivers.
10. WIN.COM executes SYSTEM.INI if present.
11. WIN.COM loads the GUI by loading KRNL32.DLL, GDI.EXE, and USER.EXE.
12. WIN.COM executes WIN.INI if present.
13. WIN.COM runs applications with shortcuts in the *StartUp* folder.

- Windows 9x offers several alternative boot modes for troubleshooting.
- Safe mode starts up the GUI with a minimal set of drivers.
- Logged mode logs each step of the process in BOOTLOG.TXT.
- Step-by-step confirmation steps through the startup line-by-line.
- Command prompt only boots to a DPMI command prompt.
- Safe mode command prompt only boots to command prompt and bypasses all startup files.

## Windows NT, 2000, and XP Boot Process

- NT versions start up very differently from Windows 9x. The system file set is almost completely different.
- Here is the Windows NT/2000/XP boot process summarized:
  1. BIOS performs a POST and then searches for the MBR.
  2. The MBR loads NTLDR (NT Loader).
  3. NTLDR switches the CPU into 32-bit protected mode.
  4. NTLDR reads BOOT.INI and displays a menu from which the user can choose the OS if more than one is installed.
  5. NTLDR runs DTDETECT, which detects installed hardware and sends the information to the Registry.
  6. NTLDR reads NTOSKRNL.EXE into memory.
  7. NTLDR locates the drivers for the hardware reported in the Registry, and then hands over control to NTOSKRNL.EXE.
  8. NTOSKRNL.EXE loads the device drivers and the GUI.
- To prepare for the A+ exam, make sure you know the order in which NTLDR, NTDETECT, and NTOSKRNL execute, and which file interacts with BOOT.INI.
- Windows NT 4.0 has only one boot alternative: you can boot to VGA mode.

- Windows 2000 and XP allow booting into safe mode (several variations), and allow boot logging and VGA startup modes.
- You can also boot to the Last Known Good Configuration to bypass recent problems introduced into the Registry.

## Troubleshooting Windows 9x Startup Problems

- *No Operating System Found* indicates that there is no bootable disk.
- *Error in CONFIG.SYS line xx* indicates that a driver called for in CONFIG.SYS has been removed or is corrupt.
- *Bad or Missing Command.Com* indicates that COMMAND.COM has been deleted or is corrupt.
- HIMEM.SYS must load in order for Windows 9x to work. It can be loaded from CONFIG.SYS or Windows can load it itself.
- If startup gets stuck at the Windows splash screen, the problem may be a corrupt paging file (virtual memory). Fix this by turning off virtual memory and then turning it on again (rebooting between) from within safe mode.
- A Windows protection error occurs when a virtual device driver encounters a problem.
- A general protection fault occurs when two programs try to use the same memory space.

## Troubleshooting Windows 2000/XP Startup Problems

- Try using safe mode if Windows will not start normally, and correct whatever driver or program is causing the problem if you can determine it.
- You can also try repairing the Windows installation using an Emergency Repair Disk (ERD), or work from the Recovery Console.
- A STOP error is usually the result of an incompatible piece of hardware or a corrupted driver.

## Controlling What Loads at Startup

- The System Configuration Editor (SYSEDIT) opens several legacy initialization files in a single Notepad-like window.
- The System Configuration Utility (MSCONFIG) lets you turn off individual lines in the startup files to troubleshoot startup problems.

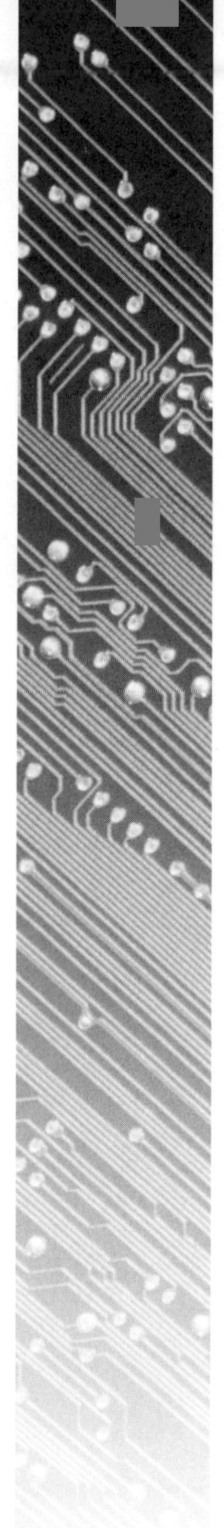

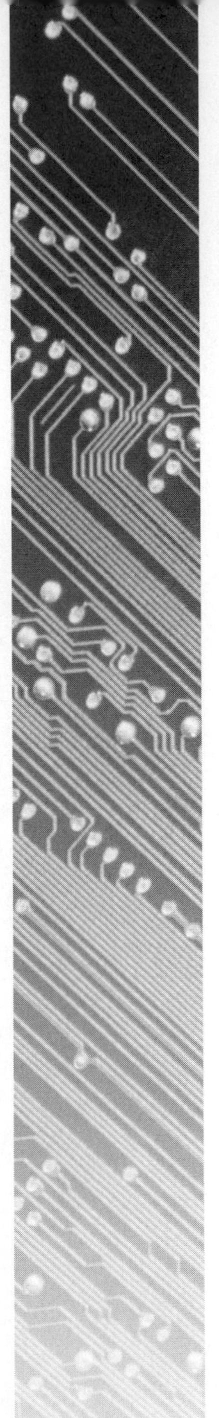

## Using a Windows 9x Startup Disk

- A startup disk is a bootable floppy from which you can start the PC.
- It contains the startup files plus some essential command-prompt utilities.
- The startup disk creates a RAM disk out of system memory and decompresses some of the utilities onto it.
- To create a startup disk in Windows, use Add/Remove Programs in the Control Panel (Startup Disk tab).
- To use a startup disk to repair a system, boot the PC and try to access the hard disk (C). If you cannot, use FDISK to examine the partitions and repartition/reformat as needed.

## Using a Windows 2000 Emergency Repair Disk

- An ERD is not a startup disk; it is not bootable. It contains data that increases the success of a repair when used in conjunction with the Windows Setup CD.
- To create an ERD, use the Backup utility in Windows (Start/Programs/Accessories/System Tools/Backup).
- To use an ERD, boot from the Windows Setup CD. At the opening screen choose Repair, and then key **R** again to choose the emergency repair process. Key **F** to select Fast Repair, and then follow the prompts.

## Using the Recovery Console in Windows 2000/XP

- The Recovery Console is a command-line interface similar to what you get when you boot from a startup floppy under Windows 9x.
- To boot to the Recovery Console you can boot from the Windows Setup CD and choose R for Repair and then C for Recovery Console.
- You can also install the Recovery Console program on the hard disk so you do not need the CD to access it. To do so, from the CD, key **\i386\winnt32 /cmdcons** using the *Run* command. Then follow the prompts.

## Common Shutdown Problems

- AT systems do not shut off automatically; they display a message that it is now safe to shut off.
- ATX systems should shut off automatically. If they do not, check ACPI settings in BIOS or try a BIOS update.

- If an application's not responding prevents Windows from shutting down, click End Task. If the same problem reoccurs, troubleshoot what may be loading at startup through MSCONFIG.
- If the Power button will not shut off the PC, hold it for five seconds.
- A known problem exists with Windows 98 Second Edition shutdown; download a patch from Microsoft to correct it.
- A corrupt sound file for the Exit Windows system event can cause a lockup at shutdown.

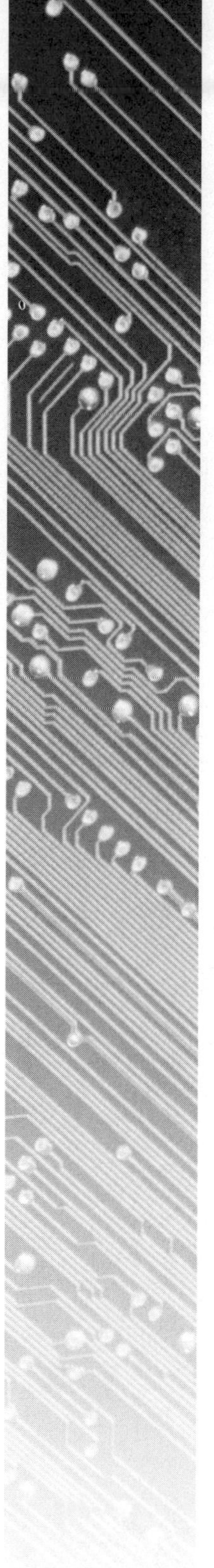

# PRACTICE TEST

On a blank sheet of paper, write the answers to the following multiple-choice questions and explain why each answer is correct.

1. What files must be present on an MS-DOS or Windows 9x bootable floppy disk?
   a. COMMAND.COM, CONFIG.SYS, and AUTOEXEC.BAT
   b. BOOT.INI, IO.SYS, and MSDOS.SYS
   c. WIN.COM, BOOT.INI, and CONFIG.SYS
   d. IO.SYS, MSDOS.SYS, and COMMAND.COM

2. Can you access a Windows 2000 hard disk from a Windows 98 bootable floppy?
   a. no in all cases
   b. yes in all cases
   c. yes, but only if the hard disk uses FAT or FAT32
   d. yes, but only if the hard disk uses NTFS

3. Which of these lines would *not* appear in a typical CONFIG.SYS file?
   a. LOADHIGH=C:\MOUSE\MOUSE.COM
   b. DOS=HIGH,UMB
   c. FILES=30
   d. DEVICEHIGH=C:\WINDOWS\HIMEM.SYS

4. When you REM a line in AUTOEXEC.BAT, what happens?
   a. The line is deleted the next time the PC starts up.
   b. The line is disabled but not deleted.
   c. The line takes precedence over earlier lines in the file, executing first.
   d. The line falls back in priority so that all non-REM lines execute before it.

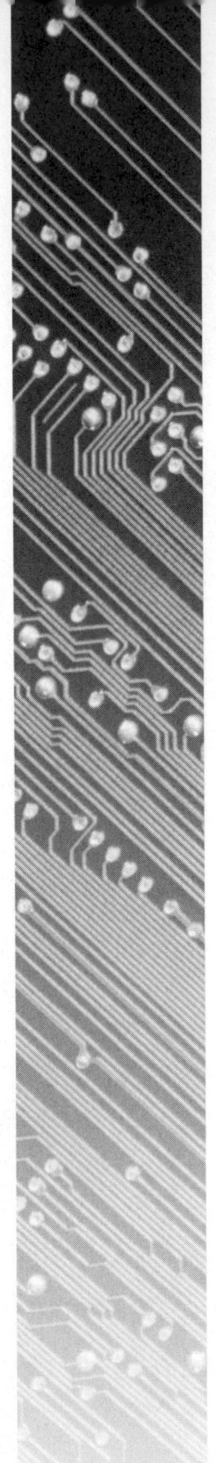

5. In what initialization file would the MSCDEX.EXE utility typically be loaded?
   a. CONFIG.SYS
   b. AUTOEXEC.BAT
   c. WIN.INI
   d. SYSTEM.INI
6. What version of Windows uses the Registry to store system settings?
   a. Windows 3.1
   b. Windows 95
   c. Windows 2000
   d. both c and d
7. What function does MSDOS.SYS serve under Windows 9x?
   a. It loads the MS-DOS kernel.
   b. It loads real-mode device drivers.
   c. It performs the POST.
   d. It is a text-based configuration file read by IO.SYS.
8. What file stores the Windows splash screen?
   a. LOGO.SYS
   b. IO.SYS
   c. WIN.SYS
   d. SPLASH.SYS
9. What is the name of the file that loads the 32-bit device drivers into memory in Windows 9x?
   a. WIN.COM
   b. KRNL32.DLL
   c. VMM386.VXD
   d. GDI.EXE
10. If you want to enter Windows in safe mode, what key do you press when you see the Starting Windows message?
    a. F1
    b. F8
    c. F5
    d. Esc
11. What video mode is used in safe mode?
    a. 800 x 600, 16-color
    b. 640 x 480, 16-color
    c. 640 x 360, 16-color
    d. 800 x 600, 256-color

12. In what order do the Windows 2000 files load?
    a. NTLDR, BOOT.INI, NTDETECT, NTOSKRNL
    b. NTDETECT, NTLDR, BOOT.INI, NTOSKRNL
    c. BOOT.INI, NTLDR, NTOSKRNL, NTDETECT
    d. BOOT.INI, NTLDR, NTDETECT, NTOSKRNL

13. Which of these Windows versions does not include safe mode as a startup option?
    a. Windows NT 4.0 Workstation
    b. Windows 95
    c. Windows 2000
    d. Windows XP

14. What type of file causes a Windows protection error?
    a. SYS
    b. VXD
    c. DLL
    d. INI

15. What utility allows you to use check boxes to disable individual startup commands for troubleshooting?
    a. MSCONFIG
    b. SYSEDIT
    c. EDIT
    d. WININIT

16. Why does Windows 9x create a RAM disk when it starts up?
    a. It makes the system run faster because RAM is faster than a hard disk.
    b. It eliminates the need for HIMEM.SYS because of its RAM usage.
    c. Utilities compressed on the startup disk are extracted onto the RAM disk.
    d. It creates the extra drive letter needed to reinstall Windows if needed.

17. How do you create an ERD in Windows 2000?
    a. through Add/Remove Programs
    b. through the Backup utility
    c. through My Computer
    d. None of the above; Windows 2000 does not use ERDs.

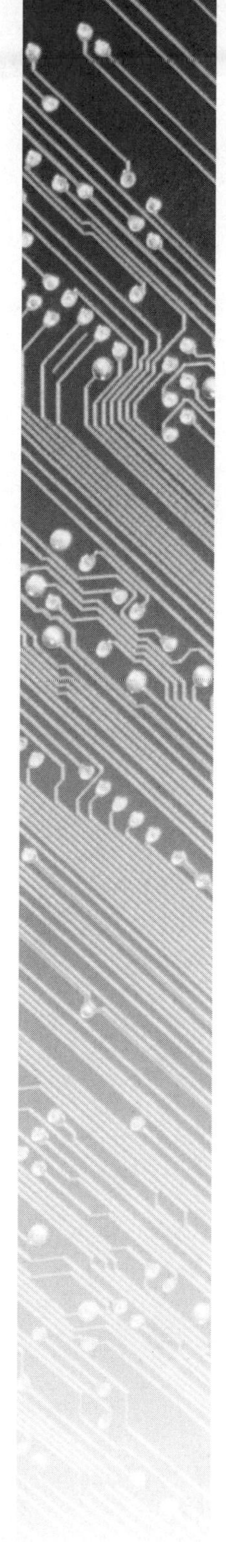

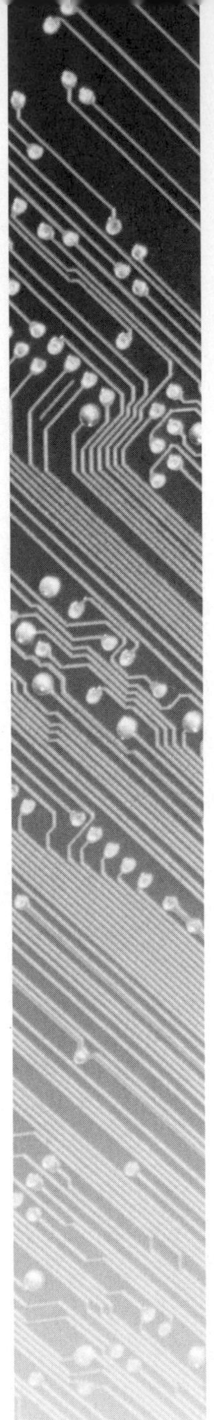

18. How do you use an ERD?
    a. Boot from it.
    b. Open it in My Computer and run Repair.exe.
    c. Go through Windows Setup using the Repair option.
    d. Any of the above

19. What does the Recovery Console offer that using an ERD does not?
    a. Fast Repair feature
    b. complete reinstallation of Windows
    c. GUI-based repair interface
    d. command-line interface

20. Which of these files is required for Windows 9x to load?
    a. HIMEM.SYS
    b. EMM386.EXE
    c. SYSTEM.INI
    d. CONFIG.SYS

# TROUBLESHOOTING

1. A client calls you complaining that when he starts up his PC, he sees an error message about COMMAND.COM being missing. He is using Windows 2000. What is probably happening?
2. A client has been making changes to the Registry—against your advice—and now Windows 2000 will not start up. What do you recommend?
3. A client's PC has crashed due to a boot sector virus. Explain how you would clean out the virus and reinstall Windows 2000.

# CUSTOMER SERVICE

1. A client has created an ERD as part of the Windows 2000 setup process, but complains that it is not bootable and does not contain a backup of the Registry. How can you explain this?
2. A client is having trouble starting Windows normally and has booted into safe mode. But now she calls you puzzled, wondering what she should do now that safe mode is on-screen. What can you advise?
3. A client has just upgraded from Windows 95 to Windows 98 Second Edition, and now Windows does not shut down properly. What can you suggest?

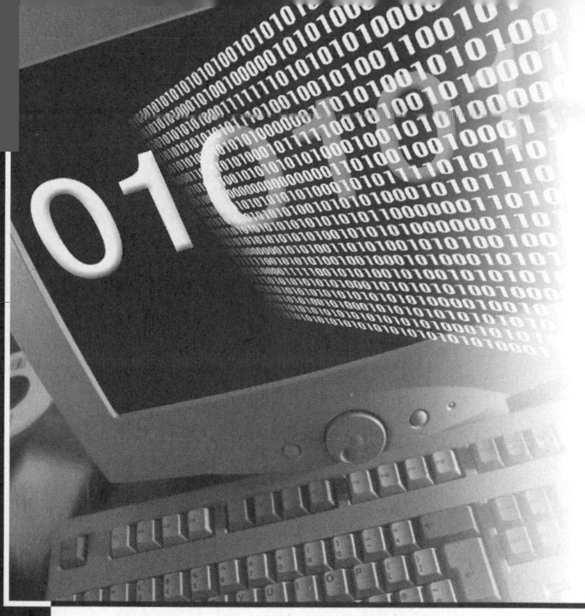

# 28 Working with Applications

## ON THE TEST

**A+ Operating System Technologies Examination**

- **Objective 1.1:** Identify the operating system's functions, structure, and major system files to navigate the operating system and how to get to needed technical information.
- **Objective 1.2:** Identify basic concepts and procedures for creating, viewing and managing files, directories and disks. This includes procedures for changing file attributes and the ramifications of those changes (for example, security issues).
- **Objective 2.4:** Identify procedures for loading/adding and configuring application device drivers, and the necessary software for certain devices.
- **Objective 3.2:** Recognize common problems and determine how to resolve them.

## ON THE JOB

Generally speaking, end users care about their computers for one reason only: the ability to run applications. In other words, they are concerned primarily with the computer's ability to help them perform useful everyday tasks such as word processing, data calculation, graphics creation, and Internet access. Anytime you can facilitate that, you are supplying invaluable tech support. Some of the activities involved with this chapter's content may include:

- installing new Windows applications
- removing Windows applications
- installing an MS-DOS program
- configuring an MS-DOS program to work within Windows
- troubleshooting problems related to applications

# Installing Windows Applications

Application setup is fairly easy these days, so many end users will install their own applications. However, a PC technician should be thoroughly familiar with the procedures for doing so, not only in the simple situations but also in the more unusual ones where the setup program is not self-explanatory, where security settings impede the install, or where there is no setup program at all.

## Installing a Typical Windows Application

A typical Windows application comes on a CD-ROM with Autorun capabilities; when you insert the CD, the setup program starts automatically. Turn off the antivirus software and close down any running programs; then continue with the installation by following the prompts.

If the setup program (or a menu containing it as an option) does not start automatically, the Autorun feature may have been turned off for the CD drive. Double-click the CD drive icon in My Computer to display it.

If a file management window appears when you double-click the icon, that means the disc has no *Autorun.inf file*. If that is the case, look for a Setup.exe file and double-click it to get started.

**Autorun.inf file**

A file containing instructions for automatic execution each time Windows detects that the CD has been inserted into a CD drive. For Autorun.inf to work, the Autorun feature must be enabled for the CD drive or you must double-click the CD icon in My Computer.

If you have downloaded the program from the Internet, it will be in one of two formats:

- A file with an .exe extension. Double-click that file to run Setup and extract all of the program and support files needed.
- A file with a .zip extension. Unzip the files in it (see the following section) into a temporary folder, and then locate and double-click Setup.exe within it.

There is no consistency among setup programs. After the setup program for the application starts, simply follow whatever prompts are presented.

## Working with ZIP Files

A *ZIP file* is a compressed archive containing one or more files. ZIP files are like envelopes that transport a group of files as a single package and compress each one to keep the size of the ZIP file as small as possible.

**ZIP file**

A file with a .zip extension. A compressed archive containing one or more files.

## In Real Life

> Do not confuse a ZIP file with a Zip disk. A Zip disk is a removable disk cartridge that fits into a 100MB or 250MB Zip drive, manufactured by Iomega. A Zip disk is not compressed; it is simply an alternative to floppy disks for storage.

### *Extracting ZIP Files in Windows XP*

If you have Windows XP, support for ZIP files is built in. You can browse their content just like a folder, but you cannot run the setup program from within the file; you must first extract it to a normal folder on the hard disk.

There are a couple of ways to extract a ZIP file containing a program you want to install in Windows XP. To extract a file manually, complete these steps:

1. Create a temporary folder to hold the setup files.
2. Open the ZIP file in a file management window by double-clicking it. Its content appears.
3. Select all of the content by pressing Ctrl + A, then copy it to the clipboard (Ctrl + C).
4. Display the temporary folder you created, and paste the files into it (Ctrl + P).
5. Locate and double-click Setup.exe.

To extract a file automatically using a wizard, complete the following steps:

1. Open the ZIP file in a file management window by double-clicking it. Its content appears.
2. In the left-hand pane, click the *Extract All Files* hyperlink. An Extraction Wizard window appears. Click Next.
3. Key the path to which the files are to be extracted. The default is to create a new folder within the current one. If you need to browse for a location, click Browse (see Figure 28.1).
4. Click Next and then click Finish. The files are extracted.

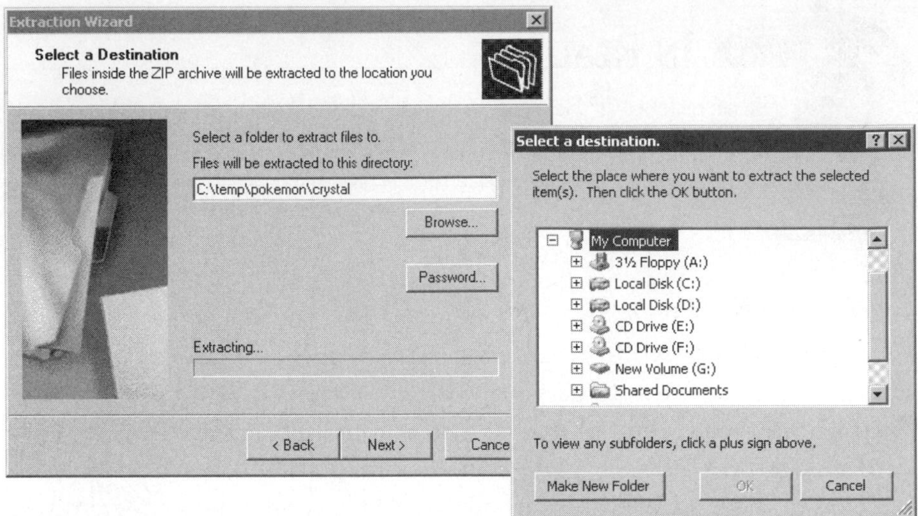


**FIGURE 28.1**
Extracting ZIP Files with the Extraction Wizard in Windows XP

### *Extracting ZIP Files in Other Windows Versions*

Other Windows versions do not have built-in support for ZIP files, so you must install a third-party utility to handle them. The most popular by far is WinZip (available as shareware from www.winzip.com). After installing it, you can handle a ZIP file in the following manner:

1. Double-click the icon for the ZIP file. If you are using a trial version of WinZip, a box appears asking you to register. Click I Agree to continue.
2. A window appears showing the content of the ZIP file (see Figure 28.2). Click the Extract button.

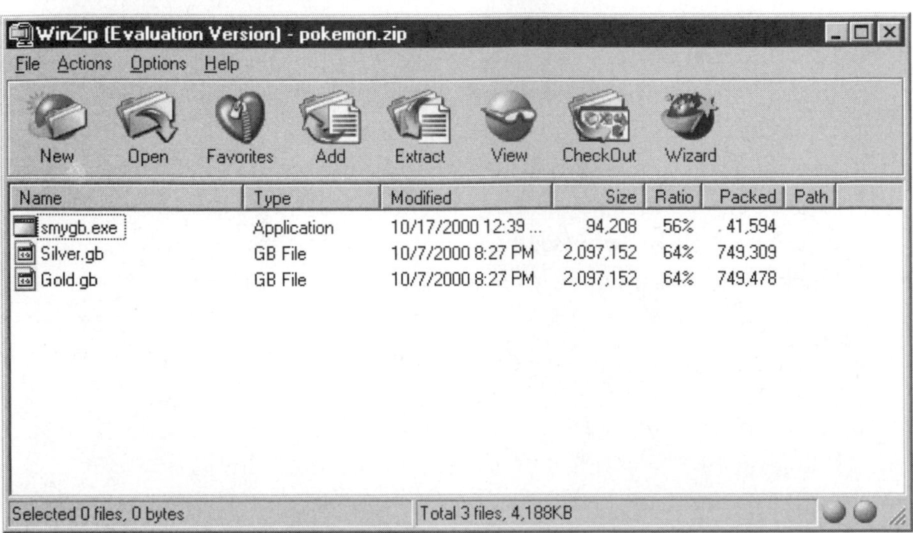


**FIGURE 28.2**
Use WinZip to view and extract files from a ZIP file.

3. An Extract dialog box appears, as in Figure 28.3. Enter the path to which you want to extract.

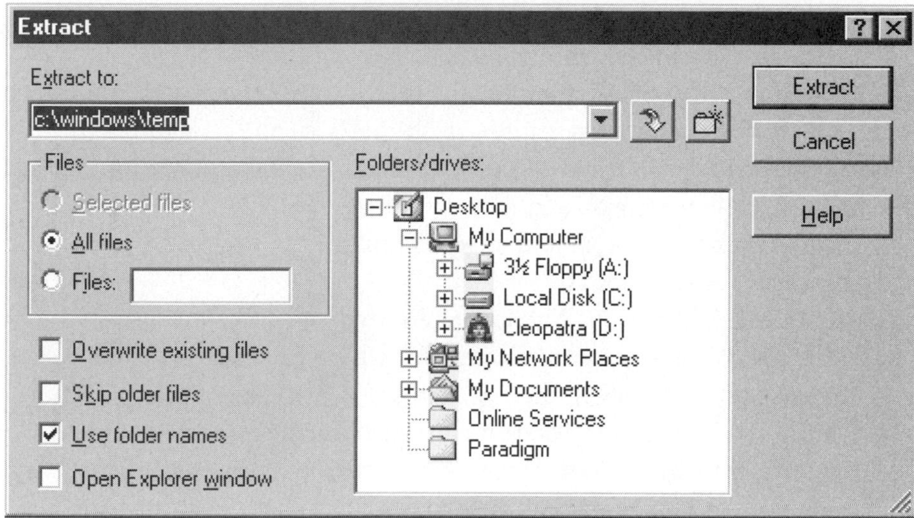


**FIGURE 28.3**
The Extract dialog box lets you specify where and how to extract the files.

4. Mark the check boxes and option buttons for any special extraction features you want, then click Extract.
5. Close WinZip.

## Installing an Application That Has No Setup Utility

Almost all Windows programs have a setup program. The setup program serves several purposes, including extracting and copying files to the hard disk, making Registry edits, and setting up a shortcut for the application on the Start menu and/or the desktop.

However, you may occasionally encounter a very simple Windows-based program that does not have a setup program. This is much more common for 16-bit than for 32-bit Windows programs. In such a case, all that is normally required is to double-click the executable file from a file management window. You do not have to edit the Registry for such programs.

If the program is a single file, simply move or copy it where you want it. If it is a zipped collection of files, unzip them into a new folder you create for this purpose.

You can create a shortcut to make it easier to run the application if you wish. Hold down Alt as you drag the executable file from a file management window to the desktop. (Or, right-drag it to the desktop and then select Create Shortcut Here from the menu that appears.)

You can also create a shortcut on the Start menu for the application. To do so:

1. Create a shortcut on the desktop (see above).
2. Drag that shortcut onto the Start button and pause a moment without releasing the mouse button. The Start menu opens.
3. Keep dragging, pausing on menu levels to make them open, and drop the shortcut where you want it on the Start menu's structure.

You can also add a shortcut to the Start menu through a more formal method. The following works in most Windows versions:

1. Right-click the Taskbar and choose Properties.
2. Select the Advanced tab.
3. Click the Add button. The Create Shortcut Wizard runs.
4. Key the path to the executable file for which you want a shortcut. Browse for it if needed, then click Next.
5. Select the folder on the Start menu where the new shortcut should appear (see Figure 28.4). If you want to create a new folder, click the New Folder button and key its name. Click Next when finished.
6. Key a name for the shortcut, then click Finish.

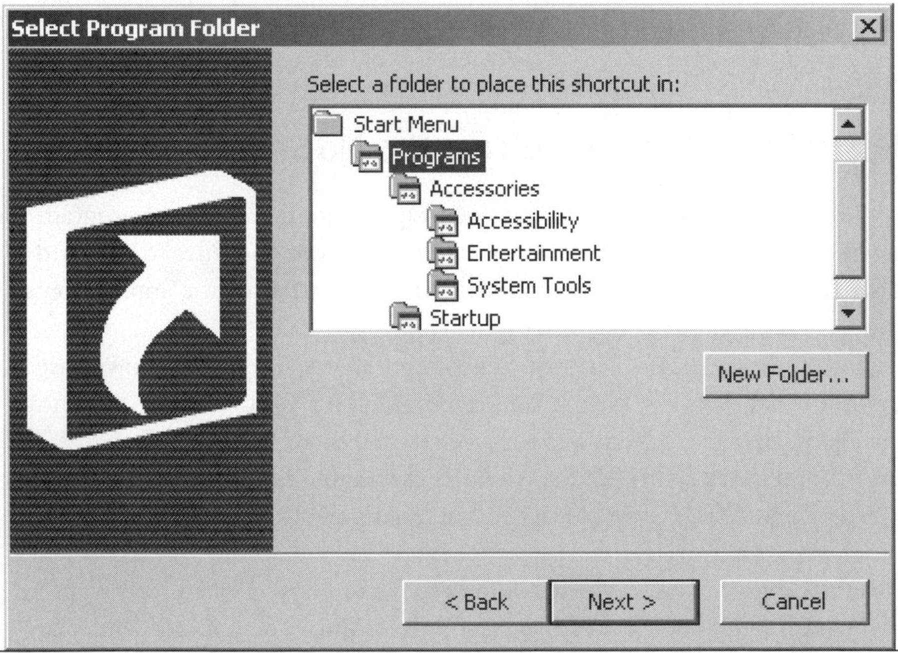


**FIGURE 28.4**
Creating a Shortcut on the Start Menu with the Create Shortcut Wizard

The above method is more time-consuming than the drag-and-drop method, but it has the advantage of allowing creation of new folders on the Start menu as needed (see step 4).

Windows XP includes the wizard, but it works only if you are using the Classic Start menu:

1. Right-click the Taskbar and choose Properties.
2. Select the Start Menu tab.
3. Click Classic Start Menu and then click Customize.
4. Complete steps 3–6 above.

Yet another way to add an item to the Start menu's structure is to use Windows Explorer. Right-click the Start button and choose Explore. This opens the Start menu's folder structure in Windows Explorer. Create a shortcut and drag it into the desired folder. See "Reorganizing the Start/Programs Menu" later in this chapter for more details about modifying the Start menu.

## Working around Installation Security Issues

In NT-based versions of Windows you occasionally might encounter problems with setup programs failing to run, or failing to complete successfully, because you do not have the appropriate security permission on that PC to install programs that modify the Registry as part of their setup (and these days almost every program does that).

To install applications, you might need to log on using an account that has Administrator privileges. That means you might need to use the Start/Shut Down/Log Off command to switch the logged-on user. A few programs might require you to log on as *the* administrator, rather than just *an* administrator—in other words, to use the user name "Administrator."

You do not have to log off the current user in order to run a program as an administrator, however; you can use the Run As command. This is a great shortcut because you can run a program as a higher-level user without having to shut down the activities of the already-logged-in user. To use the Run As command, complete these steps:

1. Right-click the executable file (usually Setup.exe) and choose Run As. The Run As dialog box opens.
2. Click The following user option. Then enter the user name and password you want to use when installing the program (see Figure 28.5).
3. Click OK to run the setup program.

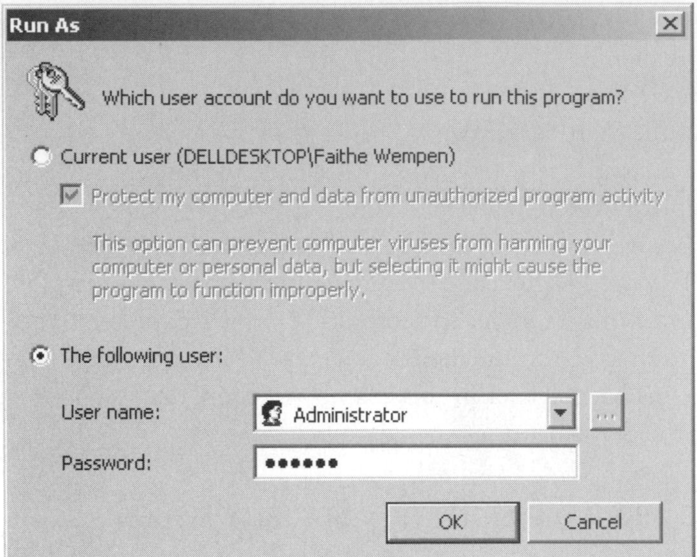


**FIGURE 28.5**
Run a setup program as someone else if the currently logged-on user does not have sufficient permission to run it.

## Other Potential Problems with Installing Applications

Here are a few last things to watch out for when installing applications:

**Other running programs.** Shut down all running programs before installing something new. If there are any files that the two applications share, those files will not be in use and will be able to be updated.

**Antivirus programs.** Turn off any antivirus software before installing new applications, or if it will not turn off altogether, disable it. Some antivirus programs proactively watch for system changes and prevent them, and may prevent part of the setup program from running.

**Hardware incompatibility.** Check the system requirements for the application before attempting to install it. If the system meets the requirements but the application still will not install, or will not run correctly after installation, check the manufacturer's Web site to find out if there are any known issues or work-arounds with certain hardware.

**Patches and updates.** If the application will not install or run after installation, check the manufacturer's Web site to see whether a program patch is available that corrects any problems that users have encountered since the original release.

**Viruses.** Certain types of retroviruses can prevent antivirus applications from installing correctly. If an antivirus application will not install, visit the Web site of the application manufacturer (for example, www.symantec.com for Norton Antivirus) to look for a removal tool for this specific type of virus.

## Controlling Whether an Application Loads at Startup

Some applications set themselves up to load automatically at startup. You can turn off that feature, and you can also add applications to the startup routine that do not already appear there.

### Making an Application Load at Startup

To make an application load at startup, create a shortcut to its executable file in the *StartUp* folder on the Start menu. See the section "Installing an Application That Has No Setup Utility" earlier in this chapter for instructions on adding shortcuts to the Start menu, or use the following steps:

1. Create a shortcut on the desktop.
2. Drag that shortcut to the Start button but do not release the mouse button. Pause a moment and the Start menu will open.
3. Point to Programs (or All Programs in Windows XP) and pause. Wait for the menu system to open.
4. Point to StartUp and pause. Wait for the menu to open.
5. Point to a spot on the StartUp menu and release the mouse button. The shortcut is placed on that menu.

### Preventing an Application from Loading at Startup

A variety of applications set themselves up to load at startup, and many times it causes more problems than benefits. Every application that loads at startup places a drain on the system resources (primarily the available RAM), and when several work together they can severely impact system performance. Therefore, it is a good idea to prevent any unneeded applications from loading at startup.

Many of the automatically loaded applications have icons in the notification area (system tray). Some of these enable you to display a configuration dialog box for the application by right-clicking and selecting Properties (or Preferences or Configure, or some similar command). In this Properties dialog box, there may be an option for preventing the application from loading automatically. This option will go by different names in different programs; look for words like "Disable" or "Startup Preferences" (see Figure 28.6).

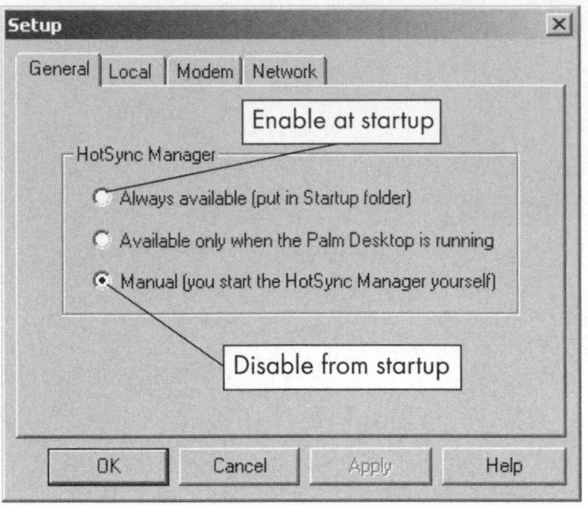


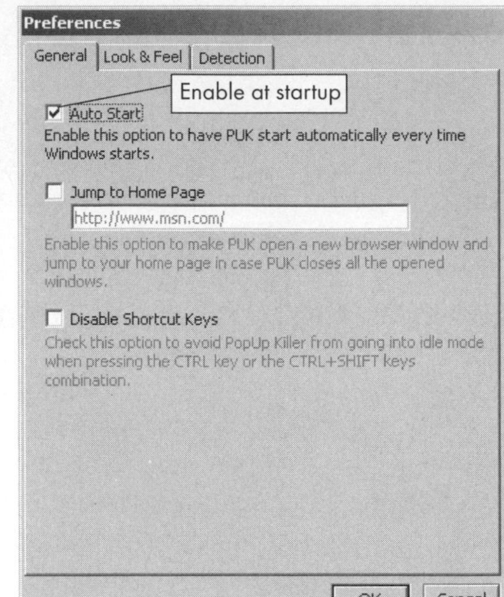


**FIGURE 28.6**
Examples of Settings in Application Properties That Determine Whether the Application Loads at Startup

If you cannot find the setting for an application that controls its automatic loading at startup, there are a couple of other places you can look:

- ***StartUp* folder.** Look on the Start menu. Delete the shortcut from the *StartUp* folder for any applications that you do not want to run automatically.
- **WIN.INI.** Sixteen-bit Windows programs sometimes load at startup because they are called for in the LOAD= or RUN= line near the top of the WIN.INI file. Delete those references (or rem them out with a semicolon in front of the line).
- **System Configuration Utility (MSCONFIG).** Run this utility, as described in Chapter 27, and disable any startup items you do not want, such as applications.
- **Registry (last resort).** Use the Registry Editor (Appendix D) to search for references to an application that loads at startup and remove those references. Use extreme caution, as with any Registry edits.

# Removing Windows Applications

Some applications have their own Uninstall program; others rely on Add/Remove Programs in Windows. Still others have no obvious removal method, so you must remove them manually.

## Removing an Application with Its Own Uninstall Program

When an application comes with its own Uninstall, you should use it rather than going through Add/Remove Programs. An application's own Uninstall will usually be more thorough (in removing unneeded files and Registry entries), since it is designed specifically for that application. It may have additional rollback features, such as restoring an older version of a system file that was replaced when the application was installed.

To determine whether an application has its own Uninstall, look in its folder on the Start menu. In Figure 28.7, for example, the game *The Sims* has its own Uninstall. Just select it from the menu and then follow the prompts. You might be asked to reinsert the application's CD.

**FIGURE 28.7**
Use the Uninstall that comes with an application if possible.

## Removing an Application through Add/Remove Programs

Almost all 32-bit Windows programs (and some 16-bit programs) can be removed through the Add/Remove Programs applet in the Control Panel. Unless there is an Uninstall for the application (as in the preceding section), this is the best way to remove an application.

### *Removing an Application in Windows 9x*

To remove an application in Windows 9x, complete the following steps:

1. From the Control Panel, double-click *Add/Remove Programs.*
2. On the Install/Uninstall tab, click the application to be removed and then click Add/Remove (see Figure 28.8).
3. Follow the prompts that appear. The steps vary for different applications.

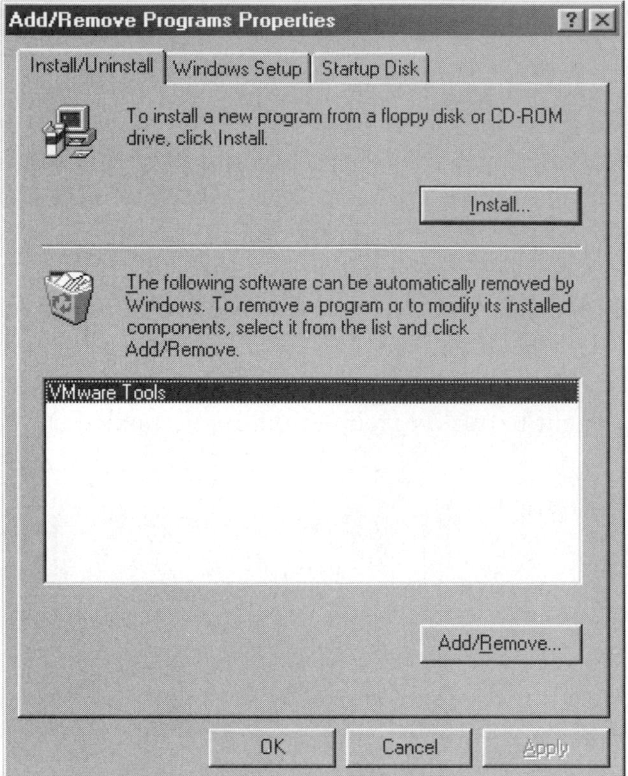


**FIGURE 28.8**
Start an Uninstall from the Install/Uninstall tab of the Add/Remove Programs dialog box.

### *Removing an Application in Windows 2000/XP*

To remove an application in Windows 2000 or XP, complete these steps:

1. From the Control Panel, double-click *Add/Remove Programs.*
2. The Change or Remove Programs list appears. If it does not, click the *Change or Remove Programs* icon at the left.
3. Click the program you want to remove, and then click the Change/Remove button (see Figure 28.9). Depending on the program, there might be separate buttons for Change and Remove; if so, click the Remove button.
4. Follow the prompts that appear. The steps vary for different applications.

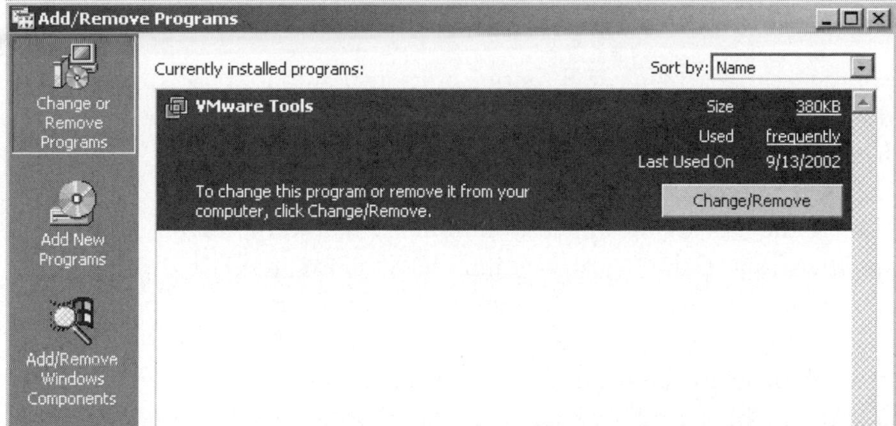


**FIGURE 28.9**
Start an Uninstall from the Change or Remove Programs list in Windows 2000 or XP.

## Troubleshooting Application Removal Problems

Most applications are able to uninstall intelligently, including removing Registry entries, because of an information file. It is either a log file (such as INSTALL.LOG) or a Microsoft Installation file with an .msi extension. This file contains information about the changes that were made to the system when the application was initially installed, so that all of those changes can be reversed when it is removed.

If the information file has been moved, deleted, or corrupted, Windows cannot usually remove the program through Add/Remove Programs. If you see an error message as you are uninstalling that says a log or MSI file cannot be located, this is probably the case. Occasionally in Windows 2000 or XP, the MSI file may have been stored in the folder containing the settings for the logged-on user who performed the installation, while a different logged-on user is now trying to run the uninstall. In such a case Add/Remove Programs might not be able to find the MSI file. Try logging on as the user who originally installed the application and then try uninstalling again.

### In Real Life

You can use a utility called TweakUI (available for download from most shareware sites) to edit the list of installed applications in Add/Remove Programs. This way you can remove an item from the list that will not uninstall because of an error. In Windows XP, when an error occurs while uninstalling, a message box offers to remove it from the list for you.

### Manually Removing an Application

If a program has no Uninstall routine of its own and does not appear in the Add/Remove Programs applet in Windows, or produces an error message when you try to uninstall it, you have several alternatives:

- Leave the application installed. It probably will not harm the system.
- Delete the files for the application from the hard disk, leaving the pointers to it in the Registry and in the Windows interface. Again, they probably will not harm the system, and you will have freed up most of the hard disk space that the application occupied. This is a rather crude way of manually removing the application.
- Delete the files (see above) and delete all shortcuts to the application from the Start menu and the desktop. This leaves only the stray mentions of the application in the Registry. It is not the best uninstall procedure, of course, but it does the bulk of the job.
- Do all of the above and then manually edit the Registry to remove all traces of the application. This is an ambitious task and, if performed incorrectly, can disable the system, so proceed with caution. See Appendix D for Registry editing help.

If you do decide to remove the application from the Registry, look for it under HKEY_LOCAL_MACHINE\Software in a folder with the manufacturer's name. The shortcut to it on the Start menu would be found in HKEY_CURRENT_USER\Software\Microsoft\Windows\CurrentVersion\Explorer\MenuOrder\StartMenu\Programs. Use the Find feature in the Registry Editor to locate all instances of the name.

## Reorganizing the Start/Programs Menu

As mentioned earlier, the Start menu's Programs list comes from a set of folders on the hard drive. You can modify the menu structure by modifying that set of folders, moving items from one location to another, creating new folders, or deleting folders.

To access the folder structure, right-click the Start button and choose Explore (or Explore All Users). In different Windows versions the folder set is located in various places. In Windows 9x it is located within the *Windows* folder; in Windows 2000/XP it is in the *All Users* subfolder within the *Documents and Settings* folder, as in Figure 28.10.

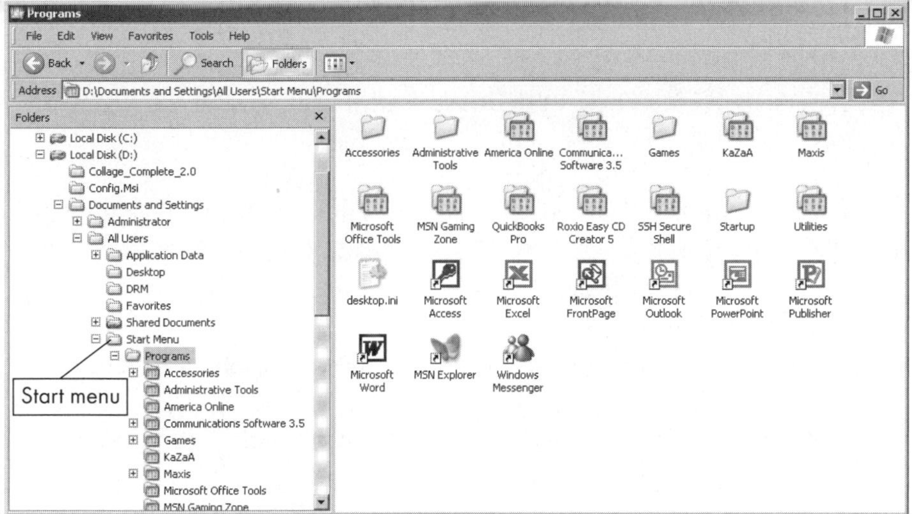


**FIGURE 28.10**
The folder structure for the Start menu is editable in Windows Explorer (Windows XP shown).

In Windows 2000 and XP there are two sets of folders for the Start menu: one for All Users and one for the individual user logged on at the moment. The All Users set contains applications that are accessible to all users of the local PC; the set for the individual user contains applications that are available only when the current user is logged on. Some applications enable you to specify which availability you want when you install them; others assume that All Users is your choice.

You can also modify the Start menu through the Taskbar properties, as you saw earlier in the chapter. Right-click the Taskbar and choose Properties, and then click the Advanced (or Start Menu) tab.

Yet another way to modify the Start menu is with drag and drop. In all versions except Windows 95 you can move items around on the Start menu by dragging them.

## Adding and Removing Windows Components

Windows components are applications that come with Windows. They have their own special utility for installing and uninstalling.

There are a number of choices for which Windows components you want. The most common ones install by default when you install Windows, but you can add or remove them at any time. The list of available components varies for every Windows version, but the interface for adding and removing is similar across all versions. Windows 9x has many optional components of interest to end users, whereas the optional components in

Windows NT/2000/XP are mostly special-purpose security or networking drivers and utilities.

## Adding and Removing Windows Components in Windows 9x/Me

To add or remove Windows components in Windows 9x or Me, complete the following steps:

1. From the Control Panel, double-click *Add/Remove Programs.*
2. Select the Windows Setup tab.
3. Scroll through the categories and their current installation statuses, as in Figure 28.11:
   - A check box with a check mark and a white background indicates all components are already installed.
   - A check box with a check mark and a gray background indicates some components are already installed.
   - A check box with no check mark indicates that no components are installed.

Some of the categories are not really categories, but simply individually installable components. If you click an item and the Details button is unavailable, it is a single item rather than a category.

**FIGURE 28.11**
Categories of Components to Install or Remove in Windows 98

4. Select a category and then click the Details button to see a list of the items in that category. Each component in the list has its own check box that shows its current status.
5. Mark or clear check boxes to install or remove components as desired. Click OK to go back to the list of categories and then repeat step 4 for another category.
6. When finished, click OK from the list of categories to install or remove your selections. If prompted to insert the Windows CD, do so.

## Adding and Removing Windows Components in Windows 2000/XP

To add or remove Windows components in Windows 2000 or XP, follow these steps:

1. From the Control Panel, double-click *Add/Remove Programs.*
2. Click the Add/Remove Windows Components button. The Windows Components Wizard runs.
3. Select the components you want to install or remove. As with Windows 9x (see the preceding section), there are categories of components; within each category, the Details button shows the individual items (see Figure 28.12).
4. When finished selecting components, click Next. If prompted to insert the Windows CD, do so. Then follow the prompts to complete the installation or removal.

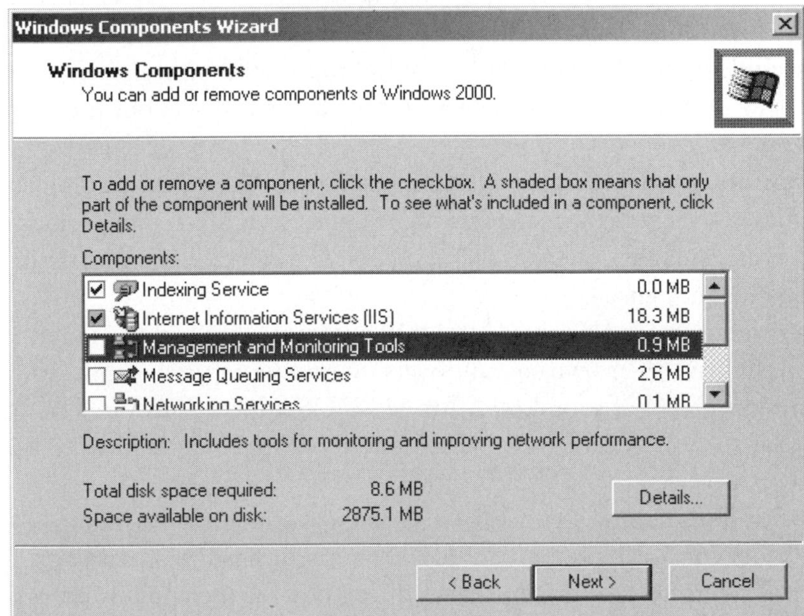


**FIGURE 28.12**
Categories of Components to Install or Remove in Windows 2000.

Notice that in Figure 28.12 all of the categories pertain to messaging and networking; there are no optional user components to install or remove in Windows 2000 (for example, Outlook Express, Paint, Notepad, etc.). In Windows XP there is a single category called Accessories and Utilities that contains many of the end user optional components.

## Working with MS-DOS Applications

Depending on the application and on the Windows version, an MS-DOS-based application might run flawlessly under Windows with the default settings, might run with a few tweaks to the default settings, or might not run at all; it is often a matter of trial-and-error.

Some problems you may encounter running MS-DOS applications include:

- **CONFIG.SYS and AUTOEXEC.BAT modifications.** Some MS-DOS applications have setup programs that modify these startup files. The modifications are probably not necessary, and may even introduce problems.
- **Memory issues.** Some MS-DOS programs run in real mode and use only 640KB of RAM; others run in protected mode and want to use more. Some want extended (XMS); others want expanded (EMS). Windows should be able to determine the requirements and provide the RAM needed, but it does not always work with the default settings.
- **Resource sharing.** Most MS-DOS applications were written with the assumption that only one application would be run at a time. Therefore, they do not have any programming to help them share system resources gracefully with other applications. Windows should be able to segment the MS-DOS program in its own separate address space, but it does not always work.
- **Proprietary video drivers.** MS-DOS programs that operate at higher display resolutions than standard VGA come with drivers for various old video cards. If the system has a much newer video card, compatibility problems may ensue.
- **Proprietary sound drivers.** MS-DOS programs that include sound typically have their own sound drivers. SoundBlaster is the most common model of sound card that MS-DOS applications support. As long as the sound card is SoundBlaster compatible, it should work—in theory, anyway.
- **Working directory.** Some MS-DOS programs require a working directory for storing temporary files. You might need to specify a working directory in the Properties dialog box for the application in

Windows. (We will look at this shortly.)

- **Shortcut keys.** The shortcut keys used in an application may conflict with the key assignments in Windows. You can set aside certain key combinations for the application's use through its Properties dialog box in Windows.
- **Problems switching back and forth.** Switching away from a running MS-DOS program and then returning to it may cause display problems in the DOS program. There are settings in the Properties dialog box that may help.
- **Stated incompatibility with Windows.** Some DOS programs refuse to run if they detect that Windows is running. This was a valid safety precaution with earlier Windows versions, but is largely a non-issue today because Windows works so differently than it did in the days of Windows 3.1 and MS-DOS. You can set up the Properties to make Windows hide itself from this sort of check.
- **Crashes under Windows.** If a program simply will not run under Windows, you can try booting to MS-DOS to run it. You can boot from a DOS startup disk, or you can use the MS-DOS mode in Windows 9x, which was covered in Chapter 27.

In most cases all of these problems can be overcome with the right configuration settings. See "Configuring DOS Applications" later in this chapter. However, before you assume that a problem exists, try installing and running the MS-DOS application under Windows using the default settings, as described in the following section.

## Installing an MS-DOS Application

DOS applications do not require any Registry edits. You can create shortcuts for them on the desktop or Start menu, but this is optional; if you run the application only occasionally, you may prefer to simply double-click its executable file from a file management window whenever you want to use it.

Some DOS applications have no setup program per se. You copy them into a folder on the hard disk, and then run them from there. Others have setup programs that make changes to the startup files (AUTOEXEC.BAT and CONFIG.SYS), create a series of subfolders and copy files into them, and run compatibility checks on the hardware to make sure it is sufficient to support the application.

### *Running Setup from Windows*

To install a DOS application that has a setup program, find the setup program in Windows and double-click it. The setup program's name may not be obvious; in the early days of MS-DOS there was no standard naming convention. Consult the documentation for the application if it is available.

> **WARNING**
>
> If the setup program offers to make changes to the system files, always choose No. If that is not possible, immediately after the installation you should open AUTOEXEC.BAT and CONFIG.SYS in a text editor and remove the lines that were added by the setup program.

### *Running Setup from a Command Prompt*

If the setup program does not run from Windows Explorer, try opening a command-prompt window and running it from there. To do so, choose Start/Programs/Accessories/Command Prompt (in Windows NT/2000/XP) or Start/Programs/Accessories/MS-DOS Prompt (in Windows 9x/Me). Then change to the drive and folder containing the setup file, key its name, and press Enter.

Running from a command prompt can be useful because the command-prompt window remains on the screen after the program terminates. If the program terminates abnormally with an error message, you can see that error message. In contrast, when you run a DOS program by double-clicking it from Windows Explorer, that window closes when the program terminates, so if there was an error message, you would not get to see it.

### *Testing the Application under Windows*

After you run the setup program, try starting the application from its executable (EXE) file. Some applications start from a batch file (BAT) instead, which usually just contains the name of the EXE file along with some switches or parameters that set a particular mode. For example, suppose a paint program's executable file is PPAINT.EXE. There might be a batch file called PPAINT.BAT that contains the line *ppaint.exe /640* that starts the application in 640 x 480 VGA video mode. Use the batch file rather than the EXE file if one is available.

## In Real Life

If the EXE and the BAT file have the same name, and you just key the name without the extension at the command prompt, the BAT file will execute. MS-DOS (and Windows at a command prompt) has an order of preference for program files: BAT, then COM, then EXE.

If the application works by running it from within Windows, then all you need to do is create a shortcut for it on the desktop and/or Start menu. If the application does not run, see "Configuring DOS Applications" later in this chapter for help.

### *Creating the Windows Shortcuts*

To create a shortcut in Windows, hold down the Alt key as you drag the icon for the executable to the desktop. When you release the mouse button, a shortcut will appear. You can then drag it onto the Start menu as discussed earlier in the chapter.

The shortcut will have the same properties as the original, so do not create the shortcut until you have the settings just right for the original EXE file. See the next few sections to learn about the properties you can set for a DOS-based executable file.

## Understanding PIFs

In 16-bit Windows versions (e.g., Windows 3.1), *Program Information Files* (PIFs) are used to store settings for MS-DOS applications that are to be run under Windows. Rather than setting properties for the executable file itself, you create a PIF file for it and set the properties for the PIF. A utility called PIF Editor creates and modifies these files.

**Program Information File (PIF)**

A shortcut for an MS-DOS application that stores any nonstandard properties governing the way the application will start and run.

In Windows 9x/Me, when you edit the properties of an MS-DOS executable file, a PIF file is created in the same location. For example, if you edit the properties of EDIT.COM, a new file called EDIT.PIF is created. It is like a shortcut to EDIT.COM, and you can use it as you would a normal shortcut. However, unlike a normal shortcut, it retains a link to the original, and if you make further changes to the properties of the original, those changes are reflected in the PIF's properties (see Figure 28.13). In Windows 2000 and XP, PIFs still exist and work the same way but they do not have the .pif extension.

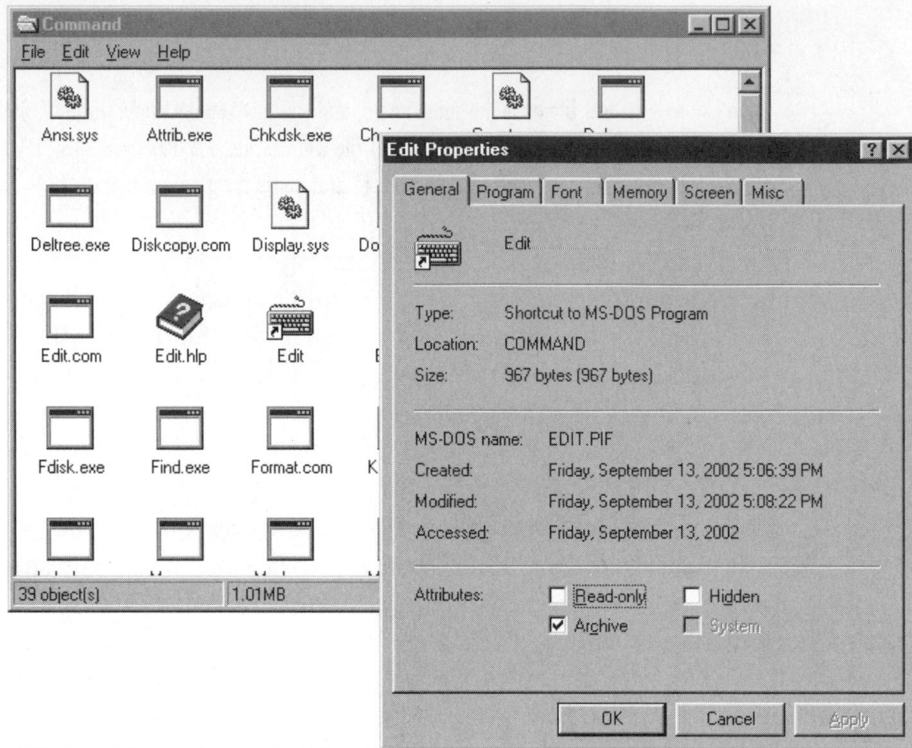


**FIGURE 28.13**
A PIF is a shortcut to an MS-DOS application.

When you want to change the properties for an MS-DOS executable, you can open the Properties dialog box for either the executable itself or its associated PIF; changes made in either location affect both.

## Configuring DOS Applications

The Properties dialog box for a DOS-based executable file is very different from that of a Windows-based executable. There are many more tabs and options, all designed to help you blend the DOS program smoothly into the Windows interface. The following sections look at these settings and explain how to use them to troubleshoot specific problems.

### *Program Settings*

On the Program tab you specify how the program will execute initially. It includes the path to the executable file, the working directory, a shortcut key that will start the application, and more (see Figure 28.14). Table 28.1 describes the various options.

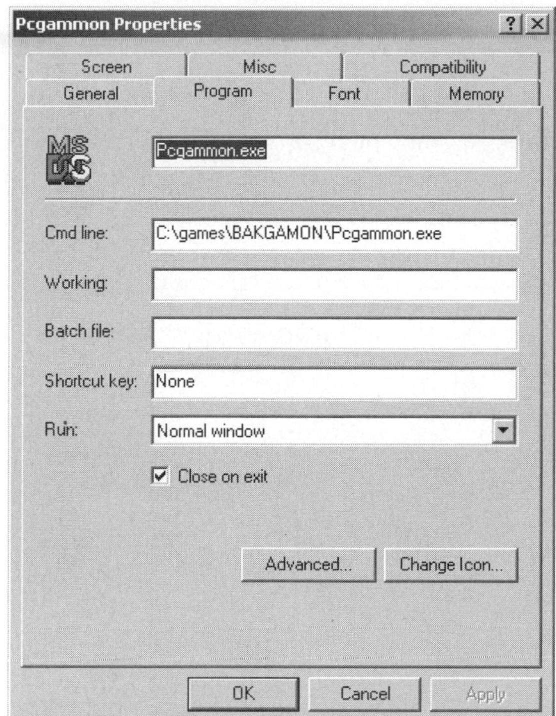


**FIGURE 28.14**
The Program Tab for an MS-DOS Application

| Setting | Purpose |
|---|---|
| Cmd line | The path to the executable file. |
| Working | The working directory (folder) for the application. If an application produces an error message telling you it cannot find certain associated files it needs to run, enter the path to the same folder in which the executable resides. |
| Batch file | A batch file that should run at startup. Rarely used. |
| Shortcut key | A shortcut key combination that starts the application from Windows (you assign it if you want it). |
| Run | Choose Normal, Maximized, or Minimized as the startup mode. This setting is applicable only if the program is set to run in a window (on the Screen tab, discussed later). |
| Close on exit | When checked, closes the MS-DOS window when the program terminates. When cleared, leaves the window open at a command prompt (useful for reading error messages that appear after the program ends). |
| Advanced | In Windows 9x, allows you to set up the application for MS-DOS mode (see "Running an Application in MS-DOS Mode" later in this chapter). In Windows 2000/XP, allows you to select custom MS-DOS initialization files. |
| Change Icon | Allows you to select a different icon to be associated with the application. |

**TABLE 28.1**
Program Settings for an MS-DOS Application

**Text-mode application**

An application that relies on the standard Extended ASCII character set for its display, rather than a graphic mode.

### *Font Settings*

On the Font tab you choose the font to be used at command prompts displayed in the window, and also in *text-mode applications*. You can choose Bitmap Only, TrueType Only, or Both Font Types; this governs which fonts appear on your list of choices. You can then select a font based on its size. The sizes are listed as number x number, such as 2 x 4 or 3 x 5. This refers to the height and width of the characters (see Figure 28.15).

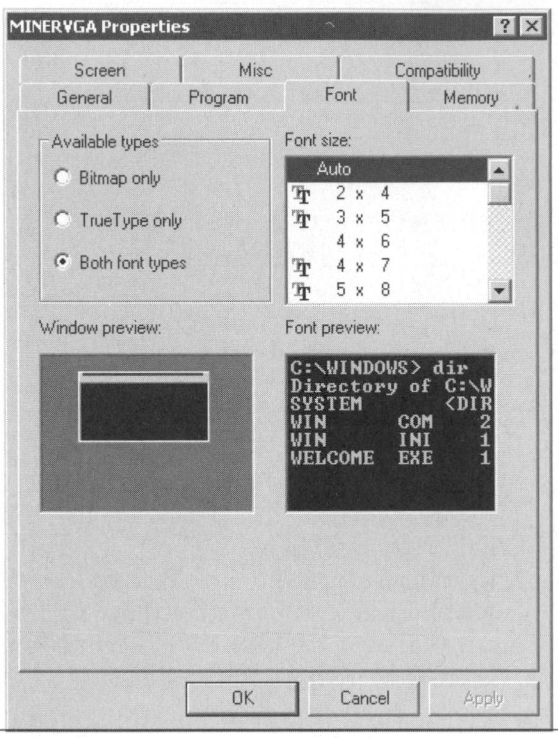


**FIGURE 28.15**
The Font Tab in the Properties Dialog Box for an MS-DOS Application

Auto is the best choice unless you have a reason to want a different size. Some applications are written assuming that a certain font size will be used, and if you use any other font size they do not look right.

### *Memory Settings*

Settings on the Memory tab control how Windows allocates memory to the application as it starts and runs. Auto is the best setting in almost all cases. Table 28.2 lists and explains the settings on this tab.

| Setting | Purpose |
|---|---|
| Conventional Memory: Total | Specifies the maximum amount of conventional memory this program can use. There is usually no reason to limit it; Auto is the default. |
| Conventional Memory: Initial Environment | Specifies the amount of conventional memory allocated to the application when it starts up. Again, Auto is the default. |
| Conventional Memory: Protected | This check box prevents the program from performing nonstandard operations, to which Windows might object, on the memory allocated to it. Some programmers of MS-DOS programs handle memory usage in unusual ways, which is fine when running the program under DOS but might cause problems when running it under Windows. Try enabling this if the application keeps terminating with errors when you try to run it. |
| Expanded (EMS) Memory | Specifies the amount of expanded memory allocated to the application. Auto is the default. Set it to 0 to allow no EMS. |
| Extended (XMS) Memory | Specifies the amount of extended memory allocated to the application. Auto is the default. Set it to 0 to allow no XMS. |
| Uses HMA | Specifies whether the application can use the high memory area if it wants to. |
| MS-DOS Protected Mode (DPMI) Memory | Specifies the amount of DPMI memory the program can use. This is an issue only when run under Windows 9x; Windows NT/2000/XP do not use DPMI. |

**TABLE 28.2**
Memory Settings for an MS-DOS Application

### *Screen Settings*

The Screen tab enables you to control the video mode in which the application runs and the way Windows allocates memory to its display. The most common setting here is Usage; you can choose Full Screen or Window. If you choose Window the program will run in a window on the desktop; Full Screen makes it look more like it would appear running under DOS. (To return to Windows from Full Screen, press Alt + Tab.) Table 28.3 outlines this and the other settings.

| Setting | Purpose |
|---|---|
| Usage | Choose Full Screen or Window. Window may be more taxing on system RAM; choose Full Screen for video most like the original. |
| Initial Size | Windows 9x only. Enables you to specify an initial size for the window, in number of lines. |
| Display Toolbar | Windows 9x only. Displays a toolbar below the Title bar when the application is running in a window. |
| Restore Settings at Startup | If you are running the application in a window (see above), this setting remembers the size and position of the window when you exit the program and restores the settings the next time you start it. |
| Fast ROM Emulation | Specifies whether the display driver should emulate any of the video functions in ROM. |
| Dynamic Memory Allocation | For applications that can operate in either text or graphics mode, this feature allows the program to release the extra memory needed for graphics mode when it switches to text mode, freeing it up for other applications. |

**TABLE 28.3**
Screen Settings for an MS-DOS Application

### *Miscellaneous Settings*

The Misc tab contains a variety of unrelated settings for dealing with the mouse, keyboard, screen saver, and so on. Table 28.4 lists and explains them (see Figure 28.16).

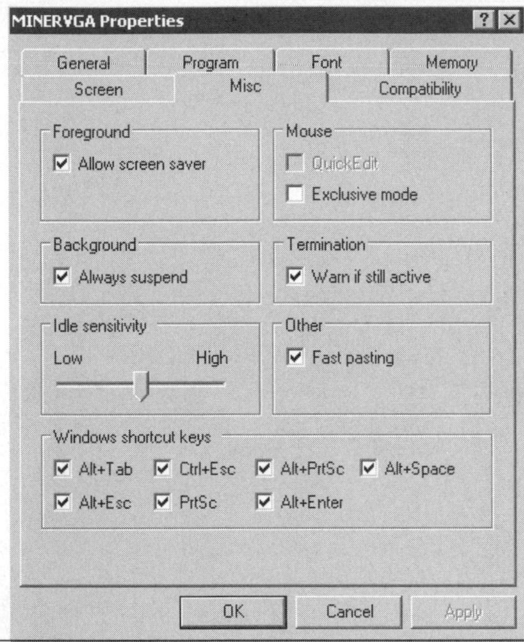


**FIGURE 28.16**
Miscellaneous settings cover keyboard, mouse, and screen saver.

**TABLE 28.4**
Miscellaneous Settings for an MS-DOS Application

| Setting | Purpose |
|---|---|
| Allow screen saver | Some MS-DOS programs will not restore their display after the screen saver has been enabled; you can clear this check box to prevent that from being a problem. |
| QuickEdit | When enabled, you can use the mouse to select text for copying and cutting to the Windows clipboard. This is an option only under Windows 9x. When disabled, you must use the Mark command in the window's control menu to select text to be cut or copied to the Clipboard. |
| Exclusive mode | Dedicates the mouse exclusively to this application. This is not normally a good idea because the mouse then stops working as a regular pointer in Windows, but it might be necessary if the mouse is not working correctly in the application. |
| Always suspend | When active, suspends the application when it is not active rather than allowing it to keep running in the background. |
| Warn if still active | Displays a warning message if you try to close the window while the application is still running. |
| Idle sensitivity | This slider controls how long the application will wait for input before reducing the resources assigned to it so that other running applications will have more resources. Low sensitivity makes it wait longer. |
| Fast pasting | Enables a faster method of pasting into the application. The default is On, but clear this check box if you have problems with pasting. |
| Windows shortcut keys | When both Windows and an application have the same shortcut key assignments, Windows wins. If you want the MS-DOS application to use the shortcut keys, clear the check box for a particular key combination. |

### *Compatibility Settings*

Compatibility mode is a new feature in Windows XP. It applies not only to MS-DOS applications but also to Windows-based programs that predate Windows XP. The Compatibility tab contains options that enable you to run the application in an OS environment that emulates an earlier version of Windows (NT 4, 95, 98, or 2000), or that uses a reduced-quality video mode. This may be useful for troubleshooting problems with applications that used to run under earlier Windows versions but will not run under Windows XP. Windows XP also has a Program Compatibility Wizard on the Accessories menu. Compatibility features are not covered on the current A+ exam.

## Running an Application in MS-DOS Mode

MS-DOS mode is a last resort for running an MS-DOS program that will not run any other way under Windows 95 or 98. It works by deleting part of Windows out of memory, down to an environment that more closely resembles MS-DOS, and then running the application in that environment. It is not available in Windows Me, NT 4, 2000, or XP. When the application terminates, Windows reloads.

If an application refuses to run under Windows 95 or 98, try MS-DOS mode by doing the following:

1. Display the properties for the application.
2. On the Program tab, click Advanced. The Advanced Program Settings dialog box appears (see Figure 28.17).
3. If the application will not run because it detects that Windows is running, mark the Prevent MS-DOS Based Programs from Detecting Windows check box.
4. To try MS-DOS mode, mark the MS-DOS mode check box.
5. If you want a warning to appear before the application enters MS-DOS mode, mark the Warn before entering MS-DOS mode check box.
6. If you want to use the standard startup options when entering MS-DOS mode, leave the Use current MS-DOS configuration option selected. Alternatively, choose Specify a new MS-DOS configuration and then edit the CONFIG.SYS and AUTOEXEC.BAT content listed.
7. Click OK. Then try running the program. If it does not work, you can come back to this tab and tweak the AUTOEXEC.BAT and CONFIG.SYS files.

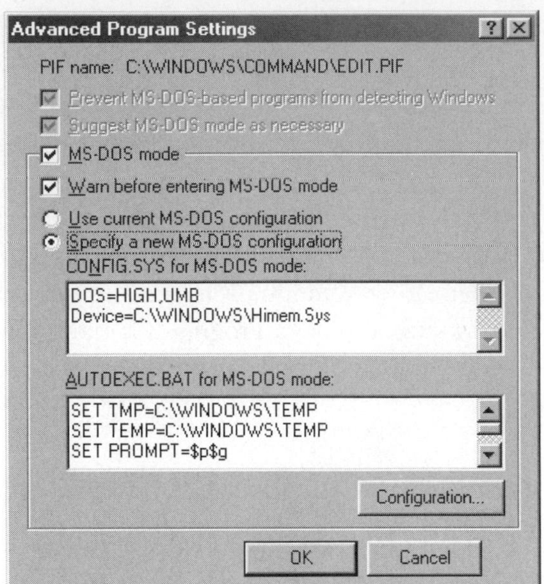


**FIGURE 28.17**
Setting Up for MS-DOS Mode in Windows 98

The AUTOEXEC.BAT settings listed in the dialog box in Figure 28.17 might not come from the regular AUTOEXEC.BAT file. If there is a DOSSTART.BAT file present in the *Windows* folder, it takes the settings from there instead as the defaults. See the following section for more information.

## Using DOSSTART.BAT

DOSSTART.BAT is a batch file that substitutes itself for AUTOEXEC.BAT whenever you run a program in MS-DOS mode or whenever you restart the PC in MS-DOS mode through the Start/Shut Down command. DOSSTART.BAT is useful because it can load utilities that are needed in MS-DOS mode but not in normal Windows operation, such as MSCDEX.EXE or a mouse utility like MOUSE.COM.

Depending on the system, DOSSTART.BAT might or might not exist. If items were removed from AUTOEXEC.BAT during Windows 95 or 98 Setup, those lines might have been moved to DOSSTART.BAT. If you did a clean install of Windows 95/98, you probably will not have a DOSSTART.BAT unless you created it manually.

To create a DOSSTART.BAT file, start with the current AUTOEXEC.BAT if there is one and then add (or un-rem) lines in it that support MS-DOS mode. You can do this by opening AUTOEXEC.BAT in Notepad and then saving it as C:\Windows\DOSSTART.BAT.

DOSSTART.BAT does not exist and cannot be used in Windows 2000 or XP.

## Troubleshooting Problems with Applications

The following sections explain several types of application errors and provide troubleshooting guidelines for them. The error message that appears will tell which type of error it is.

### General Protection Fault (GPF)

As explained in Chapter 27, this error occurs when an application tries to do something that would compromise the stability of Windows itself or of another application. For example, a GPF might occur when an application tries to directly access a hardware device or tries to use an area of memory that another application is already using. This usually occurs only with 16-bit applications or applications that have internal programming flaws.

A GPF is a " blue screen of death" error, in computer slang, because the error message appears in white letters on a bright blue background. Some other error types (mostly serious ones) also appear on blue screens, but the GPF is the most common.

When a GPF occurs, make a note of the name of the file that caused the error and restart your computer. The problem may not recur. If it does recur repeatedly and the same file is the cause every time, try reinstalling the associated program or using the EXTRACT command to reinstall the file from the Windows CD (if it is a Windows file).

### Illegal Operation

An illegal operation is similar to a GPF except it is confined to a single application. An illegal operation occurs when an application tries to do something that it cannot do, such as access a system file that is missing or corrupted. An illegal operation message typically appears in a Windows dialog box (not a blue screen), and results in the application's being terminated.

When an illegal operation occurs, restart the application. If the same error occurs again, restart the PC. If the error continues to reappear, reinstall the application. If that does not help, check with the application's manufacturer to see whether an update or patch is available that will solve the problem.

Sometimes illegal operation errors can be the result of corrupt or incompatible video or sound card drivers, so check for updates of those drivers too if the problem persists.

## Invalid Working Directory

A working directory is a folder where the application stores its temporary files as it works, and where it looks for the support files it needs to operate. By default, Windows uses the same folder for the working directory as that in which the executable file resides. When you view the properties for an executable file, one of the settings on the Program tab is Working, which is where you can specify a working directory.

The most common cause of an invalid working directory error is that the working directory is a network location that is currently offline. The error can also occur if the working directory has been moved or deleted. If it has been moved or deleted, recreate it. If a network location is unavailable, troubleshoot the network access problem.

As noted above, MS-DOS applications have a Working setting on the Program tab; you can enter a working directory there. Windows application shortcuts have a Start In text box that serves a similar purpose; you can enter a different working directory there.

## Application Not Responding (System Lockup)

This is not an error message, but a condition in which the application stops responding. It might be limited to a single application or it might affect the entire system.

When an application stops responding, the best course of action is to restart Windows immediately. You sometimes can terminate the unresponsive application and continue working, but other errors are likely to occur.

Use the following procedure to perform a controlled shutdown/restart when encountering an unresponsive application:

1. If possible, switch away from the unresponsive application, to any other applications that are open. Save your work in each of them and shut them down. The reason: sometimes when you terminate an unresponsive application, it sets off a chain reaction of errors that affect other applications, so closing all other applications before you attempt to terminate it can minimize the amount of unsaved data you might lose. If you cannot switch away from the unresponsive application, go on to step 2.
2. Display the Task Manager and attempt to shut down the unresponsive application. The specifics for displaying Task Manager depend on the Windows version; see the following sections for details. If you cannot display Task Manager, go on to step 3.

3. Restart Windows with the Start/Shut Down command or by clicking the Shut Down button in the Task Manager. If that is not possible, go on to step 4.
4. If the system is locked up and will not shut down normally, press the Reset or Power button on the PC. Then run ScanDisk (Windows 9x) or Check Disk (Windows 2000/XP) when Windows restarts to make sure there are no file system errors caused by the improper shutdown. The utilities may run automatically; see Chapter 30 for more information about them.

The underlying cause of an application's not responding may include any of the following:

- One-time problem that might not reoccur
- Error in the programming; look for an update online
- Incompatibility between a hardware driver and the application
- Conflict with some other application

### *Working with Task Manager in Windows 9x*

The Task Manager in Windows 9x appears as a Close Program window when you press Ctrl + Alt + Delete. To shut down an unresponsive application:

1. Press Ctrl + Alt + Delete.
2. In the Close Program window (Figure 28.18), select the application. It might or might not say *Not Responding* next to it.

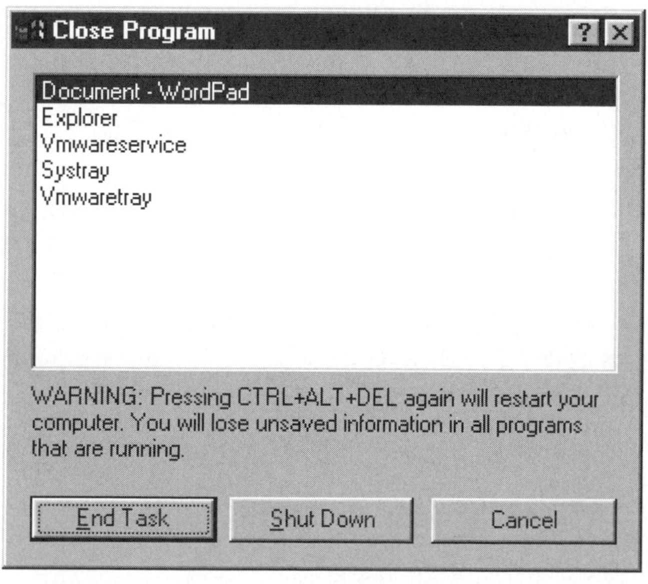


**FIGURE 28.18**
In Windows 9x, shut down an unresponsive application in the Close Program window.

3. Wait a few seconds. The application may shut down immediately and disappear from the list in the Close Program window, or a warning box may appear stating that the program is not responding, as in Figure 28.19. If the latter happens, click the End Task button in that window to shut it down.
4. In the Close Program window, shut down any other applications that say *Not Responding* next to their names. If there are none, click Shut Down to shut down the PC; then restart it.

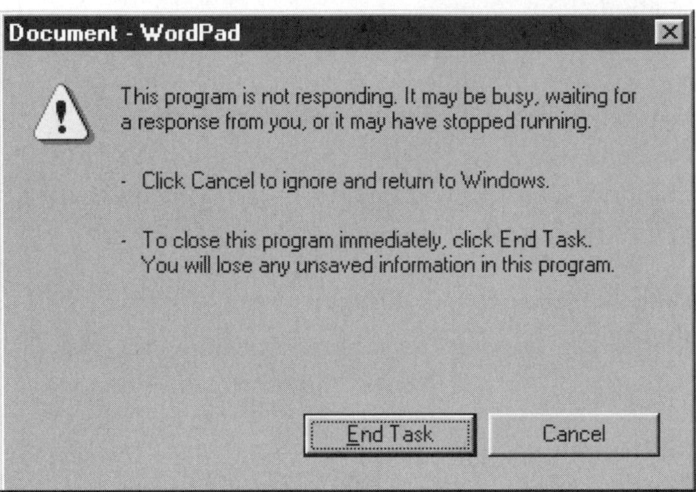


**FIGURE 28.19**
End the task if a warning box appears indicating it is unresponsive.

### *Working with Task Manager in Windows 2000/XP*

Ctrl + Alt + Delete has more than one function in Windows 2000/XP, so it does not immediately bring up a task list. Use the following steps to shut down an unresponsive application in Windows 2000/XP:

1. Press Ctrl + Alt + Delete. A Windows Security dialog box appears.
2. Click the Task Manager button. The Windows Task Manager window appears.
3. Click the unresponsive application in the task list. It may or may not report *Not Responding* in the Status column (see Figure 28.20).
4. Click End Task. The application may terminate immediately or a warning box like the one in Figure 28.19 might appear; if it does, click End Task (or End Now; the wording might vary slightly).
5. Shut down any other unresponsive applications, and then click Shut Down to shut down the PC. Restart the PC.

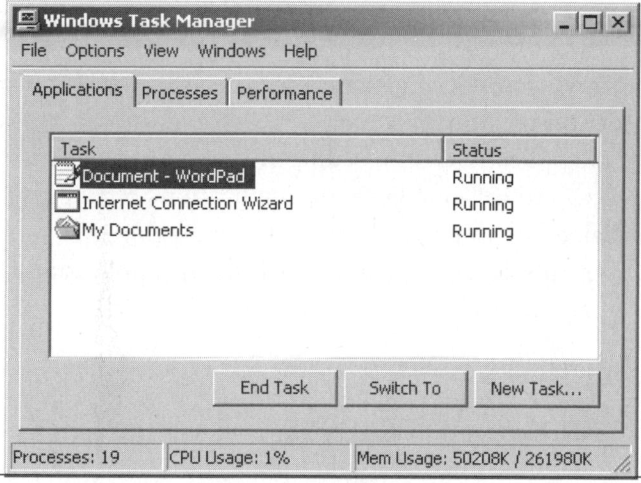


**FIGURE 28.20**
Shut down an unresponsive Windows 2000/XP application in the Windows Task Manager window.

# STUDY GUIDE

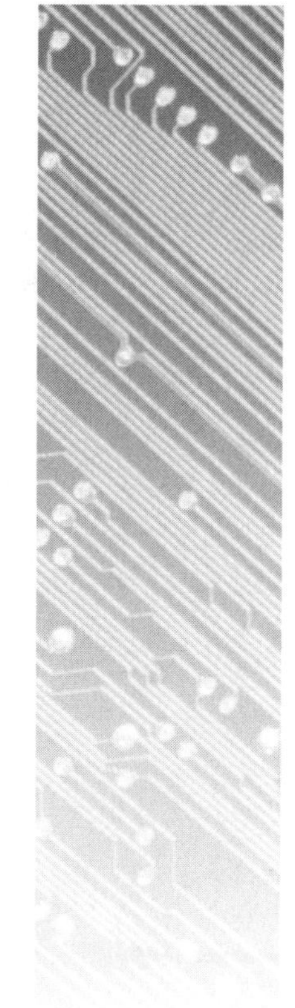

Use the following summaries to review the key concepts of this chapter.

## INSTALLING WINDOWS APPLICATIONS

- A typical Windows application installs via a Setup.exe program. It may run automatically when you insert the CD, or you might need to double-click the CD icon in My Computer.
- A downloaded application will be either in EXE or ZIP format. An EXE file is either a self-extracting compressed archive or a setup program. A ZIP file is a compressed archive containing the files needed for setup.
- WinZip is a ZIP utility that enables Windows to compress and decompress ZIP files. Windows XP supports ZIP format natively so WinZip is not needed.
- An application that has no setup utility usually requires no Registry edits. Simply create a shortcut to its executable file on the desktop and/or the Start menu.
- If you do not have the appropriate permission to install an application when logged on as the current user, right-click the Setup file and choose Run As to run as an administrator.
- Shut down all running programs before running a setup program, to avoid conflicts.

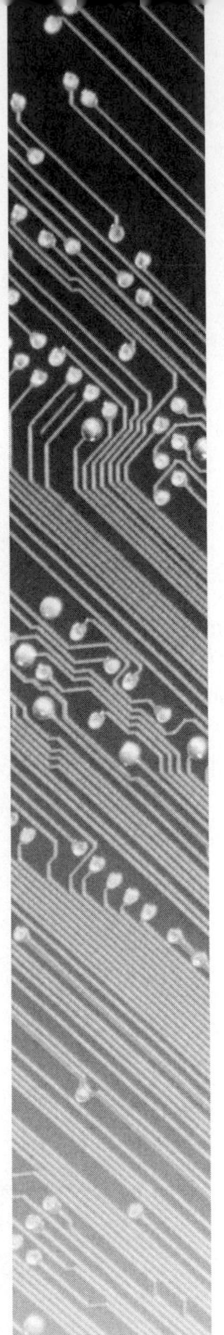

## Controlling Whether an Application Loads at Startup

- To make an application load at startup, place a shortcut for it in the *StartUp* folder on the Start menu.
- To prevent an application from loading at startup, remove its shortcut from the *StartUp* folder, or change the application's settings in its Properties dialog box to prevent automatic loading.
- If neither of the above works, you can disable the application from the System Configuration Utility (MSCONFIG) or edit the Registry manually.

## Removing Windows Applications

- Use an application's own Uninstall routine if possible.
- If there is no Uninstall, use Add/Remove Programs through the Control Panel to remove an application.
- Only as a last resort should you manually delete an application's files from the hard disk.

## Reorganizing the Start/Programs Menu

- Most Windows versions enable you to drag and drop shortcuts on the Start menu to reorganize it.
- You can also right-click the Taskbar, choose Properties, and then select the Advanced tab to add or modify items on the Start menu.
- You can right-click the Start button and choose Explore to view the Start menu's content in a file management window.

## Adding and Removing Windows Components

- Windows comes with a variety of optional components you can install or remove.
- Double-click the *Add/Remove Programs* icon in the Control Panel.
- In Windows 9x/Me, select the Windows Setup tab and mark or clear check boxes for the options you want.
- In Windows 2000/XP, click the Add/Remove Windows Components button and then mark or clear check boxes for the options you want.
- A check box with a gray background indicates that some but not all options in a category are already installed.

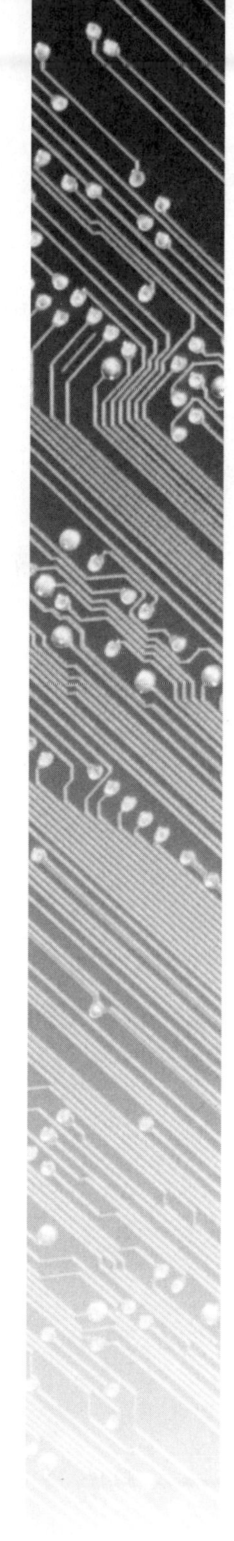

## Working with MS-DOS Applications

- Some MS-DOS applications run well under Windows; others do not. It is largely a matter of trying them under various Windows versions to see what works.
- When you install an MS-DOS application, the setup program may want to modify CONFIG.SYS or AUTOEXEC.BAT; do not let it do so if possible.
- Other common problems with running MS-DOS applications might include video and sound incompatibilities and problems switching back and forth between the application and Windows.
- Most problems can be corrected by adjusting the properties for the MS-DOS program's executable file.
- A Program Information File (PIF) is a shortcut that stores the settings for an MS-DOS program running under Windows. It is created automatically when you make a change to the executable file's properties.
- Windows XP has a Compatibility tab in the Properties dialog box for executable files that enables you to run the application in a simulated version of an earlier Windows version.
- MS-DOS mode enables Windows 95 and 98 to more closely resemble MS-DOS for the benefit of specific applications. Choose Restart in MS-DOS mode from the Shut Down menu or set up an application to use it by choosing Advanced from the Program tab of its Properties dialog box.
- DOSSTART.BAT is a substitute for AUTOEXEC.BAT that executes when you run MS-DOS mode on Windows 95 or 98.

## Troubleshooting Problems with Applications

- A General Protection Fault (GPF) occurs when an application tries to do something that would compromise the stability of another application or of Windows. It typically presents a blue-screen error message.
- An illegal operation is similar to a GPF except it is confined to a single application, and results in a Windows-based error message box and the application's being terminated.
- After a GPF or illegal operation, you should restart the PC.
- A working directory is the directory (folder) an application uses for its temporary storage as it operates. This can be specified in the properties for the executable file. If that directory is unavailable, an Invalid Working Directory error appears.

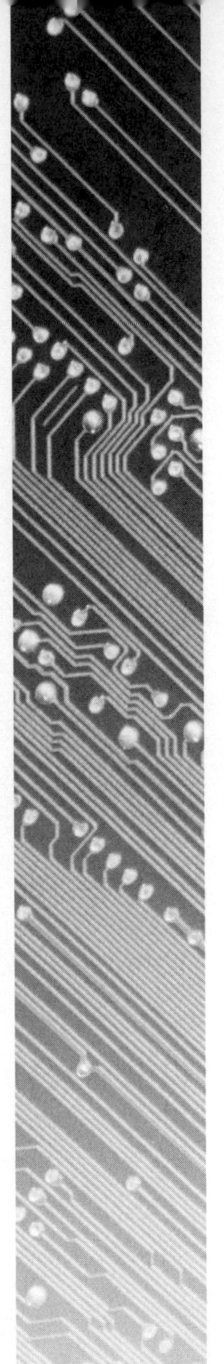

- When an application stops responding, save your work in any other running applications if possible; then use Task Manager to shut down the application, and restart Windows.
- Press Ctrl + Alt + Delete in Windows 9x to open the Close Program window; this is the same as the Task Manager in Windows 9x.
- In Windows 2000/XP press Ctrl + Alt + Delete and then click the Task Manager button.

# PRACTICE TEST

On a blank sheet of paper, write the answers to the following multiple-choice questions and explain why each answer is correct.

1. What file must be present on a CD in order for the setup program to run automatically when you insert a CD in the drive?
   a. Setup.exe
   b. Autoplay.exe
   c. Autorun.inf
   d. The files on the CD have nothing to do with it.

2. What is a ZIP file?
   a. a compressed archive containing one or more files
   b. a partition compressed with DriveSpace
   c. a 100MB or 250MB floppy disk that fits in a Zip drive
   d. None of the above

3. What is the best way to modify the Registry when installing a 16-bit Windows application that does not come with a setup program?
   a. REGEDIT
   b. MSCONFIG
   c. SYSINFO
   d. You do not have to edit the Registry for such an application.

4. How can you place a shortcut on the Start menu for an application that does not come with a setup program?
   a. It cannot be done.
   b. Drag it onto the Start button from the desktop or a file management window.
   c. Right-click the Start button and choose Add.
   d. Right-click the Taskbar and choose Add.

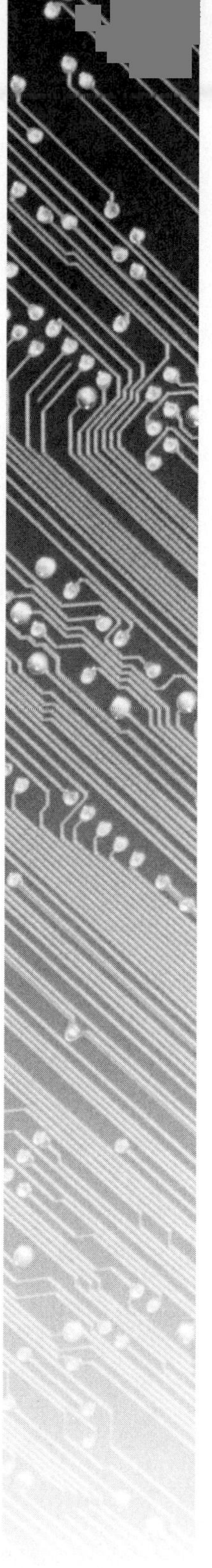

5. To run a setup program as an administrator, you must
   a. log off the current user and log on as Administrator.
   b. log off the current user and log on as any user with Administrator access.
   c. right-click the setup program and choose Run As, then enter the user name and password for a user with Administrator access.
   d. Any of the above will work.

6. Why should you shut down other running programs before installing an application?
   a. shared files may be in use and unable to be updated if you do not
   b. to avoid potential virus infection
   c. to free up system resources
   d. All of the above

7. Why should you disable the antivirus program before installing an application?
   a. It might be using shared files that need to be updated.
   b. The antivirus program might think the setup program is a virus and prevent it from running correctly.
   c. The antivirus program uses a great many system resources that the setup program needs to run correctly.
   d. There is no reason to disable the antivirus program.

8. In what folder should you place a shortcut for a program that you want to load at startup?
   a. *System tools*
   b. *StartUp*
   c. *MSCONFIG*
   d. *Win.cnf*

9. In what utility can you prevent items from loading at startup by clearing check boxes?
   a. REGEDIT
   b. SYSEDIT
   c. SYSUTIL
   d. MSCONFIG

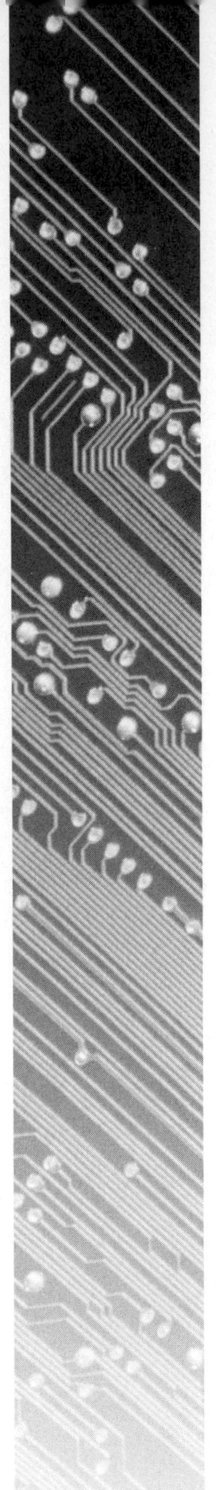

10. What file does Windows rely on to tell it how to uninstall a program through Add/Remove programs?
    a. INSTALL.LOG
    b. a Microsoft Installation file (.msi extension)
    c. UNINSTALL.LOG
    d. either a or b

11. Which Control Panel applet allows you to add and remove Windows components?
    a. Add/Remove Programs
    b. Windows Setup
    c. Windows Components
    d. Add New Programs

12. When adding or removing Windows components, what does a gray background in a check box for a category mean?
    a. Some components cannot be installed.
    b. Some components are already installed, but not all of them.
    c. All of the components in the category are already installed.
    d. There are no components in the category.

13. What is the best way to edit the Registry when installing an MS-DOS program under Windows?
    a. REGEDIT
    b. REGEDT32
    c. MSCONFIG
    d. You do not have to edit the Registry for MS-DOS programs.

14. If the setup utility for a DOS program modifies any system files automatically, which files are those likely to be?
    a. WIN.INI and SYSTEM.INI
    b. AUTOEXEC.BAT and CONFIG.SYS
    c. IO.SYS and MSDOS.SYS
    d. MSCDEX.EXE and MSDOS.SYS

15. What is a PIF?
    a. a file containing settings for running a DOS program under Windows
    b. an INF file containing system startup instructions for Windows 95
    c. a driver that allows hardware to interact directly with MS-DOS programs
    d. an information file for 16-bit Windows applications running under 32-bit Windows versions

16. How do you set up an application to run in MS-DOS mode through the program's Properties dialog box?
    a. Click the Advanced button on the Program tab.
    b. Click the MS-DOS button on the General tab.
    c. Click the MS-DOS button on the Advanced tab.
    d. Click the Advanced button on the Screen tab.

17. The Font setting for an MS-DOS application applies to what type of application?
    a. graphics mode
    b. text mode
    c. bitmap
    d. All of the above

18. What is the purpose of DOSSTART.BAT?
    a. Along with IO.SYS and MSDOS.SYS, it starts up an MSDOS system.
    b. It substitutes for CONFIG.SYS when booting into MS-DOS mode.
    c. It substitutes for IO.SYS when booting into MSDOS mode.
    d. It substitutes for AUTOEXEC.BAT when booting into MS-DOS mode.

19. Which type of error is likely to cause a blue-screen error message?
    a. illegal operation
    b. General Protection Fault
    c. error in CONFIG.SYS
    d. Invalid directory

20. What key combination opens the Close Program window in Windows 9x to shut down an unresponsive application?
    a. Ctrl + Break
    b. Ctrl + Alt + Insert
    c. Ctrl + Delete
    d. Ctrl + Alt + Delete

# TROUBLESHOOTING

1. You are installing a new application under Windows 2000, and the setup program for it seems to proceed normally until the final step. Then a message appears that you do not have the appropriate security settings to modify the Registry, and it terminates. What can you do?

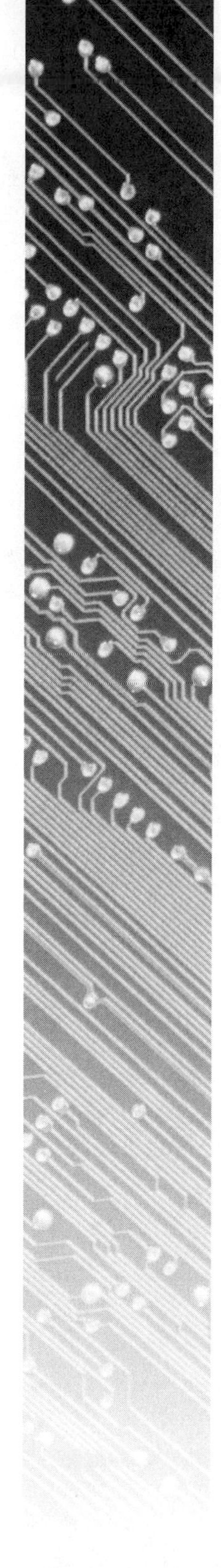

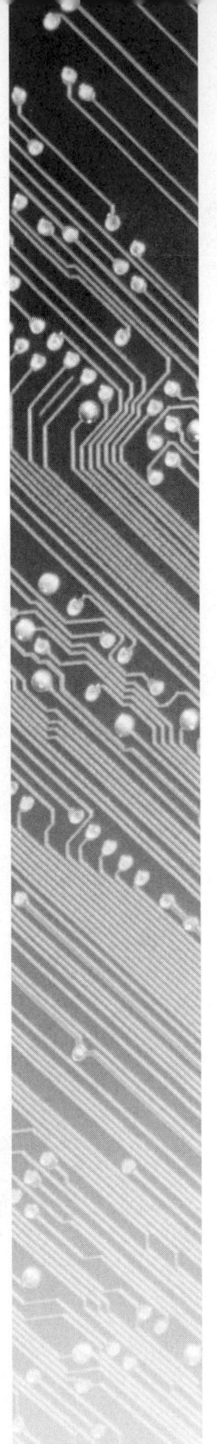

2. You are trying to get an old MS-DOS game to run under Windows 2000, but are not having much luck. When you try to run it from its executable file, a DOS window opens and some text appears, but the window closes again so quickly that you cannot read it. Explain how you would prevent that window from closing so you can see what error it is sending you.
3. You have tried to get a DOS program to run under Windows, but it will not. You set it up to run in MS-DOS mode, and it does run that way, but the mouse does not work. Explain how you could fix this problem.

# CUSTOMER SERVICE

1. A client wants to install a new application, but when he puts the CD in the drive nothing happens. Describe how you would coach him to start the setup program for the application.
2. A client calls you saying she has received a program file with a .zip extension and does not know what do to with it. Describe how you would coach her to unzip and install the file.
3. A client wants to transfer some games from an old Windows 3.1 PC to his new Windows XP PC. He does not have the original setup disks for them. What do you suggest?

# 29 Managing Files

## ON THE TEST

**A+ Operating System Technologies Examination**

- **Objective 1.1:** Identify the operating system's functions, structure, and major system files to navigate the operating system and how to get to needed technical information.
- **Objective 1.2:** Identify basic concepts and procedures for creating, viewing and managing files, directories and disks. This includes procedures for changing file attributes and the ramifications of those changes (for example, security issues).

## ON THE JOB

PC technicians must have a thorough understanding of file management under a variety of operating systems, including MS-DOS, Windows 9x, and Windows NT, 2000, and XP. This chapter assumes that you are already proficient at tasks such as moving, copying, renaming, and deleting files; these are tasks that you will likely need to train end users to perform. It also helps you understand file systems and introduces command-line file management.

Some of the tasks for which this chapter will prepare you include the following:

- selecting an appropriate file system for a PC, given its OS and compatibility requirements
- explaining the Windows file management interface to end users
- teaching end users how to move, copy, delete, and rename files and folders
- configuring the Recycle Bin
- adding or removing file attributes such as Read-Only and Archive
- enabling NTFS compression or encryption
- troubleshooting file management error messages

- backing up and restoring files
- working with a command prompt

## Understanding File Systems

**File system**

A logical method of storing data on a disk. Examples include FAT and NTFS.

A *file system* is a logical method of storing data on a disk. The file system determines what identifiers will be used to mark the beginning and end of a file, what information will be stored in the master listing of the disk content, what properties can be assigned to files and folders, and much more.

Different operating systems support different file systems. For example, Windows 95 supports FAT16 for hard drives, while Windows 2000 supports a much wider array of file systems for hard drives, including NTFS 5, FAT16, and FAT32. The "for hard drives" part is significant because other drive types have their own file systems. For example, floppy disks use FAT12 and CDs use CDFS.

### How File Systems Store Data

Because disk storage is random access, files do not need to be stored in any specific physical location; the File Allocation Table (FAT) keeps track of what is stored where. For example, in Figure 29.1 the File Allocation Table knows the file name and the starting cluster. That cluster holds the data for the first part of the file and a pointer to the cluster containing the second part. The next cluster contains more of the data file and either another pointer to another cluster or an end-of-file marker.

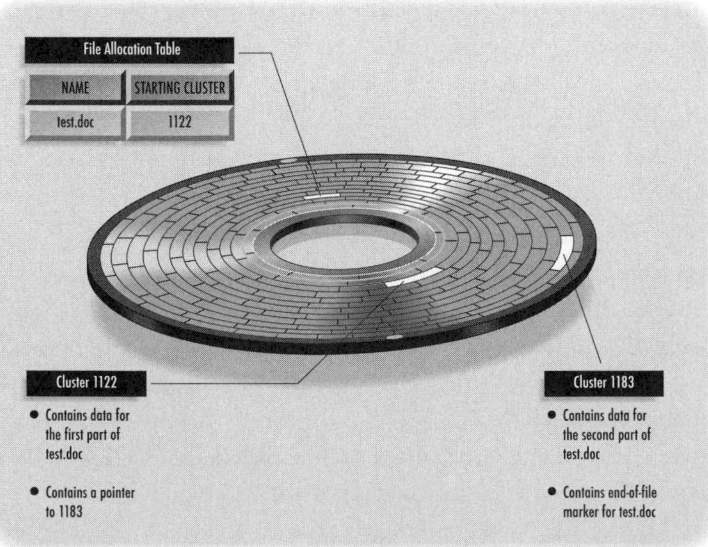


**FIGURE 29.1**
How a FAT-Based Disk Stores Data

The File Allocation Table does not store information about every file on the whole disk; it keeps track only of the root directory (that is, the top-level folder). Other folders appear as simple entries in FAT. When the operating system calls for a file within one of those folders, FAT passes on the request to the folder. The folder maintains its own directory of where the files within it are stored (see Figure 29.2).

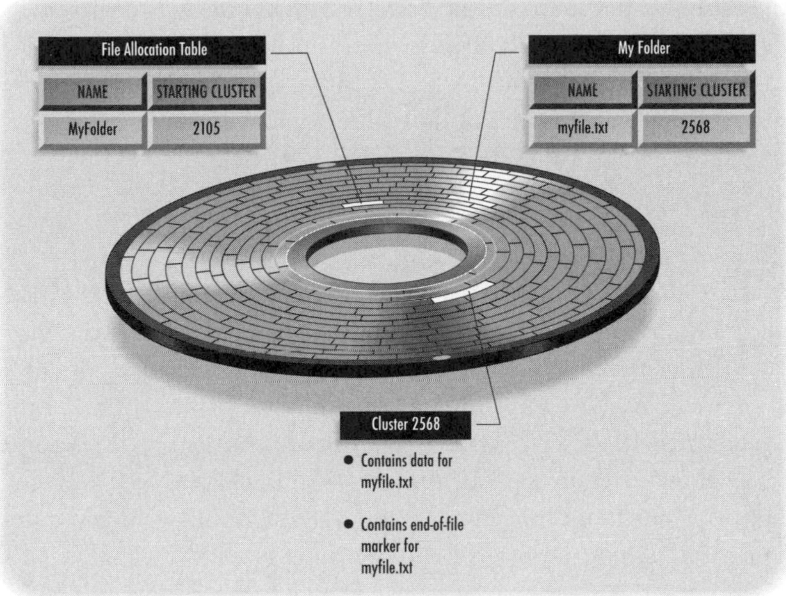


**FIGURE 29.2**
The Path to C:\MyFolder\myfile.txt

Figures 29.1 and 29.2 show a FAT system; other file systems work similarly but with some minor variations.

## File Systems on MS-DOS and Windows PCs

In earlier chapters we looked at several of the major file systems, including FAT, FAT32, and NTFS, in the context of partitioning and formatting drives. The following sections cover each of the systems and note the differences among them.

### *FAT (FAT16)*

*FAT* was the original file system used for MS-DOS and the original version of Windows 95. All other Windows versions support it, for backward compatibility. It is a 16-bit file system, so it supports up to 2GB of data per logical drive. At the time it was created that seemed ample, but as technology advanced, users wanted larger drives.

**FAT (also called FAT16)**

The original 16-bit file system for MS-DOS; also used in Windows 95 and supported by nearly all operating systems for backward compatibility.

Why a 2GB limit for FAT16? The maximum number of addressable locations that can be stored with 16-bit binary numbers is 65,526 (2 to the 16th power). As you learned earlier in the book, when we were discussing drive formatting, a drive can be formatted using any of several different cluster sizes. If each cluster is 32KB in size (the largest size possible), times 65,556, 2GB of space results.

Recall from our earlier discussion of clusters that the larger the cluster size, the more wasted space on the drive. That is because two files cannot share a cluster. If a file is only 8KB in size, it must have its own 32KB cluster, wasting 24KB of space. A FAT16 drive can use a smaller cluster size, such as 8KB, but because of its 16-bit limitation the drive size is then much smaller (65,526 times 8KB, or about 524MB).

### *FAT32*

**FAT32**

A 32-bit version of the FAT file system, provided with Windows 95 OSR2 and higher.

*FAT32* is an improved version of FAT16. Its main benefit is that it uses 32-bit binary numbering to define the addressable clusters, so the maximum drive size can be much larger while still maintaining a relatively small cluster size. The 32-bit addressing means that there can be over 250 million addressable clusters. At 4KB per cluster (a small, efficient cluster size), that equates to about 2 terabytes (TB) of data. Windows 95 OSR2 and all Windows versions that came after it support FAT32 (including Windows 98, 2000, and XP). Windows NT 4.0 does not support FAT32.

### *FAT12*

**FAT12**

A 12-bit file system used on floppy disks, supported by all operating systems.

*FAT12* is the file system used on floppy disks. As you might expect from the name, it uses a 12-bit addressing system. Floppy disks address each sector individually; each 512-byte sector is its own cluster. That means there can be a maximum of 4,096 sectors per disk, and a disk can contain up to 2,097,152 bytes (about 2MB)—in theory. When formatted, however, a standard floppy disk holds 1.44MB. All operating system versions support FAT12, but only for floppies.

**New Technology File System (NTFS)**

A 32-bit file system for NT-based versions of Windows.

### *NTFS 4*

**NTFS 4**

The version of the New Technology File System (NTFS) that comes with Windows NT 4.0.

The *New Technology File System* (NTFS) is a 32-bit file system; version 4 was introduced with Windows NT 4.0. *NTFS 4.0* predates FAT32; it offered 32-bit file system support back when FAT16 was the only other choice. It also has some features that none of the FAT file systems offer, such as file compression, the ability to set permissions for individual files, and the ability to create a *spanned disk*. Only Windows NT 4.0 can read NTFS 4 disks. Windows 2000 and XP can convert an NTFS 4 disk to NTFS 5 (see below).

**Spanned disk**

A logical drive that uses space on more than one physical disk.

### *TFS 5*

*NTFS 5* was introduced with Windows 2000, and continues in Windows XP. It is an improved version of NTFS 4, and offers additional features such as file encryption, disk quotas, and dynamic disks.

**NTFS 5**

The version of the New Technology File System (NTFS) that comes with Windows 2000 and XP.

### *HPFS*

The *High Performance File System* (HPFS) was the native file system for IBM's OS/2 operating system. It can support logical drives of up to 64GB, and has some minor advantages over FAT in the way it indexes files on a disk. However, since few PCs use OS/2 anymore, it is all but obsolete.

**High Performance File System (HPFS)**

A file system used by the OS/2 operating system; now obsolete.

**TRY IT!**

Identify the file systems used on all of the drives in all the PCs you have available. Is each of them using the file system that you would have chosen for them? If not, what would you have chosen differently, given each PC's operating system and purpose?

## Using the Windows File Management Interface

The file management interface in Windows includes any window in which you see a list of files and folders. In early Windows versions (95, for example) there were several different interfaces that were basically separate. For example, *My Computer* was separate from *Windows Explorer*. There was no easy way to switch between them. In later versions they have become much more integrated. For example, in Windows XP the only difference between My Computer and Windows Explorer is whether or not the folder tree is displayed (by clicking the Folders button on the toolbar).

**My Computer**

A file management window with a single pane that shows icons for all of the local drives on the system.

As an experienced computer user, you probably already know about the various entry points into the file management system in Windows, including the ones listed in Table 29.1. Review any that are not familiar to you.

**Windows Explorer**

A file management window that contains a folder tree, enabling the user to switch quickly to other drive and folder locations.

Even though there are many entry points into the file management system, there are essentially two ways of working with files: through a single-pane window (such as My Computer, My Documents, and My Network Places) or through a double-pane window with folder tree at the left (such as Windows Explorer). The following sections examine these two interfaces in more detail.

| Window | Description | Windows 9x/Me | Windows 2000 | Windows XP |
|---|---|---|---|---|
| My Computer | Displays icons for all local drives | Double-click *My Computer* on desktop | Double-click *My Computer* on desktop | Click Start/My Computer |
| Windows Explorer | Displays the My Documents window with a folder tree on the left; from here you can navigate to other folders | Click Start/Programs/ Windows Explorer (95/98) or Start/Programs/ Accessories/ Windows Explorer (Me) | Click Start/Programs/ Accessories/ Windows Explorer | Click Start/All Programs/ Accessories/ Windows Explorer |
| My Documents | Displays the My Documents window in a single pane | Double-click *My Documents* on desktop | Double-click *My Documents* on desktop | Click Start/My Documents |
| Network Neighborhood or My Network Places | Displays icons for network resources such as workgroups and computers; with My Network Places also displays shortcuts to network locations | Double-click *Network Neighborhood* (95/98) or *My Network Places* (ME) on desktop | Double-click *My Network Places* on desktop | Click Start/My Network Places |

**TABLE 29.1**
File Management Entry Points in Windows

## My Computer

When working with a single-pane file management window such as My Computer, you see the content of only a single folder at a time. To move or copy from that location to some other location, you must either use the Clipboard or open a second window containing the destination location, as in Figure 29.3.

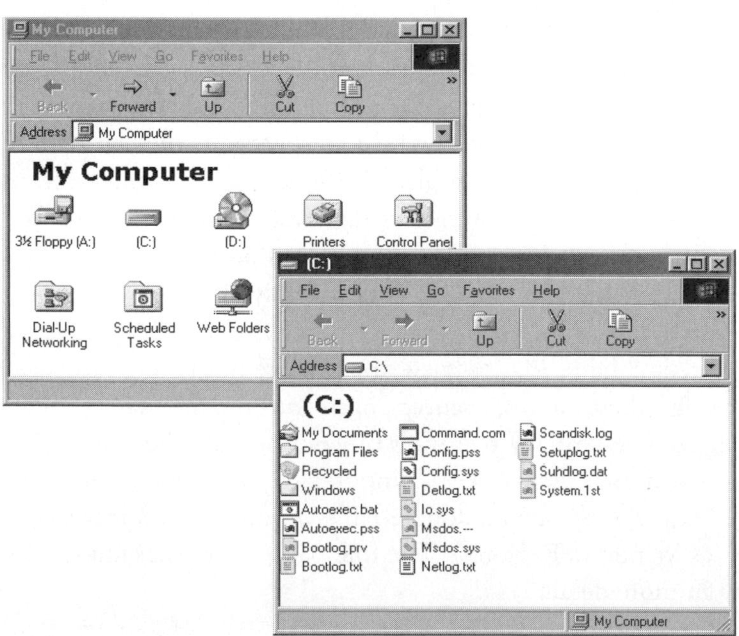


**FIGURE 29.3**
When working with single-pane file listings, you must open two separate windows if you want to move or copy with drag and drop.

When you double-click on a drive or folder in a single-pane window, the new location either opens in a separate window or replaces the previous content of the current window, depending on how Windows is configured. Table 29.2 explains the default settings and the ways to change them in various Windows versions.

| Windows Version | Default Setting | How to Change It |
|---|---|---|
| Windows 95 | Separate windows | Click View/Options, select Folder tab |
| Windows 98 | Same window | Click View/Folder Options, select Classic Style |
| Windows Me | Same window | Click Tools/Folder Options, select General tab |
| Windows 2000 | Same window | Click Tools/Folder Options, select General tab |
| Windows XP | Same window | Click Tools/Folder Options, select General tab |

**TABLE 29.2**
Choosing Whether Double-Clicking a Folder in a Single-Pane File Listing Opens a New Window

You do not have to change the default setting in order to get a different result when you double-click a folder or drive, however. You can use these shortcuts:

- Hold down the Ctrl key to open the drive or folder in a new single-pane window.
- Hold down the Shift key to open the drive or folder in a Windows Explorer (two-pane) window.

In Windows 98 and higher, a single-pane window sometimes actually has a second pane, but it is not a folder tree. Depending on the folder settings, the size of the window, and the selected folder or file, information about the selected item may appear to the left of the main listing (see Figure 29.4). Even if this extra information appears, it is still considered a single-pane file listing because the second pane does not provide access to additional locations to or from which you can drag and drop.

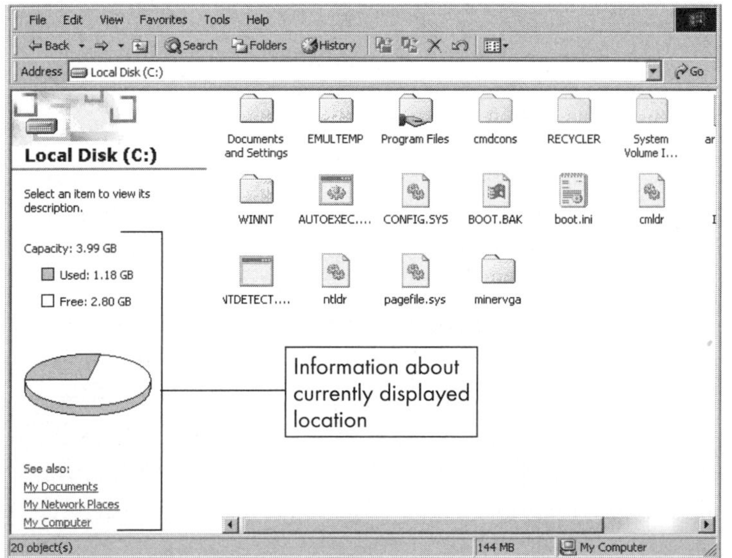


**FIGURE 29.4**
Some single-pane file listings in Windows 98 and higher contain some extra information to the left about the selected item(s).

You can make this extra information pane disappear by resizing the window so that it is smaller from side-to-side. You can also turn it on/off in the following ways:

- In Windows 98, choose View/As Web Page. This affects an individual folder/drive only.
- In Windows Me, 2000, and XP, choose Tools/Folder Options, and on the General tab change the setting in the Web View section. This affects all file management windows.

## Windows Explorer

Windows Explorer is a file management window that contains a folder tree pane at the left, as in Figure 29.5. It is a very handy tool for those who like to manage files via drag and drop because it enables more than one location to be visible at a time.

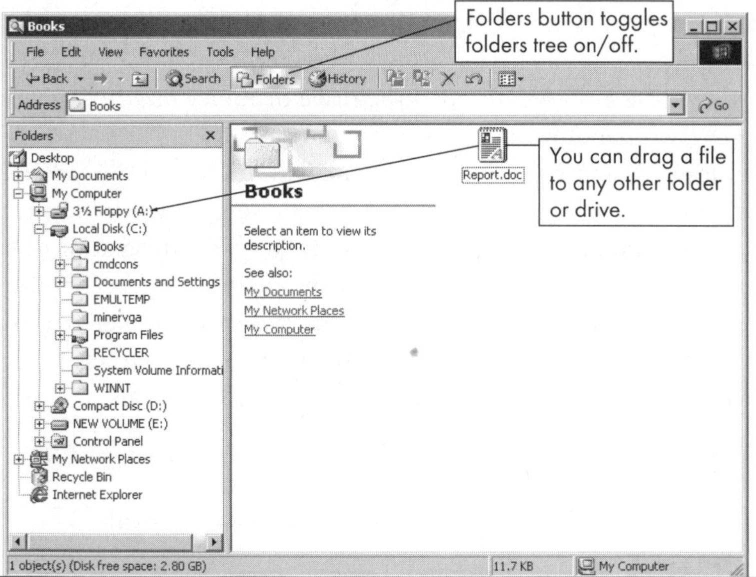


**FIGURE 29.5**
A Typical Windows Explorer Window

For example, suppose you want to move a file from the *C:\Books* folder to the A drive. With Windows Explorer, complete the following steps:

1. Display the *C:\Books* folder's content.
2. Select the file.
3. Drag the file to the A drive on the folder tree and drop it there.

You could not do that in a single-pane file management window; you would first have to open another window containing the A drive's content.

In Windows 2000, Me, and XP, a Folders button appears on the toolbar in all file management windows; this button toggles the folder tree on and off, enabling users to switch freely between Windows Explorer and a single-pane file window.

## File Management Skills to Master

The A+ exams test your abilities as a PC technician, not as an end user, so there are certain skills you are assumed to have mastered. One of these is basic file management. You will not see questions specifically about moving,

| Activity | Mouse Method | Keyboard Method | Menu Method |
|---|---|---|---|
| Select a single file | Click it | Arrow keys | |
| Select multiple contiguous files | Click on the first one, hold down Shift, click on the last one; OR drag across a group of files; OR drag a box around a group | Select first one, hold down Shift, and use arrow keys to extend selection | |
| Select multiple noncontiguous files | Click on the first one, hold down Ctrl, click on additional ones | Select first one, hold down Ctrl, use arrow keys to move to another one, press spacebar to select it | |
| Select all files in current location | | Press Ctrl + A | Choose Edit/Select All |
| Delete | Right-click and choose Delete; OR drag to Recycle Bin | Press Delete key | Choose File/Delete |
| Rename | Right-click and choose Rename; OR click in name | Press F2 | Choose File/Rename |
| View file properties | Right-click and choose Properties; OR hold down Alt and double-click file | | Choose File/Properties |
| Copy between locations on the same disk | Hold down Ctrl as you drag and drop; OR right-click and choose Copy, then right-click the destination and choose Paste; OR click the Copy button on the toolbar, then display the destination and click the Paste button on the toolbar | Press Ctrl + C to copy and then Ctrl + V to paste | Choose Edit/Copy, and then display the destination and choose Edit/Paste; OR in some Windows versions, choose Edit/Copy to Folder |
| Copy between locations on different disks | Same as above except you do not have to hold down Ctrl | Same as above | Same as above |
| Move between locations on different disks | Hold down Shift as you drag and drop; OR right-click and choose Cut, then right-click the destination and choose Paste; OR click the Cut button on the toolbar, then display the destination and click the Paste button on the toolbar | Press Ctrl + X to cut and then Ctrl + V to paste | Choose Edit/Cut, and then display the destination and choose Edit/Paste; OR in some Windows versions, choose Edit/Move to Folder |
| Move between locations on the same disk | Same as above except you do not have to hold down Shift | Same as above | Same as above |
| Create a shortcut | Hold down Alt as you drag and drop; OR right-click and choose Create Shortcut | | Choose File/Create Shortcut |

**TABLE 29.3**
File Management Skills

copying, selecting, and so on, because the test designers felt that these were skills they could take for granted. If you do not have those skills already, you will need to do some extra studying to prepare yourself. Table 29.3 provides a list of the file management skills you will need.

**TRY IT!**

1. Review My Computer, My Documents, Network Neighborhood, My Network Places, and Windows Explorer, and make sure you understand how each of them works in each Windows version.
2. Copy several files from the hard drive to a floppy disk using Windows Explorer.
3. Display the floppy drive's content in My Computer, and from there rename one of the files.
4. Delete all of the files from the floppy disk.

## Working with the Recycle Bin

You are probably already familiar with the basic workings of the Recycle Bin. It is a safety feature of Windows that helps prevent data loss due to accidental deletion. When users delete from a file management window, the deleted item is not immediately erased. Instead it is moved to the Recycle Bin, where it sits until one of these things happens:

- It is individually deleted from the Recycle Bin.
- The entire Recycle Bin is emptied.
- The hard disk starts running low on disk space, so files begin to be automatically deleted from the Recycle Bin.
- The Recycle Bin reaches its maximum size, so the oldest files (that is, those with the longest time in the Recycle Bin) begin to be automatically deleted.

The A+ exam assumes that you already know how to do the basic end user tasks associated with the Recycle Bin. These are summarized in Table 29.4.

| Activity | Mouse Method | Keyboard Method | Menu Method |
|---|---|---|---|
| Place a file into the Recycle Bin | Drag the file to the Recycle Bin; OR right-click it and choose Delete | From a file management window, select the file and press Delete | Choose File/Delete |
| Bypass the Recycle Bin, deleting a file immediately | | From a file management window, select the file and press Shift + Delete | |
| Retrieve a deleted file from the Recycle Bin | Drag the deleted file out of the Recycle Bin; OR in some versions of Windows, click the *Restore This Item* hyperlink in the Recycle Bin window | | From the Recycle Bin, choose File/Restore |
| Permanently delete a file in the Recycle Bin | From the Recycle Bin, right-click the item and choose Delete | From the Recycle Bin, press the Delete key | From the Recycle Bin, choose File/Delete |
| Empty the entire content of the Recycle Bin | Right-click anywhere in the file listing for the Recycle Bin and choose Empty Recycle Bin; OR in some versions of Windows, click the *Empty Recycle Bin* hyperlink in the Recycle Bin window; OR from the desktop, right-click the Recycle Bin icon and choose Empty Recycle Bin | | From the Recycle Bin, choose File/Empty Recycle Bin |

**TABLE 29.4**
Recycle Bin Skills

## TRY IT!

1. Copy one of the graphics files from the *WINDOWS* (or *WINNT*) folder, and then send the copy to the Recycle Bin.
2. Restore the file from the Recycle Bin.
3. Move the file to a floppy disk and delete it from there. Does it go to the Recycle Bin? Why or why not?
4. Make another copy of the original graphics file.
5. Hold down the Shift key as you delete the copy. Does it go to the Recycle Bin? Why or why not?

To control how the Recycle Bin works, display its properties. (Right-click the *Recycle Bin* icon on the desktop and choose Properties.)

From the Recycle Bin Properties dialog box, you can choose to configure each local hard disk separately or configure them as a whole. If you choose to do them separately, you then adjust other settings on the tabs for the individual drives instead of on the Global tab as in Figure 29.6.

There are three settings you can change for the Recycle Bin:

- **Do not move files to the Recycle Bin.** This turns off the Recycle Bin; when users delete from file management windows, the files are immediately deleted. You can still drag and drop files to the Recycle Bin, however.
- **Maximum size of Recycle Bin.** This slider adjusts the maximum amount of disk space to be allocated to storing files in the Recycle Bin. If the volume exceeds the limit set, the files that have been in the Recycle Bin the longest time are automatically deleted.
- **Display delete confirmation dialog.** This turns on/off the confirmation box that appears whenever you delete files from a file management window. This option appears only on the Global tab; it applies to all drives. You cannot have different settings for different drives.

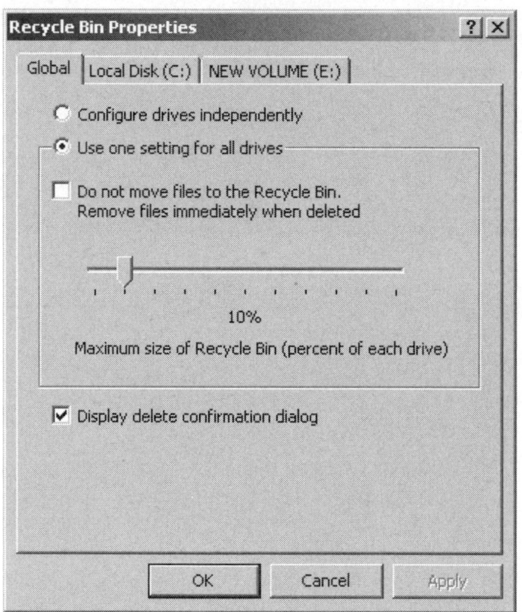


**FIGURE 29.6**
Change the Recycle Bin's properties if desired.

## Working with Basic File Attributes

**File attributes**

On/off flags for a file or folder that report its status or condition, such as read-only, archive, hidden, or system.

A file can have any or all of these *file attributes:*

- **Read-Only:** The file is locked and cannot be changed or deleted. It can be viewed, opened, and printed, however.
- **Hidden:** The file does not appear in normal file listings. If you have set up Windows to display hidden files (Tools/Folder Options), hidden files appear with dimmed icons, indicating their hidden status.
- **Archive:** The file has been changed since it has been backed up. Backup utilities set the Archive attribute to Off; then, when the file is modified,

the operating system sets it to On. This enables the system to tell which files have changed since your last backup.

- **System:** The file is a system file, required for proper system operation.

In Windows 95 you can view and change the attributes assigned to a file from its Properties dialog box, as shown in Figure 29.7.

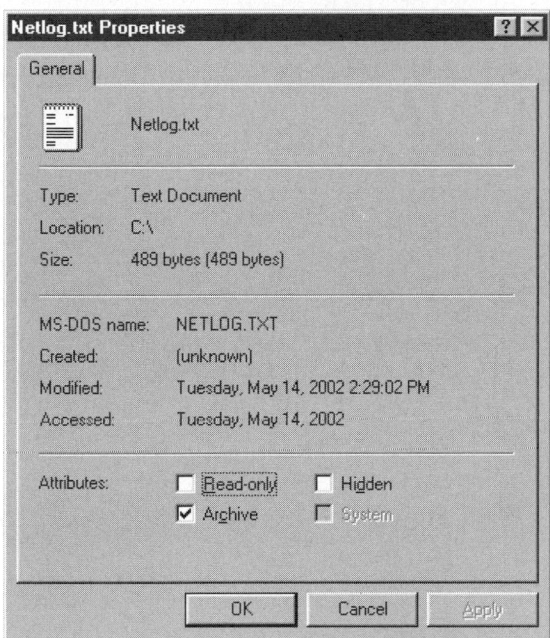


**FIGURE 29.7**
View and change a file's attributes through its Properties dialog box.

Another name for an attribute is a flag. You might occasionally hear the Archive attribute referred to as the Archive flag, for example.

In later versions of Windows the Archive and/or System attributes might not be available in the file's Properties dialog box. Table 29.5 lists the attributes and which Windows versions allow you to change them from that location.

| | Read-Only | Hidden | Archive | System |
|---|---|---|---|---|
| Windows 95 | Yes | Yes | Yes | Visible but cannot be changed |
| Windows 98 | Yes | Yes | Yes | Visible but cannot be changed |
| Windows Me | Yes | Yes | Yes | No |
| Windows 2000 | Yes | Yes | Yes* | No |
| Windows XP | Yes | Yes | Yes | No |

*In Windows 2000, on an NTFS drive, instead of an Archive check box there is an Advanced button. Click on that and then mark or clear the File is Ready for Archiving check box.

**TABLE 29.5**
File Attributes Available to Be Set

You can also view and set file attributes from a command prompt, using the ATTRIB command. Key **ATTRIB**, the first letter of the attribute you want to turn on or off (preceded by a plus or minus sign), then the file name (or wildcard specification) to which it should apply. For example, to turn on the Hidden attribute for C:\BOOK.TXT, key **ATTRIB +H C:\BOOK.TXT**. To turn off the Read-Only attribute for C:\BACKUP\SAVE.DOC, key **ATTRIB -R C:\BACKUP\SAVE.DOC**. To turn off both the Read-Only and the System attributes for all files in the *C:\BACKUP* folder, key **ATTRIB -R -S C:\BACKUP*.***. For a full description of the syntax of the ATTRIB command, key **ATTRIB /?** at a command prompt. We will discuss command prompt syntax and wildcards in greater detail later in the chapter.

**TRY IT!**

1. View the attributes for several files through their Properties dialog boxes in Windows.
2. Find a file that has the Archive attribute turned off, and turn it on through the file's Properties dialog box.
3. Open a command prompt and use the ATTRIB command to turn the Archive attribute back on for that file.
4. Return to Windows and redisplay the Properties dialog box for that file to confirm that the Archive attribute is back on.

## NTFS File Attributes

Drives that use the NTFS file system have some special attributes you can set; the following sections explain them.

### NTFS Compression

Compression is available in NTFS 4 and higher. It compresses a file to save disk space, and then decompresses it on-the-fly whenever the user or an application opens it. This is all transparent to the user. The drawback to compression is that it makes files open and save slightly more slowly than normal.

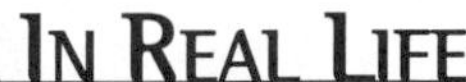

## IN REAL LIFE

There are many other types of compression. As just two examples, there is whole-drive compression, as with DriveSpace (see Chapter 30), and there is compression that packages multiple files in an archive package, as with ZIP files. Neither of these has any relationship to NTFS compression, which can apply to individual files and folders invisibly on a hard drive.

### *Compression in Windows NT 4.0*

In Windows NT 4.0, when you format a hard disk you can mark an Enable Compression check box in the Format dialog box that will set up the entire drive to use NTFS compression. You can also turn on/off compression for the entire drive from the drive's Properties dialog box, as in Figure 29.8. All files and folders also have a Compress check box in their Properties dialog box.

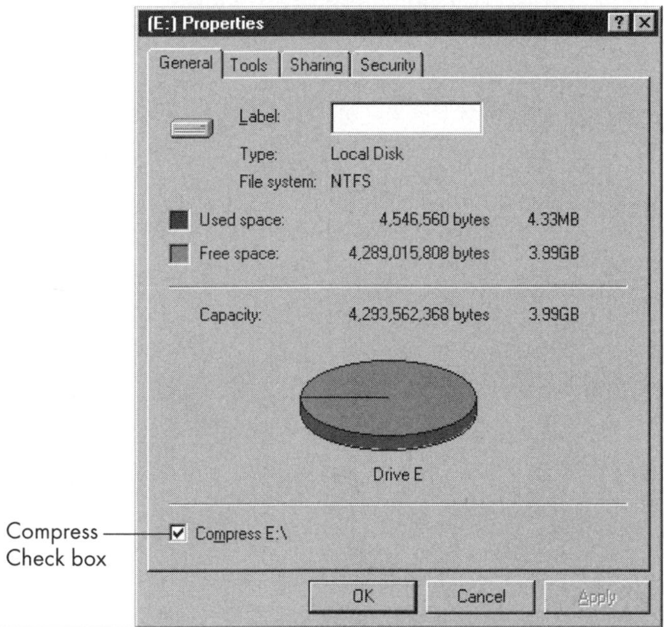


**FIGURE 29.8**
Compression is enabled/disabled in Windows NT 4.0 through a simple check box in the Properties dialog box.

### *Compression in Windows 2000 and XP*

In Windows 2000 and XP, you can enable or disable compression by completing the following steps:

1. Display the Properties dialog box for the file, folder, or drive.
2. On the General tab, click the Advanced button. The Advanced Attributes dialog box opens.

3. Mark the Compress contents to save disk space check box (see Figure 29.9).
4. Click OK twice to close all open dialog boxes.

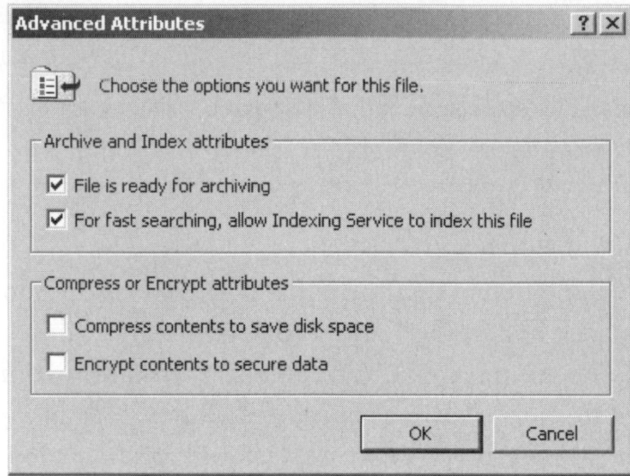


**FIGURE 29.9**
Compression is enabled/disabled in Windows 2000 and XP through the Advanced Attributes dialog box.

In Windows 2000 and XP you can configure Windows so that compressed files and folders appear with their names in blue rather than the standard black. This makes it easier to remember which items you have compressed in case you ever want to decompress them. To reconfigure the label color:

1. From any file management window, choose Tools/Folder Options.
2. On the View tab, insert a check mark next to *Display compressed files and folders with alternate color* (in Windows 2000, see Figure 29.10) or *Show encrypted or compressed NTFS files in color* (in Windows XP).
3. Click OK.

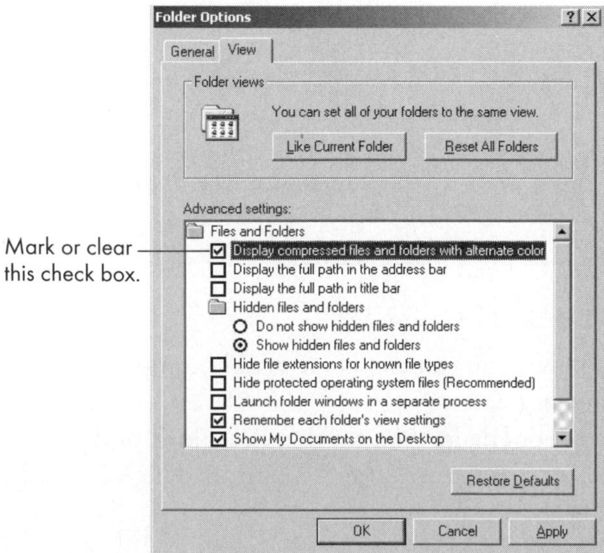


**FIGURE 29.10**
You can set up compressed files to appear in an alternate color (usually blue) through the Folder Options dialog box (Windows 2000 shown).

## TRY IT!

1. Create a new folder called *Compressed* in the root directory of one of the hard drives.
2. Set the file's NTFS attributes to include compression.
3. If it is not on already, turn on the folder option that allows the compressed items to appear in an alternate color.
4. Copy a data file (from any application) and paste it into the *Compressed* folder. Does it also become compressed? How can you tell?
5. Change the properties for the folder so that it is no longer compressed. Is the file decompressed too? How can you tell?

## NTFS ENCRYPTION

Encryption, also called *Encrypting File System* (EFS), was a new feature in NTFS 5 (Windows 2000). It enables user-based security for files and folders on the local PC. It is available in Windows XP Professional but not Windows XP Home Edition.

**Encrypting File System (EFS)**

A feature in NTFS 5 that enables users to secure files on the local drives by user logon.

Suppose two people use the same PC, and each logs on with a different user name. One user could encrypt the content of a certain folder so that only she could access it. If the other user attempted to browse it using a file management window, access would be denied.

**WARNING**

Most Windows experts agree that it is a bad idea to encrypt individual files, even though it is possible to do so. It is too easy to forget which files are encrypted and which are not. Instead, encrypt folders and place the files to be encrypted into one of those folders. As long as the file remains in the folder, it remains encrypted; if it is moved to an unencrypted folder, it becomes unencrypted.

To encrypt a folder:

1. Display the Properties dialog box for the folder.
2. On the General tab, click the Advanced button. The Advanced Attributes dialog box opens.
3. Mark the Encrypt contents to secure data check box (see Figure 29.11).
4. Click OK. If you chose a folder containing subfolders, a dialog box appears asking whether you want to apply the change to only the selected folder or to all of its content. Make your selection and click OK. Depending on the content of the selected folder, it may take a

few minutes for the new attribute setting to be applied to all the subfolders and files.

5. Click OK to close the Properties dialog box.

You cannot both encrypt and compress a folder or file; when you select one, the other becomes unselected.

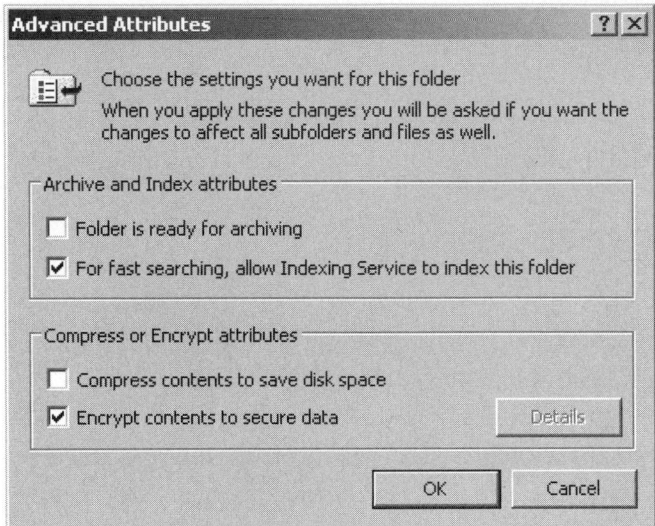


**FIGURE 29.11**
Enable encryption from the Advanced Attributes dialog box.

**WARNING**

Encryption under NTFS uses an encryption key that is stored on the hard disk. You can back up the encryption key to a floppy or some other location, but if anything happens to it, your data becomes irretrievable. Therefore, do not use encryption unless it is really needed. Limit its use to only the few truly sensitive files that you need to protect.

In Windows XP, encrypted items can be set up so that their names appear in a different color. For compression it was blue; for encryption it is green. See the steps at the end of the preceding section to set that up. Encrypted items in Windows 2000 do not appear in a different color.

Here are some suggestions for encryption:

- Do not encrypt the Windows XP system folder *(WINNT)*. Encryption slows down the process of opening and saving files, and it would make Windows run more slowly. Windows will warn you if you try to encrypt this folder.
- Do not encrypt the folders where most of the data files are kept (such as *My Documents*). If something happens to the PC such that you have to reinstall Windows, you might lose the encryption key stored on the hard disk that would enable you to access those files. Create a special folder

for encrypted files, and place there only the files that specifically need encryption.

- Do not encrypt files; encrypt folders only.
- Encrypt the *Temp* folder. This prevents other end users from browsing temporary files that might contain fragments of data. If the system crashes and you have to reinstall Windows, the fact that the temp files are irretrievable is not important.

**TRY IT!**

1. Create a new folder called *Encrypted* on the hard disk. If needed, set up the folder options so that the encrypted folder's name appears in a different color from other folders.
2. Copy several data files into the *Encrypted* folder.
3. Log off Windows, and log on as a different user.
4. Attempt to open one of the data files. What happens?
5. Log off Windows, and log back on as yourself.
6. Attempt to open one of the data files. What happens?
7. Turn off encryption for the folder. Then delete it and all of its contents.

## Troubleshooting File Management Error Messages

Here are some of the most common problems users encounter with file management.

**General Failure reading drive X.** This usually means the disk is not formatted or has gone bad and the drive is completely inaccessible. It may be a virus infection, a physical problem such as a loose cable or failed drive, or a catastrophic failure of the disk's table of contents (such as the File Allocation Table on a FAT16 or FAT32 drive). A disk recovery application may be useful if the data the disk contained was important.

**Data Error reading (or writing) drive X.** Usually indicates a physically bad area of the disk. Run ScanDisk or Check Disk on it (see Chapter 30) and use the Thorough option to check the disk surface.

**Sector not found error.** This usually means that the logical file system is malfunctioning for the disk. It can occur if you specify the wrong hard drive type in BIOS Setup, for example, so that a drive tries to read sectors that do not exist.

**Access Denied.** There is a permission setting that is preventing you from modifying a file. Usually it means that the file has the Read-Only attribute set or that the whole disk is write-protected (for a floppy).

**Insufficient Disk Space or Disk Full.** Either the disk is full, or the root directory is full.

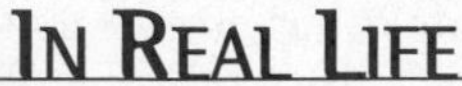

IN REAL LIFE

Why would the root directory be full but not the disk itself? This is primarily an issue with floppy disks. The File Allocation Table holds the entries for the content of the root directory, but each folder keeps its own listing for its contents. The FAT has a limited number of spaces available for data, and if the disk contains more files in the root directory than there are spaces to track in the FAT, the disk will appear to be full even if its space is not completely occupied by files.

## Backing Up and Restoring Files

Regular backup is essential for good data security, but unfortunately most people do not follow a regular backup regimen. As a PC technician you will not only be responsible for backing up your own data, but also for teaching and encouraging end users to back up their data, and perhaps even for implementing a department-wide or company-wide backup program.

There are many ways to back up data.

**Copying files to another drive.** This other drive could be a secondary local hard disk, a network drive, a floppy, a writable CD, a Zip disk, or some other type of disk. *Advantages:* It is easy, no special application is required, and the files do not require any special treatment if you ever need to restore them. *Disadvantages:* No compression, so the files take up as much space on the backup disk as they did originally. Also, there is no way to separate the files that have been changed since the last backup from the files that have not been changed (determined by the Archive attribute).

**Copying an entire drive.** This is sometimes called ghosting, after a popular program called Norton Ghost that performs this function. It copies the entire hard drive, sector by sector, onto another one. *Advantages:* You do not have to worry about whether you copied all of the important files because it copies them all. *Disadvantages:* It takes a long time, and requires a spare hard disk (unless you copy to a writable CD, which is possible with some software) and a separate application not included with Windows. Useful for transferring data from an old PC to a new one, but not particularly good for daily, weekly, or monthly system backups.

**Using a backup application.** Backup programs provide a full-featured backup experience. You can select the files you want to back up, separate files that have changed since the last backup from those that have not, compress the backed-up files, span multiple disks, and save the configuration data for a backup job to use it again. *Advantages:* Provides great flexibility, and the files are compressed to save space on the backup media. *Disadvantages:* The backed-up files cannot be used as-is; you must use the same backup program (and same Windows version) to restore them if you ever need access to them.

There are many backup applications available; one of the most popular is Microsoft Backup. The features, interface, and flexibility of Microsoft Backup vary dramatically among versions. Early versions, such as the one in Windows 95, did not support most tape drives, and many people struggled with its confusing interface. Most of the Windows versions that followed contained improved versions of Microsoft Backup that added support for high-capacity backup drives such as tape drives and CD-R/CD-RW. In the following section we will look at the version of Microsoft Backup included in Windows 2000.

## Backing Up Files with Microsoft Backup

Microsoft Backup is a feature-rich, complex application with many options. You can choose which files to back up, where to back them up, what compression settings to use, and so on. The following steps show how to perform a simple backup of an entire drive. You will want to experiment with the application on your own system to discover other features. These steps cover Microsoft Backup in Windows 2000 only; you will find that the versions included in various Windows versions are different.

To perform a full backup in Windows 2000, follow these steps:

1. Choose Start/Programs/Accessories/System Tools/Backup.
2. Click the Backup Wizard button. The wizard runs; click Next to begin it.
3. Leave the default option selected: Back up everything on my computer. Click Next.
4. Key the path and file name for the backup file to create. The location can be any drive on your system, or any folder on any drive. This allows the flexibility of backing up to a network location, for example. Click Next.
5. Click Finish. The backup begins. Follow the prompts, inserting other blank disks if needed, until it completes successfully.
6. When a confirmation box appears reporting the backup has completed, click Close.
7. Exit the backup application.

You can also use the backup program manually; the wizard is not the only way to operate it. To do so, click the Backup tab after starting the program rather than clicking the Backup Wizard button.

## Restoring Files with Microsoft Backup

Restoring is a much less common activity than backing up, so fewer people are familiar with it. The wizard in Microsoft Backup makes it fairly easy, however. Follow these steps:

1. Choose Start/Programs/Accessories/System Tools/Backup.
2. Click the Restore Wizard button. The wizard runs; click Next.
3. Mark the check box for the folders you want to restore. The folder tree works just like the one in Windows Explorer; click a plus sign to expand a branch or a minus sign to collapse one (see Figure 29.12). Click Next.

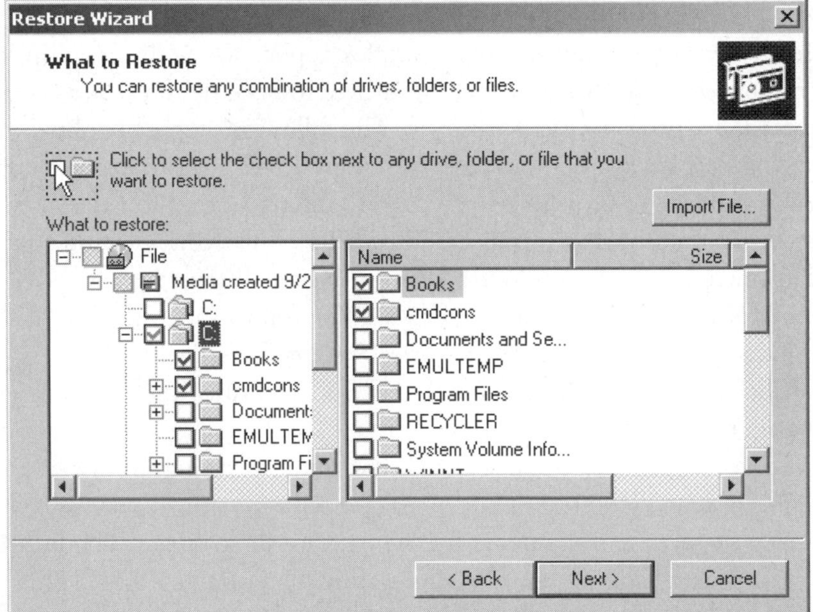


**FIGURE 29.12**
Choosing Which Files to Restore from Microsoft Backup

4. Click Finish. A message box appears asking for the backup file name. It is probably already correct. Change it if needed, and then click OK.
5. Wait for the backup to complete. When confirmation appears that it is finished, click Close.
6. Exit the Backup application.

## TRY IT!

1. Back up your important data files to another disk using Microsoft Backup.
2. Restore those files, again using Microsoft Backup.

# Working with a Command Prompt

You have had some experience working with a command prompt in other chapters of this book, such as when you used FDISK and FORMAT to prepare a hard disk, or when you used IPCONFIG to diagnose network problems. The following sections go into more detail about command prompt usage and list some useful commands you might want to memorize.

## Getting to a Command Prompt

Windows 9x has two modes, as you learned in Chapter 26: a graphical user interface (GUI) and a DOS protected-mode interface (DPMI). The DPMI is a command-line interface. You can get to this protected-mode command prompt in any of these ways:

- Press F8 when booting and select one of the command-line startup options (see Chapter 27).
- Restart the PC in MS-DOS mode (Windows 95/98 only).
- Choose Start/Programs/MS-DOS Prompt.
- Choose Start/Run, key **COMMAND**, and then click OK.

NT-based versions of Windows do not have a DPMI, but they do provide a command prompt interface. To go to it, do one of the following:

- Choose Start/(All) Programs/Accessories/Command Prompt.
- Choose Start/Run, key **CMD**, and then click OK.

If you are running the command prompt in a window, as in Figure 29.13, you can close the window at any time to get rid of it. If the command prompt is running in full-screen mode on top of Windows, key **EXIT** and press Enter to return to Windows.

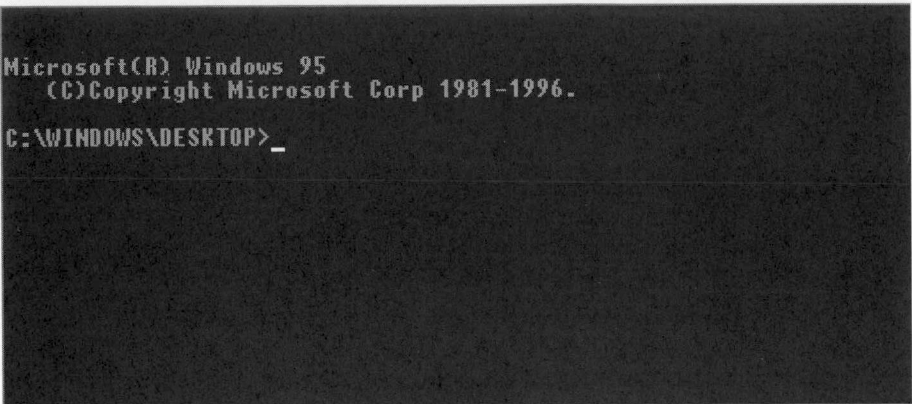


**FIGURE 29.13**
You can display a command prompt window from within the Windows GUI.

## Changing Drives and Directories

The command prompt contains the full name of the current directory (folder). In Figure 29.13 it is C:\Windows\Desktop. To change to a different directory, use the CD command (which stands for Change Directory).

Changing directories works only within a single drive letter; if you need to change drives, you must key the drive letter followed by a colon. For example, to change to the C drive, key **C:**.

To change to a different directory on the same drive, key **CD** followed by the full path (excluding the drive letter). For example, to change to the \WINDOWS\SYSTEM directory, key **CD \WINDOWS\SYSTEM**. To go up one level in the folder tree (for example, to change from \WINDOWS\SYSTEM to \WINDOWS), key two periods: **CD..**. To jump to the root directory of the drive, key a slash: **CD ** . In all of these commands the space between CD and the slash or periods is optional.

When the directory to which you are changing is at a lower level of the same branch in the tree, you do not have to key the \ sign. So, for example, to move from \WINDOWS to \WINDOWS\SYSTEM, you could key **CD SYSTEM**.

### In Real Life

The prompt should always list the current drive and directory, but if it does not for some reason, key **PROMPT $P$G.**

## TRY IT!

1. Display a command prompt.
2. Change to a different drive. Repeat until you have changed to all of the available drives; then end up at your C drive.
3. Use the DIR command to get a listing of files in the current folder.
4. Use the CD command to change to the root directory of the drive.

## Understanding Command Syntax

Most commands have rules for their usage. The rules, which include what options are permissible and in what order they should appear, are known as the command's *syntax*.

To get help with a command's syntax, simply key the command followed by the /? *switch*. A switch is an option that includes a slash in it, such as /?. The command syntax will tell you what switches are permitted. Figure 29.14 shows the information provided for the CD command used in the preceding section, for example. As you can see, an alternative to CD is CHDIR; they both do the same thing.

**Syntax**

The rules governing what parameters a command will take and in what order they should appear in a command line.

**Switch**

A command parameter or option that begins with a slash (/).

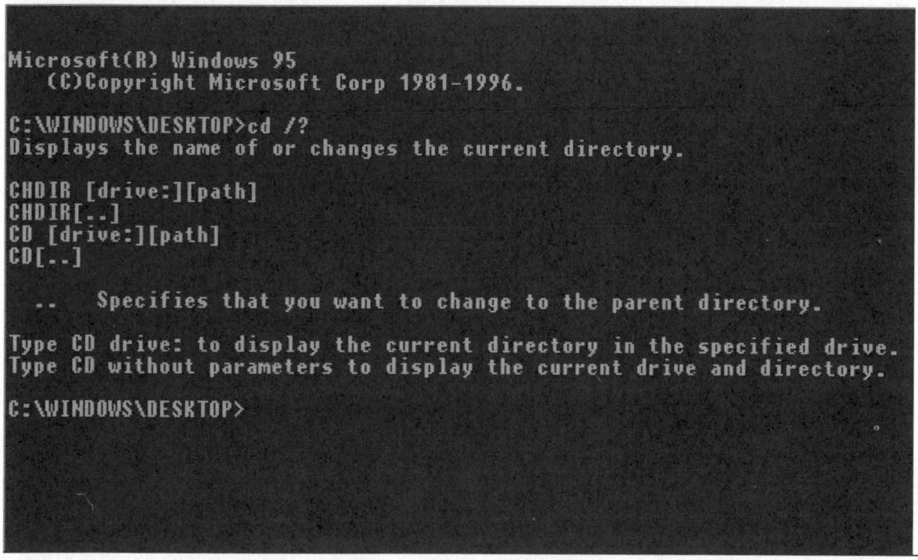

```
Microsoft(R) Windows 95
   (C)Copyright Microsoft Corp 1981-1996.

C:\WINDOWS\DESKTOP>cd /?
Displays the name of or changes the current directory.

CHDIR [drive:][path]
CHDIR[..]
CD [drive:][path]
CD[..]

  ..   Specifies that you want to change to the parent directory.

Type CD drive: to display the current directory in the specified drive.
Type CD without parameters to display the current drive and directory.

C:\WINDOWS\DESKTOP>
```

**FIGURE 29.14**
Get help with a command by keying it followed by /?.

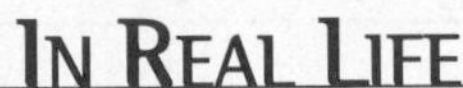


Different versions of MS-DOS and Windows have different syntax for some commands. For example, if you were to key **CD /?** in a Windows XP command prompt window, the syntax presented would include a /D switch that allows you to change the drive at the same time you are changing the directory. If you are trying to use a command for which you think you have memorized the syntax, and it does not work, check the command syntax with /? to make sure that the syntax you are using matches the capabilities of the OS version.

Optional parameters are enclosed in square brackets. However, even though each parameter individually may be optional, in some cases the command will not work unless at least one parameter is included.

Another example (see Figure 29.15) shows the syntax for the DIR command, which displays a directory listing. This is the Windows 2000 version of the DIR command, but all other versions are similar.

```
C:\>dir /?
Displays a list of files and subdirectories in a directory.

DIR [drive:][path][filename] [/A[[:]attributes]] [/B] [/C] [/D] [/L] [/N]
  [/O[[:]sortorder]] [/P] [/Q] [/S] [/T[[:]timefield]] [/W] [/X] [/4]

  [drive:][path][filename]
              Specifies drive, directory, and/or files to list.

  /A          Displays files with specified attributes.
  attributes   D  Directories                R  Read-only files
               H  Hidden files               A  Files ready for archiving
               S  System files               -  Prefix meaning not
  /B          Uses bare format (no heading information or summary).
  /C          Display the thousand separator in file sizes.  This is the
              default.  Use /-C to disable display of separator.
  /D          Same as wide but files are list sorted by column.
  /L          Uses lowercase.
  /N          New long list format where filenames are on the far right.
  /O          List by files in sorted order.
  sortorder    N  By name (alphabetic)       S  By size (smallest first)
               E  By extension (alphabetic)  D  By date/time (oldest first)
               G  Group directories first    -  Prefix to reverse order
  /P          Pauses after each screenful of information.
  /Q          Display the owner of the file.
  /S          Displays files in specified directory and all subdirectories.
  /T          Controls which time field displayed or used for sorting
  timefield   C  Creation
              A  Last Access
              W  Last Written
  /W          Uses wide list format.
  /X          This displays the short names generated for non-8dot3 file
              names.  The format is that of /N with the short name inserted
              before the long name. If no short name is present, blanks are
              displayed in its place.
  /4          Displays four-digit years

Switches may be preset in the DIRCMD environment variable.  Override
preset switches by prefixing any switch with - (hyphen)--for example, /-W.

C:\>_
```

**FIGURE 29.15**
The Syntax for the DIR Command under Windows 2000

Notice that some of the parameters in Figure 29.15 have nested items within them. For example, the /A switch is used along with a colon (:) and one or more letters representing attributes. Suppose you want to see all of the files in the current directory that have the Read-Only attribute; you might use the command **DIR /A:R.**

Do not be intimidated by the number and complexity of the syntax parameters for these example commands. Most people use very few of the available parameters for a command. You do not have to memorize the syntax because it is always available for reference with the /? switch.

## Understanding Wildcards

Commands that include a file name in their syntax can be used to act on an individual file or a group of files at once. If you want to act on a group of files, you use a wildcard, a character that stands for one or more characters generically. There are two valid wildcard characters. A question mark (?) stands for any single character; an asterisk (*) stands for any number of characters. For example, CO? would include every three-character file name in which the first two letters were CO, while CO* would include any names that began with CO regardless of the file name length.

Table 29.6 shows some additional wildcard examples.

| File specification | Includes | But does not include |
|---|---|---|
| A*.DOC | Amy.doc, Amherst.doc, A.doc | Amy.txt, Betty.doc, Amherst.grp |
| A???.DOC | Ants.doc, Army.doc, Also.doc | Amy.doc, Amherst.doc, Alls.txt |
| ??D.* | And.txt, And.doc, Atd.xls | All.txt, Anderson.doc |
| *. | And, Book, Cheers | And.doc, Book.txt, Cheers.xls |

**TABLE 29.6**
Wildcard Examples

**TRY IT!**

**Use a wildcard specification to see a list of all of the files in the *C:\WINDOWS* or *C:\WINNT* folder that begin with the letter *W*, have six letters in total, and have any extension. What command would you use?**

## Viewing Multiple Screens

Whenever a command results in more text than can fit on the screen at once, it scrolls by quickly, and you do not have the chance to read some of it. To fix this problem you can add the | MORE parameter to the end of most commands. This forces the command to display its results one screenful at a time. The | symbol is known as the "pipe" symbol. There are other commands you can use with it besides MORE, but MORE is by far the most common.

For example, suppose you want help with the XCOPY command, but XCOPY /? results in more text than will fit on one screen. You can key **XCOPY /? | MORE** to get a multipage listing, as in Figure 29.16. Depending on the command, it may advance page-by-page or line-by-line.

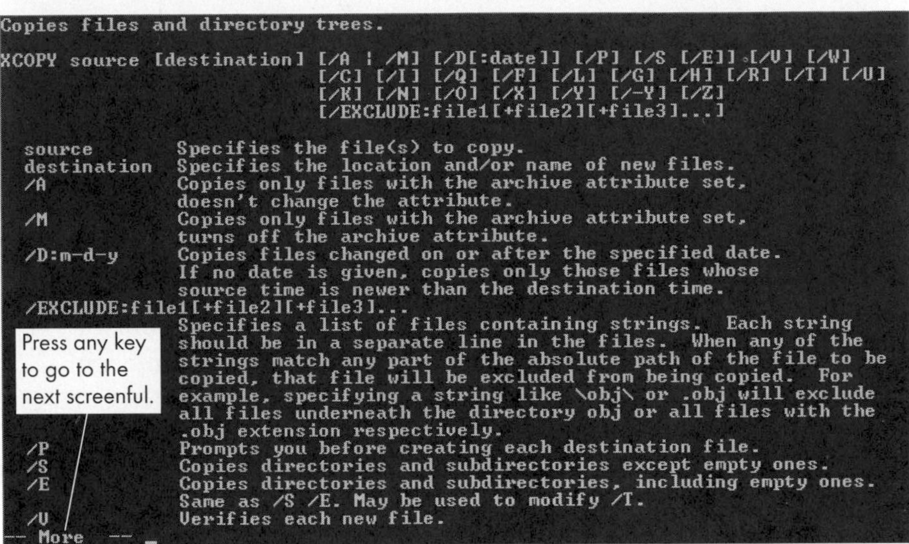

Copies files and directory trees.
XCOPY source [destination] [/A | /M] [/D[:date]] [/P] [/S [/E]] [/V] [/W]
[/C] [/I] [/Q] [/F] [/L] [/G] [/H] [/R] [/T] [/U]
[/K] [/N] [/O] [/X] [/Y] [/-Y] [/Z]
[/EXCLUDE:file1[+file2][+file3]...]
source Specifies the file(s) to copy.
destination Specifies the location and/or name of new files.
/A Copies only files with the archive attribute set, doesn't change the attribute.
/M Copies only files with the archive attribute set, turns off the archive attribute.
/D:m-d-y Copies files changed on or after the specified date. If no date is given, copies only those files whose source time is newer than the destination time.
/EXCLUDE:file1[+file2][+file3]...
Specifies a list of files containing strings. Each string should be in a separate line in the files. When any of the strings match any part of the absolute path of the file to be copied, that file will be excluded from being copied. For example, specifying a string like \obj\ or .obj will exclude all files underneath the directory obj or all files with the .obj extension respectively.
/P Prompts you before creating each destination file.
/S Copies directories and subdirectories except empty ones.
/E Copies directories and subdirectories, including empty ones. Same as /S /E. May be used to modify /T.
/V Verifies each new file.
-- More --
Press any key to go to the next screenful.


**FIGURE 29.16**
The | MORE addition to a command displays its results one screenful at a time.

Some commands also support a /P switch that also allows you to control multiple screenfuls of command results. For example, the DIR command can display a listing of the current directory's content one "page" at a time by adding the /P switch.

## TRY IT!

From the WINDOWS or WINNT directory, try the following commands, and note how the results differ:

a. DIR
b. DIR /W
c. DIR /P
d. DIR | MORE

## Command Examples

Now that you understand how to display a command prompt, change directories, and get syntax help, we will discuss some common commands you might use.

### *DEL*

DEL deletes files, as its name implies. The syntax is simple: DEL *file*. It does not work with directories (folders); for that you must use the RD command.

### *DELTREE*

This command deletes everything in a directory and removes the directory itself. It is not available in some OS versions; if it does not work, you must use a combination of RD and DEL to accomplish the same purpose.

### *MD*

MD, which stands for Make Directory, is used to create a new directory within the current one. For example, to make a directory called MYFILES in the C:\ root directory, first use CD to change to that directory (**CD** will do it) and then key **MD MYFILES**.

### *RD*

RD, which stands for Remove Directory, is used to delete directories. It works only if the directory is empty, however; you must first use DEL to clear out the directory's content.

### *SETVER*

The SETVER command was very useful under MS-DOS but is seldom used in Windows. It was a rudimentary attempt to trick applications into running under a version of MS-DOS different from the one for which they were originally designed.

If you need to use SETVER to make an application run, you must load SETVER.EXE in CONFIG.SYS. Then you can use the SETVER command at a command prompt to add or remove applications from SETVER's list.

To find out what applications are already on the SETVER list, key **SETVER** by itself and press Enter. To add an item to the SETVER list, key the syntax **SETVER *file n.nn***. For example, suppose you have an MS-DOS game called CRASH.EXE that requires MS-DOS 5.0. You could add it to the SETVER list with the command **SETVER CRASH.EXE 5.0**.

### *COPY*

COPY is one of the commands used most often. That is because when a PC has serious problems that prevent it from booting to Windows, a common activity is to copy files from the hard disk to a floppy to rescue them before reformatting the drive.

The basic syntax for the COPY command is simple: COPY *from to*. Include the entire path for each unless the location is the current directory. So, for example, to copy MYFILE.TXT from C:\Docs to A:\, you would use the line **COPY C:\DOCS\MYFILE.TXT A:**. If the current directory happened to be C:\DOCS, you could use as a shortcut **COPY MYFILE.TXT A:**. If you want to change the name of the file as you copy it, you can include a new name in the destination. For example, to rename the copy BACKUP.TXT, use **COPY MYFILE.TXT A:\BACKUP.TXT**.

For the complete syntax for the file, key **COPY /?** as with any other command.

### *XCOPY*

XCOPY is just like COPY except it copies entire directory structures, not just files. For example, suppose you have a folder that contains three subfolders; using XCOPY on the top-level folder would copy it, all of its files, and all of its subfolders. Its syntax is somewhat more complex in its available options.

### *MEM*

MEM reports the amount of RAM that the operating system recognizes. The command all by itself provides a short report, as in Figure 29.17.

```
D:\>mem


    655360 bytes total conventional memory
    655360 bytes available to MS-DOS
    598736 largest executable program size

   1048576 bytes total contiguous extended memory
         0 bytes available contiguous extended memory
    941056 bytes available XMS memory
           MS-DOS resident in High Memory Area

D:\>_
```

**FIGURE 29.17**
The MEM command reports the system's RAM usage and availability.

There are three switches available: /D (Debug), /P (Program), and /C (Classify). Of these, /C is the most useful for the average PC technician; it provides detailed information about where each application is loaded. You can use it to determine which real-mode device drivers are loaded in conventional memory under MS-DOS, for example, so you can modify CONFIG.SYS and AUTOXEC.BAT to make them load into high memory or upper memory.

### *PROMPT*

The PROMPT command, mentioned earlier in the chapter, determines what will appear at the prompt. By default, the prompt includes the current drive and directory followed by a > symbol: **C:\>**. You can make the prompt appear in a variety of other ways, however. You can include text of your own, or any of over a dozen predefined variables. For example, to display a prompt like **John Smith>**, use a command like **PROMPT John Smith $G**. The text appears as specified, and $G is a code that stands for the > symbol. Table 29.7 provides a list of codes that work with the PROMPT command.

| Code | Purpose |
|---|---|
| $A | Ampersand & |
| $B | Pipe \| |
| $C | Left parenthesis ( |
| $D | Current date |
| $E | Escape code |
| $F | Right parenthesis ) |
| $G | Greater-than sign > |
| $H | Backspace (erases previous character) |
| $L | Less-than sign < |
| $N | Current drive letter |
| $P | Current drive and complete path |
| $Q | Equals sign = |
| $T | Current time |
| $V | Windows version number |
| $_ | Carriage return and linefeed (starts a new line) |
| $$ | Dollar sign |

**TABLE 29.7**
PROMPT Command Codes

You can get very creative with your prompts! For example, the prompt shown in Figure 29.18 was created with the following PROMPT command:

**$B Welcome to $B$_$B  My PC!  $B$_Current Time: $T$_$P$G**

```
¦ Welcome to ¦
¦   My PC!   ¦
Current Time: 20:45:22.09
D:\>_
```

**FIGURE 29.18**
A Custom-Made, Unusual Command Prompt Built with the PROMPT Command

## TRY IT!

Create your own custom command prompt. What information from Table 29.7 would you like to include? If you were using the command prompt extensively, what information would you find it useful to show? Most people like to see the current drive letter and path, for example ($P).

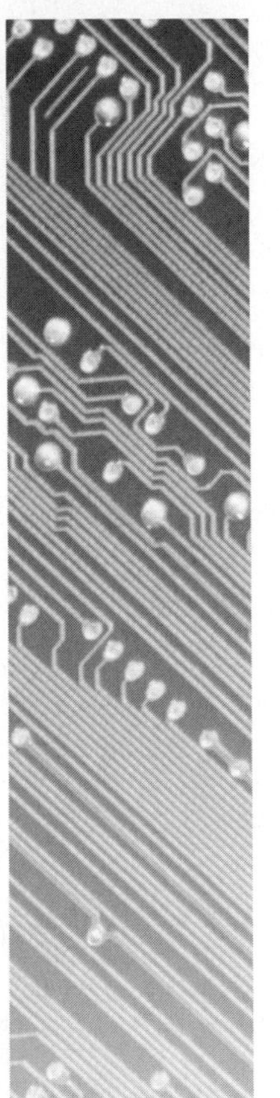

# STUDY GUIDE

Use the following summaries to review the key concepts of this chapter.

## UNDERSTANDING FILE SYSTEMS

- A file system is a logical method of storing data on disk. It determines what identifiers mark the beginning and end of a file, what information is stored in the FAT or other directory of disk content, and what properties can be assigned.
- Different OSes support different file systems. All versions of MS-DOS and Windows support FAT (FAT16), a 16-bit file system.
- FAT32 is a 32-bit version of FAT, supported in Windows 95 OSR2 and higher, Windows 98, Me, 2000, and XP.
- NTFS (New Technology File System) 4 is a 32-bit file system introduced in Windows NT 4.0. It allows for larger logical drives than FAT16, and also enables file-level security and file compression.
- NTFS 5 is an update to NTFS 4 introduced in Windows 2000. Windows XP also supports it. It adds file encryption and disk quotas to the NTFS 4 features.
- FAT12 is the 12-bit system used on floppy disks.
- HPFS (High Performance File System) is the now-obsolete file system that was used for the OS/2 operating system.

## USING THE WINDOWS FILE MANAGEMENT INTERFACE

- There are many entry points into the file management system, including My Documents, My Computer, and My Network Places.
- Windows Explorer is a two-pane interface that contains a folder tree. Most other interfaces are single pane, such as My Computer.
- In newer versions of Windows you can easily switch between single- and dual-pane views by clicking the Folders button on the toolbar to turn the Folders pane on/off.

- In early Windows versions, such as 95, My Computer and Windows Explorer were completely separate.
- In Windows 95, by default, when you double-click a drive or folder in My Computer another window opens. In all later versions the default behavior is for the new content to replace the previous content in the same window.
- You can change the default behavior in all Windows versions to suit your preference through the Folder Options dialog box.
- As a shortcut, from My Computer hold down Ctrl as you double-click to open a new window.
- As a shortcut, from My Computer hold down Shift as you double-click to open a new window that contains a folder tree (Windows Explorer type window).

## File Management Skills to Master

- The A+ exams assume that you are already a proficient end user of PCs, and this includes the ability to manage files (move, copy, delete, rename, and so on).
- The exams do not specifically test those skills, but some questions may assume that knowledge.
- Skills to master include the following:
  - Selecting files
  - Deleting files
  - Renaming files
  - Viewing properties
  - Copying between various locations
  - Moving between various locations
  - Creating shortcuts

## Working with the Recycle Bin

- Deleted files move to the Recycle Bin rather than being immediately destroyed (unless the Recycle Bin has been disabled).
- They remain there until the Recycle Bin is emptied, until it reaches its maximum size, or until the hard disk starts running low on disk space.
- Recycle Bin skills you should be familiar with include:
  - Placing a file into the Recycle Bin
  - Deleting a file by bypassing the Recycle Bin
  - Retrieving a deleted file from the Recycle Bin
  - Permanently deleting a file from the Recycle Bin

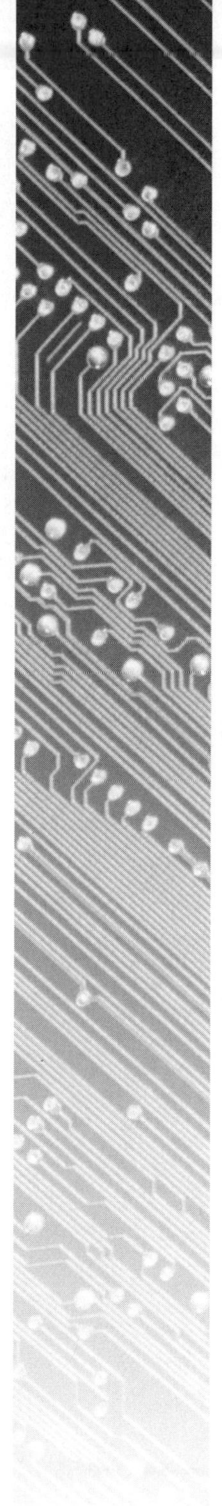

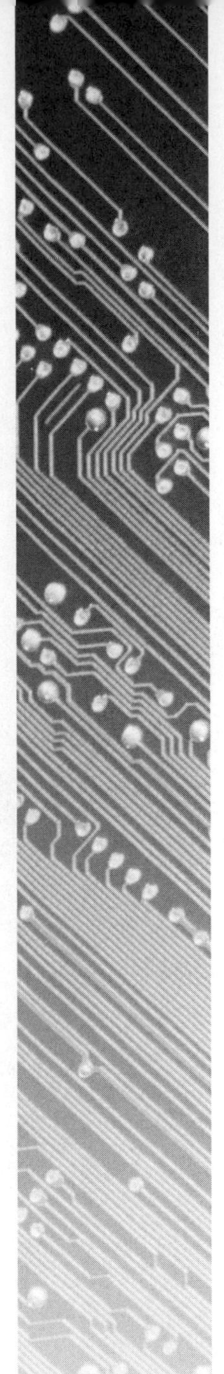

- Emptying the Recycle Bin
- Configuring Recycle Bin properties

## Working with Basic File Attributes

- The four basic attributes a file can have are Read-Only, Hidden, System, and Archive.
- Read-Only prevents a file from being changed or deleted.
- Hidden suppresses that file from normal file listings. It might still appear if Windows has been set up to display hidden files, but it will appear ghosted.
- System designates a file as a system file, necessary for the OS startup or operation.
- Archive indicates that the file has been changed since it has been backed up. Backup programs turn off the Archive attribute after backing up each file.
- A file or folder's attributes can be viewed and changed from its Properties dialog box.
- You can also use the ATTRIB command at a prompt to view or change attributes.
- With the ATTRIB command, use + or - to turn off an attribute. For example, use +H to turn on the Hidden attribute.

## NTFS File Attributes

- Drives that use the NTFS file system have some additional attributes you can set.
- NTFS compression compresses the file as it is being written to disk and decompresses it as it is being read back into memory. The process is invisible to the user.
- In Windows NT 4.0 there is a simple check box for a drive, folder, or file in the Properties dialog box that turns compression on/off.
- In Windows 2000 and XP you click the Advanced button in the Properties dialog box to open an Advanced Attributes dialog box. From there, mark or clear the Compress contents to save disk space check box.
- In the Folder Options dialog box you can choose to have compressed files and folders appear with their names in a different color from other files (blue by default) so you can easily recognize and remember them.
- Encryption prevents other users of a local PC from accessing files that one user has designated as personal. It is based on the user name used to log on.

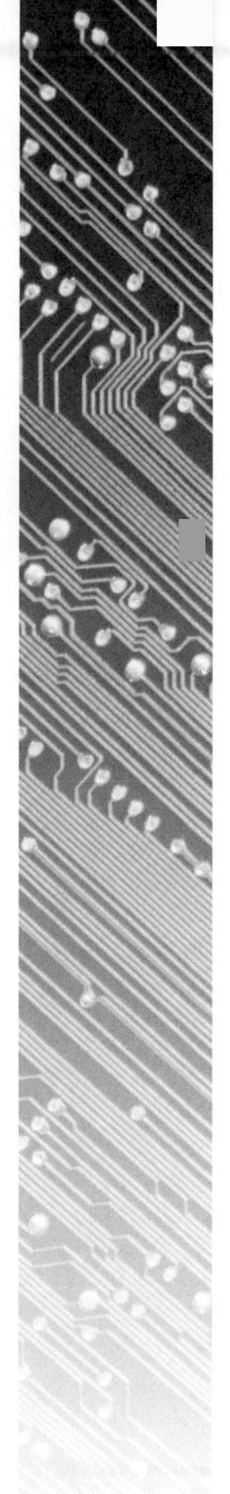

- Encryption can result in a file's becoming irretrievable in the event of a catastrophic system crash, so use it only when it is needed.
- To turn on encryption, view the Advanced Attributes dialog box for the file or folder and choose Encrypt contents to secure data.
- In the Folder Options dialog box you can choose to make encrypted items appear with their names in a different color (green by default).
- Encryption and compression are mutually exclusive.

## Troubleshooting File Management Error Messages

- A general failure means the disk is not formatted or is completely inaccessible.
- A data error means there is a bad spot on the disk physically.
- A sector not found error means that there is a disconnect between the BIOS's expectations for a drive's physical layout and its actual content.
- Access denied errors mean the disk or the file is write-protected (read-only).

## Backing Up and Restoring Files

- There are many ways to back up data. They include simple copying to other drives, ghosting a drive (making a complete copy of it on another drive), and using a backup application.
- Windows 2000 and XP come with Microsoft Backup, a backup application that works with tape drives, CD writers, hard drives, and floppy drives.
- Earlier versions of Windows included earlier versions of Microsoft Backup, but these were very different from the current versions and did not work as well.
- Microsoft Backup includes a Backup Wizard and a Restore Wizard that make creating a system or data backup as simple as following some prompts.

## Working with a Command Prompt

- You can get to a command prompt by booting from a floppy created with MS-DOS or Windows 9x, or from a window inside Microsoft Windows.
- In 9x versions of Windows, use Start/Run and then key **COMMAND**. In NT versions key **CMD**.
- Key a drive letter followed by a colon to change to it.

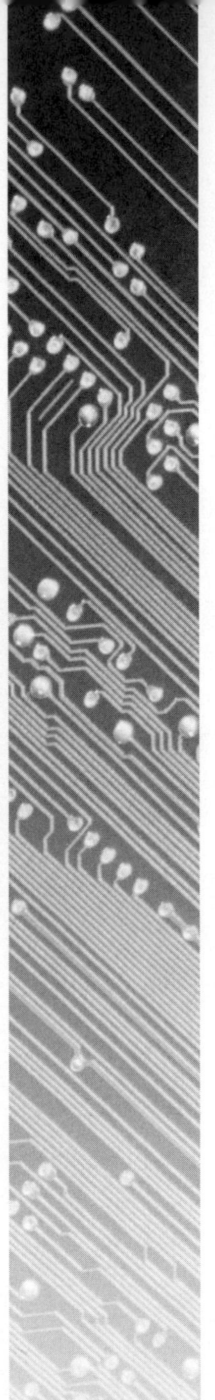

- Use the CD command to change directories.
- Use DIR to display a directory listing.
- Command syntax is the set of rules for issuing that command. It may include required or optional parameters and switches.
- A switch is a / sign followed by one or more characters.
- To get help with any command, key the command name followed by /?.
- A * wildcard stands for any number of characters; a ? wildcard stands for a single character.
- The addition of | MORE to the end of a command displays its results in multiple screenfuls rather than scrolling it all so fast you cannot read it.
- DEL deletes files.
- DELTREE deletes entire directory trees and all associated files.
- MD makes a directory.
- RD removes a directory, but the directory must be empty.
- SETVER tells MS-DOS to report a different OS version number to an application than is actually installed.
- COPY copies files and directories (folders).
- XCOPY copies entire directory tree branches of files and directories.
- MEM reports the available memory.
- PROMPT sets what characters will appear as the command prompt.

# PRACTICE TEST

On a blank sheet of paper, write the answers to the following multiple-choice questions and explain why each answer is correct.

1. Windows 2000 is able to read from drives that use which file systems?
   a. FAT16 and FAT32
   b. FAT32, NTFS 4, and NTFS 5
   c. FAT16 and NTFS 4
   d. FAT16, FAT32, and NTFS 5

2. The File Allocation Table (or equivalent) on a disk tracks the location of
   a. the starting cluster of each file on the entire logical drive.
   b. the starting cluster of each file in the root directory.
   c. all clusters of each file on the entire logical drive.
   d. all clusters of each file in the root directory.

3. Which file systems are 16-bit?
   a. FAT
   b. NTFS 4
   c. NTFS 5
   d. both FAT and NTFS 4

4. What is FAT12 used for?
   a. compact discs
   b. OS/2
   c. MS-DOS hard disks
   d. floppy disks

5. What features does NTFS 5 offer that NTFS 4 did not?
   a. compression, encryption, and disk quotas
   b. encryption, disk quotas, and dynamic disks
   c. compression and encryption
   d. dynamic disks and compression

6. Which operating system(s) support the HPFS file system?
   a. MS-DOS
   b. Windows 2000 and XP
   c. OS/2
   d. None; it is a printer language for Hewlett-Packard printers.

7. In My Computer in Windows 2000, how can you make sure that double-clicking a drive icon opens a new single-pane window rather than replacing the current window's content?
   a. hold down Shift
   b. hold down Ctrl
   c. hold down Alt
   d. No keys are necessary; it opens a new window by default.

8. Which file management window includes a folder tree by default?
   a. Windows Explorer
   b. Internet Explorer
   c. My Computer
   d. My Network Places

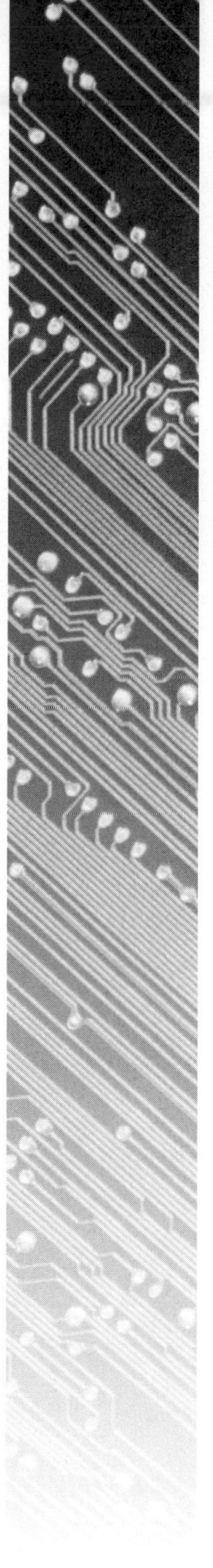

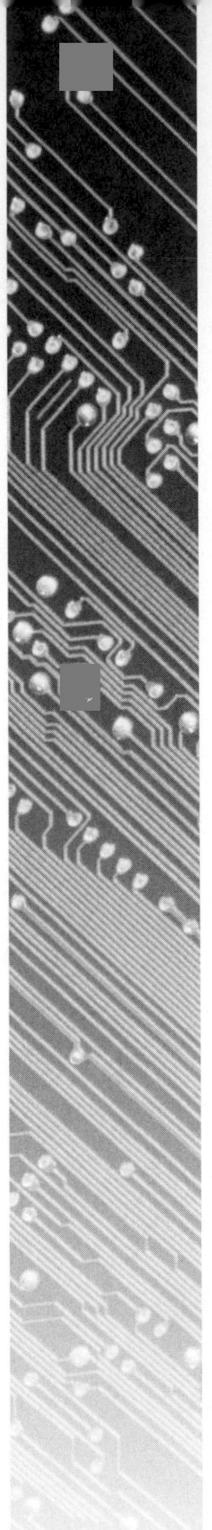

9. To select multiple noncontiguous files in a file management window, hold down the __________ key(s) as you click on the files you want.
   a. Shift
   b. Alt
   c. Ctrl
   d. Ctrl + Alt

10. What happens if you hold down the Alt key as you drag a file from a file management window to the desktop?
    a. moves it
    b. copies it
    c. creates a shortcut for it
    d. None of the above

11. How can you bypass the Recycle Bin and permanently delete a file immediately from a file management window?
    a. Press Ctrl + Delete.
    b. Press Alt + Delete.
    c. Press Shift + Delete.
    d. Right-click it and choose Delete.

12. What does it mean if a file has the Archive attribute turned on?
    a. The file has changed since it was last backed up.
    b. The file has *not* changed since it was last backed up.
    c. The file is more than one year old.
    d. The file is less than one year old.

13. When Windows is set up to display compressed and encrypted files in different colors, what does it mean when a file name appears in green letters?
    a. The file is compressed.
    b. The file is encrypted.
    c. The file is both compressed and encrypted.
    d. The file is neither compressed nor encrypted.

14. Another name for NTFS 5 file encryption is
    a. NTFS permissions.
    b. NTFS security.
    c. token-based permission.
    d. Encrypting File System (EFS).

15. What does a data error mean when reading a file from a disk?
    a. There is a bad spot on the disk where that file is stored.
    b. The entire disk is unreadable.
    c. The disk contains a virus.
    d. The disk is a FAT12 volume and you are reading it with a FAT16 drive.

16. Onto which type(s) of storage media can the version of Microsoft Backup in Windows 2000 back up files?
    a. floppy
    b. floppy or tape
    c. floppy, tape, or another local hard disk
    d. floppy, tape, another local hard disk, or a network drive

17. At the command prompt C:\Windows\System> you key **CD** and press Enter. What will the command prompt now appear as?
    a. C:\Windows>
    b. C:\>
    c. C:..>
    d. C:\Windows\System

18. At a command prompt you key **DEL C???.***. Which of these files will not be deleted?
    a. CLAM.DOC
    b. CLIENT.XLS
    c. COST.TXT
    d. They will all be deleted.

19. At a command prompt A:\> you key **FILE1.TXT C:\FILE2.TXT**. What will happen?
    a. The file FILE1.TXT, located on the A drive, will be copied to C:\ and the copy will be called FILE2.TXT.
    b. The file FILE1.TXT, located on the C drive, will be copied to A:\ and the copy will be called FILE2.TXT.
    c. The file FILE1.TXT, located on the C drive, will be copied to the same location (the C drive), and the copy will be called FILE2.TXT.
    d. An error message will appear.

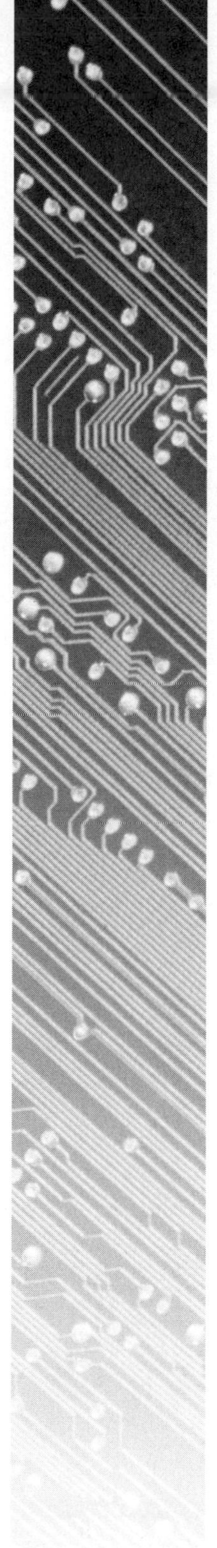

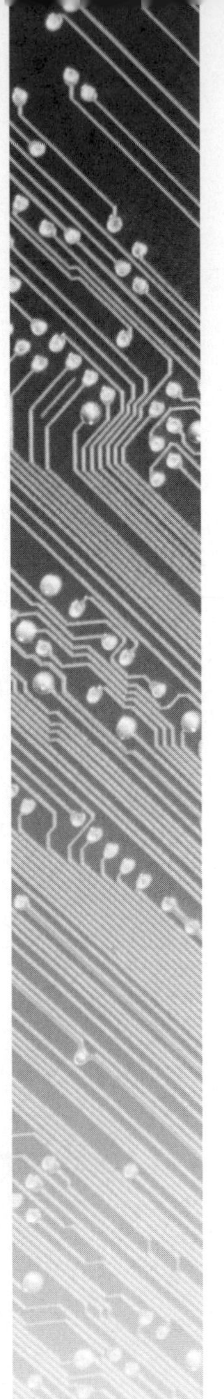

20. What is the difference between RD and DEL?
    a. RD works only on empty directories; DEL works on any directory.
    b. RD works only on empty directories; DEL works only on files.
    c. RD works on any directories; DEL works only on empty ones.
    d. RD is an MS-DOS 6.0 and above command; DEL is included with all MS-DOS and Windows versions.

## TROUBLESHOOTING

1. A client wants to move a hard disk from a PC that runs Windows 2000 to a PC that runs Windows NT Workstation 4.0. Do you anticipate any problems doing this? If so, what might they be?
2. You are cleaning up an old hard disk using a command prompt. From the C:\Files> prompt you key **DEL** *.* and press Enter. It appears that everything is deleted from the folder; checking its content with the DIR command reports File Not Found. However, when you change back to the root directory and attempt to remove the *Files* folder, an error appears that the directory is not empty. What should you check?
3. A client needs to copy several thousand small graphics files to floppy disks for storage. Some disks do not seem to be holding as much as they could, however; they show a Disk Full error message even though space remains on them. What can you suggest?

## CUSTOMER SERVICE

1. A client wants to check the status of the Archive attribute for some files in Windows 2000, but the Archive check box does not appear on the General tab of the file's Properties dialog box. What can you suggest?
2. A client calls you asking what it means when a floppy disk reports a data error. What can you tell him, and what do you recommend doing to salvage the data on it, if anything?
3. A client complains that every time she deletes a file, Windows always displays a confirmation box that she has to click on. Then she has to empty the Recycle Bin to get rid of the file permanently. She would like to be able to delete files and have them permanently deleted immediately, with no confirmation prompt. What do you suggest?

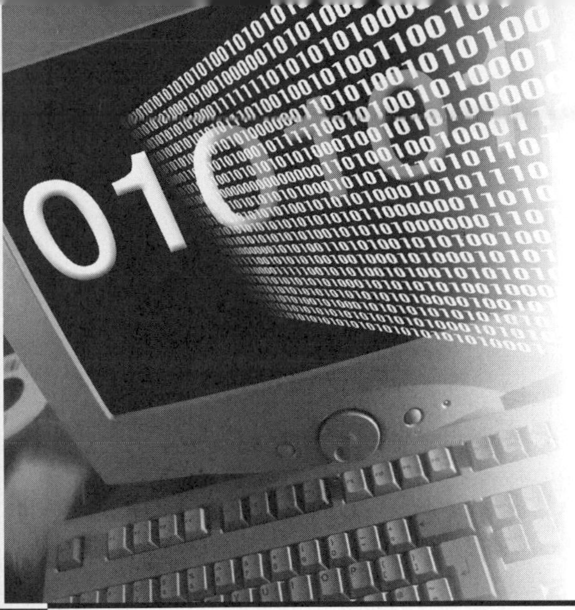

# 30 Optimizing and Troubleshooting Windows

## ON THE TEST

**A+ Core Hardware Service Technician Examination**

- **Objective 2.2:** Identify basic troubleshooting procedures and how to elicit problem symptoms from customers.

**A+ Operating System Technologies Examination**

- **Objective 1.1:** Identify the operating system's functions, structure, and major system files to navigate the operating system and how to get to needed technical information.
- **Objective 1.2:** Identify basic concepts and procedures for creating, viewing and managing files, directories and disks. This includes procedures for changing file attributes and the ramifications of those changes (for example, security issues).
- **Objective 3.1:** Recognize and interpret the meaning of common error codes and startup messages from the boot sequence, and identify steps to correct the problems.
- **Objective 3.2:** Recognize common problems and determine how to resolve them.

## ON THE JOB

This chapter provides an overview of some of the many Windows-based utilities available for troubleshooting, optimization, system information, and other functions needed by the professional PC technician as well as by the experienced end user. Some of these utilities have been introduced in earlier chapters; others may be new to you.

Some of the activities you might need to perform on the job with these utilities might include:

- diagnosing possible virus infection
- optimizing hard disk space usage and performance

- getting information about a system
- troubleshooting system and application problems
- converting from FAT16 to FAT32
- installing or removing DriveSpace
- scheduling recurring maintenance tasks

# Identifying, Removing, and Avoiding Viruses

End users will likely look to you for guidance in identifying and removing viruses on their PCs. MS-DOS and Windows do not come with any type of antivirus utility, so you must rely on third-party products such as McAfee VirusScan or Symantec Norton AntiVirus. The only reliable way to detect and remove viruses is to use one of these applications.

## Types of Virus Infections

**Virus**

A piece of programming code that causes annoyance to the PC user and/or harm to the PC or its stored data.

In the early days of personal computing there were only two types of *virus*. One type would infect .exe files, adding a foreign string to them so that when they executed, the virus would run and do its damage. The other type would travel from PC to PC via floppy disk, hidden in the boot sector, and when a PC was booted from an infected floppy, the virus would copy itself to the boot sector of the new PC.

These types of viruses still exist, but are nowhere near as common as the newer varieties. Some would argue that the newer ones are not really "viruses" per se because they lack some of the defining characteristics of a virus, such as the ability to attach itself to a program file or to infect the system area of a disk. Anyone who has ever supported users who have been victimized by one of the newer varieties would probably not quibble over the strict definition.

Some of the common virus types today include:

- **Trojan horse:** A program that appears to do something useful but actually delivers a harmful effect such as opening up a security hole, spreading itself via e-mail, or deleting or damaging files.
- **Worm:** A program that spreads by making copies of itself. It may or may not do anything additional.
- **@m:** A mailer; a type of worm that attaches itself to e-mail that you send.
- **@mm:** A mass-mailer; a type of worm that automatically sends itself to multiple addresses from your address book.
- **Back door:** A program that sends information about the infected system back to its creator, making it easy for that person to hack into the infected system and take control of it or read sensitive data.

- **Blended threat:** A combination of infection types in a single item. For example, a worm that also infects a boot sector, deletes important files, or opens a security back door would be a blended threat, as would a back-door program that distributes itself as a mass mailer. Most of the viruses circulating at this writing are blended threats, so they do not neatly fall into any one category. This also makes them more dangerous, easier to spread, and more difficult to eradicate.

## How Viruses Spread

There are still only two ways of getting a virus: booting from an infected floppy or running an infected program. However, viruses are much more sly about being "programs" these days; a virus might be contained in a Visual Basic script attached to an e-mail, for example, and named so that it resembles a graphic file, such as picture.gif.vbs. Viruses can also hide in the macros of a Word or Excel document (since a macro is technically a type of program). If there is no executable component, there can be no virus spread. Therefore, viruses cannot hide in plain-text documents, in graphic files, or in any other data files that do not contain macros. However, a virus can *affect* all of those files; some viruses delete all of the graphics files they find, for example.

Viruses also do not spread simply by browsing an infected floppy disk, either at a command prompt or through Windows. A floppy disk may contain a virus either in the boot sector or in an individual executable file. If you do not boot from the disk, the PC does not read the boot sector. If you do not run the executable file, the PC does not read it either.

**WARNING**

If you leave a floppy in the drive accidentally while booting, an error message may appear prompting you to remove the disk and then "press any key to continue." *Do not do it.* If that floppy contained a virus, at this point the virus has just been copied into RAM, but has not yet infected the hard disk. Remove the floppy and then press Ctrl + Alt + Delete to do a full reboot, wiping out the virus from RAM. Even if you are fairly sure the floppy does not contain a virus, it is better to be safe than sorry.

## Symptoms of Virus Infection

Figure 30.1 lists some unmistakable symptoms of virus infection. The symptoms listed in the figure are seldom caused by anything except viruses.

- The user received an e-mail with an odd attachment and opened it, with unexpected results like odd dialog boxes or a sudden degradation in system performance.
- Others report that they have recently received odd e-mails from the PC's user containing random attached files or a virus.
- Word will not save in DOC format, but only in DOT format. This is a symptom of a Word *macro virus.*
- There is a double extension on an attachment that the user recently opened, such as .jpg.vbs. It is much easier to spot double extensions if the display of extensions is turned on. To do that, choose Tools/Folder Options and deselect the Hide extensions for known file types check box on the View tab.
- The antivirus program is disabled for no apparent reason (perhaps with an X through its icon in the notification area), and cannot be enabled. It may report an error condition. Viruses that cause this are called *retroviruses.*
- The antivirus program will not install on the PC, or appears to install but then will not run, but other programs will install.
- Many files are missing, especially many files of a common type. For example, some viruses have a side effect of deleting all of the files of certain graphics types.
- The PC starts doing things on its own that it would normally never do, like the mouse pointer moving by itself, windows opening or closing, programs running, or the CD tray opening and closing by itself. This is a symptom of someone's actually using a back door to operate the PC, rather than a symptom of the existence of the back door itself.
- There are new users with full security permissions that neither you nor the PC's end user created. Again this is a symptom of back-door hacking, more than a symptom of a virus infection per se.
- Strange sounds or music play from the speakers for no apparent reason.
- File sizes or date/time stamps have changed for no reason.
- An application has disappeared that has not been officially uninstalled.

**Macro virus**

A virus that spreads through macros in data files such as Word or Excel.

**Retrovirus**

A computer virus that thwarts attempts to remove it, by such methods as disabling the antivirus software.

**FIGURE 30.1**
Symptoms of Virus Infection

Sometimes virus infection also causes other system problems, some of which can be mistaken for problems with applications or with Windows itself. These include overall slowdowns or lockups, spontaneous rebooting, applications not installing correctly (especially utility programs such as antivirus), extremely slow startup and shutdown, failure to start up at all, and/or an entire hard disk's losing its formatting or partition data.

Often a key to distinguishing virus-related system problems from ordinary ones is situational. What did the user do right before the problem started? If possible, check the user's e-mail box to see whether an e-mail containing a virus might still be there. Check the *Deleted Items* folder as well, and the *Sent Items* folder for evidence of the virus's having been spread to others.

For a definitive answer, you must turn to an antivirus program with updated definitions. If a reputable antivirus program will install, run, and complete a check successfully, and if its definitions have been updated within the last 24 hours, you can be fairly confident that there is no virus. Otherwise, virus infection is still a credible suspect.

## Understanding Virus Definitions

Most antivirus programs cannot detect viruses that they do not know about. There are exceptions, such as programs that monitor the file sizes and dates of essential system files and warn you if they are about to be changed. However, the vast majority of threats circulating today are not true viruses in that they do not actively infect your existing .exe files or boot sector. Instead they are Trojan horses, back-door programs, or worms, which do not usually have behaviors that trigger that kind of proactive detection. Therefore, updated *virus definitions* are your only reliable line of defense against new virus threats.

**Virus definitions**

Information about virus threats used by an antivirus program to detect and remove them.

Programs like Norton AntiVirus include automatic updating that checks for new definitions on the company's server and installs them automatically. Be warned, however, that some services (such as Symantec's Live Update) update their servers only once a week except during peak periods of virus problems, so you might not always get the latest updates by running Live Update (or whatever is the auto-updater for your software). Going to the company's Web site and comparing the date of the most recently posted definitions to the date shown in your software is one way to ensure you have the latest data. Symantec has an Intelligent Updater service that updates virus definitions every business day; this can be a good alternative for administrators with mission-critical PCs to support.

Assuming the virus definitions are up-to-date, you can be reasonably certain that if an antivirus program successfully completes a full system scan and tells you there is no virus, there probably is no virus. If you remain skeptical, check one of the major virus security Web sites after 24 hours; it is possible that a brand-new variant has slipped in, but within 24 hours other people should be reporting it and it should be all over the virus community's news.

If the antivirus program will not run or do a full system scan, or if you buy a new copy and it will not install, this is a fairly good sign that there is a virus infection. For example, many varieties of the W32.Klez.mm mass-mailing worm include commands that disable the antivirus software and make it difficult or impossible to install new antivirus software. If you think the PC might have a W32.Klez.mm virus or a variant thereof, you will need to download and run a special Klez removal tool. Symantec has a free one at its Web site at http://securityresponse.symantec.com/avcenter/venc/data/w32.klez.removal.tool.html. The company also has removal tools for many other specific viruses at http://securityresponse.symantec.com/avcenter/tools.list.html.

## Avoiding Future Virus Infections

Novice end users frequently seem prone to falling for every hoax and every encouragement to "click here." Figure 30.2 lists some tips geared toward protecting your users against their own gullibility and protecting your servers against virus attacks.

- Train your end users not to open attachments unless they are expecting them, and not to run programs they download from the Internet unless they have been scanned for viruses.
- Encourage end users to keep Windows and Internet Explorer patched with the latest security patches; if possible, set up automatic updates for Windows and IE. Simply visiting a Web site can cause infection if certain patches are not installed.
- By default, many operating systems (especially server versions) install with extra services that you do not need, such as an FTP server, telnet, and a Web server. Remove any that are not critical in order to provide fewer avenues for a threat to attack.
- Be quick to disable or block access to network services when a blended threat exploits one of them, and keep them sealed off until you can apply a fix.
- Do not boot from an unknown floppy disk. If you leave a floppy in the drive and the PC tries to boot from it, remove the floppy and do a hard reset.
- Keep patch levels up-to-date, especially on computers that host public services such as HTTP, FTP, Mail, and DNS, and are accessible through the firewall.
- Use *strong passwords* yourself, and enforce an aggressive password policy that requires complex passwords and frequent changes. This helps limit the damage in the event that a computer is compromised through a back door.
- Ask your network administrator to configure the e-mail server to block or remove e-mail that contains file attachments that are commonly used to spread viruses, such as VBS, BAT, EXT, PIF, and SCR files. Recommend to users that they send any files that legitimately need to be mailed in those formats in compressed archives (ZIP files).
- Frequently check the security advisories provided by the makers of antivirus software to find out what the latest threats are. An excellent one is the Security Advisories list from Symantec at http://securityresponse.symantec.com/avcenter/tools.list.html.

**Strong password**

A password that is very difficult to guess, involving a combination of capital and lowercase letters, numbers, and sometimes symbols as well.

**FIGURE 30.2**
Tips for Helping End Users Avoid Virus Infection

# Optimization Utilities

Optimization utilities make the PC run better. Some of them, such as Disk Defragmenter, make the PC run faster or more efficiently. Others, such as Disk Cleanup Wizard, free up hard disk space.

As with most of the other utilities covered in this chapter, there are third-party brands of these utility types available at any computer store. This chapter covers only the versions built into Windows, because those are the versions included on the A+ exams.

## Disk Defragmenter

To understand disk defragmenting, and why it improves system performance, it helps to remember something about disk storage (from Part 3). Hard disk file storage is not necessarily physically sequential. For example, suppose you have a word processing document that takes up three clusters on the hard disk. If you add another page to the document, the file might require an additional cluster. That additional cluster might be physically located in a completely different area of the disk than the original three. Such a file is *fragmented* because all of its clusters are not physically contiguous.

**Fragmented file**

A file that is not stored contiguously on a disk.

As you can imagine, moving all over the disk to pick up the fragments takes time whenever an application opens the file, which is why fragmentation slows down the system's performance.

When you defragment, a utility program rearranges the content of the hard disk so that as many files as possible are stored in contiguous clusters. This allows the files to be opened more quickly because the read/write head does not have to move around as much. Disk Defragmenter comes with all 32-bit versions of Windows (that is, Windows 95 and higher), and defragments the file system to make it more efficient.

For best performance, defragment a hard disk regularly (for example, once a month). This procedure cannot turn an old hard disk into a top performer, but it can result in a modest speedup in activities involving file opening. The frequency with which to defragment depends on how much the end user uses the PC, how many files he or she opens and changes, and how important the fastest file access may be in comparison to the inconvenience of running the Disk Defragmenter. (For greater expediency, you can set up Disk Defragmenter to run automatically with the Task Scheduler, covered later in this chapter.)

If Disk Defragmenter displays a message like *Disk Contents Changed, Restarting*, even when you have not touched the computer, programs running in the background might be interfering. Each time one of them writes to the disk, the disk content changes and the Disk Defragmenter must restart to avoid possible data corruption. Close all other open programs that you can, including any programs in the system tray.

**IN REAL LIFE**

A Microsoft Office utility called Find Fast can be the culprit in frequent restarts of the defragmenting process. This utility indexes your Office data files so they open more quickly, but it operates in the background and can interfere with the Disk Defragmenter. If the problem continues and you have Microsoft Office installed, open the Control Panel (Start/Settings/Control Panel) and double-click *Find Fast.* Select Index/Pause Indexing. Resume the indexing (by deselecting the Pause Indexing command) when you finish defragmenting, or just leave it turned off; it has no great effect on your system performance.

### *Defragmenting in Windows 95/98/Me*

To run the Disk Defragmenter in Windows 95/98/Me, follow these steps:

1. Choose Start/Programs/Accessories/System Tools/Disk Defragmenter.

**IN REAL LIFE**

You can defragment a floppy disk or other removable disk, but it is probably not worth the trouble. Most likely, you will not open files from such disks very often.

2. The Select Drive dialog box appears, asking which drive you want to defragment. You can defragment only one drive at a time. Select the hard disk from the list of drives, then click OK. If you are using the Windows 95 version of the Disk Defragmenter, a message box appears telling you how defragmented the drive is and suggesting a course of action. You do not see this in the Windows 98 or Me versions.
3. The defragmentation process may start automatically; if it does not, click Start (in Windows 95) or OK (in Windows 98 or Me) to start it.
4. Wait for the drive to be defragmented. If you want to watch the process, click Show Details to see a graphical representation of the proceedings. Click the Legend button to see a chart showing what the various colors of squares represent, as in Figure 30.3.
5. When it finishes, the program asks if you want to quit. Click Yes if all of the hard drives are done, or No to go back to step 2 and choose another drive.

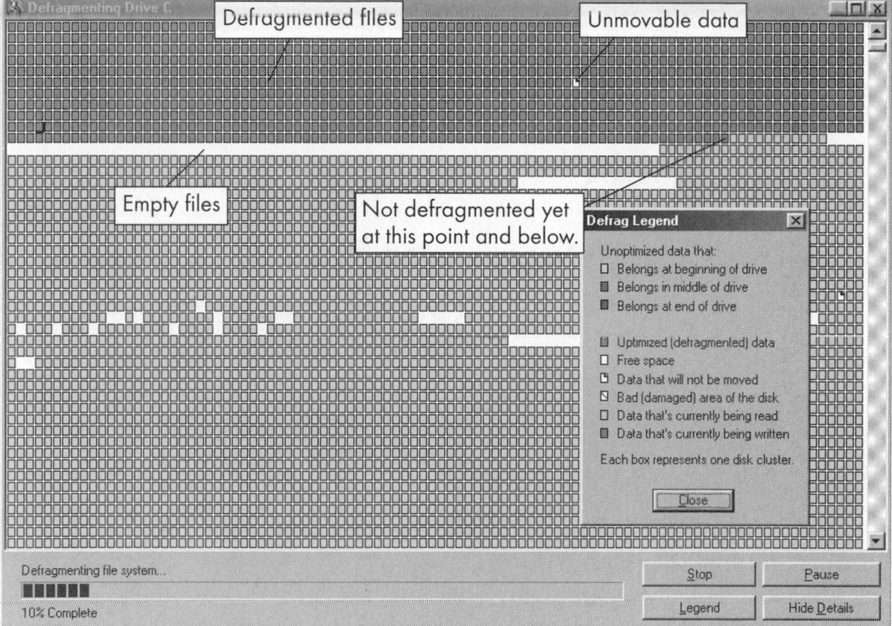


**FIGURE 30.3**
Click Show Details in Windows 9x to watch a graphical representation of the defragmenting process.

### *Defragmenting in Windows 2000/XP*

The Disk Defragmenter in Windows 2000 and XP is a little different from 9x versions, but the result is the same. To run it, follow these steps:

1. Choose Start/(All) Programs/Accessories/System Tools/Disk Defragmenter. Or you can open My Computer, right-click the drive and choose Properties, and then click Defragment Now on the Tools tab.
2. Click a drive (if more than one appears on the list) and then click Defragment. You can defragment a drive as much as you like; it will not hurt anything. But if you would rather check the drive first to make sure it needs defragmenting, click Analyze instead of Defragment, and then defragment only if Windows recommends it.
3. Wait for the drive to be defragmented (see Figure 30.4). It can take an hour or more, depending on the drive size and system speed.
4. When defragmentation is finished, a confirmation box appears; click OK to close it. Then exit the Disk Defragmenter program, or return to step 2 to choose a different drive.

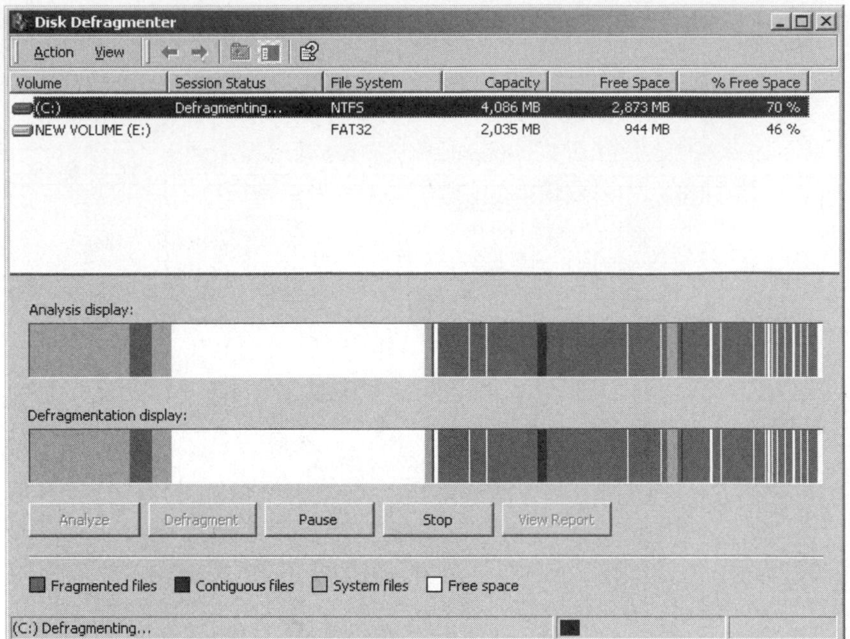


**FIGURE 30.4**
The Disk Defragmenter in Windows 2000 and XP shows a less detailed graphic of the process than in Windows 9x.

**TRY IT!**

**Check each of the local hard disks on your PC. Which ones need defragmenting? Defragment the one that needs it the most.**

## Disk Cleanup

Disk Cleanup frees up disk space by recommending files that can safely be deleted. It comes with Windows versions 98, Me, 2000, and XP. Some of the files it may suggest deleting might include the Recycle Bin contents, old System Restore saves (in Windows Me and XP), temporary files, and offline Web content. The types of data it suggests for deletion vary depending on the Windows version and on what is installed on the PC.

To use Disk Cleanup, complete the following steps:

1. Choose Start/(All) Programs/Accessories/System Tools/Disk Cleanup. A message box appears in which you can select a drive to clean up.
2. Select the drive and click OK. The utility examines the drive, looking for files that could be deleted. This takes a few minutes.
3. Disk Cleanup presents a list of file types, with check marks next to those that it recommends for deletion. You can mark or clear check boxes or click the View Files button to see exactly what files fall into a certain category (see Figure 30.5).

4. Click OK. A confirmation box appears; click Yes. Then wait for the files to be deleted. When Disk Cleanup is finished, it closes automatically.

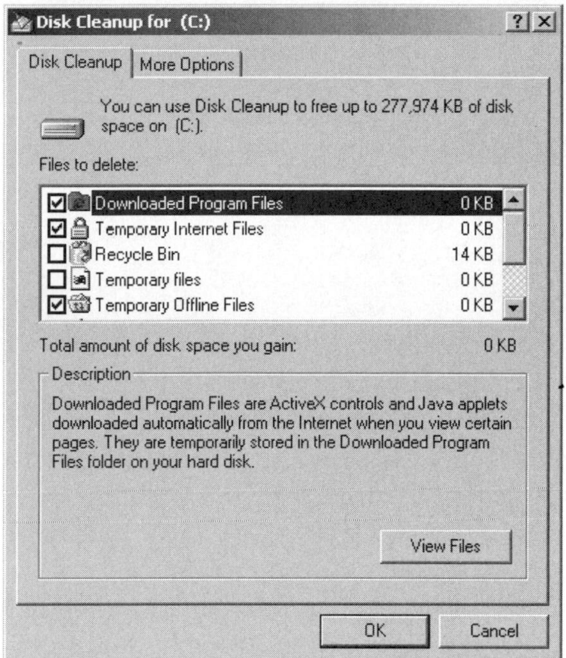


**FIGURE 30.5**
Use Disk Cleanup to free up space on a hard disk.

## TRY IT!

**In My Computer, determine which local hard disk has the least amount of free space. Then run Disk Cleanup on it. How much space were you able to free up, if any?**

## FAT32 Converter

Recall from earlier chapters that some later versions of Windows 95 supported FAT32, but there was no way of converting a drive to FAT32 without reformatting it and losing all of its data. The FAT32 Converter in Windows 98 provides a method of doing just that.

To convert a drive from FAT to FAT32:

1. Choose Start/Programs/Accessories/System Tools/Drive Converter (FAT32). Click Next to begin the wizard.
2. Select the drive to be converted (see Figure 30.6), then click Next.

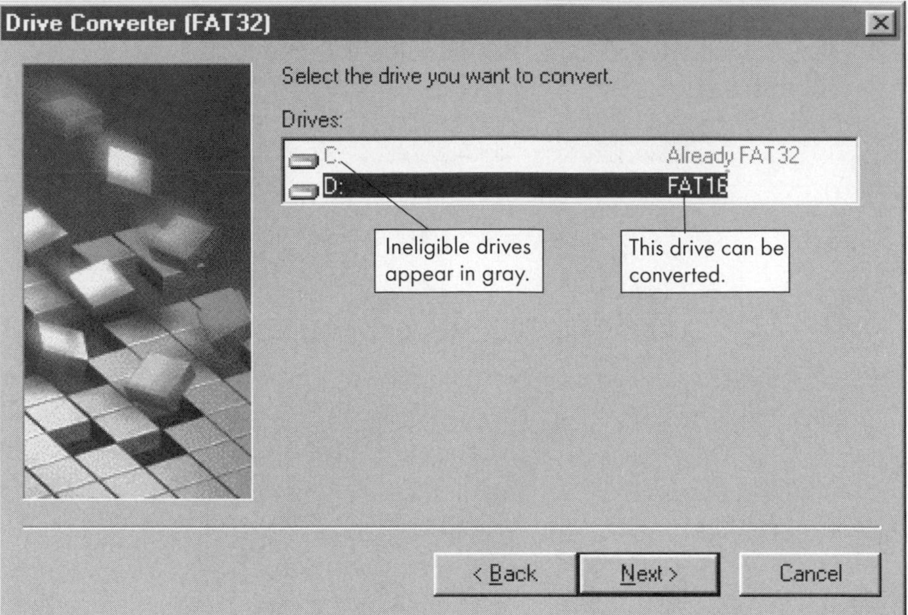


**FIGURE 30.6**
The wizard presents a list of FAT drives eligible for FAT32 conversion.

3. A warning appears. Click OK.
4. The wizard searches for applications that are known to be incompatible with FAT32. If it finds one, it displays an error message. If it does not, a message appears that you can continue; click Next.
5. A message appears urging you to back up the drive before converting it. Click the Backup button to do so, or click Next to continue.
6. A message appears letting you know that you must restart in MS-DOS mode to perform the conversion. Save your work in any running Windows applications, shut them down, and then click Next.
7. Wait for the PC to restart in MS-DOS mode and perform the conversion. Information appears on-screen as it works, as in Figure 30.7.
8. Windows restarts automatically when the conversion is finished, and automatically runs Disk Defragmenter on the newly converted drive. Then a confirmation box appears letting you know the conversion was successful. Click Finish.

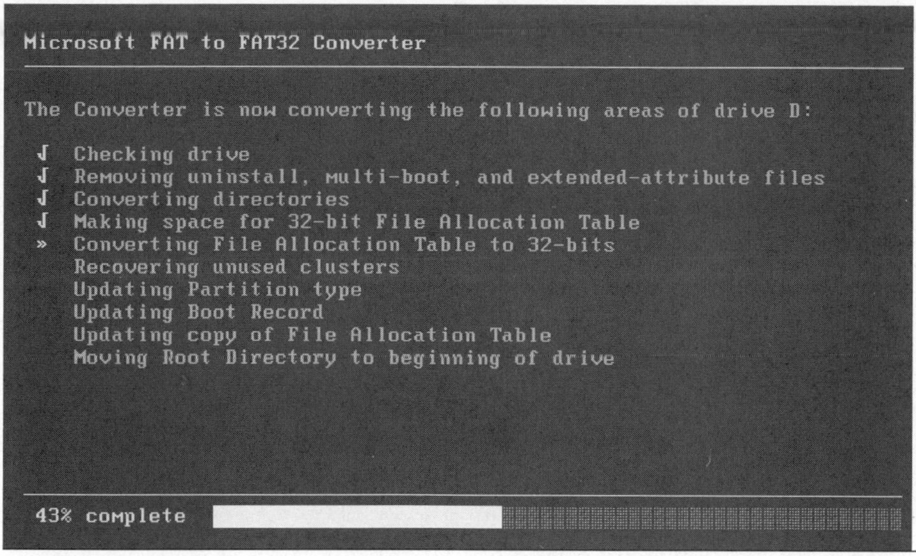

```
Microsoft FAT to FAT32 Converter

The Converter is now converting the following areas of drive D:

 √  Checking drive
 √  Removing uninstall, multi-boot, and extended-attribute files
 √  Converting directories
 √  Making space for 32-bit File Allocation Table
 »  Converting File Allocation Table to 32-bits
    Recovering unused clusters
    Updating Partition type
    Updating Boot Record
    Updating copy of File Allocation Table
    Moving Root Directory to beginning of drive

  43% complete
```

**FIGURE 30.7**
The FAT32 Converter during the Conversion Process

The FAT32 converter is also included in Windows Me, but it does not appear on the menu system. It is a command-line utility only. To use it, from a command prompt window or the Run command, key **CVT *x*:** where *x* is the drive letter to convert.

## DriveSpace

DriveSpace (called DoubleSpace in early versions) is a way of increasing the amount of data that a hard disk will hold by manipulating the way the drive stores data. It is an obsolete system, but you might encounter it on MS-DOS, Windows 95, or Windows 98 systems. DriveSpace works only with FAT drives (not FAT32); that is one reason it has fallen out of use. Another is that compressing a drive with DriveSpace has some negative effects, such as slowing down drive access time and taking twice as long to defragment.

DriveSpace was introduced under the name DoubleSpace in MS-DOS 6.20. Because of some copyright problems, DoubleSpace was removed from MS-DOS 6.21, and then reintroduced with a new compression algorithm and retitled DriveSpace in MS-DOS 6.22.

Windows 95 and 98 include a Windows-based DriveSpace utility program that can create and manage DriveSpace drives. Windows Me also has a DriveSpace utility but it cannot compress drives; it can only manage the settings for drives that are already compressed.

**WARNING**

**Before you use DriveSpace to alter a drive, you should back up any important files onto another drive. The drive compression process is fairly reliable, but it is not 100 percent safe. Disk problems have been known to occur during compression. Also, be aware that with a compressed drive, it is harder to recover from errors than on a regular, uncompressed drive.**

On systems with Windows 98, a later version of Windows 95, or Windows 95 with the Windows 95 Plus Pack installed, there is an additional program called Compression Agent. (It is on the System Tools submenu along with DriveSpace.) You can use it for greater control over your compressed drive. For example, you can specify some infrequently used files for additional compression or specify some often-used files to leave uncompressed. This utility is mostly for advanced users who love to tweak settings; average users will not find any great benefit from using it.

Windows 95 installs the DriveSpace and Compression Agent tools automatically, but Windows 98 does not. In Windows 98 you might need to install them through Add/Remove Programs (they are in the System Tools category).

### *How DriveSpace Works*

Hard disks store data very reliably, but there is often wasted space between files. DriveSpace removes all of the wasted space in the file storage system by storing the files using a different method. The DriveSpace program fools the system into thinking that a file is a disk, and it puts all of the files from the hard disk into that big disk-like file. Because it is really a file, it is not constrained by the inefficient filing system on a real disk, so it can store the hard disk content more efficiently.

Let us assume the hard disk is drive C. DriveSpace creates a big file on C and calls it H. The operating system treats this file like an extra hard disk. Then, one by one, the program moves the files from C to H, gradually increasing the size of H until H takes up almost all of the space on C. Now this massive file is consuming the C drive, and within that file is drive H and all of the programs that used to be on C.

There is one last step: All of the programs are expecting to be on C. If they are on a drive called H, they might not work properly. So DriveSpace swaps the letters; that is, your original C drive is renamed H, and the new H drive is called C. Now all of the programs are running smoothly because they think they are still on C. This process is completely automatic.

### *Compressing a Drive with DriveSpace*

Here are the steps for using the Windows 98 version of DriveSpace to compress a drive. The steps for Windows 95 are similar. Just follow the prompts.

1. Choose Start/Programs/Accessories/System Tools/DriveSpace. A dialog box appears listing the drives on the system.
2. Click the drive you want to compress. Then choose Drive/Compress (Windows 98). A window appears showing how much space you will gain by compressing the drive (see Figure 30.8).

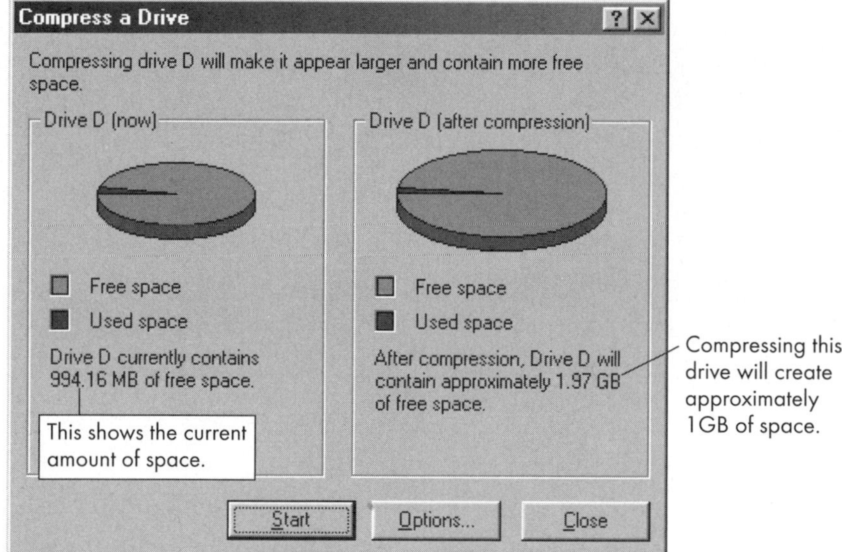


**FIGURE 30.8**
Find out how much benefit you will get from compressing the drive before you do it.

3. Click Start. A warning appears reminding you to update your Startup floppy. If you want to update it now, click Yes and follow the prompts to do so. Otherwise, click No to continue with the disk compression.
4. A box appears giving you the opportunity to create a backup of the disk contents (a good idea) or to continue the compression. Click Compress Now to go on.
5. Wait for the utility to compress the drive and defragment it.

After it finishes, you will notice a new drive on the system—a host drive for the compressed one. The host drive is actually the original uncompressed drive; the new compressed "drive" is actually a file on the host drive.

## System Information Utilities

In earlier chapters we have discussed several of the most important Windows-based utilities for gathering system information. This section briefly reviews them.

### Device Manager

Device Manager lists the hardware installed in the system and enables you to disable, remove, and add hardware and to change the resource assignments. It is covered in detail in Chapter 14.

Device Manager is accessed differently in Windows 9x versus 2000/XP. In Windows 9x it is a separate a tab in the System Properties dialog box, but in Windows 2000/XP you must click the Hardware tab in the System Properties dialog box and then click the Device Manager button. Figure 30.9 shows the Windows XP version.

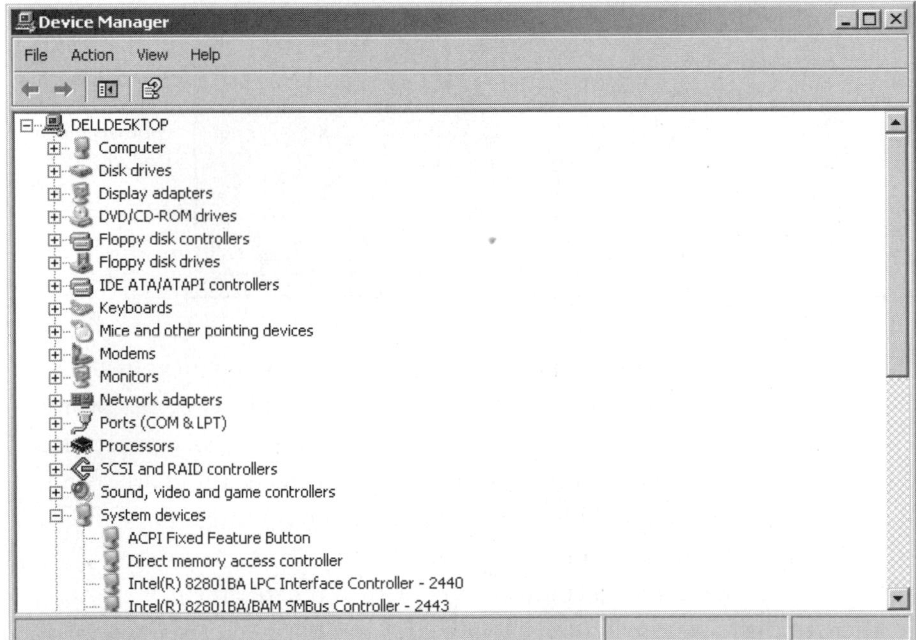


**FIGURE 30.9**
Device Manager allows you to adjust Windows settings for hardware.

## COMPUTER MANAGEMENT

Computer Management is a utility in Windows 2000 and XP that provides a single point of entry for many different administrative utilities. To open Computer Management:

1. From the Control Panel, double-click *Administrative Tools.*
2. Double-click *Computer Management.*

Computer Management displays the various utilities and categories in a folder tree at the left. To use a utility, click its name. (You might need to expand the tree by clicking a plus sign.) Figure 30.10 shows the Device Manager being displayed through Computer Management. Compare this to Figure 30.9, which shows it in a stand-alone window.

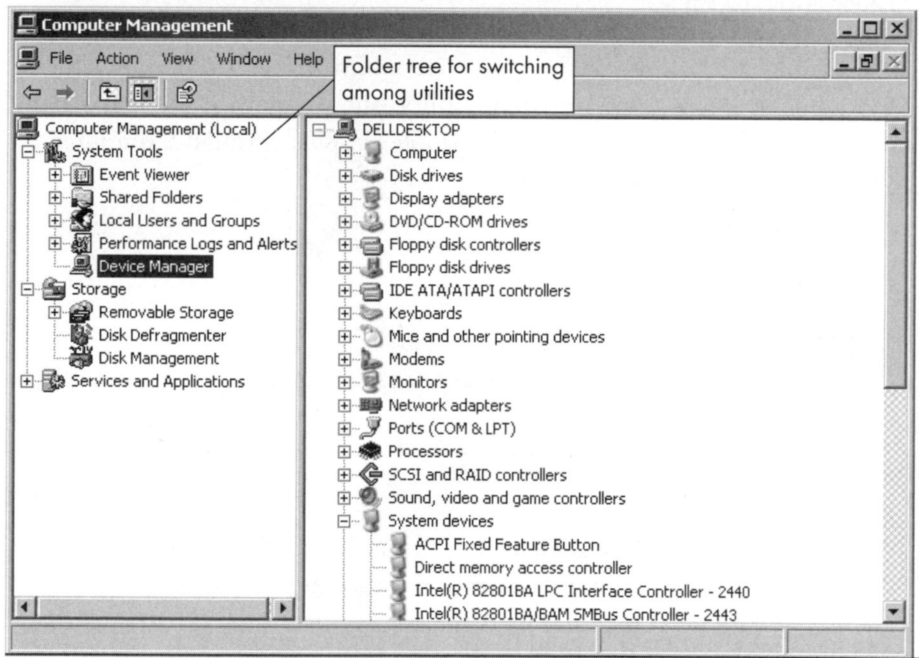


**FIGURE 30.10** Computer Management lets you access many different utilities through a single window.

Table 30.1 shows the utilities available in the Computer Management window and the uses to which you might put them. Several of these are discussed in greater detail later in the chapter. You can also create your own version of the Computer Management window by setting up a Microsoft Management Console (MMC), described later in the chapter.

| Utility | Description |
|---|---|
| Event Viewer | A list of system event messages, useful for troubleshooting problems. |
| Shared Folders | A list of which folders are shared and by whom, useful for security and troubleshooting. |
| Local Users and Groups | A list of the users and groups authorized to use the local PC. |
| Performance Logs and Alerts | Allows you to set up alert conditions to warn you of system problems. |
| Device Manager | Displays and configures hardware. |
| Removable Storage | A list of removable drives, if any (excluding floppies). |
| Disk Defragmenter | Optimizes disk storage. |
| Disk Management | A central utility for partitioning, formatting, and working with drives. |
| Services and Applications | Specialized settings and utilities for services, Windows Management Instrumentation (WMI), and indexing. All are beyond the scope of this book. |

**TABLE 30.1**
Computer Management Utilities

## Disk Management

Disk Management is one of the most-used components in Computer Management. It is also a stand-alone utility, but Windows 2000 and XP do not include it on any menus so most people access it through Computer Management.

### In Real Life

If you want to run Disk Management by itself, choose Start/Run and key **diskmgmt.msc**. You can also set up a shortcut to that file on the desktop or on the Start menu.

We looked at Disk Management in Chapter 12; recall that in Windows 2000 and XP it is the primary means of partitioning and formatting drives. It reports the status of each drive, its file system, its overall capacity, the amount of space remaining on it, and other facts (see Figure 30.11). To work with a disk, select it and then use the menu system, or right-click it and use the shortcut menu.

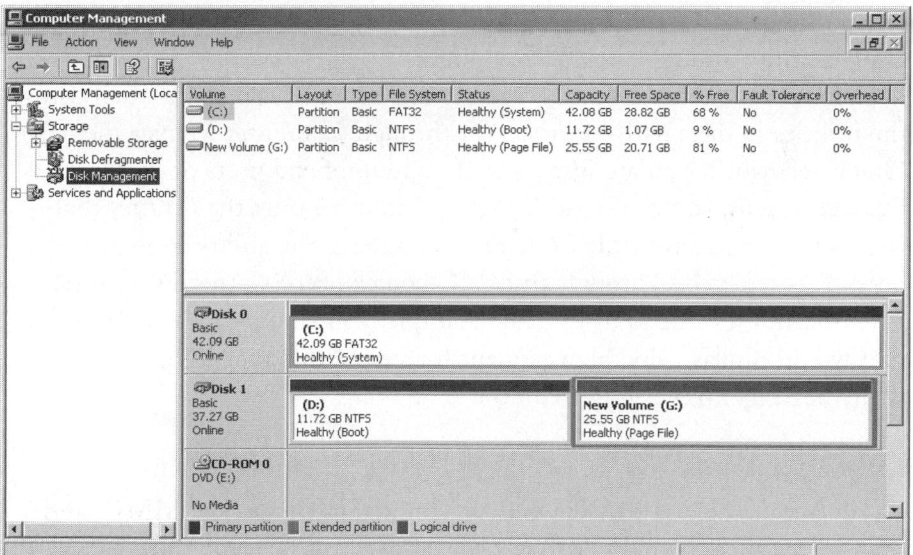


**FIGURE 30.11** Disk Management offers an array of commands and options for configuring local hard disks.

Disk Management is a powerful tool, and there are many things you can do with it that are not covered on the A+ exam. For example, you can convert a disk to a Dynamic disk, and from there you can set up spanned, striped, or RAID-5 volumes. You may want to experiment with Disk Management on your own, after your A+ exam preparation.

**WARNING**

**Do not experiment with converting to a Dynamic disk on a disk that contains the only copy of critical data. Back it up first. Problems encountered during the conversion process are rare, but when they occur they can be catastrophic.**

## TRY IT!

1. Open Computer Management and select Disk Management. What is the status reported for each of the disks in Disk Management? It should be Healthy.
2. Look at the Event Viewer. What are some of the errors that have recently occurred? Are any of them something you should troubleshoot?

## Microsoft Management Console (MMC)

The Microsoft Management Console (MMC) is a customizable version of the Computer Management window. It starts out as a blank window, into which you can add *snap-ins*. A snap-in is a utility that can be added to the MMC. Disk Management, covered in the preceding section, is one such

**Snap-in**

A utility that can be added to a Microsoft Management Console (MMC).

utility. Some of the utilities are also stand-alone applications; some are available only through an MMC window.

There are two main advantages to setting up an MMC rather than using the utilities in their native formats (or through Computer Management). One is security. If you are in charge of a group of end users or junior-level PC technicians, you can set up MMCs containing only the utilities that you want to make available to them. The other is the ability to manage other PCs remotely. Through an MMC you can access other PCs in the network, not just the local PC. For example, you could set up an MMC that would display Disk Management for several different PCs, and browse them all easily from a single window.

### *Creating a New MMC*

To open a new, blank MMC window, choose Start/Run, key **MMC**, and then click OK. A blank MMC window appears, as in Figure 30.12.

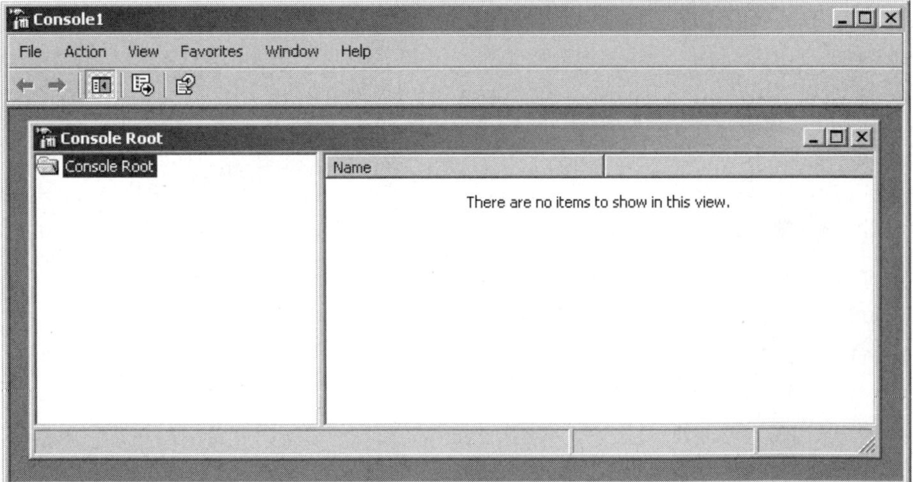


**FIGURE 30.12**
A Blank MMC Window (Windows XP shown)

### *Adding Snap-Ins to an MMC*

To add utilities to an MMC, do the following:

1. Choose File/Add/Remove Snap-In. An Add/Remove Snap-In dialog box opens. (In some versions the menu may be called Console rather than File.)
2. Click the Add button. A list of available snap-ins appears (see Figure 30.13).
3. Click the snap-in you want, and then click Add. Depending on the snap-in chosen, a message box may appear asking what computer you want it to refer to, as in Figure 30.14. You can choose another PC on the network if you like.

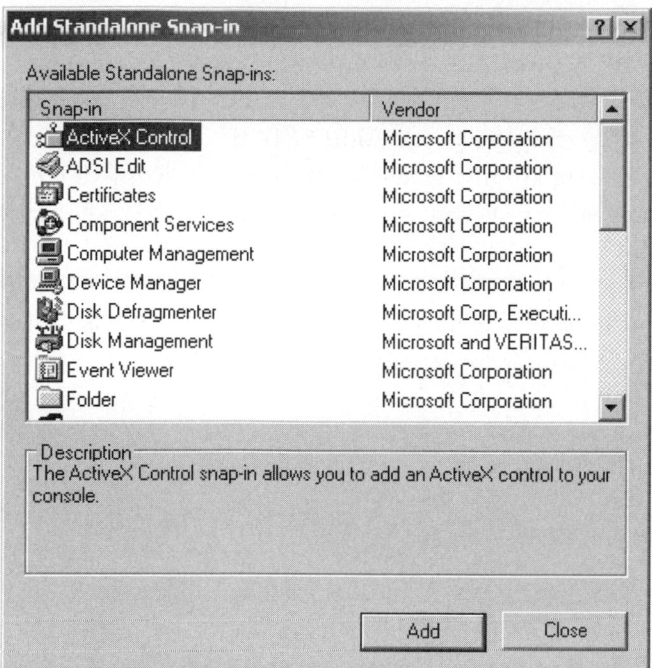


**FIGURE 30.13**
Select a snap-in to add.

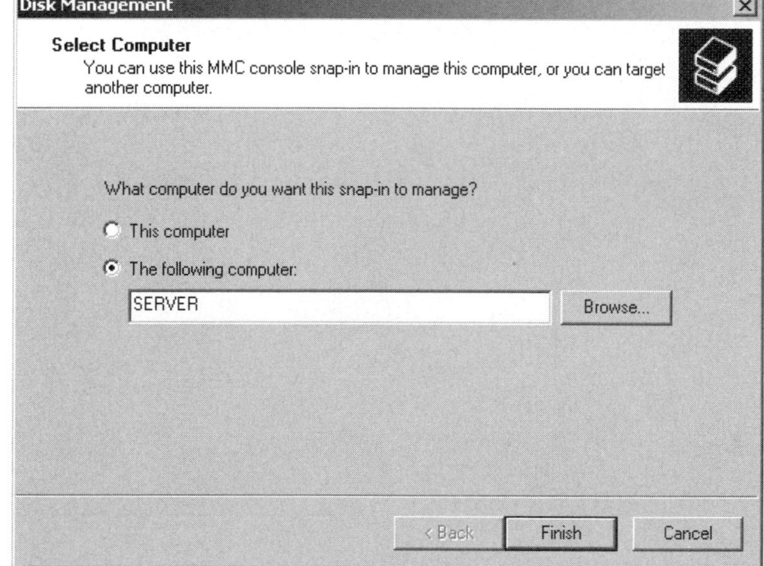


**FIGURE 30.14**
Some snap-ins can point to other PCs besides the local one.

4. Click Finish. The list of available snap-ins reappears. Repeat step 3 to add another, or click Close.
5. Click OK. The selected snap-ins appear in the MMC window.

### *Saving the MMC*

After creating a customized set of utilities in an MMC window, you will probably want to save those settings so you can use the same set again, or so you can make the set available to others. To do so, choose File/Save. The saved file will have an .msc extension, and you can copy or create a shortcut to the file anywhere that you can place any other file or shortcut.

**TRY IT!**

Create a new MMC and add three of your favorite utilities to it. Save it to the desktop using your last name as the file name; then reopen it from the desktop.

## Hardware Diagnostic Tool (HWINFO)

The Hardware Diagnostic Tool (called HWINFO) comes with Windows 98 and Me only. It provides a different view of the same information that System Information provides. Microsoft calls this an unsupported tool, and does not provide any help for it. However, you can find some basic information about it in the Microsoft Knowledge Base at Microsoft's Web site, in article Q185956, "Description of the Microsoft Hardware Diagnostic Tool."

To use HWINFO, start it with the Run command with the /UI switch: **HWINFO /UI**. Information appears in a window, as shown in Figure 30.15. The information is color-coded using the colors listed in Table 30.2. Notice that the Title bar shows Hardware Info utility for Windows, not Hardware Diagnostic Tool (Microsoft's official name for the feature).

| Color | Meaning |
|---|---|
| Green | Keys from the Registry |
| Pink | File attributes information |
| Dark Red | Configuration Manager information |
| Bold Red | Error information |
| Bold Blue | Warning information |

**TABLE 30.2**
Color Coding in the Hardware Diagnostic Tool

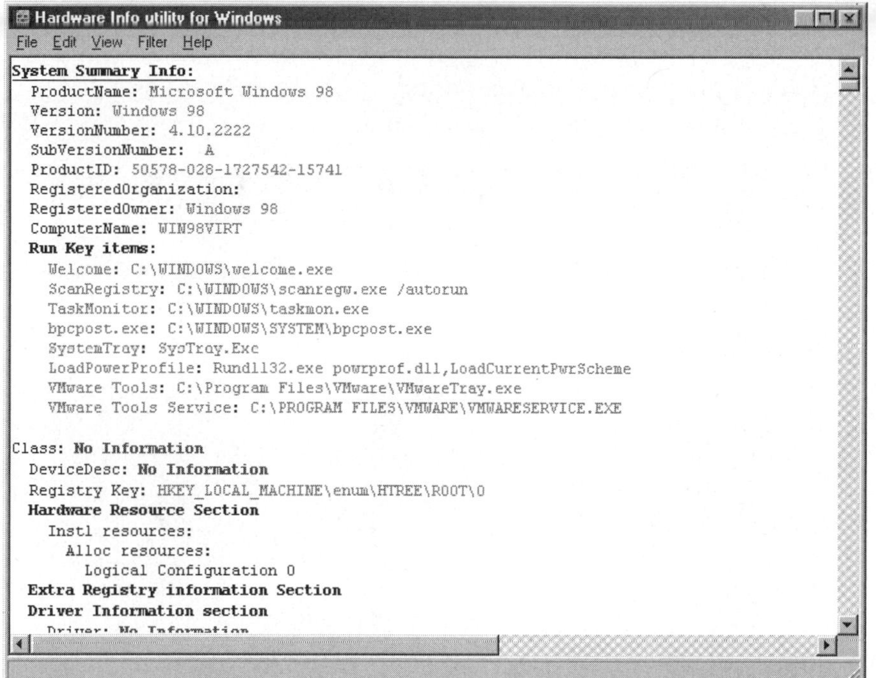


**FIGURE 30.15**
The Hardware Diagnostic Tool provides system information in a text-based color-coded fashion.

# Problem-Solving Utilities

The utilities described in the following sections are useful for finding and correcting problems on a Windows-based PC. Some of them will be familiar to you, as they were covered in greater detail earlier in the book.

## ScanDisk

ScanDisk is an MS-DOS and Windows 9x utility that checks the hard disk for errors. It can perform two types of checks: a logical check of the FAT, and a physical sector-by-sector check of the disk surface.

The MS-DOS version of ScanDisk was introduced in MS-DOS 5.0 to replace an older command-line utility called CHKDSK (short for Check Disk). To run the MS-DOS version, key **SCANDISK** at a command prompt. This also applies to the version of ScanDisk included on Windows 9x startup floppy disks.

The Windows version of ScanDisk runs automatically when Windows starts up after being improperly shut down. You can also run it at any time from the Start menu.

To run ScanDisk from within Windows and perform a complete check for errors, do the following:

1. Choose Start/Programs/Accessories/System Tools/ScanDisk. A ScanDisk window appears, as in Figure 30.16.

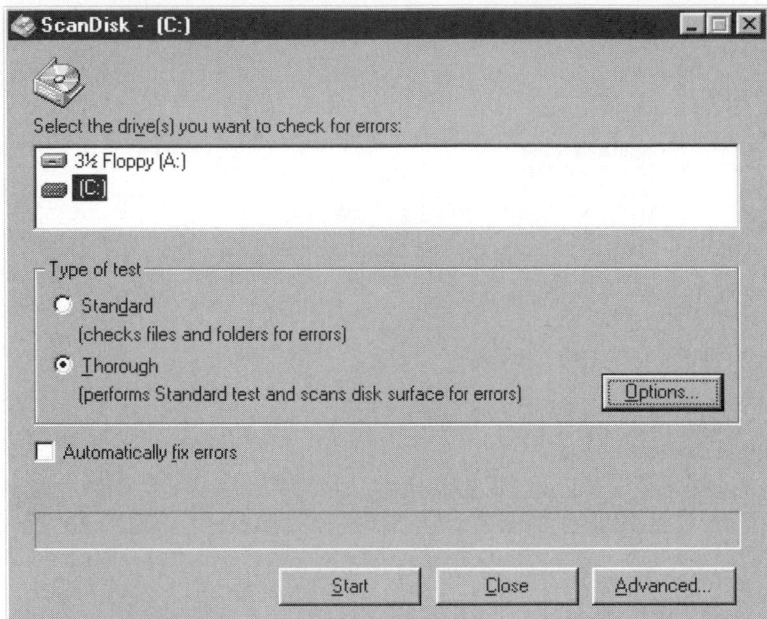


**FIGURE 30.16**
Checking for Errors with ScanDisk in Windows 95/98

**TRY IT!**

**You can also start ScanDisk from a drive's Properties dialog box, on the Tools tab.**

2. Choose Standard or Thorough. Standard does only the logical (FAT) check; Thorough does the physical check as well. It takes a long time—an hour or more in most cases—so you might want to stick with Standard unless you suspect a physical problem (for example, if you have been receiving data errors when reading or writing to the drive). If you choose Thorough, an Options button becomes available; you can click it to configure how the Thorough check takes place.
3. *Optional:* If you want the application to automatically fix any errors it finds, mark the Automatically fix errors check box. If you do not do this, a dialog box will appear for each error found, and you will need to click a button to fix it or ignore it.
4. Click Start to begin the check. When it is finished, a confirmation box appears reporting the results. Click OK to close it.

## Check Disk

Check Disk is the Windows 2000 and XP equivalent of ScanDisk. Unlike ScanDisk, it does not appear in the menu system; you must access it from the drive's Properties dialog box.

To run Check Disk from within Windows, complete these steps:

1. From My Computer, right-click the drive you want to check and choose Properties.
2. On the Tools tab, click Check Now. A Check Disk dialog box appears (see Figure 30.17).
3. If you want the utility to automatically fix any problems it finds, mark the Automatically fix file system errors check box.
4. If you want to do a thorough check (that is, check the disk physically for surface errors), mark the Scan for and attempt recovery of bad sectors check box.
5. Click Start.
6. When the check is done, a confirmation box appears letting you know. Click OK, then click Cancel to close the drive's Properties dialog box.

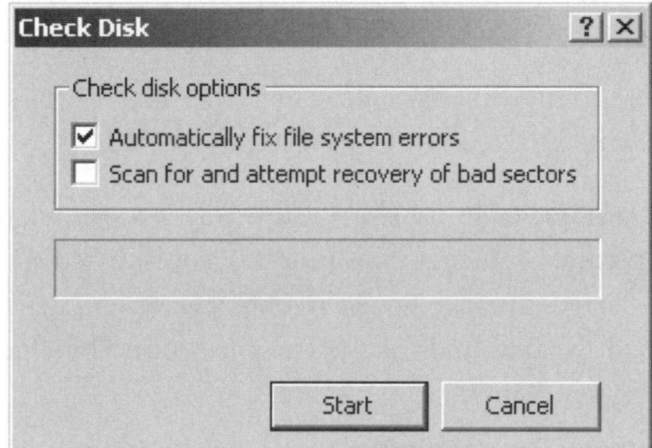


**FIGURE 30.17** Check Disk in Windows 2000 and XP checks a drive for errors.

In some cases you might not be able to check the drive because of certain running applications. In such cases Windows might offer to schedule a disk check at the next restart. You can click Yes when asked about that, and then restart the PC to perform the check.

## System Configuration Editor (SYSEDIT)

The System Configuration Editor (SYSEDIT) is a multipane Notepad window in which you can edit several text-based system files (you learned about it in Chapter 27). Run it by choosing Start/Run and keying **SYSEDIT** (see Figure 30.18).

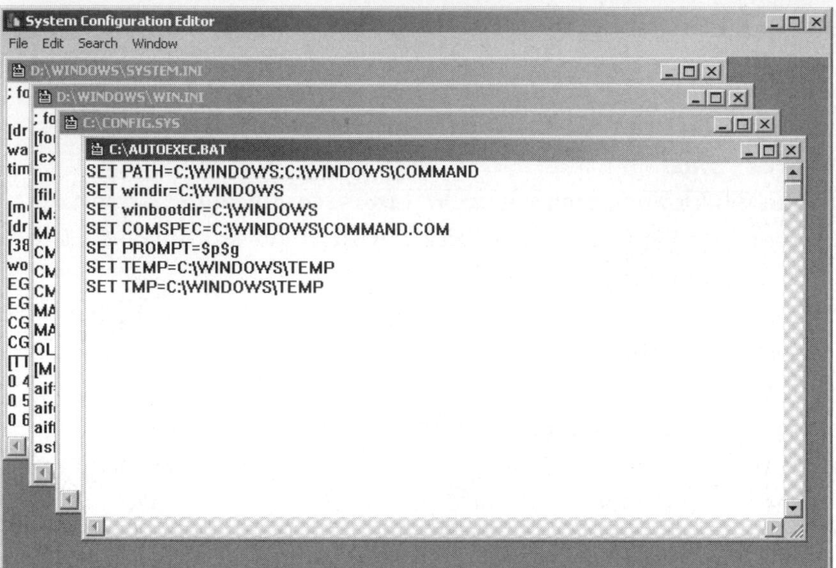


**FIGURE 30.18**
The System Configuration Editor (SYSEDIT) is a time-saver for editing text-based configuration files.

Different Windows versions show different files in the System Configuration Editor, but all versions show CONFIG.SYS, AUTOEXEC.BAT, WIN.INI, and SYSTEM.INI, all of which are included in 32-bit versions of Windows for backward compatibility.

## System Configuration Utility (MSCONFIG)

The System Configuration Utility (MSCONFIG) is a useful tool for troubleshooting startup problems in Windows, as discussed in Chapter 27. To run it, choose Start/Run and key **MSCONFIG**. It enables you to selectively disable individual lines of the startup process by clearing their check boxes (see Figure 30.19).

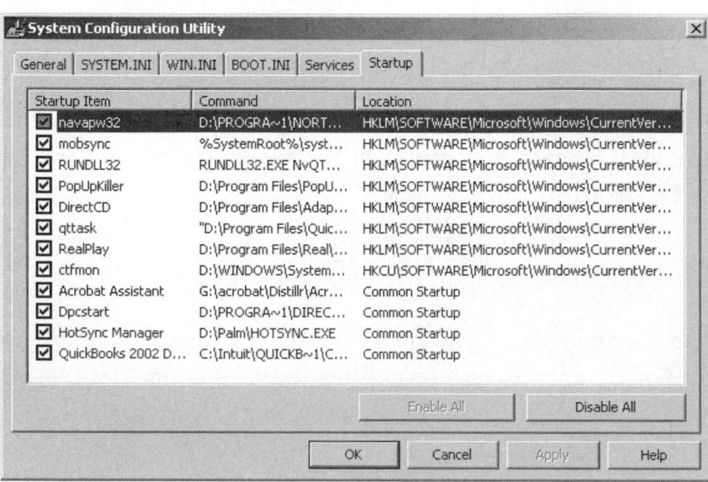


**FIGURE 30.19**
The System Configuration Utility helps troubleshoot startup problems by selectively disabling startup items.

## Registry Editor (REGEDIT or REGEDT32)

There are actually two Registry Editors included in some Windows versions: REGEDIT and REGEDT32. Both access the same Registry. Windows XP has only REGEDIT. Beginners should not make changes to the Registry (and that includes beginning PC technicians!) because of the danger of introducing errors into it. In almost all cases, for whatever you want to do to the Registry, there is a safer alternative method of accomplishing it through Windows dialog boxes. The System Configuration Utility mentioned in the preceding section is one example. You do not need Registry editing experience to pass the A+ exams. However, if you are interested in learning how to do it safely, see Appendix D.

## Registry Checker (SCANREG)

This utility, present only in Windows 98 and Me, checks and backs up the Registry. To run it, choose Start/Run, key **SCANREG**, and then click OK. Normally when Windows starts up it checks the Registry for errors, but you can use the Registry Checker while Windows is running to make sure no errors have been introduced since the last time Windows started. This might be useful, for example, if you just edited the Registry with REGEDIT and you think you might have made an error.

If the Registry Checker finds any errors, it reports them and prompts you for permission to correct them. If it does not find errors, it offers to back the Registry up, as in Figure 30.20. Click Yes and then click OK at the message that the backup has been completed.

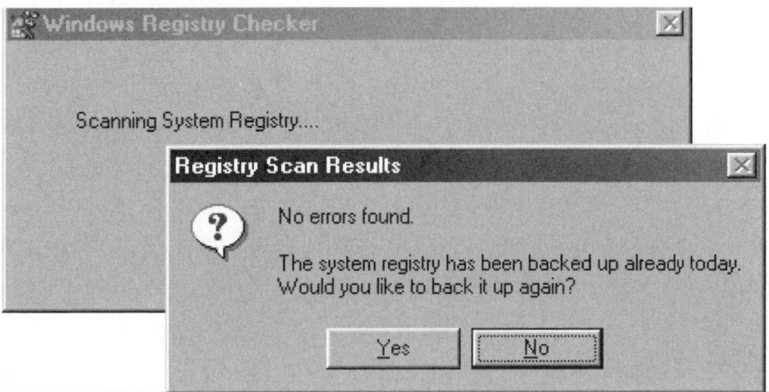


**FIGURE 30.20** The Registry Checker makes sure there are no errors in the Registry.

You can also use SCANREG from a command prompt when booting from a startup floppy. When you do so, the following switches are available:

SCANREG /RESTORE: Presents a list of available backup copies of the Registry that you can restore.

SCANREG /FIX: Repairs and compacts the Registry.

SCANREG /OPT: Removes excess space from the Registry, making it take up less space on the hard disk.

Other command-line switches are available as well; key **SCANREG /?** for a complete listing.

### Dr. Watson

Dr. Watson is a troubleshooting utility that logs extra information about system problems. When Dr. Watson is running, and the system experiences an error such as an Invalid Page Fault or General Protection Fault, Dr. Watson logs extensive information about the error. You can then either use this information yourself (if you are extremely technical and knowledgeable) or send the information to Microsoft to help them fix systemic problems with Windows.

To start it, choose Start/Run, key **DRWATSON**, and then click OK. You will not see an on-screen confirmation; the program runs in the background until an error occurs. Most people do not run Dr. Watson unless they are experiencing frequent errors; if the system is stable and reliable, having Dr. Watson running just takes up system resources.

### Automatic Skip Driver (ASD)

The Automatic Skip Driver (ASD) utility allows you to disable a driver that is preventing Windows from starting. It can be a great help when the PC will not boot normally. It comes with Windows 98 and Me only.
After the PC has failed to start, boot to safe mode and use the Run command to run ASD. It will report what driver caused the problem and offer to disable it for you.

You can run ASD at any time from the Run command, but unless a failure has occurred before there will be nothing in its log, and you will simply see a message to that effect.

## Other Utilities

CompTIA's objectives for A+ examination study include a couple of other utilities that do not fall easily into the categories discussed so far in this chapter. We will finish the chapter by reviewing them.

## Task Scheduler

The Task Scheduler enables you to set up certain routine maintenance utilities to run automatically at specified dates and times, such as Backup, Disk Defragmenter, and ScanDisk (or Check Disk). It is available in all Windows versions except 95. You can use it to schedule any installed application to run; it does not have to be a Microsoft application or even a utility program.

To schedule a task:

1. Choose Start/Programs/Accessories/System Tools/Scheduled Tasks. The Scheduled Tasks window opens.
2. Double-click *Add Scheduled Task* to run the Scheduled Task Wizard. Click Next to continue.
3. Choose the utility you want to run from the list that appears (see Figure 30.21). Click Next.

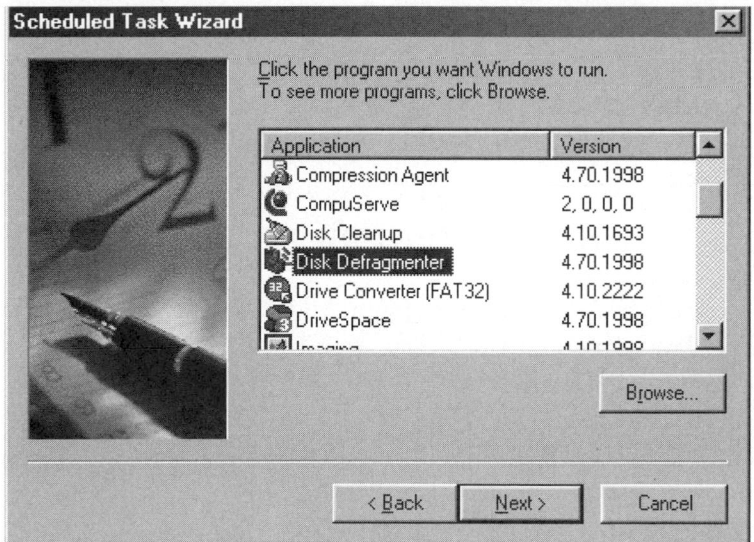


**FIGURE 30.21** You can schedule any application to run in Windows 98's Task Scheduler.

4. Specify when you want it to run (see Figure 30.22). Click Next.
5. Depending on what you chose in step 4, another screen appears asking for clarification about when you want it to run. For example, if you chose Weekly in step 4, check boxes for days of the week will appear. Make your selection and click Next.
6. In Windows 2000 and XP, an extra screen appears at this point offering to let you enter a user name and password with which to run the task. This would be useful if the security settings would not permit an ordinary end user to run that task; you could enter an Administrator name and password for it here. Click Next.

7. Click Finish. The task is now set up to run. You can change the task's parameters by double-clicking it on the Scheduled Task list at any time.

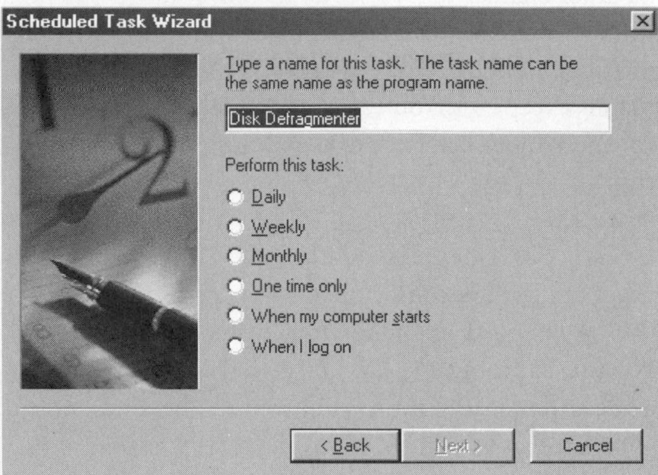


**FIGURE 30.22**
Indicate when the application should run.

**TRY IT!**

Schedule several utilities to run weekly or monthly on your PC using the Task Scheduler.

## Windows Scripting Host (WSCRIPT)

**Compiled language**

A programming language that writes programs to be run through a compiler utility, and then distributed as executable files to end users.

**Interpreted language**

A programming language that writes programs to be distributed as scripts, requiring the end user to have an interpreter installed that will run them.

**Script**

A program created with an interpreted programming language.

The Windows Scripting Host is an interpreter that helps you run Windows Script File, JavaScript, and Visual Basic scripts. Most people never need to interact with this application directly, but it is mentioned in the A+ exam objectives so you should be aware of it.

There are two types of programming languages: *compiled* and *interpreted*. When a programmer writes a program in a compiled language, he or she then sends it through a utility called a compiler that converts the program to an executable file. That executable file can be run all by itself; the end user does not need the compiler. In contrast, an interpreted language generates not executable files but *scripts*. The end user must have an interpreter program installed on his or her PC in order to run the script. The most commonly used example of an interpreted program language is Visual Basic. Another is JavaScript.

Windows Scripting Host is installed by default in Windows; files with the extensions .wsf, .js, and .vbs are associated with it. Therefore, you can double-click any such scripts to run them automatically through the Windows Scripting Host. You can also use the Run command to run a script by keying **WSCRIPT** followed by the name of the script you want to run.

# STUDY GUIDE

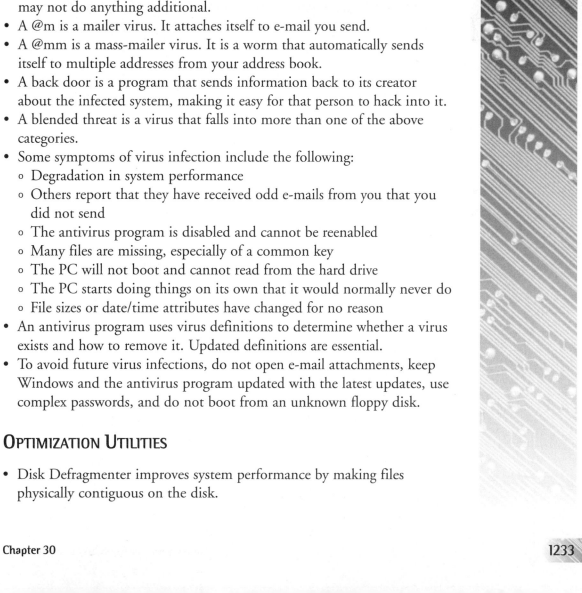

Use the following summaries to review the key concepts of this chapter.

## Identifying, Removing, and Avoiding Viruses

- A virus is a program or script that causes annoyance to the PC user and/or harm to a PC or its stored data.
- Viruses can be spread by running an infected program, by booting from an infected floppy, or by opening an infected e-mail attachment.
- A Trojan horse is a program that appears to do something useful but actually delivers a harmful effect.
- A worm is a program that spreads by making copies of itself. It may or may not do anything additional.
- A @m is a mailer virus. It attaches itself to e-mail you send.
- A @mm is a mass-mailer virus. It is a worm that automatically sends itself to multiple addresses from your address book.
- A back door is a program that sends information back to its creator about the infected system, making it easy for that person to hack into it.
- A blended threat is a virus that falls into more than one of the above categories.
- Some symptoms of virus infection include the following:
  - Degradation in system performance
  - Others report that they have received odd e-mails from you that you did not send
  - The antivirus program is disabled and cannot be reenabled
  - Many files are missing, especially of a common key
  - The PC will not boot and cannot read from the hard drive
  - The PC starts doing things on its own that it would normally never do
  - File sizes or date/time attributes have changed for no reason
- An antivirus program uses virus definitions to determine whether a virus exists and how to remove it. Updated definitions are essential.
- To avoid future virus infections, do not open e-mail attachments, keep Windows and the antivirus program updated with the latest updates, use complex passwords, and do not boot from an unknown floppy disk.

## Optimization Utilities

- Disk Defragmenter improves system performance by making files physically contiguous on the disk.

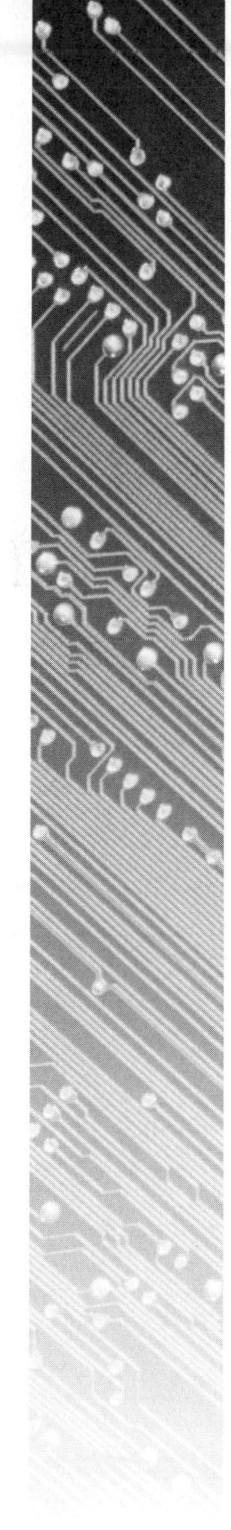

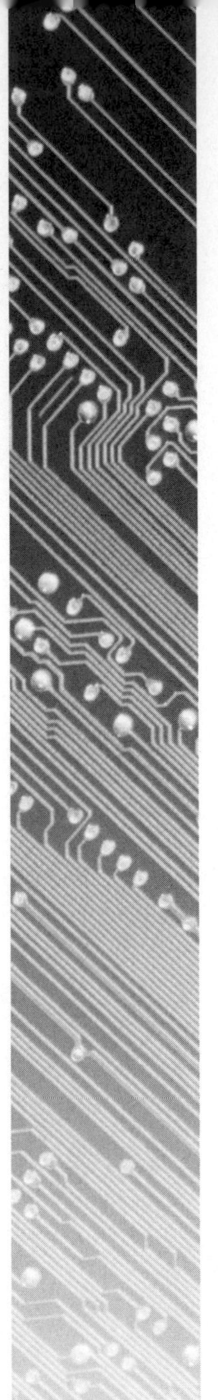

- Run Disk Defragmenter from the Accessories/System Tools menu or from the Tools tab in the disk's Properties dialog box.
- If Disk Defragmenter restarts frequently, disable all other running programs.
- Disk Cleanup frees up disk space by recommending files that can safely be deleted.
- Run Disk Cleanup from the Accessories/System Tools menu.
- FAT32 Converter converts FAT16 drives to FAT32 drives without reformatting. This utility exists only in Windows 98 and Me.
- In Windows Me the FAT32 Converter is not a Windows utility; it exists only in a command-line version. To run it, use Start/Run and key **CVT x:** where *x* is the drive letter.
- DriveSpace is a way of increasing the amount of data that a hard disk will hold by manipulating the way it stores data. It works only on FAT16 drives.
- Do not use DriveSpace unless you are running out of disk space, because it makes the drive run slower and makes utilities such as Disk Defragmenter take longer to finish.

## System Information Utilities

- Device Manager lists the hardware installed in the system and enables you to disable, remove, and add hardware and to change resource assignments.
- Computer Management is a utility in Windows 2000 and XP that provides a single point of entry for many utilities. Open it through Control Panel/Administrative Tools.
- One of the utilities in Computer Management is Disk Management, in which you can examine, partition, and format drives, as you learned in Chapter 12.
- You can also run Disk Management separately with Start/Run by keying **diskmgmt.msc**.
- The Microsoft Management Console (MMC) is a way of creating your own custom set of disk utilities, like Computer Management. Run it with Start/Run by keying **mmc**.
- Utilities added to the MMC are called snap-ins. To add one, choose File and then Add/Remove Snap-In.
- The Hardware Diagnostic Tool (HWINFO) is a Windows 98/Me utility that provides an alternative view of the same information provided with System Information. To run it, use Start/Run and key **hwinfo /ui**.

## Problem-Solving Utilities

- ScanDisk checks for logical errors in the FAT, and optionally does a physical sector-by-sector check of the disk surface. It comes with MS-DOS and Windows 9x.
- Run ScanDisk from the Accessories/System Tools menu or from the drive's Properties dialog box.
- Check Disk, which comes with Windows 2000 and XP, serves the same purpose as ScanDisk. Run it from the drive's Properties dialog box.
- The System Configuration Editor (SYSEDIT) is a multipane Notepad window in which several text-based system files open, including CONFIG.SYS, AUTOEXEC.BAT, WIN.INI, and SYSTEM.INI.
- The System Configuration Utility (MSCONFIG) enables you to selectively disable lines of the startup process. See Chapter 27.
- The Registry Editor (REGEDIT or REGEDT32) enables you to directly edit the Windows Registry. See Appendix D.
- The Registry Checker (SCANREG) exists only in Windows 98 and Me. It checks and backs up the Registry.
- Dr. Watson is a monitoring utility. It watches for errors such as Invalid Page Fault or General Protection Fault, and logs extensive information about each error.
- Automatic Skip Driver (ASD) comes with Windows 98 and Me. It allows you to disable a driver that prevents Windows from starting.

## Other Utilities

- The Task Scheduler sets up automated operation of utilities. For example, you can set up ScanDisk, Disk Defragmenter, and other utilities to run at specified days and times.
- Windows Scripting Host (WSCRIPT) is an interpreter that runs Windows Script File, JavaScript, and Visual Basic scripts. Most people never need to interact with it directly.
- To run a script, double-click the script. You can also use the Run command, keying **WSCRIPT** followed by the name of the script to run.

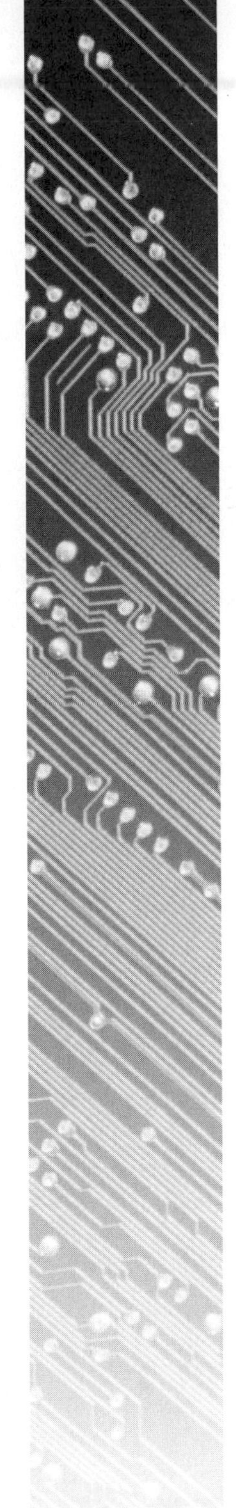

# PRACTICE TEST

On a blank sheet of paper, write the answers to the following multiple-choice questions and explain why each answer is correct.

1. Which of these could potentially cause a virus infection?
   a. booting from a floppy disk
   b. browsing the content of a floppy disk
   c. viewing a picture
   d. opening a Word document with macros disabled

2. What type of virus automatically sends itself to multiple addresses in a victim's address book?
   a. back-door virus
   b. worm virus
   c. @mm virus
   d. Trojan horse virus

3. What type of virus disables antivirus programs in an attempt to prevent its own removal?
   a. macro virus
   b. boot sector virus
   c. worm
   d. retrovirus

4. Which of these would be an example of a strong password?
   a. cat
   b. catastrophically
   c. c7td%G
   d. These are all strong passwords.

5. How do files get fragmented?
   a. disk errors
   b. making edits to an already saved file
   c. improper shutdown
   d. running a disk compression program

6. What does it mean if Disk Defragmenter keeps restarting itself?
   a. It keeps finding and correcting FAT errors.
   b. There may be power fluctuation problems.
   c. The disk is very badly fragmented.
   d. Background programs are changing the disk content.

7. Which versions of Windows include the Disk Defragmenter?
   a. 9x versions only
   b. NT-based versions only
   c. 98, 2000, and XP only
   d. all 32-bit versions (95 and higher)

8. What does the FAT32 Converter utility do?
   a. converts FAT32 to NTFS
   b. converts FAT to FAT32
   c. converts either FAT or NTFS to FAT32
   d. compresses FAT32 volumes

9. Which drive types can be compressed with DriveSpace?
   a. only FAT
   b. FAT or FAT32
   c. FAT, FAT32, or NTFS
   d. only FAT32

10. What is DoubleSpace?
    a. the FAT32 version of DriveSpace, in Windows 98 and higher
    b. the FAT version of DriveSpace, included with DOS and Windows 95
    c. a third-party utility made by Symantec as a competitor to DriveSpace
    d. the original version of DriveSpace, included with MS-DOS 6.20

11. Which of these utilities can you access from within Computer Management?
    a. Local Users and Groups
    b. Device Manager
    c. Disk Manager
    d. All of the above

12. Which of these is an advantage of using an MMC instead of Computer Management?
    a. You can view data for other computers on the network, not just the local PC.
    b. Disk information refreshes more quickly.
    c. It is easier to set up.
    d. There is no advantage; is a matter of personal preference.

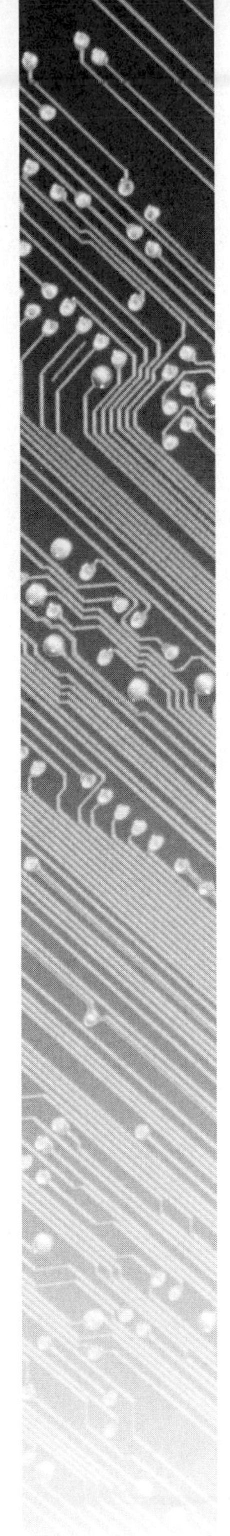

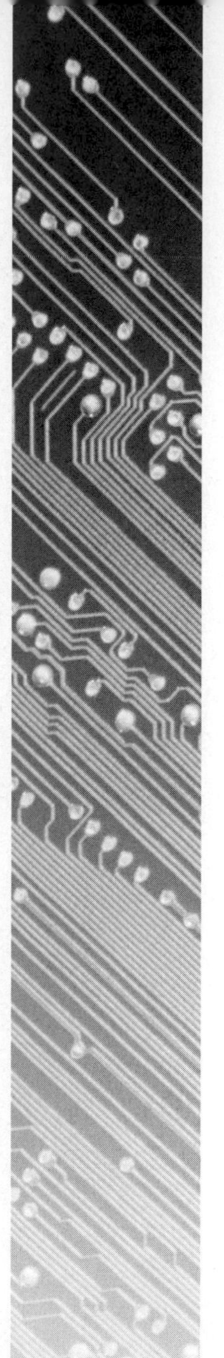

13. What does the Hardware Diagnostic Tool (HWINFO) do?
    a. allows you to selectively disable certain hardware devices
    b. provides a different view of the same data that System Information provides.
    c. skips certain drivers at startup that it finds to be causing startup problems
    d. opens a multipane Notepad window with startup files

14. Which versions of Windows come with ScanDisk?
    a. 9x versions only
    b. NT-based versions only
    c. all 32-bit versions
    d. only Windows 98, 2000, and XP

15. Which of these enables you to selectively disable startup drivers?
    a. System Configuration Editor (SYSEDIT)
    b. System Configuration Utility (MSCONFIG)
    c. Hardware Diagnostic Tool (HWINFO)
    d. Registry Checker (SCANREG)

16. Which command opens a Registry Editor window?
    a. REGEDIT
    b. REGEDT32
    c. SCANREG
    d. both a and b

17. What is Dr. Watson?
    a. a diagnostic tool that runs only in safe mode for troubleshooting startup problems
    b. an error monitoring and reporting tool that provides details about application and system crashes and problems
    c. an alternative to the Registry Editor
    d. an alternative to ScanDisk

18. What can you schedule with Task Scheduler?
    a. only Microsoft applications
    b. only ScanDisk and Disk Defragmenter
    c. only 32-bit applications
    d. any application installed on the PC

19. What type of programs does the Windows Scripting Host run?
    a. executable
    b. compiled
    c. interpreted
    d. All of the above

20. Why is using Disk Cleanup superior to emptying the Recycle Bin?
    a. It gets rid of more files than just those in the Recycle Bin.
    b. It has built-in safety precautions.
    c. It is more convenient.
    d. All of the above

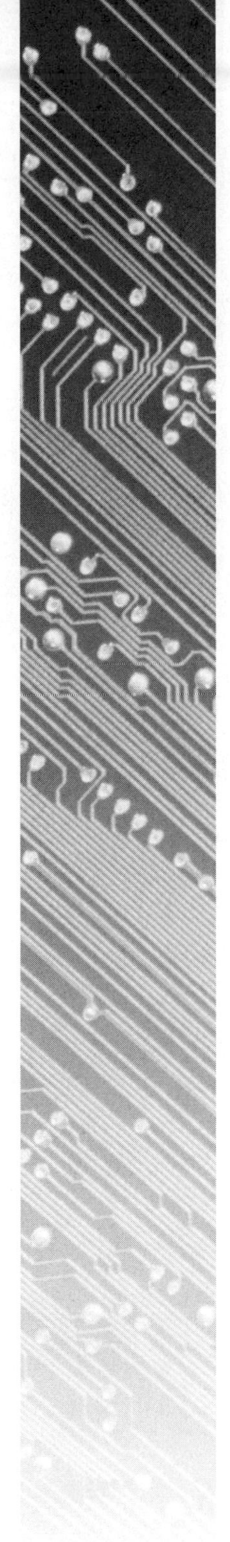

# TROUBLESHOOTING

1. A client complains that his computer is starting up very slowly, running slowly, and rebooting at random intervals. Would you suspect a virus infection? Why or why not? What would you do to troubleshoot?
2. A client wants to convert her FAT drive to FAT32, but she recently upgraded from Windows 98 to Windows Me and the FAT32 Converter no longer appears on the System Tools menu. How can she access it from Windows Me?
3. You are trying to run Disk Management with the Run command. You key **diskmgmt** in the Run text box, but get a message that the utility does not exist. What are you doing wrong?

# CUSTOMER SERVICE

1. A client thinks he may have a virus because several people have told him that they received infected e-mails from him. However, he claims that running his antivirus program shows no infection. What do you suggest?
2. A client asks whether you think defragmenting a disk is worth it, and, if so, how often she should do it. What advice can you offer?
3. A client complains that whenever she tries to run ScanDisk or Disk Defragmenter, the programs keep restarting over and over and never finish. What can you suggest?

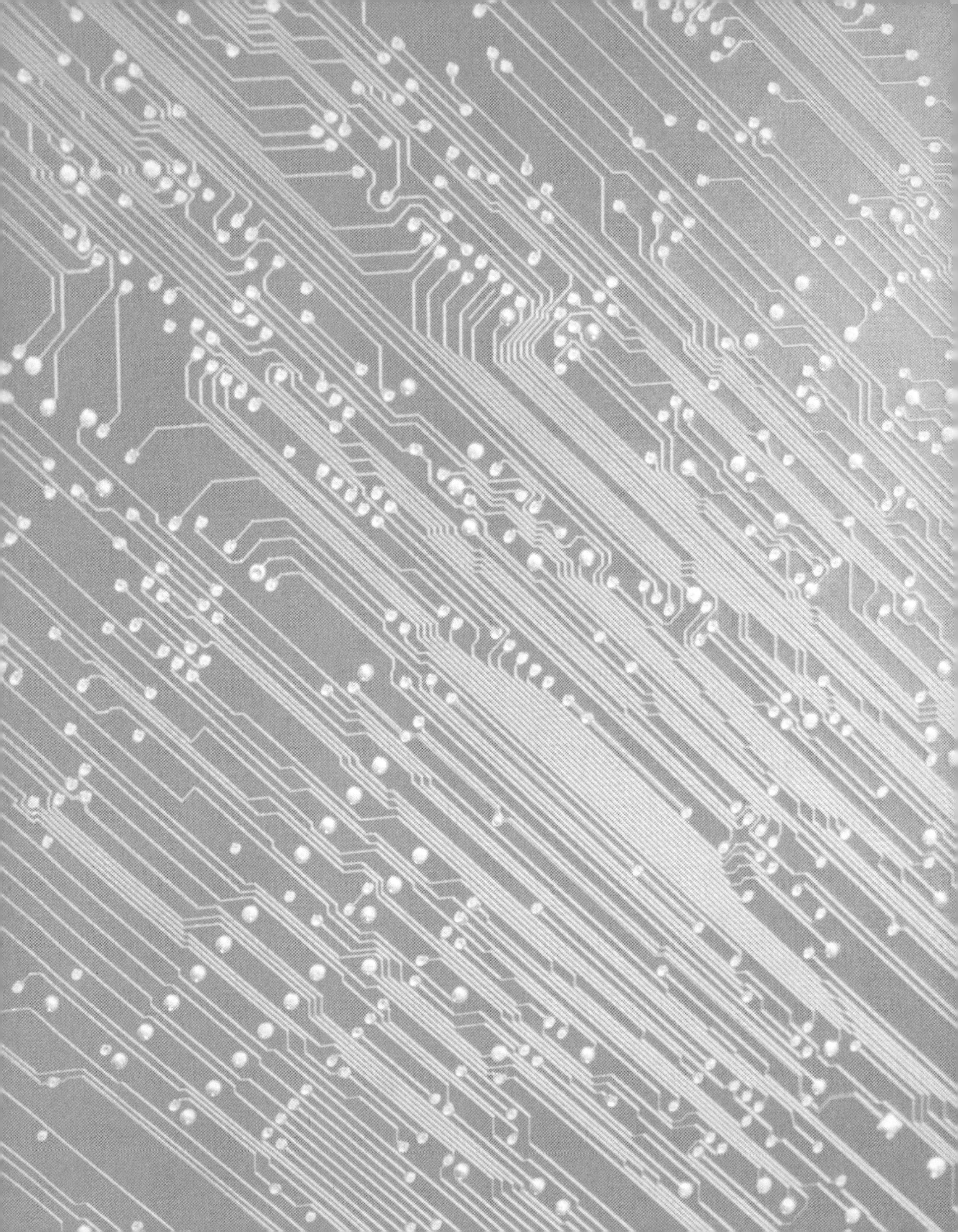

# Project Lab, Part 6
## Understanding and Using Operating Systems

These projects require a PC with Windows 95 or higher already installed. If they are available, multiple PCs, each with a different Windows version (NT 4.0, 95, 98, Me, 2000, and XP), will enhance the value of these exercises.

### PROJECT #1: UPGRADING AN OPERATING SYSTEM

Start with a PC that has installed one of the versions of Windows shown in column A below. You will also need a Setup CD for one of the Windows versions shown on the same line in column B.

| A. If the PC has this already installed... | B. Have a Setup CD for one of these versions... |
|---|---|
| NT Workstation 4.0 | 2000 or XP |
| 95 | 98, 98 Second Edition, Me, 2000, or XP |
| 98 | 98 Second Edition, Me, 2000, or XP |
| Me | 2000 or XP |
| 2000 | XP |

1. Start Windows normally.
2. Insert the Setup CD for the new version of Windows. What can you do if the CD does not autorun?
3. Follow the prompts to install the new version of Windows. Document any problems or errors you encounter.

### PROJECT #2: SETTING UP A DUAL-BOOT WINDOWS 98 AND WINDOWS 2000 SYSTEM

Start with a new hard disk, or one that does not contain anything you want to keep.

1. Boot from a Windows 98 startup disk, and use FDISK to delete all existing partitions on the drive.

2. Create a primary partition that uses approximately one-half of the available space on the drive, and an extended partition that uses the other half. Do not create any logical drives in the extended partition.
3. Format the primary partition using FAT32.
4. On the formatted volume (C), create a new directory on the drive called Winsetup, and copy all the files from the \Win98 directory on the Windows 98 Setup CD into the C:\Winsetup directory. Why is copying the files to the hard disk advantageous?
5. Start the setup program from the \Winsetup directory.
6. Follow the prompts to install Windows 98. Document any problems you encounter, and what you did to fix them.
7. Confirm that Windows 98 has been successfully installed. Troubleshoot as needed.
8. Change BIOS Setup settings to boot first from the CD, before it checks the hard disk.
9. Boot from the Windows 2000 Setup CD.
10. In the Setup program, create a new NTFS volume in the unpartitioned space. Use all remaining space.
11. Install Windows 2000 on the new NTFS volume.
12. Confirm that a menu appears when you start the PC asking which operating system you want to boot. Boot into Windows 98 and confirm that it works; then restart and boot into Windows 2000. Document any errors or problems.

## Project #3: Installing and Removing Applications

You will need the Setup CD for an application that is not already installed on your PC.

1. Using the Setup CD, install the new software. Depending on the application, it might be very simple or there might be substantial problems to overcome. Document your experience with the setup.
2. Download a shareware application from a Web site that contains a repository of shareware, such as CNet (http://www.cnet.com). Did the download come in executable format, or as a ZIP file? If it is a ZIP file, create a new folder and extract the file's content into it. Document the process you used.
3. Install the shareware application.
4. Confirm that both the application you installed from the CD and the shareware application work correctly. Troubleshoot as needed.
5. Uninstall both applications. Use the Add/Remove Programs box if possible; if not, document the alternative procedure you used.

6. Search the shareware site online again and find an MS-DOS based game. Download and install it. Document how you installed the game so that it would run under Windows. Did you need to make any changes to its properties?
7. Play the game to make sure it works. Then uninstall it. Make sure you remove all traces of it from the system.
8. Download and install a 16-bit Windows game that has its own Setup application. What changes, if any, did the application make to WIN.INI when it installed? Why would it change WIN.INI rather than the Registry?
9. Play the game to make sure it works. Then uninstall it. Were you able to uninstall it from Add/Remove Programs?

## Project #4: Working with Files

1. Create a new directory on the C drive called Practice.
2. Create a new text document in Notepad containing your name and address. Save your file as MYINFO.TXT in the *C:\Practice* folder.
3. Set the attributes for MYINFO.TXT to Read-Only and Hidden.
4. Set the Folder Options in Windows so that hidden files are displayed (if they are not already).
5. Open MYINFO.TXT in Notepad. Does it open? Why or why not?
6. Add your phone number to the file and save it. Does it save? Why or why not?
7. Change the attributes for MYINFO.TXT so that it is no longer Read-Only or Hidden.
8. Edit the file again in Notepad, adding your e-mail address (and phone number if it was not added earlier). Save your work.
9. Use Microsoft Backup to back up the *C:\Practice* folder onto a floppy disk. Then check the attributes for the file. Is the Archive attribute on or off?
10. Edit the file in Notepad again, removing your e-mail address. Then save it. Now check the attributes again. Is the Archive attribute on or off?
11. If the C drive is an NTFS drive, turn on compression for the *C:\Practice* folder.
12. Send MYINFO.TXT to the Recycle Bin.
13. Empty the Recycle Bin.
14. Rename *C:\Practice* to *C:\DeleteMe.*
15. Delete the *C:\DeleteMe* folder without sending it to the Recycle Bin.

## Project #5: Tuning Up a Windows PC

1. Check all your local hard disks for errors with ScanDisk or Check Disk (depending on your Windows version). Turn off the automatic correction of errors so you can see what errors are found. What errors were found, if any? Allow the program to correct them.
2. Use Disk Defragmenter to analyze each of the local hard drives (if you have more than one) to determine which is the most fragmented. What percentage fragmentation does it show? Then defragment the one that needs it the most.
3. Use Disk Cleanup to delete any nonessential files.

## Project #6 (Challenge): Working with FAT32 Converter and DriveSpace

For this project you will need a Windows 98 startup floppy and a hard disk that does not contain anything you need to keep.

1. Boot from the floppy, and delete all existing partitions.
2. Create a new primary partition of at least 1GB that uses FAT32.
3. Create an extended partition that contains two 500MB FAT16 logical drives. Leave any remaining space on the drive unpartitioned.

*(Hint: When you start FDISK it asks whether you want to enable large disk support or not. If you answer Yes, the drives you create are FAT32; if you answer No they are FAT16.)*

4. Install Windows 98 on the primary partition.
5. Format the two extended partition drives through My Computer in Windows. Confirm that they use FAT (FAT16). If they don't, go back to FDISK, delete them, and recreate the partitions.
6. Run the FAT32 Converter through Windows 98 to convert one of the extended partition drives to FAT32.
7. Use DriveSpace to compress the other extended partition drive.

# APPENDIX A

# A PC Technician's Toolkit

A good toolkit is an essential investment. The right tools can save you time and help you avoid damage to your equipment or injury to yourself.

Most computer stores sell toolkits of various sizes. You do not need the largest, fanciest one, as long as you have the few basic tools you need for the PCs that you will be working on. For example, Compaq laptops happen to use a small Torx screw (T-8 size), so if you work on those, you will need a T-8 screwdriver; otherwise you probably won't ever need one.

The color insert in this book shows pictures of some of the tools you may want to have in your toolkit, and the following sections describe them.

## The Basic Set

Generally speaking, a good toolkit should contain the following:

- **At least two sizes of Phillips-head screwdrivers.** You will need one of medium size for large screws, such as those holding on the cover of the computer case, plus a small one for tiny screws, such as those holding a disk drive in place. Most screws in a typical computer are Phillips (a four-prong star) rather than regular flathead screws (a straight line).

> **WARNING**
>
> Do not use a magnetized screwdriver inside the computer. Some technicians enjoy the convenience of a screwdriver with a magnetized tip for fishing screws out of crevices into which they have been dropped, but it is easy to damage disks by touching them with a magnet. If the only screwdriver you have available is magnetized, exercise extreme care not to touch its tip to any part of the PC except the screws themselves.

- **At least two sizes of flathead screwdrivers.** Although flathead screws are less common in computer equipment, you will occasionally encounter them.
- **Needle-nose pliers.** These are useful for grasping small items and for removing and replacing circuit board jumpers.
- **Tweezers.** These are also handy for grasping small items. Even better is a part retriever, which is like a tiny set of retractable claws with a spring-loaded handle.

## Handy Extras

The above list of tools constitutes the basic set; you might also want the following tools on hand:

- **Wire snips.** Use these for cutting wire and stripping insulation.
- **Small flashlight.** This is useful for seeing small or partially hidden areas inside the computer, such as the Pin 1 marking on a connector.

- **3/16-inch nut driver**. This tool helps place 3/16-inch hexagonal nuts into the computer. The nuts are used for mounting hardware on motherboards as well as serial and parallel ports.
- **Torx screwdriver or bits**. This implement has a six-pointed star-shaped screwdriver head. Torx screws are often used to secure the covers on places where the manufacturer does not want the average consumer to venture, because most people do not have this type of screwdriver.
- **Knife.** It is always useful to include a cutting blade or utility knife of some sort.
- **Soldering iron and solder.** Most of the time it is less expensive to replace a board than repair it, but if a board has the obvious problem of a resistor being broken off, you might be able to salvage it with a quick soldering job. Make sure you have solder designed specifically for electronics.
- **Chip-puller.** This is a special type of tweezers with indented ends that fit underneath chips so you can pull them straight out of non-ZIF, PGA, or SIPP slots.

## What Else Besides Tools?

Besides your toolkit, you will also want to carry a bag containing these useful items:

- **Boot disks and Setup CDs for all operating systems**. Although it is illegal to install the same copy of MS-DOS or Windows on multiple PCs, you might find it helpful to be able to boot into a particular OS version or to copy individual files from its Setup CD. For example, if a client is missing a particular file in Windows 98, you could copy it from your own Setup CD for Windows 98 without violating any licensing agreements.
- **Antistatic wrist strap.** This safety device greatly reduces the chance of static damage to components by channeling any static electric charge to the ground instead of through computer components.
- **Roll of black electrical tape**. This is helpful for wrapping wire ends and insulating components.
- **Can of compressed air.** This is useful for cleaning components, eliminating the need for hazardous liquid cleaners.
- **Soft, lint-free cloth.** Clean the monitor and other components with this.
- **Digital multimeter.** This is a meter that measures multiple types of electrical specs (ohms, amps, and volts).

## Your Spare Parts Stockpile

Finally, it is a good idea to accumulate a stockpile of spare parts if you do many PC repairs. Some suggestions are as follows:

- **Screws.** Keep a supply of various-sized screws.
- **Expansion card backplates.** Save the metal inserts that you take out of the back of a case when you put a modem or other card into the PC; you may need them again later.

- **Drive faceplates.** Save the plastic faceplates that you remove from the front of cases so you can replace them later if needed.
- **Mounting kits.** These are sometimes supplied with retail hard disks and allow you to put a 3.5-inch drive into a 5.25-inch bay. They are useful when your case has more free 5.25-inch bays than 3.5-inch bays.
- **Cables.** Save any power, IDE, floppy, CD, or other cables that you may accumulate.
- **Keyboard, mouse, and 3.5-inch floppy drive.** Keep an extra one of each of these components to help with troubleshooting problems.

## APPENDIX B

# CUSTOMER SERVICE

Earlier versions of the A+ exam had a separate section on customer service. The questions did not count toward passing or failing the exam, and the section was eliminated in the 2001 revision of the test. However, customer service is still important to any PC technician's success.

Good customer service is just basic common sense, but you would be surprised how often technically knowledgeable technicians get negative client feedback because they forget about these simple strategies.

## DRESS APPROPRIATELY

When working face-to-face with the public, respect the prevailing dress and appearance standards. If you are an in-house technician, there will probably be guidelines governing appropriate attire. If you visit clients at their offices or homes, your employer may dictate what you will wear; many companies that make service calls have some sort of uniform, such as khakis and a polo shirt with a company logo on it.

If you are in business for yourself, you can create your own dress code, but remember this: Your appearance should instill confidence and trust. You want to look knowledgeable and professional, so avoid shorts or worn jeans, tank tops, decrepit sneakers, and baseball caps.

For men, a jacket is not necessary, but a dress shirt (short-sleeved is fine) and tie can go a long way toward projecting a professional image, especially if there is something about your appearance that is nontraditional, such as long hair or tattoos. Women will probably not want to wear skirts on service calls because there is always the potential for crawling around under a desk fussing with cables; a dress shirt and pants are sufficient. Avoid large bulky jewelry, especially anything with a hoop that could get caught on equipment.

## BE PROMPT

Failure to show up on time is a common reason why clients become upset with a company's technicians. If possible, arrive within 5 minutes of your estimate. For external clients, or any site to which you must drive, allow yourself an extra 10 minutes to get there. It is much better to be 10 minutes early than 10 minutes late. If there is no way you are going to make it within, say, 15 minutes of the appointment time, call to say you are running late. This is common courtesy; you would want the same from a repair person coming to fix a household appliance, and you owe it to your own clients as well.

## Listen

When you arrive at a client site (or a client comes to you), what is the first thing you do? Check out the computer? Run a diagnostic program? No! The first thing to do is *listen*.

You can often save yourself time and effort by talking to any available persons about the nature of the problem. This is especially important when there are multiple minor problems with a PC, but only one of them is bothering the user. You do not want to do a full tune-up on the PC, especially if your time is limited, only to find out that the user just wanted the desktop wallpaper removed.

Good listening skills are also a major factor in client satisfaction. Everyone wants to be heard. By showing that you believe the client has something worthwhile to say about the problem, you are showing respect, even if you gather no useful information from the conversation.

## Ask Questions

Along with listening, good technicians ask appropriate questions that help them begin to troubleshoot even before they touch the PC. Start out with a general "What seems to be the trouble here?" and then work through as many of the following questions as are applicable:

- "What was the last thing you did before the problem started?" Do not let the answer to this lead you on a wild goose chase; the last thing the user remembers is not necessarily what caused the problem. However, if the user recently installed some new hardware or software, or updated a driver, this can give you a place to start.
- "Does the problem occur only at certain times? If so, what factors seem to influence it?" Do not take this answer at face value either; the user might say "It happens every time I drink coffee and use Word at the same time," but what really could be happening is that the user goes to get coffee 5 minutes after starting up the PC each day and a faulty cooling fan is causing overheating after 5 minutes of operation.

After determining the problem and mentally outlining your solution, turn again to the customer for more information:

- "What would you like me to do?" Strange as it may seem, not every client wants you to fix the problem. Some want only to know what is wrong and how much it would cost to fix it. It never hurts to clarify the client's wishes before you dive into a project.
- "Do you need an estimate before we proceed?" When dealing with external clients, the subject of money must invariably come up. Some people do not care how much it is going to cost; they just want the problem solved. Others are extremely price sensitive.

## Do Not Think Out Loud

As you work on a PC, your mind probably keeps up a steady internal stream of conversation. *Is it the processor? No, probably not; one of those DIMMs could be loose. Okay, it wasn't that; what could it be?* Your client does not need to hear that chatter.

Too much process talk can scare a client. When you say something like "Is it the processor?" a client is likely to hear "It is the processor!" and become extremely upset. There is no reason to put a client through that trauma. And, of course, never use profanity within a client's earshot. It is not only unprofessional, but it unnerves the client because it makes a problem sound worse than it probably is.

## Tidy Up

As you work, you will probably spread out tools, screws, extra parts, and other paraphernalia all over the place. When you finish the job, and before you walk out the door, make sure you put everything back the way you found it, and gather up all of your tools and parts. If there are old parts to junk, do not just dump them in the client's trash can; take them with you and discard them at your office.

## Thank the Client

Do not leave the site without touching base with the client. If possible, demonstrate that the problem has been solved and invite the client to try it out for himself. This is five minutes well spent: Allowing the client to try out the feature will often show you some little thing that you forgot to fix, like updating the shortcut icon on the desktop.

Ask the client if there's anything else you can help with. If the client mentions something you do not have time to fix at the moment, help the client schedule another service call. This can be a great way to promote additional business for yourself if you are self-employed! When the client is satisfied and everything is working, take your leave. The last words you say should be "Thank you." Never mind that you performed a service for the client, rather than vice versa. Just as the client is always right, the client is always bestowing a favor by using your services.

# APPENDIX C

## SUPPORTING USERS WITH DISABILITIES

Many PC users with disabilities will come to you with their own PC access systems already in place. For example, someone who has a mobility disability may already have his or her own joystick, custom keyboard, or other hardware, and may simply need it installed in Windows. Most hardware of this type is Plug and Play or requires only a simple setup from CD-ROM, just like any other new device.

In addition to specially designed devices, there are a number of features built into Windows 95 and higher to help people with disabilities use a PC more effectively. As a PC technician you should be aware of these so that you can suggest them to the end users you support when appropriate. Table C.1 lists the major accessibility features and the chapters in which they are covered in this book.

**TABLE C.1 Accessibility Features Discussed Elsewhere in the Book**

| Feature | Description | See Chapter |
|---|---|---|
| Display settings | Multiple features, including decreasing display resolution (so everything appears larger), using a High Contrast color scheme, and increasing the size of the default text in dialog boxes and title bars. | 15 |
| MouseKeys | Allows the keyboard arrow keys to substitute for a mouse, for users with mobility problems that inhibit mouse use. | 17 |
| On-Screen Keyboard | Allows the mouse to substitute for a keyboard by clicking on an on-screen image of a keyboard, for users with mobility problems that inhibit keyboard use. | 17 |
| Large pointer schemes | Makes the mouse pointer larger, so that users with visual disabilities can see it more easily. | 17 |
| Narrator | Reads text in dialog boxes and select applications, for users with visual disabilities. | 17 |
| SoundSentry | Generates a visual cue whenever Windows plays a system sound, for users with hearing disabilities. | 19 |
| ShowSounds | Turns on captioning for any applications that support it, for users with hearing disabilities. | 19 |
| ToggleKeys | Plays a sound whenever the Caps Lock, Num Lock, or Scroll Lock is pressed, for users who have trouble with accidentally pressing those keys because of a mobility disability. | 19 |

In addition to the features listed in Table C.1, there are a few other special-purpose features and utilities not mentioned elsewhere in the book. These are found on the Accessories/Accessibility menu on the Start menu.

- **Magnifier:** Magnifies whatever portion of the screen the mouse is over at the moment. Useful for users who require extra magnification to see the screen.
- **Accessibility Wizard:** A setup wizard that configures many of the features described in Table C.1 according to the user's answers to yes/no questions.
- **Utility Manager:** Provides a single interface for turning on and off Magnifier, Narrator, and On-Screen Keyboard.

# EDITING THE WINDOWS REGISTRY

The Registry is the central repository for settings in Windows. It contains vital information about the local PC, including its installed hardware and software, and information about whatever user is currently logged on, like display and keyboard preferences.

You have already edited the Registry many times, perhaps without realizing it. Anytime you change a setting using any of the Control Panel applets, those changes are written to the Registry. Setup programs for applications also edit the Registry, as does installing a new piece of Plug and Play hardware.

Sometimes, however, it can be useful to edit the Registry manually. For example, you might want to remove a reference to a driver that is causing a startup error, or you might want to make a minor change to a system setting that is not adjustable any other way.

**WARNING**

**Do not encourage end users to edit the Registry; only a trained PC technician should do it because improper Registry edits can cause the PC not to boot. Windows will not start if the Registry is corrupted, if it is missing vital settings needed for startup, or if it contains conflicting information. Further, changes to the Registry are implemented immediately; there is no "Discard Changes" feature in the Registry Editor application.**

**IN REAL LIFE**

**The REGEDT32 Registry Editor, covered in the following section, has a Save Settings on Exit feature. It is turned on by default, but can be turned off via the Options menu. Turning it off prevents changes from being immediately implemented. It also has a Read-Only mode, also accessible from the Options menu.**

## CHOOSING A REGISTRY EDITOR

In Windows NT 4.0 and 2000, there are two Registry editors: REGEDIT and REGEDT32. They both act upon the same Registry files. (Windows 9x has only REGEDIT.)

**IN REAL LIFE**

**In Windows XP, REGEDIT and REGEDT32 have been rolled into a single utility called REGEDIT that is very similar to the earlier version of the same name but incorporates some of the features of REGEDT32. There is a REGEDT32 file included with Windows XP, but its only function is to open REGEDIT, so if you run REGEDT32 from Windows XP, REGEDIT will open.**

REGEDIT is a simple dual-paned window, much like Windows Explorer. It lists all of the *keys* in a single folder tree; you expand and collapse the trees with the plus and minus signs just as you would in a Windows file management window (see Figure D.1).

**Key**

In the Windows Registry, a setting or a category of settings, represented by a folder in the hierarchical tree.

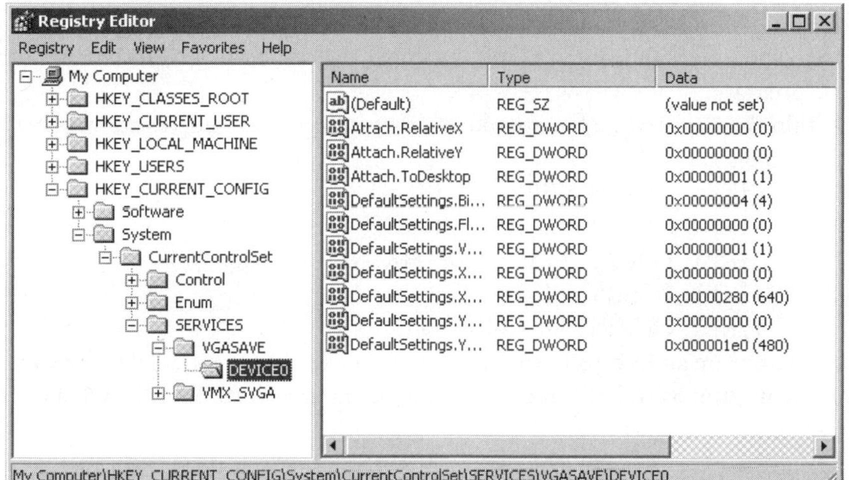


**FIGURE D.1**
The REGEDIT Registry Editor lists all keys in a single folder tree.

REGEDT32, shown in Figure D.2, uses separate window panes for each of the *root keys*. Instead of the standard plus and minus signs, the REGEDT32 editor shows plus signs directly on the folders themselves. For someone accustomed to the standard folder tree structure in Windows, this can be a bit more awkward to use. However, REGEDT32 counterbalances this awkwardness by providing some additional features that REGEDIT lacks, such as a Read-Only mode (Options/Read-Only Mode) and the ability to set security permissions for editing certain keys. Notice in Figure D.2 that REGEDT32 has a larger array of menus than REGEDIT.

**Root keys**

The top-level categories of settings in the Registry.

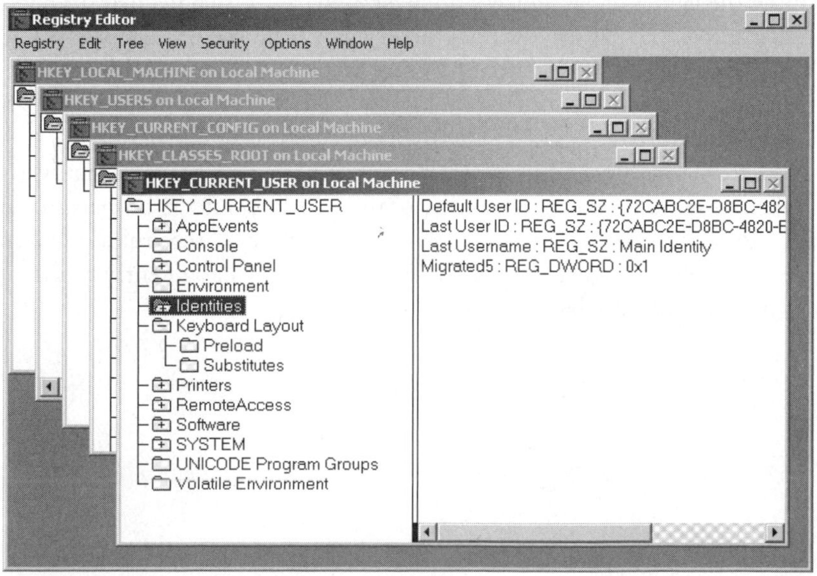

**FIGURE D.2**
The REGEDT32 Registry Editor lists each of the root keys in its own window, and offers more menu options.

## How the Registry Is Structured

As you learned in Chapter 26, the Registry is physically a set of separate files. In Windows 9x/Me it is USER.DAT and SYSTEM.DAT; in Windows NT/2000/XP it is a set of hive files: SAM, SECURITY, SOFTWARE, SYSTEM, and DEFAULT. Those file names are not important when editing the Registry, however, because the Registry Editor combines the content from all of them into a single interface.

Within the Registry are five root keys—that is, top-level folders into which all other settings fall. They are:

HKEY_CLASSES_ROOT (HKCR)
HKEY_CURRENT_USER (HKCU)
HKEY_LOCAL_MACHINE (HKLM)
HKEY_USERS (HKU)
HKEY_CURRENT_CONFIG (HKCC)

These names are all in caps in the Registry Editor, so they are traditionally written that way in print as well. Each of these keys, including all subkeys, is called a *hive*.

**Hive**

A top-level key in the Windows Registry that contains subkeys. Each of the hive names begin with the letters HKEY.

### In Real Life

**The HKEY Registry hives do *not* have an exact one-to-one relationship with the five hive files in Windows NT/2000/XP that contain the Registry settings, even though those files are commonly referred to as hive files. To find out exactly what keys correspond to what actual files, look in HKLM\System\CurrentControlSet\Control\HiveList.**

Each of the hive keys contains a variety of subkeys, embedded into multiple levels of hierarchical organization, just like subfolders within folders on a disk. Each folder is a subkey and, just as with disk storage, each key has a path containing the names of the subkeys (folders) in which it is embedded. In Figure D.1, for example, the path to the open subkey would be HKEY_CURRENT_CONFIG\System\CurrentControlSet\Services\VGASAVE\DEVICE0. In many reference books the root keys are referred to by their abbreviations, so you might see HKCC substituted for HKEY_CURRENT_CONFIG, for example.

**Value**

In the Registry, an entry within a subkey, consisting of a name, a data type, and the data itself.

Each subkey has at least one *value* in it, even if the subkey exists primarily as a folder to store subordinate keys. In many of the mid-level folders in the structure, this value does not contain any data; it exists simply because the "rules" say it must exist. For example, in Figure D.3 the HKEY_USERS key has an entry called Default that contains no data.

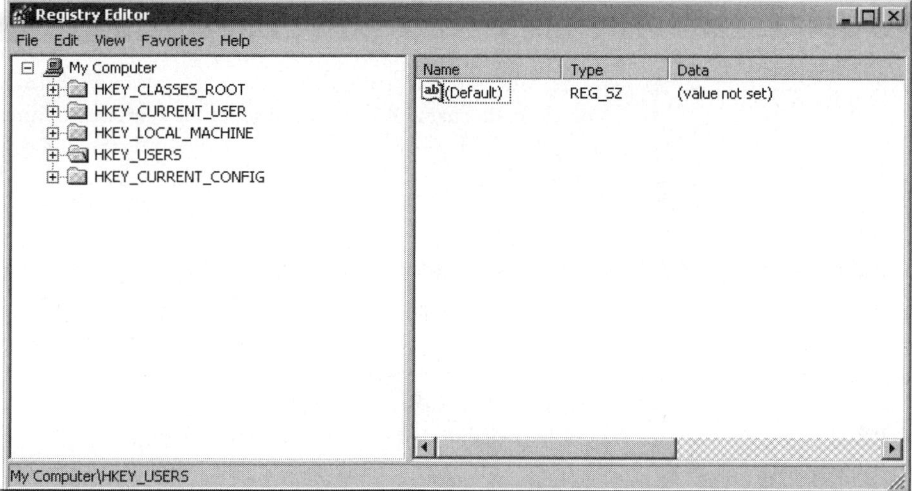


**FIGURE D.3**
Every key at every level must have at least one entry, but it need not be set to any particular value.

Each value in the Registry has three properties:

**Name**: The text-based name by which that entry is referred to by applications and by Windows itself.

**Data Type:** The type of data that the entry contains. The valid types are shown in Table D.1.

**Data:** The value, either textual or numeric.

For example, the value shown in Figure D.4 is HKCU\Printers\Settings\Wizard\Default Attributes. The name is Default Attributes, the data type is REG_DWORD, and the value is 0x00000200 in hexadecimal. The decimal equivalent is shown in parentheses after the hex value. In this case it is 512.

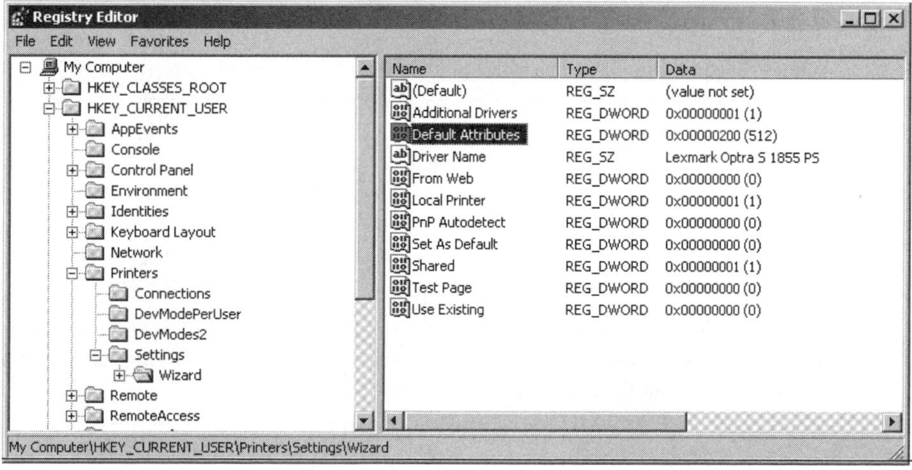


**IGURE D.4**
Each Registry entry has a name, a data type, and a data value.

**TABLE D.1 Registry Data Types**

| Type | Description |
|---|---|
| REG_SZ (String Value) | A zero-terminated string. It can be a string of any ANSI or Unicode characters (text, numbers, or symbols) of any length. The Registry Editor adds two zeros at the end of whatever value you enter, thus it is called zero-terminated. This is the most common key type, because it can hold both text and numbers. |
| REG_MULTI_SZ (Multi-String Value) | This is like REG_SZ except it is a group of zero-terminated strings that are assigned to a single entry. |
| REG_EXPAND_SZ (Expandable String Value) | This is like REG_SZ except it contains an environment variable that the system fills in based on some other value, such as %SystemRoot%. |
| REG_BINARY (Binary Value) | A binary value that contains only 0 or 1 digits. |
| REG_DWORD (DWORD Value) | DWORD is short for double-word, a 32-bit numeric value. It can hold any integer from 0 to $2^{32}$ but it is mostly used for simple binary 0 or 1 values to represent on/off or yes/no switches. |
| REG_LINK | A pointer to some other part of the Registry. This type of entry allows all the settings needed for a specific application to be "found" in a single location within the Registry, even if some of the settings are actually located in different hives. |
| REG_NONE | This type is rarely used. With this type, the actual data is not significant; Windows simply checks for the presence or absence of a value—any value at all. |
| REG_FULL_RESOURCE _DESCRIPTOR, REG_ RESOURCE_LIST, and REG_RESOURCE_ REQUIREMENTS_LIST | These types provide information about resources that various components use or require. |

## Backing Up the Registry

Before you edit the Registry, it is a good idea to back it up in its current, working state. The procedure for doing that depends on the Windows version.

In Windows XP and Me, the best option is to use the System Restore utility to create a Restore Point that includes a copy of the current Registry.

The Registry Editor also has an Export command (on the File menu) that allows you to back up all or part of the Registry. To back up the Registry with the Export command, complete the following steps:

1. In the Registry Editor, if you want to back up only a certain section of the Registry, click on the subkey that you want to back up. Everything subordinate to it will be included. If you are backing up the entire Registry you can skip this step.

2. Choose File/Export. The Export Registry File dialog box opens (see Figure D.5).
3. Open the Save as type drop-down list. You can select from a variety of types. A good choice is Registry Hive Files if you are backing up only one root key; it won't work for multiple root keys, however. An alternate choice is the default, Registration Files (REG).
4. Key a name for the backup in the File name box.
5. In the Export range section, choose All to back up the entire Registry or choose Selected branch to back up only the key selected in step 1.
6. Click Save. The selection is backed up.

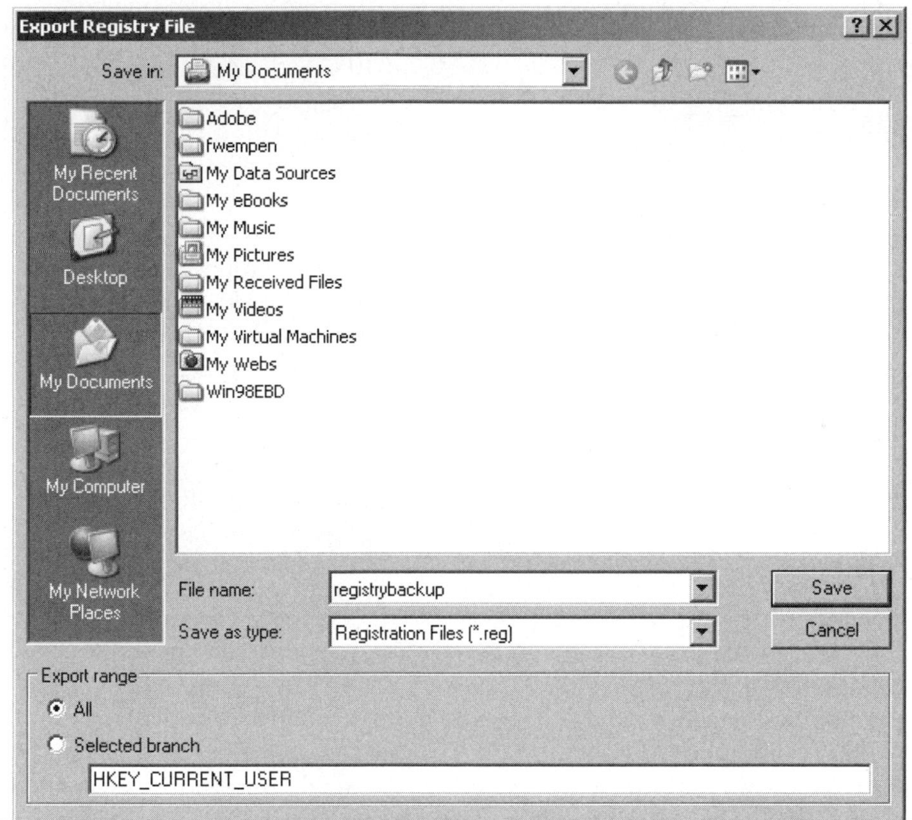


**FIGURE D.5**
Select a format in which to export (back up) the Registry.

In step 3, notice the recommendation to back up as a hive file if possible. That is because a hive file will provide the smoothest restoration if you ever need to restore your backup. Table D.2 explains the file types available.

**TABLE D.2 File Formats for Exporting Registry Keys**

| Format | Description | Notes |
|---|---|---|
| Registry Hive Files | A binary image of the selected portion of the Registry | The best choice for backup because when you restore it, if you have added keys to the Registry that are causing problems, they will be wiped out. |
| Registration Files | A text file with a .reg extension. | REG files can be read and edited in Notepad, and also imported back into the Registry. However, a REG backup will not help you if your problem is an added key because REG files merge with the existing keys in the Registry, rather than replacing them, when you import them. |
| Win9x/NT4 Registration Files (Windows 2000/XP only) | Same as Registration Files but compatible with earlier Windows versions because it does not use Unicode. | Useful for exporting a section of the Registry on a newer system and then importing it into the Registry on an older one. Not commonly done. |
| Text Files | Creates a plain-text file, not re-importable into the Registry. | Useful for capturing a snapshot of the Registry at a given time, but not useful for backup because it cannot be restored. |

Should you ever need to re-import the saved copy, use the File/Import command in the Registry Editor.

One other way to back up the Registry is through the Backup utility in Windows 2000 and XP. It includes a System State backup option; choosing this will create a copy of the registry hive files on a backup disk and in the Repair subdirectory of your Windows system folder (usually WINNT or WINDOWS). You could then use the Backup utility to restore that system state if needed.

## EDITING THE REGISTRY

The following sections outline how to find, change, add, and delete values and keys in the Registry.

### *Finding a Key or Value*

The Registry is so large that browsing for a particular value may not be easy unless you have a specific path to follow. Therefore, you will probably want to use the Find command to find the values you want. For example, suppose you are getting an error at startup because a file called scan32.dll is trying to load. You could use Find to locate all mentions of that file in the Registry and then figure out which one to delete (or decide to delete them all).

To find something in the Registry:

1. Choose Edit/Find or press Ctrl+F.
2. Type the value you want to find and then click Find Next.
3. To find another occurrence, press F3 or choose Edit/Find Next.

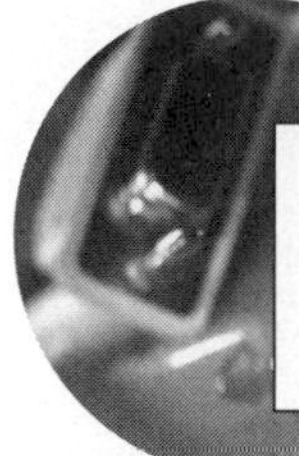

## IN REAL LIFE

**Notice that the Registry Editor window has a Favorites menu. You can add keys to it, the same as with Internet Explorer, and then easily return to those keys during another editing session.**

### *Changing a Value*

To change a value, double-click on the line you want to change. A dialog box opens for it. Enter the change in the dialog box and click OK. The name of the dialog box and the format in which it appears depend on the data type. Figure D.6 shows a representative sample of the types of boxes.

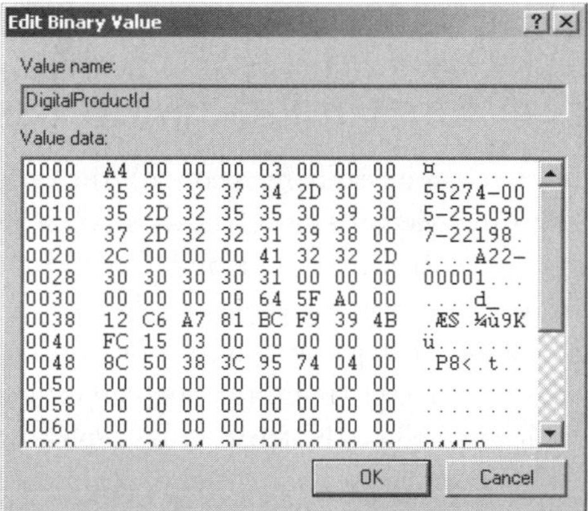


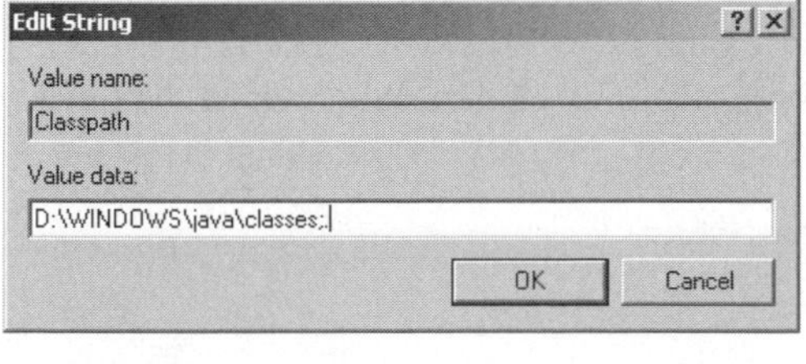


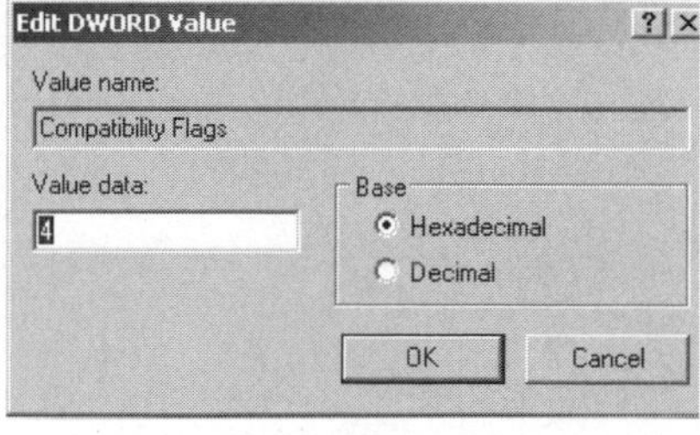


**FIGURE D.6**
Typical dialog boxes for editing Registry subkey values.

Notice in Figure D.6 that when editing a DWORD value you can choose to have it displayed in either decimal or hexadecimal. Most end users feel more comfortable working with decimal numbers, but you can work either way.

### *Adding a Registry Key or Value*

Most end users will never need to add a key or value to the Registry. Keys and values are added mainly by setup utilities and by Windows itself as needed. However, just in case you run across the odd situation in which it is necessary (for example, if you accidentally delete a key and have to re-create it), here is how to do it.

**Adding a key.** A key is a "folder" on the Registry's hierarchical tree. To create a new one:

1. Select the subkey (folder) into which the new one should be placed.
2. Choose Edit/New/Key. The new key is created.
3. Type a name for the key and press Enter.

**Adding a value.** A value is placed within whatever key is selected at the time that you issue the command to create it. As you learned earlier, a value can be of any of several types (see Table D.1). To create a new value:

1. Select the subkey (folder) into which the value should be placed.
2. Choose Edit/New and then select the data type you want. The dialog box opens for the data type you chose. Refer to Figure D.6 for some examples.
3. Enter the name and data you want, and then click OK.

### *Deleting a Key or Value*

If a particular key or value was accidentally created, or is causing a problem with Windows or an application, you can delete it. To do so, select it and press the Delete key, and then click Yes at the confirmation box.

## Using REG Files to Automate Registry Updates

Files with a .reg extension can be easily merged with the existing Registry by right-clicking them and choosing Merge. This works with REG files you create through the Export command in the Registry Editor, and also with plain-text files you create yourself and save with a .reg extension.

If you need to make a minor Registry change to many end user PCs, but you do not want the end users to use Registry Editor, you can create the change in a REG file either by creating it manually in Notepad or by exporting the section of an existing Registry that contains the setting. Then you can distribute the REG file to end users with directions for installing it using the right-click method.

Figure D.7 shows a REG file that tells Windows 98 that the user has already registered his copy of the operating system. Figure D.8 describes each of the lines in Figure D.7.

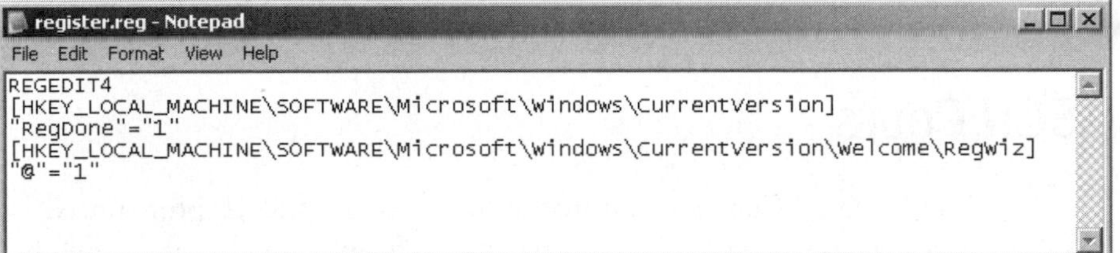
register.reg - Notepad
File Edit Format View Help
REGEDIT4
[HKEY_LOCAL_MACHINE\SOFTWARE\Microsoft\Windows\CurrentVersion]
"RegDone"="1"
[HKEY_LOCAL_MACHINE\SOFTWARE\Microsoft\Windows\CurrentVersion\Welcome\RegWiz]
"@"="1"

**FIGURE D.7**
A simple REG file that makes two changes in the Registry.

- **Header:** The header is the first line of the file, and it tells the Registry Editor that the file contains Registry settings. In Figure D.7 the header is REGEDIT4. This indicates that the file is compatible with Windows 95/98/Me or any NT-based version of Windows. If you are creating a file from scratch that would be used only in Windows 2000/XP, you could put Windows Registry Editor Version 5.00 as the header instead of REGEDIT4.
- **Key name:** Figure D.7 has two of these; each is enclosed in square brackets, and each lists the complete path to the key.
- **Name:** Value names are enclosed in quotation marks. In Figure D.7, RegDone is a name.
- **Data:** The data follows the name, with an equals sign between them. In Figure D.7, 1 is the value for RegDone.
- **Default data for a value:** If you are adding a value, and you want its default to be set to a certain setting, you use an @ sign. In Figure D.7, the fourth line specifies a new key to be created (RegWiz) and the last line sets a default value for it to 1.

**FIGURE D.8**
Changing a REG File Using Notepad

This is a very simple example that does not encompass multiple data types; if you are interested in learning to create your own REG files from scratch, you will want a more detailed book on the subject. One way to learn about the syntax involved in a REG file for various data types is to export a section of the Registry to a REG file and then examine it in Notepad.

# APPENDIX E

## ASCII CODES

The American Standard Code for Information Interchange (ASCII, pronounced "ask-key") is a standard seven-bit code for representing alphanumeric and symbolic characters on a computer. It was developed to achieve compatibility among various types of data processing equipment.

The standard ASCII character set consists of 128 decimal numbers ranging from zero through 127 assigned to letters, numbers, punctuation marks, and the most common special characters (see Table E.1).

**TABLE E.1 Standard ASCII Code Set**

| Decimal | Hex | Binary | Value | Notes |
|---|---|---|---|---|
| 000 | 000 | 00000000 | NUL | Null char. |
| 001 | 001 | 00000001 | SOH | Start of Header |
| 002 | 002 | 00000010 | STX | Start of Text |
| 003 | 003 | 00000011 | ETX | End of Text |
| 004 | 004 | 00000100 | EOT | End of Transmission |
| 005 | 005 | 00000101 | ENQ | Enquiry |
| 006 | 006 | 00000110 | ACK | Acknowledgment |
| 007 | 007 | 00000111 | BEL | Bell |
| 008 | 008 | 00001000 | BS | Backspace |
| 009 | 009 | 00001001 | HT | Horizontal Tab |
| 010 | 00A | 00001010 | LF | Line Feed |
| 011 | 00B | 00001011 | VT | Vertical Tab |
| 012 | 00C | 00001100 | FF | Form Feed |
| 013 | 00D | 00001101 | CR | Carriage Return |
| 014 | 00E | 00001110 | SO | Shift Out |
| 015 | 00F | 00001111 | SI | Shift In |
| 016 | 010 | 00010000 | DLE | Data Link Escape |
| 017 | 011 | 00010001 | DC1 (XON) | Device Control 1 |
| 018 | 012 | 00010010 | DC2 | Device Control 2 |
| 019 | 013 | 00010011 | DC3 (XOFF) | Device Control 3 |
| 020 | 014 | 00010100 | DC4 | Device Control 4 |
| 021 | 015 | 00010101 | NAK | Negative Acknowledgment |
| 022 | 016 | 00010110 | SYN | Synchronous Idle |
| 023 | 017 | 00010111 | ETB | End of Trans. Block |
| 024 | 018 | 00011000 | CAN | Cancel |
| 025 | 019 | 00011001 | EM | End of Medium |
| 026 | 01A | 00011010 | SUB | Substitute |
| 027 | 01B | 00011011 | ESC | Escape |
| 028 | 01C | 00011100 | FS | (File Separator) |

*continued*

| Decimal | Hex | Binary | Value | Notes |
|---|---|---|---|---|
| 028 | 01C | 00011100 | FS | File Separator |
| 029 | 01D | 00011101 | GS | Group Separator |
| 030 | 01E | 00011110 | RS | Request to Send<br>Record Separator |
| 031 | 01F | 00011111 | US | Unit Separator |
| 032 | 020 | 00100000 | SP | Space |
| 033 | 021 | 00100001 | ! | |
| 034 | 022 | 00100010 | “ | |
| 035 | 023 | 00100011 | # | |
| 036 | 024 | 00100100 | $ | |
| 037 | 025 | 00100101 | % | |
| 038 | 026 | 00100110 | & | |
| 039 | 027 | 00100111 | ‘ | |
| 040 | 028 | 00101000 | ( | |
| 041 | 029 | 00101001 | ) | |
| 042 | 02A | 00101010 | * | |
| 043 | 02B | 00101011 | + | |
| 044 | 02C | 00101100 | , | |
| 045 | 02D | 00101101 | - | |
| 046 | 02E | 00101110 | . | |
| 047 | 02F | 00101111 | / | |
| 048 | 030 | 00110000 | 0 | |
| 049 | 031 | 00110001 | 1 | |
| 050 | 032 | 00110010 | 2 | |
| 051 | 033 | 00110011 | 3 | |
| 052 | 034 | 00110100 | 4 | |
| 053 | 035 | 00110101 | 5 | |
| 054 | 036 | 00110110 | 6 | |
| 055 | 037 | 00110111 | 7 | |
| 056 | 038 | 00111000 | 8 | |
| 057 | 039 | 00111001 | 9 | |
| 058 | 03A | 00111010 | : | |
| 059 | 03B | 00111011 | ; | |
| 060 | 03C | 00111100 | < | |
| 061 | 03D | 00111101 | = | |
| 062 | 03E | 00111110 | > | |
| 063 | 03F | 00111111 | ? | |
| 064 | 040 | 01000000 | @ | |
| 065 | 041 | 01000001 | A | |
| 066 | 042 | 01000010 | B | |
| 067 | 043 | 01000011 | C | |
| 068 | 044 | 01000100 | D | |
| 069 | 045 | 01000101 | E | |

*continued*

| Decimal | Hex | Binary | Value | Notes |
|---|---|---|---|---|
| 070 | 046 | 01000110 | F | |
| 071 | 047 | 01000111 | G | |
| 072 | 048 | 01001000 | H | |
| 073 | 049 | 01001001 | I | |
| 074 | 04A | 01001010 | J | |
| 075 | 04B | 01001011 | K | |
| 076 | 04C | 01001100 | L | |
| 077 | 04D | 01001101 | M | |
| 078 | 04E | 01001110 | N | |
| 079 | 04F | 01001111 | O | |
| 080 | 050 | 01010000 | P | |
| 081 | 051 | 01010001 | Q | |
| 082 | 052 | 01010010 | R | |
| 083 | 053 | 01010011 | S | |
| 084 | 054 | 01010100 | T | |
| 085 | 055 | 01010101 | U | |
| 086 | 056 | 01010110 | V | |
| 087 | 057 | 01010111 | W | |
| 088 | 058 | 01011000 | X | |
| 089 | 059 | 01011001 | Y | |
| 090 | 05A | 01011010 | Z | |
| 091 | 05B | 01011011 | [ | |
| 092 | 05C | 01011100 | \ | |
| 093 | 05D | 01011101 | ] | |
| 094 | 05E | 01011110 | ^ | |
| 095 | 05F | 01011111 | _ | |
| 096 | 060 | 01100000 | ` | |
| 097 | 061 | 01100001 | a | |
| 098 | 062 | 01100010 | b | |
| 099 | 063 | 01100011 | c | |
| 100 | 064 | 01100100 | d | |
| 101 | 065 | 01100101 | e | |
| 102 | 066 | 01100110 | f | |
| 103 | 067 | 01100111 | g | |
| 104 | 068 | 01101000 | h | |
| 105 | 069 | 01101001 | i | |
| 106 | 06A | 01101010 | j | |
| 107 | 06B | 01101011 | k | |
| 108 | 06C | 01101100 | l | |
| 109 | 06D | 01101101 | m | |
| 110 | 06E | 01101110 | n | |
| 111 | 06F | 01101111 | o | |
| 112 | 070 | 01110000 | p | |

*continued*

| Decimal | Hex | Binary | Value | Notes |
|---|---|---|---|---|
| 113 | 071 | 01110001 | q | |
| 114 | 072 | 01110010 | r | |
| 115 | 073 | 01110011 | s | |
| 116 | 074 | 01110100 | t | |
| 117 | 075 | 01110101 | u | |
| 118 | 076 | 01110110 | v | |
| 119 | 077 | 01110111 | w | |
| 120 | 078 | 01111000 | x | |
| 121 | 079 | 01111001 | y | |
| 122 | 07A | 01111010 | z | |
| 123 | 07B | 01111011 | { | |
| 124 | 07C | 01111100 | \| | |
| 125 | 07D | 01111101 | } | |
| 126 | 07E | 01111110 | ~ | |
| 127 | 07F | 01111111 | DEL | |

Some notes on some of the characters in Table E.1:

- BEL (bell): Caused teletype machines to ring a bell. Causes a beep in many common terminals and terminal emulation programs.
- LF (NL line feed, new line): Moves the cursor (or print head) to a new line. On UNIX systems, moves to a new line and all the way to the left.
- FF (form feed): Advances paper to the top of the next page (if the output device is a printer).
- CR (carriage return): Moves the cursor all the way to the left, but does not advance to the next line.
- SO (shift out): Switches output device to alternate character set.
- SI (shift in): Switches output device back to default character set.

The Extended ASCII character set also consists of 128 decimal numbers and ranges from 128 through 255 representing additional special, mathematical, graphic, and foreign characters. The standard Extended ASCII character set and the one used by default in Windows are different for some characters, so there is not one universally accepted set of codes that correspond to the extended character numbers. In addition, many font sets use letters, numbers, and symbols different from the ones shown in Table E.1.

# GLOSSARY

**10Base-2** A style of bus topology Ethernet that uses coaxial cable and connects individual segments of cable and PC Network Interface Cards with T-style connectors.

**10Base-5** An old style of bus topology Ethernet that uses 0.5-inch coaxial cable (also called thicknet).

**10Base-T** A modern style of Ethernet hardware that uses UTP cable with RJ-45 connectors and a physical star topology, and transfers data at up to 10Mbps.

**100Base-T** A type of Ethernet network capable of transmitting data at up to 100Mbps and using unshielded twisted pair cables.

**386DX** An 80386 CPU with a 32-bit address bus and a 32-bit external data bus.

**386SX** An 80386 CPU with a 16-bit external data bus and a 24-bit address bus.

**3D sound** Sounds and music in a game that seem to come from all sides and seem to change depending on the position of the game character.

**3D video acceleration** Additional features in a video card that process Application Program Interface (API) commands from 3D-aware applications, helping to relieve the processing burden on the CPU.

**56KFlex** One of two early competing standards for 56Kbps modem data transfer, developed and supported by Rockwell and Lucent.

**8086** An early CPU with 16-bit internal registers, a 16-bit external data bus, and a 20-bit address bus. Never widely used or produced.

**8088** An early CPU with 16-bit internal registers, an 8-bit external data bus, and a 20-bit address bus. Used for the original IBM PCs and PC-XTs.

**AC** Alternating current. A type of electrical delivery that changes the positive and negative points many times per second (typically 60Hz). Used in household electricity.

**Accelerated Graphics Port** See *AGP.*

**Access time** The delay between a request for data and the delivery of that data from a drive.

**ACPI** Advanced Configuration and Power Interface. A set of standards for controlling Plug and Play (PnP) hardware at the OS level and managing power conservation settings.

**Active Directory** A resource management system for client/server networks based on Windows 2000 or XP servers that enables multiple domain controllers to share and constantly update a central directory.

**Active heat sink** A heat sink that includes a fan.

**Active matrix** A type of LCD screen in which each pixel has its own transistor, resulting in better display than passive matrix.

**Active partition** The primary partition that is set up to be checked for boot instructions at startup.

**Active termination** Termination achieved with voltage regulators.

**Address bus** The bus that runs between the CPU and the RAM.

**ADSL** Asynchronous DSL. A type of DSL service in which upload speed is slower than download speed.

**Advanced Configuration and Power Interface** See *ACPI.*

**Advanced Power Management** See *APM.*

**AGP** Accelerated Graphics Port. A high-speed local bus designed exclusively for video card use.

**AGP bus** The bus that connects the AGP expansion slot to the motherboard chipset.

**Alphanumeric** Derived from a combination of the words "alphabetic" and "numeric." Refers to all alphabetical characters plus all numerical digits.

**Alternating current** See *AC.*

**Amperes (amps)** A measurement of current, the rate at which a device draws electricity.

**Analog** Continuously variable data that has no precise numeric equivalent.

**Anonymous FTP** An FTP download that is available to all Internet users without them having to identify themselves.

**Aperture grille** A system of vertical wires between electron guns and phosphors for keeping the electron beams aligned on a CRT.

**API** Application Program Interface. A set of programming codes that application designers can standardize to call on specific acceleration functions in a video card or other hardware.

**APM** Advanced Power Management. The original standard for PC power management, now obsolete, replaced by ACPI.

**Applet** Slang for a small application, such as Notepad or a configuration utility for a hardware device.

**Application** Software that performs a useful end user task such as creating a document or playing a game.

**Application Program Interface** See *API.*

**ASCII characters** The set of number, letter, and symbol characters defined by the American Standard Code for Information Interchange.

**Asynchronous DSL** See *ADSL.*

**AT** (1) Advanced Technology. A style of computer introduced by IBM with the 80286 CPU. Many of its features continue to be utilized in AT motherboards. (2) The command that precedes other codes when issuing AT commands to modems. Short for "Attention."

**ATA** AT Attachment. A set of standards for IDE drives that govern their speed, performance, and interface. *AT* stands for "Advanced Technology."

**AT command set** A set of codes that tell the modem what mode to operate in and what to do. See *AT.*

**AT motherboard** A motherboard that uses a DIN-style keyboard connector and a two-part power supply connector to the motherboard, and lacks ports built into the side. Expansion slots are parallel to the narrow edge of the board. Compare to ATX motherboard.

**Attenuation** Loss of signal power in a cable carrying data, usually because the data is having to travel too far.

**ATX motherboard** A motherboard that uses a PS/2 style keyboard connector and a single-part power supply connector to the motherboard. Contains built-in ports on the side. Expansion slots are parallel to the wide edge of the board. Compare to AT motherboard.

**AUTOEXEC.BAT** A startup file used by some operating systems (such as DOS) that processes its batch of commands whenever the computer starts.

**Automatic private IP addressing** A range of reserved IP addresses (192.168.0.1 through 192.168.255.255) that Windows automatically assigns to network devices whenever it cannot find a DHCP server and does not have a fixed IP address assigned.

**AUTORUN.INF** A file containing instructions for automatic execution each time Windows detects that the CD has been inserted into a CD drive. For AUTORUN.INF to work, the Autorun feature must be enabled for the CD drive or you must double-click the CD icon in My Computer.

**Average access time** See *Access time.*

**Baby AT** A small AT motherboard, measuring 8.5 x 13 inches or less.

**Backbone** The central part of the network, through which traffic flows between remote segments.

**Back probing** A technique for taking electrical measurements while a device is running by sticking the probes in the backs of the connector holes.

**Bank** One or more memory slots on a motherboard that combine to be treated as a single logical unit when addressed by the CPU.

**Basic Input Output System** See *BIOS.*

**Batch file** A text file containing a list of commands to be executed, in the order listed, as a group or batch.

**Baud rate** The cycles per second of a modem transmission.

**Bay** A slot in a computer case for installing a disk drive.

**Beep codes** Patterns of beeps through the motherboard's speaker that provide information about errors in the boot process.

**Binary** A numbering system based on two digits: 0 and 1. Used for data input and output in PCs.

**BIOS** Basic Input Output System. Instructions on a firmware chip that tell the PC how to start up and how to interact with hardware at a base level.

**BIOS Setup program** A built-in program in a PC that enables you to configure the PC's base-level settings. See also *BIOS.*

**Bit** A single binary digit, 0 or 1.

**Bitmap font** A font in which each letter at each size is an individual graphic stored in the font file(s).

**Bits per second** See *Bps.*

**Block mode** A data transfer scheme that enables a computer to transfer data to and from the drive in blocks rather than in bytes, improving its performance.

**BNC connector** British Naval Connector or Bayonet-Neill Connector. A type of connector with a metal core and heavy outer covering. A cable television cable is one example.

**Bootable disk** A disk that contains the OS start-up files needed to bring an operating system and its associated user interface up to operational level.

**Boot sector** The first sector on a logical disk.

**Bps** Bits per second. The rate at which data is carried during a modem transmission.

**Bridge** A network device that directs traffic between network segments, screening out any traffic that is not addressed to a node within a particular segment.

**Brownout** An undervoltage condition in which a device is receiving less than the normal amount of electricity.

**Bus** (1) A data pathway between chips, slots, or other components on a circuit board. (2) A network topology that arranges the PCs in a single-file chain.

**Byte** A group of eight binary digits (bits).

**Cab files** Short for "cabinet files"; compressed archives containing files needed for Windows setup.

**Cable select** A means of determining an IDE drive's master/slave status by its position on the ribbon cable.

**Cache** A holding area for data that keeps it closer at hand for later reuse than it would normally be, improving the PC's efficiency.

**Capacitor** An electronic component that stores electrical charge and then releases it as needed.

**CardBus** A recent update to the PC Card standard that provides speed, bus, and voltage improvements.

**Cathode Ray Tube** See *CRT.*

**CAV** Constant angular velocity. A method of reading data from a CD in which the CD's spinning rate remains constant. The amount of data read changes depending on the area being read.

**CCD** Charge-coupled device. A grid of photosensitive cells that records light levels and converts it to electrical charge, which is then processed as data by a computer.

**CD** Compact disc. A disc that stores data optically in patterns of reflective land and nonreflective pits.

**CD drive** A disk drive that reads CDs. See also *CD-R*, *CD-RW*, and *DVD.*

**CD-R** Compact disc recordable. A CD-ROM drive that can also write to blank CDs. CD-R can be written only once; then the disk can only be read. See also *CD-RW.*

**CD-ROM** Compact disc read-only memory. A compact disc that cannot be written to.

**CD-RW** Compact disc rewritable. A CD-ROM drive that can write to rewritable CDs, which allow multiple rewriting. Compare to *CD-R.*

**Central Processing Unit** See *CPU.*

**Centronics** A type of connector consisting of a solid bar with pins on either side that fits into a trough-style connector and is secured with wire loops.

**Charge-coupled device** See *CCD.*

**Chipset** A set of chips that together control the traffic flow along and between buses.

**CHS** Cylinders, heads, and sectors. Three specifications for a drive that collectively determine its capacity and geometry.

**CIS** Contact image sensor. A low-end scanner technology that uses rows of LEDs to illuminate the image and capture the light reflecting from it.

**Client** (1) A PC that an end user employs to run applications, with no special network management duties. (2) Networking software for a client PC.

**Client/Server** A network that includes at least one PC dedicated for use as a server.

**Clock cycle** One tick of the system crystal's clock, resulting in one data movement into or out of the CPU.

**Clock multiplier** The multiplier by which the CPU's internal speed exceeds its external speed.

**Clock speed** The speed, in megahertz (MHz), at which the CPU's internal clock operates. See *Clock cycle.*

**Cluster** A group of sectors treated as a single storage unit.

**CLV** Constant linear velocity. A method of recording and reading data from a CD in which the amount of data read/written remains constant. The CD spins faster or slower as needed.

**CMOS** Complementary metal-oxide semiconductor. A chip that contains any exceptions to the BIOS settings made by the user through the BIOS Setup program.

**Collision** A network traffic snarl that occurs when two PCs try to send data at the same time.

**Color depth** The number of bits needed to uniquely describe each color, and the resulting maximum number of colors produced by that number of bits.

**Command line** A user interface based on typing text-based commands at a prompt. MS-DOS is one example. Also can refer to the command prompt itself.

**Compiled language** A programming language that writes programs to be run through a compiler utility, and then distributed as executable files to end users.

**Complementary metal-oxide semiconductor** See *CMOS.*

**COM port** Short for "Communications port." A generic type of serial port built into most motherboards.

**Compression algorithm** A mathematical formula that makes a file smaller by removing certain bits. These removed bits may be added back in later when the file is opened in a program that understands the compression algorithm in use, or may be lost forever, depending on the algorithm.

**CONFIG.SYS** A startup file that lists the drivers and system settings the PC should load when it starts. Used mainly in MS-DOS; not commonly used with modern versions of Windows.

**Constant angular velocity** See *CAV.*

**Constant linear velocity** See *CLV.*

**Contact image sensor** See *CIS.*

**Continuously variable** Having no fixed division between one measurement or value and the next.

**Conventional memory** The first 640KB of RAM, used for running real-mode programs.

**Cookie** A small text file stored on your hard drive that remembers settings for a particular Web site and reloads them each time you revisit that site.

**Cooperative multitasking** An early system of CPU time sharing wherein each application is in charge of pausing itself so another application can run.

**Coprocessor** See *Math coprocessor.*

**Core voltage** The electrical voltage that the CPU requires to operate.

**Cost of ownership** The total cost of an item including the costs for supplies and maintenance over its lifetime.

**CPU** Central Processing Unit. The main processing chip in a PC.

**Crosstalk** Interference between adjacent wires or cables caused by electromagnetic interference (EMI).

**CRT** Cathode Ray Tube. A traditional box type of monitor that uses electrons hitting phosphors to create the display.

**CSMA/CD** Carrier Sense Multiple Access/Collision Detection. The method used on logical bus network topologies for detecting collisions and retrying transmission.

**Current** The rate of flow of electricity, measured in amperes.

**Cylinder** All areas of a disk at a certain in/out head position, on all disk sides combined.

**Daisywheel** A disc with plastic spikes radiating from its center, with a different character at the end of each spike. In a daisywheel printer, a hammer strikes a spike, causing its letter to be pressed into an inked ribbon.

**Data transfer rate** The rate at which data can be read from a drive.

**Daughterboard** An add-on to the motherboard that provides additional connectors or interfaces, such as drive connectors.

**DC** Direct current. A type of electrical delivery in which the positive and negative poles do not change. Used in batteries. Compare to *AC.*

**DDR SDRAM** Double Data Rate synchronous dynamic random access memory. A type of RAM that operates at twice the system bus speed. See *SDRAM.*

**Decimal** A numbering system based on 10 digits. Can also refer to a period that separates digits, as in *1.2.*

**Decimal** A base-10 numbering system. The standard numbering system used by humans.

**Default gateway** The IP address of the pathway that leads out of the local subnet.

**Degaussing** Discharging any static buildup in a monitor that might be causing image distortion. Usually done by pressing a button on the monitor.

**Desktop** (1) Any nonportable PC with a case and a separate keyboard, mouse, and monitor. Compare to *Notebook PC.* (2) A nonportable PC whose case is oriented so that its largest side sits flat against the desk. Compare to *Tower.* (3) The background area of the graphical interface in Windows, on which shortcut icons sit.

**Device driver** A file that acts as an intermediary between the operating system and the device, providing translation services and a description of the device's capabilities.

**DHCP** Dynamic Host Configuration Profile. A server utility that dynamically assigns IP addresses to client PCs that request them.

**Differential SCSI** See *HVD SCSI* or *High-Voltage Differential SCSI.*

**Digital** Pertaining to exact measurements involving numbers. Contrast to analog.

**Digital camera** A camera that saves images in electronic format and feeds them into your PC instead of putting the images on conventional film.

**Digital Subscriber Line** See *DSL.*

**Digital Versatile Disc** See *DVD.*

**Digital Video Disc** See *DVD.*

**Digital zoom** On a digital camera, a zoom that magnifies the image by interpolation rather than with a real zoom lens. Compare to *Optical zoom.*

**Digitize** To convert to digital (number-based) format, such as converting a picture to a binary file on a computer.

**DIMM** Dual inline memory module. A type of RAM packaging consisting of a 168-pin rectangular circuit board onto which chips are mounted.

**DIN connector** The standard five-pin connector for an AT-style keyboard. *DIN* stands for "Deutsche Industrie Norm."

**DIP switch** A small switch on a circuit board that controls a low-level settings, much like a jumper.

**Direct current** See *DC.*

**Direct Memory Addressing** See *DMA.*

**Directory** A logical unit that organizes files into groups for easier management. Also called folder.

**DirectSound** A subset of the DirectX API that deals specifically with sound.

**Direct3D** A subset of the DirectX API that deals specifically with video.

**DirectX** A multimedia API developed by Microsoft for games and other programs to provide shortcuts for interacting with Windows.

**Disk** A platter or set of platters on which data is stored.

**DLL** Dynamic Link Library. A file containing programming codes that help applications communicate with hardware.

**DMA** Direct Memory Addressing. A drive access method that bypasses the CPU to improve performance between the device and RAM.

**DNS** Domain Name System. A server application that keeps track of the relationships between IP addresses and text names and provides translation services to PCs that request them.

**DNS Lookup** The process of looking up a domain name in a DNS server's database and sending the equivalent IP address back to the requester.

**Docking station** A stationary unit to which a notebook PC attaches to gain extra capabilities while in a fixed location.

**Domain** A client/server network controlled by a server that provides addressing services to the connected clients such as assigning IP addresses.

**Domain Name System** See *DNS.*

**DOS protected-mode interface** See *DPMI.*

**Dot-matrix printer** A printer that forms characters on the page by pushing in/out a set of metal pins and then hitting them against an inked ribbon.

**Dot pitch** The distance between two phosphors of the same color on a monitor.

**Dots per inch** See *Dpi.*

**Double Data Rate SDRAM** See *DDR SDRAM.*

**Double-scan passive matrix** See *DSTN.*

**Dpi** Dots per inch. A measurement of printer resolution.

**DPMI** DOS protected-mode interface. A command-line interface designed for use with 32-bit OSes that use protected mode for memory handling.

**Drive** The mechanical unit that reads and writes a disc.

**Drum** The large cylinder in a laser printer to which the page image is written before being transferred to paper.

**D-sub connector** A type of connector with a D-shaped metal ridge around multiple rows of pins or holes (usually two or three rows).

**DSL** Digital Subscriber Line. A broadband Internet connection type that operates through normal telephone lines.

**DSTN** Dual-scan passive matrix. A type of passive matrix LCD screen with an extra row of transistors for better performance. STN stands for Super Twisted Nematic.

**Dual inline memory module** See *DIMM.*

**Dual pipeline** A CPU that is able to process two sets of instructions at the same time. Also called superscalar architecture (although technically that refers also to quad pipeline as well).

**Duplex** The ability to transmit and receive on the same channel at the same time. Duplex settings in most terminal programs are Full Duplex and Half Duplex.

**DVD** Digital Versatile Disc. A very high capacity type of CD-ROM. When used to store movies, it is called a Digital Video Disc.

**Dvorak keyboard** A keyboard with a different arrangement of letters, designed for faster typing than with a traditional keyboard.

**Dynamic disks** A disk organization type in Windows 2000 and XP that discards the traditional paradigm of partitioning to create volumes that can be resized, combined, mirrored, or striped.

**Dynamic IP address** An IP address that is assigned to a device when it connects to the network. It retains that address for the duration of the connection and then releases it back into the pool when it logs off.

**Dynamic processing** A CPU function in Pentium Pro and higher that allows commands to run out of queue in order to minimize CPU idle time.

**Dynamic range** The ability of a scanner to distinguish between light and dark.

**EDO** Extended data out. A type of nonparity RAM used in some Pentium systems that improved on standard RAM because it needed to be refreshed less frequently. Now obsolete.

**EEPROM** Electrically Erasable Programmable Read-Only Memory. A type of chip used for the BIOS that can have its content modified by a special utility program that prompts the chip to be erased and rewritten. Also called flash ROM.

**EFS** Encrypting File System. A feature in NTFS 5 that enables users to secure files on the local drives by user login.

**EIDE** Enhanced IDE. An improved version of the original ATA standard, also known as ATA-2. Also refers to IDE devices that conform to higher ATA standards.

**EISA** Enhanced Industry-Standard Architecture. A now-obsolete early attempt at a 32-bit version of ISA.

**Electrically Erasable Programmable ROM** See *EEPROM.*

**Electromagnetic interference (EMI)** Signal interference caused by the magnetic field building up around a cable through which electricity is passing.

**Electrostatic discharge** See *ESD.*

**EMM386.EXE** A memory management utility in DOS and Windows that enables extended memory similar to either EMS or XMS.

**EMS** Expanded Memory Specification. The standard for expanded memory usage. Also called LIM.

**Emulation** A device or driver that functions the same way as another brand or model, for compatibility purposes.

**Encoding scheme** A method of minimizing the numbers of transitions involved in data storage on a disk. The most common is Run Length Limited (RLL).

**Encrypting File System** See *EFS.*

**Enhanced BIOS Services for Disk Drives** A BIOS extension that enables LBA support for drives of over 8GB.

**Enhanced IDE** See *EIDE.*

**Enhanced Industry-Standard Architecture** See *EISA.*

**EPROM** Erasable Programmable ROM. A type of ROM that can be erased with ultraviolet light and then reprogrammed to contain different data.

**Erasable Programmable ROM** See *EPROM.*

**Ergonomic** Designed to help the human body avoid unnecessary strain or stress.

**ESD** Electrostatic discharge. Static electricity, occurring when two items of unequal voltage potential touch.

**Exabyte** A trillion megabytes.

**Expanded memory** A means of providing more than 1MB of RAM to 80286 and higher systems by swapping data into and out of upper memory.

**Expanded Memory Specification** See *EMS.*

**Expansion board** A circuit card that adds new capabilities to a system.

**Expansion bus** A pathway from the main system bus to an expansion slot such as an ISA, PCI, or AGP slot.

**Expansion slot** A slot in the motherboard that accepts an expansion board.

**Extended data out** See *EDO.*

**Extended memory** Memory above 1MB in 80386 and higher systems.

**Extended Memory Specification** See *XMS.*

**Extended partition** A nonbootable partition on a hard drive that can have multiple drive letters assigned to it.

**External** A device that works from outside the PC case, rather than being installed inside it.

**External data bus** The bus that connects the address bus (the CPU and memory's bus) to the chipset on the motherboard. Also called processor bus or system bus.

**External drive bay** A bay in a PC case that is externally accessible, so the disc can be inserted/removed without opening the case.

**External speed** The speed at which the CPU actually operates, regulated by the system crystal.

**Fast page mode** See *FPM.*

**FAT** (1) The original 16-bit file system for MS-DOS; also used in Windows 95 and supported by nearly all operating systems for backward compatibility. (2) Acronym for File Allocation Table, the table listing the physical locations of the starting clusters for files stored on a disk.

**FAT12** A 12-bit file system used on floppy disks, supported by all operating systems.

**FAT16** See *FAT.*

**FAT32** A 32-bit version of the FAT file system, provided with Windows 95 OSR2 and higher.

**FDISK** Short for "Fixed Disk Utility," an MS-DOS utility program for creating and managing FAT partitions.

**Female** A connector having holes or slots into which a male connector fits.

**Fiber-optic cable** A cable that transmits data via light pulses at high speeds but is rather fragile and expensive.

**File Allocation Table** See *FAT.*

**File attributes** On/off flags for a file or folder that report its status or condition, such as Read-Only, Archive, Hidden, or System.

**File system** A logical method of storing data on a disk. Examples include FAT and NTFS.

**Firewall** Software that helps prevent hackers from breaking into a computer via its network or Internet connection.

**FireWire** See *IEEE 1394.*

**Firmware** A combination of hardware and software, such as software that is permanently stored on a BIOS chip.

**Flat shading** Filling an object with a solid color.

**Flip chip** A CPU design that places the CPU on the top of the ceramic PGA package rather than on the bottom, for easier cooling.

**Floppy drive** A disk drive that reads floppy disks.

**Flux transition** The transition on a magnetic disk between positive and negative polarity.

**FM synthesis** A sound card method of playing MIDI music by simulating the sounds made by real instruments.

**Folder** See *Directory.*

**Font** A specific typeface at a specific size with certain attributes such as bold or italic. Can also be used as a synonym for typeface.

**Footer** The error-checking portion of a data packet sent on a network, which follows the data.

**Form factor** The size and shape of a component, such as a motherboard or case.

**FPM** Fast page mode. A type of RAM found in older PCs, with speed measured in nanoseconds (ns) of delay.

**Fragmented file** A file that is not stored contiguously on a disk.

**Frame** The header and footer that accompany data when it is sent as a packet over a network.

**Frame rate** The rate at which the video card alters what it sends to the monitor, measured in hertz (Hz).

**Freeware** Software that is distributed to the public without cost or obligation.

**Frequency range** The range of sound wavelengths, measured in hertz, that a speaker can reproduce.

**Fuser** A heater in a laser printer that melts the toner so it sticks to the paper.

**Gateway** A network device that creates compatibility and connectivity between dissimilar network types.

**Gender changer** An adapter that switches between male and female connectors.

**Geometry** The definition of the number of cylinders, heads, and sectors in a disk drive.

**Gouraud shading** Applying different colors to an object and then blending them.

**Graphical user interface** See *GUI.*

**GUI** Graphical user interface. An operating system that relies on icons and a pointing device for user interaction.

**Hard disk** A stack of metal platters that store data. Roughly synonymous with hard drive.

**Hard drive** The read/write drive unit that controls a hard disk. Roughly synonymous with hard disk.

**Hardware** Physical computer equipment such as drives, circuit boards, and silicon chips.

**Hardware modem** A modem with an on-board controller, usable in any operating system.

**Hardware profile** The Device Manager settings that describe a particular hardware configuration.

**Header** The address portion of a data packet sent on a network, which precedes the data.

**Heat sink** A block of heat-conductive material placed on a CPU to channel heat away from it, either with or without a fan.

**Heat sink compound** A heat-conductive adhesive used to mount a heat sink to a CPU.

**Hermaphroditic connector** A connector that can plug into any other connector of the same type—male or female.

**Hexadecimal** A base-16 numbering system, using 0 through 9 and A through F as digits. Used for memory addressing in PCs.

**Hibernate** A power management feature of Windows that enables the computer to copy RAM contents to the hard disk and then shut down completely. Restarting is quicker than a full startup.

**High-level formatting** Preparing a disk for use by a particular operating system by creating a file system such as FAT or NTFS.

**High memory** The first 64KB above the 1MB mark.

**High-order bits** The bits sent to the CPU that represent the instructions for calculating the low-order bits.

**High Performance File System** See *HPFS.*

**High Voltage Differential SCSI** See *HVD SCSI.*

**HIMEM.SYS** A utility for managing extended memory and making it available to protected-mode programs.

**Host address** The portion of an IP address that refers to the individual network device, not the network segment on which it resides.

**Hot shoe** A metal bracket with a connector on it for attaching an external flash to a camera.

**Hot-swapping** Connecting or disconnecting a device while the PC is running. Also called hot-plugging.

**HPFS** High Performance File System. A file system used by the OS/2 operating system; now obsolete.

**HTML** Hypertext Markup Language. The programming language used to create formatted Web pages. Consists of formatting codes enclosed in brackets in plain text strings.

**HTTP** Hypertext Transfer Protocol. The protocol used by Web browsers to request and receive Web page content.

**Hub chipset** A motherboard chipset that divides operations among three chips: Memory controller hub, I/O controller hub, and Super I/O.

**HVD SCSI** A special type of SCSI incompatible with other types that allows for greater maximum distances (up to 25 meters). Also called Differential SCSI.

**Hypertext Markup Language** See *HTML.*

**Hypertext Transfer Protocol** See *HTTP.*

**ICS** Internet Connection Sharing. A feature in Windows 98 Second Edition and higher that enables a network client to share its local Internet connection with other PCs on the LAN.

**IDE** Integrated Device Electronics. A drive interface that has the drive controller built into the same unit as the disk drive itself. IDE is a common type of hard disk and CD-ROM interface to the motherboard.

**IEEE 1284** The specification governing parallel printer ports, outlining SPP, Bidirectional, EPP, and ECP modes.

**IEEE 1394** Also called FireWire. A high-speed serial connection used to connect video equipment such as digital video cameras to a PC.

**Industry-Standard Architecture** See *ISA.*

**Inkjet printer** A nonimpact sheet-fed printer that prints by forcing ink out of nozzles and onto the paper.

**Input** Incoming data from a device such as keyboard or mouse.

**Integrated Device Electronics** See *IDE.*

**Integrated Services Digital Network** See *ISDN.*

**Interlacing** Refreshing only every other line of a monitor display with each pass. Results in more screen flicker.

**Internal** A device that fits inside the PC case, such as in an expansion slot or drive bay.

**Internal speed** The speed at which the CPU can reliably operate, measured in megahertz.

**Internet** A global, decentralized, publicly accessible TCP/IP-based network.

**Internet Connection Sharing** See *ICS.*

**Internet Protocol** See *IP.*

**Internet Service Provider** See *ISP.*

**Interpolation** A method of creating extra bits of data between two ordinary bits by averaging them. Useful for increasing the resolution of pictures, for example.

**Interpreted language** A programming language that writes programs to be distributed as scripts, requiring the end user to have an interpreter installed that will run them.

**Interrupt Request** See *IRQ.*

**I/O address** A memory address reserved for transferring data to and from a device.

**I/O ports** Ports designed to transfer information into and out of the PC. Examples include serial (COM) ports and parallel (LPT) ports, as well as USB.

**IP** Internet Protocol. One of the protocols in the TCP/IP suite. See also *IP address.*

**IP address** A number that uniquely identifies a device on a network. It consists of a string of four three-digit numbers separated by periods.

**IrDA** Stands for "Infrared Data Association," the standards board that came up with the industry standard for infrared communication ports between notebook PCs, desktop PCs, PDAs, and other electronics.

**IRQ** Interrupt Request. A channel for a device to signal to the CPU that it is ready to begin a conversation.

**ISA** Industry-Standard Architecture. An older type of expansion slot that transfers data 8 bits at a time at 8MHz. Now nearly obsolete.

**ISA bus** The bus that connects any ISA slots in the motherboard to the chipset. Not present in the newer models of motherboards.

**ISDN** Integrated Services Digital Network. A type of digital telephone line with two 56Kbps data channels for Internet connection and a voice channel for regular telephone calls.

**ISP** Internet Service Provider. A company that sells Internet access to the public.

**Jumper** A metal bridge surrounded by a plastic cap that, when placed across two pins, completes a circuit between them and changes the flow of electricity on the circuit board.

**Keyframe** A frame of animation provided by the application rather than interpolated by the video card.

**LAN** Local-area network. A network in which the connected nodes are located within a limited area, such as a single building.

**Land** An area of reflectivity on an optical disc such as a CD-ROM.

**Landscape** A page orientation wherein the text runs parallel to the wide edge of the paper.

**Laptop PC** Any notebook or subnotebook PC.

**LBA** Logical Block Addressing. A means of sector translation that assigns a number to each sector and works with them individually, using a CHS table for conversion to CHS values as needed.

**LCD** Liquid Crystal Display. A flat-panel type of monitor that uses electricity passing through liquid crystals to create the display.

**Legacy** A device that uses out-of-date technology but is retained for backward compatibility.

**Letter quality** See *LQ.*

**LIF** Low insertion force. A CPU socket in which the CPU's pins are wedged into little corresponding holes and held in by the tension. An obsolete technology; zero insertion force (ZIF) is the current standard.

**LIM** Stands for "Lotus-Intel-Microsoft," the three companies that came up with the EMS memory spec. See also *EMS.*

**Line printer** A printer that receives data and transfers it to paper line-by-line.

**Liquid Crystal Display** See *LCD.*

**Local** Connected directly to the individual PC.

**Local-area network** See *LAN.*

**Local bus** A bus tied directly into the system bus, not relying on the ISA bus for data conveyance.

**Logical Block Addressing** See *LBA.*

**Logical drive** A drive letter that has been assigned to a portion of a physical disk.

**Loopback plug** A plug that connects to a parallel or serial port and routes outgoing data back into the connector for diagnostic purposes.

**Low insertion force** See *LIF.*

**Low-level formatting** The creation of the logical organization units on a disk such as tracks and sectors.

**Low-order bits** The bits sent to the CPU that represent the data to be calculated.

**Low Voltage Differential SCSI** See *LVD SCSI.*

**LPX power supply** A power supply designed for a modern baby AT-style motherboard.

**LQ** Letter quality. Generically, any printout that is as good or better than achievable with a typewriter. Also refers specifically to the output of a 24-pin dot-matrix printer.

**LS-120** A high-capacity floppy disk and drive that stores up to 120MB. Uses an IDE interface rather than a standard floppy interface.

**LVD SCSI** Low Voltage Differential SCSI. A SCSI variant that produces greater speeds and allows more devices and a greater maximum distance than Single End SCSI (SE SCSI).

**Machine language** The set of commands that the CPU understands for high-order bits.

**Macro virus** A virus that spreads through macros in data files such as Word or Excel.

**Magnetic disk** A disk that stores data in patterns of positive and negative magnetic charge. Compare to *Optical disc.*

**Male** A connector having pins that fit into holes or slots in a female connector.

**Mapping** Creating a link between a name and a location. For example, mapping a network drive makes a network drive or folder appear as a local drive letter on a client PC.

**Master** The main drive on an IDE interface cable, which takes control of all incoming instructions.

**Master boot record** See *MBR.*

**Master File Table** See *MFT.*

**Materials Safety Data Sheet** See *MSDS.*

**Math coprocessor** An extra processing chip that works with the CPU to support math calculations. Also called a floating-point unit (FPU).

**MBR** Master boot record. A reserved area of a disk containing information about the way a disk is partitioned.

**MCA** Microchannel Architecture. An early attempt by IBM at improving the ISA bus. Used a disk-based precursor to Plug and Play. Now obsolete.

**MCC** Memory controller chip. The chip that controls data flowing into and out of RAM.

**Mean Time Between Failures** See *MTBF.*

**Megapixel** A million pixels.

**Memory** A generic term meaning any electronic device (usually a microchip) that stores data in binary format.

**Memory address** The address of a particular logical memory byte.

**Memory controller chip** See *MCC.*

**Mesh** A network topology in which all computers are directly connected to every other computer to ensure reliability.

**MFT** Master File Table. The rough equivalent of a FAT, but for the NTFS file system. Stores data about the starting clusters of files and folders stored on the disk.

**Microchannel Architecture** See *MCA.*

**Mini** A type of power supply connector used to provide power to 3.5-inch floppy drives.

**Mini-DIN** Another name for the PS/2-style connector, a round connector with six pins, smaller than a DIN connector.

**MMX** Multimedia extensions. A set of CPU command features that help multimedia-intensive programs run better that are designed to take advantage of MMX functionality.

**Modem** A device that allows you to communicate with other computers through phone lines by translating digital data (PC) to analog (sound) and then back again on the other end.

**Molex connector** A connector from the power supply to a hard drive, CD-ROM, or 5.25-inch floppy drive.

**Monochrome** Consisting of only one color (plus black or white).

**Motherboard** The large circuit board in a PC that serves as the connecting point for all other components.

**Motion Picture Experts Group** See *MPEG.*

**MouseKeys** A Windows feature that enables the keyboard's arrow keys to control the mouse pointer.

**MPEG** Motion Picture Experts Group. A standards organization that creates specifications for video technology.

**MPEG-2** A standard for decoding movies on DVD discs.

**MSDS** Materials Safety Data Sheet. A document containing information about the safe handling and disposal of an item that poses a personal safety or environmental hazard.

**MTBF** Mean Time Between Failures. A measurement of the reliability of a device in terms of the average amount of time it can run before it fails.

**Multiboot** The capability of installing more than one operating system on a PC and then selecting which OS you want each time the PC starts up. Also called dual-boot.

**Multimedia** Generically refers to using more than one medium. A multimedia system typically includes a sound card, speakers, and a CD-ROM drive.

**Multimedia extensions** See *MMX.*

**Multimeter** A meter for taking multiple types of electrical measurements, usually including voltage, amperage, and resistance.

**Multiread** A technology that uses two read lasers with different wavelengths to ensure that the drive can read different types of CDs.

**Multisession recording** A method of rewriting to a CD-R after it has already been written to before by creating additional separate recording sessions.

**My Computer** A file management window with a single pane that shows icons for all of the local drives on the system.

**Near letter quality** See *NLQ.*

**NetBEUI** An older networking protocol with compact packets that is incompatible with router usage.

**Network** Two or more computers that are connected in order to share data and resources.

**Network adapter** A piece of hardware that Windows recognizes as capable of connecting to a network or the Internet, or a piece of software that simulates network hardware.

**Network address** The portion of an IP address that refers to the network segment to which the node belongs.

**Network place** A shortcut to a folder or drive that does not reside on the local PC, usually set up through My Network Places in Windows.

**New Technology File System** See *NTFS.*

**NLQ** Near letter quality. The best quality output from a 9-pin dot-matrix printer.

**NLX** See *Slimline.*

**Node** An individually addressable computer or printer connected directly to the network.

**Noninterlaced** See *Interlacing.*

**Nonvolatile** Permanent. Nonvolatile storage retains its data until it is explicitly changed; its content does not decay over time.

**Nonvolatile RAM** See *NVRAM.*

**North/south bridge** A chipset architecture that divides operations among three chips—north bridge, south bridge, and super I/O.

**Notebook PC** A portable PC that folds up into a unit the approximate size and shape of a thick writing notebook. Also called laptop.

**NTFS** New Technology File System. A file system for Windows NT, 2000, and XP that offers advantages over the traditional FAT file system.

**NTFS 4** The version of the New Technology File System (NTFS) that comes with Windows NT 4.0.

**NTFS 5** The version of the New Technology File System (NTFS) that comes with Windows 2000 and XP.

**NTFS permission** Security permission on an NTFS drive that allows different users logging in to the same local PC to view one another's files.

**NVRAM** Nonvolatile RAM. A type of RAM that does not need to be continually refreshed in order to maintain its contents.

**Object linking and embedding** See *OLE.*

**Octal** A base-8 numbering system. Not used in PCs.

**OEM** Original Equipment Manufacturer. An OEM version of hardware or software is one provided by a PC maker rather than bought in retail. It sometimes is slightly different from the retail version.

**Ohms** A unit of measurement for resistance.

**OLE** Object linking and embedding. A technology for sharing information between Windows applications that allows dynamic links between files.

**Online UPS** A UPS that runs off the battery continuously as the battery is continuously recharged.

**Open Systems Interconnection** See *OSI reference model.*

**OpenType** An improved version of TrueType.

**Operating environment** A shell that runs on top of an operating system, providing a different user interface than the operating system itself provides.

**Operating system** Software that performs housekeeping tasks that keep the PC running and provides an interface between the end user and the hardware.

**Optical disc** A disc that stores and reads data in patterns of reflectivity rather than magnetism, such as a CD.

**Optical zoom** On a digital camera, a real zoom lens, as opposed to a simulated zoom (digital zoom) that interpolates between pixels.

**Original Equipment Manufacturer** See *OEM.*

**OSI reference model** The model that describes the various layers of activity involved in sending a packet of data from one PC to another on a network. *OSI* stands for "Open Systems Interconnection."

**Outline font** A font file that contains an outline of each letter that can be sized to any dimensions and then filled in to create the characters.

**Output** Outgoing data to a device that displays results, such as monitor or printer.

**Overclocking** Pushing a CPU to run at a higher external speed than that for which it is rated.

**Packet** A logical container file for sending data over a network, containing the data itself plus a header and a footer.

**Packet writing** A scheme for writing data to CDs multiple times that creates a new table of contents with each rewriting.

**Page description language** See *PDL.*

**Page frame** A reserved 64KB area in upper memory used for swapping data into and out of expanded memory.

**Page printer** A printer that composes an entire page in memory before transferring it to paper.

**Pages per minute** See *PPM.*

**Paging file** A reserved area on the hard disk for use as virtual memory. Also called a swap file because the OS swaps data into and out of main memory from it.

**Parallel** Transmitting several bits at the same time.

**Parity bit** A bit included in a packet in modem data transfer that helps the receiving PC determine whether it has correctly received the packet by counting the number of 1s in the overall packet and determining whether it is an odd or even number.

**Parity chip** An extra RAM chip on a stick that functions as an error checker.

**Partition** A defined area of a physical hard drive on which one or more logical drives can be created.

**Passive heat sink** A heat sink that does not have a fan.

**Passive matrix** A type of LCD screen that uses one transistor for each row and each column. The least expensive kind of LCD.

**Passive termination** Termination achieved with resistors.

**PC** Personal Computer. A computer designed for the use of an individual.

**PC Card** Also called PCMCIA. A standard for connecting peripherals to notebook computers via a credit-card-size plug-in interface.

**PCI** Peripheral Component Interface. The current standard for local bus operations on a typical motherboard, connecting PCI expansion slots to the chipset.

**PCI bus** The bus that connects all of the PCI slots in the motherboard to the chipset. Also called Local I/O bus.

**PCI bus IRQ steering** A BIOS feature that allows PCI devices to share IRQs.

**PCL** Printer Control Language, the PDL used by most Hewlett-Packard laser printers and emulated by many other brands and models.

**PCMCIA** Personal Computer Memory Card International Association. A standard for expansion devices in notebook PCs. See also *PC Card.*

**PDA** Personal digital assistant. A handheld computer, usually with a touch-sensitive screen and a writing stylus.

**PDL** Page description language. The language used for communication between a printer driver and a printer.

**Peer-to-peer** A type of network that lacks a server; each of the client PCs is equally responsible for sharing the networking burden.

**Peripheral Component Interface** See *PCI.*

**Personal Computer** See *PC.*

**Personal digital assistant** See *PDA.*

**PGA** Pin grid array. A slot for a chip type of CPU on a motherboard, with concentric rings of holes into which the bottom pins on the CPU connect.

**Phase** The left-right positioning of the image within the monitor.

**Piezoelectric inkjet** An inkjet printer that uses electricity to force ink onto a page.

**PIF** Program Information File. A shortcut for an MS-DOS application that stores any nonstandard properties governing the way the application will start and run.

**Pin 1** The first numbered pin in a connector. On connectors that can physically fit in either direction, locating Pin 1 and matching it to the Pin 1 indicator on the other connector ensures that the cable is oriented correctly.

**Pin grid array** See *PGA.*

**Pin-out diagram** A diagram that tells the purpose of each pin or hole on a connector.

**PIO** Programmed Input/Output. A transfer mode (actually four different modes, PIO 0 through PIO 4) for increasing the speed at which the BIOS attempts to send and receive data for a drive. Not applicable on today's UltraDMA drives.

**Pit** An area of lesser reflectivity (lesser than a land area) on an optical disc.

**Pixel** An individual dot in a display or print image.

**Platen** The hard rubber roller behind the paper that absorbs the impact of the print head striking the ribbon and paper.

**Plug and Play** A technology for detecting hardware and installing drivers for it automatically.

**Pointer scheme** A set of mouse pointer graphics that are designed to work as a set.

**Point-to-Point Protocol** See *PPP.*

**Polarity** A positive or negative magnetic charge.

**Portrait** A page orientation wherein the text runs parallel to the narrow edge of the paper.

**Port replicator** A small docking station that exists primarily to provide easy connect/disconnect access to external ports such as external mouse, keyboard, and monitor.

**POST** Power On Self Test. The startup routine for a PC that checks its hardware and prepares to load the operating system.

**POST card** A circuit board that diagnoses motherboard problems by illuminating lights on the card or displaying an LED number code telling at what point the boot process stalls. See also *POST.*

**PostScript** A PDL developed by Adobe for use with certain high-end laser printers designed for professional desktop publishing.

**Power management** Features that help the PC extend its battery life or conserve electricity by shutting down certain components or putting them in low-power mode after a specified period of inactivity.

**Power On Self Test** See *POST.*

**Power supply** The electricity converter in a PC that steps down the voltage and converts the power to DC current for system use.

**PPM** Pages per minute. A measure of printer speed.

**PPP** Point-to-Point Protocol. A Windows-based streaming protocol used by default for Dial-Up Networking connections.

**Preemptive multitasking** A feature of Windows 9x and higher that allows Windows to control the sharing of CPU time between applications, ensuring that no one program monopolizes the CPU at the expense of all others.

**Primary corona wire** The wire in a laser printer that applies a uniform negative charge to the drum, preparing it to accept the page image.

**Primary IDE** The first IDE interface on the motherboard or expansion board.

**Primary partition** A bootable partition on a hard drive that can have only one logical drive letter.

**Primary storage** Short-term storage in a PC that is readily accessible, such as RAM.

**Primitive** An unfilled simple geometric shape.

**Print engine** The part of the printer that calculates the instructions for the print mechanism and sends instructions for moving the paper and creating the print image.

**Printer Control Language** See *PCL.*

**Printer driver** A file or group of files that take instructions from the operating system and relay them to the printer.

**Print queue** A holding area for print jobs waiting to be sent to the printer.

**Processing** Passing the data through the CPU, where it is calculated.

**Processor** See *CPU.*

**Processor bus** See *External data bus.*

**Product activation** An anticopyright-infringement feature of Windows XP and Office XP that locks that copy of the software to a particular hardware configuration.

**Product key** A string of numbers and letters used to identify your copy of a product for installation.

**Program Information File** See *PIF.*

**Programmable Read-Only Memory** See *PROM.*

**Programmed I/O** See *PIO.*

**PROM** Programmable Read-Only Memory. A type of ROM BIOS chip that cannot be modified after its initial creation.

**Protocol** The language or set of rules governing a data transmission.

**Proxy server** A server maintained by an ISP or corporation through which all Web content requests pass. The proxy server caches the most commonly accessed Web content, speeding up access to it for its clients.

**PS/2** An obsolete type of IBM PC that introduced the PS/2 port. Even though the computers are no longer made, PS/2 ports have become the standard for mouse and keyboard connectors. *PS* stands for "Personal System."

**PS/2 connector** Small, round connector consisting of five pins. Also called a mini-DIN.

**Pull** A piece of equipment that has been removed from an old system. Buying one is like buying a car part from a junkyard.

**Quad pipeline** A CPU that can process four instructions in a single clock cycle.

**RAID** Redundant Array of Inexpensive Disks. A method of creating a single logical disk out of multiple physical disks to protect the data from loss in the event of the failure of a single drive.

**RAID-5** The version of RAID supported in Windows 2000 and XP.

**RAM** Random-Access Memory. Temporary storage for data and the operating system while the PC is turned on.

**RAMDAC** The digital-to-analog converter on the video card.

**RAM disk** A virtual disk created out of RAM, used to temporarily store files. The RAM disk exists only as long as the PC remains on.

**Random-Access Memory** See *RAM.*

**Rasterization** The process of filling in a primitive with texture or shading.

**Read-Only Memory** See *ROM.*

**Read/write head** The mechanism in a disk drive that retrieves and stores data on the disk. Most magnetic disk drives have multiple heads, from 2 to 16. Optical drives usually have only one.

**Real-time clock** See *RTC.*

**Redundant Array of Inexpensive Disks** See *RAID.*

**Refresh rate** The rate at which the electron guns in a monitor refresh each pixel of the display, expressed in hertz.

**Registers** Storage areas in the CPU where it places bits as it is performing calculations on them.

**Registration** The precision with which colors align on a scanner or a printout to produce a true image.

**Registry** The configuration database that defines Windows startup configuration settings in Windows 95 and higher.

**Registry hive** A physical file containing some of the registry settings in Windows NT/2000/XP, which combines with other hives under the Registry Editor in a single interface.

**Remote** Not physically connected to the PC, accessible only through networking.

**Repeater** A network device that accepts and rebroadcasts a data signal to compensate for signal weakening caused by traveling long distances.

**Resident font** A font that is built into the printer, so it is always available.

**Resistance** The amount of obstacle placed in the electricity's path.

**Retrovirus** A computer virus that thwarts attempts to remove it, such as disabling the antivirus software.

**Rewritable CD** See *CD-RW.*

**Ribbon cable** A parallel data cable in which the wires are arranged side-by-side and each wire is separated in its own plastic-covered channel.

**Ring** A network topology in which the PCs are physically connected in a closed loop.

**ROM** Read-Only Memory. Memory that can be read but not written to.

**ROM BIOS** See *BIOS.*

**ROM shadowing** Copying the contents of ROM into RAM for faster access to it.

**Root directory** The top-level directory (folder) on a logical disk.

**Root hub** The base-level USB hub in a system, usually built into the motherboard, into which all USB devices or hubs connect.

**Router** A more sophisticated version of a bridge. It screens out traffic not addressed to a particular segment, and also plans and executes the best route to deliver a packet to the address destination.

**RTC** Real-time clock. A clock/calendar chip that keeps track of the current date and time on a PC.

**RTS/CTS** A hardware-based flow control scheme between the COM port and the modem.

**Safe mode** A way of starting up the GUI without loading nonessential drivers and applications, useful when a driver or program is preventing Windows from starting.

**Save to Disk** A BIOS-based feature that copies RAM content to the hard disk and then shuts down the PC completely.

**Scalable** Resizable to any dimensions.

**Script** A program created with an interpreted programming language.

**SCSI** Small Computer Systems Interface. A high-performance type of hard disk and CD-ROM interface to the motherboard. Can also be used for other devices as well, such as external scanners.

**SCSI ID** A unique identifying number assigned to each device in a SCSI chain.

**SCSI termination** See *termination.*

**SDRAM** Synchronous dynamic RAM. RAM that operates at the same speed as the motherboard bus.

**SDSL** Synchronous DSL. A type of DSL service in which upload and download speeds are the same.

**SEC** Single Edge Connector (or Contact). A slot for a cartridge-style CPU on a motherboard such as a Pentium II.

**Secondary IDE** The second IDE interface on the motherboard or expansion board.

**Secondary storage** Storage in a PC that does not lose its content when the power goes off.

**Sector** A segment of a track on an individual disk surface.

**Sector translation** A conversion scheme for translating the unequal number of sectors per track on the disk physically (due to zoned recording) to an equal number of sectors per track logically.

**Self-Monitoring and Reporting Tool** See *SMART.*

**SEP** Single Edge Processor. A variant of SEC that leaves the circuit board on which the CPU is mounted exposed, rather than encasing it in a plastic cartridge.

**Separator page** A page that prints before a print job reporting the user and computer that initiated the job. Used on network-shared printers to organize the printouts from multiple users.

**Serial** Transmitting one bit at a time.

**Serial Line Internet Protocol** See *SLIP.*

**Server** A PC that exists to route network traffic and provide access to shared network resources.

**SE SCSI** The standard type of SCSI.

**SGRAM** Synchronous graphics RAM. A high-speed type of RAM used in some high-end video cards.

**Shadow mask** A thin sheet of perforated metal that helps keep the electron beams aligned in a CRT.

**Share name** The name by which remote users of a shared resource will know it. This can be the same as the local name for the item or can be different.

**Shareware** Software that is distributed to the public on the honor system, with the expectation that anyone who likes and continues using the program will pay for it.

**Sheet fed** A printer that uses single sheets of paper, one sheet at a time.

**Shielded cable** A cable with an outer covering that reduces or eliminates EMI.

**Shielded twisted pair** See *STP.*

**Signal** The data being sent on a network.

**Signal regeneration** The rebroadcasting of a network signal in order to improve its strength and quality.

**Signal-to-noise ratio** The ratio of usable data signal to static interference in a transmission.

**Signed driver** A driver that has been certified to work with a particular version of Windows and device, containing a digital verification code that shows it has not been altered since its certification.

**SIMM** Single inline memory module. A type of RAM stick with 30 or 72 pins that fits into a SIMM slot on a motherboard. Now obsolete, replaced by DIMMs.

**Single Edge Connector (or Contact)** See *SEC.*

**Single Edge Processor** See *SEP.*

**Single End SCSI** See *SE SCSI.*

**Single inline memory module** See *SIMM.*

**Slave** An additional drive on an IDE interface cable besides the master, which receives instructions from the master only, not directly from the interface.

**Sleep** A power management mode for a PC that shuts off many of the components but keeps memory supplied with power so the OS remains loaded.

**Slimline** A type of PC case in which the expansion boards are mounted on a riser board so they sit parallel to the motherboard rather than perpendicular to it. Modern versions are known as NLX.

**SLIP** Serial Line Internet Protocol. A UNIX-based protocol for communicating with some UNIX-based dial-up servers.

**Slot mask** A hybrid of aperture grille and shadow mask technologies for keeping electron beams aligned on CRTs.

**Slot pitch** A measurement, like dot pitch, of the quality of a slot mask monitor. Smaller is better.

**Small Computer Systems Interface (SCSI)** See *SCSI.*

**SMART** Self-Monitoring and Reporting Tool. A technology for monitoring drive performance and reporting any irregularities or changes that might signal impending failure.

**Snap-in** A utility module that you can add to the Microsoft Management Console to make a particular tool available, such as Computer Management or Event Viewer.

**Soft font** A font that is contained in a computer file, and sent to the printer whenever a document requiring that font must be printed.

**Software** Instructions that tell the hardware what to do, such as operating systems, device drivers, and applications.

**Sound font** An effect applied to regular sound that modifies it without changing its essential character, much like a text font changes basic lettering.

**Software modem** A modem without an on-board controller, relying on Windows Software for control functions. Also called Winmodem.

**Spanned disk** A logical drive that uses space on more than one physical disk.

**SpeedStep Technology** A feature of some CPUs designed for notebook PCs that allows the BIOS to direct the CPU to run at a slower speed and use less power when the PC is running on batteries.

**Splash screen** A graphic that appears briefly as an application or OS loads, usually displaying the name of the product.

**Spool** A holding tank for print jobs waiting to be sent to the printer. Using a print spool frees up the application quicker from which you are printing to continue working on other things.

**Standby** A power management feature of Windows that enables the computer to place itself in a low power-consumption mode, keeping RAM content.

**Standby UPS** A UPS that passes regular AC current directly through to the attached devices as long as AC current is available, switching to battery when AC is not supplied.

**Stand-offs** Brass or plastic spacers that hold the motherboard away from the metal floor of the PC case.

**Start bit** The leading 0 at the beginning of a packet in modem data transfer.

**Static IP address** An IP address that is assigned to a network device for its exclusive use, and that it retains even after disconnecting and reconnecting.

**Stick** A small circuit board on which one or more RAM chips are mounted.

**Stop bit** The trailing 0 at the end of a packet in modem data transfer.

**STP** Shielded twisted pair. A type of network cabling with EMI shielding.

**Strong password** A password that is very difficult to guess, involving a combination of capital and lowercase letters, numbers, and sometimes symbols as well.

**Stylus** A pointing device, resembling a leadless pencil, with which you write or tap on a touch-sensitive screen.

**Subnet mask** A numeric code that specifies what portion of the IP address refers to the domain and what part refers to the individual node within the domain.

**Subnotebook PC** A portable PC that is smaller than a normal notebook PC.

**Subwoofer** A speaker that is dedicated to handling bass; having one makes that thump-thump effect and makes sound effects in the lower range (below 150Hz) much more dramatic.

**Surge suppressor** An electrical pass-through containing a varistor that prevents too much voltage from passing through to the devices plugged into it.

**Swap file** See *Paging file.*

**Switch** (1) An alternative to a jumper, in which tiny on/off switches substitute for jumper caps. (2) A command parameter or option that begins with a slash (/).

**Synchronous DSL** See *SDSL.*

**Synchronous dynamic RAM** See *SDRAM.*

**Synchronous graphics RAM** See *SGRAM.*

**Syntax** The rules governing what parameters a command will take and in what order they should appear in a command line.

**System BIOS** The motherboard's BIOS.

**System bus** The bus that connects the address bus (the CPU and memory's bus) to the chipset on the motherboard. Also called external data bus or processor bus.

**System crystal** The timekeeping unit on the motherboard that controls the pace of data entering and exiting the CPU.

**T1 line** A high-speed, high-bandwidth digital telephone line connection for data networks that is always on (not dial-up).

**TAPI** Telephony Application Programmers Interface. A set of codes that programmers can use to access programming libraries for working with the modem. Nearly all programs that use the modem work with the TAPI interface.

**TCP/IP** Transmission Control Protocol/Internet Protocol. The standard networking protocol for the Internet and for most Microsoft-based networks.

**Telephony Application Programmers Interface** See *TAPI.*

**Terabyte** One trillion bytes.

**Terminal program** Communication software that establishes a direct dial-up connection between two PCs in which users at each end can type messages to one another and transfer files between them.

**Terminate** To cap off a SCSI chain so the data signal stops traveling down the cable and bounces back a signal that it has reached the end.

**Terminate-and-stay-resident** See *TSR.*

**Text-mode application** An application that relies

on the standard Extended ASCII character set for its display, rather than a graphic mode.

**Texture mapping** Filling in a 3D object with a two-dimensional repeating pattern.

**TFT** Thin film transistor. A type of active matrix display that uses multiple transistors for each pixel.

**Thermal inkjet** An inkjet printer that uses heat to create vapor bubbles that force ink onto a page.

**Thick Ethernet** An older type of Ethernet network cabling, consisting of 0.5-inch coaxial cable, used in 10Base-5 networking. Also called thicknet.

**Thin Ethernet** A type of coaxial Ethernet cable used for 10Base-2 networking. Also called thinnet.

**Thin film transistor** See *TFT.*

**Timing signal** A signal in a drive that dictates the amount of time that should pass between two 1s in a row.

**Token** A permission file that is passed around a ring network. The computer that has the token is allowed to send data on the network; all others must wait until it is their turn to have the token.

**Toner** A powdered blend of metal and plastic resin particles, used in laser printers to create an image on a page.

**Topology** The physical arrangement or connectivity of a network.

**Touchpad** A touch-sensitive rectangular pad that functions as a mouse alternative for moving an on-screen pointer.

**Tower** A PC case that sits upright, with its largest side perpendicular to the floor.

**Track** A concentric ring on a disk surface.

**Trackball** A stationary device with a rolling ball on top that functions as a mouse equivalent.

**Tractor fed** A printer that uses continuous-feed paper by pulling it through with a series of gears and sprockets.

**Transfer corona wire** The wire in a laser printer that applies a positive charge to the paper so that the negatively charged toner will be attracted to it.

**Transmission Control Protocol/Internet Protocol** See *TCP/IP.*

**TrueType fonts** Scalable soft fonts in Windows and the Macintosh that work with all applications in the operating system and that can be displayed and printed at any size.

**TSR** Terminate-and-stay-resident. A type of program that runs in the background, either constantly providing a service or being ready to be activated with a certain key combination.

**Typeface** A style of lettering, not tied to any specific size of text.

**UART** Universal Asynchronous Receiver/Transmitter. A chip that converts serial data to parallel data so the CPU can use it. Its speed determines a port's maximum throughput rate.

**UATA** See *UltraDMA.*

**UDMA** See *UltraDMA.*

**UltraATA** See *UltraDMA.*

**UltraDMA** A high-speed transfer mode for disk drives that improves upon DMA and allows transfer rates of up to 100Mbps. Also called UDMA or UltraATA (UATA).

**Underclocking** Running a CPU at a lower external speed than it is capable of.

**Uniform Resource Locator** See *URL.*

**Uninterruptible power supply (UPS)** A battery backup for computer or other electrical equipment.

**Universal Asynchronous Receiver/Transmitter** See *UART.*

**Universal Serial Bus** See *USB.*

**Unshielded cable** A cable without EMI shielding.

**Unshielded twisted pair** See *UTP.*

**Upper memory** The RAM between 640KB and 1MB, reserved for system use.

**URL** Uniform Resource Locator. The complete address of a file available on the Internet, including a prefix such as *HTTP* or *FTP* that indicates the communication protocol with which to retrieve it.

**USB** Universal Serial Bus. A high-speed, Plug and Play, hot-pluggable type of serial port found in most modern PCs.

**USB function** A USB device that performs an end user function rather than simply acting as a hub.

**USB hub** A USB device whose function it is to allow other USB devices to connect to the root hub. A USB hub is like an extension cord for USB.

**UTP** Unshielded twisted pair. A type of network cabling with no EMI shielding.

**V.90** A standard for 56Kbps modem data transfer developed to bridge the two earlier competing standards of 56KFlex and X2.

**Varistor** A variable resistor, also called a MOV (metal-oxide varistor), which creates resistance against current flow when the flow exceeds a certain level. Used in surge suppressors to prevent overvoltage conditions.

**VAT** Virtual allocation table. Like a FAT, except on a packet-written CD.

**Vector font** A font consisting of mathematical equations that draw lines to create the characters.

**VESA Local Bus** See *VLB.*

**Video card** An expansion board that provides an interface between the motherboard and the monitor.

**Virtual 8086** A method of simulating multiple 8086 CPUs on a single 80386 or higher PC.

**Virtual allocation table** See *VAT.*

**Virtual machine** A simulated 8086 CPU operating in its own separate address space.

**Virtual memory** A scheme for using part of a hard disk to simulate additional RAM.

**Virtual Private Networking** See *VPN.*

**Virus** A piece of programming code that causes annoyance to the PC user and/or harm to the PC or its stored data.

**Virus definitions** Information about virus threats used by an antivirus program to detect and remove them.

**VLB** VESA local bus. The first commercially popular version of a local bus, found in many 486-class PCs. Now obsolete, replaced by PCI.

**Volatile** Not permanent. Volatile storage loses its contents if it is not constantly refreshed.

**Voltage** The strength of the electricity being delivered to a device. Standard household current is 110 volt.

**Volts** A measurement of the strength of the electricity flowing through a circuit.

**Volume boot record** Information about a particular partition and its boot files if bootable.

**VPN** Virtual Private Networking. A secure private network connection established via publicly accessible connectivity such as the Internet.

**WAN** Wide-area network. A network in which the connected nodes are spread out over a wide geographical area, such as in different cities.

**Wattage** The amount of electricity a device uses, derived by multiplying voltage by amperage.

**Waveform** A digital sound clip recorded from an analog source.

**Wavetable synthesis** A sound card method of playing MIDI music by playing back recorded clips of instruments playing the specified notes.

**Webcam** A digital video camera that connects to the PC and operates only while it is connected.

**Wide-area network** See *WAN.*

**Windows Explorer** A file management window that contains a folder tree, enabling the user to switch quickly to other drive and folder locations.

**Windows keyboard** A keyboard containing special keys used only in Microsoft Windows, such as the Menu and Windows keys.

**Wireless access point** A hub that directs the traffic between wireless Ethernet devices.

**Wizard** A step-by-step series of dialog boxes that walk a user through a setup, configuration, or troubleshooting process.

**Workgroup** A peer-to-peer network.

**Writable CD** See *CD-R.*

**Write-protect** To protect a disk from its contents being erased or modified.

**X2** One of two early competing standards for 56Kbps modem data transfer, developed and supported by U.S. Robotics.

**XMS** eXtended Memory Specification. A standard for managing extended memory.

**XON/XOFF** A software-based flow control scheme between the COM port and the modem.

**Zero Insertion Force** See *ZIF.*

**ZIF** Zero Insertion Force. A type of chip socket that has a lever that raises and lowers to secure or release the chip, so that no pressure is required to insert or remove it.

**Zip disk** A disk designed for use in a Zip drive.

**Zip drive** A disk drive that reads and writes removable 100 or 250MB Zip disk cartridges. Has no relationship to a ZIP file.

**ZIP file** A file or group of files that has been compressed using the ZIP compression algorithm and has a .zip extension.

**Zoned recording** A means of creating fewer sectors per track on the inner parts of a disk and more on the outer parts.

# INDEX

## B

## C

## D

## E

## F

## G

## M

## O



## P

## Q



## R

## T

## U

## V



## W